THE OXFORD HANDBOOK OF

SINGING

THE OXFORD HANDBOOK OF

SINGING

Edited by

GRAHAM F. WELCH

DAVID M. HOWARD

and

JOHN NIX

OXFORD
UNIVERSITY PRESS

OXFORD
UNIVERSITY PRESS

Great Clarendon Street, Oxford, OX2 6DP,
United Kingdom

Oxford University Press is a department of the University of Oxford.
It furthers the University's objective of excellence in research, scholarship,
and education by publishing worldwide. Oxford is a registered trade mark of
Oxford University Press in the UK and in certain other countries

Published in the United States of America by Oxford University Press
198 Madison Avenue, New York, NY 10016, United States of America

British Library Cataloguing in Publication Data
Data available

Library of Congress Control Number: 2018965378

ISBN 978–0–19–966077–3

Printed and bound by
CPI Group (UK) Ltd, Croydon, CR0 4YY

Preface

GRAHAM F. WELCH, DAVID M. HOWARD, AND JOHN NIX

SINGING has been a characteristic behavior of humanity across several millennia. Chorus America (2009) estimated that 42.6 million adults and children regularly sing in one of 270,000 choruses in the US, representing more than one in five households. Similarly, recent European-based data (Bartel and Cooper 2015) suggest that more than 37 million adults take part in group singing. On a much smaller scale, an in-depth case study of one small area of inner London recently discovered 51 adult amateur singing groups, representing a diverse cross-section of social groupings and musical genres (Parkinson, private correspondence). However, if we take into account the common practice of singing in schools, as part of collective events and regular music classes, these numbers increase exponentially in terms of the proportions of the total populations who sing. In England, for example, *Sing Up*—a government-funded initiative to promote regular and positive singing experiences for children—estimated that 98 percent of primary schools were taking part by 2012, embracing 17,000 schools and over four million children. Furthermore, extending the age focus to a younger phase, findings from early years and pre-school research indicate that singing by parents and caregivers is virtually ubiquitous in family settings in many countries of the world, irrespective of ethnicity and language group (see Chapters 21–24 this volume). In addition, towards the other end of lifespan, despite the physical and mental challenges of aging, older people can continue to participate in and enjoy singing, especially in groups, and often with considerable health benefits, e.g. promoting more efficient lung function and social inclusion (Skingley et al. 2011; Davidson and Garrido, Chapter 46).

The Oxford Handbook of Singing has been designed to be a comprehensive resource for anyone who wishes to know more about the pluralistic nature of singing. In part, the narrative adopts a lifespan approach, pre-cradle to senescence, to illustrate that singing is a commonplace behavior which is an essential characteristic of our humanity. In diverse ways, singing as self-expression, catharsis, communal art activity, and as a component of personal and social identity from early childhood onwards has been a locus for systematic scientific enquiry and personal commitment for each of the main and section editors and our authors over many years. The multidisciplinary components of our collective narrative, embracing different strands of the arts, humanities, and sciences, seek to marshal focused evidence which, at the same time, is underpinned by each author's sense of their own individual and emotional engagement in a particular aspect of the act of singing.

The chapter contents have been clustered into eight main sections, embracing fifty-three chapters by seventy-two authors drawn from across the world. Each chapter seeks to illustrate and illuminate a particular aspect of singing.

In Part 1, Chapter 1, Kayes provides insights into the underlying human anatomy and physiology of singing, of how singing is a physical act that requires significant coordination of many components in the human body in order to provide (a) singing's energy source from the lungs, (b) a vibrating sound source in the larynx, and (c) the subsequent frequency shaping of vocal sound into the environment. At the same time, the following two chapters (Stadelman-Cohen and Hillman, Chapter 2; Rubin and Epstein, Chapter 3) collectively recognize that certain behaviors are antithetical to the healthy voice function that underpins successful singing, particularly in the longer term, and describe the nature of common vocal threats, as well as how these might be addressed. The final chapter in this section (Lã and Gill, Chapter 4) links the information about the physical act of singing into sung performance.

Part 2 builds on the Handbook's opening chapters to provide insights into how the body's physical activity relates to the psychoacoustics of singing, of the nature of sung sound, and what we experience when we hear or listen to someone sing. Watson (Chapter 5) details the breath mechanism for singing, while Herbst, Howard, and Švec (Chapter 6), and Story (Chapter 7) review the evidence for how the voice source (larynx) is energized by the breath, and spectrally shaped and dampened by the nature and action of the vocal tract. Sundberg (Chapter 8) extends this discussion to explain the underlying vocal acoustic characteristics that lead us to experience differences between singing styles, such as between Western classical (high art) and various popular music. These adult-focused analyses are contrasted by Sergeant (Chapter 9), who discusses the acoustics of children's singing related to age and gender. The narrative focus then shifts to the particular sonic features that relate to how we perceive singing (Howard and Hunter, Chapter 10) and the impact of the local physical environment on the shaping of our perceptions (Jers, Chapter 11).

In Part 3, the authors combine to provide insights into the psychology of singing, building from Kleber and Zarate's (Chapter 12) detailed exposition of the neuroscientific research evidence into singing and the brain. The following chapters focus on diverse ways in which we might consider perception and singing. Sundberg (Chapter 13) reveals the nature of research into intonation in choral and solo singing, of the role of vibrato, and our perception of being "in-tune." Coutinho and colleagues (Chapter 14) discuss the emotional power of singing, of emotional expression, and communication, while Himonides (Chapter 15) reports on the importance of context in what counts as our perception of singing quality. Wise (Chapter 16) explains why some adults believe that they are "tone-deaf" or unable to sing, building a theoretical standpoint from empirical studies of adults and children, while Dalla Bella (Chapter 17) reveals the scientific basis for the underlying reality of relative singing competence for the majority, bringing together neuroscience and commonplace singing behaviors. Welch and Preti (Chapter 18) offer a multidisciplinary perspective on the links between singing, intra-, and interpersonal communication and identity. Part 3 ends with Cohen and Ludke's (Chapter 19) review of the impact of new technologies in gathering and analyses of singing data, illustrated by the development of a digital library as part of the international Canadian-led Advancing Interdisciplinary Research on Singing (AIRS) project.

Part 4 examines the development of singing for different age phases across the lifespan. It opens with a timely reminder by Walker (Chapter 20) of the customary scientific lens through which we view singing behaviors. He emphasizes that singing is socially and culturally located, and provides examples from diverse non-literate societies to ensure that we maintain a broad perspective on what counts as singing. The lifespan perspective opens with chapters by Woodward (Chapter 21), Trehub and Gudmundsdottir (Chapter 22), and Barrett (Chapter 23), who provide detailed accounts of the genesis of singing from pre-birth through to early childhood, and of the significance of carers and family in both exposing and nurturing singing development. Harding (Chapter 24) extends this with a more ethno-musicological perspective that compares and contrasts young children's singing encultura-tion in two contexts—inner-city London (UK) and rural West Bengal (India)—while noting (as Barrett) the impact of the child's inner creative world on the ways that they make sense of their exposure to local song repertoire. Welch (Chapter 25) considers singing as a develop-mental behavior as illustrated in research studies of school-aged children and adolescents. The challenges of adolescence in terms of physical changes in the voice mechanism and their impact on singing behaviors are examined in detail by Williams and Harrison (Chapter 26) for boys, and Gackle (Chapter 27) for girls. Each chapter reveals development trajectories that embrace characteristic phases of voice change and related vocal output. Parkinson (Chapter 28) then considers adult singing and investigates why adults choose to sing in com-munity choirs, the benefits that are reported, and also how such perceptions are impacted by gender. Part 4 closes with Davidson and Murray (Chapter 29), who consider the vocal ecology of the older singer and offer principled advice on how to promote successful singing with this age group; the chapter also acts as a bridge into Part 5 of the Handbook.

Part 5 considers education with a focus on singing pedagogy. The eight chapters com-bine to embrace an overview of what counts as effective pedagogy when we seek to promote singing in others. Nix (Chapter 30) details the process of building a secure technique and of the need for the teacher to ensure that pedagogy is grounded in the science as well as the art of singing. Relatedly, but with a focus on a perception of singing disability—the "non-singer"—Knight (Chapter 31) reviews the literature for why such attributions exist, despite singing being a species-wide ability, and of how these can be addressed by the use of appro-priate pedagogical strategies to provide access to a singing world. Callaghan (Chapter 32) examines the pedagogical requirements at the other end of the development spectrum in the nurturing of the would-be professional singer. The two chapters that follow build on this and examine in more detail how to support the mental preparation of the performer (Thomas, Chapter 33), as well as what might be experienced in the study of singing in a con-servatoire context (King and Nix, Chapter 34). Then, Fisher, Kayes, and Popeil (Chapter 35) broaden the pedagogical perspective to non-classical vocal genres under the heading of con-temporary commercial music (CCM), which includes pop, rock, jazz, folk, and musical the-ater singing styles. The authors argue that a knowledge of such genres is essential to ensure that our singing teachers have a pedagogical grounding that is sufficiently broad to meet the needs of the current wide variety of professional and amateur adult singers. Edgerton's chapter (Chapter 36) explores the demands that the singing repertoire can make on singers and details a theoretical position of how an understanding of modern psychoacoustics can be used to adapt the voice mechanism to be more efficient and effective. In the final chapter of Part 5, Yang, Carter-Ényì, Radhakrishnan, Grimmer, and Nix (Chapter 37) discuss the vocal and pedagogical traditions of Chinese, African, and Indian sung genres, explore these different traditions, and review current trends in vocal pedagogy.

In Part 6, the Handbook's focus shifts to examine the collective "choral" voice. Geisler and Johansson (Chapter 38) provide an introduction by discussing choirs as musical and societal phenomena. The authors draw on their Scandinavian-based *Choir in Focus* network to explore the variety of theoretical and disciplinary approaches that have been used to study choral activity. The remaining chapters illustrate this variety, beginning with Hill's chapter (Chapter 39) on the youth choir, drawing on empirical data collected as part of an interview study with singing teachers of youth choirs, composers, and conductors. She examines each of these perspectives in turn to tease out the distinctive nature of choral activity that characterizes this age group. In contrast, Day (Chapter 40) takes a cultural, historical, and musicological perspective by investigating the development of the so-called English Choral Tradition, a unique English singing style that arose from a particular confluence of socio-cultural and historical events. The next chapter by Durrant and Varvarigou (Chapter 41) provides theoretical and practice perspectives on choral conducting, and implications for the art of choral rehearsal, including gesture and communication. This is followed by Davidson and Faulkner's study (Chapter 42) of the theoretical links between group singing and social identity, illustrated by three case studies from Iceland and Australia. Then the choral focus shifts to a scientific understanding of how choirs address the challenge of keeping their unaccompanied singing in tune. Howard (Chapter 43) explains through a series of experiments how it is possible to predict likely shifts in pitch during sung performance. Finally, Jansson (Chapter 44) looks at the under-researched area of the conductor and examines the choral singers' perspective from a more holistic theoretical perspective of what counts as effective choral leadership.

Part 7 offers some examples of the growing research literature on the wider benefits of singing. It opens with Clift and Gilbert's (Chapter 45) review of the encouraging recent research evidence into how singing is likely to have a beneficial effect on lung function and breathing for people with respiratory illness. This is followed by Davidson and Garrido's (Chapter 46) evidence-based model of how singing can address our psychological needs through supporting our sense of relatedness, competency, and autonomy, as exampled by research into older people singing in a group context. Theorell (Chapter 47) examines the evidence for what he terms the biology of singing and illustrates the beneficial aspects of singing, such as through changes in endocrine and immunological function. Boyce-Tillman (Chapter 48) explores therapeutic approaches to singing and draws on examples from orate singing traditions to demonstrate how singing can strengthen people physically and emotionally.

Part 8 reports on the importance of technology and its development in the modern era for our understanding of singing. Technology provides core tools that are integral to many of the data-collection approaches that underpin the evidence base for the Handbook. It is fitting, therefore, to make the technology more explicit in the final Part of the Handbook. The opening two chapters by Schutte (Chapter 49, Chapter 50) rehearse scientific and clinical milestones in voice technology over the past two hundred years. He traces the design and development of diverse tools to reveal the nature of our vocal physiology, e.g. related to the structure and function of the larynx. Then, Himonides (Chapter 51) expands this literature to consider the use of modern digital technologies for the recording, archiving, and analysis of singing. It is complemented by Nair, Howard, and Welch's chapter (Chapter 52) on how voice analyses can be used practically in the voice studio to develop the singing competency of students. The last chapter of the Handbook (Chapter 53) focuses on future perspectives and is divided into seven sections, each of which offers insights into the value of technology to reveal distinctive aspects of the singing voice. Pabon reports on the use of the Voice

Range Profile, Howard discusses Hearing Modeling Spectrography and 3D Printed Vocal Tracts, Ternström reviews research into voice synthesis, and his colleagues in Stockholm, led by Askenfelt, discuss their studies of masterclass teaching at a distance. In the final two sections, Kob reports on virtual acoustics and Eckel considers the voice in computer music composition.

In summary, *The Oxford Handbook of Singing* has been conceived through various research-based disciplinary perspectives and draws from the natural, clinical, and social sciences (including psychology and education) with rich insights from the arts and humanities. Together, these elements combine to provide a holistic understanding of singing's multifaceted nature and also of its importance in what makes us human.

References

Bartel, R. & Cooper, C. F. (2015). *Singing in Europe*. Retrieved from http://www.thevoiceproject. eu/fileadmin/redaktion-thevoice/VOICE/docs/singingeurope/singingeurope_report.pdf

Chorus America (2009). *The Chorus Impact Study*. Washington DC: Chorus America.

Skingley, A., Clift, S.M., Coulton, S.P., and Rodriquez, J. (2011). The effectiveness and cost-effectiveness of a participative community singing programme as a health promotion initiative for older people: Protocol for a randomised controlled trial. *BMC Public Health* 11: 142. Available from: http://www.biomedcentral.com/content/pdf/1471-2458-11-142.pdf

Acknowledgments

As the lead editors of *The Oxford Handbook of Singing*, we are delighted to have this opportunity to acknowledge the wonderful contributions from our many expert authors, drawn from across the globe, in this final hardback edition. The Handbook has had an extended genesis over several years, with colleagues patiently drafting, scrutinizing, and updating their chapters for early online publication. Throughout, we have been supported by an excellent team from Oxford University Press under the leadership of Martin Baum. We are indebted to an expanded team of editors for the various Parts of the Handbook, as well as Eva Wilde and Karen Wise, and particularly Josephine Borradaile, each of whom has assisted at various key moments in pulling together the strands of this volume to create the final composite publication. We also acknowledge the very many thousands of anonymous volunteers of all ages who have participated in various ways in the data collection represented in the chapter narratives. The Handbook is dedicated to all those and to everyone with a curiosity about and engagement with singing.

TABLE OF CONTENTS

PART 3 THE PSYCHOLOGY OF SINGING

SECTION EDITORS: GRAHAM F. WELCH AND KAREN WISE

PART 4   THE DEVELOPMENT OF SINGING ACROSS THE LIFESPAN

SECTION EDITOR: GRAHAM F. WELCH

PART 5 SINGING PEDAGOGY

SECTION EDITOR: JOHN NIX

PART 6 THE COLLECTIVE "CHORAL" VOICE

SECTION EDITORS: URSULA GEISLER AND KARIN JOHANSSON

PART 7   THE WIDER BENEFITS OF SINGING

SECTION EDITORS: GRAHAM F. WELCH AND STEPHEN CLIFT

PART 8   SINGING AND TECHNOLOGY

SECTION EDITOR: DAVID M. HOWARD

LIST OF CONTRIBUTORS

Margaret S. Barrett is Professor and founding Director of the Creative Collaboratorium at The University of Queensland, Australia where she served as Head of School (2008–2018). Following undergraduate and graduate coursework study at The University of Tasmania in Music and Music Education, she completed a PhD at Monash University. Her research interests include: the investigation of young children's musical thought and activity as composers and notators; children's communities of musical practice; cultural psychological perspectives of musical engagement; and narrative inquiry in music education. Her research has been supported by major grants from the Australian Research Council and has been published in key journals of the discipline. Recent publications include *Narrative Soundings: An Anthology of Narrative Inquiry in Music Education* (with Sandra Stauffer, Springer, 2012) and *Collaborative Creative Thought and Practice in Music* (Ashgate, 2014). She has served as President of the International Society for Music Education (2012–2014), Chair of the Asia-Pacific Symposium for Music Education (2009–2011), and Chair of the World Alliance for Arts Education (2013–2015). She has received awards for excellence in research supervision (2016), research engagement (2016), and teaching (2006) and is a Fulbright Senior Research Fellow (2018).

Simone Dalla Bella studied cognitive psychology at the University of Padua (Italy), completed a PhD in cognitive neuropsychology at the University of Montreal (Canada), and received a Habilitation degree from the University of Warsaw (Poland). He also obtained a master's degree in piano performance from the Conservatory of Music in Mantua (Italy). He is currently full Professor in the Department of Psychology at the University of Montreal (Canada), and Co-director of the International Laboratory for Brain, Music and Sound Research (BRAMS, Montreal). His research interests concern the neurosciences of music and rhythm, with a particular focus on music disorders in the general population (tone deafness and beat deafness) and rhythm perception and production mechanisms in the general population, professional musicians, and patients with brain damage (e.g. Parkinson's disease).

The Rev Dr. **June Boyce-Tillman** MBE read music at Oxford University and is Professor of Applied Music at the University of Winchester. She has published widely in the area of education and music, most recently on spirituality. Her doctoral research into children's musical development has been translated into five languages. She has written about and organized events in the area of interfaith dialogue using music. She is an international performer, especially in the work of Hildegard of Bingen. Her large-scale works for cathedrals such as Winchester and Southwark involve professional musicians, community choirs, people with disabilities, and school children. She is the artistic convener of the Centre for the Arts as Well-being at the University of Winchester and Director of the Tavener Centre for Music and Spirituality. She is editor of a series for the publisher Peter Lang on music and spirituality.

Her most recent publications are *Experiencing Music, Restoring the Spiritual: Music as Wellbeing* (2016), (with Karin Hendricks) *Queering Freedom: Music, Identity, and Spirituality* (2018), and *Freedom Song: Faith, Abuse, Music and Spirituality: A Celebration* (2018). She is an Extra-ordinary Professor at North West University, South Africa and has included education traditions from Africa in a recent book she has edited, *Spirituality and Music Education: Perspectives from Three Continents*.

Jean Callaghan PhD holds an English Trinity College Fellowship and an Australian Licentiate in singing performance and has worked internationally as a singer. She completed undergraduate and research master's degrees at the University of Western Australia, and a DPhil at Western Sydney University. After many years as an academic, she now works freelance as a teacher, researcher, and consultant in vocal performance and pedagogy. Her research interests are interdisciplinary and concern vocal pedagogy and the relationship between music and language. Her book, *Singing & Science*, explores the relationship between voice science, neuroscience, and vocal pedagogy. She was part of the research team that developed *Sing&See* software and author, with Pat Wilson, of the extensive teachers' manual *How to Sing and See*. She has served as President of the Australian National Association of Teachers of Singing, the Australian Voice Association, and the Australian Association for Research in Music Education.

Aaron Carter-Ényì is an Assistant Professor of Music at Morehouse College in Atlanta, GA. He holds a PhD in Music Theory from Ohio State University, a Masters of Music degree in Choral Conducting from the University of Texas at San Antonio, and a Colleague Certificate from the American Guild of Organists. Aaron was a Fulbright Scholar to Nigeria in 2013 and a fellow of the American Council of Learned Societies (ACLS) in 2017. With his wife Quintina Carter-Ényì, Aaron was awarded first place in the 2015 Smartphone Application Design Competition held by the Signal Processing Committee of the Acoustical Society of America. His dissertation *Contour Levels: An Abstraction of Pitch Based on African Tone Systems* draws on two years of field research in Nigeria. Recent scholarship appears or is forthcoming in *Africa (Journal of the International African Institute)*, *Ethnomusicology*, *Music Theory Online*, and *Tonal Aspects of Languages*.

Stephen Clift is Professor of Health Education in the Faculty of Health and Wellbeing, Canterbury Christ Church University, UK, Director of the Sidney De Haan Research Centre for Arts and Health, and a Professorial Fellow of the Royal Society for Public Health (RSPH). He has worked in the field of health promotion and public health for over 25 years, and has made contributions to research, practice, and training on HIV/AIDS prevention, sex education, international travel and health, and the health promoting school in Europe. His current interests relate to arts and heath, particularly the potential value of group singing for health and well-being. The De Haan Research Centre was established in 2005 and since then has made original contributions to research on the value of singing for people with enduring mental health challenges and older people with chronic respiratory illness. The Centre conducted the first ever community-based randomized controlled trial on the value of singing for older people, with funding from the National Institute for Health Research. Stephen is one of the founding editors of the journal *Arts & Health: An International Journal for Research, Policy and Practice*. He was the founding Chair of the RSPH Special Interest Group for Arts, Health and Wellbeing. He is also co-editor with Professor Paul Camic of the Oxford Public Health Textbook on *Creative Arts, Health and Wellbeing* published in November 2015.

Annabel J. Cohen (BA McGill; PhD Queen's University; ARCT Royal Conservatory of Music, Toronto) is a Professor of Psychology at the University of Prince Edward Island, editor of *Psychomusicology: Music, Mind and Brain,* co-editor of the book *Psychology of Music and Multimedia* (Tan, Cohen, Lipscomb, & Kendall 2013, Oxford University Press) and serves on consulting boards of several other journals. She is Fellow of the Canadian Psychological Association, the American Psychological Association, and the Psychonomic Society. She has directed an international research collaboration on singing entitled Advancing Interdisciplinary Research in Singing (AIRS) supported by the Social Sciences and Humanities Research Council (SSHRC).

Eduardo Coutinho is a Lecturer in Music Psychology at the University of Liverpool (UK). His expertise is in the study of emotional expression, perception and induction through music, and the automatic recognition of emotion in music and speech. His research focuses on the emotional impact of music on listeners, namely on the link between music structure and emotion, the types of emotions induced by music, and individual and contextual factors that mediate the relationships between music and listeners. Coutinho pioneered research on the analysis of emotional dynamics in music, and made significant contributions to the field of music emotion recognition. Currently his work focuses on the application of music in Healthcare and Eldercare.

Jane W. Davidson is Professor of Creative and Performing Arts (Music) at The University of Melbourne and Deputy Director of the Australian Research Council's Centre of Excellence for the History of Emotions. Her research is broadly in the area of performance studies, with interests in emotion and expression, voice, musical development, and music and well-being. She has worked as an opera singer and music theater director and was also coordinator of vocal studies at the University of Western Australia over an eight-year period, and now leads the Master of Music Opera Performance at The University of Melbourne. She has published and performed extensively and secured a range of research grants in both Australia and overseas.

Timothy Day was educated at Oxford University where he was an organ scholar at St John's College. For many years he was a music curator in the Sound Archive of the British Library, where he inaugurated the Edison Fellowship scheme for scholars using recordings as source material and organized series of public seminars on the history of music in performance. Between 2006 and 2011 he was a Visiting Senior Research Fellow at King's College, London. He is a cultural historian who has written widely about the history of music in performance and about cathedral choirs. His fullest treatment of the topic of this essay is a monograph published by Allen Lane in November 2018, *I saw Eternity the other Night: King's College, Cambridge and an English Singing Style.*

Nicola Dibben is Professor in Music, and Faculty Director of Research at the University of Sheffield, UK. She has over sixty publication in the psychology of music and popular music studies and is former editor of the academic journals *Empirical Musicology Review* and *Popular Music*. Publications include the co-authored *Music and Mind in Everyday Life* (2010) and the monograph *Björk* (2009), the latter of which led to a collaboration on the artist's multi-media app album *Biophilia* (2011).

Colin Durrant PhD is conductor of the University of London Chamber Choir and Imperial College London Choir. He has held various positions in universities in London and the US and has published many articles on choral conducting and music education. His book *Choral Conducting: Philosophy and Practice* first appeared in 2003 and is used widely in universities around the world and is currently in its second revised edition. Colin has led conducting and choral singing workshops in the US, Australia, Singapore, Taiwan, China, Hong Kong, Malaysia, and Kenya, as well as in Europe and the UK. He is a member of the Voice Care Network of America. Colin holds a Fellowship of the Royal College of Organists and was one-time winner of the Charles Herbert Smith Organ Prize.

Gerhard Eckel is a composer and sound artist working as Professor of Computer Music and Multimedia at the Institute of Electronic Music and Acoustics (IEM) of the University of Music and Performing Arts Graz (KUG) in Austria. He also serves as Affiliate Professor at the KTH Royal Institute of Technology and as a Visiting Professor at the Royal College of Music in Stockholm. He pursues both an artistic and scientific interest in matters of sound and music and has engaged in interdisciplinary research projects for more than two decades. In the past he has worked at IRCAM, the computer music research center of the Pompidou Centre in Paris, and at the Fraunhofer Institut for Media Communication in Bonn. He is experienced in designing and coordinating publicly funded research projects in artistic, scholarly, and scientific domains. He has led research projects funded by the European Framework Programs and the Culture Programs, the Austrian Science Fund, the Zukunftsfonds Steiermark, and the Wenner Grenn Foundations Stockholm. Gerhard's artistic work focuses on sonic art, mainly in the form of sound installations and sound sculptures developed in a post-conceptual tradition. For two years he has been a member of the Executive Board of the Society for Artistic Research and its President for two years. In the context of his research projects, he organized several symposia and public project events. He is the founder of the signale^{graz} concert series at the KUG, which presents international electroacoustic music and sound art to a general public along with a varied supporting program of master classes, lectures, workshops, and soirées. In close connection to his artistic production, research projects, teaching, and management activities, he supervises artistic, scholarly, and scientific doctoral research.

Michael Edward Edgerton is at the forefront of vocal exploration by extending the technical and expressive capabilities of voice. As composer, researcher, and performer, he has presented new developments in the search for the limits of sound production. Notably, he systematically investigates vocal production using the tools of voice science and psychoacoustics, which has earned him considerable renown for those interested in the present and future of voice. As a composer, Michael's music coalesces diverse influences such as European avant-garde, American experimentalism, and world music into contexts that are informed by scientific models and metaphors. Initially stemming from his work with voice science and dynamical systems, Michael has pioneered work with multidimensionality and non-linear phenomena in music. Michael's artistic mission is to liberate those sounds that otherwise remain in danger of being overlooked or going unheard. Michael has received prizes for his compositions, which are heard around the world.

Ruth Epstein PhD MRCSLT, is Head of speech-language therapy services and Consultant speech-language therapist (ENT) at the Royal National Throat Nose & Ear

Hospital, London. She holds various honorary fellowships and Senior Lecturer positions at UCL and other academic institutions in the UK, as well as creating and running a successful MSc course in Voice Pathology since 2003 at University College London. Dr Epstein is a past-President of the British Voice Association and an elected member of CoMeT (Collegium Medicorum Theatri), the international association of laryngologists, voice scientists, and speech pathologists. She is on the Board of the World Voice Consortium. Dr Epstein has published extensively on various aspects of voice and voice therapy and her special interests are professional voice users, occupational dysphonia, and neurolaryngology.

Robert Faulkner PhD is presently Director of Music at Methodist Ladies' College, Perth and Honorary Research Fellow at the University of Western Australia. A graduate of the Royal Academy of Music, London, Robert also studied at the Guildhall School of Music and Drama, the University of Reading, and the University of Sheffield, where he completed his PhD. With extensive experience at every level of music education from kindergarten through tertiary and adult education in the UK, Iceland, and Australia, Robert has a special interest in singing. He has published a solo monograph on *Icelandic Men and Singing*, along with various other chapters and articles on the voice as a technology of Self. As a performer, Robert has conducted a wide range of choirs, including performances at prestigious international venues and in competition. Other research interests focus more broadly on a range of music education, musical development, and music psychology topics.

Jeremy Fisher is a prize-winning musician, author, and CPD-accredited performance coach. He studied oboe, piano, and accompaniment at the RNCM UK and has worked as a collaborative musician for thirty years in opera, musical theater, and on the concert platform. Books include the *Singing Express* series, *Successful Singing Auditions*, and the Amazon #1 bestseller *How To Sing Legato*. In 2016 The Wellcome Trust commissioned *This Is A Voice*—a book of exercises on speaking, singing, ventriloquism, and beatboxing. Jeremy has created a groundbreaking Voicebox Video for London's Science Museum, and more than thirty singing technique training resources for Vocal Process, including *Belting Explained* and *Understanding Head Voice*. He has presented on singing and performance techniques in the UK, Spain, Sweden, Latvia, the Netherlands, the US, and Australasia. Jeremy's vocal folds have featured on British Voice Association leaflets and have appeared on Channel 4 as an example of a healthy voice.

Lynne Gackle is the Director of Choral Activities and the Mary Jane Gibbs Chair of Choral Music at Baylor University in Waco, Texas. She conducts Baylor Bella Voce, the Baylor Concert Choir, teaches choral conducting, choral literature, and serves as the Director of the Ensemble Division. Prior to her Baylor appointment, Lynne taught at the University of South Florida, the University of Mississippi, and the University of Miami. She received her education from Louisiana State University (BME) and the University of Miami (MM and PhD). Lynne is a nationally and internationally active choral clinician and conductor. She has held various positions within the American Choral Directors Association, including President of the Southern Division and ACDA-Florida, VP of Collegiate/Community Choirs for the Texas Choral Directors Association, and is currently the National President-Elect of the American Choral Directors Association. Lynne is the editor of *Choral Artistry for the Singer* (Walton Music/GIA) and the *Lynne Gackle Choral Series* (Colla Voce). Internationally recognized for her research on the female adolescent voice, Lynne is the author of *Finding*

Ophelia's Voice, Opening Ophelia's Heart in addition to being contributing author for other books published by GIA, Oxford, and Hal Leonard/McGraw Hill. Professor Gackle was awarded Baylor's Outstanding Faculty Award in Research (2012). She holds memberships in ACDA, TMEA, TCDA, and NATS.

Sandra Garrido PhD is a pianist, violinist, and researcher. With a background in both music and psychology, she completed her PhD at the University of New South Wales. Her post-doctoral research at the Melbourne Conservatorium of Music and the ARC Centre of Excellence for the History of Emotions concerned the use of music in depression in both the modern day and historically. She is currently an NHMRC-ARC Dementia Research Fellow at the MARCS Institute for Brain, Behaviour and Development at Western Sydney University. Sandra has published over thirty academic publications, including a monograph entitled *Why Are We Attracted to Sad Music?* (2016).

Ursula Geisler PhD is Associate Professor in Musicology at the Department of Music and Art at Linnaeus University in Sweden since 2015. She has been affiliated to Lund University 2002–2013. In 2009, together with Karin Johansson from Malmö Academy of Music, she initiated Choir in Focus, the international research network on choral singing, funded by Riksbankens Jubileumsfond, the Swedish Foundation for Humanities and Social Sciences. Her inventory of choral research publications, *Choral Research: A Global Bibliography* (2010/2012) is the first attempt to make choral research visible in its disciplinary and thematic diversification. Together with Karin Johansson, she has edited and published several anthologies on choral topics, including *Choral Singing: Histories and Practices* (Cambridge Scholars Publishing, 2014). Geisler is board member of the Swedish Society of Musicology, Editor in the Swedish Royal Academy of Music's publication board, and Expert for the Norwegian National Research Council.

Rebekah Gilbert PhD graduated from the Royal Academy of Music in 1993 and worked as a professional concert and oratorio mezzo soloist in London. She has recorded at Abbey Road for EMI and the BBC. She gained her MA in Arts Management in 1994 from City University, and her Doctorate in 2012. She later studied at the London School of Sports Massage and works as a clinical sports massage therapist in Sussex. She has a strong interest in posture and performance and has recently been accepted by the British Association of Performing Arts Medicine. Rebekah has worked with Stephen Clift on a number of collaborations investigating music and well-being.

Brian P. Gill (tenor), DMA, Certificate in Vocology, 2011 Van L. Lawrence Fellowship Winner, is Associate Professor of Voice and Voice Pedagogy in the Jacobs School of Music (JSM) at Indiana University (IU). Prior to his appointment at JSM, he held the position of Music Associate Professor/Director of Vocal Pedagogy at NYU's Steinhardt School and the Voice Center (Langone Medical Center). Professor Gill has performed numerous operatic and musical theater roles, concerts, and recitals in the US and abroad. In addition to IU and NYU, Professor Gill has taught at Eastern Kentucky University, Pace University, the University of Kentucky at Lexington, and the University of Colorado at Boulder in the Continuing Education program. A sought-after master clinician/guest lecturer, Professor Gill has taught/presented throughout the US and abroad in France, Germany, Italy, Portugal, Sweden, Czech Republic, South Korea, Poland, and Taiwan. His students perform in many of the most prestigious venues throughout the world.

Sophie Grimmer has performed widely as a soloist in opera, oratorio, theater, and on the concert platform, both in the UK and abroad (English National Opera (ENO); Royal National Theatre (RNT); Banff, Canada; Aldeburgh Festival; Shakespeare's Globe; Walt Disney Concert Hall, LA), under directors such as Simon McBurney, Sir Peter Hall, and Stephen Pimlott. Informed by her performing career, she works extensively in music education as a vocal professor at Trinity Laban Conservatoire of Music and Dance in London; devised voicework director at the Royal Academy of Dramatic Art (RADA); vocal consultant for National Youth Choirs of Great Britain (NYCGB); and soloist/creative director of music projects for Glyndebourne, ENO, Oxford Lieder Festival, and elsewhere. She has been funded by the Arts and Humanities Research Council (AHRC) at the UCL Institute of Education to research voice pedagogy in the Karnatic classical tradition of South India.

Helga Rut Gudmundsdottir PhD is an Associate Professor of Music Education at the University of Iceland, School of Education. She teaches courses in early childhood music methods as well as music pedagogy for elementary and middle school. Her research focuses on young children's musical perception and development. She has been a Visiting Professor at McGill University and the University of Montreal and a visiting scholar at the BRAMS laboratories in Montreal. She was granted a Fulbright Scholar grant for the academic year 2016–2017. She is on the board of the MERYC (European Network for Music Educators and Researchers of Young Children). Dr Gudmundsdottir has developed a method in early childhood music in her home country of Iceland and runs a research-based practice that gives courses, trains teachers, and develops materials for teaching music in early childhood. She published a book and CD with Icelandic children's songs in 2015.

Valentine Harding is an early-years music practitioner and an independent researcher in ethnomusicology, with a multi-disciplinary background in mental health, counseling and psychotherapy, and music. She holds an MSc in Intercultural Psychotherapy from University College London (2002) and an MMus in Ethnomusicology from Goldsmiths College (2009). Her special interest is the music of Bengal (West Bengal and Bangladesh). She has had a long-term association with this geographical area since 1971 in other contexts as well, e.g. health and social care. She is currently working on an oral history project recording the lives of Bengali musicians living in the UK.

Scott Harrison PhD is Director of the Queensland Conservatorium at Griffith University in Brisbane, Australia. He has taught singing and music in Primary, Secondary, and Tertiary environments. He has over twenty years of experience in performance of opera and music theater as both singer and musical director. Professor Harrison's recent publications include *Perspectives on Teaching Singing* (2010), *International Perspectives on Males and Singing* (2012), *Research and Research Education in Music Performance and Pedagogy* (2013), and *Teaching Singing in the 21st Century* (2014). He has grants from the Office for Learning and Teaching and the Australia Research Council.

Christian T. Herbst PhD is an Austrian voice scientist. He has studied voice pedagogy at Mozarteum University, Salzburg, Austria, and has worked as a voice pedagogue for several years. Driven by his interest in the physics and the physiology of voice, he enrolled in a PhD program in Biophysics at the Palacky University in Olomouc, Czech Republic, from which he graduated in 2012. He currently works on Comparative Biomechanics of Mammalian Sound Production, a project funded by an *APART* grant from the Austrian Academy of

Sciences. The focus of Christian's scientific work is both on singing voice physiology and on the physics of voice production in mammals. He has received a number of international scientific awards and has published, among others, in the prestigious *Science* journal.

Joy Hill is a choral conductor at the Royal College of Music Junior Department in London, UK and is actively involved in artistic research in relation to choral performance practice. She has worked as a conductor and teacher at The Purcell School, as Senior Lecturer in Music and Music Education at the University of Roehampton and the UCL Institute of Education, and as a member of the Centre for Performance Science at the Royal College of Music. Awarded a Winston Churchill Fellowship for choral conducting in Sweden and an Arts Council England Bursary to work with choirs in Kaunas, Lithuania, Joy has long been committed to performing the work of student composers along with established contemporary composers. She has guest conducted leading youth choirs, has been a presenter and adjudicator in Japan, Estonia, Latvia, South Africa, Uganda, Slovenia, Greece, the US, and China, and is a member of the artistic committee for the World Youth Choir

Robert E. Hillman PhD, CCC-SLP is currently the Co-Director and Research Director of the Center for Laryngeal Surgery and Voice Rehabilitation at the Massachusetts General Hospital, Professor at Harvard Medical School (Surgery), and Director of Research Programs at the MGH Institute of Health Professions. His research has been funded by governmental and private sources since the mid-1980s. He has produced over 150 publications focusing on mechanisms for normal and disordered voice production, evaluation and development of methods for alaryngeal (laryngectomy) speech rehabilitation, development of objective physiologic and acoustic measures of voice and speech production, and evaluation of methods used to treat voice disorders. Dr Hillman has received over ten major awards for his work, including the Honors of the American Speech-Language-Hearing Association (2011) which is the highest award that the Association can bestow to "recognize individuals whose contributions have been of such excellence that they have enhanced or altered the course of the Professions."

Evangelos Himonides PhD held the University of London's first ever lectureship in music technology education. He is now Reader in Technology, Education and Music at University College London (UCL), where he teaches extensively on the Master's program in Music Education and supervises doctoral and post-doctoral researchers. Evangelos edits the Society for Education and Music Psychology Research (SEMPRE) conference series, is associate editor of *The Journal of Music, Technology and Education (JMTE)*, associate editor of *Logopedics Phoniatrics Vocology*, and associate editor of *Frontiers in Psychology*. Dr Himonides has developed the free online technologies for Sounds of Intent (soundsofintent. org & eysoi.org) and is a Chartered Fellow (FBCS CITP) of the British Computer Society.

David M. Howard is the Founding Head and Professor of the new Department of Electronic Engineering at Royal Holloway, University of London, which has been set up to attract more young women into engineering. Previously, David was Head of the Audio Research Group and Head of Department of Electronics at the University of York. David's research interests relate to human voice production and human hearing. Current work includes tuning in *a cappella* choral music, voice analysis and electronic synthesis, the vocal tract organ as a new musical instrument, and vocal change in boys and girls through puberty. In 2016, David was elected Fellow of the Royal Academy of Engineering. Musically, David conducts Feltham Choral and is the organist at St. Mary's Thorpe.

Eric J. Hunter PhD is an Professor at Michigan State University in Communicative Sciences and Disorders. Eric's research interests include biomechanics of speech articulators, biomechanical models of the vocal system, muscle mechanics and muscle models, voice recording, and signal processing. For the last 15 years, Dr Hunter has researched occupational voice use, specifically examining voice disorders in elementary and secondary school teachers. The goal of this research is to quantify the risk for and recovery from tissue damage, as well as to ascertain why female teachers appear to be at greater risk. Dr Hunter earned his bachelor's and master's degrees in Physics and Mathematics from Brigham Young University, with an emphasis in acoustics and vibration. He completed his training in the area of speech and hearing science and received his doctorate from the University of Iowa.

Dag Jansson is Associate Professor of Arts Management at the Oslo Business School. He earned his PhD from the Norwegian Academy of Music and his master's degree in musicology from the University of Oslo. Prior to his music and academic career, he was a business consultant and leader, educated as an engineer from the Norwegian University of Science and Technology, and earned a Master of Business Administration from INSEAD in France. He is the conductor of the chamber choir Vox Humana. In addition to having conducted other chamber choirs, he has also worked extensively with non-auditioned community choirs and workplace choirs. Based on the combined music and business experience, he has experimented with singing and conducting as part of team and leadership development programs. Esthetic leadership is also one of his ongoing research orientations. His book *Leading Musically* examines the nature of musical leadership in a choral setting and has just been published by Routledge in 2018 as part of the SEMPRE series.

Harald Jers holds master's degrees in conducting, music education/solo-singing, and physics from the University of Music Cologne, the University of Music Düsseldorf, and RWTH Aachen University (Germany). He is currently Professor of Choral Conducting at the University of Music and Performing Arts, Mannheim which includes a Conducting Centre Department, a unique institution in Europe. He teaches choral conducting, voice training, and leads all choral ensembles of the University with a special interdisciplinary research interest in choir and room acoustics. As a conductor of several orchestras and choirs, he has toured extensively through Europe, Asia, and the US and has been much in demand as leader of international master classes in conducting. He founded the chamber choir CONSONO, which has had TV and radio broadcasts, CDs, and diverse first prizes at several most respected international choir competitions. He was awarded a first prize by the Acoustical Society of America for his research in choir acoustics.

Karin Johansson is Professor of Music at Malmö Academy of Music, Lund University, Sweden. She is also a performing organist. After her PhD thesis *Organ Improvisation – Activity, Action and Rhetorical Practice* (2008), she has worked with the projects *(Re)thinking Improvisation*, funded by the Swedish Research Council, *Students' Ownership of Learning* based at the Royal Academy of Music, Stockholm, and research on higher music education, improvisation, and choral singing. Together with Ursula Geisler, she initiated the international research network Choir in Focus, funded by Riksbankens Jubileumsfond. At present, she is part of the project DAPHME (Discourses of Academization and the Music Profession in Higher Music Education), also funded by Riksbankens Jubileumsfond.

Gillyanne Kayes Gillyanne Kayes PhD is a singing voice specialist, pedagogue, and researcher, internationally recognized for her insight into function of singing voice. She has presented papers, given masterclasses, and led workshops at numerous conferences, including the Pan-European Voice Conference, the Wellcome Trust, the Physiology and Acoustics of Singing conference, the British Voice Association, and the ANATS and NEWZATS associations. Her published works include *Singing and the Actor: Successful Singing Auditions* (Bloomsbury Press), the *Singing Express* series (Harper Collins), and *This is a Voice* book commissioned by the Wellcome Trust (with Jeremy Fisher). Research publications include the *Journal of Voice* and the report from the VoiceEU project into the vocal health of amateur choral singers. Gillyanne currently holds a Visiting Professorship at the London College of Music and co-owns and runs Vocal Process Ltd., a nationally accredited voice education company providing continuing professional development for vocal trainers, choral leaders, and vocal performers.

Mary King studied English at the University of Birmingham, earned a PGCE at St Anne's Oxford, and completed the postgraduate opera course at the Guildhall School of Music and Drama. Her performing career encompasses a wide range of vocal genres, from opera, oratorio, chamber music and recital to musical theater and straight plays. She has been an Artistic Associate for English National Opera and on the faculties of the Royal Academy of Music, Royal Northern School of Music and Drama, and Guildhall School of Music and Drama. Currently, she is director of Voicelab at London Southbank Centre, has a busy teaching studio, and is a voice coach for shows in the West End of London. Publications include co-authorship of *The Singer's Handbook* (Faber, 2007) and a series of vocal repertoire collections with coaching notes, *The Boosey Voice Coach* (Boosey & Hawkes). She is a Member of Council for the Royal Philharmonic Society.

Boris A. Kleber PhD completed an MSc (2002) in Psychology at the University of Konstanz (Germany), received his doctorate in Neuroscience (2009) from the University of Tübingen (Germany), and was awarded a higher doctorate degree (Habilitation) in Psychology from the University of Tübingen (2016). His scientific interest and passion for the singing voice is strongly influenced by his early musical experiences. During his PhD, he worked with EEG Neurofeedback and pioneered fMRI research with trained singers as a model for experience-dependent plasticity of the vocal motor system. This work was crucially developed during his post-doctoral research with Professor Robert Zatorre at the Montreal Neurological Institute (QC, Canada). Since 2016, Dr Kleber has been affiliated with the Center for Music in the Brain, Aarhus University (Denmark), where he integrates his previous work on vocal motor control in trained singers with the concept of predictive coding.

Susan Knight PhD is a choral conductor, educator, researcher, and producer. She advocates singing for its intrinsic esthetic value, but also as a powerful engine for human health/enrichment and for the creation of empathic community. Published in professional journals, conference proceedings, and musical editions, Susan presents at national/international conferences and is active in governance. She is Chancellor of Memorial University (Newfoundland/Labrador, Canada) and Visiting Researcher, International Music Education Research Centre, UCL Institute of Education. Susan is Founder/Chair of

Growing the Voices, a comprehensive agency developing access to, diverse opportunities for, and increased awareness of singing's value across the lifespan. She founded *Shallaway Choir* and *Festival 500*, and has an extensive discography and filmography. Susan holds bachelor degrees (music/music education, Memorial University), an MA (University of St. Thomas. Minnesota), and a PhD (UCL Institute of Education). She has an honorary doctorate (LLB, Memorial University), and is invested in both the Orders of Canada and Newfoundland/ Labrador.

Malte Kob PhD received his Diploma in Electrical Engineering from Technical University Braunschweig where he also founded an amateur choir and started playing Jazz. His dissertation was defended in 2001 at RWTH Aachen University on singing voice synthesis. Since 2009, Malte Kob has been Professor at the Erich Thienhaus Institute of Detmold University of Music where he teaches fundamentals of electrical and acoustical engineering at Bachelor, MSc, and PhD level. His research interests range from measurement technique via voice physiology to music-room-listener interaction.

Filipa M.B. Lã PhD is an internationally recognized scientist in voice science and pedagogy, singer, and singing teacher with a background in Biology and a Masters and PhD in vocal performance studies. She is currently undertaking research at the Centre for Social Sciences and at the Institute of Interdisciplinary Research, both at the University of Coimbra in Portugal, where she investigates issues related to professional voice users' health and well-being, developing strategies to optimize voice education, and professional voice users' working conditions. Additional projects involve descriptions of cross-cultural studies in different singing styles. Her work has been recognized with several international awards, including the *Van Lawrence Award*, by the National Association of Teachers of Singing, and by The Voice Foundation in 2015.

Karen M. Ludke PhD is a Senior Lecturer in English Language at Edge Hill University, UK. After graduating from the University of Michigan, where she studied English and French, Dr Ludke completed her PhD, *Songs and Singing in Foreign Language Learning*, within the Institute for Music in Human and Social Development at the University of Edinburgh. From 2009 to 2012, she contributed to the European Commission-funded European Music Portfolio—A Creative Way into Languages project. In 2013–2014, Dr Ludke was a Postdoctoral Fellow for the Advancing Interdisciplinary Research in Singing project, working with Dr Annabel Cohen and the AIRS Digital Library team, University of Prince Edward Island, Canada. Dr Ludke's research focuses on the potential of music and singing to support language learning, and the role of individual learner differences in this process. She is a reviewer for journals including *Psychology of Music* and *Studies in Second Language Learning and Teaching*.

Lynne Murray has performed extensively as a soloist in opera, oratorio, and concert throughout Australia and in New Zealand, Germany, and the UK. Her roles include Lucia in *Lucia di Lammermoor*, the Queen of the Night in *The Magic Flute*, Sophie in *Der Rosenkavalier*, and Olympia in *The Tales of Hoffmann*. She has extensive experience as a singing teacher and has a particular interest in teaching older singers. She runs courses on vocal technique for choirs, among them Sydney Philharmonia Choirs, for whom she acts as a vocal coach. Her article on teaching older singers can be found in the 2016 edition of *Australian Voice*.

Garyth Nair PhD (deceased) was an internationally recognized voice researcher/teacher, best known for his two books, an in-depth guide to the use of spectrography in the voice studio (*Voice: Tradition and Technology*, Singular Publishing, 1998) and his compendium of voice science's practical application in the voice studio (*The Craft of Singing*, Plural Publishing, 2007). This writing led to Professor Nair presenting papers and workshops worldwide. Commenced in cooperation with, and now continued by, Dr Angelika Nair, this work branched out to include ultrasound as both voice research and biofeedback tools. He was a graduate of Westminster Choir College and New York University, and was a Professor of Music at Drew University (Madison, NJ). In addition to his work in voice science and pedagogy, Garyth enjoyed long careers as both a professional conductor and singer. Professor Nair was also a member of the *Journal of Voice* editorial board.

John Nix has a Bachelor of Music (voice performance, University of Georgia), a Masters of Music Education (arts administration, Florida State University), a Masters of Music (voice performance, University of Colorado), and a Certificate in Vocology (University of Iowa). He is Professor of Voice and Voice Pedagogy at the University of Texas-San Antonio. His mentors include Barbara Doscher (singing, pedagogy) and Ingo Titze (voice science). His students have sung with the Santa Fe, Arizona, Chautauqua, St. Louis, Nevada, Omaha, and San Antonio opera companies. In addition to his active voice teaching studio, he researches voice pedagogy, literature, and acoustics, and has produced 38 published articles and eight book chapters. Professor Nix is editor and annotator of *From Studio to Stage: Repertoire for the Voice* (Scarecrow, 2002), vocal music editor for the *Oxford Handbook of Music Education*, and one of three general editors for the *Oxford Handbook of Singing*.

Peter Pabon studied biochemistry, signal processing, and sonology at Utrecht University. His professional career started in 1983 as a part-time researcher with Professor Plomp at VU University in Amsterdam on a project called Objective Recording of Voice Quality, and he worked at Utrecht University as a teacher/researcher on (singing) voice analysis and speech and music acoustics from 1983 until 2011. He initiated a project for singing voice synthesis and analysis at the Royal Conservatoire that later resulted in a cooperative project with the singing department to monitor voice change as an effect of voice training. In 2002, he founded Voice Quality Systems, a company in which he develops the voice quality recording system Voice Profiler, which is used in many clinical centers, conservatories, and schools for professional voice training. Peter Pabon lectures at the Royal Conservatory, The Hague and is currently finishing his PhD thesis at KTH Stockholm, which has generated several papers and presentations on Voice Range Profile (VRP) recording methodology, the effects of voice training, and the spectral variation over the VRP.

Diana Parkinson is a PhD student at UCL Institute of Education undertaking research into community singing in the UK. She sings in a number of choirs and is co-chair of the Royal Free Music Society. For the last few years, she has also been working with Streetwise Opera, a charity that uses community singing to help people who have experienced homelessness to make positive changes in their lives and, as such, has seen its particular value in helping individuals overcome adversity. These experiences informed her choice of research area for an MSc in Professional Practice in Research Methods (for which she was awarded a distinction) from Middlesex University and have led to her current PhD study.

Lisa Popeil has studied piano, voice, and composition, earned an MFA in Voice from California Institute of the Arts, and has taught professionally for over forty years. Lisa is the creator of the Voiceworks® Method for singers, the *Total Singer* DVD, the *Daily Vocal Workout for Pop Singers* CD, and is co-author of the book *Sing Anything: Mastering Vocal Styles*. As a professional singer, Lisa has performed and recorded with the Pasadena Symphony, Frank Zappa, "Weird Al" Yankovic, and, in addition, her self-titled pop album was a Billboard "Top Album Pick." Her voice research projects have focused on belting voice production, vibrato, vocal registers, and the comparison of classical and commercial vocal genres. She is a member of many organizations, including the Voice Foundation (on the Advisory Board), the National Association of Teachers of Singing, SAG/AFTRA (Screen Actors Guild/American Federation of TV and Radio Artists), ASCAP (American Society of Composers and Publishers), and is a voting member of NARAS (National Academy of Recording Arts and Sciences, the Grammy® organization).

Costanza Preti PhD is an Honorary Research Associate in the Department of Culture, Communication and Media at UCL Institute of Education. She holds a Masters in Music Education, a Masters in Research Methods, and a Doctorate of Philosophy from the Institute of Education, University of London, as well as a first-class BA in Literature and the Arts from the University of Florence. Her research focuses on music and health and was funded by the UK Economic and Social Research Council (ESRC) and the Wingate Foundation. She has worked on six major research evaluation projects, including those sponsored by the Italian and English Ministries for Education. From 2014 to 2015 she was Postdoctoral Research Fellow at the Centre for Arts as Wellbeing, University of Winchester, UK.

Nandhu Radhakrishnan PhD is an Associate Professor and the Director of the Voice and Vocology Clinic at the Department of Speech and Hearing Sciences at Lamar University in Beaumont, Texas. He received his doctorate from Bowling Green State University, Ohio and completed his clinical fellowship at the University of Pittsburgh Voice Center, Pennsylvania. His areas of specialty include clinical, professional, and performance voice issues. He has published chapters and articles related to voice science and has conducted national and international workshops related to assessment and intervention of voice. He is a member of various organizations, including the Voice Foundation, Pan-American Vocology Association, and the Voice and Speech Trainers Association. Apart from his voice-related professional life, he is a stage artist, choreographer, and hobby-chef.

John S. Rubin MD FACS FRCS is a Consultant ENT Surgeon at The Royal National Throat Nose and Ear Hospital, a part of The University College London Hospital NHS Trust. He is previous Clinical Director (2003–2009), and previous Chair of the Consultant Forum (2009–2016), as well as Lead Clinician of the Voice Disorders Unit. He is Honorary Consultant ENT Surgeon at the National Hospital for Neurology & Neurosurgery, which is also a part of the University College London Hospital NHS Trust, and where he co-chairs the Voice and Swallowing Unit with Dr Ruth Epstein. John is Visiting Honorary Professor at City, University of London as well as Honorary Senior Lecturer at University College London. His particular interests lie in voice disorders and laryngeal surgery. He has written extensively, including several books, numerous articles, and chapters, and regularly lectures on voice-related topics. Mr. Rubin has served in multiple capacities on many international editorial and scientific boards and committees. He is immediate past Chairman of the Board of Trustees and Honorary Treasurer of ENT UK. He is also a past-President of the Collegium Medicorum Theatri (2009–2012 term); founding member of the European Academy of Voice and of the British Laryngological Association (where he is currently on its Board). He is President-elect and current Treasurer of the British Voice Association.

Klaus R. Scherer PhD (Harvard) has held Professorships at the University of Pennsylvania and the Universities of Kiel, Giessen, and Geneva. He is currently an Honorary Professor at the University of Geneva and the University of Munich. His extensive work on different aspects of emotion, in particular vocal and facial expression and emotion induction by music, has been widely published in international peer-reviewed journals. Klaus Scherer is a Fellow of several international scientific societies and a member of several learned academies. He founded and directed the Swiss Center for Affective Sciences, held an Advanced Grant of the European Research Council, and has been awarded honorary doctorates by the University of Bologna and the University of Bonn.

Harm K. Schutte MD-ENT PhD is retired since 2007 from the position of Professor of ENT-Phoniatrics at the University of Groningen. He was trained as a researcher on voice in the Institute of Medical Physics under Professor Dr Janwillem van den Berg, who developed the Myoelastic-Aerodynamic Theory of Voice production. Schutte did thesis work on the aerodynamic characteristics (pressure, flow, and efficiency) of voice production, including professional singing. The professional voice was subject in numerous direct in-vivo measurements of pressure below and above the glottis, along with EGG and Audio, executed together with Donald Miller in the development of VoceVista. The visual evaluation of the vocal folds vibration pattern improved significantly under the development of videokymography in Groningen.

Desmond Sergeant PhD studied voice, piano, and conducting at the Royal College of Music, London, and at the Guildhall School of Music and Drama. He gained a doctorate from the University of Reading in 1969, and has worked in higher education since 1961, teaching in Universities in England and the US. He is currently Visiting Fellow at UCL Institute of Education. He has published widely in the fields of voice research and music cognition and has special interests in childhood development of musical abilities and pre-pubertal voice development. His publications have appeared in many languages. He was the founding editor of the international research journal *Psychology of Music* and in 1987 was nominated Distinguished Foreign Scholar by the Mid-America University Association. In 2005, he was the recipient of a Lifetime Achievement Award by the Society for Education, Music and Psychology Research (SEMPRE). His works include several music-dramas for young players.

Tara K. Stadelman-Cohen BM, MS, CCC-SLP is a voice pathologist/singing health specialist at the Massachusetts General Hospital Center for Laryngeal Surgery and Voice Rehabilitation. Tara received a Bachelor's degree in music and completed her Master's degree in Communicative Disorders. She currently performs acoustic and aerodynamic analysis of voice production in addition to laryngeal endoscopy for voice assessment; she also provides voice therapy with clinical specialization in rehabilitation of the injured professional voice. She is an instructor at the Massachusetts General Hospital Institute of Health Professions in Communicative Disorders and a part-time faculty member in the vocal pedagogy programs at the Boston Conservatory of Music at Berklee, New England Conservatory, and Boston

University. Co-authored publications have appeared in the *American Speech-Language-Hearing Association (ASHA) Leader, Journal of Voice*, and *Laryngoscope*. She is a member of the American Speech-Language-Hearing Association (ASHA) and the National Association of Teachers of Singing (NATS).

Brad Story PhD is Professor of Speech, Language, and Hearing Sciences at the University of Arizona. After receiving his Bachelor's degree in Applied Physics from the University of Northern Iowa, Brad worked in industry as an engineer where he developed computer models and instrumentation systems for designing and measuring the performance of mufflers. Motivated by an interest in the production and perception of sound, he obtained the PhD degree in Speech and Hearing Science at the University of Iowa, and then held post-doctoral research positions at the University of Iowa and at the Denver Center for the Performing Arts. His current research is focused on the use of computer models to aid in understanding how the shapes, sizes, and movements of both the voice source components and the vocal tract contribute to the sounds of speech and singing. He also teaches courses in acoustics, speech science, and speech perception.

Johan Sundberg PhD was awarded a personal Chair in Professor of Music Acoustics in 1979 at KTH Stockholm (retired 2001). His main research areas are the function, acoustics, and expressivity of the singing voice and the theory of music performance. He has published more than 300 scientific articles and supervised or co-supervised more than twenty doctoral students. He is a member of the Royal Swedish Academy of Music and Doctor Honoris Causa at the University of York, UK, the National University of Athens, Greece, and l'Université de Liège, Belgium. His book *Röstlära* (*The Science of the Singing Voice*), translated into English, German, Japanese, and Portuguese, summarizes the status of voice research. He also has written a book on music acoustics (*The Science of Musical Sounds*, 1991) and has been editor or co-editor of numerous conference and seminar proceedings. He has had extensive experience also of performing music, both as a chorister and as a solo singer.

Jan G. Švec PhD is a leading Czech physicist performing basic research on human voice production. He worked as a Research Scientist at the Groningen Voice Research Lab, University of Groningen in the Netherlands and at the National Center for Voice and Speech in Denver, CO, USA. Since 2007, he has been in the Czech Republic at the Palacky University Olomouc and is also affiliated with the Voice Centre Prague. His research interests include voice measurement methodology, visualization of vocal fold vibration, non-linear dynamics of voice, singing, voice dosimetry and voice modeling. He designed videokymography, a method for high-speed visualization of vocal-fold vibrations, which is being used for advanced diagnosis of voice disorders. Jan has published over 100 scientific articles on human voice in journals and books, supervises doctoral students, collaborates with numerous research teams around the world and lectures world-wide.

Sten Ternström PhD received his MSc EE from KTH in Stockholm, joined the Music Acoustics group there in 1982, and became its Professor in 2003. His PhD thesis *Acoustical Aspects of Choir Singing* (1989) was the first major text on this subject, and its topic has remained central among his interests. Choir acoustics provides a convenient theme for pursuing diverse topics in voice analysis, voice and music synthesis, room acoustics, audio signal processing, and music perception. In parallel, he created software for voice analysis and signal processing. During the 2010s, his work has been concerned with re-search paradigms that recognize and account for the large variability between voices. Sten also teaches acoustics and audio technology in the School of Electrical Engineering and Computer Science at KTH. He is an Associate Editor of *Acta Acustica united with Acustica* and serves on several editorial boards.

Töres Theorell MD PhD is a physician with a specialty in internal medicine, cardiology, and social medicine. He has been researching stress (physiology, epidemiology, and intervention studies) since the 1960s. He was Director of the National Institute for Psychosocial Factors and Health between 1995 and 2006 and, at the same time, he was Professor of Psychosocial Medicine (mainly occupational) at the Karolinska Institute. His research interest in cul-ture and health started in the early 1980s and since then he has supervised several doctoral theses in that field. With collaborators, he has performed several studies of music and health, and published the book *Psychological Health Effects of Musical Experiences* (Springer, 2014). Recently, he has been collaborating with the Swedish Twin Registry in publishing studies on music experiences in relation to alexithymia (inability to handle emotions).

Alma Thomas holds a BA, MSc, and MPhil, and is an acclaimed sports psychologist and performance enhancement consultant currently working with the Institute of Psychology in London. She has served as the team psychologist to British Rugby Union and Rugby League teams and as a performance psychologist to the British track team at three Olympic Games and World and European Championships. Her work has covered assignments with elite performers in all fields: actors, dancers, instrumental musicians, and singers. She is the au-thor or co-author of several books on performance enhancement, including *Play the Exam Game* (1994) and *Power Performance for Singers* (1998, with Shirlee Emmons).

Sandra E. Trehub PhD studied economics and philosophy before obtaining her doc-toral degree in experimental psychology at McGill University in 1973. Since that time, she has taught and conducted research in the Department of Psychology at the University of Toronto, where she is Professor Emerita. Most of her research is conducted in laboratory contexts, but she has traveled across continents to observe cross-cultural differences in mu-sical interactions with infants. Among her scholarly honors are the Kurt Koffka Medal from Giessen University (Germany, 2012) and a Lifetime Achievement Award from the Society for Music Perception and Cognition (2013). Her research focuses largely on maternal singing and its consequences for infant development and on infants' and young children's perception of pitch and rhythmic patterns.

Maria Varvarigou PhD is a Senior Lecturer in Music at Canterbury Christ Church University, a Senior Researcher at the university's Sidney de Haan Centre for Arts and Health, and a Visiting Research Associate at UCL Institute of Education. Maria has been performing as solo singer, oboist, and chorister for many years. She has participated in several recordings of Greek traditional songs and has developed a great interest in performance practices of tra-ditional music. She completed her PhD in 2009 as a scholar of the AS Onassis Foundation. Her special areas of interest include ear-playing and performance practices of vernacular music, effective teaching and learning in higher and professional education, music and well-being, choral conducting education, and intergenerational music-making. Maria is one of the authors of the book *Active Ageing with Music* published by the IoE University Press.

Robert Walker PhD has been Director of Music in three specialist music schools in England, as well as full Professor in two universities in Canada (SFU and UBC) and Head of the School of Music and Music Education at UNSW in Australia. He is now Adjunct Professor in the School of Education at the University of New England, Australia and is recognized as a leading international scholar on musical development and culture. The author of over 100 research papers, ten single-authored books, and 25 chapters in books, Bob is now retired in rural New South Wales with his wife Myung, their parrots, DVDs, wine collection, and lovely garden.

Alan Watson PhD is a Reader in Anatomy and Neuroscience at the School of Biosciences, Cardiff University. He also runs a module at the Royal Welsh College of Music and Drama on the biological principles underlying musical performance and works with staff and students there on projects concerned mainly with breathing physiology in wind players and singers, posture, and embouchure muscle activity. He gives regular lectures for clinicians and performers at the British Association for Performing Arts Medicine and has been involved in the setting up of a Performing Arts Medicine MSc at University College London. His many public engagement activities include participation in events at the DANA Centre and Wellcome Collection and talks for the Wrexham Science Festival, the Cheltenham Music Festival, the Hay Festival, and the Menuhin Violin Competition; his book *The Biology of Musical Performance and Performance-related Injury* was published by Scarecrow Press in 2009.

Graham F. Welch PhD has held the UCL Institute of Education (formerly University of London) established Chair of Music Education since 2001. He is a Past President of the International Society for Music Education (ISME) (2008–2014) and elected Chair of the internationally based Society for Education, Music and Psychology Research (SEMPRE). He holds Visiting Professorships at universities in the UK and overseas and is a former member of the UK Arts and Humanities Research Council (AHRC) Review College for Music (2007–2015). Publications number approximately 350 and embrace musical development and music education, teacher education, the psychology of music, singing and voice science, and music in special education and disability. Publications are primarily in English, but also appear in Spanish, Portuguese, Italian, Swedish, Greek, Japanese, and Chinese. New publications in 2018 include an updated *Oxford Handbook of Music Education* (five volumes) and the *Oxford Handbook of Singing*. He is also working with Margaret Barrett (University of Queensland) on the forthcoming *Oxford Handbook of Early Childhood Early Music Learning and Development*. He was Chair of the Paul Hamlyn Foundation National Working Group on music education in England (http://www.inspire-music.org) from 2015–2017.

Jenevora Williams PhD is a leading exponent in the field of vocal health and singing teaching. After a successful career in Opera, Jenevora turned her attention to investigating healthy and efficient vocal function. Her deep understanding of the human voice is based on a combination of extensive academic study and practical experience. She was the first singing teacher to be awarded a PhD in voice science in the UK and won the 2010 BVA Van Lawrence Prize for her outstanding contribution to voice research. She is well known for her imaginative and rigorous training courses for singing teachers in the UK and Europe. As a teacher of singing, she works with professional singers of all ages, as well as working in Vocal Rehabilitation for BAPAM and the NHS in the UK.

Karen Wise PhD is Research Fellow and Lecturer in psychology and research methods at the Guildhall School of Music & Drama, London, UK. She has published on the psychology of singing and self-defined "tone deafness," and on creativity in performance. Her current externally funded research focuses on collaborative work with singing teachers and adult non-singers to investigate the journey of learning to sing in adulthood. It aims to understand the needs and development of adults who believe themselves unable to sing, and how they might best be facilitated in vocal learning and participation. Karen was previously Research Associate in the Centre for Musical Performance as Creative Practice (CMPCP) at the University of Cambridge and has held psychology teaching posts at the Royal Northern College of Music in Manchester and the University of Keele, UK. As a singer, she has performed in opera, oratorio, and recitals in the UK and Europe.

Sheila C. Woodward PhD is Professor of Music and Director of Music Education at Eastern Washington University, US. She is a native South African and earned her doctorate from the University of Cape Town. Sheila is a Past President of the International Society for Music Education and Vice President of the International Music Council. She previously served on the Editorial Board of the *International Journal of Music Education* (2010–2016) and the ISME Board of Directors (2004–2008). Her research focus is music and well-being. She explores this from before birth to adulthood, with studies on the fetus, neonate, premature infant, young child, at-risk youth, juvenile offender, and adult musician. She has published numerous articles, in addition to chapters in Benedict, Schmidt, Spruce, and Woodford's *The Oxford Handbook on Social Justice in Music Education* (Oxford, 2015) and in Malloch and Trevarthen's *Communicative Musicality: Narratives of Expressive Gesture and Being Human* (Oxford, 2009).

Yang Yang PhD is a solo singer in both Western classical and Chinese music. He received his PhD in music education from UCL Institute of Education. His doctoral research explored pedagogical challenges in the teaching and learning of traditional folk song performance (intangible cultural heritage) in higher education. This included an initial in-depth cultural inquiry into China's higher music education policies since the 1900s, as well as extensive fieldwork with associated acoustic and qualitative data analyses. He is currently a Assistant Professor at the Education University of Hong Kong, and an Honorary Research Fellow at the School of Music, University of Queensland. Recent research publications cover singing pedagogy, psycho-acoustics, music psychology, and STEAM.

Jean Mary Zarate PhD received her doctorate in neuroscience from McGill University, where she studied the neural correlates of auditory-motor integration during singing under the supervision of Robert Zatorre. She then moved to a Postdoctoral Fellowship at New York University, where she investigated the functional roles of the dorsal auditory stream with David Poeppel. She currently works as a full-time scientific editor at *Nature Neuroscience*.

PART 1

THE ANATOMY AND PHYSIOLOGY OF SINGING

CHAPTER 1

....

STRUCTURE AND FUNCTION OF THE SINGING VOICE

....

GILLYANNE KAYES

Introduction

SINGING and speaking are complex tasks involving physiological, neurological, aerodynamic, and psychological processes. When we listen to a voice, we hear and respond to its pitch, loudness, and timbre as well as to any linguistic content. Skilled singers are able to manipulate their pattern of vocal fold vibration and adjust vocal tract configuration to create their desired sound outcome (Welch 2005). The aim of this chapter, therefore, is to familiarize the reader with key structural aspects of the vocal mechanism and the physiology of vocal function as applied to singing voice.

Overview of the vocal mechanism

The voice is a complex biomechanism comprising several body systems that are adapted for singing and speech to operate as a functional unit (Titze 1994; Zemlin 1968). Phonation is not the primary function of the larynx, which serves important physiological functions such as airway protection (in swallowing), maintaining homeostasis (in respiration), and pressure-valving (in childbirth, defecation, and weight-lifting) (Hollien et al. 1999; Rubin 1998; Seikel et al. 1997). The respiratory system generates aerodynamic power for the oscillating vocal folds, giving the sound source for voiced sounds. The voice is also an acoustic instrument, in which the breath supplies the energy source, and some of the movable parts act as oscillators. The instrument of the voice, generally referred to as the vocal tract (see Figure 1.1), runs from the superior surface of the vocal folds to the exterior surface of the lips and comprises three parts:

1. Nasopharynx—extends from base of skull to soft palate.
2. Oropharynx—includes the space between the soft palate and glosso-epiglottic folds.

3. Laryngopharynx—from the glosso-epiglottic folds to the lower border of the cricoid cartilage.

Breathing and phonation are closely linked in vocal function: in singing and speech production the sound source can be "voiced"—a result of vocal fold vibration—or "unvoiced"—a result of air passing through a constriction above the vocal folds (Howard 1998). Vibration initiated by the vocal folds is known as phonation and several phonatory settings have been identified in the human voice (Abercrombie 1967; Laver 1980). A third and distinctive feature of vocal sound is the resonator, or "sound-shaper." At the level of the vocal folds, the vibration is a simple "buzz," analogous to the sound a trumpeter makes when blowing through the mouthpiece of the instrument. This basic waveform of the voice is modified by a highly moveable vocal tract that forms the upper end of the body's airway.

(Baken 1998; Sundberg 1987, 1998).

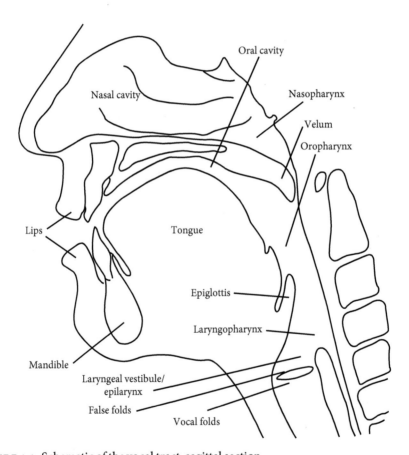

FIGURE 1.1 Schematic of the vocal tract, sagittal section.

Reproduced from Welch et al. (2000). Copyright © 2000, The VoiceCare Network.

RESPIRATION

The primary purpose of respiration is the exchange of gases between the outside atmosphere, blood, and cells. During the process of gaseous exchange oxygen must be absorbed from the atmosphere, and carbon dioxide expelled in order to maintain homeostasis within the body. Both passive and active forces are involved in respiration: surface tension in the alveoli, together with elastic forces in the alveoli walls and air passages of the chest cavity, generate the "elastic recoil" (passive); and more than twenty muscles provide the active force (Hixon 2006). Passive respiration or tidal breathing, takes place about 24,400 times a day (Bunch Dayme 2009) and is largely a reflexive action:

1. Neural impulses from the brain cause the diaphragm to contract, increasing the volume of the thoracic cavity, producing a negative pressure in the lungs relative to the outside air pressure.
2. Air is sucked into the lungs to counteract the negative pressure—*inspiration*.
3. Air pressure inside the lungs reaches the same level as outside and the airflow stops—*resting* level.[1]
4. The diaphragm relaxes and lungs and chest wall recoil—*expiration.*

The inspiratory and expiratory phases of the cycle may vary according to the task. In passive respiration they are approximately equal in time, whereas a shorter inspiratory phase and a relatively long expiratory phase may be expected in speaking (Hardcastle 1976), an effect considerably magnified in Western Lyric singing (Thomasson 2003a). However, in commercial music genres, such as Country and Western, respiratory behavior during singing is similar to that of speaking (Hoit et al. 1996).

Structural and functional elements of respiration

The respiratory system comprises structures and air passages in the torso, neck, and head. The lungs and pulmonary airways form the part of the system that receives the air and deals with gaseous exchange. The pulmonary airways (nose, mouth, larynx, trachea, and bronchial tubing system) connect air inside the body with the air outside. Movements of the rib cage, diaphragm, abdominal wall, and abdominal contents contribute to alterations in the dimensions of the insides that result in expiration or inspiration. Effectively, the respiratory apparatus operates as a negative pressure pump, sucking air into the lungs.

The diaphragm and the lungs act as a functional unit in respiration: when the dimensions of the thoracic cavity change, lung volumes will change with it. The rib cage and abdomen

---

[1] Note that the "resting level" defined by Hixon (1987), is not a temporal resting phase, since once pressures have been equalized, expiration will follow almost immediately. The temporal resting phase is more likely to occur after expiration.

form two major cavities of the torso, divided by the diaphragm. Shared boundaries and pleural linkage[2] enable these to act as a two-part unit: the rib cage, and the diaphragm-abdomen (Hixon 1987).

The rib cage wall comprises a framework of bone and cartilage that encircles the lungs and attaches to the thoracic spine at the back of the torso and to the sternum at the front. The abdominal wall encases the lower torso, wrapping around the front, sides and back to form a cylinder. The abdominal wall also attaches to the spine (lumbar, sacral, and coccygeal regions) and to the pelvic girdle. The diaphragm is a double dome-shaped sheet of muscle with a central tendon separating the thoracic and abdominal cavities (Bunch Dayme 2009; Hixon 2006). Changes in dimension of the thoracic cavity are controlled by the ribs and sternum and the diaphragm. The abdominal muscles can also act on the diaphragm to alter dimensions of the thoracic cavity during expiration. Muscles that enlarge the thoracic cavity are generally considered as muscles of inspiration, whereas those that decrease it are considered muscles of expiration. Some muscles may serve both inspiratory and expiratory functions, e.g. *latissimus dorsi* (Hardcastle 1976).

The diaphragm is the principal muscle of, and always active during, inspiration. According to Bunch Dayme (2009) the diaphragm is responsible for 60–80 percent of increased volume during deep inspiration. Although the ribs are active in passive expiration, their function is mainly to stiffen the rib cage wall to prevent the rib interspaces from being sucked inwards as pleural pressure lowers, so there will be minimal deformation of the rib cage wall (Hixon 2006). Hixon (2006) and Thomasson (2003a; 2003b) report that the diaphragm remains active for a short part of the expiratory cycle until elastic forces are balanced. In more active forms of respiration, such as are used in singing, the level of activity in the muscles of the rib cage wall, and the deformation of the rib cage and abdominal walls may alter considerably. It is thought that abdominal activity during expiration enables the diaphragm to stretch its muscle fibers, increasing their elasticity for a more effective response at inspiration, which would be advantageous to singers needing to take in large volumes of air between phrases. In terms of respiratory kinematics, both belly-in and belly out configurations have been observed in studies of expert singers (Hixon 1987; Thomasson 2003b). Figure 1.2 shows the muscles used in tidal inspiration (quiet breathing), and the main muscles of expiration.

Breath use in singing

For speaking and singing the respiratory system regulates loudness, pitch, linguistic stress, and also acts in organizing sounds into discrete units for phrases, words, and syllables. Singers may additionally impose breathing patterns to fit the phrase lengths and rhythmic structure of their musical material, making breathing for singing a "special act"

---

[2] Two membranes—the visceral and parietal pleura—link the external surfaces of the lungs to the inside of the thoracic wall, and to the superior surface of the diaphragm. A serous lubricating fluid fills the space between these two membranes, which allows for frictionless movement between them. Via this "pleural linkage," when the diaphragm contracts and the rib cage expands, the lungs expand with them.

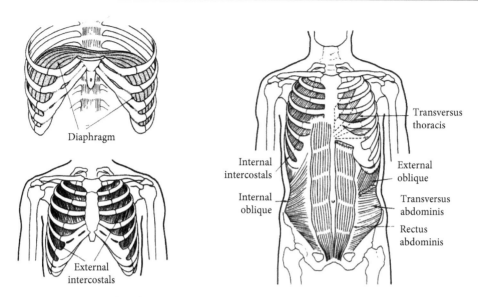

FIGURE 1.2 Muscles of inspiration (tidal breathing); main muscles of expiration.

Reproduced from Hixon et al. (1988), pp. 13 and 20. Copyright © 1988 Wiley-Liss, Inc., A Wiley Company.

of respiration (Hixon 2006). Functionally, the most important aspect of breath control in singing is to maintain an appropriate balance of subglottal pressure for the desired sound quality, dynamic level, and targeted pitch range. Subglottal pressure is a form of over-pressure, occurring when expired air flows against partially closed vocal folds. It is the principal component of vocal loudness and, to a lesser degree, of pitch (Sundberg 1987).

THE LARYNX

The larynx consists of a group of cartilages and one bone (see Figure 1.3), the latter suspended from above by the bony styloid process, which protrudes down from the skull base and attaches to the superior part of the sternum below.

As a suspensory mechanism the larynx is both moveable and flexible (Bunch Dayme 2009; Zemlin 1968) and muscular pulls can be exerted forward, backward, up, and down (Lieberman 2000).

Cartilages of the larynx

The *cricoid* cartilage forms the base of the larynx and sits on top of the trachea, connected via mucous membrane and connective tissue, which form an inner lining for both structures. The paired pyramidal *arytenoid* cartilages are positioned on the sloping upper border of the cricoid lamina. The cricoarytenoid joint allows for rocking and lateral

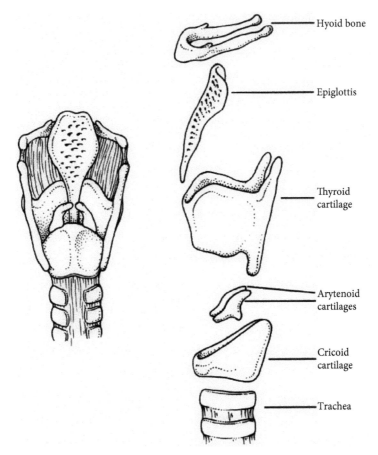

Hyoid bone

Epiglottis

Thyroid
cartilage

Arytenoid
cartilages

Cricoid
cartilage

Trachea

FIGURE 1.3 Larynx, rear and lateral view, exploded.

Reproduced from Kayes (2004), p. 20. Copyright © 2004, Bloomsbury Publishing PLC.

gliding movements of the arytenoids, rather like a saddle joint. On the apices of the ary-tenoid cartilages are two small *corniculate* cartilages, thought to act as buffers for the epi-glottis during swallowing (van den Berg et al. 1960). The *cuneiform* cartilages are paired rods of elastic cartilage that lie within the aryepiglottic fold. The *thyroid* cartilage consists of two plates of cartilage (laminae) fused at the front and wide apart at the back. In adult males the angle at which the plates are fused is more acute than in females. The thyroid has two sets of horns (cornu), both paired, with the inferior horn articulating with the cricoid cartilage. The *epiglottis,* made of soft elastic cartilage, is roughly oval in shape with a curled leaf appearance. It is attached via ligaments to the thyroid prominence and to the body of the hyoid bone above. A number of the intrinsic muscles of the larynx insert into the epi-glottis, their main function being to protect the larynx during swallowing. The horseshoe-shaped *hyoid bone* is not a structural element of the larynx but forms part of its supportive framework. As the only bone in the body not connected by a joint to any other bone, it is highly moveable. Approximately thirty muscles either originate or insert into the hyoid bone, many of which are important in speech production (Zemlin 1968). Via the hyoid bone, the larynx attaches to the muscles of the tongue, to the jaw, and to the base of the skull. Due to its positioning in relation to the larynx, the hyoid may have considerable impact on vocal function (Rubin 1998). The laryngeal structures are held together by a series of ligaments and membranes, allowing for freedom of movement while also protecting joints from over-extension.

The vocal folds

The paired *vocal folds* comprise several layers, each with different physical properties that allow for variation in the way they vibrate (Hirano 1977). The outer *epithelium* acts as a capsule to hold the shape of the vocal folds. Epithelial tissue lines nearly all of the cavities of the body, and the type that covers the vocal fold is *stratified squamous*, made up of layers of cells arranged rather like fish scales. The second layer, called the *lamina propria*, is subdivided into three sections: superficial, intermediate, and deep. The deepest layer of the vocal folds is the *thyroarytenoid* or vocalis muscle. The epithelium and superficial layer make up the *mucosa* of the vocal folds. The intermediate and deep layers make up the *vocal ligament*. A schematic view of the right vocal fold in cross section is shown at Figure 1.4, with the discrete layers indicated.

Structurally, the vocal folds also differ across their length: the *membranous portion* (beginning at the anterior commissure) making up about three-fifths of their length, and the *cartilaginous portion* (the vocal processes and medial surfaces of the arytenoids) the

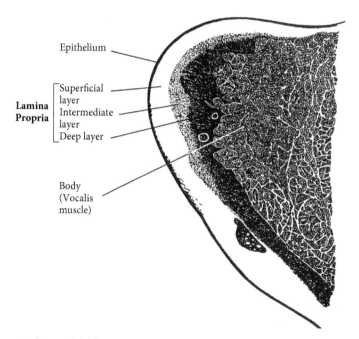

Epithelium

Lamina Propria
Superficial layer
Intermediate layer
Deep layer

Body (Vocalis muscle)

FIGURE 1.4   Right vocal fold in cross section, coronal view.

remainder. The membranous fold increases in stiffness towards both the front and back, thought to offer a degree of protection from the possible trauma of vibration (Hirano 1988). Healthy vocal folds in vibration produce a kind of "ripple wave," known as mucosal waves, which occur as the flexible cover moves across the body (Thurman and Welch 2000; Wendler et al. 2004). In louder phonation these movements are greater in amplitude from center to side, whereas in quieter phonation the amplitude of the mucosal waves will be smaller. Overall the texture of the membranous portion is that of a flexible, somewhat gelatinous, elastic membrane, making it more suitable than that of the cartilaginous portion for generating large mucosal waves. When the vocal folds vibrate but do not meet in phonation, either across their whole length or over part of their length, the resultant sound quality will be perceived as breathy, due to turbulent air noise in the sound signal. Vertical phase differences have also been observed in the vibratory patterns of the vocal folds and these have some significance in our understanding of vocal registers.

Role of intrinsic laryngeal muscles

Five key muscle groups[3] control the movements of the laryngeal cartilages:

1. Posterior cricoarytenoid muscles.
2. Lateral cricoarytenoid muscles.
3. Interarytenoid muscles, comprising transverse and oblique fibers.
4. Thyroarytenoid muscles, comprising the vocalis and muscularis.
5. Cricothyroid muscles, comprising the pars recta and pars oblique fibers.

The intrinsic laryngeal muscles serve both respiratory and phonatory functions. The four muscles (1–4) that attach to the arytenoids are all innervated by the recurrent laryngeal nerve; except for the transverse interarytenoid muscle, they are all paired. The cricothyroid muscles (5), situated outside the laryngeal cartilage, are separately innervated by the superior laryngeal nerve. Actions of these five main intrinsic muscles of the larynx are summarized below, together with commonly used acronyms.

Posterior cricoarytenoids [PCA]

i. Function mainly to open the vocal folds for breathing (abduction).
ii. Additional function is to stabilize the arytenoid cartilage, in opposition to the activity of the cricothyroid muscles.
iii. Can assist in elevation, elongation, and thinning of the vocal folds to produce higher frequencies.

---

[3] The complete list of intrinsic laryngeal muscles is more extensive and includes the aryepiglottic, thyroepiglottic, and ventricular muscles.

Lateral cricoarytenoids [LCA]

i.   Rotate the arytenoid, drawing the muscular process forward and the vocal process towards the midline, closing (adducting) the vocal fold.
ii. Also thin the vocal folds somewhat, pushing them down against the oncoming breath stream.

Interarytenoids [IA] (transverse and oblique muscles)

i.   The only unpaired muscle in the intrinsic muscle group.
ii. Acts to draw the arytenoids closer together, adducting the vocal folds at the cartilaginous portion.
iii. The oblique interarytenoids form an "X" across the posterior surfaces of the arytenoid cartilages and may have some muscle fibers continuous with the aryepiglottic muscle.

Thyroarytenoid muscles [TA] (vocalis and muscularis)

The thyroarytenoid muscle has two distinct parts: vocalis and muscularis. Their functions are quite different. The vocalis contains a high percentage of "slow twitch" muscle fibers that are well-adapted to sustained and accurate contractions for vocalizing, whereas muscularis' muscle fibers are mainly "fast twitch," suitable for rapid sealing of the larynx and more primitive vocalization (Rubin 1998).

i.   The vocalis forms the innermost (medial) layer of the vocal fold and is attached to the deep surface of the thyroid lamina and the vocal process of the arytenoid cartilage. It adducts, lowers, shortens, and thickens the vocal fold, also giving it a rounder edge.
ii. Contraction and relaxation of vocalis can significantly affect length, thickness and stiffness of the vibrating vocal folds.
iii. The muscularis attaches to the deep surface of the thyroid lamina and is lateral to the vocalis, attaching at the back to the muscular process of the arytenoid cartilage.
iv. Muscularis muscle fibers are thinner than vocalis fibers, with additional fibers running into the interarytenoid, which course vertically upwards through the laryngeal ventricle into the aryepiglottic fold. Acting as a unit, these muscles help to control and configure constriction of the aryepiglottic folds and the false vocal folds (Rubin 1998).

Cricothyroid muscles [CT]

i.   Fan-shaped muscles, diverging into two parts with oblique and anterior fibers.
ii. The largest of the intrinsic laryngeal muscles (Sataloff 1998) and the only ones that do not attach to the arytenoids.
iii. Enable movement around the cricothyroid joint, changing the position of the thyroid and cricoid cartilages relative to each other, and in so doing also alter length and tensioning of the vocal folds.

iv. A variety of configurations is possible: downward tilt of the thyroid to cricoid; up-ward tilt of the cricoid to thyroid; forward movement of the thyroid on the cricoid (Zemlin 1968). Any of these actions will increase the length and tension of the vocal folds, similar to the effect of pulling an elastic band, one strategy used by singers in pitch-raising.

The aryepiglottic and oblique interarytenoid muscles

The aryepiglottic muscles extend from the apex of the arytenoids to the epiglottis, with muscle fibers in the aryepiglottic folds; the aryepiglottic folds form the lateral rim of the entrance to the larynx, sharing muscle fibers with the oblique interarytenoids (see Figure 1.5).

   i. Act jointly to help close the larynx during swallowing (biological function).
  ii. Act jointly with the lateral cricoarytenoids to form a sphincter within the laryngeal tube (vocal function).
iii. Selective narrowing or widening of this region can produce a range of acoustic outcomes, used in singing to produce distinctive resonances (Welch et al. 2000).

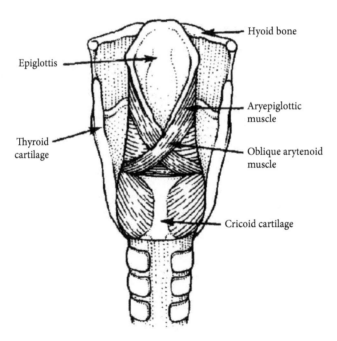

FIGURE 1.5 Posterior view of larynx, showing aryepiglottic and oblique arytenoid muscles.

The false vocal folds

Despite their name, the false vocal folds are not muscles, although some muscle fibers of the muscularis part of the vocal fold course upwards into them. Made mostly of fatty tissue and mucous glands, the false vocal folds are retracted in normal phonation (Bunch Dayme 2009). The mucous glands provide essential lubrication for the "true" vocal folds. In swallowing, the epiglottis, true and false vocal folds act together as a unit to close over the trachea so that foreign substances cannot enter the lungs.

Actions of intrinsic laryngeal muscles—discussion

Together with the biomechanical forces that govern them, the actions of the intrinsic laryngeal muscles can result in a variety of phonatory settings for controlling pitch, volume, and voice quality (Hardcastle 1976; Harris 2010; Hirano 1988). Broadly speaking, there is agreement on their main actions: enabling the vocal folds to open and close (*abduction* and *adduction*); adjusting the effective mass in vibration (resulting in *thin* or *thick* vocal folds); adjusting vocal fold length (resulting in *short* or *long* vocal folds); and adjusting tension (resulting in *stiff* or *lax* vocal folds) (Bunch Dayme 2009; Harris et al. 1998; Hirano 1988; Titze 1994; Vennard 1967; Zemlin 1968). Some researchers report that vocalists can be taught to consciously retract the false vocal folds to increase space in the laryngeal ventricle, and this is thought to be important in ensuring singer comfort in athletic voice use (Chapman 2006; Citardi et al. 1996; Mitchell at al. 2003). However, since the false vocal folds are not muscles and are therefore unable to respond to motor commands, it is likely this false vocal fold "retraction" is actually related to disengaging the muscularis so that the vocalis can work more efficiently during phonation (Harris 2010). It should be recalled that while muscles can move structures, an individual muscle is only capable of either contraction or relaxation: muscles do not extend. Extension is caused by the action of an antagonist muscle. Muscle contraction causes either a shortening of the distance between its points of origin and insertion, or an increase in its intrinsic tension (Sonninen et al. 1999). Muscles therefore rarely work in isolation: if one muscle is activated, another (or group of others) will be acting antagonistically or synergistically (Hollien et al. 1999). Dickson and Maue-Dickson (1996) reference multiple functions for many of the intrinsic muscles of the larynx, explaining that it is a matter of understanding the "functional potential" of the muscle groups involved.

Role of extrinsic laryngeal muscles

The overall role of the extrinsic laryngeal muscle group is to support and position the larynx as a whole within the neck. The larynx is therefore effectively slung from the hyoid bone by a series of muscle attachments and ligaments from above, below, front, and behind. This allows the larynx a degree of movement in all of these directions, as well as providing stabilization and support where attachments are fixed to bony structures

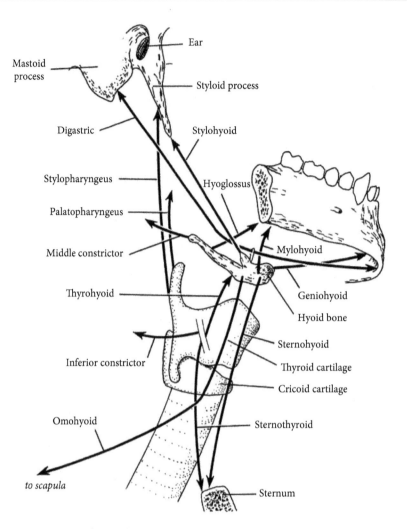

FIGURE 1.6 Direction of pull of extrinsic muscles of the larynx.

Reproduced from Bunch Dayme (2009), p. 127, DOI: 10.1007/978-3-211-88729-5, Springer Vienna,
Copyright © 2009, Springer Science and Business Media. With kind permission from
Springer Science and Business Media.

(Bunch Dayme 2009). Figure 1.6 shows a schematic view of the respective directions of muscle pull for the extrinsic muscles.

RESONANCE

Resonance can occur in any space where air molecules are directly excited by a sound source (Sundberg 1998). The shape of the structure holding the air has an important effect

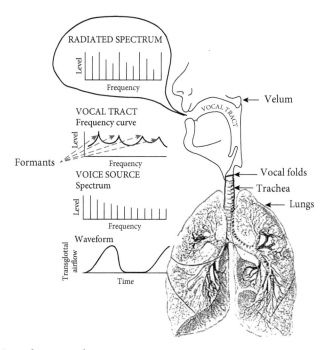

FIGURE 1.7 Sound input and output.

Reproduced from Sundberg (1987). Röstlära, 3rd edition, figure 2.10 © 2001, Proprius förlag.

on how the sound is eventually transferred from the vibrating vocal folds to the lips, and then radiated to the ear of the listener. When the harmonics of any given fundamental frequency are in close proximity to the resonant frequencies of the vocal tract, the sound levels of those harmonics are boosted, making the overall sound levels louder. The schematic diagram at Figure 1.7 shows how power generated from the lungs sets the vocal folds in vibration at a specific frequency, which is then radiated through the vocal tract, exiting through the lips.

The vocal tract is characterized by areas of resonance that enhance or damp specific frequencies, with the enhanced ones referred to as "formant frequencies."[4] The vocal tract is essentially a series of interconnected resonating "chambers," each with its own resonating frequencies. The area function of each chamber in relation to whole vocal tract length will determine the resonance characteristics of the singer's sound output. Broadly speaking, a larger chamber will enhance the lower harmonics of the spectrum, whereas a smaller chamber will enhance the higher harmonics (Sundberg 1987; Welch et al. 2000). Since the vocal tract is highly moveable, singers are able to selectively alter which harmonics are boosted and which are attenuated. The principal regions of vocal

---

[4] Formants numbered 1–5 are generally considered of most interest in singing voice with F1 and F2 defining the vowel quality and F3–F5 defining singer voice quality.

tract resonance are summarized below, together with muscle actions relevant to vocal function in singing.

Principal regions of vocal tract resonance

Pharynx

The pharynx is the most important resonator of the voice. It extends upwards into the mouth and nasal cavities, wrapping around the larynx like a muscular sleeve (see Figure 1.8).

The size and shape of the pharynx largely defines the first formant (Sundberg 1998; Titze 1994). The whole pharynx can be widened or narrowed via the three constrictor muscles: superior, middle, and inferior. Arching of the soft palate at the upper end of the pharynx will also enlarge the resonating cavity (Welch et al. 2000); the whole pharynx may also shorten or lengthen via laryngeal raising or lowering, raising or lowering all the formants respectively.

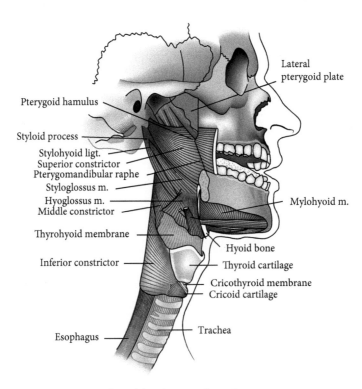

FIGURE 1.8 Constrictor muscles of the pharynx, lateral view.

Reproduced from Bunch Dayme (2009), p. 122, DOI: 10.1007/978-3-211-88729-5, Springer Vienna,
Copyright © 2009, Springer Science and Business Media. With kind permission from
Springer Science and Business Media.

Nasopharynx and muscles of the soft palate

The nasopharynx plays an important role in the mechanics of swallowing, as well as in vowel and consonant production.

1. Raising the soft palate (velum) will close off the nasopharynx from the oropharynx, which is necessary for production of orally released consonants and all non-nasalized vowels, and to create the intra-oral pressure needed to form the plosive and fricative consonants.
2. Lowering the soft palate will open the nasopharynx, allowing for a resonance coupling of the nasal and oral pharyngeal regions. A lowered velum is required for production of nasal consonants and nasalized vowels.

The soft palate itself can be raised, tensed, or relaxed. Raising the soft palate is effected by the *levator palatini* muscles creating a higher arch at the back of the oral cavity, increasing the resonating airspace. The *tensor palatini* muscles will pull the palate horizontally, producing a wider space at that point in the pharynx (Bunch Dayme 2009; Welch et al. 2000).

Oropharynx, tongue, jaw, and lips

The oropharynx offers the largest resonating space of the pharynx, extending from the soft palate to the inlet of the larynx. This area includes the soft palate, the tongue, and the jaw, all of which can act together or independently to change resonating quality (Bunch Dayme 2009). The root of the tongue and the hyoid bone are also in this region; movements of the tongue can have considerable impact on the oral pharyngeal space, either constricting or widening it (Chapman 2006; Sundberg 1998). The tongue is made up of a complex group of muscles, comprising four paired sets of intrinsic muscles (see Figure 1.9a) within the tongue body and numerous extrinsic muscles (see Figure 1.9b).

Bunch Dayme (2009) notes the following muscles from the extrinsic group as having an impact on singing:

1. *Genioglossus*—attaching to the jaw at the front (three muscle bundles form the main bulk of the tongue: acting as a whole they protrude the tongue; the anterior bundle draws the tip downwards; middle and posterior bundles draw the middle portion of the tongue down).
2. *Hyoglossus*—attaching to the hyoid below (depresses the sides of the posterior portion of the tongue).
3. *Styloglossus*—attaching to the skull above via the styloid process (contraction pulls the tongue upwards and backwards).
4. *Palatoglossus*—attaching to the pharynx behind (action depends on relative rigidity of its attachments: either pulling the soft palate downwards or raising the back and sides of the tongue). Together with the palatopharyngeus, the palatoglossus muscles form the posterior pillars of the fauces[5] of the oropharynx. These muscles, together with the levator palatinis, enlarge the resonant airspace at the back of the oral cavity.

---

[5] Also called *pillars of the fauces*.

(a)

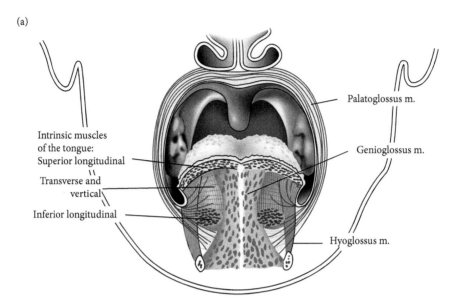

Palatoglossus m.

Intrinsic muscles
of the tongue:
Superior longitudinal

Genioglossus m.

Transverse and
vertical

Inferior longitudinal

Hyoglossus m.

(b)   Superior constrictor   Styloid process

Mastoid
process   Soft palate   Hard palate

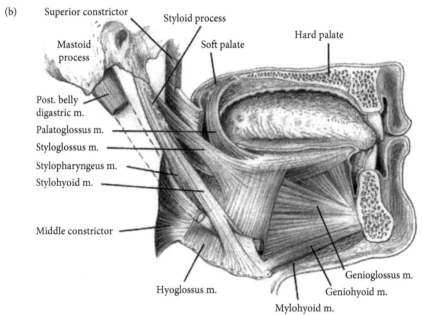

Post. belly
digastric m.
Palatoglossus m.
Styloglossus m.
Stylopharyngeus m.
Stylohyoid m.

Middle constrictor

Genioglossus m.

Hyoglossus m.   Geniohyoid m.

Mylohyoid m.

FIGURE 1.9   (a) Intrinsic muscles of the tongue and pillars of the fauces. (b) Extrinsic muscles of the tongue viewed from the right.

Reproduced from Bunch Dayme (2009), p. 155, DOI: 10.1007/978-3-211-88729-5_9,
Springer Vienna, Copyright © 2009, Springer Science and Business Media. With kind permission from
Springer Science and Business Media.

The tongue's intrinsic muscle group comprises four paired sets of muscles: *superior* and *inferior longitudinal* fibers, and *transverse* and *vertical* ones. These fibers intermingle with the fibers of the extrinsic muscles of the tongue and can alter the tongue shape: shortening and broadening (longitudinal fibers); narrowing and thickening (transverse fibers); flattening and broadening (vertical fibers). The superior longitudinal fibers can also curl the tip and sides of the tongue to form a convex shape.

The tongue plays a major role in shaping resonance of the oral cavity:

1. The second formant is particularly sensitive to tongue shape and positioning. For example, a high, fronted tongue (as in the palatal "y" sound) will raise the second formant, whereas if the tongue is "backed" close to the velar region, the second formant will be lowered (Sundberg 1987).
2. The tongue tip when advanced or retracted will raise or lower the third formant.
3. When the tongue body is pulled back it constricts the oral-pharyngeal resonating space and will raise the first formant (Sundberg 1998). This action is thought to contribute to "throaty voice quality", characterized by a raised first formant together with a lowering of the higher formants (Björkner 2008).

The jaw forms the front part of the oropharynx. The *mandible* (lower jaw) is controlled by the muscles of mastication (the *masseter, temporalis,* and *pterygoid* muscles), the most powerful muscles in the head. These muscles are in fact all elevators, rather than depressors of the mandible. The complex nature of the temporomandibular joint, by which the jaw is connected to the skull, allows for movements up, down, forward, and backward. The suprahyoid muscles (anterior belly of the digastric, the geniohyoid, and mylohyoid) all have the functional potential to lower the jaw (Dickson and Maue-Dickson 1996) but since these all attach to the movable hyoid, the hyoid must be stabilized in order for this to happen, which might compromise other laryngeal movements required for singing (Chapman 2006). Bunch Dayme (2009) stresses the importance of allowing *relaxation* of the elevator muscles so that gravity can take over when lowering the jaw for singing. According to Chapman (2006) the role of the jaw in word articulation for singing is less important than its role in resonance. Lowering the mandible will enlarge the resonating airspace in the mouth, thought to be particularly useful in high soprano singing, where the fundamental frequency may well be as high or higher than the first formant (Sundberg 1973). Together with the tongue, the main functional role of the lips in speech and singing is one of consonant articulation. Singers and speakers may also lengthen or shorten the vocal tract via lip widening or lip protrusion, thus raising or lowering all formant frequencies respectively.

The long muscles of the pharynx

Four paired longitudinal muscles help to suspend and elevate the larynx posteriorly: the *stylohyoids,* the *stylopharyngeus,* and the *salpingopharyngeus,* which joins with the *palatopharyngeus,* the latter attaching to the greater horn of the thyroid cartilage. These muscles are long and slender. Their action will contribute to raising or lowering of the larynx, thus altering the resonant airspace in the vertical dimension (Bunch Dayme 2009).

Laryngopharynx or hypopharynx

The inferior part of the pharynx includes the opening of the larynx which is formed by the epiglottis and aryepiglottic folds (Dickson and Maue-Dickson 1996). This region, also called the hypopharynx or epilarynx, extends from the inlet of the larynx to the base of the cricoid cartilage. Its borders are the free upper edge of the epiglottis (anteriorly), the aryepiglottic folds (laterally) and the interarytenoid folds (posteriorly). Selective narrowing or widening of this region has been identified with a range of acoustic outcomes such as the singer's formant (Sundberg 1974, 1998) and "twang" and "belting" voice qualities (Estill et al. 1994). Using simulated models of the vocal tract, Story et al. (1996) demonstrated that a narrowed epilarynx can act as "attractor" for all formant frequencies of the vocal tract, thus increasing sound levels of those resonances when desired.

CONTROL OF PITCH AND RANGE IN SINGING

The most fundamental element of voiced sound is produced by the vibrating vocal folds, which "chop" the air stream into short bursts of airflow. Under normal circumstances,[6] air pressure inside the lungs must be greater than outside in order for this to happen, and the glottis either closed or partially closed (Baken 1998; Sundberg 1998). This closing of the glottis interrupts the air stream, causing excitation of the vibrating air molecules in the vocal tract, and provides the raw material of voiced sound, the glottal wave. Periodicity is a feature of harmonic motion, and healthy vocal folds cycle in regular periods. A glottal wave is produced by a closed or partially closed glottis, and for each period there is a closed and open phase. The number of vocal fold cycles per second is directly related to fundamental frequency [f_o], the quantitative correlate of pitch. Due to the mechanical properties of the vocal folds and their relationship with the surrounding structures and muscle groups, the frequency of vocal fold vibration can be adjusted in more than one way.

Means of adjusting frequency

Changes of length and tensioning

Changes of length and tension in the vocal folds can be effected by the cricothyroid muscles, similar to pulling the two ends of an elastic band.

When the thyroid cartilage is tilted as shown in Figure 1.10, the longer vocal folds will present a greater surface area to the pressurized air below, making that pressure more effective in pushing the vocal folds apart during the open phase of the cycle. This allows the vocal folds to separate more quickly, shortening the cycle for pitch increase (Baken 1998). Additionally, the vocal fold cover and ligament will be more stretched, enabling the vocal folds to snap back more quickly after being "plucked," allowing for increased repetition of cycles.

---

[6] Phonation is possible during a state of "negative pressure" in the lungs in relation to outside atmospheric pressure; this usually occurs towards the end of a sung or spoken phrase.

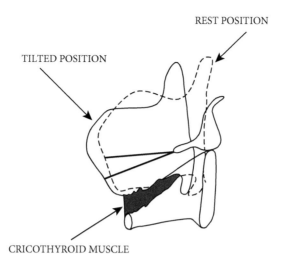

REST POSITION

TILTED POSITION

CRICOTHYROID MUSCLE

FIGURE 1.10 Schematic showing the action of the cricothyroid muscles, which lengthen and thin the vocal folds (heavy black lines).

Reproduced from Sataloff (2006), p. 71, figures 5–6, San Diego, CA: Singular Publishing Group Inc © 2006, The Authors.

An alternative mechanism for changing length and tensioning of the vocal folds is that of relaxing the vocalis muscle itself. In this instance, the PCA muscles act as antagonists to TA (Harris 1998), and the overall length of the more lax vocal folds will be greater. Since the vocal fold will also be somewhat floppier (with only the superficial layer active in vibration) it is likely to require a higher driving air pressure to vibrate faster (Roubeau et al. 1987; Sundberg 1990; Thurman et al. 2004).

Changing stiffness

The vocalis muscle is capable of both isometric and isotonic contraction (Dickson and Maue-Dickson 1996; Harris et al. 1998). Thus the frequency may be raised by increasing stiffness of the body of the vocal fold itself. In this instance the vocalis muscle will contract, working antagonistically against the CT muscles, also stiffening the vocal fold and thus contributing to a shorter vibration cycle.

Varying subglottal pressure

When the vocal folds are stretched and stiffened for pitch-raising they require a higher driving pressure from the lungs (subglottal pressure). In theory, if a singer increases subglottal pressure while holding the same pitch, there is a danger of increasing frequency as well as loudness.

It should be noted that the above mechanisms for pitch adjustment are not mutually exclusive: thus if there are changes of length and tensioning in the vocal folds, singers will need to adjust subglottal pressure (Sundberg 1990). Mainstream pedagogical and scientific literature cites the CT muscles as the primary mechanism for pitch increase (Austin

1996; Titze 1994; Titze et al. 1989; Vennard 1967), but isometric contraction has been noted in a number of studies of pitch control in both speech and singing (Lam Tang et al. 2008; Sonninen et al. 1999). It seems likely that singers of different types may favor different strategies, and at different points in their vocal range.

Registers in singing

Registration is an aspect of phonation, primarily based on changing vocal fold shapes (effective mass in vibration, length, and tension) and vibratory patterns through the singer's pitch range. Qualitative changes in sound that are heard as singers move through the vocal range are often attributed to a change of vocal register, or "register transition." Singers are known to make acoustic adjustments to facilitate or disguise register transitions, and it has been suggested that not all register changes are in fact mechanistic, but may be acoustic. Due to the difference in pitch range available to the male and female voice there is also a different use of registers between the genders, which may also be influenced by the esthetic of the musical performance culture (see Fisher, Kayes, and Popeil; Sundberg; and Herbst et al., all this volume).

CONTROL OF LOUDNESS IN SINGING

Control of subglottal pressure is considered the main contributor to changes of loudness in singing. The amplitude of the glottal wave generated by the closing glottis gives intensity, one element of perceived loudness. The larger the amplitude, the greater will be the excitation of air molecules in the vocal tract, and thus the greater the intensity (Baken 1998). Both increased lung pressures and speed of glottal closure are known to have an impact on vocal intensity. An increase in lung pressure allows for more air to be released through the glottis during the open phase; a sharper cut-off of the airflow during glottal closure will lead to greater vocal tract excitation and a steeper decreasing phase of the glottal wave, leading to a slower decay in sound intensity (Sundberg 1987). At the same time, voluntary changes must be effected in the vibrating layers of the vocal folds so that they can increase resistance to the higher airflow generated by higher lung pressure. Loudness control in singing is thus a delicate balance of aerodynamic and biomechanical factors (Sundberg 1990).

LIFE-CYCLE OF THE VOICE

As a biological instrument the voice is subject to changes during the life-cycle; these reflect overall growth, maturation, and degeneration patterns. Positioning, size, and relative stiffness of the laryngeal cartilages are important factors, as well as lung volume and the ability to control breath pressure. From infancy through childhood and up to puberty, both male and female voices will develop along similar lines, with individual differences being due to physical characteristics and voice type. The pre-pubertal laryngeal cartilages of female and male children are very similar (Thurman and Klitzke 2000). However, at puberty, the developmental paths of female and male voices diverge sharply. Growth patterns in the female voice are more linear, whereas in the male voice, growth of the laryngeal cartilages and the membranous fold is disproportionate to the rest of the anatomy (Dickson and Maue-Dickson 1996). The following section presents salient features of vocal development from infancy to adulthood, including the main differences between the male and female voice.

Infancy and childhood

Primarily designed to facilitate suckling, crying, and efficient pressure-valving, the infant larynx is functionally different from that of either the child or adult. Only from the age of one year does the mechanism begin to adapt in preparation for the onset of speech. The infant larynx is proportionally much smaller than the adult's: the cartilages are more compact and pliable and the cartilaginous portion of the larynx is proportionally longer. The larynx is positioned in line with the third cervical vertebra [c3], almost level with the jaw, allowing for a coupling of the epiglottis and soft palate so that breathing and suckling can occur simultaneously (Kahane 1983; Thurman and Klitzke 2000; Williams 2010). The vocal ligament layer of the vocal folds is not differentiated in infants and only begins to develop at ages three or four. Lung capacity in infants is not needed to facilitate speech, and lung volumes are proportionally smaller in favor of a larger digestive tract (Williams 2010).

During childhood, the larynx gradually drops in line with the 5th cervical vertebra and the vocal tract configuration becomes more adult, with increased range of movement in the cartilages. However, the cartilages are still relatively soft and less able to resist the strain of muscular pull than those of an adult. By age seven, the lamina propria will have three distinct layers, but it does not yet resemble the adult form. Although the tissues of the vocal fold layers continue to develop between ages seven and ten, they only assume adult configuration after puberty (Hirano et al. 1981; Hirano et al. 1983; Kahane 1983). As the mechanism adapts for speech and also grows with the body, the membranous fold increases in length. Between the ages of six and sixteen, average fundamental frequencies will drop, and vocal range will increase gradually but there are no sudden changes until the onset of puberty (Williams 2010). By the age of twenty the larynx will have dropped to the upper border of the 7th cervical vertebra and remains within the c7 region throughout the rest of life (Kahane 1983).

Vocal development during adolescence (mutation)

Puberty is the process of sexual development characterized by the release of testosterone in males, and estradiol and progesterone in females (Anderson et al. 2006). During this time anatomical growth spurts in height, weight, tissue, and organ size may all be expected, with the most dramatic growth spurt tending to occur between the ages of 11–15 years (Thurman and Klitzke 2000). The physiological landmark of puberty in females is the onset of menses, whereas the clearest landmarks in males are the appearance of facial hair and voice change (Thurman and Klitzke 2000). During this phase of adolescent voice change both females and males may experience vocal instability: changes of voice quality (breathiness, huskiness, or hoarseness); loss of pitch range; decreased pitch accuracy in singing; abrupt register transitions; discomfort in singing; and more effortful phonation (Cooksey 1993; Gackle 2000). Five clear stages of change have been well-documented in the male voice (Cooksey 1993), and these correlate closely with Tanner's (1964) five stages of changes in genital development. In the male voice these five stages of change are sequential and largely predictable, whereas in the female voice, the changes are more gradual and less defined, occurring in cyclic stages over several years (see Gackle, this volume).

Impact of hormonal changes in post-pubertal female voice

Female singers can expect to experience hormonal changes that fluctuate with the menstrual cycle throughout their reproductive years, and these changes are known to impact on the mucosa of the vocal folds (Abitbol et al. 1989; Abitbol et al. 1999). During the premenstrual phase of the cycle there is a predisposition to vocal fold hemorrhage due to changes in the epithelium: both estrogen and progesterone stimulation may produce thickening in the discrete layers of the vocal folds, leading to water retention, edema, and dilation of the capillaries. Typical changes observed by singers are reduced pitch range; loss of stamina; decreased ability to engage abdominal support; and huskiness or roughness in the voice quality. There is some evidence that the use of birth control medication may also affect pitch control and stability of vibrato in the upper pitch range of female singers (Lã et al. 2012). Later in the reproductive years, there is a change in the process of ovulation in females: the efficiency and regularity of oocyte (egg) maturation decreases, and the peri-menopausal phase of the reproductive cycle may begin. When menses cease, the ovaries continue to be hormonal receptors but now produce androgens instead of estrogen and progesterone. Common complaints of singers during their peri-menopausal phase are: breathiness, weakness, and instability; "cracks" appearing in the vocal range; loss of flexibility and sometimes an inability to phonate on certain pitches. Typically fundamental frequency will drop post-menopause, due to the drop in estrogen production and continued secretion of androgens (Anoop et al. 2009; Sataloff 1998).

GENDER DIFFERENCES IN ADULT VOICE

Functionally, male and female voices are the same, but their vocal tracts have different dimensions, the relative sizing of their resonating cavities are different, and there are substantial differences between them in terms of vocal fold length.

An obvious audible difference between male and female voice is that of vocal range. The average adult female speaking pitch is about 20 percent higher than the male (Fant 1966). In practical terms, this means that the adult male voice will have a pitch range of between a fifth to an octave lower than an adult female (Welch 2005). This difference is due to the disproportionate growth of the membranous vocal fold during puberty in males, resulting in a scalar difference of 1.6 between female and male voice, whereas the difference between overall larynx sizing is 1.2 (Titze 1989). Table 1.1 shows gender differences between average vocal fold lengths across the life-span.

Table 1.1 Average vocal fold lengths during life–span, in millimetres. Reproduced from Thurman and Welch (2000), p. 360. Copyright © 2000, The VoiceCare Network

	Infancy	Puberty	Adult Male	Adult Female
Total Length	6–8	12–15	17.0–23	12.5–17.0
Membranous portion	3–4	7–8	11.5–16	8.0–11.5
Cartilaginous portion	3–4	5–7	5.5–7	4.5–5.5

Adult male vocal folds will also be thicker than those of females, thought to affect depth of vibration, thus leading to a larger amplitude of vocal fold vibration visible in glottographic waveforms of male voices. Differences in vocal tract size between the genders also lead to different vocal tract formants. On average the female vocal tract is 15–20 percent shorter than that of the male, leading to formant frequency differences averaged across the vowel set of 12 percent [F1], 17 percent [F2], and 18 percent [F3] (Sundberg 1987). The average differences between the size of oral cavity and the length of pharynx between males and female are also proportionally different. Female oral cavities are around 15 percent smaller than males, whereas their pharyngeal length is around 23 percent shorter (Nordström 1977). Using magnetic resonance imaging, Story et al. (1996) found that the chamber of the epilarynx is shorter in females than males, also impacting on vowel formants and on differences in voice quality. Due to these differences, Titze (1989) has speculated that the source-filter theory of speech production might well have taken a different direction had female voice been the primary model of voice early on.

SUMMARY

Sung vocal sounds are governed by three related systems: respiratory, phonatory, and resonatory. The respiratory system generates aerodynamic power, initiating vocal fold oscillation, providing the sound source for voiced sounds. For singing, the respiratory pattern will differ from that of quiet respiration. Singers may wish to suspend respiration, change its timing, rhythm, or depth. In phonation, patterns of vocal fold vibration can be altered, resulting in different voice qualities, and vibration amplitude can be adjusted, resulting in different levels of loudness. By changing the length and tension of the vibrating vocal folds singers can access a wide range of fundamental frequencies. The vocal tract is part of both the respiratory and digestive systems and acts as a resonating airspace that can be configured by singers to create vowels and other types of voice quality. All of these may be considered functional aspects of the singing voice. Since the mechanism of the voice is characterized by numerous variables it is perfectly possible for singers to use different vocal tract configurations that lead to the same acoustic output. The voice is particularly sensitive to sex hormones, affecting the genders in different ways during their respective life-cycles. Overall the average adult male larynx is 40 percent larger than the adult female larynx, and the membranous fold is 60 percent longer. Due to these differences, it is important not to regard the female voice as a simple scaled-down version of the male vocal tract; rather, it has been suggested that the adult female provides a more reliable normative model of voice than that of the male.

KEY READING

Bunch Dayme, M. (2009). *Dynamics of the Singing Voice*, 5th edn. Wien, Austria: Springer-Verlag. Excellent appendices of Study Outlines in 5th edition.

Dickson, R.D. and Maue-Dickson, W. (1996). *Anatomical and Physiological Bases of Speech*, 2nd edn. Boston, MA: Little, Brown and Company.

Harris, T., Harris, S., Rubin, J.S., and Howard, D.M. (eds) (1998). *The Voice Clinic Handbook*. London: Whurr. Chapters 1, 2, 4, and 5 are particularly recommended. At the time of writing, a second edition of this book is pending. Chapter 8 (Singing and Therapy) now includes classical and commercial singing styles and is recommended for genre-specific information.

Joseph, J. (1982). *A Textbook of Regional Anatomy*. London: Macmillan Press. A good overview of anatomy and a useful reference text.

Laver, J. (1980). *The Phonetic Description of Voice Quality*. Cambridge, UK: Cambridge University Press. Out of print, but secondhand copies available from: <www.alibris.com> and similar. An excellent and detailed exposition of functional potential of moveable structures in the vocal tract and how these contribute to voice quality.

Sataloff, R.T. (ed.) (2006). *Vocal Health and Pedagogy: Science and Assessment*, 2nd edn, Vol. 1. San Diego: Plural Publishing Inc. Chapters 2, 3, 4, and 5 are recommended.

Thurman, L. and Welch, G.F. (eds) (2000). *Bodymind and Voice: Foundations of Voice Education*, 2nd edn, Vols 1–5. Collegeville, MN: The VoiceCare Network. A comprehensive approach to understanding of voice, from pre-birth to senescence including many user-friendly exercises for awareness.

Other learning media and web resources

Netter's 3D Interactive Anatomy
<http://www.interactelsevier.com/netter>.

Vocal Process, Looking at a Voice Voicebox video series on DVD <http://store.vocalprocess.co.uk/CompleteVoiceboxVideos>.

Blue Tree Publishing, Vocal Parts Software <http://www.bluetreepublishing.com/Details.cfm?ProdID=65>.

REFERENCES

Abercrombie, D. (1967). *Elements of General Phonetics*. Edinburgh, UK: Edinburgh University Press.

Abitbol, J., de Brux, J., Millot, G., Masson, M., Mimoun, O.L., Pau, H., and Abitbol, B. (1989). Does a hormonal vocal cord cycle exist in women? Study of vocal premenstrual syndrome in voice performers by videostroboscopy-glottography and cytology on 38 women. *Journal of Voice* 3(2): 157–162.

Abitbol, J., Abitbol, P., and Abitbol, B. (1999). Sex hormones and the female voice. *Journal of Voice* 13(3): 424–446.

Anderson, T.D., Anderson, D.D., and Sataloff, R.T. (2006). Endocrine dysfunction. In: R.T. Sataloff (ed.), *Vocal Health and Pedagogy Advanced Assessment and Treatment*, Vol. 2, pp. 67–79. Abingdon, UK: Plural Publishing.

Anoop, R., Bulbul, G., Anindita, C., and Shelly, C. (2009). A study of voice changes in various phases of menstrual cycle and in postmenopausal women. *Journal of Voice* 24(3): 363–368.

Austin, S. (1996). Principles of voice science: Studio application. *Australian Voice* 2: 1–9.

Baken, R.J. (1998). An overview of laryngeal function for voice production. In: R.T. Sataloff (ed.), *Vocal Health and Pedagogy*, pp. 27–47. San Diego, CA: Singular Publishing Group Inc.

Björkner, E. (2008). *Why so different?* PhD dissertation, Royal Institute of Technology, Stockholm, Sweden.

Bunch Dayme, M. (2009). *Dynamics of the Singing Voice*, 5th edn. Wien, Austria: Springer-Verlag.

Chapman, J. (2006). *Singing and Teaching Singing*. Oxford, UK: Plural Publishing Inc.

Citardi, M., Yanagisawa, E., and Estill, J. (1996). Videoendoscopic analysis of laryngeal function during laughter. *Annals of Otology, Rhinology and Laryngology* 105(7): 545–549.

Cooksey, J.M. (1993). Do adolescent voices "break" or do they "transform"? *Voice* 2(1): 15–39.

Dickson, R.D. and Maue-Dickson, W. (1996). *Anatomical and Physiological Bases of Speech*, 2nd ed. Boston, MA: Little, Brown and Company.

Estill, J., Fujimara, O., Erickson, D., Zhang, T., and Beechler, K. (1994). Vocal tract contributions to voice qualities. Paper presented at the Proceedings of the Stockholm Music Acoustics Conference (SMAC 93): Stockholm, Sweden: Royal Academy of Music, July 28–August 1.

Fant, G. (1966). A note on vocal tract size factors and non-uniform F-pattern scalings. *STL-QPSR* 7(4): 22–30.

Gackle, L. (2000). Understanding voice transformation in female adolescents. In: L. Thurman and G. Welch (eds), *Bodymind and Voice: Foundations of Voice Education*, 2nd edn, Vol. 4, pp. 739–744. Collegeville, MN: The VoiceCare Network.

Hardcastle, W. (1976). *Physiology of Speech Production*. London: Academic Press.

Harris, T. (1998). Laryngeal mechanisms in normal function and dysfunction. In: Harris, T., Harris, S., Rubin, J. S., and Howard, D. M. (eds), *The Voice Clinic Handbook*. London: Whurr.

Harris, T. (2010). Some laryngeal anatomy and practical mechanics. Workshop presentation at the Vocal Process Training Event: Anatomy and Physiology for Voice, January 24–25.

Harris, T., Harris, S., Rubin, J.S., and Howard, D.M. (1998). *The Voice Clinic Handbook*. London: Whurr.

Hirano, M. (1977). Structure and vibratory behaviour of the vocal folds. In: M. Sawashima and F.S. Cooper (eds), *Dynamic Aspects of Speech Production*, pp. 13–27. Tokyo: University of Tokyo Press.

Hirano, M. (1988). Vocal mechanisms in singing: Laryngological and phoniatric aspects. *Journal of Voice* 2(1): 51–69.

Hirano, M., Kurita, S., and Nasashima, T. (1981). The structure of the vocal folds. *Vocal Fold Physiology*, pp. 33–41. Tokyo: University of Tokyo Press.

Hirano, M., Kurita, S., and Nasashima, T. (1983). Growth, development and aging of human vocal folds. In: D.M. Bless and J.H. Abbs (eds), *Vocal Fold Physiology: Contemporary Research and Clinical Issues*, pp. 22–43. San Diego: College Hill Press.

Hixon, T.J. (2006). *Respiratory Function in Singing: A Primer for Singers and Singing Teachers*. Tucson, AZ: Redington Browne.

Hixon, T.J. et al. (1987). *Respiratory Function in Speech and Song*. Boston, MA: College-Hill Press/Little, Brown and Company.

Hoit, J.D., Jenks, C.L., Watson, P.J., and Cleveland, T.F. (1996). Respiratory function during speaking and singing in professional country singers. *Journal of Voice* 10(1): 39–49.

Hollien, H., Brown, O., and Weiss, R. (1999). Another view of vocal mechanics. *Journal of Singing* 56(1): 11–22.

Howard, D.M. (1998). Practical voice measurement. In: T. Harris, J.S. Rubin, D.M. Howard, and A. Hirson (eds), *The Voice Clinic Handbook*, pp. 323–380. London: Whurr.

Kayes, G. (2004). *Singing and the Actor*, 2nd edn. London: A and C Black.

Kahane, J.C. (1983). Postnatal development and aging of the human larynx. *Seminar in Speech and Language* 4: 189–205.

Lã, F.M.B., Sundberg, J., Howard, D.M., Sa-Couto, P., and Freitas, A. (2012). Effects of the menstrual cycle and oral contraception on singers' pitch control. *Journal of Speech, Language and Hearing Research* 55: 247–261.

Lam Tang, J.A., Boliek, C.A., and Rieger, J.M. (2008). Laryngeal and respiratory behavior during pitch change in professional singers. *Journal of Voice* 22(6): 622–633.

Laver, J. (1980). *The Phonetic Description of Voice Quality*. Cambridge, UK: Cambridge University Press.

Lieberman, J. (2000). Principles and techniques of manual therapy: Applications in the management of dysphonia. In: T. Harris, J.S. Rubin, D.M. Howard, and A. Hirson (eds), *The Voice Clinic Handbook*, pp. 91–138. London: Whurr.

Mitchell, H.F., Kenny, D.T., Ryan, M., and Davis, P.J. (2003). Defining 'open throat' through content analysis of experts' pedagogical practices. *Logopedics Phoniatrics Vocology* 28(4): 167–180.

Nordström, P.E. (1977). Female and infant vocal tracts simulated from male area functions. *Journal of Phonetics* 5(1): 81–92.

Roubeau, B., Chevrie-Muller, C., and Arabia-Guidet, C. (1987). Electroglottographic study of the changes of voice registers. *Folia Phoniatrica* 39: 280–289.

Rubin, J.S. (1998). The structural anatomy of the larynx and supraglottic vocal tract: A review. In: T. Harris, J.S. Rubin, D.M. Howard, and A. Hirson (eds), *The Voice Clinic Handbook*, pp. 15–33. London: Whurr.

Sataloff, R.T. (1998). Clinical anatomy and physiology of the voice. In: R.T. Sataloff (ed.), *Vocal Health and Pedagogy*, pp. 5–25. San Diego, CA: Singular Publishing.

Seikel, J.A., King, D.W., and Drumright, D.G. (1997). *Anatomy and Physiology for Speech, Language and Hearing*. San Diego, CA: Singular Publishing Group.

Sonninen, A., Hurme, P., and Laukkanen, A.-M. (1999). The external frame function in the control of pitch, register, and singing mode: Radiographic observations of a female singer. *Journal of Voice* 13(3): 319–340.

Story, B.H., Titze, I.R., and Hoffman, E.A. (1996). Vocal tract area functions from magnetic resonance imaging. *Journal of the Acoustical Society of America* 100(1): 537–554.

Sundberg, J. (1973). Observations on a professional soprano singer. *Quarterly Progress and Status Report*, pp. 14–24. Stockholm: Department for Speech Music and Hearing, Royal Institute of Technology.

Sundberg, J. (1974). Articulatory interpretation of the "singing formant." *Journal of the Acoustical Society of America* 55: 838–844.

Sundberg, J. (1987). *The Science of the Singing Voice*. Dekalb, IL: Northern Illinois University Press.

Sundberg, J. (1990). What's so special about singers? *Journal of Voice* 4(2): 107–119.

Sundberg, J. (1998). Vocal tract resonance. In: R.T. Sataloff (ed.), *Vocal Health and Pedagogy*, pp. 47–65. San Diego, CA: Singular Publishing Group.

Tanner, J.M. (1964). *Growth at Adolescence*. Oxford: Blackwell Scientific.

Thomasson, M. (2003a). *From air to aria: Relevance of respiratory behaviour of voice function in classical Western vocal art*. PhD dissertation, Department of Speech, Music and Hearing, Royal Institute of Technology, Stockholm, Sweden.

Thomasson, M. (2003b). Belly-in or belly-out? Effects of Inhalatory Behavior and Lung Volume on Voice Function in Male Opera Singers. *Quarterly Progress and Status Report*, pp. 61–73. Stockholm: Department for Speech Music and Hearing, Royal Institute of Technology.

Thurman, L. and Welch, G.F. (eds) (2000). *Bodymind and Voice: Foundations of Voice Education*, 2nd edn, Vol. 2. Collegeville, MN: The VoiceCare Network.

Thurman, L. and Klitzke, C. (2000). Highlights of physical growth and function of voices from prebirth to age 21. In: L. Thurman and G.F. Welch (eds), *Bodymind and Voice: Foundations of Voice Education*. 2nd edn, Vol. 4, pp. 696–703. Collegeville, MN: The VoiceCare Network.

Thurman, L., Welch, G.F., Theimer, A., and Klitzke, C. (2004). Addressing vocal register discrepancies: An alternative, science-based theory of register phenomena. Paper presented at the Second International Conference: The Physiology and Acoustics of Singing, Denver, CO, USA, 6–9 October.

Titze, I.R. (1989). Physiologic and acoustic differences between male and female voices. *Journal of the Acoustical Society of America* 85(4): 1669–1707.

Titze, I.R. (1994). *Principles of Voice Production*. Englewood Cliffs, NJ: Prentice Hall.

Titze, I.R., Luschei, E.S., and Hirano, M. (1989). Role of the thyroarytenoid muscle in regulation of fundamental frequency. *Journal of Voice* 3(3): 213–224.

van den Berg, J., Vennard, W., Burger, D., and Shervanian, C. (1960). *Voice Production: The Vibrating Larynx*. Groningen, The Netherlands: University of Groningen Voice Research Laboratory.

Vennard, W. (1967). *Singing: The Mechanism and the Technic*, Rev. edn. New York: Carl Fischer.

Welch, G. (2005). Singing as communication. In: D. Miell, R. MacDonald and D.J. Hargreaves (eds), *Musical Communication*, pp. 239–259. Oxford, UK: Oxford University Press.

Welch, G.F., Thurman, L., Theimer, A., Grefsheim, E., and Feit, P. (2000). How your vocal tract contributes to basic voice qualities. In: G. Welch and L. Thurman (eds), *Bodymind and Voice: Foundations of Voice Education*. Vol. 2. Collegeville, MN: The VoiceCare Network. <http://www.voicecarenetwork.org/store.cfm?CID=1&prod=1>.

Wendler, J., Nawka, T., and Verges, D. (2004, 11–16 September). Videolaryngo-stroboscopy and phonetography: Basic tools for diagnostics and documentation in the voice clinic. Paper presented at the 15th European Congress of Oto-Rhino-Laryngology, Head and Neck Surgery, Rodos-Kos, Greece.

Williams, J. (2010). *The implications of intensive singing training on the vocal health and development of boy choristers in an English cathedral choir*. PhD Dissertation, The University of London Institute of Education.

Zemlin, W.R. (1968). *Speech and Hearing: Science Anatomy and Physiology*. Englewood Cliffs, NJ: Prentice-Hall.

CHAPTER 2

···

VOICE DYSFUNCTION AND RECOVERY

···

TARA K. STADELMAN-COHEN
AND ROBERT E. HILLMAN

INTRODUCTION

···

FUNCTION of the singing voice depends upon the complex and ever-changing interaction of musculoskeletal alignment, respiration, phonation, resonance, and articulation. Inefficiency in any of these areas can lead to vocal dysfunction, ranging from excessive muscle tension and fatigue to organic pathology of the vocal fold tissue. As "vocal athletes," singers require special diagnostic and treatment consideration when voice difficulties develop as they must maintain higher-than-normal levels of phonatory agility, strength, and stamina to repeatedly execute intricate laryngeal maneuvers (Zeitels et al. 2002). This chapter will highlight the functional etiologies of vocal difficulties and give prominence to organic pathologies that are more common in the singing population, with attention to the specialized recovery process necessary in an injured singer.

THEORETICAL FRAMEWORK

···

A voice disorder is diagnosed when quality, pitch, loudness, and/or flexibility differ from what is age-, gender- or culture-specific (Aronson 1990). When these parameters are altered, an individual may experience *dysphonia,* which is impaired sound. Quality may be considered rough (i.e. hoarse), breathy, harsh, strained, or gravelly; the list is extensive in describing what is scientifically labeled as noise or aperiodicity in the voice. Pitch may contain breaks; be too high, low, or monotone; demonstrate *diplophonia* (i.e. two sounds produced at once), or range may be reduced. Similarly, loudness may be too loud, too soft, or monoloud. Flexibility is decreased when the ability to easily alter the above parameters is negatively affected and the voice becomes less agile. Changes in the structure of the vibratory layers of the vocal folds, the neuromuscular function of the larynx, and/or the respiratory system may cause changes in quality, pitch, loudness, and flexibility.

Musculoskeletal alignment, vocal subsystems, and articulation

Musculoskeletal imbalance

The effects of musculoskeletal alignment, respiration, resonance, and articulation on phonatory ability are understandable given that a singer's voice does not depend solely upon the vocal apparatus (see also Rubin and Epstein, this volume). Maintaining optimal posture involves a balanced arrangement of the body with respect to gravity (Kuchera and Kuchera 1997), and any habituated musculoskeletal imbalance affects the body of the singer's "instrument," potentially creating vocal dysfunction. The larynx, vocal tract (i.e. the larynx, pharynx, and oral and nasal cavities), and articulators are connected to the sternum, cervical spine, and skull. Further, the respiratory mechanism is connected to the spinal column, ribs, and pelvis. Misalignment of the spine contributes to muscle imbalance as the various axes of movement are negatively affected. For example, scoliosis can affect respiratory function as rib circumference can be altered from the left to the right side of the body (Stokes et al. 1989) and affect laryngeal position due to its connection to various muscles of the neck (e.g. the sternothyroid muscle). Scoliosis can also alter the movement of the ribs and place the respiratory muscles at a mechanical disadvantage (Koumbourlis 2006). A neck injury altering mobility of the vertebrae, especially the cervical vertebrae, can contribute to increased tension of the paralaryngeal muscle or even affect laryngeal nerve function and negatively affect voicing. While physical asymmetry warrants attention, reduction of excessive muscle tension within the aligned position is also of importance; if the body is not free to move, the singer will be compromised. Physical therapy, chiropractic and osteopathic medicine, therapeutic massage, and the Alexander Technique are several of the approaches used by singers to improve physical symmetry and overall function.

Respiration

Much attention is generally given to the respiration of the singer, as breath is the foundation of voice and the source of power for the larynx (see also Watson, this volume). At a basic level, respiration is an interaction between biochemical (i.e. oxygen and carbon dioxide exchange), biomechanical (i.e. structural), and psychosocial features (i.e. emotional state) (Chaitow et al. 2002). It is not surprising that singing is affected by overall respiratory health. For example, smoking contributes to deteriorated respiratory function as evidenced by a lower vital capacity (i.e. the maximum amount of air that can be expelled from the lungs), presumably due to increased bronchial reactivity and/or mild airway obstruction (Awan and Alphonso 2007).

Normal respiration involves varying types of activity, such as a combination of clavicular, thoracic, and abdominal movements, which are dependent upon the respiratory needs of the physical activity being performed at that moment. Brief paradoxical motion of the diaphragm (i.e. moving down during phonation) and rib movement to offset increasing pressure has been found when singing (Collyer et al. 2008; Thorpe et al. 2001; Titze et al. 1999). This is not considered pathological, but rather is an advanced method of managing the complex demands of singing. It is important to note that individual variances amongst singers are the norm at all skill levels, and may be related to an individual's unique physiology and the required musical demands. Note that a singer's respiratory technique may unfortunately be erroneously blamed for inefficient vocal function; for example, if a breathy voice is heard, the singer may be instructed to, "send more support." Difficulty present at the level of the vocal folds could be contributing to the lack of this clarity, and often the use of more respiratory drive creates further dysfunction via excessive muscle activity. In turn, the larynx can affect respiratory function. Paradoxing of the vocal folds during which there is closure upon inspiration can contribute to respiratory distress, such as stridor and shortness of breath (Christopher et al. 1983).

Phonation

At the laryngeal level, phonation is dependent upon adequate mobility of the vocal folds, the straightness of the edge of the vocal fold, symmetry between the left and right vocal folds, presence of the mucosal wave (i.e. a wave-like deformation of the upper layers of vocal fold tissue) that indicates overall tissue health/pliability, and the extent of any excessive muscle tension at or above the level of the vocal folds (see Herbst et al., this volume). Vocal dysfunction can occur when one or more of these factors is altered or signs of excessive muscle tension are evident.

Vocal loading is defined as excessive stress placed on the laryngeal mechanism (Morrow and Connor 2011) and is affected by the duration, loudness, and frequency of phonation. Inappropriate loading can contribute to fatigue of the laryngeal muscles and/or changes in the lamina propria such as edema or organic pathology (Hunter and Titze 2009). Fatigue is defined as an inability to continue a task at a specific level (Edwards 1981), and more specifically, vocal fatigue represents poor adaptation that is present following prolonged use of the voice (Scherer et al. 1991; Welham and Maclagan 2002). With vocal misuse, an individual engages in negative vocal habits (e.g. extensive loud talking, throat clearing, yelling, etc.), which increase the shearing forces on the mucosa above its capacity or engages unnecessary or excessive muscle activity. Importantly, deterioration in vocal function is not necessarily the direct result of an inefficient technique or misuse, but potentially due to over-use, including non-singing vocal activities. In this scenario, actual technical skill may be adequate although the paralaryngeal musculature and vocal fold mucosa is worked beyond its conditioned level. Vocal misuse and overuse factor into what is termed *phonotrauma* (Verdolini 1999), which may contribute to benign pathology.

Vocal symptoms due to increased vocal loading and resultant vocal fatigue include altered speaking pitch, loss of vocal stamina, loss of low or high notes, delay in voicing onset, deteriorated quality, increased vocal effort, and neck/throat discomfort (Scherer et al. 1991; Titze 1984), although this list is not exhaustive. Attention to recovery, such as allowing time to rest the voice, is important to reduce any long-term negative effects from inappropriate vocal loading. Also, if singing demands increase, speaking responsibilities may have to decrease in order to not cross the threshold where injury may occur.

Monitoring the vocal load of singers is an ongoing challenge. While strength and stamina of voicing can be targeted to a degree with conditioning, there remains a physiological and genetic difference amongst singers (Titze 2001) which may contribute to personal vocal limitations. Recognizing these limitations that are potentially ever-changing due to changes in environment, sleep patterns, nutrition, and systemic health is important when determining vocal demands in order to maximize vocal health and prevent injury.

Resonance

Vocal resonance is affected by how sound travels through a singer's vocal tract. A change in resonance, or the timbre of voice, occurs by shaping the flexible tract from the vocal folds to the lips. Interaction between the larynx and vocal tract contributes to one's signature vocal quality and also affects vocal intensity (see also Story and Sundberg, both this volume). Inefficient resonant production is considered to lead to excessive vibratory sensations experienced in the throat. For the utmost efficiency in speaking and singing it is beneficial to employ appropriate oral resonance (i.e. a forward focus or sensations felt in the palate, tongue, and lips) through vocal training, as the vocal folds are barely touching with this technique, thereby minimizing excessive stress and maximizing vocal output (Lessac 1987; Verdolini et al. 1998).

Articulation

Articulation of the tongue and jaw also affects voicing efficiency. Temporomandibular joint dysfunction (TMJD) and excessive tone of the chewing muscles can alter mandibular movement, which can affect laryngeal function via the tongue, hyoid, and occipitocervical joint (i.e. the area between the cervical spine and skull) (Piron and Roch 2010). This can be particularly problematic in a singer who has to continually increase his or her oral cavity space to maximize resonance and/or general articulation. Treatment of TMJD can involve massage, oral appliances, or surgical management. Minimizing any resultant tongue or jaw tension via increased awareness of structure and function, in addition to paralaryngeal massage and manipulation, can also reduce negative muscular effects on phonation (Aronson 1985; Lieberman 1998; Roy et al. 1997).

VOCAL AGING AND ITS EFFECT
ON SUBSYSTEM FUNCTION

Aging is a process that affects all organs, although its manner and extent are highly individualized due to numerous factors including genetics and lifestyle. A voice change attributable to aging is termed *presbyphonia*. Specific to vocal function, aging affects respiration, the lining and musculature of the vocal tract, and the vocal folds. The etiology of presbyphonia may be multifactorial because of comorbidities in other physical systems involved in voicing (Johns et al. 2011). Respiratory changes include reduced vital capacity of the lungs (Sperry and Klich 1992) and reduced compliance of the ribs and connective tissue

(Estenne et al. 1985). The pharyngeal muscles may also weaken (Zaino and Benventano 1977). Under laryngeal videostroboscopy, one might visualize a lack of vocal fold closure resulting in a spindle-shaped gap (bowed or atrophic appearance), discoloration (increased yellow hue), and edema (Thomas and Stemple 2007). The spindle-shaped lack of closure is often associated with an apparent stiffening (e.g. sulcus) and/or loss of the tissue layer on the medial surfaces of the vocal folds that accounts for most of the normal vibratory function (superficial lamina propria). Perceptual changes can include altered pitch (increased pitch in males, decreased pitch in females), roughness, breathiness, reduced loudness, and increased strain (Gorham-Rowan and Laures-Gore 2006; Thomas and Stemple 2007). The negative vocal effects of aging can sometimes be addressed via vocal fold augmentation if closure is a factor (Ford 2004) and via behavioral methods to improve muscle strength and balance (Berg et al. 2008).

Hormonal changes are also evident in both men and women with aging. Loss of estrogen in the female voice during menopause can reduce the thickness of the laryngeal mucosa in addition to muscle bulk and alter range, agility, and intensity (Abitbol et al. 1999). Hormone replacement therapy has been beneficial in reducing this laryngeal sensitivity in some women (Sataloff et al. 1997), although this controversial regimen may affect other bodily systems when implemented (Heman-Ackah 2004). The male voice is prone to be affected by decreasing levels of sex hormones with aging, contributing to elevated speaking pitch and an altered range (Gugatschka et al. 2010).

Lifestyle, good nutrition, physical activity, and vocal activities such as singing can probably delay the general age-related decline of function. In fact, trained vocal performers often experience less deterioration in function solely attributable to aging than their non-trained peers. Davidson and Murray, this volume, give further information on the topic of vocal aging.

MIND, BODY, VOICE

It is generally accepted there is great connection between the mind, body, and voice, especially in a performer (see chapters by Kleber and Zarate, Ginsborg, Thomas, and Davidson, all this volume). As suspected, a singer's voice is related to the health and vitality of his or her whole body. Physically, a vocal athlete must ensure they get adequate nutrition, rest, and recovery, similarly to any other athlete, in order for best performance to occur. It is often during times of increased demands and/or stress that eating well, hydration, and sleeping for an appropriate number of hours receive less attention. Inadequate nutrition can contribute to physical fatigue (Robson-Ansley et al. 2009) and dehydration affects the mucosa of the vocal folds, alters the thickness of secretions, and increases overall vocal effort (Verdolini et al. 2002). Further, sleep is the time when the body recovers from physical demands—the blood supply available to the muscles increases, delivering extra amounts of oxygen and nutrients, and human growth hormone is secreted, stimulating tissue growth and muscle repair.

The emotional health of a singer is also important. There are voice disorders that can be directly related to emotional stress without any structural change in the vocal folds. Dysfunction can range from muscle tension causing vocal fatigue to *aphonia*, which is complete loss of voice. Muscle tension, along with generalized anxiety, are primary psychosomatic manifestations in individuals with what is considered a "functional" or non-organic voice disorder (i.e. there is an absence of a structural or neurological pathology) (Butcher et al. 2007). It is important for a singer to recognize emotional stressors and minimize any physical manifestations such as neck, shoulder, tongue, and/or jaw tension.

Performance anxiety can affect subsystem efficiency, as evidenced by altered respiratory rate, restricted breathing, and impaired memory (Claire 1991). Anxiety specifically related to performance can be addressed via psychotherapy, and if deemed necessary, pharmaceutical management, in order to prevent longer-term vocal dysfunction caused by muscle tension (see Thomas, this volume).

Further, singers may experience underlying psychological issues such as depression or other clinical diagnoses (e.g. bipolar disorder) which may need to be pharmaceutically managed. Attention to the overall emotional and physical health of a singer plays a significant role in the function of the vocal apparatus and should be appropriately monitored and addressed.

LARYNGOLOGICAL ASSESSMENT: THE FIRST STEP

Appropriate musculoskeletal alignment and overall function in the above-mentioned voice subsystems all contribute to effective performance. While minor day-to-day variance in voicing can be normal, a general rule of thumb is to seek medical assessment when quality or function has remained changed for 3 weeks; this time frame is when most symptoms have resolved from a viral illness, which is the most common short-term cause of alteration of quality, although performers may benefit from earlier assessment (Schwartz et al. 2009). Changes in quality can typically be identified by the human ear, although due to the vocal skill of a singer he or she could potentially sustain a pathological change of the vocal folds and still sound "normal" as advanced compensatory measures may be applied to improve function. Importantly, a singer may possess a voice signature that includes a pathological quality, such as breathiness, for artistic purposes, although it could be a specific feature in that person's singing only and not present in speech; therefore, it is important for a singer to understand what is typical for their particular instrument without comparison to others in order to avoid potential difficulty and/or extended injury.

Determining the cause of any deterioration in voicing begins with a thorough history and physical examination that encompasses pertinent past medical history, vocal history, voice demands, description of the difficulty, and videostroboscopic visualization of the structure and function of the larynx. This examination is best carried out by a laryngologist who is sensitive to the unique demands of singers (Stadelman-Cohen et al. 2009). While vocal fold structure can be grossly visualized using a mirror placed at the back of the mouth, this is not considered comprehensive in assessing vocal function. It is important to undergo videostroboscopy to see the mucosal wave for an accurate understanding of tissue pliability and vibratory symmetry, the straightness of the vocal fold edge and its effect on closure, and overall abduction/adduction (i.e. opening and closing of the vocal folds). This can be completed transorally (through the mouth) or transnasally (through the nose). With a transoral examination, articulatory function and vocal maneuvers are restricted as the tongue is extended and a rigid scope is placed at the back of the mouth. Both speaking and singing voice function can be assessed with transnasal endoscopy as the scope does not interfere with articulatory function, which yields the most unimpeded view. Often, assessment of singers involves both methods of visualization. Based on the immediate demands of the singer, the specific difficulty upon presentation, and the findings from laryngological assessment, treatment will follow one or more combination of approaches involving medical, surgical and/or behavioral treatment.

THE VOICE TEAM

The voice team can involve numerous disciplines based on the particular needs of the injured singer. At a minimum, the team involves a laryngologist and speech pathologist. A singer may also utilize a singing voice teacher or voice coach well versed in working with injured voices. It is also becoming increasingly common to encounter speech pathologists with a background in voice training. A *singing voice specialist* is expected to possess knowledge of vocal structure, function, and pathology, although there are no present standards of certification at the time of writing. Other medical professionals may include a gastroenterologist, neurologist, psychiatrist, allergist, radiologist, pulmonologist, and primary-care physician. Ongoing collaboration between these medical and non-medical professionals, while respecting the importance of patient confidentiality, is necessary to ensure that all aspects affecting vocal function have been considered when deterioration is present.

SPEECH PATHOLOGY ASSESSMENT

Objective voice measurements obtained at a voice clinic, such as acoustic and aerodynamic testing, can be affected by muscle imbalance, organic pathology, or respiratory function. Data can yield important information about the possible cause of the dysfunction and potential treatment targets.

Acoustic assessment

Acoustic testing is typically designed to provide objective measures that correlate with how the voice is perceived by listeners, and to quantify some vocal limits. Measures of fundamental frequency (in Hz) are related to the perception of pitch and measures of sound pressure level (in dB) are related to the perception of loudness. These measures are also used to quantify the maximum ranges in pitch and loudness that the singer can achieve. Voice quality is more complex, typically involving measures that are designed to quantify the levels of perturbation (e.g. jitter and shimmer) and/or noise (e.g. noise to harmonic ratio and cepstral peak prominence) in the voice acoustic signal (Mehta and Hillman 2008). The perception of abnormal roughness or breathiness is generally associated with a decrease in the periodicity of vocal fold vibration and/or incomplete glottal closure creating noise due to air turbulence. Pathology can also alter the fundamental frequency of the speaking voice, making it too low or too high; for example, increased mass such as extensive edema can lower speaking frequency, and extensive scarring of vocal fold tissue can raise the frequency. Truncation of frequency or intensity range along with maximum sustained phonation may also be evident due to reduced tissue pliability or altered vocal fold closure.

Aerodynamic assessment

The goal of clinical aerodynamic testing is to obtain indirect estimates of laryngeal function via non-invasive oral measurements including: (1) average airflow through the glottis (transglottal airflow) from oral airflow during vowel production, and (2) air pressure below the vocal folds (subglottal pressure) from intraoral pressure during bilabial obstruent consonants. Aerodynamic measurements may indicate excessive or too little airflow depending upon the closure patterns of the vocal folds and the respiratory effort provided. If the vocal folds do not completely close, increased airflow measurements can be observed, and if the voice is strained or pressed, insufficient airflow may be present due to increased compression of the vocal fold. An elevated subglottal pressure is common with muscle tension and pathological voices, in order to drive less pliable tissue into motion. Conversely, if the vocal folds cannot approximate, it is difficult to build up enough subglottic pressure below the vocal folds. Subglottic pressure can affect both loudness level and pitch control in a singer.

Subjective testing

Subjective assessment may also be utilized to understand the full impact of the vocal difficulty on the injured singer, for example the Voice-Related Quality of Life (V-RQOL; Hogikyan and Sethuramon 1999) or the Singing Voice Handicap Index (SVHI; Cohen et al. 2007), in addition to further qualifying perceptual changes by a speech pathologist, such as the Consensus Auditory–Perceptual Evaluation of Voice (CAPE-V; Kempster et al. 2009). Additional assessment may include a hearing screening and evaluation of the structure and function of the oral mechanism to ensure there are no confounding factors in deteriorated voicing.

VOICE DISORDERS

A four-category system will be utilized to organize voice disorders outlined in this chapter (Rosen and Murry 2000). This system includes: (1) non-organic disorders, (2) organic disorders, (3) movement disorders of the larynx, and (4) systemic diseases which affect the voice-production system.

Non-organic voice disorder

Vocal deterioration can occur in the setting of no obvious organic pathology as excessive or imbalanced patterns of muscle activation may contribute to vocal symptoms observed by the singer (Hillman et al. 1989). Vocal fatigue is a common symptom that can occur from muscle imbalance within the extrinsic and/or intrinsic laryngeal musculature or mechanical fatigue within the lamina propria (Titze 1984; Welham and Maclagan 2002).

The supra- and infrahyoid extrinsic musculature assists in laryngeal positioning and therefore alters the length of the vocal tract, assists in respiratory function, and acts as a secondary mechanism when achieving higher or lower pitch (Sonninen 1968). Excessive tonicity in these muscles can negatively alter vertical laryngeal freedom and the positioning of the hyoid bone in relation to the thyroid lamina, which can result in lack of vocal flexibility (Sundberg and Askenfelt 1983). A tense sternocleidomastoid muscle can also affect the upper thoracic movement necessary in a singer, especially if he or she is singing and dancing simultaneously, as this muscle activity is necessary during periods of high lung activation (Watson et al. 2012).

Imbalanced patterns of muscle activation predictably affect intrinsic laryngeal configurations evident during videoendoscopy, yielding a diagnosis of muscle tension dysphonia (MTD) (Morrison et al. 1983). Muscle tension can be experienced in isolation (i.e. primary difficulty) or as a consequence of organic pathology (i.e. secondary/reactive) (Belafsky et al. 2002; Halum and Koufman 2005; Roy 1994; Verdolini et al. 2005). The five intrinsic muscles position the vocal folds in relation to the thyroid and cricoid cartilages and affect closure and vibratory patterns. Muscle tension as witnessed via videostroboscopy is most commonly seen as compression above the vocal folds where either the ventricular (i.e. false) folds compress and/or the arytenoids and epiglottis excessively squeeze together. Additional signs of imbalance include excessive medial compression of the vocal folds, lack of closure yielding variations of a glottic gap, increased closure force of the vocal folds during onset, and phase asymmetry of the mucosal wave (Koufman and Blalock 1982; Morrison 1997; Morrison and Rammage 1994). This activity may be perceived by the singer as increased vocal effort or strain and affect overall strength and stamina of voicing.

Involuntary register changes or breaks can be a form of non-organic vocal dysfunction specific to singers. Balanced intrinsic muscle coordination is necessary for the negotiation of registers (Hirano et al. 1970; Kochis-Jennings et al. 2011). Further, interaction between vocal tract resonances and the vibratory behavior of the vocal folds can also affect register transition and overall vocal timbre (Titze 2000).

Organic vocal fold changes

Increased voice demands, illness, and idiopathic reasons can all contribute to a voice disorder involving organic change of the vocal fold. Whether these changes are from phonotrauma (Verdolini et al. 1999) or due to mechanical (e.g. laryngeal trauma) or chemical (e.g. smoking) causes, the remodeling of injured tissue has been insufficient over time (Branski et al. 2006). The most common discrete lesions encountered in performing vocalists are fibrovascular nodules (Zeitels et al. 2002), polyps (Zeitels et al. 2002), ectasias/varices (Zeitels et al. 2006), and cysts (Burns et al. 2009). Vocal fold pathology can be benign or malignant; benign pathological tissue demonstrates disordered epithelium or variation in the mass and/or stiffness of the lamina propria, while cancer can invade much more of the laryngeal structure and beyond.

The degree of vocal dysfunction depends on whether the organic change affects a discrete area of the mucosal wave or the entire vocal fold. Pathology on the leading edge of the vocal fold can affect vocal fold closure, which in turn affects the quality of voicing (e.g. bilateral nodules may result in an hourglass closure pattern allowing increased airflow to create a breathy quality). Vocal fold symmetry is also important as the different mass and/or stiffness properties created by a lesion can create phase asymmetry in the mucosal wave and thus affect quality. A growth within the vocal fold, such as a cyst, can produce an absence or reduction of the mucosal wave in that area contributing to increased roughness of voice and altered vocal control. Pre-menstrual changes can contribute to venous dilation and/or edema resulting in a short-term increase in vocal instability and vocal fatigue (Abitbol et al. 1999) due to the added mass. Both the vibratory behavior of the vocal fold mucosa and overall glottic closure are paramount to appropriate aerodynamic and acoustic efficiency of the singing voice.

Table 2.1 provides examples of organic pathologies, their description and potential treatment.

Table 2.1 Organic pathologies

Pathology	Description	Treatment
Edema	A swelling of the mucosa; an early response to vibratory trauma, whether from voice use or a viral illness. These signs can dissipate within hours to days if further trauma is avoided	Voice rest typically resolves short-term edema
Reinke's edema/ polypoid degeneration	Diffuse gelatinous fluid in the space of Reinke within the superficial lamina propria (SLP). Causative factors include long-term smoking, hypothyroidism, and vocal misuse	Surgical management may be warranted
Acute laryngitis	Due to a viral, bacterial or fungal infection. Inflammation occurs in the SLP	Treatment is a combination of voice rest, possible antibiotics, corticosteroids, and/or anti-fungal medication
Erythema	Capillary dilation with increased blood flow; an early response to trauma; may accompany edema	Treatment is a combination of medical or behavioral therapy
Nodules	Typically bilateral. This pathology involves benign edematous (early) or fibrous (late) changes which occur in the superficial lamina propria at the junction of the anterior and middle third of the vocal fold. The pathology affects mucosal wave propagation and increases localized areas of stiffness	Treatment involves behavioral therapy and/or surgical management
Cyst	Typically unilateral, although can be bilateral. Involves a fluid-filled sphere-like mass, which occurs in the SLP but can invade deeper layers as well. This pathology affects mucosal wave propagation and increases localized areas of stiffness	Management is a combination of behavioral therapy and surgical intervention
Polyp	Typically unilateral. This pathology occurs on the epithelial surface and can be hemorrhagic or filled with keratin	Treatment is typically surgical management and behavioral therapy

Table 2.1 Continued

Pathology	Description	Treatment
Ectasia	Unilateral or bilateral. Involves a collection of localized blood vessels, which increases the risk of a vocal fold hemorrhage	Treatment is behavioral or surgical with laser coagulation
Hemorrhage	Unilateral or bilateral. This pathology is a result of acute phonotrauma from broken blood vessel(s) contributing to an active bleed in Reinke's space of the SLP	Treated with voice rest
Sulcus	Unilateral or bilateral. Involves a loss of SLP contributing to a deficit or divot in the vocal fold as the mucosal cover can be scarred to varying depths including down to the underlying vocal ligament. This pathology increases vocal fold stiffness which can interfere with vibration and closure	Behavioral therapy, vocal fold injections, lasers, or epithelium-freeing techniques may be attempted to improve function, but there is currently no routine approach that has proven efficacy
Laryngocele	Air sac located in the ventricle (space between true and false vocal folds), which bulges outward during higher-pressure activities. Typically, this does not affect vocal function unless the sac comes in contact with the true vocal folds	Treatment includes behavioral therapy to target aspects of muscle tension and/or surgical management
Laryngeal web	Disrupted mucosa near the anterior commissure, which can be congenital or traumatic in origin. If extensive, this pathology shortens the overall vibratory capability of the vocal folds	Often there is no vocal or respiratory difficulty if the web is small, although surgical management can be completed to separate the fused tissue when extensive
Vocal fold granuloma	Epithelialized granulation tissue typically on the vocal process of the arytenoid; can be unilateral or bilateral and is caused by intubation, laryngopharyngeal reflux, and/or phonotrauma	Treatment is typically a combination of medical, behavioral, and/or surgical management
Mucosal tear	Mucosal tears typically result from vocal misuse contributing to a separation of vocal fold tissue	Treatment is a combination of voice rest and behavioral therapy
Mucosal bridge	Laryngeal lesions of a genetic origin	Treatment is a combination of behavioral therapy and surgery. (see Sulcus above)
Laryngeal cancer	Malignant lesion that can affect the glottis, subglottis, and supraglottis, and can range from a small growth to a large invasive tumor. There is a synergistic relationship of smoking and alcohol use contributing to the development of cancer	Management includes surgery, radiation therapy and/or chemotherapy
Dysplasia	Abnormal, pre-malignant tissue growth typically caused by smoking, environmental pollutants and/or reflux	Management is surgical
Recurrent respiratory papilloma	Benign epithelial growth that is reddish and wart-like in appearance, caused by strain of the Human Papilloma Virus. This pathology can occur throughout the respiratory and vocal tract	Management is surgical

Movement disorders of the larynx

Laryngeal movement disorders result from altered function of the nervous system contributing to (1) reduced or absent abduction or adduction of the vocal folds and/or (2) reduced muscular control of voice. This type of disorder can be short-term, such as after a viral illness, or take up to 12 months to resolve following a surgical procedure which has temporarily stretched a laryngeal nerve (e.g. thyroidectomy). A movement disorder can also be permanent, especially when associated with a progressive neurological disorder or when the recurrent or superior laryngeal nerve has been severed during a surgical procedure in the neck or chest.

With a laryngeal movement disorder, a variety of difficulties may be visualized with endoscopy: lack of movement in one or both vocal folds; sluggish or spasmodic abduction or adduction; height differences between the two vocal folds; vocal fold bowing; altered pitch control; and hyperfunction of the supraglottic structures (Rubin 2007). Laryngeal electromyography (EMG) may be utilized to assess the electrical activity of contracted muscles in either the recurrent or superior laryngeal nerves to assist in diagnosis.

Table 2.2 contains examples of laryngeal movement disorders, their description, and their potential treatment.

More generalized neurological disorders can also affect the voice even though the primary dysfunction does not reside in the larynx. Examples include multiple sclerosis, dystonia, Parkinson's disease, essential tremor, and amyotrophic lateral sclerosis. These systemic disorders affect laryngeal function via the neuromuscular pathway, interfering with the ability to control muscle movement.

Other systemic diseases affecting the voice

Singers challenged with asthma or allergies can have respiratory systems that are at times compromised. Asthma can diminish vocal strength and stamina by weakening the power source to the larynx. Asthma involves inflamed and narrowed airways, and air exchange can become difficult. Further, asthma may contribute to increased hyperfunction of the articulatory and strap muscles in addition to vocal fatigue (Spiegel et al. 1998). Allergies can involve irritated and inflamed tissues throughout the respiratory and vocal tract, affecting respiration, vocal fold tissue, and resonance. Medical management is often warranted in both asthma and allergies depending upon the severity of symptoms.

Enlarged tonsils and/or adenoids can negatively affect velopharyngeal function and overall resonance (Kummer et al. 1993). In addition to affecting vocal function, symptoms associated with tonsillitis or adenoiditis may alter a person's quality of life. With careful consideration, tonsillectomy and adenoidectomy can be performed safely in singers despite their specialized requirements for pharyngeal function (Jarboe et al. 2001).

Laryngopharyngeal reflux (LPR) or gastroesophageal reflux disease (GERD) can affect both respiratory and laryngeal function. Performers are susceptible to LPR/GERD due to the increase in intra-abdominal pressure that occurs with singing (Cammarota et al. 2007). GERD occurs when stomach acid frequently moves through the lower esophageal sphincter

Table 2.2 Laryngeal movement disorders

Disorder	Description	Treatment
Paresis	Unilateral or bilateral. This disorder involves weakness observed in the recurrent laryngeal nerve (RLN) or the superior laryngeal nerve (SLN) which affects vocal fold motion, strength or pitch control	Treatment typically is behavioral therapy
Paralysis	Unilateral or bilateral. Involves absence of nerve function in either the RLN or SLN. It is also theoretically possible for the cricoarytenoid joint to be immobile, but is a much less likely etiology	Treatment is a combination of behavioral therapy and surgical management
Spasmodic dysphonia	Involves involuntary muscular spasms when the vocal folds either open (abductor spasmodic dysphonia) or close (adductor spasmodic dysphonia). A mixed presentation may also occur	This disorder has been responsive to ongoing botulinum toxin (Botox) injections, and the frequency of injections depends upon the severity of the dysphonia
Laryngeal tremor	Involuntary rhythmic oscillations ranging from 3–7 Hz	Medications may assist some individuals although success is limited
Paradoxical vocal fold motion (PVFM) or vocal cord dysfunction (VCD)	Presents with normal vocal fold structure but altered function often exacerbated by allergies or laryngopharyngeal reflux. This occurs when the vocal folds close, typically during the inspiratory cycle, creating a narrowed airway. It can be misdiagnosed as asthma. Stridor, a high-pitched wheeze, may be experienced upon inspiration	PVFM/VCD is typically responsive to medical management if reflux is present, behavioral voice therapy, and psychological counseling, if warranted, as it can occur following periods of trauma or increased stress

into the esophagus, often contributing to heartburn. With LPR, the contents of the stomach reflux all the way up the esophagus, beyond the upper esophageal sphincter, and come into contact with the delicate laryngeal tissues or upper airway. Heartburn may or may not be experienced with LPR (Koufman et al. 2002). Laryngeal findings associated with LPR include laryngeal and vocal fold edema, erythema, thicker mucus, and hypertrophied tissue in the posterior arytenoid region (Belafsky et al. 2001). Performers may notice increased laryngeal mucus, throat clearing, coughing, and postnasal drip, which are due to increased abdominal movement, dietary habits involving specific foods that increase reflux tendencies, the timing of meals (e.g. prior to singing or late at night), and overall stress. Symptoms can typically be adequately managed with dietary restrictions, the use of antacids, histamine-2 blockers, and/or proton-pump inhibitors (PPIs).

Endocrine influences may also be present, such as issues with thyroid function or sex hormone imbalances. Change in speaking pitch, stability of the voice, and breathy or rough qualities may occur (Sataloff et al. 1997).

IMPLICATIONS FOR PRACTICE

Medical and surgical management of the disordered voice

Based upon the type of vocal fold injury, medical or surgical management may be warranted. At the simplest level, variable amounts of prescribed voice rest, encompassing days or weeks, can allow for inflammation such as edema or erythema to recede and tense musculature to relax. More extensive voice rest is also often indicated post-operatively to allow for wound healing; the length of rest prescribed varies greatly among surgeons, typically lasting from several days to 2 weeks. At the present time, there is no conclusion regarding the ideal length of post-operative voice rest (Behrman and Sulica 2003; Ishikawa and Thibeault 2008; Koufman and Blalock 1989). Further, a performer must be considerate of detraining with voice rest and should be mindful of the possible need for retraining in order to return to a previously established level of endurance, strength, and flexibility (Sandage and Pascoe 2010).

The use of medication, whether prescription or over-the-counter, can be beneficial, although particular agents should be used cautiously when possible. The cost–benefit ratio should be determined when attempting to address symptoms while maintaining vocal health as medications can affect the voice via fluid shifts, airflow, proprioception, and coordination. Further, medications affect individuals differently; guidance under a physician is indicated for any singer. The website of the National Center for Voice and Speech (NCVS) gives a list of commonly prescribed medications and their potential effect on vocal function (see Further resources).

If an organic pathology is present, phonomicrosurgery, which involves operating with the aid of a microscope and specialized instruments, can be a viable way of improving the voice or fully returning to baseline function. Informed consent for surgery is extremely important and engenders a mutual responsibility for the decision to pursue an invasive elective procedure (Zeitels et al. 2002). Choosing a surgeon with extensive experience in phonomicrosurgery is of utmost importance, as instrumental resection of the pathology needs to be completed with as much preservation of the healthy epithelium and superficial lamina propria as possible. Laser treatment (e.g. with a pulsed-potassium-titanyl-phosphate (KTP) laser) can also be beneficial in coagulating leaky blood vessels contributing to a vocal fold hemorrhage or for effectively treating surface disease such as dysplasia without substantial photothermal trauma (Zeitels et al. 2006).

The use of injectable materials can be a treatment option if there is incomplete closure of the vocal folds (Mallur and Rosen 2010) although, again, with any elective procedure the decision to use one of these agents should be very carefully considered. Deep injections into the paraglottic space of agents such as hyaluronic acid (e.g. Restylane), fat, or collagen can improve vocal fold closure, although the effects are largely temporary depending primarily on how long the selected material lasts in the body. In cases of persistent lack of closure due to immobility of the vocal fold, a more permanent procedure to improve vocal fold contact is an option (e.g. medialization laryngoplasty with Gore-Tex; McCulloch and Hoffman 1998), although this procedure cannot be expected to regain the significant loss of singing function that occurs with this diagnosis.

Vocal emergencies

Team management of voice disorders in singers is perhaps most important in vocal emergencies, which typically arise when a performer becomes ill immediately before or during a performance. A thorough voice history, present voice demands, current voice changes such as quality, effort, range, etc., are typically compiled in addition to completion of videostroboscopic assessment. Medical assessment by the laryngologist must determine if a pathology exists that would make it dangerous for the singer to continue singing, thereby requiring a decision to postpone or cancel a performance and go on complete voice rest.

The onset of vocal difficulty can provide clues as to the etiology of the difficulty and ensure appropriate management (Klein and Johns 2007). For example, a sudden onset during phonation can be indicative of a vocal fold hemorrhage. Viral or bacterial respiratory tract infections can create nasal congestion, coughing, secretions, and edema; changes in vocal function will occur around the time of the illness and at times can even last beyond the experienced illness.

The medical team works with the performer to optimize vocal hygiene, laryngeal biomechanics, and general management if the singer makes an informed decision to continue performing or to determine when it is alright to return to full voice demands after time off.

Speech/voice therapy of the disordered voice

Behavioral therapy provided by a speech pathologist plays a role in recovery by either rebalancing subsystem function or maximizing voicing in the post-operative mechanism. Any inefficiency in musculoskeletal alignment, respiration, phonation, resonance, and articulation is targeted within therapy to improve performance. Each area may be addressed in isolation or the coordination amongst subsystems may be a focus. In addition to these physiological targets, basic vocal hygiene, education in maximizing vocal function, and counseling may be addressed.

There are a vast number of therapeutic approaches that can be implemented as treatment is not a one size fits all approach; the specific vocal difficulty guides rehabilitation in addition to the singer's goals in returning to baseline function. Attention is always given to evidence-based treatment in a medical voice session, which indicates controlled experiments have yielded data supporting the use of a specific approach. This assists in distinguishing rehabilitative therapy from the more habilitative nature of singing lessons where a baseline function is to be surpassed.

Research advances to restore vibratory function to damaged vocal fold tissue

There is currently no proven efficacious medical treatment for restoring pliability to vocal folds that have lost their normal vibratory function due to damaged mucosa, i.e. scarring/stiffening of the superficial layers of the vocal folds. This continues to be the leading cause of dysphonia among professional and non-professional voice users.

The need for methods to restore vocal fold pliability has generated an increasing number of efforts to develop biological and/or synthetic remedies. In addition to continued attempts to develop surgically based remedies (including new laser techniques), these proposed therapies include the use of synthetic biomaterials (some based on natural extracellular matrix components such as hyaluronic acid and collagen), cells (stem cells or fibroblasts), autologous tissue (fat or fascia), scaffolds (synthetic or tissue based), growth factors, and other chemical agents, such as steroids and phytochemicals. Although all of these approaches have demonstrated some positive results in animal studies, and there have been some small-scale pilot studies of several types of treatments in humans, much more research and development of these new technologies is required.

Summary

Singers, or "vocal athletes," require ongoing biomechanical conditioning to perform at a satisfactory level. Improving education regarding potential physiological inefficiencies, possible signs of injury, and basic laryngeal pathology should allow those involved in the art of singing to be proactive in prevention of injury and maximize the understanding of challenges facing the injured singer.

Importantly, injuries can be part of a physical system that is asked to engage in extensive, complex tasks that increase normal wear on ligaments, joints, muscles, and vocal fold mucosa. When an injury occurs, a vocal athlete should be viewed as any other professional athlete who has experienced difficulty with no generalized stigma attached regarding their technical skill.

If a singer should experience a decline in function, medical assessment from a laryngologist familiar with the vocal demands associated with performing is paramount. Decline in function can range from acute illness affecting respiratory and vocal mucosa, muscle inefficiency such as excessive tension or fatigue, to actual organic change of vocal fold tissue. Based on the laryngological assessment, medical, surgical, and/or behavioral management may be warranted to improve or restore the ability that has been lost. With effective collaboration of the voice team and a strategy tailored to the individual singer, appropriate treatment will ideally promote the singer's return to established singing activities and avoidance of further injury.

Further resources

Further reading

Colton, R., Casper, J., and Leonard, R. (2011). *Understanding Voice Problems*, 4th edn. Baltimore, MD: Lippincott Williams and Wilkins.

McCoy, S. (2012). *Your Voice: an Inside View. Multimedia Voice Science and Pedagogy*, 2nd edn. Princeton, NJ: Inside View Press.

Malde, M., Allen, M., Alexander Zeller, K. (2008). *What Every Singer Needs to Know About the Body*, San Diego, CA: Plural Publishing.

Sundberg, J. (1987). *The Science of Singing*. Dekalb, IL: Northern Illinois University Press.

Thurman, L. and Welch, G. (2000). *Bodymind and Voice: Foundations of Voice Education.* Collegeville, MN: The Voice Care Network.

Website

The National Center for Voice and Speech (NCVS): <http://www.ncvs.org/>

References

Abitbol, J., Abitbol, P., and Abitbol, B. (1999). Sex hormones and the female voice. *Journal of Voice* 13(3): 424–446.

Aronson, A.E. (1985). *Clinical Voice Disorders: an Interdisciplinary Approach.* New York: Brian C. Decker.

Aronson, A.E. (1990). *Clinical Voice Disorders: an Interdisciplinary Approach,* 3rd edn. New York: Theime Medical.

Awan, S. and Alphonso, V. (2007). Effects of smoking on respiratory capacity and control. *Clinical Linguistics and Phonetics* 21(8): 623–636.

Behrman, A. and Sulica, L. (2003). Voice rest after microlaryngoscopy: current opinion and practice. *Laryngoscope* 113: 2182–2186.

Belafsky, P., Postma, G., and Koufman, J. (2001). Validity and reliability of the reflux findings score (RFS). *Laryngoscope* 111: 1313–1317.

Belafsky, P., Postma, G., Reulbach, T., Holland, B., and Koufman, J. (2002). Muscle tension dysphonia as a sign of underlying glottal insufficiency. *Otolaryngology–Head and Neck Surgery* 127: 448–451.

Berg, E., Hapner, E., Klein, A., and Johns, M. (2008). Voice therapy improves quality of life in age-related dysphonia: a case–control study. *Journal of Voice* 22(1): 70–74.

Branski, R., Verdolini, K., Sandulache, V., Rosen, C., and Hebda P. (2006). Vocal fold wound healing: a review for clinicians. *Journal of Voice* 20(3): 432–442.

Burns, J.A., Hillman, R.E., Stadelman-Cohen, T., and Zeitels, S.M. (2009). Phonomicrosurgical treatment of intracordal vocal-fold cysts in singers. *Laryngoscope* 119(2): 419–422.

Butcher P., Elias A., and Cavalli, L. (2007). *Understanding and Treating Psychogenic Voice Disorder: a CBT Framework.* Chichester: John Wiley and Sons.

Cammarota, G., Masala, G., Cianci, R., et al. (2007). Reflux symptoms in professional opera choristers. *Gastroenterology* 132(3): 890–898.

Chaitow, L., Bradley, D., Gilbert, C. and Ley, R. (2002). The structure and function of breathing. In: *Multidisciplinary Approaches to Breathing Pattern Disorders,* pp. 1–41. Edinburgh: Churchill Livingstone.

Christopher, K.L., Wood, R.P., Eckert, R.C., et al. (1983). Vocal-cord dysfunction presenting as asthma. *New England Journal of Medicine* 308: 1566–1570.

Claire, J. (1991). Understanding and treating performance anxiety from a cognitive-behavior therapy perspective. *NATS Journal* 47(4): 27–30.

Cohen, S., Jacobson, B., Garrett, D., et al. (2007). Creation and validation of the singing voice handicap index. *Annals of Otology, Rhinology and Laryngology* 116(6): 402–406.

Collyer, S., Thorpe, C., Callaghan, J., and Davis, P. (2008). The influence of fundamental frequency and sound pressure level range on breathing patterns in classical singing. *Journal of Speech, Language, and Hearing Research* 50: 612–628.

Current Opinion in Otolaryngology and Head and Neck Surgery (2010). [Nine papers in the section on 'Laryngology and bronchoesophagology'] 18(6): 475–525.

Edwards, R.H.T. (1981). Human muscle function and fatigue. In: R. Porter and J. Whelean (eds), *Human Muscle Fatigue: Physiological Mechanisms*, pp. 1–18. London: Pitman.

Estenne, M., Yernault, J., and DeTroyer, A. (1985). Rib-cage and diaphragm-abdomen compliance in humans: effects of age and posture. *Journal of Applied Physiology* 59(6): 1842–1848.

Ford, C. (2004). Voice restoration in presbyphonia. *Archives of Otolaryngology Head and Neck Surgery* 130: 1117.

Friedrich, G., Dikkers, F.G., Arens, C., et al. (2013). Vocal fold scars: current concepts and future directions. Consensus report of the phonosurgery committee of the European laryngological society. *European Archives of Otorhinolaryngology* 270: 2491–2507.

Gorham-Rowan, M. and Laures-Gore, J. (2006). Acoustic-perceptual correlates of voice quality in elderly men and women. *Journal of Communication Disorders* 39(3): 171–184.

Gugatschka, M., Kiesler, K., Obermayer-Pietsch, B., et al. (2010). Sex hormones and the elderly male voice. *Journal of Voice* 24(3): 369–373.

Halum, S.L. and Koufman, J.A. (2005). The paresis podule. *Ear, Nose, Throat Journal* 84: 624.

Heman-Ackah, Y. (2004). Hormone replacement therapy: implications of the women's health initiative for the perimenopausal singer. *Journal of Singing* 60(5): 471–475.

Hillman, R.E., Holmberg, E.B., Perkell, J.S., Walsh, M., and Vaughan, C. (1989). Objective assessment of vocal hyperfunction: an experimental framework and initial results. *Journal of Speech and Hearing Research* 32(2): 373–392.

Hirano, M., Vennard, W., and Ohala, J. (1970). Regulation of register, pitch, and intensity of voice. *Folia Phoniatrica* 22: 1–20.

Hogikyan, N.D. and Sethuramon, G. (1999). Validation of an instrument to measure voice-related quality of life (V-RQOL). *Journal of Voice* 13: 557–569.

Hunter, E. and Titze, I. (2009). Quantifying vocal fatigue recovery: dynamic vocal recovery trajectories after a vocal loading exercise. *Annals of Otology, Rhinology and Laryngology* 118(6): 449–460.

Ishikawa, K. and Thibeault, S. (2008) Voice rest versus exercise: a review of the literature. *Journal of Voice* 24(4): 379–387.

Jarboe, J., Zeitels, S., and Elias, B. (2001). Tonsillectomy and adenoidectomy in singers. *Journal of Voice* 15(4): 561–564.

Johns, M., Arviso, L., and Ramadan, F. (2011). Challenges and opportunities in the management of the aging voice. *Otolaryngology–Head and Neck Surgery* 145(1): 1–6.

Kempster, G.B., Gerratt, B.R., Verdolini Abbott, K., Barkmeier-Kraemer, J., and Hillman, R.E. (2009). Consensus auditory-perceptual evaluation of voice: development of a standardized clinical protocol. *American Journal of Speech-Language Pathology* 18(2): 124–132.

Klein, A. and Johns, M. (2007). Vocal emergencies. *Otolaryngological Clinics of North America* 40: 1063–1080.

Kochis-Jennings, K.A., Finnegan, E.M., Hoffman, H.T., and Jaiswal, S. (2011). Laryngeal muscle activity and vocal fold adduction during chest, chestmix, headmix, and head registers in females. *Journal of Voice* 26(2): 182–193.

Koufman, J.A. and Blalock, P.D. (1982). Classification and approach to patients with functional voice disorders. *Annals of Otology, Rhinology, and Laryngology* 91: 372–377.

Koufman, J.A. and Blalock, P.D. (1989). Is voice rest never indicated? *Journal of Voice* 3: 87–91.

Koufman, J., Belafsky, P., Bach, K., Daniel, E., and Postma, G. (2002). Prevalence of esophagitis in patients with pH-documented laryngopharyngeal reflux. *Laryngoscope* 112: 1606–1609.

Koumbourlis, A.C. (2006). Scoliosis and the respiratory system. *Paediatric Respiratory Reviews* 7(2): 152–160.

Kummer, A., Billmore, D., and Myer, C. (1993). Hypertrophic tonsils: the effect on resonance and velopharyngeal closure. *Plastic Reconstructive Surgery* 91(4): 608–611.

Kuchera, M. and Kuchera, W. (1997). General postural considerations. In: R. Ward (ed) *Foundations for Osteopathic Medicine*, pp. 969–977. Baltimore: Williams and Wilkins.

Lessac, A. (1987). *The Use and Training of the Human Voice: a Practical Approach to Speech and Voice Dynamics*. New York: Drama Book Publishers.

Lieberman, J. (1998). Principles and techniques of manual therapy: applications in the management of dysphonia. In: T. Harris, J.S. Rubin, D.M. Howard (eds) *The Voice Clinic Handbook*, 1st edn, pp. 91–138. London: Whurr Publishers.

McCulloch, T. and Hoffman, H. (1998). Medialization laryngoplasty with expanded polytetrafluoroethylene. Surgical technique and preliminary results. *Annals of Otology, Rhinology, and Laryngology* 107: 427–432.

Mallur, P. and Rosen, C. (2010). Vocal fold injection: review of indications, techniques, and materials for augmentation. *Clinical and Experimental Otorhinolaryngology* 3(4): 177–182.

Mehta, D. and Hillman, R.E. (2008). Voice assessment: updates on perceptual, acoustic, aerodynamic and endoscopic imaging. *Current Opinion in Otolaryngology Head Neck Surgery* 16: 211–215.

Morrison, M.D. (1997). Pattern recognition in muscle misuse voice disorders: How I do it. *Journal of Voice* 11: 108–114.

Morrison, M.D. and Rammage, L. (1994). *The Management of Voice Disorders*. San Diego, CA: Singular Publishing.

Morrison, M., Rammage, L., Gilles, M., Pullan, C., and Hamish, N. (1983). Muscular tension dysphonia. *Journal of Otolaryngology* 12(5): 302–306.

Morrow, S.L. and Connor, N.P. (2011). Comparison of voice-use profiles between elementary classroom and music teachers. *Journal of Voice* 25(3): 367–372.

Piron, A. and Roch, J. (2010). Temporomandibular dysfunction and dysphonia (TMD). *Revue de Laryngologie, Otologie Rhinologie* 131(1): 31–34.

Robson-Ansley, P.J., Gleeson, M., and Ansley, L. (2009). Fatigue management in the preparation of Olympic athletes. *Journal of Sports Science* 27(13): 1409–1420.

Rosen, C.A. and Murry, T. (2000). Nomenclature of voice disorders and vocal pathology. *Otolaryngology Clinics of North America* 35(5): 1035–1046.

Roy, N. (1994). Ventricular dysphonia following long-term endotracheal intubation: a case study. *Journal of Otolaryngology* 23: 189–193.

Roy, N., Bless, D., Heisey, D., and Ford, C. (1997). Manual circumlaryngeal therapy for functional dysphonia: an evaluation of short- and long-term treatment outcomes. *Journal of Voice* 11(3): 321–331.

Rubin, A. (2007). Neurolaryngologic evaluation of the performer. *Otolaryngology Clinics of North America* 40: 971–989.

Sandage, M. and Pascoe, D. (2010). Translating exercise science into voice care. *SIG3 Perspectives on Voice and Voice Disorders (ASHA)* 20(3): 84–89.

Sataloff, R., Emerich, K., and Hoover, C. (1997). Endocrine dysfunction. In: *Professional Voice: the Science and Art of Clinical Care*, 2nd edn, pp. 291–298. San Diego, CA: Singular Publishing Group.

Scherer, R.C., Titze, I.R., Raphael, B.N., Wood, R.P., Ramig, L.A., and Blager, R.F. (1991). Vocal fatigue in a trained and an untrained voice user. In: T. Baer, C. Sasaki, and K. Harris (eds)

Laryngeal Function in Phonation and Respiration, pp. 533–555. San Diego, CA: Singular Publishing Group.

Schwartz, S., Cohen, S., Dailey, S., et al. (2009). Clinical practice guideline: hoarseness (dysphonia). *Otolaryngology–Head and Neck Surgery* 141: S1–S31.

Sonninen, A. (1968). The external frame function in the control of pitch in the human voice. *Annals of the New York Academy of Science* 155: 68–90.

Sperry, E. and Klich, R. (1992). Speech breathing in senescent and younger women during oral readings. *Journal of Speech and Hearing Research* 35: 1246–1255.

Spiegel, J., Sataloff, R., Cohn, J., and Hawkshaw, M. (1998). Respiratory dysfunction. In: R. Sataloff (ed.), *Vocal Health and Pedagogy*, pp. 147–159. San Diego, CA: Singular Publishing Group.

Stadelman-Cohen, T., Burns, J., Zeitels, S., and Hillman, R. (2009). Team management of voice disorders in singers. *The ASHA Leader*, 24 November.

Stokes, I.A.F., Dansereau, J., and Moreland, M.S. (1989). Rib cage asymmetry in idiopathic scoliosis. *Journal of Orthopaedic Research* 7(4): 599–606.

Sundberg, J. and Askenfelt, A. (1983). Larynx height and voice source: a relationship? In: D.M. Bless and J.H. Abbs (eds) *Voice Physiology*, pp. 307–316. San Diego: College-Hill Press.

Thomas, L. and Stemple, J. (2007). The aging voice: from clinical symptoms to biological realities. American Speech–Language–Hearing Association (ASHA) National Convention, Boston, MA, 17 November 2007.

Thorpe, C., Cala, S., Chapman, J., and Davis, P. (2001). Patterns of breath support in projection of the singing voice. *Journal of Voice* 15: 86–104.

Titze, I. (1984). Vocal fatigue: some biomechanical considerations. In: V.L. Lawrence (ed.), *Transcripts of the Twelfth Symposium: Care of the Professional Voice (Part One: Scientific Papers)*, pp. 97–104. New York: The Voice Foundation.

Titze, I. (2000). *Principles of Voice Production*, 2nd edn. Iowa City, IA: National Center for Voice and Speech.

Titze, I. (2001). Criteria for occupational risk in vocalization. In: *Occupational Voice: Care and Cure*, pp. 1–10. The Hague: Kugler Publications.

Titze, I., Long, R., Shirley, G., et al. (1999). Messa di voce: an investigation of the symmetry of crescendo and descrescendo in a singing exercise. *Journal of the Acoustical Society of America* 105: 2933–2940.

Verdolini, K. (1999). Critical analysis of common terminology in voice therapy: a position paper. *Phonoscope* 2: 1–8.

Verdolini, K., Druker, D., Palmer, P., and Samawi, H. (1998). Laryngeal adduction in resonant voice. *Journal of Voice* 12(3): 315–327.

Verdolini, K., Hess, M., Titze, I., Bierhals, W., and Gross, M. (1999). Investigation of vocal fold impact stress in human subjects. *Journal of Voice* 13(2): 184–202.

Verdolini, K., Young, M., Titze, I., et al. (2002). Biological mechanisms underlying voice changes due to dehydration. *Journal of Speech, Language, and Hearing Research* 45: 268–281.

Verdonlini, K., Rosen, C., and Branski, R.C. (2005). *Classification Manual for Voice Disorders-I*. Mahwah, NJ: Lawrence Erlbaum Associates.

Watson, A.H., Williams, C., and James, B.V. (2012). Activity patterns in latissimus dorsi and sternocleidomastoid in classical singers. *Journal of Voice* 26(3): e95–e105.

Welham, N. and Maclagan, M. (2002). Vocal fatigue: current knowledge and future directions. *Journal of Voice* 17(1): 21–30.

Zaino, C. and Benventano, T. (1977). Functional involutional and degenerative disorders. In: C. Zaino and T. Benventano (eds), *Radiologic Examination of the Oropharynx and Esophagus*, pp. 141–176. New York: Springer-Verlag.

Zeitels, S.M., Hillman, R.E., Desloge, R., Mauri, M., and Doyle, P. (2002). Phono-microsurgery in singers and performing artists: treatment outcomes, management theories and future directions. *Annals of Otology, Rhinology and Laryngology Supplement* 111(12): 21–40.

Zeitels, S.M., Akst, L.A., Burns, J.A., Hillman, R.E., Broadhurst, M.S., and Anderson, R.R. (2006). Pulsed angiolytic laser treatment of ectasias and varices in singers. *Annals of Otology, Rhinology and Laryngology* 115: 571–580.

....

CHAPTER 3

THE HEALTHY VOICE, LIFESTYLE, AND VOICE PROTECTION (INCLUDING EXERCISE, BODY WORK, AND DIET)

....

JOHN S. RUBIN AND RUTH EPSTEIN

INTRODUCTION

....

HEALTHY voice is an ideal that all laryngologists strive for in their patients. Yet should you put ten laryngologists in one room, the likelihood is that the definition of healthy voice would prove elusive. It has been argued that a professional singer should be able to sing for an hour without experiencing discomfort (Rubin et al. 2006), yet it has been anecdotally noted that in certain repertoires vocal discomfort may be part of performance. So how should we take this chapter forward? It is the authors' view that the best way to identify healthy voice is first to review the larynx and the vocal tract; next, to look at psychological and physiological stressors that could impact the voice; finally, to present precepts relating to vocal care. This will define the structure of this chapter.

There is a significant caveat that needs disclosure here and is hinted at above. Vocal "signature" or recognition is critical to many if not most professional voice users. As we finalize this chapter we have just recently commemorated the fiftieth anniversary of John Fitzgerald Kennedy's death. Kennedy's regional Bostonian accent was a part and parcel of his vocal signature, and his voice may well have been the key feature in his apparent victory over Richard Nixon in the pre-election debates and then his victory in the 1960 election to the Presidency of the United States.

Another example might relate to a nasal quality of the voice in a singer or public speaker, which may underpin his or her vocal/speech recognition to the public. As we think about healthy voice, we need to recall that the qualities that lead to this recognizable voice may be due to less than healthy qualities—perhaps in the instance described immediately above, a deviation of the nasal septum—and that correction of this "unhealthy" quality may in reality negatively impact upon the performer's voice by making it less identifiable. This must be considered as we undertake care of professional voice users. The overall vocal health of the voice professional is of paramount importance in our interests as clinicians, but the performer's career must always be taken into consideration as well. This is one of the features that make caring for professional voice users such a fascinating and rewarding profession.

VOICE PRODUCTION

As the reader can readily imagine, diverse elements of the body have been noted to be involved in voice production. We generally state that the entire body should be considered to represent the vocal organ (Rubin et al. 2006). Nonetheless it is traditional to divide the vocal tract into areas supplying the power source; the true vocal folds themselves, and the resonators. A discussion of each area will now follow.

The Power Source

The fundamental issue involved when considering the power source is the development of a reliable source of air under pressure that can then be presented to the glottis. Thus the lungs and adjacent pleura, and rib cage are immediately implicated. On inspiration, the diaphragm contracts due to phrenic nerve excitation. The diaphragm is actually two dome-shaped muscles that have a depressed region on which the heart rests; it separates the abdominal contents from the lungs. Contraction of the diaphragm causes it to straighten and flatten, thereby compressing the abdominal contents while simultaneously expanding the thorax. This creates negative intra-thoracic pressure causing air to enter. On quiet inspiration the volume of air inhaled is approximately half a liter. As the lungs fill up, the vagus nerve fibers involved in the respiratory reflex are stimulated, thereby preventing further inspiration (Boileau Grant and Basmajian 1965; Bunch 1995; Dickson and Maue-Dickson 1982). Quiet expiration follows, in association with generalized chest wall and soft tissue relaxation and diaphragm relaxation and reposition (Dickson and Maue-Dickson 1982). This tends to occur on average twelve to eighteen times per minute, and is, by and large, an unconscious behavior controlled at the level of the brain stem.

The lungs are lined or rather enveloped by the pleura, a two layer membranous sac, one side of which is attached directly to the chest wall. The pleura secretes surfactant, a substance that reduces surface tension between the lungs and the rib cage (Boileau Grant and Basmajian 1965; Gray 1995). The rib cage consists of twelve paired ribs that insert posteriorly into the vertebrae (spine). Anteriorly, the first rib connects directly to the manubrium sternae, while the second through seventh ribs increase in length and connect individually by a mobile cartilaginous joint with the sternum. The ribs thereafter decrease in length, with ribs eight through ten having a shared cartilaginous attachment to rib seven (and thus to the sternum), while ribs eleven and twelve do not connect anteriorly to the sternum (Boileau Grant and Basmajian 1965). Ribs five through seven allow the chest wall excursion in a lateral as well as antero-posterior direction. Ribs eight through ten are not directly attached to the sternum, and thus have wide movement possibility. These latter ribs have been described as having a "bucket-handle" type of movement (Bunch 1995; Dickson and Maue-Dickson 1982).

Intercostal muscles

There are three layers of muscles that are found between the ribs: the external, internal, and innermost. Their major function is chest wall stability. However, due to their relative position, the external intercostals are inspiratory muscles as determined by EMG (Dickson and Maue-Dickson 1982; Taylor 1960), whilst the internal intercostals insert on the lower ribs and are believed to be active in expiration.

Expiration

Expiration is necessary for phonation. Elastic recoil of the chest wall is essential to passive expiration. Controlled expiration requires further expiratory muscle activity, as observed by Agostini and Hast 50 years ago (Agostini and Mead 1964; Hast 1966). Dickson notes that the expiratory muscles become of particular importance when exhalation continues below 35 percent of vital capacity (Dickson and Maue-Dickson 1982).

Active expiration takes advantage of elastic recoil, but also relies upon muscles that stabilize and lower the rib cage (for example the rectus abdominis), and muscles that on contraction support and compress the fascia over the abdominal viscera (for example the transversus abdominis and the internal and external abdominal obliques).

The abdominal wall muscles participate in activities such as lifting, breath-holding, and raising intra-abdominal pressure. They also contract during sneezing and coughing (Boileau Grant and Basmajian 1965). Controlled expiration, through activation of some of the abdominal wall musculature (as well as internal intercostal muscles) is required in speaking and singing, in particular when a phrase is maintained. Chapman (2012) emphasizes the importance of the abdominal wall musculature in the creation of what she describes as "primal sound."

Subglottic pressure

We have been looking at this section of phonation from a biomechanical basis. From such a perspective, phonation can be seen as the movement of the chest wall and diaphragm, thereby determining airflow and subglottic pressure. Singers require the ability to sustain the subglottic pressure. The intercostals are particularly helpful for this at high lung volumes, together with the abdominal musculature working against a relaxing diaphragm.

Airflow tends to be in the 100–200 ml/s range. Subglottic pressure creating audible results can range from approximately 2–60 cm water pressure (Proctor 1980). A moderate tone requires around 10 cm of water pressure, while a crescendo needs around 50–60 cm of water pressure. In quiet respiration approximately 35–45 percent of the maximum vital capacity is used; conversational speech uses between 35 and 60 percent of vital capacity; and loud speech can require up to 80 percent of vital capacity (Hixon 1973).

This brings us to the last concept that we shall be discussing in relation to the "Bellows," that of subglottic pressure. Development of subglottic pressure is critical to vocalizing. It is created by flow of expired air against a partly closed glottis. Its importance is twofold: the control of airflow, and the achievement of a (more or less) constant sound intensity. In assisting this process there are laryngeal mechanoreceptors that Sant'Ambrogio et al. (1983) characterized into pressure receptors, flow receptors or "drive" receptors.

Titze (1992) has identified the fact that a minimum amount of air pressure is needed to start the vocal folds vibrating (phonatory threshold pressure) and then to keep them vibrating (maintenance phonation pressure). The subglottal pressure in essence needs to push the vocal folds laterally and superiorly from below to start the vocal folds vibrating, to overcome the stiffness, mass, and damping that is inherent in the vocal folds (Titze 1992). The phonatory threshold pressure varies from about 3 cm water pressure (0.3 kPa) for lower pitches to about 6 cm (0.6 kPa) for higher pitches (Titze 1992).

Clinical aspects

What can affect the seamless functioning of the power source? Certainly any primary pathology of the lungs can alter ease or facility of expiration (for example, asthma, bronchitis, chronic obstructive pulmonary disease, and lung cancer; things that affect the function of the cilia (mucoviscidosis, smoking) or even changes in secretions relating to an upper respiratory tract infection). Issues involving the rib cage, for example scoliosis (excessive sideways curvature of the spine), trauma or surgery to the ribs will also interfere with function. Problems with the abdominal wall muscles, be this a strain, or even a diastasis (pulling apart) of the recti muscles related to pregnancy could impact on efficiency. Finally, the effects of aging on all aspects of the vocal tract are relentless and require consideration. Its effects on the power source include: calcification, loss of elasticity and compliance of the rib cage; decrease of pulmonary function of approximately 50 percent between the ages of 20 and 80; and weakness of the abdominal and intercostal musculature with loss of neural supply.

The Sound Source: the True Vocal Folds

The sound source in mammals is a mechanism for converting energy; in this instance, it is the steady pressure in a column of air under pressure streaming through a tube (the larynx) into sound waves. These sound waves (alternating peaks and troughs of pressure in the air column) are the raw material that we adapt with our resonators to create speech. Any obstruction in the airflow path, if elastic and deformable, will oscillate (for example in this instance the vocal folds) when the pressure and flow of the air column are appropriately matched to the resistance to the flow. This is the basis of the Myoelastic-Aerodynamic Theory (Van den Berg 1957, 1958). At the level of the vocal folds, the alternating waves of high/low pressure in this column of air produce what we know as vocal sound (Scherer and Rubin 1996).

The true vocal folds are a complex valving sphincter whose motions correspond to diverse activities including breathing, blowing, sucking, yawning, voiceless consonant production, musical instrument playing, coughing, throat clearing, swallowing, staccato whistling, whispering, and effortful behaviors such as lifting and defecation (Scherer and Rubin 1996). Phonatory activity involving the true vocal folds can only occur when they are held closely enough to vibrate; this only represents approximately 10–15 percent of their adductory range (Scherer 2006). The mechanical phonatory motion of the vocal folds depends upon the folds being driven by air pressures within the glottis (Gauffin et al. 1983; Ishizaka 1985; Scherer and Guo 1990; Scherer and Titze 1983), and the air pressure forces working with the biomechanical characteristics of the vocal folds (mass, stiffness, damping) to overcome the damping losses within the tissue (Alipour-Haghighi and Titze 1985; Ishizaka and Flanagan 1972; Ishizaka and Matsudaira 1972; Titze 1976; Titze 1981).

The intrinsic muscles place the true vocal folds under a degree of stretch and tension determined by the central nervous system, such that the air that is delivered under pressure from the power source (the subglottic pressure) permits them to vibrate at a certain number of times per second (the fundamental frequency). As with the lungs, elasticity and natural recoil play a major role (as noted by Van den Berg (1958) and Van den Berg et al. (1957) as aspects of the Myoelastic Theory of Vocalization), as does the phenomenon described by Bernoulli in the eighteenth century whereby pressure differential of air streaming through a confined space sets up vibrations (Van den Berg et al. 1957). The vocal folds can vibrate many hundreds of times per second; in conversational speech for adult males, this generally occurs between 75 and 450 times per second (Hertz), and for women between 130 and 520 times per second (Baken 1997; Gould 1991). Singing a concert A4 means vocal fold vibration rate of around 440 times per second.

Regular, cyclic, vocal fold vibrations with complete vocal closure are important indicators of a healthy voice. Anything that affects either the elasticity of the vocal folds, the regularity of closure, or the mucus lubricating the vocal folds will be heard as hoarseness. A myriad of processes can impact negatively on regularity of vocal fold behavior. One classification of abnormal vocal fold closure is hyperfunctional closure (best understood as the process leading to vocal fold nodules, polyps, granulomas, etc.) and the less common hypofunctional vocal fold behavior (best understood as any process, be it surgical or neural, that prevents complete vocal fold closure).

Many processes affect vocal fold closure, stiffness or regularity, and need to be closely queried in the vocal history. These will be further reviewed under the section "Vocal 'stressors.'"

The Resonators

At the level of the vocal folds, the vibrations produced create not only a fundamental frequency of the voice but also a mathematically rich and complex set of overtones or harmonics. At the folds this sounds like a buzz. The shape of the vocal tract acts upon these harmonics. In some instances they are absorbed (and thus not heard) and in some instances they are magnified by the anatomical structures that the vibrating air encounters on its way out of the body through the mouth or nose. These structures above the vocal folds are termed the resonators. Unlike a trumpet, they are soft and lubricated by mucus. There are an infinite amount of changes that can be created in the sound by subtly moving these structures.

The action of the resonators impacts on the acoustic message that the sound holds. This acoustic "package" has been characterized as the fundamental (described previously) and the formants. The formants of the vocal tract refer to its preferred resonating frequencies. They are usually referred to as F1, F2, F3, etc. For example, the formants for a neutral "schwa" vowel as spoken by an adult male whose vocal tract is 17 centimeters long (a typical length) are:

F1	first formant	500 Hz
F2	second formant	1500 Hz
F3	third formant	2500 Hz

People with vocal tracts longer or shorter than 17 cm will have different frequencies for these formants, but the pattern of 1x-3x-5x will be the same (Ladefoged 2001).

By changing the vocal tract away from a perfect tube, one changes the frequencies that are optimally resonated. That is, by moving around the tongue body and lips, one can change the position of the formants. The first and second formants are influenced by the tongue position and are enough to disambiguate the vowel. The first formant has a higher frequency for open vowels such as /a/ and a lower frequency for closed vowels such as /i/ or /u/; the second formant has a higher frequency for a "front" vowel such as /i/ and a lower frequency for a more "back" vowel such as /u/ (Ladefoged 2001, 2006). The adult male vocal tract is approximately 17–20 cm in length (Sundberg 1997). Anything that affects this anatomy will have a deleterious effect on speech (as opposed to voice, which is determined by the vocal folds). Thus pathologies such as a cleft palate allowing more air to escape through the nose, poor dentition with loss of bone in the mandible, or a tongue-tie (or many other subtle neurological effects on the movement of the soft palate or tongue) can all have a major impact on speech and articulation.

Vocal "Stressors"

This section outlines some of the "stressors" that may impact voice. By "stressor," we agree with the Business Dictionary that its definition is: a physical, psychological or social force that puts real or perceived demands on the body, emotions, mind or spirit of an individual (BusinessDictionary.com). A thorough history should give the clinician a firm basis for diagnosis of these. We shall endeavor to differentiate psychological from physiological/physical stress, although the two are interlinked. Psychological stress often has a physical/physiological presentation and physical/physiological stress often has a psychological presentation (Rubin and Greenberg 2002). The reader may immediately see the difficulty in differentiating psychological from physiological stress, as the response by the end organ (larynx, lung, or vocal tract) may be the same. For example, it is well known that the common physical attributes in response to emotional stress are hypercontraction of the extrinsic and intrinsic laryngeal muscles (Aronson 1991; Butcher 1993).

Psychological stress causes illness and can also reinforce illness through the development of illness behavior (Mechanic and Volkart 1964). Stress has been linked with multiple diseases including heart disease and stroke (Frasure-Smith and Lesperance 2008; Szekely et al. 2007). Stress, depression, and anxiety represent the majority of days lost due to illness in the UK. According to the Health and Safety Executive in 2010/11 this represented 10.8 million days (<www.hse.gov.uk>). Some forms of psychological disorders that might have an impact upon the vocal tract and voice include eating disorders, bruxism (grinding teeth), and mutational dysphonia. Some authors have characterized musculoskeletal voice related tension disorders as examples of psychological voice disorder. This however remains controversial (Aronson 1991; Rosen and Sataloff 1995; Rosen and Sataloff 1997; Rubin and Greenberg 2002).

Psychological stress and anxiety has been noted physiologically to lead to autonomic dysfunction, to alter the healing process, and to modify immunological functioning, inflammatory processes, and platelet activity (Frasure-Smith and Lesperance 2008; Szekely et al. 2007). In the vocal tract such autonomic dysfunction can lead to dry sticky mucus on the vocal folds causing pitch breaks, a tight tremulous quality to the speaking voice, and tightly held laryngeal muscles. As noted above it can lead to contraction of the perilaryngeal musculature (Aronson 1991). It also can indirectly lead to an increase in gastric acid production through stimulation of the autonomic nervous system which can in turn affect the voice (see below for more on reflux).

Many external pressures can increase stress and anxiety and thereby affect the voice. These include (but are by no means limited to) conflicts with family/friends, or problems at work relating to a boss or colleagues. House and Andrews (1988) point out that over 50 percent of individuals presenting with psychological voice disorders had experienced a difficulty or event within the previous year which involved conflict over speaking out.

When discussing psychological voice issues care needs be taken with semantics. Aronson (1991) uses the phrase "psychogenic voice disorders" on the basis that the voice disorder manifests types of psychological disequilibrium that (to paraphrase) might interfere with volitional control over phonation (Aronson 1991). This makes good sense to the authors.

Physiological/physical stressors on the voice and vocal tract are unavoidable. Throat irritation is a feature or side effect of exposure to environmental allergens, active or passive cigarette smoking, many foods and medications. Viral illnesses including upper respiratory tract infections often cause laryngitis as one feature. They are also often associated with coughing, which may be prolonged and last for weeks after resolution of the acute illness.

Other medical illnesses primarily or secondarily impacting on the vocal tract and voice typically include tonsillitis, glandular fever, asthma, gastroesophageal reflux, and bronchitis. Hormonal and endocrine issues can also have vocal impact. These may include thyroid problems, polycystic ovaries, premenstrual vocal changes, pregnancy, and menopause.

It is worthwhile to review laryngopharyngeal reflux (LPR). LPR occurs when acidic fluid, as well as other gastric products including pepsin, comes up the esophagus (reflux) and into the pharynx. This is a common problem for the general population, but it appears to be a particular problem for singers, likely due to pressure on the abdominal contents by the contraction of the abdominal wall musculature during singing. LPR causes chronic irritation of the posterior larynx, and often causes symptoms such as early morning hoarseness, throat clearing, and cough. Koufman and Wright (2006) have identified LPR as a factor or co-factor in 50 percent of voice problems. While traditional tests have established fluid with a pH of 4 or lower as being potentially pathologic, pepsin remains active at pH well above 5 (Koufman 2014) and may prove to be a cause of LPR.

Many foods can increase gastroesophageal reflux. Someone thinking they may be suffering with reflux may wish to try reducing acidic foods in their diet such as cooked tomato products and citrus products. Koufman et al. (2010) have recently published the book *Dropping Acid*, which presents a number of recipes incorporating low-acidity foods.

Many medications can also have deleterious effects on the voice. These are surprisingly common and regularly available in over the counter remedies. Both aspirin and other non-steroidal anti-inflammatories such as ibuprofen can lead to gastric irritation and thereby increase reflux. Both also have an anti-platelet effect that could increase the risk of vocal fold bruising. The half-life of ibuprofen is about six hours, but the effect of aspirin on platelet adhesion is longer-lasting, up to two weeks. Other medications that prolong bleeding include Coumadin (warfarin) and clopidogrel. All of these agents have medical indications, and a general rule of thumb is to discuss their use with your physician prior to any consideration to discontinue them. It is difficult to quantify the risk of bruising to the vocal folds.

Antihistamines and decongestants can dry the mucus that lubricates the vocal folds. Inhaled steroids can also dry this mucus, and may if used for long periods of time, slightly thin the vocal folds. Inhaled steroids can also have an impact upon the local immune system thereby increasing the possibility of the development of a fungal infection in the larynx or pharynx, particularly if the person is also taking antibiotics. Some antihypertensives can affect the voice. For example, diuretics can have a drying effect on the larynx and vocal tract; anticholinesterase inhibitors (particularly those from the first generation) can cause cough; finally, some calcium channel blockers can increase reflux. Useful references include Harris and Rubin (2006) and Schwartz et al. (2009).

Musculoskeletal problems regularly impact on the voice. Groin or abdominal muscle sprains will weaken the power source. Road traffic accidents with whiplash have been associated with neck discomfort and anecdotally with voice production issues. Even excessive exercise of the abdominal musculature may affect the voice by increasing LPR (Rubin et al. 2006).

MANAGEMENT OF VOICE PROBLEMS

The American Academy of Otolaryngology–Head and Neck Surgery (AAOHNS) clinical practice guideline on hoarseness (dysphonia), published in its journal *Otolaryngology–Head and Neck Surgery* in 2009, makes a number of evidence-based recommendations on managing hoarseness. The guideline addresses identification, diagnosis, treatment, and prevention of hoarseness. The "prevention" considerations presented include voice training, vocal hygiene, education, and environmental measures. The "treatment" interventions considered include watchful waiting/observation, education/information, voice therapy, anti-reflux medications, antibiotics, steroids, surgery, and botulinum toxin (Schwartz et al. 2009).

It is our view that optimal management requires a combined use of some or all of these modalities. We concur that prevention is always better than cure, and education/information is necessary as a cornerstone for healthy voice. Vocal hygiene is presented in the AAOHNS document under prevention, but it also forms a cornerstone of our management/treatment.

To protect the voice it is necessary to develop good and robust vocal habits. These include (but are not limited to) vocal hygiene. A central feature of vocal hygiene has always been adequate hydration (Rubin et al. 2006), and the recommendation by many physicians is that

1½ to 2 liters per day of water should be consumed. However, the supporting literature for this statement is scant at best, for example, Solomon and Di Mattia (2000) found that phonation threshold pressure (PTP) was raised after a vocally fatiguing task and that systemic hydration by drinking water seemed to attenuate this in three out of four of their subjects. Common sense as to the amount of water drunk during the day is important. Drinking too much water can also be problematic, leading to medical problems such as reflux or even to effects on the metabolic state of the body.

Diet is important, as are regular meals (rather than binge eating). It is important to allow adequate time for food to digest before undertaking activities such as exercise or lying supine, to reduce the risk of LPR. Eating a well-balanced diet with adequate calorie consumption to support activities planned is recommended as is getting enough sleep (n.b. literature on direct benefit to voicing is scant, and is not reviewed in the AAOHNS guidelines document).

Steam is very useful as a part of vocal hygiene to help thin secretions and break up sticky mucus. (Again, it is not considered in the AAOHNS guidelines of 2009.) The easiest way to steam is to shower twice daily or to steam over a basin (taking care not to burn your nose).

We recommend, as part of prevention, that irritants and stimulants should be avoided such as nicotine and caffeine (recalling that many diet sodas contain a significant amount of caffeine). If a patient presents to us with a current history of smoking we strongly recommend that this be stopped. With the advent of e-cigarettes it may become easier to stop smoking, but help is often required, and may be found through smoking cessation clinics. The AAOHNS guidelines (Schwartz et al. 2009) identified limited evidence on the benefit of avoidance of tobacco smoke (primary or secondary) but they concurred that avoidance of tobacco smoke was beneficial to decrease hoarseness, and referenced an article by Landes and McCabe (1957).

Many well-trained professional voice users use their voices extremely well during performance, only to overuse the voice after (or before) the performance (Jahn and Davies 1992). Self-awareness of voice use is important, especially in noisy environments, such as are commonly found in clubs, restaurants, and pubs. It is surprising how noisy such environments are, and there is a natural tendency to speak louder against ambient noise. Cars represent another noisy environment. Recently one of the authors (JR) identified 82 dB hertz sound level in the back of a taxi en route to a conference (JR personal observation 2013). It is best to avoid singing along with the radio en route to a performance.

Two interrelated issues of importance are time management and not overdoing ("burning the candle at both ends"). These issues are problematic from the time of school and university and persist as issues right through the most successful of careers. Mindfulness (a quality or state achieved by focusing one's awareness on the present moment while calmly acknowledging and accepting one's feelings, thoughts, and bodily sensations, used as a therapeutic technique) and finding time for oneself on a regular basis are very important to maintaining a long healthy voice career. Courses in mindfulness are readily available in a variety of countries. Many centers, readily identified online in a generic search, offer such courses, such as may be found in the UK in Oxford at the Oxford Mindfulness Centre, in south London (<http://www.beingmindful.co.uk>), in central London (<http://www.lovelifelivenow.com>), in Chelsea (<http://www.mindfree.co.uk>), etc. On-line courses are also easy to find, for example, at <http://www.bemindfulonline.com>. A caveat: the authors have not taken any of these courses or enrolled in any of these programs and thus do not recommend any one in particular; there are many more that are not listed above. Furthermore, developing the ability to say "no" is very helpful (but also in the experience of the authors very difficult).

Management should be based on a thorough history and physical examination, ideally through a multidisciplinary team. Diagnosis is necessary, and can then be followed upon by focused therapy. A multimodal approach will often include focused medical therapy as indicated, for example possibly for treatment of laryngopharyngeal reflux or allergies.

Behavioral management typically consists of voice therapy, conducted by speech and language therapists. It is preferable whenever possible to have such management performed by a speech and language therapist who has a special interest in voice disorders. Voice therapy has been demonstrated to be effective as a management modality (although surgery may be required) for individuals with hoarseness of all ages (Benninger et al. 1998; Ramig and Verdolini 1998).

But what if things go wrong? Things do go wrong, at one time or another for almost all voice professionals. A typical example of things going wrong is the development of an upper respiratory tract infection immediately before a performance. The performer will then need to balance in his or her mind the risk/benefit relating to performing while sick. This affects not only seasoned performers, but also students, who not uncommonly will feel that they "must" perform.

Some precepts if and when things go wrong include: avoid panic; do not internalize the problem; do not self-medicate; and seek help by talking to teachers, members of your family, mentors, or friends. Do not be afraid to seek medical attention. This can easily be done by contacting your general physician.

Exercise is beneficial. The vocal folds are muscles just like all other muscles in the body and will respond well to regular exercise. What needs be recalled, however, is that the abdominal muscles are massive in relation to the tiny laryngeal muscles and also benefit from regular exercise. Exercising three times weekly should be sufficient for maintaining vocal and general body tone. A vigorous walk, gentle run, or swim, would all fit the bill nicely. Counsel from an expert is always beneficial, taking into account your age, body build, and general health. This is particularly important should one decide to undertake regular exercise in a gym. High impact abdominal crunches and weight lifting can be associated with poor vocal habits including vocal grunting which should be avoided. Again, working with an experienced trainer is advisable as a program is devised.

Many performance schools now include the Alexander Technique as part of the curriculum. Body techniques such as Alexander, Pilates, and Rolfing are beneficial in promoting good body posture that is an excellent preventative to the development of a vocal pathology.

Gentle warm-ups are always a good strategy prior to singing (or using the speaking voice professionally). Cool-downs at the end of the performance are equally beneficial. Carroll (2014) recommends that cool-downs should proceed from the middle-high voice into the lower-middle voice. She suggests the use of descending scales, long expressive tones, or a soulful expressive melody like Brahms' famous lullaby. It is also important to remember to build up slowly to performance level. Much as a professional tennis player would not undertake five sets after not playing for several months, so must professional voice users slowly build themselves up, especially after an illness or absence from performance. Otherwise they will set themselves up to fail.

In summary, a healthy voice is predicated by a healthy vocal tract. Understanding how this works efficiently can only help inform the professional voice user. At one time or another every professional voice user will have issues with their voice; the key thing is to develop good regular habits to protect your voice and if things do go wrong to have available a support system.

References

Agostini, E. and Mead, J. (1964). Status of the respiratory system. In: W.O. Fenn and H. Rahn (eds) *Handbook of Physiology, Section 3: Respiration*, Vol. 1 (pp. 387–409). Washington DC: American Physiological Society.

Alipour-Haghighi, F. and Titze, I.R. (1985). Simulation of particle trajectories of vocal fold tissue during phonation. In: I.R. Titze and R.C. Scherer (eds) *Vocal Fold Physiology: Biomechanics, Acoustics and Phonatory Control* (pp. 183–90). Denver: Denver Center for the Performing Arts.

Aronson, A. (1991). *Clinical Voice Disorders*, 3rd edn. New York: Thieme Medical.

Baken, R.J. (1997). An overview of laryngeal function for voice production. In: R.T. Sataloff (ed) *Professional Voice: The Science and Art of Clinical Care*, 2nd edn (pp. 147–66). San Diego: Singular Publishing Group.

Benninger, M.S., Ahuja, A.S., Gardner, G., et al. (1998). Assessing outcomes for dysphonic patients. *Journal of Voice* 12(4): 540–50.

Boileau Grant, J.C. and Basmajian, J.V. (1965). *Grant's Method of Anatomy*, 7th edn. Baltimore: Williams and Wilkins.

Bunch, M.A. (1995). *Dynamics of the Singing Voice*, 3rd edn. Wien: Springer-Verlag.

Butcher, P., Elias, A., and Raven, R. (1993). *Psychogenic Voice Disorders and Cognitive-Behavior Therapy*. San Diego: Singular Publishing.

Carroll, L.M. (2014). The role of the voice specialist in the nonmedical management of benign voice disorders. In: J.S. Rubin, R.T. Sataloff, and G.K. Korovin (eds) *Diagnosis and Treatment of Voice Disorders*, 4th edn. San Diego: Plural Publishing.

Chapman, J.L. (2012). *Singing and Teaching Singing: A Holistic Approach to Classical Voice*, 2nd edn. San Diego: Plural Publishing.

Dickson, D.R. and Maue-Dickson, W. (1982). *Anatomical and Physiological Bases of Speech*. Boston: Little, Brown and Co.

Frasure-Smith, N. and Lesperance, F. (2008). Depression and anxiety as predictors of 2-year cardiac events in patients with stable coronary artery disease. *Archives of General Psychiatry* 65(Suppl. 1): 62–71.

Gauffin, J., Binh, N., Ananthapadmanabha, T.V., and Fant, G. (1983). Glottal geometry and volume velocity waveform. In: D.M. Bless and J.H. Abbs (eds) *Vocal Fold Physiology: Contemporary Research and Clinical Issues* (pp. 194–201). San Diego: College-Hill Press.

Gould, W.J. (1991). Caring for the vocal professional. In: M.M. Paparella, D.A. Shumrick, J.L. Gluckman, et al. (eds) *Otolaryngology*, 3rd edn (pp. 2273–88). Philadelphia: W. B. Saunders.

Gray, H. (1995). *Gray's Anatomy*, 15th edn. T.P. Pick and R. Howden (eds). New York: Barnes and Noble.

Harris, T.M. and Rubin, J.S. (2006). Medications and the Voice. In: J.S. Rubin, R.T. Sataloff, and G.K. Korovin (eds) *Diagnosis and Treatment of Voice Disorders*, 3rd edn (pp. 549–60). San Diego: Plural Publishing.

Hast, M.H. (1966). Mechanical properties of the cricothyroid muscle. *Laryngoscope* 76(3): 537–48.

Hixon, T.J. (1973). Respiratory function in speech. In: F.D. Minifie, T.J. Hixon, and F. Williams (eds) *Normal Aspects of Speech, Hearing and Language* (pp. 73–125). Englewood Cliffs: Prentice-Hall.

House, A.O. and Andrews, H.B. (1988). Life events and difficulties preceding the onset of functional dysphonia. *Journal of Psychosomatic Research* 32: 311–19.

Ishizaka, K. (1985). Air resistance and intraglottal pressure in a model of the larynx. In: I.R. Titze and R.C. Scherer (eds) *Vocal Fold Physiology: Biomechanics, Acoustics and Phonatory Control* (pp. 414–24). Denver: Denver Center for the Performing Arts.

Ishizaka, K. and Flanagan, J.L. (1972). Synthesis of voiced sounds from a two-mass model of the vocal cords. *Bell System Technical Journal* 51(6): 1233–68.

Ishizaka, K. and Matsudaira, M. (1972). Fluid mechanical considerations of vocal cord vibration. *SCRL Monograph 8* (April).

Jahn, A.F. and Davies, D.G. (1992). A clinical approach to the professional voice. In: A. Blitzer, M.F. Brin, C.T. Sasaki, et al. (eds) *Neurologic Disorders of the Larynx* (pp. 149–62). New York: Thieme Medical.

Koufman, J.A. (2014). Laryngopharyngeal reflux and voice disorders. In: J.S. Rubin, R.T. Sataloff, and G.K. Korovin (eds), *Diagnosis and Treatment of Voice Disorders*, 4th edn (pp. 457–70). San Diego: Plural Publishing.

Koufman, J.A. and Wright, S.C. (2006). Laryngopharyngeal reflux and voice disorders. In: J.S. Rubin, R.T. Sataloff, and G.K. Korovin (eds), *Diagnosis and Treatment of Voice Disorders*, 3rd edn (pp. 419–31). San Diego: Plural Publishing.

Koufman, J., Stern, J., and Bauer, M.M. (2010). *Dropping Acid: The Reflux Diet Cookbook and Cure* (Reflux Cookbooks LLC).

Ladefoged, P. (2001). *Vowels and Consonants: An Introduction to the Sounds of Language*. Maldern, MA: Blackwell.

Ladefoged, P. (2006). *A Course in Phonetics*, 5th edn. Boston, MA: Thomson Wadsworth.

Landes, B.A. and McCabe, B.F. (1957). Dysphonia as a reaction to cigarette smoke. *Laryngoscope* 67: 155–156.

Mechanic, D. and Volkart, E.H. (1964). Illness behaviour and medical diagnosis. *Journal of Health and Human Behaviour* 1: 86–94.

Proctor, D.F. (1980). *Breathing, Speech and Song*. Wien: Springer-Verlag.

Ramig, L.O. and Verdolini, K. (1998). Treatment efficacy: voice disorders. *Journal of Speech, Language, and Hearing Research* 41: 101–16.

Rosen, D.C. and Sataloff, R.T. (1995). Psychological aspects of voice disorders. In: J.S. Rubin, R.T. Sataloff, G.K. Korovin, and W.J. Gould (eds) *Diagnosis and Treatment of Voice Disorders* (pp. 491–511). New York: Igaku-Shoin Press.

Rosen, D.C. and Sataloff, R.T. (1997). Psychological aspects of voice disorders. In: R.T. Sataloff (ed.) *Professional Voice: The Science and Art of Clinical Care*, 2nd edn (pp. 305–17). San Diego: Singular Publishing Group.

Rubin, J.S. (2012). Vocal and respiratory anatomy and physiology. In: J.L. Chapman (ed.) *Singing and Teaching Singing: A Holistic Approach to Classical Voice*, 2nd edn (pp. 191–216). San Diego: Plural Publishing.

Rubin, J.S. and Greenberg, M. (2002). Psychogenic voice disorders in performers: A psychodynamic model. *Journal of Voice* 16(1): 87–91.

Rubin, J.S., Korovin, G.K., and Epstein, R. (2006). Special considerations for the professional voice user. In: J.S. Rubin, R.T. Sataloff, and G.K. Korovin (eds) *Diagnosis and Treatment of Voice Disorders*, 3rd edn (pp. 637–50). San Diego: Plural Publishing.

Sant'Ambrogio, G., Mathew, O.P., Fisher, J.T., and Sant'Ambrogio, F.B. (1983). Laryngeal receptors responding to transmural pressure, airflow and local muscle activity. *Respiratory Physiology* 54(3): 317–30.

Scherer, R.C. (2006). Laryngeal function during phonation. In: J.S. Rubin, R.T. Sataloff, and G.K. Korovin (eds) *Diagnosis and Treatment of Voice Disorders* 3rd edn (pp. 91–108). San Diego: Plural Publishing.

Scherer, R.C. and Guo, C.G. (1990). Laryngeal modeling: Translaryngeal pressure for a model with many glottal shapes. *ICSLP Proceedings, 1990 International Conference on Spoken Language Processing, Volume 1.* Japan: The Acoustical Society of Japan: 3.1.1–3.1.4.

Scherer, R.C. and Rubin, J.S. (1996). Laryngeal physiology: Normal and disordered. In: M.S. Benninger (ed.) *Benign Disorders of the Voice. 1996 Cherry Blossom Conference Continuing Education Program, 2002* (pp. 29–44). New York: American Academy of Otolaryngology–Head and Neck Surgery.

Scherer, R.C. and Titze, I.R. (1983). Pressure-flow relationships in a model of the laryngeal airway with a diverging glottis. In: D.M. Bless and J.H. Abbs (eds) *Vocal Fold Physiology, Contemporary Research and Clinical Issues* (pp. 179–93). San Diego: College-Hill Press.

Schwartz, S.R., Cohen, S.M., Dailey, S.H., et al. (2009). Clinical Practice Guidelines: Hoarseness (dysphonia). *Otolaryngology, Head and Neck Surgery* 141: S1–S31.

Solomon, N.P. and Di Mattia, M.S. (2000). Effects of a vocally fatiguing task and systemic hydration on phonation threshold pressure. *Journal of Voice* 14(3): 341–62.

Sundberg, J. (1997). Vocal tract resonance. In: R.T. Sataloff (ed.) *Professional Voice, The Science and Art of Clinical Care*, 2nd edn (pp. 167–84). San Diego: Singular Publishing Group.

Szekely, A., Balog, P., Benko, E., et al. (2007). Anxiety predicts mortality and morbidity after coronary artery and valve surgery—a 4 year follow-up study. *Psychosomatic Medicine* 69(7): 625–31.

Taylor, A. (1960). The contribution of the intercostal muscles to the effort of respiration in man. *Journal of Physiology* 200: 25–50.

Titze, I.R. (1992). Phonation threshold pressure: A missing link in glottal aerodynamics. *Journal of the Acoustical Society of America* 91(5): 2926–35.

Titze, I.R. (1981). Biomechanics and distributed-mass models of vocal fold vibration. In: K.N. Stevens and M. Hirano (eds) *Vocal Fold Physiology* (pp. 245–70. Tokyo: University of Tokyo Press.

Titze, I.R. (1976). On the mechanics of vocal fold vibration. *Journal of the Acoustical Society of America* 60(6): 1366–80.

Van den Berg, J.W., Zantema, J.T., and Doornenball, P. Jr. (1957). On the air resistance and the Bernoulli effect of the human larynx. *Journal of the Acoustical Society of America* 29: 626–31.

Van den Berg, J. (1958). Myeloelastic-aerodynamic theory of voice production. *Journal of Speech and Hearing Research* 1: 227–44.

<http://www.BusinessDictionary.com>. Accessed April 10, 2014.

<http://www.bemindfulonline.com>. Accessed April 10, 2014.

<http://www.hse.gov.uk>. Accessed April 10, 2014.

<http://www.lovelifelivenow.com>. Accessed April 10, 2014.

<http://www.mindfree.co.uk>. Accessed April 10, 2014.

CHAPTER 4

....

PHYSIOLOGY AND ITS IMPACT ON THE PERFORMANCE OF SINGING

....

FILIPA M.B. LÃ AND BRIAN P. GILL

INTRODUCTION

SINGING, like other highly skilled performance activities, involves the acquisition of a set of complex coordinated functions, normally achieved through attempts to replicate functionally efficient behaviors, within proper esthetical boundaries (Doscher 1994). This learning-practice process culminates in the realization of solid vocal technique, which facilitates heightened artistic expression (Miller 1996). However, unlike other musical instruments, many actions that lead to this vocal technique are internal. This hidden nature of the human voice has allowed imaginative theories to arise in the world of voice training which often lead to opposing practices concerning breath management, resonant strategies, and articulation (Miller 1994). Although it may achieve the intended goals, learning to sing based on such imaginative terminology may not always be directly linked with the mechanisms underlying the function of the singing voice. The result may well be a vocal technique built on non-replicable strategies, leading to instabilities that compromise the singer's abilities to communicate through music. Acquiring a solid knowledge of the physiology behind the sound seems to assist singers in acquiring an efficient and effective vocal technique (Gullaer et al. 2006; Miller 1996). This chapter explores the physiology of singing and its impacts on performance, the rationale being that, when the physiology of singing is understood, the established cyclical interplays serve the purposes of the singing gestalt (Doscher 1994): Affective and effective musical communication. Taking into account that the voice is a physiological and acoustical instrument (Miller 2004), this chapter reviews the main physiological parameters that affect singing, organizing them into three subsections: Breathing, the production of a voice source, and strategies employed to modify and enhance this source for singing. The chapter ends with a summary of the key principles and approaches discussed, reaffirming their relevance more broadly within music education.

PHYSIOLOGICAL PARAMETERS
AFFECTING SINGING

The human voice, as a musical instrument, requires concomitantly fine mastering of all constituent elements. Through practice, singers experience the complex interrelationships between all systems (Miller 1996): (i) The "fuel," or aerodynamic power necessary to produce a primary sound (achieved by efficient breathing control); (ii) the source, generated by converting aerodynamic power into acoustic power (the vibration of the vocal folds); and (iii) the modulator (or acoustic oscillator), to modify and enhance the source energy into singing through articulation (Jian 2006).

Aerodynamic power: Efficient breathing control

Breath is often regarded as the "fuel" for the voice. After all, the breath is what excites vocal fold vibration (Sundberg 1987; Titze 2000). This section focuses on the function of breathing as it relates to vocal performance (See also Chapter 5, this volume). For the sake of simplification, breathing will be broken down into four stages (Titze 2000). One could start at any point in the cycle, but here the beginning is considered inspiration. In inspiration, the abdominal muscles and internal intercostal muscles (responsible for pulling down the rib cage during expiration) must release. The diaphragm (main muscle of inspiration) activates and begins to flatten from its original double-dome shaped rest position. As the diaphragm moves down, the viscera displace downward to make room for its descent. The external intercostal muscles pull the ribs upwards, increasing the volume of the thoracic cavity, which in turn keeps air moving into the lungs (Titze 2000). During expiration (stage one), there is adequate air pressure (sometimes excess) to activate vocal fold vibration simply with the elastic recoil of the ribs and lungs, which want to return to their equilibrium from the position to which they have been moved or stretched. With a deep breath, the pressure from the recoil will be greater than desired, and the air pressure needs to be restrained somewhat by continued contraction of the diaphragm (Leanderson and Sundberg 1988) and/or activation of the external intercostals. During stage two of expiration, the end of elastic recoil is reached and the internal intercostal muscles begin to help shrink the rib cage (Titze 2000). At the final stage of expiration (stage three), the abdominal muscles begin to shrink the abdominal cavity, which drives the viscera upward against the diaphragm, moving it further towards its point of origin before its descent during inspiration (Hoit et al. 1988; Watson et al. 1989).

Appoggio

At stage one of expiration, the possibility for excess pressure cannot be over-emphasized. In singing pedagogy, there is a method used to avoid excess subglottal pressure (Psub), i.e. to avoid an excess of an "overpressure of air in the lungs" (in Sundberg 1987, p. 25) called *appoggio*. The basic concept of this technique is to "sing on the gesture of inhalation" (in Doscher 1994, p. 22), i.e. keep the external intercostal muscles engaged to keep the rib cage from recoiling too fast. In essence, the inspiratory muscles balance out the action of the expiratory muscles, so as to avoid a too rapid collapse of the thoracic cavity, as well as a rapid ascent of the diaphragm. The diaphragm stays contracted by keeping the abdominal wall out (especially the area called the epigastrium—right below the ribs in the front); expansion in this area is indicative of the diaphragm being down (Vennard 1967). Since the beginning of singing pedagogy, terminology such as *appoggio* and *support* can be found to address the coordination between laryngeal action and breathing (Stark 2003), a phenomenon of paramount importance to singing performance (Miller 2004). Nevertheless, diverging explanations are found in the literature concerning the required strategies for *appoggio* or *support*. Partially, this can be related to the fact that different muscular strategies are used in accordance with the individual characteristics of each singer (Sundberg 1987). Also, breathing patterns differ greatly among individuals, as different strategies of inhalation and exhalation exist (Leanderson and Sundberg 1988). These facts perhaps have encouraged the many breathing methods employed by different schools of singing: Abdominal or belly breathing (also known as diaphragmatic breathing); thoracic breathing; a combination of both abdominal and thoracic; and clavicular breathing (Miller 1977). It is universally agreed that clavicular breathing, associated with a panic reaction or hyperventilation, is not advantageous to singing; it may lead to tensions in the neck and in the pharynx that may affect resonance (Appelman 1967). In relation to other breathing methods, one might argue that a combination of thoracic and abdominal breathing seems the most efficient method as it aligns nicely with the normal breathing cycle and does not restrict the movement of the rib cage wherein lie the lungs. This combination may lead to maximum expansion of the thoracic cavity as it allows the sternum to move up and forward (antero-posterior expansion), the ribs to move up and out (transverse expansion), and the diaphragm to move down (vertical expansion). With this increased expansion, a singer has more fuel at her or his disposal to maintain a healthy vibration at the vocal fold level. However, as pointed out before, there is no universal consensus on which breathing behavior is the most efficient (Miller 1977). Consensual opinions are only reached when it comes to the fact that less efficient phonation can become more efficient by simply altering respiratory habits (Leanderson and Sundberg 1988).

To phonate, a singer needs to increase the pressure inside the lungs, i.e. alveolar pressure, which is roughly equivalent to Psub, one of the main physiological parameters of voice control in singing; it controls loudness (louder singing requires higher Psub) and it affects pitch (when Psub increases, fundamental frequency (f_o) is raised, although not significantly) (e.g. Sundberg et al. 2005). Each note in a musical phrase will have its own Psub, according to the loudness and the f_o required. For this reason, singers need to be constantly monitoring and adapting Psub (Sundberg 1987). Thus, one might argue that the terms *appoggio* and *support* could be also finely described as *pre-tone breath management*.

Changes in subglottal pressure

Changes in Psub occur due to changes in the rib cage volume, by means of muscular forces, elastic forces, and gravitation (Sundberg 1987). Muscular forces involve the contraction and relaxation of respiratory muscles: The external and internal intercostal muscles, a paired muscle group responsible for inspiratory and expiratory forces, respectively, and the diaphragm and the abdominal wall, also a paired group of muscles that lead to inhalation and exhalation, respectively (Leanderson and Sundberg 1988). The elastic forces play a major role in Psub variations. The lungs possess a passive expiratory force that is higher with higher lung volumes (Sundberg 1992). In other words, the natural movement for the lungs is to shrink after inhalation (Proctor 1980). The same happens with the rib cage when it deviates from its resting volume after an inhalation; thus, both lungs and rib cage generate a passive expiratory force when expanded from resting volume (Sundberg 1992). Unlike speech, singing often requires, at the beginning of a phrase, high lung volumes. Thus, singers need to learn how to balance this passive exhalatory force by muscular forces in order to sing pianissimo dynamics at high lung volumes, as when the lungs are filled with air, this passive force generates a high pressure (Proctor 1980). In such cases, singers need to contract the principal inhalatory muscles (i.e. diaphragm and external intercostals). With a decrease in lung volumes as the musical phrase progresses, this need progressively decreases until passive exhalatory forces generate a subglottal pressure lower than the one needed for the tone produced. From then on, the strategy will be to activate the expiratory muscles in order to maintain sufficient thoracic pressure to move air out of the lungs and maintain vocal fold vibration (Sundberg 1992). Summarizing, to sing a pianissimo, singers need to recruit a compensatory activation of inhalatory muscles, whereas when singing a fortissimo the normal exhalatory process may suffice, especially when the lungs are at their full volume capacity. Gravitation is another parameter affecting Psub. In an upright position, gravity works as an inhalatory force by pulling down the diaphragm; on the other hand, in a supine position, gravity acts as a force on the abdominal content, facilitating the recoil of the diaphragm into the thoracic cavity. A supine position of the body heightens awareness of the contraction of the diaphragm and encourages a less forceful contraction of the abdominal wall, thus being a possible strategy for singers who tend to over-contract the abdominal wall during singing. One concludes that posture affects lung volume and indirectly Psub (Sundberg et al. 1991). This possibly explains why a good posture has been commonly referred to as an important asset in a singing performance (Schneider and Dennehy 1997). During inspiration in an upright position, this gravitational force also exerts a mechanical force upon the larynx, the tracheal pull (Sundberg 1987). As the diaphragm lowers and stretches the lung tissue downwards, the trachea also moves down. As it is attached to the lower portion of the larynx at the bottom of the cricoid cartilage, the larynx is necessarily pulled down with it. Consequently, the tracheal pull exerts its force upon the vocal folds, slightly abducting them (Iwarsson 2001). Due to this decrease in adduction, more air may flow through the folds during phonation (Zenker 1964). Increased cricothyroid activity with a low diaphragm, induced by high lung volume or a co-activation of the diaphragm during singing, corroborates these effects (Sundberg et al. 1988). From a vocal training standpoint, tracheal pull could be very useful for a trained singer who tends to over-adduct the vocal folds. By applying exercises starting at high lung volumes, the teacher will encourage the student to use a tracheal pull effect, finding a lower larynx position and avoiding overly adducted vocal folds (Iwarsson and Sundberg 1998). Conversely in non-trained singers, it is often found that larynx height increases with decreasing lung volumes. Attention to posture is essential when looking at breathing strategies; for example, protrusion of the chin and tilting backward of the head have been associated with a higher vertical laryngeal position (VLP) even when the breathing strategy applied was the one favoring the tracheal pull. Thus, one should bear in mind that there is a great variability for the configuration of the respiratory system just before phonation between and within subjects (Hixon et al. 1988) and that both vocal task and lung volume greatly influence vertical laryngeal position (Iwarsson 2001).

With the ever-increasing demands on singers, particularly in relation to physical demands while singing, one must consider the effects of being out of breath during phonation. Even short-term accelerated breathing challenges seem to affect the minimum lung pressure that is needed to sustain the oscillation of the vocal folds produced by flow, the phonation threshold pressure (PTP) (Sivasankar and Erickson 2009; Titze and Verdolini 2012). Accelerated breathing was found to increase PTP as well as perceived phonatory effort (Sandage et al. 2013; Sivasankar and Erickson 2009). To counteract this effect, a teacher might introduce physical exercise into the daily normal singing practice session. If a singer is trained for a specific task where aerobic physical activity is also needed, he or she might become better at negotiating possible changes in the vibratory cycle of the vocal folds associated with this accelerated breathing. In fact, female singers were found to reduce PTP after practicing vocal warm-ups with an aerobic exercise component included (McHenry et al. 2009).

Mechanical oscillator: Production of a voice source

Thanks to technological aids developed over the past 40 years, physiological events that occur cyclically within the human body can now be monitored. In the particular case of the mechanical oscillator that produces the voice source, i.e. air pressure variations generated by the vibration of the vocal folds (Sundberg 1987), a flow glottogram constitutes an excellent display of transglottal airflow over time. It reveals how the voice source behaves for each vibratory cycle. When the glottis starts to open (until it is completely open), the airflow gradually increases until it reaches a maximum that corresponds to a positive peak in the curve; as the glottis starts to close, the airflow decreases until it ceases at the moment that the glottis is completely closed, the zero line. Usually, the closing of the glottis is more rapid than the opening; thus, the slope of the flow glottogram is steeper on the falling part of the wave. Variations in the shape of the flow glottogram partially reflect respiratory and laryngeal muscle adjustments that singers learn in order to achieve a pre-phonatory control of the vocal fold mass, length, and inner tension (Sundberg 1987). These adjustments are normally achieved by regulating: (a) Psub; (b) adductory and abductory forces of the vocal folds (for breathing, the vocal folds are abducted whereas for phonation, they are adducted); and (c) tension and extension of the vocal folds. One way of training pre-phonatory control of the physiological parameters affecting the production of an efficient voice source is by practicing staccato exercises at different pitches, and using different vowels (Welch and Sundberg 2002). Exercises that focus on voice onset and offset often facilitate the learning of efficient voice source use as they encourage the synchronization between the activation of Psub, adductory forces, and vocal fold vibration. A hard attack corresponds to adducting the vocal folds before establishing a Psub and vibration of the vocal folds; a breathy voice onset often is related with an existent Psub, followed by the adduction and the vibration of the vocal folds; and a synchronized onset (a staccato onset) requires concomitant engagement of Psub, adduction and vibration of the vocal folds (Lã 2012; Sundberg 1987).

Subglottal pressure

As has already been described, Psub is extremely important to singers; its increase results in an increase in vocal loudness and, to a lesser extent, pitch (Sundberg 1987). The effects of Psub variations are far from trivial, as variations on this physiological parameter affect a number of equally important physiological events that change voice source behavior and thus regulate the properties of the final acoustic output. This complex matrix of interactions can be visualized by means of monitoring flow glottogram variations in terms of: (i) the time that the vocal folds are closed per cycle, i.e. closed quotient; (ii) peak-to-peak pulse amplitude in one vibratory cycle; (iii) glottal leakage (mean airflow during the closed phase of the cycle); (iv) maximum rate of airflow change; and (v) the dominance of the fundamental in the voice source spectrum—in other words, the level difference between the first and second harmonics of the voice source (Sundberg et al. 2005).

The relationship between Psub and closed quotient (Q_{Closed}) can be expressed as a power function: Q_{Closed} increases rapidly at low pressures and approximates to an asymptote at higher pressures (Sundberg et al. 2005). There are differences between the sexes and trained and untrained voices with regard to this relationship. Q_{Closed} seems to affect voice timbre as "it determines how great a portion of the cycle will contain a formant ringing" (in Sundberg et al. 2005, 884–885). Q_{Closed} is related to another parameter that has been used as a standard measure for assessing vocal fold contact time per cycle, i.e. contact quotient ($Q_{Contact}$). $Q_{Contact}$ is measured non-invasively by means of electroglottography (Baken 1992) or by electrolaryngography (Fourcin 2000). Previous studies have demonstrated that the time the vocal folds stay in contact per cycle increases with vocal training (Howard 1995). This is an important development as, by increasing $Q_{Contact}$, the singer reduces the loss of sound energy to subglottal dampening (Howard 1995). A longer contact time also offers the possibility of sustaining longer phrases, as air loss is smaller for cycles with longer contacting phases. However, if the contact phase is too long and the shape of the mucosal wave is not symmetrical, one might argue that the adductory forces of the vocal folds may be too strong, a sign of possible overpressurization in singing (Lã 2012). However, longer $Q_{Contact}$ might also be indicative of longer vocal folds. For example, longer $Q_{Contact}$ values are found for male singers than females; high notes such as those sung by sopranos reveal shorter $Q_{Contact}$ as compared to low notes (Howard 1995).

Peak-to-peak pulse amplitude in one cycle can also be affected by Psub variations, providing that adduction, longitudinal tension and extension of the vocal folds remain the same. The pulse amplitude in a flow glottogram represents an important phenomenon to a singer: the amount of air passing though the glottis during the opening phase of the cycle. It reflects the amplitude of the fundamental in the voice source spectrum, i.e. the greater the airflow amplitude, the stronger the voice source fundamental (Sundberg 1987). A combination of a high Psub and a high adduction force of the vocal folds (i.e. a great resistance of the glottis to the air flow) will lead to a smaller flow glottogram amplitude, hence a weak source fundamental. In addition, one should certainly take into account vocal fold morphology. Friction has an adverse effect on the vocal fold tissue and with more Psub and increased glottal resistance, friction is increased; hence, the vocal folds are at greater risk for injury. However, one should also take into account that the amplitude of the source fundamental depends not only on adductory forces but also on glottal area. Longer vocal folds tend to have larger f_o amplitudes as the glottal area is bigger which allows for more flow (Sundberg 1987).

The level difference between the first and the second harmonics of the voice source (H1–H2) is also an indicator of voice efficiency; if the level difference between the first and the second partials is negative and there is not a gain in sound level, this is indicative of a waste of Psub and adductory forces (Sundberg et al. 2005).

The maximum rate of the decrease in airflow during a period relates to the closing rate of the vocal folds and thus how quickly the airflow is shut-off, i.e. maximum flow declination rate (MFDR). This physiological event is important in singing because it corresponds to the acoustical excitation of the vocal tract. In other words, an increase of MFDR (fast closing rate of the vocal folds) will lead to an increase of sound level without necessarily increasing the collision force of the vocal folds. The phenomenon is that the dominance of the higher partials in the spectrum is greater when there is a rapid closing rate. However, it is important to emphasize that sound level is also determined by the distance between the first resonance of the vocal tract (first formant) and the closest partial (Sundberg 1987). This effect of proximity of a harmonic to a formant will be further explored in the section concerning the acoustic oscillator. Singers can increase MFDR by applying one of the following strategies: (i) increase the vibrational amplitude of the bottom relative to the top part of the vocal folds, possibly controlled by the thyroarytenoid muscle; (ii) increase the vocal tract inertance, narrowing the epilaryngeal area; or (iii) alter glottal configuration through a change in VLP (Titze 2006).

Adductory and abductory forces of the vocal folds

Changes in adductory and abductory forces are crucial for achieving different phonation types, which range from breathy, to neutral, flow and pressed phonation. Acoustically speaking, changing from one extreme of adduction to the other has a major impact as the amplitude of the fundamental can be increased by 15dB when changing from pressed to flow phonation (Sundberg 1987). The latter is the most efficient phonation mode for classically trained singers; a lower Psub combined with a moderate adduction and glottal resistance will promote the best setting for bigger amplitude excursions of the vocal folds, which close rapidly, resulting in a stronger fundamental with richness of high harmonic components. Although the amplitude of the source fundamental is not the same as of the radiated f_o (the latter also depends on the modifications of the resonances of the vocal tract through articulation), the amplitude of the voice source fundamental plays an important role in the perceived loudness and overall quality of the voice. Many singing teachers are experts at listening to the level of the source fundamental, and are able to separate the effects of physiological adjustments to the sound (such as too much or too little adduction), from the effects of adjustments that are acoustically produced (Sundberg 1987).

The relationship between adductory forces and Psub is of paramount importance to vocal health, as excessive vocal adduction is typically detrimental for the voice (Mathieson 2001). In addition, posterior glottal adduction has an impact on perceived vocal quality; with an insufficient posterior glottal closure (glottal chink), turbulent airflow in the glottis will lead to the perception of a breathy voice (Herbst et al. 2010). An increase in Psub will cause an increase in airflow only when glottal resistance is kept constant. A glottal leakage occurs when one increases Psub without compensating for the increase with the degree of adduction. Singers learn to control glottal resistance to avoid changes in voice quality. For example, an increase in glottal leakage (a decrease in glottal resistance) is observed with increasing f_o, an important consideration to avoid running into a pressed type of phonation in the higher range of the voice (Sundberg 1987). Another example is the increase in glottal resistance towards the end of a phrase as a strategy to maintain the same airflow and sound level when air pressure in the lungs is being reduced.

Adductory forces of the vocal folds can be elevated by contraction of: (i) the lateral cricoarytenoid muscles; (ii) the interarytenoid muscles; and (iii) the lateral parts of the interarytenoid muscles. The combination of practicing specific vocal exercises, verbalization of events and feedback using electrolaryngography/electroglottography was shown to be useful in reducing posterior glottal chink due to incomplete closure of the glottis (Herbst et al. 2010). Singers are trained to control forces that increase or decrease adduction in the search for the appropriate balance between air volume displacement at the glottis, glottal resistance, and Psub. During this training, it should be kept in mind that male and female singers have different relationships between the physiological parameters controlling the production of the voice source sound. Male singers have longer vocal folds than female singers (the basses displaying the longest sizes) (Roers et al. 2009), which will also be reflected in terms of glottal space (Sundberg et al. 2005). Also, sopranos will have smaller vocal folds than mezzo sopranos (Roers et al. 2009). Thus, if voice source x displays a stronger fundamental than voice source y, it does not necessarily mean that x is using flow phonation and y is not, as the amplitude of the source fundamental depends not only on the adducttory forces but also on the size of the glottis. Taking into account these considerations, one might agree that physiology is crucial to singing pedagogy. The way by which physiological events are expressed in singing modes, and in singer's sex and voice type, must guide the pedagogue and the practitioner in choosing the most appropriate physiological approaches for obtaining a certain sound, rather than producing that sound at any cost.

Tension and extension of the vocal folds

The tension and extension of the vocal folds will determine the f_o, that is to say, how many times per second the vocal folds vibrate. F_o has significant impacts on the physiology of singing performance. For example, it is highly correlated to the perception of pitch, i.e. the "height" of the voice—a perceptual evaluation of f_o—which is also influenced by the timbre and loudness of the voice (Titze 2000), and has been seen to influence the performer's expressivity (Sundberg et al. 2013a). Sharpening phrase-peak tones as compared with equally tempered tuning was shown to be an expressive tool used in classical singing.

Changes in f_o can be achieved by means of adjustments in the contraction of two important intrinsic muscles of the larynx: the thyroarytenoid (TA) and the cricothyroid (CT) muscles (Proctor 1980). The TA runs longitudinally, from the thyroid to the arytenoid cartilages, whereas the CT is located anteriorly, between the thyroid and the cricoid cartilages (Titze 2000). Generally speaking, one might say that increasing f_o involves an increase in the contraction of TA for the lower/mid range and as f_o continues to rise, there will be a point when the TA can no longer be dominant, as there is a physiological limit to the active muscle stress of the TA. Thus, f_o increases at higher frequencies are fully dependent on the dominance of CT activation.

Pedagogically there are some important considerations that one must have in mind concerning f_o changes. The first is that raising f_o can also be achieved to some extent by increasing

Psub, because less CT activity is required for singing the same f_o when Psub increases. One might argue that this is not an optimal strategy for singers, as the amplitude of vibration increases with increasing lung pressure, which may lead to an excessive collision force, one of the top risk factors for tissue injury (Titze 2000). Also, this will eliminate the possibility of singing high notes softly. The third consideration is that the cartilages and muscles vary in shape and size between singers. In some larynges, for example, the cricothyroid space is very narrow. In these cases, the range of rotation between the cricothyroid towards the thyroid cartilage is limited. Thus, not much can be done to stretch the vocal ligament when these two cartilages are in contact with each other. The tendency will be to increase muscular effort, which would also be a non-optimal strategy. A possible solution might be to assist the further elongation of the vocal folds by an external pull on the CT, either by applying a higher tracheal pull force or to raise the larynx with rising pitch (Titze 2000). Although previous studies have found that the larynx raises with raising pitch for professional singers, this phenomenon does not happen until a certain f_o has been reached, before which the larynx is kept in a lower position than the resting one (Sundberg 1987). Fourth, modifications in the relationships between CT and/or TA activation, and/or vocal loudness, may lead to a perception of different vocal qualities, or registers (Titze 2000). For those singing styles requiring evenness of timbre throughout the whole vocal range (e.g. classical singing), register events might be avoided by applying certain resonance strategies (see the section on the acoustical oscillator below). Another relevant pedagogical consideration is how a singer may avoid voice misuse when singing demanding repertoire in terms of f_o range and *tessitura*. The risk of developing a vocal injury may be decreased if singers adopt flow phonation and apply sufficient ligament stretch, by creating an optimal relation between CT (and external laryngeal muscles) and TA contraction (in the case of middle register). The tracheal pull strategy seems to be advantageous. Singers have a tendency to increase adduction on the higher end of their vocal range, leading to a strained vocal quality; the tracheal pull seems a key factor to avoid this, as it introduces a counter balancing abductory force, assisting the singer to maintain a flow phonation on the higher part of his/her vocal range (Sundberg 1992). Also, when rapid and precise movements of different parts of the human body are required, both muscles required to bring the structure into motion and those responsible for its stabilizations at a resting position are engaged (Rothenberg 1968).

Finally, cyclical f_o modulations give rise to a vocal effect that is desirable in some singing styles; vibrato. It is commonly accepted that the rate of f_o deviations from the mean f_o should be approximately 4.5 to 6.5 Hz in frequency, and approximately three percent (0.5 semitones) in extent in order to produce an esthetically agreeable vibrato (Sundberg 1987; Titze 2000). There are different ways of producing vibrato: lung pressure pulsations; jaw movement; or cyclical contraction of CT and TA muscles (Kempster et al. 1988). The latter has been referred to as preferable as an expressive tool for classical singing and for some non-classical styles, such as musical theater, jazz, and pop/rock (Tizte 2000). It is worthwhile mentioning that the vibrato extent increases with raising vocal intensity and to some extent with pitch. Signs of nervousness and/or excessive muscle tension can be revealed by a high vibrato frequency (between 6 and 8 Hz). Poor muscle tone, on the contrary, leads to a low vibrato frequency (between 2 to 4 Hz). Acceptable vibrato quality, in frequency and extent, is therefore a sign of good vocal technique and condition (Titze 2000).

ACOUSTIC OSCILLATOR: MODIFYING AND AMPLIFYING THE SOURCE ENERGY INTO SINGING

Resonance is "a condition that exists between the source of energy and the configuration of the medium such that the energy of some frequencies of vibration will be kept 'alive' in the medium while others will quickly die off" (Story 1999, p. 1). With singing, the vocal folds are the source of energy and the medium is the air inside the vocal tract. "Resonant voice" can be defined as "any voice production that is both easy to produce and vibrant in the facial tissues" (in Verdolini-Marston et al. 1995, p. 2). The sympathetic vibrations towards the front of the face are indicative of an effective resonator, whereas the ease of production is indicative of an efficient use of resonance and vibrator. Resonances of the vocal tract are called formants. The lowest two formants (i.e. F1 and F2) determine the identity of the vowel, whereas formants three (F3), four (F4) and five (F5) have more effect on timbre (or tone color) (Sundberg 1987).

The source-filter theory of voice production considers the vocal folds as the source of acoustic energy and the vocal tract (the space above the vocal folds) as the selective sound filter. While the vocal tract is considered to be a highly efficient resonator, it only allows approximately one percent (or less) of the acoustical output produced at the level of the vocal folds to be emitted from the mouth (Story 1999). The amount of output that either receives enhancement or becomes critically dampened is determined by the shape of the vocal tract, i.e. the length of the overall tube as well as its ever-changing diameter throughout the whole length of the tube (Doscher 1994). The shape and the length of the vocal tract are altered by means of articulation (Sundberg 1987).

When a singer produces a vowel sound, the contour of the tongue creates a degree of constriction in a certain area of the vocal tract. For instance, when a person sings an /i/ vowel, the blade of the tongue moves close to the hard palate creating a constriction near the outlet area of the vocal tract. Whereas, when an /a/ vowel is articulated, the back of the tongue creates a narrowing of the pharyngeal area. Furthermore, the /u/ vowel creates a constriction in the middle of the vocal tract tube when the mid part of the tongue approaches the soft palate. The lip rounding for a /u/ creates a secondary constriction right at the end of the vocal tract (Lindblom and Sundberg 2007).

It is important for a singer to be aware of the fact that the tongue plays a major role as a modifier of the vocal tract, and thus, its resonances, along with the lips, the jaw, the soft palate, and the larynx. Specific exercises to isolate the effects of these articulators in the overall sound quality during singing should be employed, especially because the singer's awareness of the movements of these hidden elements is imperfect (Gullaer et al. 2006).

There are infinite combinations of spaces in the vocal tract, but in general, the following rules apply with regard to the adjustment of formant frequencies (Titze 2000): (1) lengthening the vocal tract (e.g. rounding the lips or lowering the larynx) lowers all formant frequencies (Watson et al. 1989); shortening the vocal tract (e.g. spreading the lips or raising the larynx) raises all formant frequencies; a mouth constriction, i.e. closing the jaw and/or moving the blade of the tongue closer to the hard palate, causes a rise in F2 and a decrease in F1; and a pharyngeal constriction, i.e. opening the mouth and/or moving the back of the tongue toward the pharyngeal wall, causes a rise in F1 and a decrease in F2 (Lindblom and Sundberg 2007).

There is no disputing that resonance plays a key role in efficient and effective voice use; however, there are differing opinions regarding how resonance is employed. Presently, many studies have been carried out involving the measurement of formant frequencies and their interactions with the partials produced at the vocal fold level (Echternach et al. 2010; Henrich et al. 2011; Miller and Schutte 2005; Sundberg et al. 2013b). In general, whenever the partials from the vocal folds are in close proximity to the formant frequencies of the vocal tract, they will be boosted, i.e. gain in intensity will be achieved (Titze et al. 2008).

There is some disagreement in the voice science community regarding exactly how partials and formants interact. A theory of non-linear source-filter interaction in voice production has been developed over recent decades, tested and confirmed with experiments using, for example, physical models. In this case, the theory predicts that, when a low spectrum harmonic is just below F1 or F2, the sound pressure level (SPL) of a vowel may increase by as much as 10 dB. On the contrary, if a harmonic is just above the formant frequency, SPL may be weakened. In other words, a non-linear interaction between the vocal folds and the vocal tract may elicit a more efficient conversion of aerodynamic to acoustic energy (Titze 2004). Physiologically, this is related to the diameter of the epilaryngeal tube; when the impedances at the glottis and at the epilaryngeal tube are similar, a strong coupling occurs (Titze et al. 2008). Other authors, however, specify that for this coupling to occur, it is necessary to tune a formant to a partial; which formant coincides with which partial depends on the pitch area in which the singer is singing (Miller 2008). For example, according to Miller and Schutte (2005), when a male voice is singing an /a/ vowel in or just above the *secondo passaggio*, it is advantageous for F2 to coincide with the third partial (H3). A successful negotiation of register transitions may depend on resonant "tuning" skills rather than, or in complement with, muscular adjustment in laryngeal muscles (Miller and Schutte 2005). More recently, the results of a study analyzing the voice of professional male singers by inverse-filtering suggested that partials will get a similar boost regardless of whether the formant is just above, right on, or just below a particular partial. It was also noted that no instabilities occurred throughout the sung scales even when formants "crossed over" partials (Sundberg et al. 2013a). Additional findings showed that professional male singers lowered the first formant of the /a/ vowel in and above the *passaggio*, avoiding the boost of the H2 and allowing for F2 to boost H3 (Echternach et al. 2010; Hertegård et al. 1990; Neumann et al. 2005; Sundberg et al. 2013a; Titze and Worley 2009). An important finding was that the second formant/third partial "tuning" seemed to occur by happenstance, whereas the lowering of the first formant seemed deliberate, as when the singers were asked to sing in the same pitch range in a non-classical style the first formant was on or near the second partial (Sundberg et al. 2013a). This non-classical tuning is similar to the tuning found in the female belt voice; the first formant giving a boost to the second harmonic is considered a "yell-belt" strategy (Miller 2008; Titze and Worley 2009). These authors would like to make the distinction that, while this tuning—commonly found in musical theater, popular, folk, and world music idiom (Bozeman 2013)—may sound "yell-like," it should in no way be executed with the same subglottal pressure/glottal resistance combination by which most yells are produced, as this can damage the vocal fold tissue. In the case of front vowels (like /i/), there will be a considerable modification of the vowel in order to maintain this strategy; hence, the reason sometimes /ae/ is heard instead of /i/ in the higher range of the belt voice.

Although the general concept of formant tuning has been questioned (Carlsson and Sundberg 1992), one tuning that seems to be universally agreed upon involves the upper *passaggio* and high range of the female voice; a "tuning" of F1 to f_o occurs, so as to avoid a scenario where f_o is higher than F1 (Henrich et al. 2011; Rothenberg et al. 1987; Sundberg 1987; Titze 2008). So, how does this tuning occur? Imagine a woman is singing an /a/ vowel on a D5 which has a frequency of roughly 587 Hz. The approximate resonance properties of F1 and F2 (the vowel formants) of an /a/ vowel are 800 Hz and 1200 Hz, respectively. The second harmonic for the fundamental D5 is twice the f_o, making it approximately 1174 Hz. This frequency is in the neighborhood of F2 and will therefore be boosted by it. While ascending into the top voice it is often instinctive for a singer to continually open the mouth, the result of this will be an ever-increasing F1 frequency and if lip spreading is also occurring, it will increase all the formant frequencies. As the singer ascends a whole step higher to E5 (659 Hz)—if her lips spread—F2 will continue to enhance H2 and the rising F1 will remain somewhere between f_o and H2. Conversely, if the singer were to round the lips a bit, shaping the vowel more towards /ɔ/ (as in call or saw), all formant frequencies would lower and the result would be that F2 would no longer give a boost to H2 as its frequency would be in the region of 1100 Hz, and F1 would give a boost to f_o/H1 as its frequency would be approximately 700 Hz (which is very near the frequency of f_o/H1 on E5). This maneuver is employed by western classical singers in order to maintain an even timbre. Others suggest a passive modification of the vowel, i.e. "maintaining the tube shape while the pitch and its harmonics move" (in Bozeman 2013, p. 23), and assert that this will also help avoid a loss of timbral depth or warmth.

Another example of a resonance strategy that finds agreement between researchers is the singer's formant cluster. This phenomenon is a strategy used by classically trained male voices, developed to allow them to be heard over a loud accompaniment (Sundberg 1987). Contrary to female singers who shorten their vocal tract with increasing pitch by lowering their jaw and raising their larynx (in order to avoid a situation in which f_o is higher than F1), male singers tend to do the opposite. Male classically trained singers lower the larynx, and widen the pharyngeal wall, the laryngeal ventricle and the piriform sinus to cluster F3, F4, and F5. Acoustically, this strategy allows a boost in the spectrum energy around 2500–3000 Hz, precisely in the middle of the region where the human ear is most sensitive (1 KHz–4 KHz) (Titze 2000). For more information on hearing the singing voice, see Chapter 11, this volume.

As a general rule, a singer must learn how to adjust the resonators to create a space that is more acoustically sensitive to pitch, or part of the harmonic series of the sung pitch. "A singer who keeps a large mouth opening all the time will be wrong about 50 percent of the time. A singer who keeps a small mouth opening all the time will also be wrong about 50 percent of the time. The trick is to know when to open a little or a lot" (Emmons and Chase 2006, p. 132). Perhaps this is an over-simplification, but the spirit of the quote is clear. As different musical notes have different harmonic series, there are necessary acoustic adjustments that singers must make as they negotiate the full range of their voices. For the voice to sound full and with depth, at least one harmonic partial needs to be near F1; hence, low frequency notes do not need that much of a vowel adjustment, as harmonic partials lie within the vicinity of F1 bandwidth (i.e. the interval difference between two points identified as 3 dB lower than the peak of a resonance curve) (Titze 2000). Nevertheless, for higher frequency notes, as the harmonic partials are more widely spread, fewer will be within the range of F1 (and F2), so that more attention is needed towards strategies of modifying the vowels (Bozeman 2013). Vowels and the inherent shape they have in the vocal tract have frequencies at which strong boosts of energy are created (the aforementioned formants). Thus, one must concede that different frequency levels require different configurations of the resonators in order to facilitate effective resonance—which means vowels, with their inherent resonance properties, must be adjusted depending on the frequencies at which they are sung (Sundberg 1987).

SUMMARY

The development of voice control is a rather complex ability, as the change of one parameter leads to the adjustment of many others. Understanding the physiological interactions that dictate the quality of the primary sound is a key element for ensuring proper adjustments, i.e. the ones that increase the longevity of a healthy voice. In fact, hearing, unlike vision or proprioception, does not allow a direct translation of the source sound (Cytowic 2002). For singers, this is even more evident, considering the sound produced is heard differently by the singer than by others. The singer hears the voice as being low frequency. Additionally, the bone conduction of the vibrating vocal folds to both inner ears also presents the ears with a sound that is low frequency dominant (Howard and Murphy 2008). Thus, despite the fact that listening to a sound and imitating it constitutes one of the possible ways of learning to sing, when isolated from the other forms of learning (i.e. kinesthetic, visual, and intellectual) (McCoy 2004), this may lead to a limited use of the vocal instrument. Today, teaching singing in an integrated manner—focusing on the student and the process, instead of the teacher and the final result—is one of the major changes with regard to approaches to instrumental/vocal teaching. The teacher's role is not solely artistic anymore, but is also that of a builder, mentor, coordinator, facilitator, adviser, networker, manager, and developer (Lennon and Reed 2012). These changing roles require new pedagogical skills for teachers, namely knowledge and understanding of all phenomena involved in successful singing performance, including physiological events. One might argue that the current singing teaching paradigm is shifting from vocal coaches who are "empiricists" i.e. those who believe that singing should be largely taught through imagery, so that it becomes free, unconscious and reflexive, towards "mechanists" i.e. those who defend that vocal control is conscious, directly linked to the scientific based evidence (Burgin 1973). In addition, one might also argue that nowadays' singing curricula would benefit from embracing the fact that there is a need to have teachers specialized in different areas of knowledge: voice builders—teachers that understand the physiological, acoustical, and psychological aspects of voice function in order to transform the primary function of the vocal apparatus (i.e. airway protection) to a function of becoming a musical instrument; coaches—those who guide the students into the process of using their musical instrument to convey artistic meaning; and singing voice specialists—those who assist students who have suffered a voice injury and who guide them back to the process of music making (Gill and Herbst, 2015).

Scientific knowledge allows the singing teacher and the singer to uncover the meaning of vocabulary that has been around since the beginning of vocal pedagogy, as well as develop new vocabulary that is more firmly based in the reality of the physiology of voice production (Lã 2014). In the end, finding ways to avoid an overload of the most sensitive part of the whole singing system, the vocal folds, is imperative. Understanding the basics of voice function will guide a teacher down the path of discovery. Preservation of the vocal folds will certainly contribute to the longevity of a singing career. As singing is a multimodal activity, *pre-phonatory breath management* is essential to be prepared for such a complex endeavor. Becoming aware of the role of muscular forces, elastic forces, and gravitation in the control of Psub for a given pitch and vocal loudness is essential for achieving a final output that may serve the purpose of the desired artistic outcome. In fact, Psub influences a number of glottal parameters that are essential to a successful and long vocal career. Excessive vocal adduction is typically detrimental for the voice; and, although, for expressive purposes, the singer may want to use a wide range of different degrees of adduction momentarily, for those professionals seeking vocal efficiency, flow phonation is the best option to employ for the majority of phonation time. It is achieved by combining a low Psub with a moderate adduction and glottal resistance. The result is a strong fundamental, i.e. a big amplitude excursion of the vocal folds with rapid closure of the glottis, without employing a high collision force. This is a highly efficient manner of exciting the resonator with acoustic energy. In addition, intonation is another key element in singing performance as sharpening phrase-peak tones as compared with equally tempered tuning is perceived as conveying more expressivity in singing (Sundberg et al. 2013b). Unintentional altering of intonation, on the other hand, is often a result of poor resonance tuning (Vennard 1967). The importance of resonance awareness in singing cannot be overstated. The ever-changing shape of the vocal tract and, hence, the resonances, are under the conscious control of the singer (Culver 1956). A singer must be attuned to efficient resonance, which results in an easier sound production; this, in turn, can contribute to the longevity of a singing career. The monitoring of a vibrato quality can indicate whether a good technique has been used over the years (or is currently being used): a vibrato with too rapid a frequency may be related to excessive muscle tension, whereas a too slow vibrato rate may express voice fatigue and poor muscle tonus.

Finally, one might conclude that singing is highly idiosyncratic. Despite the fact that all singers share similar anatomical structures, the way individual genotypes transduce themselves produces different phenotypes, leading to small physiological differences in the way a singer may use the vocal instrument. This provides evidence that should encourage a singing teacher not to base pedagogical methods only on their own perceptive experiences. Moreover, the training of a singer should meet individual necessities; variables such as sex, age, personality, and body type may require different approaches.

References

Appelman, R. (1967). *The Science of Vocal Pedagogy: Theory and Application*. Bloomington: Indiana University Press.

Baken, R.J. (1992). Electroglottography. *Journal of Voice* 6: 98–110.

Bozeman, K.W. (2013). *Practical Vocal Acoustics: Pedagogy Applications for Teachers and Singers*. New York: Pendragon Press.

Burgin, J. (1973). *Teaching Singing*. Metuchen, NJ: Scarecrow Press.

Carlsson, G. and Sundberg, J. (1992). Formant frequency tuning in singing. *Journal of Voice* 6: 256–260.

Culver, C.A. (1956). *Musical Acoustics*. New York: McGraw-Hill.

Cytowic, R.E. (2002). *Synesthesia: a union of the senses*. London, Cambridge, MA: Massachussetts Institute of Technology.

Doscher, B.M. (1994). *The Functional Unity of the Singing Voice*. Metuchen, NJ: Scarecrow Press.

Emmons, S. and Chase, C. (2006). *Prescriptions for Choral Excellence: Tone, Text, Dynamic Leadership*. New York: Oxford University Press.

Echternach, M., Sundberg, J., Arndt, S., Markl, M., Schumacher, M., and Richter, B. (2010). Vocal tract in female registers—a dynamic real-time MRI study. *Journal of Voice* 24(2): 133–139.

Fourcin, A. (2000). Voice quality and electrolaryngography. In: R.D. Kent and M.J. Ball (eds), *Voice Quality Measurement*, pp. 285–306. San Diego: Singular Thompson Learning.

Gullaer, I., Walker, R., Badin, P., and Lamalle, L. (2006). Image, imagination, and reality: On effectiveness of introductory work with vocalists. *Logopedics Phoniatrics Vocology* 31(2): 89–96.

Henrich, N., Smith, J., and Wolfe, J. (2011). Vocal tract resonances in singing: Strategies used by sopranos, altos, tenors, and baritones. *Journal of the Acoustical Society of America* 129: 1024–1035.

Herbst, C.T., Howard, D., and Schlömicher-their, J. (2010). Using electroglottographic real-time feedback to control posterior glottal adduction during phonation. *Journal of Voice* 24(1): 72–85.

Hertegård, S., Gauffin, J., and Sundberg, J. (1990). Open and covered singing as studied by means of fiberoptics, inverse filtering, and spectral analysis. *Journal of Voice* 4(3): 220–230.

Hoit, J.D., Plassman, B.L., Lansing, R.W., and Hixon, T.J. (1988). Abdominal muscle activity during speech production. *Journal of Applied Physiology* 65(6): 2656–2664.

Howard, D.M. (1995). Variation of electrolaryngographically derived closed quotient for trained and untrained adult female singers. *Journal of Voice* 9: 163–172.

Howard, D.M. and Murphy, D.T. (2008). *Voice Science Acoustics and Recording*. San Diego: Plural Publishing.

Iwarsson, J. and Sundberg, J. (1998). Effects of lung volume on vertical larynx position during phonation. *Journal of Voice* 12(2): 159–165.

Jian, J. (2006). Physiology of voice production: how does the voice work? In: M.S. Benninger and T. Murry (eds), *The Performer's Voice*, pp. 23–32. San Diego: Plural Publishing.

Kempster, G.B., Larson, C.R., and Klistler, M. (1988). Effects of electrical stimulation of cricothyroid and thyroarytenoid muscles on voice fundamental frequency. *Journal of Voice* 2(3): 221–229.

Lã, F.M.B. (2012). Teaching Singing and Technology. Lecture given at XXIV. Jahreskongress des BDG 2012 gleichzeitig EUROVOX—Kongress 2012: Aspects of Singing II: Unity in Understanding—Diversity in Aesthetics. Munich, Bunderverband Deutscher Gesangspädagogen, April 12–15.

Leanderson, R. and Sundberg, J. (1988). Breathing for singing. *Journal of Voice* 2(1): 2–12.

Lennon, M. and Reed, G. (2012). Instrumental and vocal teacher education: competences, roles and curricula. *Music Education Research* 14(3): 285–308.

Lindblom, B. and Sundberg, J. (2007). The human voice in speech and singing. In: T.D. Rossing (ed.), *Springer Handbook of Acoustics*, pp. 669–712. Stanford: Springer.

Mathieson, L. (2001). *The Voice and Its Disorders*. London: Whurr Publishers.

McCoy, S. (2004). *Your Voice, an Inside View: Multimedia Voice Science and Pedagogy*. Princeton: Inside View Press.

McHenry, M., Johnson, J., and Foshea, B. (2009). The effect of specific versus combined warm-up strategies on the voice. *Journal of Voice* 23(5): 572–576.

Miller, R. (1977). *English, French, German and Italian Techniques of Singing: A Study in National Tonal Preferences and how they Relate to Functional Efficiency.* Metuchen, NJ: Scarecrow Press.

Miller, R. (1994). The mechanisms of singing: coordinating physiology and acoustics of singing. In: M. Benninger, B. Jacobson, and A. Johnson (eds), *Vocal Arts Medicine: The Care and Prevention of Professional Voice Disorders*, pp. 61–71. New York: Thieme Medical Publishers.

Miller, R. (1996). *On the Art of Singing.* New York: Oxford University Press.

Miller, R. (2004). *Solutions for Singers: Tools for Performers and Teachers.* New York: Oxford University Press.

Miller, D.G. (2008). *Resonance in Singing: Voice Building Through Acoustic Feedback.* Princeton: Inside View.

Miller, D.G. and Schutte, H.K. (2005). Mixing the registers: Glottal source or vocal tract? *Folia Phoniatrica Logopedia* 57: 278–291.

Neumann, K., Schunda, P., and Euler, H.A. (2005). The interplay between glottis and vocal tract during the male passaggio. *Folia Phoniatrica Logopedica* 57: 308–327.

Proctor, D. (1980). *Breathing, Speech and Song.* New York: Springer Verlag.

Roers, F., Mürbe, D., and Sundberg, J. (2009). Predicted singers' vocal fold lengths and voice classification: A study of X-ray morphological measures. *Journal of Voice* 23(4): 408–413.

Rothenberg, M. (1968). *The Breath-stream Dynamics of Simple-Released Plosive Production.* Basel: S. Karger.

Rothenberg, M., Miller, D.G., Molitor, R., and Leffingwell, D. (1987). The control of air flow during loud soprano singing. *Journal of Voice* 1(3): 262–268.

Sandage, M.J., Connor, N.P., and Pascoe, D.D. (2013). Voice function differences following resting breathing versus submaximal exercise. *Journal of Voice* 27(5): 572–578.

Schneider, C.M. and Dennehy, K.G. (1997). Exercise physiology principles applied to vocal performance: The improvement of postural alignment. *Journal of Voice* 11(3): 332–337.

Sivasankar, M. and Erickson, E. (2009). Short-duration accelerated breathing challenges affect phonation. *Laryngoscope* 119(8): 1658–1663.

Stark, J. (2003). *Bel Canto: A History of Vocal Pedagogy.* Toronto: University of Toronto Press.

Story, B. (1999). *A Note on Vibration and Resonance.* Denver: Wilbur James Gould Voice Research Center.

Sundberg, J. (1987). *The Science of the Singing Voice.* DeKalb, IL: Northern Illinois University Press.

Sundberg, J. (1992). Breathing behavior during singing. *STL-QPSR* 33(1): 49–64.

Sundberg, J., Leanderson, R., and von Euler, C. (1988). Activity relationship between diagphragm and cricothyroid muscles. *Speech Transmission Laboratory, Quarterly Progress and Status Report* 2–3: 83–91.

Sundberg, J., Leanderson, R., von Euler, C., and Knutsson, E. (1991). Influence of body posture and lung volume on subglottal pressure control during singing. *Journal of Voice* 5(4): 283–291.

Sundberg, J., Fahlstedt, E. and Morell, A. (2005). Effects on the glottal voice source of vocal loudness variation in untrained female and male voices. *Journal of the Acoustical Society of America* 117(2): 879–885.

Sundberg, J., Lã, F. and Gill, B. (2013a). Formant tuning strategies in professional male opera singers. *Journal of Voice* 27(3): 278–288.

Sundberg, J., Lã, F., and Himonides, E. (2013b). Intonation and expressivity: a single case study of classical western singing. *Journal of Voice* 27(3): 391–398.

Titze, I.R. (2000). *Principles of Voice Production*, Iowa City, IA: National Center for Voice and Speech.

Titze, I.R. (2004). A theoretical study of f_0-F1 interaction with application to resonant speaking and singing voice. *Journal of Voice* 18: 292–298.

Titze, I.R. (2008). Nonlinear source-filter coupling in phonation: Theory. *Journal of the Acoustical Society of America* 123: 2733–2749.

Titze, I.R. and Verdolini-Marston, K. (2012). *Vocology: The Science and Practice of Voice Habilitation*. Salt Lake City, UT: National Center for Voice and Speech.

Titze, I.R. and Worley, A.S. (2009). Modeling source-filter interaction in belting and high-pitched operatic male singing. *Journal of the Acoustical Society of America* 126(3): 1530–1540.

Titze, I.R., Riede, T., and Popolo, P. (2008). Nonlinear source–filter coupling in phonation: Vocal exercises. *Journal of the Acoustical Society of America* 123: 1902–1915.

Vennard, W. (1967). *Singing: the Mechanism and the Technique*. New York: Fischer.

Verdolini-Marston, K., Burke, M.K., Lessac, A., Glaze, L., and Caldwell, E. (1995). Preliminary study of two methods of treatment for laryngeal nodules. *Journal of Voice* 9(1): 74–85.

Watson, P., Hoit, J., Lansing, R. and Hixon, T. (1989). Abdominal muscle activity in classical singers. *Journal of Voice* 3(1): 24–31.

Welch, G. F. and Sundberg, J. (2002). Solo voice. In: R. Parncutt and G.E. McPherson (eds), *The Science and Psychology of Music Performance: Creative Strategies for Teaching and Learning*, pp. 253–268. New York: Oxford University Press.

Zenker, W. (1964). Questions regarding the function of external laryngeal muscles. In: D. Brewer (ed.), *Research Potentials in Voice Physiology*, pp. 20–40. New York: State University of New York.

PART 2

THE ACOUSTICS OF SINGING

CHAPTER 5

....

BREATHING IN SINGING

....

ALAN WATSON

INTRODUCTION

DESPITE its central role in the art of singing, the question of how singers breathe continues to be a source of much confusion. Accounts in books on singing pedagogy are often confusing and sometimes in conflict with descriptions of respiration in textbooks on anatomy and physiology. It is therefore not surprising that the authors of a physiological study of breathing in singers commented that " 'subjects' descriptions of how they thought they breathed during singing bore little correspondence to how they actually breathed." (Watson and Hixon 1985). Part of the problem is that singers' accounts are frequently based solely on their subjective sensations and this can give rise to misleading conclusions. Furthermore, the language used in singing textbooks is sometimes almost Delphic in its obscurity when dealing with processes where clarity is essential. While metaphor may have a role in teaching, euphemisms are often less helpful and as Chapman (2006) points out, instructions given to students are unlikely to be effective if they are incomprehensible. An awareness of the basic mechanisms of respiration is an essential starting point for the singer, though it is also important to recognize that the peculiar demands made by singing are reflected in respiratory patterns that differ significantly from those underlying physical activities such as sport, which are better understood. Furthermore, optimal breathing strategies will vary depending on singing style and probably also on the physical characteristics of the singer. As a result it is important that singing teachers are flexible and pragmatic in their approach to this issue.

This chapter begins with a straightforward introduction to the respiratory system in order to provide a foundation from which to discuss the results of evidence-based physiological studies into how classically trained singers breathe. Though our knowledge is still far from complete, objective research has provided many new insights into the respiratory strategies used by singers and has thrown light on numerous long-standing controversies. Nevertheless, it should be recognized that they have so far involved relatively small numbers of professional singers and rarely attempt to assess the effect on the qualities of the voice perceived by listeners. A few have approached the issue of vocal characteristics by analyzing various aspects of laryngeal activity when different breathing strategies are employed, however given the complexity of the vocal system this can provide only the most rudimentary indication of their effect on the voice.

The Respiratory Apparatus

During inhalation, air is taken in via the nose and mouth and passes down through the larynx into the trachea (windpipe). At its lower end, the trachea divides into two bronchi, one running into each lung. Within the lung each divides repeatedly into progressively narrower tubes, ending finally in the terminal bronchioles from which sprout small air sacs called alveoli. Here the inhaled air is brought into very close proximity to a network of fine, thin walled blood vessels known as capillaries (Figure 5.1).

Together, the two lungs contain around 700 million alveoli which provide an enormous area for gaseous exchange (about 160 m^2 which is approximately the area of a singles tennis court). The oxygen diffuses through the liquid film that lines the alveoli and into the bloodstream where it binds to the hemoglobin in the red blood cells. Carbon dioxide produced as a result of cellular activity throughout the body is dissolved in the blood plasma. In the lungs it diffuses in the opposite direction, out into the alveoli. Only twenty-one percent of the air we inhale is oxygen; the remaining volume is composed of the inert gas nitrogen, which plays no role in respiration. In the air we breathe out, oxygen levels have typically fallen to around seventeen percent, with carbon dioxide making up four percent. If we hold our breath, it is the build-up of carbon dioxide in the bloodstream that ultimately provides the irresistible stimulation to take a breath. The concentration of carbon dioxide in the blood affects its acidity (or pH). If we hyperventilate, for example during a panic attack perhaps brought on by performance anxiety (Widmer et al. 1997), too much carbon dioxide is exhaled and the blood becomes more alkaline. This may lead to dizziness or fainting as a result of increasing heart rate and a constriction of the blood vessels running to the brain. One traditional

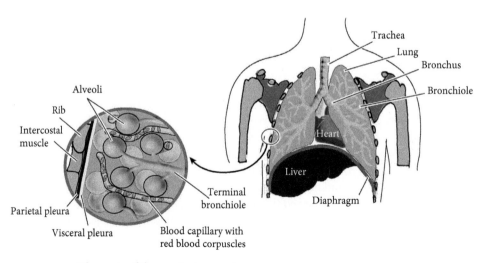

FIGURE 5.1 Elements of the respiratory system.

From Watson (2009).

remedy for this is to breathe in and out into a paper bag, as inhaling the carbon dioxide in the rebreathed air helps restore blood pH to normal levels so that the symptoms abate. This is no longer recommended as a first aid treatment however, as it can be dangerous if the individual has an undiagnosed lung or heart condition. During singing, respiration is not only used for gaseous exchange, but also to generate the necessary subglottic pressure (the pressure in the airway below the closed vocal folds of the larynx that is required to set them vibrating). During singing, subglottic pressures must be continually adjusted by the respiratory muscles to maintain a consistent vocal quality between notes of varying pitch or loudness.

The lungs themselves contain no respiratory muscles, but expand and contract due to movements of the walls of the chest cavity. Some of the muscles responsible lie within these structures, but others are to be found in the abdominal wall, the neck, and to a lesser extent, the back. For the lungs to expand and contract during breathing, they must therefore remain in contact with the chest walls and be able to glide over them during breathing. This is achieved in the following manner. Each lung is covered by a thin smooth membrane (the visceral pleura), while a similar membrane (the parietal pleura) lines the inside of the chest cavity. A thin layer of liquid between the two layers of pleura holds them together by surface tension and also allows them to glide smoothly over each other. A similar principle is at work when a tax-disk holder is stuck to a car windscreen by coating its plastic surface with a thin film of water. If air gets in between the two layers of pleura, the lung collapses away from the chest wall creating an emergency situation, because it can no longer be inflated.

MUSCLE ACTIVITY DURING NORMAL BREATHING

If we sit quietly without breathing and with all our respiratory muscles relaxed (for example at the end of a sigh), the lungs will be partly filled. The volume they contain is called the functional residual capacity (Figure 5.2).

To increase this volume we must use our inspiratory muscles, and to decrease it, recruit our expiratory muscles. If we take the deepest possible breath, then exhale as much as we can, the volume of air expelled from the lungs is our vital capacity, which is the maximum that is available to sustain a single spoken or sung phrase. The lungs are not empty at the end of this action as the chest is not flat. There remains what is known as the residual volume, which could only be expelled if the lungs were to collapse away from the ribs (see above) or the ribs were physically crushed. Vital capacity is strongly correlated with height and to a lesser extent with age (Quanjer et al. 1993); for example a twenty-year-old Caucasian woman in good health would have a predicted vital capacity of 3.6 liters if she is 160 cm tall, and of 4.6 liters if her height is 180 cm. The comparable figures for a male would be 4.6 liters and 5.8 liters, respectively. However, differences in chest shape mean that healthy individuals can differ significantly from the predicted values. During what is known as tidal breathing (Figure 5.2) when we are sitting silently at rest, the regular inward and outward flow of air (tidal volume) is typically only around 500 mL. In tidal breathing, air is drawn in actively due to respiratory muscle activity, but expiration is passive, driven by the elasticity of the lungs and so ends at the functional residual capacity. This tendency of the lungs to collapse is a consequence of the surface tension of the fluid film that lines the alveoli. Because of their small size, this is very considerable. In fact, in order to be able to inflate the lungs at all, the

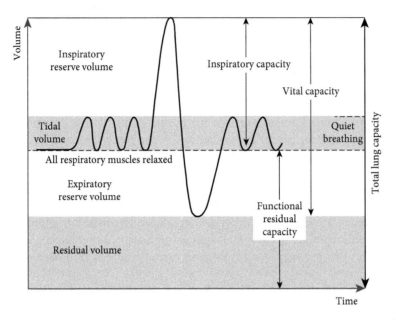

FIGURE 5.2 Diagram explaining lung function parameters. During normal quiet breathing only the tidal volume is used. With a maximal intake of breath the inspiratory reserve volume is used. If the breath is then driven out completely, we pass through the tidal volume band into the expiratory reserve volume. This exhalation uses all of the vital capacity. It leaves the residual volume which cannot be expelled because the lateral walls of the chest are supported by the ribs. As the outer surface of the lungs are held in contact with the ribs via the pleural membranes, the lungs cannot collapse completely.

From Watson (2009).

alveoli must secrete a surfactant (a detergent-like molecule) to reduce the surface tension but even so, it is still not completely abolished.

During singing, both inspiration and expiration are driven by muscle activity. The experienced singer adjusts the volume of each breath to the length and demands of the phrase being sung, so that excess stale air (air with a high carbon dioxide level) does not have to be expelled at the end of the phrase, before the next inhalation. In describing the role of the muscles responsible for respiration, we will first consider the major players in order to present a clear account of the basic mechanism. We will then turn our attention to the so-called accessory respiratory muscles. These are muscles which have other major actions not related to breathing. Finally, we will examine patterns of respiratory muscle activity that are particularly associated with singing.

Inspiration

Breathing is the consequence of regulating the volume and pressure in two chambers; the first is the chest (or thorax) which contains the lungs. These are open to the atmosphere via the trachea and mouth. The second is the abdominal cavity, which is effectively a sealed chamber. The primary respiratory muscles lie in the walls of these two cavities. Separating the two chambers is the diaphragm, the muscle which causes the most confusion among singers (Bunch 1997). When relaxed, the diaphragm is a thin, dome-shaped sheet of muscle which is pushed up into the chest cavity. Its long fibers run from the edges of the dome, where they are attached to the lumbar vertebrae and the inside of the lower ribs, to its rounded apex at the central tendon. Physically bound to its lower surface is the liver, which has a mass of around 0.8–1.5 kg. This pulls downwards on the diaphragm, although any movement can be restricted by the presence of the visceral organs that fill the abdominal cavity.

When the diaphragm contracts, the dome flattens, causing the floor of the chest to descend and hence increasing its volume. This lowers the pressure within the lungs so that air flows in through the nose and mouth until the pressure between the inside and outside equalizes (Figure 5.3).

Many singers and wind players also believe that the diaphragm is an involuntary muscle, but this is incorrect. It is what is known as a striated muscle, the same type that moves the joints of the skeleton, and the fact that it is under conscious control can be demonstrated by this simple exercise. Place your hand over your belly button and push it outwards by making the abdominal wall bulge. The only muscle that can bring this about is the diaphragm (Leanderson and Sundberg 1988) and it does so by pushing downwards on the abdominal contents. The ability of singers to consciously alter the way they use the diaphragm has also been demonstrated using biofeedback, i.e. by letting them observe real-time recordings of electrical signals within the muscle as they sing and then asking them to modify the pattern

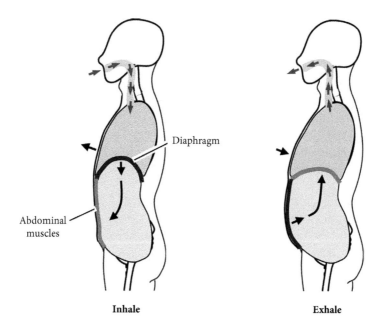

Diaphragm

Abdominal muscles

Inhale   **Exhale**

FIGURE 5.3 The actions of the diaphragm and the abdominal muscles during normal breathing. Where shown dark, the muscles are active and where light, they are inactive. Arrows pointing towards and away from the chest indicate the actions of the internal and external intercostal muscles on the ribs.

Adapted from Watson (2009).

of contraction (Sundberg et al. 1986). Of course, we often use the diaphragm unconsciously during breathing, but the same is true of the other respiratory muscles and indeed for striated muscles in general, e.g. those of the legs during walking. What is different about the diaphragm is that we receive no conscious sensation from it (von Euler 1968) and learn of its activity only through its effects on other structures.

If the muscles of the abdominal wall are not relaxed sufficiently during inhalation and it cannot bulge outwards, the descent of the diaphragm is impeded because the abdominal organs can only be compressed to a limited extent. As a result, the volume of the inhalation is reduced. As the abdominal muscles also play a role in maintaining posture, there is a tendency for them to remain in a more contracted state than is strictly necessary. For this reason, some teachers specifically instruct singers to relax the abdominal muscles quickly at the onset of inhalation (Chapman 2006). Chapman calls this the SPLAT maneuver (Singers Please Loosen Abdominal Tension). The ability of the singers she trains to do this has been confirmed objectively (Thorpe et al. 2001) and it has also been observed in other classically trained singers (Hixon 1987; Watson and Hixon 1985). Though some classical sources warn against allowing excessive distension of the abdominal wall (Slater 1911), this does not imply that it should be held rigid during inhalation by abdominal muscle contraction.

The other key muscles of inhalation are the intercostal muscles. These comprise three layers of short muscles that run between adjacent ribs. The external intercostal muscles contribute to inspiration. The role of the two internal layers of intercostals has historically been a source of great debate but there is now clear evidence that they contribute to expiration (De Troyer et al. 2005; Sears 1977; Sears and Davis 1968) as is unequivocally demonstrated in Figure 5.7. At rest, the ribs slope downwards and when the external intercostal muscles contract, they rotate upwards and outwards to increase chest volume (Figure 5.4). The upward movement (sometimes called the pump handle effect) increases the distance between the sternum and the spine, while the outward movement (likened to that of a bucket handle rising to a horizontal position) increases the lateral dimension of the chest. Though it may seem counterintuitive, the diaphragm also expands the lower part of the ribcage as it contracts and descends, though it tends to compress the upper part (De Troyer et al. 2005). This is because its fibers, which are curved around the liver, tend to straighten as they come under tension creating leverage that raises the ribs and swings them outwards. Taken together, the diaphragm and intercostal muscles increase lung volume by increasing all three dimensions of the chest.

Some teachers refer to "dorsal breathing" or "singing with the back" when discussing inhalation; for example Miller alludes to it in his account of the German school of singing pedagogy (Miller 1997). What this might refer to in physiological terms is unclear; it has been suggested that it may draw attention to the fact that rib cage expansion includes the dorsal region of the chest (Leanderson and Sundberg 1988). There is little evidence that back muscles play a significant role in inhalation. It is possible that during inhalation, some sensation may arise in the back as certain *expiratory* muscles come under tension, e.g. the lateral abdominal wall muscles (which extend into the back), or an accessory respiratory muscle called serratus posterior inferior. Latissimus dorsi, which is a large superficial muscle in the back, may also be a source of sensation. Though mainly involved in expiration, it may become active during inspiration as the lungs near full vital capacity. The major roles of all of these muscles are discussed later. There is no physiological evidence that muscles whose primary role is to support the back are involved, other than indirectly through their influence on posture.

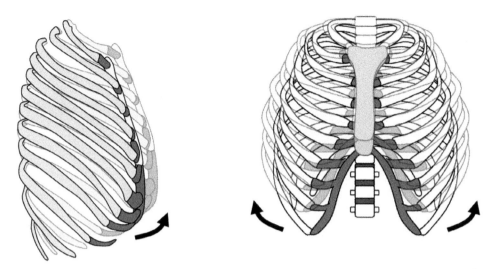

FIGURE 5.4 The upward and outward movements of the ribs during inhalation.

Singers may use a large percentage of their vital capacity when performing long or demanding phrases or when projecting the voice, but often have only a very short time to inhale if the melodic line is not to be disrupted. The ability to perform rapid and efficient inhalation is at a premium (Thomasson 2003) as the volume of air required for each breath is considerably greater than for speech (Watson 2009).

Expiration

Much of the power driving forced expiration comes from the muscles of the abdominal wall. These are the rectus abdominis and the lateral abdominal muscles (Figure 5.5). The rectus abdominis (popularly known as the "six pack") is made up of a series of muscle blocks running from the sternum and the short segments of cartilage that connect it to the ribs (the costal cartilages), down to the front of the pelvis. The lateral abdominal muscles comprise three thin sheets (the external oblique, internal oblique, and transversus abdominis). The attachment of each is slightly different, but together they run between the lower ribs, the upper edge of the pelvis, a sheet of fibrous tissue covering the muscles of the back (the thoracolumbar fascia), and the edge of the rectus abdominis muscle. The fibers in each layer run in a different direction which enhances their combined ability to contain abdominal pressure and resist herniation. The outermost layer (external oblique) runs downwards and forwards while the fibers of the underlying internal oblique run at right angles to this; downward and backwards. The fibers of the deepest layer (transversus abdominis) are almost horizontal.

The lateral abdominal muscles act in concert (De Troyer et al. 2005; Kera and Maruyama 2005) to draw the walls of the abdominal cavity inwards and compress the visceral organs. The lower regions of lateral abdominal muscles have been shown in some studies to be more active than the upper regions, whether in normal breathing or during speech or singing (Watson et al. 1989). As the abdominal contents are relatively incompressible and the muscles of the pelvic floor form an unyielding platform, this forces the *relaxed* diaphragm

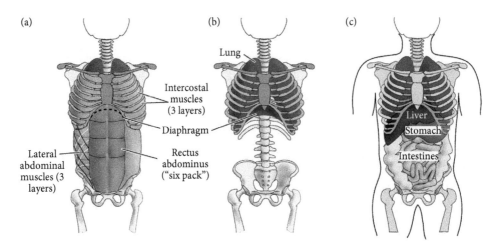

FIGURE 5.5 The principal muscles of respiration (a), the skeleton (b), and contents (b,c) of the chest and abdominal cavities.

From Watson (2009).

upwards into the chest like a piston in a cylinder. At the same time, the internal intercostal muscles pull the ribs downwards and inwards, further increasing the pressure within the lungs and driving the air out. During phonation, the vocal folds of the larynx are brought into contact with each other (a movement known as adduction), and forcing a stream of air between them causes them to vibrate rapidly (Titze 2008). This is the origin of the sound (the voice source). How firmly they are adducted is one factor that determines the driving pressure that is needed to set them vibrating and affects the perceived volume and spectral qualities of the sound produced. This subglottic pressure is monitored by sensory nerve endings in the mucosal lining of the larynx beneath the vocal folds (see Sundberg 1987).

Some singing teachers suggest that the rectus abdominis either plays no part in breathing in singers (Bunch 1997), or that its use should be discouraged (Chapman 2006). The general concept receives some support from a study which revealed that though there certainly is activity in rectus abdominis during speech and singing, it is lower than that in the lateral abdominal muscles (Watson et al. 1989). However it may nevertheless be the first abdominal muscle to be recruited during phonation as lung volume falls (Draper et al. 1960). Projected singing (which involves higher flow rates than when the voice is not projected) requires greater involvement of the abdominal muscles (Thorpe et al. 2001), which may explain why their activity was found to be greater in young professional opera singers than in vocal students (Pettersen and Westgaard 2004). There have been relatively few studies into the role of the inner intercostal muscles but their action can often be deduced from observations of changes in chest circumference. For example, when the singing line requires an abrupt increase in subglottic pressure, there is generally a simultaneous decrease in the dimensions of both the chest and abdomen which indicates that the internal intercostal muscles are activated simultaneously with the abdominal muscles, however the greater power generated by the latter may subsequently result in a transient upward movement of the chest before the dimensions of both decline gradually to maintain the vocal line (Thorpe et al. 2001).

In addition to expiratory muscle activity, passive forces also contribute to raising subglottal pressure. As the alveoli increase in volume during lung inflation, work must be done to overcome the surface tension of the liquid film that coats their walls. When the muscles of inhalation relax, surface tension causes the alveoli to collapse. This is known as elastic recoil and it makes a significant contribution to subglottic pressure at high lung volumes, a phenomenon we will return to later.

Accessory Muscles of Respiration

A number of other muscles are known or have been suggested to contribute to respiration (Campbell 1970). For the most part these make a smaller contribution than those we have encountered so far and they are often better known for roles other than breathing. For this reason they are called accessory respiratory muscles (Figure 5.6). This distinction is perhaps debatable as the abdominal muscles, which are the main driving force for expiration, also have a postural role. The contribution of some accessory muscles at least are clearly important for singers.

Two sets of inspiratory accessory muscles are found in the neck, the scalenes and the sternocleidomastoids. Both have postural roles, stabilizing the position of the head. The scalenes run from the lower vertebrae of the neck to the first or second ribs. When those on one side act alone, they tilt the neck to the side, but when both sides act simultaneously they can pull the rib cage upwards. The sternocleidomastoid muscles run from the skull, just behind the ear, to the sternum and the adjacent part of the collar bone (clavicle). Acting individually, these rotate the head to the opposite side. When they act together they can thrust the head forward or shorten the neck, both of which may have a negative

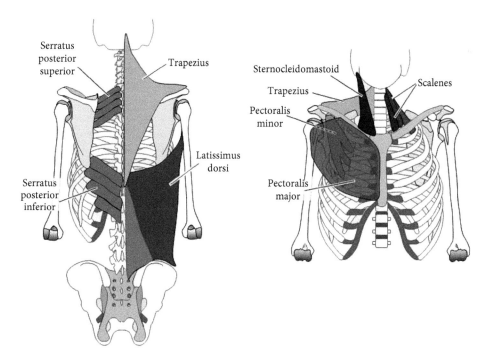

FIGURE 5.6 The main accessory muscles of respiration.

impact on the voice (Chapman 2006; Jones 1972; Quarrier 1993), however, if this move-ment is resisted by muscles in the back of the neck, they also pull the rib cage upwards. Both sets of muscles are active during inhalation, the scalenes from around twenty-five percent vital capacity and the sternocleidomastoid at higher lung volumes (typically above seventy percent) (Raper et al. 1966). In singers, these muscles are often recruited during inhalation at much lower lung volumes though the pattern of activity varies be-tween individuals for reasons that are currently unclear (Pettersen 2005; Pettersen and Westgaard 2005).

Singers also show bursts of activity in these muscles during phonation which are likely to reflect their involvement in reducing subglottic pressure at high lung volumes by resisting elastic recoil (i.e. respiratory braking, see below) (Pettersen et al. 2005). Because contrac-tion of the sternocleidomastoid is easy to observe with the naked eye (if you doubt this, observe its activity in thin female news readers!), it receives more attention in singing texts than do the scalenes, whose actions are not so easy to see. Some authors suggest that ster-nocleidomastoid activity is indicative of clavicular breathing (Bunch 1997), however, due to the site of its attachments, the muscle cannot actually raise the shoulders. In clavicular breathing, elevation of the shoulders is mainly brought about by the upper fibers of the tra-pezius muscle, which runs from the base of the skull and vertebrae of the neck and thorax, to the shoulder blade (scapula). Its influence on the chest posture is brought about indi-rectly via the muscles running between the scapula or clavicle and the ribs (see Watson 2009). In its role as an accessory respiratory muscle, trapezius is normally engaged only at the end of maximal inhalations (Campbell 1970). In singers paradoxically, it has been suggested to have an expiratory effect as it can apparently compress the upper part of the chest when the shoulders are pulled backwards and upwards (Pettersen and Westgaard 2004). However, when singers are trained to relax trapezius through biofeedback, no com-pensatory activity is seen in other respiratory muscles, suggesting that it makes little, if any, positive contribution to the mechanism of singing breathing. Tension in trapezius is often stress related and reducing this as part of a general strategy for anxiety management also involving other muscles in the neck (such as the intrinsic and extrinsic muscles of the larynx) will have a positive impact on vocal function.

Pectoralis major has also been mooted as an accessory muscle of inhalation (Campbell 1970). Its fibers run from the sternum (breast bone), the costal cartilages, and the collar bone (clavicle), to the inner surface of the upper arm (humerus). It is therefore capable of pulling the chest wall upwards and outwards though it appears to act in this way only at the end of a maximal inspiration. Pettersen (2006) has made a preliminary study of its activity in singers, and in some he observed peaks of activity during inhalation that occurred simultaneously with those in the sternocleidomastoid, but in other singers this did not occur.

It is not uncommon for singing texts to suggest that students should tense the muscles of the pelvic floor (Chapman 2006; Miller 1997), sometimes quaintly described as "sitting on the breath" or "squeezing the dime." Less colorfully, it may be said rather cryptically to "maintain abdominal balance" (Bunch 1997). Presumably this means to resist any bulging downward of the floor of the abdomen, however this muscular layer is generally unyielding and its integrity is not something that wind players concern themselves with although they generate much greater intra-abdominal pressures, The pelvic floor muscles contribute to the urethral and anal sphincters and one possible origin for this concept may be that if the mus-cles become damaged or weakened due to childbirth or age, sneezing or laughing can cause a small escape of urine (stress incontinence). Though this might give the impression that they are unable to contain the pressure within the abdomen, this is not really the case. Brass musicians are not asked to tense the pelvic floor so it would seem unlikely that this is necessary to resist the much lower abdominal pressure generated in singing. Nevertheless, is there any evidence that activity in these muscles is correlated with respiration? Recent studies reveal rhythmic activity in pelvic floor muscles in phase with expiration, however this is again to ensure continence (Hodges et al. 2007) rather than to resist any downward movement of the pelvic floor.

Other muscles sometimes referred to in singing texts include transversus thoracis, levator costarum, serratus posterior (superior and inferior) for inhalation, and quadratus lumborum in expiration. Many of these are weak and lie in positions that make it hard to record their activity during respiration, but their contributions are generally thought to be minor (Campbell 1970; Chapman 2006; Miller 1997; Vennard 1967; Williams and Gray 1989). However the thin serratus posterior inferior muscle, though it probably contributes little to pulling the ribs downwards, may when stretched be one source of sensations in the lower back that influence the output of other muscles (Vilensky et al. 2001). The role of latissimus dorsi, which often attracts the interest of singers, will be discussed later.

Control of Subglottic Pressure during Singing

The primary role of the respiratory apparatus during singing is to regulate subglottic pressure, therefore it makes a major contribution to vocal support. To singers, this concept of support also embodies other qualities such as voice manageability, timbre, and vocal projection which are dependent on a range of additional factors such as the position of the larynx and how it is used, and vocal tract conformation. The term is rarely defined explicitly and its precise meaning clearly varies not only between different singing traditions (Miller 1997) but also between individual singers (Griffin et al. 1995). Its use in this chapter will therefore be confined to the control of subglottic pressure.

If we take a deep breath and then abruptly and completely relax the inspiratory muscles (as in a sigh), the chest falls rapidly and air is quickly expelled from the lungs due to elastic recoil, until functional residual capacity is reached (Figure 5.2). This passive expiration lasts only a second or two during which airway pressure falls continuously in an uncontrolled fashion. If we wish to sing a steady note of constant pitch and volume, we need to maintain a consistent subglottic pressure for its entire duration. This requires a continuous adjustment in the level of inspiratory and expiratory muscle activity. At the start of the note, the elastic recoil forces generate pressures that are generally too high and so must be resisted by gradually reducing the level of activity in the *inspiratory* muscles until the recoil forces equal the pressure required. This is known as respiratory braking. Subsequently, expiratory muscle activity is gradually recruited to maintain the pressure at the required level. That this actually occurs during singing is clearly demonstrated in Figure 5.7, which shows the progressive decline in activity of the inspiratory external intercostal muscles, followed by a gradual increase in activity in the expiratory internal intercostals.

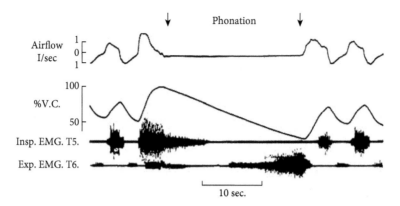

FIGURE 5.7 Activity in the intercostal muscles (electromyograph (EMG) recording) when singing a loud sustained tone. To sustain a constant airflow there is initially a gradual decline in activity in the external intercostals (Insp. EMG) representing respiratory braking, followed by a gradual increase in activity in the internal intercostals (Exp. EMG) in the later part of the breath.

From Sears and Newsom Davis (1968).

Prolonged respiratory braking must be brought about by muscles that control the fall of the chest or ribs (e.g. the external intercostals, scalenes, or sternocleidomastoids). It might be thought that the diaphragm has but a small role in such behavior as at the end of inhalation it is at, or close to, its lowest and most contracted state, however, prior to the onset of phonation, subglottic pressure must be raised to the level necessary to support the note to be sung. To achieve this, the abdominal muscles must first be engaged to push the (usually) relaxed diaphragm upwards—as part of an activity known as pre-phonatory posturing (see below). From this position, the diaphragm *can* be used in respiratory braking but only in short pulses as it will only reduce subglottic pressure if as it flattens, it increases lung volume faster than the descending chest walls reduce it. Such activity can be used to facilitate large downward pitch changes or abrupt reductions in voice intensity (Leanderson and Sundberg 1988). Another example of respiratory braking by the diaphragm can be seen in Figure 5.8, which shows its involvement in creating the trillo, a Renaissance ornament in which the same note is rapidly repeated. The braying sound this produces is vividly described by its alternative name—the goat's trill! The figure shows that the trillo is generated by a constant fluctuation in subglottic pressure. During the first half of the exhalation, this results from pulses of diaphragmatic activity, but as these die away in the second half, the abdominal muscles take over as the driving force. One would predict that the transition between the two phases will occur at the point where elastic recoil pressure reaches the level needed to generate the note. Some singers may also use the diaphragm in this way during coloratura singing, using the drops in subglottic pressure to separate the notes, while others rely solely on activity in the abdominal muscles to create discrete pressure pulses to initiate each note (Leanderson and Sundberg 1988; Leanderson et al. 1987).

Despite the recent increase in objective analysis of respiratory muscle activity during singing, much remains to be explored and established ideas still need to be challenged. This is amply demonstrated in a recent investigation into the role of latissimus dorsi (Watson

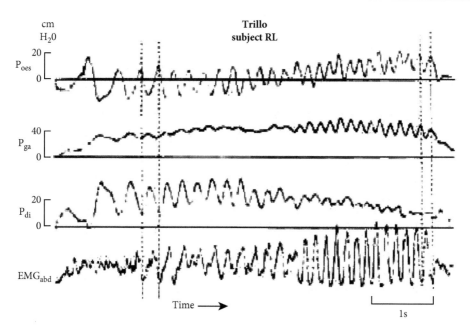

FIGURE 5.8 The involvement of the diaphragm and abdominal wall muscles underlying performance of the Renaissance trillo. Esophageal pressure (P_{oes}) gives an indication of fluctuations in subglottic pressure. During the first half of the breath this is generated by fluctuations in transdiaphragmatic pressure (P_{di}) which is a consequence of rhythmic contraction of the diaphragm. Later the trillo is driven by pulses in abdominal pressure which can be followed by recording gastric pressure (P_{ga}). This is a consequence of activity in the lateral abdominal muscles (EMG_{abd}).

From Leanderson and Sundberg (1988).

et al. 2012). A number of singing texts refer to it (Husler and Rodd-Marling 1976; Vennard 1967) though most are either unclear about its role or suggest that it might contribute to inhalation during that *bête noir* of singers: clavicular breathing (Miller 1997). The muscle arises from the fibrous sheet of tissue overlying the deep muscles of the back (the thoraco-lumbar fascia) and runs to the upper arm (humerus) forming the back wall of the armpit (axilla). Its main role is to pull the arm downward, e.g. when climbing or swimming, however it is also attached to the sides of the lower ribs which gives it some influence over respiration. It is active in coughing (forced expiration), during which the muscle pulls the ribs downwards, but it is also engaged at the end of very full inhalations. Its involvement in inhalation is usually attributed to muscle fibers running upwards from ribs up to the arm, but if the muscle is actually examined, the attachments to the ribs appear to run downwards into the body of the muscle and not upwards. Instead it is likely that when the chest is held high by other muscles, the downward pull of latissimus dorsi pulls the ribs outwards like a guy rope. During speech, it is only active towards the end of the expiration (Draper et al. 1960). Given these observations, a recent study of its role in singing produced unexpected results (Watson et al. 2012). Conscious engagement of the muscle was correlated with increased chest expansion, something that has been linked to projected singing (Thorpe

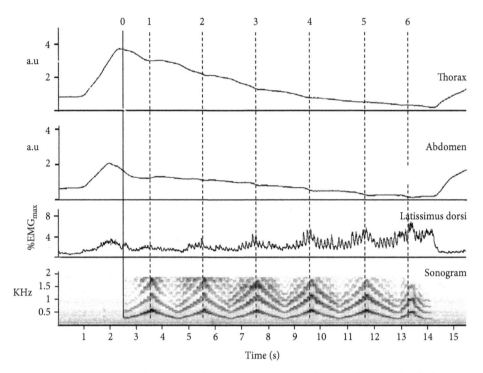

FIGURE 5.9 Activity in latissimus dorsi (electromyograph (EMG) recording) during a coloratura exercise comprising ascending and descending scales on each vowel, ending in an arpeggio (as revealed by the sonogram). Pulses in the muscle correspond to each note and these increase in amplitude as lung volume declines. The magnitude of the pulses also rises and falls with pitch. The upper two traces show changes in chest and abdominal circumference at the same scale in arbitrary units (a.u.) The singer (a mezzo soprano) employs the "noble" posture, i.e. belly-in strategy. Inward movement of the abdomen is used to raise subglottic pressure to an appropriate level before phonation begins (indicated by the line 0). Chest circumference slowly declines during the exercise but the slope increases as pitch rises and decreases as it falls. The dashed lines (1–6) mark the initiation of the highest note in each cycle. A similar pattern in abdominal wall contraction is at first slight, but becomes more marked (cycles 4, 5, and 6) as the chest reaches its limit of inward and downward movement.

From Watson et al. (2012).

et al. 2001). However during coloratura singing, pulses of activity coincided with the onset of each note. These increased in amplitude as lung volume declined but also rose and fell in line with pitch (Figure 5.9), implying that they contributed to the increase in subglottic pressure that supports each note.

During sustained projected notes, the muscle also pulsed in phase with the vibrato, supporting an oscillation in both frequency and intensity (Figure 5.10). In these activities the muscle would not be acting alone. Indeed in some (but not all) of the singers, similar activity during vibrato was detectable in sternocleidomastoid. Previous studies strongly implicated the intrinsic laryngeal muscles in the production of vibrato as well as infrahyoid muscles (such as sternothyroid) which control the vertical position of the larynx. Many dismissed the

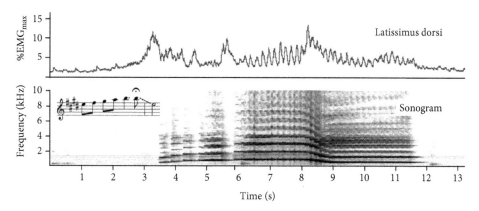

FIGURE 5.10 Activity in latissimus dorsi (electromyograph (EMG) recording) during last phrase of the Rossini aria "Una voce poco fa" (see music inset) sung by a mezzo soprano using the projected voice at performance volume. During the last two held notes, pulses in the muscle occur in phase with the vibrato, which can be seen as oscillations in the sonogram.

From Watson et al. (2012).

possible involvement of respiratory muscles in vibrato (see Hirano et al. 1995). Nevertheless a few studies have suggested that the diaphragm or abdominal wall muscles can make a contribution in some singers at least (Appleman and Smith 1971, 1985; Vennard 1967) though as none of these sources present actual data to support their conclusions more work is needed on this subject.

SINGING POSTURE

Variability in how different individuals achieve the same ends is a recurring theme in studies of respiration in singers. Though respiratory movements are not stereotyped in the strictest sense of the word as the control of each breath must match the phrase being sung, breathing patterns in individuals repeating the same phrase are highly consistent (Thorpe et al. 2001). This applies not only to the exhalation that supports phonation, but also the inhalation that precedes it. As a result, it is assumed by many that inhalatory behavior is important for vocalization (Thomasson and Sundberg 2001) but precisely why is unclear. It may be linked to the necessity of bringing the chest and abdomen into an optimal configuration for the onset of phonation. The fact that inhalation is associated with changes in laryngeal configuration (e.g. vocal fold abduction) and position may also be a factor. Inhalatory behaviors in singers will no doubt partly reflect how they have been taught, but are also likely to have been molded by subsequent experience perhaps involving optimization for the style of singing and the singer's body type.

The directions given to singers concerning breathing frequently make reference to both static and dynamic aspects of posture. Here we will confine ourselves to a consideration of those relating to chest and abdominal movement or position, as sufficient objective information is available on this subject to come to some conclusions. Two opposing strategies are sometimes invoked in discussing breathing posture in singers (Leanderson and Sundberg 1988; Titze 2000) though in terms of what singers actually do, it might be better to consider them as two ends of a continuum. In the first the emphasis is on keeping the chest high and stable leaving the diaphragm and abdominal muscles to draw air in or drive it out. This strategy may be referred to as "pear shape up" (referring to the combined shape of the chest and abdominal cavities), "belly in", or "noble" posture. In the other strategy, less emphasis is placed on chest stability and more on maintaining abdominal pressure with the abdominal wall being allowed to expand on inhalation and remaining relatively expanded even at the onset of phonation. This is known as the "pear shape down" or "belly out" posture because the relative proportions of the chest and abdomen are to some extent reversed. As a result of the abdominal distension, the diaphragm is flatter at the onset of phonation, though this may also be partly a result of keeping it contracted during expiration as well as during inspiration. In trying to make sense of these postures, it is first necessary to examine what actually happens rather than the singer's intention, as these are sometimes at variance (Watson and Hixon 1985).

Even in singers who use the "belly in" strategy, the chest falls significantly during phonation (Sears 1977) and this can clearly be seen in Figure 5.9. Though trained singers show a greater range of abdominal movement when singing than untrained singers, the greatest contribution to the decline in lung volume during a sung phrase and to its increase during inhalation comes from the chest (Griffin et al. 1995; Thomasson and Sundberg 2001). This should not be surprising because the range of movement (and hence volume change) that the abdominal wall can achieve is limited. Hixon et al. (1988) go so far as to state that the abdominal wall (presumably by driving the relaxed diaphragm upwards and thus stretching it) creates a platform against which the rib cage acts to deliver the driving pressure for phonation. Nonetheless, the emphasis on raising the chest relatively high and tensioning the abdominal wall in this posture, in preparation for phonation has certain consequences. Pushing the diaphragm upwards counteracts the downward pull of the liver, which hangs from its lower surface, thus reducing the load on the inspiratory muscles. Having the diaphragm in the stretched state may also be advantageous if it is needed to take rapid breaths at moderate to high lung volumes. The inner intercostal muscles are also stretched and so can exert fine control over subglottic pressure to control pitch or dynamics and fluctuations in chest circumference (Watson and Hixon 1985). Chest wall movements that are consistent with such a strategy can be seen in Figure 5.9, in phase with rising and falling pitch during the first part of a coloratura exercise.

The belly-out strategy advocated by some other schools of singing (Miller 1997) encourages a constant and paradoxical engagement of the diaphragm during phonation that opposes the contraction of the abdominal muscles. It can be demonstrated that some singers actually do this, and one observable consequence is that their abdominal pressure is considerably elevated (Leanderson et al. 1987). Others advocate against this approach and use breath training techniques such as the "Accent Method" which dictate that in line with normal breathing, diaphragmatic activity should strictly alternate with that of the abdominal activity (Chapman 2006). This leads us to question whether there is a rational explanation for co-activating the diaphragm and abdominal muscles during phonation. It has been proposed that this "facilitates subtle, rapid and precise adjustments in subglottal pressure . . . ." (Collyer et al. 2011) which is more or less what was attributed to the expiratory intercostal muscles in the "belly in" strategy!

If we look for other arguments in favor of the belly-out posture, one possibility is that it helps to keep the lower end of the rib cage expanded, an effect of diaphragmatic activity that we have already encountered. Another possibility is that for endomorphic (plump) singers in whom the mass of the abdomen is high, adjusting the opposing forces of the diaphragm and abdominal muscles might be advantageous for fine control of abdominal movement. Hoit and Hixon (1986) proposed that speech breathing in endomorphs (plump individuals) is predominantly driven by abdominal movement, while in ectomorphs (slight individuals), chest movement dominates. However, they used a very small number of subjects and a more extensive investigation did not confirm this conclusion (Manifold and Murdoch 1993), though this too has been challenged on methodological grounds (Hoit 1994). Vennard (1967) also suggested that breathing in men is more abdominally driven than in women, however his evidence is purely anecdotal. The possible influence of body type on breathing in singers clearly deserves further attention.

In some singers, activation of the diaphragm during phonation is associated with a shift from pressed to flow phonation and an increased stability of formant frequencies (Sundberg et al. 1986) which would be seen as an advantage in classical singing, though no explanation or causal link has been put forward. Formants are vocal tract resonances and tuning these (usually by manipulating the dimensions of the throat and mouth aperture, and the position of the tongue) is crucial for acoustically efficient projection of the voice.

It has been argued that at high lung volumes, the flatter diaphragm typical of the belly-out strategy will exert a greater downward pull on the larynx than the belly-in strategy. This would promote a lower laryngeal position, something which is also associated with vocal projection in classical singing and is therefore encouraged. Attempts to verify this have been unsuccessful however. While one study found no dependence of laryngeal position on anterior abdominal wall behavior (Thomasson 2003), another contradicted the hypothesis by reporting that the belly-out strategy was associated with a higher larynx; however, it appears likely that this anomalous result was due to postural changes in the head and neck (the reasons for which were unclear) rather than having any direct relationship to the position of the diaphragm (Iwarsson and Sundberg 1998). Furthermore there were no significant differences between the two postures in subglottic pressure or a range of parameters derived from flow glottogram recordings that measure the pattern of airflow through the glottis (the space between the vocal folds) as they oscillate during singing (Thomasson 2003). Subjective comparisons by a panel of expert vocal judges also failed to demonstrate a consistent influence on vocal quality between the two strategies. Not surprisingly, the singing was sometimes judged to be poorer when the performers used the pattern that was not habitual to them (Collyer et al. 2011), a result that was also reflected in changes seen in the flow glottogram (Thomasson 2003). All this leaves the controversy of the relative merits of these two breathing strategies in some disarray, and in practical terms, it is probably unhelpful to view the belly-in, belly-out postures as separate options rather than as the opposing ends of a range.

IMPLICATIONS FOR PRACTICE

A good understanding of the physiological basis of respiration and of the more arcane breathing strategies that underlie singing, are essential prerequisites for accurate and effective communication between teacher and pupil as well as a necessary basis for personal exploration. One of the reasons why scientifically objective studies of breathing are so important is that the sensations we receive from the respiratory system are incomplete and may lead us to inappropriate conclusions. While it will be useful to refer to these sensations when guiding others, their limitations must be appreciated. It is also important to realize that some instructions that are often given to singers such as "keep the chest high" are relative rather than absolute and that a rigid adherence to a dogma without understanding the underlying principles will ultimately be counterproductive. A recurrent theme arising from research into breathing in singers is that different individuals achieve similar ends by different means. While differences in vital capacity are easily appreciated, the possibility that age, gender, and body type or body shape may have a bearing on which strategies are optimal is less widely recognized. What works for the teacher may not work for the pupil.

Turning to the involvement of individual muscles during breathing, the role of the diaphragm is both central and complex. In functional terms it is unequivocally a muscle of inhalation but how it is actually used is highly variable and depends not only on the particular breathing strategy being used, but also the nature of the singing task. Its tonic co-contraction with the abdominal muscles during exhalation is associated particularly with the belly-out strategy, but excessive activity of this type is likely to be tiring as both sets of muscles will be working harder than is strictly necessary and will generate high abdominal pressures. Many muscles that play a significant role in respiration also have postural functions that may impact on singing. For example, the sternocleidomastoids are important muscles of inhalation, but constant over-activity is associated with forward head thrusting. This is often stress related and linked to tension in other muscles such as those in and around the larynx where excessive tension must be avoided. The singer therefore needs to disengage these two functions and ensure good posture is maintained by a balanced but not excessive activity in opposing postural muscle groups. Breathing is only one element of singing technique, and we see in the concept of support that it must be integrated with good use of the voice source and efficient vocal projection if a satisfactory outcome is to be achieved. While the expiratory muscles control subglottic pressure, the actual level required depends on these other factors, thus breathing technique cannot be viewed in isolation.

Finally, it is clear that many questions concerning the control of respiration in singers remain unanswered, though techniques for studying them are now readily available. It is important that singers become involved in this research to ensure that future studies focus on the issues that are of most practical relevance. However, in doing so they should always be prepared to challenge established dogma so that teaching can be based on objective principles.

SUMMARY

This chapter provides an overview of the principles of normal breathing and how it is modified during singing. Inhalation is a consequence of increasing the dimensions of the chest, brought about by contraction of the diaphragm and external intercostal muscles. At high lung volumes, muscles such as the sternocleidomastoids and the scalenes also contribute significantly to expanding the chest. Subglottic pressure is generated during exhalation by the muscles of the abdominal wall (especially the lateral abdominal muscles) which drive the relaxed diaphragm upwards, and the internal intercostal muscles which pull the ribs downwards. When the lungs are fully inflated and the inspiratory muscles relax, air can be driven out by elastic recoil forces, and in order to control subglottic pressure these must be resisted (respiratory braking) by a gradual reduction in inspiratory muscle activity. This is followed by an incremental recruitment of the muscles of exhalation. How different patterns of activity in these and other muscles contribute to particular aspects of singing such as the trillo, coloratura, and vibrato were described and the way in which the same ends can be achieved by different means was explained. One consistent trend which emerges from studies of breathing is that different singers can achieve the same ends by different means. Two opposing breathing strategies used by singers ("belly-in" and "belly-out") are analyzed and compared and an objective assessment of their properties is presented. This reveals that despite each having strong advocates, the differences between them in terms of outcome are at best subtle. This seems to imply either that both can be used successfully, or that one or other may be the most favorable strategy for a particular individual. Though some possible reasons for this are put forward, there is currently insufficient information available to assess their validity. Furthermore, it may be better to view them as two ends of a continuum, rather than as separate options.

REFERENCES

Appleman, D. and Smith, E. (1971). Cinefluoroscopic observations of abdominal muscular functions in their relation to the support vibrato syndrome in singing. *Journal of the Acoustical Society of America* 49: 137.

Appleman, D. and Smith, E. (1985). Cinefluoroscopic and electromyographic observations of abdominal muscular function in its support of vibrato. In: V. Lawrence (ed) *Transcripts of the fourteenth symposium: Care of the professional voice* (pp. 79–82). New York: The Voice Foundation.

Bunch, M. (1997). *Dynamics of the Singing Voice*. New York: Springer.

Campbell, E.J.M. (1970). Accessory muscles. In: E.J.M. Campbell, E. Agostoni, and J. Newsom Davis (eds) *The Respiratory Muscles: Mechanics and Neural Control*, 2nd edn (pp. 181–93). London: Lloyd-Luke.

Chapman, J.L. (2006). *Singing and Teaching Singing: A Holistic Approach to Classical Voice*. San Diego, CA: Plural Publishing.

Collyer, S., Kenny, D.T., and Archer, M. (2011). Listener perception of the effect of abdominal kinematic directives on respiratory behavior in female classical singing. *Journal of Voice* 25(1): e15–24.

De Troyer, A., Kirkwood, P.A., and Wilson, T.A. (2005). Respiratory action of the intercostal muscles. *Physiological Reviews* 85(2): 717–56.

Draper, M.H., Ladefoged, P., and Whitteridge, D. (1960). Expiratory pressures and air flow during speech. *British Medical Journal* 1(5189): 1837–43.

Griffin, B., Woo, P., Colton, R., Casper, J., and Brewer, D. (1995). Physiological characteristics of the supported singing voice. A preliminary study. *Journal of Voice* 9(1): 45–56.

Hirano, M., Hibi, S., and Hagino, S. (1995). Physiological aspects of vibrato. In: P.H. Dejonckere, M. Hirano, and J. Sundberg (eds) *Vibrato* (pp. 9–32). San Diego: Singular.

Hixon, T.J. (1987). *Respiratory Function in Speech and Song.* Boston: College-Hill Press.

Hixon, T.J., Watson, P.J., Harris, F.P., and Pearl, N.B. (1988). Relative volume changes of the rib cage and abdomen during prephonatory chest wall posturing. *Journal of Voice* 2(1): 13–19.

Hodges, P.W., Sapsford, R., and Pengel, L.H. (2007). Postural and respiratory functions of the pelvic floor muscles. *Neurourological Urodynamics* 26(3): 362–71.

Hoit, J.U. (1994). A critical analysis of speech breathing data from the University of Queensland. *Journal of Speech and Hearing Research* 37(3): 572–80.

Hoit, J.D. and Hixon, T.J. (1986). Body type and speech breathing. *Journal of Speech and Hearing Research* 29(3): 313–24.

Husler, F. and Rodd-Marling, Y. (1976). *Singing: The Physical Nature of the Vocal Organ: A Guide to the Unlocking of the Singing Voice.* London: Hutchinson.

Iwarsson, J. and Sundberg, J. (1998). Effects of lung volume on vertical larynx position during phonation. *Journal of Voice* 12(2): 159–65.

Jones, F.P. (1972). Voice production as a function of head balance in singers. *Journal of Psychology* 82: 209–15.

Kera, T. and Maruyama, H. (2005). The effect of posture on respiratory activity of the abdominal muscles. *Journal of Physiology, Anthropology and Applied Human Science* 24(4): 259–65.

Leanderson, R. and Sundberg, J. (1988). Breathing for singing. *Journal of Voice* 2(1): 2–12.

Leanderson, R., Sundberg, J., and von Euler, C. (1987). Role of diaphragmatic activity during singing: a study of transdiaphragmatic pressures. *Journal of Applied Physiology* 62(1): 259–70.

Manifold, J.A. and Murdoch, B.E. (1993). Speech breathing in young adults: effect of body type. *Journal of Speech and Hearing Research* 36(4): 657–71.

Miller, R. (1997). *National Schools of Singing: English, French, German, and Italian Techniques of Singing Revisited.* Lanham, MD: Scarecrow Press.

Pettersen, V. (2005). Muscular patterns and activation levels of auxiliary breathing muscles and thorax movement in classical singing. *Folia Phoniatrica et Logopedica* 57(5–6): 255–77.

Pettersen, V. (2006). Preliminary findings on the classical singer's use of the pectoralis major muscle. *Folia Phoniatrica et Logopedica* 58(6): 427–39.

Pettersen, V. and Westgaard, R.H. (2004). Muscle activity in professional classical singing: a study on muscles in the shoulder, neck and trunk. *Logopedics Phoniatrics Vocology* 29(2): 56–65.

Pettersen, V. and Westgaard, R.H. (2005). The activity patterns of neck muscles in professional classical singing. *Journal of Voice* 19(2): 238–51.

Pettersen, V., Bjorkoy, K., Torp, H., and Westgaard, R.H. (2005). Neck and shoulder muscle activity and thorax movement in singing and speaking tasks with variation in vocal loudness and pitch. *Journal of Voice* 19(4): 623–34.

Quanjer, P.H, Tammeling, G.J., Cotes, J.E., Pedersen, O.F., Peslin, R., and Yernault, J.C. (1993). Lung volumes and forced ventilatory flows. Report Working Party Standardization of Lung

Function Tests, European Community for Steel and Coal. Official Statement of the European Respiratory Society. *European Respiratory Journal Supplement* 16: 5–40.

Quarrier, N.F. (1993). Forward head posture in vocal performance. *Medical Problems of Performing Artists* 8: 29–32.

Raper, A.J., Thompson, W.T. Jr., Shapiro, W., and Patterson, J.L. Jr. (1966). Scalene and sterno-mastoid muscle function. *Journal of Applied Physiology* 21(2): 497–502.

Sears, T.A. (1977). Some neural and mechanical aspects of singing. In: M. Critchley and R.A. Henson (eds) *Music and the Brain: Studies in the Neurology of Music* (pp. 78–94). London: Heinemann Medical.

Sears, T.A. and Davis, J.N. (1968). Control of respiratory muscles during voluntary breathing. *Annals of the New York Academy of Sciences* 155(A1): 183–90.

Slater, D.D. (1911). *Vocal Physiology and the Teaching of Singing. A complete guide to teachers, students and candidates for the A.R.C.M., L.R.A.M., and all similar examinations.* London: J.H. Larway.

Sundberg, J. (1987). *The Science of the Singing Voice.* DeKalb, IL: Northern Illinois University Press.

Sundberg, J., Leanderson, R., and Voneuler, C. (1986). Voice source effects of diaphragmatic activity in singing. *Journal of Phonetics* 14(3–4): 351–7.

Thomasson, M. (2003). Belly-in or belly-out? Effects of inhalatory behavior and lung volume on voice function in male opera singers. *TMH-QPSR* 45: 61–73.

Thomasson, M. and Sundberg, J. (2001). Consistency of inhalatory breathing patterns in professional operatic singers. *Journal of Voice* 15(3): 373–83.

Thorpe, C.W., Cala, S.J., Chapman, J., and Davis, P.J. (2001). Patterns of breath support in projection of the singing voice. *Journal of Voice* 15(1): 86–104.

Titze, I.R. (2000). *Principles of Voice Production.* Iowa City: National Center for Voice and Speech.

Titze, I.R. (2008). The human instrument. *Scientific American* 298(1): 78–85.

Vennard, W. (1967). *Singing: The Mechanism and the Technic.* New York: C. Fischer.

Vilensky, J.A., Baltes, M., Weikel, L., Fortin, J.D., and Fourie, L.J. (2001). Serratus posterior muscles: anatomy, clinical relevance, and function. *Clinical Anatomy* 14(4): 237–41.

von Euler, C. (1968). The proprioceptive control of the diaphragm. *Annals of the New York Academy of Sciences* 155(A1): 204–5.

Watson, A.H.D. (2009). *The Biology of Musical Performance and Performance-related Injury.* Lanham, MD: Scarecrow Press.

Watson, P.J. and Hixon, T.J. (1985). Respiratory kinematics in classical (opera) singers. *Journal of Speech and Hearing Research* 28(1): 104–22.

Watson, P.J., Hoit, J.D., Lansing, R.W., and Hixon, T.J. (1989). Abdominal muscle activity during classical singing. *Journal of Voice* 3(1): 24–31.

Watson, A.H., Williams, C., and James, B.V. (2012). Activity patterns in latissimus dorsi and sternocleidomastoid in classical singers. *Journal of Voice* 26(3): e95–105.

Widmer, S., Conway, A., Cohen, S., and Davies, P. (1997). Hyperventilation: a correlate and predictor of debilitating performance anxiety in musicians. *Medical Problems of Performing Artists* 12: 97–106.

Williams, P.L. and Gray, H. (1989). *Gray's Anatomy.* Edinburgh: Churchill Livingstone.

CHAPTER 6

···

THE SOUND SOURCE IN SINGING
Basic Principles and Muscular Adjustments for Fine-tuning Vocal Timbre

···

CHRISTIAN T. HERBST, DAVID M. HOWARD,
AND JAN G. ŠVEC

INTRODUCTION

···

VOICE timbre is the one of the central qualities in singing. On a global or long-term level, singers and their teachers are most concerned with "building the instrument," i.e. by establishing motor control and behavioral patterns which allow voice production within the limits of "acceptable" or "beautiful" singing in their chosen style. This process is nicely reflected by the German term *Stimmbildung* (Engl.: voice building—see Gill and Herbst 2016). On the other hand, singers must also be able to vary voice timbre on an *ad hoc* level, allowing for artistic expression. Here, muscular fine-control and agility are paramount qualities of a "good" voice. Concerning this matter, vocal pedagogue and singer Richard Miller suggests: "Vocal timbre that results from a well-formed, well-coordinated instrument, without maladjustment of any of its physical parts or function, stands the best chance of qualifying under the artistic criteria for tonal beauty, as found in Western culture" (Miller 1986, p. 205).

The sound source of the voice is—with a few exceptions—created by vibrating laryngeal tissue (i.e. the vocal folds), which converts a steady airflow supplied by the lungs into a sequence of flow pulses. The acoustic pressure waveform resulting from this sequence of flow pulses excites the vocal tract, which filters them acoustically; the result is radiated (mostly) from the mouth, and also (partly) from the nose (Story 2002). This description of the voice production mechanism suggests three basic physiological layers for sound production: the respiratory system, the larynx, and the vocal tract, sometimes termed the *power source, sound source,* and *sound modifiers* respectively (Howard and Murphy 2007). This three-part system is shown anatomically and schematically in Figure 6.1.

The most obvious method for voice timbre modification is via the sound modifiers, by introducing changes into the vocal tract shape (Ladefoged 2001). Fine-tuning the vowel color in relation to the sung pitch is a well-established concept for varying the vocal timbre

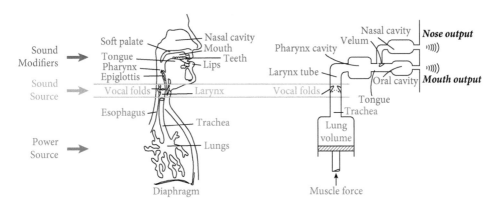

FIGURE 6.1 Human vocal organs and a representation of their main acoustical features.

After Rossing (1990), Figure 15.1.

to optimize sound output (Coffin 1980; Echternach et al. 2010, 2011; Henrich et al. 2007; Joliveau et al. 2004; Miller 2008; Miller and Schutte 2005; Story 2004; Sundberg 1972, 1974, 1977; Sundberg and Skoog 1997; Wendler 2008). In the mid-nineteenth century, however, Manuel Garcia was already suggesting that the sound quality can be influenced independently both in the larynx and via adaptations of the vocal tract (Garcia 1847a, 1894). Garcia's farsighted observations have had an impact on many pedagogic schools of thought, such as Barbara Doscher's *Functional Unity of the Singing Voice*. Doscher suggests that voice timbre can either be influenced in the larynx by the firmness of glottal closure (*ringing* vs. *veiled* quality), or by adjusting the resonance tube, i.e. the vocal tract through change of the antagonistic vertical positions of soft palate and larynx (*bright* vs. *dark* quality) (Doscher 1994).

In this chapter, we will follow that lesser explored aspect of timbre variation in singing—specifically that which is achieved by adjusting the laryngeal configuration, as opposed to changing vocal tract settings. In particular, it will be shown how relatively small muscular adjustments in the larynx can influence the vibratory properties of the vocal folds, and hence the quality of the output sound.

In other words, the goal of this chapter is to describe the physiological and physical underpinnings of the sound source in singing. Even though its text includes the occasional pedagogical suggestion when deemed appropriate, it is a scientific treatise and not a description of a pedagogical method. As such, this chapter may aid the pedagogue or therapist to better understand one particular aspect of voice production, especially when considering the "why?" (rather than the "what?," "when?," or "how?") of an exercise. That said, we readily concede that in teaching and therapy, the bigger, holistic picture should never be discarded (Herbst 2017). One should always bear in mind that there is a human attached to the larynx.

EXPLANATION OF FRAMEWORK/PRINCIPLES

Timbre vs. voice source spectrum

When describing the quality of a sung sound, one must distinguish between a *subjective* psychoacoustic level (i.e. the **voice timbre**) and an *objective* physical level (i.e. the **sound** spectrum). Voice timbre is formally defined as *"that attribute of auditory sensation in terms of which a listener can judge two sounds similarly presented and having the same loudness and pitch as dissimilar"* (ANSI 1994, p. 35). By this definition, its perception can vary from individual to individual (thus, timbre cannot be measured objectively). The sound spectrum, on the other hand, is determined by the frequency and amplitude (and phase) of each component of a complex vibration (Rossing 1990). In other words, the spectrum *is a physical property that can be characterized as a distribution of energy as a function of frequency* (Roads 1996, p. 536).

Vocal fold vibration

Most commonly, the voice source is created by the vibrating vocal folds and their interaction with the glottal airflow. In some singing styles, other structures such as the ventricular folds, the aryepiglottic folds, and the arytenoid cartilages can also constitute part of the vibrating system (Bailly et al. 2010; Fuks et al. 1998; McGlashan et al. 2007; Sakakibara et al. 2004). The primary sound source in singing is created by flow-induced self-sustained oscillations of laryngeal tissue, driven by air coming from the lungs. In other words, the steady (DC) tracheal airflow is converted into a time-varying glottal flow. This phenomenon has been described in the myoelastic-aerodynamic theory of voice production (Van den Berg 1958). Here, vocal fold vibration is facilitated by (1) a time-varying glottal shape: *convergent* (as seen in the frontal plane) in the opening phase, allowing maximum energy transfer from the air stream into the tissue; and *divergent* in the closing phase, creating a drop of intraglottal pressure that aids vocal fold closure; and (2) an inert supraglottal air column (i.e. a delayed vocal tract response caused by an inert acoustic load), also aiding in the closure of the vocal folds (Titze 1988b).

This basic mechanism of voice production is fundamentally different from other sound production mechanisms seen in mammals, such as (presumably) purring in cats. In purring, phonation is assumed to be caused by a centrally driven periodic laryngeal modulation of respiratory flow (Sissom et al. 1991). The intermittent activation of intrinsic laryngeal muscles (induced by a very regular, stereotyped pattern of muscular activity occurring c. 20–30 times per second) is hypothesized to result in glottal closure and the development of a transglottal pressure that generates sound when dissipated by glottal opening (Remmers and Gautier 1972). Despite early claims (Husson 1950), there is no evidence of such a sound production mechanism in humans (Van den Berg and Tan 1959).

In comparison to the rate of vibration during flow-induced sound production (c. 40 to over 2000 Hz (Baken and Orlikoff 2000, Echternach 2013), the speed and frequency at which the intrinsic laryngeal muscles move is relatively small. According to Hunter et al. (2004), cyclic vocal fold posturing movements in humans can only be achieved up to c. 10 times a second. Therefore, the active muscular positioning adjustments of the vocal folds (i.e. adduction and choice of register, see below) are not to be confused with the much faster passive vocal fold oscillations, which are governed by aerodynamic and mechanical principles. Nevertheless, as will be shown later, the active muscular configuration of the vocal folds via intrinsic laryngeal muscles has a basic influence on the vibratory property of the vocal folds.

There are several properties of the voice that can be measured by analyzing the sound source: (1) regularity, (2) fundamental frequency, and (3) the spectral slope of the voice source spectrum.

Regularity

The output of the voice source is a series of pressure disturbance events. It can be considered to be periodic if these events repeat. The time for which each repeated event lasts is known as the *period* (typically labeled T or T_0), i.e. the duration of one glottal cycle. It is, however, in the nature of the (biological) voice source signal that this condition can never be strictly satisfied. The voice source is therefore at best *nearly periodic* (Titze 1995).[1] As a vibrating physical system, it has a time-varying *fundamental frequency* or f_0, i.e. the number of oscillations per second, or ($f_0 = 1/T$), measured in hertz (Hz) (Rossing 1990). f_0 can in most cases be perceived as a certain *pitch*, formally defined as *"that attribute of auditory sensation in terms of which sounds may be ordered on a scale extending from low to high"* (ANSI 1994, p. 34). It should be borne in mind that f_0 and pitch are not necessarily correlates, since the first is a property of a vibrating physical system (and thus objective), and the latter is a psychoacoustic (and thus subjective) perceptual quality (Howard and Angus 2009); in some circumstances, loudness and/or timbre can change our perception of pitch even when f_0 remains constant.

Deviations from the (nearly) periodic case manifest themselves as *perturbations* (i.e. temporary changes from an expected behavior), *fluctuations* (more severe deviations from a pattern), *jitter* (a short-term, cycle-to-cycle perturbation in the fundamental frequency), *tremor* (low-frequency fluctuation), and *vibrato*, i.e. a modulation of the fundamental frequency at rates of 4–7 Hz (Hirano et al. 1995).

The classification of voice signals also encompasses signals with subharmonic structure as well as chaotic signals with no apparent periodic structure (Fitch et al. 2002; Sprecher et al. 2010; Titze 1995). A detailed discussion of non-linear phenomena and chaos in voice production is beyond the scope of this chapter. For more information, the reader is referred to further literature (Herbst et al. 2013; Herzel 1993; Titze et al. 1993; see also Edgerton, this volume). The paper by Herbst et al. (2013) introduces the so-called "phasegram," a novel visualization method for non-linear phenomena and chaos in vibrating systems. This publication also contains some tutorial-style information on non-linear phenomena in voice, including an annotated sample of involuntary voice breaks of a baritone singing a *messa di voce* in his *primo passaggio*.

Airflow

As a first approximation, there is a rather simple relation between the acoustic glottal airflow and the created sound: the acoustic air pressure is proportional to the first mathematical derivative (i.e. the rate of change) of the time-varying glottal airflow. However, research from the last two decades suggests that the actual sound generation process is more complex: Both aero-acoustic (airflow-related) sources and mechanical (vibrational) sources contribute to the generated sound (Alipour et al. 2011), and vortices arising after separation of the airflow jet from the glottis may contribute to sound radiation, due to the interaction with the

---

[1] In voice science, the term "quasi-periodic" is sometimes used interchangeably. In physics, a quasi-periodic signal is defined as the superposition of two or more periodic signals with non-integer ratio frequencies (Bergé et al. 1984). To avoid confusion, we recommend using the term *"nearly-periodic"* for voice signals with an apparent periodic structure.

supraglottal vocal tract (Barney et al. 1999). Since the fluid-induced aspect of sound production contributes considerably more to the generated acoustic energy than the vibration-induced part (Alipour et al. 2011), the remainder of this section will, for the sake of simplicity, concentrate on this aspect of sound generation.

The vibrating vocal folds are contacting and de-contacting more or less periodically, allowing pulses of air to pass from the trachea into the pharynx.[2] Interactions between air and tissue result in synchronized tissue velocity and glottal air pressure variations. The interruption of the flow at the instant of vocal fold closure sets up damped acoustic oscillations in the supraglottal as well as in the subglottal system of the trachea, bronchi, and lungs (Fant 1979). The period T at which the glottal pulses repeat is inversely proportional to the f_o of phonation, whereas the detailed shape of these airflow pulses has an impact on the quality (and hence the timbre) of the created sound.

Based on the time-varying glottal airflow, each glottal cycle can be divided into (1) a (quasi) *closed phase* where the glottis (the space between the vibrating vocal folds) has reached its minimum during the glottal cycle. In this phase of the vibratory cycle, the airflow has either totally stopped due to full vocal fold contact, or air escapes at some rate if there is incomplete glottal closure; (2) an *open phase*—see Figure 6.2. The ratio between

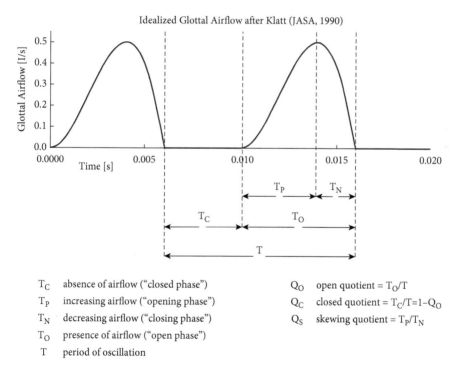

T_C	absence of airflow ("closed phase")	Q_O	open quotient = T_O/T
T_P	increasing airflow ("opening phase")	Q_C	closed quotient = $T_C/T = 1-Q_O$
T_N	decreasing airflow ("closing phase")	Q_S	skewing quotient = T_P/T_N
T_O	presence of airflow ("open phase")		
T	period of oscillation		

FIGURE 6.2 Idealized glottal flow waveform, synthesized with the model described in Klatt and Klatt (1990).

[2] Glottal flow consists of two aspects (Titze 2000): transglottal flow (air that is forced through the glottis); and displacement flow in the glottis (air that is squeezed out in all directions by the closing vocal folds).

closed phase and the period, usually expressed as a percentage, is called the closed quotient (Q_C or CQ), and the ratio between the open phase and the period is the open quotient (Q_O or OQ). The open phase can conceptually be divided into a portion where the airflow increases (commonly called *opening phase*), and a portion where the airflow decreases (*closing phase*). In most cases of phonation, the closing phase is shorter than the opening phase, resulting in a skewing of the glottal waveform (Rothenberg 1973). The ratio between the opening and the closing phases of the glottal pulse can be expressed as the *skewing quotient* (Q_S). The open quotient and the skewing quotient are important quantities, since they define the shape of the glottal waveform (Doval et al. 2006; Titze 2000).

Airflow and the voice source spectrum

The rapid termination of glottal airflow at the instant of vocal fold closure in each glottal cycle creates strong high-frequency acoustic pressure components that excite the vocal tract resonances (Miller 1959; Rothenberg 1973; Sundberg 1981b). This is particularly the case if the closing phase is abrupt, i.e. if the first derivative of the glottal flow (the rate of change of the airflow) has a strong negative peak at the moment of vocal fold closure, resulting in a large *maximum flow declination rate* (MFDR) (Holmberg et al. 1988)—see Figure 6.3. The MFDR (and thus the timbre of the sound) is heavily influenced by both the open quotient and the skewing quotient (Fant 1979).

The distribution of energy in the source spectrum, i.e. the amplitude of the individual harmonics, decays uniformly in the frequency domain with increasing prevalence

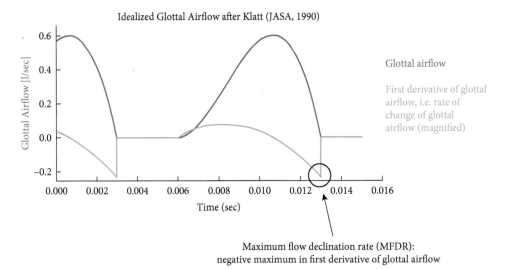

FIGURE 6.3 Relation of glottal airflow (blue) to its first derivative (orange), i.e. its rate of change. The negative maximum of the first derivative is the maximum flow declination rate (MFDR). The MFDR occurs at the point in time where, caused by abrupt cessation of glottal airflow during glottal closure, most of the acoustic energy is being created during a glottal cycle.

(Rothenberg 1981b). The energy distribution is termed *spectral slope* and is measured in negative decibels (dB) per octave. The spectral slope depends on the sharpness of the cessation of airflow, becoming less negative (i.e. flatter) the more abrupt it is. Typical spectral slope values would range from –6 dB/octave for *brassy* phonation (with more high-frequency components in the spectrum) to –18 dB/octave for *flutey* (without noise components) or *breathy* phonation (with noise components in the glottal source created by turbulent airflow in the insufficiently adducted glottis) (Fant 1979; Titze 2000)—see Figure 6.4. The model shown in the figure suggests that there is a direct relationship between the spectral slope and the abruptness of glottal closure (which is partly influenced by the duration of the closed phase, and hence the closed quotient). A theoretical study of glottal flow models revealed that a low-frequency spectral peak (also termed "glottal formant") is found in the glottal flow spectrum. Its center frequency is controlled by the open quotient, and its bandwidth and amplitude are influenced by the asymmetry coefficient (Doval et al. 2006).

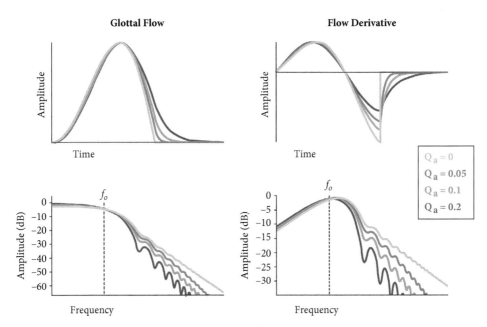

FIGURE 6.4 Effects of asymmetry of airflow waveform on created spectrum (taken from Doval et al. 2006). Top row: waveforms of glottal flow (left) and its derivative (right) for a generic glottal flow model. The varied parameter is the return phase quotient (Q_a),[3] which is defined as the ratio between the return phase time constant and the duration between the glottal closure instant (GCI) and the end of the period. Bottom row: energy spectra of the glottal flow waveform (left) and of its derivative (right). Note that a smaller Q_a (and hence a smaller open quotient) results in a flatter spectral slope. Data from Doval et al. (2006), Figure 6.13. In summary, the data suggests that the spectrum contains stronger high-frequency components (i.e. it has a flatter spectral slope) as the closing phase gets shorter and the closed phase and the closed quotient increases.

---

[3] In the generic glottal flow model, the return phase quotient is formally defined as: $Q_a = T_a / [Q_c T]$, where T_a is the time constant of the exponential decay in the return phase, Q_c is the closed quotient, and T is the period (Doval et al. 2006).

Level 1 source-filter interaction

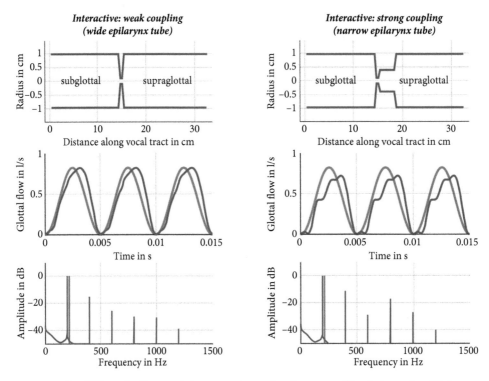

FIGURE 6.5 Effect of epilarynx tube geometry on level 1 source-filter interaction (Data was taken from Titze 2008, Figures 1 and 2). Top: Two different vocal tract configurations were used for the simulations (left: wide epilarynx tube, Ae = 3.0 cm²; right: narrow epilarynx tube, Ae = 0.5 cm²); Middle: three cycles of glottal airflow for computational models driven with a sinusoidal glottal area function (red). Note that the source-filter interaction results in a skewed waveform (blue) where the closing phase is considerably shorter than the opening phase. Bottom: Spectrum of glottal flow for the two simulation condictions (blue). The hypothetical result without interaction is superimposed (red).[4] The interaction effect is stronger in the model with the narrow epilarynx tube, where the increased input impedance to the vocal tract causes stronger harmonics and effectively introduces a closed phase into the simulated glottal flow (even though the sinusoidal driving function had no closed phase).

A vocalist has three main options for influencing the shape of glottal flow waveform and thus the timbre of the sound source:

1. Introducing changes into the quality of vocal fold vibration and glottal airflow through adjustments of intrinsic laryngeal musculature, which will be discussed in the reminder of this chapter.

2. As a by-product of intensity regulation via the respiratory system: an increase of subglottal pressure is likely to result in an increased closed quotient (particularly at

---

[4] The energy component in the spectral of the non-interactive scenario (red) has been shifted slightly to the right, in order to display both the results of the interactive (blue) and the non-interactive case in each panel.

lower intensities) and an increase of the maximum flow declination rate (Sundberg et al. 2005), thus introducing stronger high-frequency partials into the sound source spectrum.

3. Via non-linear source-filter coupling (Flanagan 1968), i.e. by increasing the vocal tract inertance by narrowing the epilarynx tube, or by moving a formant (subglottal or supraglottal) just above f_o (Rothenberg 1981a, 1981b; Titze 2004a, 2004b). The possible influences of supra- and subglottal vocal tract have been classified as (Titze 2008):

   - *Level 1* interactions, where the positive reactance of the vocal tract (caused by the inertance of the air column) influences the wave shape of the glottal air pulse. This effectively introduces additional harmonics into the *glottal wave shape* (and as a consequence also into the acoustic output) which would not be present without an attached vocal tract—see Figure 6.5.
   - *Level 2* interactions, where a change of the vocal tract reactance (via the vocal tract geometry) directly influences the mechanics of *vocal fold vibration*. This can have a possible effect on both fundamental frequency and the amplitude and mode of vocal fold vibration (Titze 2008)—see Figure 6.6.
   - Story et al. (2000) suggest a third level of interaction (partly biomechanical and partly neurological), which might be useful to explain intrinsic vowel pitch.

OVERVIEW OF AREAS OF KNOWLEDGE

Glottal adduction

The primary function of the larynx is to facilitate breathing and to protect the lungs from intruding items. In the breathing position, the vocal folds are *aBducted*, allowing for airflow during both inhalation and exhalation (see Figure 6.7, 1st image of sequence at t = 0 ms.). For voice production, the vocal folds have to be *aDducted* to enable their flow-induced oscillation. The positioning of the vocal folds is performed in the larynx via the paired arytenoid cartilages (the posterior portion of the membranous vocal fold is attached to the vocal process of the arytenoid cartilage). The lateral cricoarytenoid muscles (LCA) bring the vocal processes together by a forward rocking motion of the arytenoids on the cricoarytenoid joint; the interarytenoid muscles (IA) seal the posterior part of the glottis. Both, the LCA and IA muscles, are aDductors. An antagonist aBductory function is provided mainly by the posterior cricoarytenoid muscles (PCA), by moving the vocal processes apart. Figure 6.7 shows the transition from breathing to phonation.

The relevance of glottal adduction in singing was expertly observed more than 170 years ago by Manuel Garcia:

> When one very vigorously pinches the arytenoids together, the glottis is represented only by a narrow or elliptical slit, through which the air driven out by the lungs must escape. Here each molecule of air is subjected to the laws of vibration, and the voice takes on a very pronounced brilliance. If, on the contrary, the arytenoids are separated, the glottis assumes the shape of an isosceles triangle, the little side of which is formed between the arytenoids. One can then produce only extremely dull notes, and, in spite of the weakness of the resulting sounds, the air escapes in such abundance that the lungs are exhausted in a few moments.
>
> (Garcia 1847b, p. 152)

Level 2 source-filter interaction

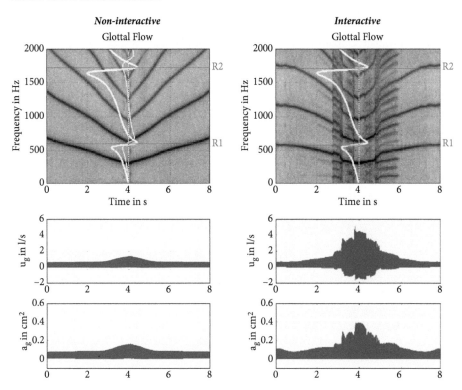

FIGURE 6.6 Effect of level 2 source-filter interaction in a simulation of downward and upward f_o glide produced with a 175 point-mass self-oscillating biomechanical model of the vocal folds (Data and graphs from Titze (2008), Figures 10 and 12). Comparison of two simulation conditions: without (left) and with (right) supraglottal source-filter interaction. Top: spectrogram with vertically superimposed reactance curves as white lines—thick: supraglottal (displayed in both simulation conditions); thin: subglottal (only displayed in non-interactive condition). The first (c. 600 Hz) and second vocal tract resonance (c. 1750 Hz) are represented as horizontal red lines (R1 and R2, respectively). Middle: Glottal flow envelope. Bottom: glottal area envelope. The interactive case differed from the non-interactive simulation by several features: (a) the lower fundamental frequency in the onset of the simulation (570 Hz instead of 700 Hz) was caused by the inertive reactance of the vocal tract, adding mass to the coupled oscillating systems; (b) the interactive case resulted in a larger glottal flow amplitude and glottal area; (c) the interactive case exhibited bifurcations and subharmonic regimes, as the first (i.e. the fundamental) and the second harmonic both went from higher to lower inertive reactance in the bifurcation regions.

In this most significant and farsighted statement, Garcia describes how voice timbre can be influenced by controlling a physiologic parameter—the adduction of the arytenoids. In addition, Garcia hints at the inverse relation between glottal adduction and airflow rates, and the fact that the maximum phonation duration is dependent on the degree of glottal adduction (see Herbst 2017, for a deeper discussion).

The degree of closure in the posterior part of the glottis can be increased by contraction of the LCA and IA muscles (Baken and Isshiki 1977; Broad 1968; Fried et al. 2009; Hunter

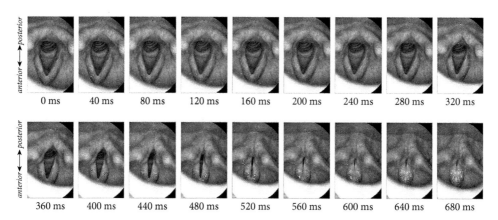

FIGURE 6.7 Videolaryngoscopic recording of an adductory gesture and phonation onset performed by a male adolescent singer (15 yrs) phonating at pitch Db3 (c. 139 Hz). Phonation onset occurred around t = 520 ms.

et al. 2004; Letson and Tatchell 1997; Sataloff 1997; Van den Berg et al. 1960; Zemlin 1998). During phonation, a supplementary role in arytenoid adduction/abduction is played also by the thyroarytenoid (TA) and cricothyroid (CT) muscles; for details see Zemlin (1998).

An incomplete adduction of the cartilaginous portion of the vocal folds can be described laryngoscopically as a "posterior glottal chink" (PGC) (Södersten et al. 1995). Variation of the cartilaginous adduction is an important modulator in both speech and singing, i.e. in the production of breathy, normal, and pressed or creaky voice (Ladefoged 2001; Zemlin 1998). While in breathy voice the arytenoid cartilages are set apart, in pressed voice they are usually squeezed together.

The degree of vocal fold adduction has a major influence on glottal airflow. Figure 6.8 shows typical time-varying airflow rates for four types of phonation: "breathy," "normal," "flow," and "pressed" (Sundberg 1981a). Acoustically, the most important feature is the steepness of the waveform at the closing phase of the glottal cycle, indicating how rapidly the airflow is terminated. This parameter is closely related to the maximum flow declinatione. A glottal flow waveform with a steeper closing phase will result in an acoustic output with a larger degree of high-frequency energy (and hence a flat spectral slope), as is the case in "flow" phonation. In "breathy" phonation, on the other hand, the closing phase of the glottal flow waveform has a more gradual slope, thus suggesting that the created sound will be less brilliant.

The overall airflow, and hence the amount of air used per unit of time, can be determined by averaging the airflow graphs in Figure 6.8 over time. It appears that "flow" phonation, while being the most efficient type from a spectral point of view, uses overall less air than "breathy" phonation. Consequently, maximum inter-breath phrase duration is increased. This is in direct agreement with Garcia's quote from the beginning of this chapter.[5]

---

[5] Sundberg's model consists of three ideal phonation types ("breathy," "flow," and "pressed") and focuses on the glottal wave shape and the MFDR. Garcia's quotation, on the other hand, is based on direct laryngeal observation, and suggests a dichotomy of aBducted vs. aDducted phonation. These two models should be related to each other with caution: It is unclear whether Garcia's "vigorous pinching of the arytenoids" is equivalent to "flow" or "pressed" phonation, or some mixture thereof.

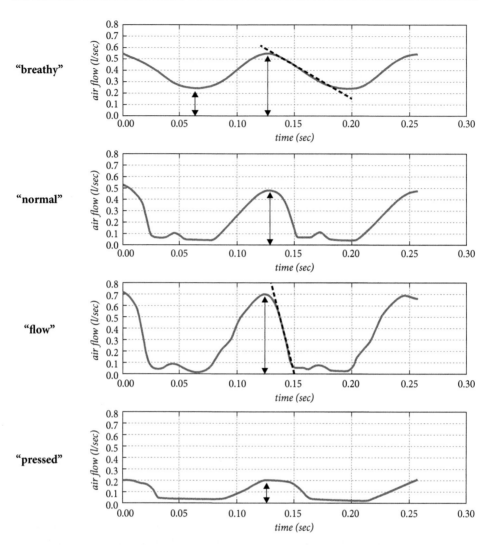

FIGURE 6.8 Airflow rates for one cycle of phonation in four different qualities (Data taken from Sundberg (1981a)): "breathy," "normal," "flow," and "pressed" (data was obtained by direct measurement and subsequent inverse filtering of the airflow waveform). Both the pulse amplitude and the closed phase duration change for different adduction settings. Note that in the given example the "breathy" case the airflow never goes below 0.2 l/sec (dark arrow), indicating incomplete glottal closure. The rate of change in the closing phase (i.e. the steepness, illustrated here by dashed orange lines for the two extremes, i.e. "breathy" and "flow" phonation) varies considerably depending on phonation type, having an effect on the steepness of the spectral slope of the acoustic output.

An excessive degree of breathiness is often observed in (young) female amateur singers.[6] From a pedagogic point of view, the shift from "breathy" to "flow" phonation has three positive effects: (1) a brighter, more "resonant" voice timbre; (2) getting rid of unwanted noise components in the sound source; (3) longer phrase durations. In case of breathy untrained singing, strengthening glottal adduction is thus likely to be more efficient than working on breathing strategies by inhaling even more before starting a phrase. Herbst, Howard et al. (2010) have suggested that the degree of posterior adduction can be increased in the voice studio if:

1. The perceived breathiness is caused by a posterior glottal chink, and not by an organic voice disorder.
2. A moderately low larynx position is maintained.[7]
3. The proper, pitch-dependent, registration is maintained (the singer must not confuse cartilaginous adduction and membranous medialization—see also the section "A model case from the singing studio" further below).
4. The ventricular folds are not medialized in the case of classical singing.
5. The method focuses on increased activity in the lateral cricoarytenoid and interarytenoid muscles, and not on simply increasing subglottal pressure.
6. Voice load and vocal effort is kept at a "healthy" level.
7. The method is applied within the relevant esthetic context.

Registers in singing

Vocal registers are described by different authors using one or more of the following approaches:

1. The singer's kinesthetic awareness of vibrations during sound production—e.g. *voce di petto* (chest voice) and *voce di testa* (head voice), suggested in the late sixteenth century by L. Zacconi (Stark 1999).
2. Perceptual qualities, such as timbre—see e.g. Titze 1988a or Sundberg 1983.
3. Vocal tract (or pitch) adjustments, i.e. changes in the relation of the frequencies of individual harmonics to the frequencies of individual vocal tract resonances (so-called *formant tuning*)—see e.g. Miller (2000) for an example of "full head" register in male classical singing.
4. Different vocal fold vibratory regimes—see Garcia's classical description (1847b).
5. Individual teaching systems based on pedagogic experience, such as Chapman (2006) or Sadolin (2008).

The terminology used for describing vocal registers is vast: Mörner et al. (1963) report more than 100 terms used in the literature. An overview of register theories proposed in the last 150 years can be found in Henrich (2006). Reid (2005) quotes the register definitions of nine contemporary groups of authors.

For the purpose of this chapter, the authors define a vocal register as "a series of consecutive and homogenous tones going from low to high, produced by the same mechanical

---

[6] In such cases, the observed breathiness is sometimes only one component of a bigger "package," including, amongst others, improper breathing strategies.

[7] This is not to be confused with "pushing the larynx actively down," particularly when this would lead to an unwanted tongue root constriction.

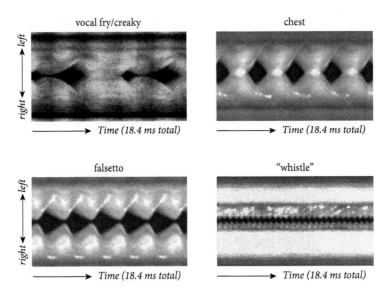

FIGURE 6.9 Videokymograms of four registers in singing (Data from Herbst et al. 2011; Švec et al. 2001; Švec et al. 2008). The measurement line was placed in the middle of the vocal folds, transversal to the glottal axis. Note the qualitative differences in the vibratory characteristics: (a) creaky voice/vocal fry: double opening, long closed phase, vertical phase differences (i.e. visible phase difference between the vibration of the upper and lower margins of the vocal folds); (b) chest/modal voice: relatively long closed phase, vertical phase differences; pronounced mucosal wave; (c) falsetto voice: no closed phase,[8] slightly reduced vertical phase differences;[9] (d) whistle register: no vocal fold contact, very limited vocal fold vibratory amplitude. Total time displayed: 18.4 ms in each case.

principle, and whose nature differs essentially from another series of tones equally consecutive and homogenous produced by another mechanical principle" (Henrich, 2006, p. 3). Based on this definition, we recognize four registers (see videokymographic images of each register in Figure 6.9):

Vocal fry[10] (also: pulse register, strohbass, Mo) is characterized by a fundamental frequency below 70 Hz (i.e. pitch C#2), where glottal pulses are perceived as localized bursts of acoustic energy followed by gaps of silence, rather than as a continuous sound: each glottal excitation pulse is dampened by the vocal tract and the trachea, thus the acoustic output goes to zero before the next pulse occurs (Titze 1988a).

The *chest* (also: modal, M1) register is closely related to speech, and is usually found in the low to mid portion of the singer's voice range, with ranges for females from about F3 (c. 175 Hz) to F4 (c. 349 Hz) with a "belting extension" to D5 (c. 587 Hz); and for males from

---

[8] Note that chest and falsetto (and even whistle) register can be produced either with glottal closure, or without, depending on vocal fold adduction (see section 3.6 further in the text).

[9] Note that in some people phonating in falsetto register, the vertical phase difference can be either greatly reduced or even missing altogether.

[10] Whereas vocal fry is not used in classical singing, it is regularly used in contemporary commercial music (particularly as an effect at note onset).

E2 (c. 82 Hz) to C5 (c. 523 Hz) (Miller 2000).[11] The chest register is usually characterized by a rich, sometimes *brassy* timbre.

Falsetto (also: head, loft, M2) register is located in the mid to upper portion of the voice range in humans, with ranges from about C4 (c. 262 Hz) to F6 (c. 1397 Hz) in females and A3 (220 Hz) to G5 (c. 784 Hz) in males (Miller 2000). Some females employ the falsetto register for speech purposes. The falsetto register is characterized by a *flutey* sound, hinting at a steeper spectral slope as compared to chest register.

Whistle register (also: flute register, flageolet, M3) is a phonation type that occurs, depending on authors, above pitches B5 (c. 988 Hz) (Švec et al. 2008), between G5 (c. 788 Hz) and D6 (c. 1175 Hz) (Miller and Schutte 1993), or above F6 (c. 1397 Hz) (Titze 2000). Phonations in whistle register are reported to be created by tightly stretched and slightly abducted vibrating vocal folds (Echternach et al. 2013; Švec et al. 2008) or by jet-induced vortices (Berry et al. 1996; Herzel and Reuter 1997; Tsai et al. 2006).

Vocal fry and whistle register can only be produced at the extreme ends of the human fundamental frequency range and are not extensively employed during singing performance, since their fundamental frequencies lie outside the typical pitch ranges for females and males (for a counter-example, see Neubauer et al. 2004; see also Edgerton, this volume). Phonations in chest and falsetto register are central to most singing styles, and consequently much more is known about them. We will therefore limit our discussion to these two registers.

Chest vs. falsetto register

Physiologically, the main difference between chest and falsetto register lies in the action of the thyroarytenoid (vocalis) mucle (TA):

In **chest register**, the TA is active, thus thickening, shortening, and medially bulging the body of the vocal fold, while slackening the vocal fold cover (Hirano 1974; Titze 2000). A vertical phase difference in vocal fold vibration is created: the inferior portion of the vocal fold *leads* the vibration, and the superior portion *follows* with a phase delay of about 60°–90° (Baer 1975).[12] This phenomenon asserts itself in the form of a mucosal wave (Hirano et al. 1981), i.e. an airflow-driven traveling wave within the surface of the vocal fold tissue, moving from the inferior to the superior portion of the vocal folds and then laterally on the surface of the vocal folds (Kumar 2018) once every glottal cycle. It is facilitated by the layered structure of the vocal folds, since these layers have different biomechanical properties: the *body*, consisting of the thyroarytenoid muscle and the deep layer of the lamina propria; and the *cover*, consisting of the epithelium and the superficial and intermediate layer of the lamina propria (Titze 2000). Both body and cover can move as separate units in vocal fold vibration (Hirano 1974). Mucosal wave speed is inversely related to vertical phase delay. A strong, relatively slow mucosal wave, as seen in chest register, will both help to stabilize vocal fold vibration (1) by aiding the energy transfer from the air stream into the tissue during the opening phase of vocal fold vibration (Titze 1988b); and (2) by

---

[11] The pitch ranges indicated for different registers vary slightly from author to author.
[12] In more recent research, a greater spread of vertical phase difference values has been reported (Jiang 1998, 2008).

prolonging the closed phase of vocal fold vibration. From an acoustic point of view, a longer closed phase (and thus a larger closed quotient) will enhance the output of high-frequency energy (Flanagan 1958). In the open phase of vocal fold vibration, a considerable portion of the high-frequency energy generated by vocal fold vibration (and carried by the vocal tract's formants) is absorbed within the subglottal vocal tract and the lungs. A longer closed phase will thus aid in creating a "brighter" voice timbre (Rothenberg 1973).

In **falsetto register** both vocal fold body and cover are stretched (Hirano 1974). This is accomplished by the action of the cricothyroid muscle which is situated between the cricoid cartilage and the thyroid cartilage, thus narrowing the cricothyroid space and elongating the vocal folds by tilting the thyroid cartilage forward (Zemlin 1998). Here, the TA is relaxed or only slightly active. Due to a higher longitudinal tension in the vocal folds, their vibration is smaller in amplitude but higher in frequency. A mucosal wave is less likely to be seen because the superficial vocal fold layer is under increased tension (Hirano 1974), both reducing the vibratory amplitude and increasing the mucosal wave speed. This effectively shortens the closed phase, and no or little vertical phase difference is found in the tissue vibration. As a consequence, the vocal fold oscillation is more likely to be influenced by the vocal tract settings (Titze 2008). The relatively longer open phase will cause less abrupt changes of airflow, which acoustically translates into a steeper spectral slope, thus limiting the high-frequency energy output (i.e. a more "flutey" sound). See Figure 6.10 for a comparison of chest and falsetto register phonation.

Registers and eigenmodes of vocal fold vibration

Physically, the vibration of the vocal folds can be explained as a superposition of independent characteristic vibratory patterns, called eigenmodes (Berry et al. 1994; Švec 2000; Titze 2000). Any vibratory pattern of the vocal folds can be explained by its decomposition into a multitude of these eigenmodes. There are two eigenmodes which play a dominant role in stable phonation: the so-called x-10 mode, where the inferior and the superior portions of the vocal fold vibrate in phase; and the x-11 mode, where the inferior and the superior portions of the vocal fold vibrate 180 degrees out of phase (Berry et al. 1994; Döllinger and Berry 2006). The x-11 mode (representing the vertical phase difference seen in vocal fold vibration, due to the occurrence of the mucosal wave) is considered to be dominating in the chest register, and the x-10 mode would be stronger in the falsetto register (see Figure 6.11, and also Figure 3 in Herbst et al. 2014). In the light of this theory, the mechanism of abrupt chest-falsetto register transitions can be explained as a spontaneous shift in dominance between different eigenmodes of the vocal folds (Tokuda et al. 2007).

Blending the registers

Some singing styles (such as yodeling) are characterized by abrupt (voluntary) register transitions, resulting in abrupt timbral changes. In other styles (like classical singing and some subtypes of musical theater singing), these abrupt timbral and register changes are to be avoided, since they would violate the style's esthetic principles. This is reflected in Lilli Lehmann's quite extreme postulate: "In singing pedagogy, registers should neither exist

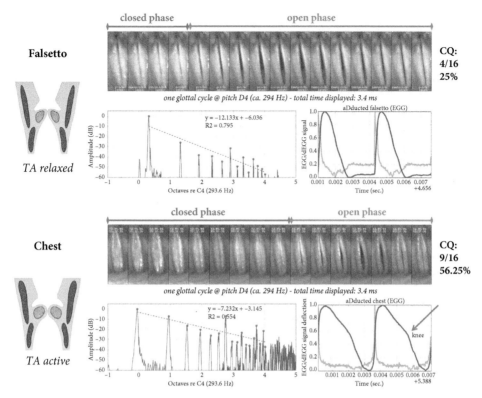

FIGURE 6.10 Comparison of phonation in chest and falsetto register (male singer phonating with "endoscopic" vowel /i/ at pitch D4—c. 294 Hz). Data displayed for each of the two registers: schematic illustration of TA muscle in coronal section of larynx; videostrobolaryngoscopic images displaying one complete glottal cycle; acoustic spectrum with estimated spectral slope; two cycles of the EGG[13] (blue) and dEGG[14] (gold) waveform. The chest register phonation has, in comparison with the falsetto register: more bulged vocal folds; a longer closed phase; a flatter spectral slope (i.e. stronger high-frequency partials); a "knee" in the electroglottographic (EGG) waveform (Titze 1990), which is typical for phonation in chest register.

nor should they be created. As long as the term 'register' is used, registers will not vanish"[15] (Felsner 2008, p. 63). Nawka and Wirth (2008) suggest that in trained classical singers, registers (and their boundaries and transitions) should not be perceivable at all.[16]

---

[13] Electroglottography (EGG) is a non-invasive method to measure the time-varying relative vocal fold contact area: see e.g. Baken and Orlikoff (2000) for details.

[14] The DeGG signal is the first mathematical derivative of the EGG signal. It exhibits positive peaks at the instances of maximum increase rate in relative vocal fold contact area (VFCA), and negative peaks at the instances of maximum decrease rate of VFCA.

[15] "In der Ausbildung der Stimme sollen Register weder existieren noch geschaffen werden. Solange der Begriff verwendet wird, werden auch Register nicht verschwinden." English translation by author CTH.

[16] "Beim ausgebildeten Sänger dürfen die Register nicht als solche erkennbar sein. Bereits beim tiefsten Ton des Stimmumfanges müssen die Klangcharakteristika des obersten Tonbereichs mitschwingen," p. 99.

mode x-10
"Falsetto-like"

mode x-11
"Chest-like"

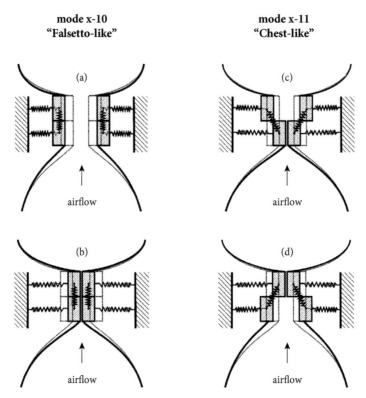

FIGURE 6.11 Simplified schematic illustration of two characteristic eigenmodes of vocal fold vibration: x-10 (A and B) and x-11 (C and D). The vocal folds are shown at two opposite phases of a vibratory cycle.

Image taken from Švec (2000).

There is an obvious discrepancy between the physical/physiological reality (voice registers do indeed exist) and the esthetical boundary conditions imposed by certain singing styles (registers and their transitions should not be audible). It is apparent that accomplished singers must have a means to navigate between chest and falsetto register without introducing abrupt timbral changes when changing either fundamental frequency or vocal intensity.

Many authors have argued for the existence of a so-called "mid register" or "voix mixte," which Seidner and Wendler (2004)[17] call into question as a "pedagogical fiction" and a mere "principle of operation." The physiological groundwork for understanding this phenomenon has been laid by Van den Berg (1963), who called the "mid register" not an "independent" register, but a "mixture" of chest and falsetto register: in chest register the longitudinal tension lies mainly in the muscular portion of the vocal fold, and in falsetto register the tension

[17] "Das sogenannte Mittelregister wird in Publikationen derart unterschiedlich definiert, dass eine Stellungnahme schwerfällt. Muß dieses Register nicht als eine überwiegend gesangspädagogische Fiktion, als ein Bekenntnis oder Arbeitsprinzip aufgefasst werden, um die stets vorhandenen Register mit Aufmerksamkeit und Konsequenz an- oder auszugleichen?" p. 103.

5s mainly borne by the vocal ligament. The mid register is a "mixture of longitudinal tension in vocal muscles and vocal ligaments," resulting in a "medium number of partials." A skilled singer can navigate between chest and falsetto without producing breaks, by fine-tuning the action of the cricothyroid muscle[18] vs. thyroarytenoid muscle, and with the aid of minute adjustments of arytenoid adduction and subglottal pressure (Van den Berg 1963). In other words, the middle (or mixed) register can be defined as "a mixture of qualities from various voice registers, cultivated in order to allow consistent quality throughout the frequency range" (Sataloff 1998, p. 370).

In contrast to these observations, some authors maintain that voix mixte sounds are always clearly produced in a given laryngeal "mechanism" (Castellengo et al. 2004), i.e. either M1 (chest) for males and M2 (falsetto) for females. Voix mixte is supposedly not the result of an intermediate laryngeal process, unlike the acoustic characteristics would suggest (Roubeau et al. 2009). The necessary adjustments for unifying chest and falsetto register would, according to this theory, have to be made mainly in the vocal tract.

In the light of the observations made by Miller and Schutte (2005), it would seem that both strategies (adjustments at the laryngeal level, and resonance adjustments by changing vocal tract geometry) can be employed to successfully navigate the transition between chest and falsetto register. In fact, the voice as a vibrating system is the result of a complex interaction between three sub-systems, each having its own physical properties: the vocal folds (Švec et al. 2000); and the supra- and subglottal vocal tract (Titze 2004b, 2008). Each of these components has a general tendency to vibrate/exhibit resonance in its own set of frequencies (i.e. eigenmodes). Since these systems are coupled, they are in constant "negotiation" with each other. Depending on the properties of the individual sub-systems, vocal fold vibration is either stable or tends to exhibit abrupt changes when the singer introduces changes in pitch or vocal intensity—see Švec et al. (1999).

In Figure 6.12, ascending scales sung by two sopranos are shown. The untrained singer produced an abrupt, involuntary register transition from Bb3 to C4 (clearly observable in the change of the electroglottographic (EGG) contact phase duration, a slight pitch jump, and an audible timbral change—see Herbst 2019 for an in-depth discussion of electroglottography). The trained soprano, on the other hand, managed the transition from chest to falsetto register without audible timbral changes. In the latter case, the gradual change of the EGG waveform (as can be seen in both the extracted waveshapes and the dEGG wavegram[19]) suggests a "blending" of registers from Bb3 to G4, a region which corresponds with the singer's primary register transition (zona di passaggio).

---

[18] Elevating the cricoid arch and depressing the thyroid lamina, and thus actively lengthening the vocal folds and increasing their tension.

[19] In an EGG wavegram, the EGG signal is decomposed into consecutive individual cycles, each of which is normalized in both duration and amplitude, and is displayed on the y-axis, going from the bottom to the top. Overall time is shown on the x-axis. In a dEGG wavegram, the first derivative of the EGG signal is used as the input signal. In such a display, the contacting and de-contacting phases for each glottal cycle are approximated by (1) one or more dark horizontal lines at the lower end of the graph (contacting phase), and (2) one or more light horizontal lines in the upper section of the graph (decontacting phase). As such, the wavegram allows for the intuitive assessment of the time-varying contact phase of phonation over a longer period of time, indicating changes of vocal register—for details see Herbst et al. (2010).

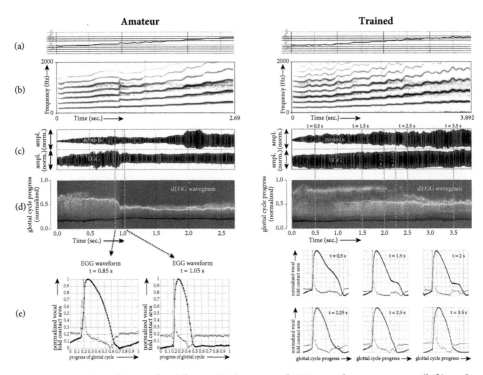

FIGURE 6.12 Ascending scales (Bb3 to Bb4) on vowel /A/ sung by an amateur (left) and a trained classical singer who was avoiding an abrupt register transition (right). (a) fundamental frequency displayed in musical notation; (b) narrow-band spectrograms (Notice the abrupt change of fundamental frequency and dEGG wavegram appearance around t = 1 s in the example on the left, whereas no such abrupt change is visible in the example on the right); (c) acoustic signal and EGG signal; (d) dEGG wavegrams. Overall time is displayed on the x-axis, and normalized intra-cycle time is shown on the y-axis. The black line at the lower end of the graph roughly indicates glottal closure, and the white line is generally related to the opening of the vocal folds; (e) electroglottographic (EGG) waveforms (black) and their first mathematical derivative (dEGG) (gray) representing one glottal cycle each. (Notice the abrupt changes of fundamental frequency and within the dEGG wavegram pattern around t = 1 s in the example on the left, whereas no such abrupt change is visible in the example on the right.)

Data taken from Herbst, Fitch et al. (2010).

Cartilaginous adduction vs. membranous medialization

The glottis can be conceptually divided into two parts: the *membranous glottis* (i.e. the portion made up of the vocal folds from the anterior commissure to the tip of the vocal processes); and the *cartilaginous glottis* (i.e. the most posterior part of the glottis, consisting of the arytenoid cartilages and their vocal processes)—see Figure 6.13. The degree of adduction of the **cartilaginous glottis** is maintained by the LCA, IA (and PCA) muscles. This maneuver, termed *cartilaginous adduction*, is realized through choice of quality of phonation along the dimension of "breathy," "flow," or "pressed." The **membranous glottis** can be adducted mainly though contraction of the TA (vocalis) muscles,

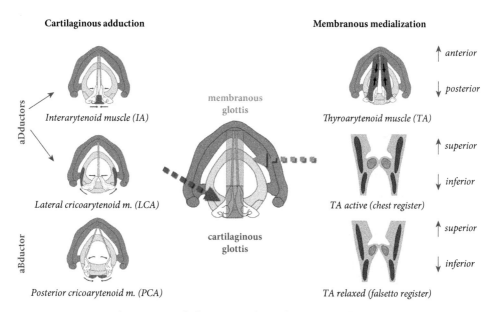

FIGURE 6.13 Membranous medialization and cartilaginous adduction. Except where explicitly stated (i.e. the lower two schematics on the right-hand side), the larynx is depitcted in horizontal orientation.

which cause the vocal folds to bulge medially, thus reducing the width of the glottis anteriorly. This maneuver is called *membranous medialization through vocal fold bulging* (short: *membranous medialization*) (Herbst et al. 2011), and it can be influenced by the singer through the choice of register (falsetto or chest). Lindestad and Södersten (1988) called this adjustment "centrally located medial compression of the vocal folds"(p. 138). This maneuver (controlled by contraction of the thyroarytenoid muscle) is to be distinguished from the posterior "medial compression" (controlled by the lateral cricoarytenoid muscles) described by Van den Berg (1960), the latter of which is comparable to cartilaginous adduction as described here.

Both trained and untrained singers can separately influence the degree of cartilaginous adduction and membranous medialization, thus being able to create four distinct voice qualities in the glottis (Herbst et al. 2009; Herbst et al. 2011)—see Table 6.1.

Table 6.1 Four distinct phonation types, as created by different degrees of cartilaginous adduction and membranous medialization

Voice quality	Cartilaginous adduction	Membranous medialization
aBducted falsetto	--	--
aDducted falsetto	++	--
aBducted chest	--	++
aDducted chest	++	++

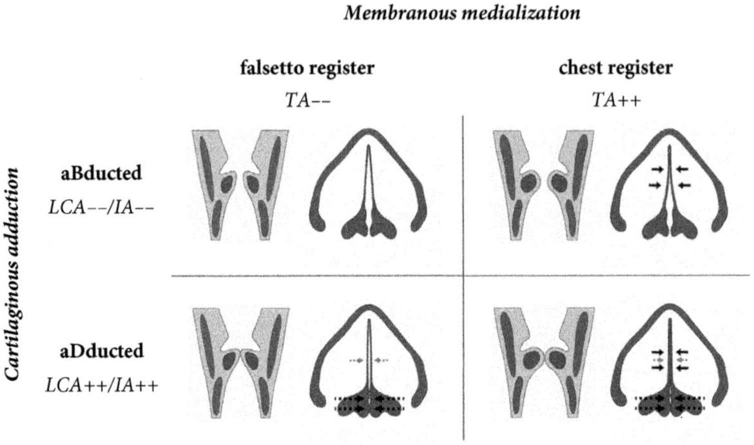

FIGURE 6.14 Schematic illustration of the effect of cartilaginous adduction and membranous medialization through vocal fold bulging in singing. For each adduction type, two schematic graphs are shown: sagittal view of larynx with schematic drawings of thyroid cartilage, cricoid cartilage, and TA muscle (left); top view of vocal folds, arytenoids and thyroid cartilage (right). The arrows indicate the primary changes in the vocal fold position for each case.

Schematically, the adduction and glottal configuration of the four phonation types is displayed in Figure 6.14. Figure 6.15 documents examples of these four phonation types as sung by a classically trained baritone.

The main difference between the **aBducted** and the **aDducted** phonation types can be observed in the posterior glottis: The aBducted phonations are generally produced with a slight posterior glottal gap (Södersten et al. 1995), and the vocal processes of the arytenoid cartilages vibrate together with the membranous portion of the vocal folds. Phonations that are created with aDducted arytenoid cartilages on the other hand, generally have a more adducted posterior glottis with no glottal gap. In many cases and particularly for phonation in chest register, a full glottal closure can be observed, and the vocal processes are pressed together and not vibrating (Herbst et al. 2011) The observed phenomena vary from subject to subject depending on individual anatomy.

The main difference between the phonations in the two different registers (**falsetto** and **chest**) is seen in (a) larger vertical phase differences of vocal fold vibration; (b) a prevalence of mucosal waves; and (c) the duration of the closed phase. It was observed that chest phonations generally have longer closed phase, ranging from c. 10–50% in the aBducted case, to about 50–75% in the aDducted case. Falsetto phonations, on the other hand, are either produced without glottal closure (0% closed phase in the aBducted case[20]), or with a shorter closed phase (max. c. 50% in the fully aDducted phase) as in chest register (Herbst et al. 2011). The observed values differed from individual to individual.

---

[20] In this case, the EGG waveform would assume the shape of a sinusoid, superimposed with random fluctuations (i.e. noise). Such a signal is not suitable for calculating the EGG contact quotient and can hence not be used to estimate the duration of vocal fold contact (Herbst and Ternström 2006, Herbst et al. 2017).

There is a certain overlap of closed quotient values for chest and falsetto register. In extreme cases, we could observe that some subjects had a longer closed phase in aDducted falsetto as compared to the aBducted chest register. This is due to the fact that the adduction of the membranous portion of the vocal folds is influenced by both membranous medialization and cartilaginous adduction. The effect of the vocal fold bulging caused by contraction of the thyroarytenoid muscle in chest register can be counteracted by a decreasing adduction in the posterior glottis, allowing for a "breathy chest" phonation. The resulting glottal configuration is, in its extreme case, comparable to the one observed in hyper-functional breathy voice or muscle tension dysphonia—see Morrison et al. (1983). On the other hand, falsetto register (where the thyroarytenoid muscle is relaxed) can be produced with full closure of the posterior glottis, such as in the mid- and upper range of trained female classical singing, and in counter-tenor singing.

The timbral effect of variations of the closed phase can be observed in the spectra shown in the bottom of Figure 6.15: when going from aBducted falsetto to aDducted chest, the ever-increasing duration of the closed phase correlates with a decreasing spectral slope, resulting in stronger high-frequency components in the acoustic signal for phonations with more cartilaginous and/or membranous adduction (i.e. a "heavier registration").

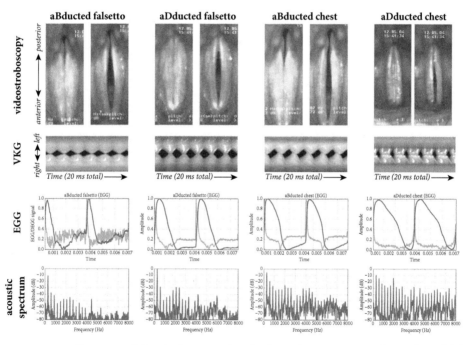

FIGURE 6.15 Images and signals documenting the four phonation examples aBducted falsetto, aDducted falsetto, aBducted chest, aDducted chest. From top to bottom: [Row 1] pairs of videostroboscopic images at the phases of maximum vocal fold contact and maximum glottal opening; [Row 2] videokymographic images at the place of maximal vibration amplitude of the vocal folds; [Row 3] EGG signals (blue) and their first derivative (orange) for two glottal cycles each, normalized both in amplitude and time; [Row 4] acoustic spectrum for each phonation type.

Two degrees of freedom at the sound source—a pedagogical model

Since cartilaginous adduction and membranous medialization can be controlled separately by both trained and untrained singers, these two physiological parameters can be displayed in a two-dimensional plane in order to create a pedagogical model for sound quality adjustments made on the laryngeal level—see Figure 6.16. This model consists of four quadrants, representing the four sound qualities described above.

Different singing styles can be mapped onto the model, showing their main mechanism of production, such as:[21]

- **aBducted falsetto:** e.g. untrained female classical singing (high *tessitura*); "naïve" male falsetto; "lighter" registration (both male and female) in pop and jazz.
- **aDducted falsetto:** e.g. trained female classical; counter-tenor.
- **aBducted chest:** e.g. untrained naïve singing (lower range); "lighter" registration (both male and female) in pop and jazz.
- **aDducted chest:** e.g. trained male classical; belting; blues; rock.

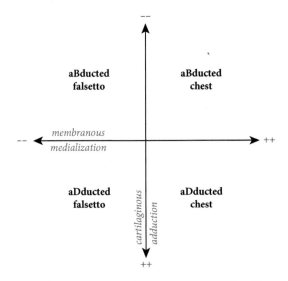

FIGURE 6.16 Relationship between the two types of adduction (membranous medialization and cartilaginous adduction) and the four phonation types described here (aBducted falsetto, aDducted falsetto, aBducted chest, aDducted chest). This pedagogical model is not limited to distinct (and possibly extreme) phonation types. Rather, it encourages gradual, fine-controlled adjustments along the two major dimensions, in order to increase timbral variability for enhanced artistic expression.

---

[21] This is a non-exhaustive list, intended solely to provide some basic orientation. Please note that some of the singing styles could also make use of other phonation types. Please refer also to the subheading entitled "Relating the two types of adduction to other systems" in this chapter, where known voice pedagogues associate the four phonation types with their own terms used in teaching.

The model is in no way restricted to the production of four distinct phonation types. On the contrary, gradual adjustments along the two major axes (cartilaginous adduction and membranous medialization) are possible, in analogy to Van den Berg's "mid register." These fine-controlled muscular adjustments allow experienced singers to create a large variety of sound timbres at the glottal level, increasing their expressional freedom within the esthetical boundary conditions of their chosen singing style. In addition, the model can provide pedagogical strategies, suggesting physiological adjustments to successfully create desired singing styles.

A model case from the singing studio

A typical example for the application of the model described here would be the mid range of female classical singers. We postulate that in classical singing (as opposed to other singing styles, such as belting) the desired quality above the *primo passaggio* (around pitch D4, c. 295 Hz[22]) would have to be aDducted falsetto[23], since (1) chest phonation is usually restricted to the lower range; and (2) the breathy phonation created by aBducted falsetto is both acoustically inefficient and outside the esthetical boundaries of classical singing. Nevertheless, untrained female singers have a tendency to produce sounds above the *primo passaggio* in either aDducted chest register, or in aBducted falsetto. In other words, they either "push" the chest register up (usually at the risk of an abrupt register transition at the upper end of the chest register range), or they produce soft, breathy falsetto sounds, in both cases severely limiting the dynamic range and timbral variability of the voice at those particular pitches.

The difficulty of switching from aDducted chest to aDducted falsetto can be explained physiologically: when changing from chest to falsetto register, the TA muscle relaxes and thus the membranous medialization is reduced. The resulting decrease of overall vocal fold adduction could be counteracted by an increase of cartilaginous adduction via the LCA and IA muscles, in order to keep the timbral change at a minimum. Such a maneuver (decreasing TA while increasing LCA and IA activity, respectively) is, however, both ambivalent and complex: since the three involved muscles are all innervated by the recurrent laryngeal nerve, the required level of fine control might be hard to reach and control accurately by some singers.

A valid pedagogical strategy would try to establish the aDducted falsetto at higher pitches (around Bb4 to F5), via calling (but not shouting) at vowel /u/, or using "primal sounds" (Chapman 2006). This sound quality could then be applied to other vowels, and to pitches all the way down to the *primo passaggio*. Once this is achieved, a smooth transition from aDducted falsetto to aDducted chest can easily be achieved in most cases, provided that the point of transition is not chosen to be too high (i.e. at or below pitch D4 for most singers).

---

[22] Depending on anatomy and *Fach*, but hardly exceeding the range of C4 to F4.

[23] We readily acknowledge that many pedagogues use the term "head" or "mixed head" for the range immediately above the *primo passaggio* in classical female singing. However, in order to maintain the simplicity of the model proposed here, the latter is limited to the two registers chest and falsetto. Please note that this model allows for gradual changes of muscle activity, effectively creating a "mixed register"; see the discussion which appears in the third paragraph of the subheading entitled "Blending the registers" in this chapter.

When attempting to achieve a successful transition from (aDducted) chest to aDducted falsetto on ascending scales, on the other hand, there is the danger that the singer may "get stuck" in the chest register.[24] In order to avoid this, it is advisable that ascending scales are only sung when:

1. The student reliably succeeded in producing aDducted falsetto in and above the *primo passaggio* on descending scales; and
2. The student managed the falsetto-chest register transition at the *primo passaggio* without abrupt timbral changes.

Relating the two types of adduction to other systems

In the pedagogical literature, several systems have been proposed to describe the creation of different timbral qualities on the laryngeal (i.e. sound source) level. Four known voice pedagogues have been invited to relate their pedagogical system to the model described in this chapter. They were asked to describe the four (extreme) voice qualities aBducted falsetto, aDducted falsetto, aBducted chest, and aDducted chest as performed by a female elite singer, documented by laryngovideostroboscopic recording (see Multimedia sample 1— [http://www.christian-herbst.org/media/MM_small.avi—MultimediaSample1.avi]).

The contributions of the four voice pedagogues are listed alphabetically in Table 6.2.

Table 6.2 Contributions of five voice pedagogues (alphabetically listed), relating their pedagogical system to the model described in Figure 6.16

	aBducted falsetto	aDducted falsetto	aBducted chest	aDducted chest
Jeanie LoVetri (LoVetri 2003; Lo Vetri et al. 1999)	breathy head	clear head mix	very breathy mix	clear light chest
Donald Miller (Miller 2008)		see comments below		
Lisa Popeil	breathy[1], pop semi-lean[2], light blend[3]	blowy[1], pop semi-lean[2], medium blend[3]	very breathy[1], full lean[2], light blend[3]	clean[1], full lean[2], medium blend[3]
Cathrine Sadolin (Sadolin 2008)	neutral with air	neutral without air	neutral with air (more air)	curbing
Kim Steinhauer (Estill et al. 2005; Steinhauer and Estill 2008)	stiff-thin	thin	stiff-thick	thick

[24] During one single phrase it is always easier to start with the newly trained behavior (in this case aDducted falsetto) and gradually change to the more habitual behavior, than the other way round.

The following passage contains explanatory information, as provided by each contributor (Text in italic font is information provided by the four voice pedagogues):

Jeanie LoVetri

- *aBducted falsetto: What I call head register, and since the folds do not close, it is breathy. Volume is moderate. High transglottal airflow.*
- *aDducted falsetto: This is head, also, but clearer and stronger, drawing it towards a mix. More vocal fold closure, probably more closed quotient. Argument could be made that this is head register depending on the song or performance context, that is, specifically how it is used musically.*
- *aBducted chest: This sounds louder to me, implying that air is being forced through the folds deliberately. It has more noise in it, due to the breathiness.*
- *aDducted chest: This is a clearer "light" chest tone, also possibly called mix, depending on the context in which it would be used in a song or performance context, specifically how it is used musically.*

The above description relies on an evaluation of the voiced sound through the auditory perception of the use of vocal registers named chest, head, and mix. Chest corresponds to TA activity, head to CT activity, and mix is a balance between, involving open/closed quotient, airflow parameters, and subglottic pressure. The balance between chest and head registers (TA and CT dominance), provides a third quality which is called "mix," a term created by the Broadway community decades ago. This can be something that is not quite "all chest" and not quite "all head." It involves auditory perception of register quality for its own sake, separate from vowel sound quality (vocal tract enhancement). It includes evaluation of the tone for breathiness and nasality and for overall constriction of the final sound.

Donald Miller

The distinction between membranous and cartilaginous adduction, which Christian Herbst has carefully articulated, has important consequences for singing pedagogy. What he calls aBducted falsetto and chest has not claimed much attention hitherto in the pedagogical literature, primarily because that literature has been largely concerned with voice production suitable for large spaces with substantial instrumental accompaniment, epitomized by opera. The high-frequency component of the singing voice makes it viable in this acoustic environment. That component, in combination with the requisite loudness that is enabled by relatively high subglottal pressure, generally requires cartilaginous adduction. It was not for nothing that the famous teacher and early observer of laryngeal action Manuel Garcia considered learning to "pinch the glottis" to be an early and primary goal of singing instruction.

Widespread use of aBducted falsetto and chest among singing professionals has been made possible by amplification. Microphones, both displayed and hidden, have removed the necessity of firm closure of the posterior glottis in the field that has been labeled contemporary commercial music (CCM). At the same time, amplification has opened professional singing to a wide range of expressive vocal sounds ordinarily limited to intimate surroundings. Illuminating the physiology of such voice production is an important step in integrating instruction in CCM within the theoretical framework that has, with increasing scientific accuracy, accumulated around "classical" singing technique. The sounds and the goals of CCM and classical instruction have important differences, but the vocal instrument and its basic mechanics remain the same.

In the common parlance that has evolved around the "classical" singing voice and its instruction there are important register distinctions that are not primarily phenomena of the glottal source. Those that have attracted the most attention in singing pedagogy concern the second "passaggio" between about 300 and 400 Hertz (D4–G4) in the male voice, and one octave higher in the female voice. The determinative mechanism in both cases is a change in the dominant resonance of the vocal tract that occurs with a change in fundamental frequency, a change that positions a different harmonic for full enhancement by one of the first two formants (resonances) of the vocal tract (see Miller 2008, chapters 8 and 9). Register terminology can be confusing on this point: in common parlance "head" is sometimes used as synonymous with what is designated as the "falsetto" voice source in this article, especially in female voice; in male voice, on the other hand, "full head," or "voce piena in testa," is characterized by membranous medialization.

Lisa Popeil

The terms detail (1) the level of ad/abduction, using a scale of five terms: pressed, hard, clean, blowy, and breathy; (2) the posture of thyroid/cricoid cartilage which results in forwardness or backness of the sensation of headiness; and (3) the balance between the activity of the TA vs. CT; for example, "heavy blend," "medium blend," and "light blend." The term "full lean" refers to a mechanism involving the forward pull of the hyoid bone, and probably the thyroid cartilage as well, useful in the production of high chest voice. The term "full lean" is therefore not synonymous with chest voice in general.

Cathrine Sadolin

For a description of the two sound qualities *neutral* and *curbing*, see Sadolin (2008).

Kim Steinhauer

Christian Herbst's hypothesis concerning the relationship between true vocal fold cartilaginous and membranous configurations and corresponding timbres complements the voice production framework established in the Estill Voice Model. Estill's four vocal fold options, Thick, Thin, Stiff, and Slack, integrate tension and mass properties necessary to produce a myriad of voice qualities. Herbst's important research connects succinctly the physiologic maneuvers of the arytenoids and vocal folds with the perceptual output of voice quality.

CONCLUDING REMARKS

A *good* singing voice has a wide dynamic and tonal range, controlled pitch, and the freedom to create various voice timbres at will during a performance. These features are all related to the anatomical, physiological, and biomechanical properties of the larynx. The quality of a singer's artistic performance is heavily influenced by his/her ability to gradually and separately control physiologic variables concerning the voice source.

The *timbre* of the voice is a perceptual quality, which has its physical counterpart in the *acoustic spectrum*. Voice timbre can be both influenced via adjustments of the vocal tract, or directly at the sound source, i.e. in the larynx. Concerning the latter case, we have seen that muscular adjustments on a physiological level will influence the quality of a mechanical and aerodynamical phenomenon: flow-induced self-sustaining oscillations of laryngeal tissue, driven by air coming from the lungs, which create a train of airflow pulses. The wave shape of these glottal airflow pulses plays a central role in relating the quality of the vocal fold vibration to the acoustic output, and hence to the voice timbre.

The wave shape of the glottal flow pulse is mainly influenced by (1) adjustments of the supra- and subglottal vocal tract (particularly in the epilaryngeal tube) which is non-linearly coupled to the sound source; (2) *cartilaginous adduction* (controlled through the degree of breathiness); and (3) *membranous medialization* (controlled via the choice of chest vs. falsetto register in singing).

A pedagogical model that incorporates the latter two physiologic parameters (cartilaginous adduction and membranous medialization) consists of four quadrants: aBducted falsetto, aDducted falsetto, aBducted chest, and aDducted chest. Since membranous medialization and cartilaginous adduction can be gradually changed (via the thyroarytenoid muscle and the adductory muscles, i.e. the lateral cricoarytenoid and the interarytenoids, respectively), the model is in no way restricted to four extreme phonation types, but rather allows for fine-controlling the glottal configuration and hence the voice timbre.

The model serves a two-fold purpose: On a global level, various singing styles can be mapped onto the four quadrants, providing a framework for putting their physiological sound source configurations in relation to the acoustic output. In the singing studio, the model gives pedagogues the opportunity to build—via acoustic assessment—working hypotheses about individual singers' habitual choice of cartilaginous adduction and membranous medialization. The model suggests possible physiologic strategies for correcting the student's degree of intrinsic laryngeal muscle contraction (TA, IA, and LCA muscles) if these deviate from what is required in the targeted singing style.

This approach fits very well into the greater picture regarding the development of vocal pedagogy: in analogy to medicine, where a certain therapy is only prescribed if (1) the status of the patient is clear and (2) the clinician has understood the underlying principles and models, vocal pedagogy is likely to become more physiologically oriented in the coming years. Certain pedagogical interventions will then only be made, if the singing teacher/vocal coach comprehends both the physical/physiological underpinnings and the acoustical consequences of the intervention (see Gill and Herbst 2016). Such an approach is ideally well balanced with the teacher's intuition and esthetic opinion.[25]

[25] This work was supported by the European Social Fund and the state budget of the Czech Republic, project no. CZ.1.07/2.3.00/30.0004 "POST-UP" (author CTH) and the European Social Fund Project OP VK CZ.1.07/2.3.00/20.0057 (JGS).

ADDITIONAL MAJOR SOURCES FOR FURTHER READING

Chapman, J. (2006). *Singing and Teaching Singing: A Holistic Approach to Classical Voice*. San Diego: Plural Publishing.

Doscher, B.M. (1994). *The Functional Unity of the Singing Voice*. Metuchen, NJ: Scarecrow Press.

Miller, D.G. (2008). *Resonance in Singing*. Princeton, NJ: Inside View Press.

Stark, J.A. (1999). *Bel Canto: A History of Vocal Pedagogy*. Toronto: University of Toronto Press.

Sundberg, J. (1987). *The Science of the Singing Voice*. Dekalb, IL: Northern Illinois University Press.

Titze, I.R. (2000). *Principles of Voice Production*. Iowa City, IA: National Center for Voice and Speech.

WEBSITES AND OTHER RESOURCES

Sources of information

Acoustics Group, University of New South Wales: Voice Acoustics: An Introduction, http://www.phys.unsw.edu.au/jw/voice.html

National Center for Voice and Speech: How Humans Speak, Sing, Squeak and Squeal, http://www.ncvs.org/ncvs/tutorials/voiceprod/tutorial/index.html

W.R. Zemlin Memorial Website (larynx anatomy), http://zemlin.shs.uiuc.edu/

The Bureau of Glottal Affairs, http://www.surgery.medsch.ucla.edu/glottalaffairs/index.htm

Software

VoceVista ("developed primarily for singing teachers to analyze the singing voice"), http://www.vocevista.com

Praat: doing phonetics by computer, http://www.fon.hum.uva.nl/praat/

Madde. An additive, real-time, singing synthesizer, http://www.speech.kth.se/music/downloads/smptool/

SFS/RTGRAM—Windows Tool for Real-time Speech Spectrogram Display, http://www.phon.ucl.ac.uk/resource/sfs/rtgram/

VRRRP!!—a free and simple software tool to create and display voice range profiles, http://www.vrrrp.org

REFERENCES

Alipour, F., Brücker, C., Cook, D.D., Gömmel, A., Kaltenbacher, M., Mattheus, W., Mongeau, L., Naumann, E., Schwarze, R., Tokuda, I., and Zörner, S. (2011). Mathematical models and numerical schemes for the simulation of human phonation. *Current Bioinformatics* 6: 323–343.

ANSI (1994). American national standard: Acoustical Terminology. Technical Report S1.1-1994. (Melville, NY: Acoustical Society of America).

Baer, T. (1975). *Investigation of phonation using excised larynxes*. Doctoral dissertation, MIT, Cambridge, MA.

Bailly, L., Henrich, N., and Pelorson, X. (2010). Vocal fold and ventricular fold vibration in period-doubling phonation: physiological description and aerodynamic modeling. *Journal of the Acoustical Society of America* 127: 3212–3222.

Baken, R. and Isshiki, N. (1977). Arytenoid displacement by simulated intrinsic muscle contraction. *Folia Phoniatrica* 29: 206–216.

Baken, R.J. and Orlikoff, R.F. (2000). *Clinical Measurement of Speech and Voice*, 2nd edn. San Diego: Singular Publishing.

Barney, A., Shadle, C.H., and Davies, P.O.A.L. (1999). Fluid flow in a dynamic mechanical model of the vocal folds and tract. I. Measurements and theory. *Journal of the Acoustical Society of America* 105: 444–455.

Berry, D., Herzel, H., Titze, I. R., and Krischer, K. (1994). Interpretation of biomechanical simulations of normal and caotic vocal fold oscillations with empirical eigenfunctions. *Journal of the Acoustical Society of America* 95: 3595–3604.

Berry, D., Herzel, H., Titze, I., and Story, B. (1996). Bifurcations in excised larynx experiments. *Journal of Voice* 10: 129–138.

Broad, D. (1968). Kinematic considerations for evaluating laryngeal cartilage motions. *Folia Phoniatrica* 20: 269–284.

Castellengo, M., Chuberre, B., and Henrich, N. (2004). Is voix mixte, the vocal technique used to smoothe the transition across the two main laryngeal mechanisms, an independent mechanism? In: *Proceedings of the International Symposium on Musical Acoustics (ISMA2004, Nara, Japan)*, March 31–April 3.

Chapman, J. (2006). *Singing and Teaching Singing: A Holistic Approach to Classical Voice*. San Diego: Plural Publishing.

Coffin, B. (1980). *Coffin's Overtones of Bel Canto*. Metuchen, NJ: Scarecrow Press.

Döllinger, M. and Berry, D. (2006). Visualization and quantification of the medial surface dynamics of an excised human vocal fold during phonation. *Journal of Voice* 20: 401–413.

Doscher, B.M. (1994). *The Functional Unity of the Singing Voice*. Metuchen, NJ: Scarecrow Press.

Doval, B., d'Alessandro, C., and Henrich, N. (2006). The spectrum of glottal flow models. *Acta Acustica united with Acustica* 92: 1026–1046.

Echternach, M., Sundberg, J., Arndt, S., Markl, M., Schumacher, M., and Richter, B. (2010). Vocal tract in female registers—a dynamic real-time MRI study. *Journal of Voice* 24: 133–139.

Echternach, M., Sundberg, J., Baumann, T., Markl, M., and Richter, B. (2011). Vocal tract area functions and formant frequencies in opera tenors' modal and falsetto registers. *Journal of the Acoustical Society of America* 129: 3955–3963.

Echternach, M., Döllinger, M., Sundberg, J., Traser, L., and Richter, B. (2013). Vocal fold vibrations at high soprano fundamental frequencies. *Journal of the Acoustical Society of America* 133: EL82–EL87. doi: 10.1121/1.4773200.

Estill, J., Klimek, M.M., Obert, K.B., and Steinhauer, K. (2005). *The Estill Voice Training System*. Pittsburgh, PA: Estill Voice International.

Fant, G. (1979). Glottal source and waveform analysis, *Speech Transmission Laboratory/Quarterly Progress and Status Report* 1/1979: 85–107.

Felsner, M. (2008). *Operatica: Annäherungen an die Welt der Oper*. Würzburg: Königshausen and Neumann.

Fitch, W.T., Neubauer, J., and Herzel, H. (2002). Calls out of chaos: the adaptive significance of nonlinear phenomena in mammalian vocal production. *Animal Behavior* 63: 407–418.

Flanagan, J. (1958). Some properties of the glottal sound source. *Journal of Speech and Hearing Research* 1: 99–116.

Flanagan, J. (1968). Source-system interaction in the vocal tract. *Annals of the New York Academy of Sciences* 155: 9–17.

Fried, M.P., Meller, S.M., and Rinaldo, A. (2009). Adult laryngeal anatomy. In: M.P. Fried and A. Ferlito (eds), *The Larynx*, 3rd edn, pp. 85–100. San Diego: Plural Publishing.

Fuks, L., Hammarberg, B., and Sundberg, J. (1998). A self-sustained vocal-ventricular phonation mode: acoustical, aerodynamic and glottographic evidences. In: *Royal Institute of Technology—Speech, Music and Hearing Quarterly Progress and Status Report* (Stockholm) 3/1998: 49–59.

Garcia, M. (1847a). *Mémoire sur la voix humaine présenté à l'Académie des Sciences en 1840.* Paris: Imprimerie d'E. Duverger.

Garcia, M. (1847b). *Traité complet de l'art du chant.* Paris: Schott.

Garcia, M. (1894). *Hints on singing.* London: Ascherberg, Hopwood and Crew.

Gill, B.P. and Herbst, C.T. (2016). Voice Pedagogy—What Do We Need?. *Logopedics Phoniatrics Vocology* 41(4): 168–173.

Henrich, N. (2006). Mirroring the voice from Garcia to the present day: some insights into singing voice registers. *Logopedics Phoniatrics Vocology* 31: 3–14.

Henrich, N., Kiek, M., Smith, J., and Wolfe, J. (2007). Resonance strategies used in Bulgarian women's singing style: a pilot study. *Logopedics Phoniatrics Vocology* 32: 171–177.

Herbst, C.T., Ternström, S., and Švec, J.G. (2009). Investigation of four distinct glottal configurations in classical singing—a pilot study. *Journal of the Acoustical Society of America* 125: EL104–EL109.

Herbst, C.T., Fitch, W.T., and Švec, J.G. (2010). Electroglottographic wavegrams: a technique for visualizing vocal fold dynamics noninvasively. *Journal of the Acoustical Society of America* 128: 3070–3078.

Herbst, C.T., Howard, D.M., and Schlömicher-Thier, J. (2010). Using electroglottographic real-time feedback to control posterior glottal adduction during phonation. *Journal of Voice* 24: 72–85.

Herbst, C.T., Qiu, Q., Schutte, H.K., and Švec, J.G. (2011). Membranous and cartilaginous vocal fold adduction in singing. *Journal of the Acoustical Society of America* 129: 2253–2262.

Herbst, C.T., Herzel, H., Švec, J.G., Wyman, M.T., and Fitch, W.T. (2013). Visualization of system dynamics using phasegrams. *Journal of the Royal Society Interface* 10(85). doi: 10.1098/rsif.2013.0288.

Herbst, C.T., Lohscheller, J., Svec, J.G., Bernadoni, N.H., Weissengruber, G., and Fitch, W.T. (2014). Glottal opening and closing events investigated by electroglottography and super-high-speed video recordings. *Journal of Experimental Biology* 217(6): 955–963.

Herbst, C.T. (2017). A review of singing voice sub-system interactions—towards an extended physiological model of "support". *Journal of Voice* 31(2): 249.e13–249.e19.

Herbst, C.T., Schutte, H.K., Bowling, D.L., and Svec, J.G. (2017). Comparing chalk with cheese—The EGG contact quotient is only a limited surrogate of the closed quotient. *Journal of Voice* 31(4): 401–409.

Herbst, C.T. (2019). Electroglottography—an update. *Journal of Voice*, in press.

Herzel, H. (1993). Bifurcations and chaos in voice signals. *Applied Mechanics Review* 46: 399–413.

Herzel, H. and Reuter, R. (1997). Whistle register and biphonation in a child's voice. *Folia Phoniatrica et Logopaedica* 49: 216–224.

Hirano, M. (1974). Morphological structure of the vocal cord as a vibrator and its variations. *Folia Phoniatrica* 26: 89–94.

Hirano, M., Kakita, Y., Kawasaki, H., Gould, W.J., and Lambiase, A. (1981). Data from high-speed motion picture studies. In: K.N. Stevens and M. Hirano (eds), *Vocal Fold Physiology*, pp. 85–93. Tokyo: University of Tokyo Press.

Hirano, M., Hibi, S., and Hagino, S. (1995). Physiological aspects of vibrato. In: P.H. Dejonckere, M. Hirano, and J. Sundberg (eds), *Vibrato*, pp. 9–33. San Diego: Singular.

Holmberg, E., Hillman, R., and Perkell, J. (1988). Glottal airflow and transglottal air pressure measurements for male and female speakers in soft, normal, and loud voice. *Journal of the Acoustical Society of America* 84: 511–529.

Howard, D.M. and Murphy, D.T. (2007). *Voice Science, Acoustics, and Recording*. San Diego: Plural Publishing.

Howard, D.M. and Angus, J.A.S. (2009). *Acoustics and Psychoacoustics*. Oxford: Oxford University Press.

Hunter, E.J., Titze, I.R., and Alipour, F. (2004). A three-dimensional model of vocal fold abduction/adduction. *Journal of the Acoustical Society of America* 115: 1747–1759.

Husson, R. (1950). Ètude des phénomènes physiologiques et acoustiques fondamentaux de la voix chantée. Thesis, Université de Paris, Faculté des sciences. (Paris: La revue scientifique).

Joliveau, E., Smith, J., and Wolfe, J. (2004). Acoustics: tuning of vocal tract resonance by sopranos. *Nature* 427: 116.

Klatt, D. and Klatt, L. (1990). Analysis, synthesis, and perception of voice quality variations among female and male talkers. *Journal of the Acoustical Society of America* 87: 820–857.

Kumar, S.P., Phadke, K.V., Vydrová, J., Novozámský, A., Zita, A., Zitová, B., and Švec, J.G. (2018). Visual and automatic evaluation of vocal fold mucosal waves through sharpness of lateral peaks in high-speed videokymographic images. *Journal of Voice*. pii: S0892-1997(18)30144-9. doi: 10.1016/j.jvoice.2018.08.022.

Ladefoged, P. (2001). *A Course in Phonetics*. Orlando, FL: Harcourt.

Letson, J.A., Jr. and Tatchell, R. (1997). Arytenoid movement. In: R.T. Sataloff (ed.), *Professional Voice: The Science and Art of Clinical Care*, pp. 131–145. San Diego: Singular Publishing Group.

Lindestad, P.A. and Södersten, M. (1988). Laryngeal and pharyngeal behavior in countertenor and baritone singing: a videofiberscopic study. *Journal of Voice* 2: 132–139.

LoVetri, J., Lesh, S., and Woo, P. (1999). Preliminary study on the ability of trained singers to control the intrinsic and extrinsic laryngeal musculature. *Journal of Voice* 13: 219–226.

LoVetri, J. (2003). Female chest voice. *Journal of Singing* 60: 161–164.

McGlashan, J., Sadolin, C., and Kjelin, H. (2007). Can vocal effects such as distortion, growling, rattle and grunting be produced without traumatizing the vocal folds? In: *7th Pan-European Voice Conference (PEVOC)*, Groningen, Netherlands, August 29–September 1.

Miller, D.G. and Schutte, H.K. (1993). Physical definition of the "flageolet register". *Journal of Voice* 7: 206–212.

Miller, D.G. (2000). *Registers in singing: empirical and systematic studies in the theory of the singing voice*. Doctoral dissertation, University of Groningen, Groningen, Netherlands.

Miller, D.G. and Schutte, H.K. (2005). "Mixing" the registers: glottal source or vocal tract? *Folia Phoniatrica* 57: 278–291.

Miller, D.G. (2008). *Resonance in Singing*. Princeton, NJ: Inside View Press.

Miller, R. (1986). *The Structure of Singing: System and Art in Vocal Technique*. New York: Schirmer Books.

Miller, R.L. (1959). Nature of the vocal cord wave. *Journal of the Acoustical Society of America* 31: 667–677.

Mörner, M., Fransson, F., and Fant, G. (1963). Voice register terminology and standard pitch. *Speech Transmission Laboratory/Quarterly Progress and Status Report* 4: 17–23.

Morrison, M., Rammage, L.A., Belisle, G.M., Pullan, C.B., and Nichol, H. (1983). Muscular tension dysphonia. *Journal of Otolaryngology* 12: 302–306.

Nawka, T. and Wirth, G. (2008). *Stimmstörungen. Lehrbuch für Ärzte, Logopäden, Sprachheilpädagogen und Sprechwissenschaftler*. Köln: Deutscher Ärzte-Verlag.

Neubauer, J., Edgerton, M., and Herzel, H. (2004). Nonlinear phenomena in contemporary vocal music. *Journal of Voice* 18: 1–12.

Reid, C.L. (2005). Voice science: an evaluation. *Australian Voice* 11: 6–24.

Remmers, J.E. and Gautier, H. (1972). Neural and mechanical mechanisms of feline purring. *Respiratory Physiology* 16: 351–361.

Roads, C. (1996). Spectrum analysis. In: C. Roads (ed.), *The Computer Music Tutorial*, pp. 533–612. Cambridge, MA: MIT Press.

Rossing, T. (1990). *The Science of Sound*. New York: Addison-Wesley.

Rothenberg, M. (1973). A new inverse-filtering technique for deriving the glottal air flow waveform during voicing. *Journal of the Acoustical Society of America* 53: 1632–1645.

Rothenberg, M. (1981a). Acoustic interaction between the glottal source and the vocal tract. In: K.N. Stevens and M. Hirano (eds), *Vocal Fold Physiology*, pp. 305–328. Tokyo: University of Tokyo Press.

Rothenberg, M. (1981b). The voice source in singing. In: *Research Aspects on Singing*, pp. 15–33. Stockholm: Royal Swedish Academy of Music.

Roubeau, B., Henrich, N., and Castellengo, M. (2009). Laryngeal vibratory mechanisms: the notion of vocal register revisited. *Journal of Voice* 23: 425–438.

Sadolin, C. (2008). *Complete Vocal Technique*. Copenhagen: Shout Publishing.

Sakakibara, K.-I., Fuks, L., Imagawa, H., and Tayama, N. (2004). Growl voice in ethnic and pop styles. In: *Proceedings of the International Symposium on Musical Acoustics (ISMA2004)*, pp. 135–138. Nara, Japan, March 31–April 3.

Sataloff, R.T. (1997). Clinical anatomy and physiology of the voice. In: R.T. Sataloff (ed.), *Professional Voice: The Science and Art of Clinical Care*, pp. 111–130. San Diego: Singular Publishing Group.

Sataloff, R.T. (1998). *Vocal Health and Pedagogy*. San Diego: Singular Publishing Group.

Seidner, W. and Wendler, J. (2004). *Die Sängerstimme*. Berlin: Henschel Verlag.

Sissom, D., Rice, D., and Peters, G. (1991). How cats purr. *Zoological Society of London* 223: 67–78.

Södersten, M., Hertegard, S., and Hammarberg, B. (1995). Glottal closure, transglottal airflow, and voice quality in healthy middle-aged women. *Journal of Voice* 9: 182–197.

Sprecher, A.J., Olszewski, A., Jiang, J., and Zhang, Y. (2010). Updating signal typing in voice: addition of type 4 signals. *Journal of the Acoustical Society of America* 127: 3710–3716.

Stark, J. (1999). Registers: some tough breaks. In: *Bel Canto—A History of Vocal Pedagogy*, pp. 57–90. Toronto: University of Toronto Press.

Steinhauer, K. and Estill, J. (2008). The Estill Voice Model™: physiology of emotion. In: K. Izdebski (ed.), *Emotions of the Human Voice*. San Diego, CA: Plural.

Story, B., Laukkanen, A.M., and Titze, I.R. (2000). Acoustic impedance of an artificially lengthened and constricted vocal tract. *Journal of Voice* 14: 455–469.

Story, B. (2002). An overview of the physiology, physics and modeling of the sound source for vowels. *Acoustical Science and Technology* 23(4): 195–206.

Story, B. (2004). Vowel acoustics for speaking and singing. *Acta Acoustica United with Acoustica* 90: 629–640.

Sundberg, J. (1972). An articulatory interpretation of the singing formant. *Speech Transmission Laboratory/Quarterly Progress and Status Report* 1: 45–53.

Sundberg, J. (1974). Articulatory interpretation of the "singing formant." *Journal of the Acoustical Society of America* 55: 838–844.

Sundberg, J. (1977). The acoustics of the singing voice. *Scientific American* 236: 82–91.

Sundberg, J. (1981a). *Research Aspects on Singing.* Stockholm: Royal Swedish Academy of Music.

Sundberg, J. (1981b). The voice as a sound generator. In: *Research Aspects on Singing*, pp. 6–14. Stockholm: Royal Swedish Academy of Music.

Sundberg, J. (1983). Chest wall vibrations in singers. *J Speech Hear Res* 26(3): 329–340.

Sundberg, J. and Skoog, J. (1997). Dependence of jaw opening on pitch and vowel in singers. *Journal of Voice* 11: 301–306.

Sundberg, J., Fahlstedt, E., and Morell, A. (2005). Effects on the glottal voice source of vocal loudness variation in untrained female and male voices. *Journal of the Acoustical Society of America* 117: 879–885.

Švec, J.G., Schutte, H.K., and Miller, D.G. (1999). On pitch jumps between chest and falsetto registers in voice: data from living and excised human larynges. *Journal of the Acoustical Society of America* 106: 1523–1531.

Švec, J.G. (2000). *On vibration properties of human vocal folds: voice registers, bifurcations, resonance characteristics, development and application of videokymography.* Doctoral dissertation, University of Groningen, Groningen, Netherlands.

Švec, J.G., Šram, F., and Schutte, H.K. (2001). Development and application of videokymography for high-speed examination of vocal-fold vibration. In: B. Palek and O. Fujimura (eds), *LP'2000*, pp. 3–10. Prague, Czech Republic.

Švec, J.G., Sundberg, J., and Hertegard, S. (2008). Three registers in an untrained female singer analyzed by videokymography, strobolaryngoscopy and sound spectrography. *Journal of the Acoustical Society of America* 123: 347–353.

Titze, I. R. (1988a). A framework for the study of vocal registers. *Journal of Voice* 2: 183–194.

Titze, I.R. (1988b). The physics of small-amplitude oscillation of the vocal folds. *Journal of the Acoustical Society of America* 83: 1536–1552.

Titze, I.R. (1990). Interpretation of the electroglottographic signal. *Journal of Voice* 4: 1–9.

Titze, I.R., Baken, R.J., and Herzel, H. (1993). Evidence of chaos in vocal fold vibration. In I.R. Titze (ed.), *Vocal Fold Physiology: Frontiers in Basic Science*, pp. 143–188. San Diego: Singular Publishing Group.

Titze, I.R. (1995). *Workshop on Acoustic Voice Analysis: Summary Statement.* Iowa City, IA: National Center for Voice and Speech.

Titze, I.R. (2000). *Principles of Voice Production.* Iowa City: National Center for Voice and Speech.

Titze, I.R. (2004a). A theoretical study of F_0-F_1 interaction with application to resonant speaking and singing voice. *Journal of Voice* 18: 292–298.

Titze, I.R. (2004b). Theory of glottal airflow and source-filter interaction in speaking and singing. *Acta Acoustica united with Acoustica* 90: 641–648.

Titze, I.R. (2008). Nonlinear source-filter coupling in phonation: theory. *Journal of the Acoustical Society of America* 123: 2733–2749.

Tokuda, I., Horáček, J., Švec, J.G., and Herzel, H. (2007). Comparison of biomechanical modeling of register transitions and voice instabilities with excised larynx experiments. *Journal of the Acoustical Society of America* 122: 519–531.

Tsai, C., Yio-Wha, S., Hon-Man, L., and Tzu-Yu, H. (2006). Laryngeal mechanisms during human 4-kHz vocalization studied with CT, videostroboscopy, and color Doppler imaging. *Journal of Voice* 22: 275–282.

Van den Berg, J. (1958). Myoelastic-aerodynamic theory of voice production. *Journal of Speech and Hearing Research* 3: 227–244.

Van den Berg, J. and Tan, T.S. (1959). Results of experiments with human larynxes. *Practica Oto-Rhino-Laryngologica* 21: 425–450.

Van den Berg, J. (1960). *Introduction to the instructional film "Voice Production. The Vibrating Larynx"* (booklet accompanying the film), Groningen, Netherlands: University of Groningen.

Van den Berg, J., Vennard, W., Burger, D., and Shervanian, C.C. (1960). *Voice production. The vibrating larynx* (instructional film). Groningen, Netherlands: University of Groningen.

Van den Berg, J. (1963). Vocal ligaments versus registers. *NATS Bulletin* 19: 16–31.

Wendler, J. (2008). Singing and science. *Folia Phonatrica* 60: 279–287.

Zemlin, W.R. (1998). *Speech and Hearing Science: Anatomy and Physiology*. Boston: Allyn and Bacon.

CHAPTER 7

··

THE VOCAL TRACT
IN SINGING

··

BRAD STORY

INTRODUCTION

··

> The upper part of the larynx, together with the pharynx . . . and mouth, constitutes
> a passage-way, or tube, of variable size and shape, through which the vibrating
> current of air is passed. It is here that the voice is moulded, so to speak, on its
> way to the ear, and the shape of the passage-way largely determines the quality or
> timbre of the voice.
>
> (Bell 1911, p. 18)

CREATING music with an instrument requires the use of a precision device (e.g. violin, trumpet, etc.) that has been handcrafted or manufactured for the exclusive purpose of generating sounds with a specific quality or timbre. In contrast, creating music by singing requires humans to utilize the same anatomical structures that are used to perform other functions such as speaking, breathing, chewing, and swallowing. Thus, a singer cannot customize the structure of the instrument, but rather can only modify, through training and learning, the ways in which it is used. This results in an acoustic waveform that is a complex aural portrait consisting of the elements of song (notes, tempo, melody, etc.) superimposed on a unique acoustic "background" or "setting" determined by the singer's anatomy and use of it. Specifically, singing is dominated by *voiced* sounds that are initiated by the vibration of the vocal folds. These vibrations create a source of oscillating airflow that acoustically encodes information relevant to the vibratory character of the vocal fold tissue. In turn, this time-varying airflow induces a pressure wave that propagates through the airspace of the vocal tract formed by the relative positions of the tongue, jaw, lips, and velum, and acquires information about the shape of the airspace that is eventually carried along to a listener's ear. The final output signal contains acoustic features that reveal information about the generation of the sound at its source as well as the vocal tract structure through which the source sound has traveled.

Precise control of the vocal tract configuration is of critical importance for producing the desired acoustic characteristics of singing. The pattern of acoustic resonances generated by a given vocal tract shape influences vowel identity and sound quality (timbre). This chapter will focus on how the vocal tract shape can be globally shaped for vowel production and lo-cally tuned (i.e. modified) in subtle ways to enhance the signal radiated from a singer to an audience. Specifically, the vocal tract shape contributions to vowel production, the "singing formant," and harmonic/formant alignment will be addressed.

REPRESENTATIONS OF THE HUMAN VOCAL TRACT

From an articulatory perspective, singing is often discussed in terms of the individual articulators (see Figure 7.1). For instance, the tongue position could be said to be forward and high for production of the vowel /i/ or backward and low for an /a/, the lips may be rounded when producing /u/ but spread for an /i/, or the larynx may be raised or lowered to alter the color of a given vowel. From an acoustic perspective, however, it is not the tongue, mandible, larynx, lips, and velum that are individually relevant, but rather how their relative positions contribute to the overall shape of the airspace that extends from the vocal folds to the lips. This airspace is called the *vocal tract*, and it is the structure that generates the acoustic char-acteristics of the sound pressure produced by a singer. Thus, precise control of the vocal tract shape is essential for producing a desired quality of sound.

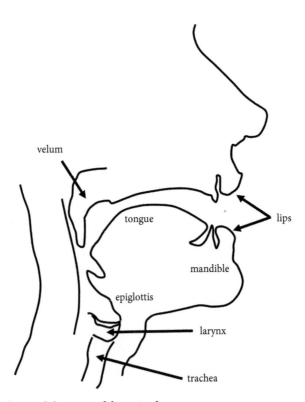

FIGURE 7.1 Midsagittal diagram of the articulators.

Imaging the vocal tract

The vocal tract can be represented in several forms, and each is useful for different reasons. Shown in Figure 7.2 are four representations of the vocal tract of an adult male producing the vowel/a/. The first, shown in Figure 7.2a, is a midsagittal slice obtained with X-ray computed tomography (CT) (Story 1995). The vocal tract extends from the glottis (airspace between the vocal folds) to the lip aperture, and can be clearly seen in black (as can the tracheal and some

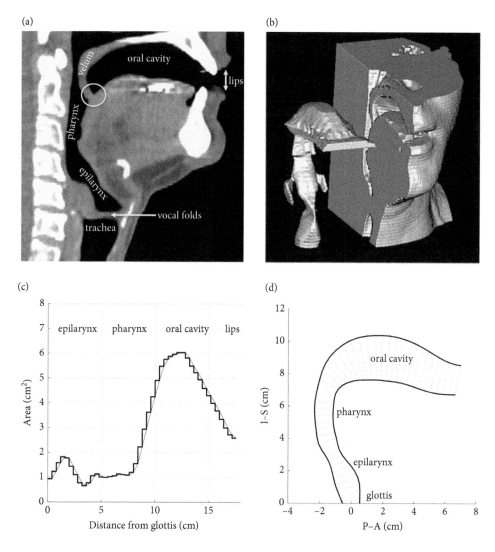

FIGURE 7.2 Four graphical representations of the vocal tract of an adult male speaker based on images from X-ray CT. (a) Single midsagittal slice of an /a/ vowel with various parts of airspace labeled; (b) 3D reconstruction of the vocal tract; (c) area function measured from the 3D reconstruction in (b); and (d) pseudo-midsagittal plot generated from equivalent diameters of the area function.

of the nasal airspaces). Three sections of the vocal tract are marked as *epilarynx, pharynx,* and *oral cavity*. In this particular case, the velum has been lowered enough that its most inferior portion appears to be in contact with the tongue surface; the lowered velar position also creates a small open space that connects the vocal tract to the nasal airspaces thus producing a nasalized vowel, albeit unintended here.

Although a midsagittal view is useful for relating the articulator positions to the vocal tract shape, it cannot provide the variation in cross-sectional area along the vocal tract length. There have been many attempts to transform *cross-distances* measured in the midsagittal plane to *cross-sectional areas* via functions such as $A = kd^\alpha$, where d is cross-distance, and α and k are empirically-derived constants (c.f., Baer et al. 1991; Heinz and Stevens 1964; Sundberg 1987). Although useful for working with midsagittal data, such transformations are not actual measurements of the cross-sectional area variation along the tract length. Instead, a volume of slices containing the relevant portions of the head and neck is needed such that the vocal tract can be reconstructed as a 3D object. Figure 7.2b demonstrates a 3D reconstruction based on the same image set containing the midsagittal slice (Figure 7.2a). The vocal tract is shown displaced from the tissue and bone, and represents the true shape of the airspace in three dimensions. The most inferior portion is the upper part of the trachea, which then narrows at the location of the vocal folds; the wing-like structures connected to the lower part of the vocal tract are the piriform sinuses.

Vocal tract area functions

Acoustic characteristics of the vocal tract are typically studied by simplifying the 3D shape to an *area function*. This is obtained by measuring the cross-sectional area of oblique sections perpendicular to a centerline extending from the glottis (vocal folds) to the lips. The area function for the 3D vocal tract (Figure 7.2b) is plotted in Figure 7.2c. The stairstep quality of the plot demonstrates that the area function discretizes the vocal tract into a series of concatenated "tubelets"; however, it is often more visually appealing to simply plot a continuous line through the data points as is also shown in the figure. It is noted that the piriform sinuses are not represented by the area function; they can be separately measured (c.f., Dang and Honda 1997; Story et al. 1996, 1998), but will not be considered in this chapter. It is also the case that the area function representation does not explicitly include the 90-degree bend in the vocal tract. Although the bend is of great biomechanical importance for efficiently changing the vocal tract shape, it does not affect the acoustic characteristics significantly, at least in the typical frequency range of interest for singing and speaking (i.e. less than 5000 Hz). It is, however, often more intuitively appealing to see the vocal tract shape presented in an anatomically relevant coordinate system. Figure 7.2d illustrates the same area function as in Figure 7.2c but shown as equivalent diameters plotted along the 2D vocal tract centerline. The light dashed lines are the diameters and the heavy solid lines generate an outline of the vocal tract shape. Since this does not represent a true midsagittal plane it will be referred to here as a *pseudo-midsagittal* plot (c.f., Story et al. 2001). Pseudo-midsagittal plots and area functions will be used in subsequent sections to describe and explain the relation of the vocal tract structure to acoustic characteristics.

MODEL OF HUMAN SOUND PRODUCTION

Vowels and vowel-like sounds are produced by the combination of a sound source and a sound filter (e.g. Fant 1960), where the source signal is the succession of airflow pulses generated by the periodic opening and closing of the space between the vocal folds (i.e. the glottis) as they vibrate. This signal is typically referred to as the glottal flow, where the temporal duration of each flow pulse determines the fundamental frequency (f_o) of a particular vowel sound. In addition to the f_o, the source signal contains a series of harmonic components that are related to the f_o by integer multiples (e.g. the second harmonic is $2f_o$, the third harmonic is $3f_o$, . . .). The primary filter is the vocal tract which, as discussed in the previous section, is comprised of the epilaryngeal, pharyngeal, and oral cavities. Any particular shape of the vocal tract produces a pattern of acoustic resonances. As the source signal (wave) travels through the vocal tract, the resonances have the effect of enhancing the amplitude of some harmonics of the source while suppressing others. Hence, the output sound results from the interaction of the source with the filter.

The source-filter representation is illustrated graphically in Figure 7.3 with signals generated by a speech production model. The particular model used is based on the author's previous research. A description of the model is outside the scope of the current chapter but interested readers can find components of it in Story (1995, 2004, 2013) and Titze (2006). Two flow pulses (cycles) of the glottal airflow signal $u_g(t)$ are plotted in the upper left panel; for this example, they are repeated every 4.5 milliseconds, which is equivalent to a fundamental frequency of 220 Hz (A_3 on the equal-tempered scale). A vocal tract shape $A(x)$ is shown in pseudo-midsagittal form in the upper middle panel of the figure; for demonstration purposes it has been configured to have a fairly uniform cross-section along the entire tract length. The glottal flow pulses enter the vocal tract at the point labeled "glottis" and generate sound pressure waves that propagate through it, reflecting and transmitting various amounts of energy at any change in cross-sectional area. The pressure that is finally generated at the lip end of the vocal tract radiates outward from the singer. An output pressure waveform $p(t)$ is shown in the upper right panel and is analogous to a signal that could be obtained with a microphone held near a singer's lips. Note that effect of the vocal tract as a filter is to transform the relatively simple glottal flow signal into a more complex pressure wave that carries with it "information" about the shape of the vocal tract.

The second row of plots in Figure 7.3 demonstrates the spectral (frequency and amplitude) characteristics of the source signal, the vocal tract, and the output sound pressure signal, respectively, from left to right. The spectrum of the glottal flow is shown in the lower left panel and is denoted as $U_g(f)$. The fundamental frequency (f_o) is indicated by the first peak in the spectrum which, for this case, is 220 Hz. The peaks that occur successively, as frequency increases, are the "harmonics" of the glottal flow signal and are related to the f_o by integer multiples; the second harmonic ($2f_o$) is labeled in the figure. The amplitude of the harmonics tends to decrease with an increase in frequency. If one were to listen to the glottal flow signal in isolation it would have a buzz-like quality.

The resonance frequencies of the vocal tract are indicated by the peaks in the spectrum shown in the lower middle panel. In studies of both speech and singing, these peaks are typically referred to as the *formant frequencies*, hence the labels of F1–F5. Note that this spectrum

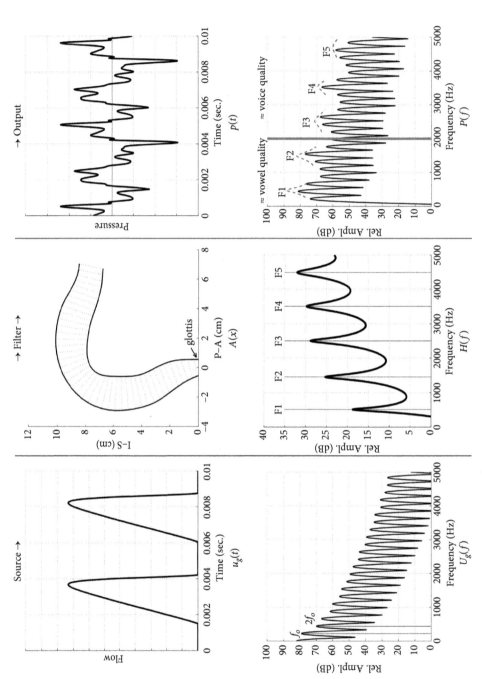

FIGURE 7.3 Illustration of the source-filter representation of vowels. The upper row shows the source waveform, a vocal tract shape for a neutral vowel, and the output waveform, all in the time domain. The second row shows the frequency domain representation of each of the quantities in the first row. The gray vertical line marks a conceptual boundary between the part of the spectrum related to phonetic qualities and that part related to voice quality.

does not represent the frequency and amplitude content of any particular sound, but rather the effect that the vocal tract shape would have on *any* sound that travels through it. For this reason, it is referred to as the frequency response of the vocal tract filter and is denoted as *H(f)*. Because the vocal tract shape in this case is fairly uniform, the resonance or formant frequencies are nearly equally spaced at intervals of 1000 Hz along the frequency axis. This could be considered a neutral vowel.

The output pressure spectrum *P(f)*, shown in the lower right panel, is the combination of the glottal flow spectrum and frequency response of the vocal tract. Mathematically, *P(f)* is the product of $U_g (f)H(f)$ (because the spectra are shown logarithmically in dB, the amplitude at each frequency in the output spectrum is the sum of the amplitudes of each frequency in the other two lower panels). The fundamental frequency and all of the harmonics are present in the output spectrum, but their amplitudes have been modified by the vocal tract resonances (formant frequencies); harmonics near a formant frequency are enhanced in amplitude, while those distant from the formants are suppressed. In other words, the harmonics of the glottal flow spectrum *sample* the frequency response of the vocal tract to express, in the output, both the harmonic content of the glottal source and the acoustic resonance pattern of the vocal tract shape.

It is noted that the terms formant and resonance can create some confusion if not properly defined. Fant (1960) discussed the differences of the two words where *formant* is defined as a peak of enhanced spectral energy in the output spectrum and *resonance* is a natural frequency of the vocal tract. Since that time it has been generally accepted that a formant measured from a spectrum (or spectrogram) is an estimate of a resonance frequency. Stevens (2000, p. 131) states that:

> The poles represent the complex natural frequencies of the vocal tract. The imaginary parts indicate the frequencies at which oscillations would occur in the absence of excitation and are called the formant frequencies. They are normally designated as F1, F2, . . . Fn, in increasing order of frequency.

Thus, in most cases the resonance frequencies of the vocal tract are essentially the formants. This definition, however, is largely based on speech research rather than singing, and there are some situations of the latter that may generate spectra with the appearance of a single broad formant that is in fact generated by close proximity of several resonances.

CONTROLLING THE VOCAL TRACT FOR SINGING

> Vocalization being essentially vowelization, it is the vowel that is the real carrier of the tone. Consonants . . . are to be respected, but they must not become predominant within the line . . . [and] need not play villain to the heroic vowel.
>
> (Miller 1996, p. 20)

Singing is dominated by vowels because they are produced with open vocal tract configurations that allow for a continuous flow of sound. In contrast, most consonants, in one way or another, require a severe constriction of the vocal tract and create a partial or complete interruption of the sound stream. Thus, the musical features that characterize singing are largely expressed through the precise control of the vocal tract during vowel production.

Vowel identity is largely based on the first two formant frequencies (Hillenbrand et al. 1995; Peterson and Barney 1952), although the third formant may also contribute in some cases. To demonstrate how the vocal tract can be shaped for different purposes, an artificial division has been superimposed on the output spectrum in Figure 7.3 (lower right panel). The gray vertical line located at 2000 Hz is intended to suggest that much of the vocal tract shaping for vowel quality (i.e. phonetic aspects) is directed at positioning F1 and F2, whereas the contribution of the vocal tract to voice quality, or what is often referred to as "timbre," is represented in the upper formants F3, F4, and F5. The next several sections explore how each of these spectral regions can be controlled by overall shaping of the vocal tract for particular vowels, as well as precise, but subtle, tuning of various parts of the vocal tract to enhance the sound quality.

Shaping the vocal tract for production of vowels

Using the neutral vocal tract shape of Figure 7.3 as a starting point and reference, three new tract shapes have been generated that shift the F1 and F2 formant frequencies into positions along the frequency axis that would roughly correspond to the vowels /i/, /a/, and /u/. The pseudo-midsagittal plots and frequency response functions for each are shown in Figure 7.4, where the dashed lines indicate the shape or frequency response of the neutral reference.

These particular shapes were created with a computer algorithm that carefully altered the vocal tract configuration until a desired set of F1 and F2 formant frequencies were achieved (Story 2006) (for these cases, the other formants were unconstrained). The /i/ vowel in the upper row of Figure 7.4 is characterized acoustically by a low F1 and a high F2, which is produced, relative to the neutral shape, by constricting the oral cavity and expanding the pharynx. In contrast, the /a/ vowel has a high F1 and and low F2, and is produced by expanding the oral cavity and constricting the pharynx. Both F1 and F2 have relatively low values for the /u/ vowel and are generated by constricting a section of the vocal tract near the lips and in the velar region, as well as slightly expanding both the oral cavity and the lower part of the pharynx.

It is sometimes necessary in singing to modify a vowel in order to accommodate a particular note. For example, if a musical score prescribed that the note F_4, which requires a fundamental frequency of 349 Hz, be sung as an /i/ vowel, a singer could not use the /i/ vocal tract shape in Figure 7.4 without sacrificing vowel identity and possibly stability of phonation (Titze and Story 1997). This is because the F1 of that vocal tract configuration is 300 Hz, which is below the f_o of the prescribed note. The solution is to slightly modify the /i/ shape such that F1 is increased just enough to be at a higher frequency than the target f_o. A modification of the /i/ vowel is shown in Figure 7.5, where the oral cavity has been expanded to release the primary constriction and the pharynx has slightly enlarged. These changes have the main desired effect of shifting the F1 from 300 Hz to 450 Hz.

Although these particular vocal tract shapes were generated through artificial means, they demonstrate the typical canonical configuration for these vowels. The main point is

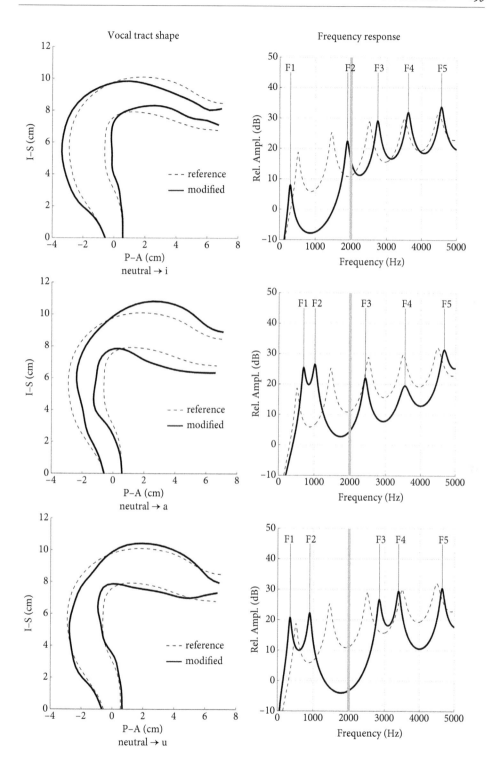

FIGURE 7.4 Three examples of imposing large global changes to the neutral vocal tract to produce the corner vowels /i/, /a/ and /u/. In each case the dashed line represents the neutral tract shape or its frequency response, and the solid lines correspond to the vowels.

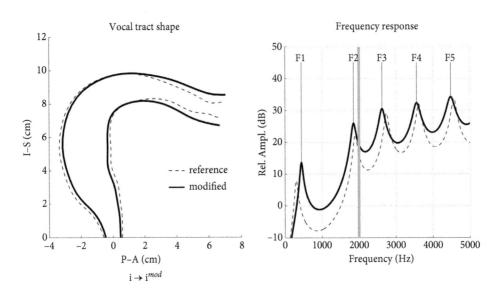

FIGURE 7.5 Demonstration of modifying an /i/ vocal tract shape (left panel) to raise F1 (right panel). The dashed lines in the left and right panels represent the /i/ vocal tract shape and frequency response, respectively, from Figure 7.4. The solid lines represent a modification to the vocal tract shape that shifts F1 upward in frequency.

that positioning the first two formant frequencies for vowel production requires fairly large changes in the cross-sectional area over most of the vocal tract length. That is, shifting from one vowel to another necessitates global changes in vocal tract shape. Interestingly, the epilaryngeal portion of the vocal tract was left nearly unchanged relative to the neutral shape when creating the three new vowels. As will be demonstrated in the next section, it is this region of the vocal tract that can be used to "tune" the overall sound quality while maintaining the desired vowel.

Tuning the vocal tract to enhance sound quality

The overall sound quality of the voice can be significantly influenced by the relative locations of acoustic resonances F3, F4, and F5. It is in this region of the spectrum that the so-called "singer's formant" or "singing formant" typically appears. An example can be seen in the long-time average spectrum (LTAS) shown in Figure 7.6 for a tenor. This "formant" is a broad peak of spectral energy but is generally produced by a cluster of two or more resonances of the vocal tract that are in close proximity to each other.

Bartholomew (1934) seems to have been the first to quantitatively describe the spectral prominence at about 2800–2900 Hz in vowels sung by males. He called it the "high formant" and suggested that it exists "regardless of whether produced by a tenor or baritone . . . and regardless of fundamental pitch $[f_o]$, the vowel or intensity." Although somewhat perplexed by its apparent existence in all the male singers he studied, Bartholomew narrowed the origin of the high formant to the portion of the vocal tract between the "rima glottidis [glottis]" and the top rim of the "laryngo-epiglottal funnel," or essentially what has been termed the

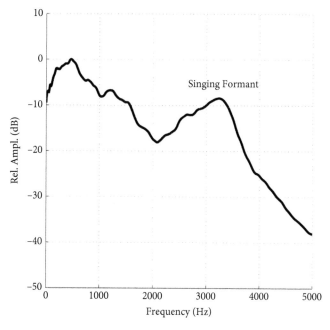

FIGURE 7.6 Long time average spectrum (LTAS) of a tenor. A singing formant is apparent in the range of 2500–3500 Hz.

epilarynx in this chapter. The notion that a fixed resonator produces the singing formant was questioned by Lewis (1936), who performed spectral analysis on recordings of several male singers. His data showed a spectral prominence in the 2800–3200 Hz range but it was suggested that the resonance frequencies contributing to the prominence shifted along the frequency axis depending on speaker and vowel. Winckel (1954) commented on a portion of the spectrum around 3000 Hz that he called the "carrying region" and suggested that it corresponded to "the active radius of the singing voice." What he meant by "active radius" is not clear but perhaps was a reference to the epilaryngeal region.

Sundberg (1974) proposed that the "singing formant" (as he called it) or later the "singer's formant" was generated by the epilarynx tube which can act nearly as an independent resonator if the ratio of its cross-sectional area to that of the pharyngeal entry is 1:6 or less. A singer can control the shape of this resonator by lowering the larynx or constricting the epiglottal and lower pharyngeal regions. The effect of an epilaryngeal tube resonator is demonstrated in Figure 7.7. The left panel shows a pseudo-midsagittal plot of an idealized vocal tract configured first as a uniform conduit (dashed line) with a 5 cm^2 cross-section, and shown again with the same vocal tract shape but with the epilaryngeal portion constricted to be 0.5 cm^2 (solid line). The frequency response functions in the right panel indicate how the constricted epilarynx generates a spectral prominence by moving F3 and F4 toward each other, relative to the initial uniform vocal tract. The close proximity of these formants causes their respective filter skirts to overlap and create a cumulatively greater amplitude response than when they are separated by a greater distance. The gray line shows the frequency response for the epilarynx tube alone whose resonance can be calculated with the formula for a closed-open tube, $F = c/4L$. In this example, $L = 3.2$ cm which gives $F = 2734$ Hz when the

(a)   (b)

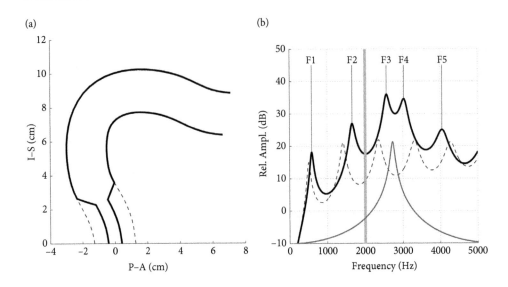

FIGURE 7.7 Idealized vocal tract modification to generate a singing formant. (a) Uniform tube (dashed) and the uniform tube with a narrowed epilarynx (solid); (b) frequency response functions of both the vocal tract shapes in (a) using the same respective line styles; the gray line represents the frequency response of the epilaryngeal tube in isolation.

speed of sound is $c = 35000$ cm/s. Conceptually, one could think of this situation as F3 and F4 being "attracted" toward the first resonance frequency of the epilaryngeal resonator.

Clearly a narrowed epilaryngeal tube is a possible mechanism for producing a singing formant, and measurements of such a narrowing have been reported in several studies (e.g. Echternach et al. 2011; Story et al. 1996, 2001; Story 2005, 2008). Other researchers, however, have reported a singing formant to exist in the spectra of singers without an apparent lengthening and narrowing of the epilarynx. Using magnetic resonance imaging (MRI), stroboscopy, and acoustic analysis, Detweiler (1994) showed that the singers in her study produced a spectral prominence in the 2800–3200 Hz range, but did not achieve a 1:6 ratio of cross-sectional area of the epilarynx to the lower pharynx. In addition, Wang (1986) showed that a spectral prominence could be achieved with both high and low larynx positions. Both studies suggest that the singing formant can be produced by some modification of the vocal tract other than lengthening and narrowing the epilarynx.

A different approach to understanding the singing formant can be developed by consideration of acoustic sensitivity functions. Choosing the /a/ vowel configuration from Figure 7.4 as a starting point, several steps will be described that allow for modification to the shape so that a singing formant will be generated (note that the frequency response in Figure 7.4 for the /a/ shows F3, F4, and F5 to be widely spaced rather than clustered as is desired for the singing formant). Acoustic sensitivity functions (Fant and Pauli 1974) can be calculated for each formant of any given area function as the difference between the potential and kinetic energy that exists along the vocal tract length (and then normalized to the total energy). When viewed as a function of distance from the glottis they can be used to predict how a particular change to the vocal tract shape will shift a particular formant.

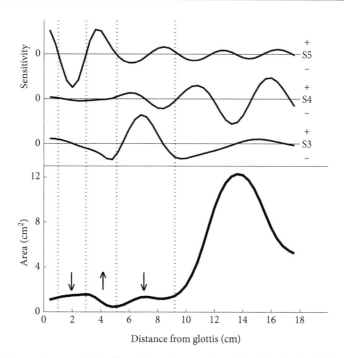

FIGURE 7.8 Acoustic sensitivity functions (upper three lines) calculated for the /a/ area function plotted in the lower part. This is the same /a/ vocal tract shape as that in Figure 7.4. The arrows indicate constrictions and expansions that are predicted to increase F3, decrease F5, and leave F4 unchanged.

Sensitivity functions for the third, fourth, and fifth formants (labeled S3, S4, and S5) of the /a/ vowel are plotted in the upper part of Figure 7.8, and the area function is shown in the lower part. They have been plotted such that constricting the vocal tract in any region where a sensitivity function is positive will cause that particular formant frequency to increase, and expanding the same region would lower the formant frequency. Conversely, constricting the vocal tract in any region where there is negatively valued sensitivity will lower the formant frequency. As an example, the arrows in Figure 7.8 indicate how three portions of the vocal tract could be modified in order to shift F3 upward and F5 downward, while leaving F4 nearly unchanged. Constricting the region centered around 2 cm from the glottis will primarily lower F5 because the S5 function is negative; S3 has equal parts negative and positive, and S4 is nearly zero, hence F3 and F4 will be unaffected. Expanding the next region (centered at 4 cm) will also lower F5 because S5 is positive (increasing the area in a region with positive sensitivity will lower the formant). In addition, this same expansion will increase the F3 frequency because S3 is negative in this region; F4 will again be unchanged because the S4 sensitivity is essentially zero. Constriction of the region between 5 and 9.2 cm will primarily increase F3 since S3 is positive; this constriction will have little effect on F4 and F5 since both S4 and S5 are nearly equal parts negative and positive.

An automated technique was used to determine the degree of constriction or expansion needed in each of the three regions to shift the formants to specified locations, or to leave them unchanged (Story 2006). The result is demonstrated in the upper row of Figure 7.9. The pseudo-midsagittal view (upper left) shows the reference /a/ as a dashed line and the modi-fied version as the solid line; the arrows indicate the same constrictive and expansive actions as in Figure 7.8. As can be seen in the frequency response functions (upper right panel) these fairly subtle modifications do indeed shift F3 upward and F5 downward, while leaving F4 (as well as F1 and F2) at nearly the same frequency as in the reference case. This has the effect of creating a cluster of the upper three formants that enhances the amplitude from approx-imately 2900–4000 Hz, but preserves the locations of F1 and F2 to maintain the /a/ vowel.

The modified /a/ vowel (henceforth referred to as a_1^{mod}) provides the beginnings of a singing formant cluster. Bringing the upper formants even closer together, however, could potentially provide greater amplitude enhancement in the 3000 Hz region. The middle row of Figure 7.9 shows a next step in which the vocal tract has been further modified so that F4 is moved downward in frequency toward F3 while all other formants are unchanged; this new shape is called a_2^{mod}. Accomplishing this required slightly more expansion and constriction of the three regions that produced a_1^{mod}, along with very subtle changes in the oral cavity, as can be seen in the middle left pseudo-midsagittal plot (the dashed line is still the original reference /a/ vowel). The frequency response function clearly shows that F4 has been shifted downward by these additional shape changes.

A final step is to bring F5 down into a tight cluster with F3 and F4, and again preserve the locations of F1 and F2 for vowel quality. This is shown in the bottom row of Figure 7.9, where the vocal tract shape, a_3^{mod}, now includes a narrow epilaryngeal tube terminated by a large expansion, much like the idealized singing formant example discussed previously. There are also other subtle expansions and constrictions along the entire vocal tract. These modifications do have the effect of driving F3, F4, and F5 into a tight cluster that could serve to enhance the output pressure amplitude in the 3000 Hz region of the spectrum. To dem-onstrate, a vowel was simulated with a_3^{mod} as the vocal tract shape, and the input glottal flow was exactly the same as in Figure 7.3. Both the glottal flow spectrum and the output pres-sure spectrum are plotted in the upper row of Figure 7.10. The singing formant enhances the amplitudes of the 12th–16th harmonics and raises them to levels just slightly lower than the harmonics in the region of F1 and F2. This is no easy feat considering the upper harmonics in the glottal flow are on the order of 30 dB lower in intensity than those at the low frequency end.

These spectra would be representative of a note sung without any variation (i.e. straight tone). It is more typical, however, that a singer would impose at least some amount of vibrato on a note. Vibrato is a periodic variation of the fundamental frequency above and below the target f_o for a desired note. Shown in the bottom row of Figure 7.10 are a succession of glottal flow (source) and output spectra of a simulated vowel with vibrato. Because all harmonics are related to the f_o by integer multiples, the vibrato sweeps each harmonic back and forth through a range of frequencies. This has the effect, over time, of more thoroughly sampling the resonance pattern produced by the vocal tract than does a perfectly steady f_o, as can be seen in the output spectra (lower right) where the lower formants as well as the singing formants become more clearly visible with the time-dependent spectra.

The latter case exemplifies how the term "formant" can become problematic. From the perspective of the output pressure spectrum (Figure 7.10), clearly a prominence exists around 3000 Hz that could be called *a* formant. However, from the frequency response of the area function for a_3^{mod} there are most definitely three resonances that contribute to the spectral prominence, and they have been called the F3, F4, and F5 formants. Thus, the term

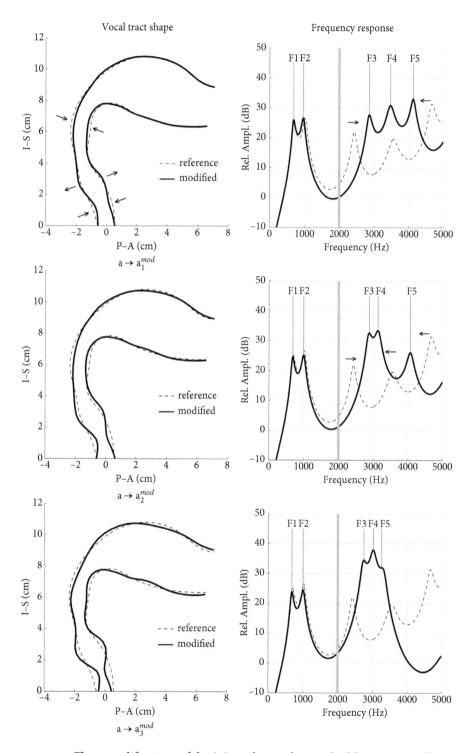

FIGURE 7.9 Three modifications of the /a/ vocal tract shape to build up a singing formant. The dashed lines in the left and right columns represent the vocal tract shape and frequency response, respectively, of the reference (initial) condition. The solid lines are the modifications as described in the text.

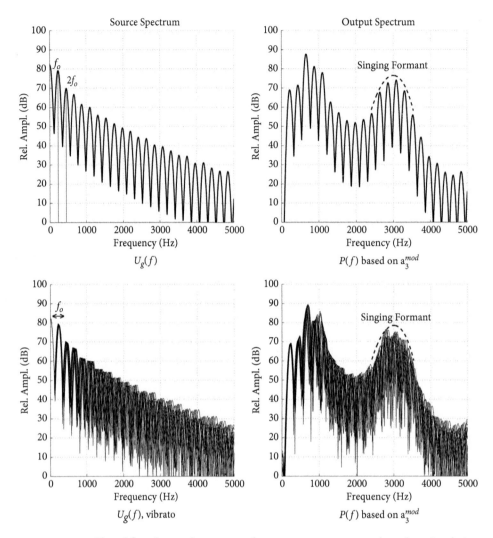

FIGURE 7.10 Glottal flow (source) spectra and output pressure spectra based on simulating a vowel with the A^{mod} vocal tract shape. In the top row the f_o is 220 Hz with no variation; the harmonics are enhanced in amplitude in the region of F1 and F2, and also in the singing formant region. In the bottom row the f_o is again 220 Hz but with vibrato; this sweeps the harmonics back and forth through the vocal tract resonances.

"singing formant" or "singer's formant" must not be thought of as a vocal tract resonance, but rather a special case where several resonances occupy a similar region of the spectrum.

The examples shown in this section have demonstrated how a singer might *tune* the vocal tract shape for a given vowel to enhance the sound quality while maintaining the acoustic features characteristic of the vowel. Clearly much of this tuning can be accomplished with modifications to the epilarynx, essentially transforming it into a tube-like resonator as suggested by Sundberg (1974) (e.g. Figure 7.7). The sensitivity function approach, however, indicated that while the epilarynx is of primary importance, the collective effect of quite subtle expansions and constrictions along the tract length can significantly alter the locations of F3, F4, and F5. The sensitivity functions themselves provide some insight into the "controls" of the resonant part of the vocal instrument. That is, they relate possible constrictions or expansions of a given vocal tract shape to the direction of change of individual formant frequencies. These latter demonstrations were performed deliberately without any modification to the overall vocal tract length to emphasize that a singing formant can be created from cross-sectional area modifications alone, although in practice a vocalist would likely make use of both length and area modification. In a conceptual sense, the series of vocal tract modifications shown in Figure 7.9 can be thought of as a simulation of a singer learning how to control the upper formants for *tuning* voice quality while not disturbing the overall *shaping* needed for production of the vowel.

This section will end with an additional example of subtle vocal tract modification. The demonstrations in Figure 7.9 could be questioned with regard to whether they are in fact physiologically realistic. For instance, can a real singer actually impose the series of constrictions and expansions needed to create the cluster of upper formants? The vocal tract shape shown in Figure 7.11 (upper left) was *measured* from a 3D reconstruction of a singer's vocal tract configured as an /a/ vowel. The image set from which the measurement was made was collected in a magnetic resonance imaging scanner, and the analysis was essentially identical to that shown previously in Figure 7.2. The singer was a baritone who, from previous acoustic analyses, was known to have a prominent singing formant in the 3000 Hz region of the spectrum. The vocal tract shape indicates many of the same type of constrictive and expansive features as were generated in the earlier demonstration shapes. For instance, the epilaryngeal region is narrow and is terminated with a large expansion; the pharynx and oral cavity additionally possess subtle wave-like features similar to those in the tract shapes of Figure 7.9. The frequency response function in the upper right panel shows that F1 and F2 are in locations typical of an /a/, but, other than the moderate clustering of F4 and F5, there does not appear a strong singing formant. Although a rather disappointing result at first, subtle modifications imposed on the measured shape, as presented in the lower left panel, bring F3, F4, and F5 into a fairly tight cluster that would generate a singing formant (lower right panel). These small changes are certainly within the range of measurement error for this type of data collection, and further emphasize the precise and delicate nature of tuning the vocal tract for sound quality.

Tuning a female vocal tract for a singing formant

Although the basic notions of vocal tract modification discussed in the previous section could, in principle, be applied to a female vocal tract, there are aspects of female singing that suggest the approach to tuning may be somewhat different. The primary difference between a male and female vocal tract is the overall length; the tract length for a typical adult male is about 17.5 cm, whereas for an adult female it is around 15 cm. Nonetheless, the global *shaping* required for vowel production is similar regardless of the tract length; for example, expansion of the oral cavity and constriction of the pharynx are needed to produce an /a/ vowel. Further, the higher notes sung by females may require some extreme shape modifications to ensure that the first formant is higher than the target note (e.g. Titze et al. 2011). It is something of an open question, however, whether female singers, especially sopranos, can

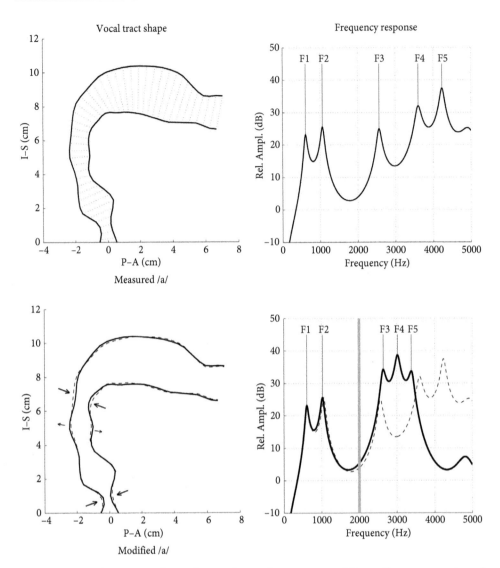

FIGURE 7.11 The top row shows the vocal tract shape measured from 3D reconstruction of a singer's /a/ vowel and corresponding frequency response function. The bottom row shows the slight modifications necessary to bring the F3, F4, and F5 formants into a cluster centered at 3000 Hz.

produce or make use of a singing formant. Weiss et al. (2001) reported that sopranos seem to produce a spectral prominence of 2600–4600 Hz for low- and mid-frequency notes (i.e. 261 Hz and 622 Hz, respectively). Because the prominence was typically broader than a singing formant observed for male vocalists, the authors suggested that the physiological origin of the soprano singing formant was different than that of males.

The purpose of this section is not to give a thorough review of the female vocal tract, but rather to provide another demonstration of vocal tract tuning, this time for a vowel configuration measured from a soprano singer. The vocal tract shape shown in Figure 7.12a is that of an /a/ vowel sung on the note D_5 (587 Hz). This was originally reported as an area function in Story (2004) and has been plotted here with exactly the same scale as the pseudo-midsagittal plots shown for the male vocal tract in previous figures. The frequency response calculated for the tract shape is plotted in Figure 7.12b, and clearly shows that F3 and F4 have been driven toward each other to produce a two-formant cluster. The effect of this cluster can be seen in the spectrum of the singer's recording of this vowel as shown in Figure 7.12c; the amplitudes of harmonics 5–8 are enhanced in the spectrum. Although the epilarynx portion is fairly narrow it gradually diverges toward the wider pharyngeal portion of the tract, providing little evidence for an epilaryngeal tube resonator as the source of the singing formant. An acoustic sensitivity function analysis of this vocal tract shape suggested that both F3 and F4 were highly sensitive to cross-sectional area changes in the region at about the mid-point where there is a fairly tight constriction (indicated by the circle in Figure 7.12a) suggesting that further constriction would move F3 and F4 even closer together and releasing the constriction would move them apart. To test the prediction, this region of the tract was increased in area (i.e. constriction was slightly released) as shown in Figure 7.12d, and indeed such an increase has the effect of moving F3 down and F4 up in frequency (Figure 7.12e), slightly detuning the singing formant. Additional expansion of this region would move F3 and F4 farther apart.

This example shows yet another subtle tuning maneuver that could alter the sound quality. The point at which the constriction was made is in the velar region. Although speculative at this point, it appears that such a constriction might be created by muscular action of both the tongue and velum, providing control of F3 and F4.

Summary

More than a century ago Alexander Graham Bell wrote, regarding the vocal tract, that "It is here that the voice is moulded, so to speak, on its way to the ear, and the shape of the passageway [vocal tract] largely determines the quality or timbre of the voice" (Bell 1911). Certainly this statement is as true today as it was then, and one might think that after a hundred years of subsequent research all things would be known about the relation of the vocal tract shape to the acoustic characteristics it produces. But research is often focused, for good reason, on understanding particular aspects of a system. With regard to the vocal tract much effort has been expended in studying those acoustic characteristics that are phonetically relevant; for vowels, this primarily means the first two or three formant frequencies. Less effort has been put toward the study of how the vocal tract imparts acoustic characteristics related to voice quality, for either singing or speech.

As has been demonstrated in this chapter, enhancement of voice quality typically requires subtle but precise modifications of the vocal tract shape. This is in direct contrast with the more global shape changes needed for shifting from one vowel to another. In light of this apparent division between the qualities needed for vowel identity vs. the desired qualities of the sound itself (musical or otherwise), a conceptual model was introduced that differentiated *shaping* from *tuning*. Shaping involves large movements of the articulators that create major changes in cross-sectional area along nearly the entire vocal tract length. In contrast, tuning

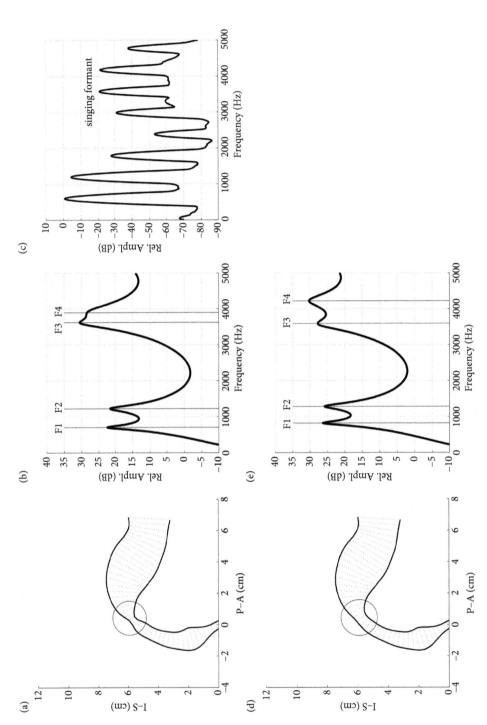

FIGURE 7.12 Demonstration of a singing formant produced by a soprano vocal tract: (a) measured vocal tract shape for an /a/ vowel sung at 587 Hz; (b) frequency response function for vocal tract shape in (a); (c) spectrum of a recorded /a/ vowel produced by the soprano; (d) vocal tract shape modified such that the constriction indicated by the circle was slightly released; (e) frequency response of the modified vocal tract shape in (d).

refers to small localized modifications of a particular vocal tract shape already in place for a specific vowel, but can alter the positions of the formants in such ways that the output is significantly enhanced in quality, and may also facilitate the efficient transfer of energy from laryngeal source to the radiated sound at the lips. There is still much to be learned about the tuning aspect of the vocal tract for purposes of voice quality.

ACKNOWLEDGMENTS

Portions of this work were supported by grant R01 DC011275 from the National Institutes on Deafness and Other Communication Disorders.

REFERENCES

Baer, T., Gore, J.C., Gracco, L.C., and Nye, P.W. (1991). Analysis of vocal tract shape and dimensions using magnetic resonance imaging: Vowels. *Journal of the Acoustical Society of America* 90: 799–828.

Bartholomew, W.T. (1934). A physical definition of "good voice-quality" in the male voice. *Journal of the Acoustical Society of America* 6: 25–33.

Bell, A.G. (1911). *The Mechanism of Speech*, 5th edn. New York: Funk and Wagnalls.

Dang, J. and Honda, K. (1997). Acoustic characteristics of the piriform fossa in models and humans. *Journal of the Acoustical Society of America* 101(1): 456–465.

Detweiler, R. (1994). Investigation of the laryngeal system as the resonance source of the singer's formant. *Journal of Voice* 8(4): 303–313.

Echternach, M., Sundberg, J., Baumann, T., Markl, M., and Richter, B. (2011). Vocal tract area functions and formant frequencies in opera tenors' modal and falsetto registers. *Journal of the Acoustical Society of America* 129(6): 3955–3963.

Fant, G. (1960). *Acoustic Theory of Speech Production*. The Hague: Mouton.

Fant, G. and Pauli, S. (1974). Spatial characteristics of vocal tract resonance modes. *Proceedings of Speech Communication Seminar 74* (Stockholm, Sweden, August 1–3): 121–132.

Heinz, J.M. and Stevens, K.N. (1964). On the derivation of area functions and acoustic spectra from cineradiographic films of speech. *Journal of the Acoustical Society of America* 36(5): 1037–1038.

Hillenbrand, J., Getty, L.A., Clark, M.J., and Wheeler, K. (1995). Acoustic characteristics of American English vowels. *Journal of the Acoustical Society of America* 97(5): 3099–3111.

Lewis, D. (1936). Vocal resonance. *Journal of the Acoustical Society of America* 8: 91–99.

Miller, R. (1996). *On the Art of Singing*. New York: Oxford.

Peterson, G.E. and Barney, H.L. (1952). Control methods used in a study of the vowels. *Journal of the Acoustical Society of America* 24(2): 175–184.

Stevens, K.N. (2000). *Acoustic Phonetics*. Cambridge, MA: MIT Press.

Story, B.H. (1995). *Physiologically-based speech simulation using an enhanced wave-reflection model of the vocal tract*, PhD dissertation. Iowa City: University of Iowa.

Story, B.H., Titze, I.R., and Hoffman, E.A. (1996). Vocal tract area functions from magnetic resonance imaging. *Journal of the Acoustical Society of America* 100(1): 537–554.

Story, B.H., Titze, I.R., and Hoffman, E.A. (1998). Vocal tract area functions for an adult female speaker based on volumetric imaging. *Journal of the Acoustical Society of America* 104(1): 471–487.

Story, B.H., Titze, I.R., and Hoffman, E.A. (2001). The relationship of vocal tract shape to three voice qualities. *Journal of the Acoustical Society of America* 109: 1651–1667.

Story, B.H. (2004). Vowel acoustics for speaking and singing. *Acta Acustica/Acustica* 90(4): 629–640.

Story, B.H. (2005). Synergistic modes of vocal tract articulation for American English vowels. *Journal of the Acoustical Society of America* 118(6): 3834–3859.

Story, B.H. (2006). A technique for "tuning" vocal tract area functions based on acoustic sensitivity functions. *Journal of the Acoustical Society of America* 119(2): 715–718.

Story, B.H. (2008). Comparison of magnetic resonance imaging-based vocal tract area functions obtained from the same speaker in 1994 and 2002. *Journal of the Acoustical Society of America* 123(1): 327–335.

Story, B.H. (2013). Phrase-level speech simulation with an airway modulation model of speech production. *Computer Speech and Language* 27(4): 989–1010.

Sundberg, J. (1974). Articulatory interpretation of the "singing formant." *Journal of the Acoustical Society of America* 55(4): 838–843.

Sundberg, J. (1987). From sagittal distance to area: A study of transverse, vocal tract cross-sectional area. *Phonetica* 44: 76–90.

Titze, I.R. and Story, B.H. (1997). Acoustic interactions of the voice source with the lower vocal tract. *Journal of the Acoustical Society of America* 101(4): 2234–2243.

Titze, I.R. (2006). *The Myoelastic Aerodynamic Theory of Phonation*. Iowa City: National Center for Voice and Speech.

Titze, I.R., Worley, A.S., and Story, B.H. (2011). Source-vocal tract interaction in female operatic singing and theater belting. *Journal of Singing* 67(5): 561–572.

Wang, S. (1986). Singer's high formant associated with different larynx position in styles of singing. *Journal of the Acoustical Society of Japan* 7(6): 303–314.

Weiss, R., Brown, W.S., and Morris, J. (2001). Singer's formant in sopranos: fact or fiction? *Journal of Voice* 15(4): 457–468.

Winckel, F. (1954). Scientific appraisal of singing voices. *Nature* 173: 574.

CHAPTER 8

THE ACOUSTICS OF DIFFERENT GENRES OF SINGING

JOHAN SUNDBERG

INTRODUCTION

MAN is a most inventive creature. The use of the breathing and chewing organ is just one example of this, although a very striking one. Phylogenetically the task of these organs is essential to maintain life, but they are used as a well-controlled acoustic instrument, not only for spoken communication, but also for esthetical purposes in singing. Interestingly, the ways in which the voice is used in different cultures varies widely, and many of these ways deviate substantially from how the voice is used in speech.

The human voice has attracted great interest among researchers, mainly as an instrument for speech production. However, during the last half century a great number of research articles have been published which also analyze the voice as a music instrument, i.e. singing. Most research has been devoted to the classical Western style of singing, but over the last half century other styles of singing have attracted voice researchers' attention, e.g. belt, musical theater, rock, folkloristic. The aim has been to describe acoustic properties as well as sound production characteristics, but a major problem has been that the same term does not always refer to the same style. A solution may be to define styles of singing in terms of the total phonatory and articulatory potentials of the voice.

Basic voice research continues to inform our understanding of how the voice works and how the sound quality changes when the physiological control parameters are changed. In this chapter a description of production changes and the resulting sound quality variations will first be provided. Then, some examples of voice use in different singing styles will be reviewed.

THEORETICAL FRAMEWORK AND BASIC PRINCIPLES

Function

The human voice organ consists of three components, as is illustrated schematically in Figure 8.1. One is the breathing apparatus, which acts as a compressor: it compresses the air contained in the lungs. The second is the vocal folds, which act as a sound generator: by vibrating they chop the airstream from the lungs into a sequence of air pulses, which is actually a sound. It sounds like a buzz and contains an unbroken series of harmonic partials. The third part is the vocal tract, which consists of the pharynx and mouth cavities; it acts as a resonator, or a filter, which shapes the sound generated by the vocal folds. When the velopharyngeal port is open, as when producing nasal sounds, the velum is lowered, opening the airway to the nasal cavity, or the nasal tract. Then, also the nasal tract is included in the resonator system.

Of the three parts, only the vocal folds and the vocal tract contribute directly to forming vocal timbre. In other words, the acoustic characteristics of the voice are determined by two factors: (1) the voice source, i.e. the pulsating airflow passing through the slit between the vocal folds, known as the glottis, and (2), the vocal tract.

The voice source is a pulsating airflow, as shown in Figure 8.2. It is controlled by three major parameters: (1) subglottal pressure for varying vocal loudness; (2) stretching and

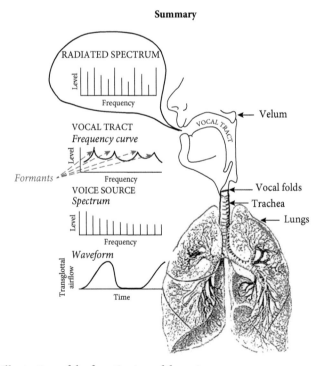

FIGURE 8.1 Illustration of the functioning of the voice organ.

After Sundberg 1987.

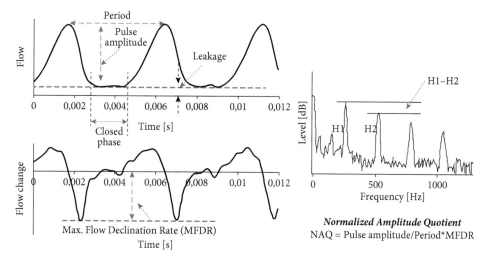

FIGURE 8.2 Voice source parameters derived from a flow glottogram and its derivative (upper and lower left panels) and from its spectrum (right panel).

stiffening the vocal folds for regulating the fundamental frequency f_o; and (3) vocal fold adduction for varying type of phonation.

The acoustic consequences of varying these control parameters are not quite independent. An increase of subglottal pressure accelerates the decline of flow during the closing of the glottis. This causes an increase of sound level and a less steeply sloping spectrum. A rise of subglottal pressure also raises f_o somewhat, everything else being constant. Stretching and stiffening the vocal folds causes f_o to rise, but may also affect the degree of glottal adduction. Adducting the folds more firmly causes a lengthening of the closed phase and a reduction of the peak airflow amplitude of the glottal vibratory cycle. This in turn mainly leads to a weakening of the voice source fundamental.

The resonances of the vocal tract are called formants and the shape of the vocal tract frequency response curve is determined by the frequencies of these formants. The curve rises to peaks at the formant frequencies and the peaks are separated by valleys, as shown in Figure 8.3. The closer two formants are in frequency, the higher their peaks in the frequency curve and the more shallow the valley between these peaks. Five formants are important to voice timbre, referred to as F1, F2, F3, F4, and F5.

The frequencies of the formants are determined by the shape of the vocal tract which can be varied by the articulators: the lip and jaw openings, the position of the tongue body and the tongue tip, and the position of the larynx. The articulatory configuration can be described in terms the area function, which shows how the cross-sectional vocal tract area varies along the vocal tract length axis.

Some articulators are particularly efficient in tuning certain formant frequencies. A widening of the jaw opening expands the vocal tract in the lip region and constricts it in the laryngeal region, which raises F1. In vowels produced by male adults, F1 varies between approximately 200 and 800 Hz. F2 is particularly sensitive to the tongue shape. In male adults it varies within a range of about 500 to 2500 Hz. F3 is especially sensitive to the position of the tip of the tongue or, when the tongue is retracted, to the size of the cavity

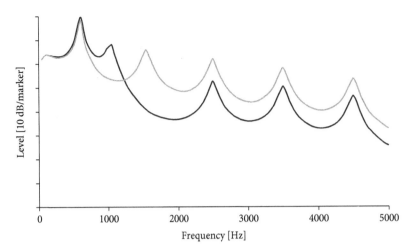

FIGURE 8.3 Idealized spectrum envelopes resulting from changing F2 from 1500 Hz to 1050 Hz, while keeping the remaining formants at 500 Hz, 2500 Hz, 3500 Hz, and 4500 Hz.

between the lower incisors and the tongue. In vowels produced by male adults, F3 varies between approximately 1600 and 3500 Hz. The relationships between the vocal tract shape and the fourth and fifth formants (F4 and F5) are more complicated and difficult to control by specific articulatory means. However, they seem to be very dependent on vocal tract length and also on the configuration in the deep pharynx. In vowels produced by adult males, F4 is generally in the vicinity of 2500 to 4000 Hz and F5 approximately 3000 to 4500 Hz.

As formants determine the frequency curve of the vocal tract it is evident that the formant frequencies have a great effect on the spectrum. At intermediate degrees of vocal loudness, the spectrum envelope of the voice source slopes off at a rate of approximately twelve decibels (dB) per octave, if measured in airflow units. However, the slope decreases if vocal loudness is increased. The spectrum of a radiated vowel is characterized by peaks and valleys, because the partials lying closest to a formant frequency get stronger than adjacent partials in the spectrum. In this way, the vocal tract resonances "form" the vowel spectrum (this probably is the reason why they are called formants).

Recalling that formants are vocal tract resonances, we realize that it is by means of vocal tract resonances that we form vowels. F1 and F2 generally define vowel quality completely according to a code, as is illustrated in Figure 8.4. Thus, if F1 is near 300 Hz and F2 near 700 Hz or 2000 Hz, the resulting vowels are /u/ as in the English word *boot*, and /i/ as in the word *beat*, respectively, and if they are near 700 Hz and 1100 Hz, the resulting vowel is /a/ as in the word *spa*.

Summarizing, the acoustical properties of the voice are controlled by the combination of voice source and formant frequencies. The former is controlled by subglottal pressure, tensing and stretching of the vocal folds, and by glottal adduction and the latter by vocal tract shape, i.e. by articulation. Contributions to a description of how the voice is used in a particular style can therefore be in terms of any of these parameters.

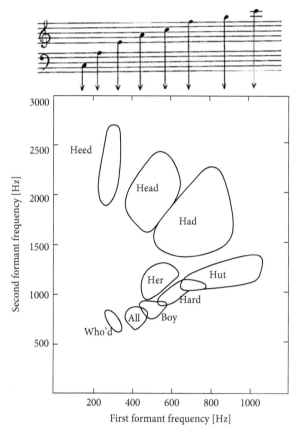

FIGURE 8.4 Typical mean values for the two lowest formant frequencies for various spoken vowels as produced by male and female adults. The first formant frequency is given in musical notation at the top.

After Sundberg 1987.

REVIEW OF RESEARCH

Classical Western Operatic Singing

Singing at Super Pitches

In speech f_o is mostly lower than the normal value of F1: in female and male adults mean f_o is generally in the neighborhood of 200 and 100 Hz, respectively, while the lowest F1 value of vowels is about 250 Hz (see Figure 8.4). This frequency approximately corresponds to the pitch of C4. In singing, by contrast, f_o is often higher than this pitch. In such cases singers have been found to modify F1 to a greater or lesser degree.

It is difficult to measure formant frequencies when f_o is high, since the partials are then widely spaced along the frequency continuum. Under these conditions special tricks are needed for measuring formants, and several have been tried. One is to excite the vocal tract by means of a vibrator held against the neck while the singer is silently articulating a vowel (Sundberg 1975). Alternatively, ingressive phonation during vowel articulation has been tried (Schutte et al. 2005). Another method is to take an X-ray or MR picture of the vocal tract in profile and then estimate the area function, which, in turn, can be used for calculating the formant frequencies (Fant 1960). A third method is to excite the singer's vocal tract during singing with a low frequency complex tone, obtained from a signal generator, and measure the vocal tract response to this sound (Henrich et al. 2011).

The results from investigations using either of these different methods of measurement agree quite well in certain respects. Figure 8.5 shows typical results, obtained from a single professional soprano. The framed data points to the left in the graph pertain to the subject's speech. A general principle seemed to be that f_o is not allowed to pass F1, so F1 is raised whenever needed to avoid that situation. At high pitches, F2 is lowered in front vowels, while in back vowels it is raised to a frequency just above the second spectrum partial; F3 is lowered, and F4 is raised. These findings seem representative of classically trained singers.

Widening the jaw opening is an efficient articulatory method for increasing F1. However, in most vowels also a widening of a narrow tongue constriction will lead to the same effect (Sundberg 2009).

All singers except perhaps basses encounter the situation that the normal F1 value is lower than f_o, at least for some vowels when sung at high pitches. As F1 differs between

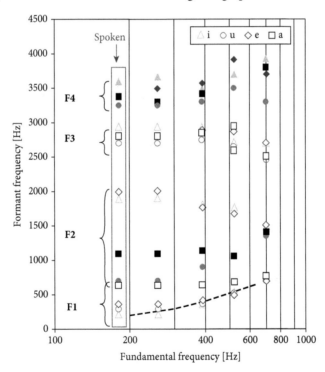

FIGURE 8.5 Formant frequencies for the indicated vowels observed in a soprano singing at the indicated f_o values and pronouncing the same vowels in speech. The framed values to the left show the subject's formant frequencies in neutral speech; in the right part of the graph the dashed curve represents f_o.

After Sundberg 1987.

vowels, the case depends on the vowel, as can be seen in Figure 8.4. In the highest range of a baritone, the vowels /i/ and /u/ would need pitch-dependent F1. Similarly, in the top part of an alto's range, all vowels except /a/ and /ae/ need modification of F1. However, according to Miller and Schutte (1993) sopranos have their F1 below f_o in the so-called flageolet or whistle register.

The benefit of the principle of avoiding f_o>F1 is a significant gain in sound level, sometimes more than 10 dB. As this gain is produced by resonance rather than by vocal effort, the principle can be seen as an example of vocal economy or efficiency.

It is often assumed that successful male singers tend to tune F1 and/or F2 to spectrum partials, also when f_o is far below F1 (see, e.g. Miller 2008). Henrich and associates (2011) observed several examples of such formant tuning in both male and female singers. On the other hand, Titze (2008) found that tuning F1 or F2 to spectrum partials entails the risk of phonatory instability. Measurements on professional operatic tenors and baritones by Sundberg and associates (2011) and by Echternach and associates (2010) found support neither for the assumption that singers deliberately tune F1 or F2 to partials, nor for the idea that they avoid such coincidences.

Singer's Formant Cluster

An important characteristic of male operatic singers is a marked spectrum envelope peak near 3000 Hz, mostly referred to as the singer's formant. Figure 8.6 shows a typical example. First observed by Bartholomew (1934), it has attracted many voice researchers' attention. It is typically present in all voiced sounds and it can be explained as a resonatory phenomenon caused by a clustering of F3, F4, and F5 (Sundberg 1974). Such a clustering

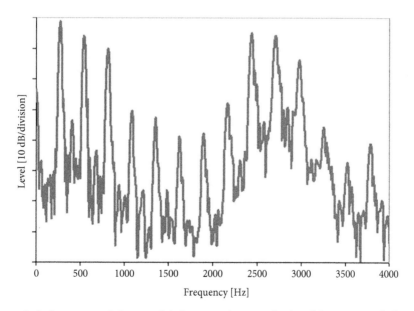

FIGURE 8.6 Spectrum of the vowel /u/ as sung by a professional baritone and showing a highly prominent singer's formant cluster.

can result when the exit of the larynx tube (or epilaryngeal tube) is narrow as compared to the cross-sectional pharynx area at that level. When this exit is narrower than one-sixth of the pharyngeal area, the resonance of the larynx tube is almost entirely independent of the rest of the vocal tract.

Under certain conditions the larynx tube resonance can appear at a frequency, such that it forms a formant cluster together with the normal third and fourth formants. Thus, male opera singers often have five formants in the frequency range where male untrained voices have four. It seems that in many singers this effect is obtained by a lowering of the larynx. As the spectrum peak is produced by clustering three formants, the author has suggested that it should be called the singer's formant cluster.

The acoustic consequence of clustering formants is that the spectrum partials in the frequency range of the cluster are enhanced in the radiated spectrum. In other words, the singer's formant cluster is compatible with the normal concept of voice production, provided a clustering of the higher formants is achieved.

The center frequency of the singer's formant cluster typically varies depending on the voice category (see Figure 8.7). In bass singers, it is often found around 2.4 kHz, in baritones around 2.6, and in tenors around 2.8; but there are great individual variations (Dmitriev and Kiselev 1979). These frequency differences, although seemingly very small, contribute significantly to the timbral differences between these voice categories (Berndtsson and Sundberg 1995).

The level of the singer's formant cluster varies with loudness of phonation. An SPL increase of 10 dB is typically accompanied by about 15 dB increase of the singer's formant cluster (Sjölander and Sundberg 2004). This effect on the overall spectrum slope is produced by the voice source.

The presence of the singer's formant cluster helps the singer's voice to cut through a loud orchestral accompaniment. The strongest partials in the spectrum of a symphonic orchestra

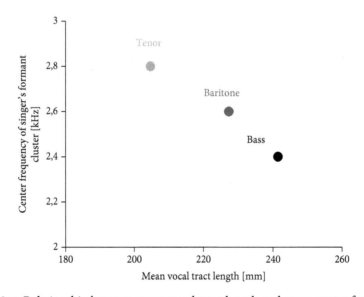

FIGURE 8.7 Relationship between mean vocal tract length and mean center frequency of the singer's formant cluster.

Adapted from Dmitriev and Kiselev 1979.

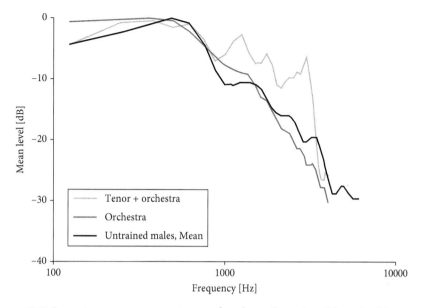

FIGURE 8.8 Long-term-average spectrum of orchestral music with and without a solo singer's voice and of untrained male voices speaking at an equivalent sound level of 80 dB at 0.3 m distance.

After Sundberg 1987.

generally occur in the range of 500 Hz to 700 Hz; above this frequency region, the levels of the spectrum components decrease by about 9 dB per octave (see Figure 8.8). The perceptual point with a singer's formant cluster is to enhance the spectrum partials in a frequency range where the competition with the sound of the accompaniment is less severe. This effect cannot be achieved by a normal speaking voice, because its long-term-average spectrum slope above 500 Hz is similar to that of a symphony orchestra. In other words, the singer's formant cluster can be seen as an example of vocal economy.

The particular vocal tract arrangements that generate vowels with a singer's formant cluster have certain consequences for F1 and F2, i.e. for vowel quality as well. In male operatic singing F2 and F3 of /i/ are low, almost as low as in the German vowel /y/. This is in accordance with the common observation that vowels are "colored" in singing. This deviation from the vowel qualities used in speech can be seen as the price that the singer pays in order to obtain his singer's formant cluster.

The singer's formant cluster seems specific to the classical operatic style of singing. It is not found among artists who sing in non-classical, pop music styles, such as country or rock. It is interesting that in these styles, the singer is provided with a sound amplification system that ensures that the voice of the soloist can also be heard over a loud accompaniment.

Choral Singing

A frequently discussed question is to what extent choral singing requires the same vocal technique as solo singing. Some claim that there are no relevant differences, whereas others see differences that are quite important to vocal technique. Because the singer's formant

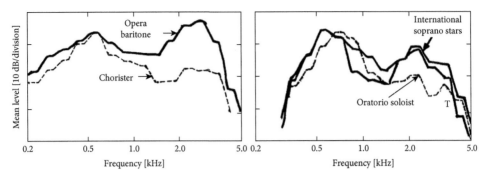

FIGURE 8.9 Long-term-average spectra of male soloists and choristers, and of female opera stars and a local soloist (left and right panels).

From Rossing et al. 1986, 1987.

cluster apparently serves to help the individual singer's voice to be heard through a loud orchestral accompaniment, it can be hypothesized that there is no need for it in choral singing. This hypothesis was supported by experiments in which male singers with considerable experience both as choristers and soloists, were asked to sing in a choral and in a solo framework (Rossing et al. 1986). In the solo singing condition, they heard through earphones the piano accompaniment of a solo song that they were to sing. In the choir singing condition, they heard the sound of a choir that they were asked to join. As shown in Figure 8.9, the subjects had a singer's formant cluster that was more prominent in the solo than in the choral condition. Also, the spectrum partials below the first formant were stronger in the choral setting. The higher level of the singer's formant cluster in solo singing was associated with a denser clustering of the third, fourth, and fifth formant frequencies. Unlike most choral singers these subjects were also performing as solo singers. Therefore, it can be assumed that the differences between solo and choir singing are generally greater than was found in this study.

A corresponding experiment was performed with soprano subjects (Rossing et al. 1987). Although soprano singers do not produce a singer's formant cluster, the result was qualitatively similar to that found for the male choral and solo singers. The mean spectrum level between 2 and 3 kHz was clearly higher when the singers sang in a solo mode. Moreover, as can be seen from Figure 8.9, two opera sopranos of world fame were found to sing with clearly stronger partials in the 2 to 4 kHz range than a singer who worked both as a choral and solo singer.

Non-classical Styles of Singing

Musical Theater

The voice timbre differences between musical theater and western opera singer voices are considerable. Figure 8.10 illustrates the differences in terms of long term average spectra, or LTAS, analyses of four baritone voices, two opera singers and two musical theater singers. There are two striking differences. The most apparent is the singer's formant cluster which

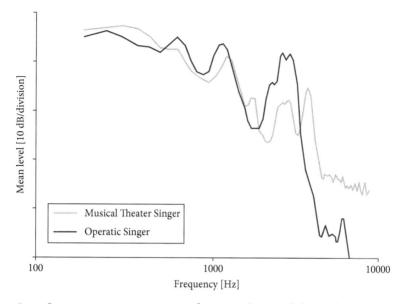

FIGURE 8.10 Long-term-average spectra of opera and musical theater baritones.

produced a marked peak near 2700 Hz in the opera singers' LTAS. The musical theater singers, by contrast, produced a less prominent but marked peak about 1000 Hz higher. These differences can be assumed to be typical and perceptually relevant.

Björkner (2008) compared subglottal pressure, voice source properties and formant frequencies in five baritone representatives of each singer group. On average the musical theater singers tended to use higher subglottal pressures than the opera singers, but systematic differences became evident after normalization of subglottal pressure. As can be seen in Figure 8.11, the opera singers exhibited lower closed quotients, stronger voice source fundamental, and, for the loudest tones, also higher NAQ values, the latter being an abduction measure defined as the ratio between the flow pulse amplitude and the product of f_o and the maximum flow declination rate. Most of these differences seemed related to the musical theater singers' use of high subglottal pressure. The differences at normalized pressures are probably relevant to the timbral differences between these two singing styles. In addition, the opera singers tended to use lower formant frequencies for the vowel /ae/ and clustered F3, F4, and F5 as needed for embellishing the timbre with a singer's formant cluster.

Broadway

Stone and associates (2003) studied formant and voice source differences between a Broadway and an operatic style of singing performed by the same female single subject. A listening test was carried out to find out how representative the examples were of the respective styles. The study revealed several measures that appeared to distinguish the two singing styles. (Note that in the Stone article, Figure 8.3, p. 288, the opera and Broadway LTAS have been switched, and in the Conclusions section, line 13, "open phase" should read "closed phase.") The long-term-average spectrum of the operatic style showed a

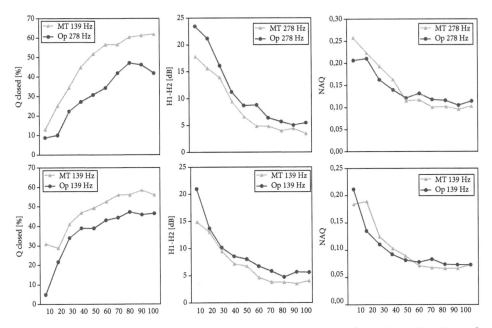

FIGURE 8.11 Averages of the voice source chracteristics closed quotient, H1–H2, and NAQ observed for the indicated normalized subglottal pressures at f_o "139 Hz and 278 Hz (lower and upper panels)" in musical theater (MT) and opera (Op) baritones. Pressures are given as % of the singer's total range for the respective pitch.

Data from Björkner 2006.

marked peak produced by a strong fundamental and weaker partials in the range of 800 to 2600 Hz (see Figure 8.12). The strong fundamental originated from the voice source which had a shorter closed phase, but also a lower F1 would have contributed. These differences suggest that glottal adduction was stronger in the Broadway than in the operatic style, the voice source characteristics of which were somewhat similar to those found in loud speech. Vibrato was found in both singing styles but less often in Broadway.

Twang

The term "Twang" is used with a number of differing meanings. Originally an onomatopoeia for the sound of a vibrating string (e.g. from a bow when shooting an arrow, or a musical instrument), it is often used for a sharp vibrating sound, characteristic of some electric guitars. In the voice area it means a special quality which seems related to strong high frequency overtones. Indeed, some authors argue that the singer's formant cluster is an example of twang. Generally, however, it refers to a special style of loud singing used as a timbral ornament in non-classical popular music.

Yanagisawa and associates (1989) examined vocal tract characteristics during twang and other vocal styles. They observed a constriction of the aryepiglottic region caused by an approximation of the epiglottis and the arytenoid cartilages. However, this characteristic was also observed in operatic style of singing so it was not specific to twang.

Titze and associates (2001) studied the "yawn-twangy" difference. Analysis of MR images of a female and a male subject who deliberately phonated in these two modes revealed that

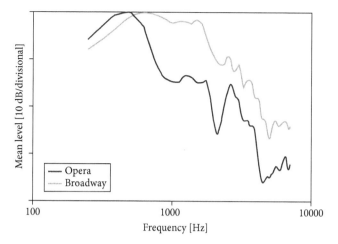

FIGURE 8.12 Long-term-average spectra of a professional singer singing the same song in operatic and Broadway style.

F1 and F2 were closer together in yawn and wider apart in twangy. Later, these findings were further analyzed in an attempt to identify the perceptual characteristics of the yawn-twangy contrast. Both phonation types were synthesized with a system combining a model of glottal airflow with an area function model of the vocal tract; the results were presented to a listening panel (Titze et al. 2003). The synthesis was a set of repetitions of the syllable /ja/ produced with a speech-like intonation. The open quotient of the voice source was varied along a continuum ranging from long to normal to short. Also varied were overall vocal tract length and pharyngeal constriction. A listening panel rated the degree of "twang" perceived in these synthesized stimuli. The results showed that all three parameters affected the mean rating values. Thus, the perception of "twang" was promoted by an increased closed quotient, by a shortening of the vocal tract, and by a narrowing of the pharyngeal area.

Sundberg and Thalén (2010) compared voice source characteristics and formant frequencies in examples sung by a professional singer in twang and in a neutral, non-twang production. An expert panel rated the "twanginess" of the examples in a listening test. SPL was higher in twang and the LTAS showed considerably more sound energy in the region 600–3000 Hz in twang than in neutral, particularly just below 2000 Hz (see right graph of Figure 8.13). The source analyses, performed by inverse filtering, revealed a weaker voice source fundamental, a longer closed phase and a lower normalized amplitude quotient in twang. These differences suggested a higher degree of glottal adduction in twang. Moreover F1 and F2 were higher in twang but F3 was lower (see right graph of Figure 8.13). The reduced frequency separation of F3 and F2 was assumed to contribute or even explain the high LTAS level just below 2000 Hz. A multiple regression analysis of the mean ratings of twanginess and the voice source and formant frequency data showed that significant contributions to perceived twanginess originated from both source and formant frequencies, with the latter seeming more important.

Belt

Belt is a type of very loud voice frequently used to intensify expressivity in genres such as musical theater and pop music singing. In operatic style it is not used. It has been investigated by several authors with respect to both its acoustic and physiological properties, but the results

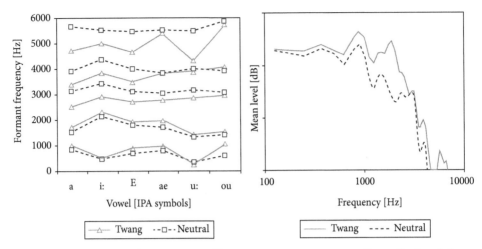

FIGURE 8.13 Formant frequencies and long-term-average spectra of a professional singer performing the same song non-nasalized in a neutral and in a twang style.

After Sundberg and Thalén 2010.

are somewhat conflicting. It is characterized by high SPL, a voice production sounding like chest register, and an f_o range mostly about C4–C5, even though Estill (1998) describes a method to produce belt tones up to much higher pitches. Anyway, belt differs substantially from classical, operatic singing, where female singers typically shift register to "middle" or "mixed" in the vicinity of E4–G#4.

LeBorgne and associates (2010) asked casting directors to evaluate the belt voice quality in song examples produced by twenty female musical theater singers, all proficient in the belt voice singing style. The listeners were asked to rate the voices along seven perceptual parameters (loudness, vibrato, ring, timbre, focus, nasality, and registration breaks), and then to give an overall score for these student belters. The results showed that vibrato and ring were the most decisive parameters to these casting directors' evaluations. These parameters also showed a strong correlation with perceived loudness.

With regard to the technique used for producing belt voice there are conflicting views. Schutte and Miller (1993) and Bestebreurtje and Schutte (2000) analyzed some recordings and also a single professional singer. They arrived at the conclusion that the characteristic loud, bright sound of the belting style was achieved by tuning F1 to $2 \times f_o$, i.e. to the second harmonic. In this way, this partial could be 20 dB stronger than the fundamental. Moreover, they found that belt was produced with a contact quotient (CQ) exceeding fifty-two percent. Lebowitz and Baken (2011) analyzed twenty singers in both legit and belt styles. They found that the contact quotient (CQ) did not differ consistently between the styles and was often also lower than fifty percent in belt voice. Further, they noted that the fundamental was always stronger than the second partial in legit but sometimes also in belt.

Titze and Worley (2009) argued that in the vowels used in belt, F1 is tuned to a frequency higher than $2 \times f_o$, i.e. above the second partial. Inferring vocal tract area functions from photos of the faces of well-known singing artists they concluded that belt is produced with megaphone-like vocal tract shape. Their reasoning appears to apply mainly to the vowels /æ/ and /a/, the high F1 of which make them particularly adequate to use in belt voice.

Some teachers of singing assume that belt can be produced in a healthy way only if a particular breathing technique is used. Using inductive respiratory plethysmography, Sundberg and Thalén (2015) analyzed the breathing strategy of six female singers, who had all been professionally performing in the belt styles for many years. They were asked to sing an excerpt of a song in belt and non-belt/neutral style. Neither for belt, nor for the non-belt style, were any consistent breathing patterns observed among the singers for lung volume change, inhalation, and phonation. Analyses of subglottal pressure and voice source revealed that belt was produced with higher pressures and higher sound levels and with firmer glottal adduction than non-belt. In four of the singers, the first formant was closer to a spectrum harmonic in belt than in neutral. Thus the results failed to corroborate the idea that belt is associated with a specific breathing behavior.

Country

The special singing style used in country music has been analyzed in a series of studies (Cleveland et al. 1997; Stone et al. 1999; Sundberg et al. 1999). Country singers were found to increase subglottal pressure with both pitch and loudness, just as classically trained singers, even though the highest subglottal pressures were higher than in classical singing. The singers' subglottal pressures were similar in speech and singing at similar degrees of vocal loudness, while the country singers' SPL tended to be somewhat lower than that produced by opera singers at comparable subglottal pressures.

LTAS characteristics of country singers' voices were found to be similar in speech and song and showed no signs of a singer's formant cluster. Rather, the LTAS curves showed a prominent peak near 3.3 kHz. Such a peak has been found also in "good" radio announcers' voices and has been referred to as the "speaker's formant" (Leino et al. 2011). The voice source properties varied both between and within the singers, suggesting a variation of the degree of phonatory pressedness. Within singer, the degree of mean perceived phonatory press increased with the center pitch of the songs performed. Thus, the singers apparently tended to sing high pitches with a firmer glottal adduction than low pitches. The closed quotient seemed rather independent of pitch but tended to increase with subglottal pressure, reaching a maximum of around 0.6 in both speech and singing. The singers also seemed to use similar or somewhat higher formant frequencies than in speech. The results suggest that, by and large, country singers use speech-like phonatory and articulatory habits.

Rock, Blues, Soul, Pop, Jazz

Different singer classifications obviously have different f_o ranges. When comparing vocal styles it therefore is often meaningful to normalize f_o range to find out what the voice characteristics are at, say, twenty, fifty, and eighty percent of the pitch range. But vocal styles do not differ only with regard to f_o range. For example, as mentioned above, male opera singers use lower subglottal pressure ranges than their musical theater colleagues, and lyric sopranos tend to use lower pressure ranges than dramatic sopranos. Therefore it is sometimes informative to also normalize pressures when comparing voice source properties. Such comparisons can then show voice properties associated with e.g. twenty, fifty, and eighty percent of the singer's pressure range when phonating at a specific percent of the pitch range. These ideas underpinned two single-subject studies of different non-classical singing styles.

The relationship between NAQ and perceived phonatory pressedness was analyzed in material collected from a single professional female singer and teacher of singing (Sundberg and Thalén 2001). In three different loudness conditions she sang a triad pattern in breathy, flow, neutral, and pressed phonation, and also in four different styles of singing: classical, pop, jazz, and blues. A panel of experts rated the degree of perceived phonatory pressedness along visual analogue scales. As illustrated in the left graph of Figure 8.14 the mean pressedness ratings correlated with the mean NAQ values ($R2 = .73$). The right graph of Figure 8.14 shows the results in terms of a "phonation map," where mean NAQ is plotted against mean normalized subglottal pressure. In the map, the styles and phonation types are clearly differentiated, with classical being close to flow phonation with a large NAQ and low pressure and blues lying close to pressed with a low NAQ and a high subglottal pressure; pop and jazz assumed values closer to flow than to pressed.

The voice types used in rock, pop, soul, and Swedish dance band were analyzed in another single-subject study (Zangger Borch and Sundberg 2011). Song examples were recorded of a male singer who had extensive professional experience of performing in these genres. In addition, he sang tones in a triad pattern ranging from low to high pitch in pressed and neutral phonation. An expert panel was then asked to classify the song samples; the result supported the assumption that the samples were typical of the styles. Formants F1 and F2 were lowest in soul, possibly reflecting a relatively low larynx position, whereas F1 was high in pop and rock. With respect to the average f_o and the average NAQ, rock and the Swedish dance band assumed extreme positions, as shown in Figure 8.15.

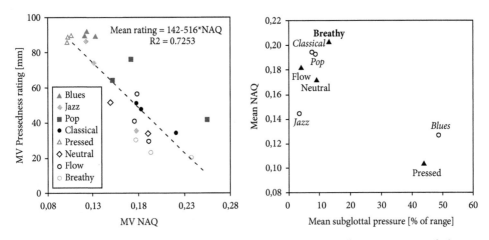

FIGURE 8.14 Left panel. Relationship between an expert panel's mean rating of phonatory pressedness and mean NAQ values. Right panel. Mean NAQ values and normalized subglottal pressures observed in a professional non-classical female singer singing in the indicated styles and with the indicated phonation types.

After Sundberg and Thalén (2010).

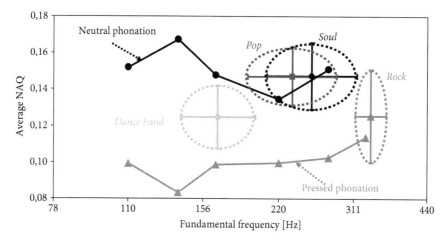

FIGURE 8.15 Average NAQ values plotted as a function of average log f_o. The black and gray curves refer to the values observed in the subject's neutral and pressed phonation. The symbols and the axes of the surrounding ellipses show the averages and the standard deviation of f_o and NAQ observed in the indicated styles.

From Zangger-Borch and Sundberg (2011).

Overtone Singing

Overtone singing is a remarkable vocal style, where the singer basically produces two tones at the same time. The explanation is that an overtone in the spectrum of a sung, constant drone tone is strongly enhanced, such that it dominates the spectrum (Bloothooft et al. 1992). Figure 8.16 shows an example where the ninth partial is enhanced so much that its level exceeds those of partials 1 and 2 by almost 15 dB. The arrows in the graph show a distribution of formant frequencies likely to produce this spectrum. While F1 is tuned to the second partial, F2 and F3 are clustered, lying at 1690 Hz and 1850 Hz, respectively, thus no more than 160 Hz apart. To enhance another partial of the drone, the formant cluster is tuned to that partial. When a lower partial is enhanced, F1 and F2 may be the crucial actors, complemented by a slight nasalization. In these ways the singer can play melodies by enhancing different overtones. It is not surprising that these extremely strong partials tend to catch a listener's attention; particularly as the drone tone does not change.

The underlying articulation seems to be a subtle adjustment of tongue body shape, form and position of the tongue tip, jaw opening, lip opening and velum. In addition, the voice source characteristics seem to be adjusted so that the fundamental is suppressed by means of a closed phase that is extended by means of a more pressed phonation.

Folk music

Henrich and associates (2007) analyzed Bulgarian singing technique as performed by a single female singer. Formant frequencies for different vowels sung at different pitches were measured from the vocal tract response to excitation at the lip opening during singing. Two different vocal qualities of this style were studied, the louder *teshka*, and the

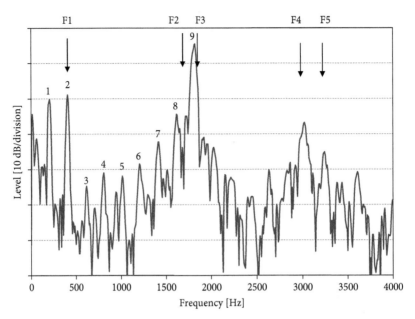

FIGURE 8.16 Spectrum of a tone produced in the overtone singing style, enhancing the ninth partial. The arrows show estimated frequencies of the indicated formants.

softer *leka*. The pitch range of the song was quite narrow, no more than half an octave, between F4 and B4. In both qualities the singer tuned the first formant close to the second spectrum partial in most vowels. This made this partial very strong and also added to the overall sound level produced. At the same time, it obviously compromised the differentiation of the various vowels.

Boersmaa and Kovacic (2006) examined the differences between three Croatian folk singing styles, *klapa, ojkanje*, and *tarankanje*, all belonging to the traditional music culture of Croatia. The *klapa* style (klapa meaning group of friends) is typically soft and slow, and usually performed *a cappella* with multiple parts in harmony; it also uses a Western European scale. The *tarankanje* style uses six narrowly spaced scale tones which do not correspond to those of the Western musical notation. It accompanies dance and the lyrics consists of strings of meaningless syllables. The ancient *ojkanje* style is sung as a loud "wild howl." It uses narrow non-Western intervals and is often perceived by outsiders as shouting or non-music. Each style was performed by the same twelve professional male singers. The thirty-six performances were analyzed in terms of LTAS. A principal-component analysis combined with a measure reflecting the overall slope of the LTAS curves allowed representation of the data in a graph with the axes spectral slope and level of an LTAS peak occurring in the frequency range of the speaker's formant. The three styles were clearly separated in this graph. The spectrum of the *klapa* style was found to be similar to that of speech. The extremely loud *ojkanje* style showed a broad speaker's formant peak near 3.5 kHz, and also a peak at twice the fundamental frequency, presumably produced by careful formant tuning. The *tarankanje* style had a flat LTAS contour, assumedly produced by vocal pressedness and nasality.

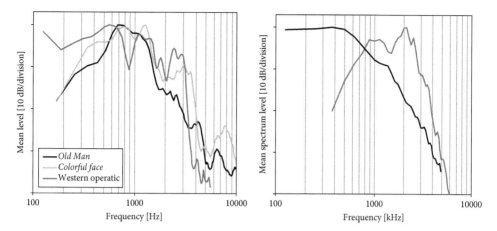

FIGURE 8.17 Left panel: LTAS curves, averaged across *Old Man* role singers and across *Colorful Face* role singers. The dark gray curve pertains to a professional Western operatic baritone singer. Right panel: The bright gray curve shows an LTAS curve for a section of an instrumental section of a Peking opera and, for comparison, the black curve shows a typical LTAS of Western symphonic orchestra.

From Sundberg et al. (2012).

Peking Opera

The timbral characteristics of classical opera singing differ considerably between the Western and the Chinese cultures. In the classical Peking opera tradition singers mostly specialize on one out of a limited number of standard roles. Voice characteristics of a group of singers specialized in the *Old Man* role and in the *Colorful Face* role have been studied (Sundberg et al. 2011). As illustraxted in Figure 8.17, the results showed no LTAS peaks comparable to a singer's formant cluster, but the LTAS of the *Colorful Face* role singers showed a spectrum peak near 3000 Hz, considerably lower than that typical of male Western opera singers and somewhat similar to the one found in musical theater singers. It is interesting that the spectral characteristics of the accompaniment are strikingly different between the Chinese and the Western opera, as illustrated in the right panel of Figure 8.17. It is tempting to speculate that Chinese opera singers would profit negligibly from a Western singer's formant cluster because of the accompaniment's strong levels at high frequencies. The spectrum of vibrato-free tones sometimes contained an unbroken series of harmonic partials reaching up to 17,000 Hz. This is in sharp contrast to what is normally seen in Western operatic singing, where the unbroken series of harmonic partials mostly reaches no higher than about 5000 or 6000 Hz. Vibrato rate of the Peking opera singers was quite slow, about 3.5 Hz, but often speeded up toward the end of the tones. This type of vibrato strongly differs from the typical rates in Western classical singing, which mostly lie between 5 and 7 Hz.

Dong and associates analyzed various aspects of singers in the classical Chinese Kunqu Opera (Dong et al. 2013, 2014a, 2014b). In this opera there is a fixed number of roles, and they perform both singing and stage speech. The analyses concerned the roles *Young Girl, Young Woman, Young Man, Old Man, and Colorful Face*. The two female roles have a pitch range comparable to those of alto, the *Young Man* is a tenor role and the *Old Man and the Colorful Face* are baritone roles. Long-term-average analysis failed to show any spectrum peak comparable to the singer's formant cluster in male Western opera singer voices, but the *Colorful Face* role singers had a peak near 3 kHz, similar to a speaker's formant. Formant tuning was observed only in one of the *Old Man* role singers and voice source analysis suggested that phonation was slightly pressed in the upper part of the pitch range.

SUMMARY

This review of several studies of singing in different styles has shown that the differences concern all the main dimensions of phonation: f_o, loudness, phonation type, and formant frequencies. Thus, the entire potential of voice quality variation is taken care of. Also, most vocal styles differ substantially from normal speech, though in quite different ways. Consider for example the extreme timbral differences between our Western classical opera voice and those performing within the Peking opera culture. Both differ hugely from normal speech but in quite different ways. It is then an interesting question what factors may determine the development of voice characteristics in different styles of singing.

One factor would be the acoustic environment. If the accompaniment is loud, the singer's voice also needs to be loud. Moreover, the vocal style must be adapted to the spectrum characteristics of the accompaniment. The singer's formant cluster is a striking example of this, located in a frequency range where the competition with the accompaniment is perhaps up to 20 dB softer than in the low frequency range. Furthermore, the absence of such a spectrum property in the Peking opera style of singing seems logical, since in that culture the mean spectrum of the accompaniment tends to be soft in the low frequency range and loud in the high frequency range. Similarly, the styles of singing used in popular music genres do not have a singer's formant cluster, but these artists sing with a microphone such that the audibility problems are solved by the PA system.

Another factor that would contribute to determining voice characteristics of styles of singing would be musical emphasis of the composition. In ballads the text is often telling a story and the musical framework is a melody that is repeated verse after verse. Here the emphasis is the lyrics, so text intelligibility is a major goal. This is likely to promote similarity with speech. In Western opera, on the other hand, the musical form is much more complex and thus plays a much more important role. This may allow greater excursions from the voice characteristics typical of normal speech, provided they are made for some other good purposes, such as audibility.

A difficulty in describing the characteristics of the styles of singing typical of different musical genres is that the same term does not always mean the same to all experts. As a consequence, experts can sometimes become involved in discussions about if this really is a typical example of a particular style of singing. Some diverging results in voice research on styles of singing may perhaps emerge from such terminological issues. Listening tests with expert panels may sometimes help. In any event, only objective data can put an end to the terminological confusion. Therefore, it seems important to relate descriptions of different styles of singing to the overall phonatory and articulatory potentials of the voice.

REFERENCES

Bartholomew, T. (1934). A physical definition of "good voice quality" in the male voice. *Journal of the Acoustical Society of America* 6: 25–33.

Berndtsson, G. and Sundberg, J. (1995). Perceptual significance of the center frequency of the singer's formant. *Scandinavian Journal of Logopedics and Phoniatrics* 20(1): 35–41.

Bestebreurtje, M.E. and Schutte, H.K. (2000). Resonance strategies for the belting style: Results of a single female subject study. *Journal of Voice* 14(2): 194–204.

Björkner, E. (2008). Musical theater and opera singing—Why so different? A study of subglottal pressure, voice source, and formant frequency characteristics. *Journal of Voice* 22(5): 533–40.

Bloothooft, G., Bringman, E., van Cappellen, M., et al. (1992). Acoustics of overtone singing. *Journal of the Acoustical Society of America* 92(4, part 1): 1827–36.

Boersmaa, P. and Kovacic, G. (2006). Spectral characteristics of three styles of Croatian folk singing. *Journal of the Acoustical Society of America* 119(3): 1805–16.

Cleveland, T., Stone, R.E., Sundberg, J., and Iwarsson, J. (1997). Estimated subglottal pressure in six professional country singers. *Journal of Voice* 11(4): 403–9.

Dmitriev, L., and Kiselev, A. (1979). Relationship between the formant structure of different types of singing voices and the dimension of supraglottal cavities. *Folia Phoniatrica* 31(4): 238–41.

Echternach, M., Sundberg, J., Markl, M., and Richter, B. (2010). Professional opera tenors' vocal tract configurations in registers. *Folia Phoniatrica* 62(6): 278–87.

Estill, J. (1998). Belting and classic voice quality: Some physiological differences. *Medical Problems of Performing Artists* 3(1): 37–43.

Fant, G. (1960). *Acoustic Theory of Speech Production*. The Hague: Mouton.

Henrich, N., Smith, J., and Wolfe, J. (2007). Resonance strategies used in Bulgarian women's singing style: A pilot study. *Logopedics Phoniatrics Vocology* 32(4): 171–7.

Henrich, N., Smith, J., and Wolfe, J. (2011). Vocal tract resonances in singing: Strategies used by sopranos, altos, tenors, and baritones. *Journal of the Acoustical Society of America* 129(2): 1024–35.

LeBorgne, W., Lee, L., Stemple, J.C., and Bush, H. (2010). Perceptual findings on the Broadway belt voice. *Journal of Voice* 24(6): 678–89.

Lebowitz, A. and Baken, R.J. (2011). Correlates of the belt voice: A broader examination. *Journal of Voice* 25(2): 159–65.

Leino, T., Laukkanen, A-M., and Leino, V.R. (2011). Formation of the actor's/speaker's formant: A study applying spectrum analysis and computer modeling. *Journal of Voice* 25(2): 150–8.

Miller, D.G. (2008). *Resonance in Singing. Voice Building through Acoustic Feedback*. Princeton, NJ: Inside View Press.

Miller, D.G. and Schutte, H. (1993). Physical definition of the "flageolet register." *Journal of Voice* 7(3): 206–12.

Rossing, T.D., Sundberg, J., and Ternström, S. (1987). Acoustic comparison of soprano solo and choir singing. *Journal of the Acoustical Society of America* 82(3): 830–6.

Rossing, T.D., Sundberg, J., and Ternström, S. (1986). Acoustic comparison of voice use in solo and choir singing. *Journal of the Acoustical Society of America* 79(6): 1975–81.

Schutte, H.K. and Miller, D.G. (1993). Belting and pop. Nonclassical approaches to the female middle voice: Some preliminary considerations. *Journal of Voice* 7(2): 142–50.

Schutte, H.K., Miller, D.G., and Duijnstee, M. (2005). Resonance strategies revealed in recorded tenor high notes. *Folia Phoniatrica* 57: 292–307.

Sjölander, P. and Sundberg, J. (2004). Spectrum effects of subglottal pressure variation in professional baritone singers. *Journal of the Acoustical Society of America* 115(3): 1270–3.

Stone, R.E., Cleveland, T., and Sundberg, J. (1999). Formant frequencies in country singers' speech and singing. *Journal of Voice* 13(2): 161–7.

Stone, R.E., Cleveland, T., Sundberg, J., and Prokop, J. (2003). Aerodynamic and acoustical measures of speech, operatic and Broadway styles in a professional female singer. *Journal of Voice* 17(3): 283–98.

Sundberg J. (1974). Articulatory interpretation of the "singing formant." *Journal of the Acoustical Society of America* 55(4): 838–44.

Sundberg, J. (1975). Formant technique in a professional female singer. *Acta Acustica united with Acustica* 32(2): 89–96.

Sundberg, J. (1987). *The Science of the Singing Voice*. DeKalb: Northern Illinois University Press.

Sundberg, J. (2009). Articulatory configuration and pitch in a classically trained soprano singer. *Journal of Voice* 23(5): 546–51.

Sundberg, J. and Thalén, M. (2001). Describing different styles of singing. A comparison of a female singer's voice source in "Classical," "Pop," "Jazz" and "Blues." *Logopedics Phoniatrics Vocology* 26(2): 82–93.

Sundberg, J., Cleveland, T., Stone, R.E., and Iwarsson, J. (1999). Voice source characteristics in six premier country singers. *Journal of Voice* 13(2): 168–83.

Sundberg, J., and Thalén, M. (2010). What is Twang? *Journal of Voice* 24(6): 654–60.

Sundberg, J., Lã, F.M.B., and Gill, B.P. (2011). Professional male singers' formant tuning strategies for the vowel /a/. *Logopedics Phoniatrics Vocology* 36(4):156–67.

Titze, I.R. (2008). Nonlinear source- filter coupling in phonation: Theory. *Journal of the Acoustical Society of America* 123(5): 2733–49.

Titze, I.R. and Worley, A.S. (2009). Modeling source-filter interaction in belting and high-pitched operatic male singing. *Journal of the Acoustical Society of America* 126(3): 1530–40.

Titze, I.R., Bergan, C., Hunter, E., and Story, B. (2003). Source and filter adjustments affecting the perception of the vocal qualities "twang" and yawn. *Logopedics Phoniatrics Vocology* 28(4): 147–55.

Yanagisawa, E., Estill, J., Kmucha, S.T., and Leder, S.B. (1989). The contribution of aryepiglottic constriction to "ringing" voice quality: A videolaryngoscopic study with acoustic analysis. *Journal of Voice* 3(4): 342–50.

Zangger Borch, D. and Sundberg, J. (2011). Some phonatory and resonatory characteristics of the Rock, Pop, Soul, and Swedish Dance Band styles of singing. *Journal of Voice* 25(5): 532–7.

CHAPTER 9

··

THE DEVELOPING VOICE

··

DESMOND SERGEANT

INTRODUCTION

IN this chapter, the complex nature of voice quality[1] is discussed, and its principal contributory elements and sources are identified. Samples of the acoustic products of speech
and singing are examined by means of computerized spectrographic analysis, and the
respective characteristics and differences that become evident in the resultant plots are
examined. The "source-filter" model (Fant 1981) is used to discuss the way in which the
waveform of the laryngeal output is modified by the configuration and resonance characteristics of the vocal tract and oral cavities to produce the phonemes of spoken and
sung words.

A developmental trajectory is traced, describing the ontogenesis of voice quality, and
the way in which patterns of normal human growth and development during the years of
childhood from birth to puberty contribute to the emergence of a personal voice characteristic is illustrated by examples of Long Term Average Spectra (LTAS) drawn from analysis of young trained and naïve singers.

Finally, gender differences that emerge as children develop towards puberty are discussed,
and the modifications of voice quality consequent on regular voice training are also
indicated.

---

[1] The term "voice quality" is customarily used in the fields of speech therapy and clinical phonetics to
refer to specific voice types such as breathy voice, tense voice, etc. which conditions are usually regarded
as primarily larynx-related rather than of supra-laryngeal or behavioral origin (Gobl and Chasaide 1992;
Mathieson 2000; Wendler et al. 1986). In this chapter, voice quality is used in its wider sense to refer to
the summation of phonological features and characteristics present in a vocal output as it is perceived by
a listener (cf. Abercrombie 1967; Laver 1980; Trask 1996), i.e. the total vocal image of a speaker or singer
(Biemans 2000).

THE ACOUSTIC FEATURES OF VOICE QUALITY

> The telephone rings. We lift the receiver:
> "Hello, John," our caller begins, "this is ... "
> ... but those few seconds of exposure to acoustic features unique to that one speaker have already been sufficient to enable us to recognize who is calling us, and the self-identification is unnecessary.

Given the very large number of voices we encounter during our daily lives, our ability to recognize individuals in this way is remarkable, yet it has been shown to be within the capabilities of surprisingly young children. Three-year-olds have been recorded as achieving 61 percent accuracy for recognition of voices of cartoon characters, rising to 81 percent and 84 percent for four and five-year-olds (Spence et al. 2002). Nursery school children have been reported to be capable of accurate identifications, even when the sound samples are reversed, though with reduced accuracy from that recorded for the original prime versions (Bartholomeus 1973). Identification rates are above chance even for non-verbal vocal "harrumps." There is some evidence of an "own-gender" superiority for recognition (Skuk and Schweinberger 2012).

The properties which enable us to make such identifications are collectively referred to as *voice quality* (Biemans 2000, p. 20; Kent and Ball 2000), but the number and diversity of its contributory elements make the term difficult to define succinctly. They may be considered to be attributable to two origins:

1. Physiological/phonational: features attributable to the speaker's physical make-up: the dimensions of the laryngeal/pharyngeal apparatus, the length of the vocal tract, and personal disposition of oral and nasal cavities, etc., all of which determine the general pitch and tonal character of a speaker's voice (Darwin et al. 2003). At least in the case of post-pubertal speakers, these all are related to overall body mass and hormonal constitution (Avery and Liss 1996; Dabbs and Mallinger 1999; Perry et al. 2001), though these relationships are rather approximate; neck circumference may be the most reliable indicator (Evans et al. 2006; Gonzalez 2004; Rendall et al. 2005; Smith and Patterson 2005).
2. Sociological/psychological: life-style and situational factors, such as first language, regional dialect, habitual articulatory and tensional usage, gender, personality, self-image, age and social-group affiliations of the speaker and also of the person addressed (Labov et al. 2013; Mathieson 2000; Scherer 1979; Scherer and Scherer 1981).

These divisions are more notional than categoric, and it might be difficult in practice to separate their respective influences in a definitive way.

Alternatively, as Biemans (2000) proposes, the characteristics of voice quality may be considered to be ordered against a comparative time frame:

- Short-term: linguistic features arising from grammatical and phonological features of a particular utterance, e.g. vowels, consonants, etc., dependent on the context and content of what is said and its informational function—whether it is declaratory or interrogative, etc.

- Medium term: paralinguistic features that shape the character of an utterance—its communicative rather than informational qualities—the adopted "*tone of voice*" or registration of a delivery, reflecting the emotional state of a speaker—anger, happiness, distress, anxiety, etc. (Gobl and Chasaide 2003; Johnstone and Scherer 1999; Pittam and Scherer 1993).
- Long term: extra-linguistic features, including those anatomically determined, such as age, gender, height and body mass, but also others relating to a speaker's habitually adopted speech style, pitch level, tempo, energy, etc.; cultural factors such as first language, regional accent, but also to socio-psychological and social-group affiliations, etc. (Coadou and Rougab 2007; Dabbs and Mallinger 1999; Pittam 1987; Pittam and Gallois 1986). These are semi-permanent features, accessible to change only over a sustained period, such as might occur with aging (Prakup 2010) or following a long-term change of spoken environment (Jacewicz et al. 2011).

Voice quality has been defined as "those characteristics that are present more or less all the time that a person is talking . . . a quasi permanent quality" (Abercrombie 1967, p. 91) and as being "the characteristic auditory colouring of an individual speaker's voice . . . and . . . an index to biological, psychological and social characteristics of the speaker" (Laver 1980, p. 1) "derived from a variety of laryngeal and supralaryngeal features" (Trask 1996, p. 381). As Baken and Orlikoff (1997) have pointed out, voice is not a tangible object or organ: it is an ephemeral product of a highly complex system of behaviors, subject to moment-to-moment variability. Measurements imposed on phenomena of phonation are therefore mapping aspects of behavior, not physical entities, and voice quality is therefore best regarded as a multi-parameter space involving many factors (Keller 2005).

Visual evidence of voice characteristics and behaviors

To illustrate some of the acoustic properties and parameters of voice quality, Jenny, a 13-year-old girl, was invited to recite a limerick which ran:

> There was a young maiden called Maggie,
> Whose dog was enormous and shaggy,
> The front end of him was ferocious and grim,
> But the back was all friendly and waggy!

The spectrogram at Figure 9.1 records the acoustic properties of her speech output at the point when she reaches the words "ferocious and grim." In the informality of the situation, she does not enunciate them exactly in the way they appear in the relentless correctness of print, it is more like "*f'rocious'n grim*." The *x* axis of the graph shows the time duration of the phonation, the *y* axis the frequencies at which its component energies occur on a scale extending from 0–8 kHz.

  The first thing that is noticeable in this spectrogram is that the data of its central panel appear to fall naturally into four distinct sectors. In the first (0–210 ms) and third (400–730 ms) sectors, the spectral energies appear widely and randomly dispersed across the frequency

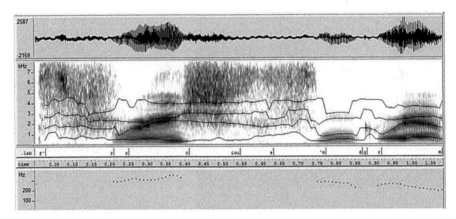

FIGURE 9.1 Spectrogram: Jenny pronounces the words *"f'rocious n'd grim."* First (top) pane: waveform bar showing spectral energies present in the vocal product as it progresses; second pane: spectral pane showing occurrence and density of acoustic phenomena across the frequency range (*y axis*); third pane: the text of the product, showing the phonemes responsible for the spectral phenomena evident in the display of the second pane; fourth pane: timescale of the phonation (total duration here: 0–1010 ms); fifth (lowest) pane: pitch (fundamental frequency) of the output (present only when the sound is *voiced*).

range, but in the second (210–400 ms) and fourth (750–1180 ms) they are closely focused within a frequency band below approximately 3 kHz, appearing on the spectrogram trace in the form of dark horizontal striations. The former two sectors represent the consonants of the utterance, the latter two the vowels. The consonants occupy approximately 70 percent of the total phonation time of the sample, the vowels just 30 percent.

The acoustic phenomena of the first sector (0–210 ms) represent the speaker's production of the initial sibilant fricative /f/ of her abbreviated *"f'-rocious,"* created by a vigorous air stream projected between the closely proximal lower teeth and upper lip, with the rear of the tongue bunched high at the rear. The third sector (400–730 ms) shows the effect of the /sh/ and /ss/ of "f'ro-*cious*," which the speaker elides to *"sh-ss,"* almost completely omitting the diphthong /iou/, creating instead a single extended sibilant fricative. This is achieved by projection of the air stream between the upper and lower teeth which are positioned close together, with the position of the tongue adjusted mid-way to separate the two elements "sh-" and "-s." The consequence of both of these consonants is creation of turbulence at high frequencies, evidenced in the spectrogram by darker shading in the upper regions of the trace (Blomberg and Elenius 1970). Both of these fricatives are examples of *voiceless* consonants.

The lowest panel of the spectrogram illustrates the pitch behavior of the voice, from which we can see that that it rose with the intuitively colorful emphasis she placed on *"fer-o-cious"* but fell at the final word *"grim."* The pitch-trace is not visible continuously throughout the graph, being present only during the vowels. Because the vocal folds (VF) are active during their production, these sounds are described as being *voiced.* At these points the vocal folds are close together in their proximal position, resisting the subglottal air pressure from the lungs below. When the pressure becomes sufficient to push the folds apart, air escapes through the space created between them; the pressure is then released, dropping to a level below the phonation threshold. This allows the muscles to recoil, and the folds to recover their proximal position. This cycle repeats itself, chopping the airflow into regular pulses, generating a regular harmonic pattern of vibration.

At the points during the two *unvoiced* consonants where the pitch trace disappears from the spectrogram, the vocal folds are abducted, and make no contribution to the sound output. The dispersion and inharmonicity of the resulting phenomena prevent their being rationalized to a consistent fundamental, f_o, and therefore also of their having a defined perceived pitch. Not all consonants are unvoiced, however. In this short sample, unvoiced elements occupy approximately 68 percent of the total phonation time, and voiced elements 32 percent.

Other features visible in the spectrogram trace include the nasally produced /n/ of the abbreviated conjunction "*nd*" (760–855 ms) and the /m/ of the final "*grim*" (1010 ms). Here the mouth is closed by lips or tongue and air emerges through the nose, and consequently a break in the pitch trace occurs (855–900 ms) marking a momentary separation of the vocal folds to accommodate the /d/ (at 860 ms) of her abbreviation of "*nd-grim*," a reflection of the amazing complexity of human speech behavior.

The waveform in the uppermost panel of the graph shows the changes in sound pressure levels energizing the phonation as it progresses. The relative width and density of the sound pressure waveform show that vowels generate considerably more spectral energy than do consonants.

Formants

The dark striations visible in the spectrogram trace at lower frequencies of the spectrum represent formants. When the transglottal airflow causes the vocal folds to vibrate, many related partials are initiated simultaneously and the waveform generated is thus harmonically rich. The lowest harmonics are strongest in the overall spectrum and the energies of the higher harmonics diminish progressively as a function of their distance from f_o (the perceived pitch). Under the source-filter theory (Fant 1981), areas above the larynx, i.e. the vocal tract (VT), and oral cavities (as shaped by the mouth, tongue, jaw, teeth, lips, and nasal passages (Lindblom and Sundberg 1971)) function as a series of infinitely flexible and finely tunable resonating chambers, the dispositions and configurations of which are adjusted by the speaker/singer in order to selectively reinforce or dampen the multiple harmonics generated by the sound source. Fant regards the chambers as comprising two elements—vertical and horizontal—to which a third, the nasal tract, must also be added (Figure 9.2).

The raw material of the voice source waveform is thus modified, shaped and increased in overall energy to create the adjusted output waveform (Figure 9.3). This is not achieved by conscious adjustment by the singer/speaker; rather, it operates by autonomic processes, as much voice behavior is habitual and is not readily accessible to conscious processes (Thurman and Welch 2000).[2]

Watts et al. (2006) describe the relationship between energies at source and output as the Singing Power Ratios (SPR), representing a measure of the amplification or

---

[2] For a more detailed description of vocal functioning, see Welch and Sundberg (2002).

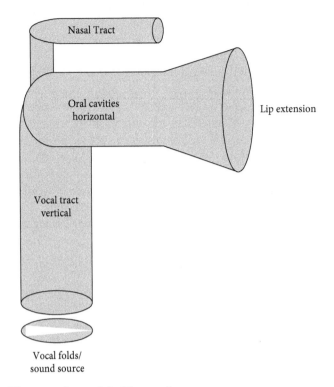

FIGURE 9.2 The two-tube model of the vocal tract.

After Fant (1981).

suppression by the vocal tract configurations of the harmonics present in the sound source waveform. They report significant differences in SPR between singers deemed "talented" and "nontalented."

The pitch height and dispersion of formants determine the resultant quality and character of the output vowel. We can see how this occurs in the spectrogram in Figure 9.1. Jenny is a well-educated young lady whose speech production is what is classified as "British Received

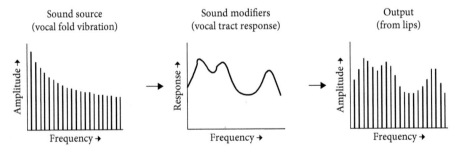

FIGURE 9.3 Source-filter theory (Fant 1981). The raw material of the voice source spectrum is modified by resonance characteristics of the vocal tract and oral cavities.

Reproduced with permission from Himonides (2008).

Pronunciation".[3] This is revealed in her enunciation of the /o/ of her *f'r/o/cious* as a dipthong; between the 250–375 ms points we can see the second formant (F2) changes pitch, moving upwards to merge with F3, which also increases in frequency, while F1 moves to a slightly lower frequency, reflecting her adjustment of the vowel quality.

The voice source and the conformations of the vocal tract are not independent but are reciprocally interactive in what is known acoustically as a "coupled system"; the vocal tract acts on and shapes the airflow and influences the mode of vibration of the vocal folds (Titze and Story 1997). Fitch and Giedd (1999) say that source and filter will be interactive if any of the resonant frequencies of the vocal tract are near the f_o of phonation. This is commonly the case in woodwind and brass instruments where the bell flare at the distal end of the instrument optimizes the selection of the multiple harmonics generated at the sound source.

The long-term average spectrum

A useful summary of the data reflected in a spectrogram can be obtained by calculating the mean energy occurring at each frequency across the spectrum range as a function of phonation time, thus creating a Long-term Average Spectrum (LTAS). This is a widely accepted and powerful procedure, at one time requiring employment of multiple filter banks, but now achievable in seconds by a modern computer. Its great usefulness is that the data it yields is largely independent of the semantic or linguistic content of a vocal product, and is even independent of the particular language of a speaker (Kitzing and Akerlund 1993; Pittam and Gallois 1986; Tarnoczy and Fant 1964). It is particularly useful in identifying those properties of a vocal product that are most characteristic of a speaker or singer's output; it conceals *what* was said, but reveals aspects of the *way* that it was said (Ternström 1993). LTAS analysis had been widely applied to analysis of speech products, but the technique is also used in the study of the spectra of singing (Sergeant and Welch 2008, 2009; White 2001).

There are some technical issues affecting the use of LTAS. Firstly, there is no generally accepted frequency range across which a spectrum should be examined: some researchers have restricted their interest to a rather narrow 0–3 kHz range, others have examined much wider ranges, for example 0–12.5 kHz (Hollien and Majewski 1977) and 0–16 kHz (DeJonckere 1983). If the range is set too narrowly, it is likely that important data will be lost.

Owing to the myriad of data that would result if every frequency point across the spectrum were to be analyzed separately, it is customary to consider the spectrum as divided into a series of successive interval bands. The bandwidth used is critical to the quality of the resulting data, and must be determined by the requirements of the particular research interest, but 500 Hz has been found to be a convenient setting.

For valid analysis, a voice product must be of sufficient duration to allow the features of a voice to be fully sampled. Products as short as three seconds have been used in some studies, but 20 seconds might represent an average duration. Jansson and Sundberg (1972) compared LTAS for 100-second samples of music with progressively abbreviated samples of the same material, and found that reductions as short as two and ten seconds showed unexpectedly good agreement with the originals. However, vowel sounds are typically more extended in

---

[3] Otherwise known as Standard Southern British English (SSBE).

singing than in speech, and consonants are shorter; this offers advantages of greater stability of spectra, so the use of shorter samples of singing is therefore justified.

Since voice is not an objective entity, attribution of spectral phenomena to causal vocal behaviors can be problematic (Eskenazi et al. 1990); relating measured values of acoustic phenomena to the psychological perceptions they evoke is even more hazardous. Parameters of voice quality do not lend themselves to precise scaling, and there is no agreed thesaurus of descriptors that can be applied to them, with the consequence that judgments have rarely shown high levels of inter-listener agreement. As a result, voice conditions that are labeled as "breathy," "harsh," tense, or "creaky," have no precisely defined boundaries or population norms. Voice characteristics are highly personal, and between-speaker variance is rarely limited to a single parameter (Mendoza et al. 1996; Whiteside et al. 2002; Zetterholm 1998).

Speech versus song

Several important characteristics differentiate the acoustics of running speech and reading from those of singing, especially in respect of pitch behavior and intonation.

Fundamental frequency

In addition to the physiological dispositions that influence a speaker's fundamental speaking frequency (SFF), individuals also vary considerably in their adopted intonational habits, and this will be reflected in the overall average f_o of their speech output. The average pitch of the vocal output of a singer, however, is not dependent on personal tendencies of intonational behavior: it is determined by the rise and fall of the melodic line of the song and its *tessitura*. Freedom to vary pitch is limited to that moment before the start of a song when an unaccompanied singer determines the pitch level at which the song will be performed. Thereafter, supposing the performance is competent, the pitches of subsequent sounds will follow accordingly, as the melody unfolds, in relation to the chosen starting pitch. There is therefore no measure that can be applied to singing that is equivalent to a Speaker's Fundamental Frequency (SFF) of speech. A measure of f_os in song will yield only values for relative presence or absence of the scalar degrees in the melody.

Intonation

Intonation fulfills important linguistic functions in speech communication, enhancing and qualifying informational content by directing attention to points of emphasis, communicating implication and affect (Pollermann and Archinard 2002; Scherer and Scherer 1981; Weusthoff et al. 2013) and marking differences between declaratory and interrogatory meanings. In speech, loudness and pitch are typically interdependent—a rise in pitch customarily equates with increased emphasis, and therefore also with increased loudness (Banse and Scherer 1996; Böhme and Stüchlick 1995; Gramming et al. 1988; Pittam and Scherer 1993)—but in singing they are separate phonatory parameters, under independent control, as, for example, when a singer performs an ascending melodic passage *diminuendo* (Sundberg 1990).

Two further factors differentiate acoustic spectra of speech and song. In running speech, words are chosen solely on their appropriateness to the meaning to be conveyed: in the case of reading, they have already been scripted by the writer against similar criteria. In song, word usage is subject to greater constraints. The first is that words of a song typically introduce rhyming, marked by regular repetition of vowels and consonants located at phrase endings, something that would occur only in the context of an unusually alliterative or assonant passage of speech. The consequence for acoustic analysis and averaging of spectra in LTAS is repeated re-sampling of the phenomena occurring at these points.

The second factor is that the relative durations of phonemes in spoken vocalizations are determined by the semantic choices and personal speech style of a speaker. Durations of syllables in song, in contrast, are subject to the rhythmic and metric structure of the music; emphasis is achieved by assignment of important words to notes of longer duration, or to those occurring at metrically stressed points or phrase peaks. Given that it is difficult for a singer effectively to sustain a vocal tone on a consonant, vowels are normally assigned to notes of longer duration, and this necessarily determines the ways in which spectra of vowels and consonants are represented in an LTAS plot.

For these several reasons the acoustic features of song are not wholly comparable to those of speech even when both forms are products of a single speaker/singer (Tsai 2012); Wendler et al. (1980) comment that the physiological correlates of speech and singing may quite possibly represent different phenomena.

At Figure 9.4, long-term average spectrograms for mean energy values across the spectrum obtained for singing and speaking are compared. Fifty trained choristers, 25 boys, 25

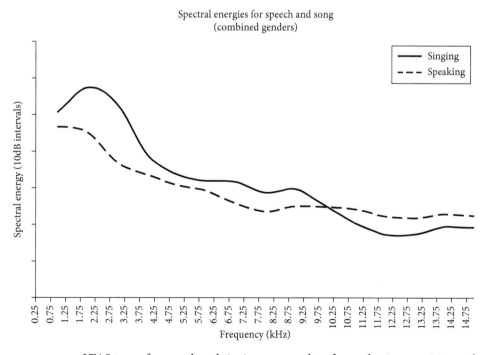

FIGURE 9.4 LTAS traces for speech and singing: mean values for 50 choristers reciting and singing the words of a carol.

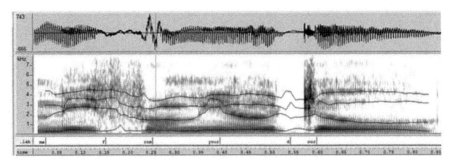

FIGURE 9.5 Spectrogram: Eleanor recites words from the carol: "...*me from your door.*"

girls aged between 8 and 13 years, each individually recited the words of a verse of a traditional Christmas carol "*This is the truth sent from above*"[4] and then sang the same words to
the carol melody. The LTAS traces which represent the mean values of their two categories
of vocal products show that the high frequency characteristics (between 10–15 kHz) attributable to prominence of consonants of speech are much reduced in singing, in which the more
extended vowels generate greater energy at lower frequencies (1–3.5 kHz), especially in the
pitch regions where vowel formants are represented (e.g. as indicated by the four fine horizontal "hairpin" lines in the spectrogram at Figure 9.1).

Differences in the respective spectra of speech voice and singing also become apparent
from comparison of the two spectrograms for a single speaker/singer at Figures 9.5 and 9.6.
Here, Eleanor, an 11-year-old choral singer (one of the 25 singers above) recited the words
of the carol "*This is the truth . . .*" (Figure 9.5) and then sang the words to the carol melody
(Figure 9.6). The melody notes at this point are shown at Figure 9.7. The spectrograms show
her output when she reaches the end of the third line, at the words "... *me from your door.*"

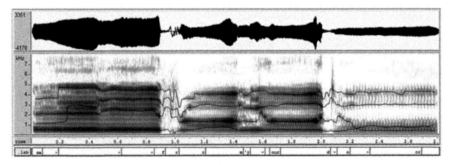

FIGURE 9.6 Spectrogram: Eleanor sings the words "...*me from your door*" to the carol melody.

---

[4] Herefordshire carol, collected by Ralph Vaughan Williams. From *Eight Traditional English Carols*,
Vaughan Williams, Stainer and Bell. Verse 1:

> This is the truth sent from above,
> The truth of God, the God of Love,
> Therefore don't turn me from your door,
> But Hearken all both rich and poor.

me   -   from   your   door,

FIGURE 9.7 Melody notes of the carol to which Eleanor sings the four words "...me from your door."

Table 9.1 Proportions of time of spectrograms of Figure 9.5 and 9.6 occupied by voiced/unvoiced and vowel/consonant sounds

Proportion of phonation time		
	Sung	Spoken
Voiced	87%	74%
Unvoiced	13%	26%
Vowels	90%	59%
Consonants	10%	41%

The first difference evident in the spectrograms is the comparative phonation times for the two products: 2.8 seconds for singing (at a flowing *andante*), compared with only 850 ms for recitation of the words. The relative densities of the two sound pressure waveforms (uppermost pane) testify to the greater spectral energies of the sung tones, and the greater subglottal pressure and airflow required to sustain them.

The respective proportions of voiced versus unvoiced sounds, vowels, and consonants in these two outputs by the same person are compared in Table 9.1.

THE DEVELOPMENTAL PROCESSES

A number of studies have reported that the spectra of children's vocal products differ from those of adults. Whiteside et al. (2002), for example, found evidence of what they interpreted to be maturational changes in samples of children between ages of six and ten years. When their participants were reassessed after a 42-month interval, changes were found in most of the measured parameters, though there was much individual variation in patterns of voice development, a feature also reported by Mendoza et al. (1996).[5] White (1999) reports that energy values across the spectrum differ between boys and girls, and that neither datasets are consonant with those for adults of corresponding sexes. The years between ages four and 11 encompass a major period of general physical growth, but from the perspective of voice

[5] Lee et al. (1999) report that inter-singer/speaker variability reduces between ages nine and 12, converging with adult values, though not fully established until 12 years.

development, this can conveniently be considered as having two broad phases: a prelimi-nary phase from the neonatal infant to 18–24 months and a second extending through the prepubertal years (Vorperian and Kent 2007). In neither of these phases can their patterns of development be regarded as linear and, importantly, Titze (1994) stresses that at no stage of these developments can children be thought of merely as being miniature versions of adults, nor can childhood vocalizations be regarded as scaled-down imitations of those of adults.

The air resource

As part of normal growth patterns, the length and width of lungs increase substantially, and in a broadly linear manner until around 14 years, at which age they begin to approximate to adult conformations, with female values tending to reach a plateau while those for males continue to increase until age 16. As a consequence of their more limited lung and ribcage volume, younger children necessarily use higher percentages of their lung capacity—estimated to be up to 50–60 percent—in the activities of speech and singing than do adults. It is only after approximately 12 years of age that the relative lung volume utilized decreases proportionally, and normal adult breathing patterns are established (Polgar and Weng 1979; Stathopoulos 2000; Stathopoulos and Sapienza 1997). Children have to work much harder than adults to achieve a given level of output.

Changes also take place in the dimensions and functioning of the larynx, and these con-tinue through and after puberty, bringing concomitant adjustments in patterns of phona-tion. Compared to that of an adult, not only is the overall size of the vocal apparatus smaller, but children's vocal tissue also has a less developed and somewhat different structure; laryn-geal cartilages are more plastic and less rigid and the inner structure of the vocal folds is dif-ferent (Kahane 1978, 1982). These structural differences are an additional cause of the greater breath demands of childhood phonation, adding to the demands on resources to meet subglottal pressure requirements. As the child approaches puberty and adult-like breathing behaviors develop, the airflow to the glottis becomes proportionately less demanding of res-piratory resources, and maintenance of subglottal pressure becomes less effortful. A conse-quence of this development is an overall increase in intensity of the vocal product.

The voice source

In optimal modal (normal) voice the arytenoid cartilages bring the vocal folds together into crisp contact, with the lateral edges of the folds meeting cleanly along their full length. Their tension appropriately adjusts autonomically to meet the anticipated transglottal airflow, en-abling a regular excitation of the folds in which open and closed phases of the glottal cycle are clearly defined, generating a harmonically rich waveform in which higher harmonics are clearly specified (Holmes 1976). Laver (1994) specifies four conditions for efficient modal voice:

1. Only the true vocal folds must be in vibration.
2. Their vibratory pattern must be regularly periodic, without audible roughness or disperiodicity.
3. Vibration must be efficient in air usage without presence of audible friction.

4. The degree of muscle tension in all phonatory systems must be moderate.

But glottal behaviors do not always meet these criteria; incompetent or incomplete closure of the folds is commonly found, usually reported as taking the form of a small gap or chink between the vocal folds as they are primed at the start of each vibratory cycle. Typically, this is located at their posterior end (Figure 9.8). Although full glottal closure is not achieved, the vocal folds are sufficiently approximated to allow their agitation in response to the subglottal pressure from below, but because of the insufficiency of their contact, the wave-form generated is less regular and the harmonics are less clearly specified. The gap remaining open between the folds also allows air that, in a fully efficient operation, would be engaged by the action of the vocal folds to transmit acoustic energy into the vocal tract and oral and nasal cavities. The consequences are twofold: loss of efficiency in the vibratory cycle of the vocal folds and friction between the escaping air and the tissue surfaces of the vocal tract. An element of disharmonicity is thus introduced into the spectra of the vocal output in the form of high-frequency noise, effectively masking high-frequency harmonics with the random products of the friction. Other measurable parameters of normal phonation spectra have also been found to be disturbed by incomplete glottal closure, including mag-nitude of the closed quotient, jitter, shimmer, harmonic-to-noise ratio, and signal-to-noise ratio for glottal area function (De Krom 1994; Inwald et al. 2011; Lofquist and Manderson 1987; McGowan and Nittrouer 1988; Mendoza et al. 1996; Pabon et al. 2000; Shirastev and Sapienza 2003; Shoji et al. 1992; Södersten and Lindestad 1990).

An intrinsic interrelationship among factors here becomes apparent: optimal energy of airflow through the glottis induces better priming of the vocal folds, improved efficiency of their motion, and more precise closure, which brings more positive specification of harmonics in the waveform that is generated. This in turn brings increased definition and prominence of formants, and the greater spectral energy at frequencies above the funda-mental will be evident in the spectrogram and LTAS curve. At the same time, high-frequency fricatious noise in the pharyngeal tube and oral/nasal cavities caused by leakage through the glottal gap will be reduced. These factors will be evidenced by a steeper spectral slope of the LTAS curve, though the change will be non-uniform owing to its dependency on pitch height of the fundamental frequency of the phonation, and also to the considerable levels of inter-personal variation. The perceived auditory effect of these shifts will be increased loud-ness, and enhancement of voice quality through improved definition and contrasts among

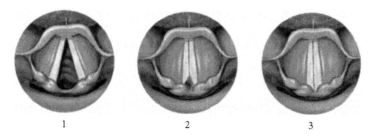

1   2   3

FIGURE 9.8 Degrees of glottal closure: (1) complete abduction; (2) closure, but with poste-rior glottal chink; (3) complete adduction.

Adapted with permission from Himonides (2008, p. 24, Fig. 21).

spectral phenomena (DeJonckere et al. 2001; Fant 1960; Gauffin and Sundberg 1989; Henrich et al. 2005; Holmberg et al. 1995; Huber et al. 1999; Hurme 1980; Kitzing and Akerlund 1993; Linville 1992; Nordenberg and Sundberg 2004; Rothenberg 1979; Schneider and Bigenzahn 2003; Schneider et al. 2010; Seshadri and Yegnanarayana 2009; Smith et al. 1995; Södersten and Lindestad 1990; Södersten et al. 1995; Sulter and Abers 1996; Sundberg 1995).

There is good agreement that the voice quality described as "breathiness" is attributable to incomplete glottal closure (Fritzell et al. 1986; Hanson and Chuang 1999; Klatt and Klatt 1990; Omori et al. 1998; Sapienza and Hoffman 2000; Shoji et al. 1992). There is corroborative evidence that the relatively shorter length of the membranous vocal fold tissue characteristic of the childhood larynx is also associated with incomplete closure. Stathopoulos and Sapienza (1997) have reported a characteristically larger posterior glottal chink in children than is generally found in adults. Similar evidence is provided by Smith-Vaughan (2007), Pabon et al. (2000), and McAllister et al. (1994), the latter workers finding incomplete closure to be present in so many of their young subjects as to cause them to speculate that what may be regarded as a form of vocal fold dysfunction in adults could be considered a normal condition for child voice. Mendoza et al. (1996) make similar observations but report that inter-singer variability, particularly in respect of patterns of high-frequency noise, was present in their samples to the extent that consistent patterns were sometimes hard to detect.

Given that, as discussed above, the airflow required for child voice is proportionally greater than that for adult voice, the elements of fricatious air noise present in the spectra of children is likely also to be higher.

Vocal tract

Non-invasive methods of digital imagery have brought better understanding of sequences of skull and vocal tract growth. Vorperian et al. (2005) report from an extensive MRI study, that VT length increases from 6–8 cm in infants to 15–18 cm in adult women and men, and these values are similar to those cited by Menard et al. (2004). Growth brings about complex reshaping of the face and the cranial base, affecting the growth and flexion of the upper jaw and mandible, and these developments have important repercussions on the position and dimensions of the vocal tract and glottis relative to vertebrae (Boë et al. 2008; Mugitani and Hiroya 2012).

Development is rapid from birth to infancy, with descent of the hyoid bone and larynx bringing a coupling between fundamental frequency of cry with resonance frequencies, and thus the first development of intentional articulatory phonational behavior (Wermke et al. 2002), which continues through the first five years of life. It is followed by a period of slower growth during middle childhood, with a final period of rapid growth after the onset of puberty towards achievement of adult proportions. The rate of growth is not uniform, however, but is markedly subject to growth spurts which tend to be particular to the individual (Gollin 1981; Sguoros et al. 1999; Vorperian and Kent 2007; Vorperian et al. 1999).

The irregularity of these growth patterns is due to the fact that the vertical (pharyngeal) and horizontal (oral-nasal) segments of the vocal tract (Figure 9.2) do not develop in tandem with age. At infancy, the horizontal oral cavity is longer than the vertical pharyngeal tube, but by puberty these proportions are reversed. Growth is therefore biased, less change taking place in the horizontal than in the vertical plane, with the consequence that shifts in voice pitch do not progress in synchrony with changes in the formant properties of the output, effectively causing a decoupling between fundamental frequency and resonance frequencies. A period of rapid growth in the lower face between seven to nine years follows, which affects the shape of the palate more than its size, continuing until around age 12 (Kent and Vorperian 1995; Kuhl et al. 1997; Menard et al. 2004; Vorperian and Kent 2007; Vorperian et al. 2007, 2005, 2011; White 1999). The ratio of pharynx height to oral cavity length, important factors for speech and voice quality, decreases significantly from 1.5 to 1 between birth and six to eight years, but thereafter remains stable. Cen et al. (2011) comment that the sequences of these changes are of some complexity.

With progressive elongation of the vocal tract across the period of childhood, it could reasonably be expected that the frequencies of the fricatious noise resulting from the abrasion of aspirative airflow against the pharyngeal wall would decrease proportionally, and this would be evidenced in the LTAS curves by their migration to lower frequencies (Smith and Patterson 2005). Sapienza and Hoffmann (2000) see a positive relationship between glottal air leakage, the presence of high-frequency noise, and the listener's perception of breathiness. It could also be anticipated that the high-frequency elements observed in LTAS for younger children would migrate to lower frequencies in tandem with increases in pharyngeal length (Smith and Patterson 2005).

Experimental evidence

In an extended study (Sergeant and Welch 2008, 2009), developmental changes in the singing voices of children between the ages of four and 11 years were traced. Three hundred and twenty children (mean age seven years 11 months) learned two songs composed for the purpose; these shared common pitch ranges (A_3 = 220 Hz to B_4 = 439 Hz), tonalities, numbers of notes, and melodic configurations, and used gender-neutral words. The songs were taught to the children by the teachers who were normally responsible for music education in the 13 London schools these children attended. After the end of the teaching sessions, each child individually sang one of the songs in a relaxed and informal situation.[6] No starting pitch was provided, and each singer spontaneously selected his/her own comfortable pitch level. Each child's performance was digitally recorded using a suitably positioned tie microphone.

Each vocal sample was then subjected to analysis by LTAS over a spectral range of 0–20 kHz, taking measurements at the center point of 500 Hz bandwidths. The spectral range for examination was set to this unusually wide range to avoid possible loss of data at high frequencies. On inspection, although the spectrograms showed that elements of energy present in the traces for most children extended up to 16–17 kHz, above that point energies were minimal, and analyses were therefore concentrated on a spectrum range of 0–15 kHz.

The mean pitches at which the songs were recovered from the young singers were slightly below the pitch at which they had been presented. The lowest pitch recorded was

---

[6] A problem for sampling and measuring the voice output of children is that however carefully the data collection is contrived, in-test behavior may be untypical of output at other unstructured times (Hunter 2008, 2009). Voice data are therefore valid for the situation in which they are collected, but may not share identical characteristics with samples collected in other situations.

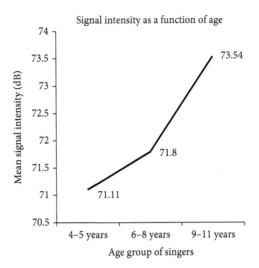

FIGURE 9.9 The relationship of vocal intensity to age. Values for age groups are statistically different: 4–5/6–8 years p<0.05; 6–8/9–11 years $p<0.001$.

64 cents below B_2 (a girl) and the highest 35 cents above A#$_4$ (a boy). A highly significant association between increasing age and extension of vocal range for singing was evident, but not until the age of ten did a majority of the children achieve the full pitch range of the songs, and at that age the mean pitch at which the songs were sung moved nearer to pitch of presentation.

A strong association was evident between overall intensity of vocal output and chronological age (Figure 9.9), but although this indicated the presence of the anticipated continuous developmental trend, it was not uniformly linear, reflecting the irregularity of the underlying patterns of physical growth. Three age-bands proved the best fit for the data: 4–5 years, 6–8 years, and 9–11 years. As intensity level of vocal output is a critical factor for evaluation of LTAS data, comparisons of LTAS curves were therefore made observing these self-defining age groups.

Spectral energies below 5.75 kHz were found to increase significantly between the ages of four and 11 years, these shifts being particularly prominent for the older age groups, but energies at frequencies above that point of the spectrum decreased proportionately (Figure 9.10). The predicted progressive shifts of spectral energies from higher frequencies to lower points of the spectral curve as a function of increasing age were therefore confirmed in these data.

The LTAS curves that are compared at Figures 9.11 and 9.12 show that although there was evidence that the shifts had begun to take place between the ages of four and six, for most children the period between eight and 11 was the most operative period of change.

Breath noise was found to be a prominent feature of the voice samples of a large majority of these children. The frequencies of the disharmonic elements could be approximately estimated from noise elements of inhalation. Most children required three intakes of breath to sustain their song performances, and these were commonly characterized by prominent noise at high frequencies. Measurements taken from the spectrograms showed these noise elements to extend considerably higher than could be interpreted as representing harmonic

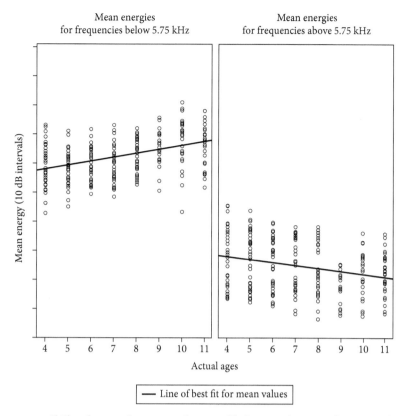

FIGURE 9.10 Shifts of spectral energies above and below 5.75 kHz as a function of age.

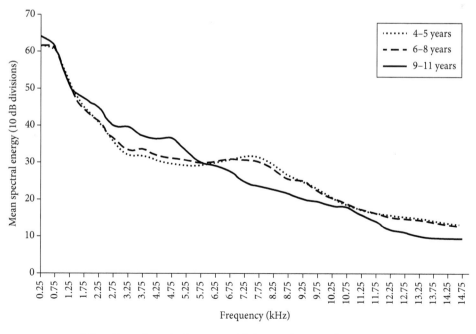

FIGURE 9.11 Migration of spectral energy with increasing age: three age groups.

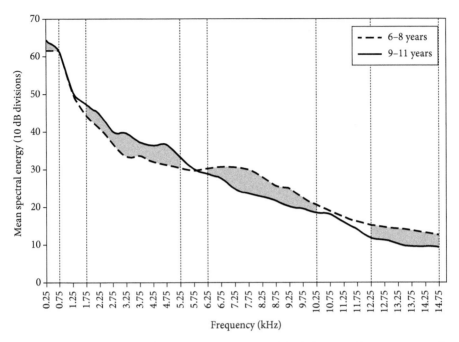

FIGURE 9.12 Energy shifts for oldest age groups (shaded areas show regions where differences reached statistical significance).

or formant areas, sometimes creating a plateau of energy between 2–18 kHz. A necessary caveat here is that spectral phenomena of inhalation might not be identical to those of exhalation, as airway configurations may not be identical for both airflow directions. Consistent with the observations of Mendoza et al. (1996), there was much inter-singer variability—so that the distributions of high-frequency fricatious noise were found to be specific to individual speakers.

Gender differences in voice quality

The presence of gendered information in adult speech, sufficient to enable listeners to make reliable sex-of-speaker judgments, has been amply demonstrated, with recognition rates ranging from 81 percent up to 95–100 percent (Caruso et al. 1994; Sachs et al. 1973; Schwartz and Rine 1968; Watts 2013; Wu and Childers 1991). In the case of adult speakers, where the characteristic octave differential in f_o is present, these high rates are unsurprising, but recognition rates for children, reported between 56.1–81 percent, also indicate the presence of sex-specific characteristics (Brend, 1971; Gelfer and Bennet 2013; Ingrisano et al. 1980; Karlsson and Rothenberg 1987; Meditch 1975; Perry et al. 2001; Rothenberg 1979; Sachs et al. 1973; Weinberg and Bennet 1971; Wolfe et al. 1990). The criterial information on which the gender decisions are resolved has been attributed variously to differences in vocal tract length, glottal conformation and behavior, presence of spectral noise, breathiness, etc. (Bachorowski and Owren 1999).

Sex-specific qualities are also present in children's singing voices, with identification rates of around 71 percent (Sergeant et al. 2005), but ease of identification tends to be related to the extent of voice training a singer has received. Trained singers have been found to be more gender-confusable than naïve singers though gender-recognition rates are influenced by the training environment, the sex of the choir trainer, and the choice of repertoire employed in discrimination tests (Howard et al. 2002; Mecke and Sundberg 2010; Moore and Killian 2000; Sergeant and Welch 1997).

Fricatious noise in the vocal product proved to be the most salient cue in sex-of-singer recognition of our naïve singers. Breathiness has so frequently been observed to be a characteristic of female voice that some writers have regarded incomplete glottal closure as a normal condition for women (Eustace et al. 1996; Södersten and Lindestad 1990; Sulter and Abers 1996) whereas males generally achieve more competent closure (Alku and Vilkman 1996; Bruckert et al. 2006; Hanson and Chuang 1999; Holmberg et al. 1995; Klatt and Klatt 1990; Price 1989). Two possible explanations have been proposed for these differences: Murry et al. (1998) have pointed out the association between degree of glottal closure and vocal competency, and that degree of closure can be improved by increased subglottal pressure; Schneider and Bigenzahn (2003) have confirmed that this is a relevant factor in women's speech and singing. It has therefore been argued that women generally are prone to lower levels of vocal competency, though the evidence of Bennett and Weinberg (1979) that voice source characteristics played only a minor part in sex identification of their participants appears to be negative to the proposition. An alternative explanation is that the differences have socio-phonological origins, in that women may aim for a softer, less positively projected production, and may subconsciously reduce the level of glottal excitation in order to match a perceived model of *woman-speak*. This explanation is supported by evidence that vocal-tract behaviors such as degree of jaw opening, mandible movement, and shaping of lips are highly relevant to gender identification (Bennett and Weinberg 1979; Lindblom and Sundberg 1971). Differences in vocal tract length may also have behavioral origins in the gestural character of the vocal product: the way speakers may manipulate speech to portray certain images, and the possibility that boys may habitually use smaller jaw opening, lower head elevations resulting in smaller extension of the vocal tract, lower larynx positions, and rounding of lips (Nolan 1983; Sachs et al. 1973); as Huckvale (2013, p. 221) remarks, "every conceivable way in which vowels vary appears to be used for the purpose of signalling speakers' social characteristics."

PUBERTY AND MUTATION: CHANGING VOICE CHARACTERISTICS

Intuition might persuade us to expect gradual changes to be apparent in childrens' voices as they grow towards puberty, and that these might primarily become evident through a perceptible lowering of average fundamental frequency. In the case of speech output, research evidence confirms this, but although a drop in voice pitch is universally noted for both sexes, it has been reported to be slightly earlier for girls, circa seven to eight years, than for boys, eight to nine years (Hacki and Heitmüller 1999; Robb and Saxman 1985; Whiteside and

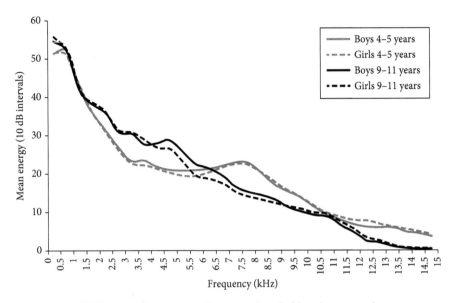

FIGURE 9.13 LTAS curves for youngest (4–5 years) and oldest (9–11 years) age groups.

From Sergeant and Welch (2008).

Hodgson 1999) with beginnings of major male voice mutation delayed until between ten and 11. Precise values vary somewhat between findings, doubtless due to environmental, racial, or sampling differences (Awan and Mueller 1996; Vuorenkoski et al. 1978). Bennett (1983) suggests that in any longitudinal study of child voice, changes in average speaking pitch will be evident. Linders et al. (1995) found mean f_0 for girls at 244 Hz (overall range 183–331 Hz) and boys f_0 250 Hz (205–293 Hz).

Equivalent evidence of voice ranges for singing cannot realistically be offered owing to the complication of the dependency of average pitch on the chosen test material—the song. Evidence from studies using voice range profiling is the nearest alternative. The data such studies generate are extensive, and it is not possible to include a review here.[7] There is, however, general agreement that age-related changes in voice characteristics affect both speech and song products, with a constant relation between the two activities (Rinta and Welch 2008). Capabilities in both forms increase with age, but not in a uniform way. The LTAS curves at Figure 9.13 show that for untrained singers, changes in spectra are attributable more to age then to sex of singer.

Effects of voice training

Voice training will obviously bring about changes in singing behaviors which will affect development of breathing patterns, bringing increased subglottal pressure and enhanced vocal fold activity. Articulatory changes will affect deployment of laryngeal structures and oral

---

[7] Schneider et al. (2010) provide a detailed resource.

and nasal cavities, and these will be evident particularly in relative strengths of formants. In terms of changes in acoustic spectra, precise outcomes of training will depend on the target musical genre and style towards which the training is aimed (Barlow and Howard 2002; Barlow and LoVetri 2010; Björkner 2006; Cleveland et al. 2001; Herbst et al. 2009; Howard 2009; Howard et al. 2012, 2002; Kato et al. 2006; Pittam et al. 1990; Sergeant and Welch 1997; Sundberg et al. 2012). Singing styles are so various, it is not realistic to pose generalizations; indeed, the range is so extensive that it might first be necessary to determine criteria for what vocal outcomes qualify as *singing* (Sundberg et al. 2012).

Operatic and music theater singing styles, for example, generate different acoustic spectra reflected in differences in strength of voice fundamental (Björkner 2006), extent of excursion of vibrato (Stone et al. 2003), relative variations in open/closed quotient, and in muscle tension (Koufman et al. 1996; Smith-Vaughan 2007). Boersma and Kovačić (2003, 2006), Barlow et al. (2007), and Kovačić et al. (2003) have all shown that different styles of folk singing in Croatian musical culture also evoke different acoustic characteristics.

In Western classical styles of singing, the effects of training on the young voice have been reported to include:

- increased demands of subglottal pressure (Sundberg 1995) and increase in overall vocal intensity (Barrichelo et al. 2001; Pollerman and Archinard 2002; Sulter and Abers 1996);
- extension of vocal range (Mendes et al. 2003; Siupsinskiene and Lycke 2011) (Pribuisiene et al. (2011) report 26 semitones compared with only 22 for untrained prepubertal voices);
- improved glottal closure, bringing better specification of harmonics in the glottal waveform;
- ability to reflect degrees of emotionality;
- changes in timing parameters (Pollerman and Archinard 2002);
- changes in relative durations of vowels and consonants;
- changes in muscular tension, especially relating to musical styles (Koufman et al. 1996).

At Figure 9.14, LTAS curves for young trained choristers (ages eight to 13 years) are compared. These indicate that boys show higher levels of energy in the frequency regions 1.75–5.75 kHz, i.e. the region in which second, third, and fourth formants might be expected to be present. Higher levels of energy are present for girls between 5.75–8.25 kHz. This is too high to be attributable to formants, and suggests that the breathiness that characterizes untrained female voice persists even when there has been sustained training.

The distinctive characteristic that marks the adult trained singer is the so-called "singer's formant"—a spectral peak with a center frequency of 2.5 kHz for males and 3.16 kHz for females, varying somewhat with voice classification (Bloothooft and Plomp 1986; Sundberg 2001), which is reported to be evident also in the speech of trained singers (Barrichello et al. 2001; Bole 2006; Lundy et al. 2000). Acquisition of the singer's formant may require several years of training (Mendes et al. 2003), and we should therefore not expect its presence in younger singers; however, the data of Figure 9.14 suggest that it may be in the early stages of acquisition at least in boy choristers, and the closely bunched resonations around 3 kHz in the spectrogram of our young female singer, Eleanor, at Figure 9.6, support this idea. Recent data presented by Howard et al. (2013) also indicate its presence in the voices of young trained singers, though at a somewhat higher frequency band (circa 4 kHz) than with adults.

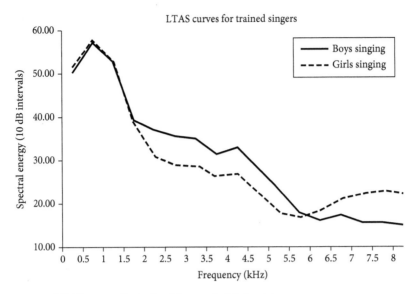

FIGURE 9.14 LTAS curves for trained boy and girl choristers.

The role of learning in acquisition of voice quality

The purpose of this chapter has been to review developmental patterns relevant to voice quality, beginning with the immediately neonatal period through to the major maturational changes at the onset of puberty. Although this developmental path can be seen to be continuously progressive, its trajectory proves to be of considerable complexity, proceeding by spurts and pauses, in which little regularity or simultaneity can be discerned.

Notwithstanding the critical importance of physical development for voice quality, an account which confined its attention solely to cataloging morphological changes and their consequent acoustic outcomes would be incomplete. Voice quality, as it is perceived by the listener, is not dependent solely on the physiological properties of the vocal tract: the functions of phonatory behavior in human social communication and interaction, and the development of correlated neural capabilities are essential parts of the story.

A fragment of conversation overheard following a performance by a young singer that *"she has a beautiful voice"* seemed to imply that the young artist's happy condition was the result of a fortuitous concatenation of laryngeal and vocal tract conformations, occurring naturally as part of her physical make-up, just as one might equally well have said of her "she has a fine head of hair!" Genetic endowment undoubtedly plays an important part in determining voice quality, but there are many other factors that contribute equally. A full discussion of these would be lengthy, and beyond the capabilities of a single chapter to report, but the salient issues for consideration are summarized here.

Of particular concern are the ways in which vocal tract and articulator settings are initially acquired and then become established as characteristic qualities of a person's phonation. It is well known that the prosodic features of a mother's speech, especially the intonation patterns, are perceived, learned, and remembered while the infant is still *in utero*, and immediately after birth these same patterns are identifiable as features of the newborn's phonatory behaviors (Abrams et al. 1998; Mampe et al. 2009; Querleu et al. 1984; Sohmer and Freemen 2001; Sohmer, et al. 2001; Voegtline et al. 2013). The earliest postnatal interactions with the mother are conducted via the phenomenon of "*motherese*," a universal cross-cultural paralinguistic prosodic code shared between mothers and their babies. The acoustic characteristics that distinguish *motherese* from modal adult female vocal behaviors have been widely researched and are generally agreed to be a higher-than-normal f_o, more extended pitch excursions, greater variability of f_o, shorter utterances, longer pauses, and ritualistic repetitions. The linguistic content of the maternal input to the communicative dyad is also simplified (Fernald and Kuhl 1987; Fernald and Simon 1984; Grieser and Kuhl 1988; Shute and Wheldall 1989; Trehub et al. 1993).

Around the age of 12–16 months, as communicative intent develops, phonatory behaviors begin to change in form, separating into the two discrete social forms of *speech* and *song*. In the propositional/informational context of *speech*, pitch variability, extent of pitch excursion, and contour become progressively constrained and limited (Knower 1941), especially in the case of boys, but song-directed behaviors retain the greater pitch variability, flexible prosodies, and rhythmicity associated with heightened emotionality.

Pre-speech vocal behaviors are thus bi-potential, containing the basic elements of both forms, but realization into their respective communicative forms will be dependent on the presence of appropriate stimulation in the environment. Through interaction with the mother, the infant rehearses settings and gestures of larynx, vocal tract, oral cavities, and tongue, acquiring articulatory skills of tongue and glottis and varied voice onset timings (VOTs) that lead to achievement of reliable production of the vowel/consonant effects that are the essential features of language (Nakata and Trehub 2004). But whereas speech-directed interaction can be expected to develop between all mother–child dyads as a matter of course, mothers are likely to differ widely in the extent to which the features of their vocal output promote the development of song-directed behaviors in the infant. In this the regularity and quality of parental singing habits will be of critical importance. Individual parents will differ widely in vocal tract settings they employ: their flexibility and agility, rapidity of adjustment, control and precision of pitching, accuracy of pitch intervals, consistency of tonality, rhythmic exactness, and also of song repertoire. The extent to which singing-related vocal tract and articulator settings are promoted and acquired will thus differ considerably between children.

As phonatory behaviors develop, correlative neural networks will be established, linking cognitive, motor, and auditory areas of the brain. As trial-and-error vocal enterprises develop into habitual schemas, they become established as autonomic systems, and are progressively mapped onto the brain. In the acoustic environment of the mother tongue, selective bonding takes place between motor schemas and linguistically relevant neural networks, building ever more extended groupings, at which point language acquisition becomes possible (Oller et al. 2013). The parental mother tongue thus acts as a magnet in language acquisition—the Perceptual Magnet-Effect (PME) (Kuhl, 2004, 2000; Kuhl et al, 2008; Naatanen 2001; Wheeler 1983).

If we mentally rehearse how it would feel to recite the limerick verse about Maggie and her dog, described at the beginning of this chapter, although we might feel our behavior to be essentially that of speech, the regularized rhythmic patterns and stresses and the stereotypical pitch prosody of the limerick recitation style show that many features of speech are also characteristic of song. So, in the same way that neural networks for language develop, mapping similarly takes place with song-schemas, increasing in complexity, ultimately embracing the tonal, scalic, and rhythmic organizations of the many grammars that characterize music and song.

The case of singing is therefore special, in that acoustic-vocal-motor schemas that determine singing voice quality and which overlap with musico-structural systems are woven into the neural networks for speech and language, a view supported by numerous studies (Brown et al. 2004, 2006; Callan et al. 2006; Gordon et al. 2010; Jeffries et al. 2003; Riecker et al. 2000; Serrien et al. 2006; Sparing et al. 2007; Tierney et al. 2013). Schön et al. (2010), interpreting fMRI evidence from tasks involving spoken words, sung words, and vocalise, observed widespread interactions between linguistic and musical dimensions of sung words. This argues against previously generally accepted ideas of domain specificity and discrete laterality, indicating instead selective engagement of shared bilateral neural networks according to task.

We may conclude, then, that voice quality and what may be regarded as "a beautiful voice" are the consequence of a concatenation of physical structures, vocal motor skills, and vocal tract resonance and articulator settings acquired early in life through interactions with specific qualities in the environmental input, leading to the establishment of appropriate neural networks, and overlaid, of course, by extended training.

REFERENCES

Abercrombie, D. (1967). *Elements of General Phonetics*. Edinburgh: Edinburgh University Press.

Abrams, R.M., Griffiths, S.K., Huang, X., Sain, J., Langford, G., and Gerhardt, K.J. (1998). Fetal music perception: the role of sound transmission. *Music Perception: An Interdisciplinary Journal* 15(3): 307–317.

Alku, P. and Vilkman, E. (1996). A comparison of glottal voice source quantification parameters in breathy, normal and pressed phonation of female and male speakers. *Folia phoniatrica et logopedica* 48(5): 240–254.

Avery, J.D. and Liss J.M. (1996). Acoustic characteristics of less masculine-sounding male speech. *Journal of the Acoustical Society of America* 99: 3738–3748.

Awan, S.N. and Mueller, P.B. (1996). Speaking fundamental frequency characteristics of white, African, American and Hispanic kindergartners. *Journal of Speech and Hearing Research* 39(3): 573–577.

Bachorowski, J.-A. and Owren, M.J. (1999). Acoustic correlates of talker sex and individual talker identity are present in a short vowel segment produced in running speech. *Journal of the Acoustical Society of America* 106(2): 1054–1063.

Baken, R.J. and Orlikoff, R.F. (1997). Voice measurement: is more better? *Logopedics Phoniatrics Vocology* 22(4): 147–151. doi:10.3109/14015439709075328

Banse R. and Scherer, K.R. (1996). Acoustic profiles in vocal emotion expression. *Journal of Personality and Social Psychology* 70(3): 614–636.

Barlow, C. and Howard, D.M. (2002). Voice source changes of child and adolescent subjects undergoing singing training—a preliminary study. *Logopedics Phoniatrics Vocology* 27(2): 66–73.

Barlow, C., LoVetri, J., and Howard, D.M. (2007). Voice source and acoustic measures of girls singing classical and contemporary commercial styles. In: A. Williamon and D. Coloimbra (eds), *Proceedings of the International Symposium on Performance Science, 2007, Porto, Portugal*, pp. 484–488. Utrecht: European Association of Conservatoires (AEC).

Barlow, C. and LoVetri, J. (2010). Closed quotient and spectral measures of female adolescent singers in different singing styles. *Journal of Voice* 24(3): 314–318.

Barrichelo, O., Huer, R.J., Dean, C.M., and Sataloff, R.T. (2001). Comparison of singer's formant, speaker's ring and LTA spectrum among classical singers and untrained normal speakers. *Journal of Voice* 15(3): 344–350.

Bartholomeus, B. (1973). Voice identification by nursery school children. *Canadian Journal of Psychology* 27(4): 464–472.

Bennett, S. and Weinberg, B. (1979). Acoustic correlates of perceived sexual identity in children's voices. *Journal of the Acoustical Society of America* 66(4): 989–1000.

Bennett, S. (1983). A 3-year longitudinal study of school-aged children's fundamental frequencies. *Journal of Speech and Hearing Research* 26: 137–142.

Biemans, P. (2000). *Gender Variation and Voice Quality*. Doctoral thesis, Utrecht University.

Björkner, E. (2006). Music theatre and opera singing, why so different? Aspects of voice characteristics in operatic and musical theatre singing. *Journal of Voice* 22(5): 533–540.

Blomberg, M. and Elenius, K. (1970). Speech analysis: statistical analysis of speech signals. *Quarterly Progress Reports, KTH* 1: 1–8.

Bloothooft, G. and Plomp, R. (1986). The sound level of the singer's formant in professional singing. *Journal of the Acoustical Society of America* 79(6): 2028–2033.

Boë, L.-J., Captier, G., Granat, J., Deshayes, M.-J., Heim, J.-L., Birkholz, P., Badin, P., Kielwasser, N., and Sawallis, T. (2008). Skull and vocal tract growth from fetus to 2 years. *Journal of the Acoustical Society of America* 124(2): 1192–1206.

Boersma, P. and Kovačić, G. (2003). Long-term average spectra in professional Croatian folk singing: a comparison of the klapa and dozivacki styles. In: *5th Pan European Voice Conference*, Graz, Austria, pp. 219–225. Zagreb: HOEMU.

Boersma, P. and Kovacic, G. (2006). Spectral characteristics of three styles of Croatian folk singing. *Journal of the Acoustical Society of America* 119(3): 1805–1816.

Böhme, G. and Stüchlik, G. (1995). Voice profiles and standard voice profiles of untrained children. *Journal of Voice* 9: 304–307.

Bole, I.V. (2006). The speaker's formant. *Journal of Voice* 20(4): 555–578.

Brend, R. (1971). Male–female intonation patterns in American English. In: *Proceedings of the 7th International Congress of Phonetic Sciences*, pp. 866–869. The Hague: Mouton.

Brown, S., Martinez, M.J., Hodges, D.A., Fox, P.T., and Parsons, L.M. (2004). The song system of the human brain. *Cognitive Brain Research* 20(1): 363–373.

Brown, S., Martinez, M.J., and Parsons, L.M. (2006). Music and language side by side in the brain: a PET study of the generation of melodies and sentences. *European Journal of Neuroscience* 23(10): 2791–2803. doi:10.1111/j.1460-9568.2006.04785.x

Bruckert, L., Lienard, J.S., Lacroix, A., Kreutzer, M., and Leboucher, G. (2006). Women use voice parameters to assess men's characteristics. *Proceedings of the Royal Society Biological Science* 273(1582): 83–89.

Callan D.E., Tsytsarev, V., Hanakawa, T., Callan, A.M., Katsuhara, M., Fukuyama, H., and Turner, R. (2006). Song and speech: brain regions involved with perception and covert production. *NeuroImage* 31(3): 1327–1342. doi:10.1016/j.neuroimage.2006.01.036

Caruso, A.J., Mueller, P.B., and Xue, A. (1994). Relative contributions of voice and articulation to listener judgements of age and gender: preliminary data and implications. *Journal of Voice* 3: 1–9.

Cen, L., Dong, M., and Chan, P. (2011). Segmentation of speech signals in template-based speech-to-singing conversion. Available at: http://www.apsipa.org/proceedings_2011/pdf/APSIPA094.pdf. Accessed June 14, 2014.

Cleveland, T.F., Sundberg, J. and Stone, R.E. (2001). Long-term-average spectrum characteristics of country singers during speaking and singing. *Journal of Voice* 15: 54–60.

Coadou, M. and Rougab, A. (2007). Voice quality variation in English. In: *Proceedings of the Congress of ICPhS*. August 6–10, Saarbrücken, Germany, pp. 2077–2080.

Dabbs, J.M. and Mallinger, A. (1999). High testosterone levels predict low voice pitch among men. *Personality and Individual Differences* 4: 801–804.

Darwin, C.J., Brungart, D.S., and Simpson, B.D. (2003). Effects of fundamental frequency and vocal-tract length changes on attention to one of two simultaneous talkers. *Journal of the Acoustical Society of America* 114(5): 2913–2922.

De Krom, G. (1994). Spectral correlates of breathiness and roughness for different types of voice fragments. *Journal of Speech and Hearing Research* 37: 985–1000.

DeJonckere, P.H. (1983). Recognition of hoarseness by means of LTAS. *International Journal of Rehabilitation Research* 6: 343–345.

DeJonckere, P.H., Bradley, P., Clemente, P., Cornut, G., Crevier-Buchman, L., Friedrich, G., De Heyning, P. van, Remacle, M., and Wosiard V. (2001). A basic protocol for functional assessment of voice pathology, especially for investigating the efficacy of phonosurgical treatment and evaluating new assessment techniques. *Oto-Rhino-Laryngology* 258(2): 77–82.

Eskenazi, L., Childers, D.G., and Hicks, D.M. (1990). Acoustic correlates of voice quality. *Journal of Speech and Hearing Research* 33: 298–306.

Eustace, C.S., Stemple, J.C., and Lee, L. (1996). Objective measures of voice production in patients complaining of laryngeal fatigue. *Journal of Voice* 10(2): 146–153.

Evans, S., Neave, N., and Wakelin, D. (2006). Relationships between vocal characteristics and body size and shape in human males: an evolutionary explanation for a deep voice. *Biological Psychology* 72(2): 160–163.

Fant, G. (1960). *Acoustic Theory of Speech*. The Hague: Mouton.

Fant, G. (1981). The source filter concept in voice production. *Quarterly Progress Reports, KTH* 22: 21–37.

Fernald, A. and Simon, J. (1984). Expanded intonation contours in mothers' speech to newborns. *Developmental Psychology* 20: 104–113.

Fernald, A. and Kuhl, P. (1987). Acoustic determinants of infant preference for motherese speech. *Infant Behavior and Development* 10(3): 279–293. doi:10.1016/0163-6383(87)90017-8

Fitch, T. and Giedd, J. (1999). Morphology and development of the human vocal tract: a study using magnetic resonance imaging. *Journal of the Acoustical Society of America* 106(3): 1511–1522.

Fritzell, B., Hammarberg, J., Gauffin, J., Karlsson, I., and Sundberg, J. (1986). Breathiness and insufficient vocal fold closure. *Journal of Phonetics* 14: 549–553.

Gauffin, J. and Sundberg, J. (1989). Spectral correlates of glottal voice source waveform characteristics. *Journal of Speech and Hearing Research* 32: 556–565.

Gelfer, M.P. and Bennet, Q.E. (2013). Speaking fundamental frequency and vowel formant frequencies: effects on perception of gender. *Journal of Voice* 27(6): 556–566. doi:10.1016/j.voice.2012.11.008

Gobl, C. and Chasaide, A.N. (1992). Acoustic characteristics of voice quality. *Speech Communication* 1(4–5): 481–490.

Gobl, C. and Chasaide, A.N. (2003). The role of voice quality in communicating emotion mood and attitude. *Speech Communication* 40(1–2): 189–212.

Gollin, E. (1981). *Developmental Plasticity: Behavioral and Topical Aspects of Variations in Development*. New York: Academic Press.

Gonzalez, J. (2004). Formant frequencies and body size of speaker: a weak relationship in adult humans. *Journal of Phonetics* 32: 277–287.

Gordon, R., Schön, D., Magne, C., Astesano, C., and Besson, M. (2010). Words and melody are intertwined in perception of sung words: EEG and behavioural evidence. *PLoS ONE* 5(3): e9889.

Gramming, P., Sundberg, J., Ternström, S., Leanderson, R., and Perkins, W.H. (1988). Relationships between changes in voice pitch and loudness. *Journal of Voice* 2: 118–126.

Grieser, D.L. and Kuhl, P.K. (1988). Maternal speech to infants in a tonal language: Support for universal prosodic features in motherese. *Developmental Psychology* 24(1): 14–20. doi:10.1037/0012-1649.24.1.14

Hacki, T. and Heitmüller, S. (1999). Development of the child's voice: permutation, mutation. *International Journal of Pediatric Otorhinolaryngology* 49(1): S141–S144.

Hanson, H.M. and Chuang, E.S. (1999). Glottal characteristics of male speakers: acoustic correlates and comparison with female data. *Journal of the Acoustical Society of America* 106 (2): 1064–1077.

Henrich, N., D'Alessandro, C., Doval, B., and Castellengo, M. (2005). Glottal open quotient in singing: measurements and correlation with laryngeal mechanisms, vocal intensity, and fundamental frequency. *Journal of the Acoustical Society of America* 117(3 pt 1): 1417–1430.

Herbst, C.T., Ternström, S., and Švec, J.G. (2009). Investigation of four distinct glottal configurations in classical singing—a pilot study. *Journal of the Acoustical Society of America* 125(3): 104–109.

Himonides, E. (2008). *The Psychoacoustics of Vocal Beauty: A New Taxonomy*. PhD Thesis, University of London, Institute of Education.

Hollien, H. and Majewski, W. (1977). Speaker identification by long-term spectra under normal and distorted speech conditions. *Journal of the Acoustical Society of America* 62(4): 975. doi:10.1121/1.381592

Holmberg, E.B., Hillman, R.E., Perkell, J.S., Guiod, P.C., and Goldman, S.L. (1995). Comparisons among aerodynamic, electroglottographic, and acoustic spectral measures of female voice. *Journal of Speech and Hearing Research* 38(6): 1212–1223.

Holmes, J.H. (1976). Formant excitation before and after glottal closure. *IEEE International Conference on ICASSP* 1: 136–142. doi:10.1109/ICASSP.1976. 1170095

Howard, D.M., Welch, G.F., and Szymanski, J.E. (2002). Can listeners tell the difference be-tween boys and girls singing the top line in cathedral music? In: C. Stevens et al. (eds), *Proceedings of 7th International Conference on Music Perception and Cognition, July 17–21*, Sydney, Australia, pp. 403–406.

Howard, D.M. (2009). Acoustics of trained versus untrained singing voice. *Current Opinion in Otolaryngology and Head and Neck Surgery* 17(3): 155–159. doi:10.1097/MOO.0b013e32832aft11b

Howard, D.M., Daffern, H., and Brereton, J. (2012). Quantitative voice quality analysis of a so-prano singing early music in three different performance styles. *Biomedical Signal Processing and Control* 7(1): 58–64.

Howard, D.M., Williams, J., and Herbst, C.T. (2013). Ring in the solo child singing voice. *Journal of Voice* 26 (2): 161–169. doi:10.1016.jvoice.2013.09.001

Huber, J.E., Stathopoulos, E.T., Curione, G.A., Ash, T.A., and Johnson, K. (1999). Formants of children, women, and men: the effects of vocal intensity variation. *Journal of the Acoustical Society of America* 106(3): 1532–1542.

Huckvale, M. (2013). An introduction to phonetic technology. In: M.J. Jones and R.-A. Knight (eds), *Bloomsbury Companion to Phonetics*, pp. 208–226. London: Bloomsbury Academic.

Hunter, E. (2008). Children's voices: a new tool for measuring children's voices could improve diagnosis and treatment. *Journal of the Acoustical Society of America* 124: 2497.

Hunter, E. (2009). A comparison of a child's fundamental frequencies in structured elicited vocalizations versus unstructured natural vocalizations: a case study. *International Journal of Otorhinolaryngology* 73(4): 561–571.

Hurme, P. (1980). Auto-monitored speech level and average speech spectrum. *Papers in Speech Research* 2: 121–127.

Ingrisano, D., Weismer, G., and Schucker, G.H. (1980). Sex identification of preschool children's voices. *Folia phoniatrica et logopedica* 32: 61–69.

Inwald, E.C., Dollinger, M., Schluster, M., Eysholdt, U., and Bohr, C. (2011). Multiparametric analysis of vocal fold vibrations in healthy and disordered voices in high-speed imaging. *Journal of Voice* 25(5): 576–590.

Jacewicz, E., Fox, R.A., and Salmons, J. (2011). Regional dialect variation in the vowel systems of typically developing children. *Journal of Speech, Language and Hearing Research* 54: 448–470. doi:10.1044/1092-4388(2010/10-0161)

Jansson, E.V. and Sundberg, J. (1972). Long-time-average-spectra applied to analysis of music. *Quarterly Progress Reports, KTH* 13(4): 40–45.

Jeffries, K.J., Fritz, J.B., and Brauar, A.R. (2003). Words in melody: an H2150 PET study of brain activation during singing and speaking. *NeuroReport* 14(5): 749–754.

Johnstone, T. and Scherer, K.R. (1999). The effects of emotion on voice quality. In: C.S. Stevens et al. (eds), *Proceedings of XIVth International Congress of Phonetic Sciences*, University of California-Berkeley Department of Linguistics, pp. 2029–2032.

Kahane, J.L. (1978). A morphological study of human prepubertal and pubertal larynx. *American Journal of Anatomy* 151: 11–20.

Kahane, J.L. (1982). Growth of the human prepubertal and pubertal larynx. *Journal of Speech and Hearing Research* 25: 446–455.

Karlsson, I. and Rothenberg, M. (1987). Sex differentiation cues in the voices of young children of different language backgrounds. *Journal of the Acoustical Society of America* 81: S68. doi:10.1121/1.2024359

Kato, K., Hirawa, T., Kawai, K., Yano, T., and Ando, Y. (2006). Investigation of the relation between (τe)min and operatic singing with different vibrato styles. *Journal of Temporal Design and Architectural Environment* 6(1): 35–48.

Keller, E. (2005). The analysis of voice quality in speech processing. *Lecture Notes in Computer Science* 3445: 54–73.

Kent, R.D. and Vorperian, H.K. (1995). Development of the craniofacial-oral-laryngeal systems: a review. *Journal of Medical Speech-Language Pathology* 3: 145–190.

Kent, R.D. and Ball, M.J. (2000). *Voice Quality Measurement*. San Diego, CA: Singular Publishing Company.

Kitzing, P. and Akerlund, L. (1993). Long-time average spectrograms of dysphonic voices before and after therapy. *Folia phoniatrica et logopedica* 45: 53–61.

Klatt, D.H. and Klatt, C.L. (1990). Analysis and synthesis of voice quality variations among female and male talkers. *Journal of the Acoustical Society of America* 87(2): 820–857.

Knower, F.H. (1941). Analysis of some experimental variations of simulated vocal expressions of the emotions. *Journal of Social Psychology* 14: 369–372.

Koufman, J.A., Radomski, T.A., Joharji, G.M., Russell, G.B., and Pillsbury, D.C. (1996). Laryngeal biometrics of the singing voice. *Otolaryngology, Head and Neck Surgery* 115(6): 527–537.

Kovačić, G., Boersma, P., and Domitrović, H. (2003). Long-term average spectra in professional folk singing voices: a comparison of the Klapa and Dozivački styles. *Proceedings of the Institute of Phonetic Sciences, University of Amsterdam* 25: 53–64.

Kuhl, P.K., Andruski, J.E., Chistovich, L.A., Kozhevnikova, E.V., Ryskina, V.L., Stolyarova, E.L. Sundberg, U., and Lacerda, F. (1997). Cross-language analysis of phonetic units in language addressed to infants. *Science* 277: 684–686.

Kuhl, P.K. (2000). A new view of language acquisition. *Proceedings of the National Academy of Sciences* 97(22): 11850–11857. doi:10.1073/pnas.97.22.11850

Kuhl, P.K. (2004). Early language acquisition: cracking the speech code. *Nature Reviews Neuroscience* 5(11): 831–843. doi:10.1038/nrn1533

Kuhl, P.K., Conboy, B.T., Coffey-Corina, S., Padden, D., Riveraq-Gaxiola, M., and Nelsom, T. (2008). Phonetic learning as a pathway to language: new data and native language magnet theory expanded (NLM-e). *Philosophical Transactions of the Royal Society B: Biological Sciences* 363(1493): 979–1000. doi:10.1098/rstb.2007.2154

Labov, W., Rosenfelder, I., and Fruelwald, J. (2013). One hundred years of sound changes in Philadelphia: linear incrementation, reversal, and reanalysis. *Language* 89(1): 30–65.

Laver, J. (1980). *The Phonetic Description of Voice Quality*. London: Cambridge University Press.

Laver, J. (1994). *Principles of Phonetics*. London: Cambridge University Press.

Lee, S., Potamianos, A., and Narayanan, S. (1999). Acoustics of children's speech: developmental changes of temporal and spectral parameters. *Journal of the Acoustical Society of America* 105(3): 1455–1468.

Lindblom, B.E.F. and Sundberg, J. (1971). Acoustical consequences of lip, tongue, jaw and larynx movement. *Journal of the Acoustical Society of America* 50(48): 1166–1179.

Linders, B., Massa, G.G., Boersma, B., and Dejonckere, P.H. (1995). Fundamental voice frequency and jitter in girls and boys measured with electroglottography: influence of age and height. *International Journal of Pediatric Otorhinolaryngology* 33(1): 61–65.

Linville, S.E. (1992). Glottal gap configurations in two age groups of women. *Journal of Speech and Hearing Research* 35: 1209–1215.

Lofquist, A. and Manderson, B. (1987). Long-time average spectra of speech and voice analysis. *Folia phoniatrica et logopedica* 39: 221–229.

Lundy, D.S., Roy, S., Casiano, R.R., and Evans, J. (2000). Acoustic analysis of the singing and speaking voices of singing students. *Journal of Voice* 14(4): 490–493.

Mampe, B., Friederici, A.D., Christophe, A., and Wermke, K. (2009). Newborns cry melody is shaped by their native language. *Current Biology* 19(23): 1994–1997.

Mathieson, L. (2000). Normal-disordered continuum. In: R.D. Kent and M.J. Ball (eds), *Voice Quality Measurement*, pp. 3–12. San Diego, CA: Singular Publishing Company.

McAllister, A., Sederholm, E., Sundberg, J., and Gramming, P. (1994). Relations between voice range profiles and physiological and perceptual voice characteristics in ten-year-old children. *Journal of Voice* 8(3): 230–239.

McGowan, R.S. and Nittrouer, S. (1988). Differences in fricative production between children and adults: evidence from an acoustic analysis of /sh/ and /s/. *Journal of the Acoustical Society of America* 83(3): 230–239.

Mecke, A.-C. and Sundberg, J. (2010). Gender differences in children's singing voices: acoustic analyses and results of a listening test. *Journal of the Acoustical Society of America* 127(5): 3223–3231.

Meditch, A. (1975). The development of sex-specific speech patterns in young children. *Anthropological Linguist* 17: 421–465.

Menard, L., Schwartz, J.-L., and Boe, L.-J. (2004). The role of vocal tract morphology in speech development. *Journal of Speech, Language and Hearing Research* 47: 1059–1080.

Mendes, A., Rothman, H.B., Sapienza, C., and Brown, W.S. (2003). Effects of vocal training on the acoustic parameters of the singing voice. *Journal of Voice* 17(4): 529–543. doi:10.1067/S0892-1997(03)00083-3

Mendoza, E., Munoz, J., and Navaringa, N.N. (1996). The long-term average spectrum as a measure of voice stability. *Folia phoniatrica et logopedica* 48: 57–64.

Moore, R. and Killian, J. (2000). Perceived gender differences and preferences of solo and group treble singers by American and English children and adults. *Bulletin of the Council for Research in Music Education* 147: 138–144.

Mugitani, R. and Hiroya, S. (2012). Development of vocal tract and acoustic features in children. *Acoustic Science and Technology* 33(4): 216–220.

Murry, T., Xu, J.J., and Woodson, G.E. (1998). Glottal configuration associated with fundamental frequency and vocal register. *Journal of Voice* 12(1): 44–49.

Naatanen, R. (2001). The perception of speech sounds by the human brain as reflected by the mismatch negativity (MMN) and its magnetic equivalent (MMNm). *Psychophysiology* 38(1): 1–21. doi:10.1111/1469-8986.3810001

Nakata, T. and Trehub, S. (2004). Infants' responsiveness to maternal speech and singing. *Infant Behaviour and Development* 27(4): 455–464.

Nolan, F. (1983). *The Phonetic Basis of Speaker Recognition.* London: Cambridge University Press.

Nordenberg, M. and Sundberg, J. (2004). Effect on LTAS of vocal loudness variation. *Logopedics Phoniatrics Vocology* 29(4): 183–191.

Oller, D.K., Buder, E.H., Ramsdell, H.L., Warlaumont, A.S., and Choma, L. (2013). Functional flexibility of infant vocalizations and the emergence of language. *Proceedings of National Academy of Sciences* 110: 6318–6323.

Omori, K., Slavit, D.H., Kacker, A., and Blaugrund, S.M. (1998). Influence of size and etiology of glottal gap in glottic incompetence dysphonia. *The Laryngoscope* 108(4): 514–518. doi:10.1097/00005537-199804000-00010

Pabon, P., McAllister, A., Sederholm, E., and Sundberg, J. (2000). Dynamics and voice quality information in the computer phonetograms of children's voices. In: P.J. White (ed.), *Child Voice*, pp. 86–100. Stockholm: KTH.

Perry, T.L., Ohde, R.N., and Ashmead, D.H. (2001). The acoustic bases for gender identification from children's voices. *Journal of the Acoustical Society of America* 109(6): 2988. doi:10.1121/1.1370525

Pittam, J. (1987). The long-term spectral measurement of voice quality as a social and personality marker: a review. *Language and Speech* 30(1): 1–12.

Pittam, J. and Gallois, C. (1986). Predicting impressions of speakers from voice quality acoustic and perceptual measures. *Journal of Language and Social Psychology* 5: 233–247.

Pittam, J., Gallois, C., and Callan, V. (1990). The long-term spectrum and perceived emotion. *Speech Communication* 9(3): 177–187. doi:10.1016/0167-6393(90)90055-E

Pittam, J. and Scherer, K.R. (1993). Vocal expression and communication of emotion. In: M. Lewis and J.M. Haviland (eds), *Handbook of Emotion*, pp. 185–197. New York: Guilford Press.

Polgar, G. and Weng, T. (1979). The functional development of the respiratory system: from the period of gestation to adulthood. *American Review of Respiratory Disease* 120: 625–695.

Pollermann, B.Z. and Archinard, M. (2002). Acoustic patterns of emotions. In: E. Keller, G. Bailly, A. Monoghan, J. Terken, and M. Huckvale (eds), *Improvements in Speech Synthesis*, pp. 237–245. Chichester: John Wiley and Sons.

Prakup, B. (2010). Acoustic measures of the voices of older singers and non-singers. *Journal of Voice* 26(3): 341–350.

Pribuisiene, R., Uloza, V., and Kardisiene, V. (2011). Voice characteristics of children aged between 6 and 13 years: impact of age, gender, and vocal training. *Logopedics Phoniatrics Vocology* 36(4): 150–155. doi:10.1002/0470845945

Price, P.J. (1989). Male and female voice source characteristics: inverse filtering results. *Speech Communication* 8: 261–277.

Querleu, D., Lefebvre, C., Tirtan, M., Renard, X., Morillon, M., and Crepin, G. (1984). Reaction of the newborn infant less than 2 hours after birth to the maternal voice. *Journal of Gynecological and Obstetric Biology and Reproduction* 13: 125–134.

Rendall, D., Kolias, S., Ney, C., and Lloyd, P. (2005). Pitch and formant profiles of human vowels and vowel-like baboon grunts: the role of body size and voice acoustic allometry. *Journal of the Acoustical Society of America* 117: 944–955.

Riecker, A., Ackerman, H., Wildgrüber, D., Grzegork, D., and Wolfgang, G. (2000). Opposite hemispheric lateralization effects during speaking and singing at motor cortex, insula and cerebellum. *NeuroReport* 11(9): 1997–2000.

Rinta, T. and Welch, G.F. (2008). Should singing activities be included in speech and voice therapy for prepubertal children? *Journal of Voice* 22(1): 100–112.

Robb, M.P. and Saxman, J.H. (1985). Developmental trends in vocal fundamental frequency of young children. *Journal of Speech, Language and Hearing Research* 28: 421–427.

Rothenberg, M. (1979). Some relations between glottal airflow and vocal fold contact area. *Proceedings of Conference on Assessment of Vocal Pathology. ASHA Reports*, No. 11, pp. 88–96.

Sachs, J., Lieberman, P., and Erikson, D. (1973). Anatomical and cultural determinants of male and female speech. In: R.W. Shuy and R.W. Fasold (eds), *Language Attitudes: Current Trends and Prospects*, pp. 74–84. Washington, DC: Georgetown University Press.

Sapienza, C.M. and Hoffman, B. (2000). Documentation of clinical features. In: P. White (ed.), *Child Voice*, pp. 105–128. Stockholm: KTH.

Scherer, K.R. (1979). Personality markers in speech. In: K.R. Scherer and H. Giles (eds), *Social Markers in Speech*, pp. 147–209. London: Cambridge University Press.

Scherer, K.R. and Scherer, U. (1981). Speech behaviour and personality. In: K. Scherer, U. Scherer, and J. Darby (eds), *Speech Evaluation in Psychiatry*, pp. 115–135. New York: Grune and Stratton.

Schneider, B. and Bigenzahn, W. (2003). Influence of glottal closure configuration on vocal efficiency in young normal-speaking women. *Journal of Voice* 17(4): 468–480.

Schneider, B., Zumtobel, M., Prettenhofer, W., Aichstill, B., and Jocher, W. (2010). Normative voice range profiles in vocally trained and untrained children aged between 7 and 10 years. *Journal of Voice* 24(2): 153–160.

Schön, D., Gordon, R, Campagne, A., Magne, C., Astesano, C., Anton, J.-L. and Besson, M. (2010). Similar cerebral networks in language, music and song perception. *NeuroImage* 51(1): 450–461.

Schwartz, M.F. and Rine, H. (1968). Identification of speaker sex from isolated whispered vowels. *Journal of the Acoustical Society of America* 44: 1736–1737.

Sergeant, D.C. and Welch, G.F. (1997). Perceived similarities and differences in the singing of trained childrens' choirs. *Choir Schools Today* 11: 9–10.

Sergeant, D.C., Sjölander, P.J. and Welch, G.F. (2005). Listeners' identification of gender differences in children's singing. *Research Studies in Music Education* 24(1): 28–39.

Sergeant, D.C. and Welch, G.F. (2008). Age related changes in Long Term Average Spectra of children's voices. *Journal of Voice* 22(6): 657–670.

Sergeant, D.C. and Welch, G.F. (2009). Gender differences in the Long Term Average Spectra of children's singing voices. *Journal of Voice* 23(3): 319–336.

Serrien, D.J., Ivry, R.B., and Swinnen, S.P. (2006). Dynamics of hemispheric specialization and integration in the context of motor control. *Nature Reviews Neuroscience* 7: 160–166.

Seshadri, G. and Yegnanarayana, B. (2009). Perceived loudness of speech based on the characteristics of glottal excitation source. *Journal of the Acoustical Society of America* 126(4): 2061–2071.

Sguoros, S., Natarajan, K., Hockley, A.D., Goldin, J.H., and Wake, M. (1999). Skull base growth in childhood. *Pediatric Neurosurgery* 31: 2061–2071.

Shirastev, R. and Sapienza, C.M. (2003). Objective measures of breathy voice quality obtained using an auditory model. *Journal of the Acoustical Society of America* 114: 2217–2224.

Shoji, K., Regenbogen, W., Vu, J.D., and Blaugrund, S.M. (1992). High frequency power ratio of breathy voice. *Laryngoscope* 102: 267–271.

Shute, B. and Wheldall, K. (1989). Pitch alterations in British motherese: some preliminary acoustic data. *Journal of Child Language* 16(3): 503. doi:10.1017/S0305000900010680

Siupsinskiene, N. and Lycke, H. (2011). Effects of vocal training on singing and speaking voice characteristics in vocally healthy adults and children based, on choral and non-choral data. *Journal of Voice* 25(4): 177–189. doi:10.1016/j.voice.2010.03.010.Epub2010 aug11

Skuk, V.G. and Schweinberger, S.R. (2012). Gender differences in familiar voice recognition. *Hearing Research* 296: 131–140.

Smith, D.R.R. and Patterson, R.D. (2005). The interaction of glottal-pulse rate and vocal-tract length in judgements of speaker sex and age. *Journal of the Acoustical Society of America* 118: 3177–3186.

Smith, M.E., Ramig, L.O., Dromey, C., Perez, K.S., and Ramandan, R. (1995). Intensive voice treatment in Parkinson disease: laryngostroboscopic findings. *Journal of Voice* 9(4): 453–459.

Smith-Vaughan, B.J. (2007). *The impact of singing styles on tension in the adolescent voice.* PhD thesis, University of North Carolina-Greensboro.

Södersten, M. and Lindestad, P.-A. (1990). Glottal closure and perceived breathiness during phonation in normally speaking subjects. *Journal of Speech, Language and Hearing Research* 33: 601–611.

Södersten, M., Hertegard, S., and Hammaberg, B. (1995). Glottal closure, transglottal airflow, and voice quality in healthy middle-aged women. *Journal of Voice* 9(2): 182–197. doi:10.1016/S0892-1997(05)80252-8

Sohmer, H., and Freemen, S. (2001). The pathway for the transmission of external sounds into the fetal inner ear. *Journal of Basic Clinical Physiology and Pharmacology* 12(2 Suppl): 91–99.

Sohmer, H., Rerez, R., Sichel, J.-Y., Priner, R., and Freeman, S. (2001). The pathway enabling external sounds to reach and excite the fetal inner ear. *Audiology and Neuro-Otology* 6(3): 109–116.

Sparing, R., Meister, G., Wienemann, M., Buette, D., Stadgen, B., and Boroojerdi, B. (2007). Task-dependent modulation of functional connectivity between hand motor cortices and neural networks underlying language and music: a trans-cranial magnetic stimulation study in humans. *European Journal of Neuroscience* 25(1): 319–323.

Spence, M.J., Rollins, P.R., and Jerger, S. (2002). Children's recognition of cartoon voices. *Journal of Speech, Language and Hearing Research* 45(1): 319–323.

Stathopoulos, E.T. (2000). A review of the development of child voice: an anatomical and functional perspective. In: P.J. White (ed.), *Child Voice*, pp. 1–12. Stockholm: KTH.

Stathopoulos, E.T. and Sapienza, C.M. (1997). Developmental changes in laryngeal and respiratory function with variations in sound pressure level. *Journal of Speech, Language and Hearing Research* 40: 595–614.

Stone, R.E., Cleveland, T.F., Sundberg, J., and Prokop, J. (2003). Aerodynamic and acoustical measures of speech, operatic and Broadway vocal styles in a professional female singer. *Journal of Voice* 17(3): 283–297.

Sulter, A.M. and Abers, F.W.J. (1996). The effects of frequency and intensity level on glottal closure in normal subjects. *Clinical Otolaryngology and Allied Sciences* 21(4): 324–327. doi:10.1111/j.1365-2273.1996.tb01079.x

Sundberg, J. (1990). What's so special about singers? *Journal of Voice* 4: 107–119.

Sundberg, J. (1995). Vocal fold vibration patterns and modes of phonation. *Folia phoniatrica et logopedica* 47(4): 218–228.

Sundberg, J. (2001). Level and centre frequency of the singer's formant. *Journal of Voice* 15(2): 176–186.

Sundberg, J., Gu, L., Huang, Q., and Huang, P. (2012). Acoustical study of classical Peking opera singing. *Journal of Voice* 26(2): 137–143.

Tarnoczy, T. and Fant, G. (1964). Some remarks on the average speech spectrum. *Quarterly Progress Reports, KTH* 5(4): 13–14.

Ternström, S. (1993). Long-time average spectrum characteristics of different choirs in different rooms. *Voice* 2: 55–77.

Thurman, L. and Welch, G.F. (2000). *Bodymind and Voice: Foundations of Voice Education.* Iowa City: National Center of Voice and Speech.

Tierney, A., Dick, F., Deutsch, D., and Sereno, M. (2013). Speech versus song: multiple pitch sensitive areas revealed by naturally occurring musical illusion. *Cerebral Cortex* 23(2): 249–254.

Titze, I.R. (1994). *Principles of Voice Production.* Englewood Cliffs, NJ: Prentice Hall.

Titze, I.R. and Story, B.H. (1997). Acoustic interactions of the voice source with the lower vocal tract. *Journal of the Acoustical Society of America* 101(4): 2234–2243.

Trask, R.L. (1996). *A Dictionary of Phonetics and Phonology.* Abingdon, UK: Routledge.

Trehub, S.E., Unyk, A.M., and Trainor, L.J. (1993). Maternal singing in cross-cultural perspective. *Infant Behaviour and Development* 16(3): 285–295.

Tsai, W.-H. (2012). Singer identification based on spoken data in voice characterisation. *Transactions on Audio, Speech and Language Processing* 20(8): 2291–2300. doi:10.1109/TASC.2012.2201473

Voegtline, K.M., Costigan, K.A., Pater, H.A., and DiPietro, J.A. (2013). Near-term fetal response to maternal spoken voice. *Infant Behaviour and Development* 36(4): 526–533.

Vorperian, H.K., Kent, R.D., Gentry, L.R., and Yandell, B.S. (1999). Magnetic resonance imaging procedures to study the concurrent anatomic development of vocal tract structures: preliminary results. *International Journal of Pediatric Otorhinolaryngology* 49(3): 197–206. doi:10.1016/S0165-5876(99)00208-6

Vorperian, H.K., Kent, R.D., Lindstrom, A.M., Kalina, C.M., Gentry, L.R., and Yandell, B.S. (2005). Development of vocal tract length during early childhood: a magnetic resonance imaging study. *Journal of the Acoustical Society of America* 17: 338–350.

Vorperian, H.K. and Kent, R.D. (2007). Vowel acoustic space development in children: a synthesis of acoustic and anatomic data. *Journal of Speech, Language and Hearing Research* 50(6): 1510–1545.

Vorperian, H.K., Wang, S., Chung, M.K., Schimek, E.M., Durtschi, R.B., Kent, R.D., Ziegert, A.J., and Gentry, L.R. (2007). Anatomic development of the oral and pharyngeal portions of the vocal tract: an imaging study. *Journal of the Acoustical Society of America* 125(3): 1666–1678.

Vorperian, H.L., Wang, S., Schimek, E.M., Durtschi, R.B., Kent, R.D., Gentry, L.R., and Chung, M. (2011). Developmental sexual dimorphism of the oral-pharyngeal portion of the vocal tract: an imaging study. *Journal of Speech, Language and Hearing Research* 54: 995–1010.

Vuorenkoski, V., Lenke, H.L., Tjernlund, P., Vuorenkoski, L., and Perheentupa, J. (1978). Fundamental voice frequency during normal and abnormal growth and after androgen treatment. *Archive of Disease in Children* 53: 201–209.

Watts, D. (2013). Sociolinguistic variation in vowels. In: M. Ball and F. Gibbon (eds), *Handbook of Vowels and Vowel Disorders*, pp. 207–228. Abingdon, UK: Psychology Press.

Watts, C., Barnes-Burroughs, K., Estis, J., and Blanton, D. (2006). The singing power ratio as an objective measure of singing voice quality in untrained talented and nontalented singers. *Journal of Voice* 20(1): 82–88. doi:10.1016/j.jvoice.2004.12.003

Weinberg, B. and Bennett, S. (1971). Speaker sex recognition of 5–6 year old children's voices. *Journal of the Acoustical Society of America* 50: 1210–1213.

Welch, G.F. and Sundberg, J. (2002). Solo voice. In: R. Parncutt and G.E. McPherson (eds), *The Science and Psychology of Music Performance*, pp. 253–268. New York: Oxford University Press.

Wendler, J., Doherty, E.T., and Hollien, H. (1980). Voice classification by means of long-term speech spectra. *Folia phoniatrica et logopedica* 32: 51–60.

Wendler, J., Rauhut, A., and Kruger, H. (1986). Classification of voice qualities. *Journal of Phonetics* 14: 483–488.

Wermke, K., Mende, W., Manfred, C., and Bruscaglioni, P. (2002). Developmental aspects of infant's cry melody and formants. *Medical Engineering and Physics* 24(7): 501–514.

Weusthoff, S., Baucom, B.R., and Hahlweg, K. (2013). Fundamental frequency during couple conflict: an analysis of physiological, behavioural, and sex-linked information encoded in vocal expression. *Journal of Family Psychology* 27(2): 212–220.

Wheeler, M.P. (1983). Context-related age changes in mothers' speech: joint book reading. *Journal of Child Language* 10(1): 259–263. doi:10.1017/S0305000900005304

White, P.J. (1999). Formant frequency analysis of children's voices using long-term average spectrum. *Journal of Voice* 13: 570–582.

White, P.J. (2001). Long-term average spectrum (LTAS) analysis of sex-and-gender-related differences in children's voices. *Logopedics Phoniatrics Vocology* 26(3): 97–101.

Whiteside, S.P. and Hodgson, C. (1999). Acoustic characteristics in 6–10-year-old children's voices: some preliminary findings. *Logopedics Phoniatrics Vocology* 24(1): 6–13.

Whiteside, S.P., Hodgson, C., and Tapster, C. (2002). Vocal characteristics of pre-adolescent children: a longitudinal study. *Logopedics Phoniatrics Vocology* 27: 12–20.

Wolfe, V.I., Ratusnik, D., Smith, F., and North, G. (1990). Intonation and fundamental frequency of male-to-female transsexuals. *Journal of Speech and Hearing Disorders* 55: 43–50.

Wu, K. and Childers, D.G. (1991). Gender recognition from speech: Part 1: coarse analysis. *Journal of the Acoustical Society of America* 90: 1820–1840.

Zetterholm, E. (1998). Prosody and voice quality in the expression of emotions. In: R. Mannell and J. Robert-Ribes (eds), *Proceedings of the 7th Australian International Conference on Speech Science and Technology*, November 30, Sydney, Australia, pp. 109–113. Sydney: Australian Speech Science and Technology Association.

CHAPTER 10

PERCEPTUAL FEATURES IN SINGING

DAVID M. HOWARD AND ERIC J. HUNTER

INTRODUCTION TO HEARING

FOR singers, hearing is a critical component for voice production in terms of how they monitor their own vocal output, how they monitor the outputs from any other musicians involved in the performance, and how they appreciate the acoustic nature of the space in which they are performing. Hearing is rarely specifically mentioned in the context of singing or musical training; it is essentially simply taken for granted as one of the human senses that is always switched on to function as an element of the human perceptual system monitoring the world around us. Human hearing is rather like human voice production in that, while they are both typically taken for granted, one is very aware of them when they go wrong and stop working normally.

Human hearing is the sense via which we pick up the sounds around us. These sounds are acoustic pressure variations that travel in the air from the sources of sound (such as musical instruments, singers, loudspeakers, environmental sounds, domestic appliances, heavy machinery, or traffic) through the local environment, being reflected off its surfaces until they reach the listeners' ears. Having two ears enables us to localize the direction from which sounds are coming, particularly horizontally, but also to a lesser degree vertically.

Human hearing anatomy

The human ear is usually considered in three parts known as the *outer, middle*, and *inner* ears, which relate to sound transmission that is (1) acoustic in air, (2) mechanical via bones, and (3) mechanical to electrical via neural transduction respectively (see Figure 10.1). The incoming sound reaches the eardrum acoustically via the external tube known as the ear canal, or *external auditory meatus*. The eardrum is the boundary between the outer and middle ears, and mechanical vibrations of the eardrum set the three bones of the middle ear—the *malleus* (hammer), *incus* (anvil), and *stapes* (stirrup)—into vibration, transmitting the sound to the *oval window* of the snail-shaped *cochlea*. The oval window is the boundary between the middle and inner ears. Within the cochlea, individual frequency components

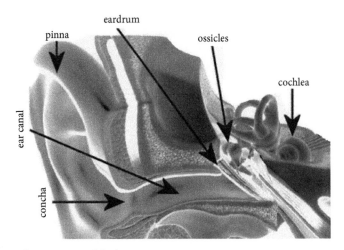

FIGURE 10.1 The anatomy of the human ear.

Adapted from Howard and Angus 2009.

in the incoming sound are isolated due to the mechanical action of the *basilar membrane* within the cochlea. This in turn responds to individual frequency components in a sound at different positions or *places* along its length, thereby triggering responses in hair cells at that position that fire electrically to transmit the response to the brain via the neurons of the VIIIth nerve.

In terms of those parts of the hearing system that are relevant to hearing singing, the first resonant frequency of the ear canal of the outer ear, which is around 2.5 to 4 kHz, is responsible for defining the frequency region within which humans are most sensitive for sound. This is directly linked to the *singer's formant cluster* (see Sundberg, The Acoustics of Different Genres of Singing, this volume), a resonance peak associated particularly with the voice of an opera soloist as a result of the acoustic properties of his epilarynx tube. By focusing sound energy into this frequency region, opera soloists are taking advantage of the most sensitive region in all listeners' hearing to be heard above an orchestra and to communicate their message.

The most important part of the hearing system that is relevant to hearing singing is the combined actions of the basilar membrane and the neural transduction to higher centers. Additionally important is cognitive function in terms of the way that the essential musical properties of pitch, loudness, and timbre are perceived as well as how singing is heard, how voice is perceived in the context of environmental factors, and the effect of high-frequency energy. These are the topics of this chapter.

PERCEIVING ESSENTIAL MUSICAL PROPERTIES

Hearing pitch

When different notes with the same loudness and duration are played on a musical instrument, we hear a change in pitch. This change is generally described as a raising or lowering of pitch with some notes being higher or lower than others. The formal definition of *pitch* as stated by the American National Standards Institute (ANSI) is "that attribute of auditory sensation in terms of which sounds may be ordered on a scale extending from high to low" (ANSI 1973).

It is important to note that assigning a pitch to a note is a *subjective* experience in that a human subject is involved, and a complete understanding of exactly how various acoustic features of a musical note contribute to the perception of pitch does not currently exist. In the context of singing performance, this is important to be aware of because even the smallest pitch changes can have a direct effect on the overall musical listening experience for performers and audience alike, especially in terms of overall tuning, due to fine changes in intonation. Awareness of this and what aspects of the acoustic output can have an effect on the perceived pitch is an extremely useful performance device, since singers change a number of acoustic features in their sung output for various reasons, such as vowels and consonants to convey the text, dynamic changes to perform the score, and modifications to the high-frequency content for sound projection. These changes can have a direct effect on the pitch perceived by other singers and listeners alike. This is particularly important since it impacts directly on overall tuning of the notes of the singer's part, as well as intonation between parts in *a cappella* singing (see Howard, Intonation and Staying in Tune in a *Cappella* Choral Singing, this volume).

Fundamental frequency and pitch

Having noted that there are a number of acoustic features in a sound that can affect how its pitch is perceived, the single most important acoustic change in a pitched sound that affects its perceived pitch directly is the number of repeating cycles per second, or the *fundamental frequency* (denoted herein as f_0). Since f_0 can be measured directly scientifically, it is an *objective* measure, and the unit used for the number of cycles per second is *Hertz*, or *Hz*. It should be noted that there are sounds for which a pitch is perceived, but for which there is no periodic acoustic signal, such as chimes, or the response one might give if asked to state which of the consonants in the two words "see" and "she" has the highest pitch (the majority response is that "ss" has a higher pitch than "sh"). In the context of hearing singing pitch, we are only interested in the former, or sounds that have repeating cycles.

Accounting for our ability to perceive the pitch of sung notes is based on finding the f_0 of the sound. This is grounded in an understanding of how the inner ear transforms the incoming acoustic signal into neural impulses; the perceptual processes for all human senses have neural impulses as their inputs. The information provided via neural impulses is twofold: (1) the particular *place* along the basilar membrane at which the hair cells respond to incoming sound by firing gives the frequency of the energy in the input (this is referred to as the *place* theory); and (2) the detailed nature of the basilar membrane response waveform in terms of how it varies with time provides *temporal* detail of the energy in the input (this is known as the *temporal* theory).

Harmonics of the fundamental and pitch perception

A sound that has a clear pitch associated with it has a repeating waveform, and the underlying frequency components will be harmonically related; that is, they must be exact integer (2^*f_0, 3^*f_0, 4^*f_0, 5^*f_0 . . . or the 2nd, 3rd, 4th, 5th . . . harmonics) multiples of the f_0. It is worth noting that the fundamental itself is $1*f_o$ and therefore is alternatively known as the *first harmonic*. To avoid any confusion with the use of the term overtones, it should be noted that the 1st overtone is the first tone that is *over* the f_o or the 2nd harmonic; thus, the 2nd overtone is the 3rd harmonic and so forth.

Any model of pitch perception has to be based on the neural firings that emerge from the inner ear in response to the input sound. The *place* mechanism signals to the brain the frequencies of individual components in the input sound directly. Therefore, models of pitch can be based on this. An early model of pitch perception proposed by Ohm in 1843, known as Ohm's *acoustical law* to differentiate it from his electrical law, suggests that a pitch corresponding to a certain frequency can only be heard if the acoustical wave contains power at that frequency. This implies that it is the presence of the lowest frequency component (f_o) that provides the basis for pitch perception. This is fine providing f_o is present in a sound, which it usually is. However, if the f_o is absent (perhaps it has been filtered out), Ohm's law suggests that the perceived pitch would be the next lowest component or $2*f_o$ which would be an octave higher. In practice, this is not what happens; the pitch remains the same, but the f_o is missing. The explanation for pitch perception in the case of such sounds with a missing f_o is that the minimum frequency spacing between any two adjacent harmonics must be f_o, and this provides a secure basis for explaining pitch perception.

This is fine providing that individual harmonics are isolated by the basilar membrane frequency analysis, but it turns out that they are not. This is a direct consequence of the way the basilar membrane functions, where it is most discriminating for low-frequency components compared to higher frequency components. Thus, in pitch perception there is a frequency above which individual harmonics are not isolated, namely the 6th to 7th harmonic, no matter what the f_o is. Therefore, explaining pitch perception based on spacing between individual harmonics is only valid up to the 6th or 7th harmonic. Place theory cannot explain a perceived pitch for sounds with no harmonics below the 7th. Such sounds do not occur in nature, in the singing voice, or in the output from acoustic musical instruments. Nevertheless, they can readily be synthesized electronically and, therefore, explored. It turns out that a pitch is readily perceived for such sounds, and therefore further explanation is necessary.

The basis for this ability lies in the nature of the outputs along the basilar membrane where harmonics are not isolated; more than one harmonic is being indicated by the vibration pattern of the basilar membrane at any position. Since the components are harmonics, it will be two or more harmonics that are "seen." These will form a "beat" waveform in which the amplitude rises and falls at their difference frequency, which for any two adjacent harmonics will be f_o. Consequently, the stimulating waveform on the basilar membrane is a beat waveform at the f_o, and this will be the case at all positions along the basilar membrane above approximately the frequency of the 7th harmonic. The beating will be at the f_o in all cases. Hence, since neural firing occurs in synchrony with the stimulating waveform, the neural firing will be at the f_o. This is known as the *temporal theory* of pitch perception.

Perceiving differences in pitch

Thus, there is a basis for explaining pitch perception for any sound based on harmonics. For singers, a critically important aspect of pitch perception is its role in enabling in-tune singing. To do this, a singer has to be able to process an external reference pitch—from other singers or accompaniment, as well as from their own pitch—and make a relative judgment

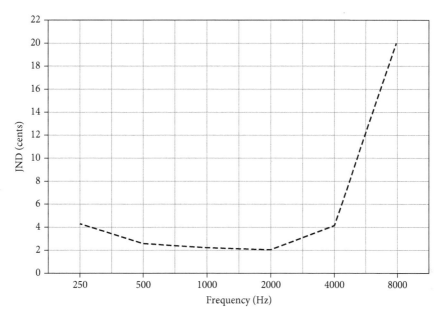

FIGURE 10.2 Just noticeable difference (JND) for pitch as a function of fundamental frequency for a 200 ms sinewave and frequencies indicated on the X axis.

Data based on Moore 1973.

between them. Note-pitching accuracy when singing relies on being able to hear one's own output as well as some reference which might be another singer or the accompaniment. The minimum pitch difference one can distinguish between two notes is known as the *just noticeable difference*, or *JND*. For sinewaves, the JND varies with fundamental frequency, as shown in Figure 10.2 where the JND is expressed in cents (one hundredths of a semitone). It is interesting to note that the number of discrete pitch steps in human hearing is around 1400, whereas the number of distinct musical notes on the equal tempered scale within the usable hearing range is 120. It should be noted that pitch perception in the context of speech is not the same as pitch perception in the context of singing (Zatorre and Baum 2012).

If two notes are heard together, the pitching accuracy improves due to an undulating interaction between the notes known as *beating*, which is the basis used for tuning musical instruments such as a guitar, flute, or violin. For singers, however, beating cannot be taken advantage of as a rule due to the potential presence of large pitch variation known as vibrato. This is particularly common in opera singers and can vary by up to a semitone up and down at a rate of around 5.5 times a second, or 5.5 Hz, and small pitch changes exhibited by all singers, known as *flutter*. Any pitch variation such as flutter or vibrato will itself cause a variation in beating for notes close together in pitch, making tuning changes very difficult. When a singer is tuning to another singer, these issues are compounded.

Hearing loudness and decibels

Loudness is a subjective measure and, like pitch, it too requires a human subject to make the judgment. The formal definition of *loudness* as stated by the American National

Standards Institute (ANSI) is "that intensive attribute of auditory sensation in terms of which sounds may be ordered on a scale extending from soft to loud" (ANSI 1973). The energy level in an acoustic signal can be measured objectively, and this is usually quoted in decibels (dB). The main thing to bear in mind when using dB is that it indicates how much greater (positive dB value) or smaller (negative dB value) a measurement is compared to a reference level. A value of 0 dB indicates that the signal of interest has exactly the same level as the reference (it is zero dB, so neither greater nor smaller than the reference). The reference level has to be defined, and there are specific dB scales that are used that include their reference values.

dB(SPL)

An important dB scale in acoustics is the dB(SPL), or dB Sound Pressure Level scale, which has a defined reference of 10 micro Pascals (essentially the quietest sound level young humans can on average hear at a frequency of 1 kHz, as hearing acuity worsens in later life). The dB scale is a logarithmic scale that is used because it approximates to the way our senses perceive stimuli, whether sound, light, taste, smell, or touch. For sound, this is relevant to our perception of both pitch and loudness; a fixed perceived change in pitch (musical interval such as an octave, perfect fifth, major third) or loudness (doubling or halving) results from a particular dB change. Being a logarithmic scale, a particular dB variation is equivalent to a fixed *ratio* variation of the stimulus itself (doubling, trebling, quadrupling, etc.). Perceived equal steps in loudness change are a result from changing the input signal level by a constant number of dB (this is a property of the logarithm; adding logarithmic values is equivalent to multiplying the original values, while subtracting logarithmic values is equivalent to dividing the original values).

Changes in power and pressure

As useful rules of thumb (see Table 10.1), a zero dB change is equivalent to a ratio of 1 for any quantity as indicated above (here for both pressure or power), a –3 dB or +3 dB change is equivalent to a halving or doubling in *power* respectively, a –6 dB or +6 dB change is equivalent to a quartering or halving quadrupling in *pressure* respectively, a -10 dB or +10 dB change is equivalent to a tenfold increase/decrease in *power* respectively, and a –20 dB or +20 dB change is equivalent to a tenfold increase/decrease in *pressure* respectively. Other ratios can be gained from these rules of thumb, particularly the ratio changes for +/–3 dB. An example that can be compared with Table 10.2 would be a +9 dB change expressed as a power ratio, which would be equivalent to changing by +3 dB three times (9 = 3*3) which would give a doubling, followed by another doubling followed by another doubling, or 2*2*2 (or 2^3) giving a power ratio for a +9 dB change of 8.

Perception of loudness

Human perception of loudness changes with frequency in terms of how we hear sounds that we judge to be equally loud. The plots in Figure 10.3 show the typical nature of equal loudness curves for human hearing. Each of the dashed lines in the figure show the sound

Table 10.1 Useful decibel (dB) values and their equivalent pressure and power ratios

Decibels (dB)	Pressure ratio	Power ratio
−20	0.100	0.010
−10	0.316	0.100
−9	0.355	0.126
−6	0.501	0.251
−3	0.708	0.501
0	1.000	1.000
+3	1.413	1.995
+6	1.995	3.981
+9	2.818	7.943
+10	3.162	10.000
+20	10.000	100.000

level in dB(SPL) required for a sinewave at a particular frequency to sound equally loud to listeners. Thus a sinewave at 100 Hz with a level of around 76 dB(SPL) sounds equally loud to a sinewave at 1 kHz with a level of 70 dB(SPL). These equal loudness contours have their own unit: the "phon." The number of phons is defined as the loudness of a sinewave at 1 kHz at that number of dB(SPL). Figure 10.3 shows equal loudness contours at 10, 30, 50, 70, 90, and 110 phons, and for each plot, the dB(SPL) value at 1 kHz equals the number of phons of the particular curve. Notice that the ear is definitely not a hifi sound-receiving organ with a flat frequency response! It is also worth noting that the phon curves become flatter (there is less overall dB(SPL) variation) for higher phon values; this is therefore termed a "non-linear" phenomenon.

Changing perceived loudness

Another feature of loudness relates to what change in level is required for a listener to hear a fixed change, for example a doubling, in loudness. This can be explored by playing sounds of known dB(SPL) levels to listeners alongside a reference sound and asking listeners to indicate how much louder they think the test sound is compared to the reference. For example, a listener might be asked to take the reference sound level as being 100, and if they think the

Table 10.2 The phon and sone scales

Phons	40	50	60	70	80	90	100
Sones	1	2	4	8	16	32	64

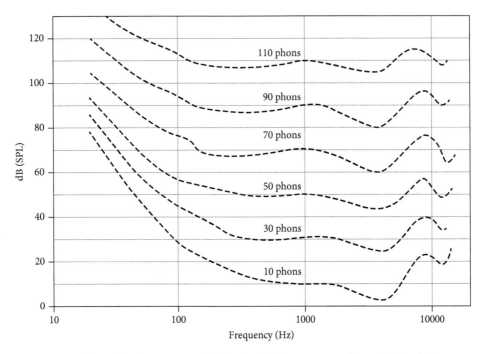

FIGURE 10.3 Equal loudness curves indicating the frequency and amplitude of sinewaves that would sound equally loud on average to listeners; these curves define the *phon* scale, where the number of phons is equal to the dB(SPL) level of a 1 kHz pure tone.

test sound is twice as loud, they should put 200, half as loud, they should put 50, and so on. The result of this experiment turns out to indicate that we need, on average a 10 dB change in sound level to perceive a doubling in loudness. This is somewhat surprising since, as indicated above, a doubling in sound intensity or pressure arises from a +3 dB or +6 dB increase respectively. There is an absolute scale of loudness known as the *sone* scale, and 1 sone is defined as the perceived loudness of a 1 kHz sine wave at 40 dB(SPL). Thus the relationship between sones and phons can be easily established as shown in Table 10.2.

Hearing timbre

If asked about relevant things to listen carefully for when performing, a majority of musicians will probably have no difficulty naming and/or understanding what loudness/dynamics and pitch means. However, when it comes to *timbre*, things are far less clear. While the word *timbre* is commonly used, providing an explanation of what it means is much harder. Loudness and pitch can both be described with reference to a perceptual rating scale in one dimension (e.g. *soft* to *loud* for loudness and *low* to *high* for pitch), but no such one-dimensional rating scale exists for timbre. The timbre of a sound relates to a perceived difference between two sounds when they are heard at the same pitch, the same loudness, and the same duration. Thus if the note A4 (440 Hz), the A above middle C, is played at the same pitch, loudness, and duration on a violin, oboe, clarinet, trumpet, or flute, or is sung by a soprano or alto on different vowels, and differences can be perceived, these notes differ in their timbre. The formal definition of *timbre* as stated by the American National Standards Institute (ANSI) is "Timbre is that attribute of auditory sensation in terms of which a listener can judge two sounds that are perceived as being different but which have the same perceived loudness and pitch as being dissimilar" (ANSI 1973).

Onset, steady state, and offset

A musical note can be considered in three parts: the *note onset*, the *steady state*, and the *note offset*. The acoustic aspects that are different between sounds that differ in timbre are (1) the spectrum of the sound (the frequency components, usually harmonics for pitched sounds, of the sound); (2) the time envelope (or amplitude of the sound) from the initial onset to the end of the note offset; and (3) any more rapid variation in the time envelope during the steady-state part (such as vibrato—fundamental frequency modulation—or tremolo—amplitude modulation). When the steady-state parts of a note are observed, even for instruments where one might expect it to be particularly steady, such as a single note on a single stop of a pipe organ, one finds that the so-called steady-state portion is not particularly steady in practice.

In terms of hearing timbre, this is based on the frequency analysis of the incoming sound that is carried out by the basilar membrane (see "Harmonics of the fundamental and pitch perception") within the inner ear. Thus the importance of the frequency components in a sound as carrying information about timbre is not a surprise. The importance of the time envelope of the sound for timbre perception demonstrates the importance of time analysis of incoming sounds, something that the human ear is particularly good at. The note onset, such as a plucked string, the first (quite complex) sound a bow makes on a string, the initial sound made when a brass player starts a note (often referred to as a *consonantal* attack), the initial strike of a drum stick on a drum head or a piano hammer on its string(s) are all vital acoustic cues to timbre and instrument identification.

Any judgment of timbre differences has to be made subjectively and, therefore, with human subjects taking part in listening tests. Timbre is often studied by asking subjects to rate different sounds using adjective pairs of opposites such as: dark to bright, dull to clear, non-wooden to wooden, non-metallic to metallic, static to dynamic, cold to hot or pure to rich. While, in principle, one might reasonably expect listeners to have some consensus in such experiments, it is not always the case that there is strong agreement. Listening is a personal matter and the mapping of everyday adjectives onto descriptors of sounds is not, for most people, an everyday task.

Choral blend and timbre

In terms of singing, especially in a choral situation, blend becomes particularly important. Good blend results from all singers producing individual vowels that are acoustically close to each other; this is a matter of timbre—appropriate intonation (pitch) and dynamic (loudness) are assumed. This involves careful listening to other singers since there are a number of variants of any given vowel, as exemplified by different accents within a language, and if a mixture of these is produced together, they do not result in good overall blend. Such variations between vowels result in acoustic spectral differences that are therefore perceived as timbral differences.

To date there is no one model of timbre and no single rating scale. Thus timbre remains as one subjective perceptual quantity that is not fully understood nor explained acoustically, but one that is critical to musical listening for performer and audience alike.

HEARING SINGING (OVERLAPPING THE SPECTRAL RANGE OF THE VOICE AND THE EAR)

If there is singing to be heard, its characteristics (e.g. pitch, loudness, timbre) can be identified and described. But how is singing *heard*? To better understand how singing is heard as a whole, let us look at how singers adjust their production in situations where they may (consciously or unconsciously) hear singing.

Trained singers have learned (whether consciously or not) to accommodate their production for the audience and/or the ensemble they are singing in. The goal of such a modification is dependent on what the singer hears or what they hope the audience may hear. For example, Rossing et al. (1986, 1987) demonstrated that trained singers produce different volumes and timbre depending on the situation (e.g. choral settings vs. solo settings). Further, the use of the *singer's formant* (Sundberg 1972, 1974, 1978) allows a singer to be *heard* above an orchestra or other accompaniment (Oliveira-Barrichelo et al. 2001). The singer's formant is a vocal tract resonance or enhancement of vocal output between 2.5 and 4 kHz; this seems to be the clustering of vocal tract formants 3, 4, and 5, which is why it is also called the *singer's formant cluster*. The convenience of this enhancement of vocal output between 2.5 and 4 kHz is that it matches the first resonance of the ear canal and, thus, the most sensitive frequencies of the human hearing range. In other words, the boost of sound from a singer employing this technique happens to affect the frequencies to which the human ear is most sensitive. This can be further illustrated in Figure 10.4.

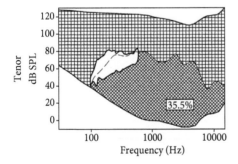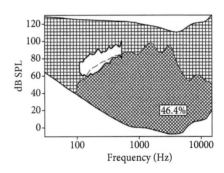

FIGURE 10.4 Hearing region (checkerboard pattern) with maximum spectral level (diagonal cross-hatch) and voice range profile (white) for two tenors, with an amateur shown on the left and a professional on the right. The percentage of the hearing range overlapped by the spectral level is shown in a box.

From Hunter, E.J. and Titze, I.R. (2005). Overlap of hearing and voicing ranges in singing. *Journal of Singing* 61(4): 387–392. Used with permission.

The overall average dynamic range of human hearing (from the lowest audible sound to the highest non-painful sound) is shown in Figure 10.4 where sound level (dB(SPL)) is plotted against frequency (Hz). Plotted within this hearing range is the voice range profile (dynamic range and pitch range—in white) of both an amateur (left) and professional (right) tenor. But this pitch and loudness range is only part of the hearing range and does not include the effects of the higher harmonics of the fundamental frequency. To illustrate the overall effect of song including the harmonics, also plotted in Figure 10.4 is the average spectral (all frequencies) output of the two singers (diagonal cross-hatch). When including the harmonics, a better idea of how singing can be picked up by the ear emerges. Consider the right side of Figure 10.4, which shows a professional tenor who produced voice that was rich in the frequencies where the ear requires the least sound to be heard. In this example, the professional singer's vocalization covered nearly half (46.4 percent) of the hearing range. Additionally, this overlap between the singer's formant and the sensitive part of the ear only describes part of how singing may be perceived.

Considering the singer's formant cluster and the most sensitive part of the audible spectrum is only one part of the story. In the study by Hunter and Titze (2005) from which Figure 10.4 above was reproduced, singers generated voice frequencies that overlapped with more than 45 percent of the entire hearing range of the ear (both dynamically and spectrally). When comparing different voice types, the mezzo-soprano and tenor singers in the study produced the widest range of frequencies in the range where the ear is most sensitive. This was calculated by looking at the dynamic range of the full spectrum (Figure 10.4, diagonal cross-hatch) that a singer could produce and the average dynamic range of the ear. The results for several singing types are shown in Figure 10.5 below, where the percentage of the hearing range overlapped by the sung sound is shown.

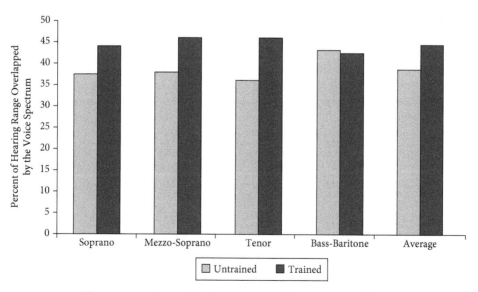

FIGURE 10.5 The average voice-to-hearing range overlap percentage for eight singers, four trained and four untrained.

After Hunter and Titze 2005.

Because of the nature of the hearing mechanism (including the brain), the increased overlap a sound would have over what is perceivable would likely be identified as a sense of richness or quality to a sound. In fact, two studies illustrate that the effect of the singer's formant makes a large and significant contribution to the overall perception of a sung vowel's loudness. Building on Hunter and Titze (2005), a follow-up study (Hunter et al. 2005) made an attempt to quantify this overlap using principles of psychoacoustics and the perception of a sung vowel's loudness. In the latter study, the sung spectrum was overlapped with the overall hearing spectrum, as discussed previously (Figure 10.4, diagonal cross-hatch), but with some additional analysis. This additional analysis converted the sung spectrum to a perceptual scale (first to phon, then to sone) so that an estimated perceived loudness difference between an untrained and trained singer could be illustrated. The contributions of effects, such as the singer's formant mixed with the sensitivities of the auditory system, helped trained singers produce 20–40% more units of loudness (called sones—see Table 10.2 above) than untrained singers (Figure 10.6a). The overall effect (in units of phon—see Figure 10.3 above) is shown in Figure 10.6b.

Therefore, in trying to understand the hearing and perception of singing, there is a symbiotic relationship between the performer and the hearer. Singers are taught or learn to maximize vocal output in light of the perception level of the ear. This allows for the question: Was the production of the singer's formant adopted specifically to exploit the most sensitive parts of the ear? Further expanding this topic could lead to questions concerning the depth of connectivity between the auditory and vocal systems, or perhaps even the joint evolution of the systems.

Perceiving voice, environmental factors

Much of how the sensitivity of the ear function overlaps with the singing voice and perception also depends on the acuity of a listener's perception of the acoustic environment. Additionally, how a performer perceives an environment may affect how they adapt their voice production to that environment. Historically, most studies of human perception of voice in an environment have been focused on how people adjust their voice in noise, with the implication that the adjustment is to allow a listener to perceive and understand voice better. The adjustment of voice production in a noisy environment is called the Lombard Effect or Lombard Reflex (Junqua 1993). Generally speaking, if a normal hearing vocalist is in an environment with elevated noise, the vocalist will naturally change their voice. This is usually done with elevated loudness, but a raised pitch and change in timbre can also be used. These effects can be similar to that of instructed or situational production (e.g. baby talk, clear speech; Burnham et al. 2002; Ferguson 2004).

How a vocalist adjusts to a room acoustic has more recently been quantified in terms of what has been dubbed *room gain*, which is analogous to the sound strength parameter from the international standard ISO 3382 (ISO 1997). This parameter represents the increase in the loudness that is caused by the room. However, when performing in a room with higher room gain, the voice power level should decrease (Brunskog et al. 2009; Pelegrin-Garcia et al. 2011a, 2011b). Most vocalists would rate a room with low gain as a "dead" room, while a room with higher gain would be considered a "live" room. This was previously thought to

(a)

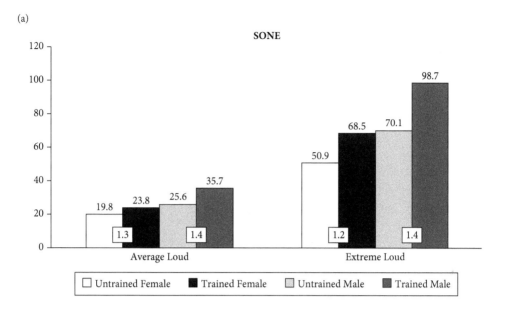

(b)

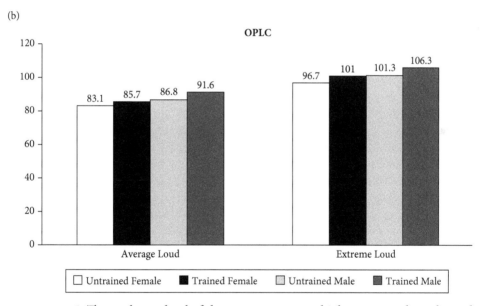

FIGURE 10.6 The total sone level of the spectra across multiple sung vowels, males and females, and trained and untrained singers is shown in the upper figure (a). In the lower figure (b), estimated total phon levels for all the vowels are shown. Extreme loud is taking the maximum spectral component across productions sung by the participants. Average loud is from the average spectral level across all productions.

be linked to the reverberation time of a room, but there is no evidence of a direct correlation between room gain and reverberation time.

This effect has been captured in a study of how vocalists adjust the performance of the same repertoire when going from a studio to a stage, where their vocal range was enhanced in a performance setting (Emerich et al. 2005). Such changes can be perceived as what has been termed vocal effort, a perceptual cue of a listener's estimate of the distance between the vocalist and the listener (Traunmuller and Erickson 2000).

The effect of high-frequency energy

Human hearing can extend up to 20 kHz, as can the spectral energy from human vocal production. Traditionally, higher-frequency sounds above 8 kHz have been more or less ignored when it comes to perceptual research (Monson et al. 2014). This is partly because so much of voice can be explained using lower frequencies. Nevertheless, our understanding of the effects of high frequencies has been increasing recently.

We have known for several years that trained singers produce high-frequency energy which may be useful to a listener. For example, in 1957, Fry and Manen showed that high-frequency acoustic energy differences were present as a singer changed the "production mood" (e.g. trying to portray aggressiveness, joyfulness, and fearfulness). Monson et al. (2011) illustrated that listeners could distinguish sound with such high-frequency energy changes, further showing that the sensitivity to the changes increased during real singing rather than just steady-sung vowels. This sensitivity to high-frequency changes affects listeners' perception of music, particularly its "naturalness" (Moore and Tan 2003).

Therefore it is possible that much of the quality of a singing voice could be this (often unstudied) high-frequency energy. Perhaps the perception of this high-frequency energy is what is judged by a listener as the outcome of training. Titze and Jin (2003) found that in trained singers, a fairly consistent peak of acoustic energy appears around 10 kHz. In a trained child soloist, listeners often describe the voice as "pure" or "clean." This judgment could be based on high-frequency energy appearing in the 7.5 to 11 kHz range in child soloists (Howard et al. 2014), giving a child soloist a unique perceptual quality.

Other qualities which have not been directly tied to singing, but which would have an effect on singing perception include: frequencies above 5 kHz and their correlation with perception of breathiness; ratings of naturalness affected by frequencies between 7 kHz and 11 kHz; listener preference and pleasantness for sounds including 10 kHz frequencies; increased ability to localize sounds; and intelligibility. (For an in-depth review of these correlates, see Monson et al. 2014.)

CONCLUSION

For singers, hearing is a critical component in how they monitor their own vocal output, how they monitor the outputs from any other musicians that they are performing with, and how they adapt to the acoustic nature of the space in which they are performing. Often taken for granted until there is a problem, hearing is rarely specifically mentioned in the context of singing or musical training.

The perception of sound, especially as related to the function of the auditory system, is complex. The sound we hear is not simply the output from singers/musicians. It is first modified by the acoustic characteristics of the environment. Before the sound is perceived by the brain, its frequency is shaped by the acoustic properties of the ear. Further, given that we rely on the frequency components in sounds for timbre and pitch perception, our hearing systems have to adapt as they receive inputs that are different, depending on the performing environment.

There are also a number of perceptual features that are specifically important in singing, for performers and audience alike. First, a singer's perception of their own acoustic output, as well as that of other singers/musicians, is a critical component of voice production. They must also monitor how these are affected by the acoustical characteristics of the performance environment. Second, singers must understand and utilize how sound is perceived by listeners. For those who perform without amplification, this is done by focusing acoustic energy specifically into the frequency region where all human ears are most sensitive, related to the singer's formant cluster. While this helps a singer be heard, it also affects how a singer perceives their sound in the acoustic space.

Recent studies have allowed us better to describe these perceptual features. Nevertheless, many of these features have been inherently recognized and utilized previously in vocal training pedagogy. For example, the singer's formant clustering in performing practice evolved independently of the cluster being labeled, measured, and described quantitatively. However, with an understanding of the physiological basis for these pedagogical techniques, these features can be better utilized.

References and further reading

American National Standards Institute (1973). *American National Psychoacoustical Terminology.* S3.20. New York: American Standards Association.

Brunskog, J., Anders, C.G., Bellester, G.P., and Calbo, L.R. (2009). Increase in voice level and speaker comfort in lecture rooms. *Journal of the Acoustical Society of America* 125(4): 2072–2082.

Burnham, D., Kitamura, C., and Vollmer-Conna, U. (2002). What's new, pussycat? On talking to babies and animals. *Science* 296(5572): 1435.

Emerich, K.A., Titze, I.R., Švec, J.G., Popolo, P.S., and Logan. G. (2005). Vocal range and intensity in actors: a studio versus stage comparison. *Journal of Voice* 19(1): 78–83.

Ferguson, S.H. (2004). Talker differences in clear and conversational speech: vowel intelligibility for normal-hearing listeners. *Journal of the Acoustical Society of America* 116(4, Pt. 1): 2365–2373.

Howard, D.M. and Angus, J.A.S. (2009). *Acoustics and Psychoacoustics*, 4th edn. Oxford: Focal Press.

Howard, D.M., Williams, J., and Herbst, C.T. (2014). "Ring" in the solo child singing voice. *Journal of Voice* 28(2): 161–169.

Hunter, E.J. and Titze, I.R. (2005). Overlap of hearing and voicing ranges in singing. *Journal of Singing* 61(4): 387–392.

Hunter, E.J., Švec, J.G., and Titze, I.R. (2005). Comparison of the produced and perceived voice range profiles in untrained and trained classical singers. *Journal of Voice* 20(4): 513–526.

ISO 3382:1997 (1997). *Acoustics—measurement of the reverberation time of rooms with reference to other acoustic parameters.* Geneva: International Organization for Standardization.

Junqua, J.A. (1993). The Lombard reflex and its role on human listeners and automatic speech recognizers. *Journal of the Acoustical Society of America* 93(1): 510–524. doi:10.1121/1.405631.

Monson, B.B., Lotto, A.J., and Ternström, S. (2011). Detection of high-frequency energy changes in sustained vowels produced by singers. *Journal of the Acoustical Society of America* 129(4): 2263–2268.

Monson, B.B., Hunter, E.J., Lotto, A.J., and Story, B.H. (2014). The perceptual significance of high-frequency energy in the human voice. *Frontiers in Psychology* 5: 587. doi: 10.3389/fpsyg.2014.00587.

Moore, B.C.J. (1973). Frequency difference limens for short-duration tones. *Journal of the Acoustical Society of America* 30(3): 610–619.

Moore, B.C.J. and Tan, C.T. (2003). Perceived naturalness of spectrally distorted speech and music. *Journal of the Acoustical Society of America* 114: 408–419.

Oliveira-Barrichelo, V., Heuer, R. J., Dean, C. M., and Sataloff, R.T. (2001). Comparison of singer's formant, speaker's ring, and LTA spectrum among classical singers and untrained normal speakers. *Journal of Voice* 15(3): 344–350.

Pelegrin-Garcia, D., Smits, G., Brunskog, J., and Jeong, C.H. (2011a). Vocal effort with changing talker-to-listener distance in different acoustic environments. *Journal of the Acoustical Society of America* 129(4): 1981–1990.

Pelegrin-Garcia, D., Fuentes-Mendizabal, O., Brunskog, J., and Jeong, C.H. (2011b). Equal autophonic level curves under different room acoustics conditions. *Journal of the Acoustical Society of America* 130(1): 228–238.

Rossing, T.D., Sundberg, J., and Ternström, S. (1986). Acoustic comparison of voice use in solo and choir singing. *Journal of the Acoustical Society of America* 79(6): 1975–1981.

Rossing, T.D., Sundberg, J., and Ternström, S. (1987). Acoustic comparison of soprano solo and choir singing. *Journal of the Acoustical Society of America* 82(3): 830–836.

Sundberg, J. (1972). An articulatory interpretation of the "singing formant." *Speech Transmission Laboratory/Quarterly Progress and Status Report, Stockholm* 1: 45–53.

Sundberg, J. (1974). Articulatory interpretation of the "singing formant." *Journal of the Acoustical Society of America* 55(4): 838–844.

Sundberg, J. (1978). Synthesis of singing. *Swedish Journal of Musicology* 60(1): 107–112.

Titze, I.R. and Jin, S.M. (2003). Is there evidence of a second singer's formant? *Journal of Singing* 59(4): 329–331.

Traunmuller, H. and Erickson, A. (2000). Acoustic effects of variation in vocal effort by men, women, and children. *Journal of the Acoustical Society of America* 107: 3438–3451.

Zatorre, R.J. and Baum, S.R. (2012). Musical melody and speech intonation: singing a different tune? *PLoS Biol* 10 (7): e1001372. doi:10.1371/journal.pbio.1001372.

CHAPTER 11

....

THE IMPACT OF LOCATION
ON THE SINGING VOICE

....

HARALD JERS

INTRODUCTION

....

In concerts or rehearsal situations solo singers or choirs are surrounded by a room, which greatly influences the perception of sound by the audience. Due to the geometry and acoustic properties of a stage with walls, ceiling, and floor, as well as bigger obstacles, each room has its own special character as an acoustic system. Hence every position of a singer in the room in relation to positions of listeners in the audience has an important effect on the performing singers and the perceived sound.

A solo singer or a choir concert in a room can be analyzed as a sound source in an acoustic system with the audience as the receiver. Frequency-dependent reflection, absorption, diffraction, or refraction influence the energy distribution and timbre in the room. The sound in a performance space can be distinguished between a near field very close to the singer and a far field. The distance at which the far field can be assumed is strongly dependent on the acoustics of the room. Especially for singers singing with instruments or within a choir, the differentiation between those sound fields is important for hearing oneself and the other players or singers. Furthermore the seating position of the listener in the audience will have an influence on listener perception.

In this acoustic system another important influence is the sound sources themselves. The sound of a singer, which mainly comes from the singer's mouth, is directional. In summary, the sound is omnidirectional for lower frequencies but is more focused into a narrow stream projecting to different directions around the singer for higher frequencies. Thus the position of the singer is of major interest, because the emitted sound spectrum in the room varies with the location. For a choir with several singers, the arrangement of the voice sections and the influence of the acoustic diffraction and reflection of adjacent singers affect the way of singing within the choir. This also leads to different impressions in the audience.

Using this knowledge, intuitive behavior and performance practice can be explained and new adaptations can be suggested for solo singers and choirs. These concern singing technique, choir formation and spacing, sound propagation and likewise the interpretation of the music reaching the audience.

THEORETICAL FRAMEWORK AND PRINCIPLES

Sound Propagation

Each singer generates sound with her/his voice, and from an acoustic point of view it can be thought of as a sound source producing a variation of acoustic pressure in the air. This acoustic energy is radiated in the form of pressure waves in all directions; its energy is reduced by the square of the distance from the source (e.g. Howard and Angus 2009). The sound propagation is modified by walls, ceiling, floor, and furnishings. To understand the distribution of the sound field in a room and how it is influenced by the properties of the room, the sound propagation can be described by a physical model relating to sound radiation. A change in the direction of a sound wavefront is called reflection when the wave returns, in the same way that light is reflected: the angle at which the wave is incident on the surface equals the angle at which it is reflected. Furthermore sound waves are reduced in energy after contact with objects in the room or its bounding walls, ceiling, and floor; this is called absorption. When absorbed, the acoustic energy changes into another form of energy. Porous materials such as carpets or curtains are very effective sound absorbers compared with stone walls. The absorptivity of a given material is frequency dependent; for example, porous absorbers are most effective at high frequencies; this is in stark contrast to resonant panels called Helmholtz resonators which absorb mainly the low frequencies of a sound (see Table 11.1 for a list of common materials in performance spaces).

Another wave phenomenon of sound propagation is called diffraction, which describes the change in direction of waves as they pass around a barrier in their path or through an

Table 11.1 Sound absorption coefficients of different materials typical for concert halls, average of octave-frequency-bands. (From the material database of the Physikalisch-Technischen Bundesanstalt, Braunschweig, Germany)

Description	Frequency (Hz)					
	125	250	500	1000	2000	4000
Coarse stone floor, sandstone	0.02	0.02	0.03	0.04	0.05	0.05
Carpet thin, cemented to concrete	0.02	0.04	0.08	0.20	0.35	0.40
Glass window	0.35	0.25	0.18	0.12	0.07	0.04
Walls (average total residual absorption of 15 halls, without seating/audience)	0.14	0.12	0.10	0.09	0.08	0.07
Audiences, seats fully occupied, medium upholstered	0.54	0.62	0.68	0.70	0.68	0.66

opening. This means that sound has the ability to travel around corners or obstacles. The amount of diffraction increases with increasing wavelength and decreases with decreasing wavelength. When the wavelength of the wave is smaller than the obstacle, no noticeable diffraction occurs and the sound is effectively shadowed by the obstacle. Diffraction is commonly observed as we notice that we can hear sounds from around a corner or through door openings, such as when we hear others singing in adjacent rooms.

Basics of Room Acoustics

In a room, or in particular in a performance space, there are many possibilities for reflection, absorption, and diffraction. For a certain spatial disposition of a singer on stage in a concert hall, the sound perceived by accompanying musicians, other singers, the conductor, or members of the audience has three components. The sound that comes along the shortest path toward the listener is called the *direct sound,* and it travels from the source in a straight line to the receiver. A short time later the listener will receive sounds that have been reflected one or more times from nearby surfaces such as the walls, floor and ceiling, or other objects within the space. These are called *early reflections* and they typically have a delay compared with the direct sound that is less than 50 ms. Early reflections are clearly separated both in time and direction, and these will vary if the singer moves on the stage. Early reflections provide information to the listener about the size of the performing space and the position of the singer within the space. Following the early reflections, once the number of reflections has increased, sound is arriving at the listener's ears from all directions; this is the *reverberant sound*, which results from the *diffuse field* of all the later reflections. These later reflections die down rapidly and the time taken for them to reduce in energy by 60 dB is called the *reverberation time*. The reverberation time depends on the volume of the space and the area and effectiveness of the absorbing materials in the room. A large space with very good reflecting surfaces, such as a church, tends to have a longer reverberation time, while well-furnished smaller spaces tend to have shorter reverberation times (see Figure 11.1 for a diagram of possible reflections and a graph of the intensity of the three components of a perceived sound over time).

The intensity of the direct sound decreases only with distance, and this is independent of the properties of the room. The first and early reflections are important for the perception of liveliness and can be helpful for good intelligibility of the text in singing. The intensity of the diffuse field in the reverberation tail is usually much the same throughout the room. The many reflections merge into a practically uniform sound field which has no direction of its own, giving no information about the location of the singers. The distance from the sound source at which the intensities of the diffuse field and the direct sound are equal is called the *reverberation radius* or the *critical distance* of the room, and it will affect how each singer hears other singers in a choir or how instrumentalists hear each other on stage. If the musician-to-musician spacing is smaller than the critical distance of the room, the sound of the neighboring musician will tend to dominate the overall sound of the whole group. Outside the critical distance, each musician will generally receive the entire sound of the group rather than sounds of single players or singers. This situation is similar to that of a listener in the audience, who will mainly perceive the group as a whole and not the individual players or singers because the listener is a considerable distance away from the

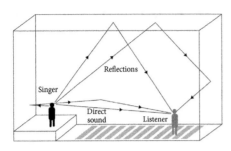 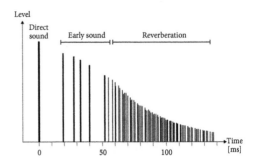

FIGURE 11.1 Mirror reflecting sound rays as model of sound distribution in rooms (left image). The resulting reflectogram gives the temporal sequence and energy of sound waves arriving at the listener (right image).

performers compared with the critical distance. For an acoustically "dry" concert hall with modest reverberation, one might recommend a spacing between musicians of a meter or more, while for a more reverberant church a distance of rather less than a meter would be appropriate.

Sound Propagation of Singers

Every sound source has its own characteristic projected sound radiation as a function of frequency. This can be perceived in everyday situations by the different sound timbres of speakers or singers depending on the direction from which one is listening to them. When the person turns around, this change of timbre is readily noticeable. This so-called directivity has different characteristics depending on frequency, and it is solely dependent on the geometry and acoustic properties of the human body. The influence of diffraction and reflection on the human body differ for each frequency due to dimensional differences. For example, low-frequency components (longer wavelengths) will be mainly influenced by the upper torso, whilst the nose, mouth, and ears affect mainly middle and high frequencies. The sound of the singing voice comprises both low frequencies around the fundamental tone and lower overtones as well as high frequencies for high overtones and consonants or noises, which leads overall to a very complex directivity pattern. Hence every frequency of a tone or noise produced by the voice has its own specific directivity characteristics in three dimensions. The sum of all natural tones of the singing voice in combination with its respective directivity implies a complex total propagation behavior, which is different for each vowel or consonant.

Perception Effects

It is not only sound production and sound propagation that are important for the perception of singing; the ear itself as a complex system with numerous functions has an important influence on the perception of the sound. To start with the outer ear, the external pinna more effectively collects high-frequency sounds above 4500 Hz from in front rather than from behind because of its position and shape. This helps us to locate sound sources and to have orientation on stage of where the accompanying musicians are. The auditory canal acts as an acoustic resonator whose resonant characteristic is most sensitive to sound in the 2500–4000 Hz range, which is the frequency domain of higher partials of singing and instruments and is of primary importance for the perception of timbre in music.

At the boundary of the outer and middle ear, the tympanic membrane is responsible for the conversion of acoustic pressure variations to mechanical variations, which are transmitted via the auditory ossicles to the oval window. The ossicles also act as a protective device against loud sounds, which is necessary for preserving the sensitive hearing system. Within the inner ear, the basilar membrane in the cochlea executes an analysis of the distinct frequencies of incoming sounds. Thus the human peripheral system is usually quoted as having a frequency range of 20 Hz to 20 kHz, subject to individual differences and the tendency that the upper cut-off reduces with age. The system is also frequency dependent with respect to sound pressure, with the greatest sensitivity found in the 3–5 kHz range. Lower and higher frequencies have to be at greater sound pressure levels to be heard.

A very significant feature of the peripheral hearing system is the *masking effect*, where individual frequency components of a complex sound can mask other components in the sound. The masking effect is greater when the sound pressure level of the component which causes the masking is higher than the masked tone, and vice versa when the frequency of the masked tone is above rather than below the masking tone. This could be important in the perception of a singer, for example when components fall in the spectral dips of formant peaks (see Story, this volume). In this case these components will not contribute to the perceptual process, regardless of whether the masked components come from the singer's own voice or from another sound.

Apart from the basics of perception, many systematic investigations have been carried out concerning the effect of the acoustic environment of a room on the perception of a musical performance. In one experiment, recordings of the same music samples in different concert halls with dummy heads were judged by different test subjects. Sound fields were synthesized and varied under special circumstances, and visitors to different concert halls were asked for their views after the performances. By this procedure, the perceptual dimensions of space effects were determined, generating metrics that correlate well with these perceptual qualities and enable predictions of the subjective sound impression. Four aspects have proved to be decisive:

1. First, there is the power and intensity of the sound experience, and associated with this a feeling of intimacy and closeness to the source of the sound. A good predictor of this is the so-called strength, G. It gives a ratio of the sound intensity measured from a source in the room in question to the intensity that the same sound source would produce in a reverberation-free environment at a distance of 10 m. The strength is an indication of how many decibels a sound source will be amplified by the sum of all reflections at the listener's seat.

2. A second aspect is the reverberation of the room, i.e. the time after which sound events fade away. The reverberation can be predicted very well using the reverberation time T, which is defined as the time for a sound to decrease by 60 dB in intensity. Closely linked to the reverberation time are "clarity" and "distinctness" which allow us to distinguish between two successive sound events.

3. A third aspect is the overall timbre of the room. This is usually the ratio of the reverberation times at low frequencies (octave bands at 125 and 250 Hz) to the reverberation
   times at medium frequencies (octave bands at 500 and 1000 Hz) and is determined as
   the bass ratio (BR).

4. A fourth aspect is spatial impression. This refers to the fact that musical instruments
   on stage are perceived to be of a certain size and do not appear as intermittent sound
   sources (apparent source width). For the prediction of this sound source-related
   impression of sound quality, the proportion of lateral sound reflections in the total
   sound energy within the first 80 ms after the arrival of direct sound is used (the early
   lateral energy fraction, LF). However, spatial impression also describes the feeling
   of the listener of being surrounded by the sound field (listener envelopment), which
   is covered by a number of metrics. But the relationship of these to the perceptual
   effect—compared with the parameters for strength, reverberation, and timbre—is
   statistically only moderately well described. Some more research in this field of room
   acoustics is needed.

Major Research Areas

The Singer and The Room

From the above-mentioned basics of acoustics and sound propagation, one can already see
interesting consequences emerging for the location of the singer on stage and for the listener
in the audience. The further away the singer is from the audience the weaker the perceived
sound, but the reverberant sound remains unaffected. Thus the relation of the intensity of direct and reverberant sound changes at different positions in the audience without changing
any aspects of the sound source on stage. But the balance of direct and reverberant sound is
important for a pleasant acoustic environment. Additional acoustic energy, which means
raising the overall amplitude and singing more loudly, only enhances the perceived loudness
not the intelligibility. Due to the fact that early reflections support the direct sound, both
components are important for clarity of speech and intelligibility. They should not be too
weak in comparison with the reverberant part, which could blur the consonants of the text
and rapid formant transitions of the vowels. It should be noted, however, that strong discrete
early reflections could confuse the listener with relation to the direction of the sound. To
avoid the resultant further difficulties of understanding the lyrics the early reflections should
be diffuse. Furthermore it should be kept in mind that reverberation is a function of frequency. Thus modification of the reverberation time by changing reflection and absorption
behavior always refers to different frequencies. The reverberation time at high frequencies
can be reduced with the addition of porous materials such as carpets, curtains, or soft
furnishings. For low frequencies, the addition of wood paneling will increase the absorption.

In addition, concert halls can exhibit acoustic problems due to the large size of the space.
If two walls in a big hall are precisely parallel with smooth surfaces *flutter echoes* very often
occur; this term describes sound bouncing to and from the walls. This can be very disturbing
for the performers and the audience and can easily be detected by handclaps in the hall.

Another problem within a big hall can occur when two spaces are acoustically open to each other. This is often the case in churches with a transept and a nave or when the space under the balcony in a concert hall connects with the main hall. The sound energy will decay at different rates in each of the spaces and the resulting reverberant sound has one or more breaks. A similar unnatural reverberation condition is caused when most of the absorption takes place on two surfaces facing each other, for example acoustic tiles on the ceiling and absorbing carpets on the floor. The sound decay between those absorbing surfaces would be quick, but slow for the remaining walls.

Stage Acoustics for Singers

To determine the best position on stage and preferred listener conditions in concert halls, several authors have investigated the subjective acoustic needs of performers of classical music and the objective properties of the sound field in laboratory experiments or *in situ*. The musicians in these experiments played in orchestras, ensembles, or performed as soloists. All those involved seemed to have an agreement on one main musical issue: getting the right balance between hearing oneself (feedback) and hearing others (reference). Briefly, the results show that small reverberant rooms will lead to difficulty hearing oneself, while larger rooms with few reflections will lead to difficulty hearing others. A lack of feedback often leads to intonation difficulties, while difficulty hearing others leads to problems with timing and synchronization within the ensemble or between soloist and accompaniment. Lindqvist-Gauffin and Sundberg (1974) investigated "self-hearing" in terms of its role in monitoring the singing voice, and concluded that singers rely more upon bone-conducted than air-conducted aspects of the feedback system. They pointed out that the air-conducted signal would tend to be less reliable, since it can be altered by room acoustics and masked by background noise. In addition, they suggested that the bone-conducted signal would not only seem to have greater reliability but would be further enhanced by the accompanying vibratory sensation in the skull.

Marshall et al. (1978), Gade (1989), Marshall (1993), Naylor and Craik (1988), and Noson et al. (2000) all investigated the acoustical conditions preferred for ensembles. The findings of these works seem to agree that: the level of supportive feedback is controlled by the stage volume; reflectors behind a choir improve the balance with an orchestra; a delay within the ensemble should not exceed 20 ms, especially for fast tempo singing; and whereas the frequency components of 500–2000 Hz are most important, below 500 Hz they may be detrimental for ensemble performance. Early reflections arriving 10–40 ms after the direct sound improve the acoustic conditions and reverberation seems not to be important for an ensemble, but is preferable for soloists. Ueno and Tachibana (2003) used a digital sound field simulation technique to investigate preferable conditions for ensembles, and found relationships between physical characteristics and psychological judgments by musicians. Early reflections increase the ease of hearing the sound of other players but can cause excess loudness when the reflections are too strong. In ensemble performance, musicians are less sensitive to a change of reverberation time but are more conscious of the magnitude of reverberation for hearing each other. Extensive investigations by Dammerud (2009) into orchestra stage acoustics show that the direction and delay of early reflections appear to be highly relevant, which agrees with the other results.

These results show a conflict between the need for early reflections on stage and in the audience. A possible compromise could be surfaces behind the performers, in which reflected sound waves pass the singer on their way back to the audience. Thus the sound energy can be used for both purposes. But the reflection should not be too late or it can irritate the singer. To keep within a sufficient maximum delay of 20 ms, the distance can be calculated using the path of travel to the wall and back again. With an approximate sound velocity of 340 m s^{-1} the reflecting surface should be within 3.4 m. Setting up reflecting screens or positioning the singer near to a room boundary would be a sufficient solution.

Directivity of a Singer

Not only is the sound production of the singing voice important for a concert performance, but the propagation of the sound is also critical. The directivity of singers has been investigated under different measurement conditions by many different researchers (e.g. Cabrera et al. 2007; Jers 2005; Marshall and Meyer 1989). This subsection gives a summary of the average results from their investigations. To get an overview of the propagation of the human voice, some details of the frequency domain have been summarized in Table 11.2. For frequencies below 500 Hz propagation is nearly omnidirectional. The directional behavior increases for frequencies between 800 and 2000 Hz, and propagation is mainly to the front downwards as well as sideways. To the back the energy decreases, apart from a local maximum in the center to the back because of constructive interference. For frequencies from 2000–5000 Hz the main propagation is frontal upwards and sideways, with very little energy to the back. In this frequency domain in particular we find the singer's formant, which is of special importance for the position of the singer in a concert situation. Frequencies above 5000 Hz are attenuated and less notable, but possess strong directionality to the front.

Directivity of the Singing Voice

Most of the investigations discussed only found small differences between different vowels, and these were mainly at higher frequencies. This can be explained by the slight differences in the mouth shape used to produce different vowels. To understand the meaning of

Table 11.2 Directivity of sound propagation from singers according to frequency

Frequency range (Hz)	Main propagation properties
80–500	Nearly omnidirectional
500–2000	Mainly front down, more and more sound to the top front and right and left, reduced propagation to the back but local maximum at the exact back due to constructive interference
2000–5000	Apart from propagation to the front top a lot of propagation to the right and left, rapidly decreased propagation to the rear

directivity for a performance situation it should be borne in mind that each frequency of the spectrum of a singer at any moment has its own propagation pattern. Thus, as can be seen in Figure 11.2, all partials of a sound of a singer at one moment are propagated differently according to their directivity properties and build up a complex sound distribution around the singer. In this context, it can be concluded that there is a different sound field around the singer for varied vowels and sounds because the partials of sounds may differ considerably in their spectral constitution, causing dissimilar excitation of frequencies with uneven directivity patterns.

For solo singers, directivity will have important consequences for their position on stage or in a concert hall. Situations where there is distance of 5–10 m between a singer and reflecting surfaces like walls, ceiling, and floor will avoid too strong a reduction of sound energy towards listeners in the audience. Similar absorbing material in the indicated directions would cause a distinct decay of energy, which would give the impression in the audience of a weak and poor sound.

For choral singing the directivity results justify the use of risers. As the main propagation is in a frontal-downwards direction the risers should exhibit a step height of about 30–40 cm to facilitate sufficient propagation over the heads of the audience in the first rows.

It is important for the intonation accuracy of a choir and solo singers that the acoustic feedback is good enough to enable singers to hear themselves sufficiently. The results of directivity measurements of singers can give some information about this. The feedback can be divided into three components: (1) direct airborne sound, (2) reflected airborne sound, and (3) bone-conducted sound. The directivity is directly related to the first two components. The direct airborne sound (1) from the mouth to the ears experiences diffraction around the head. Thus high frequencies diffract less than do low ones, which leads to a low-frequency bias of this component. The reflected airborne sound (2) returns to the singer after convolution with the impulse response of the room. The combination of directivity and the singer's distance and direction in relation to reflecting surfaces influences this impulse response and may provide important feedback. The bone-conducted sound (3) is particularly rich in low frequencies (Howell 1985). This may provide the singer with a cue to separating their voice

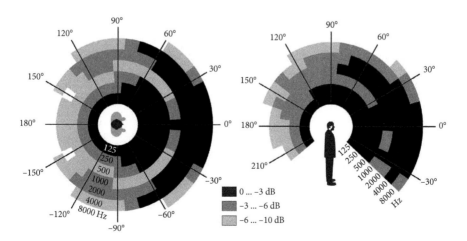

FIGURE 11.2 Principal radiation regions of the singing voice (in octave bands).

from that of other singers, because bass sounds are more likely to be from their own voice rather than that of their neighbors.

Adjacent Singers

Jers (2007) published the results of an experiment on how the directivity of a singer changes in the presence of adjacent singers, in the context of a choir singing with row and block formations. For this investigation, a human-like wooden torso of a singer with an internal loudspeaker was built to serve as a sound source with human directivity properties. This had already been used for room acoustic measurements. To serve as the adjacent singers, dummy human torsos were used and placed at several positions around the "artificial singer." The influence of lateral singers seemed to be of less importance, but frontally placed singers influenced the directivity, especially for higher frequencies. Due to a shadowing effect to the front the reduction of the sound pressure level stretched to 20–25 dB, while due to reflections it increased to the back by up to 10 dB. This further emphasizes the importance of risers for choirs in concert situations.

Choir Formation and Spacing

In a choir or ensemble with many singers, hearing oneself is an important issue if choral singing is to have accurate intonation and precise timing, among other necessary attributes. For this purpose Ternström (1995) developed and analyzed the self-to-other ratio (SOR), which is an abstract measurement of sound pressure level (SPL) and describes the ability to hearing oneself in comparison to the rest of the choir. This ratio was obtained by factoring in the absorption and reverberation of the room determined in a laboratory measurement setup via binaural microphones calibrated for SPL and worn in the outer ears during live choral singing; more recently a synthesized choir has been the reference. Ternström (1994) found that averaged SORs can vary over 6 dB and that the SOR increases (1) when room absorption increases, (2) when spacing increases, and (3) when the number of singers decreases. Sopranos tend to have higher SOR, i.e. sopranos sing more loudly than other voices, since vocal power increases with phonation frequency, and basses tend to have a lower SOR. The masking effect of one's own voice is greatest at low frequencies. For choirs with two or more rows, lower SOR values were obtained in the center of the choir and a higher SOR was obtained at the sides.

Related to this, some empirical research has been conducted concerning the formation of a choir. But here some musical performance terms which are sometimes used differently and their associated meanings have to be distinguished. *Choir formation* concerns the physical positioning of sections in a choir, in other words which voice part is positioned where within the choir (see Table 11.3). The term *spacing* denotes the distance between adjacent choristers in an ensemble, regardless of the formation employed. *Placement* is a description of the dispersal and order of choral singers within their voice section, i.e. who stands next to whom within the section.

In a choir, a group of many singing sound sources, the acoustic relation between direct sound and the diffuse field is enormously important. The distances between the sound

Table 11.3 Advantages and disadvantages of commonly used choral formations

Formation	Pros	Cons	Schematic of formation
Block sectional	Sound is often louder than in column sectional formation Suitable for homophonic pieces	Singers at the edges of a voice section may have difficulties hearing other singers in their group Singers in the middle of a section may have difficulties discerning their own voice against their section colleagues	TTTTTTTBBBBBB TTTTTTTBBBBBB SSSSSSAAAAAA SSSSSSAAAAAA
Column sectional	Especially advisable for polyphonic music to perceive entrances and good balance of voice sections	Some voice sections are separated by a large distance	SSSAAATTTBBB SSSAAATTTBBB SSSAAATTTBBB SSSAAATTTBBB
Mixed SATB quartets	Promotes self confidence Voices mix more at audience level and the sound often louder Singers can easily hear other voice sections; often improves intonation	Needs prior training Singers should be experienced Singers may "feel alone" Difficult for the conductor to address voice sections	SATBSATBSATB BTASBTASBTAS SATBSATBSATB BTASBTASBTAS

SATB, soprano, alto, tenor, bass.

sources will affect how the singers hear the rest of the choir. If the singer-to-singer spacing in the choir is smaller than the reverberation radius of the room, the sound of the neighboring singers will tend to dominate over the sound of the whole choir. Outside the reverberation radius, each singer will generally receive the entire sound of the choir rather than the sounds of single singers. This situation is similar to a listener in the audience, who will mainly perceive the choir as a whole and not the individual singers. For a "dry" concert hall with modest reverberation, one might recommend a spacing between singers of a meter or more. The distance can be adjusted by increasing the spacing between the singers, depending on the amount of reverberation. Inside the choir, this would reduce the dominance of the nearby singers and lead to a better balance in the sound of the choir as a whole. However, for a church with typical values of less than 1–2 m for the reverberation radius, a distance of rather less than a meter would be appropriate, because it matters little where in the choir the singers are placed in terms of hearing the neighboring singers. In most positions singers will generally perceive the sound of the whole choir. In very large cathedrals with long reverberation the diffuse field can be weaker still and poor in early reflections. Here it can be helpful to provide reflectors around the choir so that the singers can hear the sound of the whole choir and not just their immediate neighbors.

Daugherty (1999), Lambson (1961), and Tocheff (1990) researched the preferences within choirs and in the audience with respect to choir formation and spacing. Choral singers often preferred spread spacing and reported less vocal tension, better vocal production, and being able to hear themselves better. For this reason they also preferred a mixed formation rather than sectional formation. Audiences likewise preferred spread spacing, but in certain circumstances they preferred sectional formation. It seems that spacing makes the greatest contribution to a preferred choral sound for choristers and audiences, and not the formation as one might expect. The preferences are related to the spacing dimensions. All the research shows the same tendencies: that weaker singers prefer a sectional formation; that males especially prefer the middle section; and that stronger females like the mixed formation, especially along the outer edges (see Table 11.3 for the pros and cons of various common choral formations).

Conclusions

We can summarize the discussion of this chapter by the following points:

1. The sound of singers and choirs is influenced by many room-related acoustic factors having to do with sound propagation and auditory perception. Some of these factors are of minor importance, but some can influence the musical result very strongly.
2. The position of solo singers on stage may influence the musical result significantly. A position which takes into account the reflection of walls may lead to the impression in the audience of a louder voice, and hence to a more relaxed voice usage for the singer(s).
3. Voice training in general and an increased singer's formant in particular will improve the audibility of the voice, both because of higher sound pressure level and because of a more directed sound propagation of the corresponding frequencies.
4. Choirs should use risers to lift up the rear rows by an angle of at least 30° so that the sound of the back rows will not be reduced too much.
5. The formation of choirs on stage influences how the individual members hear each other: in reverberant rooms the position of the singer is not so important, but in less-reverberant rooms a greater distance between singers enables them to control their own voices better and also influences the perception in the audience.
6. The position of choirs in relation to the surrounding reflecting walls should be taken into account. On the one hand it will help the singers to hear each other better, on the other hand there will be much more sound energy directed to the audience.

Other Resources

Daugherty, J.F. (2002). Choir spacing and formation: choral sound preferences in random, synergistic, and gender specific placements. *International Journal of Research in Choral Singing*, 1(1): 48–59.

Howard, D. (2001). Room acoustics: how they affect vocal production and perception. In: P. Dejonckere (ed.), *Occupational voice: Care and Cure*, pp. 29–46. The Hague, Netherlands: Kugler.

References

Cabrera, D., Davis, P.J., and Connolly, A. (2007). Vocal directivity of eight opera singers in terms of spectro-spatial parameters. *19th International Congress on Acoustics, Madrid, 2–7 September 2007*. Available at: http://www.sea-acustica.es/WEB_ICA_07/fchrs/papers/mus-06-005.pdf. (Accessed 5 February 2014.)

Dammerud, J.J. (2009). *Stage Acoustics for Symphony Orchestras in Concert Halls*. PhD dissertation, University of Bath, Bath, UK.

Daugherty, J.F. (1996). *Spacing, Formation, and Choral Sound: Preferences and Perceptions of Auditors and Choristers*. PhD dissertation, Florida State University, Tallahassee, FL, USA.

Daugherty, J.F. (1999). Spacing, formation, and choral sound: preferences and perceptions of auditors and choristers. *Journal of Research in Music Education* 47(3): 224–238.

Gade, A.C (1989). Investigations of musician's room acoustic conditions in concert halls. II: Field experiments and synthesis of results. *Acustica* 69: 249–262.

Howard, D.M. and Angus, J.A.S. (2009). *Acoustics and Psychoacoustics*, 4th edn. Oxford: Focal Press.

Howell, P. (1985). Auditory feedback of the voice in singing. In: P. Howell, I. Cross, and R. West (eds), *Musical Structure and Cognition* (pp. 259–286). London: Academic Press.

Jers, H. (2005). Directivity of singers. *Journal of the Acoustical Society of America* 118: 2008.

Jers, H. (2007). Directivity measurements of adjacent singers in a choir. *19th International Congress on Acoustics, Madrid, 2–7 September 2007*. Available at: http://www.sea-acustica.es/WEB_ICA_07/fchrs/papers/mus-03-003.pdf. (Accessed 5 February 2014.)

Lambson, A.R. (1961). An evaluation of various seating plans used in choral singing. *Journal of Research in Music Education* 9(1): 47–54.

Lindqvist-Gauffin, J. and Sundberg, J. (1974). Masking effects of one's own voice. *Quarterly Progress and Status Report, Speech Transmission Laboratory, Royal Institute of Technology, Stockholm, Sweden* 15(1): 35–41.

Marshall, A.H (1993). An objective measure of balance between choir and orchestra. *Applied Acoustics* 38(1): 51–58.

Marshall, A.H. and Meyer, J. (1989). The directivity and auditory impressions of singers. *Journal of Research in Singing* 8(1): 1–24.

Marshall, A.H, Gottlob, D., and Alrutz, H. (1978). Acoustical conditions preferred for ensemble. *Journal of the Acoustical Society of America* 64(5): 1437–1442.

Naylor, G.M. and Craik, R.J.M. (1988). The effects of level difference and musical texture on ease of ensemble. *Acustica* 65: 95–100.

Noson, D., Sato, S., Sakai, H., and Ando, Y. (2000). Singer responses to sound fields with a simulated reflection. *Journal of Sound and Vibration* 232(1): 39–51.

Ternström, S. (1994). Hearing myself with others: sound levels in choral performance measured with separation of one's own voice from the rest of the choir. *Journal of Voice* 8(4): 293–302.

Ternström, S. (1995). Self-to-other ratios measured in choral performance. In: M.J. Newman (ed.), *Proceedings of the 15th International Congress on Acoustics*, Vol. II (pp. 681–684). Oslo: Acoustical Society of Norway.

Tocheff, R.D. (1990). *Acoustical Placement of Voices in Choral Formations*. PhD dissertation, Ohio State University, Columbus, OH, USA.

Ueno, K. and Tachibana, H. (2003). Experimental study on the evaluation of stage acoustics by musicians using a 6-channel sound simulation system. *Journal of the Acoustical Society of Japan* 24(3): 130–138.

PART 3

THE PSYCHOLOGY OF SINGING

CHAPTER 12

··

THE NEUROSCIENCE
OF SINGING

··

BORIS A. KLEBER AND JEAN MARY ZARATE

INTRODUCTION

THINK about the physiological events that occur as a singer begins a vocal warm-up routine. Producing a simple "ah" on one particular note requires the coordination of numerous muscle groups involved, from inhalation to the approximation of the vocal folds and movement of articulators (i.e. mouth, jaw, tongue, lips). (For a more detailed review on the physiological basis of singing, see Lã and Gill, this volume.) Now, imagine the continued coordination of these muscle systems as the singer begins to sing scales with different vowels or syllables, short melodic phrases, and finally an entire piece of music. Depending on the amount of training a singer has, he or she may be aware of the present state of the vocal system at any given moment while singing, either via auditory or somatosensory feedback or even a combination of both feedback types. However, the singer is usually unaware of the neural networks that govern and coordinate all of these muscle groups, or what happens in these networks when auditory or somatosensory feedback notifies the singer of vocal errors, or if feedback is compromised even temporarily. For instance, when a singer initially produces a note that is slightly off-pitch, how do these neural networks work in order to correct the error? Perhaps in a choral situation, if a singer cannot hear himself or herself during a performance, what changes in the brain occur for a singer to maintain the intended vocal output? If a singer cannot obtain an accurate sense of the vocal tract via somatosensory feedback, either due to illness or some other reason, how do the neural networks respond? In the present chapter, the authors will attempt to define the basic neural networks involved in singing, discuss how these networks may change due to extensive vocal training and practice, and present recent findings that illustrate how the networks respond to alterations to auditory and kinesthetic feedback.

BRAIN REGIONS INVOLVED IN SINGING

Neural Control of Vocalization in Primates and Humans

To produce vocalizations including speech and song, the control of all muscles along the vocal tract (e.g. for respiration, vocal fold motion, and articulation) requires the concerted effort of a vast network of brain regions. Primate research forms the foundation for our understanding of the neural control of vocalization. For example, extensive research in squirrel monkeys has determined that the reticular formation—a neural region located in the medulla and pons between the spinal cord and the midbrain—produces vocalizations when electrically or chemically stimulated (Jürgens and Richter 1986), due to its direct connections to phonatory (i.e. vocalization-related) muscles (Thoms and Jürgens 1987). Thus, the reticular formation may coordinate all muscle groups involved in generating complete vocal patterns (Jürgens and Hage 2007). Two separate neural networks can stimulate the reticular formation and thus control vocalization (for a review, see Jürgens 2009). The first network (see Figure 12.1a), which consists of the anterior cingulate cortex (ACC) and periaqueductal gray (PAG), is attributed with the initiation or readiness of vocalizations (Jürgens 2009). The second network, which is associated with generating learned vocalizations, consists of the primary motor cortex (M1) and two sets of brain regions (putamen and globus pallidus in one set, pontine gray and cerebellum in the other) that modulate or fine-tune the vocal motor program relayed from M1; the modified vocal motor program is then sent back via the thalamus to M1 for execution (see Figure 12.1b) (Jürgens 2009; Simonyan and Jürgens 2003).

In contrast to two separate networks for vocal control in animals (Jürgens 2009), in humans, the networks described above are organized in a hierarchy of various control levels, starting from simple utterances to highly complex (i.e. learned) vocal motor patterns (Simonyan and Horwitz 2011). As seen in the animal model above, at the most basic level of vocal control in humans, brainstem and spinal cord regions are involved in the coordination of muscles during innate non-verbal vocalizations, such as crying and laughing. The ACC and PAG network then forms a second level of neural control specifically for the initiation of vocalization and the control of voluntary utterances. Damage to the PAG would cause mutism (Esposito et al. 1999), whereas damage to the ACC would result in a loss of control over emotional intonation in speech, thus demonstrating their fundamental contribution to vocal production (Simonyan and Horwitz 2011). The highest level of vocal control in humans takes place in the M1 and its associated modulatory brain regions (i.e. putamen, globus pallidus, thalamus, pontine gray, and cerebellum); damage to these modulatory regions can cause vocal motor disorders, such as stuttering and dysarthria (Ackermann et al. 1992; Alm 2004; Jürgens 2002). Damage or removal of vocalization-associated regions within the M1 on both sides of the brain abolishes speech and song (i.e. learned or acquired vocal patterns) in humans, while preserving innate, preprogrammed vocalizations that are presumably governed by the ACC (e.g. shrieking and crying) (Jürgens 2009). Direct connections between this "vocalization" M1 area and the brainstem motor neurons that convey neural motor commands to phonatory muscles are unique to humans, which suggests that the M1 plays a major role in experience-dependent (i.e. acquired) voluntary control over vocal motor production for speech and singing.

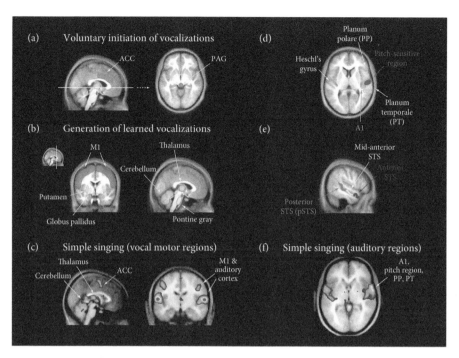

FIGURE 12.1 Vocal motor and auditory cortical regions of the brain. Note that auditory regions exist on both sides of the brain (except perhaps the pitch-sensitive region), but the illustrations only show them on one side for clarity. (a) The anterior cingulate (ACC) and periaqueductal gray (PAG) in green comprise a network involved in the voluntary initiation or readiness of vocalizations. The left brain image (a sagittal slice with the ACC) is obtained by taking a vertical slice through the brain between the eyes. The right brain image is a horizontal slice through the brain at the position indicated by the white line in the left image. (b) The coronal slice on the left results from taking a vertical slice perpendicular to the sagittal slice (inset). This image illustrates the primary motor cortex (M1, dark blue) on both sides of the brain, which is attributed with the generation of learned vocalizations. The M1's vocal motor programs are modified by the regions indicated in light blue. (c) Vocal motor regions (and auditory cortex) are engaged during singing a single note on /a/. (d) Heschl's gyrus, which is the finger-like structure on both sides of this horizontal slice, contains primary auditory cortex (A1) and a pitch-sensitive region. The planum polare and planum temporale, both of which are in the superior temporal gyrus, surround Heschl's gyrus. (e) From this sagittal (or side view) from the right, we see the entire temporal lobe, with three different sections of the superior temporal sulcus (STS). This sulcus separates the superior temporal gyrus (immediately above the STS) from the middle temporal gyrus below. (f) Auditory cortical regions recruited during singing a single note.

Data from Zarate and Zatorre (2008).

Positron emission tomography (PET) and functional magnetic resonance imaging (fMRI) studies from the last twenty years have reported that many of the brain regions discussed above are recruited during various speech and song production tasks, including: word or letter generation (Paus et al. 1993); syllable repetition (Riecker et al. 2005); repeatedly singing a note (Perry et al. 1999) or sustaining a single note (Zarate and Zatorre 2008); singing vowel changes on a single note with different rhythmic groupings (Jungblut et al. 2012); repeating syllables, spoken words, and sung or hummed melodies (Özdemir et al. 2006); speaking or singing lyrics of a well-known song (Jeffries et al. 2003); reciting the months of the year or singing a familiar melody (Riecker et al. 2000); telling a story (Schulz et al. 2005); improvising word phrases, melodies, or harmonies (Brown et al. 2004; Brown et al. 2006); and singing an Italian aria (Kleber et al. 2007). Figure 12.1c illustrates only some of the vocal motor regions that are active during singing a single note: multiple motor cortical areas such as the M1 and ACC, the thalamus, and the cerebellum.

Thus far, the authors have discussed both speech and song studies to outline the brain regions associated with general vocal control in humans, since both speaking and singing share common mechanisms involved in vocal production. From this point forward, this chapter will focus more on singing-relevant tasks and examples to address how different types of feedback are used to regulate singing performance.

Auditory Feedback Processing during Singing

In general, auditory feedback can be used to evaluate and regulate vocal output. Arguably for singers, the most crucial component of auditory feedback would be their vocal fundamental frequency (i.e. vocal pitch). When a sung melody reaches the ear, each of the different frequencies within the melody is converted to neural signals on the basilar membrane of the cochlea, which is located in the inner ear (Hudspeth 2000). The frequency characteristics that are required to perceive individual pitches are processed in various neural regions of the ascending auditory pathway before they are further processed in the primary auditory cortex, which can be found within Heschl's gyrus in the temporal lobe (Figure 12.1d). Pitch information may be handled by higher-order auditory cortex—that is, cortex that processes more complex characteristics of auditory signals—located in lateral Heschl's gyrus (Figure 12.1d), a pitch-sensitive area reported to be involved in pitch perception (Brown et al. 2004; Griffiths 2003; Griffiths et al. 1998; Patterson et al. 2002; Penagos et al. 2004; Puschmann et al. 2010). This brain region may also be involved in organizing pitches in a hierarchical fashion, since epileptic patients with this cortical area either damaged or removed (via surgery) displayed much higher pitch-discrimination thresholds than controls when indicating the direction of pitch change between two notes (Johnsrude et al. 2000). More complex auditory stimuli and tasks, such as processing melodic phrases within a sung melody, engage additional auditory cortical areas along the superior temporal gyrus that are adjacent to Heschl's gyrus (i.e. planum polare and planum temporale) (see Figure 12.1d) (Griffiths and Warren 2002; Patterson et al. 2002; Zatorre et al. 1994). When pitch comparisons are performed within either a sequence of random notes or short melodies, recruitment of additional cortical regions is observed both within and outside the temporal lobe (e.g. auditory and frontal lobe regions), presumably during working memory processes that keep track of multiple pitches (Zatorre et al. 1994). For an in-depth discussion of the cortical processing of music, please refer to Zatorre and Zarate (2012, pp. 261–94).

Although Heschl's gyrus, superior temporal gyrus (STG), planum polare, and planum temporale may be involved in processing pitch changes, yet another acoustic feature from a sung melody—the vocal timbre—may be processed by additional regions within the temporal lobe. The superior temporal sulcus (STS; Figure 12.1e) has been reported to respond to vocal sounds, when compared to non-vocal sounds (Belin et al. 2000). Furthermore, the STS can be subdivided into different regions for processing specific vocal features (Figure 12.1e): (1) the anterior STS has been shown to be involved in voice recognition, and thus can be used to determine vocal identity; (2) the mid-anterior STS preferentially responds to the spectral characteristics of voices, compared to speech sounds created from white noise; and (3) the posterior STS (pSTS), which is recruited during recognition of unfamiliar voices, may be involved in analyzing spectral changes in voices over time to establish an unfamiliar vocal identity (Kriegstein and Giraud 2004). Further evidence for the pSTS's role in spectral analyses of voices stems from its increased activity due to detecting changes in either speaker identity or the amount of spectral details presented within vocal stimuli (Warren et al. 2006). Figure 12.1f depicts the auditory cortical regions that are active during a simple singing task (sustaining a single note) from Zarate and Zatorre's (2008) study.

Somatosensory Feedback Processing during Singing

The obvious role of auditory feedback in vocal production has led to the widely held view that vocal accuracy is maintained by acoustically monitoring one's own vocalization. However, auditory feedback is not the only source by which humans control the vocal system. When you hum softly and put your hand on your neck or cheek, you may pick up vibrations with your fingertips. As you purse your lips to sing an "oh" or open your mouth to form an "ah," you may recognize different sensations in your mouth associated with each vowel. While focusing on your throat, you may feel distinct sensations when comparing quiet breathing with producing a vocal tone. These sensations are known collectively as somatosensory feedback, which includes the sense of movement (kinesthesia) and position (proprioception); this type of feedback provides the brain with information about the current state of the respiratory, laryngeal, and orofacial systems (Smith and Zelaznik 2004), and thus plays a crucial role in the coordination of muscles and accuracy of motor commands.

Somatosensory feedback originates from sensory receptors that respond to touch, position, and vibration, which are located in joints, muscles, and mucosal tissue of the vocal tract. These receptors are primarily involved in laryngeal reflexes and respiratory control (Abo-el-Enein 1966; Smotherman 2007). However, they also are involved crucially in the motor management of intrinsic laryngeal muscles, such as rapid motor control of flow-induced vocal fold oscillations during singing and speaking (Titze and Hunter 2004; Wyke 1974a,b). Sensory receptors also help coordinate supralaryngeal (i.e. articulatory) gestures that generate vocal-tract shapes, which modulate the spectral properties of the primary sound generated at the glottis, thus affecting both vocal timbre and intelligibility (Jurgens 2002; Lametti et al. 2012; Perkell et al. 2007). The neural signals that comprise somatosensory feedback from the laryngeal-orofacial system and the respiratory system are generated by these receptors and are sent to primary somatosensory cortex (S1) and the insula, respectively (Ackermann and Riecker 2004, 2010; Jürgens, 2002). Neuroimaging studies of speech motor control have proposed a common system for the neural control of voluntary exhalation and phonation, as both tasks are tightly interrelated and engage overlapping areas in S1 and M1 (Loucks et al. 2007; Simonyan et al. 2009). As such, an area specifically associated with laryngeal sensations and motor control has been found in both the S1 (Grabski et al. 2012) and M1 respectively (Brown et al. 2008; Brown et al. 2009), thus highlighting the presence of a somatotopic (i.e. body-part specific) somatosensory-motor representation for vocalization. In these studies, participants performed various vocal tasks, such as glottal stops, vocalizations, lip protrusion, and tongue movement in order to distinguish between the cortical representation of the larynx and the articulators. The insula is a higher-order area that integrates both sensory and motor information (Ackermann and Riecker 2004; Bamiou et al. 2003; Lewis et al. 2000; Riecker et al. 2000; Rivier and Clarke 1997), and has been associated with interoception—the perception of your current physiological state—based on sensory integration (Craig 2003, 2009) and the self-awareness of actions (Karnath and Baier 2010). In particular, the anterior portion of this region seems to contribute to the coordination of vocal tract movements during singing (Riecker et al. 2000) and also might play a role in respiration during vocalizations (Ackermann and Riecker 2010).

A Model for Vocal Motor Control
and Feedback Processing in Singing

The complex processes that occur within vocal motor, auditory, and somatosensory systems described above are thought to become automatic for speech towards the end of adolescence (Smith and Zelaznik 2004). Current neural network models of speech motor acquisition (Guenther and Vladusich 2012; Hickok 2012; Houde and Nagarajan 2011; Tian and Poeppel 2010) provide a theoretical framework to explain how we develop voluntary control over intentional vocal utterances, including singing. These models propose that external sensory feedback is required first to establish a relationship between motor commands and sensory consequences. During this stage, auditory feedback influences the attempted reproductions of the desired sound by detecting auditory errors and subsequently triggering corrective vocal motor commands; the integration of auditory feedback and vocal motor corrections will be discussed further in the next section. After the mapping between auditory and motor processes has been solidified, a feedforward model makes predictions about the current state of the vocal tract components and the sensory consequences of vocal tract movements. The cerebellum and premotor areas—cortical areas that select or prepare motor programs for M1—are associated with this feedforward prediction model, which becomes more and more accurate with each repetition until it generates little to no auditory error. At this stage, auditory feedback is used mainly to update the prediction model and/or to perform corrections in case of prediction errors or perturbations. Simultaneously, the somatosensory control subsystem within S1 and other related cortical regions develops a somatosensory representation for the auditory-motor mapping that was learned. The somatosensory representation develops later in vocal learning and thus requires more practice and time, during which the somatosensory inputs can fine-tune aspects of feedforward auditory predictions; particular auditory targets can also co-activate the corresponding somatosensory targets (Hickok et al. 2011). Lametti et al. (2012, p. 9357) suggest that an individual's learning experience with somatosensory versus auditory feedback during speech development could shape the sensitivity to a particular type of feedback. This difference could be of potential interest to voice teachers, who may focus on only one of these sensory streams in their didactic approach.

AUDITORY-VOCAL MOTOR CONTROL IN SINGING

At times, singing requires monitoring of auditory feedback and precise vocal motor control to make sure that the vocal output matches the intended notes or melodies. Until recently, the neural substrates that integrate the vocal motor system with auditory feedback processing (a process also known as audio-vocal integration) for singing have not been explored. Animal research suggests two possible junctions (one subcortical, i.e. not located in the cerebral cortex, and one cortical) between the vocal motor and auditory systems where audio-vocal integration can occur. The PAG (Figure 12.1a) within the midbrain can both elicit vocalizations when stimulated and respond to external auditory events (Dujardin and Jürgens 2005; Suga and Yajima 1988) due to its connections with the subcortical auditory system (Dujardin and Jürgens 2005). In humans, voiced speech specifically recruits the PAG (relative to whispered speech), which implies that producing voiced utterances requires this region (Schulz et al. 2005). Animal vocalizations are elicited also when the ACC is stimulated (Gooler and O'Neill 1987; Müller-Preuss and Jürgens 1976; Müller-Preuss et al. 1980). In the echolocating bat, the ACC has been reported to contain a frequency-sensitive map from which specific sites emit particular vocal frequencies upon stimulation (Gooler and O'Neill 1987), which is probably due to frequency-organized input from auditory cortical regions that connect to the ACC (Barbas et al. 1999; Huffman and Henson 1990). Additionally, the ACC has connections with auditory regions along the STG and dorsal bank of the STS and modifies the activity within these regions; in many animals, stimulation of the ACC reduces the activity within auditory cortex just prior to vocalization (Barbas et al. 1999; Eliades and Wang 2003; Müller-Preuss et al. 1980). As mentioned earlier, the insula integrates inputs from different modalities (e.g. auditory, visual, somatosensory, motor, etc.) (Ackermann and Riecker 2004; Bamiou et al. 2003; Lewis et al., 2000; Riecker et al. 2000; Rivier and Clarke 1997), and may also be involved in this process (Figure 12.2a) due to its connections to auditory cortical regions and ACC (Augustine 1996; Mesulam and Mufson 1982; Mufson and Mesulam 1982). The anterior insula may be involved specifically in audio-vocal integration since its activity is enhanced in humans during speech or singing when compared with mentally rehearsed or internal speech or singing (Riecker et al. 2000); this suggests that voiced utterances may specifically engage the anterior insula. Briefly summarized, both the PAG and a cortical network—auditory cortex within STG/STS, anterior insula, and ACC—may be involved in audio-vocal integration by virtue of their functions and shared connections with each other (Figure 12.2b). Due to limitations of current neuroimaging techniques, the role of the PAG in audio-vocal integration has yet to be fully investigated (see Zarate et al. 2010a); thus, we will focus on the cortical areas: auditory cortex, anterior insula, and ACC.

Zarate, Zatorre, and colleagues tested non-musicians and singers (with an average of over ten years of singing experience) with various singing tasks in fMRI studies to outline the functional network for "simple singing" (i.e. sustaining a target note on /a/) and audio-vocal integration (Zarate and Zatorre 2008; Zarate et al. 2010a). To probe brain regions that integrate auditory feedback with vocal pitch control, the authors employed a variation of the

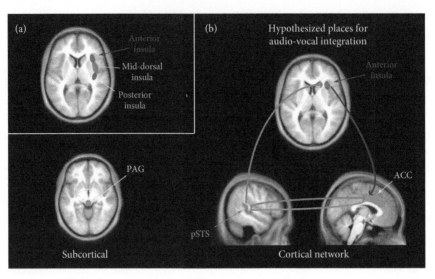

FIGURE 12.2 (a) Three subdivisions of the insula. (b) The places where audio-vocal integration for singing can occur in the brain. The hypothesized subcortical substrate is the periaqueductal gray (PAG), and the proposed cortical network consists of the posterior superior temporal sulcus (pSTS), anterior insula, and the anterior cingulate cortex (ACC).

pitch-shift paradigm (for more details, see Burnett et al. 1998; Hain et al. 2000; Larson 1998) in which auditory feedback was pitch-shifted by ± 200 cents (i.e. a whole step in Western music) in real time and sustained during singing tasks. During the "ignore" task, participants were instructed to disregard the pitch-shifted feedback and maintain the original note they were producing; this task resembled a choral singing situation in which neighboring singers who sing different harmonic lines need to ignore the other singers' vocal pitches and concentrate on their intended notes. In the "compensate" singing task, participants had to fully correct for the pitch-shifted feedback. For example, as they were singing to match a D#4, auditory feedback was shifted down by 200 cents to a C#4, and participants had to adjust their vocal pitch up to an F4 to cancel out the pitch shift (and maintain it for the duration of each trial), such that their feedback sounded like the intended target note (D#4) again. The investigators designed this task to simulate an instance in which auditory feedback informs a singer that a currently produced note is incorrect, and he or she must therefore adjust the vocal pitch until the auditory feedback matches the expected note. Importantly, the authors expected that performing this task would recruit the hypothesized cortical network for audio-vocal integration (auditory cortex, anterior insula, and ACC) during vocal pitch regulation.

In both groups, both pitch-shifted singing tasks engaged the intraparietal sulcus and dorsal premotor cortex, regions involved in transformations of sensory input for motor preparation (Astafiev et al. 2003; Grefkes et al. 2004; Tanabe et al. 2005) and selecting motor programs involved in sensory-motor associations (e.g. "green light" means "go") (Chouinard and Paus 2006; Petrides 1986), respectively. Zarate and Zatorre (2008) suggested that the intraparietal sulcus was involved in extracting information about the pitch shift (see Foster and Zatorre 2010), and that pitch-shift information was sent to the dorsal premotor cortex for the selection and preparation of the correct vocal motor program for the task (e.g. ignore the shift and maintain a steady vocal pitch, or adjust vocal pitch to correct for the pitch shift) (Zarate and Zatorre 2008; Zarate et al. 2010a). Interestingly, the compensation task recruited different neural substrates for audio-vocal integration in each group. The non-musicians relied more on the dorsal premotor cortex (see Figure 12.3a), presumably to associate a pitch shift with a corrective adjustment in vocal pitch (Zarate and Zatorre 2008). In contrast, singers engaged auditory cortex within the pSTS, intraparietal sulcus, anterior insula, and ACC (Figure 12.3b) for this task more than non-musicians (Zarate and Zatorre 2008; Zarate et al. 2010a). Zarate and colleagues suggested that within singers, the auditory cortex and intraparietal sulcus jointly process and extract pitch-shift information, which is then sent via the anterior insula to the ACC for initiation of a vocal correction (Zarate 2013; Zarate and Zatorre 2008; Zarate et al. 2010a). Furthermore, the authors suggested that these particular regions comprised an experience-dependent network that would be recruited increasingly to integrate auditory feedback with vocal pitch control as a function of more vocal training and practice (Zarate et al. 2010a).

To test the working hypothesis that auditory cortex, IPS, anterior insula, and ACC would be engaged only with more musical training and practice, Zarate et al. (2010b) trained one group of non-musicians to improve their auditory skills and then tested them against a control group of non-musicians with no training to determine: (1) whether singing accuracy subsequently improved due to auditory training; and (2) whether the experience-dependent

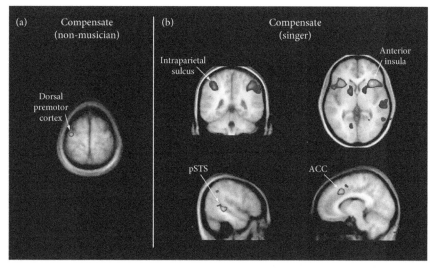

FIGURE 12.3 Maps of cortical activity measured during the "compensate" singing tasks from Zarate and Zatorre's (2008, 2010a) fMRI studies. (a) Non-musicians recruited the dorsal premotor cortex as they voluntarily adjusted their vocal pitch in response to pitch-shifted auditory feedback; this region may form the basic, experience-independent neural substrate for audio-vocal integration. (b) After extensive vocal training and practice, singers recruit the experience-dependent cortical network—posterior superior temporal sulcus (pSTS), intraparietal sulcus, anterior insula, and anterior cingulate cortex (ACC)—for audio-vocal integration to voluntarily regulate their vocal pitch.

network for audio-vocal integration was recruited during vocal pitch regulation. In this study, the investigators employed melodic singing tasks to target regions associated with this process, since accurate production of novel melodies requires audio-vocal integration in a similar fashion to voluntarily correcting for pitch-shifted feedback; the auditory feedback of the currently produced note may be monitored in order to produce the correct pitch interval to the next note. Although non-musicians who underwent auditory training displayed enhanced auditory discrimination skills and training-induced changes in auditory task-associated neural activity (Zatorre et al. 2012), they did not show significant improvements in singing performance or recruit the experience-dependent network for audio-vocal integration (Zarate et al. 2010b). Zarate et al. (2010b) proposed that auditory training alone is not sufficient to improve vocal performance or recruit the experience-dependent network for audio-vocal integration (auditory cortex, IPS, anterior insula, and ACC) during voluntary vocal pitch regulation; perhaps only improving both auditory and vocal motor skills simultaneously via extensive training (e.g. voice lessons) would elicit improvements in vocal performance and engage the outlined cortical network for audio-vocal integration.

Somatosensory-vocal Motor Control in Singing

As discussed above, skillful singing requires extensive training to fine-tune neural mechanisms for better vocal regulation of pitch and other vocal characteristics such as timbre (Titze 2008; Zatorre and Baum 2012). With respect to the role of somatosensory feedback in singing skill development, evidence from both behavioral and neuroimaging studies suggests that the somatosensory feedback circuit becomes increasingly important with singing expertise (Jones and Keough 2008; Kleber et al. 2010a; Mürbe et al. 2004). In a series of neuroimaging experiments with trained singers, Kleber et al. (2010a) further investigated the role of somatosensory feedback in the neural control of singing. The investigators used fMRI to compare brain activation patterns of professional classical singers, conservatory-level vocal students, and students with no singing experience. All participants sang excerpts of the Italian aria "Caro mio ben" inside the MRI machine. Shared activation during singing in all groups is shown in Figure 12.4a and included the basic singing network. However, results from this study revealed substantial experience-dependent differences. In both vocal students and opera singers (Figure 12.4b), increased activation was found in S1 and somatosensory association cortex in the inferior parietal lobe compared to non-singers. The location of activity within S1 is comparable to the somatotopic representation of the larynx reported elsewhere (Brown et al. 2008; Grabski et al. 2012). As shown in Figure 12.4d, correlation of accumulated singing practice with brain activity during singing confirmed the behavioral relevance of this experience-dependent activation pattern. Thus, these results strongly support the idea that the development of singing expertise coincides with the development of enhanced somatosensory processing; this, in turn, contributes significantly to the fine-tuning of vocal motor sequences, and possibly represents more accurate somatosensory targets and enhanced feedforward commands of vocal tract adjustments based on somatosensory expectations (Kleber et al. 2010a).

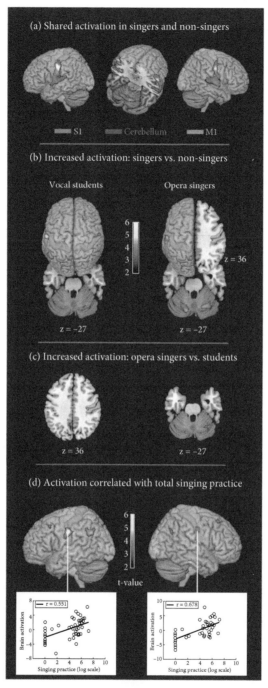

FIGURE 12.4 Maps of cerebral activity during overt singing of an Italian aria from Kleber and colleagues' fMRI study (2010a). (a) Shared network of neural activation during overt singing in both trained singers and non-singers comprised the constituents of the singing network. Note that the strongest activation (yellow) falls into the somatotopic representation of the larynx in S1 and M1. (b) A direct comparison of vocal students with non-singers

In addition, the cerebellum was more active in trained singers compared to non-singers (Figure 12.4b) particularly in the most experienced opera singers. As shown in Figure 12.4c, the comparison of opera singers with vocal students confirmed increased cerebellar activation in this highly experienced group, together with stronger engagement of right S1/M1 during singing. The cerebellum contributes substantially to the encoding of internal models (i.e. the neural representation of learned movements) by integrating sensory feedback with feedforward information (Itoh et al. 2001), via inputs from auditory and somatosensory regions and premotor cortical areas (Grodd et al. 2005; Schmahmann and Pandya 1997); approximately 80–90 percent of the cerebellum's involvement in motor tasks is attributed to the processing of sensory information (Jueptner et al. 1997). Cerebellar functions include the fine regulation of motor control, such as the temporal organization of speech movements (Braitenberg et al. 1997) and the online sequencing of syllables into smooth and rhythmically organized utterances (Ackermann 2008). Damage to the cerebellum leads to poorly coordinated speech and inconsistent articulation (Ackermann et al. 1992). Therefore, increased cerebellar activity in trained singers could indicate enhanced coordination of singing-related movements based on increased somatosensory processing.

Further evidence for enhanced somatosensory processing in trained singers comes from analyses of structural brain differences (Halwani et al. 2011; Kleber et al. 2010b). Halwani et al. (2011) used diffusion tensor imaging (DTI) to investigate macro- and microscopic differences in white-matter fiber tracts in trained singers, instrumentalists, and non-musicians. More specifically, they focused on the arcuate fasciculus (AF), a fiber-tract bundle that connects temporal and frontal brain regions and has been implicated in vocal motor control as well as musical functions (Loui et al. 2009; Schlaug et al. 2009; Wan and Schlaug 2010). For example, diminished white-matter volume in right AF was associated with impaired sound perception and singing accuracy (Loui et al. 2009). Conversely, subjects with musical training (both vocal and instrumental) show larger bilateral AF volumes relative to non-musicians, which points towards a general role of the AF in matching sounds with actions (Halwani et al. 2011). When they compared singers and instrumentalists directly, Halwani et al. (2011) found increased white-matter fiber tract

---

FIGURE 12.4 Continued

(left) and opera singers with non-singers (right) revealed substantial experience-dependent differences. Both trained groups showed increased activation of S1 somatosensory association cortex in the inferior parietal lobe, and the cerebellum compared to non-singers. (c) Opera singers showed additional activation within cerebellum and right S1/M1 when compared to vocal students. (d) A correlation of brain activation during singing with accumulated singing practice showed that more experienced singers recruited more activity in S1 (larynx area) and somatosensory association area in the inferior parietal lobe. These results confirm an experience-dependent role of somatosensation in classical singing. Accumulated singing practice included the time since commencement with formal singing training combined with an estimate of the hours spent singing per week. Please note that the corresponding value in the singing practice scale was log-transformed for statistical reasons.

volume in dorsal and ventral AF branches of singers, as well as decreased dorsal-branch fractional anisotropy (FA), a measure that represents fiber tract integrity; increased FA can indicate greater fiber alignment within a tract, while decreased FA may imply more fibers cross the tract of interest. The dorsal AF branch, which showed the most significant difference in fiber-tract volume between singers and instrumentalists, connects the STG (i.e. auditory regions) with premotor areas in the inferior frontal gyrus and thus might contribute to auditory-motor mapping of vocal output. On the other hand, the reduced FA values in singers' dorsal AF branch (relative to instrumentalists), was observed near the motor and somatosensory cortical regions, which suggests that more fibers cross to and from somatosensory areas. Halwani et al. (2011) concluded that this kind of enhanced connectivity might reflect increased sensitivity to proprioceptive feedback from larynx, lungs, and articulators in response to specialized vocal training.

Another common analysis of differences in cortical brain structure, known as voxel-based morphometry (VBM) (Ashburner and Friston 2000), has already revealed several task-related structural changes in instrumental musicians relative to non-musicians, such as increased gray-matter volume in premotor, primary motor, auditory, somatosensory, and visual-spatial brain areas (Bermudez et al. 2009; Gaser and Schlaug 2003; Han et al. 2009). Kleber et al. (2010b) applied this method to trained singers' neuroanatomical data and found increased gray-matter density in the right S1, S2, and inferior parietal cortex of trained singers, compared to non-singers. The locations of structural changes were similar to previously described areas representing laryngeal/orofacial functions (Grabski et al. 2012), thus supporting claims that: (1) experience-dependent structural changes in the brain can be driven by vocal-skill learning; and (2) somatosensory feedback, which is processed in these structurally changed brain regions, plays a crucial role in singing development.

To explicitly test whether somatosensory feedback significantly contributes to singing-skill development, Kleber et al. (2013) studied the effects of altered somatosensory feedback—via topical anesthesia of the vocal fold surface—on pitch control as a function of singing expertise. In an MR scanner, trained singers and non-singers sang ascending and descending musical intervals under two conditions: normal feedback and altered somatosensory feedback. Recordings of pitch reproduction inside the scanner were analyzed offline and were correlated with singing-related brain activation in both groups and conditions. Distinct activation patterns were observed after anesthesia in each group: trained singers displayed less activity in the cortical network for voluntary (i.e. learned) voice control in trained singers (M1, S1), but only subcortical motor control areas including the putamen and globus pallidus showed decreased activity in non-singers. In addition, trained singers were less affected by anesthesia than non-singers, and therefore sang more accurately under both normal and anesthesia conditions. Interestingly, the right anterior insula showed a differential response between groups (Figure 12.5): under vocal-fold anesthesia, singers exhibited less activity in this region, while non-singers displayed more insular activity. Furthermore, the time courses of cortical activity between the right anterior insula and S1, M1, and auditory cortex was less correlated in singers under anesthesia, suggesting that the anterior insula worked less cohesively with the other regions during singing under anesthesia; in contrast, the time courses of neural activity between anterior insula and the other regions was more correlated in non-singers. Finally, correlations between pitch accuracy and activation in right anterior insula revealed that trained singers sang more accurately

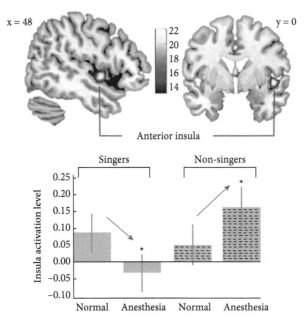

FIGURE 12.5 Singers and non-singers responded differently to singing with and without topical anesthesia of the vocal folds, as data from Kleber, Zatorre, and colleagues (2013) show. The right anterior insula was identified as the principal area dissociating the effect of anesthesia as a function of expertise. In singers, anesthesia resulted in decreased activation whereas in non-singers it resulted in increased activation. The anterior insula may play a crucial role in gating feedback processes, probably due to its ability to integrate multiple sources of sensory input. These results suggest that extensive experience in singing may establish highly accurate feedforward models that act independently, at least temporarily, from external sensory feedback.

only when their insular activity was decreased under anesthesia, which implies that this region played a key role in modulating somatosensory feedback integration as a function of experience. Although the anterior insula is capable of integrating sensory and motor information, as discussed earlier, when somatosensory feedback is unavailable (e.g. due to anesthesia), more experienced singers may "disengage" the anterior insula and rely on established feedforward predictions to prevent the loss of sensory feedback from significantly influencing their vocal accuracy.

Together with the auditory-motor data reviewed above, specifically from Zarate's "ignore" singing condition (Zarate and Zatorre 2008; Zarate et al. 2010a), these results suggest that extensive experience in singing may establish highly accurate feedforward models that act independently, at least temporarily, from external sensory feedback. The right anterior insula has not yet been included in models of vocal-skill acquisition, but it may play a crucial role in gating feedback processes, probably due to its ability to integrate multiple sources of sensory input. This feedback-gating process would be beneficial for singers, who may have to sing under varying acoustic feedback situations and often also against competing sound from large orchestras.

MENTAL IMAGERY AND SINGING

Musicians utilize auditory imagery when they reflect on a musical work, mentally rehearse a performance, and analyze or compose a new score, regardless of the presence of an instrument (Haddon 2007). However, you do not have to be a musician to imagine your favorite musical piece and create a very real experience of hearing that song in your mind. Perception and imagination share a number of qualities, which leads to the definition of mental imagery as a quasi-perceptual, conscious experience in the absence of external stimulus input that may incorporate all physical senses (Gregg 2007). Indeed, musical imagery can be surprisingly accurate when compared with the real stimulus (Halpern et al. 2004; Janata and Paroo 2006). Non-musicians, who were asked to mentally recall pitches of notes that corresponded to words taken from different sections of a familiar song, showed response times that varied systematically with the number of beats separating those words in the real tune (Halpern and Zatorre 1999). Several such shared features between imagery and perception have been identified, involving tempo (Halpern 1988), pitch (Halpern 1989), timbre (Halpern et al. 2004), and loudness (Bailes et al. 2012). In order to conjure up highly accurate musical images, humans crucially depend on recollection from memory and expectancy based on explicitly and implicitly acquired knowledge of the music to be imagined. At the cognitive level, this includes familiarity with the structure of a piece and its musical features, while at the perceptual level, this requires the development of sensory skills through practice. Experienced musicians possess superior auditory skills compared to non-musicians (e.g. Pantev et al. 2001). These training-related advantages also seem to benefit musical imagery, since musicians outperform musically naïve subjects in musical imagery and even show enhanced accuracy on tasks that involve the imagination of everyday non-musical sounds (Aleman et al. 2000). In addition to musical imagery, there is also motor imagery of one's own actions, which is defined as the mental rehearsal of a first person action-representation without movement (Jeannerod and Decety 1995). This involves a covert reflection of overt behavioral performance including the mental representation of associated physical sensations (Decety and Grezes 1999; Decety et al. 1994; Langheim et al. 2002). Analogous to research on auditory imagery, studies on motor imagery have demonstrated that the duration of imagined first person actions was equivalent to the time necessary for completing the actual performance (Decety 1996; Langheim et al. 2002), thus suggesting common mechanisms for both motor imagery and actual motor planning (Jeannerod and Decety 1995).

Over the last decade, neuroscientific research has greatly improved our understanding of imagery by identifying its underlying neural correlates. Evidence from these studies converges on one major finding: mental imagery has the capacity to engage neural networks that are also involved in actual perception and motor control (Herholz et al. 2008; Herholz et al. 2012; Kleber et al. 2007; Zatorre et al. 2007). Musical imagery has been shown to reliably engage the auditory cortex in the absence of sound (Bunzeck et al. 2005; Halpern and Zatorre 1999; Halpern 2001; Halpern et al. 2004; Herholz et al. 2012; Schurmann et al. 2002; Shergill et al. 2001; Zatorre and Krumhansl 2002), including a set of sound-responsive regions distributed throughout the planum polare and planum temporale of the superior temporal gyrus (see Figure 12.1d) (Herholz et al. 2012). The frontal lobe, which possesses direct connections to auditory areas, seems to play a pivotal role during imagery by supporting the retrieval of familiar melodic memories that are encoded in auditory cortical areas. In addition, recent studies suggest that the parietal lobe subserves the common experience of kinesthetic feelings during speech motor imagery, based on internal feedforward mechanisms in the somatosensory control system (as discussed earlier in this chapter), which may generate an estimation of somatosensory consequences of intended motor commands (Tian and Poeppel 2010). Tian and Poeppel supported this view with their observation that the parietal lobe, where S1 and other related somatosensory regions are located, was active prior to both execution and imagery of vocal responses.

Subvocalization (i.e. silently singing along), also referred to as audiation, is often reported during musical imagery and entails kinesthetic aspects of song production. As such, subvocalization has been associated with activation in areas typically engaged in overt motor tasks; these areas involve the frontal and parietal lobes as well as other motor control areas (e.g. premotor cortex, supplementary motor area (SMA), and the cerebellum), thus supporting a role of sensory-motor interactions in musical imagery (Herholz et al. 2012; Zatorre et al. 2007). To directly assess brain activity during overt singing and subvocalization, Riecker and colleagues (2000) asked participants to overtly or covertly (i.e. subvocalize) speak the months of the year or sing a non-lyrical tune while in an MR scanner. Both overt and covert speech and song recruited sensorimotor areas and the cerebellum, which demonstrates that mental imagery of singing engages cortical regions that are implicated in overt singing. Kleber et al. (2007) were specifically interested in the neural correlates of mental singing performance in musically trained participants. Sixteen music university vocal students enrolled in the voice performance program and professional opera singers performed (either overtly or imagined) excerpts from the aria "Caro Mio Ben" (by Tommaso Giordani) in the MR scanner. Results from this study revealed that most areas recruited during overt singing (Figure 12.6a) were also active during imagined performance (Figure 12.6b), including M1 and S1 on both sides. The activation pattern during imagery also included further motor areas, such as the ACC, insula, globus pallidus, the putamen, and phonatory motor regions in the brainstem, as well as areas associated with language production. When activation patterns during imagined and overt singing were directly compared (Figure 12.6c), imagery showed stronger activation in frontal and parietal lobes (involved in memory retrieval and feedforward motor control), as well as SMA, premotor cortex, and ACC, which are required for motor planning and the initiation of vocal motor patterns.

In summary, these data suggest a tight relationship between overt and imagined vocal production in singers, perhaps due to its more body-core centered nature, involving muscles and internal organs for vocal production that also support vital body functions. Together with data suggesting enhanced feedforward motor control in trained singers discussed earlier, Kleber et al. (2007) concluded that imagined singing might be useful for rehearsing the vocal motor network to achieve expert vocal performance. Similarly, mental rehearsal of manual motor tasks can improve the dynamics (Yaguez et al. 1998), velocity, and smoothness of sequential movements trajectories (Lacourse et al. 2005). Furthermore, mental imagery combined with physical practice can improve pianists' ability to learn an unfamiliar piece of music without auditory feedback (Highben and Palmer 2004). As such, imagined musical performance may thus aid in exploration and recruitment of task-related motor commands, based on previously developed internal feedforward mechanisms, which implies that kinesthetic experience must be developed through practice before motor imagery can efficiently improve behavior (Fourkas et al. 2008).

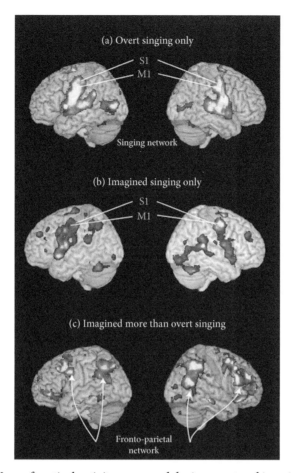

FIGURE 12.6 Maps of cortical activity measured during overt and imagined singing tasks from Kleber and colleagues' (2007) fMRI study. (a) Brain maps showing cortical activation in trained singers during overt singing of the Italian aria "Caro Mio Ben." (b) Imagined singing of the same aria engages many areas that were also active during overt performance, including S1, M1, premotor, and somatosensory association cortex in the inferior parietal cortex. (c) Direct comparisons between imagined and overt singing reveals strong activation in frontal and parietal sites. Frontal cortical areas play a role during imagery by supporting the retrieval of melodic memories that are encoded in auditory cortical areas, whereas the parietal lobe subserves the common experience of kinesthetic feelings during motor imagery.

CONCLUSION

When you think again about the physiological events that occur as you begin your vocal warm-up routine, you may now have a different view about what is going on. In this chapter, the authors have introduced you to the human brain as the central organ for controlling vocal production, and provided you with detailed information on how neural networks integrate sensory information to coordinate the complex mechanisms underlying vocalization. Much of the available information about the basic neural network for vocal control comes from research in primates, whose ability to learn a new vocal sequence is very limited. The human laryngeal-motor cortical pathway, on the other hand, may represent a major evolutionary development that enables us to learn a large repertoire of new vocal expressions throughout our lifetime (Simonyan et al. 2012). Due to technological advances in cognitive neuroscience, researchers are now better able to observe what occurs in singers' brains as they sing or speak. This provides scientists and teachers alike with a fascinating insight into the specific roles of the various neural structures engaged in vocalization.

In contrast to motor control in speech, few studies have used fMRI techniques to investigate singing. In this chapter, the authors have focused on recent fMRI experiments to discuss the neuroscience of singing in general, and to examine the development of singing skills as a means to better understand the neural basis of vocal learning in particular. The real-world applications of these studies may still be too limited to be of immediate use for the professional or aspiring singer, but they explain several important differences between trained and non-trained vocalists. As we increase our knowledge about the neural networks underlying human vocal control (and singing in particular), we can use this knowledge to address topics of greater interest, such as voice dysfunction, voice rehabilitation, and vocal training methods.

References

Abo-el-Enein, M.A. (1966). Laryngeal myotatic reflexes. *Nature* 209(5024): 682–6.

Ackermann, H. (2008). Cerebellar contributions to speech production and speech perception: psycholinguistic and neurobiological perspectives. *Trends in Neurosciences* 31(6): 265–72.

Ackermann, H. and Riecker, A. (2004). The contribution of the insula to motor aspects of speech production: a review and a hypothesis. *Brain Language* 89(2): 320–8.

Ackermann, H. and Riecker, A. (2010). The contribution(s) of the insula to speech production: a review of the clinical and functional imaging literature. *Brain Structure and Function* 214(5–6): 419–33.

Ackermann, H., Vogel, M., Petersen, D., and Poremba, M. (1992). Speech deficits in ischaemic cerebellar lesions. *Journal of Neurology* 239(4): 223–7.

Aleman, A., Nieuwenstein, M.R., Bocker, K.B., and de Haan, E.H. (2000). Music training and mental imagery ability. *Neuropsychologia* 38(12): 1664–8.

Alm, P.A. (2004). Stuttering and the basal ganglia circuits: a critical review of possible relations. *Journal of Communication Disorders* 37(4): 325–69.

Ashburner, J. and Friston, K.J. (2000). Voxel-based morphometry—the methods. *NeuroImage* 11(6 Pt 1): 805–21.

Astafiev, S.V., Shulman, G.L., Stanley, C.M., et al. (2003). Functional organization of human intraparietal and frontal cortex for attending, looking, and pointing. *The Journal of Neuroscience* 23(11): 4689–99.

Augustine, J.R. (1996). Circuitry and functional aspects of the insular lobe in primates including humans. *Brain Research Review* 22(3): 229–44.

Bailes, F., Bishop, L., Stevens, C.J., and Dean, R.T. (2012). Mental imagery for musical changes in loudness. *Frontiers in Psychology* 3: 525.

Bamiou, D.E., Musiek, F.E., and Luxon, L.M. (2003). The insula (Island of Reil) and its role in auditory processing. Literature review. *Brain Research Reviews* 42(2): 143–54.

Barbas, H., Ghashghaei, H., Dombrowski, S.M., and Rempel-Clower, N.L. (1999). Medial prefrontal cortices are unified by common connections with superior temporal cortices and distinguished by input from memory-related areas in the rhesus monkey. *Journal of Computational Neurology* 410(3): 343–67.

Belin, P., Zatorre, R.J., Lafaille, P., Ahad, P., and Pike, B. (2000). Voice-selective areas in human auditory cortex. *Nature* 403(6767): 309–12.

Bermudez, P., Lerch, J. P., Evans, A.C., and Zatorre, R.J. (2009). Neuroanatomical correlates of musicianship as revealed by cortical thickness and voxel-based morphometry. *Cerebral Cortex* 19(7): 1583–96.

Braitenberg, V., Heck, D., and Sultan, F. (1997). The detection and generation of sequences as a key to cerebellar function: experiments and theory. *The Behavioral and Brain Sciences* 20(2): 229–45.

Brown, S., Martinez, M.J., Hodges, D.A., Fox, P.T., and Parsons, L.M. (2004). The song system of the human brain. *Cognitive Brain Research* 20(3): 363–75.

Brown, S., Laird, A.R., Pfordresher, P.Q., et al. (2009). The somatotopy of speech: Phonation and articulation in the human motor cortex. *Brain and Cognition* 70(1): 31–41.

Brown, S., Martinez, M.J., and Parsons, L.M. (2006). Music and language side by side in the brain: a PET study of the generation of melodies and sentences. *European Journal of Neuroscience* 23(10): 2791–803.

Brown, S., Ngan, E., and Liotti, M. (2008). A larynx area in the human motor cortex. *Cerebral Cortex* 18(4): 837–45.

Bunzeck, N., Wuestenberg, T., Lutz, K., Heinze, H.J., and Jancke, L. (2005). Scanning silence: mental imagery of complex sounds. *NeuroImage* 26(4): 1119–27.

Burnett, T.A., Freedland, M.B., Larson, C.R., and Hain, T.C. (1998). Voice f_0 responses to manipulations in pitch feedback. *Journal of Acoustical Society of America* 103(6): 3153–61.

Chouinard, P.A. and Paus, T. (2006). The primary motor and premotor areas of the human cerebral cortex. *Neuroscientist* 12(2): 143–52.

Craig, A.D. (2003). Interoception: the sense of the physiological condition of the body. *Current Opinion in Neurobiology* 13(4): 500–5.

Craig, A.D. (2009). How do you feel—now? The anterior insula and human awareness. *Nature Reviews. Neuroscience* 10(1): 59–70.

Decety, J. (1996). The neurophysiological basis of motor imagery. *Behavior and Brain Research* 77(1–2): 45–52.

Decety, J. and Grezes, J. (1999). Neural mechanisms subserving the perception of human actions. *Trends in Cognitive Sciences* 3(5): 172–8.

Decety, J., Perani, D., Jeannerod, M., et al. (1994). Mapping motor representations with positron emission tomography. *Nature* 371(6498): 600–2.

Dujardin, E. and Jürgens, U. (2005). Afferents of vocalization-controlling periaqueductal regions in the squirrel monkey. *Brain Research* 1034 (1–2): 114–31.

Eliades, S.J. and Wang, X. (2003). Sensory-motor interaction in the primate auditory cortex during self- initiated vocalizations. *Journal of Neurophysiology* 89: 2194–207.

Esposito, A., Demeurisse, G., Alberti, B., and Fabbro, F. (1999). Complete mutism after midbrain periaqueductal gray lesion. *Neuroreport* 10(4): 681–5.

Foster, N.E. and Zatorre, R.J. (2010). A role for the intraparietal sulcus in transforming musical pitch information. *Cerebral Cortex* 20(6): 1350–9.

Fourkas, A.D., Bonavolonta, V., Avenanti, A., and Aglioti, S.M. (2008). Kinesthetic imagery and tool-specific modulation of corticospinal representations in expert tennis players. *Cerebral Cortex* 18(10): 2382–90.

Gaser, C. and Schlaug, G. (2003). Gray matter differences between musicians and nonmusicians. *Annals of the New York Academy of Sciences* 999: 514–17.

Gooler, D.M. and O'Neill, W.E. (1987). Topographic representation of vocal frequency demonstrated by microstimulation of anterior cingulate cortex in the echolocating bat, Pteronotus parnelli parnelli. *Journal of Computational Physiology [A]* 161(2): 283–94.

Grabski, K., Lamalle, L., Vilain, C., et al. (2012). Functional MRI assessment of orofacial articulators: Neural correlates of lip, jaw, larynx, and tongue movements. *Human Brain Mapping* 33(10): 2306–21.

Grefkes, C., Ritzl, A., Zilles, K., and Fink, G.R. (2004). Human medial intraparietal cortex subserves visuomotor coordinate transformation. *NeuroImage* 23(4): 1494–506.

Gregg, M. (2007). Theoretical and practical applications of mental imagery. In: A. Williamon and D. Coimbra (eds), *International Symposium on Performance Science* (1, Porto: European Association of Conservatoires) pp. 295–300.

Griffiths, T.D. (2003). Functional imaging of pitch analysis. *Annals of New York Academy of Science* 999: 40–9.

Griffiths, T.D. and Warren, J.D. (2002). The planum temporale as a computational hub. *Trends in Neuroscience* 25(7): 348–53.

Griffiths, T.D., Buchel, C., Frackowiak, R.S., and Patterson, R.D. (1998). Analysis of temporal structure in sound by the human brain. *Nature Neuroscience* 1(5): 422–7.

Grodd, W., Hulsmann, E., and Ackermann, H. (2005). Functional MRI localizing in the cerebellum. *Neurosurgery Clinics of North America* 16(1): 77–99, v.

Guenther, F.H. and Vladusich, T. (2012). A neural theory of speech acquisition and production. *Journal of Neurolinguistics* 25(5): 408–22.

Haddon, E. (2007). What does mental imagery mean to university music students and their professors? In: A. Williamon and D. Coimbra (eds), *International Symposium on Performance Science* (1, Porto: European Association of Conservatoires) pp. 301–6.

Hain, T.C., Burnett, T.A., Kiran, S., et al. (2000). Instructing subjects to make a voluntary response reveals the presence of two components to the audio-vocal reflex. *Experimental Brain Research* 130(2): 133–41.

Halpern, A.R. (1988). Mental scanning in auditory imagery for songs. *Journal of Experimental Psychology* 14(3): 434–43.

Halpern, A.R. (1989). Memory for the absolute pitch of familiar songs. *Memory and Cognition* 17(5): 572–81.

Halpern, A.R. (2001). Cerebral substrates of musical imagery. *Annals of the New York Academy of Science* 930: 179–92.

Halpern, A.R. and Zatorre, R.J. (1999). When that tune runs through your head: a PET investigation of auditory imagery for familiar melodies. *Cerebral Cortex* 9(7): 697–704.

Halpern, A.R., Zatorre, R.J., Bouffard, M., and Johnson, J.A. (2004). Behavioral and neural correlates of perceived and imagined musical timbre. *Neuropsychologia* 42(9): 1281–92.

Halwani, G.F., Loui, P., Ruber, T., and Schlaug, G. (2011). Effects of practice and experience on the arcuate fasciculus: comparing singers, instrumentalists, and non-musicians. *Frontiers in Psychology* 2: 156.

Han, Y., Yang, H., Lv, Y.T., et al. (2009). Gray matter density and white matter integrity in pianists' brain: a combined structural and diffusion tensor MRI study. *Neuroscience Letters* 459(1): 3–6.

Herholz, S.C., Halpern, A.R., and Zatorre, R.J. (2012). Neuronal correlates of perception, imagery, and memory for familiar tunes. *Journal of Cognitive Neuroscience* 24(6): 1382–97.

Herholz, S.C., Lappe, C., Knief, A., and Pantev, C. (2008). Neural basis of music imagery and the effect of musical expertise. *The European Journal of Neuroscience* 28(11): 2352–60.

Hickok, G. (2012). Computational neuroanatomy of speech production. *Nature Reviews Neuroscience* 13(2): 135–45.

Hickok, G., Houde, J., and Rong, F. (2011). Sensorimotor integration in speech processing: computational basis and neural organization. *Neuron* 69(3): 407–22.

Highben, Z. and Palmer, C. (2004). Effects of auditory and motor mental practice in memorized piano performance. *Bulletin of the Council for Research in Music Education* 159: 58–65.

Houde, J.F. and Nagarajan, S.S. (2011). Speech production as state feedback control. *Frontiers in Human Neuroscience* 5: 82.

Hudspeth, A.J. (2000). Hearing. In: E.R. Kandel, J.H. Schwartz, and T.M. Jessel (eds), *Principles of Neural Science*, 4th edn (pp. 590–613). New York: McGraw-Hill.

Huffman, R.F. and Henson, O.W., Jr. (1990). The descending auditory pathway and acousticomotor systems: connections with the inferior colliculus. *Brain Research Review* 15(3): 295–323.

Itoh, K., Fujii, Y., Suzuki, K., and Nakada, T. (2001). Asymmetry of parietal lobe activation during piano performance: a high field functional magnetic resonance imaging study. *Neuroscience Letters* 309(1): 41–4.

Janata, P. and Paroo, K. (2006). Acuity of auditory images in pitch and time. *Perception and Psychophysics* 68(5): 829–44.

Jeannerod, M. and Decety, J. (1995). Mental motor imagery: a window into the representational stages of action. *Current Opinion in Neurobiology* 5(6): 727–32.

Jeffries, K.J., Braun, A.R., and Fritz, J.B. (2003). Words in melody: an H 2 15 O PET study of brain activation during singing and speaking. *NeuroReport* 14(5): 749–54.

Johnsrude, I.S., Penhune, V.B., and Zatorre, R.J. (2000). Functional specificity in the right human auditory cortex for perceiving pitch direction. *Brain* 123: 155–63.

Jones, J.A. and Keough, D. (2008). Auditory-motor mapping for pitch control in singers and nonsingers. *Experimental Brain Research* 190(3): 279–87.

Jueptner, M., Ottinger, S., Fellows, S.J., et al. (1997). The relevance of sensory input for the cerebellar control of movements. *NeuroImage* 5(1): 41–8.

Jungblut, M., Huber, W., Pustelniak, M., and Schnitker, R. (2012). The impact of rhythm complexity on brain activation during simple singing: an event-related fMRI study. *Restorative Neurology and Neuroscience* 30 (1): 39–53.

Jürgens, U. (2002). Neural pathways underlying vocal control. *Neuroscience Biobehavior Review* 26(2): 235–58.

Jürgens, U. (2009). The neural control of vocalization in mammals: a review. *Journal of Voice* 23(1): 1–10.

Jürgens, U. and Richter, K. (1986). Glutamate-induced vocalization in the squirrel monkey. *Brain Research* 373(1–2): 349–58.

Jürgens, U. and Hage, S.R. (2007). On the role of the reticular formation in vocal pattern generation. *Behavior Brain Research* 182(2): 308–14.

Karnath, H.O. and Baier, B. (2010). Right insula for our sense of limb ownership and self-awareness of actions. *Brain Structure and Function* 214(5–6): 411–17.

Kleber, B., Birbaumer, N., Veit, R., Trevorrow, T., and Lotze, M. (2007). Overt and imagined singing of an Italian aria. *NeuroImage* 36(3): 889–900.

Kleber, B., Veit, R., Birbaumer, N., Gruzelier, J., and Lotze, M. (2010a). The brain of opera singers: experience-dependent changes in functional activation. *Cerebral Cortex* 20(5): 1144–52.

Kleber, B., Moll, C., Veit, R., et al. (2010b). Increased grey-matter density in right somatosensory and auditory cortices of trained classical singers. *Human Brain Mapping* (Barcelona).

Kleber, B., Zeitouni, A.G., Friberg, A., and Zatorre, R.J. (2013). Experience-dependent modulation of feedback integration during singing: role of the right anterior insula. *The Journal of Neuroscience* 33(14): 6070–80.

Kriegstein, K.V. and Giraud, A.L. (2004). Distinct functional substrates along the right superior temporal sulcus for the processing of voices. *NeuroImage* 22(2): 948–55.

Lacourse, M.G., Orr, E.L., Cramer, S.C., and Cohen, M.J. (2005). Brain activation during execution and motor imagery of novel and skilled sequential hand movements. *NeuroImage* 27(3): 505–19.

Lametti, D.R., Nasir, S.M., and Ostry, D.J. (2012). Sensory preference in speech production revealed by simultaneous alteration of auditory and somatosensory feedback. *The Journal of Neuroscience* 32(27): 9351–8.

Langheim, F.J., Callicott, J.H., Mattay, V.S., Duyn, J.H., and Weinberger, D.R. (2002). Cortical systems associated with covert music rehearsal. *NeuroImage* 16(4): 901–8.

Larson, C.R. (1998). Cross-modality influences in speech motor control: the use of pitch shifting for the study of f_0 control. *Journal of Communication Disorders* 31(6): 489–502.

Lewis, J.W., Beauchamp, M.S., and DeYoe, E.A. (2000). A comparison of visual and auditory motion processing in human cerebral cortex. *Cerebral Cortex* 10(9): 873–88.

Loucks, T.M., Poletto, C.J., Simonyan, K., Reynolds, C.L., and Ludlow, C.L. (2007). Human brain activation during phonation and exhalation: common volitional control for two upper airway functions. *NeuroImage* 36(1): 131–43.

Loui, P., Alsop, D., and Schlaug, G. (2009). Tone deafness: a new disconnection syndrome? *The Journal of Neuroscience* 29(33): 10215–220.

Mesulam, M.M. and Mufson, E.J. (1982). Insula of the old world monkey. III: Efferent cortical output and comments on function. *Journal of Computational Neurology* 212(1): 38–52.

Mufson, E.J. and Mesulam, M.M. (1982). Insula of the old world monkey. II: Afferent cortical input and comments on the claustrum. *Journal of Computational Neurology* 212(1): 23–37.

Müller-Preuss, P. and Jürgens, U. (1976). Projections from the "cingular" vocalization area in the squirrel monkey. *Brain Research* 103(1): 29–43.

Müller-Preuss, P., Newman, J.D., and Jürgens, U. (1980). Anatomical and physiological evidence for a relationship between the "cingular" vocalization area and the auditory cortex in the squirrel monkey. *Brain Research* 202(2): 307–15.

Mürbe, D., Pabst, F., Hofmann, G., and Sundberg, J. (2004). Effects of a professional solo singer education on auditory and kinesthetic feedback—a longitudinal study of singers' pitch control. *Journal of Voice* 18(2): 236–41.

Özdemir, E., Norton, A., and Schlaug, G. (2006). Shared and distinct neural correlates of singing and speaking. *NeuroImage* 33(2): 628–35.

Pantev, C., Engelien, A., Candia, V., and Elbert, T. (2001). Representational cortex in musicians. Plastic alterations in response to musical practice. *Annals of the New York Academy of Sciences* 930: 300–14.

Patterson, R.D., Uppenkamp, S., Johnsrude, I.S., and Griffiths, T.D. (2002). The processing of temporal pitch and melody information in auditory cortex. *Neuron* 36(4): 767–76.

Paus, T., Petrides, M., Evans, A.C., and Meyer, E. (1993). Role of the human anterior cingulate cortex in the control of oculomotor, manual, and speech responses: a positron emission tomography study. *Journal of Neurophysiology* 70(2): 453–69.

Penagos, H., Melcher, J.R., and Oxenham, A.J. (2004). A neural representation of pitch salience in nonprimary human auditory cortex revealed with functional magnetic resonance imaging. *The Journal of Neuroscience: the Official Journal of the Society for Neuroscience* 24(30): 6810–15.

Perkell, J.S., Lane, H., Denny, M., et al. (2007). Time course of speech changes in response to unanticipated short-term changes in hearing state. *The Journal of the Acoustical Society of America* 121(4): 2296–311.

Perry, D.W., Zatorre, R.J., Petrides, M., et al. (1999). Localization of cerebral activity during simple singing. *NeuroReport* 10: 3979–84.

Petrides, M. (1986). The effect of periarcuate lesions in the monkey on the performance of symmetrically and asymmetrically reinforced visual and auditory go, no-go tasks. *The Journal of Neuroscience: the Official Journal of the Society for Neuroscience* 6(7): 2054–63.

Puschmann, S., Uppenkamp, S., Kollmeier, B., and Thiel, C.M. (2010). Dichotic pitch activates pitch processing centre in Heschl's gyrus. *NeuroImage* 49(2): 1641–9.

Riecker, A., Ackermann, H., Wildgruber, D., Dogil, G., and Grodd, W. (2000). Opposite hemispheric lateralization effects during speaking and singing at motor cortex, insula and cerebellum. *NeuroReport* 11(9): 1997–2000.

Riecker, A., Mathiak, K., Wildgruber, D., et al. (2005). fMRI reveals two distinct cerebral networks subserving speech motor control. *Neurology* 64(4): 700–6.

Rivier, F. and Clarke, S. (1997). Cytochrome oxidase, acetylcholinesterase, and NADPH-diaphorase staining in human supratemporal and insular cortex: evidence for multiple auditory areas. *NeuroImage* 6(4): 288–304.

Schlaug, G., Marchina, S., and Norton, A. (2009). Evidence for plasticity in white-matter tracts of patients with chronic Broca's aphasia undergoing intense intonation-based speech therapy. *Annals of the New York Academy of Sciences* 1169: 385–94.

Schmahmann, J.D. and Pandya, D.N. (1997). The cerebrocerebellar system. *International Review of Neurobiology* 41: 31–60.

Schulz, G.M., Varga, M., Jeffires, K., Ludlow, C.L., and Braun, A.R. (2005). Functional neuroanatomy of human vocalization: an H215O PET study. *Cerebral Cortex* 15(12): 1835–47.

Schurmann, M., Raij, T., Fujiki, N., and Hari, R. (2002). Mind's ear in a musician: where and when in the brain. *NeuroImage* 16(2): 434–40.

Shergill, S.S., Bullmore, E.T., Brammer, M.J., et al. (2001). A functional study of auditory verbal imagery. *Psychological Medicine* 31(2): 241–53.

Simonyan, K. and Jürgens, U. (2003). Efferent subcortical projections of the laryngeal motorcortex in the rhesus monkey. *Brain Research* 974(1–2): 43–59.

Simonyan, K. and Horwitz, B. (2011). Laryngeal motor cortex and control of speech in humans. *The Neuroscientist: a Review Journal Bringing Neurobiology, Neurology and Psychiatry* 17(2): 197–208.

Simonyan, K., Horwitz, B., and Jarvis, E.D. (2012). Dopamine regulation of human speech and bird song: A critical review. *Brain and Language* 122(3): 142–50.

Simonyan, K., Ostuni, J., Ludlow, C.L., and Horwitz, B. (2009). Functional but not structural networks of the human laryngeal motor cortex show left hemispheric lateralization during syllable but not breathing production. *The Journal of Neuroscience: the Official Journal of the Society for Neuroscience* 29(47): 14912–23.

Smith, A. and Zelaznik, H.N. (2004). Development of functional synergies for speech motor coordination in childhood and adolescence. *Developmental Psychobiology* 45(1): 22–33.

Smotherman, M.S. (2007). Sensory feedback control of mammalian vocalizations. *Behavioral Brain Research* 182(2): 315–26.

Suga, N. and Yajima, Y. (1988). Auditory-vocal integration in the midbrain of the mustached bat: periaqueductal gray and reticular formation. In: J.D. Newman (ed.), *The Physiological Control of Mammalian Vocalization* (pp. 87–107). New York: Plenum Press.

Tanabe, H.C., Kato, M., Miyauchi, S., Hayashi, S., and Yanagida, T. (2005). The sensorimotor transformation of cross-modal spatial information in the anterior intraparietal sulcus as revealed by functional MRI. *Brain Research and Cognitive Brain Research* 22(3): 385–96.

Thoms, G. and Jürgens, U. (1987). Common input of the cranial motor nuclei involved in phonation in squirrel monkey. *Experimental Neurology* 95(1): 85–99.

Tian, X. and Poeppel, D. (2010). Mental imagery of speech and movement implicates the dynamics of internal forward models. *Frontiers in Psychology* 1: 166.

Titze, I.R. (2008). Nonlinear source-filter coupling in phonation: theory. *The Journal of the Acoustical Society of America* 123(5): 2733–49.

Titze, I.R. and Hunter, E.J. (2004). Normal vibration frequencies of the vocal ligament. *The Journal of the Acoustical Society of America* 115(5 Pt. 1): 2264–9.

Wan, C.Y. and Schlaug, G. (2010). Music making as a tool for promoting brain plasticity across the life span. *The Neuroscientist* 16(5): 566–77.

Warren, J.D., Scott, S.K., Price, C.J., and Griffiths, T.D. (2006). Human brain mechanisms for the early analysis of voices. *NeuroImage* 31(3): 1389–97.

Wyke, B.D. (1974a). Laryngeal myotatic reflexes and phonation. *Folia Phoniatrica* 26(4): 249–64.

Wyke, B.D. (1974b). Laryngeal neuromuscular control systems in singing. A review of current concepts. *Folia Phoniatrica* 26(4): 295–306.

Yaguez, L., Nagel, D., Hoffman, H., et al. (1998). A mental route to motor learning: improving trajectorial kinematics through imagery training. *Behavioral Brain Research* 90(1): 95–106.

Zarate, J.M. (2013). Cortical mechanisms of integrating auditory feedback with vocal pitch control. *Proceedings of Meetings on Acoustics* 19: 060176.

Zarate, J.M. and Zatorre, R.J. (2008). Experience-dependent neural substrates involved in vocal pitch regulation during singing. *NeuroImage* 40(4): 1871–87.

Zarate, J.M., Wood, S., and Zatorre, R.J. (2010a). Neural networks involved in voluntary and involuntary vocal pitch regulation in experienced singers. *Neuropsychologia* 48(2): 607–18.

Zarate, J.M., Delhommeau, K., Wood, S., and Zatorre, R.J. (2010b). Vocal accuracy and neural plasticity following micromelody-discrimination training. *PLoS One*, 5(6): e11181.

Zatorre, R.J. and Baum, S.R. (2012). Musical melody and speech intonation: singing a different tune. *PLoS Biology* 10(7): e1001372.

Zatorre, R.J. and Krumhansl, C.L. (2002). Neuroscience. Mental models and musical minds. *Science* 298(5601): 2138–9.

Zatorre, R.J. and Zarate, J.M. (2012). Cortical processing of music. In: D. Poeppel, et al. (eds), *The Human Auditory Cortex* (pp. 261–94). New York: Springer Science+Business Media.

Zatorre, R.J., Evans, A.C., and Meyer, E. (1994). Neural mechanisms underlying melodic perception and memory for pitch. *Journal of Neuroscience* 14(4): 1908–19.

Zatorre, R.J., Chen, J.L., and Penhune, V.B. (2007). When the brain plays music: auditory-motor interactions in music perception and production. *Nature Reviews* 8(7): 547–58.

Zatorre, R.J., Delhommeau, K., and Zarate, J.M. (2012). Modulation of auditory cortex response to pitch variation following training with microtonal melodies. *Frontiers in Psychology* 3: 544.

....

CHAPTER 13

INTONATION IN SINGING

....

JOHAN SUNDBERG

BACKGROUND

....

In music composition as well as in music performance the musical scale plays a fundamental role. From a physical point of view, a scale corresponds to a division of the frequency continuum into discrete steps, the scale tones. In our Western music culture, there are mostly seven of them in the octave, and the frequencies of the scale tones in other octaves are obtained by frequency doubling and halving.

In the development of these scales the widespread use of simultaneous playing of several instruments that produce harmonic spectra seems to have played an important role. Under these conditions some of the lower partials of two simultaneously sounding tones will coincide. This happens when their frequencies can be expressed as a ratio between small integers.

For example, if an instrument producing harmonic spectra plays a tone with a fundamental frequency (f_0) of 110 Hz, its overtones appear at 220, 330, 440, 550, 660, 770, 880, 990, etc. Hz. If another instrument simultaneously plays a tone a pure fifth higher, i.e. with an f_0 of $1.5*110 = 165$ Hz tone, the overtones of this tone will appear at 330, 495, 660, 825, 990, etc. Hz. In other words, if the frequency ratio is 165:110 = 3:2, which corresponds to a pure fifth, every third partial of the lower tone coincides with every second partial of the upper tone.

Coinciding partials results in a special timbral quality, referred to as consonance, and absence of coinciding partials induces the opposite timbral quality, dissonance. Thus, the interval of a fifth sounds consonant. The principle is that intervals with frequency ratios that can be written as ratios between low integers, i.e. 2:3, 3:4, 4:5, etc., sound consonant, and the lower the integers, the greater the number of coinciding harmonics, and the more consonant the interval. The octave therefore is the most consonant interval, as all partials of the upper tone are already present in the spectrum of the lower tone. A condition for this to happen is that the intervals are played exactly in tune. If not, they generate beats.

Dissonance is the other extreme. Maximal dissonance occurs when two partials are separated by an interval that equals a quarter of a critical band of hearing. These bands represent a type of analysis bandwidth of the ear (Plomp and Levelt 1965). For frequencies above about 500 Hz the critical bands are about a minor third wide. For lower frequencies it is around 100 Hz.

In this sense, our Western diatonic scale offers possibilities to play both very consonant and very dissonant intervals. It is tempting to speculate how music would have sounded if it were always played on instruments that generated inharmonic partials (Bohlen 1978; Mathews and Pierce 1989).

Consonance of intervals with coinciding partials happens when the intervals are tuned so that their frequency ratios can be written as ratios between small integers. This tuning is generally referred to as either *just* or *pure*. If the same intervals are played with almost, but not exactly the same, frequency ratios, beats appear. The reason is that the overtones do not coincide exactly. Thus, just tuning is the only one that does not give rise to beats in consonant intervals. On the other hand, in playing solo music, just tuning is often not applied. The greatest difference happens on the intervals that exist in both major and minor versions: the second, third, sixth, and seventh. The major versions are widened and the minor versions are narrowed. This tuning is referred to as the Pythagorean.

The frequencies of the scale tones in Pythagorean tuning can be obtained by piling pure fifth intervals on top of each other and then reducing the frequencies by halving, such that they all arrive in the same octave. This tuning enhances the difference between major and minor versions of intervals.

The equally tempered tuning (ETT) can be regarded as a brutal mathematical method for obtaining the frequencies of the scale tones that lie between those of the pure and the Pythagorean tunings. In the ETT, the octave interval is simply chopped into twelve intervals, all of exactly identical width. Here, all consonant intervals except the octave have only nearly, but not exactly, coinciding partials. They generate beats when the tones sound simultaneously.

Figure 13.1 compares pure and Pythagorean tunings with the equally tempered tuning. Pure tuning reduces the contrast between intervals that exist in both minor and major versions, in the sense that the minor versions of the second, third, sixth, and seventh are played slightly wide, and the major versions slightly narrow. The Pythagorean has the opposite effect, enhancing the contrast between minor and major intervals.

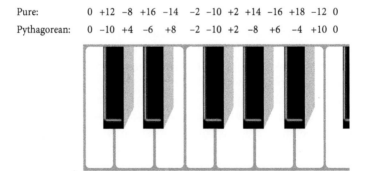

FIGURE 13.1 Deviations, in cent, from the equally tempered tuning in the pure and in the Pythagorean tunings.

Intonation in ensemble singing

Choir

Obviously, the accuracy of intonation is limited in all kinds of music performance, including choral ensembles. The accuracy can be measured in terms of the standard deviation of the f_0 values obtained from members of an ensemble.

Ternström and Sundberg (1988) glued microphones that which are sensitive only to vibrations, to the throats of six bass singers in a choir of good reputation and asked them to perform a simple eight tones cadence four times after first having rehearsed it. The maximum differences between the six subjects' mean f_0 (MF$_0$) varied between 5 and 66 cents for the various tones. The overall distribution of deviations from the group means for the eight tones was close to normal. As shown in Figure 13.2, most values of the standard deviations for the different tones lay within an interval of ±15 cent from the group mean. The average standard deviations of the eight tones were 13 cents, with extremes at 10.3 and 15.8 cents. Thus, two-thirds of the f_0 values produced by these basses agreed to within ±13 cents (corresponding to about 1 Hz at 140 Hz f_0). The largest deviation from the group average produced by individual singers was on the order of +45 cents. It is possible that smaller scatter values

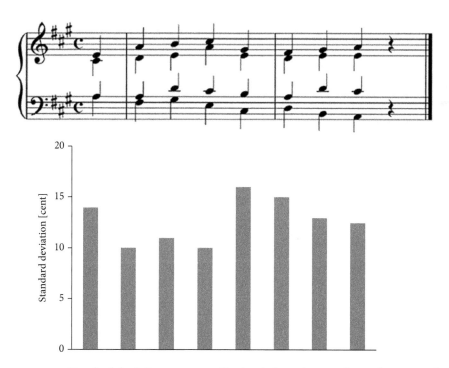

FIGURE 13.2 Standard deviations measured in the six bass singers of a good amateur choir singing four times the bass part of the cadence shown.

After Ternström and Sundberg 1988.

would have been obtained in the other choir sections, as they sing in a higher frequency range where similar errors will cause quicker and thus probably more apparent beats.

It is tempting to assume that just intonation is preferred in ensemble singing such that beats are avoided. On the other hand, beats may not be a really severe threat, since they are produced only when the f_o is perfectly constant. This condition is rarely met in music performances, where there is mostly some random variation of f_o. Further, as mentioned, just tuning has the disadvantage of being associated with intervals between successive tones that are far from the Pythagorean tuning, which seems preferred in performances of solo parts and melodies.

In the same study, Ternström and Sundberg studied also the relevance to intonation of three factors: (1) vibrato, (2) amplitude of common partials, and (3) amplitudes of partials above the first common partial. They presented synthesized tones with all combinations of these three properties to each of eighteen male choir singers who were asked to sing a major third and a fifth above the reference tones, which were presented over a loudspeaker. The standard deviation of the f_o of the tones produced was measured.

The results are presented in Figure 13.3, where significant effects are marked with asterisks and the different combinations with lower-case letters. As can be seen in the figure, all these three tone properties had significant effects on how accurately the major third and the fifth were sung, but the effect of a given property depended on what other properties the tone possessed. In any event, the results showed that the presence of common partials, an absence of vibrato, and the presence of high partials may facilitate intonation under certain conditions. In addition, it was found that intonation was facilitated when the lowest common partial was enhanced by a formant.

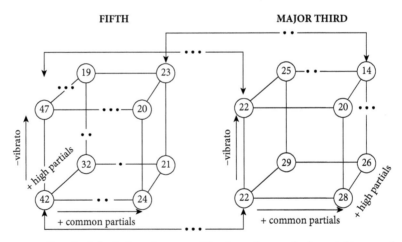

FIGURE 13.3 Standard deviations, in cent, of f_o values observed when eighteen male choral singers sang a fifth and a major third above synthesized reference tones with and without the indicated properties. Effects significant at the 5 percent, 2.5 percent, and 1 percent levels are marked with one, two, and three asterisks, respectively.

From Ternström and Sundberg (1988).

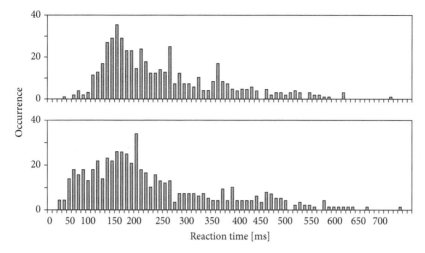

FIGURE 13.4 Distribution of reaction times for highly and moderately skilled singers (upper and lower panels).

After Grell et al. (2009).

Jers and Ternström (2005) analyzed intonation in a choir of sixteen singers. The ensemble performed in unison a music example containing half notes and quarter notes, and the males sang one octave below the females. The melody was performed in a slow and a fast tempo, average quarter note durations being about 500 ms and 750 ms. Their f_o was measured from accelerometer microphones glued to the singers' noses and recorded on separate tracks of a tape recorder. F_o was measured as the average across the entire tone. The result showed that the standard deviation of f_o of the ensemble decreased from around 25 cents to 16 cents in the slower tempo.

This effect can be assumed to reflect the time it takes for a singer to adapt to an external f_o reference. Grell and associates measured this reaction time in members of a highly skilled and a moderately skilled choir (Grell et al. 2009). They were presented with two simultaneous synthesized sung vowels forming a fifth interval. The tones were presented over loudspeakers and the task was to complement the fifth interval with a major third above the lower tone. Suddenly, the reference tones were shifted by 50 or 100 cents upward or downward and the task was to adapt to this shift in reference.

Great inter-individual variation was observed, but the most common reaction time was close to 150 ms, as can be seen in Figure 13.4. Thus, it took about 150 ms for a singer to adjust tuning to a heard reference, for example the tones from the fellow singers in a choir. This seems to explain the findings regarding the effect of tempo in the Jers and Ternström study. In that experiment the fine-tuning of the tones was averaged across the entire tone, so the mean included the fine correction of tuning that may have happened during the first 150 ms.

Barbershop

Given these results barbershop singing is an interesting case. It is traditionally performed by four singers, of which one, the lead singer, uses falsetto register, while the other singers use modal register. All singers strive to sing without vibrato, so intonation could be expected to be close to just. This hypothesis was tested in a study where two well-renowned barbershop groups were recorded by means of accelerometers glued to the external surface of the neck near the trachea (Hagerman and Sundberg, 1980). They sang examples that belonged to their standard repertoire. The results showed that the lead voice served as the tuning reference for the group. The standard deviations of f_o ranged between 4 and 17 cents, thus much less than that found in choral singing. The intervals between simultaneous tones were found to deviate systematically from their corresponding values in both just and Pythagorean intonation. The major third in major triads with the function of a dominant was found to be a slightly stretched version of a pure third, while in a tonic chord it was closer to a flattened version of a Pythagorean third. The major third in a minor triad showed the same width as the major third of major triads which included the seventh. Interestingly, the deviations from just intonation did not give rise to beats, presumably due to the finite degree of periodicity of the tones.

VIBRATO

Singing in the classical Western operatic tradition includes vibrato as an important property. It corresponds to a quasi-sinusoidal modulation of f_o. As a consequence, the frequencies of the harmonic partials also vary in phase with f_o. This also implies that the partials which undulate in frequency prevent the production of beats in mistuned, i.e. non-pure intervals. This makes intonation in singing in the classical Western operatic tradition a particularly interesting area.

A question of basic relevance is what pitch is perceived when a tone has such an undulating f_o. Experiments where musically trained subjects have matched the pitch of a synthetic sung vibrato tone with the same tone void of vibrato have indicated that the pitch corresponds to the mean f_o, averaged over a complete vibrato period (Horan and Shonle 1980; Sundberg 1978). This is true for vibrato rates in the range of about 5 to 7 Hz, which is typical in professional Western opera singing. Thus, the perceptual system appears to calculate a running average of f_o over a time window approximately fitting one vibrato period, that is, about 150 to 200 ms.

A striking application of this averaging is provided by the f_o pattern observed in legato performances of coloratura passages, i.e. sequences of short tones which are not separated by pauses. Figure 13.5 shows a typical example. Each scale tone corresponds to an f_o pattern encircling the target f_o. A similar pattern can be obtained if a vibrato-like sinusoidal modulation is superimposed on a glissando, as illustrated in Figure 13.6. If this pattern is processed with a running average function with a window of about 200 ms width, a quasi-stepwise changing f_o is obtained, as illustrated in the same Figure.

In fast staccato singing, the voiced segments of the tones are sometimes shorter than a complete vibrato cycle. Figure 13.7 shows an example. The pitch perceived of such short tones that contain incomplete vibrato cycles has been studied in detail by d'Alessandro and Castellengo (1994). They used synthesized vibrato tones where the vibrato cycle was interrupted at different places. The results showed that the pitch perceived corresponds to an f_o

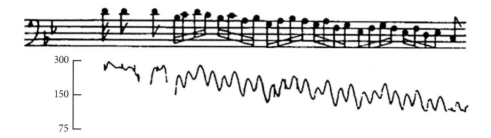

FIGURE 13.5 Fundamental frequency pattern produced by a professional singer performing the sequence of sixteenth notes shown.

After Leanderson et al. 1987.

average where more weight was placed on the final part of the event. Thus, the overall f_o pattern influences pitch perception. The authors also showed that the f_o of the perceived pitch can be approximated by an equation.

Provided that the rate lies within about 5 and 7 Hz, vibrato generally has no influence on the accuracy with which listeners perceive the pitch. This was concluded from an experiment where musically educated listeners adjusted the f_o of a vibrato free synthetic vowel such that it appeared to have the same pitch as the same vowel with vibrato (Sundberg 1978). The accuracy was found to be the same as when the same subjects repeated the experiment with vowels that lacked vibrato. On the other hand, van Besouw and associates (2008) reported that the tolerance of what was considered to be in tune was somewhat more generous for vibrato tones than for vibrato free tones. Absence of beats between vibrato tones may contribute to this effect.

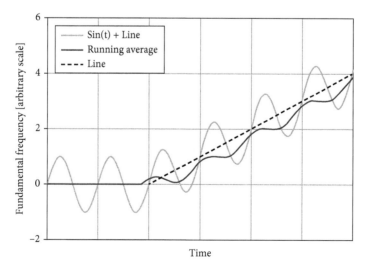

FIGURE 13.6 Gray curve: fundamental frequency pattern resulting from superimposing a sinusoidal vibrato on a glissando represented by the black dashed curve. The solid black curve shows a running average of the gray curve.

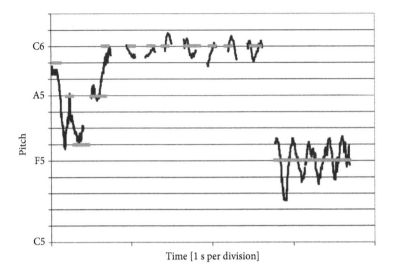

FIGURE 13.7 Fundamental frequency pattern produced in staccato performance of an excerpt from a commercial recording of the aria "Der Hölle Rache" from W.A. Mozart's opera *Die Zauberflöte*. The target values are marked with heavy gray lines.

ACCURACY

Listeners' accuracy of pitch perception is obviously crucial to the accuracy required in singing. This accuracy has been analyzed by Vurma and Ross (2006). They analyzed professional singers' performances of ascending and descending versions of three intervals: minor second, tritone, and fifth. The results showed that, on average, the singers' intonation was very close to the equally tempered tuning; the f_0 averages had a standard deviation in the vicinity of 20 cents less. Thus, on the whole the singers' mean f_0 values were less than 20 cents from equally tempered tuning. Yet there was a systematic tendency to expand the wider intervals fifth and tritone and to compress the narrow minor second interval slightly.

While Vurma and Ross investigated singers' intonation of isolated intervals, deviations from ETT seem also to depend on the musical context. Sundberg (2011) analyzed the intonation in commercial recordings of Radames' recitative preceding the "Romanze" aria in the first act of Verdi's opera *Aida*, as performed by tenors Carlo Bergonzi, Jussi Björling, Placido Domingo, Luciano Pavarotti, and Richard Tucker.

Most of these singers tended to sing the higher tones sharper than the lower tones, a tendency also observed in performances of instrumental music (Friberg 1991). For the phrase-peak tone A4 in bar 21, a general tendency was observed to sing particularly sharp relative to the ETT of the accompanying orchestra. As illustrated in Figure 13.8, some of the singers started the tone somewhat flat and gradually sharpened it towards the end of the tone, so that the following descending octave leap was stretched. The sharpening reached between 10 and 20 cents at the end of the tone. However, Björling's intonation of the phrase-peak tone A4 in bar 21 was no less than 60 cents sharp in a live recording.

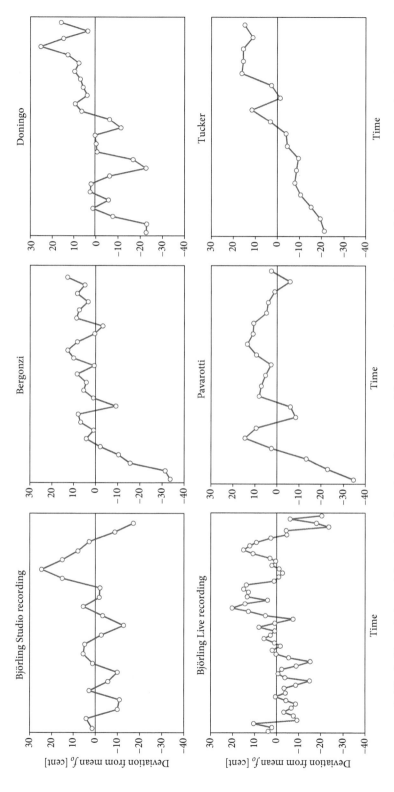

FIGURE 13.8 The indicated singers' deviations from their f_0 average of the sustained tone in bar 21. Each data point corresponds to the mean of half a vibrato cycle measured at its peak and valley.

From Sundberg (2011).

Given these observations, a relevant question is the relationship between a singer's intonation and music listeners' perception of what constitutes being out of tune. Sundberg and
associates (1996) studied the accuracy of intonation in a musical context, performances of
Franz Schubert's song *Ave Maria*. F_o data was collected from ten commercial recordings in
terms of the f_o values of adjacent maxima and minima in a sequence of complete vibrato
cycles in tones longer than an eighth note. Then the averages were calculated across each of
these tones. In calculating the corresponding ETT values, the tuning of the accompaniment
was used as the reference. Thus, if the tuning of the pitch of A4 was 443 Hz, the ETT values
for the tones were calculated using 443 Hz as the reference. The results showed a great variation, ranging from 42 cents sharp to 42 cents flat. Thus, much greater deviations from ETT
occurred in a musical context than when professional singers performed isolated intervals,
as in the Vurma and Ross study (2006).

A relevant question is to what extent these deviations were consistent. Nine of the
singers had recorded both the first and the second verse of the song, thus allowing a comparison of intonation of the same tone. The comparison was carried out for the first and
last three long tones of the first and second verse. The result is illustrated in Figure 13.9,
where the distance between the thin horizontal lines corresponds to 100 cent. In forty-
eight tones out of the total of (6 x 9) fifty-four tones, the difference exceeded ±15 cents. One
singer showed a clear tendency to sing the tones in the second verse flatter than those in
the first verse (open triangles in the graph). Thus, in most cases the deviations from the
ETT were reasonably consistent, indicating that the deviations from the ETT were similar
and quite small.

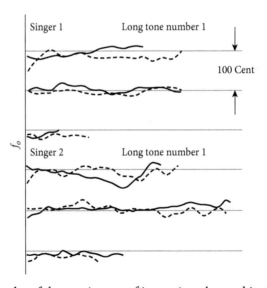

FIGURE 13.9 Examples of the consistency of intonation observed in two singers' performance of the three long tones of the first phrase in verse 1 and verse 2 (dashed and solid
curves) of Franz Schubert's "Ave Maria."

From Sundberg et al. (1996).

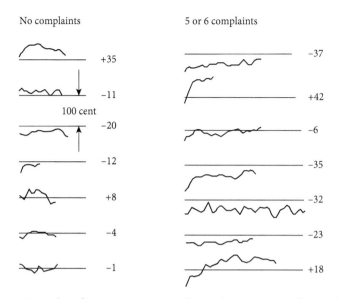

FIGURE 13.10 Examples of intonation curves observed in commercial recordings of Franz Schubert's "Ave Maria". The numbers refer to the averaged deviation in cent from ETT. All six expert listeners perceived the examples in the left column as in tune and five or six perceived the examples in the right column as out of tune.

After Sundberg et al. (1996).

A listening test was carried out with six highly experienced professional music listeners, representing different professions: teacher of singing, phonogram producer, choral conductor, and piano accompanist. They were provided with a score for each of the ten performances and were asked to circle all tones, which they perceived as out of tune.

The result showed a surprisingly great scatter. Many notes were marked as out of tune by three or four experts but not by the others. Figure 13.10 shows examples of intonation that were classified as out of tune by none of the experts and by at least five experts. Of the former tones most, but not all, were quite close to ETT, but some were clearly sharper. Of the tones perceived as out of tune, many showed an f_0 curve below the ETT value.

The mean f_0 values for the 25 long tones of the song are shown in Figure 13.11. Triangles refer to tones classified as out of tune by at least five of the six expert listeners, and tones that none of the experts complained about are represented by diamonds. In most cases, the intonation values perceived as in tune varied within a band of 20 cents. However, the center of this band deviated from the ETT value in some cases, for example for tone number 3. In addition, none of the expert listeners complained about the flat intonation of the last tone of the piece, tone number 25.

Notes number 6, 7, 18, and 21 showed exceptionally great variation of intonation of tones that none of the expert listeners perceived as out of tune, for tone 7 varying no less than between 35 cents sharp and 20 cents flat. The reason for this generosity is an open question, but it might be relevant that this tone is a suspension note, presenting the fourth that moves to the major third in the next beat. Moreover, the note initiates a chromatically falling sequence of the following melody notes appearing on stressed positions in the bar.

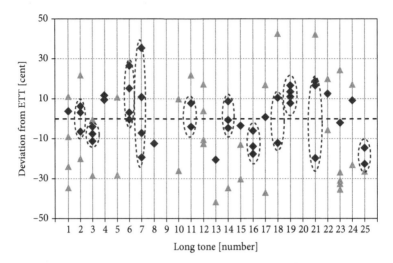

FIGURE 13.11 Mean f_o of the long tones of Franz Schubert's song "Ave Maria", measured in commercial recordings. The horizontal dashed line represents the ETT as related to the tuning of the accompaniment. Black diamonds and gray triangles represent cases perceived as in tune and out of tune by a panel of expert listeners.

From Sundberg et al. (1996).

INTONATION AND EXPRESSION

These observations suggest that intonation may serve expressive purposes. This was studied in an investigation by Sundberg and associates (2013). The material was a set of recordings where an internationally prominent baritone, Håkan Hagegård, sang eleven music excerpts from the Lieder repertoire in two ways, as in a concert and as void of musical expression as he could, a neutral version. Six excerpts had an excited character and five a peaceful, contemplative character. Intonation was compared with the ETT related to the mean intonation of the entire excerpt.

A marked intonation difference was revealed between the excited and the peaceful excerpts. In the concert versions of the excited examples, the phrase-peak tones were sung about 25 cents sharp, on average. In the peaceful examples the sharpening was close to zero in both versions. Moreover, in the excited examples, the sharpening was greater in the concert versions than in the neutral versions, as illustrated in Figure 13.12. This supported the assumption that the sharpening was used for expressive purposes in the excited excerpts.

To test this assumption the sharpening of the phrase-peak tones in the excited examples was eliminated using the Melodyne software. Thus, the intonation of these tones was flattened such that the mean f_o became in accordance with ETT. The original version and the manipulated version of the excited examples were then presented pair-wise to musicians, who were asked to decide which version in the pair sounded more expressive. The result showed that the original versions, with sharpened phrase-peak tones, were perceived as significantly more expressive than the manipulated.

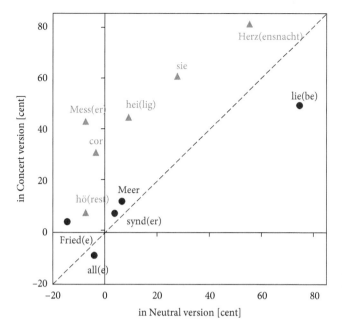

FIGURE 13.12 Deviations from ETT for the phrase-peak tones in the singer's neutral and concert versions of the excerpts. Triangles and circles refer to excited and peaceful excerpts, respectively.

From Sundberg et al. (2013).

The results of this experiment were in accordance with the assumption that tuning can be used as an expressive tool and that sharpening phrase-peak tones can be used for this purpose in excited contexts. It can also be noted that the intonation of an interval may carry some emotional information.

In view of these investigations, a relevant question is how small the intonation differences are that music listeners can notice. The answer appears to depend on the musical context and on the listening conditions.

The just noticeable difference in pitch between two tones presented in sequence approaches 10 cents. In a listening experiment Friberg and Sundberg (1994) presented three versions of short musical excerpts to musically experienced students. In one of the versions the tuning of the scale tones deviated from ETT, and the subjects' task was to tell which of the three presentations was different from the other two. When an incorrect answer was obtained the deviations were made twice as large in the subsequent presentation. The results suggested that the just noticeable difference in tuning for these listeners was about 42 cents, i.e. about four times larger than what has been found in comparison of single tones presented in succession. Thus, it seems that even musically experienced listeners may completely lack sensitivity to fine-tuning, their pitch discrimination being limited to discriminate nothing but semitones. By contrast, professional music listeners, such as teachers of singing and phonogram producers, seem to have a tolerance zone of ±10 cents, as suggested by the results shown in Figure 13.10. Thus, experience and education also appear to sharpen the auditory system with regard to fine-tuning or improve the conscious awareness of tuning differences.

And it seems likely that improved ability to detect tuning differences increases a listener's possibilities to perceive expressive components of a musical performance.

The study of phrase-peak tone intonation in sung performance of excited music excerpts suggested that sharpening such tones increased the expressiveness (Sundberg et al. 2013). Some experimental findings indeed support the hypothesis that intonation may add an emotional coloring even to an octave interval (Makeig and Balzano 1982). In any event, it seems fair to assume that an increased accuracy of pitch perception paves the way for a rich experience of emotional colors embedded in music performances.

Finally, a comment should be made regarding recording technology. In today's recording studios software packages are available that allow manipulation of vocal artists' pitch. If such corrections are made on the assumption that deviations from ETT equals singing out of tune, they may in fact have the effect of reducing the expressivity of the singer's performance. It seems important to keep in mind, that ETT cannot be accepted as the gold standard for tuning.

References

d'Alessandro, C. and Castellengo, M. (1994). The pitch of short-duration vibrato tones. *Journal of the Acoustical Society of America* 95: 1617–1630.

van Besouw, R.M., Brereton J.S., and Howard, D.M. (2008). Range of tuning for tones with and without vibrato. *Music Perception* 26: 145–155.

Bohlen, H. (1978). 13 Tonstufen in der Duodezime. *Acustica* 39(2): 76–86.

Friberg, A. (1991). Generative rules for music performance: a formal description of a rule system. *Computer Music Journal* 15(2): 56–71.

Friberg, A. and Sundberg, J. (1994). Just noticable difference in duration, pitch and sound level in a musical context. In: *Proceedings of the 3rd International Conference for Music Perception and Cognition*, pp. 339–340, Liège, July 23–27.

Grell, A., Sundberg, J., Ternström, S., Ptok, M., and Altenmüller, E. (2009). Rapid pitch correction in choir singers. *Journal of the Acoustical Society of America* 126(1): 407–413.

Hagerman, B. and Sundberg, J. (1980). F_0 adjustment in Barbershop singing. *Journal of Research in Singing* 4(1): 3–17.

Horan, J.I. and Shonle, K.E. (1980). The pitch of vibrato tones. *Journal of the Acoustical Society of America* 67: 246–252.

Jers, H. and Ternström, S. (2005). Intonation analysis of a multi-channel choir recording. *TMH-QPSR* 47(1): 001–006.

Leanderson, R., Sundberg, J., and von Euler, C. (1987). Role of the diaphragmatic activity during singing: A study of transdiaphragmatic pressures. *Journal of Applied Physiology* 62: 259–270.

Makeig, S. and Balzano, G. (1982). Octave tuning—two modes of perception. Paper presented at *Research Symposium on Psychology and Acoustics of Music*, University of Kansas, Lawrence, April.

Mathews, M.V. and Pierce, J.R. (1989). The Bohlen–Pierce Scale. In: M.V. Mathews and J.R. Pierce (eds), *Current Directions in Computer Music Research*, p. 167. Cambridge, MA: MIT Press.

Plomp, R. and Levelt, A. (1965). Tonal consonance and critical bandwidth. *Journal of the Acoustical Society of America* 38: 548ff.

Sundberg, J., Prame, E. and Iwarsson, J. (1996). Replicability and accuracy of pitch patterns in professional singers. In: P. Davis and N. Fletcher (eds), *Vocal Fold Physiology: Controlling Complexity and Chaos*, pp. 291–306. San Diego: Singular.

Sundberg, J., Lã, F.M., and Himonides, E. (2013). Intonation and expressivity: A single case study of classical western singing. *Journal of Voice* 27: 391e–397e.

Ternström, S. and Sundberg, J. (1988). Intonation precision of choir singers. *Journal of the Acoustical Society of America* 84: 59–69.

Vurma, A. and Ross, J. (2006). Production and perception of musical intervals. *Music Perception* 23: 331–344.

CHAPTER 14

··

SINGING AND EMOTION

··

EDUARDO COUTINHO, KLAUS R. SCHERER, AND NICOLA DIBBEN

INTRODUCTION

THE view that music is a powerful means of emotional expression and communication has a long-standing tradition. Indeed, composers, musicologists, philosophers and psychologists interested in music have repeatedly discussed and theorized (often controversially) the ways in which music is able to express different emotions, and to induce them in the listener (Bever 1988; Clynes 1977; Cooke 1959; de la Motte-Haber 1996; Fonagy 1981, 1983; Juslin and Västfjäll 2008; Kivy 1988; Lundin 1967; Scherer 1991; Scherer and Coutinho 2013). In this discussion, vocal music plays a very special role, particularly if we consider the connections between the evolution of non-verbal affective expression, the origins of music, and its power to produce emotions in the listener. The nature of these emotions and their components (physiological arousal, action tendencies, motor expressions, feelings) are a matter of debate (which we cannot go into in this context, but see Scherer and Coutinho 2013).

In an evolutionary context, it is instructive to review the precursors of *emotion expression* in speech and singing, in particular animal vocalizations and interjections. Scherer (1985) has reviewed research on animal communication, which demonstrates that, in many species, affective states, generally linked to changes in physiological arousal, are externalized in vocalizations and serve specific communication functions, often involving acoustic patterns that are similar across species. Closely resembling such animal affect vocalizations, one finds rudiments of non-linguistic human affect vocalizations, often referred to as 'interjections' (such as "ouch," "ai," "oh," or "yuck"). Scherer (1994) has reviewed the literature in this domain and proposed the more general notion of "affect bursts," based on a general theory of emotion processes and the role of communication. Historically, there have been many suggestions by both philosophers (e.g. Rousseau and Herder) and natural scientists (e.g. Helmholtz) that both proto-speech and proto-music have evolved from such primitive affect vocalizations. For instance, Helmholtz (1983), one of the pioneers of music acoustics, proposed that the basics of musical expression originate in the continual refinement of the natural resources of the preverbal *Affektvokalisationen* (see Scherer 1995). In the process of conventionalization and ritualization, expressive signals may have been shaped by the constraints of transmission characteristics, limitations of sensory organs, or other factors, and the resulting flexibility of the communication code may have fostered the evolution of more abstract, symbolic systems, such as language and music. This is likely to have occurred in close conjunction with the evolution of the brain—just as newer neocortical structures with highly cognitive modes of functioning have been superimposed on older "emotional" structures, such as the limbic system, the evolution of human speech as a system of discrete information encoding and transmission (and of musical scales and conventions for singing) has made use of the more primitive, analog (continuous) vocal affect signaling system as a carrier signal (see Scherer 2013a, 2013 for a more extensive discussion of this evolutionary perspective).

Vocalization, which continued to serve as the carrier for analog emotion expression, became the production system for the highly formalized, segmental systems of language and singing. As a consequence, both of these functions needed to be served at the same time. For example, in speech, changes in fundamental frequency (f_o), formant structure, or the spectral characteristics of phonation, can, depending on the language and context, serve to communicate phonological contrasts, syntactic choices, pragmatic meaning, or emotional expression. Similarly, in music, melody, harmonic structure, or timing may reflect the composer's intentions, depending on specific traditions of music, and may simultaneously induce strong emotional moods (e.g. Gabrielsson and Lindström 2010). This fusion of two signal systems, which are quite different in function and in structure, into a single underlying production mechanism, vocalization, has proven to be singularly efficient for the purpose of communication.

If the origins of music are indeed rooted in the emotional expression of the human voice, then the singing voice (or vocal music) is the most likely candidate to evoke strong emotional feelings. In this chapter, we approach this issue by providing an overview of the process of externalization of emotions by the human voice, by discussing the determinants of emotional expression in singing, and by describing the manner in which expressed emotions are encoded in the voice by singers and recognized by listeners.

The externalization of emotion by the voice

Emotions produce pervasive, although generally short-lived, changes in the organism as a whole. They represent reactions to events of major significance to the individual and mobilize the necessary and available organismic resources to cope with the respective situation, whether positive or negative. Such changes involve a complex ensemble of physiological and psychological processes and states, and one of the fundamental outcomes of an emotional episode is the production of expressive displays.

As first demonstrated in Darwin's (1998) classic work on the expression of emotion in man and animals, emotional expression serves the vital function of externalizing an individual's reaction and action propensity, and of communicating this information to the social environment. Just as emotion is phylogenetically continuous, found in more or less rudimentary form in many, particularly mammalian, species, so is emotional expression, particularly in species in which social life is based on complex interactions among individuals. All expressive modalities, particularly bodily posture, facial configurations, and vocalization, are involved in emotion communication.

Speech production is mostly controlled by the neocortex (e.g. Schulz et al. 2005). Specific motor commands produce appropriate phonatory and articulatory movements for the desired sequence of speech sounds, including intentionally produced prosodic features (intonation, voice quality). The intended vocal effects are mostly produced by phasic activation of the muscles serving phonation and articulation. The effects of emotional arousal on the vocalization process are primarily controlled by the limbic system (Jürgens 1979; Robinson 1972). They are generally produced via tonic activation in the somatic nervous system (in particular, the striated musculature) and sympathetic, as well as parasympathetic, activation of the autonomous nervous system. In addition, direct sympathetic or parasympathetic effects, such as respiratory changes and the secretion of mucus can affect the vocalization.

Since vocalization mirrors the activity of various functional aspects of the nervous and somatic systems, one would expect many different causal effects of emotion in the voice. Given the manifold determinants of voice production processes, even slight changes in physiological regulation will produce variations in the vocal output. This is shown by the fact that even if a speaker attempts to reproduce a particular utterance in exactly the same way immediately after having spoken it for the first time, some changes are likely to occur.

Despite this description, it should be mentioned that acoustic patterns are not a simple mirror of emotion-produced changes of the internal physiological system. Indeed, since vocalization has developed in part as a social communicative signaling system, the externalization of internal states has been supplemented by display mechanisms producing specific impressions in the listener (independent of internal state). For instance, in constrained (e.g. formal) situations requiring specific emotional displays (such as politeness or cheerfulness) one will likely produce the appropriate (e.g. pleasant) voice quality (in spite of one's own feelings). Indeed, human vocalization is also partially determined by such social "display rules" (Ekman 1983; Wundt 1900; see Leyhausen 1967, for a thorough discussion on the evolution of expressive communication systems).

One way of understanding the different factors influencing vocal expression of emotion is through the distinction between push- and pull-effects introduced by Scherer (Scherer 1985, 1989; Scherer and Kappas 1988). These two classes of effects distinguish between the determining factors, which operate on vocalization. Push-effects are produced by the physiological changes that accompany emotional arousal (the ones we referred to in the previous paragraphs) and that consequently change the voice production mechanism in stereotypical ways (e.g. increased tension of the laryngeal muscles, in addition to subglottal pressure and other factors, will lead to the production of higher fundamental frequency of the voice). Pull-effects, instead, are independent of the internal physiological processes in the organism. Their origin is found in external factors, such as ritualized or conventionalized acoustic patterns of communication (which are required to ensure information transfer), constraints on the acoustic signal structure imposed by a communication channel or the environment, or the need for self-presentation (given the impression formation rules of the listeners). In most cases, the acoustic structure of a vocalization, particularly in humans, is determined by both types of effects: the effects of emotion-related physiological changes internal to the organism, and effects of external constraints or social target patterns. Given the difficulty of disentangling the two types of effects, most studies so far have not differentiated between push and pull effects.

Factors determining emotional expression in singing

Having briefly outlined the process by which emotion in the voice is externalized, we describe now some factors that we identify as determining the expression of emotion in the singing voice.

Unfortunately, in the field of psychology, there are only a few cases in which the emotional expression of singers has been systematically and comprehensively studied. One reason for this may be the large number of factors that are involved. For instance, in the case of operatic singing, the expression of emotion is related to the music itself (e.g. the score, interpretation of the score, performance expression), to the psychological interpretation of both the action and the characters by the director, by the timing of the conductor, as well as the singer's intuition and empathy with the character, and the atmosphere created by the audience. Naturally, all this makes it extremely difficult to isolate the effects of the singing voice, and to apply the experimental methods that are often used in the study of emotional expression in the speaking voice (see Banse and Scherer 1996; Scherer 1986). Here, we outline three aspects of particular importance to the understanding of emotional expression in singing:

- the emotional expression of the composer's intentions (hereafter "emotional script");
- the emotional interpretation of the singer;
- the emotional state of the singer during the performance.

This chapter focuses on emotional expression in the singing voice, but not the way that people perceive those emotions or even feel them. For an exploration of the elements that construct and shape our responses, including emotional, to sung performances, refer to Himonides (2009).

Emotional script

The emotional expression in the singing voice, particularly in the lyric arts, such as operatic and classical singing, is greatly determined by the composer's score. Composers have a wide variety of musical resources available by means of which they can structure music and convey emotional meaning to listeners. These parameters (or music structural aspects) are often designated in terms of musical notations and include, among others, melody, rhythm, tempo, dynamic markings, pitch, intervals, mode, harmony, and instrumentation, which are crucial carriers of emotional meaning in music (see Gabrielsson and Lindström 2010) and, together with performance practices determining appropriate interpretation of such notation, leave only a few degrees of freedom for the artist's personal emotional interpretation of the role.

Not only will the notated music and associated performance practices limit the singers' freedom to convey emotion while singing, but in addition, the text of the libretto (or the lyrics) and annotations, establish an "emotional script," which is given to the singers and binds their performance to the way that the piece is presented emotionally by the composer and writer. These limitations to the singer's interpretation contrast, for instance, to theater, in which voice quality and prosodic aspects are designed to be relatively free, and used to show the affective state of the respective character.

In some genres an "emotional script," in the sense of a notated score, may be absent altogether, as is often the case in popular and folk genres, for instance. Nonetheless, a script of sorts still exists, albeit passed on aurally, through "sessions" and recordings. In that sense, singers of popular genres are just as beholden to lyrics, precomposed musical materials, and associated performance conventions. Where the approach differs is perhaps regarding the degree of reverence held for a composer's intentions, assuming the composer is even known (commonly not the case in folk), and is not the singer him or herself.

Artistic interpretation

Although the emotional script may often determine the emotional expression of the singer, another central aspect to this process is the singer's own interpretation of it. That includes the understanding of the moods and/or emotions expressed in a song, and, in the case of operatic singing or musical theater, the emotions that characterize a particular character.

The impact of the artistic interpretation can, nevertheless, greatly vary depending on the type of music. For instance, a pervading performance ideology in the lyric arts is that the faithful representation of the emotional qualities of the composer's work and intentions is an essential aspect of a good vocal performance (see singers' statements in Scherer 2013b). In these cases, singers agree that a strong emotional involvement with the composer's intentions (and specific role) enables them to slip into the role of the protagonist and to portray the appropriate emotional states convincingly.

However, this can be seen as just one approach to emotional expression. In the case of popular genres it is helpful to note the distinction drawn by Frith (1996) between the different layers simultaneously present in sung performance—the idea that the singer is simultaneously:

- performing him or herself, and is therefore personally expressive;
- performing a star persona;
- performing a song character.

A prevalent reception ideology associated with this, in opera or Lieder singing, as well as in pop and rock, is the idea of 'authenticity'; namely, that the singer expresses sincerely-felt emotions, most often their own, or those of a character they are portraying (Dibben 2012; Scherer 2013b). In the case of popular performance then, it is not truth to a composer's work or intention which is paramount, but, more commonly, truth to the singer's self. Hence, there can be a great deal of expressive leeway in how performers interpret the same song, and even how the same performer may perform a song on different occasions.

So far, we have treated the singer as if their interpretive choices take place outside any historical or social context, yet this is evidently not the case. As we alluded to above in relation to the emotional script, singers work within a set of performance conventions and these will influence both their emotional interpretation of the music and how they realize that interpretation. A large literature on music performance expression has shown that performers manipulate pitch, timing, dynamics, articulation, and timbre to deviate from local or broader stylistic norms (see, for instance, Sundberg et al. 2013), and do this in ways systematically related to musical structure (Windsor 2009). Models of performance expression argue that one of the purposes of such micro-variation is to convey emotion (Juslin et al. 2002). However, which parameters are varied, to what degree, and with what effect, differs according to social and historical circumstance. A good example of this in the case of singing is the use of *portamento* (the legato glide between notes). Potter (2006) shows that, having been widely used in classical singing up until the Second World War, the use of *portamento* went into decline, and is now regarded as inappropriate and even vulgar. Conversely, and not coincidentally, the use of *portamento* increased in popular genres during the same period. Potter attributes this change to the rejection of the sentimentality and emotion perceived to be conveyed by *portamento*, and its association with low-brow art. Thus, while emotional expression in singing can be thought of as arising from individual singers and performances, those individual instances are themselves shaped by larger socio-historical patterns.

Singer's affective state

The physiological changes that accompany emotional responses often affect speakers' breathing, phonation, and articulation (Scherer 1986). Analogously, one can assume that the emotional state of a singer has a similar effect on their voice. Unfortunately, there are no systematic studies of naturally occurring emotional responses by singers and the effects on their voice. Investigations of this type are even more difficult to execute in singing than in speech, because singing activity is confined to certain contexts, such as performing arts and very specific social interactions (e.g. infant-directed singing or religious ceremonies)—contrary to speech that is used systematically for interpersonal communication in most social situations (it should be noted that singing activities are also forms of communication between individuals (see Welch 2005); here, we want to emphasize that the contexts of singing and speech communication are different). It is, nevertheless, likely that the performance aspect of singing limits the range and intensity of the emotions performers feel, excluding of course non-professional performances or performances outside the stage—a caregiver singing a lullaby might certainly be experiencing calm and tenderness, a fan singing at a football match might feel strength, unity, elation, etc., while singing. Indeed, many professional singers are of the opinion that their technique would suffer if they let their emotions run wild while singing, as attested to by performances in which singers are visibly overtaken by emotions (for example, see performances by British soul singer Adele, such as "Make You Feel My Love" (2011; http://www.youtube.com/watch?v=axBMs-qK2t4)). Interviews with professional opera singers (see Scherer 2013a) show the tremendous concern of artists to find the right compromise between abandonment to emotional involvement in the service of the role and the control of physiological symptoms required for the proper technique. Singers' physiologically determined emotional states are certainly a powerful factor in determining a large number of vocal characteristics and, in some cases, may be necessary to operationalize affective intentions (see Scherer 1986).

PERCEPTION OF EMOTIONAL MEANING FROM THE SINGING VOICE

When people talk about the emotional effects of music, they usually refer to the perception or inference of emotional cues expressed in the music, and not necessarily to the induction of these or other emotional states in the listener. While it is parsimoniously accepted that music has, indeed, powerful emotional effects (particularly those related to mood induction and emotional regulation), these experiences can (and must) be clearly distinguished from the perception or interpretation of emotional content (the expressiveness of music). This duality is also valid for the expression of emotion in the speaking and singing voice, and, in this section, we focus on the perception (or decoding) of emotional content in the singing voice. In particular, we will address two central aspects: listeners' capacity to infer emotional meaning from the singing voice, and the acoustic cues used that allow listeners to recognize those emotions from the voice alone.

INFERENCE OF EMOTIONAL MEANING FROM THE SINGING VOICE

While it is legitimate and meaningful to examine whether listeners can accurately perceive particular instances of emotional meaning in the speaking voice, it is unclear if it makes sense to ask the same questions in the field of singing. Vocal music, such as *Lieder, chansons,* rock or folk songs, are forms of art, which often express diffuse and complex emotional states distinct from utilitarian or basic emotions. Even if the composer or artist intended to express a specific, clearly defined and labeled emotion, the listeners can hardly have access to that intention (except, of course, if mirrored in the lyrics or having direct access to relevant information about the artist). Moreover, the expression of the artist's intention is often complex and hard to describe with a single label. Many of the intended expressions are frequently subtle, contextual (for instance, with the lyrics), and a mixture of or a journey around several emotion categories or qualities.

Perhaps for these reasons, research studies on emotion recognition from the singing voice are scarce. Nonetheless, it is certainly possible (and it has been done) to devise research methods to infer the expressive intention of singers. For instance, similarly to studies of emotional expression in the speaking voice, which uses actors to portray particular emotions (see Juslin and Laukka 2003, for a meta-analysis), we can ask professional singers to sing pure tones or content-free syllables in such a way that they portray different types of emotions, and then present the recordings of these portrayals to a group of listeners who will judge the expressive intention of the singer. From a more naturalistic perspective, a promising possibility is to record and study several singers singing various versions of the same song, but trying to express different emotions (and perhaps with varied vocal material). By maintaining a fixed musical context, it would be possible to understand the extent to which listeners are able to distinguish these different interpretations, which differ only in acoustic characteristics of the singing voice and emotional intention.

It should also be mentioned that it would be much more difficult to address the question of how listeners can identify the emotional state of the singer (as opposed to the emotions expressed by the singer) from the voice alone. For practical and ethical reasons, it is impossible to induce distinct emotional states in psychological experiments to obtain the necessary material for such investigations. Nonetheless, it could be possible to record singers' live performances and ask them to keep a diary of the affective experiences lived in each performance. With this procedure it would be possible to evaluate listeners' ability to detect variations in singers' emotional states in their singing. If the same musical work is performed and recorded several times, it would additionally be possible to compare subtle variations in singers' affective states and their impact on the listeners' recognition of the singers' emotional state. However, it is questionable to what extent a singer's personal emotional state and dramatic interpretation may be consistently separated. Most likely, both will interact in any given performance and, in some cases such as some popular genres, the elision of the affective state of the real person singing, with that of the star persona or song character, is an important part of the reception ideology of the music (Dibben 2012).

ACOUSTIC CUES IN THE INFERENCE PROCESS

If listeners are able to recognize vocally-portrayed emotions with better than chance accuracy from the voice alone, it should be possible to determine which acoustic cues they perceive and utilize in the process of recognizing vocal expressions. Indeed, this association has been at the very center of researchers' attention, who have used various research strategies to unveil vocal expressions with distinct patterns across the emotional spectrum.

Due to the generally limited access to natural affect expression in public settings, and the practical and ethical concerns raised by inducing strong emotions in the laboratory (Scherer et al. 1991; Wallbott and Scherer 1986), very frequently researchers ask trained actors to vocally portray or simulate different emotions. These portrayals are then judged by a panel of subjects and analyzed in terms of the acoustic features associated with the expression of particular emotions. Other approaches involve instead the use of natural speech material, including excerpts from social interactions with "real-life," rather than artificially-posed emotions.

From a vocal production perspective, some researchers have also used electro-acoustic or digital equipment and/or voice experts to measure the acoustic and/or phonatory-articulatory characteristics of the vocal emotion portrayals, and to then correlate these with the listeners' judgments of underlying emotion or attitude of the speaker. Several studies of this type have also yielded important information on which vocal characteristics affect the judges' inference (Bänziger et al. 2014; van Bezooijen 1984; Wallbott and Scherer 1986).

The present state of the evidence in relation to the acoustic patterns related to the perception of specific emotions from the speaking voice is summarized in Table 14.1. The acoustic profiles shown pertain to some of the most investigated classes of emotions in vocal expressions, as reported by Juslin and Laukka's (2003) meta-analysis, and Johnstone and

Table 14.1 Emotional attributions consistently associated with acoustic parameters in multiple studies. Table adapted from Juslin & Laukka 2003 (Table 11, p. 802) and Scherer 2003 (Table 14.1, p. 233)

	Happiness/ joy	Tenderness	Anger	Fear	Sadness
Speech rate	Fast	Slow	Fast	Fast	Slow
Voice intensity	Medium-High	Low	High	Low/ High*	Low
Voice intensity variability	–	Little	Much	Much	Little
High-frequency energy	Medium–high	Little	Much	Little	Little
f_o mean	High	Low	High	High	Low
f_o variability	Much	Little	Much	Little	Little
f_o range	High		High	–	Low
f_o contour	Rising	Falling	Rising/ Falling**	Rising	Falling
Voice onsets	Fast	Slow	Fast	–	Slow
Microstructural irregularity	Very little	No	Yes	A lot	Yes

Note: f_o, fundamental frequency.
 * Except in panic fear, which is related to high intensity.
** Except (at least) in rage, which is related to falling contours.

Scherer's (2000) review. Both works include mostly intracultural studies and portrayals by actors of a few full-blown emotions.

One feature of these findings is that most emotions can be distinguished in terms of their arousal level from acoustic cues. Indeed, emotions associated with increased arousal levels (happiness/joy, anger, and fear), compared with those characterized by lower arousal level (tenderness and sadness), are associated with faster speaking rates, higher voice intensity, more voice intensity variability, higher f_o mean and range, rising f_o contours, and faster voice onsets. The acoustic characteristic of the voice that most effectively distinguishes the various emotions in terms of hedonic value is microstructural irregularity, which seems to characterize negative emotions. Thus, a recent study (Scherer et al. 2015) comparing emotional portrayals of professional opera singers in sung phrases with speech portrayals by professional actors, found that singers tend to rely more on the use of vibrato, possibly because of the restriction of other dynamic cues that are determined by the musical score (e.g. accents, intonation, and rhythm).

Unfortunately, whereas a wide range of studies have dealt with these issues in the speaking voice (see Scherer et al. 2008, for an overview), very few have focused on the singing voice. In the next few paragraphs we outline some of these studies and compare their results to studies of the speaking voice.

As in research on the speaking voice, a standard method to identify the acoustic underpinnings of emotional meaning perceived in singing is to correlate the acoustic profiles resulting from the portrayal of different emotions by singers, with listeners' judgments of emotions perceived. In one such study Kotlyar and Morozov (1976) asked 11 professional singers to perform different pieces in such a way as to portray four full-blown emotions—happiness, sorrow, fear, and anger—and neutrality. They analyzed each performance and measured syllable duration, micropauses between syllables, mean sound pressure level (SPL), tone rise, and decay time, and found characteristic combinations in these measures for the various emotions. For instance, performances recognized as sad were characterized by long syllabic durations (that is, a slow rate or tempo), angry and sad performances were associated with higher average SPL than the other emotions, and syllable onsets and decays were faster in anger than other emotions (a detailed description can be found in Sundberg 1987, pp. 152–153).

In another study, Sundberg et al. (1995) asked a professional singer (also a co-author in the publication) to sing excerpts from Lieder and opera repertoires in two contrasting fashions—(a) in a concert situation, and (b) in an emotionally neutral way. A group of experts in singing then judged both versions of each extract in terms of the degree of expressivity, and the particular emotion conveyed (secure, loving, sad, happy, scared, angry, and hateful). The acoustic analysis revealed that the level of expressivity was associated with greater f_o modulations during consonants and with a lowering of vowel formant frequencies. As regards the specific emotional qualities of the performances, renderings characterized by higher arousal levels (happy, scared, angry, and hateful) were associated with louder singing (higher SPL), faster tempi, and higher rate of loudness variation, when compared with renderings of low arousal (secure, loving, sad). These findings are in close agreement with those of Kotlyar and Morozov (1976), and show striking parallels between the expression of emotions in the speaking and singing voice. For instance, as seen in Table 14.1, joy and anger are associated with high f_o variability (assuming that f_o variability in speech is translated into vibrato extent in singing), and sadness is associated with slow speech rate and low vocal intensity. It is interesting to note that, for most performances, judges chose more than one term to characterize the emotions recognized in each performance, which as the authors note, suggests that it is difficult to describe the emotions in the singing voice using only a single emotion label.

In a study by Jansens et al. (1997), 14 professional singers (seven females) were each asked to sing the phrase "Mein Vater, mein Vater, und hörest du nicht, Was Erlkönig mir leise verspricht . . . ?" from Schubert's "Der Erlkönig" portraying four different emotions—anger, joy, fear, and sadness (the phrase was also sung neutrally). A group of listeners then rated the strength of the perceived emotions for each performance. Instead of simply correlating acoustic measures with the classes of emotions perceived by listeners, the authors performed principal component analyses on the listeners' ratings. The factors obtained (every listener had a specific loading on each factor) were interpreted as "listening strategies." Listeners who rated the performances in similar ways had similar loadings on similar factors. A combination of six factors explained circa 90 percent of the variance of the ratings for all emotions labels. These factors were then used in stepwise multiple linear regression analyses (separately for each emotion) on the acoustic measures of spectral balance, vibrato, duration, and intensity. The clearest associations were found for anger, sadness, and fear. *Anger* was associated with the presence of vibrato, whereas *sadness* was characterized by the absence of vibrato, with longer durations (slower tempi) and with low voice intensity. Fear was related to a steep spectral slope. Once again, these results are similar to those described in Table 14.1 for the speaking voice and the ones obtained in the studies described above.

Another method by which to study the link between expressed emotions and acoustics of the singing voice is to obtain recordings of the same songs performed by various singers, and analyze listeners' judgments of emotions perceived for each particular performer. By fixing the musical material in this way, it is possible to focus with more detail on aspects of voice quality and singing acoustics, and to better understand how different singers encode particular emotions in their singing. In this line of research, Siegwart and Scherer (1995) conducted digital acoustic analyses of two excerpts from the cadenza in the "mad scene" from Donizetti's "Lucia di Lammermoor" sung by five renowned singers (Toti dal Monte, Maria Callas, Renata Scotto, Joan Sutherland, and Edita Gruberova). The authors were able to show that the voice samples of the five singers differed quite substantially with respect to objective acoustic variables, and that these measures could be used to predict a high percentage of the variability in listener judgments of emotional expressiveness, and preference for a particular performer or interpretation.

Howes et al. (2004) used a similar methodology to investigate associations between acoustic cues and perceptual dimensions related to the use of vibrato in Western operatic singing. Their findings showed that the perception of the singers' vibrato by listeners did not always agree with objective acoustic measurements, but a comparison of the acoustic measurements with preference and emotion judgments indicated that at least some elements of vibrato are likely to affect listeners' perception of the singing voice and their preference for a particular singer.

Two recent publications report the results of a massive study on these issues. Eight professional opera singers were asked to sing an ascending–descending musical scale (using non-lexical vocables) to express different emotions, as if on stage. The studio recordings were acoustically analyzed with a standard set of parameters. The results show robust vocal signatures for the emotions studied. Overall, there is a major contrast between sadness and tenderness on the one hand, and anger, joy, and pride on the other. This is based on low vs. high levels on the components of loudness, vocal dynamics, high perturbation variation, and a tendency for high low-frequency energy. This pattern reveals a positive correlation between the power and arousal components of emotions and these acoustic characteristics. A multiple discriminant analysis yields classification accuracy greatly exceeding chance level, confirming the reliability of the acoustic patterns (Scherer, Sundberg et al. 2017). These recordings were then presented to more than 500 listeners/judges from different cultures with a wide range of musical preferences and degree of musical knowledge, who were asked to recognize the emotions intended by the singers. The data show that listeners are indeed able to recognize emotions expressed in singing with much better–than–chance accuracy. In addition, there were only minor effects of culture or language on the ability to recognize the emotional interpretations. Judges clearly use the differential acoustic patterns of sound generated by the singers in their performance to infer the emotion expressed, as demonstrated by comparing the recognition rates for different emotions to results of statistical classification based on acoustic parameters (Scherer, Trznadel et al. 2017).

Another relevant method to study a wide range of possible acoustic variation in the singing voice (as well as music) is to manipulate acoustic parameters in an independent manner and see how they correlate with listeners' perception of particular emotions or broad classes of affective qualities. Scherer and Oshinsky (1977) have applied such a procedure to the study of expression in instrumental music. They systematically varied several acoustic parameters (using a Moog synthesizer) of a short speech-like melody and a Beethoven melody and have shown that 66–75 percent of the variance in the emotion attributions can be explained by the manipulated acoustic cues. In the study by Kotlyar and Morozov (1976) described above, the authors have also used a similar procedure to evaluate the role of the acoustic features found to differentiate among emotions. They used electronically-generated signals to manipulate the respective features and also found that judges were able to identify the underlying affect rather well.

Another related and very promising method to systematically vary acoustic cues in the singing voice is to use synthesis (the creation of vocal samples) and resynthesis (variation of an existing vocal sample). The spectacular advances in the synthesis of the singing voice (e.g. Fonseca 2011; Goto et al. 2012; Kenmochi and Ohshita 2007; Risset 1991; Sundberg 1978) make it possible to carry out investigations in which various acoustic voice parameters, fundamental to emotional expression, can be systematically manipulated, and their effects and relevance for the recognition of emotion quantified. Unfortunately, similar techniques do not exist just yet in relation to resynthesis methods, but should they become available it would be extremely advantageous to the understanding of the expression of emotions in natural singing voices. For instance, one could find out which acoustic characteristics need to be modified to alter a singer's emotional effect (as already used in the study of vocal expression in the speaking voice; see Bergmann et al. 1988).

A related question is the extent to which the acoustic cues to emotion differ across vocal genres. For instance, popular singing is characterized by an esthetic of naturalism which manifests as a declamative style prioritizing the clarity of the text and encompassing paralinguistic features such as vocal creaks, roughness, and cries (Lacasse 2009; Moore 2012, pp. 102–103). This contrasts with classical singing, for example, in which the emphasis is on maintaining continuity and smoothness of tone, which allows more modification of vowel sounds, but fewer of the "noisy" discontinuities found in popular singing styles. In the absence of any empirical evidence we might anticipate that popular styles will show greater similarity to acoustic cues to emotion in speech than will classical vocal styles.

CONCLUDING REMARKS: APPLICATIONS IN SINGING PERFORMANCE AND VOCAL TRAINING

As is evident from what has been discussed in this chapter, research on the expression of emotions in the singing voice is still in its infancy. Nevertheless, we have described methodologies used in the study of emotional expression in the speaking voice and music, which, if applied, can lead to important developments in our understanding of singing expression. Indeed, the technical procedures for the analysis of voice parameters are relatively well developed, and there are now many methods and software tools that allow researchers to objectively analyze the singing voice in straightforward ways (e.g. Praat: Boersma and Weenink 2013; Sonic Visualizer: Cannam et al. 2010; PsySound3: Cabrera et al. 2008; MIR Toolbox: Lartillot and Toiviainen 2007; OpenSMILE: Eyben et al. 2010; WaveSurfer: Beskow and Sjölander 2000).

The application of this knowledge to singing practice is greatly dependent on the knowledge gained from study of the physiological aspects of vocal productions and the acoustic cues produced, which are drivers of listeners' perceptions of affective meaning. With such knowledge, it is possible to allow singers to practice the expression of certain emotions by systematically producing the configurations of voice parameters characteristic of particular expressions. Certainly, this would be merely a mechanical procedure by which to reproduce acoustic patterns that supposedly convey certain emotional qualities. However, there is evidence in experimental psychology that the purely mechanical production of emotion expression by proprioceptive feedback (see McIntosh 1996) can lead (at least in a rudimentary way) to physiologically measurable emotional experiences: for example, in the face (Levenson et al. 1990), even without the person knowing that his or her face shows an emotional expression (Strack et al. 1988), in body posture (Riskind and Gotay 1982), and breathing patterns (Philippot et al. 2002). It seems plausible to assume that the mechanical production of a vocal expression has similar effects, and the striking similarities between the results of the acoustic cues in emotional expression in speaking and singing suggest that this is also true in singing.

It might also be possible to create systems capable of real-time acoustic measurements of the singer's voice, which could be used to make predictions about the emotions being conveyed, and to provide feedback to singers, during practice or in performance, to allow them to fine-tune their technique. The study of expressiveness in the speaking voice and music has led to the development of various kinds of statistical, mathematical, and machine learning models, which can make very satisfactory predictions of emotional qualities or states (as perceived by humans) from voice cues alone (e.g. Batliner et al. 2011; Coutinho and Dibben 2013; Coutinho and Schuller 2017). Such systems could also be developed to predict various kinds of affective meaning or responses for the singing voice, provided more systematic work is conducted in the future regarding the link between acoustics and expressiveness in singing. Indeed, there are good reasons to believe that a reliable emotion recognition system could be developed, particularly due to the fact that many of the associations between acoustic cues and emotional qualities found for the speaking voice seem to be, at least partially, also relevant for the singing voice.

There are various specific scenarios to which such systems could be extrapolated and inform singing practice by allowing singers to explore changes in their voice and technique, to produce particular emotions or even subtle variations of the same emotion. For instance, they could be used to provide feedback in singing lessons, by allowing singers to develop their expressive skills. By complementing such a system with a formal database of prototypical expressions of emotion in singing (and perhaps speech) expressions, it would be possible to help students train their emotional interpretation objectively. In point of fact, any singer interested in developing expressive skills could use these feedback systems. Another possibility, in the realm of live performance, and particularly improvisation, would be to use feedback from emotion recognition systems to help singer and musicians to detect each other's emotions while performing, and to inform vocal and instrumental performance strategies (see Juslin et al. 2006, for an application of this concept to the communication of emotion in guitar performances).

It should be noted that the vocal apparatus of singers determines many aspects of voice quality, which are audible in singing and, in turn, affect the acoustic signal produced, as well as expressivity (see, for instance, Howes, et al. 2004; Siegwart and Scherer 1995). For instance, the length and thickness of the vocal cords and configuration of the vocal tract are crucial in determining a singer's voice quality, and alter the behavior of various acoustic features, such as the fundamental frequency and harmonics. These characteristics (which when physiologically determined cannot be intentionally manipulated or changed) are factors that determine emotional expression. A feedback system could allow singers to alter certain properties of their singing voice (those consciously controllable) and measure their emotional impact in order to achieve the intended expression.

The interest of emotion recognition in the singing voice is also pertinent to areas outside the performing arts. One possibility is to apply these methodologies to music therapy, where practitioners often focus on the relationship between musical improvisation, emotional states, and social relationships in their clients (Dvorkin 1982; Pavlicevic 1999; Stephens 1983). Real-time recognition of emotions in clients' voices while singing could be a useful tool in support of therapists' observational work and inform their strategies during specific sessions.

Most of these suggestions still belong to the future. Currently, there are only a few researchers addressing the complex issues surrounding the expression of emotions in the singing voice, and an intensive cooperation between psychologists, musicologists, and performers, is still necessary to accelerate research in this area. One example is The Swiss Center for Affective Sciences, which as part of a Music and Emotion research focus has established singing as a priority research topic. A number of interdisciplinary studies on the acoustics of emotional expression in singing and the effects on listener impressions are currently ongoing. To summarize, interdisciplinary approaches and cooperation are central aspects of a fruitful and sustainable study of the expressive powers of the singing voice.

ACKNOWLEDGMENTS

This research was supported by the National Center of Competence in Research (NCCR) Affective Sciences financed by the Swiss National Science Foundation (51NF40-104897) and hosted by the University of Geneva.

REFERENCES

Banse, R. and Scherer, K.R. (1996). Acoustic profiles in vocal emotion expression. *Journal of Personality and Social Psychology* 70(3): 614–636.

Bänziger, T., Patel, S., and Scherer, K.R. (2014). The role of perceived voice and speech characteristics in vocal emotion communication. *Journal of Nonverbal Behavior* 38(1): 31–52.

Batliner, A., Schuller, B., Seppi, D., Steidl, S., Devillers, L., Vidrascu, L., and Amir, N. (2011). The automatic recognition of emotions in speech. In: P. Petta, R. Cowie, and C. Pelachaud (eds), *Emotion-oriented Systems: The Humaine Handbook*, pp. 71–99. Berlin: Springer.

Bergmann, G., Goldbeck, T., and Scherer, K.R. (1988). Emotionale Eindruckswirkung von prosodischen Sprechmerkmalen [Emotional impression effects produced by prosodic features.]. *Zeitschrift für experimentelle und angewandte Psychologie* 35: 167–200.

Beskow, J. and Sjölander, K. (2000). WaveSurfer (Version 1.8.8) [Computer software]. Stockholm: KTH Royal Institute of Technology. Available at: M http://www.speech.kth.se/wavesurfer/ (accessed 11 July 2013).

Bever, T.G. (1988). A cognitive theory of emotion and aesthetics in music. *Psychomusicology* 7(2): 165–175.

Boersma, P. and Weenink, D. (2013). Praat: doing phonetics by computer [Computer program], Version 5.3.45. Available at: M http://www.praat.org/ (accessed 15 April 2013).

Cabrera, D., Ferguson, S., Rizwi, F., and Schubert, E. (2008). PsySound3: a program for the analysis of sound recordings. *Journal of the Acoustical Society of America* 123(5): 3247.

Cannam, C., Landone, C., and Sandler, M. (2010). Sonic Visualiser: an open source application for viewing, analysing, and annotating music audio files. *Proceedings of the ACM International Conference on Multimedia,* 1467–1468. Firenze, Italy, October 25–29.

Clynes, M. (1977). *Sentics: The Touch of Emotions.* New York: Anchor/Doubleday.

Cooke, D. (1959). *The Language of Music.* London: Oxford University.

Coutinho, E. and Dibben, N. (2013). Psychoacoustic cues to emotion in speech prosody and music. *Cognition & Emotion* 27(4): 658–684. https://doi.org/10.1080/02699931.2012.732559

Coutinho, E. and Schuller, B. (2017). Shared acoustic codes underlie emotional communication in music and speech: Evidence from deep transfer learning. *PloS One* 12(6): e0179289. https://doi.org/10.1371/journal.pone.0179289

Darwin, C. (1998) [1872]. *The Expression of Emotions in Man and Animals,* 3rd edn. P. Ekman, Ed. London: HarperCollins.

De la Motte-Haber, H. (1996). *Handbuch der Musikpsychologie.* 2. Aufl. Laaber: Laaber-Verlag.

Dibben, N. (2012). The intimate singing voice: auditory spatial perception and the performance and perception of emotion in pop recordings. In: D. Zhakarine and N. Meise (eds), *Electrified Voices: Medial, Socio-historical and Cultural Aspects of Voice-transfer,* pp. 107–122. Göttingen: V&R unipress.

Dvorkin, J. (1982). Piano improvisation: a therapeutic tool in acceptance and resolution of emotions in a schizo-affective personality. *Music Therapy* 2(1): 53–62.

Ekman, P. (ed.) (1983). *Emotion in the Human Face: Guidelines for Research and an Integration of Findings,* 2nd edn. Cambridge: Cambridge University Press.

Eyben, F., Wöllmer, M., and Schuller, B. (2010). OpenSMILE: the Munich versatile and fast open-source audio feature extractor. *Proceedings of the ACM International Conference on Multimedia,* 1459–1462. Firenze, Italy, October 25–29.

Fonagy, I. (1981). Emotions, voice and music. In: J. Sundberg (ed.), *Research Aspects on Singing,* pp. 51–79. Stockholm: Royal Swedish Academy of Music and Payot.

Fonagy, I. (1983). *La vive voix.* [The living voice.] Paris: Payot.

Fonseca, N. (2011). *Singing voice resynthesis using concatenative-based techniques.* Unpublished doctoral dissertation, University of Porto, Portugal.

Frith, S. (1996). *Performing Rites. On the Value of Popular Music.* Oxford: Oxford University Press.

Gabrielsson, A. and Lindström, E. (2010). The role of structure in the musical expression of emotions. In: P. N. Juslin and J. Sloboda (eds), *Handbook of Music and Emotion: Theory, Research, Applications,* pp. 367–400. Oxford: Oxford University Press.

Goto, M., Nakano, T., Kajita, S., Matsusaka, Y., Nakaoka, S.I., and Yokoi, K. (2012). VocaListener and VocaWatcher: imitating a human singer by using signal processing. *IEEE International Conference on Acoustics, Speech and Signal Processing,* 5393–5396.

Helmholtz, H.L.F., von. (1863). *Die Lehre von den Tonempfindungen als physiologische Grundlage für die Theorie der Musik.* Braunschweig: Vieweg. [English edn: On the Sensations of Tone as a Physiological Basis for the Theory of Music. New York, NY: Dover, 1954.]

Himonides, E. (2009). Mapping a beautiful voice: theoretical considerations. *Journal of Music, Technology & Education* 2(1): 25–54.

Howes, P., Callaghan, J., Davis, P., Kenny, D., and Thorpe, W. (2004). The relationship between measured vibrato characteristics and perception in Western operatic singing. *Journal of Voice* 18(2): 216–230.

Jansens, S., Bloothooft, G., and De Krom, G. (1997). Perception and acoustics of emotions in singing. *Proceedings of the Fifth European Conference on Speech Communication and Technology*, Vol. IV: 2155–8. Rhodes: ESCA.

Johnstone, T. and Scherer, K.R. (2000). Vocal communication of emotion. In M. Lewis and J. Haviland (eds), *Handbook of Emotion*, 2nd edn, pp. 220–235. New York: Guilford.

Jürgens, U. (1979). Vocalization as an emotional indicator. A neuroethological study in the squirrel monkey. *Behaviour* 69: 88–117.

Juslin, P.N., Friberg, A., and Bresin, R. (2002). Toward a computational model of expression in music performance: the GERM model. *Musicae Scientiae* 63–122.

Juslin, P.N., Karlsson, J., Lindstrom, E., Friberg, A., and Schoonderwaldt, E. (2006). Play it again with feeling: computer feedback in musical communication of emotions. *Journal of Experimental Psychology: Applied* 12(2): 79.

Juslin, P.N. and Laukka, P. (2003). Communication of emotions in vocal expression and music performance: different channels, same code? *Psychological Bulletin* 129(5): 770–814.

Juslin, P.N. and Västfjäll, D. (2008). Emotional responses to music: the need to consider underlying mechanisms. *Behavioral and Brain Sciences* 31(5): 559.

Kenmochi, H. and Ohshita, H. (2007). Vocaloid–commercial singing synthesizer based on sample concatenation. *Proceedings of Interspeech*, August: 4009–4010.

Kivy, P. (1988). *Osmin's Rage: Philosophical Reflections on Opera, Drama, and Text*. Princeton: Princeton University.

Kotlyar, G.M. and Morozov, V.P. (1976). Acoustical correlates of the emotional content of vocalized speech. *Soviet Journal of Physical Acoustics* 22: 208–211.

Lacasse, S. (2009). The phonographic voice: paralinguistic features and phonographic staging in popular music singing. In: A. Bayley (ed.) *Recorded Music: Society, Technology, and Performance*, pp. 225–251. Cambridge: Cambridge University Press.

Lartillot, O. and Toiviainen, P. (2007). A Matlab toolbox for musical feature extraction from audio. *International Conference on Digital Audio Effects*, 237–244.

Levenson, R.W., Ekman, P., and Friesen, W.V. (1990). Voluntary facial action generates emotion-specific autonomic nervous system activity. *Psychophysiology* 27(4): 363–384.

Leyhausen, P. (1967). Biologie von Ausdruck und Eindruck (Teil 1) [The biology of expression and impression (Part 1)]. *Psychologische Forschung* 31: 113–176.

Lundin, R.W. (1967). *An Objective Psychology of Music*. New York: Ronald Press.

McIntosh, D.N. (1996). Facial feedback hypotheses: evidence, implications, and directions. *Motivation and Emotion* 20(2): 121–147.

Moore, A.F. (2012). *Song Means: Analysing and Interpreting Recorded Popular Song*. Farnham: Ashgate.

Pavlicevic, M. (1999). Music therapy improvisation groups with adults: towards de-stressing in South Africa. *South African Journal of Psychology* 29(2): 94–99.

Philippot, P., Chapelle, G., and Blairy, S. (2002). Respiratory feedback in the generation of emotion. *Cognition & Emotion* 16(5): 605–627.

Potter, J. (2006). Beggar at the door: the rise and fall of portamento in singing. *Music & Letters* 87(4): 523–550.

Riskind, J.H. and Gotay, C.C. (1982). Physical posture: could it have regulatory or feedback effects on motivation and emotion? *Motivation and Emotion* 6(3): 273–298.

Risset, J.C. (1991). Speech and music combined: an overview. In: J. Sundberg, L. Nord, and R. Carlson (eds), *Music, Language, Speech, and Brain*, pp. 368–379. London: Macmillan.

Robinson, B.W. (1972). Anatomical and physiological contrasts between human and other primate vocalizations. In: S. L. Washburn and P. Dolhinow (eds), *Perspectives in Human Evolution*, pp. 438–443. New York: Holt, Rinehart & Winston.

Scherer, K.R. (1985). Vocal affect signalling: a comparative approach. In J. Rosenblatt, C. Beer, M-C. Busnel, and P. J. B. Slater (eds), *Advances in the Study of Behaviour*, Vol. 15, pp. 189–244. New York: Academic Press.

Scherer, K.R. (1986). Vocal affect expression: a review and a model for future research. *Psychological Bulletin* 99: 143–165.

Scherer, K.R. (1989). Vocal correlates of emotion. In: H. L. Wagner and A. S. R. Manstead (eds), *Handbook of Psychophysiology: Emotion and Social Behaviour*, pp. 165–197. Chichester: Wiley.

Scherer, K.R. (1991). Emotion expression in speech and music. In: J. Sundberg, L. Nord, and R. Carlson (eds), *Music, Language, Speech, and Brain, Wenner-Gren Center International Symposium Series*, pp. 146–156. London: Macmillan.

Scherer, K.R. (1994). Affect bursts. In: S. van Goozen, N. E. van de Poll, and J. A. Sergeant (eds), *Emotions: Essays on Emotion Theory*, pp. 161–196. Hillsdale, NJ: Erlbaum.

Scherer, K.R. (1995). Expression of emotion in voice and music. *Journal of Voice* 9(3): 235–248.

Scherer, K.R. (2003). Vocal communication of emotion: a review of research paradigms. *Speech Communication* 40(1–2): 227–256.

Scherer K.R. (2013a). Emotion in action, interaction, music, and speech. In: M. A. Arbib (ed.), *Language, Music, and the Brain: A Mysterious Relationship*, pp. 107–139. Cambridge, MA: MIT.

Scherer, K.R. (2013b). The singer's paradox: on authenticity in emotional expression on the opera stage. In: T. Cochrane, B. Fantini, and K. R. Scherer (eds), *The Emotional Power of Music*, pp. 55–73. Oxford: Oxford University Press.

Scherer, K.R., Banse, R., Wallbott, H.G., and Goldbeck, T. (1991). Vocal cues in emotion encoding and decoding. *Motivation and Emotion* 15: 123–148.

Scherer, K.R. and Coutinho, E. (2013). How music creates emotion: a multifactorial approach. In T. Cochrane, B. Fantini, and K. R. Scherer (eds), *The Emotional Power of Music*, pp. 122–145. Oxford: Oxford University Press.

Scherer, K., Johnstone, T., and Klasmeyer, G. (2008). Vocal expression of emotion. In: R. J. Davidson, K. Scherer, and H. H. Goldsmith (eds), *Handbook of Affective Sciences*, pp. 433–456. Oxford: Oxford University Press.

Scherer, K.R. and Kappas, A. (1988). Primate vocal expression of affective states. In: D. Todt, P. Goedeking, and E. Newman (eds), *Primate Vocal Communication*, pp. 171–194. Heidelberg: Springer.

Scherer, K.R. and Oshinsky, J.S. (1977). Cue utilization in emotion attribution from auditory stimuli. *Motivation and Emotion* 1: 331–346.

Scherer, K.R., Sundberg, J., Fantini, B., Trznadel, S., & Eyben, F. (2017). The expression of emotion in the singing voice: acoustic patterns in vocal performance. *Journal of the Acoustical Society of America*. 142, 1805–1815; https://doi.org/10.1121/1.5002886.

Scherer, K.R., Sundberg, J., Tamarit, L., and Salomão, G.L. (2015). Comparing the acoustic expression of emotion in the speaking and the singing voice. *Computer Speech & Language* 29(1): 218–235. http://dx.doi.org/10.1016/j.csl.2013.10.002

Scherer, K. R., Trznadel, S., Fantini, B., & Sundberg, J. (2017). Recognizing emotions in the singing voice: A path analytic approach to understanding the process of inference. *Psychomusicology*, 27(4), 244–255.

Schulz, G.M., Varga, M., Jeffires, K., Ludlow, C.L., and Braun, A.R. (2005). Functional neuroanatomy of human vocalization: an H215O PET study. *Cerebral Cortex* 15(12): 1835–1847.

Siegwart, H. and Scherer, K.R. (1995). Acoustic concomitants of emotional expression in operatic singing: the case of Lucia in Ardi gli incensi. *Journal of Voice* 9(3): 249–260.

Stephens, G. (1983). The use of improvisation for developing relatedness in the adult client. *Music Therapy* 3(1): 29–42.

Strack, F., Martin, L., and Stepper, S. (1988). Inhibiting and facilitating conditions of the human smile: a nonobtrusive test of the facial feedback hypothesis. *Journal of Personality and Social Psychology* 54: 768–777.

Sundberg, J. (1978). Synthesis of singing. *Swedish Journal of Musicology* 60: 107–112.

Sundberg, J. (1987). *The Science of the Singing Voice*. DeKalb, IL: Northern Illinois University Press.

Sundberg, J., Iwarsson, J., and Hagegard, H. (1995). A singer's expression of emotions in sung performance. In: M. Hirano and O. Fujimura (eds), *Proceedings of the Vocal Folds Physiology Conference 1994*, pp. 217–232. San Diego, CA: Singular Publishing Group.

Sundberg, J., Lã, F.M.B., and Himonides, E. (2013). Intonation and expressivity: a single case study of classical western singing. *Journal of Voice* 27(3): 391.

van Bezooijen, R. (1984). *The Characteristics and Recognizability of Vocal Expressions of Emotion*. Dordrecht: Foris.

Wallbott, H.G. and Scherer, K.R. (1986). Cues and channels in emotion recognition. *Journal of Personality and Social Psychology* 51: 690–699.

Welch, G.F. (2005). Singing as communication. In: D. Miell, R. MacDonald, and D. Hargreaves (eds), *Musical Communication*, pp. 239–259. Oxford: Oxford University Press.

Windsor, W.L. (2009). Measurement and models of performance. In: S. Hallam, I. Cross, and M. Thaut (eds), *The Oxford Handbook of Music Psychology*, pp. 323–331. New York: Oxford University Press.

Wundt, W. (1900). *Völkerpsychologie. Eine Untersuchung der Entwicklungsgesetze von Sprache, Mythos und Sitte. Band I. Die Sprache*. Leipzig: Kröner. [English edn: Element of Folk Psychology: Outline of a Psychological History of the Development of Mankind, Vol 1, Language. Redditch, UK: Read Books, 2016.]

CHAPTER 15

PERCEIVED QUALITY OF A SINGING PERFORMANCE

The Importance of Context

EVANGELOS HIMONIDES

INTRODUCTION

THIS chapter reviews earlier research by the author (Himonides 2009; Himonides 2011; Himonides and Welch 2005), in which an innovative theoretical framework was posited in relation to perceived quality in a singing performance. This work primarily focused on singing performances rather than singing performance related effects, such as visual feedback, audience dynamics, live listening logistics, and any other factor that might be part of a general "experience" but not necessarily part of the voiced/sung product. The research was purposely centered on the appraisal of recorded singing performances, so that all participants could be exposed to controlled listening experiences, and asked to rate specific aspects of the sung performances in a repeatable and replicable manner. The theoretical framework that underpins the present work offered an evidence-based understanding of the multidimensionality of perceived singing beauty as a synthesis of seven "theoretical elements," namely, musical structure (Ockelford 2005; Scherer and Zentner 2001); neuropsychobiological processing of lyrics and music (Peretz et al. 2004); human musical development (Malloch 1999; Malloch and Trevarthen 2010; Welch 2005); socio-cultural context (Durrant 2003; Durrant and Himonides 1998; Himonides 1997); listener characteristics (Sloboda and O'Neil 2001); production of the acoustic signal (Gabrielsson and Juslin 2003; Juslin 2001; Sundberg 1987); and effects of acoustic signal manipulation (Howard and Angus 2001).

It is important to clarify that although perceived beauty in singing and also assessment of the quality of a sung performance are notions that are strongly interwoven with emotion and, perhaps, the "senses," this current research attempts to offer a broader (or even a meta-) outlook on how beauty is constructed within the listener, emphasizing the importance of the specificity of context. A very comprehensive synthesis from evidence on singing and emotion is offered elsewhere (see Coutinho, Scherer, and Dibben, this volume). In relation to the senses, philosophy, and esthetics, the author subscribes to the scientific foundations of philosophy, and its ties to systematic enquiry on perception and cognition, rather than the oft self-celebratory niche of music appreciation.

In interrogating the above-mentioned seven-part theoretical model, Himonides (2009) employed a mixed-mode, methodological framework which employed a number of different empirical components (presented as research "stages"). Himonides and Welch (2005) presented findings from earlier stages of the empirical research highlighting that listeners appeared to possess co-existing conceptions of beauty in singing, namely beauty as encapsulated by a particular vocal performer and (separately) self-generated criteria of vocal beauty in the abstract (p. 64). This was somewhat reminiscent of Scherer's "plea" for a new approach to measuring emotional effects in music (Scherer 2003) at the Stockholm Music Acoustics International Conference 2003. Listeners seldom appear to shy away from providing response data; it is "how" we ask particular questions that determines what answers are going to be offered, and "what" response data will be generated by the listeners.

Himonides (2011) presented an original technological solution for increasing the specificity of response measurement. The Continuous Response Measurement Apparatus (CReMA) was developed in order to allow the synchronous recording of physiological response data (i.e. galvanic skin response and heart rate) with real-time response data offered by expert listeners on a linear position location controller. Testing of the CReMA rendered systematic and meaningful datasets, analyses of which offered additional insights into response measurement and how this informs performance assessment. A key finding of this pilot research was that very experienced listeners could produce remarkably robust datasets that showed very strong correlations between a measure of "overall perception of quality of a singing performance" and the assessment of a very particular single component/aspect of that performance in isolation, such as diction, vibrato, intonation, etc. Even more remarkably, this was found to be genre and repertoire specific. For example, at that time an exhaustive assessment of all commercially available versions of "Dido's Lament" from Purcell's opera *Dido and Aeneas* demonstrated that the particular characteristic that all expert listeners systematically recorded in strong correlation with overall quality was their perception of the quality of "vibrato."

Based on evidence that a continuous recording of an intensely focused assessment of specific attributes of a singing performance is a context-specific and also context-sensitive exercise, Himonides (2008) conducted a number of additional small-scale research investigations in order to gain additional insights into this specificity of context.

The remainder of this chapter considers two examples of short-scale unpublished empirical research as vignettes of the context-sensitive and context-specific nature of the singing voice in performance.

"THE SINGER, NOT THE SONG"

The purpose of this short-scale empirical research was to assess expert opinions on the perception of beautiful performances across different musical genres. The British Broadcasting Corporation (BBC) ran a series of five radio programs (BBC Radio 4) from January 9, 2007 to February 6, 2007. The radio series was titled "The singer, not the song," and was classified under their "factual" program category. According to the official BBC nomenclature (as published on their website[1]), the program's rationale was to analyze some of the "best" voices as well as inform listeners about "music" and "context" (i.e. the musical genre). Promotional text for the program read:

> What defines an unforgettable voice, and is a great voice born or made? In this series we will not only hear and analyze some of the best voices across the last century, but also inform about music and the context in which they are singing.
>
> (British Broadcasting Corporation 2007a)

Each of the five broadcast episodes of the series focused on a different musical genre. The first episode was broadcast on Tuesday January 9, 2007 and focused on "jazz" music. The invited experts for this episode were singer Jacqui Dankworth and trumpeter Humphrey Lyttelton. The second episode was broadcast on Tuesday January 16, 2007 and focused on "folk" music. The invited experts for this episode were Norma Waterson and Martin Carthy, who have been leading figures in the folk revival since the 1960s. The third episode was broadcast on Tuesday January 23, 2007 and focused on "blues" music. The invited experts for this episode were "blues troubadour" Eric Bibb and blues historian Tony Russell. The fourth episode was broadcast on Tuesday January 30, 2007 and focused on "rock" music. The invited experts for this episode were rock singer Paul Carrack, music magazine editor Mark Allen, and music writer/broadcaster Robert Sandall. Finally, the fifth episode of the series was broadcast on Tuesday February 6, 2007 and focused on "classical" music (with a particular focus on the "tenor voice"). The invited experts for this episode were Peter Auty, one of Britain's leading tenors (as presented in the promotional nomenclature), and singing teacher Peter Wilson.

Methods

All five episodes of the series were recorded digitally and then transcribed. The transcriptions were analyzed using ATLAS.ti version 5.0.67, Scientific Software Development GmbH (a qualitative analysis package for large bodies of textual, graphical, audio and video data) in order to explore: (1) how experts' opinions might vary across musical genres; (2) whether the distilled "themes" that resulted from the qualitative analyses of the transcripts could be mapped onto the theoretical elements of a research framework built by this author (see Himonides 2009; Himonides 2011; Himonides and Welch 2005); and (3) what the commonalities and diversities were regarding experts' opinions about sung performance quality across musical genres. Structurally, all episodes of the series were similar and addressed the series' core questions, outlined in the promotional paragraph above.

Results

The themes that emerged from the contextual analyses of the five transcribed episodes were ideas relating to:

- the cultural dimension, flagged as "culture";

---

[1] http://www.bbc.co.uk/radio4/thesingernotthesong/

- performers' or the experts' personal identities and their development, flagged as "identity";
- performers' or experts' musical development and musicianship, flagged as "musical_dev/musicianship";
- musical morphological, musicological and/or compositional aspects within the particular genres, flagged as "musical_score/style";
- the neuropsychobiological processing of lyrics and sound, flagged as "npb";
- the production of recorded performances as well as recording techniques and issues relevant to acoustics, flagged as "psychoacoustics";
- performers' or experts' personal emotional and/or psychological contexts, flagged as "psychology_emotion"; and, finally,
- the actual musical instrument (the performers' vocal instruments) and voice production, flagged as "timbre_instrument."

An overall analysis of the transcripts of all five episodes of the series rendered the following results (see Table 15.1), in terms of the frequency of appearance of the eight distilled analysis "nodes":

Further analysis

In order to gain some insights into the validity of the coding, all episodes' textual transcripts as well as the associated coding information were exported onto one eXtensible Markup Language (XML) document. The 354 individual references were assigned unique "ID" labels (from 1 to 354) and a short programming script was written (using the "AWK" programming language and the "sed" UNIX text editor), which, first, generated a random sequence of 36 unique integers (minimum value = 1, maximum value = 354) and, second, retrieved ("mined") the corresponding (to the generated numbers) textual passages from the XML

Table 15.1 The distilled "nodes" from the textual analyses

Name	Sources[1]	References
culture	5	75
identity	5	63
musical_dev/musicianship	5	57
musical_score/style	5	22
nbp	4	13
psychoacoustics	1	2
psychology_emotion	5	70
timbre_instrument	5	52

[1] The number of transcribed documents in which a particular node appears, at least once. Five individual documents were processed by the qualitative analysis software, corresponding to the number of episodes of the radio series.

Table 15.2 Descriptive statistics of judge agreement ratings

Sample	Frequency	Mean	Variance	Standard deviation	Standard-error	Minimum	First quartile	Median	Third quartile	Maximum
Judge 1 agreement	36	6.278	0.949	0.974	0.162	4.000	6.000	7.000	7.000	7.000
Judge 2 agreement	36	6.250	1.221	1.105	0.184	4.000	6.000	7.000	7.000	7.000

document and further "appended" them into a plain text digital file (the term "appended" is being used in computer programming terms; i.e. exported the passages one at a time and stored them sequentially in a plain text file).

The generated plain text file contained 36 flagged randomly selected textual passages (representing 10 percent + of the flagged body of text) and the researcher's "node allocation." This was given to two researchers (one in the field of philosophy and one in the field of music education) for validation (rating the agreement with each of the 36 codes on a scale from 1—strongly disagree to 7—strongly agree). The judges were in strong agreement (p = 0.819, α = 0.05) with the initial flagging and did not express further concerns (see Table 15.2).

As can be seen in Figure 15.1, there is an apparent overall dominance in the appearance of certain theoretical components linked to the framework proposed by this author (Himonides 2008). At the same time, the analyses demonstrate that certain elements are under-represented. For example, the "psychoacoustics" element is the only property that appears in just one of the analyzed documents (i.e. the episode that discusses "rock" music). From an inverse perspective, the only recorded episode where no mention of the neuropsychobiological processing of lyrics and sound (flagged as "npb") was made is that of

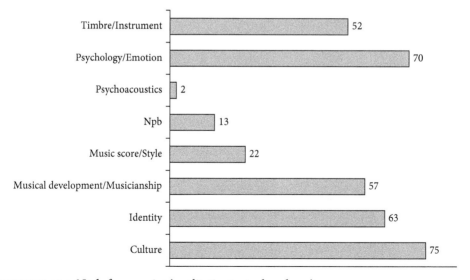

FIGURE 15.1 Node frequencies (qualitative textual analyses).

"the tenor voice." Although the latter might appear as an "odd" finding, consequent analyses (presented below) demonstrate that other themes dominated that particular discussion.

At a more microscopic level, each individual "case" (i.e. each recorded and transcribed episode) was further analyzed in terms of the distribution and frequency in appearance of individual nodes throughout the complete body of the textual transcript. All "cases" were analyzed both in terms of "node occurrence" (across program genres) but also in terms of "node coverage" (within and across genres); the findings were distilled using the "node coverage" property for within-program comparisons, as the latter is thought to provide a more accurate representation of the contextual "reality," as minor references to certain aspects might occur (thus, receiving qualitative "flags") that might occupy a small proportion of the actual discussion time (see Bandara 2006; Gable 1996).

Analyses of the five individual discourses are summarized in Table 15.3 below.

Table 15.3 A summary of the nodes' frequency of appearance and coverage

	Frequency	Coverage (%)
01 Jazz		
Culture	15	54.68
Identity	13	44.66
Musical development/musicianship	8	42.08
Musical score/style	2	2.20
Neuropsychobiological processing of lyrics	1	2.73
Psychology/emotion	9	35.59
Timbre/instrument	1	2.73
02 Folk		
Culture	21	56.27
Identity	10	28.23
Musical development/musicianship	11	24.95
Musical score/style	5	14.12
Neuropsychobiological processing of lyrics	6	17.08
Psychology/emotion	17	43.05
Timbre/instrument	7	15.83
03 Blues		
Culture	12	53.91
Identity	12	34.55
Musical development/musicianship	5	16.63
Musical score/style	3	21.48
Neuropsychobiological processing of lyrics	5	17.29

Table 15.3 Continued

	Frequency	Coverage (%)
Psychology/Emotion	15	46.15
Timbre/Instrument	9	29.41
04 Rock		
Culture	18	51.53
Identity	20	52.09
Musical development/Musicianship	15	36.62
Musical score/style	5	17.15
Neuropsychobiological processing of lyrics	1	2.40
Psychoacoustics	2	3.72
Psychology/Emotion	16	37.98
Timbre/Instrument	17	34.46
05 Tenor (classical)		
Culture	9	36.52
Identity	8	18.18
Musical development/musicianship	18	50.74
Musical score/style	7	23.13
Psychology/emotion	13	26.64
Timbre/instrument	18	70.10

For the across-genres comparison of the various "trends," the frequencies in appearance of each node were summarized, and are presented in cross-tabular format in Table 15.4 and as percentages in Figure 15.2.

The analysis suggests that different "emphases" can be associated with specific elements of the proposed theoretical framework across the different musical genres.

Statements from the experts

Experts' discussions regarding classical music (British Broadcasting Corporation 2007e) were dominantly focused on the performers' musical development, their level of musicianship as well as the musical instrument itself:

> "We've got a nice track from Franco Corelli here . . . [music] Especially at the start of the aria from *Il Dolce Bacci*—Sweet Kisses—there's a second phrase and he goes up to a top A and he 'diminuendoes' [i.e. performs a *diminuendo*] on this top A—he gets quieter on it—but he doesn't snap into a false voice of falsetto. He takes his full voice down to nothing and it's absolutely wonderful to listen to."

Table 15.4 A cross-tabular representation of nodes' frequency of appearance

Node	Blues	Classical	Folk	Jazz	Rock
Culture	12	9	21	15	18
Identity	12	8	10	13	20
Musical development/musicianship	5	18	11	8	15
Musical score/style	3	7	5	2	5
Neuropsychobiological processing of lyrics	5		6	1	1
Psychoacoustics					2
Psychology/emotion	15	13	17	9	16
Timbre/instrument	9	18	7	1	17

"His attitude to singing was—he said the first thing for singing is it's quite simple: it exists because of a low larynx and an open throat like a yawn. But the throat should not be held open rigidly. Other tenors would say it's nothing to do with the throat and it's very much to do with the mask, the head and the resonance within the head. But I think that everyone does agree that an open throat is something that you have to employ when you sing. Nothing rigid; Nothing forced."

"You can see the space on that voice—you know the loose, open throat. That was gave him [sic] the God-gift of course—and the courage—the huge courage. A tenor must have the heart of a lion, which that man had, as we can all hear. How sad it is that Nessun Dorma was written after he was around. Who knows what that would have been like."

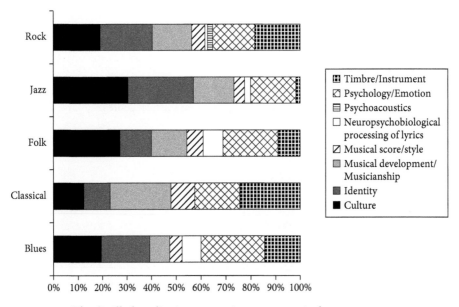

FIGURE 15.2 The distilled qualitative properties across musical genres.

"We don't write operas like this. We don't have a Verdi or a Puccini in Britain. Choral tradition in this country is wonderful but I think it's so difficult. It's impossible for a young lad learning how to sing to be in a choir with all the aspects of his technique, the freedom, the release to try and blend in with other voices. Solo singing by nature is not about blending—it's about development."

On the other hand, opinions about Jazz sung performances (British Broadcasting Corporation 2007a) are predominantly shaped by cultural and identity views:

"She's one of my favourite jazz singers, Joni Mitchell is [laughs] because it's so honest. It's so beautifully honest and she's not trying to sound like a jazz singer—in inverted commas—she's just sounding like herself. This is why I get frustrated by the compartmentalization—because she's just a great artist and she definitely lives in the present moment. And you could feel it, when you hear her sing it; you feel that you're in the room with her—and she's *living* the song in the same way that Billie Holliday does and Nancy Wilson."

"There's something about an individual voice which is just that—it's individual. And what comes with that is not only the timbre, but it's also the phrasing . . . how people think about time and how people think about a lyric and what to emphasize."

"It took me a long while to understand Billie Holliday. I used to listen to her when I was 18 or 19 and didn't really understand why. . . I kind of went along with it because everyone raved about Billie Holliday and I was like . . . huh? . . . and then when I heard this album I was in my thirties, really, and it just completely hit me and it's so . . . oh—it's just so heartbreaking. There's something so vulnerable about what she does. And so personal, so intimate."

Cultural elements appear to be very strong in the discussion about folk music (British Broadcasting Corporation 2007b). But there is also a very strong emphasis on the performers' and listeners' psychology and general emotional worlds:

"In 1957, we went down to Ken Colyer's Jazz club and in the interval there was—a lady and a man got up and she played the banjo and he played the fiddle and she started to sing and then I fell in love, really, I fell in love with that music—the yearning, the soul, everything in there that human beings have was in those songs that she sang and I was totally found. Absolutely found. I was lost and I'd been found."

"What they did was to evolve a way of group singing *semi*—well not exactly *improvised*, but they worked it out by ear and it was just tremendously powerful. I remember the first time I heard them I was in a record shop in Oxford Street and someone put this record on and—my goodness, what is that? It was tremendously uplifting, it was tremendously forceful, it was tremendously well-grounded."

"There is a difference between having a great voice and being a great singer. You can have the greatest voice in the world and not tell a story. What's the point in that? You might as well sing the telephone book. You *have* to tell the story; that's what traditional music is about. And if you don't do that, then you've failed in your job."

"The thing about this music is that it moves. What I sing today, I certainly shan't sing tomorrow because I'm older tomorrow. I hate recording; I hate it—the others will tell you. I sing it and then say 'Was that all right? Were there any bad notes, did I sing out of key or anything?' and they say 'No, that was alright' and it's like 'Right, I'm going!' [laughs]—because I can't do it over and over and over again. I think it takes the soul out of it if you keep going over and over and over and over and over again. I think recording it puts a full stop on it."

"Singing is a weird thing; singing is often a question of timing. It's why I would prefer to listen to Bob Dylan than the modern Luciano Pavarotti. Pavarotti has a gift of God as a voice—Bob Dylan hasn't. But I listen to Bob Dylan—and I *believe* him."

Blues singing appears to be mainly associated with "emotions" and "the voice" that communicates them. The Blues were presented as "the singer's music," a genre where performers speak about their own troubles, not someone else's. The very core of blues music lies in the communication of feelings and the sharing of empathy. This is evident in the experts' comments (British Broadcasting Corporation 2007c):

> "I think of the language of the Blues as being a language of the heart. It starts out maybe . . . even without words . . . it could be a moan. Spontaneous, emotional musical expression."
>
> "Magnificent, resonant voice that had a rough edge to it that was so *exciting* and just seemed like he was a man of the world who had seen it all. He seemed like a lion who just had this beautifully musical roar and one note from Howling Wolf's throat told you half the history of you know, the race, it seemed, it just was, um, so rich, with so many nuances that . . . yeah, I wanted some of that world too."
>
> "One, I think is size, the sort of sheer grandeur, breadth, and Howling Wolf has that in spades. It's a huge, great tsunami of a voice that you know, knocks houses down at hundreds of yards. It's a wonderful way of doing certain kinds of song. One of the things that Wolf started out doing, for example, was living up to his name; he sang these songs with these wolf-howls, these strange eerie cries in them that trademarked his name, so to speak, but they also fitted a certain kind of very Southern down-home Blues as in his song 'Smoke-Stack Lightening.'"
>
> "I'm Kyla Brooks, I'm a Blues singer. The best moment for me is when I can feel that the audience is with me and they're understanding the emotion that I'm trying to convey; they get what's going on inside *me*. I don't think they have to understand what you've been through—you know, you might be singing of something they have no experience of. You just get a prickly feeling and you *know* that it's working and you can just *see* it in the audience, you can feel it."
>
> "If a blues singer doesn't have some sort of story to tell then he won't have much of a future as a blues singer . . . "

Finally, the analysis suggests that rock music is a paradigm of diversity. This does not come as a surprise, as rock music may be perceived to be the offspring (or sibling) of practically all of the musical genres mentioned above. Even today, where rock music has been established as a "unique genre," we can come across submusical genres such as "blues-rock" (e.g. Allman Brothers Band, ZZ Top, Joe Bonamassa), "jazz-rock" (e.g. Weather Report, Allan Holdsworth), "folk-rock" (and its regional variations, e.g. "country-rock") (e.g. Fairport Convention, the Beatles) and even classical music influenced rock (e.g. Yngwie Malmsteen, Ritchie Blackmore). The diversity of rock music is evident in the experts' comments (British Broadcasting Corporation 2007d):

> "I went to see the Stones, recently, actually, and I originally saw them in the sixties at the Sheffield City Hall and I hadn't seen them since . . . And I thought it was probably going to be a bit of a joke, you know, a bit of a pantomime, these old guys in leather trousers. As a singer myself, I never really considered Mick Jagger to be a great singer, but I was blown away. I thought that Mick Jagger was absolutely *outstanding*. Unbelievable performer. And he left the stage for a couple of numbers and I've got to say . . . it wasn't happening, you know, until he came back!"
>
> "Freddie Mercury's voice, of course, is very difficult to disentangle from the sound of Queen and of course Queen had the most fantastically loud guitar and drums behind his voice. Again, that's the context in which his slightly camp, operatic style was listened to and appreciated. There was another aspect of Freddie Mercury's voice, which was the sheer power of it. Yes, he was very much *not* the kind of rough-and-ready sounding blues singer, but my goodness, he could blast the stadium vocally—and rock is partly about that."

"Liam Gallagher's voice has a wonderful kind of low-level projection. But what he does do is have a very menacing presence and he patrols the lip of the stage in a rather menacing and again, very theatrical way. And so he just generates this sort of rather scary vibe."

"I think rock music doesn't favour female singers as much—and there simply aren't as many of them, partly because girl singers tend to favour more emotional music—you know, they tend to be more drawn to personal songs—intimate songs, poetic songs and so there aren't that many of them—I mean, there are lots of girl singers, but they tend to drift into folk and into R&B and certainly drift into pop. You know, you've got people like Tina Turner who was actually a soul singer—the great rock grandma, you know *stomping* on stage."

"I think that Chrissie Hine is one of *the* great rock voices although she's got massive emotional range—songs like 'Stop Your Sobbing.' It's a thin line between love and hate and these beautiful soul and pop songs all in minor chords and very, very moving."

"There's a great bit in Live Aid where she [Tina Turner] does a bit with Mick Jagger—you know, it's absolutely hilarious—they're both terribly competitive and they've both decided that they're going to outshine the other one. And it gets more and more comic—wagging fingers at each other and strutting—very very camp. And yeah, let's be honest, Mick Jagger loses. He is no match for this girl. She absolutely wipes the floor with him. She's just got incredible presence and incredible projection. You just cannot take your eyes off her."

The above findings shed more light, though from a slightly different perspective on the "prism" of our present investigation. Although it is recognized that the textual analyses are a snapshot of opinions from performers and other "experts," the 75 minutes of programming reveal strong biases in the discussions, particularly across, as well as within, musical genres. Overall, socio-cultural contexts, psychobiological design and biography are strongly implicated in listener judgments.

An online-survey-based evaluation of Tibetan throat singing

The purpose of this short-scale empirical research investigation was to capture participants' opinions regarding the overall quality of a traditional Tibetan throat-singing performance, this being chosen as a sung musical genre that was likely to be unfamiliar to many listeners outside the world of ethnomusicology.

Methods

The performance was given by world-class Tibetan (Khoomii (overtone)) throat-singing specialist and clinician Michael Ormiston,[2] and filmed during a research-based visit to a special secondary school in south-west London. The performance was videotaped and later converted to digital video format (mpeg layer 2) so that it could be uploaded onto the World Wide Web. An online survey instrument was implemented for the evaluation of this performance, comprising (1) response fields regarding the respondents' sex, age, and ethnic

---

[2] http://www.soundtransformations.co.uk/Michaelbiog1.htm

background; (2) an embedded version of the digital video performance; (3) a seven-point rating scale of perceived performance quality (values: 1 = "very poor"; 2 = "poor"; 3 = "not so good"; 4 = "I cannot tell"; 5 = "fairly good"; 6 = "good"; 7 = "excellent"); and (4) an optional response field (memo box) so that people could provide comments. The online instrument was coded using XHTML (for the textual part of the instrument) and PHP (for the response data handling part of the instrument) and was deployed onto this author's personal web server. Online invitations for participation to this online instrument were communicated through "usenet" and, mainly, through the electronic newsgroups "rec.audio.pro" and "rec. audio.opinion." The survey received 177 responses.

Participant demographics

Of the 177 participants, 96 (54.24 percent) were male and 81 (45.76 percent) were female. The youngest of the respondents was 22 years old and the oldest was 64 years old. The average age of the respondent sample was 44 years (standard deviation 12 years). Of the 177 participants, 30 participants (16.9 percent) were between 20 and 30 years of age; 43 participants (24.3 percent) were between the ages of 31 and 40; 42 participants (23.7 percent) were between 41 and 50 years of age; 45 participants (25.4 percent) were between 51 and 60; and 17 participants (9.6 percent) were aged 61 years or above.

As we can see from these figures, the population is distributed quite evenly, with a small bias towards the "61+ years" and "20–30 years" age groups. This slight bias might be justifiable by the access-age statistics of the particular newsgroups where this survey had been advertised. In the specific context of the research, this was not perceived to pose a problem, as it was not intended to perform "within" and "across" groups' comparative statistics. The objective of this survey (which was to "capture" people's responses regarding the quality of a particular sung performance) as well as the findings (as presented here), support the argument that all age groups are relatively well represented.

Interestingly, the two older year groups are "led" by female participants at 70.6 percent (61+ years) and, at a weaker dominance, 51.1 percent (51–60 years). Almost all major ethnic backgrounds were represented in the acquired dataset. The biggest respondent group (93 participants, 52.5 percent) labeled themselves as "white"; the second group were the participants that labeled themselves as "Asian" (30 participants, 16.9 percent); the third group of participants labeled themselves as "Chinese" (18 participants, 10.2 percent); the fourth group of participants (16.9 percent) labeled themselves as "other"; and, finally, the two groups of participants that labeled themselves as either "mixed" or "black" each comprised 10 participants (5.6 percent). Due to the fact that this particular survey was Internet-based, it is noted that the distribution of respondents on the world map is not dissimilar from official international Internet usage statistics.[3]

This argument is based on the assumption that the majority of both European and North American populations can be classified as "white." Regarding the participants' responses about the perceived "quality" of the sung performance, the results are noteworthy in that 133 (75.14 percent) participants reported that they were not in a position to tell whether the sung performance was good quality or not. Later filtering of the responses in the "optional" commenting field of the online survey instrument also suggests that the respondents felt

[3] http://www.internetworldstats.com/stats.htm, accessed May 2008.

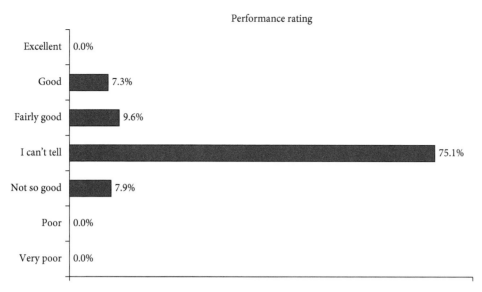

FIGURE 15.3 Tibetan throat-singing performance perceived quality rating.

that they did not possess the experiential criteria to evaluate such a performance. Some participants stated that they responded positively solely because they had never come across such a musical genre and had found this experience extremely exciting. The overall results of the survey are presented in Figure 15.3.

Results

A further analysis was undertaken within ethnic groups in order to explore whether certain groups appeared to be more "informed" about this particular type of singing. The results are reported in Table 15.5. As can be seen, there appears to be a similarity of response by ethnic group (e.g. 60–87.5 percent responded "I can't tell").

A k-samples comparison of variances (Levene's test) was performed in order to investigate whether the ratings varied homogeneously across different ethnicities. At the level

Table 15.5 Performance rating scores within the different ethnic backgrounds

Rating	Asian	Black	Chinese	Mixed	White	Other	Total
Fairly good	16.7%	10.0%	16.7%	30.0%	5.4%	0.0%	9.6%
Good	10.0%	20.0%	0.0%	10.0%	7.5%	0.0%	7.3%
I cannot tell	70.0%	70.0%	77.8%	60.0%	76.3%	87.5%	75.1%
Not so good	3.3%	0.0%	5.6%	0.0%	10.8%	12.5%	7.9%
Total	100.0%	100.0%	100.0%	100.0%	100.0%	100.0%	100.0%

Table 15.6 Descriptive statistics of the ratings across different ethnicities

Sample	Frequency	Mean	Variance	Standard deviation	Standard-error	Minimum	First quartile	Median	Third quartile	Maximum
Asian	30	4.4	0.5	0.7	0.1	3.0	4.0	4.0	5.0	6.0
Black	10	4.6	0.9	1.0	0.3	3.0	4.0	4.5	5.0	6.0
Chinese	18	4.1	0.2	0.5	0.1	3.0	4.0	4.0	4.0	5.0
Mixed	10	4.6	0.5	0.7	0.2	4.0	4.0	4.5	5.0	6.0
Other	16	3.8	0.2	0.4	0.1	3.0	4.0	4.0	4.0	4.0
White	93	4.2	0.5	0.7	0.1	3.0	4.0	4.0	4.0	6.0

of significance $\alpha = 0.05$, the inequality of variances appeared to be statistically significant ($F = 2.641$, $p = 0.027$) as ratings across different ethnicities did not vary equally. The results of the statistical test are presented in Tables 15.6 and 15.7.

Even though one would assume that Chinese or other Asian participants might be "causing" this particular "skew" in the data, as they might be more familiar with (and thus able to be more critical of) this type of genre, it is the "mixed race" group of participants that appears to behave quite "idiosyncratically" with nearly 40 percent of the mixed-race respondents replying positively to the performance. Overall, however, the findings of this short study appear to be quite robust, comprising respondents from all over the world, nearly equally distributed across genders and age groups, who were largely unable to evaluate the quality of this particular sung performance.

Participant comments

Some of the comments that were offered (in the optional comment field) were:

> "OMG [Oh My God] I have never heard anything like this before! I don't know if it's good but it certainly is unique."
> "This is really amazing! I never thought about this . . . I don't think that I can tell."

Table 15.7 Levene's test results for the ratings across different ethnicities

F (observed value)	2.599
F (critical value)	2.641
DF 1	5
DF 2	171
One-tailed p-value	0.027
Alpha	0.05

"I really don't know . . . the fact that the performer doesn't look Western might give people hints . . . but then again, I don't know."

"He is good . . . not perfect . . . I heard more good performer in Tibet. But he good."

"Fascinating!!! Absolutely fascinating!!! But is it bad quality? Is it amazing quality? I just can't tell."

"How does he do that? It's like two people singing! I thought that the voice can only sing one note at a time? Is this real?"

"He looks like he knows his stuff . . . but then again, I can't say."

"Could I email you? I would be fascinated to find out what the results are going to be . . . I couldn't tell myself."

Technology, training, context, and performance quality assessments

Vocal pitch modulation and manipulation are strongly evident in modern recording studio practice, and have been present since the early days of recording, creatively exploiting whatever technological means were at hand at a particular juncture. One example is the Beatles' song "Tomorrow Never Knows" (1966), where the recorded vocal track was fed through a Hammond revolving Leslie speaker, a technique that was consequently used by numerous other artists such as Cream, the Moody Blues, and the Grateful Dead (Everett 2008). With the advent of the modern microcomputer, and the migration of the largest proportion of recording studio practice into the digital domain, the manipulation of vocal pitch has become more controlled, systematic, and context sensitive. There is a plethora of software in the professional and "prosumer" market that enables the recordist/producer to perform sample-accurate pitch manipulation (e.g. Celemony Melodyne, Antares Auto-Tune, Roland V-Vocal) either to purely control the final vocal "product" for accuracy in intonation, or in order to evoke innovative esthetic experiences by meaningfully "abusing" the available technologies (e.g. what is known as the "Cher Effect," referring to the manipulated vocal recording in Cher's song "Believe" in 1998). Regardless of the purpose, technique, and technological means, no real systematic evidence exists concerning the implications of such interventions to the perception of performance quality and the perception of expressivity. On the other hand, there is a plethora of examples from empirical research that demonstrate that even highly skilled professional performers tend to deviate—sometimes dramatically— from fixed tuning. Furthermore, it has been demonstrated that such deviations do have an impact on people's perception of expressivity (see Sundberg et al. 2013). There is, therefore, a direct implication for music education, particularly the training of a singer/performer. An educator's role (and perhaps moral obligation) to foster the development of a singer's voice could not possibly be viewed as taking place in a vacuum, or even mapped against a table of sterilized criteria, curricular bullet points, or exam board specifications. The development of the singer needs to be seen using a context-specific as well as a context-sensitive lens. This will further ensure that the developing musician is receiving effective support that takes into consideration not only the subtleties of their genre(s), personal biography, psychological and socio-cultural worlds, level of musicianship, skill, instrument, aspirations, goals, abilities and challenges, but also the expectations and context-specific "filters" of the audiences that they aspire to reach. Hopefully, further research will help us to identify, in a more systematic manner, the particular thresholds, nuances, and style/repertoire-specific parameters. This is hypothesized to enable singers and educators to focus on these, in order to augment singing performance vocabularies and skills.

Conclusion

The specificity of context is absolutely central, not peripheral, to the perceived quality of a singing performance. This is perhaps why contemporary singing competitions (e.g. "The Voice") are produced for television and not for radio, and this is perhaps why so many heated debates can be witnessed over social media about judges' choices and decisions.

As an epilogue, it might be interesting to revisit what was reported in the January 2012 issue of *Sound On Sound* magazine. The editor-in-chief, Paul White mentioned in his leader:

> [D]uring one of our Studio SOS visits a few months back, Hugh [technical editor Hugh Robjohns] and I listened to a demo recording on which the studio owner's daughter had provided the vocals, and we both thought that he'd been too heavy-handed with Auto-Tune or some similar pitch-correction plug-in. He told us that he hadn't used any pitch-correction processing at all, that was just the way she sung. It turns out that she'd grown up on a diet of pop music in which heavy pitch-correction was the norm, and she'd learned to sing by emulating what she heard on record. I mentioned this to UK producer Steve Levine when we met to sit on a panel earlier this year and he said he'd also come across this development, specifically female vocalists who had learned to pitch very precisely and to move cleanly from one note to another without the normal glides and slides you hear in a typical unprocessed vocal.
>
> (White 2012)

This is somewhat exciting evidence of how extremely disparate assessments of the quality of a performance could change from something that sounds "wrong" or pathological to something that simply observes a novel technologically mediated esthetic paradigm. The multifaceted and extraordinary singing voice could never be assessed by an automaton, but this does not mean that we cannot develop the evidence base further in order to become more effective at fostering better singing and greater experiences through singing.

References

Bandara, W. (2006). Using NVivo as a Research Management Tool: A Case Narrative. In: A. Ruth (ed.), *Quality and Impact of Qualitative Research. 3rd Annual QualIT Conference*, pp. 6–19. Brisbane: Institute for Integrated and Intelligent Systems.

British Broadcasting Corporation. BBC Radio 4 (2007a). The singer, not the song: the jazz voice. Broadcast Tuesday, January 9, 2007, http://www.bbc.co.uk/radio4/thesingernotthesong/pip/lsbsq/, accessed June 19, 2017.

British Broadcasting Corporation. BBC Radio 4 (2007b). The singer, not the song: the folk voice. Broadcast Tuesday, January 16, 2007, http://www.bbc.co.uk/radio4/thesingernotthesong/pip/bqnpd/, accessed June 19, 2017.

British Broadcasting Corporation. BBC Radio 4 (2007c). The singer, not the song: the blues voice. Broadcast Tuesday, January 23, 2007, http://www.bbc.co.uk/radio4/thesingernotthesong/pip/bquy5/, accessed June 19, 2017.

British Broadcasting Corporation. BBC Radio 4 (2007d). The singer, not the song: the rock voice. Broadcast Tuesday, January 30, 2007, http://www.bbc.co.uk/radio4/thesingernotthesong/pip/7l4h2/, accessed June 19, 2017.

British Broadcasting Corporation. BBC Radio 4 (2007e). The singer, not the song: the classical voice. Broadcast Tuesday, February 6, 2007, from http://www.bbc.co.uk/radio4/thesingernotthesong/pip/ider2/, accessed June 19, 2017.

Durrant, C. and Himonides, E. (1998). What makes people sing together? Socio-psychological and cross-cultural perspectives on the choral phenomenon. *International Journal of Music Education* 32(1): 61–71.

Durrant, C. (2003). *Choral Conducting: Philosophy and Practice*. New York: Routledge.

Everett, W. (2008). *The Foundations of Rock: From "Blue Suede Shoes" to "Suite: Judy Blue Eyes."* Oxford, New York: Oxford University Press.

Gable, G. (1996). Integrating case study and survey research methods: an example in Information Systems. *European Foundation of Information Systems* 3(2): 112–126.

Gabrielsson, A. and Juslin, P.N. (2003). Emotional expression in music. In: R.J. Davidson, K.R. Scherer, and H.H. Goldsmith (eds), *Handbook of Affective Sciences*, pp. 503–534. New York: Oxford University Press.

Himonides, E. (1997). *What makes people sing together? Socio-psychological and crosscultural perspectives on the singing phenomenon.* Unpublished MA dissertation, University of Surrey, Guildford, UK.

Himonides, E. and Welch, G.F. (2005). Building a bridge between aesthetics and acoustics with new technology: a proposed framework for recording emotional response to sung performance quality. *Research Studies in Music Education* 24(1): 58–73.

Himonides, E. (2008). *The Psychoacoustics of Vocal Beauty: A New Taxonomy*. Published doctoral dissertation. London: University of London.

Himonides, E. (2009). Mapping a beautiful voice: theoretical considerations. *Journal of Music, Technology and Education* 2(1): 25–54. https://doi.org/10.1386/jmte.2.1.25/1

Himonides, E. (2011). Mapping a beautiful voice: The continuous response measurement apparatus (CReMA). *Journal of Music, Technology and Education* 4(1): 5–25. https://doi.org/10.1386/jmte.4.1.5_1

Howard, D.M. and Angus, J. (2001). *Acoustics and Psychoacoustics (Music Technology)*, 2nd edn. Oxford: Focal Press.

Juslin, P.N. (2001). Communicating emotion in music performance: a review and a theoretical framework. In: P.N. Juslin and J.A. Sloboda (eds), *Music and Emotion: Theory and Research (Series in Affective Science)*, pp. 309–337. New York: Oxford University Press.

Malloch, S.N. (1999). Mothers and infants and communicative musicality. *Musicae Scientiae, Special Issue* 3(1): 29–57.

Malloch, S. and Trevarthen, C. (eds). (2010). *Communicative Musicality: Exploring the Basis of Human Companionship*. Oxford: Oxford University Press.

Ockelford, A. (2005). *Repetition in Music: Theoretical and Metatheoretical Perspectives*. London: Ashgate.

Peretz, I., Gagnon, L., Hébert, S., and Macoir, J. (2004). Singing in the brain: insights from cognitive neuropsychology. *Music Perception* 21(3): 373–390.

Scherer, K.R. and Zentner, M.R. (2001). Emotional effects of music: production rules. In: P.N. Juslin and J.A. Sloboda (eds), *Music and Emotion: Theory and Research*, pp. 361–392. Oxford: Oxford University Press.

Scherer, K.R. (2003). Why music does not produce basic emotions?: a plea for a new approach to measuring emotional effects of music. In: R. Bresin (ed.), *Proceedings of the Stockholm Music Acoustics Conference 2003*, pp. 25–28. Stockholm, Sweden: Royal Institute of Technology.

Sloboda, J.N. and O'Neil, S.A. (2001). Emotions in everyday listening to music. In P. N. Juslin and J.N. Sloboda (eds), *Music and Emotion: Theory and Research*, pp. 361–392. Oxford: Oxford University Press.

Sundberg, J. (1987). *The Science of the Singing Voice*. Dekalb, IL: Northern Illinois University Press.

Sundberg, J., Lã, F.M.B., and Himonides, E. (2013). Intonation and expressivity: a single case study of classical western singing. *Journal of Voice* 27(3): 391.e1–391.e8. https://doi.org/10.1016/j.jvoice.2012.11.009

Welch, G.F. (2005). Singing as communication. In: D. Miell, R.A.R. MacDonald, and D. J. Hargreaves (eds), *Musical Communication*, pp. 239–259. New York: Oxford University Press.

White, P. (2012). Shaped by Technology, http://www.soundonsound.com/people/shaped-technology, accessed 3rd February 2013.

CHAPTER 16

···

DEFINING AND EXPLAINING SINGING DIFFICULTIES IN ADULTS

···

KAREN WISE

INTRODUCTION

···

THE voice is arguably the nexus of two fundamental human traits: The capacity for music and the capacity for language. As vocal communicators, humans are prodigious from the earliest weeks and months of life. Children exhibit through the early years an array of vocal behaviors that Young (2002) describes as a "mosaic . . . [that] includes all kinds of blending and overlapping of music and language" (p. 45). Meanwhile, research in psychology has shown that many aspects of sophisticated musical understanding are not the sole preserve of trained musicians, but are acquired on an implicit level by the vast majority of listeners (see Bigand and Poulin-Charronnat 2006, for a review). Yet against this background of universality, there is evidence that a substantial proportion of adults in Western society define themselves as unable to sing, often using the term "tone deafness" in relation to the difficulties they experience (Sloboda et al. 2005; Wise 2009).

This chapter focuses on singing difficulties in adults, in particular with singing accurately or "in tune," drawing on evidence and theory from several areas, notably music education, development, cognitive psychology, and neuropsychology. A number of pockets of research are relevant to understanding singing difficulties, including: (1) Work highlighting the psychosocial and/or cultural aspects of negative self-concepts in singing (see Knight, this volume); (2) cognitive neuropsychological work on musical deficits; and (3) small-scale intervention studies to improve the skills of non-singing or "poor pitch" singing adults. Though growing, the evidence relating to adult singing in the general population and the nature of singing difficulties experienced by adults is still relatively small, particularly in comparison to the large body of developmental and educational research into children's singing.

Singing is a complex skill involving a range of perceptual, cognitive, motor, and senso-rimotor processes, with the added challenge that many of these operate below the level of conscious awareness. Teasing out the precise nature of the relationships among a range of productive and perceptual skills is important for understanding how these are coordinated, and what goes wrong when singing difficulties are experienced. As will be shown in this chapter, there is much to be gained by integrating a developmental perspective into this work, making use of the wealth of knowledge about childhood singing development. The chapter begins by discussing the variety of terms that are used to describe musical difficulties, both in popular and scientific use. A section addressing self-perceptions of singing abilities is then followed by evidence that characterizes the singing of average adults, and a discussion of how singing difficulties have been defined and assessed in relation to this. Then the chapter considers a range of explanations for "poor pitch" singing, discussing congenital amusia (a musical developmental disorder), and the cognitive mechanisms of perception and sensorimotor coordination. Next, the distinctly different singing profiles of people with congenital amusia and those who self-define as "tone deaf" are considered from a developmental perspective, framed by knowledge gained from children's singing. Finally, the chapter moves from understanding and explaining singing difficulties to remediation, reviewing studies and teachers' accounts of training poor pitch singers, and concluding with directions for the future.

The terminology of musical difficulties

"Tone deafness" is perhaps the most commonly used lay term to describe musical difficulties. According to the Oxford English Dictionary tone deaf means "unable to perceive differences of musical pitch accurately," but in popular use it primarily describes a perceived inability to sing (Sloboda et al. 2005; Wise 2009). The terminology in the research literature is varied and reflects the complexities inherent both in accurately characterizing musical difficulties, and in determining their causes. Terms describing severe deficits in musical perception include "note deafness" (Allen 1878), "tune deafness" or "dysmelodia" (Kalmus and Fry 1980) and more recently "congenital amusia" (discussed later) (Ayotte et al. 2002), while those describing poor singing in particular include "poor pitch singer" (e.g. Lidman-Magnusson 1997; Pfordresher and Brown 2007; Welch 1979); "uncertain singer" (e.g. Porter 1977), and the Japanese "onchi" (Welch and Murao 1994), a colloquial term which roughly translates as "tone idiot" and refers to people who sing out of tune (Murao 1994). Thankfully, we no longer see such derogatory terms as "growler" and "grunter" in the literature. However, there is still a certain stigma attached to labels such as "tone deaf" and "non-singer" (see Knight, this volume).

A few studies of adult self-declared "non-singers" have shown that poor musical self-concepts are often associated with memories of negative experiences, such as being called "tone deaf" (Bannan 2000; Knight 1999; Lidman-Magnusson 1997; Richards and Durrant 2003). These studies also show that people's musical self-definition can improve when they are given support and encouragement in musical activities.

SELF-PERCEPTIONS OF SINGING ABILITIES

Evidence shows that there are significant numbers of people in Western society who consider themselves to be deficient in singing. Two surveys of university students have indicated that around 17 percent of young adults define themselves as "tone deaf" (Cuddy et al. 2005; Wise 2009). Chong (2010) analyzed 90 university students' free responses to questions about their enjoyment of singing and found that although 88.3 percent of participants gave responses that were categorized as showing enjoyment, 8.2 percent emphasized needing to be alone to enjoy singing, and 3.6 percent did not enjoy singing at all. The main reasons given for not enjoying singing were social anxiety and negative perceptions of one's own voice. For example, one participant said, "I have a bad sense of pitch and can't carry a tune," and others described their singing as "shaky," "flat," "terrible," or "inaudible."

A number of studies have taken a qualitative approach to understanding the self-concepts of those who self-define as non-singing and their relationship to singing (Abril 2007; Knight 1999; Whidden 2010). These studies emphasize negative emotional associations with singing, low assessments of one's own abilities, fear of negative social judgments or past experiences of such, and self-censoring or avoidance of singing activities. Wise (2009) investigated attitudes towards singing and self-concepts in adults self-defining as musical, non-musical or tone deaf, finding a pervasive social judgment element in people's inhibitions around singing. Some people reported not only restricting singing to when they were alone, but ensuring that they only sang when even they themselves could not hear their own voice (e.g. with the CD turned up loud, or at a sports event with a large crowd).

The accuracy of people's self-assessments, however, has sometimes been called into question. In Chong's (2010) study, some accounts also indicated a discrepancy between participants' own view of their singing and that of other people, in that others viewed them more positively than they did themselves. However, if asked to rate their own performance after specific tasks, people who consider themselves to be "tone deaf" provide accurate assessments and do not underestimate their capabilities (Wise 2009; Wise and Sloboda 2008). Furthermore, the self-defined "tone deaf" participants in these studies did perform less well than "non-tone deaf" controls in a range of singing tasks (further discussed in "Profiles of Performance"). This suggests that although some people may have an overly negative view of their singing on a global level, they are not imagining their difficulties. It also suggests that extreme negative self-views may be brought into a more realistic light by engaging with simple singing tasks.

Anecdotally, there may be other individuals whose self-perceptions are inaccurate in the sense that they sing grossly off pitch but do not consider themselves to have a singing difficulty. Such individuals may be less able to reliably self-assess. Alternatively, they may simply not have encountered the kind of negative feedback from other people that is reported by many who do self-define as non-singing or tone deaf. In any case, more research is needed separating self-judgments based on a global attribution of skill ("I just always sing off key") from those based on moment-to-moment perceptions while actually singing, which may or may not be accurate.

"Average" and "poor" singing in
the adult general population

What constitutes average singing in adults? What is impaired singing like in relation to this and how many adults are affected? These are not straightforward questions to answer, since the available data on singing in the general adult population are still relatively limited. Furthermore, the answers differ depending on the tasks used and on the definition of poor singing.

Assessing singing

The research in this area has almost exclusively used pitch accuracy as the main indicator of singing skill. There is research evidence that this is the most salient feature in a listener's impression of whether or not an individual sings well, and is related to judgments of singing ability and talent (Murry 1990; Price 2000; Watts et al. 2003). Timing, although another crucial aspect of musical performance, may not be as indicative of singing difficulties. One study assessed accuracy in timing as well as pitch in the singing of non-musician students and members of the public, finding that their timing was as accurate as that of professional singers (Dalla Bella et al. 2007). Although there are many other aspects to good singing, such as esthetic qualities and healthy voice use, these have not to date featured significantly in this area of research, probably because pitch accuracy is more readily measurable.

The singing tasks used in research broadly fall into three types: Imitation of single pitches, imitation of pitch sequences, and singing simple (usually familiar) songs from memory. Participants are invariably assessed individually; there is as yet no study to the author's knowledge that has assessed the accuracy of adult poor pitch singers in an ensemble (e.g. a choir) context. However, some studies have investigated the effects of singing in unison with another voice by presenting imitative tasks in a "sing along" format (Pfordresher and Brown 2007; Wise 2009; Wise and Sloboda 2008).

When it comes to assessing the outcome of the singing task presented, there are broadly two approaches. One is a mathematical approach based on measuring the fundamental frequency (f_0) of each tone produced, then calculating accuracy—or more specifically, deviation from a model or pitches prescribed by a musical score—in cents (100 cents = 1 semitone). The other is a perceptual approach in which listeners rate the participants' singing. The advantage of a mathematical approach is an increased objectivity in measurement and the ability to make fine distinctions between people and across different musical parameters (such as absolute versus relative pitch). The disadvantage is that some fairly arbitrary criterion has to be chosen for "inaccurate" singing, since all singing is to some extent variable. The criterion is usually a semitone, thus participants singing on average a semitone or more off pitch, either on absolute or relative (interval) levels, are designated "inaccurate" or "poor pitch" singers. The element of listener perception can be retained in assessments using rating scales, which, if they are carefully defined, and if several raters are used whose assessments are in good agreement, can provide meaningful data on the perceived accuracy of a vocal performance. The corresponding disadvantage, however, is the loss of the fine measurement scale.

In summary, although pitch accuracy is the main criterion for "good" singing as defined in the research literature, it is not a straightforward task to measure it. It is well documented that singing accuracy varies greatly according to characteristics of the task and assessment measures used, thus no one measure can fully determine an individual's level of ability.

Identifying poor pitch singers

How accurately do adults sing on average? When non-musicians or untrained singers are compared to those with training, the untrained participants often appear to be much less accurate (Amir et al. 2003; Hutchins and Peretz 2012; (Murry 1990; Murry and Zwiner 1991). However, other studies highlight wide variations in pitch accuracy among untrained singers, many of whom sing as accurately as trained singers (Dalla Bella et al. 2007; Watts et al. 2003). When it comes to determining what level of accuracy is "average" and how many adults can be considered to have singing pitching problems, the research picture is very mixed, probably due in no small part to differences in task demands and criteria for "accurate" singing.

Hutchins and Peretz (2012) classified 60 percent of their non-musician participants as inaccurate singers based on a criterion of 50 cents (half a semitone), with two-thirds of those singing an average of a semitone or more off-target and making errors on at least 65 percent of trials. The remaining 40 percent of participants sang as accurately as the comparison group of musicians. The study used a single-pitch imitation task with a synthesized complex tone; similar tasks in other studies typically cause non-musician participants to sing a semitone or more off target on average (Amir et al. 2003; Murry 1990; Murry and Zwiner 1991). However, when a human voice target is used, non-musicians can sing much more accurately, within 20–30 cents of the target (Wise and Sloboda 2008). Indeed, one study indicated a significant advantage to less skilled singers in having a human voice model as opposed to a synthesized one, reducing their pitch error in matching single pitches from 113 cents to 27 (Lévêque et al. 2012).

Based on imitation of four-note sequences with a synthesized human voice timbre, Pfordresher and Brown (2007) classified 10 of their 79 participants as inaccurate singers (over a semitone off-pitch on average) and estimated that 10–15 percent of the adult population were poor pitch singers. However, the study initially used a synthesized male voice target for all participants, requiring females either to transpose their response up an octave, or attempt to sing at a pitch that may have been too low. The authors changed this part way through the study and acknowledged that it may have caused difficulties; half the participants classified as inaccurate singers were females who had imitated the male target. Price (2000) found that female "uncertain singers" sang less accurately in response to a male voice.

In contrast, Dalla Bella et al. (2007) used a song task and naturalistic setting; the researcher asked passers-by in a Canadian public park to sing a birthday song ("Gens de pays") for him on the pretext that it was his birthday and he had made a bet with friends that he could get 100 people to sing the song for him. Forty-two participants were recruited this way while 20 non-musician university students participated in a laboratory setting. On average, these 62 "occasional singers" sang the song with more pitch errors than the four professional singers used as a comparison, but many sang as accurately as professional singers and only a few made frequent errors. However, occasional singers sang at a faster tempo than professional, and when 15 of the non-musicians were re-tested and directed to sing at a slower tempo, their performance improved to the level of the professional singers. So the authors attributed inaccurate singing largely to a speed–accuracy trade-off, but there remained two participants who sang very inaccurately despite a slower speed.

The impact of different assessment methods was highlighted by Berkowska and Dalla Bella (2013), who assessed the vocal accuracy of 50 occasional singers using a Sung Performance Battery, incorporating both imitative and song tasks. They reported the numbers of those designated poor pitch singers by a number of different measures and criteria for each task. The resulting proportion of poor pitch singers varied from 0 percent (for relative pitch accuracy in a familiar song, at the 100 cents criterion) to 84 percent (for consistency of absolute pitch over time, in an interval matching task, at the 50 cents criterion). Overall, proportions of poor pitch singers were higher when a fixed criterion of 50 or 100 cents was used, in comparison to when the criterion was set in relation to the average performance of the group. Taking a statistical criterion that is often used in psychological research to distinguish "normal" from "atypical" performance—a score of two standard deviations below the mean—2–8 percent of participants in any given task were designated poor pitch singers.

Overall then, the proportion of adult poor pitch singers varies widely depending on the task and criteria, with large variation both between and within individuals. The generally high proportions reported are somewhat discrepant with data on children's singing, which show that by age 11 only around 4 percent of children still show significant pitching inaccuracy (Welch 2009). The question remains whether this discrepancy is a result of task demands and assessment methods, or whether some people's skills deteriorate over time, perhaps due to lack of participation in singing past school age. The lack of consistency reported in 54–60 percent of occasional singers, across repeated musical intervals separated in time (Pfordresher et al. 2010), may reflect lack of practice in singing. Nonetheless, the weight of evidence is that given favorable task conditions, the majority of adults are capable of singing accurately, in many cases as accurately as professional singers.

Congenital amusia and development

A key question is whether there is such a thing as genuine tone deafness, in the sense of an innate deficit in music, which would explain the apparent difficulties some adults have in singing in tune. Recent cognitive neuropsychological research has identified a group of individuals with a musical learning disability which has been termed "congenital amusia" (Ayotte et al. 2002; Peretz et al. 2002). This is characterized by severe difficulties in musical perception, in the absence of any other perceptual, cognitive, or organic impairment. Individuals with congenital amusia perform poorly in tasks that the majority of adults find straightforward, such as recognizing familiar tunes, noticing out-of-key changes in melodies, and tapping with the beat. Congenital amusia is estimated to affect around 4 percent of the population (after Kalmus and Fry 1980), and may be heritable (Peretz et al. 2007). Amusia refers to a loss of musical skills due to brain injury or disease, in analogy to linguistic disorders (aphasias). The term "congenital" distinguishes between acquired amusia and difficulties that are apparently lifelong, but it could be argued that something like "dysmusia" might be more appropriate in line with such terms as dyslexia and dyscalculia (cf. "dysmelodia," Kalmus and Fry 1980). Congenital amusia was originally thought to stem from an inborn neurological disorder in discriminating small changes in pitch (Hyde and Peretz 2004; Peretz et al. 2002). However, the picture is now more complicated. Neurological evidence suggests that the brains of people with congenital amusia respond to small pitch changes without that information being available to the person's conscious awareness (Moreau et al. 2009; Peretz et al. 2009). Difficulties in pitch pattern perception (Foxton et al. 2004) and pitch working memory (Williamson and Stewart 2010) have also been documented, independent of discrimination deficits.

The assessment measure for congenital amusia is the Montreal Battery of Evaluation of Amusia (MBEA, Peretz et al. 2003) which tests six aspects of musical processing as follows:

Melodic processing:	1. Contour
	2. Interval
	3. Tonality (scale)
Temporal processing:	4. Rhythm
	5. Meter
Memory:	6. Incidental memory

These are theorized to be handled by specialized brain modules (Peretz and Coltheart's Model of Music Processing, 2003), and the most relevant for the present discussion are the melodic processing modules. Individuals' profile of performance across these six subtests varies, but the majority of amusics have more severe problems with melodic processing than with rhythmic processing (Peretz et al. 2008), and the test that best identifies people with amusia is the Scale test. That is, most people with amusia do not easily notice an out-of-key note introduced into an otherwise conventional melody.

The key characteristics of the melodic processing modules (contour, interval, and tonal processing) are (1) they operate sequentially each time a melody is heard and (2) that the accurate functioning of each is dependent on the earlier ones. Over time, repeated exposure to music automatically builds up mental representations of the musical language of one's own culture without specific training—in the case of tonality, the hierarchical structure of pitch relationships. It is hypothesized that the reason so many amusics perform poorly on the Scale test is that they have not established a secure mental representation of tonal relationships in music, either because the tonal processing module does not work properly, or because of a knock-on effect of a processing problem earlier in the sequence.

This processing sequence may be particularly relevant to singing development. Welch (2005) notes that the Contour-Interval-Scale sequence parallels the developmental trajectory of children's singing evidenced in his own extensive research; the relationship is illustrated in Figure 16.1 (Welch, private communication). Children learn first to reproduce the contour of melodies correctly (moving the pitches in the right direction), then become more accurate in singing the constituent intervals within phrases, and lastly achieve tonal stability

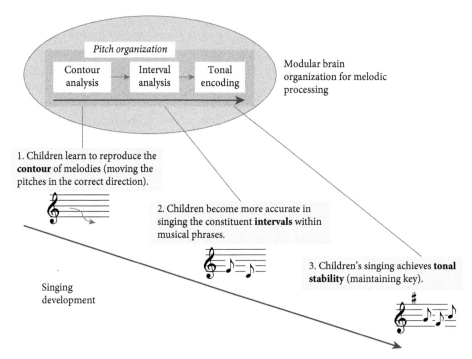

FIGURE 16.1: Diagram showing the conceptual correspondence between the developmental trajectory of children's singing (Welch 2005, private communication) related to the modular organization of melodic processing in the brain (Peretz and Coltheart 2003). Melodic processing deficits, especially in tonal processing, are characteristic of the musical developmental disorder congenital amusia.

(maintaining key). The relationship between congenital amusia and singing development has not yet been examined; at the present time the majority of the data on congenital amusia comes from adults, many of whom are relatively elderly, and there is little research on its occurrence in children (though see Lebrun et al. 2012; Mignault Goulet et al. 2012). We do not yet know how it first manifests itself or how it affects development over time; this is a ripe area for further research. However, the nature of adults' singing errors might provide some insight into both the cognitive neuropsychological basis of their difficulties and their stage of development.

SINGING AND PITCH PERCEPTION

One hypothesis about the cause of poor pitch singing that has received attention in the literature is simply that a person does not perceive pitches accurately. Due to their perception difficulties, it is expected that people with congenital amusia sing poorly. Indeed, this was part of the recruitment criteria for the first studies by Isabelle Peretz and colleagues (Peretz et al. 2002; Ayotte et al. 2002). When compared to untrained adults, people with congenital amusia do, on average, sing much less accurately in a range of tasks (Dalla

Bella et al. 2009; Wise 2009). Their singing is often characterized by contour errors, interval errors, deviation from intervals prescribed by the score (Dalla Bella et al. 2009; Wise 2009), a lack of pitch stability, and in some cases inaccurate timing (Dalla Bella et al. 2009). While children benefit from singing without words, this is often a disadvantage to amusics; only five of Dalla Bella et al.'s (2009) eleven participants were able to produce complete performances singing a song to /la/, which suggests poor memory for music without the scaffolding provided by words. Further evidence of memory being involved in amusics' singing difficulties is provided by Wise (2009) and Tremblay-Champoux and colleagues (2010).

There is some evidence that the severity of amusics' inaccuracy in singing correlates with the severity of their perceptual deficits (Dalla Bella et al. 2009). Nonetheless, in pitch matching tasks amusics often produce responses that are highly correlated with the targets, that is, they systematically represent differences in pitch, singing a relatively consistent distance from the target (usually below) (Hutchins et al. 2010). Furthermore, there is large variation between individuals, with some amusics able to sing accurately in some circumstances (Dalla Bella et al. 2009; Wise 2009), suggesting a dissociation between perception and production abilities. Amusics also respond to alterations in the feedback from their own voice (Hutchins and Peretz 2013). When singing or speaking, if the feedback from a person's own voice is shifted in pitch and relayed via headphones, the pitch they produce automatically alters in the opposite direction to compensate, even when they are unaware of the shift. About half of amusics show a normal response to both small (25 cents) and large (200 cents) shifts in auditory feedback, with only a small number showing no response at all (Hutchins and Peretz 2013). The emerging picture is that even in amusic individuals, whose musical processing is impaired, there is large variation in singing proficiency, and not all of this variation can be explained by their perceptual deficits.

Little evidence exists that singing problems in non-amusic people are connected to pitch perception abilities. Studies of children's vocal pitch matching and simple pitch discrimination have consistently failed to find any meaningful relationship between the two (Buckton 1977; Geringer 1983; Phillips and Aitchison 1997; Porter 1977; Roberts and Davies 1975). Bradshaw and McHenry (2005) found no correlation between pitch discrimination and vocal pitch matching in poor pitch singers. Two studies, by contrast, have found a relationship. In male professional musicians and non-musicians Amir et al. (2003) found that 43 percent of the variance in pitch matching accuracy was accounted for by pitch discrimination ability. Watts et al. (2005) report a figure of 42 percent for the same relationship in their study with female untrained singers. Both studies, however, had evidence to suggest that vocal accuracy was not *dependent* on pitch discrimination, with some people having accurate vocal pitching and poor discrimination (Amir et al. 2003), and others showing inaccurate vocal pitching and accurate discrimination (Bradshaw and McHenry 2005). More recently, the two very inaccurate singers in Dalla Bella et al. (2007) were found to have normal musical perception, and the authors suggested that the pitching difficulties of these two participants represented "a purely vocal form of tone deafness" (p. 1182). Data from the self-defined "tone-deaf" bear this out. While congenital amusia may affect about 4 percent of the population, the majority of the 17 percent self-defining as tone deaf score normally on the MBEA, though with a slightly lower mean score as a group (Cuddy et al. 2005; Wise 2009; Wise and Sloboda 2008). Music processing problems can only explain a proportion of singing difficulties.

Sensorimotor explanations
of singing difficulties

Given the lack of a straightforward relationship between musical perception and singing accuracy, recent research has turned its focus towards the motor and sensorimotor processes involved in singing. There is no evidence that poor pitch singing in people who are healthy is caused by a low-level motor impairment, such as the muscles of the vocal mechanism being unable to perform the movements required. Rather, it is increasingly apparent that the problem lies somewhere in the complex coordinations between perception and action, coordinations that allow a singer to imagine a pitch, plan the muscle movements necessary to reproduce it, put that plan into action, monitor the results of that action through auditory and proprioceptive feedback, and make any necessary correction if the expected results and the perceived results differ. According to most psychological theories of motor control, such sensorimotor coordination requires a mental schema (a long-term representation in memory) that "maps" perception to action. This is an abstract set of rules formed from repeated experiences of the motor task in different situations, refined according to how successful the outcome was each time. The schema thus allows a person to make a motor response to a new stimulus that has not been encountered before, for example, a schema for throwing a ball at a target will allow a person to plan and execute the movements necessary for throwing a ball of a particular weight and size in a particular direction at the desired speed, based on previous similar (though not identical) situations. The proximity of the ball to the target informs the next attempt. In singing, the challenge is that the target is not visible, but auditory, and sometimes not present but imagined (as in the case of recalling a song from memory) (see Welch 1985). Thus singers increasingly rely on proprioceptive feedback as they become more experienced (Mürbe et al. 2002, 2004) and the importance of kinesthetic mental models to singing performance has been demonstrated by recent neurological work (see, e.g. Kleber et al. 2010).

Pfordresher and Brown (2007) proposed a range of potential explanations for poor pitch singing (perceptual, memory, motor, sensorimotor) and conducted a study that aimed to distinguish between them. They concluded that a sensorimotor problem was the most likely explanation for most poor pitch singing, and suggested this may be thought of as a problem with imitation. Hutchins and Peretz (2012) compared the singing of musicians and non-musicians in a series of experiments designed to ascertain the causes of poor singing (perceptual; motor control; sensorimotor mapping). They compared participants' vocal pitch matching accuracy with their accuracy in matching pitches on a computer by using a slider to adjust the pitch. They also used two different types of stimulus tone: Synthesized voice, and the participant's own voice. Both groups of participants were most accurate in matching pitch using the slider, arguing against a perceptual explanation of singing difficulties. Non-musicians were better at vocally matching their own voice than a synthesized voice, but still not as accurate as on the slider. Again, this finding could not be explained perceptually, as synthesized tones were more accurately discriminated than actual voice tones. The authors interpreted their pattern of results as suggesting that the main factors in poor pitch singing were poor motor control and timbral translation problems in sensorimotor mapping. That is, the sensorimotor schema did not work so well when the timbre of the target was different to a participant's own voice.

A more detailed discussion of the complexities of sensorimotor mechanisms involved in poor pitch singing is beyond the scope of this chapter, but two reviews give useful summaries of the current literature, identifying the different ways in which poor singing may present itself, and examining the evidence for a range of possible underlying mechanisms (Berkowska and Dalla Bella 2009; Dalla Bella et al. 2011).

Self-defined "tone deafness," congenital amusia, and singing

A developmental view

As has already been noted, self-defined tone deafness is associated with singing difficulties, but without the perceptual deficits of congenital amusia. It is therefore useful to compare the two in order to further understand the relationships among different perceptual and productive skills. This section focuses in more detail on a research project that explored the characteristics and vocal performance profiles of both tone deafness and congenital amusia (Wise 2009; Wise and Sloboda 2008; Sloboda et al. 2005), discussing some of the findings from a developmental perspective, and drawing on the theoretical frameworks illustrated in Figure 16.1.

Taking a developmental perspective is useful because it paves the way for integrating the cognitive neuropsychological work on congenital amusia and poor pitch singing with the knowledge about singing development in childhood. This potentially allows a more holistic understanding of singing difficulties in the context of musical perceptual and vocal development across the lifespan. Congenital amusia is characterized as a learning disability, while biographical information from adult "non-singers" suggests they may have stalled in their early singing development (for example, having stopped singing because of a negative experience). In children, singing accuracy in reproducing simple songs improves with age, broadly following the contour-interval-tonality sequence outlined earlier. In addition, pitch accuracy is not the only aspect of singing that has an identified developmental trajectory. As children get older, their singing range increases, both in terms of comfortable range (Welch et al., in press) and the range of pitches in which children can sing consistently accurately, which initially may be as small as a minor 3rd (three semitones) at the low end of the usual speaking voice range (Rutkowski and Runfola 1997). These are not to be confused with the physiological limits of pitch range, which are much wider. Thus both pitch accuracy and vocal range offer insights into singing development.

To investigate singing and vocal skills in adults, Wise (2009) developed a Musical Skills Battery for use with novices (Table 16.1). This was used in conjunction with the Montreal Battery of Amusia to give a comprehensive profile of musical abilities in the self-defined tone deaf, in comparison to people with congenital amusia and non-tone-deaf controls (Wise 2009).

Table 16.1: Tasks comprising the Musical Skills Battery (Wise 2009), used in conjunction with the Montreal Battery of Evaluation of Amusia to assess self-defined "tone deafness."

	Components

Vocal tasks	1. Basic tasks in speech and singing
	   a. Imitation of exaggerated speech contours
	   b. Vocal range (slides, exaggerated speech, singing)
	   c. Pitch sustaining
	   d. Volitional movement of vocal pitch up and down

	2. Vocal imitation in two conditions—with simultaneous support of another voice ("sync") and without ("echo"):
	   a. Single pitches
	   b. Sequences (2, 3, and 5 notes)

	3. Songs
	   a. "Happy Birthday" unaccompanied
	   b. "Happy Birthday" accompanied
	   c. Own-choice song

Perception tasks	4. Pitch direction judgment
	5. Computer pitch matching
Self-report measures	6. Questionnaire (musical background; singing activities; reasons for self-defining as tone deaf)
	7. Self-ratings (in tasks 1, 2, 3, and 5)

Two measures of singing accuracy were used: (1) Mathematical measurement of fundamental frequencies (f_o) to calculate pitch deviations in both absolute pitch and interval sizes, plus a count of contour errors; (2) a rating scale reflecting Welch's (1986; 1998) developmental sequence of singing (Table 16.2), with the addition of further categories to include more subtle forms of inaccuracy. Ratings were made by two expert judges. The next section draws out aspects of the findings with regard to the developmental contour-interval-tonality sequence and vocal range.

Profiles of performance

With regard to overall singing accuracy, there are three important broad observations to make. Firstly, the self-defined tone deaf (TD) participants were very different in their performance profile to people with congenital amusia (CA). While CAs as a group sang highly inaccurately, TDs were much more similar to the non-tone-deaf controls; they sang less well by most measures, but the differences were relatively small. Secondly, the group differences notwithstanding, performance varied greatly between individuals. This variability was most pronounced in the CA group, where some individuals were wildly inaccurate, while others were as accurate as controls in some tasks. Thirdly, performance varied

Table 16.2: Perceptual rating scale developed for use by expert judges in evaluating song performances (Wise 2009).

8	All melody is accurate and in tune, and key is maintained throughout
7	Key is maintained throughout, and melody accurately represented, but some mistunings (though not enough to alter the pitch-class of the note)
6	Key is maintained throughout and melody mostly accurately represented, but some errors (notes mistuned sufficiently to be "wrong")
5	Melody largely accurate, but the key drifts or wanders. This may be the result of a mistuned interval, from which the singer then continues with more accurate intervals but without returning to the original pitch
4	Melody mostly accurate within individual phrases, but singer changes key abruptly, especially between phrases (e.g. adjusting higher-lying phrases down)
3	Singer accurately represents the contour of the melody but without consistent pitch accuracy or key stability
2	Words are correct but there are contour errors. Pitches may sound random
1	Singer sings with little variation in pitch, and may chant in speaking voice rather than singing

somewhat by task, and there were certain conditions that facilitated singing accuracy for certain groups of people.

Taking first the task of singing a well-known song from memory ("Happy Birthday"), there were clear differences between TDs, CAs, and controls according to expert blind ratings using the eight point developmental scale (Table 16.2). As shown in Figure 16.2, controls received an average rating of 6.1 (tonally stable with a few inaccuracies) while TDs were rated 4.3 (largely accurate at the interval level within phrases, but lacking tonal stability). CAs, with an average rating of 2.4, made many contour errors. Thus there appears to be a developmental distinction between CAs, TDs, and controls in the attainment of accuracy at contour, interval, and tonality levels. However, there was a large amount of individual variation, particularly among CAs, whose ratings ranged from one (simply speaking the words) to six (accuracy at a level comparable to controls). In addition, when asked to sing a song of their own choice, TDs performed better and were not statistically different from controls (Figure 16.2). There are a number of possible reasons why this may be the case, for instance that the choice allowed participants a greater degree of confidence, and/or to select a song better matched to their capabilities. Providing a piano accompaniment to "Happy Birthday" also improved the performance of both controls and TDs to a similar degree (Figure 16.2). Thus, although the difference between them remains, this suggests that TDs benefit from the same kinds of support as controls and that their singing is open to improvement.

The mathematical analysis of Vocal Imitation tasks also showed that the groups attained different levels of accuracy along the contour-interval-tonality continuum: CAs made a total of 45 contour errors (seven of 12 participants made at least three), while TDs made a total of four (two participants made two each). TDs also performed slightly less accurately than controls in both absolute pitch and interval accuracy, while being much more accurate than CAs (Figure 16.3). While TDs were singing on average within a semitone of target

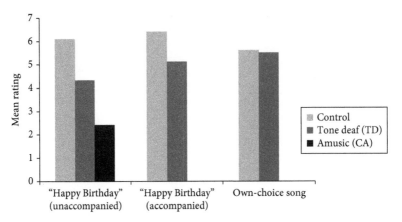

FIGURE 16.2: Mean expert ratings of performances of familiar songs, for self-defined tone deaf, amusic, and control groups. The rating scale used is shown in 16.Table 2.

Note: CAs did not sing an own-choice song or accompanied "Happy Birthday" for practical reasons.

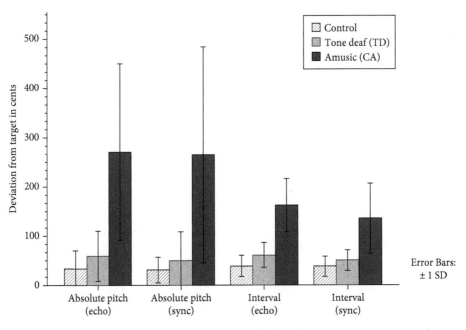

FIGURE 16.3: Accuracy in vocal imitation tasks for three groups in two conditions, measured by absolute pitch and relative pitch (interval). Echo = straightforward imitation; sync = singing along to the target as it is replayed. The figure illustrates the large discrepancy between the performance of the amusic group (highly inaccurate, and highly variable between individuals) and that of the tone deaf group, who sing only slightly though significantly less accurately than controls, and on average within a semitone of target pitches.

pitches, CAs were on average two to three semitones off pitch, with individual deviation of five semitones or more not uncommon. Here too, TDs benefited from some support in their singing. When participants had a repetition of the note or sequence to sing along to (sync condition), rather than simply imitating it solo, TDs were more accurate in absolute pitch. CAs also benefited from support; both contour and interval accuracy improved when CAs sang along with another voice. Although as a group their overall absolute pitch accuracy did not appear to improve, in fact, about half the CAs improved with support while the other half were actually disadvantaged.

With regard to vocal facility, there was evidence that TDs were at a lower stage of development than the other groups. They had a significantly smaller vocal range than controls by all three measures (Figure 16.4). In singing, TDs' capable range was an average of 13 semitones—roughly comparable to that of an eight-year-old child (Welch et al., in press). By contrast, CAs had a capable range comparable to controls, with a small number of individual exceptions. In addition, TDs showed less variability in their pitch than controls and CAs when imitating exaggerated speech; although their contours moved in the right direction, they tended to be flatter.

Finally, it is also important to consider the role of perceptual factors in the "tone deaf" profile. Only one TD and one control participant attained global MBEA scores that may have classified them as amusic. As a group, TDs were very similar in MBEA scores to the controls, and very different to the amusics, who by definition scored poorly. TDs did, however, perform slightly less well overall than controls on the MBEA, a difference that was accounted for by the Interval and Scale subtests only. Thus, it may be that TDs have slightly less developed skills in those areas. However, this was not significantly related to their singing performance. The conclusion that their difficulties are specific to singing production is reinforced by the observation that TDs also performed equally well as controls in matching pitches on a computer and in judging the direction of pitch changes, while CAs performed poorly as a group in these tasks.

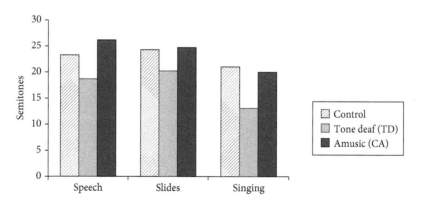

FIGURE 16.4: Vocal ranges in semitones of tone deaf, amusic and control groups, by three different measures. The tone deaf group has a significantly smaller range by all measures than the amusics and controls.

Taken overall, results place CAs at a lower developmental level of singing than TDs in accuracy, and TDs at a lower level than controls. However, the underlying reasons for the developmental differences are likely to be different. While TDs' perceptual development seems to have (largely) kept pace with their non-tone-deaf peers, their vocal development and sensorimotor skill levels have not. Further detailed analysis also showed the complex interaction of a number of perceptual and sensorimotor elements in TDs' singing difficulties, such as planning vocal responses and using sensory feedback to correct error (see Wise 2009). CAs, by contrast, are likely to be hindered by their perceptual deficits—with some participants nonetheless also exhibiting vocal range or coordination issues. Lastly, there was considerable variation between and within individuals. This heterogeneity was even more pronounced for the CAs. In each task, some amusic participants performed as well as controls, showing a broad range of competencies and preserved skills alongside some pronounced difficulties.

Remediation of poor pitch singing

Numerous education and developmental studies emphasize the potential of people with low levels of musical achievement to learn musical skills. An early study by Wolner and Pyle (1933) demonstrated that children who initially failed to discriminate between pitches as much as an octave apart learned, with training, to distinguish differences as small as 0.5 Hertz. Other examples include music education studies in the 1960s and 70s focusing on the "problem" of children who could not sing in tune (Joyner 1969; Roberts and Davies 1975, 1976), but with the emphasis firmly on remediation.

Accounts of training adult poor pitch singers shed light on the complexities of singing difficulties. Heresniak's (2004) overview of the issues in teaching those he calls adult "bluebirds" includes ten short case descriptions. These illustrate diverse poor singing behaviors, and an equal diversity of suggested explanations, from faulty cognitive schemata to extraneous physical tension. All cases showed improvement of singing skills with training, and one student who presented initially with severe pitching difficulties went on to become a professional singer. Heresniak suggested a sequence of musical tasks and questions that teachers could use to narrow down possible explanations for a student's difficulties, and decide whether to recommend a student consults another professional (e.g. audiometrist). While not an empirical paper, this account highlights the rich but as yet largely undocumented craft knowledge that teachers can bring to the understanding of singing difficulties and how to deal with them. Indeed, the empirical work in this area has usually been carried out by researchers who are singing teachers.

Mitchell (1991) adopted an empirical approach to selecting, training, and testing three poor pitch singers. He found that all three were impaired in singing simple songs, but had no difficulties identifying mistakes in familiar melodies. After a period of training all three improved in pitch matching and singing short phrases, but not in song singing. A more holistic approach was taken by Lidman-Magnusson (1994), whose action research investigated the productive, perceptual, emotional, social, and cultural "blocks" experienced by ten adult non-singers, through a period of training over many weeks. At the beginning of the project, participants presented with a variety of "symptoms" which ranged from mild (no apparent musical difficulties, but believed themselves unable to sing) to severe (e.g. extreme difficulties singing in tune). All except two performed at average or above average levels in a basic musicality test (perception and memory). At the end of the project, all participants had made some progress in their ability to sing, as judged by a group of amateur choral singers.

Anderson et al. (2012) reported the first singing intervention study with people with congenital amusia. Over a course of seven weekly group singing workshops, supported by guided practice tasks, Anderson trained five people with congenital amusia in singing as well as in musical perception and understanding. Using the Musical Skills Battery (Wise, 2009; Wise and Sloboda, 2008), she assessed participants before and after the training period. All participants made improvements in singing, particularly in well-known songs. Perceptual abilities, as measured by the Scale subtest of the MBEA, also improved, giving the first indication of possibilities for development in the core areas affected by amusia.

FUTURE DIRECTIONS

The examples of remediation discussed indicate that poor pitch singing is, to some extent at least, open to improvement. This is a rich area for further research; as Anderson et al. (2012) have noted, determining which aspects of congenital amusia may be subject to change will not only help to define the disorder, but will also inform evidence-based interventions. Conversely, carefully designed intervention studies provide one way of testing theories about the functional causes of poor pitch singing in the absence of amusia. With some exceptions, much research so far has taken a "deficit" approach, and although it does not necessarily assume that poor pitch singers cannot improve, it provides a snapshot rather than (as yet) tracking the course of adults' singing development over time. It is likely to be profitable for research to take a more explicitly developmental stance towards singing problems, that is, fully embracing the notion of congenital amusia as a developmental disorder, along with the possibility that many adults with singing difficulties, whether amusic or not, have stalled in the process of developing the necessary skills. Singing teachers, choral leaders and other voice professionals are well placed to help with the sensorimotor coordination issues that growing evidence suggests are at the heart of many people's difficulties.

Apart from simply increasing the number and scale of studies to improve the evidence base for adult singing, there are some specific issues that seem important for research to address. Firstly, what is the relationship between adult singing difficulties and early development? The contour-interval-tonality sequence paralleled in melodic processing and children's singing may be a useful starting point for investigating how singing development may be affected by specific music processing issues. Secondly, in conjunction with this, it is important to examine the role of poor vocal technique and vocal misuse, given the reduced vocal range exhibited by the self-defined "tone deaf." Problems with upper register use in singing limit many people's expressed range and vocal flexibility, while the skillful use of a pitch range outside the normal speaking voice is characteristic of higher levels of singing development in children (Rutkowski 1990). Thus far, it is not clear to what extent under-developed vocal expertise, excessive tension, or other poor vocal habits may interact with or be distinct from theorized sensorimotor bases for singing difficulties. One way of addressing these issues is to design and assess the efficacy of interventions targeted at different poor-singing patterns or "phenotypes," where these can be identified (see Berkowska and Dalla Bella 2009, 2013). In doing this we need to marshal the expertise, practical experience, and craft knowledge of voice professionals in overcoming singing difficulties, and perhaps even more importantly, systematically document effective techniques and approaches along with the developmental courses adult learners take. We also need emerging research findings to feed into practically useful resources, such as educational "toolkits," means of assessment that practitioners can employ in the teaching studio or choir rehearsal room, or even self-assessments that can be used by self-conscious individuals. Finally, and most importantly, we need collaboration between practitioners and researchers so that expertise can be shared and combined in achieving these aims.

References

Abril, C.R. (2007). I have a voice but I just can't sing: A narrative investigation of singing and social anxiety. *Music Education Research* 9: 1–15.

Allen, G. (1878). Note-deafness. *Mind* 3: 157–167.

Amir, O., Amir, N., and Kishon-Rabin, L. (2003). The effect of superior auditory skills on vocal accuracy. *Journal of the Acoustical Society of America* 113: 1102–1108.

Anderson, S., Himonides, E., Wise, K., Welch, G., and Stewart, L. (2012). Is there potential for learning in amusia? A study of the effect of singing intervention in congenital amusia. *Annals of the New York Academy of Sciences* 1252: 345–353.

Ayotte, J., Peretz, I., and Hyde, K. (2002). Congenital amusia: A group study of adults afflicted with a music-specific disorder. *Brain* 125: 238–251.

Bannan, N. (2000). Instinctive singing: Lifelong development of the child within. *British Journal of Music Education* 17: 295–301.

Berkowska, M. and Dalla Bella, S. (2009). Acquired and congenital disorders of sung performance. *Advances in Cognitive Psychology* 5: 69–83.

Berkowska, M. and Dalla Bella, S. (2013). Uncovering phenotypes of poor pitch singing: The Sung Performance Battery (SPB). *Frontiers in Psychology* 4: Article 714. doi:10.3389/fpsyg.2013.00714.

Bigand, E. and Poulin-Charronnat, B. (2006). Are we "experienced listeners"? A review of the musical capacities that do not depend on formal musical training. *Cognition* 100: 100–130.

Bradshaw, E. and McHenry, M.A. (2005). Pitch discrimination and pitch matching abilities of adults who sing inaccurately. *Journal of Voice* 19: 431–439.

Buckton, R. (1977). A comparison of the effects of vocal and instrumental instruction on the development of melodic and vocal abilities in young children. *Psychology of Music* 5: 36–47.

Chong, H.J. (2010). Do we all enjoy singing? A content analysis of non-vocalists' attitudes toward singing. *Arts in Psychotherapy* 37: 120–124.

Cuddy, L., Balkwill, L., Peretz, I., and Holden, R.R. (2005). Musical difficulties are rare: A study of "tone deafness" among university students. *Annals of the New York Academy of Sciences, The Neurosciences and Music II: From Perception to Performance* 1060: 311–324.

Dalla Bella, S., Giguere, J.F., and Peretz, I. (2007). Singing proficiency in the general population. *Journal of the Acoustical Society of America* 121: 1182–1189.

Dalla Bella, S., Giguère, J.-F., and Peretz, I. (2009). Singing in congenital amusia. *Journal of the Acoustical Society of America* 126: 414–424.

Dalla Bella, S., Berkowska, M., and Sowinski, J. (2011). Disorders of pitch production in tone deafness. *Frontiers in Psychology* 2: 164/1–164/11.

Foxton, J.M., Dean, J.L., Gee, R., Peretz, I., and Griffiths, T.G. (2004). Characterization of deficits in pitch perception underlying "tone deafness." *Brain* 127: 801–810.

Geringer, J.M. (1983). The relationship of pitch-matching and pitch-discrimination abilities of preschool and fourth-grade students. *Journal of Research in Music Education* 31: 93–99.

Heresniak, M. (2004). The care and training of adult bluebirds (teaching the singing impaired). *Journal of Singing* 61: 2–25.

Hutchins, S. and Peretz, I. (2012). A frog in your throat or in your ear: Searching for the causes of poor singing. *Journal of Experimental Psychology: General* 141(1): 76–97. doi:10.1037/a0025064.

Hutchins, S. and Peretz, I. (2013). Vocal pitch shift in congenital amusia (pitch deafness). *Brain and Language* 125: 106–117.

Hutchins, S., Zarate, J.M., Zatorre, R.J., and Peretz, I. (2010). An acoustical study of vocal pitch matching in congenital amusia. *Journal of the Acoustical Society of America* 127: 504–512.

Hyde, K. and Peretz, I. (2004). Brains that are out of tune but in time. *Psychological Science* 15: 356–360.

Joyner, D.R. (1969). The monotone problem. *Journal of Research in Music Education* 31: 115–124.

Kalmus, H. and Fry, D.B. (1980). On tune deafness (dysmelodia): Frequency, development, genetics and musical background. *Annals of Human Genetics* 43: 369–382.

Kleber, B., Veit, R., Birbaumer, N., Gruzelier, J., and Lotze, M. (2010). The brain of opera singers: Experience-dependent changes in functional activation. *Cerebral Cortex* 20: 1144–1152.

Knight, S. (1999). Exploring a cultural myth: What adult non-singers may reveal about the nature of singing. In: B.A. Roberts and A. Rose (eds), *The Phenomenon of Singing*, pp. 144–154. St John's, Newfoundland: Memorial University Press.

Lebrun, M., Moreau, P., McNally-Gagnon, A., Mignault Goulet, G., and Peretz, I. (2012). Congenital amusia in childhood: A case study. *Cortex* 48: 683–688.

Lévêque, Y., Giovanni, A., and Schön, D. (2012). Pitch-matching in poor singers: Human model advantage. *Journal of Voice* 26: 293–298.

Lidman-Magnusson, B. (1994). *Sångburen [Inhibited Singing Development].* PhD Thesis, Centre for Music Pedagogy, The Royal College of Music, Stockholm, Sweden.

Lidman-Magnusson, B. (1997). Factors influencing singing development in poor pitch singers. Proceedings of the Third Triennial ESCOM Conference, Uppsala, Sweden, June 7–12, 1997: 339–343.

Mignault Goulet, G., Moreau, P., Robitaille, N., and Peretz, I. (2012). Congenital amusia persists in the developing brain after daily music listening. *Plos One* 7 (5): e36860. doi:10.1371/journal.pone.0036860.

Mitchell, P.A. (1991). Research Note: Adult non-singers: The beginning stages of learning to sing. *Psychology of Music* 19: 74–76.

Moreau, P., Jolicoeur, P., and Peretz, I. (2009). Automatic brain responses to pitch changes in congenital amusia. *Annals of the New York Academy of Sciences* 1169: 191–194.

Murao, T. (1994). Concerning the "Onchi" in a karaoke society: Sociological aspects of poor pitch singing. In: G. Welch and T. Murao (eds), *Onchi and Singing Development: A Cross-cultural Perspective*, pp. 4–7. London: Roehampton Institute/David Fulton Publishers.

Mürbe, D., Pabst, F., Hofmann, G., and Sundberg, J. (2002). Significance of auditory and kinesthetic feedback to singers' pitch control. *Journal of Voice* 16: 44–51.

Mürbe, D., Pabst, F., Hofmann, G., and Sundberg, J. (2004). Effects of a professional solo singer education on auditory and kinesthetic feedback—a longitudinal study of singers' pitch control. *Journal of Voice* 18: 236–241.

Murry, T. (1990). Pitch-matching accuracy in singers and non-singers. *Journal of Voice* 4: 317–321.

Murry, T. and Zwiner, P. (1991). Pitch matching ability of experienced and inexperienced singers. *Journal of Voice* 5: 197–202.

Peretz, I. and Coltheart, M. (2003). Modularity of music processing. *Nature Neuroscience* 6: 688–691.

Peretz, I., Ayotte, J., Zatorre, R.J., Mehler, J., Ahad, P., Penhune, V.B., et al. (2002). Congenital amusia: A disorder of fine-grained pitch discrimination. *Neuron* 33: 185–191.

Peretz, I., Champod, A.S., and Hyde, K. (2003). Varieties of musical disorders—The Montreal Battery of Evaluation of Amusia. *Annals of the New York Academy of Sciences* 999: 58–75.

Peretz, I., Cummings, S., and Dubé, M. (2007). The genetics of congenital amusia (tone deafness): A family aggregation study. *American Journal of Human Genetics* 81: 582–588.

Peretz, I., Gosselin, N., Tillmann, B., Cuddy, L., Gagnon, B., Trimmer, C.G., et al. (2008). On-line identification of congenital amusia. *Music Perception*, 25: 331–343.

Peretz, I., Brattico, E., Järvenpää M, and Tervaniemi, M. (2009). The amusic brain: In tune, out of key, and unaware. *Brain* 132: 1277–1286.

Pfordresher, P.Q. and Brown, S. (2007). Poor-pitch singing in the absence of "tone deafness." *Music Perception* 25: 95–115.

Pfordresher, P.Q., Brown, S., Meier, K., Belyk, M., and Liotti, M. (2010). Imprecise singing is widespread. *Journal of the Acoustical Society of America* 128: 2189–2190.

Phillips, K.H. and Aitchison, R.E. (1997). The relationship of singing accuracy to pitch discrimination and tonal aptitude among third-grade students. *Contributions to Music Education* 24: 7–22.

Porter, S.Y. (1977). The effect of multiple discrimination training on pitch-matching behaviors of uncertain singers. *Journal of Research in Music Education* 25: 68–82.

Price, H.E. (2000). Interval matching by undergraduate non-music majors. *Journal of Research in Music Education* 48: 360–372.

Richards, H. and Durrant, C. (2003). To sing or not to sing: A study on the development of "non-singers" in choral activity. *Research Studies in Music Education* 20: 78–88.

Roberts, E. and Davies, A.D.M. (1975). Poor pitch singing: Response of monotone singers to a program of remedial training. *Journal of Research in Music Education* 23: 227–239.

Roberts, E. and Davies, A.D.M. (1976). A method of extending the vocal range of "monotone" schoolchildren. *Psychology of Music* 4: 29–43.

Rutkowski, J. (1990). The measurement and evaluation of children's singing voice development. *The Quarterly Journal of Teaching and Learning* 1: 81–95.

Rutkowski, J. and Runfola, M. (1997). *Tips: The child voice.* Reston, VA: Music Educators National Conference.

Sloboda, J.A., Wise, K.J., and Peretz, I. (2005). Quantifying tone deafness in the general population. *Annals of the New York Academy of Sciences, The Neurosciences and Music II: From Perception to Performance* 1060: 255–261.

Tremblay-Champoux, A., Dalla Bella, S., Phillips-Silver, J., Lebrun, M., and Peretz, I. (2010). Singing proficiency in congenital amusia: Imitation helps. *Cognitive Neuropsychology* 26: 463–476.

Watts, C., Moore, R., and McCaghren, K. (2005). The relationship between vocal pitch-matching skills and pitch discrimination skills in untrained accurate and inaccurate singers. *Journal of Voice* 19: 534–543.

Watts, C., Murphy, J., and Barnes-Burroughs, K. (2003). Pitch matching accuracy of trained singers, untrained subjects with talented singing voices, and untrained subjects with nontalented singing voices in conditions of varying feedback. *Journal of Voice* 17: 185–194.

Welch, G.F. (1979). Vocal range and poor pitch singing. *Psychology of Music* 7: 13–31.

Welch, G.F. (1985). A schema theory of how children learn to sing in tune. *Psychology of Music* 13: 3–17.

Welch, G.F. (1986). A developmental view of children's singing. *British Journal of Music Education* 3: 295–303.

Welch, G.F. (1998). Early childhood musical development. *Research Studies in Music Education* 11: 27–41.

Welch, G.F. (2005). Singing as Communication. In: D. Miell, R. MacDonald, and D.J. Hargreaves (eds), *Musical Communication*, pp. 239–259. Oxford: Oxford University Press.

Welch, G.F. (2009). Evidence of the development of vocal pitch matching ability in children. *Japanese Journal of Music Education Research* 39(1): 38–47.

Welch, G.F. and Murao, T. (1994). *Onchi and singing development: A cross-cultural perspective.* London: The Roehampton Institute/David Fulton Publishers Ltd.

Welch, G.F., Himonides, E., Saunders, J., Papageorgi, I., Vraka, M., Preti, C., and Sarazin, M. (In press). Children's singing behaviour and development in the context of "Sing Up," a national programme in England. *Music Perception.*

Whidden, C. (2010). Hearing the voice of non-singers: Culture, context, and connection. In: L.K. Thompson and M.R. Campbell (eds), *Issues of identity in music education: Narratives and practices*, pp. 83–107. Charlotte, NC: IAP Information Age Publishing.

Williamson, V.J. and Stewart, L. (2010). Memory for pitch in congenital amusia: Beyond a fine-grained pitch discrimination problem. *Memory* 18: 657–669.

Wise, K.J. (2009). *Understanding "tone deafness": A multi-componential analysis of perception, cognition, singing and self-perceptions in adults reporting musical difficulties.* PhD Thesis, Keele University. Available at: <http://ethos.bl.uk/OrderDetails.do?uin=uk.bl.ethos.502980>.

Wise, K.J. and Sloboda, J.A. (2008). Establishing an empirical profile of self-defined tone deafness: Perception, singing performance and self-assessment. *Musicae Scientiae* 12: 3–26.

Wolner, M. and Pyle, W.H. (1933). An experiment in individual training of pitch-deficient children. *Journal of Educational Psychology* 24 (8): 602–608.

Young, S. (2002). Young children's spontaneous vocalizations in free-play: Observations of two- to three-year-olds in a day-care setting. *Bulletin of the Council for Research in Music Education* 152: 43–53.

CHAPTER 17

VOCAL PERFORMANCE IN OCCASIONAL SINGERS

SIMONE DALLA BELLA

INTRODUCTION

A good deal of research and substantial work in pedagogy has been devoted to professional singing, and to the improvement of vocal technique for both teachers and students (Gabrielsson 1999; Parncutt and McPherson 2002). Basic processes, such as breath control and managing resonance, and more advanced techniques, such as those leading to vibrato and expression, are critical to reach the artistry and virtuosity typical of professional singers (e.g. Davids and LaTour 2012; Peckam 2010). Teaching programs aimed at improving these processes and techniques have measurable effects on the acoustics and on the quality of the singing voice. Starting from the seminal work of Johan Sundberg and collaborators (Sundberg 1987), there has been a growing body of evidence on the acoustical features of professional singing. For example, differences have been found between professional singers and non-singers in terms of voice quality (Sundberg 2013). Partials falling in the frequency range of 2.5–3.0 KHz (the so-called singer's formant; Sundberg 1987) are much stronger in sung vowels than in spoken vowels. Increase of the intensity of the singer's formant, the presence of vibrato, and the maximum phonational frequency range are markers of expertise (Brown et al. 2000; Larrouy-Maestri et al. 2014; Mendes et al. 2003). In spite of this general interest in the acoustics of the singing voice, only a few isolated studies have focused on the accuracy of pitch production in professional singers (Vurma and Ross 2006; Zurbriggen et al. 2006). For example, when professional singers are asked to produce pitch intervals, they can be out of tune by 20–25 cents, with respect to the equally tempered scale, an error that is typically neglected by listeners (Hutchins et al. 2012; Vurma and Ross 2006). In addition, features like the accuracy of the first note of the melody and melodic contour play a role in motor planning, as it has been observed when singers prepare to produce a melody (Zurbriggen et al. 2006).

The relative abundance of research on professional singing may lead one to think that singing is the privilege of a minority. Only a few individuals may be talented enough to undergo systematic vocal training and lessons. Moreover, it may be inferred that long-lasting and intensive training is mandatory to achieve proficient singing. These conclusions may lead to underestimating singing abilities in the majority. The layman, not used to receiving vocal training, may thus be treated as a poor singer when compared to professional vocalists. Interestingly, this view is quite widespread among non-musicians and reflects the fact that people generally tend to underestimate their ability to carry a tune. For example, based on a screening questionnaire administered to more than 1,000 students at the University of Texas in San Antonio, almost 60 percent of them reported that they could not accurately imitate melodies (Pfordresher and Brown 2007). In another study, about 17 percent of the student population self-defined as tone deaf (Cuddy et al. 2005). As a consequence, relatively little was known about singing abilities in the general population and there was a paucity of studies on "occasional singers" until about a decade ago. One of the goals of this chapter is to contrast the general belief that singing is a privilege of the few, and to build a case to show that occasional singing is widespread and that it represents a fruitful model to shed light on the cognitive and biological processes underlying singing.

Singing is one of the richest sources of information regarding the nature and origins of musical behavior. It emerges precociously and it is a universal and socially relevant activity (Mithen 2006). Singing is as natural as speaking for the majority (Dalla Bella and Berkowska 2009; Dalla Bella et al. 2007; Pfordresher and Brown 2007). It is likely that humans are hardwired for, for as early as a few months old, babies produce vocalizations that are likely to be the precursors of adult singing (Papoušek 1996). These first vocal productions emerge spontaneously by imitation of maternal singing (e.g. Trehub and Trainor 1999), and act as the building blocks of future singing skills (see also the chapter by Trehub and Gudmundsdottir in this volume). For example, by repeating short musical phrases, eighteen-month-old children start producing recognizable songs (e.g. Ostwald 1973). Based on these elementary examples of singing skills, vocal performance slowly develops over time thanks to exposure, spontaneous practice, and in some cases early musical tutoring (Welch 2006, for a review), toward the proficiency characteristic of adult performance (Berkowska and Dalla Bella 2013; Pfordresher et al. 2010). Finally, it is unlikely that singing has emerged as a cultural accident, an amusing "vocal cheesecake" crafted to tickle our auditory sensation (to rhyme Steven Pinker's comparison of music to "auditory cheesecake," intended to underline its biological uselessness; Pinker 1997). Rather, singing and vocalization, far from being a mere cultural frill, are likely to have played a role during evolution. For example, it can be observed across cultures that people enjoy singing in particular when acting in a group (e.g. during religious ceremonies, in the military). Because singing is inherently a participatory activity, it is thought to foster group bonding (see also the chapter by Davidson and Faulkner in this volume). Favoring group cohesion is one of the reasons, together with sexual selection and mood regulation, why music may have had some adaptive value during evolution (Huron 2001; Mithen 2006; Tarr et al. 2014; Wallin et al. 2000).

In sum, there is a strong motivation to examine singing abilities in the majority (i.e. occasional singers) as a way to shed light on a widespread and likely biologically rooted human ability. This chapter reviews experimental results obtained in the last decade on occasional singing in adults, coming from both experimental psychology and the neurosciences of music. It focuses first on the Song System, with a particular attention to the mechanisms supporting proficient singing in the majority and to their neuronal underpinnings. In this context, I mostly build on a schema referred to as the "Vocal Sensorimotor Loop" (VSL; Berkowska and Dalla Bella 2009a; Dalla Bella et al. 2011) which we proposed a few years ago, and which was further developed and integrated more recently by the inclusion of pitch information categorization (e.g. pitch classes based on tonality representation) and category-to-motor translations (Pfordresher et al. 2015). In the second part of the chapter I pay particular attention to the issues inherent in measuring singing proficiency in occasional singers (e.g. how to choose the appropriate metrics to define accurate and precise singing, and the cut-off criteria to qualify somebody as a good or a poor singer). Because the vast majority of studies have focused on the pitch dimension (though see, for example, Dalla Bella and Berkowska 2009; Dalla Bella et al. 2007, 2009), I will focus selectively on vocal production of pitch, without considering the time dimension. Although the question of poor singing abilities is inevitably raised throughout the chapter, the focus will remain on proficient singing (for a detailed discussion of poor singing and tone-deafness, see the chapter by Wise in this volume; for a discussion on intonation see the chapter by Sundberg, also in this volume; and for a discussion on the pedagogy of teaching "the non-singer," see the chapter by Knight in this volume).

The Song System

How singing works

The ability to sing proficiently is supported by physical mechanisms, which are governed by a complex and dedicated neural network (Berkowska and Dalla Bella 2009a; Brown et al. 2004; Zarate 2013). This is referred to as the "Song System." The lungs provide the air supply needed for vocalization; phonation is made possible by modulation by the vocal folds of the airstream coming from the lungs. The vocal tract conveys to sound the spectral and temporal features typical of sung voice (Sundberg 2013; Titze 1994). Thus, the core physical mechanisms of the Song System are respiratory, laryngeal (i.e. the vocal folds), and articulatory structures (i.e. the vocal tract). The coordination of these mechanisms is responsible for the quality of the vocal output, and allows us to distinguish a professional singer from an amateur or a novice (Sundberg 1987, 2013). In spite of their relevance for vocal performance, these physical components are not further described in the present chapter, which is more centered around the functional and neural mechanisms underlying the Song System (for reviews, see Doscher 1994; Titze 1994).

To describe the main functional mechanisms affording proficient singing I focus on an account we proposed to explain singing in tasks such as imitation (e.g. pitch- or melody-matching tasks), and singing from memory of a familiar melody (the Vocal Sensorimotor Loop—VSL; Berkowska and Dalla Bella 2009a; Dalla Bella et al. 2011; see also Zarate 2013). The purpose of the VSL is to identify the main processes in the Song System underlying pitch production during singing, and to lay out their connections. They include perceptual, motor, auditory-motor mapping, and memory components (see Figure 17.1). The role of these components can be elucidated by considering specific vocal tasks. The most common task is to sing a familiar melody from memory. To accomplish this task, the pitch information of

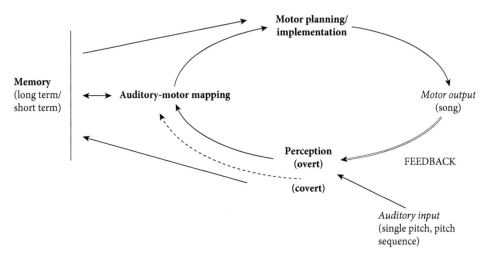

FIGURE 17.1 Schema of the Vocal Sensorimotor Loop (Berkowska and Dalla Bella 2009a; Dalla Bella et al. 2011).

Adapted from Dalla Bella (2015), with permission.

the melody to be sung, which is stored in long-term memory, is retrieved and sent to motor planning/implementation mechanisms. It is at this stage that instructions to implement a given articulatory program and commands eventually leading to phonation are executed. Note that the VSL is a typical closed-loop system, namely involving the analysis of the motor output which itself affects in real time the plan of future events in the melody. Feedback analysis, and in particular auditory-motor mapping, is a crucial aspect for accurate vocal performance (Pruitt and Pfordresher 2015). These processes allow the corrections of errors that can occur during vocal performance. Indeed, when the percept of the produced melody is compared to the memory representation of the intended melody (e.g. by referring to an inverse model of the auditory-vocal system; Pfordresher and Mantell 2014), a discrepancy is detected, and thereby the motor plan is subsequently modified. Similar processes are engaged during imitation of single pitches or of more complex sequences. Imitative tasks, however, rely more heavily on working memory and less on long-term memory than singing from memory. The VSL is underpinned by a complex neuronal network which has been detailed elsewhere (Brown et al. 2004; Dalla Bella et al. 2011; Pfordresher et al. 2015; Zarate 2013), including sensory areas (e.g. the superior temporal gyrus/sulcus), motor areas (e.g. primary motor cortex and the Supplementary Motor Area), and auditory-motor integration regions (e.g. area SPT, cortex of the dorsal Sylvian fissure at the parietal-temporal junction; Pa and Hickok 2008) (more information may be found in the chapter on the neuroscience of singing by Kleber and Zarate in this volume). An understanding of the functional and neuronal architecture of the Song System is critical for explaining poor-pitch singing. This condition can result from the disruption of one or a few components of the VSL, due to a brain insult (Ackermann et al. 2006; Berkowska and Dalla Bella 2009a; Gordon et al. 2006; Marin and Perry 1999; Stewart et al. 2009) or neurogenetic (i.e. congenital) disorders (Ayotte et al. 2002; Dalla Bella et al. 2009; Dalla Bella et al. 2011). Different sources of impairment can lead to poor singing such as impaired perception, poor motor control, sensorimotor mapping errors, or inefficient memory retrieval (Dalla Bella et al. 2011, 2012; Hutchins and Peretz 2012; Pfordresher and Brown 2007).

One peculiarity of the VSL is that it includes two parallel pathways for pitch perception. The overt pathway is engaged in those tasks where explicit judgments of pitch differences are demanded, such as in pitch discrimination tasks, or same–different tasks with melodic material. The covert pathway accounts for cases in which singers, in spite of being very inaccurate in judging pitch differences, do still exhibit proficient singing (Dalla Bella et al. 2009; Griffiths 2008; Loui et al. 2008). This condition is possible only under the assumption that pitch differences can be computed covertly by a separate mechanism. More recently (Zarate 2013), overt and covert pathways have been more specifically associated with dedicated neuronal substrates based on neuroimaging evidence (Zarate and Zatorre 2008; Zarate et al. 2010). The covert pathway is linked to the activity of the auditory cortex and of the inferior frontal gyrus, while the overt pathway involves the auditory cortex, the intraparietal sulcus, the anterior insula, the anterior cingulate cortex, and the dorsal premotor cortex.

In a recent schema of the functional architecture underlying singing accuracy (Pfordresher et al. 2015) the components of the VSL are integrated with another proposal (the Linked Dual Representation Model; Hutchins and Moreno 2013). The proposal by Pfordresher and collaborators, an outcome of the Seattle International Singing Research Symposium (17–19 October 2013, Seattle), underscores the link between more fundamental sensorimotor processes and higher-level categorization mechanisms involving long-term memory representations, which were only vaguely indicated in the VSL.

Singing accuracy and precision in occasional singers

During the last decade a few studies have been devoted to quantifying singing proficiency in occasional singers (for a review, see Dalla Bella et al. 2011). I focus here on evidence from studies where vocal performance was analyzed with quantitative acoustically-based methods (e.g. Dalla Bella et al. 2007, 2009; Murayama et al. 2004; Pfordresher et al. 2010; Terao et al. 2006). Acoustic analyses of vocal renditions yield metrics of singing proficiency in terms of both accuracy (i.e. the difference between the sung and target pitches or intervals), and precision (i.e. consistency in repeating the same pitch or interval) (Berkowska and Dalla Bella 2013; Dalla Bella 2015; Pfordresher et al. 2010).

A variety of tasks can be used to test singing proficiency. A common task, which can be easily mastered by occasional singers, is to sing a well-known song (e.g. "Happy birthday" or "Brother John") with lyrics from memory (Berkowska and Dalla Bella 2013; Dalla Bella et al. 2007, 2009). Differences can be observed when the singing of a melody is performed with lyrics or on a syllable, with the last condition typically favoring better performance (Berkowska and Dalla Bella 2009b, 2013). Another possibility is to use imitation of a single pitch, an interval, or a short novel melody, using a vowel or a syllable (pitch matching). Single-pitch matching is quite widespread (Goetze et al. 1990; Hutchins et al. 2010; Pfordresher and Brown 2007), and is treated as a core task for assessing musical talent (Watts et al. 2003). However, imitation of melodic patterns as opposed to simpler patterns or individual pitches is also a quite common task (Berkowska and Dalla Bella 2013; Pfordresher and Brown 2007; Rutkowski 1990; Rutkowski and Miller 2003). A variant of these tasks consists in presenting additional auditory feedback, when during the imitation of a pitch sequence the correct pitch or melody are delivered as one sings (Pfordresher and Brown 2007; Tremblay-Champoux et al. 2010).

Although one may be tempted to choose one of these tasks as ideal to assess singing proficiency, different tasks are likely to reflect the activity of partly independent components of the Song System. Melody imitation in the presence of augmented feedback, or singing on a syllable of a well-known song, put less demands on memory as compared to imitation of novel pitch sequences. Thus, depending on singing skills, occasional singers variably perform on different tasks (Berkowska and Dalla Bella 2013). If the goal is thus to obtain a thorough profile of singing abilities, especially in occasional singers, where there are important individual differences, the use of a rich set of tasks is highly advised (for a discussion, see Dalla Bella 2015). This approach has been adopted in recent studies, in which batteries of tests have been proposed such as the Sung Performance Battery, which includes tasks ranging from single-pitch matching to imitation and production from memory of complex pitch sequences (Berkowska and Dalla Bella 2013), and the Seattle Singing Accuracy Protocol (SSAP; Demorest et al. 2015), which includes a smaller set of core tasks.

First reports of singing accuracy (i.e. the discrepancy between the produced and the target pitch or interval) in occasional singers suggested that around 85–90 percent of the general population can sing in tune (Dalla Bella and Berkowska 2009; Dalla Bella et al. 2007; Pfordresher and Brown 2007). In one of the first studies, for example, we tested singing proficiency of a group of sixty-two occasional singers in Montreal (twenty university students tested in the lab, and forty-two participants recruited in a public park). Their performance was compared to that of four professional singers (Dalla Bella et al. 2007). Participants sang the chorus of a well-known song with lyrics. Occasional singers were less accurate in producing pitch intervals (average deviation from the correct intervals: 0.6 semitones) than professional singers (deviation of 0.3 semitones). Interestingly, occasional singers typically sing faster than professionals, a phenomenon linked to lower pitch accuracy. Reducing performance tempo had a positive effect on the performance (i.e. it increased pitch accuracy) in most of the cases. The finding that the majority can sing in tune has been confirmed by further studies, where singing from memory and imitation were compared (Berkowska and Dalla Bella 2009b, 2013; Dalla Bella and Berkowska 2009). Note, however, that the number of proficient singers can vary as a function of the measure of singing proficiency and also as a function of the task. For example, when considering pitch precision (i.e. the consistency of repeated attempts to produce a pitch) instead of accuracy, the percentage of proficient singers decreases to about 45 percent (Pfordresher et al. 2010), a value which varies as a function of the tasks and of the pitch dimension taken into account (e.g. intervals vs. pitch height, Berkowska and Dalla Bella 2013; Dalla Bella 2015). This finding suggests that precision may be considered for judging our own performance instead of accuracy. This possibility may account for the very high percentage of individuals self-reporting that they are poor singers.

Other studies targeted vocal imitation abilities. Poor performance was initially observed in single-pitch matching (Amir et al. 2003; Murbe et al. 2002; Ternström et al. 1988). Non-musicians typically deviate by 1.3 semitones on average as compared to 0.5 semitones for musicians (Amir et al. 2003; Murry 1990; Murry and Zwiner 1991; Ternström et al. 1988). More recent studies indicated, though, that low accuracy in imitating pitch does not characterize all individuals without musical training (Estis et al. 2009). Morever, poorer performance in non-musicians may partly result from using pure tones as models for imitation. Imitation of synthesized voices or sung performances led to higher accuracy, with pitch deviations of 0.5 semitones or less (Pfordresher and Brown 2007; Wise and Sloboda 2008; see also Berkowska and Dalla Bella 2013; Watts and Hall 2008). It follows that accuracy in pitch matching depends on the acoustic features of the stimulus to be imitated, showing a general advantage for the human model (Granot et al. 2013; Lévêque et al. 2012). Target stimuli which share acoustical properties with the vocal production are particularly well-suited to facilitate mapping onto sensorimotor representations, thus favoring higher accuracy.

The imitation of stimuli of increasing complexity (i.e. from single pitches to short novel melodies) has been assessed systematically more recently (Berkowska and Dalla Bella 2013; Pfordresher and Brown 2007; Pfordresher et al. 2010). For example, Pfordresher and Brown (2007) asked a large sample of university students without musical training to imitate various pitch sequences (i.e. a single repeated note, a sequence including a single change of pitch, and short four-note melodies). Most of them imitated sequences with renditions within one semitone from the target pitches. Yet they were less accurate when they imitated short melodies as compared to single pitches (as in Wise and Sloboda 2008; but see Berkowska and Dalla Bella 2013). That most occasional singers are quite accurate in imitating short unfamiliar melodies was replicated by Pfordresher et al. (2010). Nevertheless, it was found that the majority was imprecise (i.e. the standard deviation of the fundamental frequency for renditions of the same pitch class or interval exceeded one semitone). More recently, the distinction between precision and accuracy in imitation tasks as well as in singing from memory tasks has been addressed with the Sung Performance Battery (SPB; Berkowska and Dalla Bella 2013; see also Dalla Bella 2015). A group of fifty occasional singers tested with the SPB provided measures of accuracy and precision on a set of five tasks, based on the ability to reproduce target pitches (i.e. absolute pitch) or target intervals (i.e. relative pitch) presented isolately, or in the context of novel and familiar melodies. Occasional singers were more accurate and precise when imitating or reproducing from memory well-known songs than when imitating target pitches, intervals, or short novel melodies (as in Pfordresher et al. 2010). In addition, occasional singers were systematically more accurate and more precise when singing well-known melodies on a syllable than with lyrics. This finding may result from reduced linguistic memory load when singing on a syllable or to rhythmic factors due to the regularization effect of repeating the same linguistic unit (Berkowska and Dalla Bella 2009b; see also Dalla Bella et al. 2012). Note that rhythmic processing may mediate vocal performance on the pitch dimension. Better performance in a rhythmic task, such as moving to the beat of an auditory stimulus, and low rhythmic variability during singing are associated to greater singing proficiency on the pitch dimension (Dalla Bella et al. 2015).

To summarize, systematic assessments of singing accuracy and precision in occasional singers reveal that the majority is accurate across a variety of tasks. Accuracy decreases with increasing sequence length and complexity, and when the pitch material is not familiar. Even though occasional singers are quite accurate in imitating pitches, however, they may still be not very consistent over repetitions.

Measuring singing proficiency
in occasional singers: present
methodological challenges

Even though we have witnessed an increase in interest and quantitative research on singing abilities in occasional singers, there are a few challenges that deserve particular attention. Here I will focus on two methodological issues that hinder the measurement of singing proficiency and the qualification of an individual as a good or poor singer. Even when singing proficiency is measured based on acoustic methods, a panoply of metrics can be extracted from the recorded signal (e.g. pitch interval deviation, signed note error, absolute note error, note accuracy and precision, interval accuracy and precision, contour errors, pitch errors, and so forth; Dalla Bella et al. 2007; Pfordresher and Brown 2007; Pfordresher et al. 2010). Because of the diversity of metrics, there is little agreement on the measures that allow one to characterize an individual's singing abilities. Another issue concerns the criterion to adopt for teasing apart poor from good singers (Berkowska and Dalla Bella 2013; Dalla Bella 2015). For example, participants are considered to be proficient singers if their productions do not deviate from a target pitch (e.g. in a pitch-matching task) by more than a fixed value (e.g. one semitone or a quarter of tone), or by a relative criterion (e.g. with regard to a comparison group) (for a discussion, see Dalla Bella 2015). Again, there is little consensus about this criterion. These two issues are addressed in turn below.

Metrics of singing proficiency

Measures of singing proficiency based on acoustical analyses of vocal performance can be organized, for simplicity, in terms of absolute pitch (i.e. absolute difference in pitch height) and relative pitch (i.e. interval difference) metrics (see Dalla Bella 2015). Absolute pitch metrics are, for example, the mean signed note error or the mean absolute note error (Berkowska and Dalla Bella 2013; Hutchins et al. 2010; Pfordresher and Brown 2007; Pfordresher et al. 2010). The difference between the two metrics is that only the first reflects the direction of the error (i.e. whether the produced note was higher or lower than a model). Relative pitch metrics are based on the difference between two subsequent pitches (i.e. sung interval) relative to the interval in the notation, such as the absolute pitch interval error (e.g. Pfordresher and Brown 2007; Pfordresher et al. 2010; see also pitch interval deviation; Dalla Bella and Berkowska 2009; Dalla Bella et al. 2007, 2009). The aforementioned metrics vary on a continuum, expressed in cents or in semitones. More discrete measures of errors can also be computed such as the number of interval errors, defined based on a given criterion (e.g. interval departing from the target interval by more than 1 semitone), and the number of contour deviations (e.g. Dalla Bella et al. 2007, 2009). Finally, measures of accuracy and precision can be calculated for absolute and relative pitch metrics (for equations, see Berkowska and Dalla Bella 2013; Pfordresher et al. 2010; see also Dalla Bella 2015), thus providing a multidimensional profile of singing abilities.

Due to the diversity of metrics that are indicators of singing proficiency, there is little agreement on the measures of singing performance. Low pitch accuracy has been treated as an indicator of poor-pitch singing (Dalla Bella et al. 2007; Pfordresher and Brown 2007; Pfordresher et al. 2010). However, considering this metric in isolation may lead to overestimating singing proficiency, because the prevalence of poor-pitch singing is higher when considering precision instead of accuracy (Pfordresher et al. 2010). Indeed, different metrics (i.e. accuracy vs. precision, in terms of absolute or relative pitch) can lead to discordant assessments of singing proficiency and the prevalence of poor-pitch singing. This problem can be circumvented by adopting a set of metrics based on accuracy and precision, estimated in terms of both absolute and relative pitch, as a way to obtain a thorough profile of singing abilities (Dalla Bella 2015; see also Berkowska and Dalla Bella 2013). These metrics have the advantage that they can be applied to different tasks, including imitation and singing from memory tasks, thus allowing between-task comparisons.

Criteria for telling apart good and poor singers

A second issue pertains to the choice of a cut-off score to determine if a performance is typical of a good or a poor singer. The criterion can be absolute or relative. An absolute criterion applies when a production deviates on average from a target pitch (e.g. in a pitch-matching task) by more than a fixed value. Cut-off values can range from one semitone (100 cents = one-twelfth of an octave; e.g. Berkowska and Dalla Bella 2013; Pfordresher and Brown 2007; Pfordresher et al. 2010), to a quarter of a tone (50 cents; Berkowska and Dalla Bella 2013; Demorest and Clements 2007; Hutchins and Peretz 2012; Hutchins et al. 2012). The semitone cut-off is motivated by the fact that this interval is the smallest pitch difference between two subsequent tones in Western music. However, because the acceptable range of performance around the target pitch is 200 cent (e.g. see Hutchins et al. 2012), this criterion may lead one to qualify as good singers individuals who are poor-pitch singers. The more stringent 50-cent cut-off is thus proposed, which corresponds to the acceptability threshold for sung tones to be considered in tune (Hutchins et al. 2012).

Even though a fixed criterion may appear as uncontroversial, it does not do justice to the fact that norms for singing proficiency likely depend on the tested group (e.g. musicians vs. non-musicians, individuals with vocal training vs. without training, adults vs. children). For example, on average a musician with vocal training is likely to exhibit higher singing accuracy than a non-musician (Dalla Bella et al. 2007). To determine if a musician or a non-musician is a good or poor singer, different standards should be adopted. Hence, a criterion to determine singing proficiency should vary for different population groups (i.e. it should be a relative criterion). In addition, average singing accuracy and precision are affected by task factors (with worse performance in imitation tasks than singing from memory, Berkowska and Dalla Bella 2013). With a variable criterion the performance of an occasional singer is compared to that of a comparison group. A variable cut-off value can correspond to two Standard Deviations from the average of a comparison group (e.g. Berkowska and Dalla Bella 2013; Dalla Bella and Berkowska 2009). Assuming that measures of singing accuracy and precision are normally distributed, this procedure limits the incidence of poor-pitch singing to a constant percentage of individuals showing particularly poor performances.

There is currently no agreement as to whether singing proficiency in occasional singers should be assessed with an absolute or a relative criterion. It is obvious that the same performance may score as "in the normal range" with a tolerant criterion (e.g. a variable cut-off), while it will fall beyond a more stringent cut-off (e.g. 50 cents) and accordingly treated as "poor-pitch singing." The effect of different cut-offs on the assessment of good and poor-pitch singing was recently examined in fifty occasional singers with the SPB (Berkowska and Dalla Bella 2013). Three cut-offs were compared, namely two fixed (100 and 50 cents) and one relative criterion (2 SD from the average of the group). The 50-cent criterion is definitely too stringent, leading to estimates of poor-pitch singing up to 60–80 percent of the tested sample of participants. A lower incidence of poor-pitch singing is naturally observed with the 100-cent cut-off. This criterion, however, enables the identification of very few poor-pitch singers based on relative pitch. Notably, the incidence of poor-pitch singing varies as a function of the task and metrics. The variable cut-off provides a more realistic estimate of poor-pitch singing, with an incidence of 28 percent across tasks and metrics. This criterion, in addition, is well suited to uncovering individual differences among poor-pitch singers. Because of these advantages, the variable cut-off relative to a given normative population is preferred over a fixed criterion (see Dalla Bella 2015, for further discussion).

Conclusions

The majority of individuals without musical training, defined here as occasional singers, have been the object of a growing number of studies during the last decade. There is converging evidence that most occasional singers can sing accurately, although they may display low precision. Hence, proficient singing is widespread in the general population and not confined to a small group who received vocal training. Singing in tune is underpinned by functional and neuronal architectures that emerge naturally during development and engage processes ranging from auditory perception, sensorimotor integration, motor planning, and memory. These mechanisms must be functional in order to support accurate and precise singing, an ability that manifests itself across a variety of tasks and using measures issued from acoustic analysis of sung renditions. The malfunctioning of at least one of these mechanisms leads to poor singing. Identifying the origin of poor singing in the architecture of the Song System (i.e. the locus of impairment) is an important step to explaining individual differences among occasional singers. Moreover, it may play a critical role for devising remediation strategies which are theory-driven, and targeted to a particular component within the Song System (e.g. Anderson et al. 2012; Tremblay-Champoux et al. 2010).

This endeavor is not free from methodological challenges, though. Two of them concern the quantitative measures of singing accuracy and precision, and the choice of a criterion to tease apart poor from good singers. Because poor-pitch singing is a rich and multifaceted phenomenon, its assessment cannot be confined to a single task, and to the use of a single measure or criterion of singing proficiency. I suggest that the assessment of singing abilities should be based on a variety of tasks aimed at targeting the different components of the Song System and with the same set of metrics (e.g. accuracy and precision). The choice of the cut-off criterion is also critical to telling the difference between a poor and a good singer. I expressed a preference for a relative criterion (e.g. 2 SD from the average of a normative group), which takes into account both group and task factors. This multidimensional approach to singing abilities provides a detailed profile for an individual's singing abilities, and paves the way for individualized remediation strategies for poor-pitch singing.

References

Ackermann, H., Wildgruber, D., and Riecker, A. (2006). "Singing in the brain" cerebral correlates. In: E. Altenmüller, M. Wiesendanger, and J. Kesselring (eds), *Music, Motor Control and the Brain*, pp. 205–222. Oxford: Oxford University Press.

Amir, O., Amir, N., and Kishon-Rabin, L. (2003). The effect of superior auditory skills on vocal accuracy. *Journal of the Acoustical Society of America* 113(2): 1102–1108.

Anderson, S., Himonides, E., Wise, K., Welch, G., and Stewart, L. (2012). Is there potential for learning in amusia? A study of the effect of singing intervention in congenital amusia. *Annals of the New York Academy of Sciences* 1252: 345–353.

Ayotte, J., Peretz, I., and Hyde, K. (2002). Congenital amusia: a group study of adults afflicted with a music-specific disorder. *Brain* 125(2): 238–251.

Berkowska, M. and Dalla Bella, S. (2009a). Acquired and congenital disorders of sung performance: a review. *Advances in Cognitive Psychology* 5: 69–83.

Berkowska, M. and Dalla Bella, S. (2009b). Reducing linguistic information enhances singing proficiency in occasional singers. *Annals of the New York Academy of Sciences* 1169: 108–111.

Berkowska, M. and Dalla Bella, S. (2013). Uncovering phenotypes of poor-pitch singing: the Sung Performance Battery (SPB). *Frontiers in Psychology* 4: 714.

Brown, W.S., Jr., Rothman, H.B., and Sapienza, C. (2000). Perceptual and acoustic study of professionally trained versus untrained voices. *Journal of Voice* 14: 301–309.

Brown, S., Martinez, M.J., Hodges, D.A., Fox, P.R., and Parsons, L.M. (2004). The song system of the human brain. *Cognitive Brain Research* 20: 363–375.

Cuddy, L.L., Balkwill, L-L., Peretz, I., and Holden, R.R. (2005). Musical difficulties are rare: a study of "tone deafness" among university students. *Annals of the New York Academy of Sciences* 1060: 311–324.

Dalla Bella, S., Giguère, J-F., and Peretz, I. (2007). Singing proficiency in the general population. *Journal of the Acoustical Society of America* 121: 1182–1189.

Dalla Bella, S. and Berkowska, M. (2009). Singing proficiency in the majority: Normality and phenotypes of poor singing. *Annals of the New York Academy of Sciences* 1169: 99–107.

Dalla Bella, S., Giguère, J-F., and Peretz, I. (2009). Singing in congenital amusia. *Journal of the Acoustical Society of America* 126(1): 414–424.

Dalla Bella, S., Berkowska, M., and Sowiński, J. (2011). Disorders of pitch production in tone deafness. *Frontiers in Psychology* 2: 164.

Dalla Bella, S., Tremblay-Champoux, A., Berkowska, M., and Peretz, I. (2012). Memory disorders and vocal performance. *Annals of the New York Academy of Sciences* 1252: 338–344.

Dalla Bella, S., Berkowska, M., and Sowiński, J. (2015). Moving to the beat and singing are linked in humans. *Frontiers in Human Neuroscience* 9: 663.

Dalla Bella, S. (2015). Defining poor-pitch singing: a problem of measurement and sensitivity. *Music Perception* 32(3): 272–282.

Davids, J. and LaTour, S. (2012). *Vocal Technique: A Guide for Conductors, Teachers, and Singers.* Long Grove, IL: Waveland Press.

Demorest, S.M. and Clements, A. (2007). Factors influencing the pitch-matching of junior high boys. *Journal of Research in Music Education* 55(3): 190–203.

Demorest, S.M., Pfordresher, P.Q., Dalla Bella, S., Hutchins, S., Loui, P., Rutkowski, J., and Welch, G.F. (2015). Methodological perspectives on singing accuracy: an introduction to the special issue on singing accuracy (Part 2). *Music Perception* 32(3): 266–271.

Doscher, B.M. (1994). *The Functional Unity of the Singing Voice*. London: Scarecrow Press.

Estis, J.M., Coblentz, J.K., and Moore, R.E. (2009). Effects of increasing time delays on pitch-matching accuracy in trained singers and untrained individuals. *Journal of Voice* 23(4): 439–445.

Gabrielsson, A. (1999). The performance of music. In: D. Deutsch (ed.), *The Psychology of Music*, pp. 501–602. San Diego: Academic Press.

Goetze, M., Cooper, N., and Brown, C.J. (1990). Recent research on singing in the general music classroom. *Bulletin of the Council Research in Music Education* 104: 16–37.

Gordon, R.L., Racette, A., and Schön, D. (2006). Sensory-motor networks in singing and speaking: a comparative approach. In: E. Altenmüller, M. Wiesendanger, and J. Kesselring (eds), *Music, Motor Control and the Brain*, pp. 205–222. Oxford: Oxford University Press.

Granot, R.Y., Israel-Kolatt, R., Gilboa, A., and Kolatt, T. (2013). Accuracy of pitch matching significantly improved by live voice model. *Journal of Voice* 27(3): 390.e13–20.

Griffiths, T.D. (2008). Sensory systems: auditory action streams? *Current Biology* 18(9): 387–388.

Huron, D. (2001). Is music an evolutionary adaptation? *Annals of the New York Academy of Sciences* 930: 43–61.

Hutchins, S., Zarate, J.M., Zatorre, R.J., and Peretz, I. (2010). An acoustical study of vocal pitch matching in congenital amusia. *Journal of the Acoustical Society of America* 127(1): 504–512.

Hutchins, S. and Peretz, I. (2012). A frog in your throat or in your ear? Searching for the causes of poor singing. *Journal of Experimental Psychology: General* 141(1): 76–97.

Hutchins, S., Roquet, C., and Peretz, I. (2012). The vocal generosity effect: How bad can your singing be? *Music Perception* 30(2): 147–159.

Hutchins, S. and Moreno, S. (2013). The Linked Dual Representation model of vocal perception and production. *Frontiers in Psychology* 4: 825.

Larrouy-Maestri, P., Magis, D., and Morsomme, D. (2014). Effects of melody and technique on acoustical and musical features of western operatic singing voices. *Journal of Voice* 28(3): 332–340.

Lévêque, Y., Giovanni, A., and Schön, D. (2012). Pitch-matching in poor singers: human model advantage. *Journal of Voice* 26(3): 293–298.

Loui, P., Guenther, F., Mathys, C., and Schlaug, G. (2008). Action-perception mismatch in tone-deafness. *Current Biology* 18(8): 331–332.

Marin, O.S.M. and Perry, D.W. (1999). Neurological aspects of music perception and performance. In: D. Deutsch (ed.), *Psychology of Music*, pp. 653–724. San Diego: Academic Press.

Mendes, A.P., Rothman, H.B., Sapienza, C., and Brown, W.S. Jr. (2003). Effects of vocal training on the acoustic parameters of the singing voice. *Journal of Voice* 17: 529–543.

Mithen, S. (2006). *The Singing Neanderthals*. Cambridge, MA: Harvard University Press.

Murayama, J., Kashiwagi, T., Kashiwagi, A., and Mimura, M. (2004). Impaired pitch production and preserved rhythm production in a right brain-damaged patient with amusia. *Brain and Cognition* 56: 36–42.

Murbe, D., Pabst, F., Hofmann, G., and Sundberg, J. (2002). Significance of auditory and kinesthetic feedback to singers' pitch control. *Journal of Voice* 16: 44–51.

Murry, T. (1990). Pitch-matching accuracy in singers and nonsingers. *Journal of Voice* 4: 317–321.

Murry, T. and Zwiner, P. (1991). Pitch matching ability of experienced and inexperienced singers. *Journal of Voice* 5: 197–202.

Ostwald, P.F. (1973). Musical behavior in early childhood. *Developmental Medicine and Child Neurology* 15: 367–375.

Pa, J. and Hickok, G. (2008). A parietal-temporal sensory-motor integration area for the human vocal tract: evidence from an fMRI study of skilled musicians. *Neuropsychologia* 46(1): 362–368.

Papoušek, H. (1996). Musicality in infancy research: biological and cultural origins of early musicality. In: I. Deliège and J. Sloboda (eds), *Musical Beginnings*, pp. 37–55. Oxford: Oxford University Press.

Parncutt, R. and McPherson, G.E. (2002). *The Science and Psychology of Music Performance: Creative Strategies for Teaching and Learning*. New York: Oxford University Press.

Peckam, A. (2010). *The Contemporary Singer: Elements of Vocal Technique*. Boston: Berklee Press.

Pfordresher, P.Q. and Brown, S. (2007). Poor-pitch singing in the absence of "tone-deafness." *Music Perception* 25: 95–115.

Pfordresher, P.Q., Brown, S., Meier, K.M., Belyk, M., and Liotti, M. (2010). Imprecise singing is widespread. *Journal of the Acoustical Society of America* 128(4): 2182–2190.

Pfordresher, P.Q. and Mantell, J.T. (2014). Singing with yourself: evidence for an inverse modeling account of poor-pitch singing. *Cognitive Psychology* 70: 31–57.

Pfordresher, P.Q., Demorest, S.M., Dalla Bella, S., Hutchins, S., Loui, P., Rutkowski, J., and Welch, G.F. (2015). Theoretical perspectives on singing accuracy: An introduction to the special issue on singing accuracy (Part 1). *Music Perception* 32(3): 227–231.

Pinker, S. (1997). *How the Mind Works*. New York: Norton.

Pruitt, T.A. and Pfordresher, P.Q. (2015). The role of auditory feedback in speech and song. *Journal of Experimental Psychology: Human Perception and Performance* 41(1): 152–166.

Rutkowski, J. (1990). The measurement and evaluation of children's singing voice development. *The Quarterly: Center for Research in Music Learning and Teaching* 1(1–2): 81–95.

Rutkowski, J. and Miller, M.S. (2003). The effect of teacher feedback and modeling on first graders' use of singing voice and developmental music aptitude. *Bulletin of the Council for Research in Music Education* 156: 1–10.

Stewart, L., von Kriegstein, K., Dalla Bella, S., Warren, J.D., and Griffiths, T.D. (2009). Disorders of musical cognition. In: S. Hallam, I. Cross, and M. Thaut (eds), *Oxford Handbook of Music Psychology*, pp. 184–196. New York: Oxford University Press.

Sundberg, J. (1987). *The Science of the Singing Voice*. DeKalb, IL: Northern Illinois University Press.

Sundberg, J. (2013). The perception of singing. In: D. Deutsch (ed.), *Psychology of Music*, 3rd edn, pp. 69–105. San Diego: Academic Press.

Tarr, B., Launay, J., and Dunbar, R.I.M. (2014). Music and social bonding: "self-other" merging and neuro-hormonal mechanisms. *Frontiers in Psychology* 5: 1096.

Terao, Y., Mizuno, T., Shindoh, M, Sakurai, Y., Ugawa, Y., Kobayashi, S., Nagai, C., Furubayashi, T., Arai, N., Okabe, S., Mochizuki, H., Hanajima, R., and Tsuji, S. (2006). Vocal amusia in a professional tango singer due to a right superior temporal cortex infarction. *Neuropsychologia* 44(3): 479–488.

Ternström, S., Sundberg, J., and Collden, A. (1988). Articulatory f_0 perturbations and auditory feedback. *Journal of Speech and Hearing Research* 31: 187–192.

Titze, I.R. (1994). *Principles of Voice Production*. Englewood Cliffs, NJ: Prentice Hall.

Tremblay-Champoux, A., Dalla Bella, S., Phillips-Silver, J., Lebrun, M-A., and Peretz, I. (2010). Singing proficiency in congenital amusia: Imitation helps. *Cognitive Neuropsychology* 27(6): 463–476.

Trehub, S.E. and Trainor, L.J. (1999). Singing to infants: lullabies and play songs. *Advances in Infancy Research* 12: 43–77.

Vurma, A. and Ross, J. (2006). Production and perception of musical intervals. *Music Perception* 23(4): 331–344.

Wallin, N.L., Merker, B., and Brown, S. (2000). *The Origins of Music*. Cambridge, MA: MIT Press.

Watts, C., Murphy, J., and Barnes-Burroughs, K. (2003). Pitch-matching accuracy of trained singers, untrained participants with talented singing voices, and untrained participants with non-talented singing voices in conditions of varying feedback. *Journal of Voice* 17: 187–196.

Watts, C.R. and Hall, M.D. (2008). Timbral differences on vocal pitch-matching accuracy. *Logopedics Phoniatrics Vocology* 33: 74–82.

Welch, G.F. (2006). Singing and vocal development. In: G. McPherson (ed.), *The Child as Musician: A Handbook of Musical Development*, pp. 311–329. New York: Oxford University Press.

Wise, K.J. and Sloboda, J.A. (2008). Establishing an empirical profile of self-defined "tone deafness": perception, singing performance and self-assessment. *Musicae Scientiae* 12: 3–23.

Zarate, J.M. and Zatorre, R.J. (2008). Experience-related neural substrates involved in vocal pitch regulation during singing. *Neuro Image* 40: 1871–1887.

Zarate, J.M., Wood, S., and Zatorre, R.J. (2010). Neural networks involved in voluntary and involuntary vocal pitch regulation in experienced singers. *Neuropsychologia* 48(2): 1871–1887.

Zarate, J.M. (2013). The neural control of singing. *Frontiers in Human Neuroscience* 7: 237.

Zurbriggen, E.L., Fontenot, D.L., and Meyer, D.E. (2006). Representation and execution of vocal motor programs for expert singing of tonal melodies. *Journal of Experimental Psychology. Human Perception and Performance* 32(4): 944–963.

CHAPTER 18

SINGING AS INTER- AND INTRA-PERSONAL COMMUNICATION

GRAHAM F. WELCH AND COSTANZA PRETI

INTRODUCTION: THE SIGNIFICANCE OF VOICE IN THE ONTOGENY OF COMMUNICATION

VOCAL sound is one of the defining features of humanity.[1] Its commonality, plurality, and development distinguish the species. Within the wide range of sounds that humans make with their voices, there are two constellations that have the greatest socio-cultural significance: these are categorized as speech and singing. However, there is a significant overlap between the two because both sets of behaviors are generated from the same anatomical and physiological structures and initiated/interpreted by dedicated neuropsychobiological networks whose development and function are shaped by cultural experience.

Our predisposition to perceive particular vocal sounds as singing or speech is dependent on the dominant acoustic features, as well as experience. Perception begins when the sensory system is stimulated by acoustic information that is filtered according to principles of perceptual organization which group the sounds together according to key features, such as pitch range, temporal proximity, similarity of timbre, and harmonic relationships (Patel 2008).

The perception of sounds as music or language is contextualized by the listener's age, family, community membership, enculturation, and development. The first few months of life, for example, are often characterized by vocal play ("euphonic cooing," Papoušek, H. 1996) in which the growing infant's vocalizations could be interpreted as musical *glissandi*, as well as the precursors of prosody in speech. Such categorical perceptions of vocal sound as

[1] This is an updated and fully revised version of a chapter originally published as Welch, G.F. (2005). Singing as Communication. In: D. Miell, R. MacDonald, and D. Hargreaves (eds), *Musical Communication*, pp. 239–259. New York: Oxford University Press. doi:10.1093/acprof:oso/9780198529361.003.0011

being either "musical" or "speech(like)," however, are a product of the layers of enculturation that inform our socially constructed interpretations.

To the developing infant, any such distinction is relatively meaningless, because speech and singing have a common ontogeny. As far as sound *production* is concerned, infant vocal behaviors are constrained by the limited structures and behavioral possibilities of the developing vocal system (Kreiman and Sidtis 2011). The first vocalizations are related to the communication of an affective state, initially discomfort and distress (crying), followed by sounds of comfort and eustress (positive moods). The predisposition to generate vocal sounds that have quasi-melodic features first emerges around the age of two to four months (Stark et al. 1993), with increasing evidence of control during the three months that follow (Vihman 1996). These pre-linguistic infant vocalizations are characterized by a voluntary modulation and management of pitch that emulates the predominant prosodic characteristics of the mother tongue (Flax et al. 1991; Mampe et al. 2009), while also exploring rhythmic syllabic sequences with superimposed melodies and short musical patterns (Papoušek, H. 1996); for a comprehensive review on prenatal and early musical development see Parncutt (2016).

With regard to sound *reception*, hearing is normally functioning before birth in the final trimester of pregnancy (Kisilevsky et al. 2004) and the newborn enters the world capable of perceiving tiny differences in voiced sound (Trainor and Zatorre 2016). Infants are "universalists" (Trehub 2016) in the sense that they are perceptually equipped to make sense of the musics and languages of any culture. This predisposition will lead developmentally to the discrimination of vowel categories and consonantal contrasts in the native language by the end of the first year (Escudero et al. 2014). During these initial 12 months of life, it is the prosodic (pitch and rhythm) features of "infant-directed" speech (also known as "motherese" or "parentese" (Saint-Georges et al 2013; Werker and McLeod 1989)) that dominate early communication from parent/caregiver to child (Fernald and Kuhl 1987; Papoušek, H. 1996). The prosodic envelopes that define spoken phrases are thought to be essential perceptual building blocks in the infant's developing comprehension of language (Kreiner and Eviatar 2014).

The mother's infant-focused utterances are also typified by having a regulation of pulse, vocal quality, and narrative form, theorized collectively as a "communicative musicality" (Malloch 2000) that engages with an "intrinsic motive pulse," an innate ability to sense rhythmic time and temporal variation in the human voice (Trevarthen 2016). The expressive prosodic contours, pitch glides, and prevalence of basic harmonic intervals (thirds, fourths, fifths, octaves) of "infant-directed speech" (Fernald 1992; Papoušek, H. 1996) occur alongside the mother's "infant-directed singing" (Delavenne et al. 2013; see also "Mothers as Singing Mentors for Infants," by Trehub and Gudmundsdottir, this volume), a special limited repertoire of lullaby and play song which is characterized by structural simplicity, repetitiveness, higher than usual pitches (somewhat nearer the infant's own vocal pitch levels), slower tempi, and a more emotive voice quality:

> In general, the maternal repertoire of songs for infants is limited to a handful of play songs or lullabies that are performed in an expressive and highly ritualized manner. From the neonatal period, infants prefer acoustic renditions of a song in a maternal style (performances from mothers of other infants) to non-maternal renditions of the same song by the same singer. Moreover, they are entranced by performances in which they can both see and hear

the singer, as reflected in extended periods of focused attention and reduced body movement in the infant.

(Trehub 2003, p. 671)

Early vocalization is intimately linked to perception (Vihman 1996) in which the primacy of developing pitch control in infant utterances occurs alongside adult-generated sounds that are dominated perceptually by melodic contour. As such, although the "precursors of spontaneous singing may be indiscriminable from precursors of early speech" (Papoušek, M. 1996, p. 104), the weight of available evidence on the origins of language and music in the child suggests a common dominance of "the tune before the words" (Vihman 1996, p. 212) related both to the developing child's own "tunes" and the "tunes" of others.

The text that follows focuses on making sense of the nature of intra- and inter-personal communication in singing.

A THEORY OF INTRA- AND INTER-PERSONAL COMMUNICATION IN SINGING

Neuropsychobiological perspectives

Technological advances in brain imaging over the past decade have provided valuable insights into the neural basis of a variety of cognitive and affective functions, including those related to music. For example, neural areas and networks have been identified in the perception of tonal structures (Janata et al. 2002), features of musical "syntax" (Maess et al. 2001; Patel 2003), relative and "absolute" pitch processing (Zatorre et al. 1998), temporal processing (Strait et al. 2014), and how practice produces change in the motor cortex (Altenmüller and Schlaug 2015).

Hemispheric asymmetries are often evidenced, as are relative biases toward particular neural locations, depending on the type of musical behavior under consideration and the individual's relative experience and expertise in singing (see "The Neuroscience of Singing," by Kleber and Zarate, this volume). Nevertheless, findings in neurologic music therapy and brain research suggest that musical perception involves cross-hemispheric processing (Altenmüller and Schlaug 2015; Reybrouck and Brattico 2015; Rosslau et al. 2015), such that initial right-hemispheric recognition of melodic contour and meter are followed by an identification of pitch interval and rhythmic patterning via left-hemisphere systems, and even more evident in musically experienced adults. There is also evidence that specific neural circuits are devoted to dissonance computation and that these also link to the emotional systems (either in the paralimbic structures or more frontal areas) (Blood and Zatorre 2001; Blood et al. 1999; Cross 2001—see also "Singing and Emotion," by Coutinho et al., this volume).

Musical behaviors in adulthood appear to depend on specific brain circuitry that is relatively discrete from the processing of other classes of sounds (Zatorre and Krumhansl 2002), such as speech and song lyrics. A modular model of functional neural architecture has been proposed (Peretz and Coltheart 2003), based on case studies of musical impairments in brain-damaged patients, to explain neuropsychobiological musical processing, including that for singing (see Figure 18.1). Separate systems within the brain are responsible for the analyses of language, temporal organization, and pitch organization (Peretz 2012). These systems relate incoming information to existing knowledge banks (a phonological lexicon and a musical lexicon) as well as previous experience of emotional expression. Song lyrics are assumed to be processed in parallel with song melody and enacted by simultaneous cooperation between areas within the left and right cerebral hemispheres, respectively (Cogo-Moreira et al. 2013), with common cortical processing of the syntactical features of music and language (Maess et al. 2001), alongside an other-than-conscious ability to perceive underlying harmonic structures (Bigand et al. 2001). Further support for the Peretz and Coltheart model may be drawn from other neurological studies that compare song imagery (thinking through a song in memory) with actual song perception (Alonso et al. 2014; Mantell and Pfordresher 2013). Bilateral activation of the temporal and frontal cortex and of the supplementary motor area suggests that an integration of lyrics and melody in song representation is achieved through the combined action of two discrete systems for auditory-tonal and auditory-verbal working memory (Saito et al. 2012). There is also evidence that song imagery alone can activate auditory cortical regions (Oh et al. 2013).

The Peretz and Coltheart model proposes that any acoustic stimulus is subjected to an initial acoustic analysis. This is then "forwarded" to a range of discrete "modules" that are specifically designed to extract different features, namely *pitch* content (pitch contour and the tonal functions of successive intervals) and *temporal* content (metric organization = temporal regularity, and rhythmic structure = relative durational values). Both pitch and temporal outputs are further "forwarded" to a personal "musical lexicon" that contains a continuously updated representation of all the specific musical phrases experienced by the individual over a lifetime. The output from this musical lexicon depends on the task requirements. If the goal is to reproduce a heard song, then the melody from the musical lexicon will be paired with its associated lyrics whose elements are theorized as being stored in the "phonological lexicon" (Peretz and Coltheart 2003).

This is not to say, however, that the resultant sung output would necessarily be an ideal musical "match" to an original stimulus model. A significant proportion of young children often experience difficulty (and for a small minority this can be a long-term difficulty) in performing accurately both the lyrics and melody of songs from their culture (Creel 2015). Analysis of longitudinal empirical data on young children's singing development (Niland 2012; Welch et al. 2012) indicates that most young children are usually very accurate in remembering and communicating the lyrics of particular songs that they have been taught (or heard informally), but can often be less accurate in reproducing the same songs' constituent pitches (cf. Welch et al. 1997, 1998). A similar bias is reported in adult singers' ability to make fewer errors in memorizing the words of new songs compared to the musical elements (Ginsborg 2002). In relation to Peretz and Coltheart's model (Figure 18.1), the child singing data suggests that the average five-year-old's "phonological lexicon" is often more developmentally advanced than their "musical lexicon." In addition, the child data supports the model's notion of a pitch "contour" module that has a basic primacy over other perceptual pitch organization. Young children who were rated as "out of tune" when singing particular focus songs were much more pitch accurate vocally when asked to match pitch glides (*glissandi*) that had been deconstructed from the melodic contours of the same songs for the purposes of assessment of singing development.

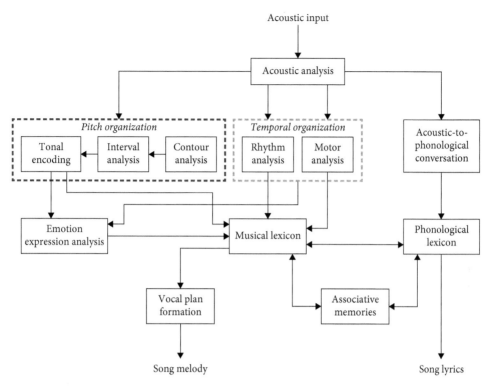

FIGURE 18.1 A modular model of music processing (adapted from Peretz & Coltheart 2003). Each box represents a processing component and arrows represent pathways of information flow or communication between processing components.

The Peretz and Coltheart neuropsychobiological model also accords with an earlier developmental model of children's singing that drew together a large number of independent studies (Welch 1986, 1998; see also Welch 2016). This developmental model and its associated literature suggest that an important phase in the child's journey toward accurate vocal pitch matching is the ability to match a song's melodic contour (Hargreaves 1996; Welch 2009a; Welch et al. 1998).

Similar findings have been highlighted in the longitudinal research evaluation of the UK Government's National Singing Programme in England "Sing Up" (see http://www.singup.org for more details) involving 11,000 pupils from over 180 primary schools across the United Kingdom (Welch 2009a; Welch et al. 2014). These results suggests that singing is subject to a developmental process in which vocal pitch matching (1) improves with age and (2) is subject to accelerated development in an appropriately nurturing environment (see also Welch 2016).

The symbiotic interweaving of singing and emotion

The Peretz and Coltheart model proposes that in parallel, but independently, outputs from the pitch and temporal perceptual modules are fed into an "emotion expression analysis" module (see Figure 18.1), facilitating an emotional response to the musical sounds. With regard to the emotional evaluation of vocal sounds, various distinct cortical and subcortical structures, primarily (but not solely) in the right hemisphere, have been identified as significant (Peretz et al. 2013). As part of our basic communication, six primary emotions—fear, anger, joy, sadness, surprise, and disgust—are all commonly expressed vocally (Titze and Martin 1998) and are differentiated by strong vocal acoustic variation (Patel 2008). Voice is an essential aspect of our human identity: of who we are, how we feel, how we communicate, and how other people experience us.

The ability to generate concurrent emotional "tags" to vocal outputs (singing and speech) is likely to relate to the earliest fetal experiences of acoustic environment, particularly the sound of the mother's voice heard in the womb during the final trimester of pregnancy. Although speech is partially muffled and the upper frequencies of the sound spectrum are reduced, the pitch inflection of the mother's voice—its prosodic contour—is clearly audible (see Parncutt 2016 for a review). The final trimester is also marked by the fetus developing key functional elements of its nervous, endocrine, and immune systems for the processing of affective states (Dawson 1994). As a consequence, a mother's vocalization with its own concurrent emotional correlate (Peretz and Coltheart 2003) is likely to produce a related neuroendocrine reaction in her developing child (Keverne et al. 1997; Seckl 1998; Thurman 2000; see also "Fetal, Neonatal, and Early Infant Experiences of Maternal Singing," by Woodward, this volume).

The filtered interfacing of the maternal and fetal bloodstreams allows the fetus to experience the mother's endocrine-related emotional state concurrently with her vocal pitch contours (see Figure 18.2). Feelings of maternal pleasure, joy, anxiety, or distress will be reflected in her vocal contours and her underlying emotional state. Given that singing (to herself, listening to the radio, in the car, with others) is usually regarded as a "pleasurable" activity, this will be reflected in a "positive body state" (Damasio 2006) that is related to her endocrine system's secretion of particular neuropeptides, such as β-endorphin, into her

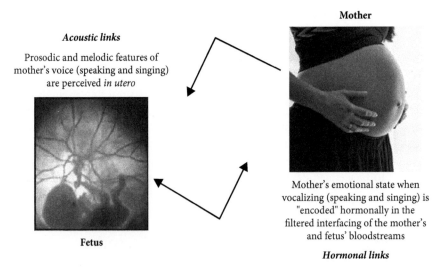

Mother

Acoustic links

Prosodic and melodic features of
mother's voice (speaking and singing)
are perceived *in utero*

Fetus

Mother's emotional state when
vocalizing (speaking and singing) is
"encoded" hormonally in the
filtered interfacing of the mother's
and fetus' bloodstreams

Hormonal links

FIGURE 18.2 The shaping of an integrated fetal emotional response to sound through concurrent experience of the mother's prosody, sung melody, and affective state.

bloodstream (Thurman 2000). Her musical pleasure (expressed vocally and hormonally) will be communicated to her fetus.

At birth, neonates are particularly sensitive to the sound of their own mother's voice, which derives from their fetal experiences of their mother's singing and reading aloud (Parncutt 2015). The perceptual salience of maternal pitch contour (Trehub 1987) is also shown in the reported ability of infants aged three to four months to imitate an exaggerated prosodic pitch contour presented by their mothers (Masataka 1992; see "Mothers as Singing Mentors for Infants," by Trehub and Gudmundsdottir, this volume), as well as an ability to imitate basic vowels at the same age after only 15 minutes of laboratory exposure (Kuhl and Meltzoff 1996). Similarly, six-month-old infants demonstrate increased amounts of sustained attention when viewing video recordings of their mothers' singing as compared with viewing recordings of them speaking (Trehub 2003).

Singing as emotional capital

Thus the child enters the world with an emotional "bias" toward certain sounds, linked to their earliest acoustic and affective experiences of the maternal vocal pitch contour. Arguably, this bias will shape the way that developing infants respond to other sounds, supplemented and expanded by concurrent auditory and affective experience of their own voices, beginning with the acoustic contours of their first cries. As suggested above, the available data suggests that there is a priming of the neuropsychobiological system from pre-birth through early infancy in which vocal melodies are associated with various emotional correlates. These associations provide a basis for musical communication across the lifespan, both in the production and reception of voice-based melodies and also for other intra-personal and inter-personal musical communications that draw on similar acoustic features.

This integration of early musical experience with its affective correlates can be construed as basic *emotional capital*, a resource which is employed as developing humans interact with, relate to, deal with, and make sense of their immediate and expanding sonic environments. Auditory experiences can be interrelated with six basic emotions that are evidenced in the first nine months of life. Initial tri-polar emotional states that relate to distress (evidenced by crying and irritability), pleasure (indicated by satiation), and being attentive to the immediate environment lead to the emergence of interest (and surprise), joy, sadness, and disgust by the age of three months, followed by emotional displays of anger and fear by the age of eight months (Lewis 1997). As mentioned above, each of these basic emotions has a characteristic vocal acoustic signature and an acoustic profile that is associated with a strong characteristic emotional state. Sounds that have similar acoustic profiles are likely to generate related or identical emotions. Musical performance relies on expressive acoustic cues, such as changes in tempo, sound level, timing, intonation, articulation, timbre, vibrato, tone attacks, tone decays, and pauses to communicate emotion, such as tenderness, happiness, sadness, fear, and anger (Juslin et al. 2010). Analyses of recorded performances indicate that virtually every performance variable is affected in ways specific to each emotion (Gabrielsson 2016). In performance, the patterns of continuous changes in such variables constitute an "expressive contour" and have been likened to the prosodic contour of speech (Juslin et al. 2010). Thus there appears to be a close correspondence between the acoustic characteristics of voiced emotion in everyday life and the expressive cues used to convey emotion in musical performance (Lavy 2001). For example, a mother suffering from post-natal depression will have a different vocal quality (quieter, lower pitched, longer pauses) than her non-depressed peers (Robb 2000). As children get older, they become more expert at recognizing and expressing intended emotion in singing as well as speaking (Gabrielsson and Örnkloo 2002). Arguably, this correspondence has its roots in mother–fetus/mother–infant vocalization and human neuropsychobiological development from the third tri-mester of pregnancy.

The acoustic features of the maternal voice and her immediate sonic environment are so-cially and culturally located, such that the initial generic plasticity demonstrated by the neo-nate for the discrimination of differences in any group of sounds is soon shaped toward a biased detection of the particular distinguishing features of salient local sounds (Soley and Sebastián-Gallés 2015). This, in turn, affects related behaviors from a very young age. For example, newborns are also able to produce different accents in their ways of crying as soon as they are born, as suggested in the analysis of the melody and intensity contours of French and German neonates (Mampe et al. 2009). The French group preferentially produced cries with a rising melody contour, whereas the German group preferentially produced falling contours.

It is hypothesized, therefore, that any auditory contour event that is perceived as "alien" to the dominant sound culture (as previously experienced) is likely to be noticed and "tagged" emotionally on a positive/negative continuum, depending on its acoustic profile. These ongoing concurrent experiences act as one of the bases for the generation of musical "preference" within the developing musical lexicon. Reported examples of early musical "preference" in relation to singing are:

- two-day-old neonates who listen longer to audio recordings of women singing in a maternal ("infant-directed singing") style than to their usual singing style (Masataka 1999);
- infant preferences for higher rather than lower pitched singing (Trainor and Zacharias 1998), which is one of the characteristics of "infant-directed singing";
- two-to-six-month-old infants that listen longer to sequences of consonant musical intervals than to sequences of dissonant intervals (Trehub 2003);
- endocrine (salivary cortisol) changes in six-month-old infants after listening to their mothers singing (Trehub 2001).

These "preferences" for particular vocal pitch contours, vocal timbres, and interval con-sonance, linked to underlying endocrine and emotional states, may also be seen as early examples of how musical experience (including singing) is multiply processed within the overall functions of the nervous, endocrine, and immune systems—the integrated human "bodymind" (Thurman and Welch 2000).

SINGING AS INTRA-PERSONAL COMMUNICATION

Sounds can be self-generated as a basis for *intra-personal* musical communication, such as the earliest melodic vocal sounds that emerge around eight weeks (Papoušek, H. 1996), the vocal play that begins around four to six months (Papoušek, M. 1996) and subsequently in pre-schoolers' spontaneous pot-pourri songs (Countryman et al. 2015; Marsh 2008) and as "outline songs" (Hargreaves 1996) that draw on aspects of the dominant song culture. The sounds can also be part of *inter-personal* communication, such as the interactive and imitative vocal play of infant and parent (Papoušek, M. 1996; Tafuri 2008), or adult-initiated song improvisations and compositions (Barrett 2006; see Barrett, this volume). As the human develops social awareness and communicative vocal skills, there is a shift from communication that is biased toward the *intra-personal* to the possibilities of *inter-personal* communication in singing, but the former will always be present.

The developing singer communicates intra-personally in a variety of ways related to the nature of the feedback system. Feedback can be auditory, visual, tactile, kinesthetic, or vestibular (Welch et al. 2005) and it is used in the construction of individual musical identity, both in the sense of "identity in music"—as a musician—as well as in the sense of "music in identity"—as a feature of an individual's overall personal identity (Hargreaves et al. 2002). At one level, there is an internal psychological feedback system that is essentially outside conscious awareness and which relates to a moment-by-moment self-monitoring of the singing behavior (cf. "vocal plan formation"— Peretz and Coltheart 2003). In the first months of infancy, this system is being developed in the vocal behaviors that are the precursors of spontaneous singing and early speech, prior to their use in the emergence of a "coalescence between spontaneous and cultural songs" (Hargreaves 1996, p. 156) from the age of two onwards.

A schema theory of singing development (Welch 1985) proposed that any initiation of a specific singing behavior (termed "voice program" in the original model), such as copying an external song model, would generate expectations of proprioceptive and exteroceptive feedback that are compared to the actual feedback received from the sense receptors and auditory environment (as both bone and air conducted sound) respectively. This internal motor behavior feedback system also provides the basis for self-reflective psychological judgments as to the "appropriateness" of any given example of singing behavior, such as its correspondence to an external song model or to an internal mental representation of a target melody's key, tonal relationships, loudness, and/or timbre. In the absence of evaluative feedback from an external source (termed "knowledge of results"), the singer has to make their own judgment of the "appropriateness" of their sung response compared to their internal model. This comparison is likely to depend on the relative developments within and between their "musical lexicon" and "phonological lexicon" (cf. Peretz and Coltheart 2003), in the sense that accurate reproduction of songs from the dominant culture requires the combination of a range of musical and linguistic skills (Davidson 1994; Welch et al. 1995, 1997, 1998). In some cases, there will be the realization of a mismatch between the intended and actual singing behavior and a subsequent correction can take place (see also "Vocal Performance in Occasional Singers," by Dalla Bella, this volume, concerning the role of a "Vocal sensory motor loop"). Awareness, however, is not a necessary guarantee of vocal accuracy or singing development. "Out-of-tune" singing can persist, for example, because singers do not know how to change their behavior, even though they may realize that something is "incorrect" or "inappropriate." It can also persist because there is no awareness that their singing behavior needs to change.

At a conscious, reflective level, the singer's intra-personal communication is a form of self-monitoring that is essential for the development of skilled performance behavior of diverse pieces in a wide variety of acoustic contexts. Adjustments, both mental and in physical coordination, may need to be made as the performer moves from the individuality of the singing studio to the more public rehearsal environment, as well as in relation to the demands of the actual performance, when stress levels may be higher (Kenny 2011) due to the efferent stimulation of the adrenal gland (Chanda and Levitin 2013; Koelsch 2014). In addition, there are other context effects. Performance behaviors are subject to social and cultural imperatives, as shown in classical singing styles by a shift in emphasis from vocal agility in the eighteenth century to vocal resonance in the late nineteenth century (Mason 2000) and by different cultural stylistics in operatic performance (Rosselli 2000). Practice, particularly deliberate practice, may be regarded as an essential feature of intra-personal communication and the development of performance expertise. Lehmann (1997) suggests that there are three necessary mental representations involved, namely concerning the desired performance goal, the current performance, and the production of the music.

At the other end of the performance skill continuum are those who are less developed as singers (see "Defining and Explaining Singing Difficulties in Adults," by Wise, this volume; see "Vocal Performance in Occasional Singers," by Dalla Bella, this volume). Some may have experienced extreme disapproval about their singing, usually from a significant person in their life (such as parent, teacher, peer) (Welch 2001, 2017). Their internal representations of themselves as (non-)singers and, by association, as (non-) musicians are constructed by their negative experience of singing, usually in childhood. This self-image is normally sustained by singing avoidance behaviors, at least in public (Knight 1999; Wise and Sloboda 2008), although there is evidence that even those who regard themselves as singing disabled can be improved in an appropriately nurturing environment (Richards and Durrant 2003; Welch 2017). Such labeling can also be environmentally and culturally sensitive, as demonstrated by the woman who had been born in Barbados and moved to the USA when she was four years of age. When questioned as to why she was convinced that she was a "non-singer," she replied: "Now that I think about it, when I go home to Barbados I am a 'singer'. I'm just not a 'singer' in this country" (Pascale 2001, p. 165). She had two different internal representations of a "singer": a USA "singer" was someone who could lead songs, sing solos, and perform easily, whereas a Barbadian "singer" was someone who could sing fast, "upbeat" songs, and who generally participated with others in singing.

However, even less skilled singers may sing alone and to themselves, either as an accompaniment to another activity (such as showering, housework, driving, deskwork, gardening) or just for its own sake. This is further indication of pleasurable intrapersonal musical communication, first evidenced in infancy, and of the interrelated nature of singing, emotion, and self. When provided with an appropriately nurturing environment, developing singers are likely to increase their range of vocal behaviors, improve their self-image, and feel generally feel better. For example, 14 weeks of individual, twice-weekly singing and speaking lessons that were aimed at generating a wider range of vocal dynamics and color, alongside greater ease in vocal production, also produced a significant reduction in stress levels (related to both physical health and cognitive stress), an increased sense of personal well-being, more self-confidence, and a more positive self-image (Wiens et al. 2001): "voice training became a metaphor of self-discovery" (Wiens et al. 2001, p. 231).

SINGING AS INTER-PERSONAL, SOCIAL, AND CULTURAL COMMUNICATION

Cross (2001) argues that the essence of music may be found in its grounding in social interaction and personal significance, as well as in its being rooted in sound, movement, and heterogeneity of meaning. Salgardo (2003) goes further by suggesting that the communication of emotion is at the heart of sung performance through the combined use of acoustical (vocal) and visual (facial) expressive cues. He undertook a series of empirical experiments to demonstrate how the singer's movements and gestures (vocally and facially) facilitate the communication of their interpretation of the intended meaning of the composer's notation, including its emotional character. Furthermore, such vocal and facial expressions in performance are similar to those used to convey emotional meaning in everyday life. Salgardo (2003) concludes that the emotions portrayed by a singer, although performed, are not "faked," but are built on the recollections of real emotions. A performance that is regarded as "authentic" or of high quality will have a close correspondence between such vocal and visual gestures and the nature of the original features of the musical structure; it is a form of corroboration.

In addition to the communication of a basic emotional state, the act of singing conveys information about *group membership*, such as age, gender, culture, and social group (see "Children Singing," by Harding, this volume). Several studies have demonstrated that listeners are able to identify and label certain features of both the singer (as a "child") and the singing (as "child-like"). Often there is an accurate correspondence between the listener assessment and the acoustic item, but this is not always the case because of the variables involved, both in relation to the listener and to the singer. As outlined above (see "singing as a physical activity"), the vocal performer's manipulation of the pattern of vocal fold vibration and the configuration of the vocal tract are basic to the act and art of singing. The acoustic output is dependent on the physiological patterning and this, in turn, is closely related to the singer's age, gender, experience, skill levels, social and cultural background, and the particular musical genre.

With regard to *age*, a study of 320 untrained child singers aged three to 12 years found a highly regular and linear relationship in listener judgments between the estimated age and the true chronological age (Sergeant and Welch 2008). Where listeners made erroneous judgments, they tended to underestimate the age of those singers aged seven years and older, irrespective of gender, suggesting perhaps that there was a categorical perception of child-like vocal quality that influenced judgments toward some notional mean age. The ability to recognize that a singer is a child is closely related to the nature of the acoustic output (Rutkowski 2015). Although development occurs across childhood, the child's vocal apparatus is significantly different in size and structure from that of the adult (Kent and Vorperian 1995; Stathopoulos 2000) and produces a relatively distinctive sung vocal timbre.

At the other end of the age continuum, older voices also have a characteristic acoustic signature both in singing and in speech that relate to changes in the underlying voice mechanism. However, there can be a significant difference between the chronological and biological ages of a singing voice (Welch and Thurman 2000). It is possible for a person to "sound" several decades younger (or older), depending on their lifelong voice use and vocal health (de Aquino and Ferreira 2016; Prakup 2012). "Older-sounding" voices may have relatively weaker vocal musculature and reduced functioning of the respiratory system, leading to qualitative changes in vocal output, such as a more "breathy" sound, reduced loudness, greater variation in pitching, and perhaps vocal tremor on sustained pitches. Nevertheless, older singers are quite capable of leading fulfilling artistic lives as vocal performers if provided with the opportunity (Silvey 2001).

In between these age extremes there are other "ages" of singing, each related to the underlying anatomical and physiological realities of the voice mechanism. These physical realities have acoustic correlates, suggesting that there are at least seven "ages" (Welch 2009b): early childhood (1–3 years), later childhood (3–10 years), puberty (8–14 years), adolescence (12–16 years), early adulthood (15–30/40 years), older adulthood (40–60+ years), senescence (60–80+) years (cf. Stathopoulos et al. 2011, see also http://www.ncvs.org/ncvs/tutorials/voiceprod/tutorial/changes.html). However, there is considerable overlap between these "ages," not least because of individual and sex differences in biological (maturational) and chronological vocal ages.

With regard to *gender*, there is evidence of differences between the sexes in vocal fold patterning across the lifespan from mid-childhood onwards (Kreiman and Sidtis 2011). Females tend to have slightly incomplete vocal fold closure, resulting in a "breathier" production that is acoustically distinctive spectrally, with more "noise" in their vocal products above 4000 Hz (Welch 2005). Males, on the other hand, tend to have stronger vocal fold closure and a steeper spectral drop-off acoustically. Gender appears to be communicated by the amount of perceived "breathiness" and the formant patterning within an overall spectral shape. The aforementioned study of untrained children's singing (Sergeant and Welch 2008) found that listeners made greater sex identification errors for boys aged below seven years. There was a highly significant linear trend in which correct sex identification was closely correlated with boys' ascending age: pre-pubescent boys became perceptibly more "masculine" in their singing as they got older. No such trend was evident with the girl singers, but there were relatively few identification errors for all age groups.

The effects of education and training on the communication of gender in singing provide similar evidence of both distinctiveness and similarity between the sexes. A range of studies (Howard et al. 2002; Welch and Howard 2002) have demonstrated that there is a slight tendency for trained male choristers to be more correctly identified than trained female choristers, but this perception accuracy is sensitive to individual performance, the particular group of singers, their age and experience, the choice of repertoire, and the individual listener. Nevertheless, both acoustic analyses and perceptual outcomes suggest that trained girl singers are capable of singing with a perceptibly "male-like" voice quality. The same singers are also capable of singing in a more characteristically "feminine" manner. There is also evidence of gender confusability in "collective" (choral) as well as solo singing (Welch et al. 2012).

The effects of *experience, training*, and *skill levels* are evidenced in studies of trained singers, child, adolescent, and adult. Singers who have undertaken classical music training tend to produce a more even timbre across their vocal range. The relatively lower larynx position creates a particular perceptual color to the trained singer's voice, although this is also culturally sensitive (such as may be evidenced in the differences between German and Italian opera performance styles). There is an intriguing interaction between *gender* and *training* at the highest sung pitches. For males, the trained *falsetto* register is distinctive, as in the countertenor voice, being a form of vocal production that uses a particular balance of muscle activity within the male larynx to produce a female sung pitch range. This style of singing is exploited in both classical and popular musics across the world and can communicate a sense of *sexual* ambiguity or androgyny (Koizumi 2001; Parrott 2015). In contrast, the highest sung female register (employing a similar voice coordination as the male—termed the "flute" or "whistle" register) presents challenges in the communication of text in singing because all vowels share approximately the same formant frequencies so that vowel intelligibility becomes problematic (Welch and Sundberg 2002).

There is an extensive literature on different musical genres and singing (for example, see Potter 2000) and there are certain key features about singing as communication with regard to *social* and *cultural* groups, which can be summarized as follows:

- Singing can be a form of group identification and social bonding (see "The Effects of Gender on the Motivation and Benefits Associated with Community Singing in the UK," by Parkinson, this volume). Examples are found in the use of specially composed company songs to reinforce a senior management's definition of company culture (Vaag et al. 2014) and in many diverse choral settings, such as bringing disadvantaged individuals together to create a "Homeless Males Choir" (Bailey and Davidson 2013), as well as in the traditional choral communities of Iceland and Newfoundland (see "Group Singing and Social Identity," by Davidson and Faulkner, this volume).
- Singing can also be a transformational activity culturally, in which members or groups evolve new musical styles or sub-genres or modify established performance practices. Examples of such communities of practice are found in the fusion music of South Asian youth groups (Farrell et al. 2000) and also in the recent influx of female singers into the traditionally all-male cathedral choir that offers the potential of a wider "vocal timbre palette" in the performance of the established repertoire (Howard and Welch 2002). Here the messages are about musical innovation, modernity, challenge, and/or social justice, such as in rap or hip hop (Forman 2000; Taylor and Taylor 2007).
- Regular singing activities can communicate a sense of pattern, order, and systematic contrast to the working day and week, such as in use of songs in the special school classroom to frame periods of activity and in the seasonally related rehearsals and performances of the amateur choir/choral society (Welch 2016).
- Singing can also be used as an agent in the communication of cultural change, such as in the identification of certain "Singing Schools" by the Ministry of Education in New Zealand (Boyack 2003) as part of their promotion of a new arts curriculum.

In each of these cases, the act of singing, whether as an individual or as part of a collective, can facilitate both musical and extra-musical communication, a sense of belonging or of being an "outsider" (cf. Becker 1963).

THERAPEUTIC USE OF SINGING

Singing has been used in recent years to mitigate the impact of major societal challenges (World Health Organization 2012). These include the perceived need to keep an expanding aging population active, or in helping to deal with an increasing onset of degenerative illnesses, such as dementia and Alzheimer's (Vella-Burrows 2012). Formalized singing activities, such as "Singing for the brain"—a popular singing program developed by the Alzheimer Society in the UK (Bannan and Montgomery-Smith 2008), have been devised and rolled out in nursing homes and community centers across the UK with the aim of bringing people together in a supportive and friendly environment, eliciting memories and words through familiar songs and music (Alzheimer's Society 2016).

The research that has supported the development of such programs suggests that—in people affected by moderate to severe stage Alzheimer's disease—musical semantic memory can be preserved (Cuddy et al. 2012). Furthermore, for this population, singing newly acquired words learnt in association with a familiar melody has repeatedly led to a better retention of words and to a consolidation in memory, compared to the learning of words without music (Moussard et al. 2012, 2014). The musical association that happens in the brain during the encoding stage appears to facilitate the learning and retention of words in people affected by dementia and Alzheimer's (Palisson et al. 2015). In addition, singing has also been linked to a general improvement of mood and quality of life in people affected by dementia (Camic et al. 2013).

The connection between singing and improvement of mood, social interaction, health related quality of life, mental health, and well-being has been consistently reported in the literature (Ahessy 2016; Clements-Cortés 2015; Pearce et al. 2016; Reagon et al. 2016; Skingley and Bungay 2010; see "Singing and Psychological Needs," by Davidson and Garrido, this volume). Some underlying explanations of these effects have been linked to the neuroendocrine production of oxytocin and cortisol (Kreutz 2014; Weinstein et al. 2016), two hormones that have been traditionally associated with social bonding and stress responses (Sternberg 2001). There has also been increasing evidence highlighting the influence of psychosocial interventions on the neuroendocrine and immune responses of people involved in music-related activities (Fancourt et al. 2014). For example, in a group of adults affected by cancer, group singing has been associated with an increase of particular cytokines[2] and a reduction of inflammation, suggesting a correlation between improved immune response to cancer and singing (Fancourt et al. 2016).

Group singing has also been shown to be effective in reducing social isolation in older people, promoting enjoyment and resulting in improved mental and physical health, as well as increased cognitive stimulation (Clift et al. 2010; Saarikallio 2011; Skingley and Bungay 2010). Specifically, Cohen et al. (2007) carried out a series of non-randomized controlled studies with 166 participants (mean age of 80 years old) taking part in singing workshops, and discovered that in comparison with a control group they reported fewer health issues, fewer falls, fewer doctor's visits, and less use of medication. Clift and his colleagues (2010), in their review of the literature on the benefit of group singing, suggested that group singing promotes social and personal well-being, encourages social participation, and reduces anxiety and depression.

Overall, active engagement with music in general and singing in particular is seen to provide a sense of purpose, community, and independence in the lives of people taking part in

---

[2] Ctyokines is a general name for a category of small proteins that are important in cell signaling. Their release has an effect on the behavior of cells around them. Their definite distinction from hormones is still part of ongoing research (Wikipedia 2016).

music-making activities (Creech, Hallam, McQueen et al. 2013; Creech, Hallam, Varvarigou et al. 2013), thus providing them with some key tools to support a healthy aging process, both physically and mentally.

CONCLUSIONS

Singing is a diverse behavior that embraces human communication that is multifaceted and concurrent, with different messages being produced and perceived at the same time, within and outside conscious awareness. The singer communicates intra-personally through the moment-by-moment acoustic stream that provides diverse forms of feedback concerning musical features, vocal quality, vocal "accuracy" and "authenticity," emotional state, and personal identity. To the external listener (parent, peer, audience), there is also inter-personal communication that is musical, referential (through the text), emotional, and extra-musical, such as in the delineation of membership of a particular social and/or cultural group. To sing is to communicate—singing as communication.

REFERENCES

Ahessy, B. (2016). The use of a music therapy choir to reduce depression and improve quality of life in older adults—a randomized control trial. *Music and Medicine* 8(1): 17–28.

Alonso, I., Sammler, D., Valabrègue, R., Dinkelacker, V., Dupont, S., et al. (2014). Hippocampal sclerosis affects fMR-adaptation of lyrics and melodies in songs. *Frontiers in Human Neuroscience* 8: 111. doi: 10.3389/fnhum.2014.00111

Altenmüller, E. and Schlaug, G. (2015). Apollo's gift: new aspects of neurologic music therapy. *Progress in Brain Research* 217: 237–252.

Alzheimer's Society (2016). Singing for the brain, https://www.alzheimers.org.uk/site/scripts/documents_info.php?documentID=760, accessed October 13, 2017.

Bailey, B. and Davidson, J.W. (2013). Emotional, social, and cognitive enrichment through participation in group singing: interviews with members of a choir for homeless men. *Phenomenon of Singing* 3: 24–32.

Bannan, N. and Montgomery-Smith, C. (2008). "Singing for the brain": reflections on the human capacity for music arising from a pilot study of group singing with Alzheimer's patients. *Journal of the Royal Society for the Promotion of Health* 128(2): 73–78.

Barrett, M.S. (2006). Inventing songs, inventing worlds: the "genesis" of creative thought and activity in young children's lives. *International Journal of Early Years Education* 14(3): 201–220.

Becker, H. (1963). *Outsiders: Studies in the Sociology of Deviance*. New York: Free Press.

Bigand, E., Tillmann, B., Poulin, B., D'Adamo, D.A., and Madurell, F. (2001). The effect of harmonic context on phoneme monitoring in vocal music. *Cognition* 81(1): B11–B20.

Blood, A.J., Zatorre, R.J., Bermudez, P., and Evans, A.C. (1999). Emotional responses to pleasant and unpleasant music correlate with activity in paralimbic brain regions. *Nature Neuroscience* 2(4): 382–387.

Blood, A.J. and Zatorre, R.J. (2001). Intensely pleasurable responses to music correlate with activity in brain regions implicated in reward and emotion. *Proceedings of the National Academy of Sciences* 98(20): 11818–11823.

Boyack, J. (2003). Hearing the voices of singing schools. *Phenomenon of Singing* 4: 26–31, http://journals.library.mun.ca/ojs/index.php/singing/article/view/557, accessed October 14, 2017.

Camic, P.M., Williams, C.M., and Meeten, F. (2013). Does a "Singing Together Group" improve the quality of life of people with a dementia and their carers? A pilot evaluation study. *Dementia* 12(2): 157–176.

Chanda, M.L. and Levitin, D.J. (2013). The neurochemistry of music. *Trends in Cognitive Sciences* 17(4): 179–193.

Clements-Cortés, A. (2015). Singing for health, connection and care. *Music and Medicine* 7(4): 13–23.

Clift, S., Hancox, G., Morrison, I., Hess, B., Kreutz, G., et al. (2010). Choral singing and psychological wellbeing: quantitative and qualitative findings from English choirs in a cross-national survey. *Journal of Applied Arts and Health* 1(1): 19–34.

Clift, S., Nicol, J., Raisbeck, M., Whitmore, C., and Morrison, I. (2010). Group singing, wellbeing and health: a systematic mapping of research evidence. *UNESCO Journal* 2: 1–25.

Cogo-Moreira, H., de Ávila, C. R. B., Ploubidis, G. B., and de Jesus Mari, J. (2013). Pathway evidence of how musical perception predicts word-level reading ability in children with reading difficulties. *PloS One* 8(12): e84375.

Cohen, G.D., Perlstein, S., Chapline, J., Kelly, J., Firth, K.M., et al. (2007). The impact of professionally conducted cultural programs on the physical health, mental health, and social functioning of older adults—2-year results. *Journal of Aging, Humanities and the Arts* 1(1–2): 5–22.

Countryman, J., Gabriel, M., and Thompson, K. (2015). Children's spontaneous vocalizations during play: aesthetic dimensions. *Music Education Research* 18: 1–19.

Creech, A., Hallam, S., McQueen, H., and Varvarigou, M. (2013). The power of music in the lives of older adults. *Research Studies in Music Education* 35(1): 87–102.

Creech, A., Hallam, S., Varvarigou, M., McQueen, H., and Gaunt, H. (2013). Active music making: a route to enhanced subjective well-being among older people. *Perspectives in Public Health* 133(1): 36–43.

Creel, S.C. (2015). Ups and downs in auditory development: preschoolers' sensitivity to pitch contour and timbre. *Cognitive Science* 40(2): 373–403.

Cross, I. (2001). Music, cognition, culture, and evolution. In: R.J. Zatorre and I. Peretz (eds), *The Biological Foundations of Music*, Vol. 930, pp. 28–42. New York: Annals of the New York Academy of Sciences.

Cuddy, L.L., Duffin, J.M., Gill, S.S., Brown, C.L., Sikka, R., et al. (2012). Memory for melodies and lyrics in Alzheimer's disease. *Music Perception* 29(5): 479–491.

Damasio, A.R. (2006). *Descartes' Error*. London: Vintage Books.

Davidson, L. (1994). Song singing by young and old: a developmental approach to music. In: R. Aiello and J. Sloboda (eds), *Musical Perceptions*, pp. 99–130. New York: Oxford University Press.

Dawson, G. (1994). Development of emotional expression and emotional regulation in infancy: contributions of the frontal lobe. In G. Dawson and K.W. Fischer (eds), *Human Behavior and the Developing Brain*, pp. 346–379. New York: Guilford.

de Aquino, F.S. and Ferreira, L.P. (2016). Vocal parameters of elderly female choir singers. *International Archives of Otorhinolaryngology* 20(1): 25–29.

Delavenne, A., Gratier, M., and Devouche, E. (2013). Expressive timing in infant-directed singing between 3 and 6 months. *Infant Behavior and Development* 36(1): 1–13.

Escudero, P., Best, C.T., Kitamura, C., and Mulak, K.E. (2014). Magnitude of phonetic distinction predicts success at early word learning in native and non-native accents. *Frontiers in
Psychology* 5: 1059. 10.3389/fpsyg.2014.01059

Fancourt, D., Ockelford, A., and Belai, A. (2014). The psychoneuroimmunological effects of
music: a systematic review and a new model. *Brain, Behavior, and Immunity* 36: 15–26.

Fancourt, D., Williamon, A., Carvalho, L.A., Steptoe, A., Dow, R., et al. (2016). Singing
modulates mood, stress, cortisol, cytokine and neuropeptide activity in cancer patients and
carers. *ecancermedicalscience* 10. doi: 10.3332/ecancer.2016.631

Farrell, G., Welch, G., and Bhowmick, J. (2000). South Asian music and music education in
Britain. *Bulletin of the Council for Research in Music Education* 147: 51–60.

Fernald, A. and Kuhl, P. (1987). Acoustic determinants of infant preference for motherese
speech. *Infant Behavior and Development* 10(3): 279–293.

Fernald, A. (1992). Meaningful melodies in mothers' speech to infants. In: H. Papoušek, U.
Jurgens, and M. Papoušek (eds), *Nonverbal Vocal Communication: Comparative and
Developmental Approaches*, pp. 262–282. Cambridge: Cambridge University Press.

Flax, J., Lahey, M., Harris, K., and Boothroyd, A. (1991). Relations between prosodic variables
and communicative functions. *Journal of Child Language* 18(1): 3–19.

Forman, M. (2000). "Represent": race, space and place in rap music. *Popular Music* 19(1): 65–90.

Gabrielsson, A. and Örnkloo, H. (2002). Children's perception and performance of emotion in
singing and speech. Paper presented at the ISME Early Chilhood Conference, Copenhagen,
Denmark.

Gabrielsson, A. (2016). The relationship between musical structure and perceived expression.
In: S. Hallam, I. Cross, and M. Thaut (eds), *The Handbook of Music Psychology*, pp. 215–232.
Oxford: Oxford University Press.

Ginsborg, J. (2002). Classical singers learning and memorising a new song: an observational
study. *Psychology of Music* 30(1): 58–101.

Hargreaves, D.J. (1996). The development of artistic and musical competence. In: I. Deliège and
J.A. Sloboda (eds), *Musical Beginnings*, pp. 145–170. Oxford: Oxford University Press.

Hargreaves, D.J., Miell, D., and MacDonald, R.A.R. (2002). What are musical identities and
why are they important? In: R.A.R. MacDonald, D.J. Hargreaves, and D. Miell (eds), *Musical
Identities*, pp. 1–20. Oxford: Oxford University Press.

Howard, D.M., Szymanski, J., and Welch, G.F. (2002). Listeners' perception of English cathedral girl and boy choristers. *Music Perception* 20(1): 35–49.

Howard, D.M. and Welch, G.F. (2002). Female chorister voice development: a longitudinal
study at Wells, UK. *Bulletin of the Council for Research in Music Education* 153/154: 63–70.

Janata, P., Birk, J.L., Van Horn, J.D., Leman, M., Tillmann, B., et al. (2002). The cortical topog-
raphy of tonal structures underlying Western music. *Science* 298(5601): 2167–2170.

Juslin, P., Liljeström, S., Västfjäll, D., and Lundquist, L.-O. (2010). How does music evoke
emotions? Exploring the underlying mechanisms. In: P. Juslin and J. A. Sloboda (eds),
Handbook of Music and Emotion, pp. 605–644. Oxford: Oxford University Press.

Kenny, D. (2011). *The Psychology of Music Performance Anxiety*. Oxford: Oxford
University Press.

Kent, R.D. and Vorperian, H.K. (1995). Development of the craniofacial-oral-laryngeal
anatomy: a review. *Journal of Medical Speech-Language Pathology* 3(3): 145–190.

Keverne, E.B., Nevison, C.M., and Martel, F.L. (1997). Early learning and the social bond.
In: C.S. Carter, I.I. Lederhendler, and B. Kirkpatrick (eds), *The Integrative Neurobiology of
Affiliation*, Vol. 807, pp. 329–339. New York: Annals of the New York Academy of Sciences.

Kisilevsky, B., Hains, S., Jacquet, A.Y., Granier-Deferre, C., and Lecanuet, J.-P. (2004). Maturation of fetal responses to music. *Developmental Science* 7(5): 550–559.

Knight, S. (1999). Exploring a cultural myth: what adult non-singers may reveal about the nature of singing. In: B.A. Roberts and A. Rose (eds), *The Phenomenon of Singing*, Vol. 2, pp. 144–154. St. John's, NF: Memorial University Press.

Koelsch, S. (2014). Brain correlates of music-evoked emotions. *Nature Reviews Neuroscience* 15(3): 170–180.

Koizumi, K. (2001). Male singers in Japanese visual rock bands: Falsetto as an alternative to shout in rock. In: Y. Minami and M. Shinzahoh (eds), *Proceedings*, pp. 148–151. Paper presented at the Third Asia-Pacific Symposium on Music Education Research and International Symposium on "Uragoe" and Gender, Nagoya, Japan, August 23–26, 2001.

Kreiman, J. and Sidtis, D. (2011). *Foundations of Voice Studies: An Interdisciplinary Approach to Voice Production and Perception.* Oxford: Wiley-Blackwell.

Kreiner, H. and Eviatar, Z. (2014). The missing link in the embodiment of syntax: prosody. *Brain and Language* 137: 91–102.

Kreutz, G. (2014). Does singing facilitate social bonding? *Music and Medicine* 6(2): 51–60.

Kuhl, P.K. and Meltzoff, A.N. (1996). Infant vocalizations in response to speech: vocal imitation and developmental change. *Journal of the Acoustical Society of America* 100(4): 2425–2438.

Lavy, M.M. (2001). *Emotion and the experience of listening to music: a framework for empirical research.* Unpublished PhD Thesis, University of Cambridge.

Lehmann, A.C. (1997). The acquisition of expertise in music: efficiency of deliberate practice as a moderating variable in accounting for sub-expert performance. In: I. Deliège and J. Sloboda (eds), *Perception and Cognition of Music*, pp. 161–187. Hove: Psychology Press.

Lewis, M. (1997). The self in self-conscious emotions. *Annals of the New York Academy of Sciences* 818(1): 119–142.

Maess, B., Koelsch, S., Gunter, T.C., and Friederici, A.D. (2001). Musical syntax is processed in Broca's area: an MEG study. *Nature Neuroscience* 4(5): 540–545.

Malloch, S.N. (2000). Mothers and infants and communicative musicality. *Musicae Scientiae* 3: 29–57.

Mampe, B., Friederici, A.D., Christophe, A., and Wermke, K. (2009). Newborns' cry melody is shaped by their native language. *Current Biology* 19(23): 1994–1997.

Mantell, J.T. and Pfordresher, P.Q. (2013). Vocal imitation of song and speech. *Cognition* 127(2): 177–202.

Marsh, K. (2008). *The Musical Playground: Global Tradition and Change in Children's Songs and Games.* New York: Oxford University Press.

Masataka, N. (1992). Pitch characteristics of Japanese maternal speech to infants. *Journal of Child Language* 19(2): 213–223.

Masataka, N. (1999). Preference for infant-directed singing in 2-day-old hearing infants of deaf parents. *Developmental Psychology* 35(4): 1001.

Mason, D. (2000). The teaching (and learning) of singing. In: J. Potter (ed.), *The Cambridge Companion to Singing*, pp. 204–220. Cambridge: Cambridge University Press.

Moussard, A., Bigand, E., Belleville, S., and Peretz, I. (2012). Music as an aid to learn new verbal information in Alzheimer's disease. *Music Perception* 29(5): 521–531.

Moussard, A., Bigand, E., Belleville, S., and Peretz, I. (2014). Learning sung lyrics aids retention in normal ageing and Alzheimer's disease. *Neuropsychological Rehabilitation* 24(6): 894–917.

Niland, A. (2012). Exploring the lives of songs in the context of young children's musical cultures. *Min-Ad: Israel Studies in Musicology Online* 10: 27–46.

Oh, J., Kwon, J.H., Yang, P.S., and Jeong, J. (2013). Auditory imagery modulates frequency-specific areas in the human auditory cortex. *Journal of Cognitive Neuroscience* 25(2): 175–187.

Palisson, J., Roussel-Baclet, C., Maillet, D., Belin, C., Ankri, J., et al. (2015). Music enhances verbal episodic memory in Alzheimer's disease. *Journal of Clinical and Experimental Neuropsychology* 37(5): 503–517.

Papoušek, H. (1996). Musicality in infancy research: biological and cultural origins of early musicality. In: I. Deliège and J.A. Sloboda (eds), *Musical Beginnings*, pp. 37–55. New York: Oxford University Press.

Papoušek, M. (1996). Intuitive parenting: A hidden source of musical stimulation in infancy. In: I. Deliège and J.A. Sloboda (eds), *Musical Beginnings*, pp. 88–112. New York: Oxford University Press.

Parncutt, R. (2015). Prenatal development. In: G. McPherson (ed.), *The Child as Musician: A Handbook of Musical Development*, pp. 3–30. Oxford: Oxford University Press.

Parncutt, R. (2016). Prenatal development and the phylogeny and ontogeny of musical behavior. In: S. Hallam, I. Cross, and M. Thaut (eds), *The Oxford Handbook of Music Psychology*, pp. 371–386. Oxford: Oxford University Press.

Parrott, A. (2015). Falsetto beliefs: the "countertenor" cross-examined. *Early Music* 43(1): 79–110.

Pascale, L. (2001). "I'm really NOT a singer": examining the meaning of the word singer and non-singer and the relationship their meaning holds in providing a musical education to schools. In: A. Rose and K. Adams (eds), *The Phenomenon of Singing*, Vol. 3, pp. 164–170. St. John's, NF: Memorial University Press.

Patel, A.D. (2003). Language, music, syntax and the brain. *Nature Neuroscience* 6(7): 674–681.

Patel, A.D. (2008). *Music, Language, and the Brain.* New York: Oxford University Press.

Pearce, E., Launay, J., Machin, A., and Dunbar, R.I. (2016). Is group singing special? Health, well-being and social bonds in community-based adult education classes. *Journal of Community and Applied Social Psychology* 26(6): 518–533.

Peretz, I. and Coltheart, M. (2003). Modularity of music processing. *Nature Neuroscience* 6(7): 688–691.

Peretz, I. (2012). Music, language, and modularity in action. In: M. Rebuschat, M. Rohmeier, J.A. Hawkins, and I. Cross (eds), *Language and Music as Cognitive Systems*, pp. 254–268. Oxford: Oxford University Press.

Peretz, I., Aubé, W., and Armony, J.L. (2013). Towards a neurobiology of musical emotions. In: E. Altenmüller, S. Schmidt, and E. Zimmermann (eds), *The Evolution of Emotional Communication: From Sounds in Nonhuman Mammals to Speech and Music in Man*, pp. 277–299. Oxford: Oxford University Press.

Potter, J. (2000). *The Cambridge Companion to Singing.* Cambridge: Cambridge University Press.

Prakup, B. (2012). Acoustic measures of the voices of older singers and nonsingers. *Journal of Voice* 26(3): 341–350.

Reagon, C., Gale, N., Dow, R., Lewis, I., and van Deursen, R. (2016). Choir singing and health status in people affected by cancer. *European Journal of Cancer Care* 26: e12568. doi:10.1111/ecc.12568

Reybrouck, M. and Brattico, E. (2015). Neuroplasticity beyond sounds: neural adaptations following long-term musical aesthetic experiences. *Brain Sciences* 5(1): 69–91.

Richards, H. and Durrant, C. (2003). To sing or not to sing: a study on the development of non-singers' in choral activity. *Research Studies in Music Education* 20(1): 78–89.

Robb, L. (2000). Emotional musicality in mother-infant vocal affect, and an acoustic study of postnatal depression. *Musicae Scientiae* 3(special issue): 123–154.

Rosselli, J. (2000). Song into theatre: the beginnings of opera. In: J. Potter (ed.), *The Cambridge Companion to Singing*, pp. 83–95. Cambridge: Cambridge University Press.

Rosslau, K., Steinwede, D., Schröder, C., Herholz, S.C., Lappe, C., et al. (2015). Clinical investigations of receptive and expressive musical functions after stroke. *Frontiers in Psychology* 6. doi.org/10.3389/fpsyg.2015.00768

Rutkowski, J. (2015). The relationship between children's use of singing voice and singing accuracy. *Music Perception* 32(3): 283–292.

Saarikallio, S. (2011). Music as emotional self-regulation throughout adulthood. *Psychology of Music* 39(3): 307–327.

Saint-Georges, C., Chetouani, M., Cassel, R., Apicella, F., Mahdhaoui, A., et al. (2013). Motherese in interaction: at the cross-road of emotion and cognition? (A systematic review). *PLoS One* 8(10): e78103. doi:10.1371/journal.pone.0078103

Saito, Y., Ishii, K., Sakuma, N., Kawasaki, K., Oda, K., and Mizusawa, H. (2012). Neural substrates for semantic memory of familiar songs: is there an interface between lyrics and melodies? *PloS One* 7(9): e46354. 10.1371/journal.pone.0046354

Salgardo, A. (2003). *A psycho-philosophical investigation of the perception of emotional meaning in the performance of solo singing (19th century lied repertoire)*. Unpublished PhD thesis, University of Sheffield.

Seckl, J.R. (1998). Physiologic programming of the fetus. *Clinics in Perinatology* 25(4): 939–962.

Sergeant, D. and Welch, G.F. (2008). Age-related changes in long-term average spectra of children's voices. *Journal of Voice* 22(6): 658–670.

Silvey, P. (2001). Perspectives of aging adult choral musicians: implications for meaningful life-long participation in ensemble singing. In: A. Rose and K. Adams (eds), *The Phenomenon of Singing*, Vol. 3, pp. 199–218. St. John's, NF: Memorial University Press.

Skingley, A. and Bungay, H. (2010). The Silver Song Club Project: singing to promote the health of older people. *British Journal of Community Nursing* 15(3): 135–140.

Soley, G. and Sebastián-Gallés, N. (2015). Infants prefer tunes previously introduced by speakers of their native language. *Child Development* 86(6): 1685–1692.

Stark, R.E., Bernstein, L.E., and Demorest, M.E. (1993). Vocal communication in the first 18 months of life. *Journal of Speech, Language, and Hearing Research* 36(3): 548–558.

Stathopoulos, E.T. (2000). A review of the development of the child voice: an anatomical and functional perspective. In: P.J. White (ed.), *Child Voice*, pp. 1–12. Stockholm: Royal Institute of Technology Voice Research Centre.

Stathopoulos, E.T., Huber, J.E., and Sussman, J. (2011). Changes in acoustic characteristics of the voice across the life span: measures from individuals 4–93 years of age. *Journal of Speech, Language and Hearing Research* 54(4): 1011–1021.

Sternberg, E.M. (2001). *The Balance Within: The Science Connecting Health and Emotions*. New York: W.H. Freeman and Company.

Strait, D.L., O'Connell, S., Parbery-Clark, A., and Kraus, N. (2014). Musicians' enhanced neural differentiation of speech sounds arises early in life: developmental evidence from ages 3 to 30. *Cerebral Cortex* 24(9): 2512–2521.

Tafuri, J. (2008). *Infant Musicality*. Farnham: Ashgate.

Taylor, C. and Taylor, V. (2007). Hip hop is now: an evolving youth culture. *Reclaiming Children and Youth* 15(4): 210.

Thurman, L. (2000). The human endocrine system. In: L. Thurman and G. Welch (eds), *Bodymind and Voice: Foundations of Voice Education*, pp. 61–67. Iowa City: National Centre for Voice and Speech.

Thurman, L. and Welch, G. (eds). (2000). *Bodymind and Voice: Foundations of Voice Education.* Iowa City: National Center for Voice and Speech.

Titze, I.R. and Martin, D.W. (1998). Principles of voice production. *Journal of the Acoustical Society of America* 104(3): 1148–1148.

Trainor, L.J. and Zacharias, C.A. (1998). Infants prefer higher-pitched singing. *Infant Behavior and Development* 21(4): 799–805.

Trainor, L.J. and Zatorre, R.J. (2016). The neurobiology of musical expectations from perception to emotion. In: S. Hallam, I. Cross, and M. Thaut (eds), *The Oxford Handbook of Music Psychology*, pp. 285. New York: Oxford University Press.

Trehub, S.E. (1987). Infants' perception of musical patterns. *Perception and Psychophysics* 41(6): 635–641.

Trehub, S.E. (2001). Musical predispositions in infancy. In: R.J. Zatorre and I. Peretz (eds), *The Biological Foundations of Music*, Vol. 930, pp. 1–16. New York: Annals of the New York Academy of Sciences.

Trehub, S.E. (2003). The developmental origins of musicality. *Nature Neuroscience* 6(7): 669–673.

Trehub, S.E. (2016). Infant musicality. In: S. Hallam, I. Cross, and M. Thaut (eds), *The Oxford Handbook of Music Psychology*, pp. 387–398. New York: Oxford University Press.

Trevarthen, C. (2016). From the intrinsic motive pulse of infant actions to the life time of cultural meanings. In: B. Mölder, V. Arstila, and P. Øhrstrøm (eds), *Philosophy and Psychology of Time*, pp. 225–265. Cham, Switzerland: Springer International Publishing.

Vaag, J., Saksvik, P.Ø., Milch, V., Theorell, T., and Bjerkeset, O. (2014). "Sound of Well-being" revisited. Choir singing and well-being among Norwegian municipal employees. *Journal of Applied Arts and Health* 5(1): 51–63.

Vella-Burrows, T. (2012). *Singing and People with Dementia.* Canterbury: Sidney De Haan Research Centre for Arts and Health.

Vihman, M.M. (1996). *Phonological Development: The Origins of Language in the Child.* Oxford: Blackwell Publishing.

Weinstein, D., Launay, J., Pearce, E., Dunbar, R.I.M., and Stewart, L. (2016). Group music performance causes elevated pain thresholds and social bonding in small and large groups of singers. *Evolution and Human Behavior* 37(2): 152–158.

Welch, G.F. (1985). A schema theory of how children learn to sing in tune. *Psychology of Music* 13(1): 3–18.

Welch, G.F. (1986). A developmental view of children's singing. *British Journal of Music Education* 3(3): 295–303.

Welch, G.F., Sergeant, D.C., and White, P.J. (1995). The singing competencies of five-year-old developing singers. *Bulletin of the Council for Research in Music Education* 127: 155–162.

Welch, G.F., Sergeant, D.C., and White, P.J. (1997). Age, sex, and vocal task as factors in singing "in tune" during the first years of schooling. *Bulletin of the Council for Research in Music Education* 133: 153–160.

Welch, G.F. (1998). Early childhood musical development. *Research Studies in Music Education* 11(1): 27–41.

Welch, G.F., Sergeant, D.C., and White, P.J. (1998). The role of linguistic dominance in the acquisition of song. *Research Studies in Music Education* 10(1): 67–74.

Welch, G.F. and Thurman, L. (2000). Vitality, health and vocal self-expression in older adults. In: L. Thurman and G.F. Welch (eds), *Bodymind and Voice: Foundations of Voice Education*, pp. 745–753. Iowa City: National Center for Voice and Speech.

Welch, G. F. (2001). *The Misunderstanding of Music*. London: Institute of Education.

Welch, G.F. and Howard, D.M. (2002). Gendered voice in the cathedral choir. *Psychology of Music* 30(1): 102–120.

Welch, G.F. and Sundberg, J. (2002). Solo voice. In: R. Parncutt and G. McPherson (eds), *The Science and Psychology of Music Performance: Creative Strategies for Teaching and Learning*, pp. 253–268. Oxford: Oxford University Press.

Welch, G.F. (2005). Singing as communication. In: D. Miell, R.A.R. MacDonald, and D. J. Hargreaves (eds), *Musical Communication*, pp. 239–259. Oxford: Oxford University Press.

Welch, G.F., Howard, D.M., Himonides, E., and Brereton, J. (2005). Real-time feedback in the singing studio: an innovatory action-research project using new voice technology. *Music Education Research* 7(2): 225–249.

Welch, G.F. (2009a). Evidence of the development of vocal pitch matching ability in children. *Japanese Journal of Music Education Research* 39(1): 38–47.

Welch, G.F. (2009b). Researching singing and vocal development across the lifespan: a personal case study. In: K. Adams and L. Chisolm (eds), *The Phenomenon of Singing*, Vol. 4, pp. 178–190. St. John's, NF: Memorial University Press.

Welch, G.F., Saunders, J., Papageorgi, I., and Himonides, E. (2012). Sex, gender and singing development: making a positive difference to boys' singing through a national programme in England. In: S. Harrison, G.F. Welch, and A. Adler (eds), *Perspectives on Males and Singing*, pp. 27–43. Cham, Switzerland: Springer International Publishing.

Welch, G.F., Himonides, E., Saunders, J., Papageorgi, I., and Sarazin, M. (2014). Singing and social inclusion. *Frontiers in Psychology* 5: 803. doi: 10.3389/fpsyg.2014.00803

Welch, G.F. (2016). Singing and vocal development. In: G. McPherson (ed.), *The Child as Musician: A Handbook of Musical Development*, 2nd edn, pp. 441–461. New York: Oxford University Press.

Welch, G.F. (2017). The identities of singers and their educational environments. In: R.A.R. MacDonald, D.J. Hargreaves, and D. Miell (eds), *Oxford Handbook of Musical Identities*, pp. 543–565. Oxford: Oxford University Press.

Werker, J.F. and McLeod, P.J. (1989). Infant preference for both male and female infant-directed talk: a developmental study of attentional and affective responsiveness. *Canadian Journal of Psychology/Revue canadienne de psychologie* 43(2): 230.

Wiens, H., Janzen, H.L., and Murray, J.B. (2001). Heal the voice—heal the person: a pilot study on the effects of voice training. In: A. Rose and K. Adams (eds), *The Phenomenon of Singing*, Vol. 3, pp. 228–234. St. John's, NF: Memorial University Press.

Wikipedia. (2016). Cytokine, https://en.wikipedia.org/wiki/Cytokine, last accessed October 15, 2017.

Wise, K. (2017). Defining and explaining singing difficulties in adults. In: G.F. Welch, D.M. Howard, and J. Nix (eds), *The Oxford Handbook of Singing*. New York: Oxford University Press.

Wise, K.J. and Sloboda, J.A. (2008). Establishing an empirical profile of self-defined "tone deafness": perception, singing performance and self-assessment. *Musicae Scientiae* 12(1): 3–26.

Woodward, S. (2017). Fetal, neonatal and early infant experiences of maternal singing. In: G.F. Welch, D.M. Howard, and J. Nix (eds), *The Oxford Handbook of Singing*. New York: Oxford University Press.

World Health Organization (2012). *Dementia: A Public Health Priority* (9241564458). http://www.who.int/iris/handle/10665/75263, last accessed October 15, 2017.

Zatorre, R.J., Perry, D.W., Beckett, C.A., Westbury, C.F., and Evans, A.C. (1998). Functional anatomy of musical processing in listeners with absolute pitch and relative pitch. *Proceedings of the National Academy of Sciences* 95(6): 3172–3177.

Zatorre, R.J. and Krumhansl, C.L. (2002). Mental models and musical minds. *Science* 298(5601): 2138–2139.

CHAPTER 19

......

DIGITAL LIBRARIES FOR SINGING
The Example of the AIRS Project

......

ANNABEL J. COHEN AND KAREN M. LUDKE

Introduction

......

THE following three situations have often characterized research in singing. The first focuses on collaborative ventures. Research in singing frequently benefits from collaboration, which usually requires access to shared vocal materials. Collaborators may reside in institutions quite distant from each other. Until the twenty-first century, this often meant the need for travel in order to discuss the vocal objects of interest. The second situation focuses on the individual researcher or research team members who may record large collections of vocal performance. While the research may focus on one particular aspect of the recordings, other aspects of the collection might be of interest to many other researchers, in the same or a related discipline. Until recently, such corpora were perceived as the property of the researcher and would be associated with his or her research. When the researcher retired, the corpora retired as well. The final situation focuses on the wide variety of types of analyses on many levels and timespans to which examples of singing can be submitted. Typically, various researchers specialize in certain forms of analysis and publish their work in specialized journals. Broadly understanding the particular vocal object of analysis could benefit from simultaneous access to the variety of analyses published in diverse sources; however, accessing these sources has in the past been a time-consuming research project in itself.

All three of the cases above describe situations in which practicalities impede progress. In one case, travel is required in order to access resources. In another, resources collected by one group are tied to a particular research project. Take for example the collection of over 3,000 improvisations that Sági and Vitányi (1988) gathered systematically from 220 persons in an exploration of the natural ability to create songs in Hungary. Consider also the recordings of the developmental psychologists Papoušek and Papoušek (1981) of their child's early vocalizations, or the annual recordings at ages 5, 6, and 7 years in a longitudinal study of over 180 primary school children in London who sang two songs and their independent musical elements (Welch et al. 1998). While important findings resulted from the analyses of these corpora by the original research teams, other researchers might well discover additional information if they had access to the recordings. The benefits of this shared access is seen in rare examples when different researchers have chosen to direct their attention to the same commercially available vocal recordings, such as Schubert's *Ave Maria* (Devaney et al. 2011; Prame 1994; Sundberg et al. 2007). Imagine the value of having multiple analyses in the same online location, with specific audio resources accessible and annotatable by anyone with Internet access. Such a scenario was hardly conceivable in the twentieth century, but today, in the form of a digital library for singing, it can be a reality.

This chapter provides background on the concept of a digital library and the functions of a digital library in the support of research. It then discusses the general benefits of a digital library for research on singing, and also describes the general challenges encountered in such an initiative. A particular example of the development of a digital library for singing research is then presented with specific reference to the AIRS Project (www.airsplace.ca), which aims to advance interdisciplinary research in singing.

Examples of Digital Libraries

At its most basic, a digital library is an organized collection of electronic resources related to a particular topic or area of knowledge. Beyond this, however, the term "digital library" may mean different things to different people. A highly influential paper entitled "What are digital libraries: Competing visions" contrasts the perspectives of researchers who see digital libraries as "content collected on behalf of user communities" with the view of practicing librarians who "view digital libraries as institutions or services" (Borgman 1999, p. 227).[1] Some digital libraries, or repositories as they are often called, are dynamic, allowing for the inclusion of new data (such as commentary, annotations, or analyses) over time, and others

---

[1] The much quoted definition of the term "digital libraries" developed by the NSF-sponsored Social Aspects of Digital Libraries workshop (Borgman et al. 1996) is as follows:

1. Digital libraries are a set of electronic resources and associated technical capabilities for creating, searching and using information. In this sense they are an extension and enhancement of information storage and retrieval systems that manipulate digital data in any medium (text, images, sounds; static or dynamic images) and exist in distributed networks. The content of digital libraries includes data, metadata that describe various aspects of the data (e.g. representation, creator, owner, reproduction rights) and metadata that consist of links or relationships to other data or metadata, whether internal or external to the digital library.

2. Digital libraries are constructed, collected and organized, by (and for) a community of users, and their functional capabilities support the information needs and uses of that community. They are a component of communities in which individuals and groups interact with each other, using data, information and knowledge resources and systems. In this sense they are an extension, enhancement and integration of a variety of information institutions as physical places where resources are selected, collected, organized, preserved and accessed in support of a user community. These information institutions include, among others, libraries, museums, archives and schools, but digital libraries also extend and serve other community settings, including classrooms, offices, laboratories, homes and public spaces (as quoted in Borgman 1999, p. 234).

are fixed, serving as an archive of previously collected information. There are increasing numbers of digital repositories for archiving musical materials, sound, and speech. The functionality of a digital repository depends on the initial design, the type of content included, and the ways of describing each resource through relevant metadata. Any library is useful only to the extent that its content is accessible. The digital libraries for music and sound described in this section are remarkable for the accessibility of their data (available to a significant number of users) and the consequent ability to revolutionize research and scholarship in their specific fields. This list of examples is not exhaustive, but we also include a few repositories that provide useful prototypes for a digital library that supports singing research, even when they were not designed with that purpose in mind and have some features that also do not lend themselves to that purpose.

Sheet Music Consortium

http://digital2.library.ucla.edu/sheetmusic/

This is a resource developed to enable greater access to printed sheet music in digital format, for academic researchers as well as students and members of the public. Hosted by UCLA, this consortium's database contains more than 225,000 items. The word "consortium" is rightly chosen to represent the 35 different digital libraries for sheet music available through the site. About 80 percent of these individual sheet music libraries are part of university libraries in the United States. Across all of these corpora, one may find an entire collection of 18 songs inspired by the sinking of the Titanic, and two songs commemorating the sinking of the Lusitania (an ocean liner torpedoed several years later). More generally, both classical and popular genres are well represented, and pedagogical works spanning the last two centuries can be found. While such information can be invaluable to certain kinds of research in singing, there are no audio recordings, and functions such as downloading the digital content, adding, or searching user-generated metadata are not available (although one can copy page by page, and there is a type of advanced search). In addition, access to some content depends on the copyright restrictions for the specific repository that hosts the sheet music.

The British Library Sound Archive

http://sounds.bl.uk/

This resource of the British Library contains over 89,000 selected recordings of "music, spoken word and human and natural environments." A number of collections of songs of ethnomusicological interest can be found here: for example, songs of the Dinka of South Sudan. Song and singing play a special role in the lives of the Dinka people, and the songs were recorded for the purpose of exploring the relation between the Dinka song and language (Ladd 2013). This specific collection is not dynamic, but other collections are. For example, a collection of children's games and songs (see http://sounds.bl.uk/Oral-history/Opie-collection-of-children-s-games-and-songs-) resulting from the dedicated efforts of Iona and Peter Opie (1985) primarily in the 1970s provides an "Add a note" link on the image of the sound file, which, pending approval, can be stored with the file. While some of these digitized recordings are almost 50 years old, their fate is much less precarious than songs stored on analogue tape or other media. The British Library aims to address the critical fragility of its old analogue audio resources. There is a costly race against time to preserve degrading cylinders, recorded disks, and tapes through a massive digitization project.

The Library of Congress in Washington, DC

https://www.loc.gov/

The US Library of Congress lists a total of over 400,000 results for the word "song" in its catalogue and over 125,000 items that are available online. Some materials are available in collections such as the "Coal River Folklife Collection" and "California Gold: Northern California Folk Music from the Thirties Collected by Sidney Robertson Cowell." The vast majority of the song-related content is in the form of digitized sheet music (also accessible in the Sheet Music Consortium described earlier), but there are also approximately 5,000 audio recordings and 1,000 video recordings available online. However, due to copyright restrictions, most of the material is not available for download for further data analysis.

The Smithsonian Institution and the Folkways project

http://www.si.edu/

The Smithsonian Institute, also based in Washington, has collected vast archives of historical and scientific materials, datasets, art, and other cultural artifacts such as audio and video recordings, with more than 1.3 million accessible online (http://collections.si.edu/search/). A search on "singing" produces over 1,200 examples, many of which are audiovideo recordings that are immediately playable. The Smithsonian Folkways project (http://www.folkways.si.edu/browse-collection/smithsonian) contains folk music collections from the United States and around the world, such as the Archives and Research Centre for Ethnomusicology (A.R.C.E.) (www.folkways.si.edu/archives-and-research-centre-for-ethnomusicology-arce/smithsonian), which holds recordings of Indian music. Many of these recordings are albums available for sale (through Smithsonian Folkways, the non-profit record label of the Smithsonian Institution), with short excerpts of every song accessible for previewing. Smithsonian Folkways also hosts the UNESCO Collection of Traditional Music, which "contains music recordings from more than 70 nations" that were mostly collected as field recordings.

DigiCult and Europeana

http://www.europeana.eu/portal/

As part of the Community Research and Development Information Service (CORDIS), the Digital Heritage and Cultural Content (DigiCult) program (http://www.echo.lu/digicult/) has funded many digitization projects designed to share and archive important cultural material from all member countries of the European Union. Now housed under the Creativity strand of the European Commission's ICT program (http://cordis.europa.eu/

fp7/ict/creativity/creativity_en.html), it aims to fund projects including leading-edge ICT research and innovation and to provide policy support. A search of the European Digital Library, Europeana (http://www.europeana.eu/portal/), for the word "song" produces more than 80,000 results, some including audio recordings, while others provide links to libraries and online repositories that host the digital audio content. Searching for the word "song" in other European languages also results in thousands of audio recordings of sung material. However, many of these materials are not available for download and data analysis due to copyright restrictions.

Variations—Digital Music Library of Indiana University

www.dlib.indiana.edu/projects/variations3

In the late 1990s, the University of Indiana started a project that aimed to provide online access to the library's collection of sound recordings and to "integrate a database of music information objects (text, images, scores, sound, and a catalogue) with a graphically oriented hypermedia user interface" (Dunn and Mayer 1999, p. 12). The Variations Project (http://variations. indiana.edu/index.html) enabled scholars and music students to access a variety of information related to a particular musical "object" in one online location. This successful project has continued to grow, with the open-source Variations3 in 2009 (http://www.dlib.indiana. edu/projects/variations3/) allowing other institutions to take advantage of the University of Indiana's digital library for music. In addition, the Variations3 project created a new metadata model "centered on the notion of the musical work" to "improve the music search experience for users over traditional catalog systems." (Indiana University Digital Library Program 2009). In 2011 the Variations on Video project began as a multi-institutional endeavor to update the existing technology and add videos, as well as enhance the search capabilities and experiment with enabling end-users to enrich the basic metadata about musical works.

It has been said, when it comes to computing, "if you can do music, you can do anything" (Ichiro Fujinaga, personal communication 2008). In 2010, the Variations Project led the way to an expanded system that went far beyond its focus of supporting the streaming of music for university courses to supporting both university teaching and research needs, which were more and more centered on audio and video. Called the Avalon Media System, this free, "open source system for managing and providing access to large collections of digital audio and video" (http://www.avalonmediasystem.org/) aims to enable libraries to create online audiovisual archives which researchers, students and members of the public can access. A consortium of 12 educational, media, and open-technology institutions have developed the system, under the leadership of the libraries of Indiana University and Northwestern University in the USA.

CNRS Musée de l'Homme audio archives database

http://archives.crem-cnrs.fr/

As described by Khoury and Simonnot (2014), "(t)he online Web-based platform for the French CNRS-Musée de l'Homme audio archives offers access to about 28,000 published and unpublished recordings of music" from around the world. The catalogue is organized according to four hierarchical levels, from highest to lowest: the Archive Series, Corpus, Collection, and Item levels. The sound file is the lowest-level unit and is ingested at the "item" level. Associated items are placed within a collection, the main level of entry into the database. Because someone or an institution has taken responsibility for the gathering or depositing of data, all of the collections by this person or institution are organized into a separate corpus identified by a theme or geographical area, and all corpora associated with that individual or institution are part of the highest-level category, the series. Thus the highest level is designated with respect to the originator who holds or held responsibility for the corpus. Additional contextual information about the individual or institution is attached to these highest levels of series and corpora.

Cornell Lab of Ornithology, Macaulay Library

http://macaulaylibrary.org

The Macaulay Library claims to be "the world's largest and oldest scientific archive of biodiversity audio and video recordings" (Cornell University Lab of Ornithology 2016). Its original focus on birdsong was later expanded to the sounds of all living species. Originating in the late 1920s, the first recordings were audiovisual and were made with new film technology. Eventually various audiotape recording techniques provided better archiving potential, leading to an entirely audio collection of the rest of the twentieth century. In the twenty-first century, recognizing that audio represents only one aspect of behavior, video regained interest at the same time that digitized audiovisual recording became feasible. The library for sound now welcomes video recordings. It is noted that this largest sound repository has only 16 audio recordings of humans, compared to over 3,500 for other primates, and almost 135,000 of birds of many species including storks (49), penguins (154) and passerines (almost 95,000).

CHILDES—Children's Language Data Exchange System

http://childes.talkbank.org/

Child language and speech development has been greatly advanced by the Children's Language Data Exchange System (CHILDES), which was co-founded by Brian MacWhinney and Catherine Snow (MacWhinney and Snow 1985; MacWhinney 2000, 2014), who have both contributed to empirically based child language theory for over four decades. More than 100 researchers have transcribed children's spoken discourse in accordance with codes specially created for CHILDES. A common coding system for sounds, grammatical features, words, and utterances, as well as higher-level descriptors of the data (age of speaker, gender, other interlocutors, location/context) was designed to allow for the flexible search and analysis of samples. In recent years, through Talkbank, a more general, higher-order content management system for communications research of all types, content in the database includes audio and video recordings. The CHILDES database has led to over 5,000 published research papers, primarily in the field of developmental psycholinguistics. The success of this digital library in serving the community of researchers of early child discourse suggests the possibility that a similar digital library might have equal success in serving the community of researchers interested in how children acquire the ability to sing and in communication through singing more generally. A "CHIMES" digital library could in theory provide a foundation for a massive outpouring of research on the acquisition of singing.

Singing corpus

http://sldr.org/voir_depot.php?id=774&lang=en&sip=1

A corpus consisting of two songs ("Happy Birthday" and a specific romantic melody) sung by 50 trained vocalists, from 19 to 66 years of age, was collected by Pauline Larrouy-Maestri (2012) from the School of Psychology at Liège University in Belgium. The first song was initially sung naturally, and then with an operatic performance style. The second song was sung three times: first naturally, second, with an operatic technique, and finally humming (with a closed mouth). The corpus is hosted by the Speech and Language Data Repository (SLDR/ORTOLANG) and this "Happy Birthday" corpus (along with a wide range of language archives) is available for download by researchers who register to become part of this group. Submitting the 200 songs (i.e. all but hummed versions) to acoustical analysis, Larrouy-Maestri et al. (2014) showed that vocal technique rather than melodic style impacted the acoustical parameters measured (e.g. energy distribution, vibrato characteristics) as well as musical features such as the average tempo, and loudness (sound pressure level), and were also able to develop a profile of the operatic singing technique. An earlier corpus created by Larrouy-Maestri (2011) includes the recordings of "Happy Birthday" performed by 166 French occasional (untrained) singers, ranging in age from 14 to 76 years. These recordings were submitted to acoustical analysis of note accuracy and were also judged for accuracy by 18 experienced vocalists or instrumentalists, which revealed congruence between the objective and subjective measures. As these databases would be available to others with legitimate research interests in singing, it would be possible for other researchers to analyze the materials in other ways (e.g. the choice of starting note; correlation of various measures with age; the role of voice quality or rhythmic accuracy on the subjective judgments), including ideas suggested by Larrouy-Maestri et al. in their publication (2014).

Developing and maintaining the valuable digital repositories described above requires the commitment of technical expertise and time; steady financial support from major granting agencies, foundations, universities, and industry; the application or adaptation of new technologies and infrastructure; and dedicated space. None of the existing digital libraries for sound could fulfill all the functions required by a dynamic digital library that would support the singing research conducted by AIRS collaborators' international, multimodal, interdisciplinary research. However, the various functions that these digital libraries serve suggest that this endeavor is within the capability of current technology.

Development of the AIRS Digital Library

The Advancing Interdisciplinary Research in Singing (AIRS) project began a major collaborative research initiative on singing (Cohen 2008, 2011), with over 70 investigators and many more students from around the world. The AIRS project aimed to conduct interdisciplinary research on singing from the perspectives of development, education and well-being. A digital library was required to facilitate distant AIRS members' work on the same data, such as the analysis of examples from voice studios around the world, stage performances, playgrounds, public places, solos, groups, classrooms, intergenerational or multicultural choirs, therapeutic settings, or new tests of singing skills (Cohen 2008; Vincent et al. 2011). Plans also included tools for annotation and analysis along with relevant documents and images. This section describes the preliminary prototypes, stages of development, and the current functional implementation of the AIRS Digital Library. It is noted that although singing is primarily an acoustic and auditory phenomenon, video records of the singer(s) are very valuable. Their benefit, however, must be weighed against challenges arising from ethical considerations and digital storage requirements. Issues of ownership and data sharing are also raised, as well as practical matters of choice of platform, storage, formats, backup, human resources, and long-term preservation.

One should not underestimate the time to develop a user-friendly, comprehensive digital library, particularly a dynamic one in which users can not only access data but can also add new data collections and comment or add to existing datasets. Khoury and Simmonot (2014) comment on seven years of work by engineers of the CREM (the Laboratory for Musical Acoustics) and web developers (from the Parisson Company) which led to a content management system and architecture to support the audio archives database for the Musée de l'homme. Once established, two full-time engineers with an ethnomusicological background manage the system with the additional help of part-time employees and students.

Fenlon et al. (2014) also describe the process of designing resources for researchers, including those in the digital humanities. They point out that at the heart of much research is the creation of collections of information. Support for research entails enabling researchers to build, access, and share these collections. The authors report on their focus group study which asked researchers to speak about their needs as builders of collections. The findings highlight the difficulty of designing digital resources to meet the unique and changing requirements of the individual researcher. Needless to say, the establishment of a digital library for AIRS was ambitious and has understandably undergone several iterations in its efforts to serve the interdisciplinary research team.

Functionality of the AIRS Digital Library

The AIRS Digital Library was developed to have the following functionality:

1. Long-term storage of vocal recordings at reasonably high resolution, including data collected in laboratory studies, solo (voice studio) and choral pedagogy, choir rehearsals, singing in natural settings (e.g. school playgrounds) and therapeutic settings (e.g. homes for seniors), and singing and speech data for the same individual.

2. Allow researchers to add information (e.g. annotation) or link to their data analyses (e.g. acoustic) so that they can build on one another's work and so that knowledge can accumulate rather than be duplicated. One example of singing contains more information than any researcher can fully analyze. By uploading new knowledge and tools along with examples, a multidisciplinary team can better develop our understanding of the nature and benefits of singing.

3. Provide examples for educators, music therapists and others:

   (a) Songs and singing examples with information about the cultural context that gives meaning to the songs or through which the songs bring cultural understanding;

   (b) Pedagogical examples of models (e.g. singing lessons within a voice studio) that can be used for serious voice study or voice pedagogy study (i.e. how to teach singing);

   (c) Materials for use in intergenerational singing (e.g. in homes for seniors or community choirs) or for developing international or multicultural choirs;

   (d) Singing exercises for various health disorders (e.g. lung diseases, Parkinson's disease, speech and language pathology).

4. Provide a place for rare, potentially otherwise perishable, cultural archives (e.g. native songs that exist only as oral tradition) that can be used for studies of song and cultural evolution (although there may be more appropriate ethnomusicological repositories).

5. Provide tools for analyzing or transforming vocal audio or notational data, both for particular individuals and groups: acoustical, anthropological, linguistic, (musical) structural, psychological, and sociological analyses. Specific procedures or tools developed by one researcher or research group (e.g. Ness et al. 2010) can be made available in one place for all researchers.

6. Provide search features using an appropriate, well-designed metadata scheme and leading-edge open-source technology. Using an open-source platform to hold the digital material allows for greater flexibility in the included information and annotation features.

In the AIRS project, each singing-related research question fits into a research framework that focuses on development, education, and well-being, along with sub-categories for each theme (see Table 19.1). A fourth primary research outcome of the project is the AIRS Digital Library itself. A key component of metadata for the AIRS Digital Library is to assign every resource to at least one theme or sub-theme using the hierarchical structure of this AIRS Research Framework.

AIRS Digital Library Prototypes

A first prototype of the AIRS Digital Library, devised with the help of the UPEI Robertson Library using the Drupal open-source software content-management environment, provided a further breakdown within each of the nine sub-themes: Experiments, Studies, Demonstrations, and Miscellaneous. Navigating to a particular category within a sub-theme led to another drop-down menu, which listed all of the experiments, studies, etc., for which data existed. Navigation to an experiment with the AIRS Test Battery of Singing Skills (Cohen et al. 2009), for example, produced a further menu that revealed the code name for a participant, one of five sessions, and the 11 different components for each test session. Each

Table 19.1 Structure of AIRS Research into three primary themes each with three
          sub-themes

Development	Education	Well-being
Perception and Production of Singing	Learning to Sing Naturally	Singing and Cross-cultural Understanding
Multimodal Aspects of Singing	Formal Teaching of Singing	Singing and Intergenerational Understanding
AIRS Test Battery of Singing Skills	Using Singing to Teach	Singing and Direct Benefits to Mental and Physical Health

component revealed an audiovisual clip of a participant in the study performing a particular singing skill, such as creating a song, singing a familiar song, learning a new song, or carrying out a language task. An ingestion system enabled the uploading of each segment and the provision of searchable metadata. While the ingestion process was slow, the primary issue was that this database was not built for scale. Its great value was in the establishment of a working prototype, whereby audiovisual information from a research study could be uploaded through a hierarchy of structural levels for sharing across a network of individuals.

In 2012, Nyssim Lefford conducted a formal survey of the needs of AIRS researchers regarding data types, quantity, and file formats. With this information, a new Digital Library prototype (version 1.0) was developed and included a wider variety of data. The model was developed using Drupal and was highly accessible, available as part of the AIRS website to anyone with a user ID and password. The prototype held mainly textual information, such as descriptors of datasets and links to the content owner (i.e. an individual AIRS researcher). While AIRS DL 1.0 contained a wide variety of singing research examples, the search features were limited.

The third AIRS Digital Library (version 2.0) was developed later in 2012 and improved permission features by enabling a sub-group of researchers to share otherwise confidential data. This prototype also added advanced search features, based on custom metadata options that reflected content types important to the AIRS user community. Each content type was associated with a custom set of metadata fields, some of which were common to all content types while others were unique to a particular content type. As an example, the Bibliography content type had metadata fields including: Title, AIRS Theme, Researchers/authors, Publication date, Keywords, Format, and Permissions, whereas the Interview content type also included fields such as Subject/Country and Authority lists.

AIRS Digital Library version 3.0

In 2014–2015, the AIRS Digital Library version 3.0 was built using an open-source Drupal website integrated with Fedora (or Flexible Extensible Digital Object Repository Architecture), together known as Islandora. Islandora was developed as a digital asset management framework by Mark Leggott, Donald Moses, and their team at the UPEI Robertson Library (www.islandora.ca).

This version of the AIRS Digital Library has benefited greatly from earlier versions in terms of both structure and functionality. However, an important advantage of version 3.0 is that the AIRS Digital Library is now integrated with the main AIRS website, using the same login ID and password to determine user access (viewing, downloading, and editing capabilities) for a file or the saved information about a file. Some of the AIRS Digital Library files can be viewed and downloaded by the general public (without logging in) whereas other files are available only to people who have the appropriate AIRS login credentials, only to people in a particular AIRS sub-theme, or only to specifically identified individuals (e.g. collaborators on a research project that is still in progress). Achieving this level of control over user access permissions was an essential requirement for AIRS researchers, in part due to the sensitivity of participants who are singing (who themselves have the ethical right to define who has the right to see their data), in part due to the fact that the data are not just audio but also video, and in part because the researchers themselves wanted a secure and private workspace for their particular team. However, this does not mean that the researchers would never share information with other AIRS members or beyond to the public arena for research and educational purposes. Figure 19.1 shows four sample screenshots from video

FIGURE 19.1 Sample screenshot from video clips related to a cross-cultural study of singing which involved children in Brazil, Kenya, China and Canada. Top left shows Brazilian children singing and top right, an individual child modeling the pronunciation of the first line of the song [with kind permission of Alda de Jesus Oliveira, from the Quadcultural Songbook study under direction of Lily Chen-Hafteck]. Bottom left shows children from Kenya singing and bottom right, an individual child modeling the pronunciation of the first line of the song. [With kind permission of Elizabeth Andang'o, from the Quadcultural Songbook study.]

clips related to a particular cross-cultural study that involved children in Brazil, Kenya, China, and Canada.

There are multiple ways to access the resources held in the AIRS Digital Library. Users may browse items that have been grouped by theme or sub-theme, or they can search for individual files using the basic and advanced search functions. Depending on the search terms and the metadata included for particular files, the search functions will return a different number of results; if too many files are found, it is possible to refine the search criteria (e.g. by date of publication) by choosing that option on the search results screen.

Examples of singing data for the AIRS Digital Library include:

- audio recordings of individuals and small groups singing
- audio and audiovideo recordings of 4–9-year-old children from the AIRS Test Battery of Singing Skills (ATBSS)
- citations linking to published resources related to the AIRS themes and sub-themes
- image files of poster presentations about singing that have been given by AIRS members
- PDF files of singing-related research papers that have been published by AIRS members
- video recordings of voice lessons in the teaching studio
- video recordings of adults (young and older) obtained from the ATBSS.
- video recordings of AIRS annual meetings (presentations and performances)
- video recordings of successive rehearsals of a choir
- audiovisual materials supporting a multi-national project.

For those who wish to contribute to the AIRS Digital Library, there are several ways to upload different types of files, including a batch upload option. Registered users may upload as many items to the AIRS DL as they wish, provided that they include the required metadata for each one. An online webform for uploading individual files makes it clear to the user which information about the resource must be provided. The required information includes the file type, the title, the type of resource, the AIRS theme or sub-themes, and copyright and user access information. For batch uploads, only one file type (e.g. .pdf) can be uploaded at a time. The metadata for each file is first entered into rows of a special Excel spreadsheet and then a macro is used to convert a Word file into multiple plain text files with the metadata for each resource. These individual text files are then combined into a .ZIP file along with each of the .pdf files corresponding to the metadata, and then uploaded to the repository. For more information, see the AIRS Digital Library at http://airsplace.ca/about/digital-library.

As previously mentioned, one of the advantages of the AIRS Digital Library is that it enables researchers in any location to access and contribute to the project, including the analysis of others' collected data. For example, in a project measuring how singing leads to the development of gross and fine motor skills, for which video recordings of children's singing and clapping games were collected, the same data could potentially be used by later investigators along with a larger corpus of children's singing to chart the natural development of singing accuracy for rhythm or pitch amongst children of different age ranges or in different cultures.

Figure 19.2 shows how the data for a particular research study might be found within the current structure of the AIRS Digital Library. Clicking on the folder for Theme 1–Development reveals a deeper level, consisting of three different sub-themes, which then leads to a level listing the surnames of different researchers working in that sub-theme.

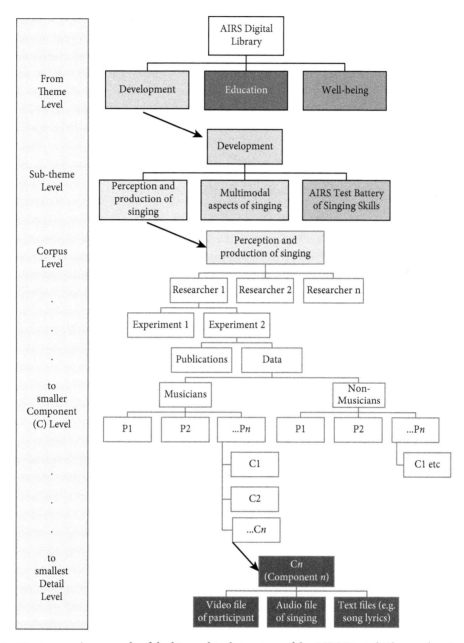

FIGURE 19.2 An example of the hierarchical structure of the AIRS Digital Library, showing the highest level of the three themes, the next level of the breakdown of the sub-themes within that research theme, several researchers contributing to that sub-theme at the next level, an experiment carried out by a researcher, a further breakdown into publications and data, the latter broken further into the data of musicians and non-musicians, and a folder for each of the participants (e.g. P1, P2, . . ., P*n*), various sung components for each participant, and finally video, audio, and text files for each component.

Underneath this level may be folders that list different projects, for example, a particular research study, experiment, or demonstration. In this project, an "experiment" refers to the acquisition of data through a formal set of procedures that allow various conditions to be compared in the testing of hypotheses, whereas a study might be more exploratory, following a process more likely to be carried out in the arts and humanities than in the sciences, and the data analysis might be more amenable to qualitative as opposed to quantitative techniques. A study might entail the collection of a particular kind of singing data (e.g. from particular choirs of interest at successive rehearsals) that would provide a resource for those researchers or others to use later. The particular example represented in Figure 19.2 shows an Experiment, but similar concepts could apply to the other research categories, each of which may have many types of data and files associated with a particular project within that sub-theme.

After choosing "Experiment 2," in this example the user can view a further sub-level for Publications or documents associated with the Experiment or data derived from the experiment, found in the Data folder. The diagram expands the Data category, which in this case is further divided into two categories, musicians and non-musicians, and within each category a folder is included for each individual participant. Within the participant folders are files for each task completed, called components (C_1, C_2 ... C_n). Within each component, the data types acquired in this example experiment include video, audio, and text files. This is the lowest level shown; however, additional levels could be added to further analyze the data files. For example, the segmentation of each note in the audio file for each participant could be added, furthering the pitch analysis conducted by ear or by a computer algorithm. Thus, other researchers can build on the data and analysis provided in this study, or check the accuracy of a new method compared to previous analysis techniques.

Conclusion

Data collected in research is costly and time consuming. Moreover, its funding typically comes from government resources, which in turn have come from taxpayers. Other institutions may have also provided resources. Looked at in this way, all research outcomes might be regarded as jointly owned by the researchers who dedicated their time and intelligence to the work, and the organizations and government institutions that supported the work. Recognizing research as a public resource, funding agencies such as the Wellcome Trust in Britain, the National Institutes of Health in the United States, the Social Sciences and Humanities Research Council of Canada (SSHRC), the Natural Sciences and Engineering Research Council of Canada (NSERC), and the Canadian Institute for Health Research (CIHR) have instituted a requirement to provide open access to all publications arising from their funding. This requirement, however, only goes so far. A further step is to publish the data along with the research publication. Beyond this, provision of the statistical tests carried out on the data would add a further level of information. But ultimately, access to raw data, such as audiovisual recordings of singing, may be of greatest benefit to the research community.

There are, however, costs in providing access to data through a digital library. As mentioned earlier in this chapter, simply depositing information in a digital resource is of no use unless the resource is searchable. The infrastructure must also be organized so as to effectively serve end-users, and it must be maintained over time. In addition, safeguards must be put in place such that the use of data is properly managed and acknowledged, in the same way that using information from a published article entails acknowledging the work through a complete reference. The AIRS Digital Library has been developed with ideals in mind of maximizing data sharing, reuse, transparency of workflow, linkage of data to publications, and broad dissemination of findings. While the process of development is complex, we believe that ultimately there will be extraordinary benefits for progress in our field of research on singing in its many aspects.

In closing, we point to a few questions that the AIRS Digital Library (and singing-related DLs in general) can hopefully help us answer. Some are feasible with the data and analysis tools we already have, whereas others are projects for the future.

- To what extent does the natural development of children's singing correspond to the rate of their development of speech, and how does vocal training support these skills?
- Can we identify different levels of singing ability in order to target age- and skill-appropriate group training for use in school, extracurricular, or community settings?
- What are effective techniques for training singers in the voice studio?
- What are effective techniques for choral leadership?
- How can singing be best exploited to teach other skills, for example, language?
- Can we use the relatively intact ability of individuals with Alzheimer's disease and dementia to sing old favorite songs to improve relationships between these individuals and those who help care for them?
- To what extent does enjoyment in singing depend on your cultural understanding (whether of your own or another culture), as represented in the song being sung?
- Can singing the songs of another culture increase an individual's positive attitude toward members of that culture?

Author Note: A portion of this work was presented at the International Congress on Acoustics in 2013 as represented in a conference proceedings paper (Cohen et al. 2013). This was prior to the work of Karen Ludke as postdoctoral fellow who, over an eight-month period, managed the recent development of AIRS DL 3.0 between December 2013 to August 2014.

ACKNOWLEDGMENTS

Many thanks go to Tom Germaine, Ryan Sampson, George Tzanetakis, Ichiro Fujinaga, Mike Forrester, Nyssim Lefford, Theresa Leonard, the Islandora team (Mark Leggott, Donald Moses et al.) at the Robertson Library, Bing-Yi Pan, Polina Proutskova, and Coralie Vincent for their valuable contributions to this endeavor, which have greatly aided us in creating the third version of the AIRS Digital Library. The Social Sciences and Humanities Research Council is gratefully acknowledged for its support of the AIRS Major Collaborative Research Initiative, which is directed by Annabel J. Cohen since 2008.

References

Borgman, C.L., Bates, M.J., Cloonan, M.V., Efthimiadis, E.N., Gilliland-Swetland, A., Kafai, Y., Leazer, G.L., and Maddox, A. (1996). *Social Aspects of Digital Libraries: Final Report to the National Science Foundation*, pp. 227–234.

Borgman, C.L. (1999). What are digital libraries? Competing visions. *Information Processing and Management* 35: 227–243, https://www.ischool.utexas.edu/~i385d/readings/Borgman-1999-What_Are_Digital_Libraries.pdf.

Cohen, A.J. (2008). Advancing interdisciplinary research in singing through a shared digital repository. *Acoustics '08 Paris (2nd joint conference of the Acoustical Society of America and the Association of European Acoustics)*. Paris, June 29–July 4, 3177–3181 (CD-ROM).

Cohen, A.J. (2011). Research on singing: Development, education and well-being, Introduction to the special volume on the Psychology of Singing. *Psychomusicology: Music, Mind & Brain* 21: 1–5.

Cohen, A.J., Armstrong, V., Lannan, M., and Coady, J. (2009). A protocol for cross-cultural research on acquisition of singing. *Neurosciences and Music III—Disorders and Plasticity: Annals of the New York Academy of Sciences* 1169: 112–115.

Cohen, A.J., Vincent, C., Moses, D.S., Fujinaga, I., Lefford, N., Leonard, T., and Tzanatakis, G. (2013). A digital library to advance interdisciplinary research in singing. International Congress on Acoustics ICA 2013 5aMUb1. *Proceedings of Meetings on Acoustics*, 19, 035079. doi: 10.1121/1.4801078.

Cornell University Lab of Ornithology (2016). "About the Macaulay Library." http://macaulaylibrary.org/about.

Devaney, J., Mandel, M.I., Ellis, D.P.W., and Fujinaga, I. (2011). Automatically extracting performance data from recordings of trained singers. *Psychomusicology: Music, Mind & Brain* 21: 108–136.

Dunn, J.W. and Mayer, C.A. (1999). "VARIATIONS: A Digital Music Library System at Indiana University." In: *DL99: Proceedings of the 4th ACM International Conference on Digital Libraries*, 1999, 12–19. http://www.acm.org/pubs/articles/proceedings/dl/313238/p12-dunn/p12-dunn.pdf.

Fenlon, K., Senseney, M., Green, H., Bhattacharyya, S., Willis, C., and Downie, J.S. (2014). Scholar-built collections: a study of user requirements for research in large-scale digital libraries. *Proceedings of the American Society for Information Science and Technology* 51: 1–10. doi: 10.1002/meet.2014.14505101047.

Indiana University Digital Library Program (2009). http://www.dlib.indiana.edu/projects/variations3/index.html.

Khoury, S. and Simonnot, J. (2014). Applications and implications of digital audio databases for the field of ethnomusicology: a discussion of the CNRS-Musée de l'homme sound archives. *First Monday* 19: 10–16. doi: http://dx.doi.org/10.5210/fm.v19i10.5554.

Ladd, D.R. (2013). Singing in tone languages: phonetic and structural effects. Text of talk presented at the 27th annual meeting of the Phonetic Society of Japan, Kanazawa, http://www.lel.ed.ac.uk/~bob/TALKS/japan.tone-song.public.pdf.

Larrouy-Maestri, P. (2011). *Happy birthday corpus*. http://sldr.org/sldr000774/en.

Larrouy-Maestri, P. (2012). *Trained singers corpus*, http://sldr.inist.fr/voir_depot.php?id=792&lang=es&sip=1&olac=1.

Larrouy-Maestri, P., Magis, D., and Morsomme, D. (2014). Effects of melody and technique on acoustical and musical features of western operatic singing voices. *Logopedics, Phoniatrics Vocology* 39(3): 126–129.

MacWhinney, B. and Snow, C.E. (1985). The Child Language Data Exchange System. *Journal of Child Language* 12: 271–295.

MacWhinney, B. (2000). *The CHILDES Project: Tools for Analyzing Talk*. Mahwah, NJ: Erlbaum.

MacWhinney, B. (2014). What we have learned. *Journal of Child Language* 41(Suppl. S1): 124–131.

Ness, S., Tzanetakis, G., and Biro, D.P. (2010). Computer-assisted cantillation and chant research using content-aware web visualization tools. *Multimedia Tools and Applications* 48: 207–224.

Opie, I.A., and Opie, P. (1985). *The Singing Game*. Oxford: Oxford University Press.

Papoušek, M. and Papoušek, H. (1981). Musical elements in the infant's vocalization: their significance for communication, cognition, and creativity. *Advances in Infancy Research* 1: 163–224.

Prame, E. (1994). Measurements of the vibrato rate of ten singers. *Journal of the Acoustical Society of America* 94: 1979–1984.

Sági, M. and Vitányi, I. (1988). Experimental research into musical generative ability. In: J.A. Sloboda (ed.), *Generative Processes in Music: The Psychology of Performance, Improvisation, and Composition*, pp. 179–194. Oxford: Clarendon Press.

Sundberg, J., Trovén, M., and Richter, B. (2007). Sopranos with a singer's formant? Historical, physiological, and acoustical aspects of castrato singing. *Speech, Music and Hearing, KTH, CSC Computer Science and Communication* 49: 1–6.

Vincent, C., Lane, J., and Cohen, A.J. (2011). *Le projet AIRS de recherche sur l'acquisition de la voix chantée. Research on the Acquisition of Singing: The AIRS Test Battery and Digital Library*, 9th Pan European Voice Conference PEVOC9, Marseille.

Welch, G. Sergeant, D.C., and White, P.J. (1998). The role of linguistic dominance in the acquisition of song. *Research Studies in Music Education* 10: 67–74.

PART 4

THE DEVELOPMENT
OF SINGING ACROSS
THE LIFESPAN

CHAPTER 20

....

SOCIO-CULTURAL, ACOUSTIC, AND ENVIRONMENTAL IMPERATIVES IN THE WORLD OF SINGING

....

ROBERT WALKER

INTRODUCTION

....

ALTHOUGH all humans share the same or very similar physical attributes in their vocal mechanism, the sheer flexibility of the vocal tract and its articulators has allowed for a surprising variety of vocal usage across the world. This enormous diversity can be explained to some extent in terms of acoustic science which expresses mathematically the nature of the particular sound pressure wave caused by the effects of various muscular mechanisms within the vocal tract on the column of air emanating from the lungs. Such detail indicates how the particular sounds studied are produced in a particular human. Some researchers have gone further in the study of particular vocal tracts and musical instruments in order to discover the extent of the range of sounds each might be capable of producing, irrespective of whether or not such sounds are used in musical practices. Much of this work has been carried out at the University of New South Wales by Joe Wolfe and his "Acoustics Group" in the School of Physics (Joliveau et al. 2004; Tarnopolsky et al. 2005). But it is argued that it is not possible to predict, or explain epistemologically, particular vocal behaviors as they might occur in musical practices purely from such scientific studies demonstrating the extent of the possibilities for the variety of sounds a vocal tract might be capable of. It is clear from the different choices of types of vocal sounds found in the cultures described in this chapter that human societies have not explored in their choice of vocal sounds the many possibilities an individual is capable of and then selected some and rejected others. Instead, the choice of vocal sounds accepted by a particular society is guided by complex interactions between belief, environment, and socio-political considerations.

The reason, of course, is that music is a product of the complex interactions between the individuals producing sounds and those listening to and interpreting such sounds as a form of communication within a specific social and cultural group of people. Humans do not just produce sounds for their own sake: we utilize sounds in music as symbols for and references to beliefs, events, objects, community values, and traditions as well as many types of metaphor and semantic signaling. Vocal music, as well as instrumental music, is a form of expression which relates to the complexities of lifestyle and the meanings evoked by the processes of acculturation and enculturation which have evolved within specific socio-cultural and geographical contexts. What might be perceived as random noise making to one cultural group can be regarded as highly sophisticated musical activity containing deeply held meanings to another. And this would have little to do with the actual physical properties of the sounds involved: any humanly produced sound can be regarded as musical, and therefore culturally significant.

Goodale (1995) cites an interesting example of this when she describes how the Kaulong people of Papua New Guinea ridiculed the drumming of the Yoruba people of Nigeria when she played recordings to them, saying that the Yoruba people obviously had no idea how to play the drums. To most Western ears Yoruba drumming sounds immensely complex and highly musical in a technical sense; nevertheless, the sounds which had great cultural significance to the Yoruba people meant little or nothing to the Kaulong. A more obviously disjunct pairing might be the throat singing, or *katajjaq* (a type of vocal activity which is actually voiceless and more resembles white noise than singing), practiced by the Inuit people, mostly women, of northern Canada, and the *bel canto* singing style of eighteenth- and nineteenth-century Italian opera. The former sounds like air rushing through a tube because the vocalist deliberately opens the vocal folds widely in order to ensure they are undisturbed, while the latter utilizes the vocal tract-inspired amplifications of the vibrations generated in the vocal folds in order to produce a sound containing the fullest range of frequencies in the spectrum. Clearly, these two examples demonstrate more or less opposing ends of the physical capabilities of the human vocal tract for producing sound. And while studies of the physics of the vocal tract in action might suggest such variation as being possible, the data produced cannot provide musical or other reasons for each to occur as a practice in any human society.

Two distinct methods of explaining or describing musical sounds have been posited: the scientific and the cultural. This is in order to make a clear distinction between the materialistic and the idealistic, or perhaps more appropriately between the objective and the subjective. It is also to outline the main feature of this chapter, which is to elevate the idealistic and subjective above the materialistic and objective in dealing with vocal music-making.

Rea (2002) in his book *World Without Design: the Ontological Consequences of Naturalism* argues that there is no generally accepted precise definition of naturalism. Additionally, he states that the metaphysical form of rationalism argues that "the sciences paint a complete and accurate ontological picture of the world; there are quarks, molecules and organisms, but not ghosts and gods" (Cross 2003). As Cross further points out, Rea suggests that

> epistemological naturalism fares no better. If it is at the mercy of future developments in science, it cannot follow science wherever it leads. But if it is immune to empirical results, then it is self-refuting, because it is just the sort of hypothesis that epistemic naturalism insists must be grounded on scientific investigation rather than armchair theorizing.

The point in citing Rae, and Cross's commentary, is to provide a supporting argument for elevating the role of qualitative investigations into the socio-cultural and environmental contexts within which vocal music occurs above that of scientific ones. It is also to suggest that the former can best be utilized as a means of understanding what any objective definitions of the sound pressure waves found in vocal music might mean semantically. But most importantly, qualitative investigations provide valuable insights into appreciating and becoming aware of the spiritual, esthetic, and ontological significance of the sounds for members of an individual culture.

The complexities of the vocal mechanism and the many diverse influences affecting what a social group might decide is suitable and acceptable as music in vocal tract behavior, render the approach of what philosophers call materialism or scientific naturalism a rather barren *modus operandi* for understanding vocal music if utilized with no supporting information from the socio-cultural and geographical realms. In particular, such an approach can only describe what currently exists. It cannot enable us to predict, for example, that there should, somewhere on earth, be a vocal practice such as that of the Canadian Inuit purely because objectively the human vocal tract might be capable of such a practice. Nor can it predict, to give another example, where the appearance might occur of the type of vocal music found in Korean *pansori*. Both of these practices make the throat the focus of vocal sound production in ways which are unique to the specific culture. Until we found such practices existing in a human society it would be unknown as music and, I argue, impossible to predict purely from studies of the acoustic properties of the potential capabilities of a human vocal tract in producing sound pressure waves. This is because particular human societies develop particular vocal sounds within a specific socio-cultural knowledge system, not as pure sound but as reflections in sound, idealistically, of the belief system evolved within that cultural system.

EXAMPLES OF CULTURAL DIVERSITY

Katajjaq: The Throat Music of the Women of the Inuit People

We might regard such a practice as that of *katajjaq* as highly unusual purely because only the Inuit people have developed its use in their cultural practices. But if we recognize the effects of isolation of the Inuit caused by their location in the frozen tundra of northern Canada, we can see why it is an unusual practice. Their traditional lands are not on any well-used trade route and the climate is very inhospitable with temperatures well below freezing for most of the year. They live above the tree line, an area where few human groups have settled over time and very few people would visit. So it would be unlikely that they would encounter many other human groups traveling through their territory; in which case, there would be little or no effects of acculturation through contact with other cultures. In more temperate climates there are often many different cultures living comparatively close to each other and acculturation processes ensure that musical practices are often shared and developed across different cultural groups. Geographical location, then, is one important factor in the use of different vocal postures for producing musical sounds.

Korean *Pansori*

Pansori is performed by both male and female singers with a drummer as accompaniment. Training for the *pansori* singer is extremely arduous, and it takes several years for a *pansori* expert to emerge. The purpose of such training is to produce what to some would seem to be a most raucous, loud, and dramatic sound. One activity in training is to stand near a waterfall and attempt to make vocal sounds louder than the waterfall (Chang 1983). Often this causes bleeding in the throat, but it is nevertheless regarded as essential. *Pansori* is a form of one-person opera where highly dramatic and emotional scenes are portrayed by the singer whose voice often ranges over two or more octaves, with loudness levels often ranging from *fff* to *pp* as they take the listener on a highly emotional journey into the human psyche. This is folk music performed mostly in the open air. Often it can be seen at local markets where many people from the outlying locations gather, and sometimes more recently in concert halls.

Tuvan Shepherds and Their Throat Music

Another highly unusual vocal practice which relies on only part of the potential sounds that the human vocal tract is capable of is another form of what is generally known as throat singing: that practiced by the nomadic shepherds in the Tuva region of southern Siberia. The Tuvinian shepherds have perfected over centuries a method of vocal activity whereby they sing a low frequency at around 100 Hz, and then enhance the energy levels around the second speech formant regions for the vowels /e/ and /i/, approximately 1500 and 2000 Hz, respectively. This gives the impression that they are producing two different vocal pitches simultaneously: a low-pitched fundamental plus these higher spectral pitches which the singer can manipulate and vary in frequency across the formant regions. One might predict the possibility of the human vocal tract being capable of this ability, but not where or when its particular practices might occur in a human society. Somehow, this acoustic configuration has the reverberant capacity to travel across hillsides, leading to speculation about how isolated Tuvinian shepherds might have experimented with such sounds over centuries to develop an important form of communication in such matters as commerce and social issues, capable of being transmitted over long distances.

The Personal and Private Songs of the Kwakiutl and Haida People

The development of such sounds capable of being heard in the open air is common practice among many other socio-cultural groups across the planet. In British Columbia, Canada, for example, the Kwakiutl people and the Coast Salish people express their communion with the natural world by singing down the deep fjords of the mountainous western coastal areas of British Columbia between Vancouver and the Alaskan border. The basic vocal posture in this singing practice is a neutral vowel sound very like the /ʌ/ as it appears in words such as "up," but this vowel sound is extended and amplified in the vocal tract at the junction of the oral cavity and the pharynx. Acoustic analysis shows that formants often appear to be merged.

In some ways it resembles the cries of the raven and the crow as they fly overhead in this terrain. Both the raven and the crow are sacred birds for many of the indigenous people of British Columbia for whom they are important totems, and with whom they identify emotionally, spiritually, and physically by imitating their behavior. In traditional dances at feasts and other important occasions of celebration or remembrance, both the Kwakiutl and Coast Salish cover themselves with feathers or imitation wings as they act out their commitment and their close relationship to their bird totem. Statistically, arguments have been postulated that these singers, as well as the Australian Aborigines, produce acoustic pitch sensations but not musical pitch since their focus is more with manipulations of spectral content (Walker 1997). Spectral energy can sometimes give the impression of melodic content whereby, for example, the /i/ vowel (as in heed), with second and third formants at 2300 and 3200 Hz, can sound like a higher pitch than the /u/ sound (as in who'd) with its spectral energy concentrated at much lower levels with second and third formants at 800 and 2050 Hz, respectively (Pierce 1992, p. 50).

Several singers, both Kwakiutl and Salish, mostly living around the Prince Rupert area of northern British Columbia, and who practice this traditional singing down the fjords of this area have reported that these ancient practices traditionally enabled the singers to forecast weather changes by listening to the ways in which their voices echoed down the hillside towards the sea (Walker 1986, 1990, p. 190). One such singer in Prince Rupert reported that these songs were all about nature, the weather, the ways in which birds fly in the differing wind conditions, and human links to these aspects of life which traditionally dominate their existence. Such information about birds flying and wind directions are crucial to the lifestyle of these people, in particular the relevance to fishing, their most important source of food (Walker 1986, 1990).

The indigenous people of the Pacific Northwest have a rich tradition of singing in their rituals, celebrations, and what we would call partying, the *potlatch*. One of the most important early ethnomusicologists was Dr Ida Halpern (Halpern 1967, 1981) who reported many social and religious aspects of the music of the Pacific Northwest. One was the important concept of song ownership, whereby songs were the private property of individual Kwakiutl or Haida singers. No one else could sing them without permission and to do so would be regarded as an insult. The concept of private ownership of songs had implications for such things as melody, rhythmic structure, and intonation, since there was little or no involvement of a community in the making of these songs, and hearing their performance was regarded as a privilege for the community to relish and treasure. Such songs were handed down through generations, and often through dreams or trances where long dead ancestors would share a song with the recipient to treat as his own. Singing was generally a male activity, and all songs were inevitably accompanied by small hand drums.

The Kwakiutl and Haida song men all reported that they could not sing without the drum with which they would accompany themselves (personal interviews 1983–84; Walker 1990, p. 199). Their songs had many meanings and functions, especially at the great *potlatch* ceremonies or the *hamatsa* secret society rituals. Some songs given in dreams or trances were especially linked to *hamatsa* rituals. The *potlatch* is what we would call a major party where many other groups would be invited often over a period of several months. Everyone would bring gifts, usually blankets, and dance, song, and feasting were major activities. The *hamatsa* rituals have an ancient origin linked to the myth of a human eating giant flesh-eating ravens. Young men would be sent out into the forest to encounter these mythic creatures and to learn to live off the sustenance provided by the forest. Generally speaking, the person in a tribe regarded as the greatest songman was often the chief. Chief Tom Willie, a Kwakiutl chief from Vancouver Island who had over 350 songs in his head, was regarded as a national Canadian treasure. During a visit to Simon Fraser University, Vancouver, he was asked to sing six of his songs three times each, all of which were recorded. Acoustic analysis of each repeat showed each time the exact same pitches were replicated. His singing voice was a sort of extension of his speech where spectral frequency was focused around the first natural speech formant for males. No acoustic information could possibly explain the mystical, magical, and supernatural meanings which these songs held for Tom Willie and the Kwakiutl people (Walker 1990, p. 196).

The Polyphonic Yodeling of the Ituri Forest People

The Ituri people live in the forest of central Africa in the Democratic Republic of the Congo. The forest is their home, their spiritual guide, and their source of energy, pride, and sense of identity. The singing of the Ituri is best described as high-pitched yodeling, but it includes different parts sung by different individuals entering the singing game at different times (Turnbull and Chapman 1958). The effect is that of high-pitched polyphony and it is mostly performed by women as they work their way through the forest performing various important tasks required for daily subsistence (Turnbull 1962). The vocal sounds seem to penetrate the forest canopy well and carry over long distances. The semantic purpose of this exciting performance behavior is to placate the gods of the forest with whom the Ituri people live in harmony and absolute trust, and to ensure good returns in hunting and the growth of the various crops they cultivate. Turnbull reports that it is very difficult to understand what this means if one is not a member of the tribe. The Ituri beliefs are complex and very ancient, having been reported by Plato in *Atlantis* as an example of a people who are perfectly integrated into their environment. The style of singing reflects the equality each individual feels in that there are no solos and each singer contributes as they feel fit. The Belgian ethnologist Jean-Pierre Hallet (Hallet and Pelle 1973) speculates that the lifestyle of the Ituri people became the model for the idea of the Garden of Eden.

Noise Singing in Contemporary Rock Music

Our contemporary world of popular music in all its various styles and fashions contains vocal sounds almost as contrasting as those outlined above. A most important difference, however, is the use of the microphone in popular music to amplify the sung sound which otherwise would not carry far beyond the singer. More recently, the practice of using software which can alter all aspects of the sound prior to it being heard beyond the mixing process is common both in the concert location and the recording studio. The relatively gentle and melodious sounds of Elvis Presley or Roy Orbison, melodious in the Western sense that the pitches they sing conform to the diatonic scale system, contrast with the comparatively raucous and noise-containing vocals of Meatloaf or Motörhead. These examples were chosen deliberately in order to contrast a singing style in popular music which is Western in its singing style and musical content with one which is clearly non-Western in both, and where noise, rather than a Western sense of musical pitch, is regarded as highly important. The special and distinct vocal characteristics of both these types of sound can be enhanced electronically in the mixing process.

In the same way that one cannot predict the emergence of a particular type of vocal sound as music within a particular human culture without the supporting socio-cultural context and significance of such a vocal sound, one cannot readily predict the rise to fame and fortune of particular styles of vocal music in the popular sphere, even given the context of what became known as *youth culture* (see later in this section). However, the situation in the popular music world is different from that in the real world. When a new type of popular music emerges, such as that where noise and vocal shouting are predominant, it sets a precedent where new groups can enter the scene in the knowledge that support has already been generated by targeted advertising. Popular music does not work in the same way as the music of specific socio-cultural groups living in specific geographic areas.

Popular music stars become popular among the adolescent community for reasons which are not clear. There would appear to be no musical or socio-cultural reason why Meatloaf or Elvis should become as popular as they did. And we can only comment on potential reasons after the event: we cannot predict the event. However, the fashions in popular culture generate their own supporters through high-pressure sales techniques and the formation of fan clubs.

The major component in the type of vocal sound found in the music of Meatloaf, Motörhead, and others who are similar, is generated vocally rather than electronically. Some have labeled this practice *noise rock* from its emergence during the 1960s and 1970s and especially during the 1980s when it became more prevalent. It is caused by a form of shouting which heavily modulates most of the frequency spectrum produced by the vocal folds such that within particular bandwidths most of the frequencies are sounding simultaneously over a wide frequency band. When this is amplified the effect can be overwhelming, especially when feedback and electronic distortions are applied. The result is a type of sound which can mask any pitched sounds. The effect is that of a very rough sound often without any semblance of musical pitch, but which is designed to produce maximum impact through heavy amplification.

Meatloaf visited Australia in July 2011, and a television reporter waiting outside his dressing room to interview him colorfully described his warming up exercises as a mixture of cats screaming in pain and cattle being tortured. The socio-cultural context of the popular musician, whatever the genre, is strongly supported by the mass entertainment industry and its intrusive use of advertising and personality creation. A virtual world of social and political interaction is invented by various entertainment media which acts much like a real world except that it is a one way process—from the star to the individual only with no two-way interaction as in real life social communication. However, this virtual world for young people does have a social force in real life in the emergence of what became known as youth culture and the emerging acceptance that adolescence be regarded as a special stage in human development.

The concept of *youth culture* as an entity separate from what one might consider to be the main *culture* involving all members of a human group began with Hall (1904) and his conviction that adolescence, being a time of stress, rebellion, and emotional outbursts caused by sexual awakening, merited its consideration as a separate period of human development from childhood and adulthood. Muuss (1996, p. 1) described Hall as "the father of a scientific psychology of adolescence." But although youth culture, as culture, as opposed to adolescence as a stage in development, had a different genesis, the two often became fused in the public consciousness, especially during the 1950s and 1960s when some early signs of violent behavior from teenagers became a problem in the United States, to be followed across the English speaking world in the UK and elsewhere. During the 1940s in the United States and the 1950s in the UK and other English-speaking countries two developments emphasized the separateness of the adolescent years; one was the growing affluence of this age group, the other was the extension of the years of attendance at high school whereby teenagers suddenly found themselves relatively isolated from society in a school classroom. Previously, they would have been at work and treated as adults (Aries 1962; Palladino 1996). However, Fowler (2008) presents a different picture of youth culture in his thorough examination of the youth cults in the UK beginning with the Edwardian era and ending with the Mods and Rockers of the 1960s. Fowler describes a cultural movement involving young people which extended well beyond the concept of the adolescent to eventually involve youth from several different countries mixing and learning about each other through joint adventures and activities.

Nevertheless, there is little doubt that from the 1940s and the bobby soxers, groups of young girls who idolized Frank Sinatra, to the 1950s and the development of the transistor radio enabling teenagers to listen alone to their own choice of music, popular music became a major force in the lives of teenagers. Many researchers report that popular music is one of the most important sources of emotional sustenance in a teenager's life (Macdonald et al. 2002; Neufeld and Mate 2004; North et al. 2000; Steele and Brown 1995). It was this sustenance which accounts for the rise of and continued support for popular music stars. This became the *raison d'être* for popular music in all its forms and provided the socio-cultural context within which popular music stars were worshiped and idolized by young people. Followers of pop stars become attracted to particular ones and not others. They form fan clubs, either officially or incidentally, and as Frith (1996) points out, they regard themselves as firm members of the particular fan club whose duty it is to defend the musical "turf" of their star performer with pride and often physical violence against "non-believers." Large amounts of money are involved in the world of popular music, and those who manage pop stars have the task of speculating on the potential of unknowns to achieve stardom and make a lot of money.

THE INFLUENCE OF MATHEMATICS, SCIENCE, AND PHILOSOPHY

In contrast to the vocal music produced in the indigenous cultures mentioned above, the vocal music of cultures where complex theory lies at the heart of socio-cultural practices and beliefs betrays different epistemological origins. We refer here exclusively to the religious and art music of Western culture, and not the diverse field of popular music. The growth of technology, socio-political and socio-cultural influences on Western music has had direct effects on the practices of singing.

The ancient cultures of China and Egypt were both based on mathematical and philosophical theory arguing about the nature of the universe and the place of humans in the cosmic scheme. The science and philosophy developed by these two ancient cultures became part of the foundation of Western culture as this earlier knowledge became absorbed into early Western thought. The beginnings of modern Western thought and practice were formed through their grounding in the Hellenist culture of ancient Greece over 2000 years ago, followed by its subsequent absorption by Rome. Ancient Rome then absorbed Christianity during the third and fourth centuries AD, to eventually become transformed into what we know as Western culture. In its modern version this ancient knowledge emerged during the Renaissance in a profound and systematic reinvention of ancient Greek and Roman philosophy, science, and mathematics. This turned into the Enlightenment of the seventeenth and eighteenth centuries, which was followed by what some regard as its antidote, Romanticism and Idealism, during the nineteenth century and into the twentieth, when skepticism took over. These important developments had profound effects on the evolution of the art of vocal music in Western culture.

The Renaissance, which spread over several hundred years, was a pivotal event in Western culture. Apart from the activities of many travelers throughout medieval times across the Middle East and Europe from Spain, Africa, Egypt, and Greece, the Ottoman expansion across the Middle East and into Europe (beginning in the Balkans during the thirteenth century AD and continuing until the twentieth century) was an important catalyst. These Muslims were not ignorant of the wealth of ancient mathematical and philosophical practices. Brotton (2006, p. 28) states that while Sultan Mehmed II was conquering Constantinople in 1453, he employed Italian scholars who "daily read to him from the ancient historians" of Rome and Greece. In fact the Muslim communities across the Middle East, and especially in Spain, were highly sophisticated, having invented the use of +, −, and × in their trade, as well as algebra generally. The point is that there was no divide between Muslim and Christian communities in terms of the sophisticated use of mathematics, science, and philosophy: all had access to these disciplines.

There was wide dissemination of this knowledge across Europe and the Middle East. One of the most important developments which spurred on the process of renewal and reappraisal was the invention of printing in the fifteenth century. Brotton (2006, p. 39) comments that at the beginning of the fifteenth century books and literacy were the preserve of a tiny elite, but by the end of the sixteenth century "the printing press had created a revolution in both elite and popular apprehensions of reading, writing, and the status of knowledge." Thus, the Renaissance was the result of many diverse events, especially during the fifteenth and sixteenth centuries, which together had major effects on life across Europe and the Middle East.

Musical Intervals

A major component in the belief systems of ancient Greece, Rome, and their subsequent rebirth in the modern West was an acceptance of supernatural beings and the powers they enjoyed. The realm of perfection, which Plato defined mathematically, was the ideal to which all activity in philosophy, science, and mathematics, and consequently music, aspired.

Plato described Pythagoras' accidental discovery of the ideal proportions in music (2:1; 3:2; 4:3) in a myth whereby Pythagoras heard the perfect sounds of the intervals produced by these proportions (octave, 5th, and 4th respectively) as he passed by a blacksmith's forge. Throughout the modern history of Western theory the ideal of musical perfection, expressed mathematically, was an important driving force. It was the quest to achieve this ideal music which has driven Western musical theory and the evolution of music in Western culture over the last 1000 years (Walker 2004). Importantly for modern music, these three intervals suggest the tonic, dominant, and subdominant, the three chords which form the basis of the diatonic key system. In Plato's scheme, however, these numbers had cosmic significance and even today they are described as "perfect" intervals. But there were more ancient origins of such ideas, and these ideas or concepts traveled across the various trade routes to became commonplace across the ancient world. It was as though the fashion across this world was to speculate through mathematics about the magical properties of the movement of the planets and how the "music" produced in the heavens affected human behavior.

Belief in the powers of supernatural entities characterized the Egyptian scheme of things where music was an important tool in communicating with the various gods, especially the sun god Ra. Mathematical perfection for the music of ancient China was closely linked to the division of the octave into 12 equal parts (Kuttner 1965; Walker 1990). The ability of musical sound to imitate nature, especially flora and fauna, was regarded as the main source of Chinese musical expression. Vocal music copied the instrumental music defined by mathematical models for scales, and the imitative use of sounds also became a model for singing. In this way, vocal music evolved in imitation of instrumental music.

The evolution of Western music followed a similar pathway from its origins in ancient Greece through to today. Vocal music in Western culture evolved from complex theory relating musical sound to the cosmic movements of planets and their relationship to human behaviors. The origins of Western musical theory are complex, widespread across the ancient world, and emanate from many varied cultural traditions in music and mathematics. Through Pythagorean philosophy and mathematics emerged the earliest attempts at the science of acoustics. Pythagoras acquired this ancient knowledge during his travels, along with the so-called Pythagoras' theorem which was known in ancient China and to the ancient Sumerians more than a 1000 years before Pythagoras lived (Boyer 1968; Bunt et al. 1976; Gillings 1962; Scott 1960).

The Roman statesman Boethius (AD 480–525) in his *De Institutione Musica* collated and summarized much of the theory concerning music from the ancient world and was largely responsible for the main tenets of this mass of music theory surviving through the "dark ages" until the Renaissance. This ancient theory classified music into distinct types: *musica mundana*, the universal music of the spheres; *musica humana*, the internal music of the human body; and *musica instrumentalis*, the music of singing and instrumental performance. These distinctions reflected the ancient view of the world and the place of humans within it. However, the idea of different types of music with different powers and different functions eventually became the complex differentiation we make today between, for example, sacred music and entertainment, or art music and popular music, program music and so on, each with its own vocal style.

It was something of a mystery to ancient cultures as to why certain intervals sounded more harmonious or pleasant, or unpleasant, than others, and mathematics was their means for solving this problem. The fact that numbers in the ancient world were regarded as highly symbolic, containing magical powers linked to the planets and their movements, meant that musical sounds also assumed these expressive qualities. The series 1, 2, 3, 4, the sum of which equals 10, was itself regarded as sacred in forming the *tetractys*, a triangular shape with four points as the bottom line, three above it, two above that, and one at the top. The *tetractys* was the sacred symbol of the Pythagoreans and the theoretical musical sounds generated by these proportions were regarded as "perfect" because they reflected the movements of the planets in their journey across the universe and the sounds created by their movements created the "music of the spheres" (Christenson 2002; Reese 1940; Walker 1990).

Equal-tempered Scales

One particular aspect of this ancient belief in the power of the *tetractys* led eventually to the diatonic system and the chromatic scale: how to produce the sounds implied by the ratios. This arose out of the problem of dividing the monochord into 12 equal parts so that from a single string one could play the sounds of these intervals. It is relatively easy to divide the string into two equal parts to form the octave (the whole string versus half), and similarly for the 5th (the whole string versus two-thirds) and the 4th (the whole string versus three-quarters). But to produce all three intervals from one set of divisions of the monochord was extremely difficult because it relied on the division of the octave into 12 equal parts: a very difficult task utilizing proportional mathematics.

The Chinese eventually achieved success in 1584 when Zhu Zaiyu, a Ming prince, correctly calculated how to divide the octave into 12 equal parts where the ratio produces 1.0595 as the semitone (Cho 2003; Goodrich 1976; Kuttner 1975). This knowledge was eventually transmitted to Europe by Italian merchants (Goodrich 1976). It eluded the hundreds of monks in European monasteries throughout the medieval period trying to solve it through proportional mathematics. In 1636, the French mathematician Marin Mersenne produced the same calculation. The invention of logarithms in the eighteenth century made this calculation much easier and led the way towards the establishment of equal temperament and the chromatic scale in Western music. Tuning and the construction of scales in vocal performance became strictly delineated by this powerful mathematical tradition in music where musical instruments were the reliable source of tuning accuracy for voices to emulate. These developments also facilitated the establishment of the central concept of pitch, including the phenomenon of absolute pitch (Sergeant 1983; Solomons 2002). The important difference between the indigenous singers mentioned above and Western singers is the imposition externally of pitch and melody in the practices of the latter and the freedom to invent entirely personal and otherwise unknown melodic content in the former.

Development of Musical Notation

But there were other, equally powerful, influences on vocal music in Western culture. Music, by which was meant the mathematical theory of harmonics, became one of the main subjects in education from the earliest times through its inclusion in the *quadrivium* comprising arithmetic, geometry, music, and astrology, the four basic subjects of medieval education established by Boethius, and leading to the serious study of philosophy. The adoption of

Christianity by Rome also elevated vocal music in importance through its growing use in worship. Much of this initially was based on Jewish traditions, but it soon developed a specific Christian tradition of singing, especially after Pope Gregory (590–604) reorganized the singing at the mass and other daily services by systematizing the various melodies available, all of which were learned orally. Guido d'Arezzo (990–1050) is credited with the invention of modern staff notation which replaced the old system of *neums* enabling singers to read the melodies they sang from notations instead of learning them by rote. These were important events affecting the practices of vocal music in the West.

Architecture and Vocal Music

Another highly important influence on vocal music was the development of buildings in which vocal music was performed. The castle, a fortified building housing a local nobleman with his guards and household became a place where the wandering minstrels could obtain accommodation in return for the entertainment they provided. They would perform in the large dining area of a castle, and sometimes would become permanent employees at certain courts. The music they performed was popular, melodic, and relatively easy to sing. The monastery was another institution where singing was important, but this involved the more complex vocal music of the mass and other daily services sung by monks.

Monasteries would include churches large enough to contain the whole membership. In turn these large buildings would require the ability to project the voice across large spaces. With the construction of large cathedrals from the twelfth and thirteenth centuries onwards, vocal music assumed a major role in the general development of Western musical art. From chant, where everyone sang the same melody, part singing evolved between the ninth and twelfth centuries into highly complex rhythmic and polyphonic structures. This necessitated the ability to sing in tune so that the combination of parts would sound harmonious. Thus, the importance of tuning became an essential focus in vocal music in these buildings. As the organ evolved into a relatively easily playable keyboard instrument by the fifteenth century, so the art of tuning between both organ and choir became crucial, again affecting the practices of vocal music. Voice production during these times was often a matter of imitating instruments, since wind and string instruments played the same parts as those of the choir. Many compositions of the sixteenth and seventeenth centuries still had the instruction "fit for voices or viols" at the head of the score, indicating that there was little difference between vocal and instrumental music up to the end of the sixteenth century.

The ability to sing in tune within the acoustic confines of building, in combination with the externally imposed tuning systems and scales, became the defining feature of Western vocal music—as opposed to the personal internal tuning systems of the indigenous vocal music described above. With the huge size of the new cathedrals and monastic churches, a new type of vocal production was necessary in order to carry over the large distances. Here, it is important to mention that women were not allowed to sing in Western religious worship at this time. Only men and boys sang the complex music which by the sixteenth century had become highly sophisticated. This only changed in many cathedral choirs late in the twentieth century when girls were introduced.

The sixteenth century was an important turning point for the art of vocal music. The use of polyphony had reached important milestones of sophistication, especially in the vocal settings of the mass and motet where each voice was required to blend into the harmonious whole. But it also marked the gradual evolution from the old ecclesiastical modes to the new emerging diatonic system of major and minor. In fact, several compositions of the sixteenth century were, for all intents and purposes, written in a major key, with some almost entirely in a minor key. Thomas Tallis, for example, wrote lengthy passages in a major key in such works as the 40-part motet *Spem in Alium*, the Christmas motet *Haec Dies*, and the *Lamentations of Jeremiah*. This content affected the singing style: it should be harmonious, aimed at blending the parts, with no leading voices dominating.

Instrumental Developments and Vocal Music

The seventeenth century saw instrumental music rise to greater prominence than vocal music, even to the point where discussions took place concerning the relative merits of each. The impact on vocal music was considerable, whereby singers, performing music for the new instrumental ensembles, found themselves imitating the sounds of instruments rather than enhancing the purely vocal styles which had emerged up to that point. In the reformed churches of England and Germany, no such controls existed. So by the end of the seventeenth century composers were introducing operatic-style works into liturgical use, such as the verse anthem and the cantata. Henry Purcell's *My Beloved Spake* is a good example, involving string orchestra, tenor, bass, and alto soloists, vocal quartets, and a large four-part chorus. Indeed, J. S. Bach expected no less from his singers than he did from his instrumentalists in technique, pitch range, and rhythmic complexity.

The rise of symphonic music during the eighteenth and nineteenth centuries was matched by the rise of Italian opera during the same period. Each had a major impact on the development of the art of vocal music, especially solo singing and choral music. By the eighteenth century the oratorio had become a hugely expressive work involving large orchestras, choir, and soloists. Inevitably this type of choral singing evolved further in copying instrumental music as the symphony orchestra developed. The introduction of choirs into the symphonic structure, as in Beethoven's Ninth Symphony (1825) and Mahler's *Resurrection Symphony* (1894) and *Symphony of a Thousand* (1907), were inevitable developments. In Italian opera the idea of *verismo* emerged during the late nineteenth century and the new enlarged symphony orchestra provided composers with a huge range of instrumental colors. Singers were expected to express their feelings as realistically and as charismatically as possible in arias which tested the voice to its limits. In Puccini's *La Boheme*, Rodolfo's aria "Che gelida manina" and Mimi's "Mi chiamano Mimi," and Canio's "Vesti la giubba" from Leoncavallo's *Pagliacci* are prime examples of how operatic singing style evolved further to match the composer's demands. The new operatic singing style was perhaps best exemplified initially by Enrico Caruso (1873–1921) and Nellie Melba (1859–1931), both of whose power and sweetness of tone set the standard for the future.

Commensurate with the rise of the huge symphonic forces of the concert hall and opera house was the size of these venues. By the early nineteenth century musicians performed to audiences of several thousand in some concert halls and opera houses. For the solo singer this brought about a major change in vocal technique in order to be heard above large orchestras and choirs. The generation of the singer's formant (Sundberg 1987), high levels of spectral energy around 2500–3200 Hz caused in part by enlarging the pharynx opening and lowering the larynx, enabled male singers to carry over larger distances and to be heard more clearly above a large orchestra where the average spectral peak was much lower in frequency.

In contrast, the more intimate *lieder* and *melodie* involving a soloist and pianist provided a more intimate approach to vocal music, whereby the singer's role was to imbue the vocal sounds with all the expressiveness and drama implied in the poetry. The greatest poets expressing innermost thoughts of humanity, as opposed to the deity, in situations which mattered to them (such as love, loss, anger, cruelty, etc.) were set to music by the finest composers of the time, including Beethoven, Schubert, Schumann, Brahms, Wolf, and Mahler in Germany, and Berlioz, Gounod, Faure, Chausson, Ravel, and Debussy in France.

Religion, Humanism, and Vocal Music

The previous section ("Instrumental developments and vocal music") offered a very brief summary of some important compositions reflecting the greater and different demands made on singers of art music. However, an important backcloth to this development is the effect of philosophical ideas about the nature of humanity in relation to God and the art of music. Humanism describes a movement from the fifteenth and sixteenth centuries onwards which focused on how humans behave, on human expressiveness, human intelligence, sensibilities, and, eventually, during the nineteenth century on the idea that there was no God, just humanity (Nietzsche 1968). As a result one can trace a gradual change in musical expressiveness, especially in vocal music, from expressions of religious worship and adulation towards humanity expressing thoughts and feelings which were important in the daily lives of humans, and where the human was more of an autonomous being than a servant of God. This shift to expressing human thoughts and feelings was responsible for many developments in expanding vocal technique in terms of pitch range and expressiveness, through opera, lieder, oratorio, and symphonic works with large choirs and soloists. The idea of *verismo* in opera is an important product, but the twentieth century saw an inevitable reaction in the use of *Sprechstimme*, a mixture of speech and pitched vocal tone in Schoenberg's *Pierrot Lunaire* (1912).

HUMANITY AND VOCAL MUSIC

Although the commentary on vocal music in Western culture has taken up greater space above than that of any other culture, it would be a mistake to assume this to be an indication of its superiority. It is true that the evolution of Western culture over the last 2000 years has seen profound changes in the way all humans regard their place on the planet and within the cosmos, which has affected practically everyone. In comparison, non-literate, agrarian, and hunting societies developed no similar overwhelming epistemological tools. However, considering the crucial importance of the role of vocal music in expressing deeply felt spiritual, esthetic, and emotional beliefs of individuals, but shared by the social group in which they live, both the non-literate cultures mentioned earlier and Western culture share the same bonds of sentience existing between the vocal sounds emanating from the human producing them and the particular cultural practice within which the vocal music has evolved. This fact defines the semantic equality between the two types of culture as far as the role of vocal music is concerned.

The fact that substantially different environments, epistemologies, levels of literacy, and scientific knowledge delineate important contextual differences does not change this basic relationship between the intimate vocal sound and the individual for whom such sounds have highly significant meaning and profound effects on the listener. The nature of these meanings and emotional effects differ according to cultural context and interpretation, but not their impact on the human recipient. For these reasons it is impossible, as well as pointless, to speculate about whether or not one cultural practice is worth more than another, and certainly not because of the power or sophistication of the knowledge base of a particular culture. The singing of a Kwakiutl songman in the rain forests of the Pacific Northwest is as valuable and powerful a symbol of human thought and sentience as the highly trained (in the Western classical sense) tones of a Western opera singer. Each may be explained differently in terms of its philosophical, religious, esthetic, or social importance and acoustic properties, but each represents different, yet equal, attempts of humanity in particular situations and contexts to express vocally their understanding and explanation of the world and their place in it as they see it.

The point that has been made in this chapter is not just simple relativism, but rather the issue of relevance for the individual human and the culture in which they live. Clearly, the science of the Ituri forest people would not produce an airplane that could fly, and in this particular sense Western science would have to be considered superior. However, in the sense of humans responding to their environment, developing a workable way of living comfortably within its confines, evolving an epistemology which fits that environment, and above all developing a relationship with the forces beyond comprehension, such as that wielded by the gods of the Ituri forest home or the spirits of the Pacific Northwest rain forests, the power of vocal music assumes great significance in objectifying these processes and beliefs, and in providing an important social focus for the particular socio-political group. To this extent there is little difference between modern humans with their great cathedrals and concert halls and highly complex music designed to fill such buildings and promote reflection in the audience on the unknowable and unknown and the ancient forest people of the Ituri Forest or the other indigenous groups mentioned above also attempting to make contact with the invisible and unintelligible powers that control their lives.

The only cuckoo in the nest mentioned above is that of popular music written and aimed specifically at the teenager. This is because it is a product of an invented emotional state, a deliberate creation of an ersatz culture designed essentially to persuade young people to spend money and to become infatuated with the contrived and spurious gods of pop culture. As such, this creation is not a product of the natural processes of cultural development and complex interactions of socio-political forces which have, over time and space, contributed towards the evolution of a particular epistemology involving ways of explaining the human situation within particular environments.

References

Aries, P. (1962). *Centuries of Childhood* (trans. R. Baldwick). London: Jonathan Cape.

Brotton, J. (2006). *The Renaissance: a Very Short Introduction*. Oxford: Oxford University Press.

Boyer, C.J. (1968). *A History of Mathematics*. New York: Wiley.

Bunt, L.N.H., Jones, S., and Bedient, R. (1976). *Historical Roots of Elementary Mathematics*. Englewood Cliffs, NJ: Prentice Hall.

Chang, S. (ed.) (1983). *Education in Korean Music: Part 3: Traditional Korean Music*. Seoul: Si-Sa-Yong-O-Sa Publishers Korea Inc.

Cho, G.J. (2003). *The Discovery of Musical Equal Temperament in China and Europe in the Sixteenth Century*. Lewiston, NY: Edwin Mellen Press.

Christenson, T. (ed.) (2002). *The Cambridge History of Music Theory*. Cambridge: Cambridge University Press.

Cross, T. (2003). Review of *World Without Design: the Ontological Consequences of Naturalism*. *Notre Dame Philosophical Reviews*, 14 July 2003. Available at: <http://ndpr.nd.edu/news/23646-world-without-design-the-ontological-consequences-of-naturalism/>

Fowler, D. (2008). *Youth Culture in Modern Britain, 1920–1970: from Ivory Tower to Global Movement*. London: Palgrave Macmillan.

Frith, S. (1996). *Performing Rites*. Cambridge MA: Harvard University Press.

Gillings, R.J. (1962). *Mathematics in the Time of the Pharaohs*. Cambridge MA: MIT Press.

Goodale, J.C. (1995). *To Sing with Pigs is Human: the Concept of Person in Papua New Guinea*. Seattle: University of Washington Press.

Goodrich, L.C. (ed.) (1976). *Dictionary of Ming Biography, 1368–1644, Volume II*, pp. 462–470. The Ming Biographical History Project of the Association for Asian Studies. New York: Columbia University Press.

Hall, G.S. (1904). *Adolescence*. New York: Appleton.

Hallet, J.-P. and Pelle, A. (1973). *Pygmy Kitabu*. New York: Random House.

Halpern, I. (1967). Indian music of the Pacific Northwest coast. *Notes for Ethnic Folkways Album FE 4523*. New York: Folkways Records.

Halpern, I. (1981). Kwakiutl Indian music. *Notes for Ethnic Folkways Album FE 4122*. New York: Folkways Records.

Joliveau, E., Smith, J., and Wolfe, J. (2004). Tuning of vocal tract resonances by sopranos. *Nature* 427: 116.

Kuttner, F.A. (1965). A musicological interpretation of the twelve *lus* in China's tonal system. *Ethnomusicology* 9(1): 22–38.

Kuttner, F.A. (1975). Prince Chu Tsai-Yü's life and work: a re-evaluation of his contribution to equal temperament theory. *Ethnomusicology* 19(2): 163–206.

Muuss, R. (1996). *Theories of Adolescence*. New York: McGraw-Hill.

MacDonald, R.A., Hargreaves, D.J., and Meill, D. (2002). *Musical Identities*. Oxford: Oxford University Press.

Nietzsche, F. (1968). *The Will to Power* (transl. W. Kaufmann and R.J. Hollingdale). New York: Vintage Books.

Neufeld, G. and Mate, G. (2004). *Hold on to Your Kids: Why Parents Matter*. Toronto: Knopf.

North, A.C., Hargreaves, D.J., and O'Neill, S.A. (2000). The importance of music to adolescents. *British Journal of Educational Psychology* 70: 255–272.

Palladino, G. (1996). *Teenagers: an American History*. New York: Basic Books.

Pierce, J.R. (1992). *The Science of Musical Sound*. New York: Freeman and Company.

Rea, M. (2002). *World Without Design: the Ontological Consequences of Naturalism*. Oxford: Oxford University Press.

Reese, G. (1940). *Music in the Middle Ages*. London: Dent.

Scott, J.F. (1960). *A History of Mathematics From Antiquity to the Beginning of the 19th Century*. London: Taylor and Francis.

Sergeant, D. (1983). The octave—percept or concept. *Psychology of Music* 11(1): 3–19.

Solomons, R. (2002). *Absolute pitch: a widespread latent ability responsive to training using a new chroma isolation method*. PhD Thesis, University of New South Wales.

Steele, J.R. and Brown, J.D. (1995). Adolescent room culture: studying media in the context of everyday life. *Journal of Youth and Adolescence* 24(5): 551–575.

Sundberg, J. (1987). *The Science of the Singing Voice*. Dekalb, IL: Northern Illinois University Press.

Tarnopolsky, A, Fletcher, N., Hollenberg, L., Lange, B., Smith, J., and Wolfe, J. (2005). The vocal tract and the sound of a didgeridoo. *Nature* 436: 39.

Turnbull, C. (1962). *The Forest People*. New York: Simon and Schuster.

Turnbull, C. and Chapman, F.S. (1958). Pygmies of the Ituri forest. *Folkways Records FE4457*. New York: Folkways Records.

Walker, R. (1986). Music and multiculturalism—a comparative study of Kwakiutl and Western singing styles. *International Journal of Music Education* 8: 43–52.

Walker, R (1990). *Musical Beliefs: Mythic, Psychoacoustic and Educational*. New York: Columbia University Press.

Walker, R. (1997). Visual metaphors as music notations for sung vowel spectra in different cultures. *Journal of New Music Research* 26(4): 315–345.

Walker R. (2004). Cultural memes, innate proclivities and musical behaviour: a case study of the Western traditions. *Psychology of Music* 32(2): 153–190.

Willie, Chief Tom (1981). *Smithsonian Folkways Recordings of Kwakiutl Indian Songs*. Washington: Smithsonian Museum.

CHAPTER 21

FETAL, NEONATAL, AND EARLY INFANT EXPERIENCES OF MATERNAL SINGING

SHEILA C. WOODWARD

THE UBIQUITY OF SINGING

THE development of singing originates before birth in the intimacy of a mother who is musically embracing the child in her womb with her songs. Across every culture, investigators report mothers singing to their infants and lullabies to have distinctive, recognizable qualities (Trehub and Schellenberg 1995; Trehub and Trainor 1998; Trehub et al. 1993a). Whether believed to be instinctive or cultural, this natural manifestation of the "biological phenomenon of love" is "expressed and exchanged" through "emotionally meaningful 'rhythms and modes' that are jointly created and sustained by mothers and their infants in ritualized, evolved interactions" (Dissanayake 2000, p. xi).

Singing belongs to all. It is not the exclusive privilege of highly educated musicians. Musicality is expressed as a natural human intelligence (Gardner 1983) and as a "human phenomenon, dwelling within even the very young and awaiting the call to expression" (Campbell 1998, p. 226). The biological life forces of the mother's body nurture the physical development of the child in her womb, while the songs that live in her maternal breath embody her thoughts, feelings, and emotional expressions. Her songs are love embodied in sound (Dissanayake 2009). Whether self-consciously tentative or confidently bold, anxious for what lies ahead or welcomingly warm, a mother singing to the fetus in her womb or to her newborn is forging bonds (Dissanayake 2009) that may have long-term implications for future relationships and child development (Alhusen et al. 2013).

Music is widely understood to convey expression and emotion (Juslin and Persson 2002; Juslin and Västfjäll 2008; Koelsch 2013). Its role in communication may be less than in the literal way that speech is viewed as a more efficient (less ambiguous) day-to-day means to communicate between those using a shared language. Nevertheless, music (including singing) can have a powerful role in the broader sense of the communication of emotions, ideas, images, or representations, such as where it occurs naturally between those sharing a musical culture. In the immortalized words of Victor Hugo, "Music expresses that which cannot be said, and on which it is impossible to remain silent" (Hugo, trans. 1907, p. 58). For pre-linguistic infants, the affective messages, which are conveyed through speech and singing, are paramount in achieving maternal infant communication (Fernald 1991; Papoušek 1992; see also "Mothers as Singing Mentors for Infants" by Trehub and Gudmundsdottir in this volume).

The earliest infant vocalizations are characteristically musical (Papoušek 1996), such that adult differentiation between infant speaking and singing appears inappropriate, as the two are imperceptively intertwined. Bannan and Woodward (2009) discuss the origins of human musical nature and spontaneity of musicality. Everyday life teaches us that the impulse to vocalize is a common human trait that may be reinforced or sedated by the environment (Blacking 1973). Against a backdrop of speculation that music may have evolved through early mother–infant interactions, this early form of human musical communication is considered to be intimate in nature (Dissanayake 2009; Malloch and Trevarthen 2009). Dissanayake (2009) proposes this theory with emphasis on "(a) the noteworthy nature of the signals presented by the mother; (b) the infant's strong and untaught receptivity to the signals; and (c) the infant's active contribution to the communication" (p. 23).

The communicative expressions between mother and infant are believed to involve sympathetic responses that occur through delicate expressions and sensitive awareness that supersede merely perceptive and discriminatory processes and positively impact maternal-infant bonding with long-term implications (Alhusen, Hayat, and Gross 2013; Dissanayake 2009; Malloch and Trevarthen 2009; Trevarthen 1977 1979; see also "Mothers as Singing Mentors for Infants" by Trehub and Gudmundsdottir in this volume).

THEORIES OF MATERNAL–INFANT BONDING AND ATTACHMENT

Questions have arisen about the interchangeability of the words "bonding" and "attachment." For example, a review of literature by Kinsey and Hupcey (2013) indicates that, while the concept of maternal–infant bonding has no uniform definition in the literature, it is often viewed as "a process that includes the emotional tie of a mother to her fetus" (p. 1316). They report that authors refer to the tie from the infant to the mother as "attachment" and others see these as dependent on each other. Bonding was also discussed in this review as involving the affective, behavioral, and biological domains. These were linked, for example, to oxytocin (a hormone implicated in social bonding (Kreutz 2014) and trust (Kosfeld et al. 2005)) being produced during labor and breastfeeding, and with behavioral aspects discussed as possibly being outward expressions of bonding or simply good parenting.

Bowlby's (1978) cross-cultural theory views maternal attachment as "a biologically driven construct, inherent within humans . . . [,] designed to preserve the species through nurturing and protective behaviors" (quoted in Alhusen et al. 2013, p. 521). Bowlby's ground-breaking ideas on attachment (1969/1982) have been widely explored (Ainsworth 1979, 1991; Main and Weston 1981; Kinsey et al. 2014), confirming positive physiological and emotional outcomes of attachment for infants, and—conversely—linking a lack of maternal–infant bonding with long-term complications for mother and infant (Brockington 1996). Integrating this broad field of literature, Kinsey and Hupcey (2013) developed this theoretical definition:

> Maternal–infant bonding is the maternal-driven process that occurs primarily throughout the first year of an infant's life, but may continue throughout a child's life. It is an affective state of the mother; maternal feelings and emotions towards the infant are a primary indicator of maternal-infant bonding. Behavioral and biological indicators may promote maternal–infant bonding or be an outcome of maternal/infant bonding, but are not sufficient to determine the quality of maternal-infant bonding nor are these indicators unique to the concept.
>
> (p. 1319)

More than half a century of research has been devoted to the bond formed between mother and infant, resulting in major changes regarding maternal access to newborns in hospitals (Kinsey and Hupcey 2013). Some controversy emerged in the 1970s around whether such access was essential, considering that loving parents might be able to overcome unavoidable denial of access for medical reasons. However, this issue never totally detracted from the overall acceptance within fields of medicine and psychology that early maternal–infant bonding is a positive and desirable process, and that lack of it can have major negative impact on long-term relationships and child development (Ainsworth 1979; Antonucci et al. 2004; Brockington et al. 2001; Klaus and Kennell 1982; McFarland et al. 2011).

Some authors see attachment as a bilateral relationship that develops post partum (De Jong-Pleij et al. 2013; Pretorius et al. 2006). Certainly, the uterus does not offer the post-partum environment where comfort from the mother in response to hunger or separation helps a neonate develop attachment. However, might the fetus possibly be developing a foundational form of attachment to the mother simply through the safe environment of the uterus being associated with the sounds of her voice?

The first mention of prenatal maternal bonding in the literature is believed to be in the work of Deutsch (1945). Cranley (1981) defined maternal fetal attachment (MFA) as "the extent to which women engage in behaviors that represent an affiliation and interaction with their unborn child" (p. 181) and he designed the Maternal Fetal Attachment Scale (MFAS) as a reliable measure used across many studies (Cannella 2005). Various studies have indicated that interventions promote MFA in pregnant women (Mikhail et al. 1991). (Studies particularly relating to maternal singing are addressed later in this chapter.) Another measure is the Maternal Antenatal Attachment Scale (MAAS) developed by Condon (1993). Cranley's (1981) idea that maternal awareness of the fetus increases MFA was supported by Heidrich and Cranley's (1989) study, which showed that pregnant women who reported having felt fetal movement earlier in the pregnancy had higher MFA scores than women who did not. In addition, mothers seeing ultrasound images of the fetus improved MFA, particularly when three-dimensional images had a high degree of visibility and recognition (De Jong-Pleij et al. 2013).

Attachment during the pre-, peri-, and post-partum periods has been shown in the literature to be of both short- and long-term importance, with indications that poor maternal attachment to the fetus is linked with an increased likelihood of negative neonatal outcomes. In turn, these may also be associated with less healthy maternal behaviors and reports of sadness, loss, and concern for the future (Alhusen, Gross, Hayat, Rose et al. 2012; Alhusen, Gross, Hayat, Woods et al. 2012). One longitudinal study of maternal attachment determined that women demonstrating higher avoidant attachment styles and symptoms of depression during pregnancy were more likely to have children displaying early child-hood developmental delays than women with less avoidant attachment styles (Alhusen et al. 2013). Furthermore, women reporting higher maternal–fetal attachment during pregnancy demonstrated more secure attachment styles with their children years later and the children displayed optimal development as compared with children of women reporting lower maternal–fetal attachment.

The origins of infant attachment to the mother appear to be founded in the early sensory experiences within the womb. Research has informed us that a rich sensory experience is very much a part of intrauterine existence. For example, the fetus responds to touch first on the area of the lips and cheeks from eight weeks' gestation (Hooker 1952). By 15 weeks, the fetus responds to the flavors in the amniotic fluid, with increased swallowing activity if the fluid tastes sweet and less if it tastes bitter (Liley 1972). Response to sound is observed consistently from the 22nd to 24th weeks, with some response noted by researchers from 18 weeks onwards (Graven and Browne 2008; Hepper and Shahidullah 1994; Lecanuet et al. 1995). Maternal singing is found to be beneficial in facilitating the mother–infant relationship in the neonatal intensive care unit for premature infants (Standley and Whipple 2003). This chapter will explore characteristics of maternal singing; the response of the fetus and young infant to that singing; and how both these components impact maternal–infant bonding and attachment.

QUALITIES OF MATERNAL SINGING TOWARDS THE FETUS, NEONATE, AND YOUNG INFANTS

It is well known that mothers within cultures across the world show a tendency to speak with infants in a more musical style than that used in their usual engagement with adults. This expressive speaking style has often been referred to in the literature as "motherese" (Fernald 1985). The origins of motherese are believed have evolved in prelinguistic behaviors in which mothers were "constantly modifying vocalizations and gestures to control infants," "adopting new foraging strategies that entailed silencing, reassuring, and controlling" infant behaviors (Falk 2004, p. 491). Infant-directed (ID) speech involves a more pronounced, prosodic style of speech than found in adult-directed (AD) speech (Fernald 1984; Katz et al. 1996; Papoušek 1992). The more expressive, musical style of ID speech has been described as having "smooth pitch contours, heightened pitch, expanded pitch range, vowel elongation, and slow tempo" (Bergeson and Trehub 2002, p. 72). Other investigations have confirmed ID speech tempo being characteristically slower and spanning a wider pitch contour than AD speech (Fernald and Simon 1984; Papoušek et al. 1990; Papoušek et al. 1991; see Saint-Georges et al. 2013 for a review). There is also a tendency for mothers to ask their infants questions, even though they are pre-linguistic, with the result that sentences often end in a raised pitch that elicits heightened infant attention (Stern et al. 1982). Some see this speech as transformed into melody (Fernald 1992; Papoušek et al. 1991).

The practice of mothers and caregivers singing to infants is found in cultures across the world (Trehub and Schellenberg 1995; Trehub and Trainor 1998). This singing is characteristically entwined in everyday activities of feeding, changing diapers, bathing, playing, or preparing for sleep (Trehub et al. 1993a; Trehub et al. 1997; Unyk, Trehub et al. 1992). Genres of children's music repertoire are typically found in any culture, frequently referred to as lullabies, nursery rhymes, or play songs (Campbell and Wiggins 2013).

With similar qualities to ID maternal speech, recurrent structural elements of many ID songs include relatively high pitch and slow tempo, while the songs are normally performed with heightened expressiveness and emotionality than might be found in AD singing (Trainor et al. 1997; Trehub et al. 1997). Mothers sing a children's play song of their choice more expressively when their infants are present than when they are absent (Milligan et al. 2003).

The natural, communicative way in which adults sing to infants is often through intensified expressive use of the singing voice, varying the subtleties of voice quality (see "The impact of maternal singing on maternal–infant bonding and attachment" and "Mothers as Singing Mentors for Infants" by Trehub and Gudmundsdottir in this volume). However, in comparison to ID speech, they tend to apply comparatively small variations in pitch and timing. For example, Bergeson and Trehub (2002) found that the pitch level and tempo of speech utterances were highly variable. In contrast, they found pitch and tempo to be largely maintained in song. Furthermore, their results indicated that, while mothers tend to say specific phrases very differently when repeated, they typically display less variation in their renditions of a particular song, with the tempo (about two syllables per second), rhythm, and dynamics changing very little. Several studies indicated that, typically, mothers use a higher pitch register than usual when singing to their infants than they do when speaking to infants (Bergeson and Trehub 2002; Trainor et al. 1997; Trehub et al. 1997). While there is reported to be a three- to four-semitone difference between ID and AD speech, the overall pitch of ID singing might commonly only be a semitone higher than in AD singing (Fernald and Simon 1984; Trehub et al. 1997). The fundamental pitch of speech varies more than that of singing (Patel et al. 1998; Vos and Troost 1989). These same studies also determined that mothers tend to use a slower tempo than normal when singing to infants; however, the rhythmic features of the song remain intact, preserving the musical characteristics of the songs. These differences in ID singing characteristics are suggested to be less obvious than observed in ID speech, because songs exist within structural pitch and rhythmic elements that make them recognizable and repeatable (Nakata and Trehub 2004). Therefore, the same flexibility of adjusting pitch and rhythm is not possible in the same way as in speech. While ID singing involves less variability in tempo, there is evidence of greater dynamic range than in non-ID performances (Nakata and Trehub 2011). Although maternal speech towards infants may vary widely in content, it may be reasonably argued that there may be a strong degree of repetition in the specific choice of songs mothers sing from their cultural surroundings.

Mothers are not the only adults who display a distinctive style of ID singing; it has been observed in other family members, too (O'Neill et al. 2001). While much research tells us about the characteristics of maternal ID singing, other investigations provide evidence of fetal, neonatal, and infant experience of that singing and of the maternal–infant bonding inherent in maternal singing. These are offered in the immediate next section and the section titled "The impact of maternal singing on maternal–infant bonding and attachment" against the backdrop of theories presented earlier in this chapter of early intelligence, perception, and learning, as well as maternal–fetal bonding and attachment that go far beyond goals of survival, problem solving, object use, or language acquisition.

FETAL, NEONATAL, AND EARLY INFANT RESPONSE
TO THE MOTHER'S VOICE

The fetus develops within a blanket of sound consisting predominantly of background white "noise" from the mother's body, random intestinal gurgles, and rhythmic pulses of maternal cardiovascular sounds (Querleu et al. 1988). The Woodward intrauterine recordings of maternal singing (and other musical sounds) transmitting into the uterus (Woodward 1992; Woodward and Guidozzi 1992) have allowed the auditory environment of the fetus to be described in detail. These recordings demonstrated that pure tone sounds are transmitted into the human uterus with little attenuation of lower frequencies and sharply increasing attenuation up to 35dB of frequencies from about 400 Hz to 1000 Hz. There is little attenuation in the range of the fundamental frequency of the human voice (125–350 Hz) and the mother's singing voice emerges clearly above background uterine sounds. From her recordings, Woodward (1992) determined the timbre, melodic pitches, and rhythms of the maternal voice which transmit distinctly into the uterus. The higher frequencies of consonants (about 1500 Hz or above) were strongly attenuated. Knowing that fathers, siblings, and others might be interested in knowing to what extent their voices also reach the fetus, data analyses revealed that similar characteristics were noted in the intrauterine recordings of the father's singing and another female singing (both at a distance of one meter away from the mother), with vowel sounds being well-evident, but not consonants. All songs in the Woodward investigations were sung at normal conversational level (about 60 dB). Having established that the pregnant mother's singing voice reaches the fetus in her womb, very different kinds of investigations are valuable in indicating fetal hearing of her voice.

Auditory cognitive perception awakens and matures during the experience of sound. Therefore, maternal singing and the fetal processing of this are an integral part of the human journey towards singing. Science is confirming much of what pregnant mothers notice of fetal movement associated with external sounds from about midway through the pregnancy (such as a loud door bang or music at a live concert) (see Ullal-Gupta et al. 2013, for a review). Just how early does the fetus perceive sound in the womb? Auditory response emerges much later than fetal tactile response, the latter having been noted from as early as eight weeks while the former was reported as strongly evident in the last three months of pregnancy, with some evidence of hearing as early as 18 weeks (Graven and Browne 2008; Grimwade et al. 1971; Hepper and Shahidullah 1994; Lecanuet et al. 1995). By the later stage of pregnancy, the fetus has a mature auditory system with reliable perception and response to sound (Birnholz and Benacerraf 1983; Hepper and Shahidullah 1994; Querleu et al. 1988; Zimmer et al. 1993;). The presence of fluid (which we know is a strong conductor of sound) in the outer and inner ear of the fetus has led scientists to conclude that the acoustic energy that exists inside the uterus easily reaches the fetal cochlear receptors (Lecanuet and Schaal 1996). The fetus discriminates differences in frequency, timbre, loudness, and duration, which are all necessary for perceiving both speech and singing (Shahidullah and Hepper 1994; Shannon et al. 1995; Smith et al. 2002; Zatorre et al. 2002). Various studies indicate an ability of the late gestation fetus to distinguish changes in the gender of a speaker, between the mother's voice and that of another female, and between two different low-pitched notes (Kisilevsky et al. 2003; Lecanuet et al. 1993; Lecanuet et al. 2000). Sophistication of fetal experience of maternal speech and singing and higher-order processing of sound is determined by fetal responses in the third trimester (DeCasper et al. 1994; Jardri et al. 2008; Lecanuet et al. 1993; Moon et al. 1993).

The fetus displays a number of responses to music, such as altered behavioral states (James et al. 2002). The rhythmic rocking of a mother in a rocking chair leads to significant stimulation of fetal heart rate (Lecanuet and Jacquet 2002). There is a strong startle response to noise (Woodward 1992; Woodward and Guidozzi 1992). However, there is evidence that this goes beyond auditory perception and discrimination to auditory memory and learning. For example, in the late utero stages, startle response to sound will habituate with repeated stimulation (James 2010; Leader et al. 1982). Having determined that altered fetal behavioral states to music exposure are carried forward to the newborn period, James et al. (2002) suggest that "a simple form of fetal programming or learning has occurred" (p. 431). Auditory memory of prosodic patterns is observed in repeated exposure (DeCasper and Spence 1986b; DeCasper et al. 1994). Kisilevsky et al. (2009) suggest that their findings on fetal sensitivity to properties of maternal speech and language

> provide evidence of fetal attention, memory, and learning of voices and language, indicating that newborn speech/language abilities have their origins before birth. They suggest that neural networks sensitive to properties of the mother's voice and native-language speech are being formed.
>
> (p. 59)

Investigating the neural basis of fetal learning, Partanen et al. (2013) show direct neural evidence of neural memory traces being formed through auditory learning before birth and that the human fetus learns speech-like auditory stimuli. Their findings indicate that prenatal auditory experiences have a "remarkable influence on the brain's auditory discriminatory accuracy, which may support, for example, language acquisition during infancy" (p. 15145). Evidence of speech perception and learning capabilities continue in the neonatal stage in responses to recordings of the mother's voice (Moon and Fifer 1990; Moon et al. 1992). Newborn discrimination of speech prosody is indicated in sensitivity to the rhythm of words created through stress patterns (Sansavini et al. 1997).

The role of familiarity on impacting early preference is widely indicated, as in the study by DeCasper and Fifer (1980), which determined that newborns modify behavior to activate the mother's voice rather than that of another female. This study indicated evidence of fetal auditory memory and the development of preference for familiar sounds by the neonatal stage. Not only hearing, but other senses are also involved in the early development of familiarity. Pregnant women develop distinctive patterns of volatile compounds that contribute towards helping newborns recognize their own mother's smell, and are suggested to impact maternal infant bonding (Vaglio 2009). Breastfeeding neonates discriminate between their mother's axillary odor and odors produced by another woman (Cernoch and Porter 1985) and show increased mouthing response to the mother's smell (Sullivan and Toubas 1998). Newborns turn their head towards a breast pad worn by the mother and decrease activity to the presence of her odor (Macfarlane 1975; Schaal et al. 1995). Neonates spend longer periods looking at the face of their mother rather than that of another woman (Bushnell et al. 1989).

Not only do neonates prefer speech to non-speech sounds (Vouloumanos and Werker 2007), they also prefer the mother's native language to a foreign language, indicating memory of her speech heard before birth (Byers-Heinlein et al. 2010; Fifer 1987; Fifer and

Moon 1995; Mehler et al. 1978; Mehler et al. 1988; Moon et al. 1993). DeCasper and Spence (1986a) determined neonatal preference for a story by Dr. Seuss's *The Cat in the Hat*, which had been read repeatedly during the pregnancy, rather than another story by the same author. This finding was confirmed by DeCasper et al. (1994).

It has been argued that music reinforces learning from infancy and throughout life (Standley 1996). Standley (2012) presented premature infants with commercially recorded female singing of lullabies that was activated through the sucking of a pacifier. Results indicated a clear learning curve, with a consistent increase in sucking during stimulation periods. The researcher concluded: "it was obvious that infant learning and discrimination of music occurred" (p. 380). An earlier study of similar recordings determined that music served as reinforcement of sucking behavior and the transfer from non-nutritive to nutritive sucking (Standley 2003), assumedly contributing toward infant well-being.

Furthermore, infants appear to be emotional beings capable of recognizing emotional cues and of experiencing empathy. For example, infants engage in the emotional connections inherent in vocal expressions, as evidenced in their preference for positive vocal expressions over neutral vocal expressions (Singh et al. 2002). They also prefer positive facial expressions rather than neutral expressions (Kuchuk et al. 1986). A mother's facial expression during singing conceivably contributes towards a multisensory experience that, at any given moment, may also include expressive vocal sounds, affectionate touching, maternal smell, and even the taste of her milk, if occurring during feeding. The sustainability of preference for the multisensory familiarity of maternal singing beyond the neonatal period was explored by De L'Etoile (2006) who found that ID singing is far more effective in sustaining six-to-nine-month infant attention than listening to recorded music.

Relating back to the previous discussion on the musical characteristics of maternal ID speech, it is not surprising that infant attention to ID speech is heightened over AD speech (Fernald 1985). Mothers naturally respond to the more attentive body language of their infants by adjusting their ways of communicating to boost such infant responses (Fernald and Kuhl 1987) The infant responses are attributed to the more expressive mannerisms typical of ID speech when compared with the more subdued expressions found in everyday AD speech (Trainor et al. 2000), and to positive rather than neutral affect (Singh et al. 2002). Furthermore, infants pay more attention to the wider pitch range of motherese than is typical of regular speech (Cooper and Aslin 1990; Fernald 1991; Fernald and Kuhl 1987; Grieser and Kuhl 1988; Werker and McLeod 1989). Heightened infant responsiveness reinforces maternal use of a higher pitch register than in AD speech (Fernald 1992; Trehub and Trainor 1998).

Infants are more attracted to maternal singing than to maternal speech (Nakata and Trehub 2004). ID singing is seen to more effectively regulate infant stress than ID speech (Ghazban 2013). Pitch level and tone of voice are important in infant preferences for singing (Trainor 1996). Infants respond with more intensity to higher-pitch renditions of the same song (O'Neill et al. 2001; Trainor and Zacharias 1998). While the differences in ID and AD singing may be less pronounced than in speech, ID singing is shown to elicit more neonatal attention than AD singing (Masataka 1999). The tendency of some mothers to engage in singing as a playful, arousing activity with their infants, while others sing for calming effect, may be linked to cultural practices in infant caregiving, such as the infant being left to sleep alone, or sleeping with the mother (Trehub et al. 1993b).

Orienting response (such as decreased motor activity and heart rate) is found in the fetus to the maternal spoken voice (Hepper et al. 1993). Fetuses from 36 weeks of gestation show a calming, orienting response to maternal reading aloud when the mothers were previously awake and talking (Voegtline et al. 2013). However, in the same study, fetuses whose mothers had previously been resting and silent responded with elevated heart rate and increased movement, indicating a mild startle response. Orienting response in the fetus to the maternal voice is consistent with the investigation by Fifer and Moon (1994) and confirmed in the review of research by Lecanuet and Schaal (1996). Calming effect is also demonstrated in newborns exhibiting lowered heart rate to the mother's voice (Ockleford et al. 1988), fewer movements (Fernald 1989), and more cardiovascular and behavioral stability (Filippa et al. 2013). These calming responses to the maternal spoken voice are similar with regards the maternal singing voice.

The capacity of maternal singing previously heard *in utero* to soothe an infant indicates its importance in early cognitive and emotional development (Longhi 2008; Trehub 2003). Arousal regulation, distress aversion, and the fostering of interpersonal bonds are all evident in infant response to ID maternal singing (Trehub and Trainor 1998). ID singing appears to be frequently used by mothers in modulating (calming) infant arousal (Trainor 1996; Trehub and Schellenberg 1995; Trehub et al. 1993b). The effectiveness of music in reducing dangerously high arousal levels of neonates in intensive care units has been demonstrated (Cassidy and Stanley 1995; Lorch et al. 1994). Even normal, non-distressed infants indicate lowered arousal levels as measured in salivary cortisol changes (Shenfield, Trehub, and Nakata 2003). While maternal speech is also noted to reduce infant arousal, impact is more sustained for maternal audiovisually-based singing (Shenfield et al. 2003). Similarly, infants show more sustained attention to extended audiovisual episodes of maternal singing than to comparable episodes of maternal speech (Nakata and Trehub 2004). The elicitation of infant attention and intense engagement through maternal singing appears to be linked to pronounced movement reduction (Bacher and Robertson 2001; Casey and Richards 1991; Field et al. 1989).

The impact of maternal singing on maternal–infant bonding and attachment

Dissanayake (2009) suggests that the origins of communicative musicality occur through the mutuality of maternal–infant musical experience, that is, making meaning through the combination of love, art, and intimacy, where everyday interactions are elevated from the ordinary to the extraordinary. The impact of maternal singing on maternal–infant bonding and attachment occurs within this realm of communicative musicality (c.f. Malloch and Trevarthen 2009). First, associations between higher-pitched and slower vocalizations have been found with happiness and affection (Scherer 1981). It is suggested, therefore, that the naturally higher pitches and slower vocalizations used by mothers when singing to their infants may well be an indication of their happiness and affection, both of which would conceivably promote maternal–infant bonding. Second, the regularity of the beat within any song is described to promote coordination with movement and is suggested to enhance coordination of emotional communication between mother and infant (Nakata and Trehub

2004; Trehub 2003). Third, there is the tonal quality of how a mother sings to her child. The unique prosodic qualities of her singing encourages a reciprocal relationship (Abromeit 2003). Newborn adult-like processing of pitch intervals is suggested to "underlie attachment to and communication with the caretaker" (Stefanics et al. 2009). Fourth, the familiarity of maternal songs may impact bonding and attachment (Trehub et al. 1997). Maternal repertoire of songs in infant communications may be more limited than the variety of speech that might normally be covered in daily spoken interactions (Nakata and Trehub 2004). As a result, infants may develop more familiarity with specific songs than with specific speech (Bergeson and Trehub 2002; Trehub et al. 1997). Furthermore, the ritualistic styles of singing particular songs are suggested to bring comfort and pleasure through this experience of familiarity (Bergeson and Trehub 2002). Benefits of well-being to newborns in experiencing familiar maternal speech and singing may be indicated, considering the preference of newborns for the mother's voice, for her language, for a story read by her repeatedly during the pregnancy and for a lullaby sung before the birth (DeCasper and Fifer 1980; Hepper et al. 1993; Satt 1984; Standley and Madsen 1990). Furthermore, neonates prefer a song sung by the mother during pregnancy with the "la" syllable (rather than the words) to an unfamiliar melody also sung to the "la" syllable (Panneton 1985), confirming the ability to develop familiarity with the tonal and rhythmic patterns of a melody. These four components of infant experience of maternal singing appear to be key in the impact on mother–infant bonding. Whipple's (2000) study also confirms links between singing and mother–infant bonding.

Young infants are shown to respond to the emotional content of music, showing preference for happy voice quality (Corbeil et al. 2013). Six women attending antenatal classes at a metropolitan maternity hospital in Ireland were taught to sing three lullabies during four group sessions (Carolan et al. 2012). Instead of using traditional Irish lullabies, the musicians chose lullabies not known to any of the participants, each selected for its "flowing melody and meaningful lyrics" (p. 322). Interviewed several months later, the women reported that the songs provided a means for articulating the deep emotions that they were feeling, and induced peaceful relaxation and feelings of closeness to their babies. The women also reported the impact they perceived being experienced by their infants—noticing apparent recognition of the lullabies, and responses in movement and vocalizations. They believed that early cognitive development was being impacted positively and that these early musical experiences would foster a lifelong appreciation for music. The researchers highlighted that teaching and encouraging pregnant women to sing lullabies was a low-cost approach to reducing maternal stress that was enjoyable to the women. This confirmed an earlier report by the same authors indicating that singing lullabies during pregnancy promoted relaxation and bonding, as well as being a tool for caregiving after birth (Carolan et al. 2011). In an Australian pilot study, women were shown how to use lullabies in creating a safe and calm environment for their infants (MacKinlay and Baker 2005). The 18 mothers' reports of how singing lullabies to their infants positively impacted their own emotional and physical well-being indicates further indirect benefit regarding infant well-being.

The range of benefits of maternal singing to the infant goes well beyond bonding and attachment matters. However, these aspects may indirectly impact such bonding and attachment through the enhanced well-being of the child. Live music and singing have been increasingly incorporated in research studies pertaining to music therapy and the premature infant (Hanson-Abromeit et al. 2008; Haslbeck and Costes 2011; Malloch et al. 2012; Teckenberg-Jansson et al. 2011). Recorded lullabies played to incubated infants are reported to result in a reduction in time to achieve sufficient weight gain for discharge (Chapman 1975). Lullabies presented during kangaroo care[1] are shown to enhance preterm infant behavioral state stability (more quiet sleep and less crying) and significantly lower maternal anxiety (Lai et al. 2006). Standley (1998) determined enhanced developmental gains in premature infants receiving live singing along with multimodal stimulation. In a much larger, multisite study, premature infants receiving developmental multimodal stimulation that included live singing or live singing with guitar accompaniment had positive neurodevelopmental gains, as measured by significantly shorter length of stay (Walworth et al. 2012). Premature infants receiving music stimulation gained more weight per day than infants not referred for intervention (Caine 1991; Coleman et al. 1997). Similarly, those born at 24–28 gestational weeks were discharged earlier than infants in the same age range (Standley and Swedberg 2011). Additionally, there has been increasing interest since the early 1990s in testing the efficacy of music interventions for premature infants' numerous outcomes (Standley 2001). In her 2002 meta-analysis of 10 studies, Stanley determined an overwhelming homogeneity of findings suggesting "that music has statistically significant and clinically important benefits for premature infants in the NICU" (p. 107). A marked reduction of distress has been noted in premature infants undergoing medical procedures (Burke et al. 1995). The music of Mozart was found to lower resting energy expenditure in healthy preterm infants (Lubetsky et al. 2010). Another study confirmed this, but did not find any such effect with the music of Bach (Keidar et al. 2014). Noise, however, is suggested to be a hazard for the fetus and newborn (Committee on Environmental Health 1997). Loud noises in the NICU impact behavioral and physiological responses of infants (Zahr and Balian 1995). Hypoxemia occurs in infants in conjunction with sudden loud noise, and measures have been taken to quantify and lower ambient noise levels in the NICU (Long et al. 1980).

Premature infancy or illness that results in neonates being assigned to the NICU may result in additional stressors and vulnerability for the parent, including feelings of guilt, of parental isolation from the infant, loss of control over infant care, and feeling inconsequential to the baby's well-being (Fendwick et al. 2001). However, O'Gorman (2007) points out that that, as long as stress is manageable, attachments can still be formed and the stress may be a contributing factor in further strengthening bonds. Her case study involving recordings of parental singing, as well as live therapist and parental ID singing, demonstrated a positive impact on infant emotional well-being (soothing) and on parental feelings of empowerment (being able to connect with and demonstrate care for their infant) (Crittenden 1999). Overall, evidence suggests that a baby's ability to form attachments is connected with the caregiver's capacity to comfort and protect. Parent–infant interactions are ideally reciprocal, synchronous, and coherent (Tronick 1989).

The communicative musicality model is promoted in music therapy interventions to improve physiological and behavioral outcomes in the premature infant, in supporting the parents, and in promoting parent–infant attachment (Haslbeck 2012, 2014). Studies have involved parents singing for their infants in facilitating the infant–parent attachment process (Loewy 2011; Shoemark 2011). A range of studies has addressed interactive and individualized music therapy approaches in the NICU (Cevasco 2006; Malloch et al.

---

[1] Kangaroo care is a method of the adult carer (mother/father) holding a baby to their chest that involves skin-to-skin contact.

2012; Shoemark and Grocke 2010; Teckenberg-Jansson et al. 2011; Whipple 2008). Van de Carr's Prenatal University stimulation program (Van de Carr and Lehrer 1998) was based on the theory that purposeful interaction (including musical interaction) with the fetus by the mother, father, and siblings leads to increased maternal–infant bonding, paternal–infant bonding, and sibling–infant bonding. Follow-up interactions with parents and infants were found to support the theory (Van de Carr and Lehrer 1998).

CONCLUSION

This review cannot end without at least briefly raising the question of whether the technology-rich world with instant music access at the touch of a screen is impacting on the prevalence of maternal ID singing. Furthermore, it is conceivable that the lack of access to an extended family that is reported to be typical of modern urbanized communities across much of the world might be impacting on whether young mothers have parents and grandparents teaching them the lullabies and children's songs of their culture. Scant research in this area indicates the need for more exploration of these questions. A recent study of 500 pregnant women from the Marburg region of Germany determined that women over 30 years of age sang significantly more often compared with women of 30 or fewer years of age, as did multiparous women (having more than one child) in comparison with nulliparous women (Arabin and Jahn 2013). Furthermore, women with university education sang more than those with secondary or lower education. In all these comparisons, the older women, the more educated women, and those who had multiple births sang more lullabies and children's play songs than younger, less educated, and nulliparous women respectively. In contrast, a study of 52 mothers with a child of one year or younger, living in Florida, USA, found that younger mothers and those in a lower income bracket were more likely to sing prenatally (Sirak 2012). Further studies in this area would be valuable. It is heartening to see programs across the globe that foster singing practice in pregnant women, such as the *Coorie Doon* project of Helen McVey, from Enterprise Music Scotland, which supports young mothers composing new lullabies to sing to their babies (Pickering 2015). Another is the program in Ireland (mentioned previously) that teaches women lullabies (Carolan et al. 2012).

This review has highlighted the ubiquity of singing across cultures, as well as the global phenomenon of maternal–infant communication through singing, which has roots in ancient traditions (Skeles 1996). Evidence has been presented of the characteristically song-like nature and musical attributes of ID speech (Dissanayake 2000; Fernald and Simon 1984; Trehub, et al. 1997) and the enhanced qualities of ID singing (Trainor et al. 1997; Trehub et al. 1997). Multiple studies as reviewed here indicate benefits of maternal singing for both mother and infant, including facilitating enjoyment, offering a means for expressing emotions, fostering maternal–infant attachment, reducing maternal and infant stress, and furthering infant cognitive development. The power of maternal singing in soliciting attention, fostering calming, and impacting development is attributable not just to the music itself, but also to the emotional and social interaction involved in maternal singing (Trehub 2003; see "Mothers as Singing Mentors for Infants" by Trehub and Gudmundsdottir in this volume). Theories presented here inform our current thinking on the role of maternal singing on maternal–infant attachment and bonding with links to infant perception, memory, learning, and the development of early preference (DeCasper and Fifer 1980; Hepper 1996; Hepper 2005; O'Gorman 2007). Theories on the ameliorative effects of maternal singing on the psychophysiological well-being of infants provide additional interest in terms of how these may indirectly impact maternal–infant bonding (Standley 2002).

Areas of knowledge informing this investigation have included psychology, audiology, neurology, biomedical science, developmental science, sociology, cultural studies, philosophy, music therapy, and music education, amongst others. Key sources have included evidence-based literature that is supported predominantly by experimental research. Implications for the benefits of maternal singing during and after pregnancy emerge that are applicable across interdisciplinary fields. In summary, fetal and neonatal experience of the maternal singing voice is shown to involve detailed discrimination, memory, and learning pertaining not only to musical components, but also to the communicative nature of the interactions involved. The author has endeavored to emphasize the overriding importance of the messages that are conveyed to the infant through maternal singing. As eloquently expressed by Dissanayake (2009, p. 27) "This view of human music as rooted in communicative musicality helps us to appreciate music's unique emotional and transformative power in human experience."

FURTHER READING

Arabin, B. (2002). Music during pregnancy. *Ultrasound in Obstetrics and Gynecology* 20: 425–430.

Fonagy, P. (2001). *Attachment Theory and Psychoanalysis*. New York: Other Press.

Nocker-Ribaupierre, M. (2004). The mother's voice: A bridge between two worlds. In: M Nocker-Ribaupierre (ed.), *Music Therapy for Premature and Newborn Infants*, pp. 97–112. Gilsum, NH: Barcelona Publishers.

REFERENCES

Abromeit, D.H. (2003). The newborn individualized developmental care and assessment program (NIDCAP) as a model for clinical music therapy interventions with premature infants. *Music Therapy Perspectives* 21(2): 60–68. doi:10.1093/mtp/21.2.60

Ainsworth, M.D. (1979). Infant-mother attachment. *American Psychologist* 34: 932–937.

Ainsworth, M.D. (1991). Attachments and other affectional bonds across the life cycle. In: C.M. Parkes, J. Stevenson-Hinde, and P. Maris (eds), *Attachment across the Lifecycle*, pp. 32–51. London, Routledge.

Alhusen, J., Gross, D., Hayat, M. Rose, L., and Sharps, P. (2012). The role of mental health on maternal-fetal attachment in low-income women. *Journal of Obstetric, Gynecologic, and Neonatal Nursing* 41: E71–E81.

Alhusen, J., Gross, D., Hayat, M., Woods, A.B., and Sharps, P. (2012). The influence of maternal-fetal attachment and health practices on neonatal outcomes in low-income, urban women. *Research in Nursing and Health* 35: 112–120.

Alhusen, J., Hayat, M., and Gross, D. (2013). A longitudinal study of maternal attachment and infant development outcomes. *Archives of Women's Mental Health* 16(6): 521–529.

Antonucci, T.C., Akiyama, H., and Takahashi, K. (2004) Attachment and close relationships across the life span. *Attachment and Human Development* 6: 353–370.

Arabin, B. and Jahn, M. (2013). Need for interventional studies on the impact of music in the perinatal period: results of a pilot study on women's preferences and review of the literature. *Journal of Maternal-Fetal and Neonatal Medicine* 26(4): 357–362.

Bacher, L.F. and Robertson, S.S. (2001). Stability of coupled fluctuations in movement and visual attention in infants. *Developmental Psychobiology* 39: 99–106.

Bannan, N. and Woodward, S.C. (2009). Spontaneity in the musicality and music learning of children. In: S. Malloch and C. Trevarthen (eds), *Communicative Musicality: Exploring the Basis of Human Companionship*, pp. 465–494. Oxford: Oxford University Press.

Bergeson, T.R. and Trehub, S.E. (2002). Absolute pitch and tempo in mothers' songs to infants. *Psychological Science* 13(1): 72–75.

Birnholz, J.C. and Benacerraf, B.R. (1983). The development of human fetal hearing. *Science* 222(4623): 516–518. PMID 6623091

Blacking J. (1973). *How Musical is Man?* Seattle: University of Washington Press.

Bowlby, J. (1978). Attachment theory and its therapeutic implications. In: S.C. Feinstein and P.L. Giovacchini (eds), *Adolescent Psychiatry: Developmental and Clinical Studies*, Vol. 6, pp. 5–33. New York: Jason Aronson.

Brockington, I.F. (1996). *Motherhood and Mental Health*. New York: Oxford University Press.

Brockington, I.F., Oates, J., and George, S. (2001). A screening questionnaire for mother-infant bonding disorders. *Archives of Women's Mental Health* 3: 133–140.

Burke, M., Walsh, J., Oehler, J., and Gringas, J. (1995). Music therapy following suctioning: four case studies. *Neonatal Network* 14(7): 41–49.

Bushnell, I.W., Sai, F., and Mullin, J.T. (1989). Neonatal recognition of the mother's face. *British Journal of Developmental Psychology* 7(1): 3–15. doi:10.1111/j.2044-835X.1989.tb00784.x

Byers-Heinlein K., Burns T.C., and Werker J.F. (2010). The roots of bilingualism in newborns. *Psychological Science* 21(3): 343–348. doi:10.1177/0956797609360758

Caine, J. (1991). The effect of music on the selected stress behaviors, weight, caloric and formula intake, and length of hospital stay of premature and low birth weight neonates in a newborn intensive care unit. *Journal of Music Therapy* 28(4): 180–182.

Campbell P.S. (1998). *Songs in their Heads: Music and its Meaning*. Oxford: Oxford University Press.

Campbell, P.S. and Wiggins, T. (eds) (2013). *The Oxford Handbook of Children's Musical Cultures*. New York: Oxford University Press.

Cannella, B. (2005). Maternal-fetal attachment: an integrative review. *Journal of Advanced Nursing* 50(1): 60–68.

Carolan, M., Barry, M., Gamble, M., Turner, K., and Mascarenas, O. (2011). Singing lullabies in pregnancy: what benefits for women? *Women and Birth* 24: S29.

Carolan, M., Barry, M., Gamble, M., Tumer, K., and Mascarenas, O. (2012). Experiences of pregnant women attending a lullaby programme in Limerick, Ireland: a qualitative study. *Midwifery* 28: 321–328.

Casey, B.J. and Richards, J.E. (1991). A refractory period for the heart rate response in infant visual attention. *Developmental Psychobiology* 24: 327–340.

Cassidy, J.W. and Stanley, J.M. (1995). The effect of music listening on physiological responses of premature infants in the NICU. *Journal of Music Therapy* 32(4): 208–227.

Cernoch, J.M. and Porter, R.H. (1985). Recognition of maternal axillary odors by infants. *Child Development* 56: 1593–1598. [PubMed] PMID: 4075877

Cevasco, A.M. (2006). *The effects of mothers' singing on full-term and preterm infants and maternal emotional responses* (doctoral dissertation). Retrieved from ProQuest Dissertations Publishing. (3232373)

Chapman, J.S. (1975). *The relation between auditory stimulation of short gestation infants and their gross motor limb activity* (unpublished doctoral dissertation). New York University, New York.

Coleman, J.M., Pratt, R.R., Stoddard, R.A., Gerstmann, D.R., and Abel, H.H. (1997). The effects of male and female singing and speaking voices on selected physiological and behavioral measures of premature infants in the intensive care unit. *International Journal of Arts Medicine* 5(2): 4–11.

Committee on Environmental Health (1997). Noise: a hazard for the fetus and newborn. *American Academy of Pediatrics. Pediatrics* 100: 724–727.

Condon J.T. (1993). The assessment of antenatal emotional assessment: development of a questionaire instrument. *British Journal of Medical Psychology* 66: 167–183.

Cooper, R.P. and Aslin, R.N. (1990). Preference for infant-directed speech in the first month after birth. *Child Development* 61: 1584–1595. Medline. PMID: 2245748

Corbeil, M., Trehub, S.E., and Peretz, I. (2013). Speech vs. singing: infants choose happier sounds. *Frontiers in Psychology* 4: 372.

Cranley, M. (1981). Development of a tool for the measurement of maternal attachment during pregnancy. *Nursing Research* 30: 281–284. [PubMed] PMID: 6912989

Crittenden, P.M. (1999). Danger and development: the organization of self-protective strategies. In: J. Vondra and D. Barnett (eds), *Atypical Attachment in Infancy and Early Childhood among Children at Developmental Risk*, pp. 145–171. Monographs of the Society for Research on Child Development.

De Jong-Pleij, E.A.P., Ribbert, L.S.M., Pistorius, L.R., Mulder, E.J.H., and Bilardo, C.M. (2013). Three-dimensional ultrasound and maternal bonding, a third trimester study and a review. *Prenatal Diagnosis* 33: 81–88.

De l'Etoile, S.K. (2006). Infant behavioral responses to infant-directed singing and other maternal interactions. *Infant Behavior and Development* 29(3): 456–470.

DeCasper, A.J. and Fifer, W.P. (1980) Of human bonding: newborns prefer their mothers' voices. *Science* 208(4448): 1174–1176. 10.1126/science.7375928 [PubMed] PMID: 7375928

DeCasper, A.J. and Spence, M.J. (1986a). Newborns prefer a familiar story over an unfamiliar one. *Infant Behavior and Development* 9: 113–150.

DeCasper, A.J. and Spence, M.J. (1986b). Prenatal maternal speech influences newborns' perception of speech sounds. *Infant Behavior and Development* 9: 133–150. doi:10.1016/0163-6383(86)90025-1

DeCasper, A.J., Lecanuet J.P., Busnel, M.C., Granier-Deferre, C., and Maugeais, R. (1994). Fetal reactions to recurrent maternal speech. *Infant Behavior and Development* 17: 159–164.

Deutsch, H. (1945). *The Psychology of Women: A Psychoanalytic Interpretation*, Vol 2. *Motherhood*. New York: Grune and Stratton.

Dissanayake, E. (2000). *Art and Intimacy: How the Arts Began*. Seattle, WA: University of Washington Press.

Dissanayake E. (2009). Root, leaf, blossom, or bole: concerning the origin and adaptive function of music. In: S. Malloch and C. Trevarthen (eds), *Communicative Musicality: Exploring the Basis of Human Companionship*, pp. 17–30. New York: Oxford University Press.

Falk, D. (2004). Prelinguistic evolution in early hominins: whence motherese? *Behavioral and Brain Sciences* 27(1): 491–541.

Fendwick, J., Barclay, L., and Schmieder, V. (2001). Struggling to mother: a consequence of inhibitive nursing interactions in the neonatal nursery. *Journal of Perinatal and Neonatal Nursing* 15(2): 49–64.

Fernald, A. (1984). The perceptual and affective salience of mothers' speech to infants. In: L. Feagans, C. Garvey, and R. Golinkoff (eds), *The Origins and Growth of Communication*, pp. 5–29. Norwood, NJ: Ablex.

Fernald, A. and Simon, T. (1984). Expanded intonation contours in mothers' speech to newborns. *Developmental Psychology* 20: 104–113.

Fernald, A. (1985). Four-month-old infants prefer to listen to motherese. *Infant Behavior and Development* 8: 181–195. CrossRef doi.org/10.1016/S0163-6383(85)80005-9

Fernald, A. and Kuhl, P.K. (1987). Acoustic determinants of infant preference for mother's speech. *Infant Behavior and Development* 10: 279–293.

Fernald, A. (1989). A cross-language study of prosodic modifications in mothers and fathers to preverbal infants. *Journal of Child Language* 16: 477. [PubMed] PMID: 2808569

Fernald, A. (1991). Prosody in speech to children: prelinguistic and linguistic functions. *Annals of Child Development* 8: 43–80.

Fernald, A. (1992). Meaningful melodies in mothers' speech to infants. In: H. Papoušek, U. Jürgens, and M. Papoušek (eds), *Nonverbal Vocal Communication: Comparative and Developmental Approaches*, pp. 262–282. Cambridge: Cambridge University Press. Google Scholar.

Field, T., Healy, B.T., and LeBlanc, W.G. (1989). Sharing and synchrony of behavior states and behavior states and heart rate in nondepressed versus depressed mother-infant interactions. *Infant Behavior and Development* 12: 357–376.

Fifer, W. (1987). Neonatal preference for mother's voice. In: N.A. Krasnagor, E.M. Blass, M.A. Hofer, and W.P. Smotherman (eds), *Perinatal Development: A Psychobiological Perspective*, pp. 111–124. Cambridge, MA: Academic Press.

Fifer, W.P. and Moon, C.M. (1994). The role of the mother's voice in the organization of brain function in the newborn. *Acta Paediatrica Supplement* 397: 86–93. [PubMed] PMID: 7981479

Fifer, W.P. and Moon, C.M. (1995). The effects of fetal experience with sound. In: J.P. Lecanuet, N.A. Krasnegor, W.P. Fifer, and W.P. Smotherman (eds), *Fetal Development: A Psychobiological Approach*, pp. 351–366. Hillsdale, NJ: Lawrence Erlbaum.

Filippa, M., Devouche, E., Arioni, C., Imberty, M., and Gratier, M. (2013). Live maternal speech and singing have beneficial effects on hospitalized preterm infants. *Acta Paediatrica* 102(10): 1017–1020.

Gardner, H. (1983). *Frames of Mind: The Theory of Multiple Intelligences*. New York: Basic Books.

Ghazban, N. (2013). *Emotion Regulation in Infants Using Maternal Singing and Speech* (dissertation). Ryerson University, Toronto, Ontario, Canada.

Graven, S.N. and Browne, J. (2008). Auditory development in the fetus and infant. *Newborn and Infant Nursing Reviews* 8(4): 187–193. doi:10.1053/j.nainr.2008.10.010

Grimwade, J., Walker, D., Bartlett, M., Gordon, S., and Wood, C. (1971). Human fetal heart rate change and movement in response to sound and vibration. *American Journal of Obstetrics and Gynecology* 109: 86–90. [PubMed] PMID: 5538975

Grieser, D.L. and Kuhl, P. (1988). Maternal speech to infants in a tonal language: support for universal prosodic features in motherese. *Developmental Psychology* 24: 14–20.

Hanson-Abromeit, D., Shoemark, H., and Loewy, J. (2008). Music therapy in the newborn intensive and special care nurseries. In: D. Hanson-Abromeit and C. Colwell (eds), *Medical Music Therapy for Pediatrics in Hospital Settings: Using Music to Support Medical*

Interventions. Silver Spring, MD: American Music Therapy Association. 10.1093/mtp/21.2.60 [Cross Ref] doi:10.1093/mtp/21.2.60

Haslbeck, F.B. and Costes, T. (2011). Advanced training in music therapy with premature infants—impressions from the United States and a starting point for Europe. *British Journal of Music Therapy* 25(2): 19–31.

Haslbeck, F.B. (2012). Music therapy for premature infants and their parents: An integrative review. *Nordic Journal of Music Therapy* 21(3): 203–226. doi:10.1080/08098131.2011.648653

Haslbeck, F.B. (2014). The interactive potential of creative music therapy with premature infants and their parents: a qualitative analysis. *Nordic Journal of Music Therapy* 23(1): 36–70. doi:10.1080/08098131.2013.790918

Heidrich, S.M. and Cranley, M.S. (1989). The effect of fetal movement, ultrasound scans and amniocentesis on maternal-fetal attachment. *Nursing Research* 38(2): 81–84.

Hepper, P., Scott, D., and Shahidullah, S. (1993). Newborn and fetal response to maternal voice. *Journal of Reproductive and Infant Psychology* 11: 147–153.

Hepper P.G. and Shahidullah, B.S. (1994). Development of fetal hearing. *Archives of Disease in Childhood* 71: 81–87. [PMC free article] [PubMed] PMID: 7979483 PMCID: PMC1061088

Hepper, P.G. (1996). Fetal memory: does it exist? What does it do? *Acta Paediatrica Supplement* 416: 16–20.

Hepper, P.G. (2005) Unravelling our beginnings. *Psychologist* 18(8): 474–477.

Hooker, D. (1952). *The prenatal origin of behavior* (thesis). University of Kansas, Kansas.

Hugo, V. (1864). *William Shakespeare*. Translated by Nottingham Society (1907) Part I, Book II, Ch 4, p. 58. http://www.gavroche.org/vhugo/shakespeare/

James, D.K., Spencer C.J., and Stepsis, B.W. (2002). Fetal learning: a prospective randomized controlled study. *Ultrasound in Obstetrics and Gynecology* 20: 431–438. doi:10.1046/j.1469-0705.2002.00845.x

James, D.K. (2010). Fetal learning: a critical review. *Infant and Child Development* 19(1): 45–54. doi:10.1002/icd.653

Jardri R., Pins, D., Houfflin-Debarge, V., Chaffiotte, C., Rocourt, N., Pruvo, J. P., . . . Thomas, P. (2008). Fetal cortical activation to sound at 33 weeks of gestation: a functional MRI study. *NeuroImage* 42: 10–18. 10.1016/j.neuroimage.2008.04.247 [PubMed] [Cross Ref] PMID: 18539048 doi:10.1016/j.neuroimage.2008.04.247

Juslin, P.N. and Persson, R.S. (2002). Emotional communication. In: R. Parncutt and G. E. McPherson (eds), *The Science and Psychology of Music Performance*, pp. 219–236. Oxford: Oxford University Press.

Juslin, P. and Västfjäll, D. (2008). Emotional responses to music: the need to consider underlying mechanisms. *Behavioral and Brain Sciences* 31: 559–621.

Katz, G.S., Cohn, J.F., and Moore, C.A. (1996). A combination of vocal Fo dynamic and summary features discriminates between three pragmatic categories of infant-directed speech. *Child Development* 67: 205–217.

Keidar, H. R., Mandel, D., Mimouni, F.B., and Lubetzky, R. (2014). Bach music in preterm infants: no "Mozart effect" on resting energy expenditure. *Journal of Perinatology* 34: 153–155.

Kinsey, C. and Hupcey, J. (2013). State of the science of maternal–infant bonding: a principle-based concept analysis. *Midwifery* 29: 1314–1320.

Kinsey, C., Baptist-Roberts, K., Zhu, J., and Kjerulff, K. (2014). Birth-related, psychosocial, and emotional correlates of positive maternal-infant bonding in a cohort of first-time mothers. *Midwifery* 30: 118–194.

Kisilevsky, B.S., Hains, S.M.J., Lee, K., Xie X, Huang, H., Ye, H.H., . . . Wang, Z. (2003). Effects of experience on fetal voice recognition. *Psychological Science* 14(3): 220–224. [PubMed] PMID: 12741744 doi:10.1111/1467-9280.02435

Kisilevsky, B.S., Hains, S.M.J., Brown, C.A., Lee, C.T., Cowperthwaite, B., Stutzman, S. S., . . . Wang, Z. (2009). Fetal sensitivity to properties of maternal speech and language. *Infant Behavior and Development* 32(1): 59–71. [PubMed] PMID: 12741744 doi:10.1111/1467-9280.02435

Klaus, M. and Kennell, J. (1982). *Parent-Infant Bonding*. St. Louis, MO: Mosby.

Koelsch, S. (2013). Emotion. In: *Brain and Music*, pp. 203–235. Hoboken, NJ: John Wiley and Sons.

Kosfeld, M., Heinrichs, M., Zak, P.J., Fischbacher, U., and Fehr, E. (2005). Oxytocin increases trust in humans. *Nature* 435: 673–676.

Kreutz, G. (2014). Does singing facilitate social bonding? *Music and Medicine* 6(2): 51–60.

Kuchuk, A., Vibbert, M., and Bornstein, M.H. (1986). The perception of smiling and its experiential correlates in three-month-old infants. *Child Development* 57: 1054–1061. [Medline] PMID: 3757600

Lai, H., Chen, C., Peng, T., Chang, F., Hsieh, M., Huang, H., and Chang, S., et al. (2006). Randomized controlled trial of music during kangaroo care on maternal state anxiety and preterm infants' responses. *International Journal of Nursing* 43(2): 139–146.

Leader, L. R., Baillie, P., Martin, B., and Vermeulen, E. (1982). The assessment and significance of habituation to a repeated stimulus by the human fetus. *Early Human Development* 7: 211–219.

Lecanuet, J.P., Granier-Deferre. C, Jacquet, A.Y., Capponi, I., and Ledru, L. (1993). Prenatal discrimination of male and female voice uttering the same sentence. *Early Development and Parenting* 2: 217–228.

Lecanuet, J. P., Granier-Deferre, C., and Busnel, M.C. (1995). Human fetal auditory perception. In: J.P. Lecanuet, W.P. Fifer, N.A. Krasnegor, and W.P. Smotherman (eds), *Fetal Development: A Psychobiological Perspective*, pp. 239–363. Hillsdale, NJ: Lawrence Erlbaum.

Lecanuet, J. and Schaal, B. (1996). Fetal sensory competencies. *European Journal of Obstetrics and Gynecology and Reproductive Biology* 68: 1–23. [PubMed] PMID: 8886675

Lecanuet, J.P., Graniere-Deferre, C., Jacquet, A.Y., and DeCasper, A.J. (2000). Fetal discrimination of low-pitched musical notes. *Developmental Psychobiology* 36(1): 29–39. PMID: 10607359

Lecanuet, J.P. and Jacquet, A.Y. (2002). Fetal responsiveness to maternal passive swinging in low heart rate variability state: effects of stimulation direction and duration. *Developmental Psychobiology* 40(1): 57–67.

Liley, A.W. (1972). The foetus as a personality. *Australian and New Zealand Journal of Psychiatry* 6: 99.

Loewy, J.V. (2011). Music therapy for hospitalized infants and their parents. In: J. Edwards (ed.), *Music Therapy and Parent-Infant Bonding*, pp. 179–192. Oxford: Oxford University Press.

Long, J.G., Lucey, J.F., and Philip, A.G. (1980). Noise and hypoxemia in the intensive care nursery. *Pediatrics* 65: 143–145.

Longhi, E. (2008). Emotional response in mother-infant musical interactions: a developmental perspective. *Behavioral and Brian Sciences* 31(5): 586–587.

Lorch, C.A., Lorch, V., Diefendorf, A.O., and Earl, P.W. (1994). Effect of stimulative and sedative music on systolic blood pressure, heart rate, and respiratory rate in premature infants. *Journal of Music Therapy* 31(2): 105–118.

Lubetsky, R., Mimouni, F.B., Dolberg, S., Reifen, R., Ashbel G., and Mandel, D. (2010). Effect of music by Mozart on energy expenditure in growing preterm infants. *Pediatrics* 125(1): e24–28. doi: 10.1542/peds.2009-09

MacKinlay, E. and Baker, F. (2005). Nurturing herself, nurturing her baby: creating positive experiences for first-time mothers through lullaby singing. *Women and Music: A Journal of Gender and Culture* 9: 68–89.

Main, M. and Weston, D. (1981). The quality of the toddler's relationship to mother and father as related to conflict behavior and readiness to establish new relationships. *Child Development* 52(3): 932–940. doi:10.2307/1129097

Malloch S. and Trevarthen, C. (2009). Musicality: communicating the vitality and interests of life. In: S. Malloch and C. Trevarthen (eds), *Communicative Musicality: Exploring the Basis of Human Companionship*, pp. 1–11. New York: Oxford University Press.

Malloch, S., Shoemark, H., Crncec, R., and Burnham, D. (2012). Music therapy with hospitalized infants: the art and science of communicative musicality. *Infant Mental Health Journal* 33(4), doi:10.1002/imhj.21346

Masataka, N. (1999). Preference for infant-directed singing in 2-day-old hearing infants of deaf parents. *Developmental Psychology* 35: 1001–1005.

McFarland, J., Salisbury, A.L., Battle, C.L., Hawkes, K., Halloran, K., and Lester, B.M. (2011). Major depressive disorder during pregnancy and emotional attachment to the fetus. *Archives of Women's Mental Health* 14: 425–434. [PubMed] PMID: 21938509 PMCID: PMC3248759 doi:10.1007/s00737-011-0237-z

Macfarlane, A.J. (1975). Olfaction in the development of social preferences in the human neonate. *Ciba Foundation Symposium* 33: 103–117. [PubMed] PMID:1045976

Mehler, J., Bertoncini, J., and Barriere, M. (1978). Infant recognition of mother's voice. *Perception* 7: 491–497.

Mehler, J., Jusczyk, P.W., Lambertz, G., Halsted, N., Bertoncini, J., and Amiel-Tison, C. (1988). A precursor of language acquisition in young infants. *Cognition* 29(2): 143–178. [PubMed] PMID: 3168420

Mikhail, M.S., Freda, M.C. Merkatz, R.B., Polizzotto, E., and Merkatz, I.R. (1991). The effect of fetal movement counting on maternal attachment to fetus. *American Journal of Obstetrics and Gynecology* 165: 988–991.

Milligan, K.A.L., Trehub, S.E., Benoit, D., and Poulton, L. (2003). Maternal attachment and the communication of emotion through song. *Infant Behavior and Development* 26: 1–13.

Moon, C. and Fifer, W.P. (1990). Syllables as signals for 2-day-old infants. *Infant Behavior and Development* 13(3): 377–390. [Cross Ref] doi:10.1016/0163-6383(90)90041-6

Moon, C.M., Bever, T.G., and Fifer, W.P. (1992). Canonical and non-canonical syllable discrimination by two-day-old infants. *Journal of Child Language* 19: 1–17. [PubMed] [Cross Ref] doi:10.1017/S030500090001360X

Moon, C.M., Cooper, R.P., and Fifer, W.P. (1993). Two-day-olds prefer their native language. *Infant Behavior and Development* 16(4): 495–500. [Cross Ref] doi:10.1016/0163-6383(93)80007-U

Nakata, T. and Trehub, S.E. (2004). Infants' responsiveness to maternal speech and singing. *Infant Behavior and Development* 27: 455–464.

Nakata, T. and Trehub, S.E. (2011). Expressive timing and dynamics in infant-directed and non-infant-directed singing. *Psychomusicology: Music, Mind and Brain* 21(1): 45–53.

Ockleford, E.M., Vince, M.A., Layton, C., and Reader, M.R. (1988). Responses of neonates to parents' and others' voices. *Early Human Development* 18: 27–36.

O'Gorman, S. (2007). Infant-directed singing in neonatal and paediatric intensive care. *Australian and New Zealand Journal of Family Therapy* 28(2): 100–108.

O'Neill, C.T., Trainor, L.J., and Trehub, S.E. (2001). Infants' responsiveness to fathers' singing. *Music Perception* 18: 409–425.

Panneton, R.K. (1985). *Prenatal auditory experience with melodies: effects on postnatal auditory preferences in human newborns* (unpublished doctoral thesis). University of North Carolina at Greensborough.

Papoušek, M., Bornstein, M.H., Nuzzo, C., Papoušek, H., and Symmes, D. (1990). Infant responses to prototypical melodic contours in parental speech. *Infant Behavior and Development* 13: 539–545.

Papoušek, M., Papoušek, H., and Symmes, D. (1991). The meanings of melodies in motherese in tone and stress languages. *Infant Behavior and Development* 14: 415–440.

Papoušek, M. (1992). Early ontogeny of vocal communication in parent–infant interactions. In: H. Papoušek, U. Jurgens, and M. Papoušek (eds), *Nonverbal Vocal Communication: Comparative and Developmental Approaches*, pp. 230–261. Cambridge: Cambridge University Press.

Papoušek, H. (1996). Musicality in infancy research: biological and cultural origins of early musicality. In: I. Deliège and J. Sloboda (eds), *Musical Beginnings. Origins and Development of Musical Competence*, pp. 37–55. Oxford: Oxford University Press.

Partanen, E., Kujala, T., Naatanen, R., Liitola, A., Sambeth, A., and Huotilainen, M. (2013). Learning-induced neural plasticity of speech processing before birth. *Proceedings of the National Academy of Sciences of the United States of America* 110(37): 15145–15150. [PMC free article] doi:10.1073/pnas.1302159110

Patel, A.D., Peretz, I., Tramo, M., and Labreque, R. (1998). Processing prosodic and musical patterns: a neuropsychological investigation. *Brain and Language* 61: 123–144.

Pickering, D. (2015). Coorie Doon at North Edinburgh Arts. *North Edinburgh News*.

Pretorius, D.H., Gattu, S., Ji, E.K., Hollenbach, K, Newton, R., Hull, A., . . . Nelson, T.R. (2006). Preexamination and postexamination assessment of parental–fetal bonding in patients undergoing 3-/4- dimensional obstetric ultrasonography. *Journal of Ultrasound in Medicine* 25(11): 1411–1421.

Querleu, D., Renard, X., Versyp, F., Paris-Delrue, L., and Crèpin, G. (1988). Fetal hearing. *European Journal of Obstetrics and Gynecology and Reproductive Biology* 28: 191–212. [PubMed] [Cross Ref] doi:10.1016/0028-2243(88)90030-5

Saint-Georges, C., Chetouani, M., Cassel, R., Apicella, F., Mahdhaoui, A, Muratori, F., and Coh, D. (2013). Motherese in interaction: at the cross-road of emotion and cognition? (A systematic review). *PLoS One* 18(8): 10. doi:10.1371/journal.pone.0078103

Sansavini A., Bertoncini A., and Giovanelli G. (1997). Newborns discriminate the rhythm of multisyllabic stressed words. *Developmental Psychology* 33(1): 3–11. [PubMed] [Cross Ref] doi:10.1037//0012-1649.33.1.3

Satt, B.J. (1984). *An investigation into the acoustical induction of intrauterine learning* (doctoral dissertation). Retrieved from ProQuest Dissertations Publishing (8418310).

Schaal, B., Orgeur. P., and Rognon, C. (1995). Odor sensing in the human fetus: anatomical, functional and chemo-ecological bases. In: J.P. Lecanuet, N.A. Krasnegor, W. Fifer, and W.P. Smotherman (eds), *Prenatal Development: Psychobiological Perspectives*, pp. 205–237. Hillsdale, NJ: Lawrence Erlbaum.

Scherer, K.R. (1981). Speech and emotional states. In: J.K. Darby, Jr. (ed.), *Speech Evaluation in Psychiatry*, pp. 189–220. New York: Grune and Stratton.

Shahidullah, S. and Hepper, P.G. (1994) Frequency discrimination by the fetus. *Early Human Development* 36: 13–26.

Shannon, R.V., Zeng, F.G., Kamath, V., Wygonski, J., and Ekelid, M. (1995). Speech recognition with primarily temporal cues. *Science* 270(5234): 303–304.

Shenfield, T., Trehub, S.E., and Nakata, T. (2003). Maternal singing modulates infant arousal. *Psychology of Music* 31(4): 365–375.

Shoemark, H. and Grocke, D. (2010). The markers of interplay between the music therapist and the high risk full term infant. *Journal of Music Therapy* 47(4): 306–334.

Shoemark, H. (2011). Contingent singing: the musicality of companionship with the hospitalized newborn infant. In: F. Baker and S. Uhlig (eds), *Therapeutic Voicework in Music Therapy*, pp. 229–249. London: Kingsley.

Singh, L., Morgan, J.L., and Best, C.T. (2002). Infants' listening preferences: baby talk or happy talk? *Infancy* 3: 365–394.

Sirak, C. (2012). *Mothers' singing to fetuses: the effect of music education* (master's thesis). Available from ProQuest Dissertations and Theses database (UMI No. 1519318).

Skeles, C. (1996). *Music, Motion, and Emotion: The Developmental-Integrative Model in Music Therapy*. St. Louis, MO: MMB Music.

Smith, Z.M., Delgutte, B., and Oxenham A.J. (2002). Chimaeric sounds reveal dichotomies in auditory perception. *Nature* 416: 87–90.

Standley J.M. and Madsen, C.K. (1990). Comparison of infant preferences and responses to auditory stimuli: music, mother and other female voice. *Journal of Music Therapy* 27(2): 54–97.

Standley, J.M. (1996). A meta-analysis on the effects of music as reinforcement for education/therapy objectives. *Journal of Research in Music Education* 44(2): 105–133.

Standley, J.M. (1998). The effect of music and multimodal stimulation on physiologic and developmental responses of premature infants in neonatal intensive care. *Pediatric Nursing* 24: 532–538.

Standley, J.M. (2001). Music therapy for the neonate. *Newborn and Infant Nursing Reviews* 1(4): 211–216.

Standley, J. M. (2002). A meta-analysis of the efficacy of music therapy for premature infants. *Journal of Pediatric Nursing* 17(2): 107–113.

Standley, J.M. (2003). The effect of music-reinforced non-nutritive sucking on feeding rate of premature infants. *Journal of Pediatric Nursing* 18(3): 169–173.

Standley, J.M. and Whipple, J. (2003). Music therapy for premature infants in the neonatal intensive care unit: health and developmental benefits. In: S.L. Robb (ed.), *Music Therapy in Pediatric Healthcare: Research and Evidence-based Practice*, pp. 19–30. Silver Spring, MD American Music Therapy Association.

Standley, J.M., and Swedberg, O. (2011). NICU music therapy: post hoc analysis of an early intervention clinical program. *The Arts in Psychotherapy* 38: 36–40.

Standley, J.M. (2012). A discussion of evidence-based music therapy to facilitate feeding skills of premature infants: the power of contingent music. *The Arts in Psychotherapy* 39: 379–382.

Stefanics, G., Haden, G., Sziller, I., Balazs, L., Beke, A., and Winkler, I. (2009). Newborn infants process pitch intervals. *Clinical Neurophysiology* 120(20): 304–308.

Stern D.N., Spieker S., and MacKain K. (1982). Intonation contours as signals in maternal speech to prelinguistic infants. *Developmental Psychology* 18: 727–735. doi:10.1037/0012-1649.18.5.727

Sullivan, R.M. and Toubas, P. (1998). Clinical usefulness of maternal odor in newborns: soothing and feeding preparatory responses. *Biology of the Neonate* 74(6): 402–408.

Teckenberg-Jansson, P., Huotilainen, M., Pölkki, T., Lipsanen, J., and Järvenpää, A.L. (2011). Rapid effects of neonatal music therapy combined with kangaroo care on prematurely-born infants. *Nordic Journal of Music Therapy* 20(1): 22–42.

Trainor, L.J. (1996). Infant preferences for infant-directed versus noninfant-directed playsongs and lullabies. *Infant Behavior and Development* 19: 83–92.

Trainor, L.J., Clark, E., Huntley, A. and Adams, B. (1997). The acoustic basis of preferences for infant-directed singing. *Infant Behavior and Development* 20(3): 383–396.

Trainor, L.J. and Zacharias, C.A. (1998). Infants prefer higher-pitched singing. *Infant Behavior and Development* 21: 799–805.

Trainor, L.J., Austin, C., and Desjardins, R. (2000). Is infant-directed speech prosody the result of the vocal expression of emotion? *Psychological Science* 11(3): 188–195.

Trehub, S.E., Unyk, A.M., and Trainor, L.J. (1993a). Adults identify infant-directed music across cultures. *Infant Behavior and Development* 16: 193–211.

Trehub, S.E., Unyk, A.M., and Trainor, L.J. (1993b). Maternal singing in cross-cultural perspective. *Infant Behavior and Development* 16: 285–295.

Trehub, S.E. and Schellenberg, E. (1995). Music: its relevance to infants. *Annals of Child Development* 11: 1–24.

Trehub, S.E., Unyk, A M., Kamenetsky, S.B., Hill, D.S., Trainor, L.J., Henderson, J.L., and Saraza, M. (1997). Mothers' and fathers' singing to infants. *Developmental Psychology* 33: 500–507. 10.1037/0012-1649.33.3.500 Medline

Trehub, S.E. and Trainor, L.J. (1998). Singing to infants: lullabies and play songs. *Advances in Infancy Research* 12: 43–77.

Trehub, S.E. (2003). The developmental origins of musicality. *Nature Neuroscience* 6(7): 669–673.

Trevarthen, C. (1977). Descriptive analyses of infant communicative behavior. In: H.R. Schaffer (ed.), *Studies in Mother–Infant Interaction*, pp. 227–270. New York, NY: Academic Press.

Trevarthen, C. (1979). Communication and cooperation in early infancy: a description of primary intersubjectivity. In: M. Bullowa (ed.), *Before Speech: The Beginning of Human Communication*, pp. 321–347. Cambridge: Cambridge University Press.

Tronick, E.Z. (1989). Emotions and communication in infants. *American Psychologist* 44(2): 112–119.

Ullal-Gupta, S., Vanden Bosch der Nederlanden, C.M., Tichko, P., Lahav, A., and Hannon, E.E. (2013). Linking prenatal experience to the emerging musical mind. *Frontiers in Systems Neuroscience* 7(48). doi:10.3389/fnsys.2013.00048

Unyk, A., Trehub, S.E., Trainor, L., and Schellenberg, G. (1992). Lullabies and simplicity: a cross-cultural perspective. *Psychology of Music* 20: 15–28.

Vaglio, S. (2009). Chemical communication and mother–infant recognition. *Communicative and Integrative Biology* 2(3): 279–281. PMC2717541

Van de Carr, F.R. and Lehrer, M. (1998). Prenatal university: commitment to fetal-family bonding and strengthening of the family unit as an educational institution. *Journal of Prenatal and Perinatal Psychology and Health* 12(3–4): 119–134.

Voegtline, K.M., Costigan, K.A., Pater, H.A., and DiPietro, J.A. (2013). Near-term fetal response to maternal spoken voice. *Infant Behavior and Development* 36(4): 526–533. doi:10.1016/j.infbeh.2013.05.002

Vos, P.G. and Troost, J.M. (1989). Ascending and descending melodic intervals: statistical findings and their perceptual relevance. *Music Perception* 6(4): 383–396. doi:10.2307/40285439

Vouloumanos, A. and Werker, J.F. (2007). Listening to language at birth: evidence for a bias for speech in neonates. *Developmental Science* 10(2): 159–164. [PubMed] [Cross Ref doi:10.1111/j.1467-7687.2007.00549.x

Walworth, D., Standley, J., Robertson, A., Smith, A., Swedberg, O., and Peyton, J. (2012). Effects of neurodevelopmental stimulation on premature infants in neonatal intensive care: randomized controlled trial. *Journal of Neonatal Nursing* 18: 210–216.

Werker, J.F. and McLeod, P.J. (1989). Infant preference for both male and female infant-directed talk: a developmental study of attentional and affective responsiveness. *Canadian Journal of Psychology* 43: 230–246.

Whipple, J. (2000). The effect of parent training in music and multimodal stimulation on parent-neonate interactions in the neonatal intensive care unit. *Journal of Music Therapy* 37(4): 250–268.

Whipple, J. (2008). The effect of music-reinforced non-nutritive sucking on state of preterm, low birthweight infants experiencing heelstick. *Journal of Music Therapy* 45(3): 227–272.

Woodward, S.C. (1992). *The transmission of music into the human uterus and the response to music of the human fetus and neonate* (unpublished dissertation). University of Cape Town, South Africa.

Woodward, S.C. and Guidozzi, F. (1992). Intrauterine rhythm and blues? *British Journal of Obstetrics and Gynaecology* 99: 787–790.

Zahr, L.K. and Balian, S. (1995). Responses of premature infants to routine nursing interventions and noise in the NICU. *Nursing Research* 44: 179–185.

Zatorre, R.J., Belin, P., and Penhune, V.B. (2002). Structure and function of auditory cortex: music and speech. *Trends in Cognitive Sciences* 6(1): 37–46.

Zimmer, E., Fifer, W., Kim. Y., Rey, H., Chao, C., and Myers, M. (1993). Response of the premature fetus to stimulation by speech sounds. *Early Human Development* 33: 207–215. [PubMed] PMID: 8223316

CHAPTER 22

MOTHERS AS SINGING MENTORS FOR INFANTS

SANDRA E. TREHUB AND HELGA RUT GUDMUNDSDOTTIR

INTRODUCTION

THIS chapter focuses on maternal singing in the everyday lives of infants, its functions, intentional or otherwise, and its consequences for the onset and nature of early singing. Mothers in most cultures are the principal caregivers of children from birth until at least two years of age. In many cultures, fathers, siblings, and grandparents also play an important role in infant care. For our purposes, however, the mother serves as a proxy for the primary caregiver, whether she plays that role alone or in concert with others, or whether others assume the primary caregiving role.

In the first few months, mothers' efforts are aimed largely at promoting infant health and well-being by feeding, regulating arousal, and ensuring adequate rest. Once infants gain the ability to remain awake, quiet, and alert, mothers increasingly engage in interactions in which melodious talk and singing figure prominently. Such vocal behaviors are influenced by culture, infants' presumed needs, and mothers' specific caretaking goals. By singing in a way that brings comfort and joy to infants, mothers provide intuitive rather than deliberate mentoring. During the first year, their singing exerts its most noticeable effects on infant attention and affect while also enhancing mother-infant bonds. In the second year, the fruits of maternal mentoring become evident in toddlers' singing.

Framework

The perspective adopted here is that maternal singing to infants is, first and foremost, a caregiving tool aimed primarily at emotion regulation in those whose self-regulatory skills are extremely limited. Studies of informal singing in adulthood, even in childhood, tend to be concerned primarily with pitch accuracy, or singing in tune, and, at times, with timing accuracy, or singing in time (e.g. Dalla Bella et al. 2007; Pfordresher et al. 2010; Welch 1985). By contrast, studies of maternal singing focus on expressive features that convey maternal feelings or intentions (e.g. Rock et al. 1999; Trehub et al. 1997) and their consequences for infants (e.g. Masataka 1999; Trainor 1996; Trainor et al. 1997). Because maternal singing commonly occurs in face-to-face contexts, visual gestures are an integral part of the performance (Longhi 2009), even though scholars often ignore such non-vocal features. Infants not only hear maternal singing; they see and feel the multimodal performances orchestrated by their primary attachment figure. Infants' and toddlers' subsequent reproduction of maternal songs may be motivated, in large measure, by their propensity for imitation (Gergely and Csibra 2006; Over and Carpenter 2013).

Singing to infants: what, when, and how?

Mothers everywhere sing to infants in the course of caregiving, but what they sing, when they sing, and how they sing vary across cultures. Because maternal singing is a form of nurture, the nature of that nurture is influenced by cultural values and circumstances. For example, as agrarian societies in the developing world experience high levels of infant mortality and economic challenge, which in turn promote high birth rates, caregiving is geared to infant survival and almost constant physical contact between mother and infant (Hrdy 2009; LeVine 1988). Holding or carrying infants maximizes safety in sub-optimal environments while providing contact comfort. Where high contact prevails, lullabies seem to be the songs of choice, serving the important function of promoting infant tranquility and sleep (Trehub and Prince 2010; Trehub and Trainor 1998; Trehub et al. 1993). Lullaby singing in those cultures typically occurs with little or no face-to-face contact because infants are in slings, hammocks, or cradles, sometimes with their faces covered to eliminate visual stimulation (e.g. Trehub and Prince 2010).

Freedom from the physical and economic stresses of agrarian life allows middle-class American and European mothers to focus on mental and social stimulation as well as protection for infants. They "childproof" their homes, making liberal use of secure devices (e.g. seats, swings, bouncers) that allow them to engage in vocal and visual play without physical contact (Richman et al. 1988). These mothers talk much more than they sing to infants (Eckerdal and Merker 2009). The melodious or music-like properties of their speech have been described elsewhere (e.g. Bergeson and Trehub 2007; Fernald 1991; Trehub et al. 2010). When they sing, these mothers mostly choose play songs (Trehub et al. 1997), with lullabies incorporated, at times, into pre-sleep routines.

North American surveys reveal more frequent singing by mothers with high levels of education (Custodero et al. 2003; Ilari 2005). Diaries of singing to infants reveal that mothers' frequency of singing often exceeds their estimates, especially for mothers who initially claim to be infrequent singers (Trehub et al. 1997). According to the diary reports, singing to infants four months and older occurs primarily in the context of play and secondarily as an accompaniment to routine caregiving tasks such as diaper-changing, feeding, and bathing. Although mothers know many children's songs, they generally sing only a few, singing those few songs repeatedly. When queried about their song choices, mothers often claim that they simply sing their infant's favorite songs.

Acoustic analyses and independent ratings of maternal singing reveal that mothers sing more expressively, more slowly, and at a higher pitch level when they sing to their infant than when they sing informally on their own (Trainor, 1996; Trainor et al. 1997; Trehub et al. 1993). When they attempt to reproduce their manner of singing to infants in the absence of the infant, the renditions lack the expressiveness of renditions sung directly to infants (Trehub et al. 1997). Examination of the visual gestures that accompany maternal vocalizations indicates that mothers smile much more when they sing than when they talk to infants (Trehub et al. 2016). Smiling not only adds visual interest to maternal vocalizations; it also makes those vocalizations sound happier (Tartter and Braun 1994). In effect, smiling can be heard as well as seen; for examples of maternal singing, see Video 1 <https://vimeo.com/98542581> and Video 2 <https://vimeo.com/98535122>.

Maternal songs are more like rituals than spontaneous performances in the sense that repetitions of the same song on different occasions are unusually stable, featuring nearly identical pitch level and tempo (Bergeson and Trehub 2002) and individually distinctive visual gestures (Trehub et al. 2013). There is no indication that mothers are aware of the stability of their performances, which contributes to the uniqueness and memorability of maternal songs. Mothers seem to be equally unaware that they emphasize the temporal structure of songs by marking phrase boundaries with pauses or phrase-final lengthening (Delavenne et al. 2013; Longhi 2009; Trainor et al. 1997) or that they emphasize the pitch structure of songs by singing higher pitches more loudly than lower pitches (Nakata and Trehub 2011). In essence, their singing to infants has intuitive didactic components.

Mothers are also sensitive to feedback from infants. As noted, they sing more expressively in infants' presence than in their absence (Trainor 1996; Trehub et al. 1993, 1997). Even when infants are present, mothers sing less expressively when their view of infants is obscured (Trehub et al. 2016).

Infants' responsiveness to singing

Maternal singing sounds pleasant to adults largely because of its positive emotional expressiveness. It is even more engaging to infants. For example, newborns and six-month-old infants listen longer when unfamiliar women sing in a maternal style rather than a non-maternal style (Trainor 1996; Masataka 1999). Evidence of such listening dispositions in hearing newborns who have deaf, signing parents (Masataka 1999) suggests an innate bias for positive vocal expressiveness. Just as infants listen preferentially to speech that is happy-sounding (Kitamura and Burnham 1998; Singh et al. 2002), their choice of listening to speech or singing by an unfamiliar person who speaks or sings in a foreign language is determined by its happy-sounding qualities rather than its musical or speech status (Corbeil et al. 2013).

To date, infants' responsiveness to singing has been examined primarily with audio recordings from unfamiliar women (Corbeil et al. 2013; Masataka 1999; Trainor 1996). One would expect familiar songs by a familiar singer (e.g. mother) to have much more dramatic effects. In fact, live maternal singing modulates infant arousal, with arousal reductions for infants with higher initial levels and modest arousal increases for those with lower initial levels (Shenfield et al. 2003). Infants are attentive to audiovisual recordings of maternal speech, but they are much more attentive to comparable recordings of maternal singing (Nakata and Trehub 2004). Undoubtedly, maternal smiling during singing (Trehub et al. 2016) adds to its engaging qualities.

It is clear that maternal singing has salutary effects on the arousal and attention of infants who are initially content, but what about infants who are distressed? In the first year of life, when self-regulatory skills are limited, caregivers' management of infants' negative emotions is crucial (Kopp 1989). Mothers' success in regulating these negative emotions is thought to have implications for the subsequent development of self-regulation skills (Thompson 1994). Interestingly, when 10-month-old infants are acutely distressed, their arousal and distress are reduced more rapidly and more completely by multimodal maternal singing (face-to-face singing with contact) than by multimodal maternal speech (Ghazban 2013). Interestingly, playful or arousing maternal singing is more effective than soothing maternal singing (i.e. lullabies) in reducing infants' distress. Infants in those circumstances become progressively more absorbed by mothers' rhythmic singing, which seems to offer welcome distraction from their distress. In short, lively maternal singing makes happy infants happier and transforms distressed infants into happy infants.

Other indications of infants' sensitivity to music

Perhaps it is not surprising that infants are sensitive to expressive variations in singing. What is more surprising is the scope and precision of their music perception abilities. After infants hear several repetitions of a brief non-vocal melody (five to ten notes), they are able to notice a small pitch change (e.g. one semitone) in a single note of the melody, even when the altered melody is presented in a different key (Trainor and Trehub 1993; Trehub et al. 1986). For infants, the pitch contour of a melody (i.e. pattern of directional changes) seems to be its most salient feature (Trehub et al. 1985, 1987). At times, however, infants can detect interval changes when the melodic contour remains unchanged (Cohen et al. 1987; Trainor and Trehub 1993).

Infants' perception of musical rhythm and meter is equally impressive. For example, they detect changes in rhythmic grouping (Chang and Trehub 1977; Thorpe et al. 1988) even in the context of concurrent tempo changes (Trehub and Thorpe 1989). They focus on relative rather than absolute durations, as is the case for adults. Moreover, they more readily detect pitch or timing changes in melodies with "good" rhythms (as judged by Western adults) than in those with "bad" rhythms (Trehub and Hannon 2009). It is possible, indeed likely, that these infant skills do not depend upon learning, arising instead from inherent preferences for temporal regularity. In addition, infants are more accurate at detecting timing changes to patterns with duple rather than triple meter (Bergeson and Trehub 2006). Enhanced processing of patterns with duple meter could arise from greater exposure to duple meter in maternal songs or to the greater simplicity of duple over triple meter.

In other situations, the role of exposure is clear. For example, infants' perception of metrically ambiguous patterns is influenced by the pattern of movement that they experience while listening (Phillips-Silver and Trainor 2005). For example, infants who are bounced on every second beat subsequently respond to a duple version of the pattern as familiar, and those bounced on every third beat respond to a triple version as familiar. By six or seven months of age and thereafter, spontaneous movement to rhythmic music becomes increasingly common (Zentner and Eerola 2010). Although early movement to music is rhythmic, it is not coordinated with the musical rhythm or beat. The early swaying, kicking, and bouncing to music is a precursor to the dancing that is commonly observed in toddlers, as can be seen in Video 3 at <https://vimeo.com/98542344>.

Infants as super-listeners

Exposure to music, whether formal (e.g. music lessons) or informal (e.g. enculturation by incidental listening), increases listening proficiency and memory for culturally relevant musical features (Bigand and Poulin-Charronnat 2006). Such selective attention skills are advantageous when listening to music in a familiar style, but they can be disadvantageous when listening to music that is foreign or unfamiliar in style. For example, adults readily detect a small pitch change (less than a semitone) in music based on the familiar major scale, but they fail to detect a comparable change in music based on an unfamiliar scale (Trehub et al. 1999). Their implicit knowledge of major scale structure interferes with the perception of melodies with different pitch organization. By contrast, nine-month-old infants detect both types of changes because they are not yet attuned to the pitch structure of Western music. In this instance, ignorance of the conventions of Western music is advantageous.

In the rhythmic domain, Western adults detect metrical changes in the context of Balkan music with simple meter (i.e. duple or triple) but not complex (non-Western) meter, whereas six-month-olds detect changes in both metrical contexts (Hannon and Trehub 2005a). This is another favorable consequence of infants' ignorance of Western musical structure. By the time infants are 12 months of age, they perform like Western adults, succeeding with simple meter and failing with non-Western meter (Hannon and Trehub 2005b). The preferential processing of Western metrical structure by 12-month-olds indicates that their musical enculturation is under way. Nevertheless, their implicit knowledge of Western music is fragmentary and superficial rather than deeply entrenched like that of adults. One consequence is that infants retain greater perceptual flexibility than adults, which means that they are more receptive to foreign musical materials. For example, limited exposure to music with complex metrical structure enables 12-month-olds but not adults to succeed on the complex-meter task (Hannon and Trehub 2005b). In effect, six-month-olds outperformed adults on a task involving complex meter, and 12-month-olds learned the task more readily than adults.

Children as vocal imitators

It is clear that infants are keen music listeners, especially for singing, but what assists them in the transition to song production? The ability to copy what they hear is critical, but even more critical is the motivation for such imitation. Children's imitation of others' actions is often aimed at attaining some goal (e.g. a desired object) rather than being focused on the behavior for its own sake, as is the case with singing. At times, children only copy actions that are relevant to achieving a goal but, at other times, they reproduce irrelevant as well relevant actions (Whiten et al. 2009). Some scholars contend that the propensity for exact copying arises from an innate system for facilitating the transfer of information from one person to another (e.g. Gergely and Csibra 2006). Others emphasize the social functions of imitation, for example, the conscious or unconscious desire to be like other valued persons, to be liked by them, or to communicate affiliation or liking (Over and Carpenter 2013). The onset of singing may be triggered not only by the availability of a model and the requisite vocal skills but most especially by identification with the mother, a desire to be like her, and to join in her joyous vocal activity. The mother, for her part, provides appropriate models of singing by virtue of the limited number of songs that she sings repeatedly in a highly stereotyped manner (Bergeson and Trehub 2002).

THE PATH TO SINGING

Before the onset of meaningful speech and often continuing through the single-word phase, infants produce rhythmic babbling (Dolata et al. 2008), which consists initially of reduplicated syllables (e.g. *bababa*), and subsequently of varied syllables (e.g. *badagoo*). As early as eight months of age, the babbling of infants from different backgrounds differs noticeably in intonation (e.g. rising versus falling pitch), rhythm, and component vowels, reflecting differences in the ambient language (Lee et al. 2010; Levitt and Wang 1991; Rvachew et al. 2006; Whalen et al. 1991). There are claims that infants and toddlers engage in song babbling, a form of pre-singing that is distinct from speech babbling (Moog 1976), but there is little consensus about its age of onset or distinctiveness from speech babbling (Dowling 1988). Nevertheless, there is preliminary evidence that nine- to 11-month-old infants use different vocal modes in response to caregivers' speech or singing (Reigado et al. 2011).

The path from song babbling to singing is unclear. What is clear, however, is that mothers' role as singing mentor undergoes considerable change as infants' response to maternal singing changes gradually from attention capture and stillness to more active engagement that includes movement (e.g. rhythmic movement induced by excitement) and vocalization (e.g. vocalizations of approval). These infant signals prompt mothers to encourage fuller participation, first, by inviting infants to reproduce their pantomimed actions for some songs (e.g. "Itsy, Bitsy Spider," "The Wheels on the Bus," "If You're Happy and You Know It") and then by inviting their participation in rudimentary vocal duets. The earliest duets take the form of the mother pausing at the end of each line of a highly familiar song so that the toddler can fill the gap with a sound resembling the missing "word," as can be seen in Video 4 at <https://vimeo.com/98542342>.

Initially, the toddler fills the gap with a single sound (e.g. *tah* for *star*), often ignoring the target pitch, which may stem from the mother's primary focus on the lyrics as she plays this game. Her pronunciation of words is more precise at this phase than it was a month or two earlier, perhaps reflecting her initial view of singing as a pleasurable and fruitful means of promoting language acquisition. The duets, which are highly energizing for mother and infant, become increasingly frequent, extending to other songs. The gaps to be filled become progressively larger, eventually leading to simultaneous singing of entire songs. Such synchronous singing, like other forms of synchronous activity, promotes cooperative behavior not only in toddlers but also in preschool children (Kirschner and Tomasello 2010) and adults (Wiltermuth and Heath 2009). As soon as the mother witnesses the toddler's pleasure in singing, she encourages singing for its own sake. She models songs without correcting the toddler's missteps and exposes the toddler to more and more singing, including recordings of children's songs. Ultimately, the toddler needs no prompting to initiate independent singing.

The nature of toddlers' singing

Some classifications of toddlers' spontaneous singing include chants as well as melodic singing, the former being more speech-like than the latter and relying more on rhythm than on melody (Björkvold 1992; Moorhead and Pond 1941; Sundin 1998). Although there is disagreement on the nature of toddlers' singing, there is general consensus that toddlers engage in singing or song-like behavior throughout the day (Björkvold 1992; Whiteman 2001), with considerable individual variation (Whiteman 2001; Young 2002). Toddlers reproduce songs from their everyday environment, and they also invent their own songs (Barrett 2011; Björkvold 1992; Whiteman 2001; Young 2002), with standard and invented songs typically featuring words, pseudo-words, or speech syllables (Whiteman 2001).

The singing of two- to three-year-olds is often characterized as lacking fixed pitches and scale structure (Davidson 1985), having a very compressed pitch range (Davidson et al. 1981), being rhythmic but largely monotonic (McKernon 1979), or having an extremely rough approximation to the contour of the target song (Davidson et al. 1981). Although these problems are thought to stem from physical constraints, it is puzzling that the constraints underlying toddlers' small singing range (Davidson et al. 1981; Werner 1917) do not preclude a larger vocal range during non-singing vocalizations (Fox 1990; Mang 2001; Reigado et al. 2011).

Physical constraints on early song production may be accorded an oversized role in early singing development, with cognitive constraints playing an even greater role. For example, toddlers are more accurate at matching pitches and tonal patterns when words are absent (Flowers and Dunne-Sousa 1990; Levinowitz 1989; Welch et al. 1998). Producing a familiar song with words adds to children's cognitive load because words and tunes must be retrieved from memory to serve as internal models, after which their production must be planned and produced. Even adults' production of pitches is less accurate when they sing a familiar song with words rather than on a neutral syllable such as "la" (Berkowska and Dalla Bella 2009). Their accuracy also decreases as the length or complexity of the target material increases (Pfordresher and Brown 2007; Wise and Sloboda 2008). In other words, the material sung (e.g. single pitches, single intervals, unfamiliar or familiar melodies, lyrics or no lyrics, examiner-selected or self-selected songs) and the conditions of singing (e.g. copying or singing from memory, comfort in the presence of others) influence the proficiency of singing observed in those contexts.

Well into the preschool period, linguistic dominance is thought to prevail (Welch et al. 1998), with the child's initial songs described as verbal chants with few melodic components. That situation may be relevant to song production or song learning in formal settings such as schools, but it does not seem to reflect the capabilities observed at home, where singing and language acquisition proceed informally and in parallel, guided by maternal mentoring. Home recordings of individual toddlers two years or younger reveal recognizable melodies sung without words (Barrett 2011; Stadler-Elmer 2012). In another study involving home recordings from 24 children of 16 months to three years of age, adults were highly accurate at identifying familiar tunes ("Happy Birthday," "Twinkle, Twinkle Little Star") sung in an unfamiliar language (Gudmundsdottir and Trehub 2018). The toddlers in question were relatively accurate at reproducing the melodic contours and rhythms of the songs (please see Video 5 <https://vimeo.com/98557103> and Video 6 <https://vimeo.com/98557102>).

Surprisingly, they used a pitch range of 6–17 semitones for an average range of 9.75 semitones. Their range approximates the average notated range of 10.5 semitones for the target songs, but it is in marked contrast to the singing range of 2–7 semitones that is commonly reported for preschool and kindergarten children (Flowers and Dunne-Sousa 1990; Rutkowski and Miller 2003; Welch 1979; Welch et al. 1996).

Toddlers' singing range, as observed in the home setting, calls into question the very small singing range reported for older children. The apparent skill deficiencies of older children may be attributable to the test materials (e.g. songs acquired in school, educator-selected rather than child-selected songs), the context of evaluation (e.g. school versus home), and the prevailing atmosphere (e.g. pressured versus leisurely). It is also possible that singing in school settings does not make use of the child's most comfortable vocal register (Welch 1979) or the vocal register used at home, which may be closer to the child's speaking range. Children's "natural" vocal register may not be ideal in terms of conventional standards of singing, but its use in the early years may prevent the disconnect between singing at home and at school.

Just as the nature and pace of language acquisition vary considerably across children (Nelson 1973), the acquisition of singing may show comparable individual variation, depending, in part, on the home environment. A longitudinal study of three families, two of whom were considered "musical," revealed musical babbling at 9–10 months of age in the two infants from musical homes and in-tune singing by two years of age for the child from the most musical family (Kelley and Sutton-Smith 1987). Some toddlers may show a words-first or melody-first pattern, but it is possible that a number of toddlers focus on lyrics in some contexts and on melody in others, depending on the song and situation. For an example of a "words-first" strategy, see "Toddler Chanting Words," Video 7, at <https://vimeo.com/98557104>, and for examples of a "melody-first" strategy, see "Toddlers Singing Melody" Video 8 <https://vimeo.com/98557104> and Video 9 <https://vimeo.com/98330008>. In any case, whether words or melodies appear first may be of less importance than understanding the reciprocal influences of toddlers' developing speech and singing abilities. To date, no research has addressed this critical question.

The notion of linguistic dominance is consistent with the prevailing belief, in popular culture as well as science, that language acquisition is rapid and effortless but music acquisition is effortful and protracted (e.g. Pinker 1997). Children take several years to understand the intricacies of their native language, which is also the case for the nuances of their musical culture. Perhaps it is inappropriate to apply very different evaluative standards to the linguistic and musical elements in young children's singing. Toddlers and preschoolers commonly mispronounce the words of songs, but the words are typically considered acceptable, even correct, if they are barely intelligible. Their melodies, by contrast, are not evaluated in terms of identifiability, but rather by conventional adult standards involving contour, intervals, and key stability. Such divergent standards for verbal and melodic aspects of sung performances may create the illusion that young children's progress in speech proceeds rapidly but progress in singing proceeds at a snail's pace.

It is also important to consider young children's conception of songs and singing and their limited knowledge of the musical conventions of their culture. For children who have yet to master most of the social and linguistic conventions, how can we expect them to understand the features of songs that require precise reproduction (e.g. contour, intervals, rhythm) and those that are free to vary (e.g. tempo, timbre, dynamics)? Presumably, they must first gain implicit knowledge of the conventions of Western tonal music, which can be accomplished by incidental exposure (Bigand and Poulin-Charronnat 2006). Focusing on precision may come at the cost of the exuberance that is the hallmark of toddlers' and preschoolers' singing.

Singing in moments of solitude

As noted, toddlers sing more frequently and more proficiently when they are in the familiar surroundings of their own home. Although singing is an inherently social activity, toddlers also engage in solitary singing (Davidson et al. 1981), either during play when others are out of sight or as part of their pre-sleep monologues (Dean 2017; Sole 2017). They sometimes invent songs during these periods of solitude (Davidson et al. 1981; Sundin 1998). Such vocal play may function as practice or exercise of their developing skills. Solitary singing in toddlers also indicates that it has become functional for emotional self-regulation. The opacity of toddlers' intentions and the theoretical biases of observers preclude objective interpretation of these solitary productions (Mang 2005; Young 2002). It is possible, however, that acoustic analyses of these productions could indicate whether such melodic play includes elements of the ambient tonal system.

ARE ALL MOTHERS SINGING MENTORS?

Middle-class mothers in the developed world typically sing to their infants in the ways described even if they are not inclined to sing in other contexts. Nevertheless, some mothers sing to infants infrequently, if at all. The factors associated with diminished talking to infants—poverty, depression, and low educational attainment, among others—are also associated with diminished singing to infants. Young children from socially disadvantaged families receive dramatically less verbal input than do children from more advantaged families (Hart and Risley 1995), and their vocabulary at 24 months of age lags six months behind their peers (Fernald et al. 2012). What is critical is not the overall amount of speech in the environment (i.e. overheard speech) but rather the amount directed specifically to infants and toddlers. The quantity of infant- or child-directed speech predicts the efficiency of language processing and vocabulary size at 24 months of age (Weisleder and Fernald 2013), which are linked to subsequent academic achievement. Limited exposure to maternal singing, in itself, may seem trivial, but it may reflect caregiving that features limited one-on-one interaction and limited sensitivity to infants' and toddlers' social, emotional, and intellectual needs.

Some circumstances that preclude or limit vocal interactions with infants need not have unfavorable consequences. For example, deaf, signing mothers do not engage in infant-directed speech or singing, but they provide other sensitive, one-on-one interactions with infants. Their signed communications with infants incorporate slower tempo and more exaggerated movements than their signed communication with adults, resulting in visual stimulation that is highly engaging to hearing as well as deaf infants (Masataka 1996, 1998). In effect, infants of deaf signing parents receive rhythmic dance-like gestures rather than the rhythmic singing provided by hearing parents. In short, sensitive mothering can occur in the absence of specific behaviors such as maternal speech and singing so long as there are other means of communicating expressively with infants.

IMPLICATIONS FOR MUSIC EDUCATORS

In the course of being sensitive caregivers, mothers sing to their infants, first for the sole purpose of soothing or amusing them, later for encouraging collaborative and independent singing. Mothers model singing as pleasure, comfort, shared feelings, and common purpose. Singing continues to function in that manner, even outside the home, as long as the spirit of the endeavor continues to have priority over the precision of execution. Increasing precision is typically a natural consequence of practice, even the very informal practice of singing for pleasure. Despite high self-reports of inaccurate singing (Pfordresher and Brown 2007), the overwhelming majority of adults sing in tune (Dalla Bella et al. 2007), which means that most maternal singing is likely to be in tune, and it is even more likely to be temporally regular or in time (Nakata and Trehub 2011). The small minority of infants and toddlers who hear out-of-tune singing still benefit from the expressiveness of their mothers' multimodal performances. After all, maternal singing is primarily an introduction to the pleasures of singing and secondarily an introduction to the music of the mother's culture. Nevertheless, the one-on-one context optimizes infants' and toddlers' opportunities for learning. With some exceptions, toddlers' singing capabilities may be related to the amount of maternal singing that they have experienced as well as the extent of their participation in maternal duets.

Maternal mentoring is, first and foremost, about sensitive caregiving and only incidentally about singing. For toddlers, singing is associated with joy, comfort, and security. Subsequent mentoring under the auspices of music educators may have the best chance of success if relationship building and relationship maintenance continue to have priority over skill building.

ACKNOWLEDGMENT

The authors acknowledge the assistance of the Social Sciences and Humanities Research Council of Canada and AIRS (Advanced Interdisciplinary Research in Singing).

FURTHER READING

Adachi, M. and Trehub, S.E. (2012). Musical lives of infants. In: G.E. McPherson and G.F. Welch (eds), *The Oxford Handbook of Music Education*, Vol. 1, pp. 229–247. New York: Oxford University Press.

Campbell, P.H. and Wiggins, T. (2013). *The Oxford Handbook of Children's Musical Cultures.* New York: Oxford University Press.

Hrdy, S.B. (2009). *Mothers and Others: The Evolutionary Origins of Mutual Understanding.* Cambridge, MA: Harvard University Press.

Trehub, S.E. (2003). The developmental origins of musicality. *Nature Neuroscience* 6: 669–673.

Websites

Video examples mentioned in the text:
Video 1 <https://vimeo.com/98542581>
Video 2 <https://vimeo.com/98535122>
Video 3 <https://vimeo.com/98542344>
Video 4 <https://vimeo.com/98542342>
Video 5 <https://vimeo.com/98557103>
Video 6 <https://vimeo.com/98557102>
Video 7 <https://vimeo.com/98557104>
Video 8 <https://vimeo.com/98557104>
Video 9 <https://vimeo.com/98330008>

References

Barrett, M.S. (2011). Musical narratives: A study of a young child's identity work in and through music-making. *Psychology of Music* 39: 403–423.

Bergeson, T.R. and Trehub, S.E. (2002). Absolute pitch and tempo in mothers' songs to infants. *Psychological Science* 13: 72–75.

Bergeson, T.R. and Trehub, S.E. (2006). Infants' perception of rhythmic patterns. *Music Perception* 23: 345–360.

Bergeson, T.R. and Trehub, S.E. (2007). Signature tunes in mothers' speech to infants. *Infant Behavior and Development* 30: 648–654.

Berkowska, M. and Dalla Bella, S. (2009). Acquired and congenital disorders of song performance: A review. *Advances in Cognitive Psychology* 5: 69–83.

Bigand, E. and Poulin-Charronnat, B. (2006). Are we "experienced listeners"? A review of the musical capacities that do not depend on formal musical training. *Cognition* 100: 100–130.

Björkvold, J.R. (1992). *The Muse Within: Creativity and Communication, Song and Play from Childhood through Maturity*. New York: Harper Collins. [Original version published in Norwegian, 1989.]

Chang, H.W. and Trehub, S.E. (1977). Infants' perception of temporal grouping in auditory patterns. *Child Development* 48: 1666–1670.

Cohen, A.J., Thorpe, L.A., and Trehub, S.E. (1987). Infants' perception of musical relations in short transposed tone sequences. *Canadian Journal of Psychology* 41: 33–47.

Corbeil, M., Trehub, S.E., and Peretz, I. (2013). Speech vs. singing: Infants choose happier sounds. *Frontiers in Psychology* 4: 372.

Custodero, L.A., Britto, P.R., and Brooks-Gunn, J. (2003). Musical lives: A collective portrait of American parents and their young children. *Applied Developmental Psychology* 24: 553–572.

Dalla Bella, S., Giguère, J.F., and Peretz, I. (2007). Singing proficiency in the general population. *Journal of the Acoustical Society of America* 121: 1182–1189.

Davidson, L. (1985). Tonal structures of children's early songs. *Music Perception* 2: 361–374.

Davidson, L., McKernon, P., and Gardner, H. (1981). The acquisition of song: A developmental approach. In: *Documentary report of the Ann Arbor Symposium: Applications of psychology to the teaching and learning of music*, pp. 301–315. Reston, VA: Music Educators National Conference.

Dean, B.K. (2017). *A hidden world of song: Spontaneous singing in the everyday lives of three- and four-year-old children at home.* Unpublished doctoral dissertation, University of Exeter, UK.

Delavenne, A., Gratier, M., and Devouche, E. (2013). Expressive timing in infant-directed singing between 3 and 6 months. *Infant Behavior and Development* 36: 1–13.

Dolata, J.K., Davis, B.L., and MacNeilage, P.F. (2008). Characteristics of the rhythmic organization of vocal babbling: Implications for an amodal linguistic rhythm. *Infant Behavior and Development* 31: 422–431.

Dowling, W.J. (1988). Tonal structure and children's early learning of music. In: J.A. Sloboda (ed.), *Generative Processes in Music: The Psychology of Performance, Improvisation, and Composition*, pp. 113–128. New York: Clarendon Press.

Eckerdal, P. and Merker, B. (2009). Music and the "action song" in infant development: An interpretation. In: S. Malloch and C. Trevarthen (eds), *Communicative Musicality: Exploring the Basis of Human Companionship*, pp. 241–261. New York: Oxford University Press.

Fernald, A. (1991). Prosody in speech to children: Prelinguistic and linguistic functions. *Annals of Child Development* 8: 43–80.

Fernald, A., Marchman, V.A., and Weisleder, A. (2012). SES differences in language processing skill and vocabulary are evident at 18 months. *Developmental Science* 16: 234–248.

Flowers, P.J. and Dunne-Sousa, D. (1990). Pitch-pattern accuracy, tonality, and vocal range in preschool children's singing. *Journal of Research in Music Education* 38: 102–114.

Fox, D.B. (1990). An analysis of the pitch characteristics of infant vocalizations. *Psychomusicology* 9: 21–30.

Ghazban, N. (2013). *Emotion regulation in infants using maternal singing and speech.* Unpublished doctoral dissertation, Ryerson University, Toronto.

Gergely, G. and Csibra, G. (2006). Syvia's recipe: The role of imitation and pedagogy in the transmission of human culture. In: N.J. Enfield and S.C. Levinson (eds), *The Roots of Human Sociality: Culture, Cognition, and Human Sociality*, pp. 229–255. Oxford: Berg Publishers.

Gudmundsdottir, H.R. and Trehub, S.E. (2018). Adults recognize toddlers' song renditions. *Psychology of Music* 46: 281–291.

Hannon, E.E. and Trehub, S.E. (2005a). Metrical categories in infancy and adulthood. *Psychological Science* 16: 48–55.

Hannon, E.E. and Trehub, S.E. (2005b). Tuning in to musical rhythms: Infants learn more readily than adults. *Proceedings of the National Academy of Sciences* 102: 12639–12643.

Hart, B.M. and Risley, T.R. (1995). *Meaningful Differences in the Everyday Experience of Young American Children.* Baltimore, MD: Brookes.

Hrdy, S.B. (2009). *Mothers and Others: The Evolutionary Origins of Mutual Understanding.* Cambridge, MA: Harvard University Press.

Ilari, B. (2005). On musical parenting of young children: beliefs and behaviors of mothers and infants. *Early Child Development and Care* 175: 647–660.

Kelley, L. and Sutton-Smith, B. (1987). A study of infant musical productivity. In: J.C. Peery, I.W. Peery, and T.W. Draper (eds), *Music and Child Development*, pp. 35–53. New York: Springer-Verlag.

Kirschner, S. and Tomasello, M. (2010). Joint music making promotes prosocial behavior in 4-year-old children. *Evolution and Human Behavior* 31: 354–364.

Kitamura, C. and Burnham, D. (1998). The infant's response to maternal vocal affect. *Advances in Infancy Research* 12: 221–236.

Kopp, C.B. (1989). Regulation of distress and negative emotions: A developmental view. *Developmental Psychology* 25: 343–354.

Lee, S., Davis, B., and MacNeilage, P. (2010). Universal production patterns and ambient language influences in babbling: A cross-linguistic study of Korean-and English-learning infants. *Journal of Child Language* 37: 293–318.

LeVine, R.A. (1988). Human parental care: Universal goals, cultural strategies, individual behavior. *New Directions in Child Development* 40: 3–12.

Levinowitz, L.M. (1989). An investigation of preschool children's comparative capability to sing songs with and without words. *Bulletin of the Council for Research in Music Education* 100: 14–19.

Levitt, A.G. and Wang, Q. (1991). Evidence for language-specific rhythmic influences in the reduplicative babbling of French- and English- learning infants. *Language and Speech* 34(3): 235–249.

Longhi, E. (2009). "Songese": maternal structuring of musical interaction with infants. *Psychology of Music* 37: 195–213.

Mang, E. (2001). A cross-language comparison of preschool children's vocal fundamental frequency in speech and song production. *Research Studies in Music Education* 16: 4–14.

Mang, E. (2005). The referent of children's early songs. *Music Education Research* 7(1): 3–20.

Masataka, N. (1996). Perception of motherese in a signed language by 6-month-old deaf infants. *Developmental Psychology* 32: 874–879.

Masataka, N. (1998). Perception of motherese in Japanese Sign Language by 6-month-old hearing infants. *Developmental Psychology* 34: 241–246.

Masataka, N. (1999). Preference for infant-directed singing in 2-day-old hearing infants of deaf parents. *Developmental Psychology* 35: 1001–1005.

McKernon, P.E. (1979). The development of first songs in young children. *New Directions for Child and Adolescent Development* 3: 43–58.

Moog, H. (1976). *The Musical Experience of the Pre-School Child*. London: Schott Music.

Moorhead, G.E. and Pond, D. (1941). *Music of Young Children*. Santa Barbara, CA: Pillsbury Foundation for Advancement of Music Education.

Nakata, T. and Trehub, S.E. (2004). Infants' responsiveness to maternal speech and singing. *Infant Behavior and Development* 27: 455–464.

Nakata, T. and Trehub, S.E. (2011). Expressive timing and dynamics in infant-directed and non-infant-directed singing. *Psychomusicology: Music, Mind Brain* 21: 45–53.

Nelson, K. (1973). Structure and strategy in learning to talk. *Monographs of the Society for Research in Child Development* 38: 1–135.

Over, H. and Carpenter, M. (2013). The social side of imitation. *Child Development Perspectives* 7: 6–11.

Pfordresher, P.Q. and Brown, S. (2007). Poor-pitch singing in the absence of tone deafness. *Music Perception* 25: 95–115.

Pfordresher, P.Q., Brown, S., Meier, K.M., Belyk, M., and Liotti, M. (2010). Imprecise singing is widespread. *Journal of the Acoustical Society of America* 128: 2182–2190.

Phillips-Silver, J. and Trainor, L.J. (2005). Feeling the beat: Movement influences infant rhythm perception. *Science* 308: 1430.

Pinker, S. (1997). *How the Mind Works*. New York: Norton.

Plantinga, J., Trehub, S.E., and Russo, F. (2011, June). Multimodal aspects of maternal speech and singing. Presented at Meetings of Neurosciences and Music IV, Edinburgh, Scotland.

Reigado, J., Rocha, A., and Rodrigues, H. (2011). Vocalizations of infants (9-11 months old) in response to musical and linguistic stimuli. *International Journal of Music Education* 29: 241–255.

Richman, A., Miller, P.M., and Solomon, M.J. (1988). The socialization of infants in suburban Boston. *New Directions in Child Development* 40: 65–74.

Rock, A.M.L., Trainor, L.J., and Addison, T.L. (1999). Distinctive messages in infant-directed lullabies and play songs. *Developmental Psychology* 35: 527–534.

Rutkowski, J. and Miller, M. S. (2003). A longitudinal study of elementary children's acquisition of their singing voices. *Update: Applications of Research in Music Education* 22: 5–14.

Rvachew, S., Mattock, K., Polka, L., and Ménard, L. (2006). Developmental and cross-linguistic variation in the infant vowel space: The case of Canadian English and Canadian French. *Journal of the Acoustical Society of America* 120: 2250–2259.

Shenfield, T., Trehub, S.E., and Nakata, T. (2003). Maternal singing modulates infant arousal. *Psychology of Music* 31: 365–375.

Singh, L., Morgan, J.L., and Best, C.T. (2002). Infants' listening preferences: Baby talk or happy talk? *Infancy* 3: 365–394.

Sole, M. (2017). Crib song: Insights into functions of toddlers' private spontaneous singing. *Psychology of Music* 45: 172–192

Stadler-Elmer, S. (2012). Characteristics of early productive musicality. *Problems in Music Pedagogy* 10: 9–23.

Sundin, B. (1998). Musical creativity in the first six years. In: B. Sundin, G.E. McPherson, and G. Folkestad (eds), *Children Composing: Research in Music Education*, Vol. 1, pp. 35–56. Lund, Sweden: Malmo Academy of Music, Lund University.

Tartter, V.C. and Braun, D. (1994). Hearing smiles and frowns in normal and whisper registers. *Journal of the Acoustical Society of America* 96: 2101–2107.

Thompson, R.A. (1994). Emotion regulation: A theme in search of definition. *Monographs of the Society for Research in Child Development* 59: 25–52.

Thorpe, L.A., Trehub, S.E., Morrongiello, B.A., and Bull, D. (1988). Perceptual grouping by infants and preschool children. *Developmental Psychology* 24: 484–491.

Trainor, L.J. (1996). Infant preferences for infant-directed versus noninfant-directed playsongs and lullabies. *Infant Behavior and Development* 19: 83–92.

Trainor, L.J. and Trehub, S.E. (1993). What mediates infants' and adults' superior processing of the major over the augmented triad? *Music Perception* 11: 185–196.

Trainor, L.J., Clark, E.D., Huntley, A., and Adams, B. (1997). The acoustic basis of preferences for infant-directed singing. *Infant Behavior and Development* 20: 383–396.

Trehub, S.E. and Hannon, E.E. (2009). Conventional rhythms enhance infants' and adults' perception of musical patterns. *Cortex* 45: 110–118.

Trehub, S.E. and Prince, R. (2010). Lullabies and other women's songs in the Turkish village of Akçaeniş. *UNESCO Observatory E-journal*, Vol 2(1): 1–19.

Trehub, S.E. and Thorpe, L.A. (1989). Infants' perception of rhythm: Categorization of auditory sequences by temporal structure. *Canadian Journal of Psychology* 43: 217–229.

Trehub, S.E. and Trainor, L.J. (1998). Singing to infants: Lullabies and play songs. *Advances in Infancy Research* 12: 43–77.

Trehub, S.E., Hannon, E.E., and Schachner, A. (2010). Perspectives on music and affect in the early years. In: P.N. Juslin and J.A. Sloboda (eds), *Handbook of Music and Emotion: Theory, Research, Applications*, pp. 645–668. Oxford: Oxford University Press.

Trehub, S.E., Plantinga, J., and Russo, F.A. (2016). Maternal vocal interactions with infants: Reciprocal visual influences. *Social Development* 25: 665–683.

Trehub, S.E., Schellenberg, E.G., and Kamenetsky, S.B. (1999). Infants' and adults' perception of scale structure. *Journal of Experimental Psychology: Human Perception and Performance* 25: 965–975.

Trehub, S.E., Thorpe, L.A., and Morrongiello, B.A. (1985). Infants' perception of melodies: Changes in a single tone. *Infant Behavior and Development* 8: 213–223.

Trehub, S.E., Thorpe, L.A., and Morrongiello, B.A. (1987). Organizational processes in infants' perception of auditory patterns. *Child Development* 58: 741–749.

Trehub, S.E., Unyk, A.M., and Trainor, L.J. (1993). Maternal singing in cross-cultural perspective. *Infant Behavior and Development* 16: 285–295.

Trehub, S.E., Cohen, A.J., Thorpe, L.A., and Morrongiello, B.A. (1986). Development of the perception of musical relations: Semitone and diatonic structure. *Journal of Experimental Psychology: Human Perception and Performance* 12: 295–301.

Trehub, S.E., Plantinga, J., Brcic, J., and Nowicki, M. (2013). Cross-modal signatures in maternal speech and singing. *Frontiers in Psychology* 4: 811.

Trehub, S.E., Unyk, A.M., Kamenetsky, S.B., Hill, D.S., Trainor, L.J., Henderson, J.L., and Saraza, M. (1997). Mothers' and fathers' singing to infants. *Developmental Psychology* 33: 500–507.

Weisleder, A. and Fernald, A. (2013). Talking to children matters: Early language experience strengthens processing and builds vocabulary. *Psychological Science* 24(11): 2143–2152.

Welch, G.F. (1979). Vocal range and poor pitch singing. *Psychology of Music* 7: 13–31.

Welch, G.F. (1985). A schema theory of how children learn to sing in tune. *Psychology of Music* 13: 3–18.

Welch, G.F., Sergeant, D., and White, P. (1996). The singing competences of five-year-old developing singers. *Bulletin of the Council for Research in Music Education* 127: 155–162.

Welch, G.F., Sergeant, D.C., and White, P.J. (1998). The role of linguistic dominance in the acquisition of song. *Research Studies in Music Education* 10: 67–74.

Werner, H. (1917). Die melodische Erfindung im fruhen Kindesalter. *Bericht der Kaiserlichen Akademie, Wien* 182: 1–100.

Whalen, D.H., LeVitt, A.G., and Wang, Q. (1991). Intonational differences between the reduplicative babbling of French and English learning infants. *Journal of Child Language* 18: 501–516.

Whiteman, P.J. (2001). *How the bananas got their pyjamas: A study of the metamorphosis of preschoolers' spontaneous singing as viewed through Vygotsky's Zone of Proximal Development.* Unpublished doctoral dissertation, University of New South Wales, Australia.

Whiten, A., McGuigan, N., Marshall-Pescini, S., and Hopper, L.M. (2009). Emulation, imitation, over-imitation and the scope of culture for child and chimpanzee. *Philisophical Transactions of the Royal Society B* 364: 2417–2428.

Wiltermuth, S.S. and Heath, C. (2009). Synchrony and cooperation. *Psychological Science* 20: 1–5.

Wise, K. and Sloboda, J. (2008). Establishing an empirical profile of self-defined "tone deafness": Perception, singing performance, and self-assessment. *Musicae Scientiae* 12: 3–23.

Young, S. (2002). Young children's spontaneous vocalizations in free-play: observations of two-to-three-year-olds in a day care setting. *Bulletin of the Council for Research in Music Education* 152: 43–53.

Zentner, M. and Eerola, T. (2010). Rhythmic engagement with music in infancy. *Proceedings of the National Academy of Sciences* 107: 5768–5773.

CHAPTER 23

SINGING AND INVENTED SONG-MAKING IN INFANTS' AND YOUNG CHILDREN'S EARLY LEARNING AND DEVELOPMENT

From Shared to Independent Song-making

MARGARET S. BARRETT

INTRODUCTION

THE phenomenon of singing and song-making has been acknowledged as universal in human society through the work of anthropologists (Dissanayake 2000, 2006, 2009, 2012), archeologists (Mithen 2005, 2009), ethnomusicologists (Blacking 1976), and evolutionary theorists (McDermott 2009). Given the seeming ubiquity of singing and song-making in human society, there have been claims for music's evolutionary role (Dissanayake 2006, 2009, 2012; Huron 2003; Mithen 2005, 2009) and its centrality to human development.

Studies of music in families (Barrett 2009, 2006; Boer and Abubakar 2014; Custodero and Johnson-Green 2008; Custodero et al. 2003) have highlighted the ways in which music functions as a ritual medium for a range of purposes. Such use of music has been reported to produce social cohesion, emotional well-being, and positive psychological benefits for the individual child and those with whom s/he interacts as they engage in mutually reinforcing singing and song-making experiences (see also "Mothers as Singing Mentors" by Trehub and Gudmundsdottir, and "Children Singing: Nurture, Creativity, and Culture" by Harding in this volume). Musical family rituals have been defined as "a set of musical behaviors (engagement and listening) that are reported within a family context and hold symbolic meaning for the family members" (Boer and Abubakar 2014, n.p.).

Much early research in the developmental psychology of music has taken place in laboratory settings. While aspects of the musical macro-cultures that child participants experience might well be retained through the choices of music and presentation in these settings, the decontextualized nature of the laboratory removes the powerful shaping forces of the intersecting multiple systems (Bronfenbrenner 1979; Rogoff 2003) in which infants and children normally experience music. These include the relational features of engagement with others, the situational prompts and facilitators for music-making, and the spaces and places in which music-making occurs. For example, specific music-making events might be associated with particular individuals and/or groups (the songs that grandma sings with the child, as opposed to those that siblings sing with the child), be prompted and supported by particular objects and routines (songs sung when playing with particular toys, or participating in routine behaviors such as brushing the teeth), or be linked to particular places and spaces (songs sung in the bath, in the car, or in worship).

Initially, research in developmental psychology focused on issues of musical perception (Deutsch 2013; Dowling and Harwood 1986; Hallam et al. 2008; Trehub et al. 1997). Later work sought to explore issues of musical production (or re-production) and, subsequently, generation ("original" musical works). This acknowledgment that young children not only attend to music as audience members, but also are actively engaged in music-making as performers and producers of "new" music has expanded the research lens through which young children's musical development has been investigated. In this chapter, I explore the ways in which young children (aged approximately 16–48 months) engage with singing as both performers and producers of songs. Specifically, the chapter seeks to address the following questions:

- What is young children's invented song-making?
- When and how does singing and invented song-making emerge?
- What prompts and supports early singing and invented song-making?
- What function does early singing and invented song-making have in young children's early learning and development?
- How might young children's early singing and invented song-making be supported and developed?

What is young children's invented song-making?

In the kitchen

Jay is an early riser according to his mother, Erica. While the rest of the house slumbers on, including his baby brother Adam, Jay is up and active in the house. His early morning solitary play is often accompanied by song and music-making, drawing on a repertoire of songs that he has accumulated from singing sessions in the local library, CDs, Children's MTV, a Kindermusik program, and the diverse "record collections" of his mum and dad and grandparents. At the age of three, Jay's singing is not restricted to the known and familiar: he often sings invented songs, songs that reflect his thoughts at the time concerning his location, his relationships with self and others, his activities, and his state of mind.

This morning is no exception. Erica, alerted to Jay's whereabouts by the sound of singing and a curious rhythmic drumming sound, grabs the video camera and heads to the kitchen. As she rounds the bench, camera rolling, Jay's song becomes loud and clear:

> "Here we are, in the kitchen,
> every-body, Ah, Ah, Ah,
> Here we are, in the kitchen,
> play with oh and (unclear),
> Here we go sing in the kitchen,
> everybody sing in the kitchen . . . "

His singing is loud and confident, and the rising melody is on pitch. As he sings he steps rhythmically from side to side, raising each leg high and lowering to the floor in time to the pulse of his singing. In each hand, he grasps an egg carton; they are raised in front of his face, cymbal-like, and he beats them together marking the rhythm of "in the kitchen" over his stepped performance of the underlying pulse.

> *He breaks off to ask:*
> "Where's Adam, mum?" *referring to his baby brother.*
> "We're just going to get Adam up now, OK?" *she responds.*
> "Here we go" *he reprises before dropping the egg cartons to the floor and heading for the corner cupboard.*
> "I need some more" *he concludes.*

(Barrett 2012)

This event takes no longer than 34 seconds, captured fortuitously by Jay's mother as part of her family's participation in a research study that sought to understand the role of invented singing and song-making in young children's world-making and identity work (Barrett 2005–2008). Jay[1] was in one of 18 parent–child dyads who contributed to the study. Data were generated in the study through parents (1) maintaining video diaries of their child engaged in music-making in the home and community; (2) participating in interviews; and (3) maintaining "week-at-a-glance" paper diaries that mapped their child's developing song repertoire, engagement in music, including any others who participated in the music-making, and also the child's emotional state at the time. From these data, a rich story of children's early generative music-making in the form of invented song has emerged. The youngest child enrolled in the study was 16 months of age at commencement, the oldest (Jay) 37 months. The average time in which parents engaged in the study was approximately 12 months, with some generating data for greater or lesser periods. Regardless of age or circumstance, each family captured their child in the act of inventing songs.

Studies of young children's singing behaviors as childhood and non-institutionalized practices have documented some commonalities in the ways in which children generate original musical utterances. Researchers have noted that initial utterances consist of short fragmentary rhythmic and melodic phrases (Davidson 1985, 1994; Dowling 1984a, 1984b, 1999) that evolve into "pot-pourri" (Moog 1976) or "outline" (Hargreaves 1986) songs around two to three years of age. Moog's description of "pot-pourri" songs focuses on the ways in which young children create "mash-ups" of a number of known songs interpolated with

---

[1] A more complete report of Jay's singing and song-making is available in Barrett (2012).

In the Kitchen

May 2010   Jay

Here we are   in   the kitch-en   ev - 'ry bod - y   ah - ah - ah   Here we are

in   the   kitch - en   play with   oh   and   Here   we   go

sing   in   the kitch - en   ev - 'ry bod - y   sing   in   the kitch - en   er

J: Where's Adam, Mum?   Here   we   are
M: We're just gonna get Adam up. OK?   J: I need to get some more.

FIGURE 23.1 In the Kitchen—May 2010.

From Barrett (2012). Reproduced with permission.

original musical comments or asides. Hargreaves' notion of "outline" songs describes the ways the child secures the "outline" features of known melodic and rhythmic structures prior to the achievement of a fully detailed rendition of these components.

Young children's singing tends to reflect cultural differences (Mang 2001, 2002, 2006) and the repertoire to which they are exposed in family and community. For example, Mang's investigation of singing development of young children in Chinese (Cantonese)–English bilingual households demonstrated that children in bilingual tonal language households employed more "intermediate vocalizations," i.e. vocalizations that encompass some of the qualities of speech and song, than did their monolingual non-tonal language peers. For these latter, speech and song behaviors were more clearly differentiated.

In a recent longitudinal study of Italian infants' singing development, the researchers noted that singing behaviors documented as musical babbling occurred much earlier than reported elsewhere in the literature.

> the babies (aged 2–8 months) who have been exposed to musical experiences during the prenatal and neonatal stages produced vocalizations that we can consider "musical babbling" . . . vocalizations that appear earlier, in greater number and with greater musical value with respect to those children who have not had such a rich experience.
>
> (Tafuri 2008, p. 58)

Key to the differences reported in the Italian study was the children's participation in a mother and infant Music Early Learning Program (MELP) that commenced in the third trimester of pregnancy. The findings of this study underline the rich contribution of the nurturing environment to genetic endowment. Consideration of the interplay between nature and nurture in the development of singing in the human species has been the focus of a range of researchers in archeology and related fields and is addressed in the following section.

My use of the term "invented song" is intended to focus on the generative rather than reproductive intentions of the singer and the song. As evidenced in Jay's singing above (and see Figure 23.1), his song is "original" in both melody and lyrics. While its structure reflects those of many children's songs, it is not a mash-up in Moog's sense of a "pot-pourri" song, borrowing chunks of material from the repertoire. Nor is it an "outline" song in Hargreaves' sense: indeed the song is tightly structured in terms of melody and lyric fit and addresses a topic of immediate interest to Jay—his location in the family kitchen. Accordingly, I describe "invented song" as a *genre of children's early song-making that is generative in intention, draws on the musical materials of the child's cultural experience, and is used as a means to engage with and make sense of their worlds.*

When and how does singing and invented song-making emerge?

Archeologist Stephen Mithen claims that "to be human is to be musical" and that "the capacity for music is deeply embedded in the human genome: it is a part of our biology rather than merely our culture and can only have gotten there through an evolutionary process" (2009, p. 4). In claiming music as an evolutionary feature of human development, Mithen not only points to the ubiquity of music in the world's cultures, but also shapes a view that the proto-musical calls of pre-language human ancestors, specifically Plio-Pleistocene hominins functioned as signals of emotional expression and manipulation that aided communication and understanding in increasingly complex social groups. For Mithen:

> our ancestors had to be highly emotional beings to have survived; in the absence of language, musicality would have been the principal manner in which emotions would have been expressed and a response induced in others as a means to manipulate their behavior. So our minds and our bodies evolved to be emotionally sensitive to musical sounds.
>
> (2009, p. 7)

The view of music as an evolutionary adaptation has been taken up by others (Dissanayake 2006, 2009, 2012; Fernald 1992; Malloch & Trevarthen 2009a), with a specific focus on the function of infant–caregiver shared music-making in reproductive success and infant survival (Dissanayake 2009). Infants are exposed to music pre-birth as hearing is normally functional in the third trimester in the womb (Lecanuet 1996). They enter the world with experience of the sound world of the mother, and an attunement to the voice of the mother (Nakata and Trehub 2004). The ubiquity of infant-directed speech and song across the world's cultures suggests that we are biologically programmed rather than merely culturally conditioned to employ our musicality in our earliest interactions with infants. The distinctive musical features of these forms of interactions (such as heightened voice, softened timbre, enhanced melodic line) function as a means of ritualizing and "making special" simple routines and actions (Dissanayake 2000, 2009). Mothers, fathers (O'Neil et al. 2001) and other caregivers draw on their musicality as a means to establish mutuality, socialize, and bond with their infants (Papoušek 1996). Importantly, such activity is bi-directional. Infants are not merely passive recipients of such musical communication; rather, they elicit our music-making through their attention and positive reception to infant-directed speech and song. In short, infants "teach us to perform for them" (Dissanayake 2012, p. 2) by rewarding us with their delighted reception at our attempts to communicate.

The notion of "communicative musicality" has been developed to describe the musical dialogic interaction that occurs between infant and caregiver (Malloch and Trevarthen 2009b). Such interactions are imbued with mutuality, meaning, and emotion, and constitute a form of "coordinated companionship" that draws on the elements of pulse (timing), quality (expressive musical qualities of dynamics, timbre, and tone-color), and narrative (the coordination of pulse and quality in forming companionship through time) (Malloch 1999/2000). Not only do these interactions promote bonding (Trevarthen and Malloch 2000), support emotional recognition and regulation (Trehub 2003, 2009), and language and cultural learning (Barrett 2009, 2016a), they also "prepare infants to be musical" (Dissanayake 2012, p. 4).

While many of the infant's early vocalizations function as signals to parents and carers concerning emotional and physiological states (hunger, being wet, tiredness), they also function as a means of conveying contentedness, and eliciting attention and playful engagement from the mother or carer. These improvised duets also lay down the basis for later music-making as the adult singer "mentors" the child (see "Mothers as Singing Mentors" by Trehub and Gudmundsdottir in this volume) in the musical and linguistic features of songs of the culture.

Old MacDonald

Amy is seated in her high chair at the kitchen table, a plate of red grapes in front of her. She throws a grape down on the plate and pushes back against the table with both hands. Her father says "Right" in a determined tone and commences singing Old MacDonald. As he sings the first phrase, Amy begins to move in the chair, bouncing from side to side in time to her father's singing, supporting herself with her hands on the arms of the chair. By the second phrase, Amy is looking towards him in expectation:

"and on that farm he had a . . . "

In the pause, Amy interjects "chicken" before her father continues with the phrase. Her movement settles as the next phrase approaches and she joins into the gaps he leaves in the song for her to insert the relevant animal noise. Her "buck buck" sounds for the chicken are sung and she flaps her arms in time, like chicken wings, for the remainder of the verse.

The second verse commences and again Amy's father pauses for her to insert the name of the animal. After giving it some thought, she calls out

"Chicken!"

"We've already had a chicken, can't he have something else?" her father asks.

"Duck" is Amy's next contribution and her father continues to sing the verse waiting for her to add the "quack quack" sounds as required. As the verse finishes Amy begins to "Moo" in anticipation of what might come next.

"And on that farm he had a . . . "

"Duck"

"We've just had a duck."

Her father resumes the verse.

"And on that farm he had a . . . "

"Chicken"

"We've done a chicken", he explains patiently.

Her father starts again.

"And on that farm he had a . . ." he sings.

"Cow" Amy adds quickly.

"Cow!" her father repeats triumphantly. And with evident relief he completes the phrase "E I E I O"!

Amy smiles broadly as her mother is heard laughing in the background. Amy joins in enthusiastically to the "Moo Moo" sounds, improvising an accompaniment through the remainder of the verse, again to the amusement of her parents.

A further verse of the song is begun and again Amy's contribution is "Chicken." As she speaks her father calls out quickly "Koala!!" and continues the verse. Amy calls out "Wake up" for the sleepy Koala at the relevant point of the song, raising her arms in time. She begins to tease her father, mouthing the words "wake up" to him rather than singing or saying them, again to the amusement of both parents. All are involved in the shared music-making as the singing continues. Through the last phrase of the verse, her father sings with a ritardando signaling the end. But it's not the end for Amy: she calls out "pig."

"Pig?" he inquires. "Oh." He takes up the chorus "With a ngh ngh here and a ngh ngh there, here a ngh, there a ngh, everywhere a ngh, ngh."

Amy shapes her mouth to make the pig noises and startles herself on the third attempt with a massive snort. She shrieks with delight as her father continues the sounds of the pig. Before he can finish the song, she turns towards the table again and commands imperiously:

"Milk."

The song is over.

The above vignette (2 minutes and 18 seconds) was captured on camera by Amy's parents at approximately 20 months of age. The study strand from which this data has been extracted sought to capture aspects of musical parenting in the home and community and involved some 17 families from across Australia (Barrett and Welch 2013–2016). While the initial prompt for this singing interaction appears to have been to re-focus Amy on the task at hand—finishing her meal—as the song unfolds much more is occurring here. Through her father's careful prompting, Amy is practicing her vocabulary, specifically, farmyard animals and their sounds. She is also singing, interpolating her contributions into the musical structure of the song. In this process she is demonstrating her understanding of how a song goes, her grasp of melody and pulse as expressed in her movement accompaniments, her understanding of phrasing and structure, and her role in the joint performance of the song. Importantly, her efforts to contribute to her father's musical game are received with humor and appreciation by all members of her family. With the above taken into consideration, the joint singing of "Old MacDonald" is much more than the performance of a musical favorite: it has become a vehicle for strengthening social and emotional ties, learning about aspects of the world in which Amy lives, and accumulating cultural knowledge.

As Amy becomes more independent and mobile, she takes up these early shared lessons concerning language, music, and the function of song in her life in her independent musical and linguistic practice.

Crib songs

> Amy is settled in her cot in her darkened bedroom, the nightly ritual of a story and song completed. The sound of her singing has brought her father to the bedroom door in an attempt to capture her song on video. Amy sings:
>   "Yes he fix it . . . all day town."
> She sings through fragments of current favorite songs, "The wheels on the bus" and "Bob the Builder", in a musical mash-up of her own. After a pause she begins again:
>   "Hmmm. Take on the bus, round and round, All day long."
> The refrain "All day long" is sung with the marked rhythmic emphasis of the original model. Amy pauses. Words disappear from her singing and she begins to hum. Without words, the melodic line is less effortful, more fluid, as she improvises around the melodic shapes of the refrain, "All day long."

In the above, Amy is engaging in the practice of a "crib narrative" (Nelson 1989). Studies of these narratives have documented the ways in which music is a prime organizing feature in a process in which "a melodic rhythm is established and then words are 'backfilled' into it" (Dore 1989, p. 249). These sung crib narratives function as a means of practicing language, of self-comfort, and, I suggest, as a transition from the shared music-making of "communicative musicality" to children's independent invented song-making. What prompts this early singing and invented song-making?

WHAT PROMPTS AND SUPPORTS EARLY SINGING AND INVENTED SONG-MAKING?

Social interactions are powerful prompts and supports for young children's early engagement in singing. Parents, carers, and siblings initiate interactions in social settings as a means to induct the child into the cultural practices of their world, of which song is one. The child's earliest experiences of song are those encountered in the womb where s/he is both an audience and sometimes active participant in the musical experiences and music-making of the mother, and the focus of such music-making (see Tafuri 2008). Mithen (2009) argues that music is part of our biology rather than merely our culture, an argument that suggests that the child emerges into the world primed for music activity. Following birth, the child's experiences of song are those shared rituals of singing and soothing, of communicative musicality, and the use of cultural "standards" such as lullabies in the parenting and caring practices employed with the child (Trevarthen 2002, 2010). As the child develops and grows, song is employed to mark significant transitions in life, including birthdays (of the child and others), religious worship and festivals, and observance of national events.

Families develop private rituals that are marked by song, such as singing as part of car journeys, singing to soothe and calm, singing to change moods, singing to accompany activity such as preparing meals, bathing, getting changed, getting dressed, and settling down to sleep. These activities also function as a form of musical parenting as parents draw on the resource of joint music-making in structuring their child's day and activities. In these home settings, young children's attempts at singing are supported in and through family joint singing and structured prompting—as illustrated in the vignette above featuring Amy and her father.

While family and carers provide live models of what constitutes singing and demonstrate a repertoire of songs, young children also encounter song in a wide variety of fora beyond the family. Music has become a ubiquitous part of the contemporary world: it is employed as an overt and covert marketing tool through its uses in media advertising on television and radio, as a backdrop to shopping in department stores, supermarkets and malls, and as an accompaniment to eating in restaurants, cafés, and food halls of all descriptions. Public transport often features a soundscape of diverse musical inputs to which the child contributes (Custodero et al. 2016), as does the family car.

Increasingly, children's toys are manufactured with a soundtrack in which music is featured. Attendance at sports events is often a musical occasion as music is used in a range of forms including the performance of the national anthem, the use of music to mark key events in the game, as half-time entertainment, and as a means of identifying and expressing affiliation with a team through the singing of team songs or chants. Public play environments often feature a musical soundtrack that accompanies the movements and actions of play equipment. In short, there is barely a public setting in which music is not somehow featured as part of the environment (DeNora 2000, 2011).

For increasing numbers of children, the childcare center and pre-school provide further settings beyond the home in which they may encounter music, singing, and song-making. The OECD data for 2014 states that, on average across the OECD, 70 percent of three-year-olds and 84 percent of four-year-olds are enrolled in pre-primary education (OECD 2014a). Data in relation to children under the age of three enrolled in childcare is reported as widely variable. The OECD average for 2010, for example, is reported as 33 percent, covering a range from less than 10 percent of children under three enrolled in childcare in the Slovak Republic to the highest levels in Denmark, where 70 percent of children under three are enrolled in childcare (OECD 2014b). Childcare in these measures includes:

> Childcare at a day-care center, childcare by a professional child-minder at the child's home or at a child-minder's office, and education at pre-school or equivalent (e.g. kindergarten, nursery school, asilo nido) . . . the child-minder category may include a relative, friend, neighbor or baby sitter . . . (who) . . . received a payment for this activity.
>
> (OECD 2014b, p. 5)

These settings provide another context in which young children may encounter music. For example, music may be employed in childcare and pre-school settings to soothe at nap time, to mark transitions in the day (through using a packing-up song), as an early learning tool (through the use of naming songs such as "Head, Shoulders, Knees and

Toes"), to create a sense of community through collective singing and movement, and as a medium for structured and free play (Barrett et al. 2018). It should be noted that in the absence of a formal curriculum for these settings, the music experiences presented to children largely reflect the musical capabilities of the childcare workers. With the documented decline of music education in the training and professional learning experiences of early childhood professionals (see Australian Government Department of Education, Science and Training 2005 and Suthers 2007 for examples in Australia), increasingly childcare workers are relying on commercial products, primarily CDs and DVDs, as the basis for music engagement and education (Suthers 2004), as are parents (de Vries 2007).

Beyond childcare and pre-school, parents are increasingly purchasing music services for their children. There has been a proliferation of commercial Music Early Learning Programs (MELPs) for the birth-to-five age group (Abad and Barrett 2016). For infants and toddlers (0–36 months), these programs provide a context in which mother/carer and child participate in a range of music activities, including joint singing, moving, and listening to music, instrumental play, and musical storying. These settings can also assist parents in developing a repertoire of songs and musical ideas and strategies to supplement their parenting in the home environment (Barrett 2009).

Children are alert and receptive to the many uses and contexts of music-making and engagement outlined above. Their attention to these can be observed in the ways in which they adapt and adopt features of the range of musical genres to which they are exposed in their own singing and invented song-making. In a study of the invented song-making of a two-year-old girl, for example, her invented songs drew on the structures and performance traditions of a diverse range of musical genres that included the classic Australian rock favorites of her father and the more standard repertoire of songs written for children and experienced by her in the MELP (a Kindermusik program) that she attended (Barrett 2011). Analysis of her song production indicated a capacity to move seamlessly between these genres and to incorporate key musical features of these in her own music-making.

As outlined above, children's experience of singing and song-making is seemingly ubiquitous. Potentially every aspect of a child's life from waking and sleeping, bathing and dressing, eating, transitioning from one activity to another, playing, traveling, shopping, comforting, and celebrating can be accompanied by music, singing, and song-making. Consequently, the musical richness of the child's environment is a key aspect of the developing capacity to sing and invent song. Recent research has emphasized the benefits of shared music-making for young children. In a study of 3031 Australian children participating in *Growing Up in Australia: The Longitudinal Study of Australian Children* (LSAC), findings indicated that frequency of shared home music activities as reported by parents was associated with positive measures of children's vocabulary, numeracy, attentional and emotional regulation, and prosocial skills as measured at age five by teachers' report and direct testing (Williams et al. 2015). This research emphasizes the importance of shared music-making as encompassing more than exposure to music as sound— it also includes the opportunity to sing and make music with and for self and others in relationships. These prompts and supports also point to the many functions of singing and invented song-making in the lives of young children.

What function does early singing and invented song-making have in young children's early learning and development?

Young children's generative musical narratives fulfil a range of purposes including: (1) establishing the mutuality of the infant–caregiver relationship in communicative musicality (Malloch and Trevarthen 2000); (2) establishing the basis of playground interactions (Bjørkvold 1989; Marsh 2008); (3) establishing social bonds and communicating feeling-states (Campbell 2011; Papoušek, H. 1996; Papoušek, M. 1996); (4) participating in family rituals (Barrett 2009); (5) trialing different ways of being in the world with self and others (Barrett 2005, 2009); and (6) undertaking identity work (Barrett 2011, 2012a, 2016b). To these purposes might be added the role of song-making and vocalization in underpinning early music and language development (Barrett 2016a). Importantly, young children's singing and song-making may also be regarded as a cultural tool (Vygotsky 1986) through which they narrate their experience of the world.

Bear's not there

> Ginnie is in the bedroom of the tiny apartment where she lives with her mother and older brother Caleb. The curtains are drawn against the fading light of a hot Brisbane day. It is 5:49:05 pm and the children are playing in the brief lull before their evening meal at 6 pm. Ginnie's loud singing has brought her mother to the bedroom door, video-camera in hand. Caleb, aged four, stands quietly by his bed, watching his sister as she inspects the assortment of books and objects on the chest of drawers and then the bedroom floor. She has a small ninja toy clasped in one hand and sings an invented song that mixes melody and rhythm from the "Little, Little Star" song, with occasional references to "bears" and things "not there." She turns to look down on the collection on the floor, stoops to pick up a book and looks at it briefly before throwing it back on the floor. She starts singing a new phrase, "And then the bear . . . ," stooping to pick up another book " . . . walked away," before throwing it back to the ground. The next phrase, "Bear's not there . . . ," accompanies her as she walks to her brother's bed. "The bear's not there," she announces, and leans on the bed.
>
> In the next video clip, commencing at 5:49:23, Ginnie is still by the bed, picking through her brother's collections and singing clearly "Bear's not here." Her brother interrupts her "No! No!", moving her away from his things, and she moves towards the door rubbing her eyes, clearly tired.
>
> The next video clip, commencing at 5:50:08, shows Ginnie at a toy stand placed between the end of her cot and the doorway. She plays with the ninja toy, placing it on the top of the toy stand while singing:
>
>> "Kangaroo, and Teddy Bear.
>> Rockaby the bear
>> Bear's not asleep.
>> Kangaroo, and (indistinct)

Rockaby Bear . . .
Bear's not sleepy,
Shh, Shh, Shh."

She kneels on the floor, searching through the different levels of the stand, the
ninja now abandoned on the top level. She pauses, then sings "Pinky (her bear)
I love . . . you."

In this vignette, captured as part of a study of musical parenting in Australian families (Barrett and Welch 2013–2016), Ginnie is using invented song and singing in a range of ways: it is an accompaniment to activity as she searches through her toys in the bedroom for her bear; as the search continues, the song becomes a means for her to reflect on her activity ("Bear's not there . . ."). Finally, as she abandons the ninja toy while looking through the toy stand, she uses her singing as a means of stating her feelings for her bear, Pinky: singing has become a means of self-comfort. This practice of narrating experience through the medium of song has been observed in the song practices of other children (Barrett 2016a) and is, I suggest, a means by which children engage in "culture in the small," in the local settings "where cultures pass on their evaluative messages" (Bruner 2006, p. 4). Such practices also contribute to children's identity work as a "small story" narrative practice through which children present in-the-moment narratives of their experiences, thoughts, and feelings (Barrett 2016b).

From the above, it is evident that young children's early singing and song-making fulfills a number of functions in children's development. Singing and song-making is both the focus of young children's playful activity, and its accompaniment. Drawing on singing and song-making as a cultural tool, children use song to both learn about and explore their "culture in the small," comment on their experiences of these worlds, and develop a repertoire of music as a continuing cultural resource. How might this important early childhood practice be fostered?

How might young childrens' early singing and invented song-making be supported and developed?

I have described children's invented song-making as a *genre of children's early song-making that is generative in intention, draws on the musical materials of each child's cultural experience, and is used as a means to engage with and make sense of their world.* Understood as a genre that is employed by children in their early learning in and about the world, distinction needs to be made between learning to sing as a personal expression and means of social and cultural engagement, and mastery of the discipline of music. While these two aims are not mutually exclusive, recognition of the multiplicity of functions of singing and invented song-making in young children's lives suggests that supporting and developing invented song-making differs from building children's skills as singers in command of a known and shared body of repertoire. The former focuses on the child's use and interests, while the latter seeks to bring the child to engagement and interaction with the skills, techniques, and repertoires of singing as a mainstream cultural practice. In the former, we are interested in songs made *by* children, while in the latter we are interested in their mastery of songs made *for* children.

Supporting and developing children's singing and mastery of songs made *for* children suggests an emphasis on assisting them to sing in time, in tune, with a faithful rendition of the melodic line and an accurate presentation of the words. This approach assumes that these features are at the foreground of children's engagement in singing and invented song-making. However, children's comments on the process of invented song-making suggest otherwise (see Barrett 2006). When we focus on children's invented song-making, on songs made *by* children, the interest becomes one of engaging with the child's multiple uses of songs as outlined above, facilitating children's access to multiple musical models, encouraging them in their inventiveness, and engaging playfully in the use of singing and song-making. This latter returns us to the use of singing and invented song-making as a central component of family (and childcare and pre-school) routines. I do not suggest the abandonment of singing and teaching the rich repertoire of children's songs: rather, that we should expand our singing and pedagogical practices to embrace children's invented song-making.

Concluding remarks

Sprinkle song

> Tom (aged 30 months) is seated at a table in the family room. A sheet of paper covered with blue splodges and a good helping of paste from a bottle of "clag" (just visible in front of him) rests on the table surface. He clasps a jar of silver "sprinkles" in his left hand and is shaking this in time to his singing. He swaps the jar to his right hand and continues singing.

Tom[2] sings to accompany activity (see Figure 23.2). He sings to describe and comment on his activity, that of shaking silver sprinkles onto his painting. Singing functions also as a means of locating him in his world. Viewed from another perspective, Tom's singing reveals an understanding of musical phrase and song structure, a grasp of rhythmic and melodic patterning, and a capacity for inventiveness. What would happen were we to recognize and embrace young children's capacity to invent songs and draw on this to structure a richer continuing music education?

---

[2] This vignette was generated from the Music Early Learning Programme strand of Barrett and Welch (2013–2016).

Sprinkles Song

sprin-kles, sprin-kles, sprin-kles, sprin-kles, sprin-kles, sprin-kles, sprin-kles, sprin-kles, sprin-kles, sprin-kles,

sprin-kles, sprin-kles, sprin-kles, sprin-kles, sprin-kles, sprin-kles, sprin-kles, sprin-kles, sprin-kles, sprin-kles,

sprin-kles, sprin- DONE!

FIGURE 23.2 Sprinkles Song.

Research reported in this chapter has been supported by the Australian Research Council Discovery grant scheme (Barrett, 2005–2007 DP0559050; Barrett and Welch 2013–2016 DP130102488).

References

Abad, V. and Barrett, M.S. (2016). Families and music early learning programs: boppin' babies. In: S. Jacobsen and G. Thompson (eds), *Models of Music Therapy with Families*, pp. 135–152. London: Jessica Kingsley.

Australian Government Department of Education, Science and Training (2005). *Augmenting the Diminished—National Review of School Music Education.* Canberra, Australia: Department of Education, Science and Training, Australian Government.

Barrett, M.S. (2005–2008). *Young children's world-making through music: Young children's identity construction in and through music.* Funded by the ARC Discovery Program Grant no DP0559050.

Barrett, M.S. (2006). Inventing songs, inventing worlds: the "genesis" of creative thought and activity in young children's lives. *International Journal of Early Years Education* 14(3): 201–220.

Barrett, M.S. (2009). Sounding lives in and through music: a narrative inquiry of the "everyday" musical engagement of a young child. *Journal of Early Childhood Research* 7: 115–134.

Barrett, M.S. (2011). Musical narratives: a study of a young child's identity work in and through music-making. *Psychology of Music* 39(4): 403–424.

Barrett, M.S. (2012). Mutuality, belonging and meaning-making: pathways to developing young boys' competence and creativity in singing and song-making. In: S. Harrison, G.F. Welch, and A. Adler (eds), *Perspectives on Males and Singing*, pp. 167–187. Dordrecht: Springer.

Barrett, M.S. (2016a). Attending to "culture in the small": a narrative analysis of the role of play, thought, and music in young children's world-making. *Research Studies in Music Education* 38(1): 41–54.

Barrett, M.S. (2016b). Laying the foundations for narrative identities in and through music. In: R. McDonald, D. Hargreaves, and D. Miell (eds), *Oxford Handbook for Music Identity*, pp. 63–78. Oxford: Oxford University Press.

Barrett, M.S., Flynn, L., and Welch, G.F. (2018). Music value and participation: An Australian case-study of music provision and support in Early Childhood Education. *Research Studies in Music Education* 40(2): 226–242.

Barrett, M.S. and Welch, G.F. (2013–2016). *Being and Becoming Musical: Towards a Cultural Ecological Model of Early Musical Development*. Funded by the ARC Discovery Program Grant no DP130102488.

Bjørkvold, J. (1989). *The Muse within: Creativity and Communication, Song and Play from Childhood through Maturity* (trans. W.H. Halverson). New York: HarperCollins.

Blacking, J. (1976). *How Musical Is Man?* London: Faber and Faber.

Boer, D. and Abubakar, A. (2014). Music listening in families and peer groups: benefits for young people's social cohesion and emotional well-being across four cultures. *Frontiers of Psychology*, http://dx.doi.org/10.3389/fpsyg.2014.00392, accessed October 4, 2015.

Bronfenbrenner, U. (1979). *The Ecology of Human Development: Experiments by Nature and Design*. Cambridge, MA: Harvard University Press.

Bruner, J.S. (2006). Culture, mind and narrative. In: J.S. Bruner (ed.), *In Search of Pedagogy (Volume II): The Selected Works of Jerome S. Bruner*, pp. 230–236. Abingdon: Routledge.

Campbell, P.S. (2011). Musical enculturation: sociocultural influences and meanings of children's experiences in and through music. In: M.S. Barrett (ed.), *A Cultural Psychology of Music*. Oxford: Oxford University Press. Available at: doi:10.1093/acprof:oso/9780199214389.003.0004.

Custodero, L., Britto, P.R., and Brooks-Gunn, J. (2003). Musical lives: a collective portrait of American parents and their young children. *Applied Developmental Psychology* 24: 553–572.

Custodero, L.A. and Johnson-Green, E.A. (2008). Caregiving in counterpoint: reciprocal influences in the musical parenting of young and older infants. *Early Child Development and Care* 178: 15–39.

Custodero, L., Cali, C., and Diaz-Donoso, A. (2016). Music as transitional object and practice: children's spontaneous musical behaviors in the subway. *Research Studies in Music Education* 38(1): 55–74.

Davidson, L. (1985). Tonal structures of children's early songs. *Music Perception* 2(3): 361–374.

Davidson, L. (1994). Songsinging by young and old: a developmental approach to music. In: R. Aiello with J. Sloboda (eds), *Musical Perceptions*, pp. 99–130. Oxford: Oxford University Press.

DeNora, T. (2000). *Music and Everyday Life*. Cambridge: Cambridge University Press.

DeNora, T. (2011). *Music-in-Action: Selected Essays in Sonic Ecology*. Farnham: Ashgate.

Deutsch, D. (2013). *The Psychology of Music*, 3rd edn. San Diego: Academic Press.

de Vries, P. (2007). The use of music CDs and DVDs in the home with the under-fives: what the parents say. *Australian Journal of Early Childhood* 32(4): 18–21.

Dissanayake, E. (2000). *Art and Intimacy: How the Arts Began*. Washington, Seattle: University of Washington Press.

Dissanayake, E. (2006). Ritual and ritualization: musical means of conveying and shaping emotions in animals and humans. In: S. Brown and U. Voglsten (eds), *Music and Manipulation: On the Social Uses and Social Control of Minds*, pp. 31–56. New York: Berghahn Books.

Dissanayake, E. (2009). Root, leaf, blossom, or bole: concerning the origin and adaptive function of music. In: S. Malloch and C. Trevarthen (eds), *Communicative Musicality: Exploring the Basis of Human Companionship*, pp. 17–30. Oxford: Oxford University Press.

Dissanayake, E. (2012). The earliest narratives were musical. *Research in Music Education* 34(1): 3–14.

Dore, J. (1989). Monologue as reinvoicement of dialogue. In: K. Nelson (ed.), *Narratives from the Crib*, pp. 231–260. Cambridge, MA: Harvard University Press.

Dowling, W.J. (1984a). Development of musical schemata in children's spontaneous singing. In: W.R. Crozier and A.J. Chapman (eds), *Cognitive Processes in the Perception of Art*, pp. 145–163. Amsterdam: North-Holland.

Dowling, W.J. (1984b). Tonal structure and children's early learning of music. In: J. Sloboda (ed.), *Generative Processes in Music*, pp. 113–128. Oxford: Clarendon Press.

Dowling, W.J. and Harwood, D.L. (1986). *Music Cognition*. San Diego: Academic Press.

Dowling, W.J. (1999). The development of music perception and cognition. In: N.D. Deutsch (ed.), *The Psychology of Music*, 2nd edn, pp. 603–625. London: Academic Press.

Fernald, A. (1992). Human maternal vocalization to infants as biologically relevant signals: an evolutionary perspective. In: J.H. Barkow, L. Cosmides, and J. Tooby (eds), *The Adapted Mind: Evolutionary Psychology and the Generation of Culture*, pp. 391–428. New York: Oxford University Press.

Hallam, S., Cross, I., and Thaut, M. (2008). *The Oxford Handbook of Music Psychology*. Oxford: Oxford University Press.

Hargreaves, D. (1986). *The Developmental Psychology of Music*. Oxford: Oxford University Press.

Huron, D. (2003). Is music an evolutionary adaptation? In I. Peretz and R. Zatorre (eds), *The Cognitive Neuroscience of Music*, pp. 57–77. Oxford: Oxford University Press.

Lecanuet, J.-P. (1996). Prenatal auditory experience. In: I. Deliège and J.A. Sloboda (eds), *Musical Beginnings*, pp. 3–34. Oxford: Oxford University Press.

Malloch, S. (1999/2000). Mothers and infants and communicative musicality. *Musicae Scientiae*, Special Issue, 13–18.

Malloch, S. and Trevarthen, C. (2009a). *Communicative Musicality: Exploring the Basis of Human Companionship*. Oxford: Oxford University Press.

Malloch, S. and Trevarthen, C. (2009b). Musicality: communicating the vitality and interests of life. In: S. Malloch and C. Trevarthen (eds), *Communicative Musicality: Exploring the Basis of Human Companionship*, pp. 1–11. Oxford: Oxford University Press.

Mang, E. (2001). Intermediate vocalisations: an investigation of the boundaries between speech and song in young children's vocalisations. *Bulletin of the Council for Research in Music Education* 147: 116–121.

Mang, E. (2002). An investigation of vocal pitch behaviors of Hong Kong children. *Bulletin of the Council for Research in Music Education* 153/154: 128–134.

Mang, E. (2006). The effects of age, gender, and language on children's singing competency. *British Journal of Music Education* 23: 161–174.

Marsh, K. (2008). *The Musical Playground: Global Tradition and Change in Children's Songs and Games*. Oxford: Oxford University Press.

McDermott, J.H. (2009). What can experiments reveal about the origins of music? *Current Directions in Psychological Science* 18: 164–168.

Mithen, S. (2005). *The Singing Neanderthals: The Origins of Music, Language, Mind and Body*. Orion: London.

Mithen, S. (2009). The music instinct: the evolutionary basis of musicality. *The Neurosciences and Music 111—Disorders and Plasticity: Annals of the New York Academy of Sciences* 1169: 3–12.

Moog, H. (1976). *The Musical Experience of the Pre-school Child*, trans. C. Clarke. London: Schott.

Nakata, T. and Trehub, S. (2004). Infants' responsiveness to maternal speech and singing. *Infant Behavior and Development* 27(4): 455–464.

Nelson, K. (ed.) (1989). *Narratives from the Crib*. Cambridge, MA: Harvard University Press.

OECD (2014a). *Education at a Glance (EAG) Interim Report*, https://www.oecd.org/edu/Education-at-a-Glance-2014.pdf, accessed October 14, 2017.

OECD (2014b). *OECD Family Database*. www.oecd.org/social/family/database, accessed October 17, 2015.

O'Neil, C.T., Trainor, L.J., and Trehub, S.E. (2001). Infants' responsiveness to fathers' singing. *Music Perception* 18(4): 409–425.

Papoušek, H. (1996). Musicality in infancy research: biological and cultural origins of early musicality. In: I. Deliège and J. Sloboda (eds), *Musical Beginnings: Origins and Development of Musical Competence*, pp. 37–55. Oxford: Oxford University Press.

Papoušek, M. (1996). Intuitive parenting: a hidden source of musical stimulation in infancy. In I. Deliège and J. Sloboda (eds), *Musical Beginnings*, pp. 88–112. Oxford: Oxford University Press.

Rogoff, B. (2003). *The Cultural Nature of Human Development*. Oxford: Oxford University Press.

Suthers, L. (2004). Music experience for toddlers in day-care centers. *Australian Journal of Early Childhood* 29(4): 45–49.

Suthers, L. (2007). Early childhood music education in Australia: a snapshot. *Arts Education Policy Review* 109(3): 55–61.

Tafuri, J. (2008). *Infant Musicality: New Research for Educators and Parents*. Farnham: Ashgate.

Trehub, S., Schellenberg, G.E., and Hill, D.S. (1997). The origins of music perception and cognition: A developmental perspective. In: I. Deliège and J. Sloboda (eds), *Perception and Cognition of Music*, pp. 103–128. Hove: Taylor and Francis.

Trehub, S.E. (2003). The developmental origins of musicality. *Nature Neuroscience* 6: 669–673.

Trehub, S.E. (2009). Music lessons from infants. In: S. Hallam, I. Cross, and M. Thaut (eds), *The Oxford Handbook of Music Psychology*, pp. 229–234. Oxford: Oxford University Press.

Trevarthen, C. (2002). Origins of musical identity: evidence from infancy for musical social awareness, pp. 21–38. In R.A.R. MacDonald, D.J. Hargreaves, and D. Miell (eds), *Musical Identities*. Oxford: Oxford University Press.

Trevarthen, C. (2010). What is it like to be a person who knows nothing? Defining the active intersubjective mind of a newborn human being. *Infant and Child Development* 20(1): 119–135.

Trevarthen, C. and Malloch, S. (2000). The dance of well-being: defining the musical therapeutic effect. *Nordic Journal of Music Therapy* 9(2): 3–17.

Vygotsky, L.S. (1986). *Thought and Language*. Cambridge, MA: MIT Press.

Williams, K.E., Barrett, M.S., Welch, G.F., Abad, V., & Broughton, M. (2015). Associations between early shared music activities in the home and later child outcomes: Findings from the Longitudinal study of Australian children. *Early Childhood Research Quarterly* 31: 113–124.

CHAPTER 24

CHILDREN SINGING

Nurture, Creativity, and Culture. A Study
of Children's Music-Making in London, UK,
and in West Bengal, India

VALENTINE HARDING

INTRODUCTION

OVER a period of seven years, since I first started running group music sessions for children aged under five years in London, I have observed children's enjoyment, spontaneity, a natural sense of rhythm, and the desire to dance, from infancy upwards. Equally, I have watched the same responses to these music sessions from their parents, many of whom may not previously have spent much time singing, dancing, or playing a drum with their child. When parent and child participate and enjoy themselves together then that child's ability to learn is greatly enhanced. Over a similar period of time I have also been working with rural folk musicians in West Bengal, India. I have observed their children learning, also spontaneously and with enjoyment. These children were learning orally and informally from their parents and other adult musicians around them.

In order to study these processes in more depth, and in order to focus particularly on the role which culture plays in learning, I set up a ten-week project at a SureStart Children's Centre[1] in inner-city South London (where I work) which featured children's songs from the various cultures representative of the local community. This was followed by a six-week field trip to the rural town of Bolpur in West Bengal, India, to observe children learning music and singing in folk traditions and local schools. This chapter is an account of this research, which was undertaken from September 2012 to April 2013 in the UK and in India, with the support of SEMPRE (Society for Education, Music and Psychology Research).

---

[1] The SureStart program includes family welfare, health, and preschool education. Although targeting disadvantaged families, such children's centers are open to all families with zero to five-year-old children in the UK. SureStart is a nationwide program throughout the UK; it was initiated in 1998 under central government administration and is now controlled by Local Authorities (local government).

Both communities in this study experience economic and social disadvantage within the context of the countries in which they are located. However, children attending the SureStart Children's Centre, and school children and individuals observed in India, are still in the category of those who access schools and services. Children observed in India were all from rural communities, and all the schools I visited except one, had an intake of children from lower socio-economic backgrounds. In India today, 4 percent of children never start school, 58 percent do not finish primary school, and 90 percent do not complete a full education and do not go to college.[2] Nevertheless, children from all the schools that I visited could potentially rise above the 90 percent. In India, rural musicians acquire their skills outside of school. Learning takes place with parents at home and in the local community.

A large part of this research demonstrates how music and socio-economic status are deeply entwined, both from the point of view of how the process of musical enculturation takes place and also of how music itself emerges from varying socio-economic backgrounds. Fieldwork in India also demonstrates changing patterns due to modernization, the growth of technology, electronic instruments, and media intervention (see "Vocal Music and Pedagogy of China, India and Africa," Yang Yang et al., in this volume).

The choice of locations for this research was based on my current place of employment at a SureStart Children's Centre in South London and my ethnomusicological field of study with *Baul*[3] musicians in West Bengal. My background is multi-disciplinary and includes work in the field of mental health, counseling, and psychotherapy, as well as ethnomusicology. I have worked at this SureStart Children's Centre for nine years as a Group Facilitator specializing in parenting skills groups and as a Music Leader for Under-Fives, and I have made frequent fieldwork trips to West Bengal since 2008, this area being known to me since 1971 when I worked on a medical team in the Bangladesh Refugee Camps.

THEORETICAL FRAMEWORK

My approach in early years' music is that I view music-making as an essential parenting skill, one which gives children access to music-making of some sort, with parents themselves participating in music-making with their child. I emphasize the role of music in the process of attachment and bonding between parent and child. This means parents playing alongside, but not controlling, their children's musical creations. Music, including voice, rhythm, and movement, is a part of a child's natural psychology and self-discovery from birth. "Western" psychoanalytic theory promotes the idea of the "self" as the core of identity, the "self" being the personality with its accompanying make-up of individual and cultural influences, something the individual can get to "know" and learn to distinguish between the "true" and the "false." Psychoanalyst D.W. Winnicott noted that "it is only in being creative that the individual discovers the self" (Winnicott 1971, p. 63). He was referring here to the creativity that children use when they play. These concepts of "self" and "identity" may be viewed differently in different cultures, although not diametrically

---

[2] Information from Teach for India (<www.teachforindia.org>, November 2013).

[3] Traditional wandering musicians. See further details in the section on West Bengal.

opposed. Psychoanalyst Sudhir Kakar, for instance, notes that in the Indian concept of child-utopia children are valued as autonomous and self-directed beings, and value is placed on "precisely those attributes of the child which have not been 'socialised'" (Kakar 1981, p. 210). This has a parallel with the concept of children as members of their own culture (Blacking 1973; Campbell 2010; Nettl 1983/2005), a concept which embraces the child's inner world and does not view children solely, in the case of music, as "bearers of sophisticated traditions in the early stages of musical enculturation" (Campbell 2010, p. 102). Nurturing this period of creative play in a child's life is crucial to a child's development and future sense of identity and self-worth. However, creativity does not take place in isolation, but within a secure relationship between parent or carer and child.

In the context of the formation of children's musical cultural identities, Lucy Green in *Learning, Teaching and Musical Identity: Voices across Cultures* (2011) presents a possible hypothesis that it is harder to locate national and local musical identities in "central" (previously colonizing) countries, while local and national musics of "peripheral" (previously colonized) countries are relatively straightforward as markers of identity (Green 2011, p. 16). Over one hundred years ago in Bengal, Rabindranath Tagore[4] embraced *Baul* music and philosophy as a means to re-embrace the culture of that region in the struggle against colonialism. Tagore, and other thinkers of the Bengali Renaissance,[5] also worked with notions of cultural exchange and dialogue between India and the West. Although today national and regional identity in West Bengal is clearly seen in the teaching and learning of Tagore's music and local folk music, what is less straightforward as a marker of identity is the style of delivery and interpretation of this local music, the use of Western instruments, the lack of contextual information and practice, alongside middle-class reinterpretations and media influences. Furthermore, areas such as West Bengal are today ethnically and culturally diverse. In 2007–2008, for example, it was estimated that in Kolkata only 37 percent of the city's inhabitants spoke Bengali (Chaudhuri 2013, p. 92).

The Bengali economist and Nobel Laureate, Amartya Sen, notes that: "the confining of culture into stark and separated boxes of civilisations or of religious identities takes too narrow a view of cultural attributes" (Sen 2006, p. 103), "ignoring the other identities that people have and value, involving class, gender, profession, language, science, morals, politics" (Sen 2006, p. xvi). Sen draws attention to the appalling outcomes of presuming that people can be uniquely categorized on the basis of religion and culture and the conflicts which arise from single predominant identities that tend to drown all other affiliations (Sen 2006). Psychological historian Ashis Nandy also comments on the dialogue which arises through an exploration of cultures other than one's own and describes how this is a recognition of the self in others and a recognition of the diversity of cultural attributes which exists both within the individual and their culture of origin, particularly in the post-colonial context (Jhaveri 2013, p. 24). My emphasis is, therefore, to seek out those multiple affiliations that are present in the dialogue and exchange that take place between cultures, both in the UK and in India.

---

[4] Rabindranath Tagore (1861–1941), Bengali poet, writer, philosopher, dramatist, social reformer, artist and composer, and founder of Santiniketan School and Visva Bharati University in West Bengal.

[5] Bengali thinkers of the nineteenth century who wrote on issues of polity, morality, history, economy, and culture. They assimilated Western ideas in order to define new social horizons in India (Sengupta and Bandyopadhyay 1998).

John Blacking discusses the importance of understanding what happens to human beings when they make music, describing music as a "synthesis of cognitive processes which are present in culture and in the human body" (Blacking 1973, p. 89). This integration of the physical, emotional, and cultural is central to my understanding of the process of children's musical enculturation.

THE MUSIC ROUND THE WORLD PROJECT, LONDON, UK

The ten-week project at the SureStart Children's Centre in London was known as the "Music Round the World Project." This effort focused on children's songs from the various cultures representative of the local community. A total of twenty families attended the sessions across the ten weeks, with the numbers of families per week ranging from five to ten. Participants' countries or continents of origin included Nigeria, Algeria, Africa, Poland, South America, Great Britain, the Caribbean, Egypt, Bangladesh, Kazakhstan, Bulgaria, Russia, and Eritrea. All adult participants were female; there were no fathers or male carers. The numbers of children per family ranged from one to four. There were five core participants who attended every week, who included two Polish, one Kazakhstani, one French Algerian, and one Venezuelan. Others who attended several sessions included Russian and Bulgarian parents; thus, the group ended up with a strong Eastern European focus.

The group was co-facilitated by myself and an ethnomusicologist (Emma Brinkhurst), crèche practitioner (Sue Simmonds), and Centre Outreach Worker (Clarice Boothe). Each session included singing and arts and crafts. We asked parents to bring songs from their cultural backgrounds to the group, we used songs we already knew from various cultures, and we used educational books featuring songs from various cultures. We translated a greeting song, "Bonjour Mes Amis," into the various first languages of participants, which included French, Spanish, Polish, Russian, Eritrean, Ethiopian, Arabic, and Bengali. The arts and crafts section included making song books, musical instruments such as shakers and drums, and unrestricted drawing and painting. We had a bag of instruments, which included percussion instruments from the UK, Ghana, India, and Mexico. In addition, we used two larger drums from India and Nepal. Songs were also accompanied by myself on guitar and Emma on flute. We categorized our songs as follows: greeting songs, songs which tell a story, action and instruction songs, sounds (without words), and songs of life affirmation, and we made a CD at the end of the ten weeks for the parents and children to keep and for use by staff at the Children's Centre.

Participants welcomed the opportunity to bring children's songs from their cultures; however, very few were able to identify any. One song chosen by parents was "Frère Jacques." "Frère Jacques" was known to most participants who had sung this song in their local language at schools in countries as far apart as Poland and Africa. The Eritrean and Ethiopian versions were brought to the group by a participant who was a grandmother, the translations being biblical references about brothers Isaac and Jacob. "Frère Jacques" in Spanish was not related to the original words of this song, but was about an owl "La lechuza." The only truly original song identified by parents was a Russian song. This song was first brought in by a Polish parent who remembered it as a lullaby, although she had forgotten some of the words. However, the following week, the parent from Kazakhstan (who had not been at the group the previous week) knew this song well and told us it was a Communist Party children's song from the 1940s/1950s, and she had learned it in a militaristic style. All the Eastern European parents then said they had learnt this song at school.[6]

Pust' vsegda budjet sonlce	There will always be sunshine
Pust' vsegda budjet nebo	There will always be sky
Pust' vsegda budjet Mama	There will always be Mama
Pust' vsegda budu Ja!	There will always be Me!

The composition of this verse has been attributed to Kostya Barannikov, who may have written it in 1928 at the age of four years. The popular Russian children's author and poet Kornei Chukovsky (1882–1969), who collected children's poetry, and was also an exponent of the child's inner creative world (Morton 1971, p. xv), incorporated the boy's verse into a chapter about children composing their own verse in his book *From Two to Five*, published in 1933. The boy wrote this verse just after learning the meaning of the word "always" ("*vsegda*"), and Chukovsky praises this verse as "splendid," noting that "repetitiveness is also used [by children] to express strong emotion" (Morton 1971, p. 79). The boy and his verse were depicted in a poster in 1961 by Nikolai Charukhim, and this poster inspired another writer, Lev Oshanin, who wrote the extended version of the song, using the verse above as the chorus, which was then set to music by the composer Arkady Ostrovsky. The song was written as a children's song for peace, and subsequently became very popular.[7]

Our reaction to this song was to enjoy its child-centered and reassuring message and we saw it as something of a SureStart anthem. It stood out from traditional songs and nursery rhymes that are usually more to do with telling a story or giving instructions. There are not many nursery rhymes that carry such life-affirming messages, expressing positive secure attachments between mother and child.

Our participants' knowledge of nursery rhymes reflected a predominance of English nursery rhymes, not only, as one might expect, in use in the UK today, but also in use in other countries, particularly previously colonized countries. Nursery rhymes are an important aspect of national musical and cultural identity in many countries and they demonstrate the importance that societies attach to initiating their children at an early age into music that symbolizes and promotes cultural and national identity. Their meanings and origins also demonstrate the relationship between music and political and economic factors. Such songs carry messages of past history; they teach children the roots of the music that they will hear and/or learn in the future; and most people on a regular basis at some time in their lives are likely to have sung them, or still do sing them, or listen to them on recordings. Central countries have used them throughout colonial education systems

[6] The song reproduced here and the translation are as given by parents in the group.
[7] Information from Katya Rogatchevskaia, Lead Curator, Russian Studies, British Library, August 2014.

around the world,[8] and the former Soviet Union used songs to promote ideology and cohesion in satellite countries, as was demonstrated in the Russian song mentioned above.

In *The Oxford Handbook of Children's Musical Cultures* (2013), Patricia Campbell observes how

> Music may be used as an element of control, as children are recipients of the embedded morality of songs that were intentionally selected by parents, teachers, and caregivers to distance them from matters they perceive to be harmful to their ethical development.
>
> (Campbell and Wiggins 2013, p. 19)

Attention to ethical issues was prominent in the 1980s in the UK as a result of equal opportunities policy, and much attention was paid to the politics of children's music and the political correctness of nursery rhymes. I worked in children's centers during that time and "Baa baa black sheep" was, famously, one song that we did not sing because of the perceived racist connotations associated with "black sheep." Various unsubstantiated accounts of the origin of this rhyme include that it is a complaint against the amount of wool that went to the king ("The Master") and the over-rich nobility ("The Dame") (Baring-Gould and Baring-Gould 1967, p. 33),[9] and also the division of bags is said to refer to the export tax on wool imposed in 1275 (Opie and Opie 1997, p. 101). I have never favored altering rhymes to make them acceptable (e.g. the inclusion of white sheep and girls as well as boys), and in this case such alteration would completely obliterate the history of this song and I would rather not sing the song at all. Even though today I now know that this song is a protest against the accumulation of wealth by the rich, I still feel reluctant to sing "Baa baa black sheep." However, many parents I meet today enjoy this song. These parents may have been small children themselves living in inner-city areas in the 1980s, but the apparent ban on "Baa baa black sheep" is not something they remember. When I ask groups of parents today which song they would like to sing, someone invariably asks for "Baa baa black sheep," and it is often black and minority ethnic parents who request this. However, these requests do not mean there are no underlying feelings about this and other English songs. Parents may want their children to learn songs that they will be singing at school and in groups with other children, and they are also keen to demonstrate their efforts to integrate into life in the UK. If schools and early years groups had a greater repertoire of songs from other cultures, then these could become equally popular requests. Another interesting feature of "Baa baa black sheep" is that it has close similarities in its melody with "Twinkle twinkle little star," another universally popular children's song. Both of these nursery rhymes are based on the French folk tune "Ah! vous dirai-je maman," which has also been used by various composers including Mozart piano variations, J.C.F. Bach variations in G major, Joseph Haydn in the Andante of his 94th symphony, and Saint-Saëns in *Carnival of the Animals*. "Twinkle twinkle little star" was written as a rhyme in 1806 by Jane Taylor, and first published as a song in New York in 1881 (Fuld 1966, p. 483). Mozart wrote his piano variations in 1778, more than a hundred years before "Twinkle twinkle

---

[8] During my fieldwork, I have observed the extent to which English nursery rhymes are widely known and sung by people from previously colonized countries. They are well known and sung in schools and communities in India today.

[9] W.S. Baring-Gould and C. Baring-Gould gathered their information for *The Annotated Mother Goose* (1962/1967) from *The Real Personages of Mother Goose* by Katherine Elwes Thomas (1930).

little star" was published using the same tune (Fuld 1966, p. 484). "Baa baa black sheep" illustrates not only how choices may be made by teachers and institutions working in the apparent national interest, but also the functions of a tune.

I do not know the full extent to which nursery rhymes are used in the home, but in children's centers and nurseries many traditional rhymes are sung along with newer more recent songs, and there are also many CDs of nursery rhymes which are played in crèches and nurseries. Knowledge of nursery rhymes enhances children's phonological sensitivity, which in turn helps them to learn to read (Bryant et al. 1989). Whether or not parents, staff, and children know or understand the origins of English nursery rhymes, when we sing them we are still providing a message concerning national allegiance to children. We feed our children, consciously or unconsciously, with a great deal of English history when we teach or sing traditional English nursery rhymes. Children are being lulled to sleep on the history of the wool trade, the madness of King George, the sixteenth-century spice race which led into colonialism, the stupidity of the Grand Old Duke of York, London's stock exchange, the great fire of London, the plague, and countless other historical details about the UK. Because we do not realize half the time what we are singing about, we instead instill an abstract sense of "Britishness" into children through nursery rhymes. However, to delve more deeply into the history of some nursery rhymes reveals other factors such as anger and insurrection against the injustices perpetrated by those who held power.

Thomas, in *The Real Personages of Mother Goose* (1930), writes in a florid and poetic style that:

> these political satires, written with a merciless keen-ness of scintillating thrust and blood-letting, in the directness of their lunge at the heart of people and events, embody through many notable reigns the vices and foibles of humanity upon the throne and about the court of England.
>
> (Baring-Gould and Baring-Gould 1967, p. 12)

The impact of colonial education systems is a fact that is not ignored by some communities. At the SureStart Children's Centre in London where I work, parents of Caribbean origin are underrepresented at regular music sessions. A possible reason for staying away from these sessions is perhaps a distrust of English nursery rhymes and their meanings and usage as an element of control. Under colonialism, the use of English nursery rhymes in colonized countries was probably seen by many colonial teachers as a means to distance children from what were perceived as "harmful" local beliefs and customs, bringing children into the sphere of "civilized" Western culture. My experience in India was also to investigate the continued use of English nursery rhymes in schools today, and the prestige attached to the knowledge and use of English nursery rhymes. Clarice Boothe, outreach worker at the Children's Centre, herself of Jamaican origin, feels that Caribbean parents' views on attending music sessions need further research; this will certainly be a focus of my continued investigations in the future. These feelings are reflected in a song by Jamaican reggae artist Tarrus Riley (b. 1979) who has certainly picked up the essence of nursery rhymes in this song, "Parables":

> Read between the lines: Mister Babylon yeaaa has got the people's eyes blind folded
> Lost in a nursery rhymes culture . . .
> It looks like the three blind mice
> Dem are the big guys put the price on the rice . . .

When the dish ran away with the spoon many were left hungry . . .
You got to check those parables . . .read between the lines
Now Jack and Jill went up the hill
Robbed people against them will . . .

The parents from the "Music Round the World" project sessions emphasized that they wanted their children to learn from all cultures and they did not want their children's knowledge of music to be bound to any one culture. It is also important to stress that this project was equally about embracing local white British culture—we could all be asking the question "Who are this Jack and Jill?".[10] Arguably, white British communities are equally alienated from the original folk music of this country and its working-class origins, and, as expressed by the psychological historian Ashis Nandy (1983, p. 2), the process of colonialism has "altered cultural priorities on both sides," and therefore needs to be re-balanced on both sides.

In a survey on the current teaching practice of Fujian-Taiwan Nursery Rhymes in China, Shi Nengjing (2009) draws attention to the issues of safeguarding the intangible cultural heritage of traditional nursery rhymes, referring to them as the "united wisdom of all people" and their role of "transmitting human civilisation" (Nengjing 2009, ch. 3.5). Nengjing reflects on how this cultural heritage may be kept alive through government support, education programs, TV and media, entertainment programs, and, in the case of this region of China, maintenance of the local dialect in which these traditional songs are sung. These Fujian Nursery Rhymes, in common with many nursery rhymes, also carry political, social and moral messages: for example, consider a rhyme named "Eight honours and eight shames" (chapter 3.1). Nengjing describes this rhyme as "closely connected with the life in modern society," and the lyrics describe commitment to socialist principles.

If we want children to benefit from nursery rhymes linguistically and musically, then a positive way forward is to afford them a high status, as in this example from China, and celebrate them in a manner that gives them equal status with adult songs, recognizing their historic and cultural value. Rather than viewing nursery rhymes as medicine of which all good children should receive a dose, or conversely as bad medicine which is out of date, we need to view them as creative art. We need to free ourselves, as both Campbell and Kakar have suggested, of the socialization[11] model, and this theme is discussed further in the second half of this chapter. Perhaps a National Nursery Rhyme Week in the UK, celebrating nursery rhymes of all shapes and sizes and from all cultures, might help promote such an approach.

At the end of the "Music Round the World" project, participants expressed their enjoyment in sharing different songs and languages and meeting parents from differing cultural backgrounds. They commented that they felt valued and that the sessions gave them confidence. They saw music as an important part of their child's education and thought it helped emotional development and helped to nurture language development. Parents also

[10] Baring-Gould and Baring-Gould (1967, p. 60) refer to Jack and Jill as representations of Cardinal Wolsey and Bishop Tarbes who traveled to France together to arrange the marriage of Mary Tudor to the French Monarch. The "pail of water" is said to refer to the "holy water" of the Pope. Baring-Gould and Baring-Gould (1967, p. 15) also quote a source that refers to this song as originating from Iceland.

[11] Campbell (2010) refers to the socialization model which sees children as "unrealised adults" or waiting to "become something more than themselves" which is prevalent in Western thinking. Kakar (1981), quoted earlier, emphasizes the concept of "valuing those attributes of the child which have not been socialised."

commented that, when they were children, their families sang more traditional songs together, but that TV and computers have made this less frequent. Consequently, they welcomed the aims of this project group. An interest in learning more about the origins and meanings of songs and nursery rhymes from all cultures was registered as the most popular request for future workshops.

All parents reported that children sang songs from the group when back at home, as also do children from the regular music sessions at this SureStart Centre. There were some interesting choices here, which bring into question the assumptions sometimes made about children's capacity and the necessity of a graded structure. One Polish boy, whose attention during sessions often appeared to be miles away, was keen on singing "The banana boat song" at home. This was one song that the parents thought was a more adult song, and they were worried that their children were bored when we sang it. However, this boy appeared to have picked up this song easily, in spite of the fact that he was usually running around and playing during the session. He sang it at home, wanting his mother to join in. Another three-year-old bilingual Polish child liked to practice the songs sung in different languages, and had picked up the French and Spanish versions, as well as English and Polish, of "Bonjour mes amis." Our anxieties that some of the songs that we sang were not sufficiently easy for children seemed to be misplaced, and these examples demonstrate the importance of allowing children to learn and create in their own way, and not create rigid hierarchies between children's songs and adults' songs.

WEST BENGAL

In Bengal (West Bengal and Bangladesh)[12] we see another genre of enigmatic rhymes. These are the songs of the *Bauls* of Bengal with their roots in the esoteric and mystical traditions of Hinduism, Islam, and Buddhism. *Baul Gan* (song) represents a unique tradition from the Indian sub-continent and in 2008 was inscribed by UNESCO in their list of the Intangible Cultural Heritage of Humanity.

The philosophy espoused by *Bauls* includes a belief in the value of the human being over religious identity and a rejection of the caste system and scripture-based creeds. *Bauls* originate from communities of low socio-economic status. They are recruited from both Hindu and Muslim communities, rejecting divisions between these communities, and include women as equal partners. However, although *Bauls* have become the recognized exponents of this philosophy, it is not unique to them.

Rather, it stems from the *bhakti* (devotional) movements which extended across India during medieval times and which also gave rise to the musical tradition of *Kirtana*. This genre is one of the principal sources of and influences on all music in Bengal, and has a rich tradition of musical development continuing to the present day (Chakrabarty 1988, p. 12). Amongst numerous other genres of folk song in Bengal, two are commonly identified. These

---

[12] Bengal was originally one province, sharing a common language and culture. Bengal was partitioned in 1947 on independence from British rule into West Bengal and East Pakistan. East Pakistan subsequently gained independence from West Pakistan in 1971 and became the People's Republic of Bangladesh. References to "Bengal" throughout this chapter refer to both West Bengal and Bangladesh.

are *bhaoyaiya*, associated with herdsmen and ox-cart drivers, and *bhatiyali*, associated with the river and boatmen. Folk song in Bengal is characterized by its humanist orientation.

However, a definition of the term *Baul* is a complex issue. For example, the anthropologist Jeanne Openshaw concluded from her research that the term *Baul* is of little use from an analytical point of view (Openshaw 2004, p. 5). The term *Baul*, which is popularly translated as meaning "mad" (mad with divine love), in fact only came into use during the nineteenth century through gentrified images of these rural musicians (Openshaw 2004, p. 19). *Bauls* today include both initiates and non-initiates, and many folk musicians in West Bengal seem to hover somewhere between being *Bauls* and "folk" musicians. One fifty-two-year-old *Baul* musician I interviewed said "We are all individuals," and "Whether someone is a musician, a Baul, a sannyasin[13] or a government employee it makes no difference, we are all fighting, life is fighting [for survival]." He moved away in this statement from stating his identity either as a musician or a *Baul*, preferring to identify clearly with those who struggle to earn a living and survive.

Basu (1988, p. 96) claims that *Baul* songs in the late twentieth century are to a large extent the creations of urban-orientated culture, and have influenced the imagery, melody, and artistic techniques of many modern art songs of Bengal. More recently, Choudhury and Roy (2012, p. 12) have commented on how "modern *Bauls* tend to utilize both mysticism and economics for their survival in this competitive world and their commodification of the philosophy and music of the *Baul* cult is gradually engendering a novel form of *Baul* music." However, it must be said that there are still practitioners of *Baul* philosophy who are not in this category of "*modern Baul*," and they are wary of performance in present-day concert venues or on the world music stage.

Baul music enjoys something of an iconic status in West Bengal. However, the music of Rabindranath Tagore, who was inspired by *Bauls*, is renowned and acclaimed and could be described as the present-day "national" music of Bengal. "Amar sonar bangla" (My golden Bengal) is the national anthem of Bangladesh, and in 1947 "Jana gana mana adhinayak jaya he/ Bharat bhagya bidhata" (Hail to the custodian of the minds of its multitudes and of India's destiny) was adopted as India's national anthem on gaining independence from the British. Tagore's music has a special place in Bengali culture, which is not often shared outside of that culture. In 1915, he became the first person of Indian origin to be awarded the Nobel Prize for Literature for his prose poem *Gitanjali*. An appreciation of Tagore song, known as *Rabindrasangeet*, is hard to gain without an understanding of the Bengali language. Following in the traditions of *Puratan Bangla Gan* (Old Bengali song) (Banerjee 1988b, p. 113), Tagore composed his songs as songs, language, and music conceived together; they are not poems set to music, and neither can they be heard purely as music.

Tagore based some of his compositions on *Baul* melodies, using his own lyrics, and "Amar sonar bangla" (above) is one example of this. Another example is the well-known song by Tagore composed in 1905 "Jodi tore dak shune keyu na ashe taube ekla cholo re" (If no one responds to your call, then go your own way). During the struggle for independence, Gandhi was inspired by this song and it was sung at his prayer meetings (Som 2009, p. 104). Som also notes how this song is sung today outside Bengal on occasions emphasizing national identity (Som 2009). This song is an adaptation from the *Baul* song "Hari nam diye jogot mataley

---

[13] One who has renounced householder life in order to follow a spiritual path.

amar ekla Nitai" (My Nitai alone intoxicates the world with the name of Hari [Vishnu])[14]. The song addresses the spiritual relationship between Sri Chaitanya[15] (also known as *Gour*) and his chief follower *Nitai*. An interpretation given to me by a *Baul* informant also described *Gour* and *Nitai* as one; they are both aspects of *Krishna* (who is an aspect of *Vishnu*). Interpretation may vary according to differing cultural perspectives. The authorship of this song is attributed to Gagan Harakara, who worked as a postman, and may have been an associate or follower not of an authentic *Baul* but an "amateur *Baul*," i.e. a person, often of middle class origin, who aspires towards being a *Baul*, composing and performing in the style of a *Baul* (Openshaw 2004, pp. 28–29).

In West Bengal, appreciation and reverence for Tagore tends to come from those who have had the opportunity to study his literature, poetry, and music through access to higher education. *Baul* musicians, although they regard him, like others, as a national hero, know very little about his writing and poetry and music. Neither do they know very much about *Ragas* and Indian classical music. They never sing Tagore songs, but some have a repertoire of *Rabindrabaul* songs which are the specific *Baul* songs that Tagore adapted, as above.

Children's rhymes

Bengali children's rhymes are known as *chora*. They are rhythmic recitations rather than songs and are widely known and taught in schools. An example of *chora*, translated from Bengali, is as follows:

> The boy (khoka) goes to take fish from the river Kir
> The frog takes the fishing line
> The bird takes the fish
> The boy says, "Where does the bird live?"
> The boy calls the bird to come

These are traditional rhymes describing rural life and nature. Sometimes they include references to weddings or festivals, and many are lullabies. Tagore also composed *chora*.

There was, however, one well-known song that was the only children's song that both a *Baul* musician in Bolpur and a housewife in Nabadwip knew; they said that this was a standard song sung when children are going to sleep (it could also be used as a threat to quieten naughty children). This song is also featured in the Bollywood film *Devdas*. It is about the *bargi* (pronounced *borgui*) who were marauding Maratha horsemen:[16]

> Khoka ghumalo, para juralo,
> Bargi elo deshe

---

[14] Vishnu is the God of Preservation, and Krishna his earthly incarnation. Both gods may be referred to as "Hari." Krishna is usually depicted in the color blue in rural scenes where he is tending cows. He plays the flute and stands in a characteristic pose with one leg crossed over the other.

[15] A charismatic early sixteenth-century Vaishnava leader of the *bhakti* movement in Bengal, often regarded as the founder of Bengali Vaishnavism. A Vaishnava is a follower of the Hindu God Vishnu, or one of his "incarnations," especially, in the Bengali context, Krishna (Openshaw 2004, p. 255/260).

[16] The song reproduced here is as given by the two people mentioned as informants.

Bulbulite, dhan keyeche
Khajna debo kishe
Dhan phuralo, paan phuralo,
Ekhon upai ki?
Ar kota din, shobur koro
Roshun bunaichi

When the child sleeps, the neighborhod is at peace,
The "bargi" are in the land
The bulbul bird is eating all the rice,
We have to pay land tax.
We lost our rice and paan
Now what is to be done?
Be patient a little longer
We are planting garlic

In *History of the Bengali Speaking People*, Sengupta (2002, pp. 132–137) gives a description of the *bargi*. Alivardi Khan was a Mughal ruler in Bengal from 1740 to 1756 and the *bargi* were Maratha horsemen who invaded and plundered the land for ten years on the pretext of supporting opposition to Alivardi Khan's rule. The word *bargi* meant horseman, and the *bargi* were provided with horses and arms from the Maratha state, which, in league with the state of Orissa, was opposing Alivardi Khan's rule. Sengupta notes that "how dreaded the *bargi* were in popular view is evident from nursery rhymes which are still current in Bengal." The story also includes a legend that the Goddess Bhavani (Durga) appeared in a dream before the Maratha Emperor Shahu in Poona and asked him to rescue Bengali Hindus from the oppression of Alivardi. However, Sengupta notes that the raids affected Hindu and Muslim alike and were purely exploitative.

Bulbul translates as "nightingale" from the Persian *bolbol*. It is larger than a British nightingale and also has a lovely song. *Paan* is the vine leaf used to wrap *betel* nut. *Khajna* means land tax or rent. Locally, the people who sang this song to me thought the *bargi* were a pre-Mughal group and collected taxes on behalf of landowners. It seems more likely that this song is from the Mughal era rather than pre-Muhgal. However, if the *bargi* were raiders opposing the local ruler, as described by Sengupta, it seems unlikely that it was they who collected the taxes. The origins of this song, as in English nursery rhymes, would appear to be somewhat shrouded in history.

Individual learning in West Bengal

The younger generation

The four young people that I interviewed were all from villages and each was aiming for a musical career in folk music. They included a fourteen-year-old girl who was the only young person in her village learning music, a talented ten-year-old already holding a business card of her own and giving performances, a seventeen-year-old who was singing in a band and rapidly becoming the main wage earner for her family, and also the only young person in her village learning music, and a twenty-one-year-old younger-generation *Baul* musician.

Arati (age fourteen), Runa (age ten), and Durga (age seventeen) all learned music at home with their fathers, with some support from outside. Durga had taken some classical lessons and exams. Their repertoire included *Baul* and folk songs. Arati learned mainly *Baul* songs, since her father is a *Baul* musician, and the song referred to earlier, "Hare nam diye jogot mataley amar ekla nitai," is one which she was learning. Arati, in fact, had originally started learning *Rabindrasangeet*, but realized that a girl from her background would be unlikely to succeed in this genre, which tends to be the preserve of the middle classes. Arati said her favorite song was an invocation to the *guru* that she sang at the start of each lesson.

Natalie Sarrazin, in her account of children learning music in North India, suggests that currently pursuing the arts as a realistic livelihood is a fantasy for most young people. However, this could become more of a reality with advances in technology and the media, with their "democratising aspects" (2013, p. 264). To what extent young people like Arati, Runa, and Durga will be able to access such democratizing aspects is hard to assess. Advances in technology and the media also include changes in the use of instruments and style of musical performance, including the voice, and these often result in changes from traditional culture. An elderly *Baul* once remarked to me that no voice had remained the same since the advent of electricity, since ceiling fans "disturb the vocal cords" (vocal folds).

Arati, Runa, and Durga all appeared to be learning solely vocal and not instrumental skills, which possibly reflects the fact that, in the future, they would play with electronic musical accompaniment rather than folk instruments, and—as female performers—they would be seen to have a greater appeal as vocalists rather than instrumentalists. Each was being prepared for life as a performing musician with earning potential.

Twenty-one-year-old Lakhon, although from a family of *Bauls*, did not start learning music until the age of eighteen. After leaving school, at which he gained good exam passes, he decided to follow in the *Baul* traditions of his family. However, he started to learn *tabla*, which is not a traditional *Baul* instrument, and reflects the necessity that the family felt for him to learn an instrument that would help him access employment, since *tabla* is increasingly used by *Baul* musicians in the process of modernization. Lakhon's grandmother had embarked on extra rounds of singing for alms (*Madhukuri*)[17] in order to finance his lessons. At the age of twenty-one, Lakhon has not been able to develop his voice. However, his percussion skills, on *khol* and *kartal*,[18] are very good. He works hard at home, on daily errands, shopping, cleaning, and tending the land. Consequently, the hours spent in *tabla* practice are minimal.

The older generation

Fifty-two-year-old *Baul* musician Gopal Das reported that he was not very happy with the way that these young people were learning music, and did not see their learning as following in the true traditions of *Baul*, or other folk music in West Bengal. Safeguarding musical cultural heritage was a priority for him and he would prefer to see young people not only learning traditional instruments as well as song, but also following spiritual traditions. However, not all *Bauls* would share this opinion. Choudhury and Roy (2012, p. 16) comment

[17] *Madhukuri* translates as "honey-gathering" referring to the gathering of spiritual blessings through song, both the mendicant and the recipient gaining blessings through this process.
[18] *Khol*—traditional ceramic drum played by *Bauls; Kartal*—traditional small cymbals.

that most *Bauls* do not disapprove of the emerging style of *Baul* singing introduced by non-initiated musicians.

Although born into a family of several generations of *Baul* musicians, Gopal was self-taught until the age of eleven, when his father started teaching him. Before the age of eleven he lived with his grandmother. He had very little formal schooling. He was brought up in the tradition of the practice of *Madhukuri*, or singing for alms, which is central to *Baul* traditions, and sometimes popularly seen as their territory alone.[19] Gopal no longer sings for alms on a regular basis, but only on specific occasions such as at *Janmasthami* (Krishna's birthday) or occasionally when visiting particularly holy places, in which cases he sees *Madhukuri* essentially as a spiritual practice and not as a means of livelihood.

As a child, Gopal's main experience of music was *Kirtan*.[20] Then at the age of six he taught himself to sing two songs through listening to early recordings of the famous *Baul* singer Purno Das Baul, probably the only recorded *Baul* artist at this time. The fact that Gopal first learned from recorded material is very important to note. Purno Das particularly refined his voice for recording purposes and was the first *Baul* to tour abroad and gain an international reputation. Gopal was therefore learning, back in the 1960s, under the influence of media and technological advances. At first he performed on the street and on local buses, earning himself a few *pisa*, which he took home to his grandmother, and then, at the age of eleven, his father started to teach him.

Five schools

The five schools that I visited included two local state primary schools, one in Bolpur and one in Santiniketan.[21] The school in Santiniketan was in a Santal[22] village. The third school was a fee-paying nursery school in Santiniketan and attached to Tagore's university. This school was also important because the music and songs of Rabindranath Tagore, as noted previously, are seen by many as the "national" music of Bengal and it was the only music consistently taught in all five schools. The fourth was a traditional Hindu school for poor children. The fifth was a school in Kolkata for children from North-East India displaced through local conflict.

Boner Pukur (meaning forest pond) is a state school in a Santal village with roughly fifty pupils housed in one purpose-built schoolroom with two teachers. Singing, dancing, and

---

[19] In Mimlu Sen's book *The Honey Gatherers* (2009) *Bauls* are portrayed as "wild and free, they raised their clamour in the mansions of the rich, and roared in gaiety in the courtyards of the poor. They traveled by foot to fairs and festivals. They sang in buses and trains. Their melodies were poignant, their texts enigmatic. Garbed in long, flowing, multi-coloured robes, often living in pairs, they played their frenetic rhythms on strange, handmade instruments made of wood and clay, miming the contradictory moods of nature and of passion."

[20] A form of chanting in Bhakti devotional tradition. Kirtan also includes the telling of stories about Krishna along with exposition of the nature of Krishna and devotional living. Kirtan may be performed by individuals or groups and includes theatrical productions reenacting the life of Krishna.

[21] Santiniketan is an area adjacent to the town of Bolpur where Rabindranath Tagore lived and founded his school and Visva Bharati University. The area is now an extension of Bolpur town.

[22] The *Santals* are an indigenous *adivasi* group with their own language, religion, and culture. They are protected by law. Locally in the Bolpur district Santals are respected and co-exist peacefully with their Bengali neighbors.

playtime take place in an open space next to the forest outside the school building. Children learn traditional Bengali songs, *Rabindrasangeet* and *chora*, Santali songs, and English nursery rhymes. The other state primary school, Dharmarajtola School, is situated in Suripara, the poorer area of Bolpur town, and has two hundred children, two rooms, and five teachers (all female). There are no grounds around this school and assembly and break times are held in the small side road outside the front door with children, bicycles, motorbikes, rickshaws, cows, and hens weaving their way around each other. This school also taught Bengali songs, *Rabindrasangeet* and *chora*, and English nursery rhymes.

All my school visits in India necessitated my singing English nursery rhymes. It was a fate from which I could not escape. The teachers at Boner Pukur wanted me to teach them new English nursery rhymes. Equally, I was requested to sing *Rabindrasangeet* and *Baul* songs and I do not think I would have got much response from anyone during this research if I could not have produced a song myself. However, singing "Row the boat" at Boner Pukur School made me feel the close similarity between *Bengali Chora* and English nursery rhymes. "Row the boat" includes the philosophical touch of "life is but a dream," and all the animals in the song (adapted for children), i.e. crocodiles, lions, polar bears, and octopuses, are not indigenous to the UK. Everyone loved this song, and children responded just like children anywhere, and appreciated being given permission to scream at the crocodile ("If you see a crocodile, don't forget to scream!")

At Dharmarajtola, the teachers sang a version of "Knick knack paddywack," which had morphed into a Bengali style song. The tune was similar, but used a smaller range of notes than the version that I am familiar with and the rhythms were altered. The linguistics researcher Suresh Canagarajah refers to such linguistic adaptation as "the vibrant afterlife of English." He notes that "it is now well noted in sociolinguistic literature that mixing of codes can enable a speech community to reconcile the psychological and socio-cultural tensions it faces between two conflicting languages, and thus maintain both codes" (Canagarajah 1999, p. 75), and that "these are healthy developments that counteract the colonial and alien associations English holds in many periphery communities" (Canagarajah 1999, p. 142). This was reflected in this version of "Knick knack paddywack" sung at Dharmarajtola School, and in both this school and Boner Pukur School there were other examples of English nursery rhyme adaptation.

The Hindu ashram school, *Bharat Sevashram Sangha*, is situated in another Santal village a mile or so from the edge of Bolpur town. There are few cars or motorbikes in and around this peaceful village. The school stands in extensive grounds where crops are also grown and a herd of cows is maintained. This primary school for boys, founded eleven years ago, houses two hundred boarders from "poor" families up to the age of eleven. These may be children from different ethnic and religious groups; however, the religion practiced in the school is Hinduism. The school diet is vegetarian, although meat may be eaten off the premises. The *Sangha*'s herd of cows are treated like royalty and their sheds equipped with ceiling fans and mosquito netting over the windows. Every evening the school celebrates *Aarti* (a ceremony involving ghee oil lamps and offering light to the deity or Guru), which is performed totally by the children without adult intervention and includes performing religious ritual with accompanying drumming and cymbals. Other music learned by children includes *bhajan*[23] and *Rabindrasangeet.*

---

[23] Devotional song.

South Asian cultures have strong traditions of nurturing the child as an autonomous and self-directed being (Kakar 1981, p. 210), and this tradition was reflected in the teaching approaches at this school. Psychoanalyst Sudhir Kakar notes that, in the Hindi language, bringing up children is known as *palna posna*, meaning "protecting-nurturing," children are not "reared" or "brought up" (Kakar 1981, p. 210). Kakar also notes that in the

> Child-utopia that is reflected in Bhakti songs and poems, there is a specific stream in the Indian tradition of childhood that values precisely those attributes of the child which have not been "socialised." In this tradition it is the child who is considered nearest to a perfect, divine state and it is the adult who needs to learn the child's mode of experiencing the world [this tradition emphasizes] mutual learning and mutual pleasure in each other [i.e. parent and child] thus sharply differing from the socialization model that concentrates solely on the child and his movement towards adulthood.
>
> (Kakar 1981, p. 210)

These traditions were reflected in the educational philosophy of the *Bharat Sevashram Sangha* school, particularly in the children's autonomous conducting of religious ceremony, and also in the gentle and nurturing approaches of teachers.

The fourth school that I visited was *Ananda Pathshala* (meaning Happy Nursery) and this school is the nursery school attached to Visva Bharati University (Tagore's university). It was originally set up for the families of university employees, including all cleaners, cooks, and other laborers, as well as teaching staff. The school now also has fee-paying places for other children, the majority of whom are from middle-class families. This school differed distinctly from the other three, poorer rural schools. The class sizes were smaller and the teaching materials were of higher quality. On the day of my visit, children were being read a Bengali version of Chekhov's *White Star*, translated and improvised on the spot by their teacher. *Rabindrasangeet* is an essential part of the curriculum and I was told at *Ananda Pathshala* that they particularly teach the Tagore songs about nature. In addition, I was told, other schools did not teach these songs about nature—they were a speciality of *Ananda Pathshala*. With extensive gardens and grounds around the school children learn under the shade of banyan trees, outdoor lessons under the sky being an important aspect of Tagore's educational theory.

The fifth school that I visited was Bodhicariya Senior Secondary School in Kolkata. I have known Bodhicariya School since 2004 and first made contact with this school through Amnesty International. It was established in 1990 as a school for children from North East India displaced through local conflict. Bodhicariya School is in the Rajarhat district of north Kolkata now in the middle of the area being developed into the new Kolkata megacity.

The morning that I visited Bodhicariya School it was the annual school music exams for classes 4–8. The music exam theory paper was in English. However, students could answer in English, Bengali, or Hindi. The exam paper contained five questions:

1. Define any five of the following:- *aroho, aboroho, khali, lay, abortan, saptak, sangit, som.*[24]
2. Write a full description of *"tintal."*[25]
3. Write a *Tal* which was created by Rabindranath Tagore.

---

[24] Terms of reference used in classical music.   [25] Tintal is 16 beats.

4. Write a short note on Rabindranath Tagore's music.
5. Write any one of the following in the style of a poem:- a) Rabindrasangeet b) A patriotic song.

The theory paper was followed by a practical exam. Both theory and practicals were conducted very informally. Each student was called to the front of the class to sing to the teacher or play Hawaiian (slide) guitar; a few students played *tabla*. Both boys and girls learn singing, but usually girls learn dancing and boys Hawaiian guitar and *tabla*. Sometimes girls learn guitar. This is choice rather than policy. Dancing exams took place in another classroom; the students were all female and performed very well.

The music curriculum featured the music of Tagore and Indian classical. Folk dance and music were not a part of the curriculum, but children from ethnic minorities were given the opportunity to play and perform music from their cultural backgrounds. The Hawaiian (slide) guitar is a popular Bengali instrument. The teachers explained its advantages for beginners as an instrument which used melody, as opposed to the Spanish guitar which harmonizes. Skills from this instrument could also be applied to *sitar, sarod*, or *santoor*. The dancing included *Rabindra* dance and regional folk dance from North East India.

In *Resisting Linguistic Imperialism in English Teaching* (1999), Suresh Canagarajah discusses traditional, pre-colonial, learning methods in Sri Lanka which include the "deductive, teacher-fronted method in the *guru–shisya* [teacher–disciple] tradition," the pedagogical tradition or "dialogical learning method based on exchanges between *guru* and *shisya*," and "informal learning approaches where the learner lived with the family of the teacher and 'picked up' knowledge and skills as he or she worked in the teacher's house" (Canagarajah 1999, p. 108; see also "Vocal Music and Pedagogy of China, India and Africa," Yang Yang et al., in this volume). Canagarajah discusses how these styles were suppressed in school classrooms under colonialism. I felt that there were connections harking back to these earlier, traditional methods in the learning that I observed in schools, and the home learning was definitely based on these methods, although among folk musicians the *guru–shisya* relationship is much less formal than in classical music settings, and informal learning is far stronger. As identified by Campbell, learning is facilitated by cultural expectations, and children become competent musicians when they are in environments where music is a daily activity and is regarded as a human achievement to be carefully nurtured (Campbell 2010, p. 272). Campbell also refers to the socialization model, which sees children as "unrealised adults" or "waiting to become something more than themselves" (Campbell 2010, p. 272) which is prevalent in Western thinking. This is alien to the Indian concept of childhood as described by Kakar, and—in Campbell's view—the application of a socialization model is likely to inhibit natural creativity.

Conclusions

While we may be keen to introduce cultural identity at an early age into children's musical learning, it would appear that we are not afraid to do this through the use of complex language. It would seem that Western nursery rhymes and *Baul* songs have one thing in common, and that is their use of metaphor. Furthermore, Thomas (1930) notes that "Love, politics and religion are the three inexhaustible themes upon which the changes are incessantly rung" (Baring-Gould and Baring-Gould 1967, p. 13). Both nursery rhymes and *Baul* songs lampoon society, politics, and religion. In *Baul* songs, however, "love" takes another turn, since these songs are also expressions of esoteric practices and the nature of spiritual "love." John Blacking concludes that, under certain circumstances, a "simple 'folk' song may have more human value than a 'complex' symphony" (Blacking 1973, p. 116). However, while I completely support the notion of the human value of folk songs (including nursery rhymes), in many regions of the world the words and music of folk/nursery songs are in fact quite complex, but this does not seem to deter children from learning and making these songs their own.

Dialogue and exchange have great potential in musical education in multicultural communities of the UK today and in India. The "Music Round the World" project demonstrated that there are parents and carers from a range of ethnic and cultural backgrounds in the UK who are likely to welcome initiatives in education of this nature. In India, there is an enthusiasm and desire for the development of fusion and experimentation. Historically, Bengal has never lacked enthusiasm or ability to experiment and develop music within a Bengali context. However, as noted by Gerry Farrell in *Indian Music and the West* (1999), there has not always been an equal exchange: "The West has been encountering, but never really knowing, Indian music for almost two centuries" (1999, p. 1). India currently knows Western music better than the West knows Indian music. However, music today in local, folk, and popular traditions in both countries reflects the diversity and cultural exchange that has grown throughout the colonial era to today, and, as referred to earlier in relation to the theories of Amartya Sen and Ashis Nandy, these are identities of multiple affiliations which we all hold as a result of our shared histories.

There are still enormous social class differences in musical learning in both the UK and in India. Although there was some access to classical music in the case of Lakhon, with his grandmother fundraising for his lessons through singing for alms, his progress was also dependent on having the time to practice, and in poorer communities practice time is often in short supply. Arati and Durga were also the only young people, apparently, learning music in their villages. As in Maslow's hierarchy of needs, self-actualization is harder to achieve from a lower socio-economic background (Maslow 1943/1954)

This study has only touched on, but not fully described, the inner worlds of children's musical creation, their musical practices and cultures which they experience as a separate entity, alongside, but not directly practicing the culture of the adults around them (Campbell 2010, p. 102). Campbell notes that children are not "passive recipients of the music they value, but active agents in choosing the music they will take time to listen and respond to, to make, and to choose to preserve, reinvent, or discard" (Campbell 2013, p. 1). Campbell's view in many ways corresponds to the child-autonomous theories described by Kakar. Kornei Chukovsky, who published the verse composed by a four-year-old "There will always be sunshine" (referred to earlier in this chapter), was also an exponent of children's autonomous creativity. Writing in 1933 about the need to listen to children's speech, he commented that "by studying it, it is possible to discover the whimsical and elusive laws of childhood thinking" (Morton 1971, p. xv).[26]

---

[26] Chukovsky received an honorary degree from Oxford University on his eightieth birthday, May 20, 1962, for his "services to British Literature in the Soviet Union"—a tribute to his translations

Tagore was another exponent of the child's inner world. I shall leave the last word to him as he writes about his own experience as a child.

Writing in his auto-biographical book, *My Boyhood Days* (1941), Tagore describes how he felt that his music teacher, Jadu Bhatta, made the mistake of thinking he could teach according to his own strict methods and preconceived ideas, and not take into account the child's own creative inner world. Jadu Bhatta subsequently failed to engage with his young student:

> *"After this, when I was a little older, a very great musician called Jadu Bhatta came and stayed in the house. He made one big mistake in being determined to teach me music, and consequently no teaching took place. Nevertheless, I did casually pick up from him a certain amount of stolen knowledge. I was very fond of the song* Ruma jhuma barakhe aju badarawa..... *which was set to a Kaphi[27] tune, and which remains to this day in my store of rainy season songs".*
>
> (Tagore 1941:41. Translated from the original Bengali by Marjorie Sykes[28])

REFERENCES

Banerjee, B. (1988a). Rabindra Samgit: its distinctiveness. In: J. Banerjee (ed.), *The Music of Bengal*, p. 81. Vadodara: Yamuna Art Printers.

Banerjee, D. (1988b). On the distinctiveness of Old Bengali Songs. In: J. Banerjee (ed.), *The Music of Bengal*, p. 113. Vadodara: Yamuna Art Printers.

Banerjee, J. (1988c). *The Music of Bengal*. Vadodara: Yamuna Art Printers.

Baring-Gould, W.S. and Baring-Gould, C. (1962/67). *The Annotated Mother Goose*. New York: Bramhall House.

Basu, A.K. (1988). Folksongs of Bengal. In: J. Banerjee (ed.) *The Music of Bengal*, p. 93. Vadodara: Yamuna Art Printers.

Blacking, J. (1973). *How Musical is Man?* Seattle: University of Washington Press.

Bryant, P.E., Bradley, L., Maclean, M., and Crossland, J. (1989). Nursery rhymes, phonological skills and reading. *Journal of Child Language* 16(2): 407–428.

Campbell, P.S. (2010). *Songs in their Heads. Music and its Meaning in Children's Lives*. New York: Oxford University Press.

Campbell, P.S., and Wiggins, T. (eds) (2013). *The Oxford Handbook of Children's Musical Cultures*. New York: Oxford University Press.

Canagarajah, A.S. (1999). *Resisting Linguistic Imperialism in English Teaching*. Oxford: Oxford University Press.

Chakrabarty, R. (1988). Vaisnava Kirtana in Bengal. In: J. Banerjee (ed.), *The Music of Bengal*, p. 12. Vadodara: Yamuna Art Printers.

of Shakespeare, Swift, G.K. Chesterton, Kipling, and Oscar Wilde (in the foreword to *From Two to Five* by Frances Clarke Sayer, in the translated and edited edition of *From Two to Five* by Chukovsky (1933; Morton 1971)).

[27] Referring to the North Indian classical *raga* of that name.

[28] Marjorie Sykes (1905-1995) was a British Educationalist who went to live in India in the 1920s and joined the Indian Independence Movement, spending most of the remainder of her life in India. She wrote many books and became acquainted with many of the leading figures in Indian politics and culture, including Rabindranath Tagore and Mahatma Gandhi.

Chaudhuri, A. (2013). *Calcutta: Two Years in the City*. New York: Knopf Doubleday.

Choudhury, S. and Roy, A. (2012). *Baul* music: electronic mediation and media intervention. *Social Science Research Network*, downloaded from <http://ssrn.com/abstract=2072978>.

Farrell, G. (1999). *Indian Music and the West*. London: Clarendon.

Fuld, J. (1966). *The Book of World Famous Music: Classical, Popular and Folk*. New York: Crown Publishers.

Green, L. (2011). *Learning, Teaching and Musical Identity: Voices across Cultures*. Bloomington: Indiana University Press.

Jhaveri, S. (2013). *Western Artists and India*. London: Thames and Hudson.

Kakar, S. (1981). *The Inner World: A Psychoanalytic Study of Childhood and Society in India*. New Delhi: Oxford University Press.

Maslow, A. (1943/1954). A Theory of Human Motivation. *Psychological Review* 50(4): 370–396.

Morton, M. (trans. and ed.) (1971). *From Two to Five* by Kornei Chukovsky. Berkeley: University of California Press.

Nandy, A. (1983). *The Intimate Enemy: Loss and Recovery of Self under Colonialism*. Delhi: Oxford University Press.

Nengjing, S. (2009). *A Survey on the Current Teaching Practice of Fujian-Taiwan Nursery Rhymes in the Regional Music Education of South Fujian*. Unpublished manuscript.

Nettl, B. (1983/2005). *The Study of Ethnomusicology*. Champaign: University of Illinois Press.

Openshaw, J. (2004). *Seeking Bauls of Bengal*. Cambridge: Cambridge University Press.

Opie, I. and Opie, P. (1997). *The Oxford Dictionary of Nursery Rhymes*. Oxford: Oxford University Press.

Sarrazin, N. (2013). Children's urban and rural musical worlds in North India. In: P.S. Campbell and T. Wiggins (eds), *The Oxford Handbook of Children's Musical Cultures*, p. 249. New York: Oxford University Press.

Sen, A. (2006). *Identity and Violence*. London: Allen Lane.

Sen, M. (2009). *The Honey Gatherers* (also published as *Baulsphere*). Delhi: Random House.

Sengupta, K. and Bandyopadhyay, T. (1998). *19th Century Thought in Bengal*. Calcutta: Allied Publishers.

Sengupta, N. (2002). *History of the Bengali Speaking People*. New Delhi: UBS Publishers.

Som, R. (2009). *Rabindranath Tagore: the singer and his song*. Gurgaon: Penguin.

Tagore, Rabindranath (1941). *My Boyhood Days*, translated from the Bengali by Marjorie Sykes. (published for Visva-Bharati University, West Bengal, India).

Thomas, K. E. (1930). *The Real Personages of Mother Goose*. In: W.S. Baring-Gould and C. Baring-Gould, *The Annotated Mother Goose*. New York: Bramhall House, 1962/1967.

Winnicott, D.W. (1971). *Playing and Reality*. London: Pelican Books.

CHAPTER 25

··

SINGING AND VOCAL DEVELOPMENT

··

GRAHAM F. WELCH

INTRODUCTION

DESPITE the warmth in the room as they shook the snow off their winter coats and gathered around the kitchen table, there was a collective sense of nervousness and, in some cases, un-ease that was barely touched by the hostess' cheerful manner and greeting. Outside, the dark of a Newfoundland evening had already descended and the hostess wondered if some of the wind's icy chill was reflected in the body language. This gathering was to be the first of several sessions for the group when things usually unspoken, sometimes hidden for many decades, would be allowed to surface.

> My biggest recollection is school, of course. You went to school, the first thing the nuns would say—Anybody can sing. You'd go and you were embarrassed to tears because you knew you couldn't sing, and there was no help . . . I can remember, at least a full row, if not two, in the classroom choirs or the singing choir, that you were told to pantomime. You had to go to music, and you had to listen to all the words and be able to mouth it or lip-sync it like every-body else, but you were not allowed to sing and you weren't allowed to turn it down.
>
> (Knight 2010, pp. 108–109, interview with C., aged 50)

> I remember playing skipping and singing on the street. I can't remember the tunes now . . . I don't think I ever really thought I couldn't sing until Grade 7 and the teacher and all my friends and I were in glee club and that was a major time, she stopped and said—Somebody is tone deaf here. She said—It's you Vic, you're tone deaf. She said—You don't have any notes, you just can't sing along with the music at all . . . I can see the class, I was sitting second row back and there were kids behind me, you can imagine how embarrassed I felt. From then on, I just assumed I was tone deaf . . . I guess obviously it was traumatic, to remember after 30 years.
>
> (Knight 2010, p. 125, interview with V., aged 47)

> Then in Grade 6 [age 11] . . . I stood up to sing it and she told me to sit down, that I couldn't sing. Well, I was devastated . . . I'm sure I wanted to cry. Of course, you came home, it was no good of telling your parents at the time that something like this had happened to you . . . And she was such a powerful person in the community . . . It stayed with me for so long. It was so degrading at the time. Even in high school, if there was anything to do with music, I hated

music . . . I didn't learn it. I couldn't learn it, as I thought . . . I'm sure that [incident] affected it, in a lot of ways . . . maybe she just didn't have the knowledge and it didn't come to her—"I am doing something that's going to affect this child for most of her life." That's probably the way it was.

(Knight 2010, p. 91, interview with L., aged 42)

Over the next few weeks and months, these adults shared many similar detailed, yet negative, memories, particularly associated with their former schooldays. Despite the passing of time, these episodes of childhood were vividly recalled. A sense of embarrassment, shame, deep emotional upset, and humiliation were commonly evidenced, usually accompanied by reports of a life-long sense of musical inadequacy. For these particular Canadians, as for many other adults around the world in different cultural contexts, the associations between singing and childhood were not positive. Within the local Newfoundland culture, singing competency, either as an individual or within a group, has always had high status. Consequently, any perceived singing "failure" in childhood has often led to continued self-identify as a "non-singer" (see Knight 1999) and has reinforced a cultural stereotype of a community that is divided in two: those who "can sing" and those who "cannot"—a status associated with emotional trauma, acceptance, and a sense of "irrevocability" (Knight 1999, p. 144).

Similar findings have been reported from other studies of adults in North America, the UK, and Scandinavia. Yet, despite such experiences, there are some adults who never give up hope of improvement and there have been several successful examples of specialist choirs being started for adult "non-singers" (Mack 1979; Richards and Durrant 2003). These include a new community choir in St. John's, Newfoundland, four "beginners" choirs in one London college that have a 20-year history, various "Singing from Scratch" choirs in the Midlands and South-East of England, and similar initiatives in Sweden, the United States, Canada, Australia, and New Zealand.

The existence of such choirs for adult "non-singers" is one of a number of significant challenges to a binary "can/cannot" categorization of singing behaviors. They are part of the evidence base for singing to be considered as a normal developmental behavior that can be enhanced or hindered, particularly by the events and experiences of childhood. For example, other recent research suggests that such self-labeling in adulthood may be somewhat erroneous. An adult's perceived sense of singing inadequacy, based on their negative childhood experiences, is not necessarily borne out empirically when their singing ability is actually assessed. Several studies have reported a mismatch between perceived and actual singing ability in adults, with the behavior often being more competent than the self-perception (Cuddy et al., 2005; Knight 2010; Wise 2009). One recent study of singing ability in the general adult population, for example, found that the majority of adult participants were much more pitch accurate when they performed a well-known target melody at a slower tempo (Dalla Bella, Giguére, and Peretz 2007).

Overall, the prime source of singing "failure" for an individual is often a particular moment in childhood and/or adolescence when there is a mismatch between developing singing competences and a set singing task (Cooksey and Welch 1998; Welch 1979, 1985, 2000a, b, 2005a). Erroneous adult expectation often creates the problem. This mismatch may then become further "objectified" by continuing inappropriate comments from adults or peers, which suggests that the singing problem is evidence of an underlying disability in music. Arguably, the number of singing "failures" that are socially generated in our communities would be reduced radically if there was a greater awareness of a) how singing mastery develops, b) how children of the same age can be in different phases of development (as is considered normal with other forms of culturally biased behavior, such as reading), and c) how best to provide suitable "developmentally sensitive" singing activities. The narrative that follows reviews the nature of singing development from early childhood through to (and including) adolescence. Particular features are highlighted of how normal development may be fostered, shaped, and sometimes hindered.

Singing as a developmental behavior

Pre-birth and infancy

The foundations of singing development originate in the auditory and affective experiences of the developing fetus during the final months of gestation, particularly in relation to the earliest perception of melodic variations in the mother's voice. The amniotic fluid that surrounds the fetus is an effective transducer of the pitch contours of maternal voicing. As the mother speaks or sings, the prosodic features of her voice (melody and rhythm) are conveyed to the developing fetus by the sound waves that transfer through her body tissue and that also are reflected from surfaces in her immediate environment. At the same time, the mother's affective state as she speaks or sings is encoded hormonally in her bloodstream through neuroendocrine activity. This emotional state is believed to be experienced by the fetus relatively concomitantly with the sound of the mother's voice because of an interfacing of the fetal and maternal bloodstreams (for a more detailed review, see Welch 2005a and Welch and Preti, this volume). The outcome is an interweaving of acoustic (prosodic/melodic) and emotional experiences pre-birth that are likely to underpin the developing infant's subsequent interactions post-birth with the sounds of the maternal culture. For example, our ability to determine particularly strong emotions in vocal behaviors in speech and singing (Johnstone and Scherer 2000; Loui et al. 2013; Nawrot 2003; Sundberg 2000) is likely to originate in these earliest dual-channel (acoustic-affect) experiences and, arguably, to create a certain bias toward the association of particular vocal timbres with positive and negative feelings (termed "emotional capital", see Welch 2005a; Welch and Preti, this volume). For example, six-month-old babies exhibit endocrine (cortisol) changes after listening to their mothers singing (Trehub 2001), becoming calmed when upset and more alert when sleepy.

The first year of life is characterized by a shaping of the infant's vocal production through an interaction with the acoustic characteristics of the maternal culture. Parents, for example, typically incorporate rich musical properties when interacting with infants: they speak and sing at higher pitch levels, use a wider pitch range and longer pauses—often at a slower rate, and use smooth, simple, but highly modulated intonation contours (see Thurman and Welch 2000; Trehub and Degé 2016; Welch 2005b). At birth, neonates continue to be particularly sensitive to the sound of the human voice, while demonstrating a certain initial perceptual plasticity toward any language (Eimas 1985). For example, two-day-old neonates listen longer to women singing in a maternal style (Masataka 1999). Adult singing (both male and female) appears to be especially significant, as demonstrated in its beneficial effects on premature infants' physiological functioning through changes in heart rate and oxygen saturation, alongside a reduction in stressful behaviors (Coleman et al. 1997).

The earliest vocal behavior is crying. It contains all of the ingredients of subsequent vocalization, including singing, with variations in intensity and pitch, as well as rhythmic patterning and phrasing (Vihman 1996). At the age of two months, cooing and vowel-like sounds are already evidenced and being shaped by the maternal culture (Ruzza et al. 2003). Aspects of "musical babbling" that contain definite musical features, e.g. pitch and rhythmic patterns, are also evidenced from two months onwards (Tafuri and Villa 2002). Their incidence and quality appear to be related positively to the amount of time devoted to daily singing behaviors by the mother; the greater the amount of maternal singing, the increased likelihood of earlier musical babbling. Although maternal singing to infants is primarily a caregiving tool aimed at emotional regulation, it provides a rich musical context for mother–infant interaction where the young child is motivated to imitate and play with vocal sound (for a review, see Trehub and Gudmundsdottir 2014).

By the age of three to four months, the infant is able to imitate their mother's exaggerated prosodic contours that characterize infant–mother interaction (Masataka 1992). Vocal play emerges around the ages of four to six months (Papoušek 1996). By the age of one year, infants are sufficiently cued into the language of the maternal culture for elements to be reflected in their own vocalizations. As examples, French infants babble using French speech units, Russian infants babble using Russian, and Japanese infants using Japanese (Meltzoff 2002). In general, the first year of life is characterized by increasingly diverse vocal activity. The first vocalizations of infancy, with their communication of affective state (discomfort and distress, then also comfort and eustress), are expanded to include quasi-melodic features (two to four months), developing vocal control (four to seven months), with vocal pitch behaviors that are directly linked to the prosodic features of the mother tongue.

Early childhood and preschool

Preschool singing development is characterized by an increasing interaction with the sounds of the experienced maternal culture. This interaction is reflected in a mosaic of different singing behaviors that are evidenced between the ages of one and five years. They relate to the young child's acquisitive, playful, creative, and spontaneous nature as they engage with and make sense of their "local" musical world (e.g. Barrett 2011). The variety of vocalization includes two-year-olds' repetition of brief phrases with identifiable rhythmic and melodic contour patterns (Dowling 1999); and three-year-olds' vocal interplay between spontaneous improvisation and selected elements from the dominant song culture, termed "potpourri" songs (Moog 1976) and "outline songs" (Hargreaves 1996), in which the nature of the figurative shape of the sung melodic contour (its "schematic" contour) is thought to reflect the current level of the young child's understanding of tonal relationships (Davidson 1994).

There is evidence of increasing sophistication and complexity in relation to the learning of songs from the dominant culture by young children (e.g. Mang 2005; and developmental models by Rutkowski, 1997;[1] Welch 2002). However, the path of development is not necessarily linear for any particular individual. For example, in a US study of the spontaneous singing of two-year-olds' first songs there is evidence that "phrases are the initial musical units" (Davidson 1994, p. 117). Such phrases are characterized by limited pitch range, a certain disjunction of key/tonality, and a descending contour. In contrast, recent Italian data of two- to three-year-old children indicate that some young children appear to be much better at imitating a complete melody modeled by their mother (and also by a specialist course tutor) than matching individual phrases of the same song (Tafuri and Welch, unpublished data; see Figure 25.1; see also Tafuri 2008). These Italian children had been exposed to regular sessions of their mothers' singing since the final trimester of pregnancy, both at home and in a special infant–parent singing course organized in the local conservatoire. Yet, for other children in the same Italian group, with apparently the same levels of exposure to maternal singing, the opposite is the case. Their sung phrase accuracy is rated as better than their whole song accuracy (Figure 25.1), in line with data from the earlier US study (Davidson 1994).

For the youngest children, the boundaries between singing and speaking may be blurred, or at least ambiguous, to the adult listener, and are related to the dominance of a particular contour schema (Davidson 1994) as well as to the influence of the mother tongue. For example, a longitudinal study in Canada of young girls aged 18 to 38 months from monolingual and bilingual backgrounds reported that "intermediate vocalizations" (a type of vocal behavior at the boundary between speech and song) were more prevalent in Mandarin- and Cantonese-speaking children than in English-speaking children (Mang 2000/1). A follow-up study in Hong Kong with mono- and bilingual three- and four-year-olds confirmed these findings and revealed that, regardless of age, the manipulation of vocal pitch was used to distinguish between singing and speaking (Mang 2002). The mean fundamental frequencies (f_o) for songs were reported to be consistently higher than speech, but "own choice" songs were performed at a slightly lower pitch than a criterion song. In addition, the older English monolingual children demonstrated a wider mean f_o differentiation between their singing

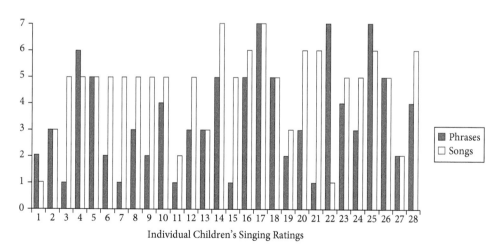

Individual Children's Singing Ratings

FIGURE 25.1 Accuracy ratings of Italian children (n=28) aged 2.6 to 3.3 years in imitating song phrases and complete songs modeled by their mothers. Ratings are based on a seven-point scale of perceived accuracy.

Data from Tafuri, J., *Infant Musicality*, 2008.

and speaking behaviors compared to their Cantonese monolingual and bilingual peers. Taken together, such examples from these diverse cultural settings remind us that singing behavior is subject to developmental processes, while also being sensitive to socio-cultural context (including task). In these examples, context also includes the presence or absence of a pitch-based language as the mother tongue in which meaning is explicitly conveyed by the shaping of melodic contour.

As might be expected from the interaction of enculturation with generative skill development in music (British Educational Research Association Music Education Review Group 2001; Welch 2005b), longitudinal data on singing development in early childhood confirm the importance of the prosodic features of the mother tongue. Spontaneous singing is characterized principally by the control of melodic–rhythmic contour patterns (Dowling 1999; Sundin 1997). For example, between the ages of one and two years, a typically spontaneous infant song consists of repetitions of one brief melodic phrase at different pitch centers. By the age of three years, three different phrases are characteristically evidenced and one-phrase singing is rare (Dowling 1988, 1999). Furthermore, case study research with two- to three-year-olds in a free-play daycare setting (Young 2002) celebrates a wide diversity in young children's spontaneous singing that is linked to context and activity while being mediated by age. This diversity includes "free-flow vocalizing" (a wordless vocal creation often associated with solitary play with no defined overall musical shape), "chanting" (often short, repeated phrases), "reworking of known songs" (the utilization of enculturated song fragments), "movement vocalizing" (either of self or objects), singing for "animation" (associated with dramatic play), and the imitation of actual sounds (defined as "comic-strip type noises," usually associated with object play). As children grow older (three to four years) and more sociable, more speaking than singing may be evidenced.

Age is also a factor in young children's perception and expression of emotion in singing; four- and five-year-olds are able to express happiness and sadness in their invented songs. In one Canadian study, children used conventional musical devices, such as a major modality and dotted or syncopated rhythms for "happy" songs, contrasted by a reduced pitch range and suppression of melodic contours in "sad" songs (Adachi and Trehub 2000). Their song texts were also contraposed emotionally, with "happy" songs focused on "friends," "family," and "sweets," but "sad" songs focused more on a negative version of these (e.g. "no family"). In contrast, older children's "sad" songs were dominated by themes related to death (Adachi and Trehub 1999). Data from Sweden (Gabrielsson and Örnkloo, 2002) confirm the growth of children's expertise with age in the recognition and expression of intended sung emotion, particularly between the ages of four and seven years.

The first years of schooling

It is common for a diverse range of singing abilities to be exhibited by children on entry to compulsory schooling. Within this diversity, it is necessary to distinguish between a) children's (developing) skill in the performance of a taught song (Rutkowski 1990, 1997; Welch 1986, 1998, 2000b, 2002; Welch, Sergeant, and White 1996, 1997, 1998) and b) children's ability to invent songs (Davies 1986, 1992, 1994). As with preschool singing behaviors, context and culture are also factors (Mang 2003; Rutkowski and Chen-Haftek 2000).

With regard to the first of these categories concerning the skilled performance of a taught song, two major US and UK studies have drawn on developmental theories to propose phased models of singing development (Rutkowski 1997; Welch 1998).[1] The US data (Rutkowski 1997) was generated through systematic evaluation of children's singing behaviors across a period of over 15 years. The emergent nine-phase model (which went through several versions)[2] suggests that children progress from speech-like chanting of the song text, to singing within a limited range ("speaking range singer"), to the demonstration of an expanded vocal pitch range that is allied to skilled competency in vocal pitch matching. This model has an affinity with that of another US-based longitudinal study (Davidson 1994), which suggests that children's singing development is linked

---

[1] Rutkowski (1997), **Singing Voice Development Measure (SVDM)**

1   "Pre-singer" does not sing but chants the song text.

1.5 "Inconsistent Speaking Range Singer" sometimes chants, sometimes sustains tones and exhibits some sensitivity to pitch, but remains in the speaking voice range (usually A3 to C4 [note: the pitch labels have been altered to bring them in line with modern conventions in which middle C=C4, 256 Hz]).

2   "Speaking Range Singer" sustains tones and exhibits some sensitivity to pitch but remains in the speaking voice range (usually A3 to C4).

2.5 "Inconsistent Limited Range singer" wavers between speaking and singing voices and uses a limited range when in singing voice (usually up to F4).

3   "Limited Range Singer" exhibits consistent use of initial singing range (usually D4 to A4).

3.5 "Inconsistent Initial Range Singer" sometimes only exhibits use of limited singing range, but other times exhibits use of initial singing range (usually D4 to A4).

4   "Initial Range Singer" exhibits consistent use of initial singing range (usually D4 to A4).

4.5 "Inconsistent Singer" sometimes only exhibits use of initial singing range, but other times exhibits use of extended singing range (sings beyond the register lift: B♭4 and above).

5   "Singer" exhibits use of extended singing range (sings beyond the register lift: B♭4 and above).

Welch (1998) A revised model of vocal pitch-matching development (VPMD)

Phase 1: The words of the song appear to be the initial center of interest rather than the melody, singing is often described as "chant-like," employing a restricted pitch range and melodic phrases. In infant vocal pitch exploration, descending patterns predominate.

Phase 2: There is a growing awareness that vocal pitch can be a conscious process and that changes in vocal pitch are controllable. Sung melodic outline begins to follow the general (macro) contours of the target melody or key constituent phrases. Tonality is essentially phrase based. Self-invented and "schematic" songs "borrow" elements from the child's musical culture. Vocal pitch range used in "song" singing expands.

Phase 3: Melodic shape and intervals are mostly accurate, but some changes in tonality may occur, perhaps linked to inappropriate register usage. Overall, however, the number of different reference pitches is much reduced.

Phase 4: No significant melodic or pitch errors in relation to relatively simple songs from the singer's musical culture.

[2] The conceptualization of development as occurring in "phases" is a common outcome of research that is undertaken over a long period with time for researcher reflection and the evaluation of new data. For example, the current author has developed and reviewed a particular model of vocal pitch matching over the past two decades (1986, 2002), which reconceptualizes the evidence and reduces the number of developmental "phases" (rather than the originally labeled "stages") from five to four.

to a schematic processing of melodic contour. Data from Harvard University's six-year *Project Zero* study of children aged between the ages of one and six years indicates five specific levels of pitch development in young children's singing, expanding from an initial melodic contour scheme with a pitch interval of a third to one that embraced a complete octave.

Within the research literature, children are sometimes reported as being more skilled when copying a sung model if they used a neutral syllable rather than attempting the song with its text (e.g. Levinowitz 1989). This finding resonates with data from a three-year longitudinal study of 184 children in their first three years of formal education in ten UK primary schools (Welch et al. 1996, 1997, 1998). The research provided detailed evidence of how singing behaviors are age-, sex-, and task-sensitive. Over the three years, the participants as a collective appeared to demonstrate little overall improvement when required to match the sung pitches of the criterion songs (two songs were specially taught and assessed each year; see Figure 25.2). However, this singing behavior was in marked contrast to their ability to learn the words of the songs, which was extremely good, even in their first term of compulsory schooling at age five (Figure 25.2: Year 1, age 5 data). Furthermore, when the pitch elements of the target songs were deconstructed into simpler musical tasks in which the children were required to match individual pitches, echo melodic contours, or copy small melodic fragments, the children were significantly more pitch accurate, as demonstrated by year-on-year improvements. There were no sex differences in their singing of these three types of deconstructed tasks: boys and girls were equally successful and demonstrated similar improvements over time. In contrast, when the *same* boys were faced with the challenge of singing a complete song, their vocal pitch became less accurate and, as a group, they demonstrated little or no improvement in song-singing across the three years. Overall, singing competency appeared to be closely related to the nature of the task, with many boys negatively affected in the task of singing a "school" song.

This is a consistent finding across twentieth-century research literature. In general, girls as a group are reported to be more advanced in their singing development than boys, with recent research indicating that this gender difference gets larger as children get older from age five through to 12 (for a review, see Welch et al. 2012).

In line with these longitudinal findings, two studies suggest that gender stereotyping may be a factor in the lack of singing development in some young boys (Hall 2005; Joyce 2005). Australian research into five-year-old boys' singing (Hall 2005) indicates that singing may be perceived as a "female" activity. UK research of nine- and ten-year-olds (Joyce 2005) across three primary schools found that only one-third of boys enjoyed singing (compared with two-thirds of girls) and that boys believed that girls were better singers.

In addition to age, sex/gender, and task, there are also contextual factors that can affect children's singing behaviors. For example, the UK longitudinal study data demonstrated a clear "school effect" (Welch 2000a). When comparing individual school data, *all* the children in one inner-city school improved their singing skills over the three years, notwithstanding their poor socio-economic environment and generally low academic attainment in other areas of the curriculum, whereas relatively few children made progress in another school, despite them having much higher socio-economic status and attainment levels. A major factor in these differences appears to have been teacher expectation. Progress was most marked where the class teacher expected and worked consistently for singing improvement

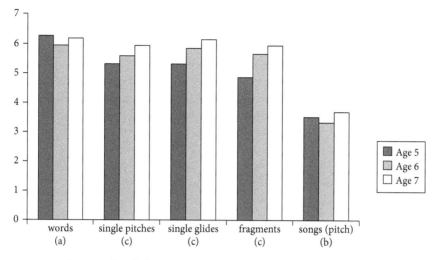

FIGURE 25.2 Longitudinal data on 5- to 7-year-old children's (n=184) rated singing abilities (maximum accuracy rating=7) for a) words of target songs (two songs were assessed each year); b) sung pitches of same complete songs; c) deconstructed pitch elements of the same songs (single pitches), simple melodic contours (glides), and simple melodic fragments.

Data from Welch, G. F., Sergeant, D. C., and White, P., The singing competences of five-year-old developing singers. *Bulletin of the Council for Research in Music Education*, 127, pp. 155–162, 1996, Welch, G. F., Sergeant, D. C., and White, P., Age, sex and vocal task as factors in singing "in-tune" during the first years of schooling. *Bulletin of the Council for Research in Music Education*, 133, pp. 153–160, 1997, and Welch, G. F., Sergeant, D. C., and White, P., The role of linguistic dominance in the acquisition of song. *Research Studies in Music Education*, 10, pp. 67–74, 1998.

with all their pupils over a sustained period. Similar findings concerning school effects on singing motivation, perceived self-identity as a singer, and overall enjoyment of singing as a school activity are also reported (Joyce 2005).

Other examples of socio-cultural differences appear in the more advanced singing skills demonstrated by a large class of first-grade Chinese (Hong Kong) children compared with their US peers (Rutkowski and Chen-Haftek 2000). Similarly, an assessment of the singing behaviors of 120 Hong Kong children aged seven to nine years from various language groups (Mang 2003, 2006), using both the Rutkowski and Welch developmental profiles, reported statistically significant effects for sex (favoring girls) as well as mother-tongue. Chinese monolingual children performed consistently better than English bilingual children, even though the criterion song was in English. This was seen as a further indication (following Mang 2006; Rutkowski and Chen-Haftek 2000) that Cantonese-speaking children achieve singing mastery earlier than their English counterparts, perhaps because the pitch centers for speech and singing of the former are more closely aligned.

Both the US- and UK-based developmental models agree that different "phases" of singing competency are likely to be exampled within any group of children entering their first school class. Some children already will be extremely competent performers of complete songs from the experienced maternal culture (both words and music), while others will be less advanced and will be in one of the "earlier phases" of singing development. This does not mean that the latter group of "developing" singers will not gain singing mastery, particularly if they are provided with an appropriately nurturing environment in which singing tasks are designed to match, then to extend, current vocal behaviors. For such children, it is likely that their preschool interactions have provided fewer opportunities to fulfill their singing potential (as outlined previously in "Early childhood and preschool").

The effects of singing alone or with a group are equivocal in the research literature. Some research evidence suggests that children may become more accurate in reproducing the musical features of a criterion song when singing in a group compared to singing alone (e.g. Buckton 1982; Greene 1993). Other research (e.g. Goetze 1985; Smale 1988) reports the opposite in favor of increased reproductive accuracy if the young child is assessed when singing alone. It may be possible to reconcile these two positions by assuming that individual singing behavior is likely to be framed by an interaction between current singing competency, the nature of the singing task, the competency of other singers in the group, and an individual's current ability to make sense of the available feedback. There is an internal psychological feedback monitoring system that is essentially outside conscious awareness, which is used for a moment-by-moment self-monitoring of the singing behavior. This system draws on information from internal sense receptors, as well as internal and external auditory information concerning the relative matching of vocal behavior with an external model (see Welch 1985, 2005a; Welch and Preti, this volume). Where the individual is able to make sense of and use these different feedback channels in combination, then singing as a member of a skilled group may promote more competent behavior. Where the individual is less able to make sense of and use this feedback, e.g. when surrounded by a less-skilled group of singers and/ or when it is difficult to "hear" their own voice, then performing in a group context may be more disadvantageous. For example, data from studies of choral acoustics indicate that auditory feedback for one's own vocal output is reduced when a) other singers are in close proximity (self-to-other ratio) and b) when nearby singers are singing, or attempting to sing, the same pitches (Daugherty 2000; Ternström 1994).

Nevertheless, it is likely that singing competency will be nurtured through exposure to frequent opportunities for vocal play within an environment that encourages vocal exploration and accurate imitation (Mang 2003; Welch 2005a; Young 2002).

The data from various studies on early singing development were collated into a theoretical protocol "baseline assessment of singing" for use with children on entry to school (Welch and Elsley 1999). This was evaluated subsequently with a small class of children (n=19) aged from three years eight months to five years ten months (King 2000). In general, the data supported key features of the model; namely, that singing competence is likely to vary at an individual level with musical task, such as in the sung reproduction of melodic contour, pitch intervals, and song text. Therefore, any assessment of singing abilities in young children should provide a mixture of tasks (such as pitch glides and pitch patterns, as well as song melodies) as a basis for diagnosis and curriculum planning. Furthermore, recent neuropsychobiological data on pitch-processing modules in the brain (Peretz and Coltheart 2003) support a hierarchical model in which melodic contour (*pace* Davidson 1994; Rutkowski 1997; Welch 1998) is analyzed before the processing of intervals and tonality (for a review, see Welch 2005a; Welch and Preti, this volume).

With regard to children's ability to invent songs, a series of studies (Davies 1986, 1992, 1994) indicates that five- to seven-year-olds have a range of song-making strategies; these include narrative songs (chant-like in nature, often with repeated figures), as well as songs that have more conventional features, such as an opening idea and a clear sense of closure, four-phrase structures, repetition, phrases that both "borrow" from the immediate musical culture and which also may be transformed (sequenced, inverted, augmented) in some way. Overall, children in the first years of schooling demonstrate a clear sense of musical form and of emotional expression in their invented songs.

Older childhood

The latter years of childhood are characterized by a general singing competency for the majority. Relatively few children are reported as singing "out-of-tune" at the age of 11 years (Howard, Angus, and Welch 1994; Welch 1979, 2000b). For example, evidence from a wide range of studies indicates that approximately 30 percent of pupils aged seven years are reported as being relatively "inaccurate" when vocally matching a melody within a Western cultural tradition. However, this proportion drops to around 4 percent of the same pupil population by the age of 11 (a proportion that is similar to that reported for the adult population—Dalla Bella et al. 2007). Within each of these and the intervening age groups, "out-of-tune" boys outnumber girls by a ratio of 2:1 or 3:1 (Welch 1979). Culture, however, continues to be significant. For example, anthropological and ethnomusicological studies have suggested that young children from the Anang in Nigeria can sing "hundreds of songs, both individually and in choral groups" by the age of five (Messinger 1958, p. 20), Venda children in South Africa were reported as both learning special children's songs and composing new songs for themselves (Blacking 1967), whereas Herati children in Afghanistan tended to focus on the imitation of adult models, with the children (particularly boys) of professional musicians' families (*sazendeh*) being immersed in the local music culture and often expected to perform professionally by the age of 12 (Doubleday and Baily 1995).

A large-scale study of children's singing development was undertaken as part of an evaluation of the impact of the UK Government's National Singing Program "Sing Up," which ran in England from 2007 to 2012. Data on the singing ability of 11,258 children aged five to 12 years were collected over a period of four years as the program was rolled out across the country. Children's singing was assessed using a protocol that combined the Rutkowski (1997) and Welch (1998) developmental profiles[1] to create a normalized singing score (out of 100). Among other findings, data analyses revealed a) that older children tended to be more advanced in their singing ability compared to younger children, and b) that those children with experience of "Sing Up" were, on average, two years in advance developmentally compared to their peers outside the program, an impact that was even more marked for the youngest children (see Figure 25.3; Welch et al., forthcoming). In general—and in line with the research mentioned previously—singing ability normally develops with age and can be enhanced if children experience an appropriately rich educational program. Moreover, there are also other potential benefits of successful singing experience in that children are more likely to have a positive self-concept and sense of being socially included (Welch et al. 2014). Among other potential benefits from singing are improved reading skills (Biggs et al. 2008; Welch et al. 2012).

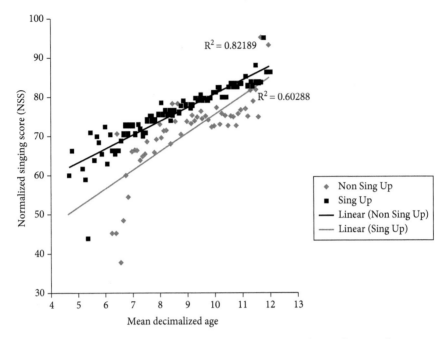

FIGURE 25.3 Mean normalized singing scores averages by decimal age and intervention ("Sing Up" versus non "Sing Up") for n=11,258 children.

Welch et al., forthcoming.

One effective means of fostering singing development is by the use of "imitation," which is a core reciprocal feature of early mother–child vocal interactions (Trehub and Gudmundsdottir 2014). This approach is also evidenced pedagogically as part of an enculturated induction into the skilled practices of expert singers in many different musical cultures, e.g. in the cathedrals where European sacred music is practiced, the choral communities of sub-Saharan Africa and Scandinavia. Cathedrals in the UK, for example, typically induct their choristers at the age of eight, so that by the age of 13 they will have had five years' immersion into a weekly (usually daily) ritual of rehearsals, performances, choral singing, and solos, embracing a wide range of compositional styles and musical genres that span over 500 years of Western classical music. Within the cathedral choir, performance skill level is signaled by singer nomenclature (such as "head chorister," "senior corner boy," "probationer") and variations in the dress code, as well as by the degree of performance involvement in particular repertoire. Novices are deliberately placed in between more skilled, older choristers and normally are required to sing only certain items during the cathedral services while they deepen and develop their performance skills through listening and observing their more accomplished peers (see Welch 2011).

Although the tradition of highly skilled boy singers in the UK may be traced back to the first foundations of English cathedrals in Canterbury (AD 597), Rochester (AD 604), and St. Paul's, London (AD 604), the "all-male" hegemony of cathedral music experienced a major challenge in 1991 with the admittance of girls to Salisbury Cathedral in the West of England. Since then, by 2009, the potential for equally skilled performance by girl choristers has been recognized through the creation of separate girls' choirs in 31 cathedrals and minsters (Welch 2011),[3] with a small number of others added since. Girl choristers are usually admitted using the same audition criteria as their male counterparts and are expected to perform the same repertoire to the same professional standard.

Evidence of the power of the musical culture in cathedrals in fostering specialist singing skills may be found both in the quality of choral outputs (e.g. national and international broadcasts by the BBC, commercial recordings, international tours, concerts) and also in the regular media-fueled controversies over whether it is possible or not to perceive differences between the singing of older female and male children (Sergeant, Sjölander, and Welch 2005; Welch and Howard 2002). With regard to perceived singer gender, a summary of recent research data (Figure 25.4) indicates that, while it is possible for an untrained solo singer's sex to be identified relatively accurately from around the age of eight onwards, it is also equally possible for trained female choristers from the age of eight to be systematically mistaken as male, depending on the particular piece of music being performed. However, once the female chorister moves into her mid-teens, the voice quality becomes more characteristically identifiable as "female" ("womanly").[4]

A key component of our ability to assign gender accurately to children's sung products relates to changes in vocal timbre as part of the aging process. A recent study of n=320 children (aged 4–11 years) revealed that, as children get older, there are significant shifts in spectral energy in their singing of the same target song. For the youngest age group (4–5 years), no gender differences were evidenced in the vocal spectrum. In contrast, significant differences emerged between genders for children aged 9–11 years, with spectral energy levels above 5.75 kHz decreasing with age and energies below 5.75 kHz increasing. However, this spectral shift occurred up to two years earlier for girls compared to boys of the same age (Sergeant and Welch 2009).

In general, children's voices tend to be higher in pitch and have a less complex acoustic make-up than those of adults. Also, there are increases in vocal pitch range, both upwards and downwards, that are closely correlated with advancing chronological age (Sergeant and Welch 2009). Nevertheless, children are able to achieve similar loudness levels as adults by using relatively more breath until the age of 12, when adult-like breathing patterns are observed (Stathopoulos 2000).

Puberty and adolescence

The onset of puberty initiates fundamental changes to the nature and quality of the singing voice for both females and males. Whereas the actual dimensions and growth of the vocal instrument are similar across sexes during childhood (Titze 1994), during puberty the male vocal tract becomes significantly longer and develops a greater circumference. In contrast,

---

[3] The data for 2009 on the numbers of cathedrals with female choristers in UK cathedrals has been collated by Claire Stewart as part of her ongoing doctoral studies at the Institute of Education into their impact on the all-male choral tradition.

[4] For a detailed review of the literature on gender and chorister voice, including similarities and differences in the underlying anatomy and physiology for singing, see Welch and Howard (2002). For data on the perceived gender of untrained children's voices, see Sergeant et al. (2005).

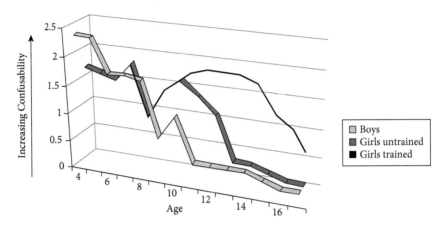

FIGURE 25.4 Confusability by age and gender of children and adolescents aged 4 to 16 years. The figure is extrapolated from measured data of perceived confusability for untrained singers (Sergeant et al. 2005) and measured data of perceived confusability for trained singers (Welch and Howard 2002). Initially, untrained young boys are confused as girls. Then, the sexes become more readily distinguishable from the age of 8/9 years. However, singing training can enable girls from 8/9 years to 14 years to sound "boy-like" in certain pieces from the repertoire. From 14 years onward, singer sex becomes more readily identifiable.

Data from Sergeant, D. C., Sjölander, P., and Welch, G. F., "Listeners' identification of gender differences in children's singing." *Research Studies in Music Education*, 25, pp. 28–39, 2005; and Welch, G. F., and Howard, D., "Gendered voice in the cathedral choir." *Psychology of Music*, 30(1), pp. 102–120, 2002.

the growth of the female vocal tract is less marked, being about 15–20 percent shorter than in the male and with a different internal ratio of resonating spaces, mainly because the female neck (pharynx) is relatively shorter compared to that of the male (Story, Titze, and Hoffman 1997). Growth typically lasts from ten to 18 years of age in females (and can begin at age seven; see Herman-Giddens et al. 1997), compared with 12 to 20 years in males (Thurman and Klitzke 2000). At the turn of the century, the highpoint of pubertal voice change was reported to be around the age of 12 to 14 years in both females and males (Cooksey 2000; Gackle 2000), a finding subsequently generally supported in more recent studies (Juul et al. 2006; Willis and Kenny 2008). Nevertheless, there is also some evidence of a trend for voice change to happen earlier than previously (Ashley and Mecke 2013; Killian and Wayman 2010). The mean average onset of voice change is likely to be between ten and 12 years (e.g. Fisher 2010), with one study reporting 80 percent of 11-year-olds showing evidence of voice change (Killian and Wayman 2010). However, ethnicity is not reported to be a significant factor in voice change (Fisher 2010).

There are relatively few major empirical studies of singing voice transformation during adolescence reported in the literature, particularly with regard to the female changing voice. Those that are available draw primarily on data from populations in the US (e.g. Cooksey 2000; Gackle 2000; Killian and Wayman 2010; Williams, Larson, and Price 1996), the UK (e.g. Cooksey and Welch 1998; Geddye, personal communication; Harries et al. 1996; Williams 2010), Japan (Norioka 1994), and Germany (Ashley and Mecke 2013;

Heidelbach 1996). The data are consistent about the presence and characteristics of adolescent voice change.

Gackle (2000, updated and revised 2014, and see Gackle, this volume) reports the outcome of her doctoral studies in Florida (during 1987), allied to almost 30 years' professional observation, to suggest that there are four distinct "phases" in female adolescent voice change (see ♀ in Figure 25.5a). In the first phase (termed "pre-pubertal: unchanged") the voice has a "clear/light, flute-like quality" with no apparent register changes. The comfortable singing range is between D4 and D5, within a wider singing range of Bb3 to F5 (and up to A5). The next phase ("pre-menarcheal: beginning of mutation"— Phase IIA) is characteristic of the beginnings of female voice mutation around the ages of 11 to 13. The comfortable range is approximately the same as previously (D4 to D5), within a slightly expanded overall range (A3 to G5). However, there is often breathiness in the tone due to inadequate closure of the vocal folds as a result of growth occurring in the laryngeal area. A singing register transition typically appears between F#4 and A#4, and some girls may have difficulties in singing lower pitches; others will experience a loss of upper range. Singing often becomes uncomfortable and effortful and a breathy voice quality is characteristic across the range. The next phase is the peak of female voice mutation ("post-menarcheal: pubertal—high point of mutation"— Phase IIb). Singing is characterized by a limited comfortable range (B3 to C5), discomfort (particularly at upper pitches), distinct voice qualities for each sung register, and with the lower part of the voice often taking on a more "alto" and often husky quality. Register changes appear between F4 and A#4 and also at D5 to F#5. The final phase ("young adult female"— Phase III) has a much-expanded comfortable singing range (A3 to G5), less breathiness, greater consistency in tone quality and registers, and greater singing flexibility and agility. Vibrato often appears at this stage and the voice has a more adult, womanly quality. Ongoing research (Welch 2004; Welch and Howard 2002) indicates that adolescent voice change is the same for relatively untrained female singers as for those who have been involved in sustained vocal performance, e.g. through membership of a female cathedral choir. However, as with adult female singers (Lã and Davidson 2005), there is always some individual variation in the impact of puberty on the singer's voice related to slight differences in the underlying endocrinological metabolism and physiological functioning.

Male adolescent voice change has a more extensive literature, both in Europe and the US. One major and influential longitudinal study was conducted by Cooksey (2000), initially based on fieldwork in California in the late 1970s, then drawing on further studies in the US during the following decade, as well as a London-based cross-cultural investigation in the 1990s (Cooksey and Welch 1998). Overall, Cooksey reports six "stages" of adolescent male singing voice change (see ♂ in Figure 25.5a) that are characterized by an overall lowering of the sung pitch range. While the rate of voice change is unpredictable for any given individual, it is reliably sequential for all.

In the first male adolescent stage ("unchanged"), the mean sung vocal pitch range is A3 to F5, with the *tessitura* pitch boundaries C#4 to A#4. The voice quality is perceived as "clear," with relatively little evidence of breathiness in the tone. The beginnings of voice change (termed by Cooksey as Stage I, "Midvoice I") are marked by a reduced vocal range (Ab3 to C5) and instability of sung pitch, particularly for the upper frequencies, which tend to be produced with increased effort, as well as tone quality that is perceived as more effortful, strained, and breathy. The sung range then descends approximately in thirds across the next three stages (see Figure 25.5a), with each stage being characterized by a reduced mean range

(a)

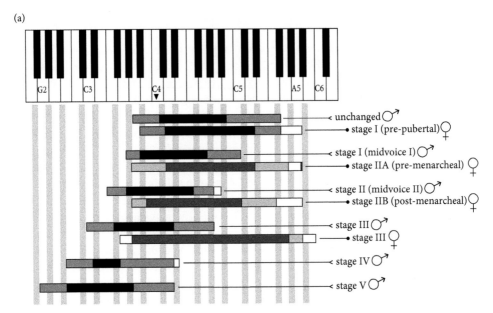

FIGURE 25.5A Stages of singing voice change for females (based on Gackle 2000) and males (based on Cooksey 2000).

Data from Gackle, L., "Understanding voice transformation in female adolescents," in: L. Thurman and G. F. Welch (eds.), *Bodymind and Voice: Foundations of Voice Education*. rev. edn, pp. 739–744, 2000; and Cooksey, J., "Voice transformation in male adolescents," in: L. Thurman and G. F. Welch (eds.), *Bodymind and Voice: Foundations of Voice Education*. rev. edn, pp. 718–738, 2000.

and relative continuing instability in the production of upper pitches, but contrasted by relative stability for the lower pitches. The pitch ranges are: Stage II ("Midvoice II"), F3 to A4; Stage III ("Midvoice IIa"), D3 to F#4; followed by Stage IV ("New Baritone," also termed "New Voice"), B2 to D#4. Within these, Stage II may be regarded as the mid-point of voice change, and this is when a falsetto register (C5 to B5) first appears and (for some) a whistle register (C6 to C7). Stage III ("Midvoice IIa") is characterized by the greatest vocal instability and the least clear vocal quality. It is only in the final stage of voice change (Stage V, "Settling Baritone," also termed "Emerging Adult Voice" G2 to D4) that the mean sung pitch range opens out again and the voice timbre begins to adopt a clearer, less breathy quality. However, the number and intensity of harmonics do not yet approximate normal adult characteristics. Nevertheless, for each stage of voice change the adolescent male has a (limited) number of pitches that can be produced comfortably and musically (see the darker shaded elements in the ranges for male voices in Figure 25.5a) and it has been possible in recent years to find a greater awareness by publishers to produce repertoire that is specially written as being suitable for these changing voices.

In general, age is a poor predictor for establishing voice change stages, with any given age group likely to encompass several stages. It is possible for an individual to pass through all stages of adolescent voice change in twelve months, but it is also possible for this process to be much slower and to last several years. Nevertheless, a summation of selected UK and Japanese data for over 3,000 males, aged nine to 14 years, provides some indication of the possible proportions of different categories of voice change by age group (Figure 25.5b),

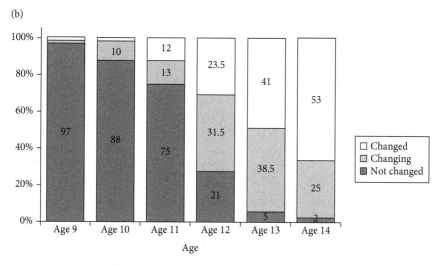

FIGURE 25.5B Extrapolated model of adolescent male voice change by age, based on UK (Geddye, personal communication) and Japanese data (Norioka 1994), total n=3,188.

Includes data from Norioka, Y., "A survey of Japanese school aged poor pitch singers,"
in: G. F. Welch and T. Murao (eds.), *Onchi and Singing Development*, pp. 49–62, 1994.

while noting that other, more recent research suggests that voice-change onset may be getting younger (Ashley and Mecke 2013; Killian and Wayman 2010). As shown, the ages of 12 to 14 have significant proportions of males whose voices are perceived to have already "changed," or are in the process of "changing," while embracing a reducing number that are still "unchanged." Ideally, choral groups of adolescent male singers in this age range are best suited, therefore, to music that has been arranged specifically for them in three parts, using the Cooksey classification guidelines (Unchanged and Stage I on a top line, Stages II and III on a middle line, and Stages IV and V on the bottom line), rather than to attempt traditional four-part music in which the *tessiturae* often are likely to be mismatched with current singing abilities.

Factors Influencing Singing Development and the Realization of Potential

As discussed, singing in one form or another is an essential feature of our musical development and behavior. In each age phase (infancy, early childhood, older childhood, adolescence), the human voice has a distinctive underlying anatomy and physiology that is capable of producing a diversity of "singing" behaviors. These increasingly explore and approximate to the particular sonic features of models that are available in the soundworlds of the experienced maternal and global cultures. In the first months of life, these "sung" products are driven by basic human needs before becoming more exploratory and melodic in nature as vocal skills develop in the acquisition and mastery of musical elements. Throughout childhood and adolescence, singing development is a product of neuropsychobiological activity, potential, and change interfaced with, and shaped by, particular socio-cultural environments in which certain patterns of sound characterize the dominant musical genres. At any age, development can be supported or hindered by a number of factors, such as the appropriateness of a given singing task set by an adult in relation to current singing capabilities, the expectations of peers, and/or the value placed on singing (and certain types of singing behavior) within the immediate culture. Opportunities to engage in vocal play and exploration, to share in singing games with peers and "experts," as well as to improvise and compose their own songs are essential features of musical cultures that foster singing development. Children who exceed the "norms" reported in the research literature are likely to have been provided with a nurturing environment that is designed to match, celebrate, enable, and extend individual singing expertise (such as evidenced in the "Sing Up" evaluation data (Welch et al., forthcoming)). Others, whose singing is perceived to be "lacking" in some way, will not have had such appropriate opportunities. For some, entry to adolescence can confirm their perceived identity as a "non-singer," and as someone for whom music is seen as an area of "failure." Yet, everyone has the potential to learn to sing—indeed, studies of singing in adults suggest that "singing in the general population is more accurate and widespread than currently believed" (Dalla Bella et al. 2007, p. 1188; see also Cuddy et al. 2005). We need, therefore, to continue to seek optimal ways to allow children and adolescents to explore and extend their singing (and musical) birthright. In this, we will reduce the need for "remedial" action in adulthood, such as the establishment of adult choirs for "non-singers." The stories of a life-long sense of singing "disability" should be confined to history.

Reflective questions

1. What is the nature of children's first experiences of singing?
2. Has your own experience of singing been positive, or not?
3. What are the key factors that can influence singing development?
4. What happens to the singing voice during adolescence?
5. How should teachers organize singing in their classes with different age groups?

ACKNOWLEDGMENT

This chapter was originally published as Welch, G. F. (2016). Singing and vocal development. In: G.E. McPherson (ed.), *The Child as Musician: A Handbook of Musical Development*, 2nd edn, pp. 441–461. Oxford: Oxford University Press.

KEY SOURCES

Dalla Bella, S., Giguére, J.-F., and Peretz, I. (2007). Singing proficiency in the general population. *Journal of the Acoustical Society of America* 121(2): 1182–1189.

Trehub, S.E. and Gudmundsdottir, H.R. (2014). Mothers as singing mentors for infants. In G.F. Welch, D.M. Howard, and J. Nix (eds), *Oxford Handbook of Singing*. New York: Oxford University Press.

Welch, G.F. (2005a). Singing as communication. In D. Miell, R. MacDonald, and D.J. Hargreaves (eds), *Musical Communication*, pp. 239–259. New York: Oxford University Press.

Welch, G.F., Saunders, J., Papageorgi, I., and Himonides, E. (2012). Sex, gender and singing development: Making a positive difference to boys' singing through a national programme in England. In S. Harrison, G.F. Welch, and A. Adler (eds), *Perspectives on Males and Singing*, pp. 37–54. London: Springer.

REFERENCE LIST

Adachi, M. and Trehub, S.E. (1999). Children's communication of emotion in song. In: S.W. Yi (ed.), *Music, Mind and Science*, pp. 454–465. Seoul: Seoul National University Press.

Adachi, M. and Trehub, S.E. (2000, April). *Preschoolers' Expression of Emotion through Invented Songs*. Paper presented at the meeting of the Society for Research in the Psychology of Music and Music Education, University of Leicester, England.

Ashley, M. and Mecke, A.-C. (2013). "Boys are apt to change their voice at about fourteene yeeres of age": An historical background to the debate about longevity in boy treble singers. *Reviews of Research in Human Learning and Music*, 1: 1–19. doi: 10.6022/journal. rrhlm.2013001.

Barrett, M.S. (2011). Musical narratives: A study of a young child's identity work in and through music-making. *Psychology of Music* 39(4): 403–423. doi: 10.1177/0305735610373054.

Biggs, M.C., Homan, S.P., Dedrick, R., Minick, V., and Rasinski, T. (2008). Using an interactive singing software program: A comparative study of struggling middle school readers. *Reading Psychology* 29(3): 195–213.

Blacking, J. (1967). *Venda Children's Songs*. Johannesburg: University of Witwatersrand Press.

British Educational Research Association Music Education Review Group (2001). *Mapping Music Education Research in the UK*. Southwell, UK: British Educational Research Association.

Buckton, R. (1982). *Sing a Song of Six-Year-Olds*. Wellington, New Zealand: Council for Educational Research.

Coleman, J.M., Pratt, R.R., Stoddard, R.A., Gerstmann, D.R., and Abel, H.-H. (1997). The effects of the male and female singing behaviours and speaking voices on selected physiological and behavioural measures of premature infants in the intensive care unit. *International Journal of Arts Medicine* 5(2): 4–11.

Cooksey, J. (2000). Voice transformation in male adolescents. In L. Thurman and G.F. Welch (eds), *Bodymind and Voice: Foundations of Voice Education*, rev. edn, pp. 718–738. Iowa City: National Center for Voice and Speech.

Cooksey, J. and Welch, G.F. (1998). Adolescence, singing development and National Curricula design. *British Journal of Music Education* 15(1): 99–119.

Cuddy, L.L., Balkwill, L.-L., Peretz, I., and Holden, R.R. (2005). Musical difficulties are rare. A study of "tone deafness" amongst university students. *New York: Annals of the New York Academy of Sciences* 1060: 311–324. doi: 10.1196/annals.1360.026.

Dalla Bella, S., Giguére, J.-F., and Peretz, I. (2007). Singing proficiency in the general population. *Journal of the Acoustical Society of America* 121(2): 1182–1189.

Daugherty, J.F. (2000). Choir spacing and choral sound: Physical, pedagogical, and philosophical dimensions. In: B.A. Roberts and A. Rose (eds), *Conference Proceedings of the International Symposium, Sharing the Voices: The Phenomenon of Singing II*, pp. 77–88. St. Johns, Newfoundland, Canada: Memorial University of Newfoundland Press.

Davidson, L. (1994). Songsinging by young and old: A developmental approach to music. In: R. Aiello and J. Sloboda (eds), *Musical Perceptions*, pp. 99–130. New York: Oxford University Press.

Davies, C. (1986). Say it till a song comes: Reflections on songs invented by children 3–13. *British Journal of Music Education* 3(3): 279–293.

Davies, C. (1992). Listen to my song: A study of songs invented by children aged 5 to 7 years. *British Journal of Music Education* 9(1): 19–48.

Davies, C. (1994). The listening teacher: An approach to the collection and study of invented songs of children aged 5 to 7. In: H. Lees (ed.), *Musical Connections: Tradition and Change*, pp. 120–127. Auckland, NZ: International Society for Music Education.

Doubleday, V. and Baily, J. (1995). Patterns of musical development among children in Afghanistan. In: E.J. Fernea (ed.), *Children in the Muslim Middle East*, pp. 431–444. Austin: University of Texas Press.

Dowling, W.J. (1988). Tonal structure and children's early learning of music. In: J. Sloboda (ed.), *Generative Processes in Music*, pp. 113–128. Oxford: Oxford University Press.

Dowling, W.J. (1999). The development of music perception and cognition. In: D. Deutsch (ed.), *The Psychology of Music*. 2nd edn, pp. 603–625. London: Academic Press.

Eimas, P.D. (1985). The perception of speech in early infancy. *Scientific American* 252(1): 34–40.

Fisher, R.A. (2010). Effect of ethnicity on the age of onset of the male voice change. *Journal of Research in Music Education* 58(2): 116–130. doi: 10.1177/0022429410371376.

Gabrielsson, A. and Örnkloo, H. (2002, August). *Children's Perception and Performance of Emotion in Singing and Speech*. Paper presented at the ISME Early Childhood Conference, Copenhagen, Denmark.

Gackle, L. (2000). Understanding voice transformation in female adolescents. In: L. Thurman and G.F. Welch (eds), *Bodymind and Voice: Foundations of Voice Education*. rev. edn, pp. 739–744. Iowa City: National Center for Voice and Speech.

Gackle, L. (2014). Adolescent girls' singing development. In: G.F. Welch, D.M. Howard, and J. Nix (eds), *Oxford Handbook of Singing*. New York: Oxford University Press. doi: 10.1093/oxford-hb/9780199660773.013.22.

Goetze, M. (1985). *Factors affecting accuracy in children's singing* (Unpublished doctoral dissertation). University of Colorado.

Greene, G.A. (1993). *The Effects of Unison Singing versus Individual Singing on the Vocal Pitch Accuracy of Elementary School Children*. Paper presented at the Southern Division of the Music Educators' National Conference.

Hall, C. (2005). Gender and boys' singing in early childhood. *British Journal of Music Education* 22(1): 5–20.

Hargreaves, D.J. (1996). The development of artistic and musical competence. In: I. Deliège and J. Sloboda (eds), *Musical Beginnings*, pp. 145–170. Oxford: Oxford University Press.

Harries, M.L.L., Griffin, M., Walker, J., and Hawkins, S. (1996). Changes in the male voice during puberty: Speaking and singing voice parameters. *Logopedics Phoniatrics Vocology* 21(2): 95–100.

Heidelbach, U. (1996). *Die entwicklung der knabenstimme zur mannerstimme bei chorsangern dargestellt am singstimmfeld* (Unpublished MD thesis). Technischen Universität Dresden, Dresden, BRD.

Herman-Giddens, M.E., Slora, E.J., Wasserman, R.C., Bourdony, C.J., Bhapkar, M.V., Kock, G.G., and Hasemeier, C.M. (1997). Secondary sexual characteristics and menses in young girls seen in office practice: A study from the Pediatric Research in Office Settings Network. *Pediatrics* 99(4): 505–512.

Howard, D.M., Angus, J.A., and Welch, G.F. (1994). Singing pitching accuracy from years 3 to 6 in a primary school. *Proceedings of the Institute of Acoustics* 16(5): 223–230.

Johnstone, T. and Scherer, K.R. (2000). Vocal communication of emotion. In: M. Lewis and J.M. Haviland-Jones (eds), *Handbook of Emotions*, pp. 220–235. New York: The Guildford Press.

Joyce, H. (2005). *The effects of sex, age and environment on attitudes to singing in Key Stage 2* (Unpublished master's dissertation). Institute of Education, University of London.

Juul, A., Teilmann, G., Scheike, T., Hertel, N.T., Holm, K., Laursen, E.M., Main, K.M., and Skakkebaek, N.E. (2006). Pubertal development in Danish children: Comparison of recent European and US data. *International Journal of Andrology* 29(1): 247–255. doi: 10.1111/ j.1365-2605.2005.00556.x.

Killian, J.N. and Wayman, J.B. (2010). A descriptive study of vocal maturation among male adolescent vocalists and instrumentalists. *Journal of Research in Music Education* 58(1): 5–19. doi: 10.1177/0022429409359941.

King, R. (2000). *An Investigation into the Effectiveness of a Baseline Assessment in Singing and some Influential Home-Environmental Factors* (Unpublished master's dissertation). Roehampton Institute London, London.

Knight, S. (1999). Exploring a cultural myth: What adult non-singers may reveal about the nature of singing. In B.A. Roberts and A. Rose (eds.), *The Phenomenon of Singing II*, pp. 144–154. St. John's, NF: Memorial University Press.

Knight, S. (2010). *A Study of Adult "Non-Singers" in Newfoundland* (Unpublished doctoral dissertation). Institute of Education, University of London.

Lã, F. and Davidson, J. (2005). Investigating the relationship between sexual hormones and female Western classical singing. *Research Studies in Music Education* 24(1): 75–87.

Levinowitz, L. (1989). An investigation of preschool children's comparative capability to sing songs with and without words. *Bulletin of the Council for Research in Music Education* 100: 14–19.

Loui, P., Bachorik, J.P., Li, H.C., and Schlaug, G. (2013). Effects of voice on emotional arousal. *Frontiers in Psychology* 4(675). doi: 10.3389/fpsyg.2013.00675.

Mack, L. (1979). *A Descriptive Study of a Community Chorus made up of "Non-Singers"* (Unpublished EdD dissertation). University of Illinois at Urbana-Champaign.

Mang, E. (2000/1). Intermediate vocalisations: An investigation of the boundary between speech and songs in young children's vocalisations. *Bulletin of the Council for Research in Music Education* 147: 116–121.

Mang, E. (2002). An investigation of vocal pitch behaviours of Hong Kong children. *Bulletin of the Council for Research in Music Education* 153(4): 128–134.

Mang, E. (2003). Singing competency of monolingual and bilingual children in Hong Kong. In: L.C.R. Yip, C.C. Leung, and W.T. Lau (eds), *Curriculum Innovation in Music*, pp. 237–242. Hong Kong: Hong Kong Institute of Education.

Mang, E. (2005). The referent of children's early songs. *Music Education Research* 7(1): 3–20. doi: 10.1080/14613800500041796.

Mang, E. (2006). The effects of age, gender and language on children's singing competency. *British Journal of Music Education* 23(2): 161–174. doi: 10.1017/S0265051706006905.

Masataka, N. (1992). Pitch characteristics of Japanese maternal speech to infants. *Journal of Child Language* 19(2): 213–223.

Masataka, N. (1999). Preference for infant-directed singing in 2-day-old hearing infants of deaf parents. *Developmental Psychology* 35(4): 1001–1005.

Meltzoff, A.N. (2002). Elements of a developmental theory of imitation. In: A.N. Meltzoff and W. Prinz (eds), *The Imitative Mind*, pp. 19–41. Cambridge: Cambridge University Press.

Messinger, J. (1958). Overseas report. *Basic College Quarterly* 4(Fall): 20–24.

Moog, H. (1976). *The Musical Experience of the Pre-School Child*. trans. by Clarke, C. London: Schott.

Nawrot, E.S. (2003). The perception of emotional expression in music: Evidence from infants, children and adults. *Psychology of Music* 31(1): 75–92.

Norioka, Y. (1994). A survey of Japanese school aged poor pitch singers. In: G.F. Welch and T. Murao (eds), *Onchi and Singing Development*, pp. 49–62. London: David Fulton Publishers.

Papoušek, M. (1996). Intuitive parenting: A hidden source of musical stimulation in infancy. In: I. Deliège and J. Sloboda (eds), *Musical Beginnings*, pp. 88–112. Oxford: Oxford University Press.

Peretz, I. and Coltheart, M. (2003). Modularity and music processing. *Nature Neuroscience* 6(7): 688–691.

Richards, H. and Durrant, C. (2003). To sing or not to sing: A study on the development of "non-singers" in choral activity. *Research Studies in Music Education* 20(1): 78–89.

Rutkowski, J. (1990). The measurement and evaluation of children's singing voice development. *The Quarterly* 1(1–2): 81–95.

Rutkowski, J. (1997). The nature of children's singing voices: Characteristics and assessment. In: B.A. Roberts (ed.), *The Phenomenon of Singing*, pp. 201–209. St. John's, NF: Memorial University Press.

Rutkowski, J. and Chen-Haftek, L. (2000, July). *The Singing Voice within Every Child: A Cross-Cultural Comparison of First Graders' Use of Singing Voice*. Paper presented to the ISME Early Childhood Conference, Kingston, Canada.

Ruzza, B., Rocca, F., Boero, D.L., and Lenti, C. (2003). Investigating the musical qualities of early infant sounds. In: G. Avanzini, C. Faienza, D. Minciacchi, L. Lopez, and M. Majno (eds), *The Neurosciences and Music*, Vol. 999, pp. 527–529. New York: Annals of the New York Academy of Sciences.

Sergeant, D.C., Sjölander, P., and Welch, G.F. (2005). Listeners' identification of gender differences in children's singing. *Research Studies in Music Education* 24(1): 28–39.

Sergeant, D.C. and Welch, G.F. (2009). Gender differences in Long-Term-Average Spectra of children's singing voices. *Journal of Voice* 23(3): 319–336. doi: 10.1016/j.jvoice.2007.10.010.

Smale, M.J. (1988). An investigation of pitch accuracy of four- and five-year-old singers. *Dissertation Abstracts International* AAT—8723851.

Stathopoulos, E.T. (2000). A review of the development of the child voice: An anatomical and functional perspective. In: P.J. White (ed.), *Child Voice*, pp. 1–12. Stockholm: Royal Institute of Technology, Voice Research Centre.

Story, B.H., Titze, I.R., and Hoffman, E.A. (1997). Volumetric image-based comparison of male and female vocal tract shapes. *National Center for Voice and Speech Status and Progress Report* 11: 153–161.

Sundberg, J. (2000). Emotive transforms. *Phonetica* 57(2–4): 95–112.

Sundin, B. (1997). Musical creativity in childhood: A research project in retrospect. *Research Studies in Music Education* 9(1): 48–57.

Tafuri, J. (2008). *Infant Musicality*. Farnham: Ashgate.

Tafuri, J. and Villa, D. (2002). Musical elements in the vocalisations of infants aged 2 to 8 months. *British Journal of Music Education* 19(1): 73–88.

Ternström, S. (1994). Hearing myself with others: Sound levels in choral performance measured with separation of one's own voice from the rest of the choir. *Journal of Voice* 8(4): 293–302.

Thurman, L. and Klitzke, C. (2000). Highlights of physical growth and function of voices from prebirth to age 21. In: L. Thurman and G.F. Welch (eds), *Bodymind and Voice: Foundations of Voice Education*. rev. edn, pp. 696–703. Iowa City: National Center for Voice and Speech.

Thurman, L. and Welch, G.F. (eds) (2000). *Bodymind and Voice: Foundations of Voice Education*. rev. edn. Iowa City: National Center for Voice and Speech.

Titze, I. (1994). *Principles of Voice Production*. Englewood Cliffs, NJ: Prentice-Hall.

Trehub, S.E. (2001). Musical predispositions in infancy. In: R.J. Zatorre and I. Peretz (eds), *The Biological Foundations of Music*, Vol. 930, pp. 1–16. New York: Annals of the New York Academy of Sciences.

Trehub, S.E. and Degé, F. (2016). Reflections on infants as musical connoisseurs. In: G.E. McPherson (ed.), *The Child as Musician*, 2nd edn, pp. 31–51. New York: Oxford University Press.

Trehub, S.E. and Gudmundsdottir, H.R. (2014). Mothers as singing mentors for infants. In: G.F. Welch, D.M. Howard, and J. Nix. (eds), *Oxford Handbook of Singing*. New York: Oxford University Press.

Vihman, M.M. (1996). *Phonological Development*. Oxford: Blackwell.

Welch, G.F. (1979). Poor pitch singing: A review of the literature. *Psychology of Music* 7(1): 50–58.

Welch, G.F. (1985). A schema theory of how children learn to sing in tune. *Psychology of Music* 13(1): 3–18.

Welch, G.F. (1986). A developmental view of children's singing. *British Journal of Music Education* 3(3): 295–303.

Welch, G.F. (1998). Early childhood musical development. *Research Studies in Music Education* 11(1): 27–41.

Welch, G.F. (2000a). Singing development in early childhood: The effects of culture and education on the realisation of potential. In: P.J. White (ed.), *Child Voice*, pp. 27–44. Stockholm: Royal Institute of Technology.

Welch, G.F. (2000b). The developing voice. In: L. Thurman and G.F. Welch (eds), *Bodymind and Voice: Foundations of Voice Education*, pp. 704–717. Iowa: National Center for Voice and Speech.

Welch, G.F. (2002). Early childhood musical development. In: L. Bresler and C. Thompson (eds), *The Arts in Children's Lives: Context, Culture and Curriculum*, pp. 113–128. Dordrecht: Kluwer.

Welch, G.F. (2004). Developing young professional singers in UK cathedrals. *Proceedings of the 2nd International Physiology and Acoustics of Singing Conference*, Denver, USA. Retrieved 3 June 2005 from <http://www.ncvs.org/pas/2004/pres/welch/welch.htm>.

Welch, G.F. (2005a). Singing as communication. In: D. Miell, R. MacDonald, and D.J. Hargreaves (eds), *Musical Communication*, pp. 239–259. New York: Oxford University Press.

Welch, G.F. (2005b). The musical development and education of young children. In: B. Spodek and O. Saracho (eds), *Handbook of Research on the Education of Young Children*, pp. 251–267. Mahwah, NJ: Lawrence Erlbaum Associates Inc.

Welch, G.F. (2011). Culture and gender in a cathedral music context: An activity theory exploration. In: M. Barrett (ed.), *A Cultural Psychology of Music Education*, pp. 225–258. New York: Oxford University Press.

Welch, G.F. and Elsley, J. (1999). Baseline assessment in singing. *Australian Voice* 5: 60–66.

Welch, G.F., Himonides, E., Saunders, J., Papageorgi, I., and Sarazin, M. (2014). Singing and social inclusion. *Frontiers in Psychology* 5(803). doi: 10.3389/fpsyg.2014.00803.

Welch, G.F., Himonides, E., Saunders, J., Papageorgi, I., Vraka, M., Preti, C., and Sarazin, M. (forthcoming). *Children's singing behaviour and development in the context of Sing Up, a national program in England.*

Welch, G.F. and Howard, D. (2002). Gendered voice in the cathedral choir. *Psychology of Music* 30(1): 102–120.

Welch, G.F., Saunders, J., Hobsbaum, A., and Himonides, E. (2012). *Literacy through Music: A Research Evaluation of the New London Orchestra's Literacy through Music Programme.* London: International Music Education Research Centre, Institute of Education, University of London.

Welch, G.F., Saunders, J., Papageorgi, I., and Himonides, E. (2012). Sex, gender and singing development: Making a positive difference to boys' singing through a national programme in England. In: S. Harrison, G.F. Welch, and A. Adler (eds), *Perspectives on Males and Singing*, pp. 37–54. London: Springer.

Welch, G.F., Sergeant, D.C., and White, P. (1996). The singing competences of five-year-old developing singers. *Bulletin of the Council for Research in Music Education* 127: 155–162.

Welch, G.F., Sergeant, D.C., and White, P. (1997). Age, sex and vocal task as factors in singing "in-tune" during the first years of schooling. *Bulletin of the Council for Research in Music Education* 133: 153–160.

Welch, G.F., Sergeant, D.C., and White, P. (1998). The role of linguistic dominance in the acquisition of song. *Research Studies in Music Education* 10(1): 67–74.

Williams, J. (2010). *The Implications of Intensive Singing Training on the Vocal Health and Development of Boy Choristers in an English Cathedral Choir* (Unpublished doctoral dissertation). Institute of Education, University of London.

Williams, B., Larson, G., and Price, D. (1996). An investigation of selected female singing- and speaking-voice characteristics through comparison of a group of pre-menarchial girls to a group of post-menarchial girls. *Journal of Singing* 52(3): 33–40.

Willis, E. and Kenny, D.T. (2008). Relationship between weight, speaking fundamental frequency, and the appearance of phonational gaps in the adolescent male changing voice. *Journal of Voice* 22(4): 451–471. http://dx.doi.org/10.1016/j.jvoice.2006.11.007.

Wise, K. (2009). *Understanding Tone Deafness: A Multi-Componential Analysis of Perception, Cognition, Singing and Self-Perceptions in Adults Reporting Musical Difficulties* (Unpublished doctoral dissertation). Keele University.

Young, S. (2002). Young children's spontaneous vocalizations in free play: Observations of two- to three-year-olds in a day care setting. *Bulletin of the Council for Research in Music Education* 152: 43–53.

CHAPTER 26

BOYS' SINGING VOICE CHANGE IN ADOLESCENCE

JENEVORA WILLIAMS AND SCOTT HARRISON

INTRODUCTION

THIS chapter focuses on physiological and sociological elements related to the singing of boys through pubertal voice change. The management of the person and the instrument is a critical element of this process. Through an extensive review of the literature, along with new material about physiological change and sociological challenges, the aim is to provide an overview of current activity, to bring out some of the important lessons for training the voice at the time of change, and to assist in educating those responsible for teaching and caring for boys' vocal development at this crucial stage.

THEORETICAL FRAMEWORK

The study of the male changing voice in adolescence has a long history. Much of the literature focuses on two distinct fields: the physiology of the changing voice, and the sociological factors pertaining to non-engagement through and after the change.

The physiology of male adolescent voice change

Male vocal mutation through puberty is generally referred to as "changing" and not "breaking." The term "breaking" voice can be construed as a negative or destructive process. It may describe the pitch instability of some boys in adolescence who will flip into falsetto intermittently; this can be observed during emotional upset or laughter. The term "changing voice" is more commonly used to describe the period of male adolescent voice mutation.

Duration of puberty can be from as little as eight months to over four years (Whiteside, Hodgson, and Tapster 2002) as well as commencing at any time between the ages of 11 and 16 (for boys). Physical growth through adolescence is in growth spurts or stages. The growth of the larynx mirrors the observable overall growth of the individual (Hollien, Green, and Massey 1994). If the individual is undergoing a growth spurt with a noticeable height gain, the larynx and its associated skeletal and muscular anatomy will be undergoing similar enlargement. This is then followed by a period of stabilization (Tanner 1964).

In the male, the thyroid cartilage grows primarily in the front-to-back direction, particularly at the anterior tip, forming the "Adam's apple." In the female, the thyroid cartilage growth remains more rounded. The male vocal folds undergo nearly twice the growth of those of the female: 65 percent increase in the male and 34 percent in the female. Within the larynx, the vocal folds of the boy increase in both length and thickness. This increased mass means that they vibrate at a lower frequency, hence the drop in speaking pitch.

Why the adult male human has evolved a speaking voice an octave lower than the female is an interesting question. The degree of growth (65 percent) is extreme when compared to all other body growth; there must have been an evolutionary benefit to this. The answer could lie in the ability of the adult male to articulate clear text very loudly. In women this is compromised by the acoustic properties of the vocal tract that make clarity of vowels at high pitches nearly impossible. Perhaps women were better off keeping their higher pitched voice to be "in tune" with their children while the men evolved to shout at each other over large distances. The setup of the adult male with a larger larynx and a longer vocal tract has the effect of making him sound larger (larger animals make deeper, louder sounds). This can have a double benefit for both intimidating other males and attracting females.

This growth pattern during adolescence is caused by hormonal levels and cannot be accelerated or decelerated except by artificial hormonal input. Delay to puberty can also be caused by severe malnutrition or severe emotional deprivation (Pozo and Argente 2002). It has been argued that extreme physical exercise, as has been observed in some child dancers and gymnasts, could delay puberty (Malina 1994). More recent literature suggests that the children and the body types for these activities are self-selecting. Children who are smaller, slimmer, and who may have a later onset of puberty are more likely to choose to be dancers or gymnasts, rather than the activity itself causing these tendencies. Changes to the onset of puberty have been observed in obese children: recent research suggests that obese girls are more likely to have early pubertal onset, but that obese boys are more likely to have delayed pubertal onset (Wang 2002). In a normal healthy individual it is an unstoppable process.

During the pubertal growth spurt, the lungs approach adult size and vital capacity. However, vital capacity and total lung volume can only be estimated to occur by the age of 18 to 20, which is generally two to three years after the end of the pubertal growth spurt (Hixon 1987). The height of the larynx in the vocal tract drops to C6 (level with cervical vertebra number 6) by puberty and C7 by about 20 years (Kent and Vorperian 1995).

Skeletal growth and muscle mass are directly related. An increase in skeletal size will result in increased muscle mass; this increased muscle mass precedes increased strength. In other words, muscles grow in length before they acquire strength. The resulting temporary decrease in coordinated motor skills can have important implications for the child singer, both in terms of pitch range and vocal agility.

Assessing the singing voice during voice change

Five distinct male adolescent stages of growth were clearly outlined by the pediatrician James Tanner in the 1960s. In the 1970s, John Cooksey assessed hundreds of boys' voices

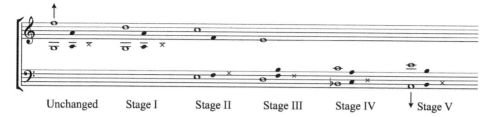

FIGURE 26.1 The pitch ranges of each stage of male voice change (Cooksey 2000).

Key: x = speech f_o, • = speech range, o = singing range

and recognized five stages of voice change. These physical and vocal changes have since been demonstrated to have a significant correlation with each other (Harries et al. 1996). The maximum change in pitch occurs at the same time as the maximum growth, between stages 3 and 4. Although the pitch of the speaking voice is mainly dependent on vocal fold length, the sudden drop in pitch observed between stages 3 and 4 is largely due to increased vocal fold mass more than sudden elongation of the vocal folds. This can be heard as a significant change in voice quality as well as pitch.

The pitch ranges in Figure 26.1 show:

- *Extended singing range* (unfilled note). This is the pitch range possible with no observable sign of strain and without using falsetto.
- *Comfortable modal singing range* (filled note).
- *Speech fundamental frequency* (cross). This can be ascertained simply by asking the boy to count backwards from 20 and observe the pitch at which his voice settles most comfortably. This is usually three to four semitones above his lowest comfortable singing pitch.

Possible signs of change to Cooksey stages I and II (Cooksey 2000)

- Growth spurt
- Change of timbre in the mid-range of the singing voice
- Decrease in control at the top of the singing range
- Change in timbre of speaking voice
- Increased variability; more "off" days.

There tends to be more stability and less individual variation in the lower pitch range limit throughout the different stages of voice maturation than in the upper pitch range limit. Therefore, it is more reliable to judge the developmental stage by the lower singing range and by the fundamental frequency of speech. Assessing this is easily done by listening to the boy speak, preferably on a rather dull task such as reciting the months of the year, or counting backwards. The pitch of his speaking voice will determine his stage of voice change, as illustrated on Cooksey's chart. Remember that these are based on averages, and that there will be many individual variations. What is crucial is that the main body of the singing with a rapidly growing and vulnerable voice is within the fundamental comfort zone—at the lower end of the pitch range.

Another feature of the rapidly growing vocal system is a change in voice quality. The voice can become rough, thin, reedy, hooty, or grating. It can become rich, full, warm, resonant, or vibrant. These are all subjective terms and of limited use for accurate description, but they can give away a great deal about the expectations of either the boy or his parents. It is absolutely essential at the time that the boy is encouraged in his singing, that he feels excited by the possibilities opening up for him.

If adolescent students are to sing solo repertoire, it is essential that they are taught appropriate vocal technique. For example, if the child plays the keyboard or the guitar without guidance, they may manage to achieve a certain amount of facility. They will, however, reach a limit to this where some technical input is necessary in order to make further progress. This will often mean a return to simple exercises and a great deal of unlearning. If children sing using their "natural" ability without expert guidance, they will inevitably develop unhelpful habits which will either limit their future development, or have to be unlearnt before they can progress. In itself this is not calamitous, but it is better if it can be avoided.

Singing in the right vocal range

A problem faced by choral directors everywhere is how to allocate parts to individual singers in order to create a balanced choral sound using the singers available. Because of the physical nature of the larynx, there will be more baritones and second sopranos than anything else. How do they create enough tenors and altos? Any sort of shoe-horning of people into less appropriate voice parts needs to be looked at carefully, so that they balance the needs of the choir with the more important needs of the individual.

First, it helps briefly to revisit the way the larynx works, in order to find out what happens when it is asked to go outside its normal comfort zone. The larynx has opposing sets of muscles (like nearly all muscle groups in the body) that work against each other in order to raise and lower the pitch. In every voice, there will be a range of pitches within which the laryngeal muscles are most comfortable, where they can operate for the longest time without tiring. An easy way to locate this is to listen to the speaking voice of a singer. If the speaking task is relatively monotonous (days of the week, months of the year, counting) then the pitch of the voice will settle into an average comfortable pitch.

Once the average speaking pitch has been established, it is generally the case that the lowest comfortable singing note will be about a third below this. This in itself would suggest the larynx is most comfortable when phonating near to the bottom of its pitch range. This does not mean that extending the pitch range is intrinsically harmful, merely that it is an unusual activity for the larynx, and that it is likely to be a learned skill.

The changes during adolescence for boys are much more radical than girls and need to be more carefully monitored and accommodated. The first issue to deal with is the one where boys continue to sing high when their speaking voice is dropping. It is often tempting to do this as a director. Boys with good vocal technique can often produce a strong and musical soprano range, even when their speaking voice would suggest young baritone. This is because the larynx is still flexible at this point; the cartilages are growing rapidly but are still softer than adult larynx cartilages (the "box" part of the voice-box). The muscles carry on with their habitual use, even though they are growing much longer. The problem here is that the demands on the larynx become more and more extreme. If the boy continues to sing soprano during voice change, at some point the whole system will collapse and the boy will have a short-term vocal collapse, regardless of any potential problems later.

The problem only occurs when the boy uses exclusive use of the upper range. Occasional use is fine; in fact, it can encourage flexibility in the upper range. So it is possible for young tenors to sing some notes in falsetto. It is a useful task for all adolescent boys to use falsetto in their warming up, and it is often an artistic requirement from time to time in pop or musical theater singing. What is crucial is that the main body of the singing with a rapidly growing and vulnerable voice is within the fundamental comfort zone—at the lower end of the pitch range.

Sociology of male adolescent singing

A historical perspective

The consideration of boys singing in their soprano range during and beyond voice change is also interesting when cultural and historical perspectives are considered. There are a number of early recordings of boy singers in British cathedral and Parish church choirs, using their upper (soprano) pitch range with a high level of vocal artistry and skill. Many of these boys were mid- or post-puberty; this can be heard on the one or two rare spoken interviews with them. It is possible that some boys are able to retain their soprano voices while their larynx is growing in power and stamina, especially if these early phases happen relatively fast. The boys on these recordings were reported to have stopped singing when their voices "broke" (often at the age of 17 or 18). As this event came some time after they had undergone adolescent voice change (probably at the age of 14 or 15), it is only possible to conjecture what may have precipitated this "breaking" and what was happening physically. It is conceivable that the reported "breaking" was a sudden inability of the laryngeal structures to sustain this thin-fold phonation as the larynx became less pliable in early adulthood. This sudden collapse of the singing voice would explain the reported phenomenon of overnight voice change. This sudden change is obviously not possible from a physical consideration; no part of the body can grow by 65 percent overnight. What was most likely is that the speaking voice was descending normally but the singing voice was maintained in the high pitch until the whole system suddenly and alarmingly gave way.

Currently, maintaining the practice of singing in the soprano range after the onset of voice change is not generally popular among boys. They normally want to be seen to be maturing alongside their peers; any late developers may feel as isolated as the few early developers.

Reluctance to sing

Related to the historical and physiological changes described above are the reasons for non-participation in male singing during adolescence and beyond. Questions have been raised about the reasons for adolescent males' reluctance to sing for almost a century: Grace (1916, p. 368) observed "a shortage of men, boys and money in choirs"; while Giddings (1915) makes mentions of a choir with 60 sopranos, 10 altos, two basses and no tenors. In 1923, Randolph (1923) asked "Why do not more men take up music?," while Damon (1936, p. 41) encountered a class of eighth-grade boys who "never sing." Winslow (1946, p. 58) described the frustration of middle school teachers noting "probably nothing perplexes the secondary school teacher more than the vocal education of boys . . . most boys enter high school with negative attitudes towards vocal music and music education in general."

While a number of studies were undertaken from the late 1970s to the mid-1990s that interrogated the sex stereotyping of musical participation (Abeles and Porter 1978; Delzell and Leppla 1992; Fortney, Boyle, and DeCarbo 1993; Griswold and Chroback 1981; O'Neill and Boulton 1995), many of these dealt only with instrumental involvement. This is perhaps due, in part, to the assumption that stereotyping and gendered attributes of musical participation are aligned. In the instrumental domain this may be so: because more school-aged girls play the flute, for example, it may be deemed to have feminine attributes. The confusability between sex stereotyping (numbers of males and females engaging in certain activities) and the gendered attributes of a particular activity (whether the activity is considered masculine or feminine) is further exacerbated in singing where the physical manifestations of the voice have a direct impact. The unchanged male voice sounds, to the untrained ear, like a female voice, and therefore singing with this voice can be considered feminine or "sissy." This is evident in the work of Hanley (1998, p. 58): "singing is viewed a feminine activity—boys who engage in singing are feminine by implication." Similarly Ashley (2006), working from a psychological perspective, focused on removing the myth surrounding the "you sing like a girl" phenomenon that confronts boys whose rates of maturation are slower than their peers.

Furthermore, the uncertainty of the change has the potential to bring about reticence on the part of boys in the change to sing. In addition, there is substantial evidence in the literature to suggest that boys who do singing through adolescence are likely to be subject to bullying. As White and White (2001, p. 40) note: "though the young man may inwardly enjoy singing, when he sits with his buddies at school or at church, he will not sing if the group believes it is not masculine or 'cool.'" Bullying can take the form of exclusion, or homophobic accusation, as found in the work of Harrison (2001, 2008). One of his participants commented:

> Then came high school. It was no longer "cool" to do music. From the moment I started high school in 1988 to the year I finished, came the taunting. The name-calling started. Poofter, Faggot, Queer. You name it, I copped it. If it wasn't for my passion to do music, I would not be where I am today. For 5 years I put up with this crap.

The calling into question of one's sexuality is one of the strongest modifiers of adolescent behavior, and singing is one of the sites at which these modifications take place. This is not a uniform trend across genres. The recent work of Harrison et al. (2013), Mook (2012), and Bennett (2012) indicates that singing popular music, barbershop, and to a lesser extent Glee phenomenon is exception to tendency. Similarly, as Faulkner (2012) and Russell (2012) point out, Western society has a series of stereotyping, gender, and sexuality constructions around singing that are not necessarily replicated in other cultures.

The interface between male singing, sex stereotyping, gender, and sexuality has been the source of several studies in the past decade (Ashley 2007; Demorest 2000; Freer 2006, 2008, 2010; Hall 2005; Harrison 2002, 2005, 2007, 2008). Common themes to emerge from these studies have included the importance of early (pre-teen) influences, peer pressure, leadership, the use of single-sex environments, the status and profile of singing, choice of repertoire, and a number of minor issues including name of the vocal ensembles and uniform choice.

Of particular note in this literature is the work of Freer (2006) and Demorest (2000) that suggests lack of male role models, the physiology of the changing voice, and issues surrounding male identity are of particular significance. Adler (2001) picks up the issue of identity, stating that since singing does not construct or defend masculinity it carries with it gender-incongruent and therefore homophobic labels. Hanley (1998) concurs, commenting that while some girls might want to be like boys, boys do not want to be like girls. Adler's (2001, p. 3) work also recognizes that boys make a decision not to sing between elementary and secondary school, in response to psychological and sociological messages that singing is not an appropriate activity for males beyond a certain age.

A relationship between the physiological and sociological aspects of boys' voice change is evident in this literature. The growth spurt, change of timbre, and decreased control of the instrument contribute to uncertainty about the reliability of the instrument in this period. This, in turn, affects confidence and social interactions. The insecurity surrounding the physical attributes of the voice, itself a symbol of changing from boyhood to manhood, causes boys to cease singing for fear of ridicule about their sexuality. This is not universal, however: it tends to be genre- and culture-specific.

METHOD

The methodology herein draws on the authors' interactions with male adolescent singers over an extended period. A mixed method approach (Creswell 2003) has been employed, initially focusing on quantitative measures of the adolescent voice change. The data for both quantitative and qualitative measures were subject to thematic analysis (Benner 1985; Leininger 1985) to identify any recurrent patterns. The themes chosen were the result of clustering linked categories identified in the student responses that conveyed similar meanings. In this instance, the work of Taylor and Bogdan (1984, p. 131) was employed to define the themes that were based on "topics, vocabulary, recurring activities, meanings, feelings."

Evidence for the implications of falsetto singing during adolescent voice

There is anecdotal evidence to suggest that boys who continue to sing in their falsetto voice, instead of dropping gently into tenor or baritone singing, may engender certain compensatory vocal behaviors. These may include a high larynx position and pharyngeal constriction as a result of continually straining for high pitches, and less effective vocal fold closure, arising from falsetto phonation. We know from medical research that muscles grow in length before strength (Malina, Bouchard, and Bar-Or, 2004). The muscles of the adolescent male larynx are growing faster than any other muscle; the male larynx increases in size by 65 percent in about two years. This suggests that, while muscles are growing rapidly, their strength and coordination may be compromised, and that activities should be less demanding of intense muscle use. Falsetto singing requires relatively small muscles to work in extreme and unrelenting contraction for the duration of the vocal line. This may possibly be compromising the healthy development of the adult voice.

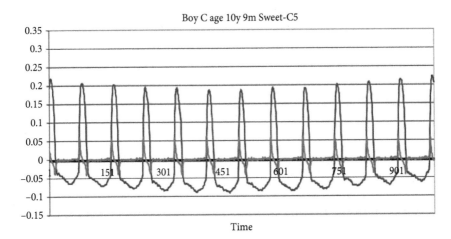

FIGURE 26.2 Boy C at the age of 10 years and nine months, treble singing. Blue line = vocal fold cycles of the word sweet on a C5 (one octave above middle C). Red line = speed of vocal fold closure (a taller line denotes a faster closure).

In order to investigate this, a study was made of several trained singers entering puberty. Electroglottogram data can show the duration of each vocal fold closure; it can also show the level of efficiency of the initial snap together of the vocal folds.

Figures 26.2 and 26.3 show the changes over time of boy C. By the age of the second recording, his speaking voice was one of a developing baritone, but he was continuing to sing soprano in his choir. There are two main changes to see: first, the duration of the vocal fold closure is longer for each cycle in the second recording; second, the efficiency of vocal fold

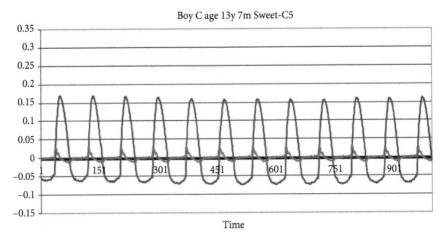

FIGURE 26.3 Boy C at the age of 13 years and seven months, falsetto singing. Blue line = vocal fold cycles of the word sweet on a C5 (one octave above middle C). Red line = speed of vocal fold closure (a taller line denotes a faster closure).

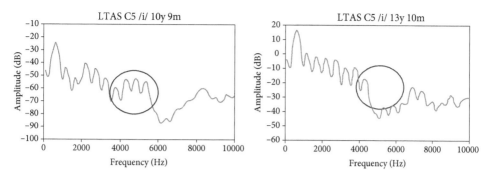

FIGURE 26.4 The long-term average spectrum of the |i| vowel in the word sweet, sung by boy C at the two ages specified on the graph. The dark grey circle shows the upper frequency boost in the treble voice that is missing in the falsetto voice.

closure is greater in the first recording. This would suggest an efficient, ringing tone in the treble singing and a pressed, dampened tone in the falsetto singing. When the long-term average spectrum is observed in Figure 26.4, it shows an upper frequency boost in the treble voice which is missing in the falsetto voice.

Although there is no evidence to show that voices can be physically damaged through the acquisition of inefficient habits of singing, there is evidence to show that these habits may inhibit future development. It is suggested that a thorough and appropriate grounding in vocal technique is essential for any singer of any age who wishes to sing at a high level of performance. With the right guidance, children can learn habits of vocal efficiency and physical economy. These will not only enable them to maximize their current situation, but will also provide a foundation for accomplished adult singing.

ILLUMINATIVE CASE STUDIES

In the second part of this chapter the qualitative accounts of adult men who were asked to reflect on their experiences as adolescents at the time of their voice change are presented. Drawing on more extensive stories of men's engagement with singing across the lifespan, these vignettes speak to their experiences at the time of adolescence. These vignettes are taken from two data generation events, ten years apart, and in that sense, they serve as longitudinal case studies (Stake 1995). The first data were generated in 2001, and the second in 2011. A pseudonym has been given to each student and the initial responses have been verified and supplemented via email.

DALTON (2001)

In my adolescent years, singing was always encouraged, and I can never remember a time that I was not a part of a choir or a school musical. During this time I can never really remember being picked upon because I was a musician; this is not to say it didn't happen to other people. I always had a great cross-section of mates who were involved heavily in other aspects of school life and I guess I looked upon my involvement in music as being my way of being involved in the life of the school. I also played sport but was never as good as some of my mates. I always found, and still do, that if you encourage your friends in whatever they do then they will encourage you in whatever you choose to do with your life. This is a sure way of finding out who your real friends are.

During my adolescent years, I developed a great love of music and it soon became my greatest concern in life. I probably didn't practice as much as I should have, but helping to develop a part of that school still to this day gives me much pride and satisfaction. Thanks mainly to the music teachers at that time, we were given the opportunity to do and see things that your average student would not. We were taken on tours, performing in competitions and concerts; we were taken to watch concerts and had nights at the opera. It was during this part of my life that I began thinking about continuing music as a full-time career, but this was not to happen right away. I did try but was rejected by the music school I applied for. There is one more thing that you never realize about being a musician while you are at school: girls love it!

DALTON (2011)

These [adolescent] were the years in which music really started to form an important part of my life. It was also the point in my life where my parents started to encourage me in my musical pursuits. Here I started to be exposed to all different types of music. Another important step was being able to actually study music in the classroom. I developed a passion for the history of music and over these years was taken on a journey through the ages discovering all things musical. I was also given the opportunity to create music. This was an important development in the psyche of me as a performer because I started to realize you could interpret music in many different ways. This is one of the most important aspects of being a musician. Being able to put your own stamp on music that has been performed thousands of times gives you a sense of ownership and also, perhaps at this age unknowingly, helps to develop music further. For me this is the age where the music teacher is most vital. These are the years when you are making decisions that affect the rest of your life. At the time of course you don't realize this, but looking back if it was not for the influence of my music teachers I would never have achieved anything close to what I have been able to accomplish. Here I discovered Musical Theater and Opera. I attended shows and performances and in my final year of school performed in a musical that really made me realize the power of music and the ability to entertain. In these years I also discovered "the" most important aspect in life, teamwork. Very few, if not any, can achieve success in life without being part of a team. Families, couples, sports teams, bands, orchestras, choruses, workplace environments, schools and universities all rely on teamwork, and that its participants all understand the importance of this and where they fit in and how they can contribute to the development of society. Eventually for me, my involvement would be in the music industry.

LAMAR (2001)

The adolescent years were very much a formation period for me as a musician, along with all areas of life; however, it was music at high school that gave me a focus for everything else. Therefore it was very important that, as an extremely enthusiastic and also quite sensitive 13-year-old, the music staff gave the right support. The Director of Music at the school was excellent in this regard. He encouraged me to compose and gave me every singing opportunity he could. He constantly guided me while never making me be something I was not.

It was the support of people like this at my school that really helped me survive at high school. The school I went to was definitely not set up with people like me in mind. My first years at the school were very tough; I was constantly bullied and victimized. I would sometimes come home from school and just start crying while trying to explain what happened. It was not so much the fact that I was a musician that made me a target, more the type of musician/person. Music was a big thing at the school at that time and many boys were involved. However, it was not because you were involved with music that made you a target for bullying; it was how much music meant to you. My life revolved around music, and when this is the case, it is only natural that you will have a different outlook on things than the vast majority of other people. The fact that I was a singer, an artistic and sensitive person, proved to be something many boys could not handle. I was teased with many slang homosexual names and questioned with regard to my sexuality.

An interesting point to note is that I feel if I had only played guitar, there would not have been so many people joking about what I did. In my first two years at the school [the time of the highest occurrence of voice mutation], whenever I performed in front of my peers I would be given a hard time, mostly about my singing. When I arrived at the school my voice was not even beginning to "break" and the fact that I was comfortable and willing to stand in front of a large group of students to sing and play my own compositions was too much for some people to handle; the more conviction one has, the more open that person is leaving themselves to others' victimizing. The problem was not being caused by a large number of students but rather a very small number. The school really should have done better in dealing with such bullies who did not only give me a hard time but many others also.

LAMAR (2011)

I think that music became all consuming, but also a refuge in my adolescent years. I remember vaguely responding to the first round of questions in this research, ten years ago, and stating that: "I didn't think it was my involvement in music that made me a target for bullies." On further reflection on (and removal from) my adolescent years, I think that, while I didn't get victimized for being primarily interested in music, I wasn't popular because of it. If I had have been half the athlete that I was a singer, I think I would have probably been much more accepted by my peers. I was much more sensitive than the average student at my high school and this certainly left me open to being victimized, but also probably contributed to my lack of interest in rugby/soccer or a host of other sports. Therefore, I was unlikely to make friends at a school where the predominant lunchtime activity involved some type of sports game. When I found it difficult to make friends at my new high school, I retreated further and further into music. Unfortunately, the music program at that time was filled with the social misfits of the school. Some of these people were kind; however, others would not accept me.

RAFFERTY (2001)

It wasn't until I was about 13 that I had really started to pursue singing. The school counselor told me about a vocal teacher. Not long after that I contacted her and we arranged lessons. I loved my lessons; she taught me about the fundamentals of good singing—the correct way in which to breathe and so on. The most important thing I got out of all of this was I had found something which I was enjoying immensely. All through most of my adolescent years I had to persevere with a lot of nasty comments and rumors from most of the mainstream students, and for a while I was alienated purely because I enjoyed singing. So having said that, my school wasn't a place for young male singers. We didn't really have a place.

I'll try to be as specific as possible. My school wasn't really a place for singers because it wasn't considered "normal" for a young man to sing. The accepted pursuits for young men were sports. And because I enjoyed singing, the large majority of the students thought I was a homosexual and because of that I didn't have a lot of friends. This was not the same for girls though; I know for a fact that they didn't have the same problems at all during their schooling. This really sad stuff happened in my earlier years though, years 9 and 10. I couldn't sit through a lunch hour or recess without people screaming things at me and throwing pieces of food at me. For a while it was really terrible.

RAFFERTY (2011)

It was during my adolescent years that my interest in music really started to take flight. I discovered that I had a voice, and so I gave up saxophone and took up singing lessons. I enjoyed singing so much that I couldn't imagine myself doing anything else. Even though I enjoyed singing as much as I did, doing it was not always easy. I had an incredibly difficult time with my peers during my secondary schooling years. Singing was not considered to be the accepted pursuit of most teenage boys.

It was also around this time that I began having difficulties with my parents (mainly with my father) with regard to my interest in music/singing. I began having singing lessons at the age of about 14 with a local teacher. She taught me in the classical style, mainly with art song and musical theater selections. My voice responded to classical training rather favorably, and it was at this point that I began to take a real interest in classical singing and perhaps auditioning for tertiary studies.

BORIS (2001)

Being a singer and clarinet player at age 12 did enable me to get a fair bit of attention from the bullies. My school didn't really have any physical bullies—they were mainly the verbal ones and they were few and far between. Perhaps the reason for this was that there were so many kids in the music program. It wasn't a minority: you know, the rare loser with braces and a tuba. There were plenty of us, and we were mostly proud to be a part of the music program because of how cool the bands, and to a lesser extent the choir, was. We were occasionally teased not because we played music but because we were in the lesser groups. Another possible factor in the reduction of bullying at my school was the fact that in year 8 a lot of "cool" kids who were in the great sport teams were also in the marching band. In 1995 if you insulted the marching band too loudly you'd probably get the shit beaten out of you by the bass drum line. They were big, big guys.

My school also didn't really tolerate bullies: if you were caught bullying you were suspended and if you kept going you were expelled—no ifs, no buts.

There was another thing my school encouraged. Getting involved in everything—don't just be a bookworm or a musician or a sportsman: diversify. It was extremely successful in creating an atmosphere where to be really good at something wasn't considered bad or nerdy, but almost cool and respectable. It didn't matter whether you were good at schoolwork or music or sport. So I guess the reason for the lack of teasing at my school was the atmosphere they created. It was a very positive atmosphere and I'm not even sure how they did it. But you never felt uncool being a musician, and I was only ever given 100 percent support from home.

BORIS (2011)

The school I went to at age 12 had a fantastic music program. Even more importantly, as I reflect, a fantastic atmosphere geared towards music and culture. As members of the various bands, orchestras, and choirs, my friends and I never really suffered bullying or abuse. I think for most students, institutions like our marching band were sources of school pride. Sure, we were never going to be the "cool" kids, but we were never ostracized either.

Throughout my adolescent years I became more involved in music primarily because of my school. The school not only encouraged participation in as many co-curricular activities as possible but also offered a great variety. As well as continuing studies with the clarinet, I joined several choirs, began to study trombone, and taught myself to play piano (mostly by listening to, and imitating, Billy Joel and Elton John). From a musical perspective I can say my adolescent years were highly positive. Since leaving high school I have never had the pleasure of performing with a choir.

COMMENTARY ON ILLUMINATIVE CASE STUDIES

Several threads emerge from these cases. These include: early influences, formal music education (incorporating teachers, the school environment, and education systems), genre, and other factors.

A number mention the role family played in their decision to participate in singing activities. Often it was a parent, but in some cases it was another relative or family friend. For others, it was a choral experience that led to a more all-embracing experience of music. In each case, there was mention of a critical incident in the adolescent years that assisted in maintaining singing through and beyond these formative years.

Formal schooling played a largely positive role in the cases cited here. There were encouraging teachers, facilitators, and enablers who provided opportunities for the young men as they went through their voice change. With one exception, Rafferty (and to a lesser extent, Lamar), the school setting was largely supportive of music making. Even in Rafferty's case, the passage of time appears to have softened his views, but he acknowledges the role his father played in discouraging his involvement in music as a career. While this is not evident in the excerpt above, Lamar now works at the school he attended in his adolescent years. He has found significant change there in the intervening ten years. Music, and the individuals who engage with it, are supported in a variety of forms.

Singing as part of a broader music education experience also appears to be a key thread. Adolescent males who experienced instrumental music and/or music of a variety of genres were more likely to stick with singing. For example, Boris, who participated in a "fantastic" music program with bands, orchestras, and choirs, felt supported in his endeavors. Similarly, Lamar played guitar and sang, and believed he would have been subjected to less bullying if he had only played guitar. Lamar also notes that a sole focus on music could be seen as unhealthy in his school context. The "social misfits" who did music only helped to contribute to a sense of isolation for all involved. The creation of a critical mass of singers, as described by Boris and Dalton, appears to provide protection from bullying and a sense of purpose and identity within the school setting. Where most of the cases refer to activities outside the classroom (i.e. co-curricular music), Dalton also recognized that in undertaking classroom music he was able to experience opera and musical theater—two things that were to influence his career as a musician beyond the adolescent years.

Above all else, there is evidence in the time-based comparison of the cases that in relation to the adolescent years, as Jerry Herman would say, "Time heals [almost] everything."

SUMMARY

The key issues to emerge from both the physiological and sociological discussions above relate to the management of the physical and social dimensions of singing through the change. This is critical not only as preparation for singing in adulthood, but also for the function singing has in the day-to-day lives of adolescents who may not sing beyond their formal schooling or church experience. The importance of role models emerges in both types of data—vocal role models and masculine role models are equally integral to boys negotiating the change. The emphasis on teachers who provide appropriate technique and a suitable atmosphere for singing should not be underestimated. The lessons from genres and cultures outside the Western classical choral tradition are also worthy of note. Knowledge of what will occur through and after the change is a powerful tool in managing the adolescent male voice, as is the sense of team, references to exemplars, and the support of family and educational institutions.

ACKNOWLEDGMENT

Portions of this chapter have been previously presented as Williams, J. (2011). "Foundations for excellence: nurturing and supporting talented young dancers and musicians." In: Mary Schwarz (ed.), *Proceedings from Music and Dance Scheme Conference*, February 28–March 1, 2011, Totnes, UK. Exeter: South West Music School.

ADDITIONAL SOURCES

Freer, P. (2006). Hearing the voices of adolescent boys in choral music: a self-story. *Research Studies in Music Education* 27: 69–81.

Harrison, S. Welch, G.F., and Adler, A. (2012). *Perspectives on Males and Singing*. New York: Springer.

Harrison, S.D. (2007). Where have the boys gone? The perennial problem of gendered participation in music. *British Journal of Music Education* 24(3): 267–280.

Williams, J. (2018). *Teaching Singing to Children and Young Adults*, 2nd edn. Braunton, UK: Compton Publishing Ltd.

Williams, J. (2006). From boys to men: the changing adolescent voice. *Church Music Quarterly* 175: 18–19.

Websites and other media

Ancell, N. (2011). *More than just a Hobby. DVD for Teachers and Choral Conductors Working with Teenage Boys*. Melbourne: Educational Media Solutions.

Boys Keep Singing <http://www.martin-ashley.com/Boys-keep-singing>.

Williams, J. <http://www.jenevorawilliams.com/>.

REFERENCES

Abeles, H.F. and Porter, S.Y. (1978). The sex-stereotyping of musical instruments. *Journal of Research in Music Education* 26: 65–75.

Adler, A. (1999). A survey of teacher practices in working with male singers before and during the voice change. *Canadian Journal of Research in Music Education* 40: 4.

Adler, A. (2001). Male gender issues in music education: a three dimensional perspective. Paper presented at *Research in Music Education Conference*, April 6–8, Exeter, UK.

Ashley, M. (2006). You sing like a girl? an exploration of "boyness" through the treble voice. *Sex Education: Sexuality, Society and Learning* 6(2): 193–205.

Ashley, M. (2007). *Exploring Young Masculinity Through Voice. Proceedings of the Art Based Education Research Conference*, Graduate School of Education, University of Bristol, July 5–7 (Bristol: University of Bristol).

Benner, P. (1985). Quality of life: a phenomenological perspective on explanation, prediction, and understanding in nursing science. *Advances in Nursing Science* 8(1): 1–14.

Bennett, A. (2012). "Let me know you're out there!" Male rock vocal and audience participation. In: S. Harrison, G.F. Welch, and A. Adler (eds.), *Perspectives on Males and Singing*, pp. 287–295. New York: Springer.

Cooksey, J. (2000). Male adolescent transforming voices: voice classification, voice skill development, and music literature selection. In: L. Thurman and G. Welch, (eds) *Bodymind and Voice: Foundations of Voice Education*, pp. 821–841. Collegeville, MN: The VoiceCare Network and the NCVS.

Creswell, J.W. (2003). *Research design: qualitative, quantitative, and mixed method approaches.* London: Sage.

Damon, I.F. (1936). The boys who did not sing. *Music Educators Journal* 21(1): 41.

Delzell, J. and Leppla, D.A. (1992). Gender association of musical instruments and preferences of fourth-grade students for selected musical instruments. *Journal of Research in Music Education* 40(2): 93–103.

Demorest, S. (2000). Encouraging male participation in chorus. *Music Educators Journal* 86(4): 39.

Faulkner, R. (2012). Icelandic men, male voice choirs and masculine identity. In: S. Harrison, G.F. Welch and A. Adler (eds), *Perspectives on Males and Singing*, pp. 215–231. New York: Springer.

Fortney, P.J., Boyle, J.D., and DeCarbo, N.J. (1993). A study of middle school band students instrument choices. *Journal of Research in Music Education* 41: 28–39.

Freer, P.K. (2006). Hearing the voices of adolescent boys in choral music: a self-story. *Research Studies in Music Education* 27: 69–81.

Freer, P.K. (2008). Teacher instructional language and student experience in middle school choral rehearsals. *Music Education Research* 10(1): 107–124.

Freer, P.K. (2010). Two decades of research on possible selves and the "missing males" problem in choral music. *International Journal of Music Education: Research* 28(1): 17–30.

Giddings, T.P. (1915). The high school chorus. *Music Supervisors Journal* 1(3): 8.

Grace, H. (1916). A choir problem of today. *The Musical Times* 57(882): 367–369.

Griswold, P.A. and Chroback, D.A. (1981). Sex-role associations of musical instruments and occupations by gender and major. *Journal of Research in Music Education* 26: 57–62.

Hall, C. (2005). Gender and boys' singing in early childhood. *British Journal of Music Education* 22(1): 5–20.

Hanley, B. (1998). Gender in secondary music education in British Columbia. *British Journal of Music Education* 15(1): 51–69.

Harries, M.L., Griffith, M., Walker, J., Hawkins, S. (1996). Changes in the male voice during puberty: speaking and singing voice parameters. *Logopedics Phoniatrics Vocology* 21(2): 95–100.

Harrison, S.D. (2001). Real men don't sing. *Australian Voice* 7: 31–36.

Harrison, S.D. (2002). Devaluing femininity: Its role in determining musical participation by boys. Paper presented at *International Society for Music Education Conference*, August 13, Bergen, Norway.

Harrison, S.D. (2005). Let's hear it for the Boys: the place of boys' music in a feminist world. In: E. Mackinlay, S. Owens, and D. Collins (eds), *Aesthetics and Experience in Music Performance*, pp. 115–122. Newcastle: Cambridge Scholars Publishing.

Harrison, S.D. (2007). Where have the boys gone? The perennial problem of gendered participation in music. *British Journal of Music Education* 24(3): 267–280.

Harrison, S.D. (2008). *Masculinities and Music*. Newcastle: Cambridge Scholars Publishing.

Harrison, S.D., Welch, G.F. and Adler, A. (eds) (2013). *Perspectives on Males and Singing*. New York: Springer.

Hixon, T.J. (1987). *Rspiratory Function in Speech and Song*. London: Taylor and Francis.

Hollien, H., Green, R., and Massey, K. (1994). Longitudinal research on adolescent voice change in males. *Journal of the Acoustical Society of America* 96 (5, Pt. 1): 2646–2654.

Kent, R.D. and Vorperian, H.K. (1995). *Development of the Craniofacial-oral-laryngeal Anatomy*. San Diego: Singular.

Leininger, M.M. (1985). Ethnography and ethnonursing: models and modes of qualitative data analysis. In: M.M. Leininger (ed.), *Qualitative research methods in nursing*, pp. 33–72. Orlando, FL: Grune and Stratton.

Malina, R.M. (1994). Physical activity and training: effects on stature and the adolescent growth spurt. *Medicine and Science in Sports and Exercise* 26: 759–766.

Malina, R., Bouchard, C., and Bar-Or, O. (2004). *Growth, Maturation, and Physical Activity*, 2nd edn. Champaign, IL: Human Kinetics.

Mook, R. (2012). The sounds of gender: textualizing barbershop performance. In: S. Harrison, G.F. Welch and A. Adler (eds), *Perspectives on Males and Singing*, pp. 201–214. New York: Springer.

O'Neill, S.A. and Boulton, M.J. (1995). Is there a gender bias towards musical instruments? *Music Journal* 60: 358–359.

Pozo, J. and Argente, J. (2002). Delayed puberty in chronic illness. *Best Practices Research in Clinical Endocrinology and Metabolism* 16 (1): 73–90.

Randolph, H. (1923). Why do not more men take up music? *Etude* 41(May 1923): 299–300.

Russell, J. (2012). Communities of singing practice in the Fiji Islands. In: S. Harrison, G.F. Welch, and A. Adler (eds), *Perspectives on Males and Singing*, pp. 189–199. New York: Springer.

Stake, R. (1995). *The Art of Case Study Research*. Thousand Oaks, CA: Sage Publications.

Tanner, J.M. (1964). The adolescent growth-spurt and developmental age. In: G.A. Harrison, J.S. Werner, J.M. Tanner, and N.A. Barnicot (eds), *Human Balance: An Introduction to Human Evolution, Variation, and Growth*. Oxford: Clarendon Press.

Taylor, S.J. and Bogdan, R. (1984). *Introduction to Qualitative Research Methods: The Search for Meanings*. New York: John Wiley and Sons.

Wang, Y. (2002). Is obesity associated with early sexual maturation? A comparison of the association in American boys versus girls. *Pediatrics* 110: 903–910.

White, C. and White, D. (2001). Commonsense training for changing male voices. *Music Educators Journal* 87(6): 39–43, 53.

Whiteside, S.P., Hodgson, C., and Tapster, C. (2002). Vocal characteristics in pre-adolescent and adolescent children: a longitudinal study. *Logopedics Phoniatrics Vocology* 27(1): 12–20.

Winslow, R.W. (1946). Male vocal problems in the secondary school. *Music Educators Journal* 34(4): 58–61.

CHAPTER 27

......

ADOLESCENT GIRLS' SINGING DEVELOPMENT

......

LYNNE GACKLE

INTRODUCTION

HISTORICALLY, a considerable amount of study has been devoted to male adolescent singing development. Information has been published concerning stages of maturation, characteristics of each stage, methods of voice classification and teaching, as well as the psychological ramifications which affect adolescent boys (Cooksey 1977a,b,c, 1978; Cooksey 1999; Cooksey et al. 1983; Cooper and Kuersteiner 1970; Groom 1979; Killian 1999; McKenzie 1956; Naidr et al. 1965; Swanson 1977). Some of these studies are longitudinal in nature, providing a much clearer and more credible body of information.

Recent studies, both in the United States and abroad, indicate that women singers significantly outnumber men singers in choral programs; some studies indicate the ratio of females to males to be as much as two to one (Bell 2004; Clift and Hancox 2010; Clift et al. 2008). In fact, girls will often number in the majority to such an extent that finding an appropriate "balance" of voices for mixed youth choir music is sometimes very difficult. In the past, however, little, if any, study was devoted to maturational effects on female adolescent singers.

In recent years, there has been an increase in information about the female voice during adolescence in research (Bottoms 1996; Fett 1994; Huff-Gackle 1987; Howard and Welch 2002; Sipley 1994; Toole 2003; Williams 1996, Willis and Kenny 2011), articles (Gackle 1991, 2006; Huff-Gackle 1985), and textbooks (Brinson 1996; Collins 1999; Gackle 2011; Hylton 1994; Phillips 1992, 2004). Much like their male counterparts, young female singers present characteristic symptoms of vocal change. These symptoms directly affect vocal technique, selection of repertoire, the development of practice/rehearsal strategies, and issues of self-concept. Recently, there has been an acknowledgment of the psychological effects of voice change in the adolescent female which may accompany the onset of puberty as well as other aspects of female adolescence. These psychological issues often affect the development of the young female singer, both vocally and emotionally (Gackle 2011; Phillips 2004, Willis and Kenny 2011).

Male and Female Voice Change: Changes of Color vs. Shades of Change

When comparing the adolescent female voice with the male adolescent voice, several characteristics become apparent. At six to eight years of age, the voices of boys and girls seem similar in tone, range, and color. In fact, one could apply a visual analogy to this aural phenomenon. For instance, the color azure (light blue) might be used as a descriptor to visually characterize the sound of the two voices in terms of color. As the boy's voice approaches mutation, there is brilliance in the boy soprano voice which one might liken to a deeper shade of blue. Clarity of tone and brilliance in certain ranges seem effortless in the young boy's voice, especially just prior to the beginning of voice mutation. The young male sopranos of the Vienna Boychoir or the American Boychoir produce a tone that leaves an indelible aural image in the mind of any listener.

However, during vocal development, the young male experiences many changes in the vocal anatomy due to the influence of the sex hormone testosterone (i.e. vocal fold length/thickness, descent of the larynx, growth of laryngeal structures, the development of the thyroid cartilage, greater vital breath capacity, increased size and space within the vocal tract, etc.). Thus, as the boy's voice changes, passing through the various stages of mutation, it also lowers approximately an octave by adulthood (J. Abitbol et al. 1999). The treble color of blue yields to a change in color—much like the changes of the color spectrum. To continue to utilize the visual analogy, the color is no longer blue, but rather progresses through different colors, perhaps green, red, or another color. Due to these physiological changes in the vocal anatomy, there is a marked contrast in timbre and pitch between the voices of the two genders.

In contrast, as the girl's voice begins to change, this characteristic brilliance of tone is not as pronounced as in the boy's voice. Just as the vocal anatomy changes in the male voice, the female voice also goes through various physiological changes due to the influence of the sex hormones estrogen and progesterone. Many of these changes are similar to her male counterpart, though not as drastic or notable (i.e. the growth of the larynx, the lengthening and thickening of the vocal folds, greater vital breath capacity, increased size and space within the vocal tract, etc.). The visual analogy for female voice change is more like shades of change within one color rather than a complete change of color. For instance, as the female voice develops, it might be characterized as azure blue changing to a deeper blue, to a royal blue, to a navy blue. . . .still a treble voice. . . .still blue, but a different shading of blue. Thus, with proper vocal training, the resulting sound of the girlchoir has a warm resonance unlike the boychoir, the women's choir, or even the children's choir. It is truly an entity unto itself.

Historically, the voices of girls were not utilized in the church liturgy. Only since 1991 have the cathedral choirs of England employed the use of girls' voices (Welch and Howard 2002). Choirs of boys and men have traditionally been recognized in religious liturgy since the time of the Levitical choirs prior to the capture and fall of Jerusalem (70 AD). According to historical commentary, Pope Sylvester (314–335 AD) founded the first ecclesiastical choral school in the Roman Catholic Church. Singing schools sprang up throughout Europe during and after the tenure of Pope Gregory (590–604 AD) and remained a musical force throughout Europe for centuries afterward (Stubbs 1917). Thus, throughout the centuries, the impetus to focus on the vocal development and training of the young female voice was simply not a consideration.

To summarize, the changes in the boy's voice are very obvious to the ear, whereas the changes in the girl's voice are more subtle and perhaps a little less obvious to the listener. Perhaps this is one reason so little attention has been given to the female changing voice by voice educators and other voice professionals. Basically, the girl's voice simply did not present the tumultuous challenges within the choral scenario as did the male changing voice.

Theoretical Framework and Principles

Adolescent female voices exhibit symptoms which are similar (though perhaps not as dramatic) to those found in the male changing voice. These characteristic symptoms (Gackle 1991, 2006, 2011) include:

(1) increased huskiness/breathiness of tone
(2) lowering of speaking voice
(3) decreased and inconsistent range (*tessiturae* tend to fluctuate)
(4) noticeable changes in timbre (tone quality)
(5) voice "breaks"/cracking (often only thought to be characteristic of boys' voices)
(6) obvious transition notes (appearance of *passaggi*) or register changes
(7) insecurity of pitch
(8) difficulty initiating phonation.

These symptoms are indicative of physiological changes which occur during female voice mutation. However, exactly why, how, and when these changes and other biological factors affect voice change in adolescent females continues to be an area of study and exploration.

Some of these physiological changes include the following.

Hormonal Changes

Puberty represents a virtual "hormonal earthquake" for the female. During the time of puberty, the secondary sex characteristics appear; they do so as a reflection of the physiological changes which are peculiar to each sex. In the Western world, the average age of puberty begins as early as eight to fourteen years of age for girls and nine to fourteen years for boys (J. Abitbol et al. 1999). Research also indicates that the onset of puberty is occurring at earlier ages (Biro et al. 2013; Herman-Giddens et al. 1997; Herman-Giddens et al. 2012; Kaplowitz et al. 2001; Wilson and Umpierrez 2008; Zuckerman 2001).

Hormonal secretions at the onset of puberty are observable in various physiological changes: skeletal growth, thelarche (breast development), and menarche (onset of menstruation) (Joseph 1965; Tanner 1972). Estrogens, which are also responsible for the growth of the breasts in young girls at puberty, in concert with progesterone, produce the characteristics of the female voice, with a fundamental frequency a musical third lower than that of a child. The combined effects of estrogen and progesterone cause the cyclical changes in the body of females during the reproductive years (J. Abitbol et al. 1999).

Vocal Fold Growth

During adolescence, the vocal folds of the female increase in size approximately three to four mm, while the vocal folds of the male adolescent increase up to one cm (Alderson 1979; Luchsinger and Arnold 1965). Kahane noted that the male vocal fold length increased by an average of 66.69 percent from prepuberty to adulthood while the female vocal fold length increased by 24.03 percent (cited in Thurman and Klitzke 2000).

Laryngeal Growth

According to J. Abitbol et al. (1999), the human larynx is a "hormone-dependent organ" (p. 431). During adolescence, the female larynx increases in size and weight, though not as dramatically as that of the male larynx. The male larynx increases more in the anterior-to-posterior dimension than the female, and thus, the two are distinctly different from each other (Kahane 1982; Weiss 1950; see also Thurman and Klitzke 2000).

Growth of the Vocal Tract

The overall vocal tract length also increases, though in males, the vocal tract becomes both longer and develops a greater circumference (Thurman and Klitzke 2000). The size of the resonator obviously yields differences in overall color or timbre. Titze (1994, p. 173), states that the vocal tract "needs to be included in a meaningful voice-classification scheme." In musical instruments, the size of the resonator has as much to do with the resulting sound as does the sound source. Thus, the growth of the vocal tract results in the deepening or richness of the voice as it approaches young adulthood.

The changes mentioned above affect various aspects of the changing voice, including speaking voice, range, registers, and timbre.

Speaking Voice

The lowering in pitch of the female speaking voice is more gradual than with boys, possibly only a semitone per year (Hollien 1978). Duffy (1958, 1970) observed a relatively gradual decrease in fundamental speaking frequency with age and also noted a difference of one semitone in average speaking fundamental frequency in thirteen-year-old pre-menarcheal and thirteen-year-old post-menarcheal females (the latter being lower). More recently, these observations were noted in the study completed by Toole (2003).

Range

The lower limit of the girl's vocal range falls approximately the interval of a third, and the upper limit rises slightly, as compared to the lower limit of the changing male voice ultimately descending an octave (Seth and Guthrie 1935). Gackle (1991, 2006) identified a decrease in vocal range to be one of the symptoms of voice change in adolescent females.

Registers

Cyrier (1981) noted that the upper transitional pitch (lift point or *passaggio* as referenced by *bel canto* singers) of the female voice tends to be higher in fourteen to fifteen-year-olds than in ten to eleven-year-old females. Gackle (1991, 2006) observed that in early mutation, a lower transition area is often evidenced first at F4—G#4. She also observed a trend in the upper register transition area to rise in pitch with age. As the voice matures, this upper register transition area begins to approximate the adult soprano *passaggio*, which is generally observed at D5—F#5. Willis and Kenny (2011) observed that weight gain was influential in the occurrence of pitch breaks in 13-year-old girls. This study found that the peak of pitch-break activity was most apparent among the girls in the weight range 56–62 kg (approximately 123–136 lbs). The study also found that pitch breaks also occurred more often around weight fluctuations (gain or loss) than when compared to the effects of gain in height.

Timbre

Breathiness of tone is at least partially due to the presence of the so-called "mutational triangle" or "glottal chink." This represents the incomplete closure of the posterior part of the glottis resulting from weaknesses in the inter-arytenoid muscles. This phenomenon is observed as an audible "rustling of wild air" through the chink (Seth and Guthrie 1935; Vennard 1967; Weiss 1950). It is interesting to note that as early as 1866, Fournier described the openness in the glottis, which was later termed the "mutational triangle" by Flateau and Glutzman (cited by Weiss 1950).

These changes indicate how and to some degree why certain characteristics of voice change are apparent in young female voices. The following information regarding pubertal sequence and its effects on the onset of menarche may shed further light when voice change is occurring in adolescent girls.

Pubertal Sequence

Tanner (1972) noted that though the sequence or stages of adolescent development remains relatively unchanged throughout the years, the age at which development begins is occurring earlier and the pace at which development proceeds is faster than reported in previous years. He noted that menarche was reported to begin at an average age of fourteen years. Currently, the average age of menarche is 12.8 years to 13.3 years (i.e. roughly around the thirteenth birthday) for girls of European descent and slightly earlier in girls of African origin (12.5 years).

Onset of Menarche and Voice Change

Laryngologists such as Brodnitz (1983) suggest that menarche and lowering of pitch in female voices are simultaneous and voice studies indicate pre-post-menarcheal differences with the same age level (Duffy 1970). Additionally, Duffy (1958) also noted a successive decrease in mean speaking fundamental frequency with age. Williams (1996) investigated singing and speaking voice characteristics through comparison of pre-menarcheal and post-menarcheal girls. Even though both the post- and pre-menarcheal girls experienced some degree of voice breaks, pitch changes, inconsistencies in speaking pitch, breathy voices and sore throats from singing, in all cases, the post-menarcheal girls identified these symptoms as happening more often than the pre-menarcheal girls.

The information on pubertal sequence indicates some important trends concerning voice change. It appears that menarcheal age appears to be decreasing by three to four months per decade. It is important to note that menarche occurs later in the development sequence, approximately two-and-a-half years after breast budding; generally, this occurs after the peak of the spurt in overall height has passed. The female growth spurt can be observed between the ages of ten and twelve, while in boys, the growth spurt tends to be between the ages of twelve and fourteen (Rogol et al. 2002).

Rutkowski (1985) utilized the voice classification stages set forth by Cooksey (1977b) to investigate their practical application in a three-year longitudinal study of ten male adolescent subjects. It was observed that the subjects generally progressed through the sequence or stages outlined by Cooksey, but noted that boys participating in the study consistently entered classifications of Midvoice II, Midvoice IIA (high point of change) and new baritone one year earlier than originally stated by Cooksey.

If a correlation exists between adolescent voice change and menarche, and the age of menarche is actually decreasing, then one might expect that voice change in females is also occurring earlier than previously expected. This information would most certainly seem to affect the repertoire selection and vocal techniques used with adolescent female singers.

PHASES OF FEMALE ADOLESCENT VOCAL DEVELOPMENT (MUTATION): A FRAMEWORK FOR UNDERSTANDING

In 1985 and 1991, the author proposed a framework for voice classification and maturation in the female changing voice from empirical evidence gathered over years of work with young female voices (Gackle, 1991; Huff-Gackle 1985). This information has subsequently been cited in several choral methods texts (Collins 1999; Hylton 1994; Phillips 1992; Phillips 2004) and has been found consistent with other research (Toole 2003; Williams 1996; Willis and Kenny (2011).

Classification of Voices According to Vocal Development

Most adolescent females are soprano or mezzo-soprano in voice type. Often, a sweet, breathy, twelve-year-old voice is assigned to sing the alto line, and therefore thinks of herself as an alto. However, since the true adult singing voice does not fully emerge until the early- to mid-twenties, to "label" the young voice according to voice part at this early stage is not advisable. One indicator of a quality voice is vocal range capability. To summarize, if a young singer has the ability to sing a low G3, it does not necessarily mean that she is an alto. Perhaps the reasons for having a girl sing the alto part lie in the fact that (1) she takes piano lessons and reads music well (therefore her skills are beneficial to the choral ensemble), and/or (2) suddenly, it has become difficult to sing in the upper register; she may even complain of discomfort in singing "high." Therefore, it seems somewhat "easier" to sing in the middle and lower range of the voice.

One of the symptoms of voice change in females is the decrease in range (Gackle 1991, 2006). Often, the high notes simply are not easily produced or are extremely breathy. In fact, during female voice change, the *tessitura* or comfortable singing range seems to fluctuate. Therefore, it may be desirous to switch the girl from a higher part to a lower (judiciously chosen) alto part during part of the voice change process. However, avoiding classification (labeling) by voice part is highly suggested. Comfortable vocalization through voice training in both directions (into the upper and lower range) to encourage range development and vocal flexibility in the developing voice is recommended.

When this text refers to classification of voices, it is important to remember that the reference is to classification according to vocal development rather than actual voice type or vocal "part" assignment. It is imperative to first determine the stage or phase of vocal development and then assign the appropriate vocal part.

Phases of Female Vocal Development

Originally, the author conceived her framework of female vocal development in terms of stages of development. More recently, a revision of this framework regards development in terms of phases rather than stages due to the gradual nature of the changing process over time. Table 27.1 provides the author's vocal development framework for female adolescent voices (Gackle 2011).

Specific Criteria for Classification of the Female Voices

The following criteria for classifying the voices according to developmental phase are provided below (Gackle 2006, 2011).

In classifying female changing voices according the vocal development, the following criteria are suggested:

- average speaking pitch (determine by having students count backwards from 10, pausing on 2 or 3)

Table 27.1. Phases of female vocal development

Phase Number	Phase Name	Speaking Fundamental Frequency (from Wilson, 1972)	Vocal Characteristics	Assignment Voice Part	Age Range (chronological ages are given as general guides and should not be used as definitive indications of each phase of change	Comments
1	Prepubertal: Unchanged	C4 (261 Hz)– D#4 (311 Hz); acceptable limits: A3 (220 Hz)–F4 (349 Hz)	Clear/flute-like quality Much like the boy voice at this age No obvious register breaks Flexible/agile	Soprano I	Up to ages 8–10 (12)	Depending upon other physiological changes (i.e. breast development, menarche) this stage could continue through age 12
2A	Pre-menarcheal: Beginning of Mutation	Bb3 (233 Hz)–C#4 (277 Hz); Acceptable limits: A#3 (233 Hz)–D4 (293 Hz)	The range of the voice is approximately the same as that in the previous phase; however, there is more breathiness of tone exhibited throughout the range; lift points (register changes) sometimes appear around F4–A#4; loss of upper range; some have difficulty in the lower pitch range	Soprano II or Soprano I (if comfortable)	Ages 11–13	First signs of physical maturation begin (breast development, height increase, other secondary sex characteristics)

2B	Post-menarcheal: Pubertal–High Point of Mutation	A3 (220 Hz)–C4 (261 Hz); Acceptable limits: G3 (196 Hz)–D4 (293 Hz)	Huskiness throughout the range. Decrease in range; loss of some pitches in the upper register. Register changes appear between F4–A#4 and also at D5–F#5. Lower notes are more easily produced; "illusion" of alto quality. Difficulty in or discomfort with singing (or phonation in general). *Tessitura* is variable; can move up or down at either end of range. Voice cracking and breathiness frequently occur. As the voice begins to leave this phase, some vibrato may appear	Soprano II or Alto	12–15	None
3	Young Adult Female	G3 (196 Hz)–B3 (246 Hz); Acceptable limits: F#3 (185 Hz)–C4 (261 Hz)	Timbre approximates young adult quality. More richness is perceived in vocal quality. Range characteristically increases. Greater consistency in registers. Decreased breathiness. Register change at D5–F#5 (adult soprano *passaggio*) is more apparent. Some vibrato may naturally appear in the voice. Greater flexibility and agility in the voice. Volume and resonance capabilities increase	Soprano I, Soprano II, or Alto; wherever the student is most comfortable or wherever "color" is desired within the ensemble	14–17 (18)	Voices in this phase can sing almost any treble vocal part for various periods of time (as long as it is comfortable for the singer and there is emphasis on vocal health). In choral scenarios, this voice can be used to "color" sections depending upon the desired tone quality in a piece of music. In addition to encouraging musical growth, most students enjoy the movement between parts because of the challenge and interest it provides. Emphasis, however, should be on vocal comfort, with no strain or tension as a result of the assigned vocal part

- vocal range/*tessitura* (have students sing throughout the range on an open vowel such as /a/ to determine lowest and highest singing pitch; note where greatest comfort is in the range)
- register development (appearance of transition notes or *passaggi*; have students sing an ascending diatonic scale or use a ascending vocal glide on open vowel such as /a/, noting where transition notes are audible
- overall voice quality (timbre)—pure vs. breathy tone

Tessitura is here defined as the range of pitches most easily and freely produced within the total vocal range. Voice quality is determined by the perceived color, weight, and overall timbre of the tone.

Using these criteria, classification can be determined relatively quickly by listening to individual students. Some teachers advocate charting vocal ranges on a periodic basis (every six to eight weeks).

Review of Current Research on Female Adolescent Singing Voice

Due to increased interest in the female changing voice over the past thirty years, researchers have begun to focus on topics such as pedagogical techniques for tone development, speaking and singing voice characteristics, the effects of vocal skills/training on singing performance as well as studies regarding self-identity and singing in adolescent females. Two longitudinal studies now exist regarding the female adolescent voice. The following is a chronological overview of research specifically regarding the adolescent female voice.

Huff-Gackle (1987) and Fett (1994) examined the effect of vocal skills instruction on singing performance and breath management. Both studies concluded that the use of vocal techniques for emphasizing proper respiration, phonation, and resonance were effective in improving singing performance and breath management as well as promoting more efficient use of the developing voice. Sipley (1994) further examined the effects of vocal exercises, knowledge of the voice and the vocal development process on tone quality and vocal self-image of adolescent girls. Subgroups received (1) no treatment (control), (2) a program of vocal exercises, (3) only information about the voice, and (4) a combination of exercises and knowledge about the voice. At the end of the treatment, group four showed significant improvement in attitudes toward their singing voice, and while no statistically significant differences in tone quality for the whole group or subgroup were found, individual subjects showed marked vocal improvement (as rated by judges' evaluations).

Bottoms (1996) investigated William Vennard's "light mechanism" principle which was offered as a means of better understanding the female adolescent voice and its typical light, breathy tone quality. One hundred adolescent subjects accomplished three tasks: one acoustical, one perceptual, and one diagnostic. The acoustical task revealed that not all adolescent females produced a weak, breathy voice, and the perceptual study found that student judges were able to correctly identify sixty-three percent of the sounds with upper partials and those without upper partials. The diagnostic study found a direct relationship between breathiness and the presence or absence of upper partials. Breathiness had the effect of reducing upper partials.

In a study by Bonnie Blu Williams (1996), the speaking fundamental frequency, physiological vocal range, singing voice quality, and self-perceptions of the speaking and singing voice between two groups of pre-and post-menarcheal girls were compared. Though no significant differences were observed on either of the physiological measures, indications were that both groups of girls were experiencing some level of vocal mutation, demonstrating that there was a loss of control of the singing and speaking voice during mutation. In all cases, the post-mutational girls identified these symptoms (voice breaks, cracks, pitch changes, inconsistencies in speaking, breathy voices, and sore throats after singing) as happening more often than did the pre-menarcheal girls.

In addition to providing a comprehensive review of recent research comparing the development of male and female voices, Welch and Howard (2002) discuss the all-male tradition of cathedral choristers and the categorical perception regarding the "uniqueness" of male choristers vs. female choristers of English cathedral choirs by listeners. Among other conclusions, it is most interesting that "in all published studies to date, trained girls' voices appear to be more likely to be mislabeled as boys" (2002, p. 117). Listeners seem to have a perceptual "stereotype" of the sound of boy choristers to which any examples (male or female) are matched. It was also noted that girl choirs can be trained to sing with a "boy-like/masculine" vocal sound since many of the choral directors are ex-choristers, well acquainted with the cathedral choral tradition.

In 2003, Toole examined various aspects of female voice mutation and their effect on vocal characteristics associated with singing. This study examined 289 female public school students (ages six to sixteen years) regarding physical characteristics, musical performance participation, and vocal tone (breathiness, existence of register change). The analysis from this study revealed that (a) the fundamental speaking frequency decreased with age, (b) mean fundamental speaking frequency and mean singing range of the study were generally lower than indicated in earlier research, (c) mean singing range expanded with age, and (d) register change became increasingly pronounced at age eleven to sixteen. Additional information of importance to music educators included the fact that participation in choral/instrumental musical ensembles was associated with increased singing range and that female voice mutation appeared gradual and highly individual.

Presently, two longitudinal studies exist concerning the voice development of female adolescent voices. The first focused on choristers at Wells Cathedral in the United Kingdom, conducted by David Howard and Graham Welch (2002). This study reports acoustic data for three individual female choristers. Data collection occurred over a three year period; the results on specific measures (i.e. larynx closed quotient (CQ), overall amplitude (dB), and long-term average spectrum (LTAS)) indicate that developmental variations exist in both individual and group performance.

The second and most recent longitudinal study by Willis and Kenny (2011) was conducted over one year and focused on the process of vocal development of twenty girls (twelve to thirteen years of age) as observed in changes in speaking fundamental frequency (SFo), vocal range and register breaks, while also examining weight, height, vocal training, and individual self-perception. The study noted that several vocal characteristics changed as the girls progressed through various weight ranges. These changes included a decrease of the vocal range during the earlier part of the study and an increase of the vocal range and pitch breaks approximating adult vocal register transitions in the later part of the study. For some girls, SFo actually increased during the study. Vocal training resulted in higher SFo, greater speech-range inflection, high vocal range, and overall, a greater confidence in the use of the voice. Interestingly, these girls were also heavier in weight. It was also noted that all girls in the study (even those who had vocal training) lost confidence in their voice-use ability during this crucial year (age twelve to thirteen years).

Review of Current Research Regarding Self-Identity, Singing, and Adolescent Females

It is interesting that young female singers experiencing mutation cite a loss of confidence in regard to their voices during this time. Often, this lack of vocal confidence is also accompanied by a lack of confidence in other areas of the adolescent girl's life.

The connection between voice change and self-identity is undeniable. The period of adolescence is often filled with feelings of inadequacy, insecurity, and an over-riding need for peer acceptance. In fact, acceptance of self is often predicated first on one's acceptance by others. Research confirms the increased incidence of negative self-image and low self-esteem, which at times places adolescents at risk for depression (Wright 2005).

There is no doubt that pre-teens and teens of both genders face specific challenges as they navigate through this maze of change known as adolescence. Physiological, psychological, emotional, relational, and cognitive development converge at this time of life in hormonal tempo unlike any other time in human development. Understanding the physiological and psychological issues which these young women face requires that educators be aware of the changes and pressures which they encounter. Though studies which focus on self-concept/self-identity and the adolescent singer (especially the female adolescent singer) are limited, perhaps the following review of literature will provide some insight on this topic as well as the need for further study.

As previously noted, there has been increased information regarding the female changing voice in choral methods texts; however, with the exception of the latest text by Phillips (2004), one "crucial chapter" has been left out (O'Toole 1998). Indeed, there is recognition by the profession that there are gender-specific issues which educators face with choral singers. However, these concerns seem to be more focused on issues which the adolescent male encounters rather than those experienced by the adolescent female.

O'Toole further observed:

> . . . expectations based on gender exist in choral practices—that is, choral directors anticipate that male and female singers will have different needs. For example, directors expect male singers to be fewer in number and more difficult to recruit than females, to have more complicated and noticeable vocal problems, and to be more of a disciplinary challenge.
>
> (1998, p. 15)

A review of the literature reveals that journal articles, professional periodicals as well as methods texts all discuss these very real concerns. However, such discussions fail to address "what it means to be a female singer who is not difficult to recruit, has few noticeable vocal problems, is well-behaved and spends most of her time waiting for directors to turn their focus from male singers" (O'Toole 1998, p. 15). Thus, the author offered the following suggestions to counter this deficit with young female singers: (1) provide more SSA/SSAA opportunities for female singers in school ensembles, (2) eliminate the perceived hierarchy of the SATB ensemble as being the "top choir" by allowing SSA choirs to tour, record, and receive the same amount of attention as the SATB choirs often do, (3) focus on repertoire that encourages positive attitudes toward females (using appropriate texts—not just stereotypical female texts or man-centered texts) as well as the inclusion of music by female composers.

The study by Sipley (1994) was discussed in the previous section. Though the author examined the effects of vocal exercises and increased vocal knowledge and awareness of individual vocal development and vocal self-image in adolescent female singers, it is important to note that there were statistically significant differences in students' attitudes (improved attitude) toward their singing voices in the treatment group which received both vocal exercises and "vocal knowledge." This type of knowledge may lead to an acceptance of some of the unsettling vocal challenges which face the adolescent female singer during voice change.

In 1997, Chinn examined the relationship between high or low cultural mistrust and vocal characteristics of African-American adolescent females. The vocal characteristics included vocal self-identification, singing style, and singing range. It was not surprising that girls who highly identified with and valued cultural musical traditions attempted to incorporate those styles into their singing. Additionally, students who highly identified with these cultural musical traditions tended to demonstrate a high level of cultural mistrust and were suspicious of Caucasian music and musical values.

Chinn also reported that the high mistrust group exhibited lower overall singing ranges (lower upper terminal pitches). The author suggests that African-American girls who have feelings of mistrust toward Caucasian institutions may also have feelings of mistrust toward the idea of "school music," especially when the music is presented in a Caucasian environment. Thus, these girls may be more resistant to the teacher's attempts to have them sing with a tonal quality which is more representative of the institution (i.e. Caucasian). This study indicated that cultural mistrust affects vocal self-identity and is linked to singing tasks. The author suggests that teachers be aware of the need for sensitivity toward such students and focus their teaching on appropriate style characteristics in a healthy manner, no matter what style is performed.

In a one year study conducted by Monks (2003), a group of thirty students (male and female, aged eleven to eighteen), were recorded at two-month intervals in order to compare vocal changes with previous research studies on adolescent vocal development. From this group, case studies were made of fifteen students which examined their self-assessments regarding their own voices at year-end as well as a performance study using video recording.

Monks observed that "The sense of vocal identity shown by these young singers reveals a close relationship with their sense of self" (2003, p. 253). The author also found that students in the study were very aware of their singing and the changes in their voices which occur at puberty and which in the final analysis, affect their performance. These findings "resonate with the research of others in the field" (2003, p. 254). Monks also stated that the information provided by the students is of great value to the choral conductor and vocal teacher in the selection of repertoire, in which rehearsal strategies are chosen, and overall communication with the adolescent singer.

Yarnell (2006) studied voice change from the viewpoint of the private voice teacher. The author studied thirty-two children (male and female, aged eleven to eighteen), over the period of one year and monitored their voice qualities and overall vocal development. The author found that her findings also matched the vocal development stages/phases outlined by Cooksey (1992) and Gackle (1991). As the author monitored the singers aurally, she also interviewed them about their own feelings and their self-understanding as to the vocal changes taking place.

In the summary of this initial study, Yarnell cited the following findings (2006, p. 82):

First stage: aged eleven to twelve. Girls were confident and seem to have an extended range, and feel "comfortable" throughout the range. However, by the end of the year, there was a loss of resonance in the voice.

Second stage: aged twelve to thirteen. Many of the students noticed little change and found that the voice was "fairly reliable" during this period. The beginnings of a breathy quality as well as some inconsistency in one subject was also noticed based on the physical maturity of the singer.

Third stage: aged thirteen to fourteen. In the majority of the singers, a breathy or "airy" tone was observed. Though not all singers experienced these symptoms, some continued with the flute-like sound characteristic of the previous stage. At times, students attempted to overcome the symptoms by employing a "belt" quality. The author indicated that this was the most difficult year from a pedagogical standpoint. The author cited issues of difficulty in maintaining interest and enthusiasm for singing when the voices are "unpredictable" and when range and vocal timbre changes so drastically. It is at this stage that teachers should be most aware of the psychological implications of self-image and self-confidence which affect the singer. She further suggested that the choice of music (choosing inspiring music with which students can relate) is very important in maintaining involvement in singing.

Fourth stage: aged fourteen to fifteen. This period is marked by students having both more confidence in their voices and more control over the voice. According to Yarnell, students start to "own" their voices.

Fifth stage: aged fifteen to sixteen. Boys in this stage of development begin to settle into their "new baritone ranges," and new timbres and wider possibilities for vocal colors are available to both male and female singers.

Even though this study was conducted over the span of only one year, with students in one school in the United Kingdom, the results seem to speak to the universality of experiences for adolescent singers in Western culture.

Finally, in an unpublished article, Gackle (2010) surveyed 391 collegiate female students and 52 high school female students from 2005–2008 using a Likert-type questionnaire. Students were requested to rate their agreement/disagreement to statements regarding specific attitudes relating to singing. Of the college students, 67.5 percent were music majors, while 32.5 percent were non-majors. Forty-six percent of the respondents had sung in choirs six to ten years, while 33 percent had sung in choirs over eleven years.

Both the collegiate and high school students indicated strong agreement with statements such as:

(1) "when I sing, I feel better about myself and my abilities" (89 percent collegiate—64 percent high school) and (2) "when I sing, I feel as though I can express my inner feelings" (86 percent–78 percent, respectively). Both collegiate and high school respondents indicated

total or strong agreement that many of the friendships in their lives were those made in choir and/or musical settings (64 percent). When students were asked to rate agreement with the statement that singing had made little or no difference in their lives, 84 percent indicated no agreement. When asked to respond to the statement that they "would seek opportunities to sing throughout life," both collegiate and high school respondents rated total or strong agreement (82 percent and 77 percent, respectively). Encouraging their own children to sing in choirs was rated with 88 percent (collegiate) and 79 percent (high school) total or strong agreement.

Though these responses were informal in nature, it appears that music, specifically singing and participation in choir, may provide a viable outlet for self-expression, a sense of belonging, and ultimately, a mechanism for encouraging positive self-concept in young females.

SUMMARY

Over the past twenty-five years, there has been an increase in information concerning the female adolescent voice. During this time, voice change in girls has been recognized and made the focus of much greater study. Both the physiological changes which occur in the young female voice as well as the psychological issues which face these young women during this time of their lives are finally becoming topics of interest to the profession. It is obvious, however, that this is fertile ground for future research. Hopefully, there are more longitudinal studies on the horizon which utilize the expertise of interdisciplinary investigator groups, (i.e. otolaryngologists, specialists in adolescent pediatrics and adolescent psychology, engineers/acousticians, and music educators). With the collective abilities of such professionals, a more thorough understanding of the adolescent female voice can be achieved. With this type of insight, vocal educators may be better prepared to aid these young women during this time of transition, both vocally and emotionally.

REFERENCES

Alderson, R. (1979). *Complete Handbook of Voice Training*. West Nyack, NY: Parker Publishing.

Bell, C. (2004). Update on community choirs and singing in the United States. *International Journal of Research in Choral Singing* 2(1): 39–52.

Biro, F.M., Greenspan, L.C., Galvez, M.P., Pinney, S.M., Teitelbaum, S., Windham, G.C., et al. (2013). Onset of breast development in a longitudinal cohort. *Pediatrics* 132(5): 1–9. <http://pediatrics.aappublications.org/ content/early/2013/10/30/peds.2012-3773.full.pdf>, retrieved December 1, 2013.

Bottoms, J.F. (1996). Investigation of William Vennard's light mechanism principle in the adolescent female voice. *Dissertation Abstracts International* 56(9): 3493.

Brinson, B. (1996). *Choral Music Methods and Materials*. New York: G. Schirmer.

Brodnitz, F. S. (1983). "On the changing voice." *National Association for Teachers of Singing 40* (2): 24–6.

Chinn, B.J. (1997). Vocal self-identification, singing style, and singing range in relationship to a measure of cultural mistrust in African-American adolescent females. *Journal of Research in Music Education* 45(4): 636–49.

Clift, S. and Hancox, G. (2010). The significance of choral singing for sustaining psychological well- being: Findings from a survey of choristers in England, Australia and Germany. *Music Performance Research* 3(1) Special Issue on Music and Health: 79–96.

Clift, S., Hancox, G., Staricoff, R., and Whitmore, C. (2008). Singing and health: A systematic mapping and review of non-clinical research. *Canterbury: Canterbury Christ Church University.* <http:// www.canterbury.ac.uk/Research/Centres/SDHR/Documents/ SingingAndHealthFullReport.pdf>, retrieved on November 30, 2013.

Collins, D.L. (1999). *Teaching Choral Music.* Englewood-Cliffs, NJ: Prentice Hall.

Cooksey, J.M. (1977a). The development of a continuing, eclectic theory for the Training and cultivation of the junior high school male changing voice. Part I: Existing theories. *Choral Journal* 18(2): 5–13.

Cooksey, J.M. (1977b). The development of a continuing, eclectic theory for the training and cultivation of the junior high school male changing voice. Part II: Scientific and empirical findings; some tentative solutions. *Choral Journal* 18(3): 5–16.

Cooksey, J.M. (1977c). The development of a continuing, eclectic theory for the training and cultivation of the junior high school male changing voice. Part III: Developing an integrated approach to the care and training of the junior high school male changing voice. *Choral Journal* 18(4): 5–15.

Cooksey, J.M. (1978). The development of a continuing, eclectic theory for the training and cultivation of the junior high school male changing voice. Part IV: Selecting music for the junior high school male changing voice. *Choral Journal* 18(5): 5–17.

Cooksey, J.M. (1992). *Working with the Adolescent Voice.* St. Louis, MO: Concordia Publishing.

Cooksey, J.M. (1999). *Working with Adolescent Voices.* St. Louis, MO: Concordia Publishing.

Cooksey, J.M., Beckett, R.L., and Wiseman, R. (1983). *A longitudinal investigation of selected vocal, physiological, and acoustical factors associated with voice maturation in the junior high school male adolescent.* Research study resulting from the report for the National ACDA (American Choral Directors Association) Convention, New Orleans, Louisiana, March 10–12.

Cooper, I.O. and Kuersteiner, K.O. (1970). *Teaching Junior High School Music: General Music and Vocal* Program, 2nd edn. Conway, AK: Cambiata Press.

Cyrier, A. (1981). A study of the vocal registers and transitional pitches of the adolescent female. *Missouri Journal of Research in Music Education* 4(5): 84–6.

Duffy, R.J. (1958). The vocal pitch characteristics of eleven, thirteen, and fifteen-year-old female speakers. *Dissertation Abstracts* 19: 599.

Duffy, R.J. (1970). Fundamental frequency characteristics of adolescent females. *Language and Speech* 13: 14–24.

Fett, D.L. (1994). The adolescent female voice: The effect of vocal skills instruction measures of singing performance and breath management. *Dissertation Abstracts International* 54(7): 2501.

Gackle, L. (1991). The adolescent female voice: characteristics of change and stages of development. *Choral Journal* 31(8): 17–25.

Gackle, L. (2006). Finding Ophelia's Voice: The female voice during adolescence. *Choral Journal* 47(5): 28–37.

Gackle, L. (2011). *Finding Ophelia's Voice, Opening Ophelia's Heart: Nurturing the Female Adolescent Voice*. Dayton, OH: Heritage Music.

Gackle, L. (2010). Student responses to questionnaire from 2005 and 2006 Florida Collegiate Women's Choir Festival, and FL-ACDA Intercollegiate Women's Honor Choir, 2007, 2008. *Unpublished raw data.*

Groom, M. (1979). A descriptive analysis of development in adolescent male voices during the summer time period. *Dissertation Abstracts International* 40: 4946A.

Herman-Giddens, M.E., Slora, E.J., Wasserman, R.C., Bourndony, C.J., Bhapkar, M.V., Koch, G.G., and Hasemeier, C.M. (1997). Secondary sexual characteristics and menses in young girls seen in office practice: A study from the Pediatric Research in Office Settings Network. *Pediatrics* 99(4): 505–12.

Herman-Giddens, M.E., Steffes, J., Harris, D., Slora, E., Hussey, M., Dowshen, S.A., et al. (2012). Secondary sexual characteristics in boys: Data from the Pediatric Research in Office Settings Network. *Pediatrics* 130(5): e1058–68. <http://pediatrics.aappublications.org/content/130/5/e1058.full.pdf+html>, retrieved on November 30, 2013.

Hollien, H. (1978). Adolescence and voice change. In: B. Weinberg and Van Lawrence (eds), *Transcripts of the Seventh Symposium Care of the Professional Voice: Part II. Life span changes in the human voice*, pp. 36–43. New York, NY: The Voice Foundation.

Howard, D.M. and Welch, G.F. (2002). The female chorister voice development: A longitudinal study at Wells, UK. *Bulletin of the Council for Research in Music Education* 153(4): 63–70.

Huff-Gackle, L. (1985). The adolescent female voice (ages 11–15): classification, placement and development of tone. *Choral Journal* 25(8): 15–18.

Huff-Gackle, M.L. (1987). The effect of selected vocal techniques for breath management, resonation, and vowel unification on tone production in the junior high school female voice. *Dissertation Abstracts International* 48(4): 862.

Hylton, J.B. (1994). *Comprehensive Choral Music Education*. Englewood Cliffs, NJ: Prentice Hall.

Joseph, W.A. (1965). A summation of the research pertaining to vocal growth. *Journal of Research in Music Education* 13(2): 93–100.

Kahane, J.C. (1982). The developmental anatomy of the human prepubertal and pubertal larynx. *Journal of Speech and Hearing* 25: 446–55.

Kaplowitz, P.B., Slora, E.J., Wasserman, R.C., Pedlow, S.E., and Herman-Giddens, M.E. (2001). Earlier onset of puberty in girls: Relation to increased body mass index and race. *Pediatrics* 108(2): 347–53.

Killian, J. (1999). A description of vocal maturation among 5th– 6th grade boys. *Journal of Research in Music Education* 47(4): 357–69.

Luchsinger, R. and Arnold, G.E. (1965). *Voice-Speech-Language: Clinical communicology: Its physiology and pathology*. Belmont, CA: Wadsworth Publishing.

McKenzie, D. (1956). *Training the Boy's Changing Voice*. London: Bradford and Dickens, Drayton House.

Monks, S. (2003). Adolescent singers and perceptions of vocal identity. *British Journal of Music Education* 20(3): 243–56.

Naidr, J., Zboril, M., and Sevcik, K. (1965). Die pubertalen veränderungen der stimme bei jungen im verlauf von 5 jahren (Pubertal voice changes in boys over a period of 5 years). *Folia Phoniatrica* 17: 1–18.

O'Toole, P. (1998). A missing chapter from choral methods books: How choirs neglect girls. *Choral Journal* 39(5): 9–32.

Phillips, K.H. (1992). *Teaching Kids to Sing*. New York: Schirmer Books.

Phillips, K.H. (2004). *Directing the Choral Music Program*. New York: Oxford University Press.

Rogol, A.D., Roemmich, J.N., and Clark, P.A. (2002). Growth at puberty. *Journal of Adolescent Health* 31(6) suppl.: 192–200.

Rutkowski, J. (1985). Final results of a longitudinal study investigating the validity of Cooksey's theory for training the adolescent male voice. *Pennsylvania Music Educators Association Bulletin of Research in Music Education* 16: 3–10.

Schiff, M.B. (1999). Sex hormones and the female voice. *Journal of Voice* 13(3): 424–43.

Seth, G. and Guthrie, D. (1935). *Speech in Childhood: Its Development and Disorders*. London: Oxford University Press.

Sipley, K.L. (1994). The effects of vocal exercises and information about the voice on the tone quality and vocal self-image of adolescent female singers. *Dissertation Abstracts International* 54(8): 2940.

Stubbs, G.E. (1917). Why we have male choirs in churches. *Musical Quarterly* 3(3): 416–27.

Swanson, F.J. (1977). *The Male Singing Voice Ages Eight to Eighteen*. Cedar Rapids, IA: Igram Press.

Tanner J.M. (1972). Sequencing, tempo and individual variation in growth and development of boys and girls aged twelve to sixteen. In: J. Kagan and R. Coles (ed.), *Twelve to sixteen: Early Adolescence*, pp. 1–24. New York: W.W. Norton.

Thurman, L. and Klitzke, C. (2000). Highlights of physical growth and function of voices from prebirth to age 21. In: L. Thurman and G.F. Welch (eds). *Bodymind and Voice: Foundations of Voice Education*, revised edn, pp. 696–703. Iowa City, IA: National Center for Voice and Speech.

Titze, I.R. (1994). *Principles of Voice Production*. Englewood Cliffs, NJ.: Prentice-Hall.

Toole, G.H. (2003). The female singing voice from childhood through adolescence. *Dissertation Abstracts International* 64(6): 2019.

Vennard, W. (1967). *Singing, the Mechanism and the Technic*. New York, NY: Carl Fischer.

Weiss, D. (1950). The pubertal change of the human voice. *Folia Phoniatrica* 2(3): 126–59.

Welch, G.F. and Howard, D.M. (2002). Gendered voice in the cathedral choir. *Psychology of Music* 30: 102–20.

Wilson, P.W.F. and Umpierrez, G.E. (2008). Insulin resistance and pubertal changes. *Journal of Clinical Endocrinology and Metabolism* 93(7): 2472–3. <http:// jcem.endojournals.org/content/93/ 7/2472.full.pdf+html?sid=38bb1806-25e4-4c4b-8154-c6a588be4cd7>, retrieved on November 30, 2013.

Williams, B.B. (1996). An investigation of selected female singing—and speaking—voice characteristics through comparison of a group of pre-menarcheal girls to a group of post-menarcheal girls. *Journal of Singing* 52(3): 33–40.

Willis, E.C. and Kenny, D.T. (2011). Voice training and changing weight—are they reflected in speaking fundamental frequency, voice range, and pitch breaks of 13-year-old girls? A longitudinal study. *Journal of Voice* 25(5): e233–43.

Wilson, D.K. (1972). *Voice Problems of Children*. Baltimore, MD: Williams and Wilkins.

Wright, E.J. (2005). Trapped in negative self-focus: The implications of emerging self-focused emotion regulation and increased depression risk following pubertal onset in females. *Proquest Dissertations and Theses*. PhD dissertation. Iowa: The University of Iowa. Section 0096, Part 0622, 223 pp. Publication Number: AAT 3172457.

Yarnell, S. (2006). Vocal and aural perceptions of young singers aged ten to twenty-one. *Journal of Singing* 63(1): 81–5.

Zuckerman, D. (2001). When little girls become women: Early onset of puberty in girls. *The Ribbon: Newsletter of the Cornell University Program on Breast Cancer and Environmental Risk Factors in New York State (BCERF)* 6(1). <http://envirocancer.cornell.edu/Newsletter/articles/v6little.girls.cfm>, retrieved on November 30, 2013.

CHAPTER 28

THE EFFECTS OF GENDER ON THE MOTIVATION AND BENEFITS ASSOCIATED WITH COMMUNITY SINGING IN THE UK

DIANA PARKINSON

INTRODUCTION

COMMUNITY singing—by which is meant any type of amateur group singing—is important. It is important not only for individuals, but for society as a whole. Research has shown that singing can have significant positive effects on the psychological and social well-being of individuals (see the review carried out by Clift et al. 2010). Equally, the contribution which singing makes to communities has been demonstrated by researchers such as Langston and Barrett, who found that "choirs and similar organizations are strong community resources, crucial in the creation of social capital that benefits the whole community" (Langston and Barrett 2008, p. 133).

Community singing has become one of the most common forms of active musical participation in Western societies. In 2009, nearly a fifth of households in the USA reported one or more adults participating in a choir (Chorus America 2009). Similarly, in Sweden, researchers found that more than one in ten people were participating in a choir or singing group (Sandgren 2009). Although there are no official records for participation in community singing in the UK, a recent report has revealed that there are at least 40 000 choirs in the UK, representing around 2.14 million singers (Voices Now 2017).

However, it has been increasingly recognized that there is a gender dimension to participation in community singing; while historically choral singing was predominantly a masculine activity until at least the eighteenth century, since the nineteenth century researchers have been reporting the phenomenon of the "missing males" in choral singing (Freer 2012; Harrison, Welch, and Adler 2012; Koza 1993). Wilson (2011) reviewed fifteen studies carried out across Canada, the USA, Germany, and the UK, and found that the mean percentage of male participation was just 35 percent. These days, it is recognized that this may threaten the continued existence of mixed-voice amateur choirs and singing groups: "if the number of male singers continues to decline, some community choirs will be unable to sustain performances of the standard choral repertoire" (Bell 2004, p. 50).

Researchers have already identified a number of issues which may help to explain the reasons for this decline. For some, the male disengagement from singing stems from childhood with "girls being more likely to participate, and boys who wish to sing or play certain instruments facing the disapproval of a 'macho' peer culture" (Ashley 2002, p. 180). For Hall (2005), this forms part of a "hegemonic masculinity" which compels boys (and girls) to adopt behaviors regarded as suitable for their sex. Others go further back, arguing that pre-birth experiences influence our future musical development (Lecanuet 1996) and that the dominant influence of the mother's voice creates a gendered experience of early sound which informs the way we view music. This theme has been further developed by researchers such as Harrison et al. (2012), who edited a collection of essays titled *Perspectives on Males and Singing*, arguing that boys and young men are strongly influenced by these perceptions of singing as a "feminine" activity. Nonetheless, some researchers have taken a different approach in explaining the gender imbalance in community singing. Green, for example, argues that, while music is a masculine domain that excludes women from many areas of musical life, women's singing represents "the greatest musical performance opportunity available to women, in both the amateur, domestic sphere and the professional, public sphere" (Green 1997, p. 33).

Most previous research in this area has focused on singing at schools or universities, and although some studies have looked at the benefits of singing to adults with long-term health conditions (e.g. Dingle et al. 2012; Särkämö et al. 2014), scant attention has been paid to adult singers more generally and how gender influences their engagement in community singing. This has been reported by Clift et al. (2012), who highlighted the lack of attention to gender as a "significant limitation of the existing corpus of work" around singing and its perceived relevance for well-being (Clift et al. 2012, p. 234). This chapter describes a recent study that sought to examine the ways in which amateur singers perceive the motivations and benefits associated with community singing and how these are affected by gender.

DESCRIPTION OF STUDY

The study focused on singers across the UK and used an online survey to gather the views and experiences of men and women singing in different types of choirs and singing groups.[1]

---

[1] Those taking part in professional ensembles and music therapy were excluded as it was felt that the participants of these groups would have very different motivations and experiences from those of amateur singers.

Taking a mixed-methods approach, it included open and closed questions in order to collect both quantitative and qualitative data. The survey was piloted with members of one choir, and once finalized was sent out nationally by posting messages on relevant Internet sites and asking music networks and choir leaders to promote the research to their members.

Overall, the survey received a total of 686 valid responses. Unsurprisingly, the gender distribution of the sample was unequal: two-thirds of participants were female (66 percent) and one third was male (34 percent). Furthermore, the majority of participants (72 percent) were aged over fifty and the vast majority (96 percent) were from Caucasian ethnic backgrounds. As previous research confirms (Bell 2004; Chorus America 2009; Clift et al. 2007), this demographic profile appears to be highly representative of the general population of people who sing in community choirs. However, despite the steps taken to reach choirs likely to have a large proportion of non-Caucasian singers, the very small proportion of non-Caucasian participants in the study is clearly not reflective of twenty-first-century Britain and therefore may not be representative of those currently involved in community singing in the UK. On the other hand, participants sang in a wide range of choirs and singing groups (see Figure 28.1); while the largest proportion sang in choral societies (34 percent), participants were also singing in rock choirs (5 percent), workplace choirs (3 percent), and gospel choirs (3 percent).

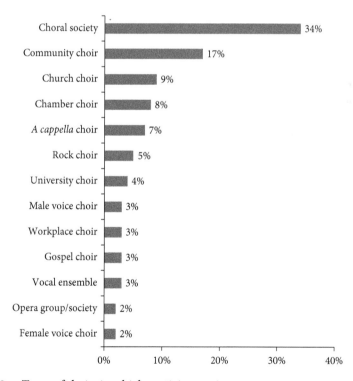

FIGURE 28.1 Types of choirs in which participants sing.

Note: Many participants sang in more than one choir; n = 937

Motivations associated with community singing

Participants were asked to indicate on a four-point scale to what extent they had been motivated to join a choir/singing group by a number of specific factors that had been identified from the literature. Their response was then examined along with their responses to an open question which asked them to describe these reasons. Three themes of particular interest emerged in participants' responses to the questions about motivation. First of all, it seemed that, unsurprisingly, almost all participants (99 percent) were motivated by musical reasons such as a desire to sing with others, or to develop their musical experience. Equally, their answers suggested that for many people (67 percent), joining a choir fulfilled a social need, such as to meet other people, to share an activity with family or friends, or to feel part of a community. Finally, a considerable number of people described personal reasons for joining a choir, such as in response to life changes or to answer a need for emotional space.[2]

Musical reasons

Participants were strongly motivated by the desire to sing as part of a group (99 percent rated this as very or quite important). In addition, over three-quarters (76 percent) said they had wanted to improve their singing voice and nearly two-thirds (62 percent) said they had wanted to improve their musical skills. Musical reasons emerged strongly in participants' responses to the open question; nearly a fifth indicated that a desire to experience music or to maintain or deepen their engagement with music lay behind their decision to join a choir. For many, this was simply because they remembered "the sheer joy of singing in a choir" while at school. Indeed, data from the survey revealed that most participants had engaged in a considerable amount of musical activity as children; nearly two-thirds (64 percent) had been involved in three or more musical activities such as learning a musical instrument, singing in a choir, or going to concerts. This reflects previous research which has shown singing at school to be a predictor of later musical activity (Cavitt 2005). For many of the participants in this study, singing in a choir had become a constant in their lives that had, over the years, become part of their identity: "I need to sing; it's part of who I am" (male, 60–69).

For others, joining a choir had been a way to bring music back into their lives. One person described how she had experienced "a burning need to get involved with music again after a gap of nearly twenty years." Others talked about joining a choir to experience specific types of music, particularly choral music, although some also had sought out groups singing gospel, folk, or rock music.

Some participants had been driven by a desire to extend their musical experiences. These participants talked about wanting to work with a particular conductor, to perform in specific venues or to sing solos as factors which had motivated them to join their current choir/group. Others simply wanted to extend their musical repertoire: "I wanted to stretch my musical awareness of composers, as it's easy to get into insular habits. Being in a choir you sing what is put in front of you, not just what you like" (female, 40–49).

---

[2] This aspect was not measured on the quantitative scale but was identified by nearly a fifth (19 percent) of participants in their qualitative responses to this question.

Alongside the drive to be involved as an individual in making music, participants also emphasized the need to sing with other people. For many, the attraction of singing in a choir was clearly driven by an understanding of the power and the beauty that can be achieved by people singing together. Participants talked about wanting to be "part of a beautiful sound" or to experience "the powerful feeling of singing harmonies."

Looking at participants' responses by gender, the qualitative and quantitative data suggested that, overall, female participants were more motivated than male participants by musical reasons. In particular, female participants were significantly more motivated than male singers to sing as part of a group and to improve their singing voice, and this was reinforced by the qualitative data.[3] On the other hand, the qualitative data revealed that male participants seemed to have been more influenced by having sung in childhood and by the need to re-engage or continue their involvement with music. It seems therefore, that although male participants placed less emphasis than women on particular musical reasons, this is nonetheless one of the more important motivators for men. This aligns with previous research (Clift and Hancox 2010; Rensink-Hoff 2011), which has suggested the importance of musical motivators for men who sing.

Social reasons

In their responses to the quantitative question, over two-thirds of participants (67 percent) said they had wanted to meet new people; female singers were significantly more strongly motivated than male singers in this respect.[4] However, social reasons emerged as a motivating factor in only a small number (7 percent) of participants' open responses. This was surprising, particularly in the light of previously published qualitative research showing that choir members rated social drivers highest alongside musical drivers (Rohwer 2010).

Nonetheless, for some people, joining a choir was clearly a way of fulfilling social needs; some participants talked about joining a choir as a way of sharing an activity with family or friends, while others saw it as a way to meet new people. Some described it as a means of developing a deeper connection to people around them, a way of increasing their "sense of belonging" or of feeling "more connected to other human beings." For others, a desire to contribute to or share in the cultural life of their community was a motivating factor, reflecting findings from previous research (McCrary 2001; Rensink-Hoff 2011), and it was particularly interesting to note that in both the quantitative and qualitative data, male participants were more likely than female participants to express this desire (although this was not statistically significant).

Personal reasons

Another strong motivating factor for many participants was the way in which joining a choir could provide a means of responding to personal challenges, particularly life changes

---

[3] Chi-square tests carried out on the quantitative data showed that female participants were significantly more motivated than male singers to sing as part of a group ($X^2(1, N = 662) = 14.39$, p <.005) and to improve their singing voice ($X^2(1, N = 654) = 14.32$, p <.005).

[4] Chi-square tests carried out on the quantitative data showed that female participants were significantly more motivated than male singers by a desire to meet new people ($X^2(1, N = 662) = 9.61$, p = <.05).

such as moving home, retirement, children leaving home, or bereavement. One participant described how joining a choir had helped her cope with the death of her first child: "I lost my first baby at eleven weeks. I was very distressed for a time then my husband suggested I join the local choral society—a decision I have never regretted" (female, 70 and over).

Other participants had sought to join a choir believing that it would benefit their physical or mental health. For example, a participant with asthma had been told by her doctor that singing would improve her breathing. Equally, several participants had felt singing in a choir would improve their mental health and/or self-confidence: "I suffer with depression, social anxiety and asthma and hoped to improve one or all of these by singing and performing in a group" (female, 30–39).

For others, joining a choir was a way to create a space in their lives that was purely their own. One male participant talked about needing to "fill a void" when he stopped playing football. Others described a need to have something outside of family, home, and work. On the other hand, some participants saw joining a choir as a way of challenging themselves to "open up new areas of experience," to develop new skills, or to seek "general enrichment." For some, this had a very specific relevance, such as overcoming bad experiences gained in childhood, or providing a safe space for self-expression: "[I wanted a choir I could join] and contribute to as me . . . a bereaved lesbian, a person who would enjoy the singing/social/political/performing parts of choir life" (female, 60–69).

Overall, this finding echoes those from previous research which identified personal development as one of the main factors in the motivation of singers (Wilson 2011). However, looking at participants' responses by gender suggests that there are gender dimensions to this which have not previously been uncovered; it appears that a need to respond to personal issues is more likely to motivate women to join a choir than men. Female participants were particularly likely to join a choir as a response to life changes or to answer a personal need for space and self-expression, while male participants were more attracted by the challenge of doing something different.

Benefits associated with community singing

Participants were also asked to rate on a scale from one (low) to ten (high) how much they felt they derived certain benefits from singing in a choir. Their responses were then examined in their light of their responses to an open question which asked them to describe how they felt they benefited from community singing. Several themes emerged particularly strongly: social connectedness; personal development; mood enhancement; emotional resilience; esthetic benefits; and health benefits.

Social connectedness

First, participants of both genders identified a feeling of social connectedness that resulted from community singing. Many people described how community singing gave them a sense of "belonging," of "fellowship," and of "being part of something." One person said simply: "It is a way in which I can feel at one with others" (female, 60–69).

Some people also described how singing enabled them to give pleasure to others, both by sharing their singing with their audiences and by supporting other people in their choirs/singing groups. Some saw their singing as a way of connecting with the community around them: "It's a way that I can give back to the community I live in" (male, 40–49).

Some participants described how singing had helped them to make "new friends and renew old friendships," while others found it helped them to share something with their partner. Equally, some people described how it helped them to feel "less alone in the world."

These findings echo those seen in previous research (Clift et al. 2010; Faulkner and Davidson 2006; Langston and Barrett 2008; Rensink-Hoff 2011; Stewart and Lonsdale 2016) in suggesting the importance of social benefits to singers and the way in which this links to their emotional well-being. However, the data appear to contradict the finding by Rensink-Hoff (2011) that female singers rated social benefits more highly than their male counterparts, as there were no significant differences in the way in which male and female participants in this study rated the benefits of community singing in terms of social connectedness. On the other hand, analysis of the qualitative data revealed that male participants were particularly likely to recognize benefits related to feeling part of something, a sense of community and of helping others.

Esthetic benefits

Being part of a choir also brings esthetic and artistic benefits (Rensink-Hoff 2011) in enabling participants to develop their musical skills and knowledge. Some people particularly appreciated the intellectual challenge involved in learning and performing new music: "I enjoy the learning of new music from scratch and the experience of continuous improvement through to the performance" (male, 60–69).

Some participants described how community singing had given them new experiences and opportunities, not only in terms of performing in different places, but also in enabling them to experience different musical genres. Others had widened their knowledge of a particular repertoire or extended their musical appreciation: "It has given me a greater understanding of choral music and enhanced my enjoyment of music in general" (female, 60–69).

A considerable proportion of participants (19 percent) identified this benefit, in line with Rensink-Hoff's study (2011) which reported that singers rated esthetic benefits highly along with social and health benefits. Furthermore, there were some indications in the qualitative data that female participants rated the benefits they derived from the challenge of learning and extending their musical skills and knowledge more highly than did the male participants.

Personal development

Participants highlighted the way in which singing had made a difference to them as individuals; many people described the importance of community singing in terms of personal fulfillment and increased confidence. In particular, many participants talked about the way in which their singing gave them an immense sense of satisfaction: "Learning, making and performing music provides me with pleasure at a profound level together with the kind of satisfaction that craft people get from completing a successful piece of work" (male, 70 or over).

For some, community singing had contributed to a greater sense of self-worth. One person explained that they needed to sing in order to feel that their life was worthwhile. Others talked about feeling valued and having a greater sense of purpose in their lives. This reflects the findings from an earlier study in which researchers noted the way in which singing adds meaning and purpose to singers' lives (Livesey et al. 2012, p. 18).

Some participants also talked about the way in which they had gained confidence; it seemed that for some people, their experience of community singing had acted as a springboard, giving them strength and self-belief to take into other areas of their lives: "It is a huge part of my personal identity. It helps my mental health and self-confidence" (female, 30–39).

Looking at participants' responses by gender, female participants rated increased self-confidence significantly higher than male participants.[5] This also came through in their responses to the open question. On the other hand, male participants were more likely to emphasise the sense of personal fulfillment they gained from community singing (although this was not statistically significant).

Mood enhancement

Another important theme to emerge was the way in which participants felt community singing lifted their spirits and brought joy into their lives. One person talked about "the amazing buzz" they got from singing while others described the way in which singing helped them to feel good about themselves, both immediately after singing and more generally: "It feels a very healthy and emotionally wholesome thing to do; the payback is much greater than simply singing with lots of people. Singing in a choir reaches parts that other things don't!" (female, 50–59).

Some people likened this to a spiritual experience; for example, one person described how singing together in harmony "sends shivers down my spine . . . It is the nearest I come to having a spiritual experience." For others, singing simply brought laughter and fun into their lives: "There is a huge amount of fun in the shared experience of rehearsing in a group" (male, 60–69).

This theme has been recognized by other researchers (see Clift et al. 2010) who have noted the importance of community singing in having a positive effect on mood. The analysis of the qualitative data also suggested that female participants were generally more likely to identify the mood-enhancing benefits of singing than men, aligning with previous research showing that women were more likely to report positive emotional states from singing (Clift and Hancox 2010; Sandgren 2009).

Emotional resilience

Although other studies have identified the benefits of singing in terms of stress reduction (see Clift et al. 2010), the way in which some participants talked about this suggested that it may have a broader effect in increasing their emotional resilience. In their responses to the quantitative question as well as to the open question, many people emphasized the way in

---

[5] An independent t-test comparing the means of both groups showed that female participants gave increased self-confidence a mean score of 8.1 compared to a score of 7.1 given by the male participants and that this was statistically significant (p<.001).

which singing helped them to cope with the stress of their lives. They described how singing allowed them to "leave behind the stresses and strains of the day," enabling them to switch off from everyday concerns. Some people suggested this contributed to better mental health and an enhanced ability to cope with life: "It gives me a great feeling of being in control of my life" (male, 50–59).

Interestingly, one male participant described it "as a way of expressing and articulating certain emotional narratives that cause disturbance if they don't find a suitable outlet/arena." For a number of participants, singing had provided a way to cope with personal challenges such as bereavement or depression. Several people described how it had provided an alternative to being "back on the tablets" while others felt that it helped make the grief they felt following the death of their partner more manageable: "After my husband died, it kept me sane and gave me the strength to cope" (female, 60–69).

For many people, singing also provided a regular activity which was important in terms of providing structure in their lives and helping them get out of the house: "Apart from doing food shopping, it's the only thing I do every week ... It's as important as eating and breathing" (female, 50–59).

As Table 28.1 shows, female participants were significantly more likely than male participants to identify benefits in terms of how community singing helped to them to feel less stressed[6] and to feel stronger/fitter[7] which again reflects previous research showing that women were more likely to report positive emotional states from singing (Clift and Hancox 2010; Sandgren 2009).

Table 28.1 Benefits of community singing by gender

	Gender	N	Mean	Std. Deviation	Signif.	t-values
Reduces stress levels	Male	217	7.67	2.265	.000	–5.503
	Female	417	8.70	1.874		
Gives me more confidence in myself	Male	215	7.07	2.226	.017	–2.406
	Female	422	8.06	1.997		
Has given me new friends/ more support	Male	219	7.07	2.207	.140	–1.497
	Female	421	7.52	2.273		
Gives me a sense of being part of a community	Male	217	7.49	2.192	.000	–4.138
	Female	420	7.77	2.281		
Makes me feel stronger/ fitter	Male	219	6.87	2.452	.364	–968
	Female	421	7.70	2.329		
Gives me personal satisfaction/fulfilment	Male	221	9.08	1.192	.000	–6.088
	Female	421	9.19	1.463		

[6] An independent t-test comparing the means of both groups showed that female participants gave reduced stress a mean score of 8.7 compared to a score of 7.7 given by the male participants and that this difference was statistically significant (p<.001).

[7] An independent t-test comparing the means of both groups showed that female participants gave improved strength/fitness a mean score of 7.7 compared to a score of 6.9 given by the male participants and that this difference was statistically significant (p<.001).

Health benefits

Finally, some participants identified health benefits from singing, particularly in terms of providing mental stimulation and helping them keep mentally active: "It stimulates the grey matter!" (female, 60–69).

Others highlighted its positive effects on respiratory problems such as asthma and in improving posture and breathing. Some people felt that it contributed to general fitness and health, particularly in terms of improving posture and providing physical exercise: "I believe it's beneficial to health and all round well-being" (male, 70 and over).

This reflects other research showing how singers perceive physical benefits from singing such as positive effects on breathing, posture, and energy levels (Beck et al. 2000; Clift et al. 2009; Grape et al. 2003; Valentine and Evans 2001). Participants' responses to the open question suggested that male participants were more ready to recognize the health benefits of community singing than their female counterparts.

Conclusion

The purpose of this particular study was to gain insight into the motivations and benefits associated with community singing and to explore the extent to which these are affected by gender. Much of what it has revealed aligns with previous research into the motivation and benefits associated with singing. In particular, this study highlighted, as others have done, the development of musical skills, personal development, and socialization as the main factors in the motivation of singers (see Rensink-Hoff 2011; Rohwer 2010; Wilson 2011). However, three themes of particular interest emerged in participants' responses to questions about their motivation for joining a choir/singing group. First of all, it seemed that many people felt a deep need to sing with others; this was generally linked to childhood experiences and appears to have been particularly influential for male singers. In addition, while female participants appeared to have been more motivated than male participants by musical reasons, the qualitative data suggested that musical reasons were nonetheless important motivators for men. On the other hand, the importance of singing as a way of responding to personal challenges also emerged through the qualitative data; this was particularly noteworthy for female participants. Social motivations also appeared to be more important for female participants, although male participants were more likely than female participants to express a desire to contribute to their community. While these themes largely reflect previous research, they also suggest that there are gender dimensions to singers' motivations which have not previously been apparent.

Similarly, the findings from this study also strongly reflect previous research which has identified areas of benefit for singers in terms of social benefits, esthetic benefits, and benefits to emotional and physical well-being (see the review carried out by Clift et al. 2010). However, some interesting themes emerged in participants' responses to the open questions around benefits. First, while participants of both genders identified the feeling of social connectedness that resulted from community singing, it seemed that the male participants were more likely to value the community aspect of singing (something which had also emerged in the analysis of male motivation for community singing), while female participants were more likely to emphasize the importance of personal connectedness such as making new friends or feeling less lonely. However, the lack of any significant differences in the social benefits identified by participants suggests that, overall, the value of community singing in bringing about social connectedness is something which transcends gender.

On the other hand, female participants seemed more likely to identify benefits associated with increased confidence, improved mood, and emotional resilience. These findings echo previous research that has found women describe greater benefits than men in terms of the emotional benefits of community singing (Clift and Hancox 2010; Sandgren 2009). Clift et al. (2012) have suggested that there might be "something more fundamental at work in the character of women's and men's emotional experiences generated by singing" (Clift et al. 2012, p. 252). As such, it may be that community singing plays a particularly vital role for some women in enabling them to use their voice and feel heard, and that this in turn leads to feelings of greater self-confidence and self-belief. This has been previously argued by Kleinerman (2007), who believes that singing gives women a voice and "to have voice is to have identity" (Kleinerman 2007, p. 17). As Kleinerman has argued, women's voices have traditionally been undervalued and dismissed; singing therefore provides a "powerful transformative learning experience, enabling women to gain their voices," which in turn encourages the growth of their identities (Kleinerman 2007, p. 20).

Overall, this study shows that community singing provides a powerful experience that has a profound impact on the people who take part. It also supports the theory that, as Belenky et al. (1986) have suggested, singing is indeed a gendered experience and has different resonances for male and female singers. While this study provides evidence to support the particular value of community singing for women, the way in which community singing may have a particular resonance for men still remains unclear. Nonetheless, both male and female participants in this study described the powerful feeling of connectedness that comes from singing together with other people, echoing the "sense of community, belonging and shared endeavour" described by Welch (2015). This strong level of entitativity may even link with research into the physical effects of singing which has shown how singers' heartbeats synchronize as they sing together (Vickhoff et al. 2013). Community singing, then, has the potential to break down social boundaries caused by gender, class, and race and enable people to experience a feeling of togetherness which is important not just to individuals but to society.

Limitations of this study

As much as I tried to anticipate issues in order that this study should be as robust as possible, it is also important to acknowledge its limitations. First, and fundamentally, I recognize that categorizing "men" and "women" as homogeneous groups can be dangerous as there is enormous diversity within each group. Second, the methodology I chose enabled me to capture views and experiences from a wide range of singers; however, it also limited the depth to which I could go in this exploration as my survey imposed my own framework on participants and provided relatively limited opportunities for participants to express themselves freely. Furthermore, by using an online survey, my research only reached those who had Internet access and therefore excluded some people who might have brought additional perspectives to the research.

Suggestions for future research

In order to develop a greater understanding of the value of community singing in bringing about both personal and social benefits, I echo the suggestion made by Stewart and Lonsdale (2016) that further investigation of the well-being effects of community singing could usefully be carried out through carrying out a comparison study involving amateur orchestral musicians. This would help to isolate the effects of group participation in a musical activity from those associated with community singing in particular.

I also feel there is much more to be learned about the way in which singing appears to be beneficial in terms of enhancing emotional resilience and personal development. A qualitative study of men's and women's experiences of community singing would no doubt bring valuable insights to this area and help to uncover more about what makes it so special to singers of both genders. Finally, it would be extremely interesting to explore further the suggestion emerging from this study that community singing has a particular relevance in enabling women to gain confidence and feel heard.

REFERENCES

Ashley, M. (2002). Singing, gender and health: perspectives from boys singing in a church choir. *Health Education* 102(4): 180–187.

Beck, R.J., Cesario, T.C., Yousefi, A., and Enamoto, H. (2000). Choral singing, performance perception, and immune system changes in salivary immunoglobulin A and cortisol. *Music Perception* 18: 87–106.

Belenky, M.F., Clinchy, B.M., Goldberger, N.R., and Tarule, J.M. (1986). *Women's Ways of Knowing*. New York: Basic Books.

Bell, C. (2004). Update on community choirs and singing in the United States. *International Journal of Research in Choral Singing* 2(1): 39–52.

Cavitt, M.E. (2005). Factors influencing participation in community bands. *Journal of Band Research* 41(1): 42–59.

Chorus America (2009). The Chorus Impact Study: How Children, Adults, and Communities Benefit from Choruses. Available at: https://www.chorusamerica.org/publications/research-reports/chorus-impact-study>. Retrieved February 10, 2014.

Clift, S., Hancox, G., Morrison, I., Hess, B., Kreutz, G., and Stewart, D. (2007). Choral singing and psychological wellbeing: findings from English choirs in a cross-national survey using the WHOQOL-BREF. In: A. Williamon and D. Coimbra (eds), *Proceedings of the International Symposium on Performance Science*, pp. 201–207. Utrecht: European Association of Conservatoires.

Clift, S., Hancox, G., Morrison, I., Hess, B., Kreutz, G., and Stewart, D. (2009). What do singers say about the effects of choral singing on physical health? Findings from a survey of choristers in Australia, England, and Germany. *Proceedings of the 7th Triennial Conference of European Society for the Cognitive Sciences of Music, Jyväskylä, Finland*. Available at: http://www.whitstablechoral.org.uk/wp-content/uploads/2009/10/microsoft_word__clift_et_al_what_do_singers_say_escom_conference_paper.pdf. Retrieved November 9, 2015.

Clift, S. and Hancox, G. (2010). The significance of choral singing for sustaining psychological wellbeing: findings from a survey of choristers in England, Australia and Germany. *Music Performance Research* 3(1): 79–96.

Clift, S., Nicol, J., Raisbeck, M., Whitmore, C., and Morrison, I. (2010). Group singing, wellbeing and health: a systematic mapping of research evidence. *UNESCO Observatory, Faculty of Architecture Building and Planning, The University of Melbourne Refereed E-Journal* 2(1). Available at: <http://education.unimelb.edu.au/_data/assets/pdf_file/0007/1105927/clift-paper.pdf>. Retrieved February 10, 2014.

Clift, S., Hancox, G., and Morrison, I. (2012). Singing, wellbeing and gender. In: S.D. Harrison, G.F. Welch, and A. Adler (eds), *Perspectives on Males and Singing*, pp. 233–256. London: Springer.

Dingle, G., Brander, C., Ballantyne, J., and Baker, F. (2012). "To be heard": The social and mental health benefits of choir singing for disadvantaged adults. *Psychology of Music* 41(4): 405–421.

Faulkner, R. and Davidson, J.W. (2006). Men in chorus: collaboration and competition in homo-social vocal behavior. *Psychology of Music* 34(2): 219–237.

Freer, P. (2012). The successful transition and retention of boys from middle school to high school choral music. *Choral Journal* 52(10): 8–17.

Grape, C., Sandgren, M., Hansson, L. O., Ericson, M., and Theorell, T. (2003). Does singing promote well-being? An empirical study of professional and amateur singers during a singing lesson. *Integrative Physiological and Behavioral Science* 38(1): 65–74.

Green, L. (1997). *Music, Gender, Education*. Cambridge: Cambridge University Press.

Hall, C. (2005). Gender and boys' singing in early childhood. *British Journal of Music Education* 22(01): 5–20.

Harrison, S.D., Welch, G.F., and Adler, A. (eds) (2012). *Perspectives on Males and Singing*, Vol. 10. Dordrecht: Springer.

Kleinerman, K.E.D. (2007). Women sing, women lead: the transformation of identity and emergence of leadership in women through voice. Available at: <http://www.queensu.ca/music/links/gems/past/5th/kleinerman5.pdf>. Accessed July 29, 2015.

Koza, J. (1993). The "missing males" and other gender issues in music education: Evidence from the "Music Supervisors" Journal 1914–1924. *Journal of Research in Music Education* 41(3): 212–232.

Langston, T.W. and Barrett, M.S. (2008). Capitalizing on community music: a case study of the manifestation of social capital in a community choir. *Research Studies in Music Education* 30(2): 118–138.

Lecanuet, J.P. (1996). Prenatal auditory experience. In: I. Deliège and J.A. Sloboda (eds), *Musical Beginnings: Origins and Development of Musical Competence*, pp. 3–34. Oxford: Oxford University Press.

Livesey, L., Morrison, I., Clift, S., and Camic, P. (2012). Benefits of choral singing for social and mental wellbeing: Qualitative findings from a cross-national survey of choir members. *Journal of Public Mental Health* 11(1): 10–26.

McCrary, J. (2001). "Good" and "real" reasons college-age participants join university gospel and traditional choral ensembles. *Bulletin of Council for Research in Music Education* 149: 23–29.

Rensink-Hoff, R. (2011). Singing for life: leisure and learning in the adult community choir. *Anacrusis* Fall 2011: 1–4. Retrieved July 23, 2015 from <http://www.choralcanada.org/Sample_Citation_Format.pdf>.

Rohwer, D. (2010). Church musicians' participation perceptions: applications to community music. *Research and Issues in Music Education* 8(1): 1.

Sandgren, M. (2009). Evidence for strong immediate well-being effects of choral singing. In: J. Louhivuori, T. Eerola, S. Saarikallio, T. Himberg, and P. Eerola (eds), *Proceedings of the 7th*

Triennial Conference of European Society for the Cognitive Sciences of Music (ESCOM 2009), pp. 475–479. Jyväskylä, Finland, August 12–16.

Särkämö, T., Tervaniemi, M., Laitinen, S., Numminen, A., Kurki, M., Johnson, J.K., and Rantanen, P. (2014). Cognitive, emotional, and social benefits of regular musical activities in early dementia: randomized controlled study. *Gerontologist* 54(4): 634–650.

Stewart, N. and Lonsdale, A. (2016). It's better together: The psychological benefits of singing in a choir. *Psychology of Music* 44(5): 1240–1254.

Valentine, E. and Evans, C. (2001). The effects of solo singing, choral singing and swimming on mood and physiological indices. *British Journal of Medical Psychology* 74(1): 115–120.

Vickhoff, B., Malmgren, H., Åström, R., Nyberg, G., Ekström, S.R., Engwall, M., and Jörnsten, R. (2013). Music structure determines heart rate variability of singers. *Frontiers in Psychology* 4.

Welch, G. (2015). Sing for your heart. Available at: <http://www.heartresearch.org.uk/hearthealth/singinggood>. Accessed March 3, 2015.

Wilson S. (2011). *Community Choir—What Motivates People to Join, Stay and Sing*. Published MEd Thesis. University of Victoria, Vancouver. Retrieved from <http://dspace.library.uvic.ca/bitstream/handle/1828/3499/Wilson_Sarah_MEd_2011.pdf>. Accessed July 23, 2015.

CHAPTER 29

···

VOICE MANAGEMENT AND THE OLDER SINGER

···

JANE W. DAVIDSON AND LYNNE MURRAY

INTRODUCTION

SINGERS have specific and highly individual learning needs, with each voice emanating from a unique, finely tuned, individual ecosystem comprised of the vocal system housed within the physical, psychological, and cultural environment of the individual singer. This chapter explores the vocal ecology of the older singer, focusing on three specific categories of singer: the professional and/or keen and successful soloist who is approaching the end of a singing career; the amateur chorister; and the community singing group participant. Unlike the soloist, the latter two may have only started singing in late adulthood. Though the current authors are both classically trained singers, their teaching covers a spectrum of styles, so for the sake of this chapter, individual genres and techniques specific to a genre are not discussed. Rather, the focus is on the main approaches that apply across all styles of singing. The term "older singer" in the context of this chapter is a reference to someone typically over 60 years of age, though the definition of "older" cannot be determined solely by age. Since people pass through hormonal, anatomical, cognitive, and social changes at different times, one 60-year-old is likely to deal with their biological age very differently from another. Physiological age is of much more importance than chronological age.

Offering appropriate support and knowledge to the older singer is a duty of any voice specialist, whether he or she is an individual teacher or a singing group facilitator. The current chapter explores the types of support older members of different musical communities may be offered. The singing teacher or vocal facilitator can collaborate with specialists such as laryngologists, speech-language pathologists, endocrinologists, exercise physiologists, and psychologists. The effects of age on the voice and the management of vocal aging have been reviewed by Sataloff and Davidson (2012), Sataloff and Linville (2005), and Sataloff (2005). The current chapter takes content from Sataloff and Davidson (2012) but also adopts a more socially informed model to explore the many factors that affect the aging singer through six case studies. This draws on the current authors' experiences and proposes strategies for the singer and the singing teacher/facilitator to consider when developing a program of vocal study. The content is by no means comprehensive, but aims to stimulate critical reflection and further inquiry.

Physical impacts of aging on the voice

Many biological structures develop into peak condition in early adulthood and then weaken as we age. Overall physical condition is not as robust, and older people may have to manage chronic conditions such as arthritis. Additionally, memory often becomes less reliable and retrieval and recall may be compromised.

There are many age-related diseases that can impact on the singer: hypertension, stroke, cancer, coronary artery disease, cerebrovascular disease, osteoporosis, vision loss, anemia, arthritis, neurological dysfunction including tremor, diabetes, and gastrointestinal disorders (with both obesity and anorexia being possible results). Another special condition that affects the voice is thyroid disease, in both hyper and hypo conditions. Symptoms include weight gain, musculoskeletal discomfort, dry skin, and changes in facial appearance—all of which can impact on the singing voice. In addition, mental slowing, loss of energy, and vulnerable psychological behavior can emerge. It is known that vocal complications generally resolve when the thyroid condition is treated, but they become increasingly difficult to diagnose if they are often confounded with other aging-related problems such as dementia (National Center for Voice and Speech Tutorials 2015).

All of the above-mentioned changes affect the voice, in terms of action either on the larynx or the voice-producing mechanism. This means that the teacher/facilitator needs to have an overall awareness of any older student's underlying medical conditions.

Physical atrophy in the ear can result not only in hearing loss, but also in pitch distortion and loudness distortion, which may also result in faulty intonation (Sataloff and Davidson 2012). The older person also experiences changes in the vocal tract. The facial muscles decrease in elasticity, there is a reduced blood supply to the area, and collagen fiber breakdown may affect connective tissue (Levesque et al. 1984). The jaw joints undergo extensive changes and the mouth becomes affected, with the mucous membranes, tongue surface, dentition, and pharyngeal and palatal muscles all experiencing atrophy (Sonies 1991). In the larynx, the cartilages ossify and calcify, and the intrinsic muscles atrophy. This can result in vocal fold "bowing" and in a soft or incomplete glottis closure, resulting in breathier voice and a reduction of power. With conditions such as arthritis, the joints stiffen and so body rigidity becomes common. The body also experiences a decrease in the capacity to contract the respiratory muscles, a loss of lung tissue elasticity, and a stiffening of the thorax. The conditions associated with these impacts include mouth dryness, swallowing difficulties, and oral discomfort. Estrogen deprivation in women as they reach menopause causes substantial changes in the mucous membranes that line the vocal tract, the muscles, and elsewhere throughout the body (Linville 2001). Female opera singers have found hormonal replacement to be a useful treatment to counter impacts of menopause such as hoarseness and the reduction of muscle tone. It seems that these can result in better control of pitch, but there are risks associated with any type of hormonal treatment and so medical advice is necessary (Sataloff and Davidson 2012).

Surprising knock-on effects of aging are that some older women are not able to phonate as quietly as younger ones. As men age, their minimum speaking volume tends to increase, meaning that older men tend to talk loudly. Overall, however, both genders experience a decrease in maximum speech intensity (Morris and Brown 1987). The teacher/facilitator needs to work with these effects. In addition to physical factors, psychological factors such as personality type and individual anxiety/arousal state are affected by aging.

Psychological factors and the aging voice

While many people have temperaments that may be resilient and psychologically robust, adapting to various age-related changes can be challenging. Some people may have fewer coping strategies than others, and find themselves vulnerable to several concomitant effects of aging, which in turn impact on the singing voice. However, reporting the older person as someone less than at their prime in terms of both physical and cognitive capabilities is a somewhat biased perspective. New theories and political approaches to aging suggest that while we may encounter both physical and cognitive atrophy, in many ways the quality of our thinking in older age becomes "better." Research by Cohen (2005) showed that as people mature, their thinking improves in three important ways. They become better at: relativistic thinking, where their understanding is based more on a synthesis of more relative concepts; dualistic thinking, where opposing views can be accepted as valid; and systematic thinking, an ability to see the bigger picture and not be trapped by narrow personal ideas. His extensive clinical and research work revealed that the mature mind is open and that older people are more liberated, especially in the mid-50s to mid-70s age group whose life question becomes: if not now, when? He also theorized that as people age they seek to share and give back to community by often restating and reaffirming major life themes. As we shall explore, being a singer or becoming a singer in this latter phase of life offers both cognitive insights and challenges.

A wealth of psychological study has revealed that individuals have both trait (persistent) and state (transient and contextual) dependent characteristics. While there are many approaches to theorizing traits, two types have been distinguished according to personality (for more detail, see Friedman 1996): Type-A (displaying concern about personal status, highly competitive, time-consciousness, impatience, aggressive, has difficulty relaxing); and Type-B (relaxed, easy-going). The Myers–Briggs inventory (Briggs and Myers 1976), perhaps the most commonly used modern psychological categorization of personality, summarizes a five-factor model: extroversion, emotional stability, agreeableness, conscientiousness, and culture. McCarthy (2017) noted the interaction between voice and the individual's personality, and stated that this needs to be addressed by the teacher/facilitator, who must be sensitive to the student's individual character. Whatever model is argued, people have different traits and characteristics and, depending on type, there may be different responses to the effects of aging. Interfacing with this information related to findings that older people are generally more flexible in their thinking (Cohen 2005), care is needed in assessing mental potentiality and flexibility. Indeed, research has shown ways in which character can impact on outcomes in music. Davidson and Coimbra (2001) found that some classical singers tended to attribute their own failures to fixed capacities, or external factors such as bad teaching. Evidently, the belief an individual holds will affect how a teacher interacts with them. A sensitive teacher will accommodate an individual's attitudes, often working to turn potential negative areas into positives (Fontana 1995).

Exploring psychological approaches with older professional opera singers, Sataloff and Davidson (2012) noted that the opera singer Shirley Verrett had modified her work as she aged. Advice that she offered to colleagues included taking regular rest and accepting the differences between one's younger and older singing voice, especially a reduction in vocal range. Memory capacity is less, performance stamina is reduced, and thus more breaks in performance might be required. Good management and a regular vocal, physical, and mental exercise regime appeared to keep Verrett's attainment and spirits high. A different investigation of older singers (Drohan 2004) indicated that those with extended careers in opera adapted techniques to maintain muscle tone as well as achieving good levels of rest appropriate to personal age-related requirements. In other words, they adopted good strategies to help them manage their goals in a positive manner.

This brief overview of the literature relating to the factors that affect the aging voice leaves us with many questions relating to how we might approach working with older singers. What options are available? How do we support and enhance the experience for the older singer? In the majority of instances, work with a singing teacher/facilitator—assisted by the additional expertise of a voice therapist, if required—should offer the most productive support mechanism for competence and enjoyment of the older singer. Of course in extreme cases, where weakness in glottal closure from vocal fold bowing or poor adductory function is excessive, surgery may be considered (Sataloff and Davidson 2012).

Voice training approaches for older singers

Of recent texts on voice training, the edited collection by Chapman (2017) combines traditional classical singing methods, scientific research, and the teacher's studio experiences. A nucleus/satellite model of teaching is promoted which embraces postural, breath, and core sound work, interfaced with speaking voice work, articulation, resonance, and matters associated with artistry, combined with performance techniques. Notwithstanding the physical changes which may accompany aging, the scope of working with an older singer to develop an efficient vocal technique will be similar to working with a younger singer; however, the process may vary considerably. As Edwin (2012) points out, both singer and teacher may need to modify their expectations, particularly in relation to vocal range and vocal tone.

Psychological approaches to shifting goals and challenges are also highlighted and critical reflection is emphasized. The application of Gardner's (1983) multiple intelligences is encouraged. It argues that we each have different and preferred means of experiencing the world, which form the bases of our intelligences. While each one of us may be stronger in one area than others, all areas can be accessed and developed. In Chapman's volume, McCarthy (2017) speaks of the teacher/facilitator as a "container," supporting a learning process in a trusted and safe space, and nowhere is this more appropriate than when working with an older student who is either a professional singer transitioning into late career, or someone coming to singing as an amateur choral singer or a member of a community singing group. The older person comes to singing with a set of problem-solving skills developed through their life experience, which may not be appropriate for singing. With respect and support, the teacher/facilitator can challenge fixed or misplaced views.

Older age is a time of significant change in relationships, social networks and roles, and is often accompanied by grief and social isolation. The singing teacher/facilitator can play an important part in facilitating the social and interpersonal aspects of singing (Rayapati 2012).

In the sub-sections that follow, we present examples developed for the sake of illustration. Thus, the students we discuss are fictional, though emanating from our own experiences as practitioners and researchers working with older singers; each student is given a name to facilitate discussion.

THE OLDER PROFESSIONAL SOLO SINGER

Older singers who have worked in many jazz and commercial styles may sustain careers without having experienced formal training. These individuals present special challenges as they age, for when problems emerge they have no technical resources to support themselves. The untrained voice can suffer hyperfunction and associated tension, meaning that, as the voice ages, extreme fatigue and ensuing injury can occur. Help in such cases is relatively easy with aerobic conditioning, strengthening of muscles of the back, abdomen, and chest, and vocal education. This work needs to include singing lessons and sometimes speaking voice training. Once the singer is assured that this sort of work will assist, training can begin, but in all cases, it must be preceded by a full medical evaluation.

Where the singer has received years of classical training, there is a technical base on which to ground an intervention specific to the age-related assistance, and much of the work is about optimizing muscles that have atrophied.

Case study 1

Henry is 66 years old and enjoyed a successful career as a solo classical singer, working mainly in opera. Ten years ago, out of choice rather than a lack of vocal engagements, he began to reduce his performance workload, preferring to be based in one place and focusing on the development of a small business. He had not had regular singing lessons since his mid-30s. He presented for assistance with two principal concerns: firstly, that although he had not noticed a "problem" himself, recent concerts had included items that he had sung out of tune; and secondly, his vibrato was beginning to widen more than he found to be acceptable.

Strategies for teaching

As explained above, as muscle loses tone, inevitably "wobble" creeps into the voice, but by working through some exercises to keep the breath flow secure and the voice mobile, Henry began to re-establish vocal stamina. In addition, a series of careful exercises working on head tone through *messa di voce* exercises (gradual crescendo from pianissimo to fortissimo, then returning to pianissimo on a sustained pitch) helped him to focus on gentle tone onset and use of the upper partials in the sound, assisting with a clearer tonal center and preventing a forced breath attack. The widened vibrato was not removed, but it was more controlled, through judicious management of technique.

The out-of-tune singing required a little detective work. On presentation, Henry seemed to have accurate hearing, in that technical exercises were "in tune"; nevertheless, to provide full information, it was decided that he should have a hearing test. This thorough and detailed appraisal revealed that, although there was some loss of hearing associated with aging at a general level, his capacity to sing accurately "in tune" should not have been unduly affected. However, more systematic work in the lessons revealed that the tuning issue was associated to some degree with feedback from the room acoustic. When Henry sang where there was a lot of reverberation (a long reverberation time), he would sing out of tune. Not being able to self-monitor effectively in a resonant room and unsure of his own volume, he would begin to push his breath flow to tighten the focus of sound to achieve more projection, but this resulted in a flattening of the pitch. He would generally sing more in tune in a very dry acoustic (a room with more absorptive wall, floor, or ceiling coverings), where there was limited "interference" in terms of room reverberation. Additionally, the vowel /ɑ/was much more prone to flatness than other vowels, owing to its open positioning and a tendency that Henry had to push his breath on that specific sound. The vowel /i/was best tuned, with the more closed mouth position making it easier from a sensation perspective to "direct" the sound and so focus on the pitch height.

Case study 2

Catherine presented for a series of lessons at 69 years of age with the specific goal of getting feedback about her voice, and also building vocal stamina to produce a CD of solo repertoire for private distribution. From her late teens to her mid-30s, Catherine had enjoyed a stellar career as a coloratura soprano, having toured in concerts, sung in operas, and recorded internationally. She then stopped singing to raise a family. At the age of 55, she began teaching and slowly developed her own voice studio. Along with this work as a teacher, she started to practice. She had not performed in public for 20 years, so the prospect of giving a live performance was deemed too anxiety provoking, but the desire to make a CD which she could craft and be able to give to her family at the celebration of her 70th birthday was highly motivating for her. She came for lessons with a program already selected.

Catherine's interpretative skills and languages were impeccable, but her voice had stiffened with age and her high notes were pinched and unattractive. She had come for lessons to help her with stamina, but the concerns she had to address were in part organic, as well as some matters that could be tackled with appropriate technical work.

Strategies for teaching

A series of gentle head tone warming-up exercises, then a program of practice that gradually increased vocalization from 15 minutes daily all the way though to an hour, helped Catherine immensely. However, the repertoire she had found very suitable at 35 years of age was not sitting as well for her. By working on exercises to identify the "core" of her voice and its scope, it was revealed that the median pitch of Catherine's speaking voice was quite low and that, allied to this, her singing voice was both more restricted and lower in *tessitura* than she had realized. It was sitting a good third lower than she had expected, so some of the repertoire she had been considering for her CD was discounted, and repertoire that fitted with her range as well as her musical preferences was found. For Catherine, it was something of a disappointment not to be able to produce the vocal fireworks associated with her younger vocal identity, but investigating repertoire she did not know, alongside learning to sing a more legato line, was both rewarding and successful. The teacher's role was one of subtle management, but collaboration with the student to fulfill her goals without undermining her confidence.

THE OLDER AMATEUR CHORAL SINGER

Choral singers represent a majority of older people who sing in contexts where they might seek out lessons or facilitation. Typically, these singers are devoted to their groups, enthusiastic about all aspects of participating, and largely untrained in the techniques of singing. Until recently, many choral conductors were also not well trained in voice technique and vocal health. Many came from instrumental backgrounds (piano or organ most commonly), and did not understand that instrumental rehearsal techniques are not always appropriate for singers. Happily, this trend is beginning to change. In any case, all choral singers, regardless of their age, can be helped through individual lessons and by avoiding singing too loudly in the noisy choral environment.

In the vignettes below, we describe students who joined a large choir that required prospective members to pass a very basic group audition, but otherwise had no prerequisites for joining, i.e. no formal former singing experience and no age limit. The choir performed usually in premier national classical performance venues and tackled an eclectic range of repertoire, which included popular choral works such as *Carmina Burana* (Orff), opera choruses such as "Va, pensiero" from Verdi's *Nabucco*, various representations of "The Village" in Britten's *Peter Grimes*, and the Verdi *Requiem*.

Case study 3

Derek, like many of our students, began singing for leisure in his mid-60s in a local community choir, and then started singing lessons in his late 60s in order to gain entry into an auditioned choir, which he did successfully seven years ago. Now 77 years old, Derek has received lessons for a decade. In part, these lessons assist with questions relating to the choral music that he is rehearsing—such as confirming notes and rhythms—and they also focus on getting Derek through the audition solo for the annual re-entry to the choir. From a vocal technique perspective, Derek has been principally focused on improving his capacity to access high notes and to sing long phrases; that is, with issues which tend to be stressed by choral directors. He is less concerned about tonal quality.

It is important to note that Derek prioritizes staying fit and healthy. His other leisure pursuits include long-distance ocean swimming and exercises at a gym, where he has focused mainly on upper body strengthening with weights. When singing, given these sporting activities and his age, he presents as quite rigid in the torso, with a classic older man's barrel chest making deep breathing difficult (Rayapati 2012). The baseline muscle tone in his upper chest, shoulders, and neck is quite high all the time, whether swimming, lifting weights, or at rest. Breathing for swimming has been so well entrained that he adopts the same posture when breathing for singing: his breath tends to be gulped or snatched, and his head reflexively turns to one side, tightening his neck. The breath is high and the shoulders lift. Clearly, one experiences the act of breathing differently when swimming compared to singing—in singing the body is generally upright, for one thing—but Derek has become so attuned to the kinesthetic awareness of breathing while swimming that the singer's relaxed low silent breath does not feel to him like breathing at all. He expects breathing—in and out—to be active, and so similarly his inclination is to attempt to push the air out, as one does in swimming.

Derek's kinesthetic awareness is not strong (this is frequently the case with older singers). He will say, after a series of short vocal exercises, "I didn't take a breath at all," when he has in fact breathed after each exercise. To assist with some reflection of his actual actions, Derek is asked to watch himself in the mirror as he sings. He is also asked to focus on just one key aspect: for example, not to raise the shoulders when breathing.

Derek's vocal tone initially was quite breathy, with a persistent hiss also apparent in his speaking voice, suggesting incomplete glottal closure. As this is consistent with age-related bowing of the vocal folds, a somewhat "chicken or egg" situation has developed in his case: pulling in of stomach muscles combined with clavicular breathing, neck tension, and forceful onset delivering too much breath to the vocal folds would also contribute to breathiness. Despite a suggestion to see an ear, nose, and throat specialist to determine the exact cause, he has thus far refused.

When Derek initially began lessons he was also having prosthetic dental work over many months, which is common with the age group. This changed the "geography" of the inside of his mouth and his perception of his sound. This was particularly problematic when attempting to address the considerable stiffness in the root of his tongue and its effect on tonal quality. His tongue pulls back as he sings, particularly on forward vowels, and the usual first step in correcting this is to direct the student to feel the tip of the tongue resting behind the lower front teeth. Derek was unable to do that as his teeth had been removed, and it was some time until they were replaced by dentures.

Strategies for teaching

Because Derek was not able to feel his teeth with his tongue, he was encouraged to sing scales and easy short vocalises with his tongue relaxed onto his lower lip, which was surprisingly successful. He also sang exercises using lingua-dental consonants (e.g. /d/, /θ/) to encourage his tongue to be more active and forward in his mouth.

Exercise is clearly part of his identity for Derek, and so he has been encouraged to include stretching and movement, which enhances flexibility, as part of his fitness regimen, and to consider reducing exercise that contributes to "over-muscling" of the upper chest and shoulders.

Reduced (although not eliminated) tension in neck, tongue, jaw, and abdomen have led to improved tone quality, and an increase of a fourth in his upper range, to B4. Lower range was initially limited to C3, which was very breathy and barely audible; exercises to reduce laryngeal tension (alternating voiced and unvoiced consonants, and judicious use of vocal fry, which initially Derek was completely unable to do) have improved both tone and range, and he now reports that he is able to sing lower than the tenors around him.

Case study 4

Gerald is a slightly built baritone who also came to singing late, in his mid-60s. He is now in his early 70s. He, too, progressed to the larger auditioned choir five years ago, and now attends one, often two, rehearsals a week. He leads an active life, and also attends a gym where he does a combination of aerobic and strengthening exercises. Arthritis causes him some discomfort in his neck and shoulders, and some of the physical warm-ups at the start of lessons needed to be modified for him. Being stiff in the upper torso has slowed his ability to change his breathing habits: he breathes clavicularly, lifting his shoulders. He was under the impression that he needed to push his breath out to make a sound, which in unskillful singers often leads to an increase in upper body tension and pressed phonation; however, Gerald allowed the rib cage to collapse and the sternum to drop, making the tone breathy.

Gerald wears hearing aids in both ears. He is inclined to speak very softly, and his singing voice until recently had also been soft, without much formant clustering in the sound. Misconceptions about how the sung sound is formed led him to attempt to start and stop the sound from the throat by stiffening the root of the tongue. When he sang, his tongue was visibly flattened and tensed, and consonants requiring an active tongue such as /l/and /n/ were not pronounced. Vowels were produced with a spread mouth position which favored the upper partials.

Strategies for teaching

Encouraging Gerald to take a low unhurried breath has been a slow process, not helped by the breathing imperatives of singing sometimes quite complex choral music. Observing the upper chest and shoulders staying stable and feeling the cyclical nature of breathing when not singing has been part of the change process.

Much lesson time has been devoted to releasing the root of his tongue, which has been achieved by relaxing it forward onto the lip, and energizing it through exercises using various lingua-dental consonants and tongue twisters.

Working on easy solo repertoire in German, with different consonant patterns from English, challenges Gerald's tongue to move in unexpected ways, while at the same time allowing him to sing repertoire which he enjoys. It also supports Gerald's choir activity, as he occasionally has to sing choral repertoire in German, which is not a language he knows.

Like many relatively untrained men, Gerald allowed his larynx to rise at the *primo passaggio* (around C4). Gerald was not aware of the position of his larynx, but his physiology is such that he is able to feel it with his finger. Once he had learned to (mostly) take a lower breath, to allow the sound simply to start rather than feeling the need to "make" it start, and his tongue was more relaxed, work could begin on keeping the larynx stable. All these factors have changed the tonal quality, which is now warmer and more resonant.

Interestingly, though, Gerald does not perceive this as an improvement, and instead hears the tone as dull or muddy. His deafness might incline him to hear himself better when he makes an overly bright, almost shrill sound. Paradoxically then, Gerald has developed a vocal technique which may mean that he hears himself less well.

However, changing one's perception and therefore expectation of one's own sound is fundamental to developing one's technique, at any age. It is important, therefore, that he hears himself sing sustained vowels in vocalises or repertoire, so that he becomes accustomed to his sound and to the sensations that go along with it. Otherwise, when singing in the choir, he may well revert to the "old" sound which he can hear.

Case study 5

Marion is a soprano in her early 60s. She began singing in choirs when she was in her mid 50s, and only recently began formal lessons. Despite her lack of vocal training, she naturally makes a firm, warm, resonant sound; however, the exigencies of singing major choral works with a "natural" technique has impacted on her breath management. When singing, Marion conveys the impression that it is quite effortful and that she does not have sufficient energy for the task. She has the typical dropped sternum and rounded shoulders of a computer user, and in singing she often gasps for breath, lifting her upper chest and shoulders, and allowing her rib cage to collapse and her sternum to drop as soon as she starts to sing. She frequently complains of feeling out of breath, even on short phrases. Although her voice will travel easily enough up to A5 when encouraged, her instinct is to lift her chest and tighten the back of her neck as the pitch ascends. She speaks with quite a closed mouth position, and it is counter-intuitive for her to release her jaw.

Like many people of middle age or older, Marion wears multifocal eye glasses. This is problematic when she sings, as she tends to tip her head back to read the music through the bottom (close vision) part of the lens, thus shortening the back of her neck, putting tension on her throat, and making it difficult to release her jaw or to keep her laryngeal position stable. This is a difficult issue to address.

Marion would dearly love to sing with the auditioned choir, partly because she has friends who do, and this is her motivation for having singing lessons. She has the musical skills and vocal tone to make her an appropriate candidate for a choir which performs a more challenging repertoire, but she finds it difficult to sing in front of others, even in a lesson, and is very anxious at the prospect of having to audition. Her drooping posture, while partly habitual, reflects her psychological state.

Strategies for teaching

Marion finds it difficult to watch herself in the mirror when she sings, but it is important to encourage her to do so, so that she can develop an awareness of what she does with her body when she sings. Singing teachers have been asking their students to observe themselves in a mirror for centuries (Farinelli is recorded as having practiced before a mirror, for example, in the early eighteenth century), but many older singers find it particularly challenging and can refuse to do so. However, it provides such useful instant feedback to the singer that it should be persevered with, but in a light-hearted way, which acknowledges that it can be uncomfortable. The student can find it easier to watch not their whole self, but to check for particular actions, such as not raising the shoulders, or a hand mirror can be used to look only at the action of the lips or tongue on a particular vowel. Marion has benefited from watching herself keeping her sternum lifted, then feeling the same thing while looking away from the mirror.

Breath management issues have been addressed through exercises and straightforward songs and vocalises, with an emphasis on maintaining the tone to the end of the phrase or note while taking the time for a low non-effortful, silent breath. Taking ample time at the ends of phrases to allow for such a breath (i.e. by breathing out of time) has both physical and psychological benefits: the breath is taken more functionally, tensions associated with habitually gasping for breath can be eliminated, and the singer learns to associate breathing not with effort and anxiety but with calmness and ease.

As Marion's breathing has become less effortful, she has less neck tension. She has found that she can release her jaw to sing upward leaps, although it will take some time to become habitual. Tipping the head to look through the bottom of her multifocals will be an ongoing issue, which can only be completely resolved by memorizing words and music, but clearly this is not always going to be possible.

Feeling less at the mercy of her vocal technique has reduced some of Marion's anxiety around singing, but anxiety over the audition remains. Role-playing the audition process and singing in small studio concerts where the audience consists of other singers in much the same position have helped, as has practicing some performance anxiety reducers such as the "power posing" advocated by Carney, Cuddy, and Yap (2010).

THE OLDER SINGER WORKING FOR HEALTH AND WELL-BEING BENEFIT

One of the current authors (Davidson) has spent a decade developing group-singing activities for older people with no previous experience in music. The participants in these groups have virtually no aspirations to sing solo or explore the choral works of the main classical repertoire; rather, their participation is for social capital, musical experience, and well-being impact. A paper with Faulkner (Davidson and Faulkner 2010) describes approaches to implementing health and well-being impact with the older participants. It includes the following approaches:

1. Warming up voice and body with gentle vocalization and physical exercises.
2. More vigorous breathing/diaphragmatic support work and physical stretching as singers become familiar with their breath mechanism.
3. Musical games for technical and social impact—tongue twisters, rounds, rhythmical movement.
4. Working at the singer's personal level of physical comfort—chairs always being available should anyone feel tired, dizzy, or uncomfortable.

5. Offering a range of invigorating, as well as soothing and comforting repertoire.
6. Providing both familiar and new repertoire.
7. Encouraging creative participation in song writing and harmonization, with unaccompanied and accompanied songs.
8. Offering critical reflective listening, with attention to pitch matching, good tone quality, and support of the singing tone, using legato, staccato, and florid exercises.
9. Working at a comfortable pace, with opportunities for hydration, rest, and refreshment breaks to encourage recovery and social exchange.
10. Introducing a program of performance opportunities which encourages memorization and motivation towards going out into the community.
11. Using strong leaders with sound knowledge of the physical and psychological concerns of the cohort.
12. Encouraging the leader's use of humor and fun to stimulate participants.

As in the cases above, the best way to highlight these processes is to discuss a vignette of one group session.

Case study 6

Fascinating Rhythms is comprised of 45 people, with attendance numbers varying between 25 and 40, depending on the overarching health of participants and whether or not they are able to get transport to attend the sessions. Its membership is two-thirds female, with the majority in their 80s. Many have illnesses such as arthritis, high blood pressure, angina, diabetes, or mild dementia, and in the past year members have been treated for heart bypass, abdominal aortic aneurysms, stroke, and cancer. These people virtually never sing solo and are exclusively taught in large group settings.

Class strategies

Once all members are present and seated, the facilitator offers a joke: everyone laughs, smiles, and acknowledges one another. They are then asked to recite a few tongue twisters, again eliciting much laughter. After this, they work on simple breathe in, sustain, and release exercises for breath control. They also do some warming and stretching of upper body, neck, and head. These include clapping and patting games. Vocalizations begin with humming and glissandi and then staccato vowel sounds on stepwise intervals up and down fifths. After approximately 10 minutes, a first song is introduced, "Edelweiss" from the musical *The Sound of Music*. It is sung in unison, and where possible, people are encouraged to harmonize. General advice is given about diction and legato, and hints about tone color are made. A further song is explored, this time Doris Day's hit "Que Sera, Sera." This is a new song, and while the singers know the melody, it is necessary to go through the words, breath points, and dynamic contrasts. A tea break follows in which snacks are shared and a forthcoming performance is discussed, with singers making arrangements for a community bus to collect them from the rehearsal venue—a local community hall. After the break, other repertoire is covered: "Tea for Two," "I've got Rhythm," and "Hello Dolly."

Tasks involve singing back phrases to remember words, working on simple choreography (specifically for the song "Hello Dolly"), which people need to repeat several times before connecting their singing part with the accompanying gestures. The choreography is relatively static, given that almost a quarter of the participants need to remain seated. By the end of the session, the song is revised and everyone finishes by laughing and applauding themselves at the skill and humor of their achievement.

CONCLUDING REMARKS

It has been the intention of this chapter to show that the highly individual learning needs of the older singer can be addressed by paying attention to the ecosystem that comprises the vocal system within the physical, psychological, and cultural environment of the individual singer. While specialists such as laryngologists, speech-language pathologists, endocrinologists, exercise physiologists, and psychologists have been recognized as important potential collaborators, the discussion has revealed how the informed teacher/facilitator can work for effective and satisfying vocal management, and well-being impact. Even with the physical limitations that aging causes, the teacher/facilitator with an overall awareness of an older student's underlying medical conditions can adapt their program to produce a positive impact. While psychological factors such as personality type influence all singers, by working with individual characteristics the teacher can assist the older singer to come to terms with some of their limitations. While the older singer may also face restricted cognitive capabilities, the relativistic thinking, dualistic thinking, and systematic thinking that emerge in later life (see Cohen 2005) indicate that older singers are often open in their thinking and not trapped by narrow personal ideas. The positive "if not now, when?" attitude found in many older people can be used to advantage, as shown in some of the teaching points discussed in the current chapter. Not covered in this chapter, but elsewhere in this *Handbook*, the emotional benefits of sung companionship are explored (see Davidson and Garrido, "Singing and Psychological Needs," and Davidson and Faulkner, "Group Singing and Social Identity"); again, these can operate as incredibly powerful motivators for engagement. The current chapter does reveal that older people are keen to engage in singing for the positive emotional outcome, such as having fun and sharing in the communion of social interaction in singing and allied activities around each singing session. As demonstrated, modification and flexibility are core strategies when working with the older singer, but both strategies need to be embraced by the singers themselves to assist in generating a positive experience.

ACKNOWLEDGMENTS

The community singing group research was supported by the Wicking Trust, Healthway, and Musica Viva Australia. Approximately 20 percent of the overall content draws on work found in Sataloff and Davidson (2012).

REFERENCES

Briggs, K.C. and Myers, I.B. (1976). *Myers-Briggs Type Indicator: Form F*. Palo Alto, CA: Consulting Psychologists Press.

Carney, D.R., Cuddy, A.J.C., and Yap, A.J. (2010). Power posing—brief nonverbal displays affect neuroendocrine levels and risk tolerance. *Journal of the Association for Psychological Science* 21(10): 1363–1368.

Chapman, J. (2017). *Singing and Teaching Singing: A Holistic Approach to Classical Voice*, 3rd edn. San Diego, CA: Plural Publishing.

Cohen, G.D. (2005). *The Mature Mind: The Positive Power of the Aging Brain*. New York: Basic Books.

Davidson, J.W. and Coimbra, D.C.C. (2001). Investigating performance evaluation by assessors of singers in a music college setting. *Musicae Scientiae* 5: 33–54.

Davidson, J.W. and Faulkner, R. (2010). Meeting in music: the role of singing to harmonise carer and cared for. *Arts and Health* 2(2): 164–170.

Drohan, M.-A. (2004). *The effect of aging on the singing voice and the vocal longevity of professional singers*. Unpublished PhD thesis. Teachers College, Columbia University.

Edwin, R. (2012) Voice pedagogy for aging singers. *Journal of Singing* 68(5): 561–563.

Fontana, D. (1995). *Psychology for Teachers*, 3rd edn. London: Palgrave Macmillan.

Friedman, M. (1996). *Type A Behavior: Its Diagnosis and Its Treatment*. New York: Plenum Press (Kluwer Academic Press).

Gardner, H. (1983). *Frames of Mind: The Theory of Multiple Intelligences*. New York: Basic Books.

Levesque, J., Coruff, P., De Rigal, J., and Agache, P. (1984). In vivo studies of the evaluation of physical properties of the human skin and aging. *International Journal of Dermatology* 23: 322–329.

Linville, S.E. (2001). *Vocal Aging*. Albany, NY: Delmar Thomson Learning.

McCarthy, M. (2017). The teaching and learning partnership. In: J. Chapman (ed.), *Singing and Teaching Singing: A Holistic Approach to Classical Voice*, pp 165–214. San Diego, CA: Plural Publishing.

Morris, R. and Brown, W. (1987). Age-related voice measures among adult women. *Journal of Voice* 1: 38–43.

National Center for Voice and Speech Tutorials on Voice Production. *Voice changes throughout life*, www.ncvs.org/ncvs/tutorials/voiceprod/tutorial/index.html, accessed 1 August 2015.

Rayapati, S. (2012) *Singing into your Sixties—and Beyond! A Manual and Anthology for Group and Individual Voice Instruction*. Delaware, OH: Inside View Press.

Sataloff, R.T. (2005). *Professional Voice: The Science and Art of Clinical Care*, 3rd edn. San Diego, CA: Plural Publishing.

Sataloff, R.T. and Davidson, J.W. (2012). The older singer. In: G. Welch and G.E. McPherson (eds), *The Oxford Handbook of Music Education*, pp. 610–625. Oxford: Oxford University Press.

Sataloff, R.T. and Linville, S.E. (2005). The effects of age on the voice. In: R.T. Sataloff, *Professional Voice: The Science and Art of Clinical Care*, 3rd edn, pp. 497–511. San Diego, CA: Plural Publishing.

Sonies, B. (1991). The aging oropharyngeal system. In: D. Ripicd (ed.), *Handbook of Geriatric Communication Disorders*, pp. 187–203. Austin, TX: Pro-ed.

PART 5

SINGING PEDAGOGY

CHAPTER 30

··

SYSTEMATIC DEVELOPMENT OF VOCAL TECHNIQUE

··

JOHN NIX

INTRODUCTION

A free voice expressing the full range of human emotions is a joy for the listener. Regardless of the genre being sung, to accomplish this artistic ideal singers must develop a reliable, flexible technique capable of meeting the style's demands. A secure technique enables singers to achieve greater artistry by freeing them from having their attention diverted from expression to the physical challenges of singing.

The acquisition of technique and the development of artistry are methodical processes. Teachers of singing must respect a hierarchy in developing a singer's voice, as each aspect of technique builds upon and interacts with previous ones. In this hierarchy, body alignment is of primary importance. Proper use of the body enables efficient respiration, phonation, resonation, articulation, and expressive gestures and movements. Respiration follows alignment as the next element; without optimal respiratory function and coordination, free phonation, resonation, articulation, and artistic phrasing are compromised. Phonation, the third aspect, transfers kinetic energy from the airstream provided by respiration into acoustic waves. The sound wave produced is complex in nature; the coordination of intrinsic laryngeal positioning muscles determines how much acoustic energy is generated and also determines the complexity and frequency of the resulting sound wave. The fourth aspect, resonation, varies greatly with the musical style. As the voice is a non-linear system (Titze 2006), resonation provides either positive or negative feedback to phonation, aiding or hindering the production and projection of sound and the use of different vocal timbres. Articulation, which provides voice with the means to communicate ideas, "rides" on all other aspects, and can, like resonation, benefit or impair breathing, phonation, and resonation. Subtle diction for singing depends upon freedom and sophisticated control of not only the articulators but also the entire vocal system.

Optimal technique is built through:

- efficient use of the body established through body work modalities (see Chapter 3);
- the careful design and appropriate usage of vocal exercises;

- the selection of an appropriate repertoire;
- the optimal structuring of practice sessions.

Teaching technique is facilitated by employing knowledge drawn from voice physiology, voice acoustics, voice development/maturation, exercise physiology, and motor learning, all of which is used in combination with that most essential tool, a discerning ear. Teachers must individualize training for each singer based on the strengths and weaknesses of the student and upon his or her learning style.

This chapter focuses upon the systematic development of vocal technique through the means outlined above. Subsequent chapters in this section address principles of teaching the so-called "non-singer" (Chapter 31), meeting the needs of professional singers (Chapters 32 and 33), teaching pre-professional singers in conservatories and artist training programs (Chapter 34), meeting the varying demands of different singing styles in the modern world (Chapter 35), extended vocal techniques (Chapter 36), and vocal styles and teaching traditions in China, Africa, and India (Chapter 37). We begin with the design of exercises.

The design of exercises

Exercises are specific patterns of pitches, vowels, consonants, and some non-speech sounds used to develop technique and to establish or renew the body–mind relationship. They can be "stand alone" patterns specifically designed by a teacher to target technical skills or they can be selected phrases or longer passages carefully excerpted for teaching purposes from the literature. Physiologically, exercises used in practice sessions should stretch tendons, ligaments, and muscles; move joints gently through their full range of motion; increase blood flow to active areas; increase the precision of muscle action; foster the balance of function between antagonistic pairs; encourage efficient, rapid transitions from one activity to another; and develop overall power (Titze 1993, 2001).

A distinction needs to be made between "warming up" and "vocalizing." Athletes and performers of all types, including singers, warm up to renew and review established skills and to prime themselves for performance. The time immediately prior to a performance is for the reassurance of skills, not swimming in unfamiliar seas. Singers vocalize to learn new skills and to transfer those skills to music performance. So instead of vocalization, *vocal skill acquisition* (Titze and Verdolini-Abbott 2011) might be a more accurate descriptor.

Singers should spend time vocalizing almost every day. The singer constantly challenging him or herself with learning new skills is the singer who avoids falling into a "rut."

Variables in the design of vocalises

Direction

Lower-range singing is marked by greater activity of the thyroarytenoid (TA) muscle and lower subglottic pressure, while higher-range singing involves (in most cases) a more active cricothyroid (CT) muscle and higher subglottic pressure. Therefore, exercises that begin high and move lower generally require higher subglottic pressure and a more active

CT muscle at vocal onset, with the CT gradually releasing and the TA gradually becoming more active as subglottic pressure decreases. Exercises that ascend require singers to start phonation with a more active TA and a less active CT, then gradually reduce TA activity and activate the CT more as the exercise continues. One must also manage subglottic pressure so as to not adversely affect intonation, as excessive pressure can make the pitch sharp. Singers of contemporary commercial music (CCM) of both genders and male operatic performers often keep the TA more active throughout ascending patterns (Titze 2000).

Pattern

Many musical terms exist to describe vocal patterns, including agility, fioratura, sostenuto, staccato, scalar, arpeggiated, conjunct, and disjunct. An agility exercise, which requires singers to rapidly move their voice through *disjunct* intervals accurately, is the vocal version of making efficient, rapid transitions from one activity to another. Agility requires very fast changes in intrinsic muscle activation and subglottic pressure. Fioratura, on the other hand, is rapid *conjunct* changes, where the magnitude of changes intrinsically is less but the speed of change is increased. Sostenuto exercises build stability of function between antagonistic pairs of muscles and encourage appropriate breath management, stable adductory behavior, and consistent laryngeal positioning. Staccato exercises require instantaneous synchronization of breath, pitch, and vowels, increasing the precision of muscle action; they are thus very beneficial for fine control of adduction.

Length

The length of an exercise can be varied for pedagogical reasons. Shorter exercises typically demand less from the respiratory and adductory musculature than do longer exercises. The longer the exercise, the more precise the postural balance, breath management, and adductory control must be.

Vowels

Vowels are a key variable in vocalises. Adjusting vowels in accordance with the location of the first two vowel formants is of particular importance to singers (see Chapters 8, 9, and 52). Vocalises must be designed in such a way to help students automatically make the necessary adjustments. The concept of inertance of the vocal tract also needs to be considered. Low first-formant vowels such as /i/ and /u/ are more inertive than more open vowels, and encourage a lighter production (Titze 1999).

Consonants

Different consonants can be used in vocalizing depending upon the needs of the student. For example, students with tongue retraction habits may profit from using tongue-fronting consonants like /t/, /z/, /d/, /l/, and /n/ as initial consonants before troublesome vowels. Students needing airflow at onset might be best served by pilot consonants which promote airflow. However, the higher air pressure of these consonants (see Table 30.1) must be taken into account. The voiced fricatives, such as /v/ and /z/ and voiced plosives

Table 30.1 Exercise variations for singing training

Exercise characteristic	Physiological and acoustical considerations	Comments on application to singing training
Ascending pattern	Increased subglottic pressure as pitch rises Classical female singers: decrease TA activation and increase CT as pitch rises CCM "belt": increased TA and CT with pitch rise Females in classical style above approx. G4 gradually open lower F1 vowels to achieve F1–1f_0 match Males generally close vowels D4–G4 to lower F1 Extrinsic muscle activation varies with style, but often increases in operatic males and CCM belt with pitch rise	Used often in music for building musical and dramatic intensity; essential to almost all styles
Descending pattern	Gradual decrease in subglottic pressure as pitch decreases; gradual decrease in CT activation with decrease in pitch Classical females descending to approximately E4 close vowels; males and females descending below E4 generally open vowels gradually	Singers often overshoot descending intervals Good for initial exercise, especially for singers with overly heavy production
Agility pattern (rapid wide pitch changes)	Rapid adjustments on TA/CT activation balance needed Some adjustments in LCA/IA/PCA may be needed as well Rapid adjustments in subglottic pressure needed Consistent function of extrinsic muscles needed for maintaining a stable laryngeal position	Often seen in *bel canto* or 20th/21st century literature Beneficial though challenging for singers with a heavy production Valuable for older singers in order to maintain flexibility
Fioritura pattern (rapid narrow pitch changes)	Very rapid and subtle adjustments needed between TA and CT, in conjunction with subglottic pressure adjustments Consistent function of extrinsic muscles needed for maintaining a stable laryngeal position	Often seen in classical and *bel canto* literature Beneficial though challenging for singers with a heavy production Valuable for older singers in order to maintain flexibility
Sostenuto pattern	Requires coordinated extrinsic muscle function for stable laryngeal position, especially at high dynamic levels Demanding for the respiratory system Requires skilled LCA/IA/PCA balance in order to provide adductory integrity and dynamic control	Often seen in classical and romantic period music Essential for developing legato

Table 30.1 Continued

Exercise characteristic	Physiological and acoustical considerations	Comments on application to singing training
Staccato pattern	Requires instantaneous adjustments of all intrinsic muscles Instantaneous adjustment of subglottal pressure with each pitch change Generally requires a slightly less open vowel than sostenuto singing	Often seen in *bel canto* or 20th/21st century literature Challenging but helpful for singers with a heavy production Recommended for older singers in order to maintain adductory control and dynamic finesse Provides an excellent means of developing efficient phonation and appoggio breathing techniques
Conjunct pattern (can be slow or fast in tempo; intervals between notes smaller than minor 3rd)	Physiological demands vary with the tempo: slow conjunct is a form of sostenuto; fast conjunct is fioratura	Excellent for addressing specific areas of a singer's voice for vowel tuning, intonation, etc.
Disjunct pattern (can be slow or fast in tempo; intervals minor 3rd or larger)	Physiological demands vary with tempo: fast disjunct is agility Demands fine control of TA/CT balance, and when performed over the primary registration bridge, some adjustment of LCA/IA/PCA may be needed For classical style in males, extrinsic muscle function important, especially in leaps up/down through the *passaggio*	Especially valuable for working on 20th/21st century literature and advanced repertoire in other musical styles
Length of exercise: (a) long, (b) short	(a) See aspects listed for sostenuto above. Longer exercises/phrases tax the extrinsic laryngeal positioning musculature, the adductory muscles, the respiratory system and postural muscles; requires balancing of the active muscular aspects and passive recoil forces of breathing (b) Less demanding on the respiratory system: demands vary with the *tessitura*—a short intense outburst can be just as taxing as a longer phrase at a lower *tessitura*	(a) Essential for developing legato, especially for the *bel canto*/romantic style (b) Better for younger or less technically advanced singers
Type of onset used: (a) fry (pulse register), (b) aspirated (h-onset), (c) balanced	(a) Features greater activity in the TA; minimal activity in the CT, IA, PCA; low subglottic pressure; constriction of the laryngeal vestibule. Possible better velar closure and reduced nasality (b) Reduced impact forces on vocal fold tissue (c) Aerodynamic and myoelastic factors coordinated	(a) Pedagogical uses detailed in Nix et al. (2005) (b) Healthier alternative for singers who are hyperfunctional with "glottal" onsets (c) Can be trained with staccato and other onset/offset exercises; see Miller (1986) for examples

(continued)

Table 30.1 Continued

Exercise characteristic	Physiological and acoustical considerations	Comments on application to singing training
Semi-occluded vocal tract postures (SOVT)	SOVT postures achieve a high maximum flow declination rate with relatively low vocal fold vibration amplitude, producing more acoustic output for less effort and reduced risk of tissue damage from impact forces Some semi-occluded postures may encourage epilaryngeal outlet narrowing, which may aid in the production of the singer's formant cluster and may aid in matching glottal impedance with vocal tract input impedance Improved breath management: a vocalist can engage greater thoracic and abdominal "support" without using a pressed phonation Lowered phonation threshold pressure (PTP): the positive pressures above the glottis lower PTP "Head voice" sensation is encouraged: due to the sympathetic vibration of the orofacial tissues and sinuses of the face and skull and a coupling of the vibration of the upper surface of the vocal folds with acoustic pressures above the glottis. A higher ratio of TA activation relative to CT activation during and after use of the semi-occluded postures. Similar to that found when contrasting "covered" with "open" singing See Titze (2004, 2006) and Bele (2005) for further information	Sensations of more consistent respiratory support, particularly found with lip buzzes and raspberries Sensations of vibration in the orofacial area, particularly while doing the voiced fricatives, the nasals, the lip buzz, raspberry and rolled r Release of habitual tensions in the tongue, lips, and jaw, particularly while doing the oscillatory and transitory semi-occlusions. Release of inhibitions Elevation of the soft palate in the non-nasal semi-occluded postures Fronting the tongue. The voiced fricative /z/, the nasal continuant /n/, the raspberry, the rolled r, /j/ glide and the voiced plosive /d/ all front the tongue See Nix (1999, 2008)
Vowels: (a) front (also known as "tongue" vowels, /i/, /e/, etc.); (b) back (also known as "lip" vowels, /a/, /o/, /u/); (c) mixed; (d) closed (refers to mouth opening); (e) open (refers to mouth opening, not pharyngeal sensation)	(a) Tongue freedom essential; slight nasalization often occurs with use; F1 and F2 widely separated (b) Degree of jaw opening and lip rounding very important for tuning; F1 and F2 closer together (c) Combines the tongue position of front vowels with the lip rounding of back vowels (d) Accurate "mapping" of the jaw joint is crucial; lower F1 (e) Degree of mouth opening used varies with pitch, dynamic range, desired vowel, duration of note, size of singer's voice; higher F1	(a) Can be paired with back vowels to help find desired *chiaroscuro* timbre (b) Can be paired with front vowels to help find desired *chiaroscuro* timbre (c) Often helpful in working with male singers in the upper range (d) Essential for work with male singers in the higher range of the Western classical style (e) Essential for work with female singers in all styles in higher range

Table 30.1 Continued

Exercise characteristic	Physiological and acoustical considerations	Comments on application to singing training
Consonants: (a) voiced, (b) unvoiced, (c) fricatives, (d) plosives, (e) affricates, (f) glides, (g) nasals	**Peak intraoral pressure:** (higher > lower) Unvoiced plosives > voiced plosives and unvoiced fricatives (e.g. compare [p] with [b], [f]) Unvoiced fricatives > voiced fricatives (e.g. compare [f] with [v]) Intervocalic plosives > pre-vocalic plosives > post-vocalic plosives (e.g. compare [aba] with [ba] with [ab]) **Airflow:** Plosives > fricatives > "vowel-like sounds" (e.g. compare [d] with [v] with [w]) Unvoiced phones > voiced cognates to those phones (e.g. compare [t] with [d], [p] with [b]) Lingua-alveolars > labiodentals See Baken and Orlikoff (2000)	As a wide variety of consonants are used in languages, singers should include different types of consonants in their vocalizing. The tongue fronting consonants [t], [d], [n], [z], [j], and [l] can be useful as pilots to back vowels which timbrally can become too dark. Similarly, lip rounding consonants such as [w] can be used as pilots to front vowels perceived to be too strident. The plosives and voiced fricatives which feature velar closure can be used as pilots in front of vowels which are undesirably nasalized For further reading see Coffin (1976), Miller (1986), and Nair (1999)
Tempo of exercise: (a) fast, (b) slow	(a) Same as found above under agility and fioratura (b) Same as found above under sostenuto and long length of exercise	Exercise tempi should be varied to develop general technical skills and to meet specific repertoire requirements Those singers who perform baroque, classical, and *bel canto* period music should make extensive use of fast tempi exercises
Dynamic level: (a) high, (b) low, (c) crescendo, (d) decrescendo, (e) *messa di voce*	(a) Higher subglottic pressure. A slightly more open vowel shape is necessary; much like sostenuto in other muscular demands. Taxing to the lamina propria, particularly when passages are repeated at this level. Demands more power from the respiratory system (b) Lower subglottic pressure. A slightly more closed vowel should be used. Intrinsic and extrinsic stability still very important. Demands more fine control in the respiratory and adductory musculature (c) Extrinsic stability necessary: increasing subglottic pressure; increased glottal resistance (although some advocate a very slight abduction). Vowel modifies from more closed to more open with increase in dynamic	All are fundamental aspects of many styles. Stability of postural, respiratory, and laryngeal function is required for high dynamic singing in CCM and operatic styles. Stability at low dynamic levels is essential for healthy choral singing and for subtlety in the art song repertoire The *messa di voce* is a quintessential sign of great artistry (or the lack thereof) and is a great tool for shaping cadences and phrases

(continued)

Table 30.1 Continued

Exercise characteristic	Physiological and acoustical considerations	Comments on application to singing training
	(d) Extrinsic stability essential: decreasing subglottic pressure; some pedagogues advocate slightly increasing adduction. Vowel modifies from more open to more closed with decrease in dynamic (e) Combines aspects of (c) and (d) from above	

TA, thyroarytenoid; CT, cricothyroid; IA, interarytenoid; PCA, posterior cricoarytenoid; CCM, contemporary commercial music; LCA, lateral cricoarytenoid.

like /b/ and /d/ might be the best compromise. One must also consider the turbulence that is created in the airstream by fricatives. In short, there are no magic consonants or vowels which help all singers. Two other important factors are habituation and generalization. As a behavior is repeated, it becomes more habituated (more automatic) and it can also become generalized (the behavior has some negative or positive effect on other behaviors and situations). With respect to singing, over time, the habilitative benefits of an articulatory pattern may change or even become negative rather than positive. A wide variety of articulation patterns which are used in a rotating fashion seems most effective. Readers are referred to more in-depth discussions of consonants in Coffin (1976), Miller (1986), Nair (1999), and Baken and Orlikoff (2000).

Tempo and note values

A slower tempo requires more stability of muscular function intrinsically and extrinsically, and a more consistent air flow, similar to that already mentioned for sostenuto patterns. A faster tempo requires more flexibility of function and more rapid muscular adjustments. Likewise, more sustained notes in an exercise tend to invite a fuller, richer timbre and more activity from the TA muscle. Teachers must always know what they are requiring of their students physiologically when they design patterns of varying lengths.

Dynamic level

The extremes of one's dynamic level require greater overall stability and control of the vocal mechanism. The higher the dynamic level, the more vowel adjustment needs to be made. Reduced dynamic levels typically require the vowel to be more closed, making the vocal tract more inertive; as the amplitude of the sound being fed into the vocal tract is increased and the complexity of the sound wave grows (because firmer adduction at the glottis generates a richer source spectrum of partials), the more a singer must tune the vocal tract to be acoustically in sync with the vibrator.

Tailoring exercises to address technical issues and to meet specific demands of the repertoire

Imagine an economic situation where personally tailored and commercially available clothes cost the same. Given the choice, one would likely choose tailored ones, as they would fit and look better. Now consider the same economic choice with one wrinkle: purchasing tailor-made clothes costs the same as commercially manufactured ones, but the buyer must do the design work for him- or herself to get the tailored ones at the same price. How many people would still choose tailored clothing?

Much the same choice exists in the singing profession. Pedagogical writers dating back hundreds of years have designed vocalises and even entire voice training systems. Through careful shopping, one can find pedagogical clothes that fit most singers reasonably well and suit most occasions. Books, CDs, DVDs, and websites exist which feature exercises and vocal methods; these can be purchased at a reasonable price. Authors of such exercise resources include Panofka, Marchesi, Coffin, and Miller, to name only a few. The choice exists, however, for knowledgeable singers and teachers to design vocalises and to formulate their own system of organizing vocalises to best fit personal needs. By designing exercises, one avoids the dangers of buying pedagogical clothing "off the rack," which includes falling into a rote approach, with little thought being put into why a specific exercise should be used, how it should be employed, or how it might be adapted to meet individual needs. As any good tailor will say, no matter how fashionable the outfit, one size does not fit all bodies and one style does not fit all ages.

As Table 30.1 indicates, there are many factors to consider in designing exercises, including intrinsic and extrinsic muscle activation, lamina propria fatigue, and musical factors (i.e. the relevance of the exercise to musical applications: does it assist in the transference of needed skills?). Consider the following analysis of two exercises:

1. For soprano, a legato arpeggio on a major chord on /ɑ/, starting on F4 and proceeding upward on scale degrees 1–3–5–8–10–8–5–3–1.

The pedagogical goal is to sing legato at a comfortably high intensity through at least one register bridge, such as might be necessary in negotiating a sweeping phrase in the music of Brahms or Strauss. To achieve this, an optimal balance between the TA and CT must occur and the singer must modify the vowel appropriately. The combination of a high frequency range and high vibration amplitude can fatigue the lamina propria. Multiple attempts at this pattern could fatigue the extrinsic laryngeal positioning muscles and the breathing musculature.

2. For mezzo soprano, a staccato agility pattern on /o/ in F major starting on C5 and proceeding on scale degrees 5–4–5–3–5–2–5–1.

The pedagogical goals are precise vocal onset/offset control and agility, such as is required in much of Rossini's vocal music. This exercise demands an instantaneous TA/CT balance for targeting each new pitch along with adduction (lateral cricoarytenoid/interarytenoid activity) in rapid alternation with abduction (posterior cricoarytenoid activity). The singer must adjust for the next pitch while the vocal folds are abducted. In addition, there must be instantaneous adjustment of subglottic pressure for each new pitch. Repeated trials of this exercise can fatigue the intrinsic muscles.

Solving technical problems with exercises

Carefully designed exercises (or selectively chosen phrases from the literature) are one means of addressing technical issues with singers. Singing teachers must develop and employ keen observational and listening skills for both functional and artistic issues in order to correctly identify the underlying cause of the vocal difficulty (not just the symptoms) and to select appropriate habilitative exercises (Nix 2002b). When choosing exercises or phrases, teachers must balance a number of factors, including how soon the singer needs to be able to perform, how well the singer copes with challenges, and how to present the singer with feedback. The timing of upcoming performances is crucial; there are exercises and teaching techniques which can provide a "quick fix" for a specific problem. However, in some cases, the quick fix is not always the best choice in the long term. The emotional stability of the singer when he or she is experiencing difficulties can be a very crucial issue in choosing how to habilitate them. During the process of remedying an issue, vocal production may initially become more unstable as old habits are given up before new habits become secure. Finally, teachers must carefully consider how to best implement corrections. Some students respond best to demonstration and imitation; others thrive with imagery or specific physical instructions. In any case, it is essential to use terminology that is as accurate as possible when describing any aspect of technique. No matter the instructional method, nebulous language that is neither specific in its directive nor based on physiological principles has little place in the modern teaching studio.

SELECTION OF REPERTOIRE

Repertoire appropriate to age, gender, and vocal development

Selecting appropriate repertoire is one of the most important responsibilities of a teacher. Repertoire must be assigned on an individual basis after carefully considering the student's age, gender, technical challenges, personality, musicianship, and developmental level. Astute repertoire selection can be used to address the technical and musical development of the singer, as well as advancing the singer's performing career in the case of students in training programs and working professionals (see Chapters 32 and 34).

Matching appropriate repertoire to a singer's abilities is a complex task. As has been said regarding the design of exercises, the first step is to assess the student's strengths and weaknesses accurately (Nix 2002b). Many of these same skills can then be combined with a solid foundation in voice anatomy, physiology, acoustics, and lifespan development and applied to accurately assessing the vocal, musical, linguistic, and expressive challenges of repertoire (Nix 2002a, 2008). Finally, the two assessments can be cross-referenced, providing teacher and student with proper repertoire without resorting exclusively to trial and error. One repertoire reference that facilitates this approach is Doscher (2002). Table 30.2 shows an assessment of a song by Haydn which was examined in the approach advocated by Nix and Doscher.

Age and gender are important criteria in repertoire selection. The music selected must match the student's physiological development. Harm can result by assigning pieces too demanding for young, developing muscles and ligaments. The adage "better a month late than a day too soon" certainly applies to assigning repertoire to beginning singers. In addition, the text of the song or aria must match the singer's emotional maturity and personality, and the age of the character (if specifically indicated) portrayed must be reasonably close to the singer's age. Regarding gender, while there are many works that can be successfully sung

Table 30.2 Evaluation of Haydn's song "Piercing eyes"

Poet	Anne Hunter
Physical issues	Age: youthful
	Length of study: intermediate to advanced beginner; 2–3 years of study
Technical issues	Registers: requires negotiation of the upper *passaggio* in female voices
	Vowels/consonants: /aːl/ diphthongs; several words with r and n, especially n-containing words as pickups to the next measure
	Length of phrases: fairly short, except for a slow scale from F4–F5
	Phrase direction: two long stepwise ascents to F5; otherwise, the piece is balanced between descending and ascending phrases
Voice classification	Melodic line often occurs around register bridges: some tricky intonation (1/2 step motion) around B4–D5 and E5/F5
	Tessitura: approximately C5
	Timbre: needs a light, bright, "innocent" voice
	Range: D4–F5
	Approach to extremes: stepwise approach to lowest note, step/leap to highest
Emotional issues	Maturity: not a really "deep" text. Youthful subject
	Temperament: a plaintive text
	Personal preferences: typical of classical period—graceful triadic melody, simple harmonically, innocent text
Musicianship	Melody: triadic and scalar figures. Melody is often doubled, except at "e'er since they played . . ." Many pickup notes
	Harmony: note harmonic tension at later repetitions of "and need no other light." Typical modulation away from tonic to dominant and back again
	Rhythms: lilting 6/8 with few difficulties
	Articulation: a few slurs
	Text: see notes above on timbre (Voice classification). Rather dated to modern readers, e.g. word order ("those eyes full well do know my heart"), use of "e'er." Some repetition of text, especially at the end of the song. Plays on the poetic tradition of eyes being likened to lights

by either gender, some pieces, because of technical demands (such as vowels chosen by the composer on crucial passages) and sentiments expressed in the text are specifically intended for one gender. For example, male classical singers have difficulty singing staccato passages in the upper fifth of their range. Seeing high-lying staccato passages in a piece would indicate that a female singer would be better suited to performing it. Female singers have difficulty executing high passages with syllabic text settings featuring closed front vowels, unless substantial modification is used. Male singers generally fare much better with such a text setting, and in this case might be recommended over females.

Developing technique and musicianship through repertoire assignment

A skillful teacher not only uses individualized exercises to address each singer's technical growth; he or she also seeks out repertoire which reinforces technical work, applies new skills to serve vocal expression development, and assists in acquiring greater musicianship. For example, imagine a young soprano who is struggling with breath management on long phrases. Wise repertoire choices for such a student would feature phrases of varying lengths and pitch directions with frequent breathing opportunities until the proper appoggio is acquired. As many pieces of this type can be found in the literature from the baroque and classical periods, while gradually developing breath capacity, the singer could also learn with the teacher's guidance about performance practice in those periods. The song by Haydn analyzed in Table 30.2 and others like it might be recommended.

ORGANIZATION OF PRACTICE

Like all athletes and skilled performers, singers must practice in order to improve and to maintain their level of proficiency. The major goals of practicing are:

- developing the necessary physical and mental skills for artistic singing;
- applying acquired skills of singing performance to artistic expression;
- physically and mentally preparing for varying performance situations.

Many factors determine who succeeds as a singer. Genetically determined body structures and a musically enriching environment in the developmental years are certainly very important. Mental factors also have a crucial impact on performance outcomes (see Chapter 33). All these factors being relatively equal, however, some singers excel while others do not. A principal reason is how they practice. Those singers who best know how to train through efficient practice will progress more rapidly and will meet performance goals more consistently.

Earlier in this chapter, Table 30.1 provided a list of the diverse physical characteristics of various vocal exercises. Singing is a highly skilled whole-body activity, so exercise physiology and motor learning principles of training can be combined with the knowledge base on voice science contained in Table 30.1 in order to organize singing training.

Applying exercise physiology and motor learning to structuring practice sessions

Exercise physiology and voice training

Four basic principles of physical training have been identified which, when carefully manipulated, can evoke training benefits (Saxon and Berry 2009; Saxon and Schneider 1995). These four are overload, specificity, individuality, and reversibility.

1. Overloading involves asking more from a muscle or group of muscles than normal. An example of overloading in singing training might be to take the three consecutive phrases at the beginning of Beethoven's "Adelaide" and doing them at a slower tempo than is needed for performance. Such practicing would tax the singer's breath management system beyond what is needed to perform the song; by so doing, the singer would gain greater ease in performing the phrases at tempo and in an artistic fashion. It is important to distinguish this example from overloading that would not be constructive, such as singing a piece which is too advanced or singing overly loud or dark.
2. Specificity means that the training must match the task or skills to be developed. Specificity of training for a singer performing Handel's "Ombra mai fu" might include practicing a *messa di voce* exercise on the /o/ vowel in the pitch range required at the start of the aria.
3. Individuality concerns adjusting the training to match the performer's age, physical development, experience, health, and skill level. The discussions earlier in this chapter about designing tailor-made exercises and matching singers and repertoire are prime examples of how singing training can incorporate this principle.
4. Reversibility is how training benefits are lost over time without continued training. An example of this in singing would be a song that a singer decides to discontinue practicing for a while; when work on the piece resumes, it is "rusty;" elements that had previously been mastered are once again awkward and in need of renewed attention.

Singers and teachers have additional variables that can be used in designing optimal practice sessions. These include practice frequency, duration of the practice session, the intensity of sessions and exercises within a session, and how quickly to advance to more difficult tasks (Saxon and Berry 2009). More will be said about these variables in the practice examples below.

One further element in organizing all practice is working from the general to the specific. When first starting to learn golf, one does not go to the course and practice a backspinning fade; rather, one receives a bucket of balls and patiently works on the fundamental mechanics of the swing. Professionals continue this pattern in how they warm up before a tournament: one sees them start with general skills on the driving range. They reinforce the fundamentals of their swing before reviewing specific or more advanced skills and starting a competitive round. The same is true for how singers should organize practice. One begins with gross motor control by using simple vocalise patterns, then gradually works towards finer elements of technique. The *messa di voce* on a challenging vowel in the *passaggio* is saved for late in the session. This general to specific hierarchy also applies to how teachers should ideally approach training young singers. Gross motor control of "the big picture" items, such as postural alignment and breathing efficiency, must be acquired before more refined sounds can be expected. This general to specific dictum applies to vocalizing, repertoire selection, and how a teacher gives feedback to a student.

As always, since singing is an artistic endeavor, a balance has to be struck between artistic and technical concepts. The technical skills acquired through carefully designed and sequenced exercises and wisely chosen repertoire are only a means to an end; making beautiful music is the goal. All singing practice should occur with an artistic goal in mind. Simultaneously, artistic expression demands that a singer have full command of his or her instrument. An analytical approach to singing training does not prevent one from being expressive; if anything, such an approach provides teacher and student with more tools for pursuing artistic goals. Just as a secure technique is developed by using specific training methods and schedules, so, too, must artistry be practiced in order for it to be reliable in performances. Best practices for this holistic view of voice training also employ principles developed in the fields of motor learning and performance psychology, most notably in the field of sports. Key aspects of motor learning and voice training are provided here; the use of performance psychology in securing peak performance is discussed in Chapter 33.

Motor learning and voice training

As the field of motor learning continues to grow, it is increasingly apparent that music teaching has been oriented towards how information is most easily delivered to students rather than how teaching could be structured for the optimal student experience. By "learning," with regard to motor learning, we mean that a permanent change in the capability for skilled movement has occurred (Maas et al. 2008). This is quite different from any temporary performance enhancement. Consider a masterclass where a singer performs better than before thanks to the guidance of a clinician. However, the next day, the singer is frustrated when recapturing the same level proves elusive. Short-term performance was enhanced, but learning did not occur. Evidence of learning includes maintenance, the retention of a skill after training, and generalization, the transfer of a skill to a related but untrained task (Maas et al. 2008). By not being able to match the level of performance in the masterclass, neither maintenance nor generalization were exhibited.

In many cases, as shown in Table 30.3, practice and feedback that promote learning frequently suppress immediate performance, and practice/feedback that promote performance often impede learning. The information may seem counterintuitive when compared with more traditional approaches to teaching.

Given the evidence to date, how might a practice session employing the ideas presented in this chapter be structured? Here is an example.

1. One or two simple conjunct descending exercises (perhaps starting with semi-occluded postures) in blocked constant fashion.
2. Three to five exercises addressing skills needed for the music to be sung done in circuit training fashion (exercise A, B, C, D, A, C, B, A, D, etc.), changing initial consonants and vowels in order to further facilitate motor learning. The difficulty level should gradually increase as the session progresses.

Table 30.3 Motor learning and singing training (based on Tables 1 and 2 in Maas et al. 2008)

Practice category	Description	Singing training example	Comments*
Blocked practice order	Desired behaviors practiced in separate blocks or groups	Ten five-note ascending scales on /i/; then ten five-note scales on /a/, i.e. AAA, BBB, etc.	Learning may best be assisted by blocked, then random practice
Serial practice order	Desired behaviors practiced in sequential order which is repeated	Five-note scale on /i/; five-note scale on /a/; five-note scale on /o/. Repeat all in order; i.e. ABC, ABC, etc.	Random and serial better than blocked for learning; little difference exists between serial and random
Random practice order	Several different desired behaviors practiced intermixed in a non-sequential fashion	Five-note scale on /i/; five-note scale on /a/; five-note scale on /u/; five-note scale on /ae/; i.e. ABA, BCA, CAB, BBC, CAA	Change of target versus unpredictability of next task seems to be the reason serial and random are better than blocked for learning
Type of behaviors practiced: constant	The exact same behavior or movement is practiced in the same context	Diction drills on /z/ between two /a/ vowels; i.e. /caza/, /raza/, /daza/, /baza/	Suppresses learning with large amounts of practice; best when used in early stages of training. Learning may best be assisted by constant, then variable, practice
Type of behaviors practiced: variable	More than one variant of a given behavior or movement is practiced. Behaviors practiced are different from each other and occur in different contexts	Scale on /i/ vowel; then an arpeggio on /i/, then staccato on /i/, then *messa di voce* on /i/	Enhances learning with large amounts of practice. Most effective when coupled with random or serial order. More similar to "real world" situations. May help children more than adults (children have less motor learning experience). Most beneficial in later stages of training
Massed practice schedule	Same amount of practice time or repetitions used as in distributed practice (below), but practiced in a relatively short time period	One 60-minute practice session per day	No clear evidence available. Some massed practice is essential for developing endurance for extended performances

(continued)

Table 30.3 Continued

Practice category	Description	Singing training example	Comments*
Distributed practice schedule	Same amount of practice time or repetitions used as in massed practice (above), but divided into several sessions spaced over a longer period of time	Six 10-minute practice sessions per day, each separated by 1 hour of other activities	No clear evidence available. Distributed practice is less fatiguing to all muscle groups and the lamina propria than massed practice
Timing of feedback: concurrent (with guidance/ cues during practice) versus non-concurrent	Real-time outcome information is either presented (i.e. immediate knowledge of results (KR) or knowledge of performance (KP)) or given after a delay	Concurrent: teacher places hand on the singer's abdominal wall to cue breathing movements. Non-concurrent: teacher allows the student to perform an entire song without comments or cues	Concurrent feedback greatly benefits performance while practicing, but suppresses learning, except when the feedback provides an external focus of attention. Non-concurrent is essentially the same as delayed feedback
Timing of feedback: delayed	Feedback (KR or KP) presented after a pause of seconds or minutes after each attempt at the desired behavior	Teacher waits before providing feedback	Even a 5-second delay appears sufficient to enhance learning. The feedback delay seems to allow the singer to evaluate performance/results based on intrinsic feedback before the teacher provides external feedback
Frequency or amount of feedback	Feedback can be provided: (a) after each effort, (b) after a specified number of efforts, or (c) randomly	(a) Teacher responds after each vocalise attempt or phrase (b) Teacher responds after every fourth repetition of a vocalise (c) Teacher uses no fixed schedule to respond to student efforts	A feedback reduction benefits learning of general motor programs. Frequent feedback benefits learning specific parameters of an action
Type of feedback: KP versus KR	KP addresses how the student undertook the task KR addresses how the student's performance met a goal	KP: "You opened your mouth quite wide when you sang that high note" KR: "You were right on the pitch on the last note of the phrase"	Both seem equally beneficial to learning. KP seems helpful when undertaking a new or unclear task, but may not be helpful to learning when providing feedback concurrent with a student's performance

Table 30.3 Continued

Practice category	Description	Singing training example	Comments*
Attentional focus: internal versus external	Internal focus brings the singer's awareness to processes and sensations of performing the task External focus brings the student's attention to a result of performing the specific task	Internal: "Pay attention to the way your tongue moves as you go from /i/ to /a/" External: "When you do this lip buzz, make sure the tissue in front of your mouth stays in motion"	Using an external focus which is relevant to the task being performed has been shown to have a strong learning advantage over using an internal focus

* Caveat: few studies have been done on motor learning and voice.

3. Selected phrases from the repertoire are mixed in with the exercises.
4. A musical selection in preparation is addressed, first through singing the entire piece or a large section non-stop, then by alternating back and forth between exercises and selected phrases as needed. The complete selection is sung non-stop once more for synthesis.
5. Warm down, using one of the first exercises from the beginning of the session; the singer evaluates how the exercise feels and sounds after having had a vocal "workout."
6. The last vocalise is alternated with speaking common phrases ("Hi, my name is . . .," "Hello, this is . . .") to transfer good habits from singing voice production into speech.

The session moves from general to specific and from reassurance of acquired skills to developing new skills; skills are transferred from exercises to vocal repertoire, and basic principles are reviewed at the end. How does one juggle optimal motor learning-based practice with the emotional well-being of the singer? Take for example a talented but self-critical singer who becomes too easily discouraged when he or she cannot succeed in short order. With this type of student, a careful balance must be struck between blocked constant and random variable practicing. Some singers need the reassurance of blocked practicing, where immediate performance is enhanced through repetitions of similar tasks, before they venture out on the limb of learning-enhancing (and perhaps more immediately frustrating) random practice. On a less drastic basis, the intentional use of limited amounts of blocked practice can be helpful for students of all temperaments.

Planning a major performance

Anyone who has sung a long operatic role or an extensive song recital can confirm that vocal endurance—as acquired gradually through periodic massed practice sessions—is a necessity in preparing for such a performance. A sample practice plan is provided below for a singer preparing a 1-hour solo recital:

1. Three months prior to the performance: distributed practice.
2. One month prior to the performance: 4 days per week distributed practice, 2 days per week massed (similar to performance conditions), 1 day per week rest (after massed practice).
3. Two weeks prior to performance: alternate 1 day distributed, 1 day massed (with all aspects as similar to actual performance as possible, including the time of day, location, room acoustics, wearing performance-related articles of clothing, etc.), saving 1 day per week for rest following a massed practice day.
4. Performance day: massed, blocked, constant warm-up of skills needed in recital; sing the recital; brief warm down afterwards.

Further information can also be found in Chapter 33 on mental preparation.

Summary of key points

1. Singing technique is built through efficient use of the body, the careful design and appropriate usage of exercises, the selection of appropriate repertoire based on factors such as age, gender, and vocal development, and the optimal structuring of practice.
2. Teachers must remain current in voice physiology, acoustics, and development/maturation, as well as exercise physiology and motor learning in order to best design and implement vocal exercises, accurately assign repertoire, and plan lessons and practice schedules.
3. Best teaching practices include the creation of individualized plans for each singer based on the strengths and weaknesses of the student and his or her learning style. These plans should include sequencing of technical skills to be developed, specific repertoire challenges, types of practicing (blocked, random, distributed, etc.) to be used, and the scheduling of performance targets.

References

Baken, R.J. and Orlikoff, R. (2000). *Clinical Measurement of Speech and Voice*, 2nd edn. San Diego, CA: Singular.

Bele, I. (2005). Artificially lengthened and constricted vocal tract in vocal training methods. *Logopedics Phoniatrics Vocology* 30: 34–40.

Coffin, B. (1976). Articulation for opera, oratorio and recital. *NATS Bulletin* 32(2): 26–41.

Doscher, B. (2002). *From Studio to Stage: Repertoire for the Voice* (edited and annotated by J. Nix). Lanham, MD: Scarecrow Press.

Maas, E., Robin, D.A., Austermann Hula, S., et al. (2008). Principles of motor learning in treatment of motor speech disorders. *American Journal of Speech-Language Pathology* 17: 277–298.

Miller, R. (1986). *The Structure of Singing.* New York: Schirmer.

Nair, G. (1999). *Voice Tradition and Technology: a State-of-the-Art Studio.* San Diego, CA: Singular.

Nix, J. (1999). Lip trills and raspberries: "high spit factor" alternatives to the nasal continuant consonants. *Journal of Singing* 55(3): 15–19.

Nix, J. (2002a). Criteria for selecting repertoire. *Journal of Singing* 58(3): 217–221.

Nix, J. (2002b). Developing critical listening and observational skills in young voice teachers. *Journal of Singing* 59(1): 27–30.

Nix, J. (2008). Vocology and the selection of choral repertoire. *Australian Voice* 13: 36–42.

Nix, J. and Simpson, C.B. (2008). Semi-occluded vocal tract postures and their application in the singing voice studio. *Journal of Singing* 64(3): 339–342.

Nix, J., Emerich, K., and Titze, I. (2005). Application of vocal fry to the training of singers. *Journal of Singing* 62(1): 53–59.

Saxon, K. and Schneider, C.M. (1995). *Vocal Exercise Physiology*. San Diego, CA: Singular.

Saxon, K. and Berry, S. (2009). Vocal exercise physiology: same principles, new training paradigms. *Journal of Singing* 66(1): 51–57.

Titze, I. (1993). Warm-up exercises. *NATS Journal* 49(5): 21.

Titze, I. (1999). The use of low first formant vowels and nasals to train the lighter mechanism. *Journal of Singing* 55(4): 41–43.

Titze, I. (2000). *Principles of Voice Production*. Iowa City, IA: National Center for Voice and Speech.

Titze, I. (2001). The five best vocal warm up exercises. *Journal of Singing* 57(3): 51.

Titze, I. (2004). A theoretical study of Fo–F1 interaction with application to resonant speaking and singing voice. *Journal of Voice* 18(3): 292–298.

Titze, I. (2006). Voice training and therapy with a semi-occluded vocal tract: rationale and scientific underpinnings. *Journal of Speech, Language and Hearing Research* 49: 448–459.

Titze, I. and Verdolini-Abbott, K. (2011). *Vocology*. Iowa City, IA: National Center for Voice and Speech.

CHAPTER 31

....

ADDRESSING THE
NEEDS OF THE ADULT
"NON-SINGER" ("NS")

....

SUSAN KNIGHT

INTRODUCTION

....

What happens to people when societies do not allow for, or encourage, the development of latent musical abilities? (Blacking 1973, p. 238)

But it was a dread that you were going to have to go to music–singing I guess . . . I really disliked it because it was an ordeal. You had to get in the back row and pretend you were singing while everybody else sang . . . but you were not allowed to sing, and you weren't allowed to turn it down. It was never "try a bit harder, or half dozen of you girls come down a little earlier or stay after class"; there was no encouragement, none whatsoever . . . There was no instruction. They worked with you to sing a song same as anybody. I guess practice makes perfect for those that could sing. But I never sing. You never hear me in the shower, accidentally, ever sing a note. Never in the car. Never even to myself."

("Carla", age 43 [attributed at age 7], in Knight 2010)

This chapter provides a background on the subject of the adult "non-singer" ("NS") in Western and Westernized (e.g. Japan) cultures, including the various meanings that may be attached to the "NS" label. It also provides evidence on the phenomenon of the adult "NS" as established in the literature. Attribution as an "NS," its subsequent profile, and ensuing challenges and needs are articulated and explained, and singing enablement strategies are presented. The chapter will conclude with a discussion of impediments to singing development and consideration of proactive strategies to prevent/diminish such barriers from forming in the first place.

The "kind" of singing referenced here in relation to the adult "NS" is *not* about performance or high standards of artistic excellence. Rather, it is about singing that is personal, casual, and often social in nature—"everyday" singing as a human capacity, or "singing for its own sake," as Wise (2009) so aptly called it. It is about the human behavior of people who sing when they gather for an occasion; of children singing as they play, by themselves and with others; of families singing around the house; of people singing by or to themselves or another for pleasure or purpose, or both, as in a lullaby; about parishioners congregating to worship together in song, or folks gathering to mourn the loss of a friend, and so forth. But principally, it is about the many who have learned, i.e. *come to believe*, for the most part quite early in their lives, that they cannot do that human thing, which is "sing."

What is meant by the term "non-singer"?

The term "non-singer" may be understood in a number of ways. The label "NS" (which is often self-ascribed) can include those who:

1. Believe that they are innately incapable of singing or learning to sing
2. Declare that they cannot sing, but actually mean they cannot sing well enough for others to hear them sing by themselves
3. Recognize that they do have a singing capacity, but because it falls short of their own notion/expectation of good singing, declare themselves as "NS." "Anyone can sing, if you want to call it singing" ("Lucy," in Knight 2010, p. 91)
4. Choose not to out of disinterest, i.e. they refer to themselves as "NS" because they do not engage in singing
5. Are thus differentiated as those who do not sing professionally, i.e. the "NS" as compared with the professional singer.[1]

This categorization is sometimes used by professional singers as a non-pejorative distinction, although it may not necessarily be perceived in such a light by those thus designated. However, it is also a term which some "lay" people, i.e. *non-professional singers*, use to clarify that they themselves, or other "lay" people, are *not (professional)* singers. While those described in categories 2–5 above could self-reference or be referenced as a "NS," such designation is in relation to the *developed*[2] degree of their singing ability. However, the first category above will be the principal focus of this chapter—those adults who believe that they are innately incapable of singing or of learning to sing.

Cultural evidence of "NS"

The reality of the adult "NS" as a culturally acknowledged phenomenon is evidenced by its significant representation in the English language. A substantial presence and acknowledgment of the perception of "NS" as a common human condition is indicated by the many colloquialisms (often pejorative) used to recognize/denote the "NS": "dis-ability" ("NS"), for example "note deafness" (Allen 1878), "tune deafness," or "dysmelodia" (Kalmus and Fry

---

[1] E.g. the title of an article by Ginsborg et al. (2011) "Have we made ourselves clear? Singers and non-singers' perceptions of the intelligibility of sung text."
[2] The term *developed* is italicized here to denote that self/other's perception of a person's singing ability is not necessarily interpreted as being a result of development, but rather is often an observation of what is believed to be an inborn, i.e. a fixed state.

1980); "droners," "grunters," and "growler" (Fieldhouse 1937); "monotone" (Joyner 1969); "poor pitch singer" (e.g. Lidman-Magnusson 1997a; Welch 1979); "uncertain singer" (e.g. Porter 1977); "backward singers," "tone dumb," "tone deaf" (Bentley 1968). Western and Westernized cultures, such as Japan, have similar terms for those they designate as "NS," for example "onchi" (Japanese, "tone idiot") (Welch and Murao 1994). This common folk acknowledgment of innate singing dis-ability as a fixed human condition will be explored later in this chapter.

Attribution and re-identifying as "NS"

We all begin life as singers, for our infant vocalization is more akin to singing than to speech. Children, that is to say people, assume that they can sing until/unless they are told or infer that they cannot.[3] Once thus attributed, they assume the newly ascribed identity of "NS," adapt to the physical, psychological, and social implications of such a categorization, and adjust their expectations and behaviors accordingly. Most significantly, further development of their singing skill is arrested.

The ensuing needs of self-perceived "NS" adults are many, and vary, but are all connected with their exclusion from a singing world and the negative emotions and social marginalization which often accompanies such exclusion. Understanding those needs and their derivation is key to meeting them, thereby opening the possibility for "NS" *re-entry* to a life with singing. So, prior to discussing singing enablement strategies and techniques, the process of "NS" attribution is explained. Clarification of this phenomenon is a crucial first step in comprehending the situation of those thus ascribed. The needs arising from the "NS" state span and intersect social, cultural, psychological, educational, and musical perspectives and are viewed through the following lens:

- common experiential profile of the adult "NS"
- relationship of "NS" self-belief to societal acknowledgment of "NS" as a fixed state
- factors affecting attribution and identity formation as "NS"
- the "NS" attribution process
- common social coping techniques of the adult "NS."

Common experiential profile of the adult "NS"

Studies producing narrative data from the lived experience of "NS" have thus far been situated in Western or Westernized cultures, but as far-flung as Australia (Ruddock and Leong 2005; Ruddock 2007a, 2007b, 2008, 2010); Sweden (Lindman-Magnusson 1994, 1995, 1997a, 1997b); Canada (Joyce 1993, 1998, 2003; Knight 1995, 1999, 2004, 2010, 2011; Whidden 2008, 2009, 2010); Finland (Numminen 2004); the UK (Richards and Durrant 2003); the USA (Abril 2007; Pascale 2002a, 2002b; Wheaton 1998); and Japan (Welch and Murao 1994). The accounts which this research provides of adult "NS" experience bear remarkable

---

[3] The literature evidences that most "NS" attributions occur in childhood or adolescence.

similarity given their comparative age span, backgrounds, and geographical disparity. From this data emerges what appears to be a common experiential profile, comprising the following characteristics:

1. "NSs" believe that they do not have the ability to sing, nor the innate capacity to learn to sing;
2. "NS" self-belief most often arose in childhood, either through an other-imposed negative, defining ensemble experience, frequently involving an authority figure, or was self-inferred by skill comparison with other/s in singing settings;
3. At attribution, this "NS" self-belief was accepted without resistance and was believed to be irrevocable. If the attributor/s was an authority in the child's life, s/he was seen as an expert, omniscient and omnipotent on this topic, and the "NS" self-belief persisted across the lifespan. Memory of the "NS" attribution endures into adulthood in detail, retaining its negative emotions on recall[4].
4. "NS" childhood singing environments involved low/absent levels of *singing development indicators*, i.e. exposure to, encouragement of, access to involvement, experience, and instruction in singing.
5. In singing settings, or anticipation thereof, "NSs" experience negative emotions about their perceived singing deficit, expressing feelings of anxiety, embarrassment, and fear of humiliation and shame around singing.

---

[4] The narratives of multiple participants described in the SCSR research evidenced common traumatic themes. These memories recounting the moment of childhood NS attribution, some held for decades, revealed a starkness of detail, as if they had been frozen in time. This phenomenon of detailed, enduring memory for traumatic events is evidenced in the literature. Neurological research helps to explain why emotional memories have the power that they do. Stress associated with emotion may affect how deeply an event is etched in the memory. Brown and Kulik (1977) suggested that a novel, shocking event activates a special brain mechanism, which they referred to as a "Now Print." Much like a camera's flashbulb, they hypothesized, the "Now Print" mechanism preserves or "freezes" whatever happens at the moment we experience the shocking event. When subjects' emotions are negatively aroused, they process more elaborately those critical details that were the source of the emotional arousal, and they maintain or restrict the scene's boundaries. A similar study found that "tunnel memory" of a traumatic or shocking event results from greater elaboration of critical details and more focused boundaries. Tunnel memory may explain the superior recognition and recall of central, emotion-arousing details in a traumatic event (Safer et al. 1998). A 2003 study (McIntyre et al. 2003), found that emotionally arousing events activated the amygdala, which then increased a specific protein—activity-regulated cytoskeletal protein (Arc')—in the neurons in the hippocampus. It is thought that Arc' helps store these memories by strengthening the synapses. Dolcos et al. (2005) found that this recall was associated with higher activity in both the amygdala and the hippocampus. The synchronicity of activity (Dolcos et al. 2005) between these two brain regions suggested that each region triggers the other, creating a self-reinforcing "memory loop" in which an emotional cue might trigger recall of the event which then loops back to a re-experiencing of the emotion of the event. Another study in 2007 added to this knowledge with a finding that emotion increases the memorability of events, because during emotional arousal, the stress hormone norepinephrine makes synapses dramatically more sensitive by increasing the number of GluR1 receptors (Hu et al. 2007). In addition, Ledoux (1998) has discovered that there are more connections leading from the amygdala to the pre-frontal cortex than the reverse, explaining why anxious memories predominate over the ability of consciousness to suppress them.

6. "NSs" report common coping strategies to shield against potential judgment, which is commonly anticipated and often experienced in social-singing situations (formal or informal). A prominent, consistent coping strategy is to pre-empt critical scrutiny by openly declaring their (perceived) singing deficit through self-deprecating humor.

7. Regret is expressed at the social marginalization/exclusion which many "NS" report experiencing as a result of their singing "dis-ability," thus producing, to varying degrees, disadvantageous effects on their lives.

8. "NSs" most often report no instruction/intervention having been given in childhood/youth to help with their singing development challenge.

While these characteristics are all significant, especially pertinent to the discussion is the third trait—immediate, unresisted acceptance of "NS" designation and belief in its irrevocability. An associated complication is the frequency of the attributor being an authority, which involves issues of trust and power as influencing factors. These will be addressed later in this section.

Relationship of "NS" self-belief to societal acknowledgment of "NS" as a fixed state

Evidence is well established that humans possess a species-wide facility for singing as a learned musical behavior featuring development across a continuum of increasing singing skill and knowledge (Welch 1986). The singing potential of individuals begins to be realized (nurtured and/or hindered), commencing in infancy, through learning encounters in particular socio-cultural contexts across and beyond childhood (Welch 1986). Singing is not only integral to all human cultures (Merriam 1964) but is also expressive of the individuals who comprise them and relate within them. The value and practice of singing is globally divergent. A culture's imperatives shape its expressions, and one of the functions that culture seems to fulfill is the determination of the ability/disability view of singing within it. Merriam (1964) remarked that whatever the cultural belief system about "talent," the power of the prevailing perspective determines who may or may not become "musical" in that society. The dramatic effect of prevailing opposite views about human musical capacity is evidenced by two different African cultures. The Venda (Blacking 1973) believe in and foster singing development in each member from birth, thus enabling inclusive success by all. But the Ewe (Merriam 1964) neither expect nor support pervasive singing development, nor do their members all develop musically. The latter societal view of singing ability relates closely to the dominant Western cultural narrative around human singing capacity as a fixed entity.

The relationship of individual "NS" self-belief to the dominant societal acknowledgment of "NS" as a fixed state lies at the core of the "NS" phenomenon in Western culture, its constituent factors comprising:

- the socially exposed nature of singing
- the dominance of folk psychology forming/perpetuating cultural assumptions
- "NS" immediate acceptance and irrevocability of such designation on attribution
- issues of trust and power influencing "NS" attribution of children
- the significance of fixed versus developmental views of singing as a human capacity.

The socially exposed nature of singing bears a close relationship to the "NS" phenomenon. Lomax (1968, p. 3) reported that "singing is a universal trait found in all known cultures as a specialized and easily identifiable kind of vocal behavior." He further defined singing as a social act:

> A specialized act of communication, akin to speech, but far more formally organized and re-dundant. Because of its heightened redundancy, singing attracts and holds the attention of groups. Whether chorally performed or not, however, the chief function of song is to express the shared feelings and mould the joint activities of some human community.
>
> (Lomax 1968, p. 3)

For the individual, some aspects of singing life are private, but most are socially located, even while individually perceived and experienced—cognitively, kinesthetically, and affectively. This reality brings implications for the individual singer, which vary according to the societal expectations around singing in her/his particular culture. Lomax expanded on the exposure which cultures impose on members, so that if a singer should:

> overstep the bounds of proper vocalizing in a given cultural context, they rouse feelings of shame, amusement or anger among the hearers. This is because singing, like speech, is a lan-guage. Therefore, its use of tone, meter and much more must be bound by formal conventions if it is to communicate effectively.
>
> (Lomax 1968, p. 11)

As Lomax explained, "overstepping the bounds" points to the expectations and accompanying sanctions around "proper vocalizing" in a given culture. The array of com-posite cultural expectations "understood" within a culture have powerful implications:

> The most important thing for a person to know is just how appropriate a bit of behaviour or communication is, and how to respond to it appropriately . . . Everyone in a culture responds with satisfaction or ecstasy to the apropos, and with scorn and resentment to the unseemly.
>
> (Lomax 1968, p. 12)

How cultural understandings form, are accepted, and serve to regulate society and the individual lives within it, relates directly to the, thus far, enduring phenomenon of the "NS."

Our everyday mental states constitute a folk theory of mind, which is an intuitive view of reality (Sellars 1956). Bruner (1990) referenced that all cultures have a folk psychology and described the concept as "a system by which people organize their experience in, knowledge about and transactions with the social world" (Bruner 1990, p. 35).

Folk psychology plays a dominant role in forming and perpetuating cultural assumptions. The function of folk psychology is to represent the prevailing notions of the general popula-tion, i.e. what people think about things. The cultural need exists to identify and explain the patterns comprising the differences in heterogeneous societies (Abrahams 1986). Dundes (1975) called these patterns *folk ideas*, or the descriptive constructs of perceived reality, and characterized a folk idea as a belief that structures attitudes—a form of cultural validation. The Western folk psychology interpretation of the nature of human singing as a fixed genetic entity is an elemental belief that has entered into our cultural narrative, reflecting cultural practice (Ayotte et al. 2002; Peretz et al. 2002; Wise 2009). So, with regard to folk psychology, the question of whether or not singing ability actually is a finite, selective inborn gift without which "NS" is an irrevocable reality is immaterial. It is the satisfaction provided by the explanation that counts.

Within a given culture, people use value-laden folk ideas (i.e. clichés, labels, slogans) to help order their personal and social lives. For instance, the fact that "NS" are well represented in the terminology of our language via the folk idiom demonstrates the pervasiveness of the "NS" concept as a perceived social reality. Folk descriptions of those who ostensibly cannot (or have not *yet*) learned to "carry a tune" can be blatant, graphic, and unflattering, as previously referenced (e.g. "tone deaf," "droners," "monotone," etc.). This serves not only to describe the phenomenon, but also to comment on its judged anomaly, and in some cases, its unseemliness (Lomax 1968). This intuitive folk view of the nature of human singing as a fixed entity (rather than a developmental acquisition of skill) reflects cultural practices (Lomax 1968).

Self-beliefs are strongly shaped by folk psychology, which in turn exerts a powerful influence on the formation and perpetuation of cultural assumptions. Therefore, it is not surprising that the culturally held sense that singing is an innate skill selectively distributed amongst the population, like the African Ewe belief system (rather than the pan-human developmental capacity view of the African Venda), is one of common awareness and generally unquestioned acceptance in Western society. Likewise, it is not difficult to see the powerful effect that a dominant cultural assumption, valid or not, can have on influencing the development of a society. While research focusing on the deficit aspect of adult "NS" singing continues (e.g. Bradshaw and McHenry 2005; Cuddy et al. 2005; Dalla Bella and Berkowska 2009; Dalla Bella et al. 2009; Foxton et al. 2004; Hyde et al. 2006; Hyde et al. 2007; Moreau et al. 2009; Peretz 2006; Peretz and Hyde 2003; Peretz et al. 2002, 2008, 2009; 2008; Pfordresher and Brown 2007; Stewart 2008), investigations evidencing development, and practices for its expanding facilitation, are also well established (and previously referenced), with a shift in conceptions of child singing development away from disability and towards competency (Welch 2001). Nevertheless, it is important and responsible to acknowledge the presence of folk psychology, which has the power and influence of myth in our society. This pervasive cultural view of singing as a "selective inborn talent" is ingrained in the Western folk psyche, and as yet, remains unequivocal on the point.

Researchers examining the phenomenon of the adult "NS" (Abril 2007; Joyce 1993, 1998, 2003; Knight 1995, 1999, 2004, 2010, 2011; Lidman-Magnussen 1994, 1995, 1997a, 1997b; Numminen 2004; Pascale 2002a, 2002b; Richards and Durrant 2003; Ruddock 2007a, 2007b, 2008; Ruddock and Leong 2005; Whidden 2008; Wheaton 1998) report that on designation of "NS" status, the designee exhibits immediate, non-resistant acceptance of this new identity as well as the belief of its irrevocability. Why such a diagnosis would be met with unquestioned acceptance can be explained by two principal factors:

- The cultural awareness that many people are perceived as "NS," i.e. that such a group exists, makes sense to the person being thus attributed. They "figure out" that they must just belong to that category:

> They got you to stand up to sing something and I croaked out something and he said "thanks a lot – go away" and that was it. It was just a traumatic experience, and you thought "well, I'm not a singer, I know that now," and you're hurt naturally, because you just thought that you could sing and now you know you can't and that's it.
>
>   ("James," recounting school choir audition at age 14, in Knight 2010)

- As previously referenced, the majority of adult "NSs" report having been attributed in childhood by an authority figure. The issues of trust and power figure prominently in why a child would readily agree with an authority diagnosis of their non-singing state in this attributional encounter.

Children trust authority figures on both interpersonal and epistemic levels (Corriveau and Harris 2012). Interpersonal trust is that which the child vests in the authority as a person—to be thoughtful, fair—to keep their promises. Epistemic trust means that children believe that the adult has expert knowledge. Children evaluate information as to its accuracy (trustworthiness) in two principal ways: a perceptually driven mode (trusting their own senses) and a socially driven mode (deferring to consensus, possibly even despite perceptual evidence available to them). Children notice who agrees with whom, and they tend to trust informants who belong to a consensus (Corriveau and Harris 2009). Therefore, because the widespread notion of human as "NS" is firmly established in the culture as a folk idea, i.e. a generally accepted popular "belief" (Ayotte et al. 2002; Wise 2009), the child is likely to encounter a wide social consensus on this point.

The issue of power (i.e. legitimate power and expert power) also affects a child's attribution as "NS" by an authority figure (Raven 1965). Legitimate power is rooted in the child's obligation to accept the authority figure's influence attempt (i.e. you are an "NS") because the child believes that the authority has a legitimate right to do so. Expert power emanates from the perception that the authority has the knowledge/expertise to make the "NS" attribution (Raven 1965). The literature evidences that most children attributed as "NS" were not offered help to improve their singing, which underscored a sense that intervention would have been useless to the child, hence validating the irrevocability of their "NS" "reality."

Self-theories of intelligence can explain the divergence of individuals' belief systems, with a consequential effect on motivation and achievement, i.e. development (Dweck 1999). Divergent stances on singing development as a human phenomenon—fixed versus developmental—may be seen as compatible if viewed in this light. Self-theories belong to the philosophical and psychological tradition in which people's beliefs form a meaning system around which they organize and understand their world. According to Dweck, people hold either an entity (fixed) or an incremental (malleable) view of intelligence and ability. Such divergence results from the motivation and subsequent achievement which are influenced by either of the two viewpoints. Dweck (1986) also demonstrated that self-beliefs are more powerful predictors of future achievement than IQ. Over time, the dominant Western cultural belief system focusing on the fixed view of human singing may gradually shift to an incremental one, as increasing scientific evidence and practical demonstration of its developmental nature combine to validate its malleable nature, and thus enter more prominently into public view and acceptance.

Factors affecting attribution and identity formation as "NS"

A multitude of interactive factors contribute to an individual's singing development as well as their attribution and identity formation as either a singer or an "NS." The developmental literature evidences that individual singing behaviors emerge from a multi-faceted interface between biological, developmental, and environmental elements across time (Welch 2006).

In addition, the nature of this interaction is non-linear, varying amongst individuals, due to the comparative differences and biases emerging from the interaction and formation of our basic neuropsychobiology—by experience, socio-cultural imperatives, and maturational processes (Altenmüller 2004). Singing is a natural human capacity the development of which is informed by the complexity of the interaction of these many factors. A disproportionately high number of young people self-designate as "NS," with this self-belief serving to stall or arrest further singing development. Investigation of the "NS" phenomenon has tended to focus on either the deficit or the developmental aspects of singing ability. However, a recent study from the deficit tradition is now considering both the detrimental effect of holding a fixed view and the opening view of a developmental possibility:

> Language from studies investigating self-perceptions of singing skill suggest that people tend to view singing as a fixed characteristic like "talent" rather than a temporary condition that could be improved at any time. It may be that accurate singing is a musical skill more akin to playing the trumpet. Nobody expects adults who haven't picked up their trumpet since 5th grade to play with any skill, but we think that we either "have" or "don't have" a singing voice.
>
> (Demorest and Pfordresher 2015, p. 301)

Complex though the array of interactive developmental factors may be, focusing on central elements in a child's experience may aid consideration of early, formative singing development. A fundamental framework comprising *singing development indicators* (Knight 2010) may aid in understanding an individual's developmental context and skill level. Five basic elements are viewed within the ambit of an overall childhood environment, i.e. not particularly family, neighborhood, or school, etc. but a combination of all environs. While these factors are offered in relation to childhood, they still apply to the adult "NSs," most of whom date their "NS" identity to the early period of their lives. These *singing development indicators* (SDI) are:

- exposure to singing
- encouragement of singing
- access to involvement in singing
- experience in singing
- instruction in singing.

Important characteristics of these SDI are their nature (presence/absence and positive-negative continua), onset (when/how early they occur in life), and the degree to which they apply all influence the capacity of an individual's singing development. Figure 31.1 depicts these five indicators in relation to singing development. These SDI[5] are described in the following.

---

[5] These elements being positively present in a child's life may be insufficient to withstand the potent influence of a negative attribution. The publicly exposed nature of singing, the trust children invest in authority figures who may/may not have the expertise accorded them, and the entrenched cultural myth of singing as an innate ability fixed at birth can combine to overcome the fragile state of a child's self-belief in their own singing capacity. Often, a child's slower natural maturational rhythm can be misinterpreted as inability to the unaware singing facilitator, whose ill-informed reaction may stall or halt a child's singing development, resulting in their mistaken acceptance/irrevocability of the "NS" label.

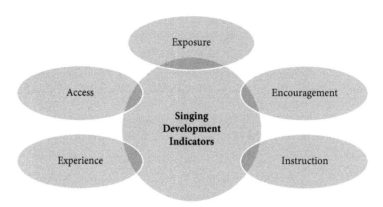

FIGURE 31.1 Singing development indicators (SDI) (Knight 2010).

- *Singing exposure*: singing to which the child is exposed, while not necessarily participant within. This could include being sung to, witnessing singing in general at home or elsewhere in the community, participant vocal play or song-singing to or with family members, friends, even pets or toys, etc.
- *Encouragement of singing*: an atmosphere and engagement with the child whereby they are actively encouraged to participate in singing through self-expression; their development of singing skills are likewise encouraged and facilitated; this includes encouragement to audit singing (e.g. lullabies, media).
- *Access to involvement in singing*: singing opportunities which are readily accessible for the child to become involved with in a participatory manner.
- *Experience in singing*: those experiences in which the child is actively singing; these experiences can range from informal (singing to oneself while playing, singing with the family in the car) to formal (congregational singing, choral singing).
- *Instruction in singing*: the age/stage-appropriate teaching of singing pedagogy, including appropriate interventions to resolve any singing development obstacles encountered.

The "NS" attribution process

The literature informs that individuals often come to acquire an "NS" label, and a self-understanding as such, in social/relational situations. Certain elements are commonly reported in what seems to be a shared *attributional process*. This process seems to proceed sequentially, and may be viewed as sub-dividing into three distinct yet linked categories—catalyzing, characterizing, and consequent elements. The model in Figure 31.2 aims to represent these categories in relation to each other. The categories are described in this section.

Catalyzing elements are circumstances and/or settings which have consistently been identified as increasing the likelihood of an "NS" attributional occurrence. For instance, an early childhood with few or no *singing development indicators*, as discussed above, would represent a *catalyzing* element. Many adult "NSs" have identified ensemble singing settings which lacked instructional intervention for singing developmental challenges as the main site for their attribution. Therefore, while the singing ensemble can be a positive site for many developing singers,

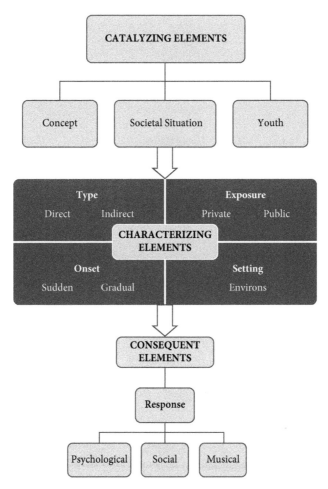

FIGURE 31.2 "NS" attribution process–a proposed model informed by Weiner's attributional theory (Knight 2010).

paradoxically, it can also serve to catalyze an "NS" attribution. Another catalyzing element is the mere fact of being young—that is, within the age bracket where most "NS" report their attribution as having occurred.

Characterizing elements describe the principal characteristics elements comprising the nature and gravity of this defining moment/experience of "NS" attribution (see Figure 31.3). There are four *characterizing elements* of an "NS" attribution. It should be noted that three of these elements (*type, exposure,* and *onset*) have an *active* and a *passive* form:[6]

---

[6] *Active forms* of the proposed elements had the following properties: *type* of attribution was **direct** (told outright by an "other" or "others" that they could not sing), *onset* was sudden and *exposure* was public, with the *setting* (e.g. school) being significant to the attributee. *Passive forms* of the proposed elements had these properties: *type* was **indirect** ("NS" was self-inferred rather than being told by another), *onset* was gradual and *exposure* was private.

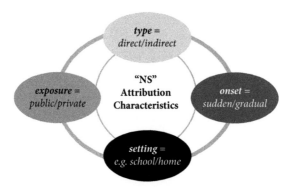

FIGURE 31.3 Proposed model of the *critical characterizing core* of NS attribution (Knight 2010).

- *Type*: can be *direct (active)* by another, or *indirect (passive)* by the attributee through inference; the *direct* type produces deeper negative effects.
- *Exposure*: can occur in *public (active)* or *private (passive)*; *public* exposure produces deeper negative effects.
- *Onset*: can occur *suddenly (active)* or *gradually (passive)*; *sudden* onset produces deeper negative effects.
- *Setting*: the environs in which attribution occurs; of various settings (family, neighborhood, etc.), school was most often identified as the setting where attribution occurred; it also was considered as the most exposed.

Active forms of *characterizing elements* reportedly produced a high degree of negative intensity, which prompted a heightened response to identity clarification, or adaptation from understanding oneself as "singer" to the newly arrived awareness as "NS." A *critical characterizing core* in its *active form*, i.e. *direct* type, *public* exposure, and *sudden* onset in a school *setting*, was described as producing a startled, alarmed, distressed state of disequilibrium in the "NS" attributees, which, to remind, were children:

> She [music teacher] said—"you don't have any notes, you just can't sing along with the music at all"... I can see the class, I was sitting second row back and there were kids behind me, you can imagine how embarrassed I felt. From that on then, I just assumed I was tone deaf... I guess obviously it was traumatic, to remember after 30 years.
> ("Vic" recounting school attribution at age 12 in Knight 2010)

Consequent elements within the model comprise the individual's response to an "NS" attribution, and are described in three categories—physiological, psycho/social, and musical reactions. The literature suggests that an adjusting process of post-attribution re-identification as "NS" seems to commonly take place, involving the reconfiguration of the previous self-understanding as "singer" to match the new mold of "NS." It could be reliably argued that identity (at any age) as a whole, and in this particular instance, the identity of being a "singer," may be in a continuous stage of construction (Elliot 1995). What seemed particular in the case of "NS" *identity clarification* was the urgent and negative nature of its reconfiguration. Varying accounts, but with similar themes, described how self-perception and operating tactics related to singing in the world, changed as a result of a realized "NS" ascription.

Common social coping techniques of the adult "NS"

Social singing following "NS" attribution is described as representing risk of exposure and potential negative judgment. A commonly reported phenomenon of the newly attributed "NS" were self-protective measures acquired to manage the risks represented by unavoidable social singing encounters. Tactics and approaches were reported to have been found to help reorient to the new self-perception of "NS" identity on both internal and external levels. Coping techniques were reported as being employed in a risk management role around dealing with the negative fallout of identity reconfiguration. Some common strategies surfaced:

- avoid singing altogether;
- if going to sing, do so privately, e.g. in the shower or in the car;
- avoid social situations involving singing, or if unable to;
- pre-empt social scrutiny/judgment by advancing self-deprecating humor about one's own singing deficit;
- feign involvement without singing, e.g. mouth the words of the song, laugh, tap feet;
- fortify social courage with alcohol consumption.

This section has aimed to clarify the concept of the adult "NS," placing it in the context of cultural realities and processes, including the forces which influence people in their becoming ascribed with that designation. It also references the consequences arising from such a designation and the subsequent needs resulting for the attributed person.

ENABLEMENT OF SINGING DEVELOPMENT FOR SELF-LABELED ADULT "NSs"

(See also the chapter by Gackle in this volume.) This section addresses the enablement of singing re-entry for those self-labeled as "NS" from a micro and a macro perspective. Challenges posed by the phenomenon of the adult "NS" in society are presented in Figure 31.4 in two concentric divisions—the immediate problem and the greater challenge.

Categories of difficulty

The immediate problem: enabling adult "NS" singing re-entry

The immediate problem is the facilitation of those "NS" who would like to re-engage their singing development where it left off, so they can enjoy a participatory singing life.

FIGURE 31.4 "NS" Singing enablement—immediate problem and greater challenge.

This problem will be addressed here. The greater challenge comes with effecting a cultural change of mind regarding the now-dominant Western cultural narrative of human singing as a *fixed* genetic entity, rather than the pan-human developmental capacity that is scientifically evidenced. This larger challenge will be dealt with directly in the next section.

The most detrimental issue posed by the phenomenon of the adult "NS" is their exclusion/marginalization from the multiple, evidenced benefits that human singing embodies. To reverse this exclusion and join/re-join a participatory singing reality, the adult "NS" must experience a learning process comprising the requisite elements shown in Figure 31.5.

FIGURE 31.5 Requisite learner elements for successful adult "NS" singing re-entry process.

Pedagogical intervention techniques enabling "NS" children and adults to rediscover their singing voice are quite similar in most but two regards:

1. Notable difference lies between their relative anxiety levels when addressing a challenged singing skill. In most cases, with children, particularly younger children, anxiety need not be present during facilitation, especially if it is carried out in a knowledgeable, supportive, and patient manner. With adult "NSs," however, contemplating an attempt to discover/rediscover singing is reported as generally being accompanied by social anxiety, trepidation, embarrassment, and a low or non-existent level of confidence accruing from their "NS" state. Therefore, crossing the threshold into possible singing re-entry requires a strong will and much courage. Despite the attendant anxiety, and almost paradoxically, adult "NSs" seeking singing re-entry often also arrive with (veiled) hope, fueled by their persistent longing to sing.

2. The second reason the challenge for adult "NS" is greater than for the child "NS" is that they are not just dealing with a slower singing development rate (as with most singing-challenged children), but with *arrested* development—an entrenched state experienced for many over multiple decades. The common emotions that adult "NS" often report as bringing to their singing facilitation are ones of shame, humiliation, embarrassment, and, most often, a belief that they will not be able to succeed in accessing their singing voice. So helping them surmount the accumulated fear and disbelief is the first task and the most difficult challenge for the singing facilitator.

> I just know I can't sing and I feel I can't get better at it. It is already in me . . . I know that you tell me that I can sing on pitch . . . you showed me when we worked together here, but I have a hard time believing that. It would have to go over all the years and times that I've been told I can't. I have a voice, I can talk and even speak in front of others with no problem, but I just can't sing.
>
> ("Melissa" in Abril 2007, p. 5)

In order for successful singing re-entry to occur, there are two basic need sets to be met: those of the adult "NS" as well as those of the singing facilitator. For the person seeking to re-enter singing, the following criteria are necessary if the intervention is to be effective:

- access to opportunities for enablement;
- courage to risk;
- empathic, aware supportive setting;
- daring to try, and keep trying, notwithstanding self-doubt/non-belief of possible success;
- opportunity to express/share their "NS" story and thus help work through and beyond its negative impact;
- effort—perseverance and patience—awareness of the time/development factor.

The singing re-entry facilitator (in school, community, etc.) also has needs which are likewise required to be met before engaging with adult "NSs" to guide the transformative experience of their singing recovery.

- knowledge, skill and experience in creating a community of mutually-supportive learners;

- capacity to build relationships that encourage confidence-building;
- keen observation and facilitation of learner needs;
- awareness, acknowledgment, attention, and accommodation of likely embedded negative "NS" emotions and mind-set;
- knowledge, skill, and experience with successfully facilitating slower-paced or stalled/arrested singing development in singers to successful independent competent singing production via developmentally appropriate instruction.

The nature of the facilitating environment is a most significant factor in optimizing the potential for successful adult singing re-entry. Managing and lessening the risk learners experience when they choose to attempt singing re-entry while boosting opportunities for developing their confidence (i.e. to dare and keep trying) stem from the kind of empathic learning community that is consciously formed (with private lessons, two can be a community). Lessons can be given privately or in small groups, depending on the individual situation. Some adult "NSs" may prefer to start the re-entry journey privately, and then move to a group setting. There is an advantage with the group lesson in which an empathic atmosphere is created. In such a setting, learners can provide each other with encouragement just by being together in their shared challenge. Whether the setting is private or group, creating a facilitating, confidence-building climate to optimize the singing re-entry process is fundamental. Overall, it is important that the learner not feel "judged" in the situation and be encouraged to share their singing journey from childhood forward, whether verbally, as a written reflection, or both.

The written reflection is a powerful learning/encouraging tool (Schon 1987). In documenting the journey of their own singing story, including current re-entry, producing written reflections widens/deepens insight into their own situation. It often helps to identify impediments or obstacles, as well as helping discover the means to overcome them. Written reflections (during and after lessons) also provide the opportunity for serial protected dialogue between learner and facilitator, who can then respond to the learner privately in written form to the contributed learner narrative. If learning is occurring in a group, the possibility of open dialogue and shared narrative (with narrator consent) affords the opportunity of creating common ground—a potent means of gaining insight, confidence, and motivation for the ongoing courage required by re-entry singers.

Specific aspects of re-entry facilitation

Some fundamental aspects of the learner climate (private or ensemble) are an airy space with room for movement and structured lessons within which are components of in-built freedom. A period of 60–90 minutes is a suggested lesson time-frame. Where group lessons are concerned, a maximum of 12–15 members is suggested, to provide a sufficiently large group for a successful sound volume as well as limiting exposure and encouraging contribution. A framework of 8–12 weekly lessons per set seems to work well. Development is an individual process, but in general, progress for re-entering singers does take time, which needs to be communicated at the outset and throughout. Setting a community atmosphere with the opportunity for shared narrative and dialogue is strongly recommended (as referenced above). The social/emotional challenge of singing re-entry far outweighs the challenge of acquiring the technical requirements for healthy vocal production. If operating with a group, opportunity for private coaching is also encouraged. If there are two facilitators, one can work with individual learners in an adjacent space for short periods, while the group remains engaged with the other facilitator. The private setting is helpful for facilitator evaluation and learner self-evaluation. It provides a safe space where the facilitator can help the learner discover how to recognize and assess their own feedback, and use it to guide and readjust their own singing development goals. In a group class, if only one facilitator is present, then singing tasks can be set with the learner recording their vocal "homework" during the period between lessons. The universality of phones having recording and transmitting devices expedites communication, and with it the learning process. Learners can work on their singing assignments and email them to facilitators between lessons. Facilitators can comment on progress and make suggestions, emailing the feedback to the learner. Similarly, the sharing of repertoire and dissemination of accompaniments, messaging, encouragement, and so forth, is easily accomplished on a one-to-one facilitator–learner basis, or to the full group. This process can be adapted in many ways, but its advantage is that there is a confidential mentored exchange happening continuously in parallel to the group lessons throughout the period of the course.

To review:

- group instruction—maximum 12–15 members;
- lesson framework—8–12 lesson set, 60–90 minutes/lesson;
- creating a community atmosphere with shared narrative and open dialogue;
- relation building to create trust between learners and facilitator/s as well as among learners;
- airy space with room to move;
- structured lessons—in-built freedom within a framework of components;
- opportunity for private coaching (e.g. record/respond) within the group framework;
- written reflection during and after class; submitted to instructor, who responds privately (share with co-learners, if consent);
- opportunity for singing in a variety of ensemble sizes.

With these needs being met in the learner–facilitator relationship, singing development is likely to be realized for most, in varying degrees and over varying time periods. As one participant in a class remarked: "In singing class, I can be overcome by emotion so easily. Just facing the years of hurt and the amazing belief that I can sing after all" (Knight 1999, p. 153)

Researchers and practitioners have identified requisite skill components for singing re-entry that proceed along a continuum of gradual development, and these are discussed below. While the fundamental physiological elements of vocal development apply to everyone (i.e. body alignment, respiration, phonation, resonation, and articulation), those facing singing re-entry experience *extra-vocal challenges* arising from their arrested singing status. For the basics of vocal development, the reader is referred to "Systematic Development of Vocal Technique" by Nix in this volume, where vocal fundamentals are addressed in detailed hierarchical sequence. These fundamentals must be applied to facilitate overall "NS" singing development progress, *parallel to meeting* the extra-vocal challenges that are addressed below.

Assessing each learner's starting point is important at the journey's outset. This evaluation must be handled sensitively, and is best organized in an individual private brief session— circa 10 minutes. Protecting the re-entry learner from scrutiny and judgment is paramount. His or her re-entry attempt requires courage. He or she will likely be hyper-vigilant about managing the risk of embarrassment, humiliation, and shame that previous singing attempts have led them to expect and (often) to experience. The assessment needs to include:

- flexibility of the vocal instrument;
- tonal memory (degree);
- capacity for pitch discrimination and pitch replication;
- pitch range;
- vocal timbre (including any sign of vocal impairment/pathology);
- any fundamental showing a deficit, e.g. postural impediment, hearing impairment, etc.;
- inner hearing/inner singing (audiation).

Documenting this data provides all involved with a point of comparison against which to measure subsequent progress. Audio recording this initial assessment is recommended.

Conceptually, whether it is a private or group learning setting, the above assessed elements need to be thoroughly explained and understood by the learner, and should form a critical ongoing focus for goal setting, self-assessment, and subsequent adjustment as the learning proceeds.

As has been referenced, the challenges which adult "NSs" face are similar to those which some children face in their journey along the singing skill continuum. In fact, we all have the child alive within us, so thinking of adult "NSs" as singing-arrested ex-children is a helpful image, as it reminds that by re-engaging, they are (simply) picking up where they left off in their singing development journey. Any child left unfacilitated to singing success becomes an adult who carries those challenges across life.

Just as the singing challenges of adults and children are similar, so are the methods to ameliorate them. The same production and perception approaches help both to progress along their skill continuum, including overcoming obstacles that have been resistant. While each person's path is unique and individual evaluation will help establish particular needs, certain patterns tend to predominate. The following goal sequence provides a framework for approaching singing recovery in the adult "NS." Learners will vary as to which point in this sequence they need to "pick up the trail" of their lost singing. Pre-lesson evaluation, as discussed above, will help to determine the most advantageous entry point. For many, they are far more advanced than they self-credit. It is not so much that they have not been able to sing for years, as it is that they believed they could not. Whatever individual elements require attention need to be gradually yet persistently addressed until satisfactorily met in each learner.

In the sequence of skill-building exercises listed below, all learners will need to be able, eventually, to demonstrate mastery of these points as they progress, and also be able to recognize them in the singing of others. Individual singing developmental rates vary across people. For some, progress to singing recovery may occur within a single set of 8–12 lessons. For others, it may require several successive lesson sets. When facilitating adult "NSs," while encouraging them, it is also important to underscore that this re-entry process requires time—therefore their patience and persistence. Decades of singing silence and self-unbelief cannot often be overcome in weeks or months, but for most, the tortoise wins the race!

Two critical elements of bedrock importance in singing re-/discovery underpin the strategic goals posted below. One is the conceptual understanding/experience of *vocal exploration* and the other is the conceptual understanding/experience of *inner hearing/inner singing*. The former facilitates development of a flexible vocal instrument, and in non-threatening and enjoyable ways. The latter not only builds coordination of vocal production to listening/hearing, but brings this all-important loop into conscious awareness. It also helps develop tonal memory, and unifies external and internal singing life. These two concepts of *vocal exploration* and *inner hearing/inner singing* are critical first elements, not only in singing recovery for adults, but also as prime building blocks in the area of singing development in young children. Sadly, both areas receive little attention in primary music education practice.

Skill building activities

Here is a suggested route for facilitating singing re-development in the adult "NS":

- Develop a *generically* flexible vocal instrument (skill to move the voice by glissando in multiple random directions) via both guided and free vocal exploration, gradually extending the range in both directions.
- "Play" with the voice, experimenting with a variety of contoured sounds, such as different types of laughter, crying, animal, and nature sound effects, etc., to increase flexibility and raise awareness of the broad dimensions of vocal expression *under one's control*. Incorporate variations in volume, range, articulation, etc.
- Develop a *particularly* flexible instrument (skill to move the voice by glissando at will in particular directions, such as ascending-descending-ascending, and eventually to stop on a given note, matching it).
- Speak common rhymes in regular speaking voice first, then more lightly, vocally "dancing" into chant; from there lighten the chant and intone more widely until the rhyme "lifts off" into improvised, intoned "melody." This natural progression bridges the natural connection between spoken and sung vocalizing. By keeping it improvisatory, or "just as it comes," no proviso exists to "keep" a particular tune, and yet the singing voice is employed. It is an important step.
- Access different vocal registers, first echoing, then intentionally initiated by learners. Define and discuss these vocal registers once experienced and manipulated by learners.
- Increase and refine the capacity for pitch discrimination, beginning with recognition of same/different two-note melodic patterns progressing from wide to narrow intervals, gradually increasing length and complexity of pattern.
- Develop the skill to listen, retain, and then echo-sing tuned replication of simple two-note descending intervals (minor 3rd) and short (three-to-four-note) melodic patterns (initially pentatonic, then diatonic).
- Develop the skill to listen, retain and then echo-sing tuned replication of simple ascending intervals and short melodic patterns (as above), moving on to bidirectional patterns.

- Develop the skill to listen, retain, and then echo-sing a tuned, sustained replication of a single note.
- Increase *inner hearing/inner singing* capacity and flexibility by singing a simple tune, switching on signal from singing aloud (i.e. "outside") to singing internally (i.e. "inside"), repeating this process throughout the song.
- Gradually increase tonal memory starting with two-note descending minor third patterns, increasing to longer (three-, four-, five-note) and bidirectional patterns of a melody by singing (repeating) it *without text*, from a partial phrase to a whole song (simple pentatonic moving toward simple diatonic, major and minor).
- Gradually increase tonal memory starting with two-note descending minor third patterns, increasing to longer (three-, four-, five-note) and bidirectional patterns of a melody by singing it *with text*, as above.
- Gradually develop skill to maintain the tonal center of a song, building toward being able to reproduce the tonic at any point in the song.
- Vocally match pitch simultaneously with another singer, starting with descending glissandi and gradually moving to ascending and bidirectional patterns.
- Replicate short to longer melodic patterns to whole phrases, to two phrases etc., echoing both another voice and a percussive melodic instrument (metallophone, piano, etc.).
- Keep in mind (both learner and facilitator) that the ear serves as important a function as the process of vocal production; it is in the consistent perception, analysis, and application of feedback that the ear and the voice together produce satisfactory and also beautiful singing.

While the exercises suggested above are to be facilitator-led initially, passing them over to being learner-led in a group setting fosters increased skill, understanding, and confidence all round.

People like to sing songs they know, so in addition to particular simple "facilitating" songs (e.g. two- or three-note, pentatonic), it is essential to offer the learner a choice of several songs (diatonic) that they choose themselves. This maintains interest and increases enjoyment as well as providing an array of material from which can be chosen, at the very least, some phrases which are developmentally appropriate to the learner's current capacity.

Implementing effective learning strategies for enabling the challenged developing adult "NS" is an area that is beginning to receive increasing attention from facilitation and research perspectives, but needs more development in pedagogical (including curricular) and resource areas. This current deficit reflects the dominant "talent account" of singing in Western culture. Facing such a powerful cultural "myth" can surely be daunting to "NSs," for the courage needed to risk trying to sing (again) as an adult "NS" is often greater than the vocal production/auditory perception changes needed to re-engage and advance that singing skill. Nevertheless, as referenced earlier, people seem to be willing to take such risks, as is evidenced by the growing appetite for "singing from scratch" programs in the UK, US, Scandinavia, New Zealand, Australia, and Canada. Expanding this pedagogical power to a readily recognized capacity that enables and *demonstrates* successful singing facilitation would provide a much-needed platform of singing access to a wider population that does not *yet* exist. This leads to the greater challenge of addressing the overall cultural "NS" problem which was referenced at the beginning of this chapter, and which will now be elaborated upon.

The greater challenge: transforming cultural mindset from fixed to developmental

The prevailing cultural narrative that singing ability is genetically fixed exerts a powerful influence on societal beliefs about the nature of human singing. This current dominant powerful folk myth of singing as an innate can/cannot state affects singing pedagogy and practices, as well as attitudes and beliefs around it. Until there is an overall shift from this fixed view to one of the pan-human capacity for *developmental* acquisition of singing skill, then the steady tide of children remaining unfacilitated in their singing development will continue to grow the adult "NS" community in an unending supply.

What follows are some approaches that engage with the greater challenge of transforming the Western cultural narrative of the nature of human singing from a fixed to an incremental view. Effecting this change of folk-mind is central to the emancipation of singing, democratizing it for current and future generations.

Unpacking the folk idea that underpins societal views of "NS" as an innate state in terms that can be popularly understood could help to debunk the myth of the "fixed state" of singing capacity. The story needs to be told of how the overriding cultural view runs counter to scientific evidence of human capacity for singing development. It could also provide (expressed in easily accessible language), ethnomusicological evidence of the correlation between cultural belief in innate human musical capacity and the demonstrated musical development of that society as a whole, both with incremental and entity belief systems (e.g. Blacking 1973; Merriam 1964; Messenger 1958; Romet 1992). Effectively communicating to society the knowledge and information that could inform and motivate their questioning of the prevailing view can happen more easily in the current capacity-enhancing reach of social media. Once the question begins to be raised, a new conversation about the democratization of singing could commence, and minds, and eventually the cultural mindset, could be changed.

Little is actually known about the incidence of self-declared "NS" in national populations, nor what percentage of reported "NS" are actually singing-challenged:

> Studies have suggested that extreme poor pitch singing of the type that may reveal a more serious audio-motor deficit is a relatively rare phenomenon . . . . yet a majority of adults still view themselves as poor singers.
>
> (Cited in Demorest and Pfordresher 2015, p. 301)

Obtaining data regarding the scope and nature of the self-labeled "NS" population would be an important initial step in understanding and addressing the scope of the problem. The few incidence surveys of adult "NSs" that have been conducted have not been national in scope, but did reveal some common and important factors (see the chapter by Wise in this volume). A disproportionate and inconsistent ratio between studies of participants self-reporting as "NS"—from 17 percent in Cuddy (2005 et al.) to 59 percent in Pfordresher and Brown (2007)—indicates the need for comprehensive surveys at local, regional, and national levels. Also, for many of those who self-reported as "tone deaf," their singing-assessment ratings indicated the opposite. There was a demonstrated trend for participants to underrate their singing performance in the self-assessment sections while the research results indicated much higher results in participants' measured singing ability. The indications are that many more think they are "NSs" (or declare as such) than is actually the case. National incidence studies of "NSs" would shed light on the scale of the issue and results could illuminate singing self-perception in relation to the prevailing cultural narrative. In addition, national results could be viewed comparatively. Most studies measuring adult singing performance are conducted via a "snapshot" assessment, whereas measuring within a pre/post singing facilitation model would demonstrate degree of developmental shift.

Another approach to countering the prevailing fixed cultural narrative would be to disseminate in scholarly and popular media the evidence of those "NSs" successfully accessing singing in later life. Such a demonstration of the developmental power of singing overcoming decades of culturally imposed singing silence is a narrative that would have wide public resonance, particularly with the current emphasis on public engagement. A companion approach to this would be proliferation and promotion of programs for "later access" to singing re-entry. This increased public awareness is an important factor for encouraging those "NSs" who might like to resume a singing life, but have felt disinclined (disempowered) to do so. Similarly powerful would be networking with researchers/practitioners involved with enabling "later singing access," to encourage and share their ideas and efforts, using social media as a tool for communication and collaboration.

Hopeful directions for change can be seen for enabling "NSs" to re-enter singing. The following bear witness to this hope:

- an expanding desire for public engagement in expressive life, worldwide (e.g. Australian National Arts Policy 2013; Brault 2010; Canada Council for the Arts Strategic Plan 2011; Ivey and the right to an expressive life 2010; Seoul Agenda on the Arts and Learning, UNESCO 2010);
- a growing research interest in the adult "NS" from a developmental and wellness perspective (see "Can Singing have a Beneficial Effect on Lung Function and Breathing for People with Respiratory Illness?" by Clift and Gilbert, "Singing and Psychological Needs" by Davidson and Garrido, and "Unchained melody: The Rise of Orality and Therapeutic Singing" by Boyce-Tillman, all in this volume);
- a proliferation of "Adults Learn How to Sing" courses, internationally, online (Skype/in person, etc.);
- community agencies encouraging/developing participatory singing (e.g. Sage Gateshead, UK);
- local-global agencies facilitating participatory singing access/opportunities on the ground and online (e.g. Growing the Voices: Festival 500).
- national/international agencies promoting community singing, e.g. Singing Cities

PREVENTION OF THE ADULT "NS" PHENOMENON

Prevention of "NS" is the last topic that will be addressed, but it could easily have been the first, as it represents the crux of the issue. While it is important to facilitate singing re-entry for "NSs," it does bring to mind the old idiom about "shutting the stable door after the horse has bolted." Some cultures are so structured that their belief systems and corresponding practices support singing for all their members in terms of exposure, access, encouragement, experience, and instruction. However, the West has generally evolved into cultures where participatory singing has become a rarity in the general population, especially after middle-school age, and since church-going has declined. A recent study (Demorest and Pfordresher 2015) in the US evidenced that while Grade 6 students demonstrated more advanced singing skills than Kindergartners, those skills had regressed in college students. This seems to reflect the "use it or lose it" axiom, since after Grade 6, opportunities to be involved in singing at school lessen and societal encouragement for singing involvement wanes.

> Music educators need to provide singing experiences for all children K–12 that can allow them to participate and continue to engage in singing. This may point to reforming educational policies that limit musical offerings after a certain age and expanding the role of participatory singing in our culture.
>
> (Demorest and Pfordresher 2015, p. 301)

Increase and strengthen participatory ensemble singing

Most people access singing as a consumer. It is a small minority who actually take part, mostly singing in a presentational mode, with a choir or other form of performance ensemble. Increasing access and opportunity for participatory singing throughout the culture, from the very first culture—the family—on through school and community life, and across the lifespan, would prevent a lot of "NS" attributing in the first place. Were participatory singing to grow, and perhaps even once again become commonplace, taking on new forms, as is the nature of transmitted culture, it would engage and involve the community and its members in far more than musical experiences. A growing movement of increased participatory singing would strengthen society as a whole. The more ubiquitous that participatory singing of any kind becomes, the greater the involvement of all across the lifespan. This in itself would do much to provide exposure, encouragement, access, and experience to all on their singing developmental path. It could even be its own unique form of instruction.

Effective teacher preparation and primary school singing facilitation

In Western culture, all children must attend school by law. This represents a great opportunity to prevent "NS" from occurring by facilitating children's singing development from their early school life onward. This means that their singing teacher/facilitator/s has to have the requisite knowledge, skill, and experience to do so. The teacher's sound understanding, training, and subsequent expertise (and the time, facilitation, and experience to acquire the same) around singing facilitation are paramount in providing little children with a fundamental grounding and guided development in appropriately sequenced singing skill acquisition. This includes knowing how to identify lags or challenges in the child's singing development path and when best and how to intervene. The developmental events and patterns along which singing travels and children's temporal journey along this path vary (Welch 2005), just as they do with acquisition of other acquired skills, i.e. walking, talking. With informed and experienced teaching, for most, singing development will proceed successfully. But there will be children who may falter, or get temporarily "stuck." In addition to being alert to signs of such possible obstacles, teachers need to know when to begin to expect such a signal and then have the confidence, time, and resources successfully to intervene and restore the developmental pattern. It follows that this must be part of the teacher preparation and lifelong professional development program for the practicing professional teacher responsible for guiding the singing development of schoolchildren. Currently, in most Western nations, this is sadly not the case. Nevertheless, this standard must be pursued. Many teachers tasked with facilitating children's singing development report feeling intimidated by the task, as they have little confidence in their own singing ability, something that often stems from negative experiences of their own early schooldays (Abril 2007). Little children, pre-service teachers, and adult "NSs" all need to be encouraged to believe in their singing selves.

> While it is important for teachers to help students improve their singing skill at a young age, it may be even more important to help them believe that accurate singing is attainable through practice even when they don't experience success early on.
>
> (Demorest and Pfordresher 2015, p. 301)

Revision of developmental singing pedagogy

Best practice would suggest a re-visioning of singing pedagogy—the introduction of a new discourse on developmental singing pedagogy, from early childhood through senescence—a "lifelong learning" approach (see also "Socio-cultural, Acoustic, and Environmental Imperatives in the World of Singing" by Walker, "Mothers as Singing Mentors for Infants" by Trehub and Gudmundsdottir, "Children Singing: Nurture, Creativity, and Culture: A Study of Children's Music-making in London, UK, and in West Bengal, India" by Harding, "Boys' Singing Voice Change in Adolescence" by Williams and Harrison, "Adolescent Girls' Singing Development" by Gackle, and "The Effects of Gender on the Motivation and Benefits Associated with Community Singing in the UK" by Parkinson). This topic is so important and broad, it needs not just a group of chapters to explore, but its own treatise. Suffice it to say that the healthy (not expert) singing of a nation, and of a long individual life, rests on the quality and experience of early singing facilitation which young children experience, particularly in the school system. If it is carefully and professionally carried out in primary school, it is likely to carry forward successfully across the lifespan, as the children will have learned how to learn about singing.

SUMMARY

This chapter has set forth a background and context for the phenomenon of the adult "NS," provided enablement techniques to facilitate the re-entry of the "NS" to singing, and addressed the problems underlying these issues, suggesting possible solutions. The reader is encouraged to engage with these suggestions and also to expand them, working with students, colleagues, and community to find new avenues of facilitating singing health and its optimal development.

Singing in public when you've always thought you couldn't must be more like undressing after you've some mutilating surgery, like a mastectomy or an amputation. You know you won't measure up, you'll be a disappointment to yourself and your audience, and, worst of all, you fear you'll be the object of malicious humour. The miracle of singing classes is the discovery that I am not disfigured, that my voice can be a source of pleasure, and amazingly, the "limb" can re-grow.

(Reclaimed Singer, quoted in Knight 1999, p. 153)

The only thing better than singing is more singing.

(Ella Fitzgerald, cited in Nicholson 1995)

REFERENCES

Abrahams, R.D. (1986). Ordinary and extraordinary experience. In E. Turner and E. Bruner (eds), *The Anthropology of Experience*, pp. 45–73. Urbana, IL: University of Illinois Press.

Abril, C.R. (2007). I have a voice but I just can't sing: a narrative investigation of singing and social anxiety. *Music Education Research* 9(1): 1–15.

Allen, G. (1878). Note-deafness. *Mind* 3: 157–167.

Altenmüller, E.O. (2004). Music in your head. *Scientific American* 14(1): 24–31.

Australian National Cultural Policy (2013). Creative Australia. http://creativeaustralia.arts.gov.au/assets/Creative-Australia-PDF-20130417.pdf

Ayotte, J., Peretz, I., and Hyde, K. (2002). Congenital amusia. A group study of adults afflicted with a music-specific disorder. *Brain* 125: 238–251.

Bentley, A. (1968). *Monotones*. Music Education Research Papers 1. London: Novello and Company.

Blacking, J. (1973). *How Musical Is Man?* Seattle: University of Washington Press.

Bradshaw, E. and McHenry, M.A. (2005). Pitch discrimination and pitch-matching abilities of adults who sing inaccurately. *Journal of Voice* 19(3): 431–439.

Brault, S. (2010). *No Culture, No Future*. Toronto: Cormorant Books.

Brown, R. and Kulik, J. (1977). Flashbulb memories. *Cognition* 5: 73–99.

Bruner, J. (1990). *Acts of Meaning*. Cambridge, MA: Harvard University Press.

Canada Council for the Arts (2011). Strategic Plan 2011–2016: *Strengthening Connections*. http://canadacouncil.ca/~/media/files/corporate-planning%20-%20en/canadacouncil_strategicplan2011_16_en.pdf (accessed November 30, 2015).

Corriveau, K.H. and Harris, P.L. (2012) Young children's trust in what other people say. In: K. Rotenberg (ed.) *Interpersonal Trust during Childhood and Adolescence*, pp. 87–109. Cambridge, UK: Cambridge University Press.

Cuddy, L., Balkwill, L-L., Peretz, I., and Holden, R. (2005). Musical difficulties are rare: A study of "tone deafness" among university students. *Annals of the New York Academy of Sciences, The Neurosciences and Music II: From perception to performance* 1060: 311–324.

Dalla Bella, S. and Berkowska, M. (2009). Singing proficiency in the majority: Normality and phenotypes of poor singing. *Annals of the New York Academy of Sciences, The Neurosciences and Music III: Disorders and Plasticity* 1169: 99–107.

Dalla Bella, S., Giguére, J-F., and Peretz, I. (2009). Singing in congenital amusia. *Journal of the Acoustical Society of America* 126: 414–424.

Demorest, S.M. and Pfordresher, P.Q. (2015). Singing accuracy development from K–adult: a comparative study. *Music Perception: An Interdisciplinary Journal* 32(3): 293–302.

Dolcos, F., LaBar, K. S., and Cabeza, R. (2005). Remembering one year later: role of the amygdala and medial temporal lobe memory system in retrieving emotional memories. *Proceedings of the National Academy of Sciences* 102: 2626–2631.

Dundes, A. (1975). Folk ideas as units of world-view. In: A. Paredes and R. Bauman (eds), *Towards New Perspectives in Folklore*, pp. 93–103. Austin, TX: University of Texas Press.

Dweck, C. (1986). Motivational processes affecting learning. *American Psychologist* 41: 1040–1048.

Dweck, C. (1999). *Self-Theories: Their Roles in Motivation, Personality and Development*. Philadelphia, PA: Psychology Press.

Elliot, D. (1995). *Music Matters*. New York: Oxford University Press.

Fieldhouse, A.E. (1937). *A study of backwardness in singing among school children*. PhD thesis, University of London.

Foxton, J.M., Dean, J.L., Gee, R., Peretz, I., and Griffiths, T.D. (2004). Characterization of deficits in pitch perception underlying "tone deafness." *Brain* 127(4): 801–810.

Ginsborg, J., Fine, P., and Barlow, C. (2011). Singers and non-singers' perceptions of the intelligibility of sung text. In: A. Williamon, D. Edwards, and L. Bartel (eds), *Proceedings of the International Symposium of Performance Science*, August 24-27, 2011, Toronto, Canada (pp. 111–116).

Hu, H., Real, E., Takamiya, K., Kang, M., Ledoux, J., Huganir, R., and Malinow, R. (2007). Emotion enhances learning via norepinephrine regulation of AMPA-receptor trafficking. *Cell* 131(1): 160–173.

Hyde, K., Zatorre, R., Griffiths, T.D., Lerch, J.P., and Peretz, I. (2006). Morphometry of the amusic brain: a two-site study. *Brain* 129: 2562–2570.

Hyde, K., Lerch, J., Zatorre, R., Griffiths, T.D., Evans, A., and Peretz, I. (2007). Cortical thickness in congenital amusia: when less is better than more. *Journal of Neuroscience* 47: 13028–13032.

Ivey, B. (2010). Expressive life, May 25–29, 2010: *An Arts Journal Weblog*. Nashville, TN: Curb Center, Vanderbilt University. Available at: http://www.artsjournal.com/expressive/ (accessed November 30, 2015).

Joyce, V.M. (1993). *Singing for our lives: women creating home through singing*. MA thesis, Faculty of Education, OISE/University of Toronto.

Joyce, V.M. (1998). Singing our way home: the strategic use of singing by women. *Sounds Australian: Journal of the Australian Music Centre* 51: 12–13.

Joyce, V.M. (2003). *Bodies that sing: the formation of singing subjects*. PhD thesis, Faculty of Education. Toronto: OISE/University of Toronto.

Joyner, D. (1969). The monotone problem. *Journal of Research in Music Education* 17 (1): 115–124.

Kalmus, H. and Fry, D.B. (1980). On tune deafness (dysmelodia): frequency, development, genetics and musical background. *Annals of Human Genetics* 43: 369–382.

Knight, S. (1995). *Diagnosis and remediation of obstructed beginning singers using a collaborative reflective action process*. Unpublished Masters's thesis, University of St. Thomas, St. Paul, Minnesota.

Knight, S. (1999). Exploring a cultural myth: what adult non-singers may reveal about the nature of singing. In: B.A. Roberts and A. Rose (eds), *The Phenomenon of Singing II*, St. John's, Newfoundland, July 2–5, pp. 144–154. St. John's, Newfoundland: Memorial University Press.

Knight, S. (2004). Border-crossing: exploring adventurous directions in cultural education. *Canadian Music Educator* 45(3): 10–15.

Knight, S. (2010). *A study of adult non-singers in Newfoundland*. Unpublished PhD thesis, Institute of Education, University of London.

Knight, S. (2011). Adults identifying as non-singers in childhood: cultural, social, and pedagogical implications. *Proceedings of the International Symposium on Performance Science*, August 24–27, Toronto, Canada, pp. 117–122.

Ledoux, J. (1998). *The Emotional Brain: The Mysterious Underpinnings of Emotional Life*. New York: Simon and Schuster.

Lidman-Magnusson, B. (1994). *Sångburen [Inhibited singing development]*. PhD thesis, Centre for Music Pedagogy, The Royal College of Music, Stockholm, Sweden.

Lidman-Magnusson, B. (1995). Inhibited singing development. Invited (unpublished) paper, *Pan European Voice Conference (PEVOC-I)*, London, 8–10 September.

Lidman-Magnusson, B. (1997a). Factors influencing singing development in poor pitch singers. *Proceedings of the Third Triennial ESCOM Conference*, June 7–12, Uppsala, Sweden, pp. 339–343.

Lidman-Magnusson, B. (1997b). Singing development: comparisons between poor pitch singers and other groups. In: B.A. Roberts (ed.), *Festival 500: Sharing the Voices, Proceedings of the Phenomenon of Singing International Symposium*. St. John's, Newfoundland, June 20–23. St. John's: Memorial University.

Lomax, A. (1968). *Folk Song Style and Culture*, 3, Publication No. 88. Washington, DC: American Association for the Advancement of Science.

McIntyre, C.K, Power, A.E., Roozendaal, B., and McGaugh, J.L. (2003). Role of the basolateral amygdala in memory consolidation. *Annals of the New York Academy of Sciences* 985: 273–293.

Merriam, A. (1964). *The Anthropology of Music*. Chicago: Northwestern University Press.

Messenger, J.C. (1958). Reflections on aesthetic talent. *Basic College Quarterly* 4: 18–24.

Moreau, P., Jolicoeur, P., and Peretz, I. (2009). Automatic brain responses to pitch changes in congenital amusia. *Annals of the New York Academy of Sciences* 1169: 191–194.

Nicholson, S. (1995). *Ella Fitzgerald: A Biography of the First Lady of Jazz*. Jackson, TN: Da Capo Press.

Numminen, A. (2004). Helping adult poor pitch singers learn to sing in tune: a study of stumbling blocks confronting developing singers and means of surmounting them. Paper presented at the 14th Nordic Musicological Congress, Helsinki, Finland, August 14.

Pascale, L. (2002a). *Dispelling the myth of the non-singer: changing the ways singing is perceived, implemented and nurtured in the classroom*. PhD dissertation, Lesley University, Cambridge, MA.

Pascale. L. (2002b). Dispelling the myth of the non-singer: embracing two aesthetics for singing. *Philosophy of Music Education Review* 13(2): 165–175.

Peretz, I., Ayotte, J., Zatorre, R., Mehler, J., Ahad, P., Penhune, V., and Jutras, B. (2002). Congenital amusia: a disorder of fine-grained pitch discrimination. *Neuron* 33: 185–191.

Peretz, I. and Hyde, K. (2003). What is specific to music processing? Insights from congenital amusia. *Trends in Cognitive Sciences* 7(8): 362–367.

Peretz, I. (2006). The nature of music from a biological perspective. *Cognition* 100: 1–32.

Peretz, I. (2008). Musical disorders: from behaviour to genes. *Current Directions in Psychological Science* 17: 329–333.

Peretz, I., Gosselin, N., Tillmann, B., Cuddy, L.L., Gagnon, B., Trimmer, C.G., Paquette, S., and Bouchard, B. (2008). On-line identification of congenital amusia. *Music Perception* 25(4): 331–343.

Peretz, I., Brattico, E., Järvenpää, M., and Tervaniemi, M. (2009). The amusic brain: in tune, out of key, and unaware. *Brain* 132: 1277–1286.

Pfordresher, P.Q. and Brown, S. (2007). Poor-pitch singing in the absence of tone deafness. *Music Perception* 25: 95–115.

Porter, S.Y. (1977). The effect of multiple discrimination training on pitch-matching behaviours of uncertain singers. *Journal of Research in Music Education* 25: 68–82.

Raven, B.H. (1965). Social influence and power. In: I.D. Steiner and M. Fishbein (eds), *Current Studies in Social Psychology*, pp. 371–381. New York: Holt, Rinehart and Wilson.

Richards, H. and Durrant, C. (2003). To sing or not to sing: a study on the development of "non-singers" in choral activity. *Research Studies in Music Education* 20(1): 78–89.

Romet, C. (1992). Song acquisition in culture: a West Javanese study in children's song development. In: H. Lees (ed.), *Music Education: Sharing Musics of the World. Proceedings of the 20thWorld Conference of the International Society of Music Education, Seoul, Korea*, July 26–August 1, pp. 164–173. Christchurch, NZ: ISME/University of Canterbury.

Ruddock, E. and Leong, S. (2005). "I am unmusical!": the verdict of self-judgement. *International Journal of Music Education* 23(1): 9–22.

Ruddock, E. (2007a). Musical communities? I'm not even in the ballpark! Unpublished paper presented at *Celebrating Musical Communities: The 40th Anniversary National Conference* Perth, Australia, July 6–8.

Ruddock, E. (2007b). *Ballad of the never picked: a qualitative study of self-perceived non-musicians' perceptions of their musicality*. Unpublished Master's thesis, School of Music, University of Western Australia.

Ruddock, E. (2008). "It's a bit harsh, isn't it!" Judgemental teaching practice corrupts instinctive musicality. Unpublished paper presented at the 30th Annual Conference: Innovation and Tradition in Music Education Research, Melbourne, Victoria, Australia, October 3–5.

Ruddock, E. (2010). Societal judgement silences singers. *UNESCO Observatory University of Melbourne Refereed Journal* 2(1). Available at: http://education.unimelb.edu.au/__data/assets/pdf_file/0007/1105936/ruddock-paper.pdf (accessed November 30, 2015).

Safer, M.A., Christiansen, S.-A., Autry, M.W., Österlund, K. (1998). Tunnel memory for traumatic events. *Applied Cognitive Psychology* 12(2): 99–117.

Schön, D.A. (1987). *Educating the Reflective Practitioner*. San Francisco: Jossey-Bass.

Sellars, W. (1956). Empiricism and the philosophy of mind. In: H. Feigl and M. Scriven (eds), *Minnesota Studies in the Philosophy of Science*, Vol. 1, pp. 126–196. Minneapolis: University of Minnesota Press.

Seoul Agenda on the Arts and Learning (2010). UNESCO Second World Conference on Arts Education, Seoul, South Korea, May 22–25, 2010. DOI http://portal.unesco.org/culture/en/files/41117/12798106085Seoul_Agenda_Goals_for_the_Development_of_Arts_Education.pdf/Seoul%2BAgenda_Goals%2Bfor%2Bthe%2BDevelopment%2Bof%2BArts%2BEducation.pdf

Stewart, L. (2008). Fractioning the musical mind: insights from congenital amusia. *Current Opinion in Neurobiology* 18: 127–130.

Welch, G.F. (1979). Poor pitch singing: a review of the literature. *Psychology of Music* 7(1): 50–58.

Welch, G.F. (1986). A developmental view of children's singing. *British Journal of Music Education* 3(3): 295–303.

Welch, G.F. and Murao, T. (1994). Onchi and singing development: pedagogical implications. In: G.F. Welch and T. Murao (eds), *Onchi and Singing Development: A Cross-Cultural Perspective*, pp. 82–95. London: David Fulton/ASME).

Welch, G.F. (2001). *The Misunderstanding of Music*. London: Institute of Education University of London.

Welch, G.F. (2006). The musical development and education of young children. In: B. Spodek and O. Saracho (eds), *The Handbook of Research on the Education of Young Children*, pp. 251–268. New York: Routledge.

Wheaton, B. (1998). Self-perceptions of singing ability for the adult self-proclaimed nonsinger. *Missouri Journal of Research in Music Education* 35: 18–27.

Whidden, C. (2008). The injustice of singer/non-singer labels by music educators. *Gender, Education, Music and Society*, 4. Available at: http://www.queensu.ca/music/links/gems/Whidden5.pdf (accessed November 30, 2015).

Whidden, C. (2009). Understanding complex influences affecting participation in singing. In: T. Reynish (ed.) *Proceedings of the Phenomenon of Singing International Symposium*, July 2–5, Memorial University 7: 142–156. St. John's: Memorial University Press.

Whidden, C. (2010). Hearing the voices of non-singers: culture, context and connection. In: L.K. Thomspon and M.R. Campbell (eds), *Issues of Identity in Music Education: Narratives and Practice*, pp. 83–109. Charlotte, NC: Information Age Publishing.

Wise, K. (2009). *Understanding tone deafness: a multi-componential analysis of perception, cognition, singing and self-perceptions in adults reporting musical difficulties*. Unpublished PhD dissertation, Keele University.

CHAPTER 32

....

TEACHING THE
PROFESSIONAL SINGER

....

JEAN CALLAGHAN

INTRODUCTION

....

THIS chapter details what is involved in teaching to meet the needs of the professional singer. In working with professional singers, the teacher assumes a slightly different role from that appropriate to dealing with beginning and developing students and amateurs. Here, the teacher is more of a senior colleague/mentor/adviser. That role includes assisting the singer to develop:

- advanced skills in relation to voice, music, text, and movement;
- effective practice techniques;
- procedures for preparing roles;
- strategies for working with others, including other singers, conductors, directors, and technical staff;
- ways of dealing with performance anxiety, focus, and performing "in the zone."

FRAMEWORK/PRINCIPLES

....

The teacher assists professional singers to develop skills to meet changing professional demands, and is often called upon to give advice on working in difficult conditions or dealing with vocal difficulties. Teachers need to assist professional singers to maintain the necessary attributes and skills throughout a career, which may entail changing professional demands, personal situations, and vocal capabilities. In this chapter, the differing demands of various genres are discussed, including expectations of skills, audition requirements, and ways of working. Particular attention is given to developing and maintaining high-level voice skills, and to casting. Teachers may be required to advise singers on building a career, structuring a retirement strategy, or making the transition to teaching or choral conducting. The necessity of maintaining vocal health under often difficult working conditions is discussed, as well as the need for good general health and psychomotor skills.

There is a great deal of literature on the singing voice and teaching singing; much has been written on musical cognition and the psychology of music; and there is a growing body of knowledge on vocal health and the treatment of vocal pathologies. This knowledge rarely comes together in a way specifically addressed to the teaching of the professional singer. In *Singing and Teaching Singing* (2016), Janice Chapman brings together some of this knowledge in writing about her own work with professional singers in the classical field. This chapter builds on this, synthesizing theoretical and practical knowledge from many sources with the author's own teaching experience to inform a comprehensive approach to the teaching of singers working professionally in a range of genres.

What makes a professional singer?

The term "professional singer" is used here to designate musicians for whom singing is the whole, or part, of their paid vocation, in order to distinguish them from amateurs. It is not just that they are paid for their work, but that they are expert performers. These are the singers who have undergone a long period of specialized education and training to make a career involving singing. This may mean working entirely as a singer or, for many, using singing as part of their career. This may include:

- opera soloists;
- opera choristers;
- music theater soloists;
- music theater ensemble singers;
- singers in other small ensembles;
- cabaret singers;
- actors (including those performing in Shakespeare comedies, Brecht plays, theater in education, youth theater, etc.);
- gig singers in contemporary commercial music (contemporary commercial music (CCM)) (e.g. jazz, rock, pop, country, dance/funk, Rhythm & Blues);
- CCM recording artists;
- recording studio session singers;
- singer/songwriters;
- singer/singing teachers;
- choral directors.

To succeed as professionals, singers must have a high level of physical, emotional, and intellectual toughness. It may be that a biological predisposition plays some part in becoming an expert singer, but the environment contributes at least 50 percent to the learning of the complex cognitive behaviors involved. The biological predisposition seems to have more to do with temperament than with talent (Williamon 2004, p. 20). Levitin (2006, pp. 200–201) suggests that the qualities needed to be a successful musician include muscle control, motor control, tenacity, patience, memory for certain kinds of structures and patterns, and a sense of rhythm and timing. Technical expertise is essential, but so are emotional communication, creativity, and musical memory.

Levitin points out that determination, self-confidence, and patience are involved in becoming good at anything. Superior memory is also vital to expertise, but only for things within the domain of expertise. One of the most important qualities is the determination that allows a singer to cope with failure and keep going. Failure may occur for all sorts of reasons, some beyond the performer's control, and teachers can help singers to analyze why failure has occurred and how to deal with it.

In any field, a minimum of 10 years of dedicated work and practice is required to become an expert. The skills acquired in those years must be continuously maintained and developed through practice (Williamon 2004, p. 20).

Different genres, different demands

Professional expectations of singers and the demands made of them differ from genre to genre. Different voice qualities, musical abilities, and skills are expected. There may be more or less emphasis on acting, movement, and spoken text. Some performances may not require an audition, some may involve a lengthy audition process. Performances may be rehearsed and delivered in different ways. Some will have long rehearsal periods, some short. Some genres and styles rely heavily on the recording studio, some hardly at all. Some are delivered from a small performance area in a pub, some in vast opera houses. Some may require eight performances a week, for a run of several years, in different theaters country-wide and sometimes internationally, while others may involve a single performance in a cabaret venue or outdoors. Some may use no amplification, some body mikes, and some general sound enhancement or reinforcement. The teacher needs to understand these expectations and demands in order to assist professional singers to meet them.

Auditions

Auditions may be required for all kinds of performances, for example, oratorio and cantata, live theater, film, television, music theater, and opera. Obviously, performers devising their own show will not need to audition, but they may want to audition supporting performers. For many events, such as singing solo parts in a choral concert, it may be just a matter of the musical director hearing the singer, at a mutually convenient time and place. Actors auditioning for a part that involves singing may be required to sing a set song, or type of song, as part of their audition. Music theater and opera have their own conventions.

Music theater

Effective singing teachers need to be familiar with facts relating to the music theater trade worldwide in order to prepare their students for work within an industry that has specific demands relating to auditioning, performing, recording, and touring. Music theater is an international multimillion dollar business, with all the inflexibilities inherent within a global industry (Wilson 2010, p. 295).

Auditions usually come through agents who have received a casting breakdown from the producers, including details of roles, characters, vocal range and style, approximate age, and sometimes physical requirements. Sometimes open auditions ("cattle calls") are advertised online, in local newspapers, and in trade publications. Singers need to be aware that while amplification is always used in music theater performances, it is never used in auditions.

Agents negotiate audition appointments for their clients, whereas singers attending open auditions need to arrive well ahead of time and wait to be heard. It can be a long wait in which the performer needs to maintain the poise to be able to stand and deliver when the moment finally comes. For such auditions, teachers need to advise students on appropriate songs that quickly convey the singer's ability and personality.

Any audition is an unnatural situation, and the first music theater audition more unnatural than most. Performers are aiming, in a very short time, to demonstrate to the panel that they could be cast for a role in the show and warrant a call-back. Sometimes clothing that hints at the role can help the director imagine the singer for a particular part, but if a number of roles seem possible, clothing that expresses something of the singer's personality and looks good on stage is appropriate. For that first round, the usual requirement is for two contrasting music theater pieces, a ballad and an up-tempo number. However, depending on the show, these could be two contrasting pieces appropriate to the style/s and era of the show. While it is advisable to prepare one song by the composer of the show, panels usually prefer not to hear a number from the show, since they probably have their own concept and want to see whether the performer fits that. Audition panels usually have a very tight schedule, so they rarely hear the whole song in first-round auditions. While 16 bars is a common request, sometimes as few as eight bars are heard. It is therefore important for the teacher to help singers identify the 16 bars that show them at their best, mark up the score so it is clear for the audition pianist, and have less experienced singers rehearse how they can concisely communicate to the pianist how they intend to perform the song.

Professional singers may need to audition at short notice and, while the requirement may be for only two songs, it is useful to take a minimum of six songs ready to sing should the panel want to hear something more. Music theater performers need to have a portfolio of audition songs, covering a wide range of classifications, such as narrative, comedy, ballad, jazz, torch song, up-tempo, rock/pop, music hall, "legit," and even operatic. Sometimes songs indicating specific locations are requested, e.g. Southern American musical or British cockney.

A recall audition after an open audition is essentially the first audition, for which singers need to be ready to sing the song they sang at the open audition, as well as two other contrasting songs. After a first private audition, often a song from the show is prescribed for the call-back; singers should also take their folder of songs in case the panel requests something else. The performer often has little time to prepare the prescribed song, so may well need help from the teacher. Casting can be a lengthy process in which as many as six recalls may be required.

Opera and oratorio

Opera and oratorio auditions can be arranged through agents or directly with a company, so auditions may mean auditioning for an agent and/or auditioning for a company. Sometimes agents or companies will be prepared to attend a performance to hear a singer. Opera companies may hold regular open auditions annually, but experienced professionals can usually make an appointment for an audition. Sometimes, the initial audition will be in a rehearsal studio and, if that is successful, a stage audition is arranged. However, depending upon the singer's reputation and the company's needs, they may go straight to the stage audition. Singers need to be prepared for strange conditions for stage auditions—the piano may be in the wings or in darkness below the stage, the set for the current production may still be in place, or there may be noises off-stage or in the auditorium.

As in music theater, the choice of audition repertoire is vital. For oratorio auditions contrasting styles (from Baroque, Classical, Romantic, and twentieth/twenty-first century periods) and languages (from Latin, Italian, German, French, and English) are expected. Contrasting material is also required for opera auditions. Often it is possible for the singer to choose the first aria and then, if the panel wants to hear more, he or she may offer a list for them to choose from.

In opera, casting depends on voice type, age, and appearance. Teachers may need to advise beginning professionals on their operatic voice classification (or *Fach* in the German system) and the range of arias appropriate to that classification. Voice type is not just a matter of "soprano" or "mezzo soprano," but also rests on range, register transitions, and vocal weight, character, and stamina. So a soprano is not just a soprano, but a soubrette soprano, a lyric coloratura soprano, a lyric soprano, a dramatic coloratura soprano, a spinto soprano, or dramatic soprano. Teachers can provide important advice here; even professional singers are not always realistic about their casting. While in small companies there may be some flexibility between categories, in larger houses casting is usually done within them. Singers need a portfolio of contrasting arias in a number of different languages. Long arias may need to be cut. For German houses, it is important to have several arias in German, and to adhere to repertoire within the *Fach*.

In repertory companies (such as German opera houses), the operas are usually scheduled years ahead, with audition panels already knowing the roles they need to cast, and looking for singers who can sing a number of the roles within their *Fach*. It is, therefore, usually advisable to present only standard repertoire arias, preferably ones that involve some dramatic development and a range of musical demands. In German houses, it is usually assumed that singers presenting an aria of a particular character can sing the whole role.

TRAINING TO MEET PROFESSIONAL DEMANDS

Vocal skills

The professional singer needs the skills necessary to produce the vocal sound appropriate to the particular genre and style, not only while standing still in a concert or recording situation, but while moving on stage. Rock singers, music theater singers, and opera singers may be required to execute demanding physical moves, while still producing the appropriate vocal tone, and producing it safely. These vocal skills need to be finely honed to meet sometimes extreme demands in relation to pitch, rhythm, range, and phrasing. Most importantly, they need to serve the singer's artistry and individual performance persona.

Vocal expertise requires integrated, embodied control of body alignment and breath management, phonation, resonance and articulation, and registration. At professional level these skills have to be so cultivated that they are automatic. Psychomotor skills are learned in three stages: cognitive, associative, and autonomous (Fitts and Posner, 1967). Experts need to have reached the autonomous stage, where the skills can be unconsciously recruited to express the meaning of music and words, and communicate that in emotional form to an audience. Yet they need enough awareness to deal with difficulties if they occur. The singer needs to balance a sense of self as performer with a feeling of belonging to the applicable musical tradition, and employing the knowledge and techniques expected by that tradition, while simultaneously being able to meet the demands of conductors, directors, sound technicians, and others.

Linguistic skills

In many genres and styles, linguistic skills and verbal expression are vitally important. In music theater and cabaret they dominate, while in opera they combine with the music as the singer's text. In some CCM, such as jazz, they can be subservient to rhythmic and musical effects, but in others such as Rhythm and Blues, they are paramount.

A particular challenge for singers is to maintain the appropriate vocal tone, while articulating words. For music theater, different dialects of English may be required. For classical singing, the expectation is expertise in singing the high forms of English, Italian, French, and German. Czech, Russian, and Spanish are also useful—and sometimes required! In larger opera companies, language coaches are usually employed. There is, however, a vast difference between making the "correct" sounds of a language and making that language sound meaningful. This is a matter of the subtle flow and stress of the language, and how it is linked to the music, which may well present challenges when associated with singing over a wide vocal range.

Musical skills

By the time they become professionals, most singers have already attained a high level of musical skills. Different genres and styles may place more emphasis on understanding harmonic structure, or devising vocal embellishments, or sight reading. Singers need to be ready to meet new musical challenges when moving to a different genre or style.

Acting and movement skills

All singers are actors, in the sense that they have a musical and verbal text to interpret and convey to an audience. As with other actors, they need to consider who they are, whom they are addressing, what they are saying, why they are saying it, when they are saying it, and so on. In both opera and music theater, the movement requirements may vary from moving on stage and interacting with other performers in a convincing way, to full-scale, demanding dance sequences. While opera singers are often required to look convincing in a company dance scene, for more skilled moves dancers are usually employed. In music theater, greater dance skills may be required, and some shows largely require dancers who have some singing ability. Many shows require performers who can meet the "triple threat," i.e. performers who are equally skilled in acting, singing, and dancing. For both opera and music theater, the skill is in managing to move on-stage, while meeting the vocal and musical demands of the score. The teacher needs to be able to advise on how to balance these competing demands.

Professional skills

Professional singers need to be fit (physically, mentally, emotionally) for rehearsals and performances, regardless of personal circumstance. They need to know how to use rehearsals to build to performance. Many need to know how to work in a recording studio. They need to be able to work with others, often under great stress. In genres such as opera and music theater there are many others—singers, actors, dancers, instrumentalists, stage directors, musical directors/conductors, repetiteurs/coaches, wardrobe, publicity, front of house. Many deal with agents, managers, and recording engineers.

Preparing for a performance

Roland (1997, p. 19) suggested a planned approach to building to a successful flow performance, including objectives for the long-term build-up to the performance, the minutes immediately before the performance, during the performance, and after-performance evaluation. While experienced performers probably do most of this, having a detailed, structured plan builds to a feeling of assurance and control (see "Mental Preparation for the Performer" by Thomas, this volume).

Practice

In the lead up to a performance singers are, of course, focused on learning music, words, and where required, stage moves. Given the emphasis on vocal skills in their training and the evident necessity for vocal virtuosity in many performances, singers routinely practice vocal technique. Williamon (2004, p. 20) identified five general characteristics of effective practice—concentration, goal-setting, self-evaluation, strategy selection, and having a view of "the big picture." Teachers can assist the singer to form a view of the big picture, and to begin preparing mentally and emotionally by listing objectives and how to achieve them.

In both opera and music theater thought needs to be given to how to learn the role, being secure about the "script," both words and music, while remaining open to incorporating the interpretation of the director in a particular production. It is important, even in the early stages, to be building the stamina needed to sing the whole role on stage.

Because of the delicacy of the vocal apparatus, singers cannot devote the same number of hours a day to physical practice that many professional instrumentalists do. What is efficacious is a mixture of physical and mental practice. In kinesthetic imagery, the movement is reproduced, virtually, in the mind. For singers, combining this kind of imagery in real time with the auditory imagery of the words and the vocal line, and then (if needed) with the stage movement, is a powerful type of practice. Combining mental practice with physical practice builds body maps for that performance. Virtuosity requires that kind of practice.

Rehearsing

The physical, mental, and emotional preparation done in private then needs to be implemented in rehearsal, with all the distractions of dealing with many different demands and sometimes very long rehearsal periods. Singers need to be self-aware enough to pace themselves, knowing when it is important for the process to be singing out, and when it is appropriate to mark. Marking (not singing full voice, and singing high-lying passages down an octave) may be employed in long production rehearsals, but this practice is only useful if it can be done accurately and with full body support, and so long as cues are clearly given to colleagues. If done too often it may compromise the learning of the full embodiment needed for the performance.

Artistry: knowledge or magic?

Whether consciously or not, what audience members are looking for is an emotional experience. Much research and training in music is focused on technical accomplishment, and this certainly is vital, but technical expertise needs to be employed in emotional communication. Quite how this is done and why some performers are better at it than others, is something of a mystery. Emotions are evoked when people process objects or situations through the senses, or when the mind conjures up from memory objects or situations, and represents them as images in the brain (Damasio 1999, p. 56). Musicians are better equipped for emotional communication than other performers in that there seems to be a linkage between movement, the brain, and music that is only now becoming proven (Levitin 2006), with emotion being linked not only to the actual sound, but also to the movement/s that make it. Singing, more than other music-making, can speak to the emotions through the link between body, language, and sound. Emotion, feeling, and consciousness are linked through the body: "their shared essence is the body" (Damasio 1999, p. 284). It is these linkages that make live performance more affecting than recorded performance.

Artistry is an ineffable thing. However, the singer must have a view of what artistry means and continually strive to achieve it. Different genres of performance provide different challenges. In classical music, for instance, where the emphasis is on realizing the composer's written intentions, the performer is always competing against predecessors to produce a more beautiful, authentic, subtle, or more captivating performance. In music theater, artistry consists of embodying the character in the performer's own individual way. In

CCM, there is more pressure to be musically creative and to have a unique voice, both in terms of approach to performance and the vocal sound. There is pressure to sound "natural," "unschooled," and instantly recognizable.

"However hard we think about artistry, we will conclude that whatever else it may be—obviously, the transcending of anxiety to start with—it is also the repository of the purely musical" (Dunsby 1995, p. 36). The joy of singing is that it is a natural activity, in all cultures, from childhood to old age. This is why singing touches people in a way that other music-making does not. For professional singers this is a two-edged sword. Singers can capitalize on this to make an emotional connection with their audience; they need great self-awareness and expertise to do this, but if self-awareness tips over into self-consciousness, the effect is lost. Performers often feel that if they think about performing too much, they will lose the magic. Rather than not thinking about it, it is more a matter of how to think about it, in terms of the emotional communication of words and music, and how these are embodied by the singer.

It is helpful to remember that sound is a temporal phenomenon, and for the skilled performer who has already acquired an arresting, individual sound, attention to that aspect of the music-making may open up artistry. Dunsby refers to the example of past masters as being "a handing-on not just of experience, but also of knowledge; not just of magic (which is what we're really after), but of how the tricks are done . . . we will never lose the magic by knowing how the tricks are done" (1995, p. 80).

Maintaining vocal health

Many professional vocalists do not earn enough to work full time as singers and often what they do to supplement their income (working in education, hospitality, sales, etc.) taxes their voice. There are others who perform at an expert level, in church or with a performing ensemble, but without pay, and others who work in other occupations to earn their living. To perform at an elite level, these singers need to develop volitional control over movements that are normally part of an unconscious and uncontrolled reflex (Jahn 2009, p. 3). Both these categories of singer are at particular risk of vocal damage. By the time a singer presents to a medical specialist, the problem may be plain. The teacher can often help early on by suggesting strategies to avoid the problem or early interventions that prevent full-scale damage. Teachers need a finely-tuned ear to detect the beginnings of vocal problems during performances or lessons, and should suggest solutions. They need to be alert to changes in vocal tone, such as breathiness or hoarseness, difficulties negotiating register changes, or limitations in range. "Because the head and neck contain representatives of other major organ systems in close proximity to the phonating larynx, singing is additionally vulnerable to a range of diseases of the respiratory, gastrointestinal, and endocrine systems" (Jahn 2009, p. 3).

Having a list of health practitioners who can help singers to avoid vocal problems or to deal with them when they begin to occur is important. This might include Feldenkrais and Alexander practitioners, massage therapists, laryngeal manipulators, Pilates and yoga instructors, respiratory specialists, speech pathologists, psychologists, and laryngologists. It is important that these practitioners appreciate that the voice is the singer, that there are many demands and stresses on professional singers, and that any kind of health problem may affect the voice or the ability to perform. In many fields, there is also blame and shame imputed to singers who have a vocal problem. To deal effectively with professional singers, health practitioners need not only to be knowledgeable in their field, but also empathetic and supportive.

Occupational disorders in singers include muscle tension dysphonia, vocal nodules, vocal hemorrhages and polyps, or general vocal deterioration. Unlike instrumental playing,

> mastering singing involves making reflexive activity voluntary and voluntary activity re-flexive. Specifically, the singer must learn to contract groups of muscles in isolation while simultaneously relaxing muscles which are either antagonistic or not involved in phonation. . . . The overall aim is to produce the greatest spectrum of vocal pitch and inten-sity with the least effort.
>
> (Jahn 2009, p. 4)

It only takes a small imbalance in these elements for vocal problems to begin. If excess muscle tension is employed, muscle tension dysphonia may result, with a loss of resonance and dy-namic range, and then hoarseness and sometimes nodules. Nodules are more common in women and children, whose vocal folds vibrate at higher frequencies. Vocal hemorrhage may result from a particular incident, such as coughing, vomiting, weight lifting, or child-birth and may be exacerbated by the use of blood thinners or by menstruation. Healing requires complete vocal rest. If the singer continues to sing, a polyp may develop. Polyps may resolve with voice rest and steroids, or may require laser removal. Young professional singers who have pushed themselves, or been pushed by management, may present with a weak and tremulous voice, as may experienced, older singers whose voices are declining. Therapy and good teaching may assist, but often the lack of control involved in general vocal deteriora-tion means the end of a career.

Singing at an expert level requires a high level of physical fitness, general health, and stamina. Performers are required to meet the demands of directors and conductors in a vo-cally efficient way. Professional singers often need to cope with extended rehearsals, heavy performance schedules, and international travel. They often work at night and may need to be away from home, family, and friends for extended periods. Illness (even minor illness) may mean loss of income and loss of face. A cold, minor bronchitis, laryngitis, gastric reflux, allergies, asthma, menstrual problems, may all affect the voice. Hearing or dental problems may have a radical negative effect. Many medications prescribed for minor health problems cause dehydration, which is disastrous for singing. It is, therefore, not surprising that profes-sional singers are often seen as very precious about their health. They need advice and sup-port from their teacher, and from sympathetic medical experts.

Elite performers are usually aware that they need to eat well (including avoiding anything that may produce even a minor allergic reaction), maintain hydration, and exercise regu-larly. However, beginning professionals may need to be reminded of this and perhaps con-sult a dietician for detailed advice. It is important to include complex carbohydrates in the diet to ensure sustained energy. A solid meal two to three hours before a performance will supply the energy required, and perhaps a little fruit or fruit juice immediately before a per-formance. Many a singer has woken the day following a performance, sure that they had sung well, and wondering why they feel hoarse. This may well be because they have yielded to the temptation to have a large meal, with alcohol, after the performance, immediately be-fore going to bed. Gastric reflux often results and has a deleterious effect on the voice.

Dealing with performance anxiety

Professional singers may be afflicted with performance anxiety at different stages of their career. The main cause is fear of negative evaluation and, if the consequences of that negative evaluation are serious, the anxiety may be more severe. Performance anxiety may strike with the first solo role, the first solo recording, the first big tour, or the comeback tour, as the voice begins to decline with aging, or when performing before a completely new audience. Singers performing in small groups, if they feel musically or vocally inadequate, may fear negative evaluation by their peers. Artists are particularly vulnerable when auditioning. Usually, performers feel less anxiety when they are performing for an audience they see as less demanding, or when they are performing music they have performed successfully many times before. In long runs of musicals this may be a problem, with singers needing strategies to ensure that they continue to bring life and fresh inspiration to each performance.

There may be underlying psychological problems affecting the performer's feeling of self-worth that lead to performance anxiety. Performers are vulnerable, with the prospect of success bringing joy and feelings of self-worth, but the prospect of failure bringing anxiety. For artists who have long-term underlying anxiety in other areas of their life, performance anxiety may be ongoing. In that case, it is a matter of seeking intensive psychological help to deal with the condition. These artists may need to evaluate whether the stresses of a performance career are worthwhile.

When artists are feeling threatened by a performance, they will mentally create one or more of these "threats":

- over-estimate their chance of failing in the performance;
- over-estimate the difficulty of the performance;
- over-estimate the consequence of potential failure;
- underestimate their ability to cope with the demands of the performance.

(Roland 1997, p. 9)

These are examples of mental responses to a performance situation. In anxiety, these mental responses trigger behavioral and physiological responses in that situation. Mental, behavioral, and physiological responses combine in what is called anxiety, nervousness, or stage fright. Mental responses are those that involve the thinking processes and are not observable by anyone except the artist. These may include loss of concentration, distraction, memory blanks, and/or thoughts about failure. Behavioral responses are those that involve actions that are observable by others. These may include tension, agitation, or acting in a panicky way. Physiological responses involve the physical changes brought about by the fight or flight response. These may include increased heart rate, nausea, hormone secretion, and high, rapid breathing (Roland 1997).

The state of arousal that may become stage fright can be interpreted as a challenge rather than a threat. That arousal immediately before a performance can help the singer become alert and focused. If the focus is on bringing to life a piece of music for an appreciative audience, then the anxiety level falls immediately and the experience is a positive one. Singers can use their expertise in breath management to control the anxiety response of fast, rapid breathing. Less experienced singers reach the peak of anxiety during the performance, which then leads to their negative predictions being fulfilled, thus fueling their performance anxiety. This is the real problem with performance anxiety—it "feeds off itself" and becomes stronger even though the "threat" has not changed (Roland 1997, p. 11).

Seeing performance as a challenge implies positive self-talk, leading to a different mindset than that involved in seeing performance as a threat and the negative self-talk implicit in that. Even highly-experienced professionals may be unaware that they are engaging in negative self-talk. Changing that mindset can accomplish significant changes in the approach to performance. Seeing performance as a challenge means the singer saying "I've chosen to undertake this performance," rather than "I want to avoid this performance;" "I'm determined to give it my best," rather than "I feel like giving up;" "I feel excited," rather than "I feel afraid."

It is important for singers to appreciate that the way they prepare for a performance (mentally, physically, emotionally) has a radical effect on their experience of the actual event and their interpretation of it afterwards. This involves having specific practice and rehearsal strategies, a pre-performance routine, strategies for dealing with anxiety at performance time, and ways to approach post-performance evaluation. At all these stages the performer needs objectives and ways of achieving them. In practicing, the singer may have the specific preparation tasks for the performance as an objective to focus on and achieve this by working out a plan to meet the technical and musical demands of this particular performance. Immediately before the performance, the singer may have as an objective to interpret arousal as excitement rather than anxiety and achieve that objective by positive self-talk such as "I can meet this challenge" and relaxed breathing. During performance, the singer may have as an objective to stay focused in the present and achieve that objective by low breathing and focusing on the flow of a particular phrase. After the performance, the singer may have as an objective to evaluate the performance honestly in order to better perform next time. This might involve making a list of what worked and what did not, and resolving to do even better next time.

Performers and athletes speak of "performing in the zone," "flow," or "peak performance." This is the experience where mind, body, emotion, soul, merge as one in the activity. A flow experience comes out of tackling a challenging activity requiring a degree of skill that has been learned, that is perceived as joyful and important, that has a definite goal or purpose, which is totally self-absorbing, that requires such control that self-consciousness disappears, that is in itself rewarding. For professional singers this means having made the detailed cognitive, physical, and emotional preparation so that in performance they can totally immerse themselves in the activity.

Managing a career

The young singer beginning a career usually has a great deal of energy, enthusiasm, and vocal clarity. It is exciting to be offered work and the teacher often needs to provide a balanced opinion on what is appropriate to the current stage of development and what is useful in building a career. Young singers usually have exciting voices, but need encouragement to develop disciplined habits of vocal and physical health and fitness, and ways of balancing their personal with their professional life. They need to be self-aware and develop habits of reflective performance and ongoing learning.

Professional singers mid-career have usually reached their vocal peak and have enough experience to be secure in what they do. They may be receiving exciting offers of work, with the main difficulty being how to decide which offers to accept, then dealing with the challenge of learning new material, traveling, and living in different cultures. Voice lessons may be neglected for long periods, and when they resume the teacher needs to be ready to build on positive developments and deal with any potentially negative ones. Sometimes, at this stage of the career, a change to a whole new style, or different type of role, or even a different *Fach*, may seem the right move. Often the teacher can offer informed input on such decisions and, if a change is made, help the singer in any vocal transitions that are required.

Aging is associated with deteriorating bodily functions—muscle and neural tissues atrophy, and the chemicals responsible for nerve transmission change; ligaments atrophy and cartilages ossify, including those in the larynx (see "The development of singing across the lifespan by Sataloff", The Oxford Handbook of Singing). The vocal folds themselves thin and deteriorate, becoming less elastic, and the vocal fold edge becomes less smooth. All these changes have a negative effect on the voice (Sataloff and Linville 2006, pp. 133–137). Changes in the oral cavity with aging may involve loss of dentition that alters occlusion and articulation, a disturbing problem for professional singers.

At what age these changes occur varies from individual to individual and, as with other psychomotor skills, singing skills may last longer in accomplished performers. Skilled professional singers may be able to maintain an acceptable performance standard for many decades, and compensate for failing vocal abilities with seasoned performance and communication skills. Maintaining physical fitness may prevent aging singers from resorting to excessive muscle use in the neck and tongue.

In female singers, the hormonal changes of menopause may have a deleterious effect on the voice. Estrogen deprivation causes substantial changes in the mucous membranes that line the vocal tract, the muscles, and throughout the body. These changes can often be forestalled through appropriate hormone replacement therapy (Anderson, Anderson, and Sataloff 2006, pp. 349–352). In other cases the teacher can often help with a transition to new repertoire, or even a new *Fach*.

The teacher can encourage singers to remain physically fit and to continue to work on vocal technique. The teacher also provides the expert ear, both in studio sessions and in the performance environment, to be able to advise on when to begin planning retirement or transition to another musical career, such as teaching or choral conducting.

The teacher's role

In working with professionals, the teacher acts as senior colleague and mentor. Singers at this level are constantly working under physical and emotional stress, often being away from family and friends for extended periods, in unfamiliar places, and working with people they have not met before. The teacher needs to be a trusted guide, someone familiar with their particular voice, their personality, strengths, and weaknesses. The teacher needs a detailed knowledge of voice generally, and this voice in particular, in order to diagnose any problems and suggest efficient solutions.

In order to appreciate the strains the singer is exposed to, the teacher needs an understanding of the operation of the particular area in which the singer is operating—the musical and vocal conventions; how auditions are conducted; and the usual working of rehearsals and performances. The teacher needs to be able to help the singer to interpret the directions or feedback supplied by coaches, musical directors, and sound technicians, which may be expressed in a language vague about the specifics of vocal sound or how to achieve it. If it is possible to observe a rehearsal or a performance in the venue, it can be very helpful in understanding the acoustic and how the singer can best deal with it. Those working with singers in CCM need a knowledge of sound equipment and microphone technique.

At the beginning of this chapter many different types of professional singers were identified. Their personal and professional differences will mean they have slightly differing needs. They will also have differing needs at different stages of their career. There are those who have been studying for some time, either in tertiary education or privately, who are now embarking on a career; there are singers who have an established career, but have not had lessons for some time; and there are those who are dealing with specific vocal difficulties. Teaching is always focused on the particular needs of the singer, but with beginners or continuing amateurs, the concern is with ensuring that the basics of breath management, phonation, register transitions, resonance, and articulation are in place and can be coordinated to meet the musical demands. Often the teacher is involved in suggesting repertoire and grading it in a way that ensures vocal and musical development, as well as enjoyment.

Singers working at a higher level already have the vocal and musical skills in place. Where they often need help is in adapting those skills to a class of repertoire they have not previously attempted, or performing in a difficult acoustic, or making a transition to a different genre. Their artistry may have been affected by personal or professional anxieties, or the difficulties of working with new people. Here, the teacher provides sympathetic, but objective ears and eyes and the focused skills to facilitate the small changes needed to put the singer back on track. The teacher must be an expert diagnostician, able through visual and aural observation to identify small changes that will make a big difference in the vocal sound, the musical interpretation, the authenticity of the foreign language diction, or the efficiency of the overall coordination. As previously stated, if it is possible to attend a rehearsal or a performance in the venue, that can provide a more realistic view than observing the singer in the teaching studio; there may be, for instance, difficulties of staging or acoustics, of which the singer is not consciously aware, but which are affecting the performance. Singers who have been traveling may benefit from being reminded of the most efficient way to prepare for performance, in terms of their physical, mental, and emotional preparation.

The teacher advises on body alignment and use (without being a physiotherapist), maintaining vocal health (without being a laryngologist), and on dealing with professional relationships and performance anxiety (without being a psychologist). Often the teacher can recommend consultations with physical or mental health professionals who understand the stresses on professional performers, are sympathetic to their needs, and are able to supply the requisite support. Often judgment is required in terms of needing to have quite an intimate knowledge of a singer, but not crossing any personal or professional boundaries.

Summary

Teachers working with professional singers have an obligation to stay abreast of a broad range of knowledge in voice and vocal pedagogy, music education, music history and style, and musical performance. They need the skills to help clients achieve their optimum level of performance. It is vital that they understand the practical workings of performance in the particular genre/s in which they work. They need a finely-tuned ear and eye to diagnose any problems that may be affecting the voice, and a list of specialists to whom singers can be referred for help with particular vocal, physical, or mental health problems.

KEY REFERENCES

Anderson, T.D., Anderson, D.D. and Sataloff, R.T. (2006). Endocrine dysfunction. In: R.T. Sataloff (ed.), *Vocal Health and Pedagogy*, Vol 2, 2nd edn, pp. 319–376. San Diego, CA: Singular Publishing Group.

Chapman, J.L. (2016). *Singing and Teaching Singing: A Holistic Approach to Classical Voice*, 3rd edn. San Diego, CA: Plural Publishing.

Damasio, A. (1999). *The Feeling of What Happens. Body, Emotion and the Making of Consciousness*. London: Vintage.

Dunsby, J. (1995). *Performing Music. Shared Concerns*. Oxford: Clarendon Press.

Fitts, P. M. and Posner, M. I. (1967). *Human Performance*. Belmont, CA: Brooks/Cole.

Jahn, A. (2009). Medical management of the professional singer. *Medical Problems of Performing Artists* 24(1): 3–9.

Levitin, D. (2006). *This is Your Brain on Music. Understanding a Human Obsession*. London: Atlantic Books.

Roland, D. (1997). *The Confident Performer*. Sydney: Currency Press.

Sataloff, R.T. and Linville, S.E. (2006). The effects of age on the voice. In: R.T. Sataloff (ed.), *Vocal Health and Pedagogy*, Vol 2, 2nd edn, pp. 109–178. San Diego, CA: Singular Publishing Group.

Williamon, A. (2004). *Musical Excellence. Strategies and Techniques to Enhance Performance*. Oxford: Oxford University Press.

Wilson, P. (2010). Showtime!—Teaching Music Theatre and Cabaret Singing. In: S. Harrison (ed.), *Perspectives on Teaching Singing. Australian Vocal Pedagogues Sing Their Stories*, pp. 293–305. Bowen Hills: Australian Academic Press.

ADDITIONAL SOURCES

Blakeslee, S. and Blakeslee, M. (2007). *The Body has a Mind of its Own. How Body Maps in your Brain Help You Do (Almost) Everything Better*. New York: Random House Trade Paperbacks.

Callaghan, J. (2014). *Singing and Science: Body, Brain & Voice*. Oxford, UK: Oxford, UK: Compton Publishing.

Callaghan, J. (2010). Singing teaching as a profession. In: S. Harrison (ed.), *Perspectives on Teaching Singing. Australian Vocal Pedagogues Sing Their Stories*, pp. 13–30. Bowen Hills: Australian Academic Press.

Callaghan, J., Emmons, S., and Popeil, L. (2012). Solo voice pedagogy. In: G. McPherson and G. Welch (eds), *The Oxford Handbook of Music Education*, pp. 559–580. New York: Oxford.

Desberg, P. and Marsh, G. (1988). *Controlling Stagefright*. Oakland, CA: New Harbinger Publications.

Gorrie, J. (2009). *Performing in the Zone*. Available at: www.thezonebook.com

Kayes, G. and Fisher, J. (2002). *Successful Singing Auditions*. London: A. and C. Black.

Legge, A. (2002). *The Art of Auditioning. A Handbook for Singers, Accompanists and Coaches.* London: Rhinegold Publishing.

Thurman, L. and Welch, G. (2000). *Bodymind and Voice. Foundations of Voice Education*, rev. edn. Collegeville, MN: The VoiceCare Network.

Wrigley, B. (1999). *Peak Music Practice Handbook.* Brisbane: Rebecca Fortescue.

WEBSITES AND OTHER RESOURCES

Australian National Association of Teachers of Singing. Available at: M www.anats.org.au/

Australian Society for Performing Arts Healthcare. Available at: M www.aspah.org.au/

Australian Voice Association. Available at: M www.australianvoiceassociation.com,au/

British Association for Performing Arts Medicine. Available at: M www.bapam.org.uk/

British Voice Association. Available at: M www.british-voice-association.com

European Voice Teachers Association. Available at: M www.evta-online.org

Journal of Singing [online]: the official journal of the National Association of Teachers of Singing. Jacksonville, The Association, c. 1995-www.nats.org/cgi/page.cgi/about_journal_singing.html

Korean Classical Singers Association. Available at: M www.ekcsa.or.kr/

McCoy, S. (2004). *Your Voice. An Inside View. Multimedia Voice Science and Pedagogy.* Princeton, NJ: Inside View Press.

Miller, D. (2008). *Resonance in Singing.* Princeton, NJ: Inside View Press. Available at: M www. VoiceInsideView.com/

Nair, G. (2007). *The Craft of Singing.* San Diego, CA: Plural Publishing.

National Association of Teachers of Singing. Available at: M www.nats.org/

New Zealand National Association of Teachers of Singing. Available at: M www.newzats.org.nz/

The Voice-Care Network. Available at: M www.voicecare.org.uk

The Voice Foundation. Available at: M www.voicefoundation.org/

CHAPTER 33

···

MENTAL PREPARATION
FOR THE PERFORMER

···

ALMA THOMAS

INTRODUCTION

EXTENSIVE evidence confirms the role of psychological factors as determinants of elite performance, especially in applied sports psychology and science literature. Psychological success factors have been identified. Orlick and Partington (1988) cite the possession of a high level of commitment, long- and short-term goals, imagery, focus, pre-and in-performance plans as factors that differentiate successful performers from less successful ones. Other research supports such findings. Gould et al. (2002), and Salmela and Durand-Bush (2002) identified personal characteristics, such as self-confidence and motivation, as well as the mental skills of imagery and self-talk, as being used by elite performers to prepare for performance and to use during performance.

While most of this research has been in the domain of sport, there is a growing body of evidence that considers the place of such psychological success factors in the domains of music and voice. Williamon (2004) states, "Increasingly . . . researchers are forging cross-disciplinary collaborations and generating innovative methods for investigating how exceptional musical performances can be produced." Applied research is now informing the training and development of practitioners at all levels and in all aspects of voice. There is, however, a word of caution from Hamilton and Robson (2006), who state "while techniques and approaches to psychological consulting are similar to working with performing artists, there are definite differences that need to be considered when comparing a vocalist to a quarterback."

One of the main differences between the sport and singing domains is that singers must learn highly technical skills, as well as accuracy, which demands more precise and deliberate practice from a younger age before they can perform. According to Ericsson et al. (2007), this may mean that because the different performance domains require different levels of specific practice, they may also require differences in psychological characteristics. Singers often face multiple stressors and demands, such as voice control, singing, acting, and awareness and maintenance of body weight.

Recent research by MacNamara et al. (2006, 2010) suggests that development programs in the arts should "place greater emphasis on the advancement and application of psychological behaviors at an early stage to optimize both the development and performance of performers." Kiik-Salupere and Ross (2009), investigating to what extent vocal teachers and students are aware of the necessity of the pre-performance psychological preparation, identified that while the teachers admitted "the majority of students have problems with performance anxiety . . . however, not enough attention is paid in lessons to the problem of dealing with pre-performance psychological skills."

Kamin et al. (2007) and MacNamara et al. (2006) established a range of psychological factors that promote the conversion of potential into talent. These include motivation, commitment, goal setting, quality practice, imagery, realistic performance evaluations, coping under pressure, and social skills. Other psychological characteristics required include factors such as attitudes, emotions, and "desires" if the young performer is to realize her potential.

It is also important to consider the influence of environmental factors within which the young singer or beginner singers of any age take part. Kemp and Mills (2002) state that "influential researchers have stressed the environmental factors that they maintain are of paramount importance in the realization of a child's musical potential." For example, home and family factors, as well as the teaching environment within which especially enthusiastic young performers find themselves, should be nurturing, rather than critical. Both parents and teachers need to provide a stimulating environment in which young performers are listened to and responded to with imagination and compassion.

This chapter outlines some of the key psychological characteristics for developing excellence, using principles established by MacNamara et al. (2010) as being important in the development of success in learning and performance. These include teaching performers to set realistic goals, techniques to combat anxiety, strategies that enhance performance (such as positive self-talk, imagery, and relaxation techniques), and dealing with environmental stress. It is recommended that teachers enable their singers at all levels, especially beginners, to become aware of and learn the importance of psychological skills in performance and practice. Incorporating these essential skills into teaching and learning sessions, and performance preparation can only enhance the quality of practice and performance. There is also evidence that such an approach, which incorporates mental training, can make sessions more fun, with less anxiety, stress, and concern about having to get things right. While all mental skill programs are individualized, one thing remains paramount—mental skills require practice. They should be practiced regularly, and the singer should be committed to them long-term. The best way to do this is within the larger program of vocal practice, incorporating mental skills from the earliest practices and lessons, both for beginners and experienced singers.

Commitment and motivation

Occasionally, during performance or practice, things seem to fall into place. Singing becomes more productive and effortless, and the singer feels completely in touch with what is happening. This can be described as a high-performance experience, which transcends normal levels of ability. In their book *The C Zone: Peak Performance Under Pressure*, Kriegel and Kriegel (1984) discuss three words that characterize such performance behavior—confidence, commitment, and control. The authors also mention that such behavior is not the province of a chosen few, but rather that every singer has the power to achieve and to tap into the potential that exists within himself, but that this cannot be achieved without the second word—commitment.

If singers are to improve, three things are required:

- a disciplined effort;
- a belief they are capable of doing well;
- a belief they have the talent to succeed.

Without the belief or faith, motivation will be in short supply, especially when progress is slow. The spark of commitment is often called desire. This is not just a hope or a wish, but an intense drive to pursue what the singer loves doing. According to Garfield and Bennett (1984), "[desire] . . . is the biggest predictor of success . . . it being a strong preference for the work." Commitment is, therefore, a commitment to the self, knowing what is wanted, meeting the needs of personal desires, and translating them into actions. A commitment is not an unintentional thing. Adhering to an improvement plan can be difficult. It demands time and trust, both in self, and in the role model of the teacher and other performers. Above all, commitment is a long-term process that demands patience.

The following commitment check exercise may help any singer. Even singers of a higher level may benefit from doing this exercise regularly, especially if they appear to be lacking in motivation.

- Make a list of the things you do each day for singing, including all significant activities.
- Mark each activity on a scale of 1–10, with the high end of the scale being reflective of a commitment to yourself, and the things you want and enjoy doing in relation to your singing.
- Review the list to see how you are spending your time.
- Notice the activities given a low score.
- Are you wasting time doing what you can already do, and avoiding the things that you may consider boring, hard-work, or simply too difficult? In other words, how committed are you to pursuing the activities you do not want to do that are necessary to your success?
- Can you make a deeper commitment to yourself, and the process of improvement?

Some singers seek the challenges of learning and persist in the face of difficulty, while others, perhaps with just as much potential, avoid challenges and withdraw when faced with difficulties. McPherson (2000) states that an important outcome of the past 20 years of research is that "motivation is no longer viewed as a distinct set of psychological processes but as an integral part of learning that assists students to acquire the range of behavior that will provide them with the best chance of reaching their full potential."

Motivation underpins the mental skills included in this chapter. It is responsible for most of a singer's thoughts, emotions, and actions. It will determine what the singer likes and does. It is still not known what extent genetics play in the motivation to sing, but there is clear evidence of the powerful contribution that the social environment makes to the motivation to succeed and the development of musical excellence (Chaffin and Lemieux 2004). Bortoli et al. (2011) state also that "High perceived competence facilitates positive expectations for success, intrinsic motivation, achievement orientated behaviors, such as engagement, effort to master skills, persistence in the face of difficulty, and choice of challenging tasks." For more information on theoretical approaches to motivation, readers are referred to Achievement-goal Theory in the work of Nicholls (1984).

Social environments that encourage and facilitate the above behaviors will enhance motivation in all performers. It is therefore important to understand and appreciate the concept of motivation. Kemp and Mills (2002), however, caution:

> ... that the first manifestations of a child's musical responses are internally motivated ... these behavioral indications of the child's motivation belong to the child and must not be high-jacked by the parent (or teacher) ... and any pressurised development will tend to destroy the child's sense of motivation.

Motivation can be internal or intrinsic. This is characterized as a feeling of pleasure and enjoyment when practicing or performing, i.e. doing it because there is a desire to do so. External or extrinsic motivation, however, is characterized as doing an activity for other people or for the extrinsic value in the activity. This extrinsic value could be termed its usefulness for the future or for monetary value, including a future career. Intrinsic motivation is essential if a singer is to develop effective practice plans, and as intrinsic motivation develops the singer requires fewer reminders from either parents or teachers to practice (see reviews by McPherson and Zimmerman 2002).

In his ground breaking studies of enhancing intrinsic motivation, Csikszentmihalyi (1990) called the complete sensation performers feel when they are totally involved, or on automatic pilot, flow. He contends that flow experiences occur when a performer's skills are equal to challenges. Consequently, flow is achieved when both skills and challenge are high. It is important for both teacher and singer to understand how to enhance the likelihood of flow occurring. The following factors are important for increasing the chances of flow:

- be well trained;
- enjoy the activity at hand;
- have a positive mental attitude;
- maintain appropriate focus;
- channel energies and remain relaxed.

In all motivational theories, the element of achievement is vital (Pintrich and Schunk 1996). How a singer explains his achievements does affect future motivation. Does the singer attribute success or failure internally or externally? For example, does he/she attribute success to his/her efforts and ability, or to a teacher's excellent teaching? Expectations are fundamental to continuing motivation. Consequently, it is important to understand how the singer attributes the cause of success and or failure. For information on theoretical approaches to Attribution Theory, see Weiner (1986, 1992).

Singers all need to feel some level of achievement, especially early in their training, and before they can develop a level of intrinsic motivation required to undertake the concentrated effort required to practice effectively. Singers learn to recognize their own successes

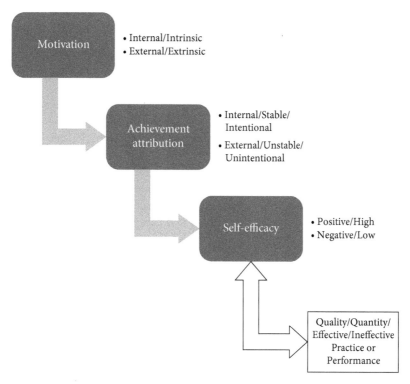

FIGURE 33.1 Motivation and practice or performance quality.

Adapted from Chaffin and Lemieux (2004).

and failures, as well as their talents and ability, mainly through positive experiences. Bandura (1997) outlines how an individual values any activity through a sense of competence or self-efficacy. Self-efficacy tends to be task specific. This includes a sense of personal responsibility to achieve, as well as the knowledge that he has the capability to develop the necessary skill, i.e. "How well can I do this?" Hackett (1995) posited: "Perceptions of personal competence are so powerful that they are theorized to influence a student's motivation and future decision to continue developing his or her skill in an area." Research in music by McPherson and McCormick (1999) supports these claims: "high levels of self efficacy strengthen confidence and guarantee perseverance, despite any future difficulties."

Figure 33.1 (amended from Chaffin and Lemieux 2004) illustrates a conceptual model of motivation, and its relationship to practice or performance quality.

GOAL SETTING

The mental skill that aids motivation is goal setting. Singers can save essential energy by pursuing the right goals and planning appropriately. Weinberg and Gould (2008) state that " . . . 90 percent of studies (within performance literature) show that goal setting has a consistent and powerful effect on behavior, whether in young children or professional people . . . Goal setting is a behavioral technique that works." Weinberg (2010) goes further by stating that "research over the past 45 years clearly shows that in approximately 90 percent of the studies, specific difficult goals lead to higher levels of task performance than easy goals, no goals, or 'do your best' goals."

Goal setting is a major element of all mental preparation programs for practice and performance. It is imperative before, during, and after any practice or performance. By setting appropriate goals and planning how to achieve them, singers give themselves every chance of being successful. Kiik-Salupere and Ross (2009) outlined the importance of mental skills training, especially goal-directed behavior, in the success of vocal performances. Goals give a singer a focus on what to attend to in practice or performance, they summon effort, prolong determination, and encourage the development of new learning strategies. However, research by Weiss and Burton (2008), and Locke and Latham (1990a,b) has clearly shown that just setting the goal will not guarantee improvements in practice or productivity. The singer, the coach, and the teacher need to use goal-setting principles and guidelines to make the most of their effectiveness.

Goal-setting principles

Research can and does provide performers, coaches, teachers, parents, and others with the science of goal setting, but it is important to also be aware of:

- situational constraints;
- individual differences.

It is therefore important that the singer knows his-/herself well, and that the coach, teacher, or parent also knows their student/child well in order to maximize the goal-setting effectiveness.

Dream goals

The journey toward excellence begins with dreams. It is important for a singer to have a dream goal, where he/she accepts the possibility of unlimited horizons in the future, a vision of what he/she wants to achieve. This, in turn, helps to stretch the limits, tap the potential, and remove barriers that could prevent the singer from moving forward.

The following questions may help a singer to get started:

- What would I like to eventually achieve in my singing performance?
- How far can I take this?
- Which singer do I aspire to be most like?

Assessment

Before singers can determine where they want to be, they must first assess their present status. Hence, an accurate assessment of self and one's current skills is an essential beginning.

Singers should be very honest, and get a teacher or parent to help with this if necessary. The following questions may help in the assessment:

- Where are you in your overall development now?
- What are your strengths?
- What do you need to improve specifically?
- What things do you need to do well in a performance or competition?

There is some evidence that individuals assess themselves harshly by only focusing on the things they believe they do badly, which is counterproductive to progress. The singer should try not to compare herself with others, but remain objective. This forms a baseline of information from which the singer can build on strengths and improve areas that need improving. It is important for the singer to note that the only thing he/she can control is in the present. Consequently, it is important that the assessment is done in the moment, and is not based upon what happened last month or what may occur next week in an audition. Singers must examine what their present priorities are. Mediocre performers categorize priorities at two extremes—either they are all important or none of them are important. There are various ways of doing this assessment, e.g. through profiling and by questionnaire (see Emmons and Thomas (1998) for an in-depth approach to these methods).

Specificity

The more specific and measurable goals are, the more they can guide and focus actions in the future. Additionally, the singer concerned knows he/she is making progress and achieving milestones toward each goal. Two main areas of importance are *appropriateness* and *attainability*. Goal setting is somewhat like being on a ladder. The rungs are far enough apart to enable the climb, but so close that they do not present a challenge or allow for progress. Effective goals are difficult enough to challenge the singer, yet realistic enough to achieve in practice and performance. Goals are of little value if they are too easy to achieve, which may cause a singer to lose interest. However, goals that are too difficult to achieve lead to frustration, a loss of confidence, and poor performance.

Goals should be stated in specific measureable and behavioral terms. For example, a goal to improve one's singing is too vague. The secret is to strike a happy medium between challenge and achievability.

There are different types of goals:

- *Outcome goals focus on an end result*: examples include the outcome of an audition, getting a role, or winning a competition. These goals are principally concerned with winning and losing. One key feature of such goals is that the singer is not in control of reaching the outcome because winning or losing depends on external factors, such as other competitors, and the opinions of judges or an impresario.
- *Performance goals focus on the singer's own performance independent of the other singers/ performers*: e.g. a performance goal may be to correct the technical phrasing in the aria "Vesti la giubba" from 68 to 76 percent. The singer would be in control of such a goal because the performance of others does not affect the goal achievement.

674   MENTAL PREPARATION FOR THE PERFORMER

- *Process goals are flexible, within the singer's control, and associated with less anxiety and better performances*: they are usually concerned with how the singer performs certain skills, whether they are physical, technical, or mental. Such goals are important in practice. An example of a process goal might be "I will practice singing the complete aria with a focus on the imagery I want to use." Process goals should be emphasized throughout all singing lessons and during all preparation for auditions and performances.

For every outcome goal, the singer should set performance goals that will lead to that outcome. All three types of goals are effective in enhancing performance and they can change behavior positively. Therefore, it is recommended that each singer should prioritize his/her goals, because different goals may be better for different situations, such as practice, auditions, or stage performances. A sample method of prioritizing goals might include the following:

a. Prioritize three goals that are the most important to the singer now. These demand determination and urgency.
b. Write down the next three goals. These goals are less urgent or are not as important as the goals in part (a).
c. The goals which are left do not have the same importance as the goals in (a) and (b), but are goals the singer may have to evaluate in the future.
d. All goals should be reviewed and evaluated weekly, monthly, and yearly if necessary.

Setting long- and short-term goals

Because changes in behavior take time, both long- and short-term goals should be set. Figure 33.2 shows a visualization of this concept. The long-term goal is placed first, while short-term goals are set on the steps leading up to the eventual achievement.

Once goals are set, they should be recorded and viewed regularly by the singer and all other members of the singer's preparation team. Above all, it is essential that the goals remain first and foremost in the singer's mind, and that they remain relevant to her. There are many ways of recording goals; one efficient way is for the singer to develop a mental log, which is used to record all the mental work to be done on each song, aria, or part. Another important issue about goals is that they should be flexible. They can be changed, amended, or even abandoned if necessary. Teachers, coaches, parents, and all other important counselors can all support and guide goal-setting programs of singers. Including other members of the singer's team provides support, empathy when needed, and fosters a compassionate, encouraging atmosphere.

MANAGING ANXIETY

Performance anxiety is a common problem amongst most performers, including singers. It affects individuals who tend to be prone to anxiety, especially in situations where they are

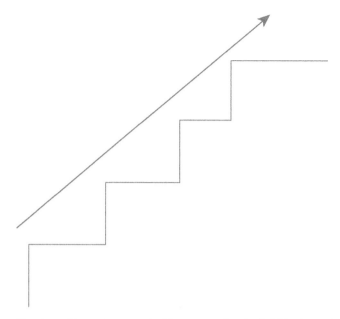

FIGURE 33.2 Short- and long-term goals. The present level of ability is on the lowest step. A sequence of progressively linked short-term goals connect stages of achievement until the long-term goal is met.

being judged, evaluated, or scrutinized publicly. Anxiety is also widely viewed as a complex psychological occurrence. As Hardy et al. (2009) state: "it is probably one of the most difficult emotions to define and diagnose." The relationship between anxiety and performance is not straight forward. While the understanding of anxiety and performance has been enhanced through the advancement of sports anxiety models, in particular the catastrophe model (Hardy 1990; Hardy et al. 1996), and the Jones (1995) control model, the empirical results have been inconsistent. New research (Hardy et al. 2009), however, is beginning to shed light on an alternative model of performance anxiety that may contribute more to the understanding of the complex relationship between anxiety and performance. At present, singers, teachers, and coaches can only utilize the evidence found in the research that has been validated, and work with the cognitive, physiological, and behavorial dimensions of anxiety. One additional point worth mention is that anxiety is one area where singers and sports performers differ. Because singing demands fine, manipulative motor skills, rather than gross motor skills as in sports, a lower threshold of anxiety tolerance is required before it can affect the singer's performance.

Wilson and Roland (2002) posited that performance anxiety can be regarded as "a form of social phobia (a fear of humiliation)," and "is an exaggerated, often incapacitating fear of performing in public." It has also been shown that high social anxiety is associated with an attentional bias toward negative information (American Psychiatric Association 1994). It is also suggested that any suppression of feelings and emotion, such as anger, worry, or fear, especially in a performance situation, can cause the emotions to be exacerbated (Wegner 1994) and that there may be a cognitive cost to engaging in suppression, as

Table 33.1 Symptoms of anxiety, categorized by anxiety source

Cognitive	Physiological	Behavioral
Indecisiveness	Pounding heart	Pacing
Worry	Profuse sweating	Actions getting faster
Feeling overwhelmed	Rapid respiration	Actions getting slower
Unable to concentrate	Muscle tension	Angry or aggressive behavior
Attention deficit	Dry mouth	
Loss of confidence	Trembling	
Forgetfulness	Frequent urination	
Fear irritability	Nausea	
	Loss of appetite	
	Sleeplessness	

Adapted from Emmons and Thomas (1998).

any intense emotions and feelings may interfere with cognitive monitoring processes (Baumeister 2007).

The symptoms of anxiety can be either physiological, cognitive (mental), behavioral, or any combination all three. Symptoms from each anxiety source are listed below in Table 33.1.

When a singer is anxious, the body's emergency system is activated. Under threatening circumstances, such as forgetting words in a major audition where he/she is being judged, the singer may wish to withdraw, become hyperactive, or show increased body tension. Hardy and Parfitt (1991) hypothesized in their catastrophe model of arousal that once arousal has passed a certain stress level, performance plummets. Arousal (see Figure 33.3 below) is a general physiological and psychological level of activation varying on a continuum from a deep sleep to extreme excitement. Hardy and Parfitt (1991) state that it is necessary to distinguish cognitive (mental) anxiety from somatic (body) distress, because it is mental aspects of anxiety that are likely to cause a catastrophe in a performance.

The important issue about arousal levels is that individual singers should be aware how much or how little arousal they require to perform well. Too little arousal and the performance will seem dull and lacklustre; too much and the performance suffers from a lack of concentration. Excessive arousal also interferes with memory, and can result in physiological effects, such as unsteadiness in hands and voice, which could be catastrophic in a performance if anxiety levels are too high. As singers are all unique individuals, each singer will require a different level of arousal to perform well. Ultimately, how the singer copes with

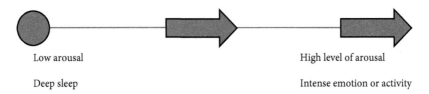

Low arousal   High level of arousal

Deep sleep   Intense emotion or activity

FIGURE 33.3 Arousal continuum.

anxiety is more important than how much anxiety the singer experiences. In other words, it is normal to have anxiety, and some is required for good performance, but it is not helpful if the singer cannot manage to control his/her anxiety.

Research indicates that the incidence of anxiety in musical performance is significant. For reviews of such work in the arts, see Kenny (2011), Van Kemanade et al. (1995), and Wesner et al. (1990). All researchers report the most troubling symptoms as poor concentration, rapid heart rate, trembling, dry mouth, sweating, shortness of breath, nausea, and dizziness. In the study by Wesner, 9 percent of students questioned in a Music Department responded that they avoided all performance situations because of anxiety. In a comparative study by Marchant-Haycox and Wilson (1992), 38 percent of singers and 47 percent of instrumental musicians reported they were affected by anxiety.

However, there is also evidence that while anxiety can be managed, it is also related to other personality traits, such as self-esteem, self-efficacy, and perfectionism. For example, a core belief of perfectionists is that they can never be good enough. They are highly self-critical and often suffer from lower than normal self-esteem. The interaction of other personality traits, including perfectionism, personal control, and performance anxiety, have been studied in the arts. Mor et al. (1995) found that "high personal and social standards together with low personal control were most strongly associated with debilitating performance anxiety." Furthermore, socially prescribed perfectionism (high standards imposed by others) was more strongly associated with debilitating performance anxiety than self-orientated perfectionism (i.e. self-imposed high standards).

The complexities of such characteristics are great and impossible to disentangle in a short chapter. However, the implications of the psychological characteristics have profound consequences on the level of anxiety in a singer's performance. Singers, teachers, and parents are advised to seek further help if there are indications that the anxiety level is extremely high, if panic attacks are evident prior to, during, or following performance, and if the singer is finding it difficult to cope in performing situations. In the excellent book, *The Psychology of Music Performance Anxiety* (2011), Kenny draws on a range of disciplines including psychology and therapeutic interventions, which may be of further help and may provide guidance in understanding and treating intense performance anxiety.

In any preparation for performance:

- It is critical for the singer to achieve a balance between skill and challenge. The singer needs to be challenged, but not beyond his/her skill level.
- Clear goal setting and focus is also a requirement.
- Feedback to the singer pre- and post-performance, lessons, and practice is vital. This allows the singer to evaluate, assess her progress, and make adjustments about future practices and performances. Extrinsic feedback and sensory information provided by an outside source can be made available at different times and in different forms. This can influence learning because it reinforces positive actions and motivates the singer to continue work towards the relevant goal. Intrinsic feedback is the sensory information that occurs from within the singer when he can hear that the sound was right or the technique felt right. The singer should always be encouraged to express how actions feel. The work of Schmidt and Wrisberg (2008) is recommended for more information of the nature of feedback in learning and performance.

If the singer is to manage anxiety and achieve the flow state (Csikszentmihalyi 1990), some of the precursors of performance anxiety have to be evaluated and appraised in order to raise awareness levels. The precursors include:

- evaluation apprehension;
- cognitive anxiety;
- self-presentation;
- some personality traits.

Strategies for managing anxiety

1. *Identify the causes of the anxiety*: is there a doubt about the singer's ability? Are situational demands the problem? Is it the consequences of any failure? Does the singer perceive him/herself negatively on a physical level (a self-presentation problem)? The work of Kenny (2011) may provide help. If change is desired, the singer should re-appraise the causes.
2. *If the cause is mental then mental skills are required to manage the anxiety*: if the cause is physiological, then physical skills are needed to manage the anxiety. The cause can also be a combination of both mental and physical issues. Cognitive anxiety begins long before physiological anxiety, so it is vital that the singer becomes aware when cognitive anxiety begins before a lesson, practice, or performance, so that management strategies can be implemented as early as possible.

Anxiety management skills

All skills in this section utilize a cognitive–behavioral approach, and these strategies can be used at a cognitive and/or a behavioral level.

Relaxation

Training in methods of relaxation skills can guide the singer's awareness of bodily and mental states, especially prior to a performance or audition. It is recommended that the singer practices the following two methods of relaxation.

- A deep method, such as progressive muscular relaxation, is recommended. It can be used as part of an anxiety-reduction program, preferably after any performance, hard practice session, or audition.
- A momentary method of relaxation, such as breathing exercises, the use of imagery, and the use of mindfulness-based stress reduction exercises are also important parts of any anxiety-reduction program. All can be used in pre-performance and performance routines, with practice, in order to reduce both physical and mental tension.

In-depth information regarding progressive muscular relaxation and breathing exercises can be found in Emmons and Thomas (1998, pp. 65–74). For mindfulness information, see Williams et al. (2007) and Chang et al. (2003).

Positive and negative self-talk

Positive self-talk is a cognitive strategy aimed at enhancing performance and reducing anxiety. Research studies have systematically supported the proposition that self-talk can be an effective cognitive strategy for skill acquisition, performance enhancement, and the management of anxiety (Hamilton et al. 2007). Self-statements are words and phrases that a singer says to him/herself, which are expressions of negative or positive personal self-worth. Self-talk can also be about situations in which the singer is performing, practicing, or being taught. Self-statements can have an enormous influence on performance levels; they mold attitudes and beliefs, and either reaffirm self-imposed limitations or guide a singer toward a breakthrough into a high-level performance. Self-talk is the mechanism that supports the principle of the self-fulfilling prophecy. The outcome in the performance is related in part to the type of self-talk being used by the singer.

Negative self-talk can range from just worrying or becoming distracted, to extremes such as anxiety and panic attacks. It sets the stage for poor performances. The more such self-talk is projected onto potential disasters, the more chance of the performance failing. Some examples of negative self-talk are:

- I should have prepared more thoroughly.
- I should have been more serious about my practice.
- If I do poorly I will disappoint my teacher and parents.
- I remember the awful experience I had the last time I auditioned in this space.

Such statements are image put-downs for the singer and affect performance effort negatively.

The skill is to cognitively re-structure what is being said or thought. A singer should write down the negative talk and then, on another piece of paper, first challenge what is written for its accuracy, then write down a positive alternative. For example:

- "I should have prepared more thoroughly" becomes "My preparation has been thorough and I am well prepared."
- "I am quitting" becomes "I love what I do; it is hard work, but it is worth it all."

Then the singer should destroy the negative self-talk list.

Positive self-talk

Positive self-talk is not about wishing or hoping, but rather a confirmation or affirmation of qualities, skills, and attributes that already exist in the singer. Positive self-talk reinforces positive performance abilities, as well as guiding the singer's focus on what he/she can do. This means that the singer's self-awareness has to be acute and realistic. Positive self-talk can be based on basic aspects of the performance or practice that confirm the singer's positive qualities. For example:

- I trust my abilities.
- I am relaxed.
- I am proud of my efforts.

Positive self-talk can also be based on specific skills and attributes needed to perform well. For example:

- My phrasing in this song is excellent.
- I can reach all the high notes in the runs in the second verse.
- I am excited about the way in which I have interpreted this song.

Process self-talk is often based on one word that can be used during a performance or practice, as it can focus the mind, and spark thoughts and feelings that can enhance performance. It is important for the singer to learn when and where this kind of affirmation can be used effectively in practice or performance. Cue words for process self-talk might include smooth, focus, relax.

As with all mental training, several guidelines exist. Key instructions include the following:

1. *Make sure all negative self-talk has been challenged and re-structured*: continue to monitor any negative words or phrases being used.
2. *Always be relaxed before using affirmations*: refer to the guidelines for imagery work below. Relaxation opens pathways to the singer's attributes and qualities that are required for performance.
3. *Construct and phrase affirmations in a positive manner without using any limitations*: e.g. use "I am a competent singer," rather than "Sometimes I am a competent singer." It is also important to avoid using double negative connotations, such as, "I will not panic today," or "I will not worry that my voice teacher is listening." Affirmations should be phrased in terms of what the singer wants to achieve.
4. *Construct affirmations in the present tense*: this is the only time period over which the singer has control. Phrasing positive self-talk in the future may turn affirmations into wishes and wants, and perhaps expectations. Such talk pushes the singer's thinking into the future and toward outcomes over which he or she has no control.
5. *Positive self-talk requires repetition*: this way it can be reinforced and strengthened. Positive self-talk is a dynamic entity, which requires constant attention. Without attention, it stagnates, weakens, and become negative and counter-productive. Kubistant (1986) states that "affirmations are like muscles;" they require work to keep them in good shape.

An important objective for positive self-talk is that it guides the singer's focus of attention onto positive aspects of her qualities, skills, and competencies. Performances at all levels are dependent upon what the singer can do, rather than what he/she cannot achieve.

Imagery and mental rehearsal

Mental rehearsal is the imaginary or cognitive rehearsal of a skill, performance, or part of a performance or song without obvious muscular movement. In all imagery work, the senses of hearing, sight, touch, taste, smell, and kinesthesia are used to create or recreate an experience that is similar to the actual physical experience. Mental rehearsal requires the singer to imagine, as vividly as possible, going through a performance or practicing in an ideal way how he/she would like the performance to occur. It is also possible for the singer to include his/her positive-self talk at the same time as doing mental rehearsal.

There are two ways of mentally rehearsing:

1. *With an external focus*: this is as if the singer were watching him/herself perform from the outside (the audience perspective).
2. *With an internal focus*: this is as if the performer were watching from within herself (on the stage looking out towards an audience).

Mental rehearsal strategies have been used for some time in sports and dance. The research supports its effectiveness as a preparation strategy and a means to reduce anxiety (Jones 1999; Taylor and Taylor 1995). The effects of mental rehearsal are such that the more the singer practices, the more likely he/she is to perform confidently in an actual performance. This is a form of neuromuscular programming.

Mental rehearsal can be used to:

- develop vocal skills and overcome technical vocal difficulties;
- improve memory and learning (especially during the early stages of learning);
- make practice more effective;
- guide attention to refocus during practice and performance;
- gain more control over arousal levels;
- enhance confidence.

The practice of using mental rehearsal to enhance performance in sport covers several decades (Butler 1996; Loer 1987; Martens 1987). This work has led to some guidelines for the use of mental rehearsal:

- Rehearsal should be undertaken in a relaxed state without any interruptions.
- Rehearsing should always be positive. If negativity appears, practice should be stopped.
- The rehearsal should be in the present, as if the singer is actively doing the performance.
- The singer should practice at her current level of performance.
- Mental rehearsal sessions should be short and regular. It is much better to do ten 3-minute sessions per day as opposed to one 30-minute session .
- Sessions should seek to use all the senses, but more importantly, they should always begin with senses the singer is already accomplished at utilizing, then continue with the development of others through experimentation. The more senses that are used, the more vivid the rehearsal.

- Singers should mentally rehearse with both an external and an internal focus. As above, practice should begin with the focus the singer can already do before practicing the other focus.

To review key aspects of imaging, singers should relax first. They need to stay positive, stay in the moment, and use all their senses. It is preferable to practice in short regular blocks of time, using both foci, to make the experience of imaging as realistic as possible.

Goal setting

Goal setting is an important skill for managing arousal levels and, hence, anxiety in performance. The guidelines listed above in goal setting should be used to help with performance anxiety.

EXPECT SUCCESS: DEVELOPING SELF-CONFIDENCE

One of the most consistent findings in the sports performance literature is the significant correlation between self-confidence and successful performance (Feltz 2007). Research has indicated that the most consistent factor distinguishing successful from less successful performers is confidence. Top performers, regardless of the activity, consistently exhibit a strong belief in themselves and their ability. Weinberg and Gould (2008) state that confidence is characterized by a high expectancy of success and it has many benefits. The benefits of confidence include:

- stimulation of positive emotions;
- assistance with concentration;
- impact upon goals;
- an increase in effort/motivation;
- an influence on psychological energy, as confident performers will rebound from adversity more readily than less confident ones.

Many studies of self-confidence feature Bandura's social cognitive theory of self-efficacy (1997), which brought together the concepts of confidence and expectations. Bandura defines self-efficacy as "the conviction that one can successfully execute the behavior required to produce the outcome." The singer can therefore achieve more by improving his self-efficacy judgments. Self-efficacy is specific in its content, and is a situation-specific form of self-confidence. Bandura's theory posits that the singer may expect self-efficacy from four main sources of information (see Figure 33.4).

Building self-confidence

People often believe that a singer naturally does or does not possess confidence. However, confidence can be acquired through planning, practice, and hard work. Performance can

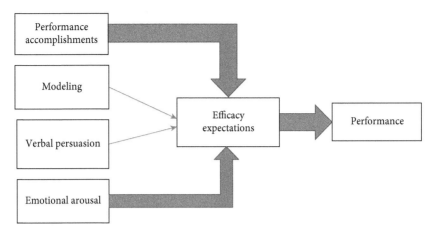

FIGURE 33.4 Relationships of performance accomplishments, modeling, verbal persuasion, emotional expectations, and performance.

Adapted from Feltz (1984).

be improved through preparation, imagery, performance accomplishments, thinking and acting confidently, and feeling physically good about oneself.

Preparation: goal setting

There is no substitute for effective and efficient planning and preparation. Being prepared gives a singer confidence so that he/she can expect success. This requires thought about pre-performance planning, during performance plans, and post-performance planning. The performance will only be as good as the preparation that went into it. The skill required is goal setting, as self-confidence has been associated with the setting of challenging goals (Bandura and Wood 1989), which in turn influence achievement behaviors.

Imagery

The use of imagery to build self-confidence is developed around the fact that the singer has seen, felt, heard, and experienced the performance in the imagination, long before the actual physical performance. If imagery principles have been followed then self-confidence is a likely outcome. The skill required is that of imagery, described earlier in the chapter.

Performance accomplishments

This concept is really quite simple. "Successful behavior increases confidence and leads to further successful behavior" (Weinberg and Gould 2008). Effective and successful practice becomes vital when developing confidence. Consistently performing well in practice develops confidence, especially in young performers who have had little or no performing experience. The skill required is positive self-talk, outlined earlier in the chapter.

Thinking and acting confidently

The more a singer acts confidently, the more likely he/she is to feel confident. Acting confidently in terms of body language can raise spirits and is important in all forms of competition, including auditions. Because thinking, feeling, and behaviors are interrelated it is important for a singer to also think he/she can and will achieve personal goals. Thinking that becomes judgmental, rather than encouraging, does not allow for development of self-confidence. The skills of imagery and positive self-talk are important, as the performer can use mental rehearsal to remember and recall good, consistent performances from the past.

Positive sense of physical well-being

It is useful if a singer can regard him or herself as an athlete, and be able to develop a positive body and appearance concept. Physical exercise, good nutrition, and healthy hygiene will allow for an added confidence in self-presentation, which can be an important issue for a singer. Once again, the skills of imagery and positive self-talk become important in such contexts.

Confident singers tend to be more skilled and effective in using cognitive coping strategies and resources that are necessary for success in performance. Bandura and Wood (1989) showed that confident individuals remain task-diagnostic, rather than self-diagnostic, and, consequently, process solutions more effectively when things are not going well.

SUMMARY OF KEY POINTS

1. Without doubt, mental skills are integral to success both in practice and performance. Prominent educators both in sport and in the performing arts have advocated their use for many years.
2. The purpose of this chapter has been to provide voice educators and singers with some illustrative mental skills that are based on recent research, to supply background on mental training, and provide examples. Teachers, coaches, and singers are encouraged to introduce the exercises presented and apply them to their practice schedules, and if necessary, adapt them through experimentation to meet individual needs.
3. While it is understood that all singers are individuals and any mental skills training will be specific to each individual, two important points remain—mental skills require regular practice and commitment from a singer, and in order for them to be effective, mental skills should be an integral part of all teaching and learning.
4. The literature in sport, and more recently, in music education and performance, is full of the benefits of using mental skills. The literature is equally full of ways in which mental skills constantly guide and enhance performances at all levels.
5. The key mental skills covered in this chapter are commitment and motivation, goal setting, managing anxiety, relaxation, imagery, and developing self-confidence.

References

American Psychiatric Association (1994). *Diagnostic and Statistical Manual of Mental Disorders (DSM- IV)*, 4th edn. Washington, DC: APA.

Bandura, A. (1997). *Self- efficacy: the Exercise of Control.* New York: Freeman.

Bandura, A. and Wood, R.E. (1989). Effect of perceived controllability and performance standards on self- regulation of complex decision making. *Journal of Personality and Social Psychology* 56: 805–814.

Baumeister, R.F. (2007). The strength model of self-control. *Current Directions in Psychological Science* 1(6): 351–355.

Bortoli, L., Bertollo, M., Comani, S., and Robazzo, C. (2011). Competence, achievement goals, motivational climate, and pleasant psychobiosocial states in youth sport. *Journal of Sport Sciences* 29(2): 171–180.

Butler, R.J. (1996). *Sport Psychology in Action.* Oxford: Butterworth-Heinemann.

Chaffin, R. and Lemieux, A.F. (2004). General perspectives on achieving musical excellence. In: A. Williamon (ed.), *Musical Excellence: Strategies and Techniques to Enhance Performance*, pp. 19–39. New York: Oxford University Press.

Chang, J.C., Midlarsky, E., and Lin, P. (2003). The effects of meditation on music performance anxiety. *Medical Problems of Performing Artists* 18(3): 126–130.

Csikszentmihalyi, M. (1990). *Flow: the Psychology of Optimal Experience.* New York: Harper Row.

Emmons, S. and Thomas, A. (1998). *Power Performance for Singers: Transcending the Barriers.* New York: Oxford.

Ericsson, K.A., Prietula, M.J., and Cokely, E.T. (2007). The making of an expert. *Harvard Business Review* 85(7–8): 114–121.

Feltz, D.L. (1984). Self-efficacy as a cognitive mediator of athletic performance. In: W.F. Straub and J.M. Williams (eds), *Cognitive Sport Psychology*, pp. 191–198. Lansing, NY: Sport Science Associates.

Feltz, D.L. (2007). Self-confidence and sports performance. In: D. Smith and M. Bar-Eli (eds), *Essential Readings in Sport and Exercise Psychology*, pp. 278–294. Champaign, IL: Human Kinetics.

Garfield, C.A. and Bennett, H.Z. (1984). *Peak Performance: Mental Training Techniques of the World's Greatest Athletes.* Los Angeles: Tarcher.

Gould, D., Greenleaf, C., and Krane, V. (2002). Arousal anxiety and sport behavior. In: T.S. Horn (ed.), *Advances in Sport Psychology*, 2nd edn, pp. 207–241. Champaign, IL: Human Kinetics.

Hackett, D. (1995). Self-efficacy in career choice and development. In: A. Bandura (ed.), *Self-Efficacy in Changing Societies*, pp. 81–106. New York: Cambridge University Press.

Hamilton, L.H. and Robson, B. (2006). Performing arts consultation: developing expertise in this domain. *Professional Psychology: Research and Practice* 37(3): 254–259.

Hamilton, R.A., Scott, D., and MacDougall, M.P. (2007). Assessing the effectiveness of self-talk interventions on endurance performance. *Journal of Applied Sport Psychology* 19(2): 226–239.

Hardy, J., Oliver, E., and Tod, D. (2009). A framework for the study and application of self-talk in sport. In: S. D. Mellalieu and S. Hanton (eds), *Advances in Applied Sport Psychology: a Review*, pp. 37–74. London: Routledge

Hardy, L. (1990). A catastrophe model of performance in sport. In: J.G. Jones and L. Hardy (eds), *Stress and Performance in Sport*, pp. 81–106. Chichester, UK: Wiley.

Hardy, L., Jones, G., and Gould, D. (1996). *Understanding Psychological Preparation for Sport.* Chichester: Wiley.

Hardy, L. and Parfitt, G. (1991). A catastrophe model of anxiety and performance. *British Journal of Psychology* 82(2): 163–178.

Jones, G. (1995). More than just a game: research developments and issues in competitive anxiety in sports. *British Journal of Psychology* 86: 449–478.

Jones, G. (1999). The acquisition and development of cognitive skills and strategies: making the butterflies fly in formation. *Sport Psychologist* 13(1): 1–12.

Kamin, S., Richards, H., and Collins, D. (2007). Influences on the talent development process of non-classical musicians: psychological, social, environmental influence. *Music Education Research* 9(3): 449–468.

Kemp, A.E. and Mills, J. (2002). Music potential. In: R. Parncutt and G.E. McPherson (eds), *The Science and Psychology of Music Performance*, pp. 3–16. New York: Oxford.

Kenny, D.T. (2011). *The Psychology of Music Performance Anxiety.* New York: Oxford University Press.

Kiik-Salupere, V. and Ross, J. (2009). *The Impact of Psychological Preparation on Vocal Performance.* Talliuallu University, Estonia: Institute of Education Research.

Kriegel, R.K. and Kriegel, M.H. (1985). *The C Zone: Peak Performance under Pressure.* New York: Fawcett Columbine.

Kubistant, T. (1986). *Performing Your Best: a Guide to Psychological Skills for High Achievers.* Champaign, IL: Life Enhancement Publications.

Locke, E.A. and Latham, G.P. (1990a). *A Theory of Goal-Setting and Task Performance.* Englewood Cliffs, NJ: Prentice-Hall.

Locke, E.A. and Latham, G.P. (1990b). Work motivation and satisfaction: light at the end of the tunnel. *Psychological Science* 1: 240–246.

Loer, J.E. (1987). *Mental Toughness Training for Sport.* Harrisburg, VA: R.R. Donnelley.

MacNamara, A., Button, A., and Collins, D. (2010). The role of psychological characteristics in facilitating the pathway to elite performance. Part 2: examining environmental and stage related differences in skills and behaviors. *Sport Psychologist* 24: 74–96.

MacNamara, A., Holmes, P., and Collins, D. (2006). The pathway to excellence: the role of psychological characteristics in negotiating the challenges of musical development. *British Journal of Music Education* 23: 80–98.

Marchant-Haycox, S.E. and Wilson, G.D. (1992). Personality and stress in performing artists. *Journal of Personality and Individual Differences* 13: 1061–1068.

Martens, R. (1987). *Coaches Guide to Sport Psychology.* Champaign, IL: Human Kinetics.

McPherson, G. (2000). *Proceedings of XXIV International Society for Music Education Research Commission, Salt Lake City, USA, July 10–15.* New York: Oxford University Press.

McPherson, G.E. and McCormick, J. (1999). Motivational and self-regulated learning components of musical practice. *Bulletin of the Council for Research in Music Education* 141: 98–102.

McPherson, G.E. and Zimmerman, B.J. (2002). Self-regulation of musical learning: a social cognitive perspective. In: R. Colwell and C. Richardson (eds), *The New Handbook of Research on Music Teaching and Learning*, pp. 327–347. New York: Oxford.

Mor, S., Day, H., and Flett, G. (1995). Perfectionism, control, and components of musical practice. *Cognitive Therapy and Research* 19(2): 207–225.

Nicholls, J. (1984). Achievement and motivation: conceptions of ability, subjective task choice, and performance. *Psychological Review* 91: 328–346.

Orlick, T. and Partington, J. (1988). Mental links to excellence. *Sports Psychologist* 2: 105–130.

Pintrich, P.R. and Schunk, D.H. (1996). *Motivation in Education: Theory, Research, and Applications*. Englewood Cliffs, NJ: Prentice-Hall.

Salmela, J.H. and Durand-Bush, N. (2002). The development and maintenance of expert athletic performance: perceptions of world and Olympic champions. *Journal of Applied Sport Psychology* 14: 154–171.

Schmidt, R.A. and Wrisberg, C.A. (2008). *Motor Learning and Performance*. Champaign, IL: Human Kinetics.

Taylor, J. and Taylor, C. (1995). *Psychology of Dance*. Champaign, IL: Human Kinetics.

Van Kemanade, J., VanSon, M.J., and Van Heesch, N.C. (1995). Performance anxiety among professional musicians in symphonic orchestras: a self-report study. *Psychological Reports* 77: 555–562.

Wegner, D.M. (1994). Ironic processes of mental control. *Psychological Review* 101: 34–52.

Weinberg, R.S. (2010). Making goals effective: a primer for coaches. *Journal of Sport Psychology in Action* 1: 57–65.

Weinberg, R.S. and Gould, D. (2008). *Foundations of Sport and Exercise Psychology*, 4th edn. Champaign, IL: Human Kinetics.

Weiner, B. (1986). *An Attribution Theory of Motivation and Emotion*. New York: Springer-Verlag.

Weiner, B. (1992). *Human Motivation: Metaphors, Theories, and Research*. Newburg Park: C.A. Sage.

Weiss, C. and Burton, D. (2008) The fundamental goal concept: the path to process and performance success. In: T. Horn (ed.), *Advances in Sport Psychology*, 3rd edn, pp. 339–375. Champaign, IL: Human Kinetics.

Wesner, R.B., Noyes, R., and Davis, T.L. (1990) The occurrence of performance anxiety among musicians. *Journal of Affective Disorders* 18: 177–185.

Williamon, A. (2004). *Musical Excellence. Strategies and Techniques to Enhance Performance*. New York: Oxford.

Williams, J.H.G., Teasdale, J.D., Segal, Z., and Kabat-Zinn, J. (2007). *The Mindful Way through Depression: Freeing Yourself from Chronic Unhappiness*. New York: Guilford.

Wilson, G.D. and Roland, D. (2002). Performance anxiety. In: R. Parncutt and G.E. McPherson (eds), *The Science and Psychology of Music Performance: Creative Strategies for Teaching and Learning*, pp. 47–61. New York: Oxford.

OTHER RESOURCES

Bandura, A. (1986). *Social Foundations of Thought and Action: a Social Cognitive Theory*. Englewood Cliffs, NJ: Prentice-Hall.

Further details of mental skills training and sports psychology can be found from the following websites:

www.psyc.unt.edu/apadiv47

www.aaasponline.org

www.psychology.lu.se/Fepsac

www.HumanKinetics.com

....

CHAPTER 34

CONSERVATORY TEACHING AND LEARNING

....

MARY KING AND JOHN NIX

INTRODUCTION

THE progression from enthusiast to professional is sometimes marked by full-time training in a conservatory. By a conservatory, we mean an institution that one enters instead of a university, although many conservatories have been absorbed by universities or have made changes in their curricula to fulfill accreditation standards set by national associations governing higher education. Many institutions offer full-time study, and while course content varies from site to site, more similarities than differences exist between schools, certainly within any one genre of singing. Immersion in full-time study brings many benefits, as students are surrounded by similarly focused individuals. Conservatories fill their teaching staffs with dedicated teachers and experienced professionals who have in-depth knowledge of what is required to move from aspiration to reality. The more informed students are about vocally suitable genres of music that pique their interest, and the more they understand how they compare to entry-level standards, the easier school selection and the course of study will be.

To maximize the benefits of conservatory training, attending at the appropriate time is vital. This start of training will vary from student to student. It is equally vital to be aware of the many advantages that conservatory training can bring, as well as the pitfalls that may trap the unwary or unprepared.

THE SELECTION PROCESS

Entry to a conservatory is typically done through a live audition at the college of choice, although this is not always the case for students wishing to study in foreign countries, in which case videos may be accepted. Policies vary with the institution and the country.

Students are required to demonstrate both sufficient natural vocal talent and technical competence. All students are measured against the faculty's opinion of national and international standards, so the competition that singers face can be extreme. Hundreds of singers might apply for as few as ten places in a program. Conservatories also must balance voice types across a year group wherever possible, although this is secondary to the talent level (e.g. they would rather have three excellent sopranos than one excellent soprano, a poor tenor, and an immature bass).

It is usual for incoming students to have some academic musical achievement; an understanding of musical theory and notation is a help, although it is possible to fast-track these skills if a student is a late starter. Many conservatories have changed their focus from purely practical to academic, or a combination of practical and academic, to articulate with the demands of being a part of a university system.

There are no fixed ages attached to courses of study, although there are guidelines. All decisions will depend on an interface between biological age, vocal development, and talent. It is important to recall that mastery of the singing voice develops much later than other instruments. While a young pianist in France might begin conservatory training at age 6, in parallel with regular school courses, a singer would not commence training intensely until many years later. As a guideline, the following ages apply:

- musical theater programs aimed at dancers may have singers as young as 16 at point of entry;
- most undergraduate programs will have singers of 18 and above (although in some countries it is quite normal for students to begin in their twenties);
- postgraduate students can range from early to late twenties;
- entry to a conservatory beyond age 30 is unusual, although not impossible, particularly with late developing lower voices or larger voices, or in the case of musical theater courses, and the majority of the student body will be in the 20–30 age range.

TRAINING PROGRESSION FOR CLASSICAL
AND MUSICAL THEATER SINGERS

A typical classical singer's training may include some or all of the following elements:

- private lessons with a teacher;
- undergraduate conservatory or university study;
- study of languages;
- postgraduate conservatory study;
- opera course in a conservatory:
  - in some countries, such as the USA, this would be combined with the postgraduate work;
  - in others, such as Sweden, opera courses are provided by a separate institution from the primary conservatory;
- opera studio;

- young artist Program (typically linked with a professional company)—in the USA, such programs can occur in summers between academic terms as early as the later stages of undergraduate study.

At any point between phases, time may be taken to add personal programs of study.
    An aspiring musical theater singer's training might include:

- private study with a singing teacher, along with group instruction in acting and dance;
- undergraduate conservatory or university study;
- public performances (paid or unpaid);
- postgraduate conservatory.

As before, at any point between phases, time may be taken to add a personally-directed program of study. Not all conservatories in all countries offer musical theater programs.

Entrance to an undergraduate program

At the undergraduate level, students will be requested to prepare a number of songs, all of which should demonstrate sufficient musical understanding, vocal quality, and some level of communicative skill. The songs should demonstrate variety in style, tempo, and character. This would be true for any genre of music at any conservatory. There may well be specific requirements that encourage this variety, such as requirements for a recitative, an operatic aria, an art song in each major foreign language, etc. For those embarking on a classical vocal pathway, students should also demonstrate sung linguistic competency in at least one other language.
    At an audition, singers typically choose their first song. Following this, the audition panel will determine whether they want to hear any more. Since the number of singers to be heard outstrips the number of places for study, most conservatories use some method of fast-tracked processing. Many schools request a pre-screening video on DVD or on-line (www.youtube.com, etc.), in order to invite only the singers they are truly interested in auditioning in person. Even with pre-screening, a faculty might hear sixty students in the morning, with several audition panels running simultaneously hearing each singer for five or ten minutes, then make a "cut," recalling only selected singers to be heard by a single panel. There are several processes that might be used with these recalled singers; for example, students might take a brief lesson with one of the faculty teachers; in other cases, sight reading and musicianship tests might be administered. In many schools, students will have a brief interview with the faculty. Singers should expect any of these, as well as more singing.
    Singers who are applying for musical theater programs at drama colleges will be required to prepare spoken monologues, and will do some form of dance or movement workshop. These are given different priorities according to the specialization of the college: a curriculum for dancers who sing and act will weight movement sections of the audition more importantly than one for actors who sing and dance. Regardless of the emphasis, all

courses for musical theater will have a high percentage of movement in the curriculum. All conservatories give clear indications of their requirements; if in doubt, prospective students should ask the auditions coordinator.

Audition processes are intense. The panel has to keep in mind every singer they hear, gathering detailed notes on the recalled singers, so that singers may be compared fairly against each other at the end of the audition period.

Postgraduate auditions

At this level, singers will present more material; up to five songs/arias might be required (although not all may be heard), and they should be varied in style, language, tempo, and character. The panel will have a methodology for refining the process; there may be several rounds, where further auditions occur on different days with specific requests made. For musical theater, singers should expect the audition to involve workshop components, as well as singing prepared pieces. These assess how people work in a group, and how they spontaneously respond to creative instructions with no time for preparation.

Postgraduate courses demand high levels of skill and achievement. Such courses are less likely to accept students purely on raw talent. Students must demonstrate that they have the vocal and physical stamina to endure intensive study; this is why auditions are lengthy, so that endurance can be judged. There must also be a sense that students have potential for further development.

Students who audition to enter a conservatory at the postgraduate level without having done a related subject as an undergraduate will be expected to demonstrate a strong level of musical understanding. Classical singers must demonstrate a facility for singing in a language that is not their native tongue and for being expressive through language, rather than merely phonetically correct. They must be physically relaxed (although energized), have no self-consciousness about performance, and they must communicate well. Many young singers get distracted by technical matters to the extent that they forget the purpose of performance, which is communication. At the postgraduate level, this technical security should have already been acquired.

Pitfalls of the conservatory selection system

The selection system for conservatory admittance is harsh. There are many more people wanting to study professionally than there are places for them to do so. Some students have not had exposure to much competition—they have been a "big fish in a small pond," and have not had the means of measuring their ability in a broader context. Students are initially heard for a short amount of time; to succeed, they already must be technically stable enough to manage nervousness. Audition panels are very experienced at listening, but inevitably some good potential is missed.

Professional conservatory training is very rigorous. Singers in particular are vulnerable, as they can seldom blame something external for poor performance (unlike a string player, for example). All skill development comes with criticism attached, although hopefully also with encouragement. Potential professional singers must be emotionally robust, incredibly self-motivated, and healthy both physically and mentally. The singers who will most profit from conservatory training will be the ones who can adapt positively to new environments, who see problems as challenges, rather than obstacles, and who are so motivated by music itself that they have the emotional resources to endure difficult times.

STRATEGIES THAT ENHANCE SUCCESSFUL CONSERVATORY SELECTION

The system of selection, which measures current achievement, as well as potential, benefits those who have had the following:

- one-on-one lessons with skilled teachers from an early age;
- good all-round acquisition of musical knowledge;
- some language training;
- exposure to competition.

Much of this training is only supplied in the private sector, although this does differ from country to country. Usually, successful singers will also have had considerable emotional and financial support. At an audition it is not always possible to see how much input students are giving, and how much has been well-drilled by teachers. This may have an impact on how well the student will develop later on in the process.

It is important that prospective students and their families understand what they are undertaking. The decision to train professionally should not be decided on a whim. Fortunately, most conservatories offer visitation days and consultations. It is wise for aspiring singers to attend these events if at all possible. The head of the department or a trusted deputy who knows the college will hear singers, and advise them whether they have professional potential. If they do, the conservatory official can advise what their entry level should be. If they do not have the potential for success, advice can be given about whether or not admittance is a realistic goal, and if so, what is needed to achieve conservatory admittance.

SELECTING AUDITION REPERTOIRE

The importance of choosing appropriate audition repertoire cannot be over-estimated. Formulating this task is challenging, but the following should be considered:

- singers should be able to perform the piece at the volume and quality intended and at any time on any day of the week;

- repertoire lists should include carefully chosen works with technical difficulties that demonstrate singer achievement level;
- repertoire lists should have musical variety (different tempi, style periods, languages, etc.);
- singers should be able to emotionally and expressively communicate each piece on the list, displaying command of lyric diction in the process;
- all selections should be age, voice type, and body shape appropriate.

This last issue is one that often causes the most problems. More naïve classical singers try to sing works by composers such as Verdi before they are ready; similarly, musical theater singers attempt songs whose lyrics are intended for singers with more life experiences. Singers must balance demonstrating current skill with showing future potential. Advice should be sought from experienced musicians. This disadvantages those living away from major population centers. Singers should determine where their national centers of excellence are located so that consultations with working professionals can occur.

References

Conservatory applications generally require written references. These will usually be from a prospective student's principal study teacher, plus one or two other professional musicians. References help the panel gain greater understanding of the auditioning student's potential and character. It gives a context to support the practical performance they hear.

At the audition

The initial sung audition is critical. It is essential for singers to make a favorable first impression. Audition panels can see beyond nervousness; they expect that some ability to control performance anxiety has been acquired, which is usually proof of technical competency, and that there is interesting potential behind those nerves. In addition, auditioning singers should dress in flattering, tasteful clothing appropriate to the type of audition. Auditions with a dance component require different wardrobe choices than would an opera audition. Singers should also be able to interact verbally with the auditioning panel in a professional manner.

Curricula and student expectations

Once singers have been selected by a conservatory and their course of study has been determined, each student will be assigned to a vocal teacher. This may or may not be a teacher the student has requested.

In the majority of cases, there is a fixed curriculum of classes, which all students in that degree track follow. The specific components, and the frequency and duration of each component will vary from school to school, and country to country, but the curriculum will include some or all of the following:

- lessons with a singing teacher;
- vocal coaching sessions (less likely at the undergraduate level in some countries);
- possible sessions with a spoken voice teacher (especially in musical theater programs);
- language and/or lyric diction classes;
- vocal repertoire classes (operatic, oratorio, and song literature);
- secondary lessons on a different instrument, most commonly piano;
- choral or ensemble participation;
- movement classes (which may include various dance styles—waltz, polka, tap, jazz, modern, and ballroom) and possibly stage combat;
- improvisation classes (physical, musical, dramatic);
- harmony/musicianship/theory classes;
- music history courses;
- outreach/community engagement participation;
- open or selective workshops or master-classes with visiting teachers/professionals;
- internal competitions;
- public performance;
- juried performances evaluated by the faculty.

In some countries, additional general education requirements (courses in math, science, and the humanities) might be included in the curriculum.

THE SINGING TEACHER

Classical singers will generally have private lessons with their singing teacher once or twice a week. The details of this study depend upon each school; lessons can be of varying lengths according to the methodology and availability of the teacher, the academic guidelines of the institution, and each student's vocal experience and stamina. This teacher is dedicated to the singer's technical, expressive, dramatic, and musical development of his or her voice. Musical theater singers may have one individual session per week with their singing teacher, and in some schools, in pairs or small groups.

Teacher/student relationships are complex, and the results are hard to predict—some teachers work well for some students, and some do not. Nevertheless, the singing teacher is the most important person at the conservatory for any developing singer. At some colleges, teachers are still actively performing; this can take them away from the conservatory for considerable stretches of time. Some institutions supply a deputy to substitute for the primary teacher during absences; at other schools, lessons will be crammed together more intensely, with longer gaps between them. The earlier a singer is in his or her development, the more this factor is likely to affect progress. Most students learn to be self-sufficient incrementally. Any changes in technical approach need to be constantly refined and assessed, which is best done when lessons are regularly spaced at frequent intervals. The most crucial gift a teacher can provide for his or her students is the gift of independence. All students must learn with their teacher's guidance how to practice effectively alone, so that forward progress continues between lessons.

In general, the best teachers are those who are the most open and responsive, and who are keen to develop each singer into the best singer he or she individually can be, rather than turning out a clone of the teacher. Also, the best singing teacher may not be or have been the best performer. What is needed in a teacher is (a) a fine diagnostic skill; (b) many creative ways of solving problems once they have been analyzed; (c) patience and persistence in addressing problems; and (d) the ability to adapt his or her teaching style to the student's best way of learning. Often it is not the technical problems themselves that are the stumbling block in learning, but the terminology or methodology of delivering possible solutions.

Successful teachers are likely to have the following attributes:

- a profound involvement with singing and music, crafted over many years, and a proven track record with the teaching of singing;
- generosity to, and a deep interest in, a younger generation developing skills;
- the ability to be reflective and self-critical (not merely critical of students);
- sound musicianship and an openness to many styles of music within one genre;
- an awareness of other vocal and musical genres, and a basic knowledge of their requirements;
- a thorough knowledge of vocal anatomy, physiology, acoustics, voice development, and voice hygiene.

THE VOCAL COACH

The vocal coach is generally a pianist who possesses a good knowledge of vocal technique. He or she works with singers to help them develop musical skills across a range of styles and languages. Usually, this instruction is delivered through a weekly private session, and involves consultation with the singing teacher so that repertoire choices are in line with the technical development that is underway. Often there will be strong links between given voice teachers and coaches, so that if a singer works with Teacher X, he or she is likely also to be placed with Coach X.

In an opera training program, the coaches are usually experienced pianists/repetiteurs who work with opera companies. They may also serve as assistant conductors. In a musical theater training program, the coaches are frequently performing musical directors who are used to shaping an entire show, as well as looking at the details of one person's performance. The best have a broad knowledge of the repertoire and a stylistic awareness that covers everything from Legit (classical) singing to Pop and Rock.

SPOKEN VOICE INSTRUCTION

Spoken voice teachers are important in the musical theater singer's training, although unfortunately they are not always involved with the classical singer's training. The length of training sessions may vary, but they usually occur once weekly. These classes are designed to develop the resonance, power, and emotional range of the spoken voice. Musical theater singers will also experience coaching (in groups or in private) in dialect and accent, which is the theatrical equivalent to the language skills needed by classical singers.

OTHER COURSEWORK

Language study

There is much debate about the best way to develop language skills in singers. Some schools expect students to do their own training in language schools (or preferably, to begin college with high competency in any one of the performance languages—Italian, German, or French). Other schools deliver spoken word and conversational skills in seminar classes on a weekly basis. Some deliver language teaching through coaching sessions on the music, correcting and teaching the language only in reference to its being sung, where rules are often slightly different from those used in conversation.

Repertoire seminars

Performance seminars, repertoire classes, concert practice, or in the musical theater school, Acting Through Song, are group classes held weekly, where students sing in front of a coach and their peers. The purpose is to develop musical knowledge through practical performing and listening, in a non-public environment. Teaching in groups allows the sharing of information; students learn from each other, and increase their understanding of the expectations of the professional environment. The teachers of these classes hail from a variety of disciplines, including professional singing, vocal coaching, opera and musical theater conducting, and stage direction. What they will have is an in-depth knowledge of all aspects of the repertoire and usually fluency in specific languages. Classical singers might have a class on French and German song repertoire once a week, but there might also be classes on Italian repertoire, early music, and other specific genres and periods. There are often rotations for singing in these classes (e.g. not everyone enrolled sings every week).

Study of another instrument

Supplementary study, which usually occurs at the undergraduate level, is often offered or expected in another instrument. These secondary studies may involve group classes (particularly with piano) and private coaching and teaching, but in shorter durations than would be used with a student whose primary instrument is that instrument. It is not unusual for a singer to graduate from a conservatory after entering on another musical instrument; the singing voice's relatively late development often leads musicians to not be aware of singing potential until serious vocal study is undertaken.

ENSEMBLE CLASSES

Choirs and vocal ensembles are brilliant ways to develop sight reading, listening skills, musicianship, and to become immersed in some of the greatest music ever written. Debate flourishes about whether these pros are outweighed by the cons—that in choirs the individual voice must be surrendered to the corporate one, and that technique can suffer as a consequence. Choir is something students might do in their first year of studies, but not thereafter. In some countries, especially the USA, scholarships often are dependent upon choral participation throughout the entire course of study, even at the graduate level.

Movement and acting instruction

Movement classes are a vital part of all vocal training. They increase physical awareness (to correct poor postural habits) and help singers become physically confident, relaxed, and self-assured, all of which are part of a performer's essential skills. Depending on the genre, this work will be given different priority. Musical theater singers might do an hour of aerobic activity daily, and follow this with supplementary classes in fencing, partner dancing, jazz, and tap classes, while dance schools teaching musical theater might work on a much heavier dance timetable, with each day including five hours of dance classes in different disciplines. For classical singers, the movement demands are less, although increasingly staging for modern opera singers indicates that a high level of physical ability provides a distinct advantage to aspiring singers.

Some schools offer classes in other physical disciplines, such as Alexander Technique, Yoga, Pilates, Feldenkrais, T'ai Chi, and Dalcroze Eurhythmics. Singing involves coordination and physical self-awareness, and the solutions to technical problems are often found away from the vocal folds and vocal tract. All these disciplines increase body awareness. They can also enhance physical and mental flexibility, relaxation, and mental focus. All involve breath and the release of abdominal tension. As directors no longer necessarily specialize in art forms, but work in theater, film, TV, and opera, there are increasing demands upon singers to be convincing on stage—indeed, for their physical attributes to be very much a part of the all-round talent base. While one rarely sees size zero singers, physical appearance weighs heavily upon casting decisions.

Improvisation

Improvisation classes are an essential part of musical theater training, helping singers develop creativity, flexibility, and quick-fire responses. They are less represented in a classical singer's training, and often much mocked by staff and students alike as being irrelevant. They are also a part of the elective courses that students might take in community outreach music.

Academic coursework in music

Musicianship and music theory are taught in different ways, depending upon the institution. Delivery methods may include weekly class meetings, written and theoretical assignments, and practical classes. All classes, individual lessons, and coaching sessions are in a sense developing understanding and skill in all areas of musicianship. The student singer may be starting music theory study late if his or her voice developed late, or if school had few musical offerings. Music is a complex, multi-layered language, and all students should be taught to be as self-reliant as possible, so that they can learn music and understand notation without the intervention of a third party.

Depending on the conservatory and the exact nature of the curriculum, there will be some level of written work, including analysis of musical content of different styles and knowledge of the history of music. For singers pursuing a performance career, rather than an academic one, this is of great contextual importance. Original work is not required.

Some conservatories offer courses in pedagogy or in teaching music in the broader community. At its simplest level, this might be studying about teaching and learning skills, in order to progress to teaching of singing to adults or children. Additionally, there is in the UK a requirement to perform outreach in the broader community. Most schools undertake initiatives to encourage skill in this type of outreach teaching. Generally, these courses are elective, rather than compulsory. Course activities may involve simple tasks, such as taking a performance to a school or hospital, or could require more protracted work with a school class that might last several weeks. Training is often delivered through workshops with experienced professionals in the field, and typically uses musical and dramatic improvisation techniques to explore music and performance. This is an area undergoing much growth in Europe and the USA, but not in Australia and New Zealand.

Performance opportunities

Across the years of development of a classical singer in a conservatory, there are numerous opportunities for public performance. These may include:

- master classes with visiting professors and performers;
- competitions in designated musical styles (i.e. opera, *melodie*, English Song, *Lieder*) that are judged internally;
- public performances of staged opera scenes;
- song recitals (sometimes shared by several students).

Some of these opportunities are open to all interested students, while participation in others may be selected on a competitive basis.

Musical theater singers are often expected to take part in public performances of "straight" plays (i.e. where there is no singing) in order to challenge their acting skills further, and will generally have the same range of performance opportunities in songs, scenes, and shows as their classical peers. Agent showcases are also a vital part of the musical theater singer's experience. Typically, each singer has about 1 or 2 minutes of solo performance time, along with participation within an ensemble comprised of their entire year cohort. Some schools will devote the entire final year of a degree curriculum to a rolling program of shows to provide multiple casting opportunities to students. This is less the norm in classical training, as agents tend to go to public performances spread out throughout the year.

Rehearsal periods

In some conservatories, especially in the UK and Sweden, with postgraduate classical courses and musical theater curricula, there will be periods of time in the academic year when the majority of regularly scheduled classes are suspended and the students go into full-time rehearsal as they would in a professional job. Sometimes one-on-one classes continue in this period, such as singing lessons and coaching sessions, and sometimes even these are cancelled. The singer is engrossed in the requirements of a particular piece of work, and possibly is working with an artistic team (a conductor, stage director, and choreographer) that is totally new to them. This variety and immediate relevance to professional development is one of the ways that conservatories try to keep motivation high. In contrast, in countries such as the USA, such work is done within the context of a summer young artist's program outside of the conservatory setting.

Study weeks

Students are expected to be personally responsible for individual practice in their own time, organized efficiently around their class schedule. Singing teaching faculty will generally provide advice to students on how they should go about practicing, although some may expect students to be both motivated to practice and skilled at knowing how to do so before they come to a conservatory. Practice rooms are often at a premium in conservatories; this reality provides another reason for conservatory singers to know what to do when practice time and space are available. Some schools now have online systems for reserving a practice room. Being able to practice effectively in a space that is not ideal, or being resourceful to find a space that is readily available outside of the college (i.e. church hall, church, friend's room) will help progress.

Some conservatories have some weeks designated as study weeks. These are often seen as catch-up times, providing more breathing space to students and faculty for the consolidation of information. Such times can also allow more time for self-generated practice, for one-time classes or week-long projects in place of the regular multi-themed course timetable. The student who cannot practice effectively will not gain much from these periods.

Mental preparation (see also Chapters 32 and 33)

Singers have to fight hard to get into conservatories; once there, all kinds of mind sets emerge, ranging from complacency to despair. Very little psychological testing is done before entry;

aptitude for study is assessed by referring to the testimonials supplied by the prospective student's former teachers.

Success in music is not merely a matter of superior talent; it is a combination of talent, motivation, mental strength and skills, health, encouragement, luck, guidance, and the ability to process information that is sometimes conflicting. In singing, as in sport, much is about mind set and motivation; self-belief is essential. Maintaining the will to keep going when progress is slow requires energy and creativity. Not all conservatories recognize this: when musicians face disappointments and hurdles, they are expected to be self-reliant—to "toughen up" or "get used to it." There is a general scarcity of mental training for musicians in many conservatory programs.

THE UNPREDICTABLE HUMAN VOICE

Voices, possibly more than any other instrument in music, are individual, with each one literally a reflection of the human genome, and their development is complex. To sing well is reasonably easy; to sing very well is hard; and to sing at the very top professional level and be consistently employed for thirty years is very difficult indeed. As with all learning, understanding deepens over time. What complicates the situation is that voices change over time and with continued training. These changes can be at a fundamental level and can occur quite unpredictably. For example, light sopranos on entry to a conservatory could develop into mezzos or dramatic sopranos over time, and they might also remain as light lyric voices just as they were at age 20. Could anyone have predicted that Joan Sutherland would have transformed from a dramatic soprano to the premiere coloratura soprano of her generation? These changes can be confusing to both students and teachers, and careful monitoring and emotional support is needed during training.

Ongoing training, advanced study, and apprenticeships

Conservatory training can take up to seven years, with undergraduate and postgraduate study, and an opera course. Some singers take all levels within the same institution, but more often, singers move to a different institution, either abroad, or within the same city or country. A fresh start can often accelerate learning.

Singers at this level must examine why they are embarking on further study. What more do they need to know? For the majority, postgraduate work will only be useful if the vocal technique is stable enough to take advantage of the increased workload and exposure to the public.

Advanced study through an opera course is an indication that the singer has decided what his or her speciality will be. Operatic voices develop over a long time: it is not unusual for basses to still be in college after age 30. In these courses, there is more time for individual work; coaching and vocal teaching remain the cornerstones of the course schedule. Preparation for and rehearsals of performances of operatic scenes and complete operas (usually one per term, although dependent on the stage of the student) now take up more time than formal classes. Students have the frequent experience of working with orchestras and conductors, directors, and choreographers, of managing costumes and props, and experiencing the gruelling demands of technical rehearsals. The teacher's role may be quite passive, such as being present at rehearsals, and providing technical and emotional support. At this point, nothing should be allowed to de-rail the singer before such performances, as agents and influential persons are often in the audience.

Some conservatories offer one-year postgraduate courses as an accelerated track for:

- those who have sung extensively, but not at a conservatory; or
- those who have been working in a semi-professional way; or
- those who have taken time out between undergraduate and postgraduate study while their voices mature or information is consolidated.

These courses are very intense, and feature very concentrated scheduling, particularly in the case of musical theater. They only suit people who have a high level of skill, a burning hunger for performance, and possess the emotional maturity to cope with the barrage of information directed at them.

There are further bridges between study and full employment. It is now common for students in their final year of study to have substantial though short-term professional engagements—an opera season, for example, or a run of a musical—while still theoretically in full-time conservatory study. These singers will have gone through rounds of auditions to receive these contracts, and will be heard alongside young professionals who have finished their training, but are seeking the same jobs.

There are concert opportunities throughout training, and singers are usually encouraged to accept such work, although they may be first required to seek the permission of their teachers and other conservatory officials; longer contracts are a more recent thing. Students might even return to college after a longer engagement and do further study. In a sense, this is the performing parallel to teaching practice (in the USA, student teaching or a teaching practicum), when studying to be a teacher, where a student might spend one term in college, one term teaching in a school, and then a final term back in college.

There are also apprentice-like schemes for shadowing professional choral and ensemble singers. These programs are not as yet consistent across the sector, and the type of experiences offered to singers are dependent upon the conservatory's philosophy as much as its funding.

Some singers take a break or pause before the next level of training, devising personal courses of study to bridge levels, as there is a large leap in expectations between postgraduate in-conservatory training, and opera studios and young artist residencies. This requires an ability to evaluate strengths and weaknesses, and then to try and fill in the gaps. It also requires the ability to work with new teachers who specialize on micro-technical matters, to work on movement, or to perform more at the professional–amateur apex in order to get more stage experience. For those who are singers who began vocal studies later, such a break can be used to fill knowledge gaps. There are companies, organizations, universities, and other higher education establishments who offer part-time (and often evening-based) study, not all of which is formally accredited. In some cases, singers may choose to get away from formal learning altogether in order to refocus intentions.

Intensive programs of study at dedicated centers like opera studios, where a very small number of singers are accepted for one or two years of work, are a feature of many countries.

There might only be ten singers in each cohort, and this limited size allows a much more individual approach, although the singers are encouraged to work as a team, with very strong bonds often developing between the year group. Voice lessons with the singer's choice of teacher are the focus of the work, but also coaching with visiting professionals from the opera world. The facilities can vary, but at best they provide dedicated space for each student to work uninterrupted whenever they like. Tuition is provided in all areas of work, and there are usually showcase-type performances, rather than whole operas, as the range of singers will be quite broad (Heldentenors mixing with soubrettes, for example). What is suited to the individual singer is the focus here, and how each singer compares with the gold standard of the best singer in that vocal *Fach*.

Studios often have regular visits from casting directors, as well as coaches, conductors, and dramatic directors. The standard required for performer entry is already something of a guarantee of quality. The further up the rungs a performer climbs, the more likely he or she will be able to secure financial support for training.

Young artist programs

Most opera companies run development programs for encouraging emerging professionals. These may be informal, such as taking a long-term interest in how a singer is going to develop, especially if the singer has a rare voice type, such as a genuine contralto or a potential Heldentenor. In this informal case, the relationship might amount to little more than occasional coaching sessions with a member of the music staff, the outcomes of which are reported back to the artistic director or the casting department. These sessions would be free to the singer in question. At the more formal end of the spectrum, there are "in house" young artist programs, which may be funded by specific individuals. This is the *crème-de-la-crème* of learning environments, and these opportunities are only offered to the very finest of singers.

For a singer to be accepted for these programs, many layers of scrutiny will be involved. There will be coaching sessions, regular auditions, and stage auditions (where the singer is on the stage of the operatic house in question, rather than in a small room where regular auditions are held). In many cases, geography permitting, potential young artists will have been heard in staged performances at their conservatories by opera company scouts, or at least will have been recommended by people who have heard them in live operatic performances. Before singers even audition, there are ways of assessing what their level is likely to be, and whether they will be of interest.

If the singer is lucky, he or she will have more intensive coaching, paid vocal lessons, and understudying of principal roles. Singers will study entire roles, rather than merely the solo highlights, regardless of whether there are actual performances in mind. This role study is dependent on the repertoire choices of the company, which will in the vast majority of cases of course have been fixed before the young artists are selected for any given year. Not all understudying will lead to "going on" in the event of an emergency; it will depend on how close the young artist is getting to the standard required.

Whenever possible, young artists will be cast in comprimari roles. This provides the experience of being in the performance and working with the very best national and international artists as a professional equal. Outside of a young artist program, most young singers work their way up through smaller companies. Progress is marked in two ways: through continuing employment in supporting roles in successively larger companies, or by performing larger roles within the same level of (smaller) company. Smaller companies in this context refers to smaller performance spaces, smaller orchestras (or even piano accompaniment), smaller budgets, smaller casts (i.e. less chorus), and lighter voices. There is a very big difference between this and the experience of the young artist, who is to some extent protected from this type of career progression.

While giving young artists no guarantees, companies selecting them are providing in-depth monitoring, feedback, and nurturing. They also provide the artists access to a vast network of other singers, conductors, pianists, directors, and audience members, all of whom could provide links to future work.

This kind of young artist program has no real parallel in the musical theater business, although it does in the acting world, in the sense of having a resident company of performers who perform a number of different roles in a single season.

Summary

There are no certainties about conservatory training. Attending a superior school provides no guarantee of success; neither does being blessed with physical beauty, possessing a wonderful singing voice, or having a wonderful skill for dramatic communication. The professional music world is highly competitive, and those who are open to the challenge tend to be physically robust, energetic, musically- and dramatically-gifted individuals who are *certain* of their need to contribute to that world.

There are many starting points for an emerging professional:

- the aural traditions of a church or the notated ones of a choir;
- being well-schooled in conventional musical theoretical tradition or self-taught and inspired by commercially successful contemporary stars.

Teachers must ensure that they can deliver a fit-for-purpose training across a wide spectrum of styles and singers, so that all the musical styles of the world can be developed and tutored at the very highest levels. This is what the conservatories of the world offer. Conservatories and their faculties must be able to adapt to a changing musical world.

Questions for further reflection and inquiry

1. How can conservatories encourage students to become more entrepreneurial and proactive in developing opportunities for themselves?
2. The learning needs of elite performers in training are highly individual. How do current curricula and educational timetables meet these needs? What adaptations are

necessary for curricula and teaching/learning schedules to become more flexible in content and delivery?

3. Many aspects of conservatory training are very traditional, with little change having occurred for many, many decades. How can innovation be best balanced with the successful traditions for the benefit of the students?

4. How can conservatory teaching faculties be fairly assessed for teaching fitness? Should conservatory faculties be populated with experienced performers, academically-trained pedagogues, or a mixture?

5. Active performers who teach in conservatories may have performing engagements, which take them away from campus for extended periods. Do students learn as well when being taught once or twice a week for ten weeks at a time compared with four times in ten days, and then not at all for weeks?

6. In some countries, conservatories are being required to become more academically-based and are less able to select based on purely vocal potential. Does this promote or hinder the widest intake of students?

ACKNOWLEDGMENT

The authors wish to recognize the following individuals who provided additional comments and perspective to this chapter: Professor Jean Callaghan (AUS), Ms Christine Debus (FR/USA), Dr Katherine Eberle-Fink (USA), and Dr Anna Hersey (SWE/DEN/USA).

SUGGESTED WEBSITES

Conservatoire National Supérieur de Musique et de Danse de Paris. Available at: M http://www.conservatoiredeparis.fr
Guildhall School of Music and Drama. Available at: http://www.gsmd.ac.uk
Hochschule für Musik und Theater Hamburg. Available at: M http://www.hfmt-hamburg.de
The Juilliard School. Available at: M http://www.juilliard.edu
Kungliga Musikhögskolan i Stockholm. Available at: M http://www.kmh.se
Oberlin Conservatory. Available at: M https://new.oberlin.edu/conservatory/
Royal Academy of Music. Available at: M http://www.ram.ac.uk
Royal Conservatoire of Scotland. Available at: M http://www.rcs.ac.uk
Toronto Royal Conservatory. Available at: M http://www.rcmusic.ca
Sydney Conservatorium. Available at: M http://music.sydney.edu.au

....

CHAPTER 35

PEDAGOGY OF DIFFERENT SUNG GENRES

....

JEREMY FISHER, GILLYANNE KAYES,
AND LISA POPEIL

INTRODUCTION

THE role of vocal pedagogy is to explore, to learn, and ultimately to be able to impart the intricacies of each vocal genre to the next generation while honoring traditions and values. This chapter acknowledges that the assessment of excellence in singing is closely linked with cultural esthetics. Each genre will be reviewed in light of its cultural expectations and how these expectations translate into style idioms and in turn have an impact on function in singing. Key aspects of pedagogical approaches of different genres will also be discussed.

GENRE AND SINGING PEDAGOGY IN THE TWENTY-FIRST CENTURY

Until very recently, singing pedagogy has been heavily influenced by the performance practice and esthetic of the Western lyric tradition, sometimes called classical music. Western lyric music seems to have held a uniquely authoritative status compared with other genres which have existed alongside it (Potter 1998), and this appears to have contributed to widespread thinking that classical is the best or, indeed, the only type of singing pedagogy. So strong is this influence that Green (2001) reports that popular musicians often feel inferior to classical musicians, and that these popular music vocalists were seeking training from classical singers.

An umbrella term, coined by pedagogues to describe what had previously been referred to as non-classical singing, is a good indicator that the hegemony of classical music is waning. The authors regard the non-pejorative term contemporary commercial music (CCM) as a useful opposite to Western lyric (LoVetri and Means Weekly 2003). It should be noted that CCM and Western lyric are each over-arching categories, containing different genres and cultures of performance practice. A recent proliferation of courses and new exam boards targeted specifically at CCM singing genres is also indicative of change. An internet survey of 805 singing teachers spanning six continents showed that 91.6 percent are teaching CCM singing genres (Fisher et al. 2011). In a 2006 workshop run by the Incorporated Society of Musicians for singers and singing teachers, focus groups identified issues that were of concern (Incorporated Society of Musicians 2006):

1. Is there a basic singing technique which is then adapted to the style? [It is assumed here that the group meant musical style which implies different musical genres.]
2. How do you change from a classical style to a pop sound?
3. Is it important for singing students to learn about different styles of singing?
4. Specialization—is it detrimental to your ability in other genres?
5. Is your voice naturally suited to one style?
6. Can or should a teacher be teaching an awareness of different vocal styles?

It is encouraging that such discussions are taking place in professional organizations, but the questions indicate only a basic understanding of the needs of CCM genres. Well-established training courses for jazz singers exist in Europe, the United States, and Australia, as do a number of specialist training courses for musical theater, but training for other CCM genres is in its infancy. To date the authors are aware of only one university validating a specialist CCM pedagogy program—Shenandoah Conservatory, Winchester, VA, USA.

Table 35.1 outlines the genres to be discussed in this chapter. In a chapter of this length it is impossible to include the multiplicity of CCM genres that exists. Therefore discussion is limited to genres that have outlasted their original era and have evolved over several decades. For this chapter we have excluded rap, as its requirements are different from genres that require sung pitch. In addition, we have excluded world music such as Chinese opera and indigenous folk singing as being outside of the scope of the chapter and beyond our expertise.

Table 35.1 Genres discussed

Western lyric	CCM
Opera	Musical theater
Art song	Jazz
Early music	Commercial
	Pop
	Rock
	R&B including soul
	Country

CCM, contemporary commercial music; R&B, rhythm and blues.

GENRE, IDIOM, VOICE

Genre specification allows for categorization of different types of music according to broad parameters, just as films are genre-categorized by producers. Some genres are linked to a historical era or a set of social circumstances, such as stories of enslavement or the youth movement of the 1960s; others may be linked to broader movements such as the Renaissance or the Enlightenment. Western lyric music is largely a written form; boundaries between the genres are well established and clearly defined by composer, country, or era. Most CCM genres are based on an aural tradition, where the material is passed on by ear or recording and is often not written down unless commercial demand requires it. Even when published, CCM musical scores rarely represent the notes performed by the original singer.

Genre

In CCM music, genre is defined by the audience (the market) (Frith 1998). An important cultural difference between the two over-arching categories is that in CCM genres it is normally the artist who is categorized, not the composed material. New bands and singer/songwriters, in order to gain an audience, will either fit existing genres or attempt to create their own. Indeed, the twenty-first century is the only century so far where new artists stand a chance of creating an entirely new genre or geographical market due to the proliferation of internet music production. This makes finding and keeping an audience much cheaper than previously.

An enormous amount of CCM is being created daily for internet sites such as iTunes, Pandora, and Spotify. Individual singers might be identified by a particular genre, but may well release a song that is categorized in a different genre. The charity album "Red Hot and Blue" released in the 1990s featured songs by Cole Porter sung by twenty singers of different genres. An established artist such as Robbie Williams may be categorized as a pop/rock singer but may also issue an entire album as a swing singer. An iconic CCM vocalist such as Aretha Franklin can rightly be termed a pop singer, a rhythm and blues (R&B) singer, a gospel singer, and even a blues shouter. There is no overall consensus regarding terminology in CCM singing, and the meaning of the terms used to discuss it may well change as individual genres evolve.

In musical theater it is the work that is categorized, not the artist, making this genre closer to its Western lyric counterpart, opera. In this sense musical theater is an outlier in the CCM category, because like opera it is a written form. Unlike opera, the same musical theater composer may well write in several genres. For example, consider some of the works of Andrew Lloyd Webber (*Jesus Christ Superstar* is a rock musical; *Phantom of the Opera* is an operetta musical) and Steven Sondheim (*Pacific Overtures* is an operatic musical; *Assassins* contains folk-pop and country influences). Moreover, musical theater composers may well include different genres within the same musical (e.g. *The Full Monty* contains folk-rock, funk, and vaudeville). This panoply of genres has an important impact on the requirements for musical theater training.

Idiom

In this chapter we use the term idiom to denote the interpretive elements of phrasing, note and word articulation, the use of dynamics, vibrato, and degree of improvisation. Word articulation is here defined as the degree of appropriate clarity of diction necessary to authenticate a genre. These idiomatic behaviors are sometimes called vocal effects.

Voice

In Western lyric pedagogy, it is conventional to refer to four established principles of voice: respiration, phonation, resonation, and articulation. In a paper produced by the American Academy of Teachers of Singing in support of CCM voice pedagogy (American Academy of Teachers of Singing 2008), the authors remark: "While it is true that all singers must breathe, phonate, resonate, and articulate, they do not necessarily approach these technical elements in the same manner." Pedagogues may use different terminology in their studios to communicate these concepts to their students. Here are some important substrata, including common pedagogical terms, of the four principles listed above:

- respiration—breath use, support, airflow, lung volume;
- phonation—pitch range, voice categorization, register, degree of vocal fold adduction;
- resonation—voice quality, formant tuning, vowel modification;
- articulation—balance of vowel to consonant, consonant placement, degree of clarity (including use of co-articulation), linguistic base (e.g. Italianate vowels, pseudo-American vowels, regional accent).

Some of the above embrace more than one category—for example, breath use implies both respiratory and phonatory behavior.

Characteristics of genre

Table 35.2 gives broad guidelines on the skill requirements and performance characteristics of each genre.

Use of voice in different sung genres

Pitch range and voice categorization

Since the nineteenth century, singers in the Western lyric tradition have been expected to sing the notes and rhythms shown in the score. A smooth and even tone across the pitch range, with the ability to grade dynamic changes, is a key skill in all Western lyric singing, and this has led to specific ways of training singers whether performing opera, early music,

Table 35.2 Culture and performance practice of different sung genres

	Culture of performance	
	Expected skills and environment	Main characteristics
Western lyric		
Opera	Acoustic. Venues are large-scale with substantial orchestral accompaniment; music reading required	Theatrical but vocal beauty over-rides intelligibility of the text. Must be audible above the orchestra. Grand emotions, refined phrasing. Performed by singers, not actors
Art song	Acoustic. Size of venue varies, often accompanied by one instrument; music reading required	Lyrics and poetic content of text important but vocal beauty still paramount. Subtle timbre changes may be used to depict mood and words. Performed by singers
Early music	Acoustic. Small-scale venues and light instrumental accompaniment; music reading required	Voice must be audible over instruments. Ornamentation based on historical records required. Subtlety and elegance of phrasing; song forms require poetic sensibility. Performed by singers
Musical theater		
1927–1964: early	Originally acoustic but modern practice includes amplification of singers and orchestra. Dance skills required. Some performers may read music	Theatrical and dramatic content more important than the voice. Intelligibility of the text is paramount. Characterization often delineated by different musical writing and voice types. Content ranges from light comedic, glamorous, and dreamlike to darker themes of war, loss of loved ones, and murder
1964 onwards: contemporary	Venues may be small (50–1700 seats), but nearly always include amplification. Dance skills not always necessary but good stagecraft is a must. Some performers may read music	As above. Dramatic contrasts within the same song now common for the same character. Many commercial forms absorbed into the genre, requiring performers to be multi-genre skilled. Performed by actors and actor–singers. Content may be comedic, satirical, dark, intellectual, political, often reflecting mores of the decade
Commercial		
Pop	Small coffee-houses to 100,000 in outdoor arenas. Amplified, with small instrumental group, often with background vocalists and dancers. Music reading not required; dancing skills often required	Simple, direct lyrical content. Simple musical setting, often not requiring range and power in vocal abilities. Emphasis on dancing and singers' appearance. Special stage effects such as lights and multimedia displays

(continued)

Table 35.2 Continued

	Culture of performance	
	Expected skills and environment	Main characteristics
Rock	Small clubs to 100,000 in outdoor arenas. Amplified, with small instrumental group. Music reading not required	Simple and sometimes undecipherable lyrical content. Simple musical setting. Requires vocal power and stamina. Special stage effects such as lights, explosions. Emotions are histrionic, sexual, rebellious, aggressive
Country	Small coffee-houses to large concert halls. Acoustic and amplified, with small instrumental group singing background vocals. Music reading not required	Simple, direct lyrical content reflecting modern-day relationship issues, work, and philosophy typical in the southern American working class. Male emotion tends towards repression; female emotion tends towards self-assertion. Musical settings simple, often not requiring vocal range or power. Emphasis on in-tune harmonic group singing; interaction with audience
R&B (including soul)	Concert halls, 100–20,000 seats. Amplified, with instrumental group, often with background vocalists and dancers. Music reading not required, dancing skills required	Repetitive lyrical motifs; rhythm-based music. Improvisational vocal and instrumental technique. Strong focus on movement and dancing. Highly sexual or romantic subject matter; emotions include assertive, exhortative, labile, ecstatic
Jazz		
Jazz	Often small-scale venues and informal atmosphere; audiences usually well-informed about the genre. Pitch accuracy, awareness of harmonic structure and rhythmic stability required. Music reading not necessarily a requirement but good musicianship is important. Strong emphasis on each performance as a new arrangement of existing material and as a collaborative effort between singer and instrumentalists	Emphasis is on ensemble rather than individual voice. Melodic and rhythmic improvisation expected. Lyrics very important; includes vocal imitation of instruments. Content may range from simple and direct to witty, clever, playful. Emotions reflect mature love, often meditative

or art song. Western lyric singers are normally categorized by voice type or *Fach*. This *Fach* system is not based simply on range; timbre and voice size are also important factors, as is vocal agility, the dramatic weight of the voice, and—often less important—the singer's appearance and personality. Richard Miller (1986, p. 161) writes that "an amazingly high percentage of all vocal writing for any category of singer is contained within the range of a tenth." In actuality, it is expected that a Western lyric singer will possess a working range of two octaves (Chapman 2006).

In writing about rock, pop, and soul singers, Zangger Borch (2005) reports that while a vocal range of about two octaves is common amongst professional vocalists, the positioning of those two octaves is not particularly important since singers will transpose songs to suit their own abilities. Inventing individual nuances, using alternative timbres within genre expectations, and putting one's own stamp on a song are requirements of these genres and are considered more important than singing in a specified range; it is also perfectly acceptable for singers to transpose songs into keys best suited to their voice. While it is impossible to generalize the expected range for songs under the umbrella of "commercial" used for this chapter, it is significant that many songs of the Great American Songbook have a written range of a tenth. Songs with a range of as little as a seventh are not uncommon in commercial genres (Bob Dylan's "Blowin' in the Wind" is a case in point).

Jazz singers may use a broad range while scatting (a form of vocal improvisation performed on nonsense syllables): ranges of two octaves are not uncommon and vocal agility is required for successful scatting, as can be heard in Ella Fitzgerald's performance of "One Note Samba" (1969) (<http://www.youtube.com/watch?v=PbL9vr4Q2LU>).

In musical theater, a singer's appearance and casting type are likely to override voice type when being chosen for roles (Kayes and Fisher 2002). In addition, musical theater is unique in its range specificity for professional audition purposes, for example, "soprano legit to high C, belt to upper E."

Registration

Register terminology in singing pedagogy is highly contentious; it is not the aim of this chapter to contribute further to these debates. Registration is an aspect of phonation, based on changing vocal fold shapes and vibratory patterns through the singer's range. The change points between registers (points of transition) may lead to changes in voice quality or loudness and sometimes to pitch instability. Singers of different musical genres will approach registration in different ways.

Scientific research has demonstrated that the vocal folds vibrate differently in the different register mechanisms, each of which has distinctive features (see Lã and Gill, and Herbst et al., this volume). In this chapter we use the French numbering system for registers as our reference point. Thus: M0 (pulse, fry, strohbass); M1 (thick, heavy, modal, chest); M2 (thin, light, loft, falsetto), M3 (whistle, flageolet, or flute) (Henrich 2006). We acknowledge that this numbering system has its limitations in view of reported performance practice: particular issues are female use of the middle register in Western lyric singing and use of a mixed register in CCM singing, and differences between falsetto and head registers. From a voice science perspective, mechanisms cannot be mixed: the patterns of vocal fold vibration that define register mechanisms are mutually exclusive. Nevertheless, the practice of middle register/*voix mixte* and mixing are widely taught, especially in the female voice in both Western lyric and CCM singing styles. Specific genre requirements of registration will be discussed in detail under the respective categories of genre.

Within the Western lyric tradition, the goal of register blending or unification is highly prized. Audible differences between the registers are considered undesirable and a significant part of a singer's training is devoted to smoothing the transitions between registers.

Among voice scientists there has been much interest in the transition point between M1 and M2, often called the primary register transition. For those researchers who have investigated Western lyric singers, sometimes comparing them with naïve singers, there has been good agreement that this primary register transition is in the region of D4 to G4 in both the male and the female voice (Miller 2000; Titze 1988). The pedagogical and musicological literature indicates that the use of chest voice above these pitches in females is unacceptable. Male singers of Western lyric music, unless they are categorized as male alto or countertenor, rarely use falsetto register in performance settings. Some pedagogues teach blending of falsetto and chest in males as a way to find head register (confusingly also called mixing), but since falsetto and chest registers are two opposing modes of vocal fold vibration it is highly unlikely that this in fact occurs; an acoustic alternation on one of the two registers is more likely. To date, no research studies have found evidence of a separate middle register (Hollien 1974).

Use of registration in CCM is often very different from that in Western lyric singing. There appears to be less need for register blending; and transitions may well be exploited for expressive purposes, resulting in audible changes in mechanism characteristic of folk traditions and non-Western styles, such as yodeling and fry. In almost all the genres, females will use M1 more than their Western lyric counterparts, and there is good evidence that they will also take M1 (chest) higher in pitch, sometimes as high as D5. Anecdotal, written, and scientific investigations confirm that this more extensive and extended use of M1 is a key difference between Western lyric singing and CCM genres (Balog 2005; Björkner et al. 2006; LoVetri 2003). Female jazz singers of the European tradition may use a breathy or clear version of M2 (e.g. Astrud Gilberto, Norah Jones), whereas their African American counterparts are more likely to use M1 (L. Gibbs, personal communication, 13 December 2011).

The use of M2 (falsetto) in males is more acceptable in CCM styles except for country and rock (although much rock screaming is done by male singers in M2). Male R&B singers will frequently use M2 and may pitch their songs close to the transition point between it and M1 for expressive effect. M2 may be used by males in musical theater provided the dramatic content of the text implies it, or where there has been cross-fertilization with commercial genres (e.g. "Bring Him Home" from *Les Miserables*; "Sherry" from *Jersey Boys*). M1 is generally used by male jazz singers although M2 might be used in improvisation.

Vocal fry (M0) and whistle register (M3) may also be used in pop, rock, R&B, country, and jazz singing. These registers are seldom used in Western lyric singing. M3 is used for melodic improvisation by females in pop and R&B; M0 is widely used for expressive reasons in country, rock, jazz, and pop to suggest resignation, distress, and lassitude.

In musical theater singing it is essential for females to be proficient in M1 and M2 if they are to work regularly (Balog 2005; Kayes and Fisher 2002; Melton 2007). Two contrasting vocal styles used in musical theater singing are belting and legit. Musical theater belting is based on M1 and legit is characterized by frequent use of M2 in females. Belting is used by both males and females in musical theater singing, and it is not uncommon to hear female singers belting as high as E5 and male singers between A4 and D5.

Like their Western lyric counterparts, teachers and singers of CCM genres also talk about mixing, particularly in regard to female singers. Some even refer to this as "The Mix." Although both terms are much used, Bourne reports that teachers also express frustration with their lack of specificity (Bourne et al. 2011). Some recent research into the vocal fold characteristics of chest, chestmix, and headmix in female commercial singers found higher levels of adduction and thyroarytenoid activity during chestmix than in headmix or head, but less thyroarytenoid activity than in chest. Cricothyroid activity was found to be similar for head, headmix, and chestmix but was greater during chestmix, especially in the higher pitches (Kochis-Jennings 2008). Therefore these register subsets may result from varying degrees of vocal fold adduction, thyroarytenoid to cricothyroid activity, and formant tuning strategies.

Voice quality

In describing voice quality, singing teachers may use the terms timbre, tone, and voice quality interchangeably. For the purposes of this chapter, the term voice quality denotes a distinctive timbre held by the vocalist over several phonetic segments (Laver 1980). Changes in voice quality can be made at the vocal folds, in the vocal tract, or by an interaction between these (see Lã and Gill, Herbst et al., Story, and Sundberg, this volume).

Western lyric singing tends to feature a warm, clear tone, with variable degrees of intensity, according to the type of repertoire performed: the sound is neither harsh nor breathy. A balance of darkness and brightness (*chiaroscuro*) is required in operatic singing, and resonance settings must enable the voice to project above an orchestra. Peaks of harmonic energy, known as formants, can be adjusted by narrowing and widening the vocal tract. Certain areas of the vocal tract are known to impact on specific formants (see Story and Sundberg, this volume).

The singer's formant, also known as *squillo* or ring, is a common resonance strategy in Western lyric singing. Its use is considered essential by Chapman (2006) for vocal efficiency and longevity in operatic singing. According to Sundberg (1998), sopranos do not use the singer's formant, but many pedagogues report teaching this resonance strategy to both males and females. Chapman (2006), for example, uses Estill's twang exercises to elicit a singer's formant via sounds such as cackling or duck quacking. The darker timbral qualities used in Western lyric singing result from lowered vowel formants. Some pedagogues will teach a form of vowel neutralization by matching all the vowels to a low-backed vowel, with jaw retraction or lip-rounding achieving much the same effect. Early music singers are less likely to use a lowered larynx, as the style does not require a darker tonal quality.

The voice qualities used in CCM are more varied than in Western lyric singing, both between the genres and within individual performances. This perception is evidenced in the audio examples of the two song transcriptions (see Figures 35.1 and 35.2). Nasality, harshness, and breathy tone are allowable; timbres may also be edgy, speech-like, twangy, creaky, wailed, and yelled; and the style of articulation can be based on vernacular speech (Jungr 2002; Potter 1998; Soto-Morettini 2006). None of these is acceptable in Western lyric singing. Conversely, the characteristic deep, covered type of chest voice used by Western lyric singers is not heard in pop, rock, jazz, or country. Some female R&B singers do use dark, covered tonal qualities (e.g. Heather Small of M People). Male American jazz singers influenced by the gospel style may produce a rounded, full-bodied tone in their lower range, often associated with classical singing (e.g. Johnny Hartman). Researchers of country singing have noted links between the phonation modes of country singers and their habitual speaking voice (Hoit et al. 1996), and research into jazz, soul, and pop singing also indicates that phonation modes match either flow or neutral on Sundberg's scale of breathy/flow/neutral or normal/pressed (Sundberg et al. 2004).

Amazing Grace Jessye Norman

FIGURE 35.1 Transcription of "Amazing Grace" performed by Jessye Norman.

Breathy tone in many CCM genres is not only acceptable but also often desirable. Baken (1998) has noted that adding a little breath into the sound will "add velvet to the tone." This velvety tone is used in jazz, musical theater, pop, and R&B singing. In both jazz and pop, breathy voice might be produced on M1 or M2 in either gender and might range from slightly breathy to an almost whispered tone. A breathy quality would result from a voice source adjustment, implying a looser adduction than in clear-toned versions of M1 or M2 and a lower subglottal pressure. Recent research indicates that this sound quality (sometime called abducted chest) can be identified as a subset of M1 (Herbst et al. 2009). This tonal quality is well suited to singing with a microphone or other forms of amplification commonly used in CCM singing (see Herbst et al. and Sundberg, this volume).

Amazing Grace LeAnn Rimes

Key: ○ = falsetto   + = vocal fold fry   ↑ = sharp note (tuning)   ⤨ = yodel down

FIGURE 35.2 Transcription of "Amazing Grace" by LeAnn Rimes.

Twang is a distinctive quality that was researched in the 1980s by Estill et al. (1994), by Titze and Story (1996), and most recently by Sundberg and Thalén (2010). Perceptually it is bright and "narrow." Twang, whether described as "edge" by Sadolin (2000), or ring or forward tone, is regarded as useful for boosting intensity in the higher part of the singing range, since it can be made with thinned vocal folds (Sundberg and Thalén 2010). Twang is commonly heard and widely taught in CCM, especially in musical theater and country singing, and in the production of rock screaming. It may also be used in R&B (especially by female singers as a component of "wailing" voice quality) and pop.

Nasality is here defined as sound generated while the velum is partially lowered during vowel production (Laver 1980). Clear, non-nasalized vowels are produced when the velum is closed. Pedagogues and singers may be unclear about the source of nasality, often confusing it with twang. According to the above definition, nasality is rarely used in Western lyric singing (unless the language of origin demanded it, e.g. French) but it appears to be acceptable in all forms of CCM, depending on context. In musical theater singing, nasality is most commonly used where singers are using a regional accent and vernacular speech. Nasality can be heard in the commercial genres either as a result of co-articulation (where the vowel blends into the nasal consonant, or vice versa) or as a choice of sound quality. The most widely reported finding of nasality is a marked drop in intensity of the first formant (Björk 1962; Fant 1960; House and Stevens 1956). Perceptually, nasality results in a slightly duller and less resonant sound. This may be desirable in some subgenres.

Belting is a sound quality that may be heard in some of the CCM genres; it is a skill requirement for musical theater singers and is also used in rock singing, which requires high-intensity sounds in the high pitch range (Zangger Borch 2005). Belting may also be heard in some R&B singing, especially in female power ballads such as the late Whitney Houston's "I Will Always Love You." The practice of belting appears to have originated in traditional blues singing (blues "shouters" or "coon belters") and would have been heard in vaudeville (USA) and British music hall singing in the early part of the twentieth century. Belting is a high-intensity sound characterized by high subglottal pressure, a fast rate of vocal fold closure, and a high larynx position (see Herbst et al. and Story, this volume). Some pedagogues report subsets of belting including heavy belt, twangy belt, brassy belt, nasal belt, and speech-like belt (Sundberg et al. 2012).

Types of formant tuning may vary between CCM genres. In musical theater, Kayes (2004) reports a technique of medialization where the differences between the vowels are made in the center of the tongue, rather than between the front and the back. The resultant higher, fronted tongue position would be likely to adjust the second (tongue body) and third (tongue tip) formants, increasing the perception of a brighter tonal quality that is very characteristic of musical theater singing. Jazz singers may seek a darker vowel timbre; this would be achieved by strategies such as laryngeal lowering or lip-rounding. Some R&B and soul singers will use the R-colored or rhotic vowels in their pronunciation, as in the American [ɑɹ] (start), and this will have the effect of lowering the third formant, contributing to a perceptually darker sound. In Western lyric pedagogy such vowel coloring would be considered unacceptable and might be referred to as an impure vowel production.

Breath management and support

It is not the purpose of this chapter to debate different approaches to breathing. The mechanics and kinematics of different breathing styles have been adequately addressed by the research of Thomas Hixon; readers are referred to his excellent and approachable *Respiratory Function in Singing* (Hixon 2006) for further information and to Chapter 5 by Watson in this volume. However, the requirements for breath management are different for many CCM genres than for those of Western lyric, and these differences are now discussed.

A key term used by teachers of Western lyric and CCM is that of support. It is not always clear what is meant by support, and historically, there has been much controversy over how it is achieved. A useful and clear definition from *Dynamics of the Singing Voice* (Bunch Dayme 2009, p. 87) allows leeway for the many approaches to support used by pedagogues of all genres: "Support of tone is dependent upon maintenance of subglottic pressure. This is done by the maintenance of postural balance, including the position of the rib cage, which in turn allows the abdominal muscles and diaphragm to function efficiently." The adductive force of the vocal folds during any sung phrase will impact on the singer's use of breath support. Although research has not yet attempted to make inferences about a singer's breath support during the different phonation modes identified by Sundberg et al. (2004), it seems highly likely that these factors are linked in practice. Pressed and breathy represent extremes on this scale of measurement: in pressed phonation the adductive force is strong during vocal fold vibration, with minimal airflow during the open phase; in breathy phonation, the adductive force is weak (the vocal folds may not in fact meet) and air flows through the glottis during this partially closed phase. Two interim phonation modes are flow and neutral. In flow phonation, the vocal folds close snugly during the closed phase, but maximum air flows through the glottis during the open phase; neutral mode is neither breathy nor pressed, but airflow is not optimized during the open phase of vocal fold vibration.

The ability to manage breath over long phrases is a highly valued goal of Western lyric singing. Singers who do so employ high volumes of air together with 'flow' phonation mode (Thomasson and Sundberg 1997). Noisy inhalation is considered a sign of poor technique; inhalation should be silent except for special dramatic effects. Breath support is also considered to have an important role in projected singing (Thorpe et al. 2001).

Although CCM genres in general are artificially amplified, personal control of dynamics is nevertheless considered an important expressive tool. Many CCM genres include shorter phrases and a more conversational style, implying smaller lung volumes than in Western lyric singing. Lung volumes and breath patterns in male country singers have been found to be the same as for their speaking voice (Hoit et al. 1996). Twang voice quality is known to increase glottal resistance, which implies a lower airflow during sound production (Kayes 2004). Breathier sounds used in CCM (decreased glottal resistance) imply the need to breathe more often during phrases. Many CCM sounds are M1-based (speech-like), implying higher subglottal pressure, which means less air will escape through the glottis during phonation. For example, Zangger Borch (2005) reports that lung pressures are high in traditional rock, moderate in pop, and moderate in soul. It may be that smaller lung volumes (shallower breaths) are more suited to these types of phonation. Research comparing male operatic and Broadway singers found that subglottal pressures tended to be higher in the Broadway singers, which implies that at least some musical theater singing is closer to pressed phonation than flow (Björkner et al. 2006).

In CCM a variety of inhalation and even exhalation sounds can be used for expressive purposes. In addition, since silent inhalation is not a valued aspect of CCM performance, many CCM singers are completely unaware of any audible breathing sounds they may produce.

Outside of country singing, little research has been done on the breathing patterns and lung volumes of CCM singers. Almost all research into breathing behaviors has focused on the Western lyric tradition, classical actors, or naïve singers. We believe that, since numerous voice qualities may occur within one song in many CCM styles, a set breathing pattern is unlikely to suffice.

Idioms of different sung genres

The following transcriptions indicate some key differences between the over-arching categories of Western lyric and CCM genres. These performances of "Amazing Grace" (first verse) by Jessye Norman (opera singer; see Figure 35.1) and LeAnn Rimes (country singer; see Figure 35.2) can be found on YouTube.

Commentary on song transcriptions

Version 1: Jessye Norman

This version can be accessed at: <http://www.youtube.com/watch?v=8bsvJfPyB5o>. The tone is sustained throughout with a fast vibrato on all long notes. Most long notes have no dynamic shaping but remain at a constant volume. Each phrase is sung at approximately the same volume with only small variations for musical shaping. The phonation is M2 with just the lowest notes in M1. The extra grace notes shown are mostly distinct pitches used as fleeting approach notes. There is an element of under-pitching the beginnings of some notes. Care is taken to voice voiced consonants, although almost never on the target pitch. The phrases are long and the speed is very slow. Many vowels are darker than standard American, presumably to increase richness of tone; on the video footage Norman's jaw appears retracted much of the time and her tongue appears low and flat in her mouth.

Version 2: LeAnn Rimes

This version can be accessed at: <http://www.youtube.com/watch?v=iT88jBAoVIM>. The tone is not sustained with frequent changes of quality and volume. The sound is M1, with occasional flips into M2 (falsetto) and onsets in Mo. There are many more extra notes, used as melody and ornamentation. Vibrato is used on long notes. Breaths are taken in the middle of phrases or words, and extra syllables are included. The singer changes her style of pronunciation at will, often using different degrees of jaw opening. Some changes of vowel pronunciation during a word (for example the word "but" in bar 11) seem to coincide with ornamentation or register change—this contributes to an enhanced expressive effect.

The yodels between M1 and M2 (chest to falsetto and back) are a particular feature of country singing, indicating that Rimes is bringing her home genre (country) into a more pop-oriented style. She is also using R&B-based style idioms including the three-note drop on the word "sound;" this feature has now been adopted by mainstream pop vocalists. The head–torso relationship is noticeably different from that of Jessye Norman, with the head tilted up and forwards, contributing to the production of brighter, higher chest sounds.

Table 35.3 details various characteristic features of genres including a variety of tone onsets, note arrivals, tone offsets and note releases, phrasing choices, linguistic bases

Table 35.3 Key idioms of different sung genres

Vocal effects	Description
Tone onsets and arrival on target pitch:	
Glottal (gentle or strong)	Glottal closure precedes the onset of expiration and phonation
Aspirate: fast or slow	Expiratory airflow precedes glottal closure and phonation onset
Glide	Glottal closure is synchronized with the expiratory airflow and phonation
Note arrival:	
Fry	Note/word begins in M0 followed by a transition to M1 or M2
Yodel down	Note/word begins in M2 followed by a transition to M1
Yodel up	Note/word begins in M1 followed by a transition to M2
Squeeze	Note/word begins with voiced constriction (false vocal folds or pharynx) then releases into target pitch
Growl	Note/word begins with pharyngeal turbulence ("looser" than squeeze) then releases into target pitch
Pitch rise (distinct note or slide)	Note/word begins on lower pitch then steps or slides up to target pitch
Pitch fall (distinct note or slide)	Note/word begins on higher pitch then steps or slides down to target pitch
Short improvisation	Two to five notes added at speed before target pitch achieved (often based on non-diatonic scales)
Combinations include:	
Aspirate fast + glottal	Note/word begins with aspiration /h/, then glottal (causing sound to stop) before target pitch achieved
Squeeze + glottal	Note/word begins with constriction, then glottal (causing sound to stop) before target note/word achieved
Aspirate fast + squeeze	Note/word begins with aspiration /h/, then constriction added before target pitch achieved
Aspirate fast + pitch rise	Note/word begins with aspiration /h/, then lower pitch rising to target pitch
Tone offsets and note releases—completion of phonation plus exit from the target pitch	
All of the tone onsets and note arrivals listed above plus:	
Aspirate (fast) + short improvisation	Note/word begins with aspiration /h/, then two to five notes added at speed before target pitch achieved
Additional vowel (uh)	Schwa added to the end of the word
Vibrato fade	Note held without vibrato, then vibrato and diminuendo added
Combinations include:	
Pitch fall + aspirate (fast or slow)	Note/word ends with a drop in pitch and aspirate offset (the "fall/exhale")
Pitch rise + aspirate (fast)	Note/word ends with a rise in pitch and aspirate offset (the "rise/exhale")

Table 35.3 Continued

Vocal effects	Description
Short improvisation	Two to five notes added at speed before target pitch achieved (usually based on non-diatonic scales)
Short improvisation + aspirate (fast)	As above plus ending in aspirate offset

Bold text indicates vocal effects rarely heard in Western lyric performances.

(accents), use of vibrato, and clarity of enunciation. Note that since these texts are delivered in versions of English, we are limiting our comments on articulation for different genres to English. Readers may assume that similar adjustments to articulation are made in different languages where these apply.

IMPLICATIONS FOR PRACTICE

Key teaching and learning differences between genres

Although all singers need to breathe, phonate, resonate, and articulate (American Academy of Teachers of Singing 2008), the different performance cultures require different approaches in teaching practice and in student learning modes.

One obvious difference is the use of perceived vocal effort: in classical voice training, disguising effort is an important technical aim, while in popular genres display of effort, in order to appear more genuine or emotional, is often highly prized (Soto-Morettini 2006). In some CCM genres there is also a counter-culture towards acquisition of vocal technique which may be considered unnecessary or even a hindrance to getting the "groove," "feel," or "soul" required for authentic performance.

Classical training

In traditional classical voice education it is not uncommon for a singer to train exclusively and for a long duration with one teacher. Progress towards excellence in the many skills required is slow, often taking years of private study for singers to be able to compete at a world-class level. As in ballet, classical singers usually continue studying and refining their craft with a teacher and/or voice coach throughout their careers.

In the early part of training, exploration of one's voice is more highly valued than imitation of celebrated classical singers in the journey towards excellence. Traditional techniques involving imagery and kinesthetic awareness of vibration in the resonators are still widely used today. Vocal training exercises are used extensively prior to song choice and early live performing in this genre is discouraged. As training progresses, especially if the student is on a path leading to an operatic career, some focus is placed on the concept of finding one's *Fach*, the subclassification of voice type based on range, voice size, and timbre. The *Fach* system allows for easy placement of professional singers into roles by opera companies.

CCM training

In CCM there are successful singers who have had little or no professional training. These singers may only seek advice when confronted with technical disability or voice loss. Until the 1990s there were few singing teachers who specialized in these genres, and many of these teachers developed their approaches outside traditional methods. Most self-titled CCM voice coaches (or vocal coaches) are consulted by clients (i.e. students) in every aspect of vocal education, including career consultation, recording techniques, vocal health advice, improvisational skills, background harmony, interpretation, creating a unique style, all in addition to technical voice training. Unless a CCM teacher is known to specialize exclusively in musical theater, jazz, country, or rock singing (and there are many specialists), students expect their CCM teacher to be a generalist and to have at least a passing knowledge of many genres of popular music from the 1920s to the present.

Singers often seek out teachers for short-term training only, to solve a technical issue or perhaps to prepare for an upcoming audition or show. Less common is long-term training with any one teacher. In fact, it is common practice for singers to seek many sources of information, learning a variety of techniques from various coaches and by attending workshops. CCM teachers who are not skilled pianists often rely on the large array of backing (karaoke) tracks available via the internet. Studios are expected to contain electronic equipment such as computers, microphones, sound systems, headphones, transposing keyboards, wireless internet access for audio and sheet music downloading, and the ability to record lessons digitally. Many CCM teachers create books, DVDs, or practice CDs marketed to the general public. With the advent of inexpensive and easy-to-use audio and video recording equipment, it is now easy for teachers to create and upload voice training lessons to such free websites as YouTube, thereby gaining credibility simply by the vast exposure afforded them.

It is not uncommon for CCM singers to attend their first voice lesson having already recorded and performed extensively for many years. They often reluctantly accept the need for vocal instruction to facilitate ongoing recording and performing opportunities. CCM singers in pop, rock, R&B, jazz, and country coming to a voice coach for the first time often express concern that vocal training might require a dramatic style change in order to achieve vocal health. Pedagogues are recommended to allay such fears by resolving issues of vocal hyperfunction without radical style or timbral changes.

Vocal exercises are used for warm-ups and for remediation of technical problems and may not be included in every lesson. Teachers often fix as they go, attending to technical issues within the context of songs. Though the concept of *Fach* is not broached in pop, rock, jazz, R&B, and country styles, it is beginning to be discussed in musical theater. Terms such as soprano belt, alto belt, and high tenor are now being heard in the musical theater community. As in opera, these *Fach* subclassifications can be useful in a singer's song choice. Picking repertoire is also based on one's casting, meaning one's look, age, and type (e.g. *ingénue*, leading man, character).

Terminology

Although there is no one system of terminology used in Western lyric singing pedagogy, there is nevertheless widespread acceptance and use of terms. With the burgeoning rise in CCM, teachers and singers have felt the need to invent their own terms to describe sounds and register events experienced in these genres. Three popular approaches are based on the work of Jo Estill (Europe and Australasia), Cathrine Sadolin (Europe), and Lisa Popeil (United States).

1. Estill researched and devised her own taxonomy of voice qualities that she considered largely independent of registers. She identified four basic voice qualities (speech, falsetto, sob, and twang) and two composite qualities (opera and belting). Estill asserts each voice quality can be maintained across the singer's pitch range, although she acknowledges certain voice qualities are more easily produced in specific parts of the vocal range (Colton and Estill 1981).
2. Sadolin teaches four distinct modes of the voice: neutral, curbing, overdrive, and edge. Sadolin implies that different modes will tend to be used by singers of different musical genres (Sadolin 2000).
3. Popeil focuses on different uses of vibrato, registers, resonance (ring, nasality, and brightness), vertical laryngeal positions, five vocal fold closures, and three pharyngeal widths, as well as the basic skills of breathing, posture, and support, and their use in American vocal styles.

Training environments and teacher experience with CCM

Singers who begin their voice study in private studio training or through participation in school or church choirs often decide to continue their solo voice education at the university or conservatory level. They may choose between degree programs focusing on musical theater, opera, jazz, commercial voice, or general voice. These training programs are described in more detail in Chapter 34. With regards to the types of training current teachers of voice are providing, a worldwide internet survey by the present authors of 805 singing teachers found that only 8.4 percent (67) of respondents indicated they received requests solely to teach classical music. Of the remaining 738 respondents teaching CCM, 40 percent did not list *any* CCM genres as their most comfortable style for teaching (Fisher et al. 2011).

Results of a 2010 survey by the National Association of Teachers of Singing (including American, Canadian, and foreign membership) working with disordered voice, revealed a high percentage of teachers in that association are teaching either classical or musical theater singing (Gilman et al. 2010): classical 98.6 percent, musical theater 93.2 percent, country 34.6 percent, gospel 33.2 percent (included here as it has affiliations with soul), rock 22.8 percent, and jazz 41.6 percent (from a total of 425 respondents). A total of 83.6 percent of 412 respondents declared themselves most comfortable working with classical music genres and 12.1 percent with musical theater. No other specified CCM genre received even a 1 percent rating other than jazz (1.2 percent). Since 58.7 percent of 416 respondents had received their training via a masters degree in music (vocal performance) and 24.5 percent via a doctorate of music/musical arts (vocal performance/vocal performance and pedagogy), we can only assume that degree programs are heavily weighted towards Western lyric singing, leaving many singing teachers ill-equipped to deal with CCM genres.

Recommendations

Given the results of these surveys it is clear the current model of vocal pedagogy as it is taught in formal educational institutions needs revision and updating to include the following:

1. Musical skills that are non-literacy based need to be valued and forms of assessment need to be devised. Class music and school choir repertoire needs to include different sung genres; it no longer serves the development of children's musical education to expose them only to folk songs.
2. More programs at conservatories and colleges should provide student modules in CCM.
3. Universities should consider including the pedagogy of multiple genres in master of music programs.
4. For those committed to the task, innovative learning styles can assist and augment traditional vocal pedagogical methods. Careful listening and thoughtful imitation of archetypal artists are valuable approaches in the quest for mastery in fast-changing modern culture.

SUMMARY OF KEY POINTS

Traditional singing voice pedagogy has been heavily influenced by the performance practice and esthetic of the Western lyric (classical) tradition. Recently, non-classical vocal genres have been termed contemporary commercial music (CCM). These genres include pop, rock, jazz, country, folk, R&B, and sometimes musical theater. Though in its infancy, the pedagogy of CCM (including belting) is of great interest worldwide.

There are numerous differences between Western lyric and CCM genres including: written versus oral tradition; historical/cultural context; use of voice, word articulation, dynamics, vibrato, phrasing; stylistic idioms; vocal registers; pitch range; resonance characteristics; and learning cultures. In summary, all teachers of singing should be educated in understanding the vocal function, performance practice, and pedagogical goals of multiple genres, even though they may eventually choose to specialize.

QUESTIONS FOR FURTHER REFLECTION

1. Can singers reasonably expect to master more than one vocal genre?
2. Which pedagogical methods are most efficacious in training multiple genres?
3. To what degree is knowledge of musical theory necessary or helpful in CCM?

4. Are there any reasons why vocal pedagogy programs should *not* include musical theater and CCM genres?
5. How can the efficacy of proprietary vocal methods be appraised?
6. How useful is voice science terminology in helping teachers communicate more effectively with students?
7. How relevant is the concept of primary register transition in view of female register use in CCM singing?
8. Are any of the phonation modes on the breathy to pressed scale unsafe to use, or is it a matter of genre, idiom, and the number of times the singer must perform each day/night?

FURTHER RESOURCES

Websites and Social Media Groups

Vocal Process: <http://www.vocalprocess.co.uk>
The Voice Centre: <http://www.voicecentre.se>
Lisa Popeil's Voiceworks®: <http://www.popeil.com>
The New Forum for Professional Voice Teachers: <https://www.facebook.com/groups/1810591335659853>

FURTHER READING

Howard, E. (2006). *Sing!* Los Angeles, CA: Vocal Power, Inc.
Stark, J. (2003). *Bel Canto: a History of Vocal Pedagogy.* Toronto: University of Toronto Press.
Benninger, M., Murry, T., and Johns, M. (eds) (2015). *The Performer's Voice*, 2nd edn. San Diego, CA: Plural Publishing.
Fisher, J. and Kayes, G. (2018). *This Is A Voice* (Wellcome Collection). London: Profile Books.
Latimerlo, G. and Popeil, L. (2012). *Sing Anything: Mastering Vocal Styles.*

REFERENCES

American Academy of Teachers of Singing (2008). *In Support of Contemporary Commercial Music (Non-classical) Voice Pedagogy* [electronic version]. Accessed 5 January 2011 from: http://www.americanacademyofteachersofsinging.org/assets/articles/CCMVoicePedagogy.pdf
Baken, R.J. (1998). An overview of laryngeal function for voice production. In: R.T. Sataloff (ed.), *Vocal Health and Pedagogy*, pp. 27–47. San Diego, CA: Singular.
Balog, J.E. (2005). A guide to evaluating music theater singing for the classical singing teacher. *Journal of Singing* 61(4): 401–406.
Björk, L. (1962). Velopharyngeal function on connected speech. *Acta Radiologica (Stockholm)* Suppl. 202.
Björkner, E., Sundberg, J., Cleveland, T., and Stone, E. (2006). Voice source differences between registers in female musical theater singers. *Journal of Voice* 20(2): 187–197.

Bourne, T., Garnier, M., and Kenny, D. (2011). Music theatre voice: production, physiology and pedagogy. *Journal of Singing* 67(4): 437–444.

Bunch Dayme, M. (2009). *Dynamics of the Singing Voice*, 5th edn. Vienna, Austria: Springer-Verlag.

Chapman, J. (2006). *Singing and Teaching Singing*. Oxford: Plural.

Colton, R.H. and Estill, J.A. (1981). Elements of voice quality: perceptual, acoustic and physiological aspects. In: N. J. Lass (ed.), *Speech and Language: Advances in Basic Research and Practice*, Vol. 5, pp. 311–403. New York: Academic Press.

Estill, J., Fujimara, O., Erickson, D., Zhang, T., and Beechler, K. (1994). Vocal tract contributions to voice qualities. *Proceedings of the Stockholm Music Acoustics Conference (SMAC 93)*, pp. 161–165 Stockholm, Sweden: Royal Academy of Music.

Fant, G. (1960). *Acoustic Theory of Speech Production*. The Hague: Mouton.

Fisher, J.P., Kayes, G., and Popeil, L. (2011). *A Survey of Singing Teachers and Vocal Coaches*. Unpublished data.

Frith, S. (1998). *Performing Rites: Evaluating Popular Music*. Oxford: Oxford University Press.

Gilman, M., Nix, J., and Hapner, E. (2010). The speech pathologist, the singing teacher, and the singing voice specialist: where's the line? *Journal of Singing* 67(2): 171–178.

Green, L. (2001). *How Popular Musicians Learn: a Way Ahead for Music Education*. Aldershot, UK: Ashgate.

Henrich, D.N. (2006). Mirroring the voice from Garcia to the present day: some insights into singing voice registers. *Logopedics Phoniatrics Vocology* 31(1): 3–14.

Herbst, C., Ternström, S., and Švec, J. (2009). Investigation of four distinct glottal configurations in classical singing— a pilot study. *Journal of the Acoustical Society of America* 125(3): 104–109.

Hixon, T.J. (2006). *Respiratory Function in Singing: a Primer for Singers and Singing Teachers*. Tucson, AZ: Redington Browne.

Hoit, J.D., Jenks, C.L., Watson, P.J., and Cleveland, T.F. (1996). Respiratory function during speaking and singing in professional country singers. *Journal of Voice* 10(1): 39–49.

Hollien, H. (1974). On vocal registers. *Journal of Phonetics* 2: 125–143.

House, A. and Stevens, K. (1956). Analog studies of the nazalisation of vowels. *Journal of Speech and Hearing Disorders* 12: 218–231.

Incorporated Society of Musicians (2006). *Bel Canto or Can Belto?* Workshop for Singers and Singing Teachers, London, UK, 12 March 2006.

Jungr, B. (2002). Vocal expression in the blues and gospel. In: A. Moor (ed.), *The Cambridge Companion to Blues and Gospel Music*, pp. 102–115. New York: Cambridge University Press.

Kayes, G. (2004). *Singing and the Actor*, 2nd edn. London: A & C Black.

Kayes, G. and Fisher, J. (2002). *Successful Singing Auditions*. London: A & C Black.

Kochis-Jennings, K.A. (2008). *Intrinsic Laryngeal Muscle Activity and Vocal Fold Patterns in Female Vocal Registers: Chest, Chest Dominant Mix and Head Dominant Mix*. Doctoral dissertation, University of Iowa, Iowa City, IA, USA.

Laver, J. (1980). *The Phonetic Description of Voice Quality*. Cambridge: Cambridge University Press.

LoVetri, J. (2003). Female chest voice. *Journal of Singing* 60: 161.

LoVetri, J.L. and Means Weekly, E. (2003). Contemporary commercial music (CCM) survey: who's teaching what in non-classical music. *Journal of Voice* 17(2): 207–215.

Melton, J. (2007). *Singing in Musical Theatre*. New York: Allworth Press.

Miller, D.G. (2000). *Registers in Singing: Empirical and Systematic Studies in the Theory of the Singing Voice.* Doctoral dissertation, University of Groningen, Groningen, The Netherlands.

Miller, R. (1986). *The Structure of Singing: System and Art in Vocal Technique.* New York: Schirmer.

Potter, J. (1998). *Vocal Authority.* Cambridge: Cambridge University Press.

Sadolin, C. (2000). *Complete Vocal Technique.* Copenhagen, Denmark: Shout Publishing.

Soto-Morettini, D. (2006). *Popular Singing: a Practical Guide to Pop, Jazz, Blues, Rock, Country and Gospel.* London: A & C Black.

Sundberg, J. (1998). Vocal tract resonance. In: R.T. Sataloff (ed.), *Vocal Health and Pedagogy,* pp. 47–65). San Diego, CA: Singular.

Sundberg, J. and Thalén, M. (2010). What is "Twang"? *Journal of Voice* 24(6): 654–660.

Sundberg, J., Thalén, M., Paavo, A., and Vilkman, E. (2004). Estimating perceived phonatory pressedness in singing from flow glottograms. *Journal of Voice,* 18(1): 56–62.

Sundberg, J., Thalén, M., and Popeil, L. (2012). Substyles of belting: phonatory and resonatory characteristics. *Journal of Voice* 26(1): 44–50.

Thomasson, M. and Sundberg, J. (1997). Lung volume levels in professional classical singing. *Logopedics Phoniatrics Vocology* 22: 61–70.

Thorpe, C. W., Cala, S.J., Chapman, J., and Davis, P.J. (2001). Patterns of breath support in projection of the singing voice. *Journal of Voice* 15(1): 86–104.

Titze, I.R. (1988). A framework for the study of vocal registers. *Journal of Voice* 2(4): 1–12.

Titze, I.R. and Story, B.H. (1996). Acoustic interactions of the voice source with the lower vocal tract. *Journal of the Acoustical Society of America* 101(4): 2234–2243.

Zangger Borch, D. (2005). *Ultimate Vocal Voyage.* Bromma, Sweden: Notfabriken Music Publishing AB.

CHAPTER 36

THE EXTRA-NORMAL VOICE

MICHAEL EDWARD EDGERTON

Introduction

THIS chapter will present a description of new directions in voice exploration. Focused on scaled and multidimensional networks, the extra-normal voice presents the next step in the evolution of exceptional voice practice. In general, this development presumes to inhabit a greater area of topology in order to extend the biomechanical limits of production. Technically, such activity is mediated via the inherent non-linearity of the acoustic framework that is intentionally desynchronized from normal, in order to present extra-complex sonorities that exceed a single fundamental frequency with a gently sloping spectra, such as is normally seen in speech and song (Titze 1994). Such sonorities will feature the perception of multiple pitches, spectral reinforcement/manipulation, subharmonics, sustained pitch and noise, noise sonorities, and transient and unstable sonorities, among others (Neubauer et al. 2004).

Multiple parameters

Since we are not able to externally manipulate voice, such as with a clarinet, trombone, or violin, the identification of individual parameters for performer manipulation is not a trivial issue. Even though the number of elements involved in sound production is enormous, simplified models provide powerful conceptual tools by which performers can reliably predict the results of even extreme parametric change (Behrman 1999; Tigges et al. 1997). One such model, based on an acoustic framework, consists of a driving force, a source of acoustic generation, a resonant environment, and a system of articulation (Backus 1969; Fant 1960; Fletcher and Rossing 1998).

With voice, the source generation and resonant cavity are weakly coupled, so that vocal fold oscillation is considered to be functionally separate from the resonant cavity of the vocal tract (Risset 1978; Sundberg 1977). Evidence of such separation is seen with the ability humans have to change pitch (source change), while keeping a vowel steady (resonator steady), or vice-versa. Embedded within the power, source, resonator, articulation framework are numerous factors that are manipulated by humans during phonation. These include:

- airflow through the glottis;
- the tension of the folds;
- the amount of coupling between the resonator and the sound source;
- sound intensity;
- subglottal pressure;
- pitch range to voice type;
- front to back tongue placement [bright/dark];
- torso tension;
- glottal valving;
- nasality;
- phase within breath cycle (i.e. end of breath);
- laryngeal height;
- sensation of placement of sound;
- respiratory support/function;
- open to close ratio in each glottal cycle (brassy/ordinary);
- presence or absence of the singer's formant;
- physical action;
- air direction (Edgerton et al. 2003).

As will be elaborated upon further in the discussion of non-linear phenomenon, it has been shown that the production of an esthetically-pleasing tone by instruments and voices is the result of keeping parameters within certain values/ratios (Benade 1960, 1975; Bouhuys 1965). However, recent studies in bioacoustics show that when parameters are shifted to non-idiomatic ratios, bifurcations may occur (Berry et al. 1996). In voice, these non-idiomatic ratios may be accessed through methods that shift any single parameter within continua encompassing minimal to maximal values (Edgerton et al. 2003). This means, for example, that vocal fold tension may shift between an extremely lax glottis to a hyperpressed glottis in order to produce a variety of extra-complex sonorities.

A heightening of individual parameters involved in sound production was implicated by James Tenney in a discussion of the two primary factors responsible for producing a gestalt factor of cohesion and segregation:

> The factor of similarity applies not only to pitch and timbre, but also to the other parameters—dynamic level, envelope, temporal and vertical density, etc.—and in fact it may be said to function with respect to any attribute of sound by which we are able, at a given moment, or within a given time-span, to distinguish one sound or sound-configuration from another.
>
> (Tenney 1988)

In this way, a performer may manipulate any element to produce an audible change of sound quality. Crucially, due to the inherent non-linearity of voice, this does not imply that a large parametric change will produce a correspondingly large change in the acoustic output; nor that a small parametric change will produce only a small change in its output. Furthermore, within any single parameter, each performer has the opportunity to scale each parametric space, utilizing the amount of effective steps between minimal and maximal values, determined by an appropriate amount of variation in each context.

Non-linear phenomena

The human voice production system can be considered to consist of non-linearly coupled oscillators (e.g. left and right vocal folds, each with the potential for different modes of vibration, the ventricular folds, and aerodynamic oscillators). Generally, egressive airflow driven by lung pressure is disrupted by the vocal folds to produce phonation. The interaction of air and tissue properties are highly non-linear and must be proportionally regulated in order to produce normal voice. However, when any robust element is desynchronized from ordinary, non-linear phenomena begin to appear.

For voice, non-linear phenomena have been reported for newborn cries (Mende et al. 1990), pathological voices (Titze et al. 1993; Ward et al. 1969), extra-normal extended vocal technique (Edgerton et al. 2003; Neubauer et al. 2004), animal vocalizations (Fletcher and Tarnopolsky, 1999), and in speech (Titze et al. 1993). Furthermore, it has been reported that non-linear vocal phenomena carry functional and communicative relevance for animals and humans (Fitch et al. 2002; Kohler 1996).

Dynamic systems

Understanding the dynamics of voice requires an introduction to a few basic concepts of dynamic systems. According to the theory of non-linear dynamics, all systems feature qualitatively different dynamic regimes, or attractors. The attractors relevant for voice include *limit cycle* (periodic oscillation or, for voice, pitch), *folded limit cycle* (period doubling or, for voice, subharmonics), *torus* (for voice, two independent frequency contours), and *chaos* (Lorenz Strange Attractor, which for voice involves highly irregular, aperiodic and noise-like behavior). Attractors represent a particular state for external parameters, such as vocal fold tension or subglottal pressure during phonation. Then when the system parameters (pitch, formants, subglottal pressure or the varying interaction with supraglottal tissue structures) begin to vary past a particular threshold, transitions may occur between the different attractor states. These transitions are known as bifurcations that include:

- Hopf bifurcation, a transition from a steady state to a limit cycle;
- period doubling bifurcations, transitions from a limit cycle to folded limit cycles;
- secondary Hopf bifurcation, a transition from a limit cycle to a torus, due to the excitation of another independent oscillation;
- cascades of subharmonic bifurcations, which often are precursors of deterministic chaos, such that small parameter shifts induce jumps to non-periodic oscillations (Herzel et al. 1994; Mende et al. 1990; Titze et al. 1993; Wilden et al. 1998).

A useful tool for visualizing such transitions can be seen with bifurcation diagrams (Glass and Mackey 1988), which display dynamical behavior resulting from one or two varying system parameters. Such diagrams were calculated for a simplified two-mass model of vocal folds (Steinecke and Herzel 1995) and continuum models (Berry et al. 1994). Furthermore, bifurcation diagrams were developed from excised larynx experiments (Berry et al. 1996), and analyzed for a voice with unilateral paralysis (Mergell at al. 2000). However, in contrast to bifurcation diagrams obtained from mathematical models or experimental set-ups where single system parameters can be varied, the measurements of the varying system parameters in *extra-complex* sonorities produced by voices and instruments are highly complex and variable, making the correspondence between discrete parameter change and resultant bio-acoustic product less exact. Further compounding this analytical complexity, while musical instruments, such as a string instrument, control many of the variables externally, with voice exact parametric behavior is more difficult to track and measure. However, we can still speculate on parametric change from a few hints like pitch, formants, and subglottal pressure (Neubauer et al. 2004).

In the literature covering dynamic systems, cascades of subharmonics and tori are predicted to be precursors of chaos (Williams 1997). However, recent voice research has shown that attractor states do not solely progress via linear bifurcation processes, but may occur in any order (Edgerton et al. 2001).

SUBHARMONICS

In addition to the non-linear phenomena mentioned above, there are numerous examples of exceptional voice featuring intended dynamical behavior (Barnett 1972; Chase 1975; Clark 1985; Jensen 1979; Kavasch 1980; Large and Murray 1979; Lee et al. 1998; Newell 1970). For example, subharmonics in voice occur not only at period-doubling ratios of 1/2, but also at 1/3, ¼, and 1/6 (Edgerton 2013; Fuks et al. 1999; Stratos 1978), and it may even be possible to feature other subharmonic intervals. In a remarkable demonstration of subharmonics on the violin, a descending series of subharmonics were produced beginning at a minor third below and moving chromatically to a minor sixth below, alternating at each step with the fundamental frequency of string vibration (Kimura 1999). For voice, the production of imitated-Tibetan chant subharmonics have been reported to involve two different methods—one using the combination of vocal folds in conjunction with the ventricular folds, and a second utilizing vocal fold asymmetry in which a normal vocal fold tone is combined with what feels like a resonant vocal fry (Edgerton et al. 1999).

TORI

Tori have been reported in voice as two or more simultaneous and independent frequency contours that occur through a variety of vocal fold asymmetries (left-right, multiple mode, vortex-induced; Neubauer et al. 2004). In an often reported study, a subject had precise control over both frequency contours simultaneously in biphonic voice by producing oblique (upper contour remains the same, lower contour begins, and ends on the same pitch with a lower neighbor tone in between) and contrary motion (both voices moving outward and returning to initial interval of a major third). The subject was viewed with high-speed photography, from which the physical properties of vocal fold oscillation could be measured, and found that the biphonic voice was produced with the left and right vocal folds vibrating at different frequencies (Ward et al. 1969). In a completely different way, tori may be produced with aerodynamic forces, such as with vortex-induced vibrations produced at the superior boundary of the vocal folds, known as a glottal whistle or M4. In this production, two or more independent frequency contours are able to move in parallel, similar, oblique, and contrary motion that may feature voice crossing (Stratos 1978).

CHAOS IN VOICE

The Lorenz Strange Attractor or chaos in voice may be represented by complex, wideband, and noisy signals that are produced through factors related to aerodynamic or tissue vibration. One such strange attractor occurs with the combination of high airflow, lax vocal fold vibration, and relatively high pitch. In this production, the mode of vibration features incomplete closure, allowing the high airflow to continue as a separate, perceptual entity. Added to this noise and pitch sonority is a subharmonic, normally at the octave (Edgerton et al. 2001). A second chaotic attractor combines high air pressure with ventricular and vocal fold vibration. In this production, a pressed glottal pitch is combined with moderately-tight ventricular fold constriction in order to produce a clearly-defined harmonic tone with the simultaneous occurrence of a broadband tone from approximately 1.5–2 kHz. Both elements are stable and reproducible at will (Edgerton 2013). The use of the ventricular folds to produce the low frequency component of a subharmonic has been reported in Tibetan chant, the Kargyraa method of Tuvan overtone singing, and by Xhosa singers (Levin and Edgerton 1999; Sakakibara et al. 2001, 2004). However, in this production, a singer uses his ventricular folds to produce relatively high frequencies from approximately F6 to B6 that resemble high velocity clicks that seem to result from an extremely sharp glottal closing phase (Blonk 1997).

COMMON EXTENDED VOCAL TECHNIQUES

Table 36.1 provides a description of a number of commonly used extended techniques called for in contemporary scores.

Table 36.1 Commonly used extended vocal techniques

Extended vocal technique	Description	Further details on production or use
Sprechgesang	Uses normal voice, although in a contextually progressive manner, which exists somewhere midpoint in the continuum between speech and song. It is most often associated with Arnold Schoenberg (i.e. *Pierrot Lunaire*).	More sustained than normal speech, and a wider fundamental frequency range, but not sung on precise pitches.
Reinforced harmonic singing (also known as Tuvan throat singing or as overtone singing)	Vocal phenomenon in which a person produces a melody resting entirely on the harmonics of its associated fundamental frequency. The melody is sculpted out of a fundamental frequency by boosting the amplitude of a single harmonic, while damping adjacent harmonics.	Achieved by narrowing the bandwidth and increasing the amplitude of either the first or second formant in order to focus on a single harmonic. In practice, throat singers from Tuva use primarily harmonics 6–12, with the 13th commonly being used as upper grace notes to the 12th (Bloothooft et al. 1992; Kob 2004; Levin and Edgerton 1999).
Undertone singing (subharmonic, imitated-Tibetan chant)	Undertone singing in which multiple tones are produced with one or more prominent frequencies that are lower than the fundamental frequency of vocal fold oscillation, in both harmonic and non-harmonic ratios with the fundamental.	Numerous methods available. This chapter focuses on a single technique—that of imitated-Tibetan chant. Generally, chant combines the vocal folds with ventricular folds, or an asymmetry of vocal fold phonation featuring the combination of what feels to the singer like a normal tone with a vocal fry. The pitch profile often features a 1:2 harmonic ratio with little pitch movement of the fundamental or subharmonic. When using the ventricular folds, supra-glottal closure occurs at every other closure of the vocal folds. A typical fundamental pitch would be C3 (130.8 Hz), with the false folds vibrating one octave below at C2 (65.4 Hz). Spectral analysis shows that when a singer switches into chant mode, the number of frequency components doubles, verifying that the second source is periodic and half the normal pitch (Fuks et al. 1999; Levin and Edgerton 1999; Tigges et al. 1997). During the performance of Tibetan chant, a singer often reinforces the tenth harmonic to produce a bell-like sonority. Although the octave below is the most frequently used undertone, a twelfth below, and other lower undertones are also possible (La Barbara 2003).

Table 36.1 Continued

Extended vocal technique	Description	Further details on production or use
Registral and oscillatory movement	Often occurs during ethnic voice performance, such as with P'ansori music from Korea.	One performer, Kim So-Hee, was known for her ability to produce rapid and wide-ranging pitch changes that involve what appeared to be a shift in register while changing the extent of vibrato from moderate to large (Kim 1988).
Vocal fry	Non-periodic, low frequency components that produce a pulsing of the glottal signal. f_0 is sufficiently low enough (<70 Hz) that acoustic energy in the vocal tract dies out before the next impulse begins, leaving a perceptible gap or silence (Titze 1994).	Consists of an alternation between large and small glottal excursions. Generally, vocal fry occurs low in range, but when combined with higher pitch, the fry may produce intermittent subharmonics (Dejonckere and Lebacq 1983; Herzel 1993; Mazo et al. 1995).
Creaky voice	Consists of low frequency tones at the lowest end of phonation; creaky voice features damped single or double pulses (Laver 1980)	Often used term, although some overlap of meaning may occur between this term and vocal fry.
Growl	Audio signal of this technique consists of alternating pulses of high and low peak-to-peak amplitude (Rose 1988).	Phonation mode that features a rough tone with perhaps ventricular fold and aryepiglottic influence.
Ingressive phonation	Vocal sounds or even words can be produced while a singer is inhaling. The durations of ingressive phonation can exceed 20 seconds.	Phonation during inhalation. Multiphonic production is available for most singers, though with less control compared to egressive methods (Edgerton 2005).
Yodeling	Part of the vocal tradition of Alpine music of Austria. Also found in American Country-Western music and in some Mariachi styles.	Performed by rapidly alternating between a singer's modal/chest and falsetto/head voice, often facilitated by the use of rapidly alternating higher F1 vowels /a, o, e/ with low F1 vowels such as /u/ and /i/.
Screaming		High frequency and high intensity phonation, often accompanied by high amounts of noise elements.

Multiphonic combinations/multiple sound sources

Multiple sound sources have been identified as important resources for contemporary, avant-garde music since the 1950s, when Bartolozzi began to systematize a theory behind the production of multiphonic sonorities (Bartolozzi 1969). Such innovations led to the development of expanded sound resources for voice through important works, such as Davies's "Three Songs for a Mad King," Ligeti's "Aventures" and "Nouvelle Aventures," and Lachenmann's "temA," among others. All of these works featured expanded vocal resources and were important in the development of an extended vocal technique (Griffiths 1981).

Multiple sound sources have been reported in the scientific and medical literature, not as the components of a desired musical expression, but rather as part of a dysfunctional make-up (see also "Voice Dysfunction and Recovery" by Stadelman-Cohen and Hillman in this volume). A variety of multiple sound sources have been described (Herzel et al. 1994; Large and Murray 1979; McKinney 1982; Nonomura et al. 1996; Terrio and Schreibweiss-Merin 1993). Although artistic use is far removed from dysfunction, the understanding of multiple sound source production can be increased if research in vocal physiology and anatomy are thoroughly examined.

Information about the mechanics of multiple sound sources can be found in the literature on diplophonia (Ward et al. 1969). Both physiological and acoustic information can be used to make inferences of the bases of diplophonic patterns (Gerratt et al. 1987, 1988; Marasovich et al. 1993; Ward et al. 1969). This research suggests there are several causes of diplophonia, including:

- unilateral vocal fold polyps causing different vibratory patterns of the two folds;
- the ventricular folds acting as an additional sound source;
- congenitally absent or rudimentary vocal folds;
- asymmetrical loading of mucus on the vocal folds;
- adolescent voice change;
- the voluntary control of asymmetrical vocal fold vibration.

However, in addition to articles that focus on dysfunctional production, there is a growing body of literature, which suggests multiple sound sources are intentionally used in the production of numerous types of extended vocal techniques (Anhalt 1984; Barnett 1972; Chase 1975; Clark 1985; Herzel and Reuter 1997; Herzel et al. 1994; Jensen 1979; Kavasch 1980; Large and Murray 1979; Newell 1970; Wishart 1983).

Depending on the artistic context, multiple sound sources may occur at any level of the vocal tract. Two related taxonomies that may be applied to combinatorial principles of multiple sound sources are those based on functional use during voice production that include (a) degree of voicing (voiced versus unvoiced), or (b) sources based within the categories of power, source, articulation, and resonance.

DEGREE OF VOICING

First, combining elements according to the degree of voicing is a highly effective and powerful conceptual mode. In this framework, the underlying principle involves a simple additive procedure that combines two separate sources. For instance, it is possible to combine sources:

1. Voiced and voiced, such as with Tibetan chant (glottal pitch + ventricular folds, or glottal pitch + vocal fry), or two separate non-harmonic components produced via vocal fold asymmetries, among others.
2. Voiced and unvoiced, such as glottal pitch + lip buzz, or vocal fry + bilabial buzzes, among others.
3. Unvoiced and unvoiced, such as pharyngeal articulation + lip buzz, or whistle + sustained oral cavity frication, among others (Edgerton 2005).

An alternative framework places combinations of voice and/or vocal tract manipulation within an acoustic framework of power, source, articulation and resonance, as can be seen in Table 36.2.

An example of combinatorial principles in composition may be seen in *Anaphora* for solo voice, which is a study of 56 classes of vocal multiphonics (Edgerton 2001). In this composition, each class of multiphonic is expected to produce a wide variety of outputs encompassing timbral and/or dynamical change. In Figure 36.1, the first page of *Anaphora* is

Table 36.2 Multi-phonic combinations within an acoustic framework

	Power	Source	Articulation	Resonance
Power	Nasal air frication + Lingual-dental air frication	Lingua-dental whistle + Air sonority	Rear tongue flutter + Air frication at lower teeth, tongue	Oscillation of nasal filter open and close + Moderate airflow
Source	High airflow + Vocal fold pitch (subharmonics)	Tibetan Chant and variants (vocal folds + ventricular folds)	Voice + Repeated tongue clicks	Throat/overtone singing (pressed voice + Radical filtering)
Articulation	High airflow + Bilabial frication (with voice)	Voice + Sustained tongue frications	Bilabial whistles or "pops" + Front tongue flutter	Lingual-pharyngeal articulation + Open v-p port to produce rising and lowering pitch through nasal cavity
Resonance	High airflow + Unvoiced vowels /i-e-a-o-u/	"Turkey" glottal stops + Registral jumps	Percussive cheek tap + Rapid lingual movement (w rounded lips) to produce sense of pitch change	Airflow through nasal port + Airflow through oral cavity

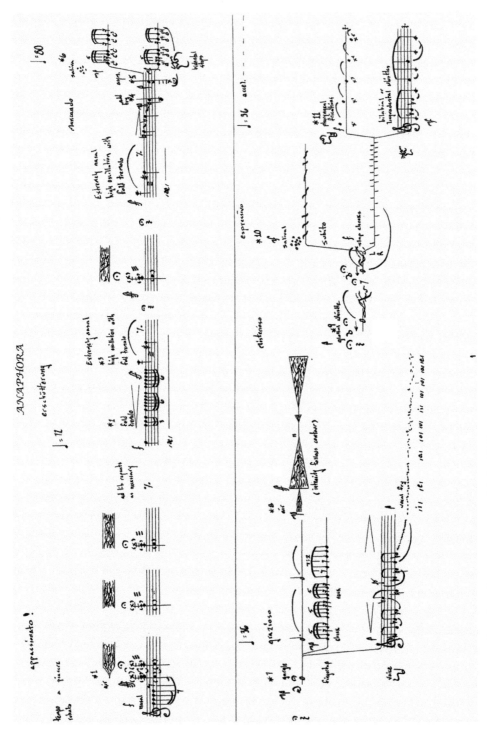

FIGURE 36.1 *Anaphora* by Edgerton, page 1. © Michael Edgerton.

shown with 11 of the 56 multiphonic combinations indicated on the score. The combinations are as follows:

1. Lax vocal fold pitch (a5) + extremely high perceptible airflow, producing subharmonics, non-harmonic tones, and air noise.
2. Vocal fold tremolo + pressed vocal folds, producing isolated registral flips higher and lower.
3. Vocal fold tone + nasal placement + pressed production, producing a high oscillation nearly resembling the gobble call of a turkey.
4. Vocal fold tone + vocal fry, producing a chant-like production.
5. Asymmetry of vocal fold production, producing a time-varying biphonic sequence (torus).
6. Saliva + bidental stops, producing a sustained liquid approximant with sharp percussive articulation.
7. Gargle + finger tap on cheeks + ordinary vocal fold tone, producing complex sequences with much diversity if water is used artistically.
8. Variation of perceptual airflow + vocal fry, producing a cloud of varied glottal pulses often with transients appearing.
9. M4 or vortex-induced glottal whistle.
10. Saliva ejections + slap cheeks, producing a two part noise sonority with time-variance.
11. Pharyngeal frication with bilabial or labial-dental whistle, producing an almost bird-like interruption on the more prominent whistle; however, if pharyngeal frication is dominant the sonority will become unstable and chaotic with multiple noises overpowering slight pitched whistles.

SCALED MULTIDIMENSIONAL NETWORKS

During the production of normal voice in song, numerous parameters combine to form the timbral identity of the singer. Normally, such parameters feature limited excursion within any multidimensional topology. However, when one or more robust element is desynchronized from normal, timbral changes and bifurcations to other sound classes (attractor states) may occur. Such desynchronization may vary parametric change between minimal and maximal values, for example, with airflow through the glottis (none to maximum flow) or vocal fold tension (extremely lax to hyperpressed). Of course, the value of shifting elements between minimal and maximal values is to more fully exploit the biomechanical potential of voice, as well as to offer the ability for increased coherence of procedure across multiple variables.

An example of multidimensional scaling in practice was reported in a study of excised laryngeal experiments (Berry et al. 1996). In this study, two elements were scaled experimentally, which included asymmetrical vocal fold tension (micrometer asymmetry) and subglottal pressure. Shown in bifurcation diagrams, the authors found that variations of asymmetrical vocal fold tension and subglottal pressure produced chest-like vibrations, falsetto-like vibrations, vortex-induced vibrations (whistle-like) and instabilities. Specifically, they found that an increase in subglottal pressure at low to medium vocal fold asymmetries did not result in instabilities, but remained in chest-like vibrations. However, as micrometer asymmetry increased, coupled with the increase of subglottal pressure, falsetto-like, whistle-like, and instabilities began to appear. The results provide experimental evidence that even small parametric change may result in qualitative variation in voice.

In music composition, perhaps the first explicit use of scaled, multidimensional use was identified by Hübler in a paper discussing expanded string technique (Hübler 1984). Other composers and performers who have exploited multidimensionality in limited, mostly non-scalable ways include composers Scelsi, Ferneyhough, Schnebel, Wishart and performers Stratos, Minton, and Blonk, among others (Aurbacher-Liska 2003; Blonk 1997; Minton 1998; Stratos 1978; Wishart 1983).

As multidimensional networks offer the potential for traversing a greater topology of production and output, it is appropriate to mention that numerous approaches are used by composers and performers today. In terms of multidimensionality, there seem to be two extremes in use today: first, parametric change focused on a single region, behavior, or idea, or secondly, parametric change spread amongst multiple regions, behaviors, or elements

PARAMETRIC CHANGE: SINGLE IDEA

An example of scaled, multidimensional networks during sound production in voice focused on a single region, behavior, or idea may be seen in *Rhotic* by Jaap Blonk (Blonk 1997). This composition/performance features numerous modifications to the letter /r/ (rhotic consonant) that include the phonetic variants alveolar trill, alveolar approximant, alveolar flip/tap, retroflex fricative, retroflex approximant, retroflex flap, as well as uvular trill and uvular frications, among others (Ladefoged 1996).

In this performance, four broad anatomical categories were used—manipulation of airflow, laryngeal behavior, the upper vocal tract (filter and articulation), and bilabial influence. Even as an incredible diversity of manipulation is produced, it is striking that most of the procedures still carry a clear and recognizable relationship to /r/ or its variants. However, not all manipulations carry either the same perceptual or generative relation to /r/; some are more closely-related, others moderately-related, yet others more distantly-related. In general, this performance involved the manipulation of one or two elements simultaneously in order to present the perception of nearly constant change using small changes in the total timbral space.

The initial idea in *Rhotic* consists of an unvoiced, /r/ colored tongue-tip trill, which is combined with slight bilabial opening and closing in order to produce a sense of pitch contour (pitch rising as lips broaden, pitch lowering as lips close). In principle, such filtering applied to either voiced or unvoiced sounds may produce a secondary pitch movement, similar to the Kargyraa method of Tuvan throat singing in which the controlling formant (F1) used to reinforce successive harmonics is primarily affected by the lip opening (Levin and Edgerton 1999). To this initial idea, Blonk added slight tongue movement with increased lingual pressure.

Throughout *Rhotic*, one has the feeling of nearly constant, small-scale parametric change. Some of the dominant procedures used to alter the initial idea and the perception of /r/ include:

- tongue vibration, front and back;
- lips opening and closing to filter noise sonorities (tongue trill, ventricular fold clicks, vocal fry) to produce pitch contours;
- non-modal vocal fold production including asymmetries, vocal fry, hyperpress, creaky voice, and rough voice;

- tongue movement to color sound and alter vowel;
- dramatic timbre change through mimicry, such as with child's voice and a sound that nearly resembles Donald Duck;
- ventricular folds producing harsh and sharp clicks;
- air as a separate, perceptual property.

In this performance, Blonk was investigating the variety of manipulations that could be made to /r/ while still retaining its core perceptual quality. As previously mentioned, some productions are closer to /r/ than others. Therefore, since consonance/dissonance as understood within common-practice harmony plays little role here due to the prominence of noise-based filtering procedures and sonorities combining pitch and noise, it was decided that an analysis suggesting a perceptual distance from /r/ would be of value for performer and listener. This analysis rests upon judgments of the manipulations to be closely-related, moderately-related, distantly-related and not-related to /r/. A complete mapping of these relationships may be seen in Figure 36.2. To better explain this mapping, one example for each perceptual distance within the categories air, laryngeal, oral/nasal/pharyngeal, and bilabial is presented below.

For the category air, one example of closely-related manipulations are crescendi/decresendi of air, while a moderately-related manipulation was not used in this performance. An example of a *distantly-related manipulation* is ingressive airflow to produce a heavy air noise sonority, and *manipulations with no relationship* to /r/ include extremely high airflow with no /r/ coloring.

For the category laryngeal, an example of a *closely-related manipulation* is unvoiced, modal voice, falsetto voice, etc.; *moderately-related manipulations* include rough voice with slight bits of vocal fry; one *distantly-related manipulation* is the use of a high-pitched, nearly glottal whistle (M4) and biphonic, and an example of a *manipulation with no relationship to /r/* is the use of the ventricular folds with an extremely pressed glottis.

For the category oral/nasal/pharyngeal, a *closely-related manipulation of resonance* is the retroflex /r/, while an example of a *closely-related manipulation of articulation* is a front tongue trill; a *moderately-related manipulation of resonance* is represented by an exaggerated lingual pressure, while a *moderately-related manipulation of articulation* is represented by lingual accents with increased pressure. A *distantly-related manipulation of resonance* might consist of vowel changes with the vocal folds + the ventricular folds in combination, with noise from the ventricular folds providing a secondary pitch movement in conjunction with bilabial movement, while a *distantly-related manipulation of articulation* could be represented by a rear-tongue vibration with movement up and down; finally, *manipulations of resonance with no relationship* to /r/ might consist of large vowel changes losing /r/ coloring, and *manipulations of articulation with no relationship* to /r/ could be represented by back and front tongue vibration together.

For the category bilabial, *closely- and moderately-related manipulations* are represented by lip broadening/lessening; *distantly-related manipulations* were not used in this performance, and *manipulations with no relationship* to /r/ are represented by a loose bilabial flutter with no /r/ coloring.

Transformations amongst multiple elements

Figure 36.3 presents a musical excerpt that condenses multiple elements in an extremely short time span for demonstration purposes only, that would in practice need slightly longer for many of the extra-normal techniques to develop. In this excerpt a network of nine elements

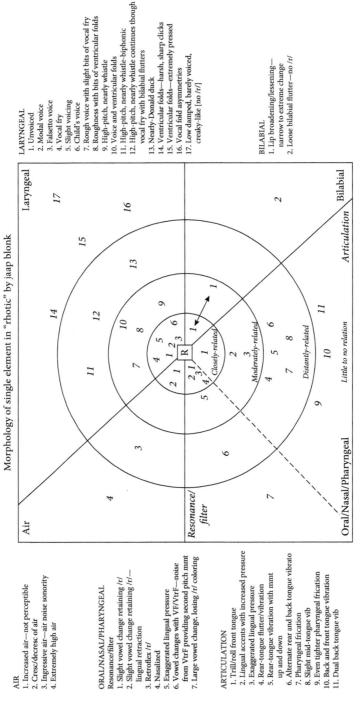

Morphology of single element in "rhotic" by jaap blonk

AIR
1. Increased air—not perceptible
2. Cresc/decresc of air
3. Ingressive air—air noise sonority
4. Extremely high air

ORAL/NASAL/PHARYNGEAL
Resonance/filter
1. Slight vowel change retaining /r/
2. Slight vowel change retaining /r/—lingual retraction
3. Retroflex /r/
4. Nasalized
5. Exaggerated lingual pressure
6. Vowel changes with VF/VtrF—noise from VtrF providing second pitch mmt
7. Large vowel change, losing /r/ coloring

ARTICULATION
1. Trill/roll front tongue
2. Lingual accents with increased pressure
3. Exaggerated lingual pressure
4. Rear-tongue flutter/vibration
5. Rear-tongue vibration with mmt up and down
6. Alternate rear and back tongue vibrato
7. Pharyngeal frication
8. Slight mid-tongue vib
9. Even tighter pharyngeal frication
10. Back and front tongue vibration
11. Dual back tongue vib

LARYNGEAL
1. Unvoiced
2. Modal voice
3. Falsetto voice
4. Vocal fry
5. Slight voicing
6. Child's voice
7. Rough voice with slight bits of vocal fry
8. Roughness with bits of ventricular folds
9. High-pitch, nearly whistle
10. Voice and ventricular folds
11. High-pitch, nearly whistle–biphonic
12. High-pitch, nearly whistle continues though vocal fry with bilabial flutters
13. Nearly-Donald duck
14. Ventricular folds—harsh, sharp clicks
15. Ventricular folds—extremely pressed
16. Vocal fold asymmetries
17. Low damped, barely voiced, creaky-like [no /r/]

BILABIAL
1. Lip broadening/lessening—narrow to extreme change
2. Loose bilabial flutter—no /r/

FIGURE 36.2 Map of /r/ manipulation relationships for *Rhotic* by Jaap Blonk. © Michael Edgerton.

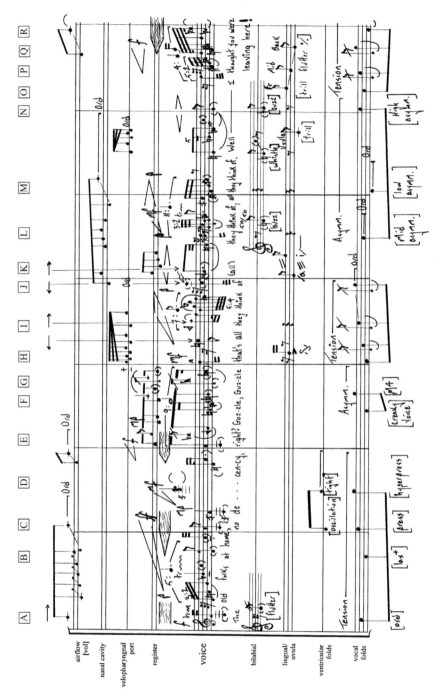

FIGURE 36.3 Demonstration Excerpt featuring transformations among multiple elements. © Michael Edgerton.

are chosen to accompany the five-line rhythm and pitch staff. The notion is that every parametric change from ordinary will produce a change of timbre or even acoustic class.

Beginning with an already complex pitch and rhythm line, the modifications to tone are grouped into 18 sections labeled A through R that are located above the airflow indications. Since the score features a modified tablature notation, descriptions will carry more than a single expectation of sound output, of which some alternatives will also be presented.

1. *High airflow and ordinary vocal fold tension:* air noise with subharmonic multiphonic may alternate with single pitches; lip flutter will be rough; beginning with extreme airflow each successive level will feature a crescendo of air noise.

2. *Lax vocal folds and air crescendo at moderate, moderate-high, and extremely high flows:* at moderate-high to high airflow, noise will begin to appear, as will subharmonics; also due to vocal folds laxness, other non-harmonic tones may appear due to air-induced and transient vocal folds asymmetries.

3. *High airflow, pressed vocal folds, and oscillating ventricular folds:* the tone will begin to be choked with transient register flips; due to oscillation of the ventricular folds, subharmonics may appear. The ventricular folds may add subharmonics, and due to the high airflow, air noise may become prominent; and if a sharp closing phase of the ventricular folds is used, loud percussive clicks may be produced.

4. *Hyperpressed vocal folds and tightly closed ventricular folds, adding high airflow:* this will produce an extra-complex tone with two separate components—a harmonic tone with harmonic four being the strongest harmonic (and also potentially containing a subharmonic), while also containing a broad-band tone from approximately F6–C7. The tone may feature harmonic and/or subharmonic jumps.

5. *High airflow and ordinary vocal fold vibration with mid-register placement, changing to high register, then low register:* the result is high air noise with potential subharmonics leading to phonation in chest register, then modal register. The different registers may produce different subharmonics.

6. *Creaky voice in medium register leading to low register:* low transient pitches (perhaps with multiple non-harmonic tones) may be present. The notated pitches may sound at an octave. The timbral changes should occur with the change of register; even though the phonation uses creaky voice, the performer should keep the idea of register change, as this will produce transient interval movement.

7. *Glottal whistle and pitch change with register change:* the glottal whistle will potentially produce unstable, multiphonic, and time-varying sonorities. This leads to pitch and register change that may affect resonator, glottal pressure, and airflow volume to produce additional time-variant behavior, such as the simultaneous combination of normal tones with the glottal whistle, an alternation between a normal tone with glottal whistle, or multiple glottal whistles.

8. *Lax to ordinary vocal folds, and rapid opening and closing of the velo-pharyngeal port with ingressive airflow:* at the beginning, a rapid opening and closing of the nasal port may produce registral jumps of an octave or more with sharp clicks, with the lax folds helping to allow pitch movement; this is followed in the score by a /ʃ/ in combination with opening and closing the nasal port to produce a pulsing of noise, leading to the pitch E5 produced on an ingressive breath with continued nasal port opening and closing to result in unstable pitches and noise.

9. *Pressed vocal folds with transition to hyperpressed vocal folds with rapid opening and closing of the velopharyngeal port:* the vocal folds will produce a brassy sound with harmonics being reinforced in the change from open to closed nasal port.

10. *Hyperpressed vocal folds and ingressive airflow:* hyperpressed vocal folds on ingressive airflow will produce a high-pitched and glassy tone, perhaps even a glottal whistle; multiple pitches may result.

11. *Hyperpressed to ordinary vocal fold vibration with lingual oscillation /a – i/, register change and nasality:* a biphonic sequence may appear. The frequency contour(s) may feature time-variance due to the change of register and tongue movement. At ordinary vocal fold tension, biphonation will stop and the sound will feature timbral changes due to the nasal and register behavior.

12. *Middle to high pitch asymmetry, changing to ordinary vocal fold vibration and nasal change and lip buzz:* depending on the ability of the singer, a clear biphonic sequence may appear; alternatively, a tone in mid-range may appear with either spectral manipulation or subharmonics, or alternatively may feature perceptually rough difference tones between biphonic tones A and B. Nasality should help to stabilize the multi-phonic potential of the asymmetrical vibration. The lip buzz should be loose, allowing the vocal folds' asymmetry to propagate outside the lips; at the end, the lip buzz and voice tone should carry equal weight.

13. *Asymmetry with increased nasality, changing to ordinary vocal fold vibration with bilabial/ linguadental whistle and uvula trill, and opening and closing of the nasal port:* the low asymmetry may produce clearly identified frequency contours or even a wide-band clustering of low tones, while the increasing nasality will help to perceptually isolate the multiple components produced by the vocal fold asymmetry. This is followed by the whistles, which will produce combinatorial multiphonics or difference tones, while the uvula trill will add percussive strokes onto the rapidly changing nasal to non-nasal production.

14. *High asymmetry with lip buzz leading to ordinary vocal fold vibration:* multiple high pitches should occur.

15. *Ordinary vocal fold tension and front tongue trill with transition:* the front tongue trill will continue through the rest.

16. *Pressed vocal fold and mid-tongue flutter with transition:* a strong and irregular mid-tongue flutter will inhibit accurate pitch production, which should become noisy and rough.

17. *Hyperpressed vocal fold tension with rear-tongue flutter and increasing airflow:* hyperpressed vocal fold tension will inhibit clear pitch definition producing a noisy tone with perhaps wideband components, and rear-tongue flutter will produce a strong noise, while the increasing airflow will begin to produce air noise.

18. *Lax vocal folds with tongue flutter and high airflow:* this will produce a strong air noise with a strong subharmonic, featuring percussive strokes.

Summary

In conclusion, the voice is capable of incredible diversity that this chapter only begins to address. In current artistic practice the biomechanical limits of voice are being explored by engaging with multidimensionality that allows inherent non-linear properties to be engaged through methods that desynchronize one or more elements within scaled networks from *ordinario* sound production. The nature of these explorations are diverse with no central mandate amongst those continuing such forward leaning practices. However, it may be acknowledged that two extremes include parametric change based on a single idea, and parametric change utilizing transformations amongst multiple elements.

REFERENCES

Anhalt, I. (1984). *Alternative Voices: Essays on Contemporary Vocal and Choral Composition.* Toronto: University of Toronto Press.

Aurbacher-Liska, H. (2003). *Die Stimme in der Neuen Musik.* Heinrichshofen: Florian Noetzel Verlag.

Backus, J. (1969). *The Acoustical Foundations of Music.* New York: W.W. Norton.

Barnett, B.M. (1972). *Aspects of Vocal Multiphonics.* Master's Thesis. University of California, San Diego, La Jolla.

Bartolozzi, B. (1969). *Metodo per Oboe.* Milan: Edizioni Suvini Zerboni.

Behrman, A. (1999). Global and local dimensions of vocal dynamics. *Journal of the Acoustical Society of America* 105: 432–434.

Benade, A. (1960). *Horn, Strings and Harmony.* Garden City: Doubleday Anchor Books.

Benade, A. (1975). The wolf tone on violin family instruments. *Catgut Acoustical Society Newsletter* 24: 21–23.

Berry, D.A., Herzel, H., Titze, I.R., and Krischer, K. (1994). Interpretation of biomechanical simulations of normal and chaotic vocal fold oscillations with empirical eigenfunctions. *Journal of the Acoustical Society of America* 95: 3595–3604.

Berry, D.A., Herzel, H., Titze, I.R., and Story, B.H. (1996). Bifurcations in excised larynx experiments. *Journal of Voice* 10: 129–138.

Blonk, J. (1997). *Vocalor,* compact disc. Amsterdam: Staalplaat.

Bloothooft, G., Bringmann, E., van Capellen, M., van Luipen, J., and Thomassen, K. (1992). Acoustics and perception of overtone singing. *Journal of the Acoustical Society of America* 92(4:1): 1827–1836.

Bouhuys, A. (1965). Sound-power production in wind instruments. *Journal of the Acoustical Society of America* 37: 453–456.

Chase, A.M. (1975). *Aspects Involving the Performance of Contemporary Vocal Music.* Master's Thesis. University of California, San Diego, La Jolla.

Clark, E.M. (1985). *Emphasizing the Articulatory and Timbral Aspects of Vocal Production in Vocal Composition.* DMA Thesis. University of Illinois, Urbana.

Dejonckere, P.H. and Lebacq, J. (1983). An analysis of the diplophonia phenomenon. *Speech Communication* 2: 47–56.

Edgerton, M.E. (2001). *Anaphora.* Musical Score. Paris: Babelscores.

Edgerton, M.E. (2005). *The 21st-Century Voice. Contemporary and Traditional Extra-Normal Voice.* Lanham, MD: Scarecrow Press.

Edgerton, M.E. (2013). *Music within the Continuum.* Saarbrücken: Lambert Academic Publishing.

Edgerton, M.E. (2016). The Old Folks at Home. Musical Score. Paris: Babelscores.

Edgerton, M.E., Khidr, A., and Bless, D. (1999). Multiple sound sources of the vocal tract, an analysis of [imitated-Tibetan] chant. *National Center for Voice and Speech, Status and Progress Report* 13: 131–140.

Edgerton, M.E., Neubauer, J., and Herzel, H. (2001). The influence of nonlinear dynamics and the scaling of multidimensional parameter spaces in instrumental, vocal and electronic composition. *Proceedings of 4th Generative Art Conference*, Politecnico di Milano University, Milan.

Edgerton, M.E., Neubauer, J., and Herzel, H. (2003). Nonlinear phenomena in contemporary music. *Perspectives of New Music* 41(2): 30–65

Fant, G. (1960). *The Acoustic Theory of Speech Production*. The Hague: Moulton.

Fitch, T., Neubauer, J., and Herzel, H. (2002). Calls out of chaos: the adaptive significance of nonlinear phenomena in mammalian vocal production. *Animal Behavior* 63(3): 407–18.

Fletcher, N. and Rossing, T. (1998). *The Physics of Musical Instruments*. New York: Springer-Verlag.

Fletcher, N. and Tarnopolsky, A. (1999). Acoustics of the avian vocal tract. *Journal of the Acoustical Society of America* 105: 35–49.

Fuks, L. (1999). *From Air to Music—Acoustical, Physiological and Perceptual Aspects of Reed Wind Instrument Playing and Vocal Ventricular Fold Phonation*. Stockholm: Royal Institute of Technology.

Gerratt, B.R., Precoda, K., and Hanson, D.G. (1987). *Diplophonia: features in the time domain*. Annual Convention of the American Speech-Language-Hearing Association, American Speech-Language- Hearing Association, New Orleans, November 13–16.

Gerratt, B.R., Precoda, K., Hanson, D.G., and Berke, G.S. (1988). Source characteristics of diplophonia. *Journal of the Acoustical Society of America* 83(suppl. 1): 66.

Glass, L. and Mackey, M. (1988). *From Clocks to Chaos: The Rhythms of Life*. Princeton: Princeton University Press.

Griffiths, P. (1981). *Modern Music: The Avant-Garde Since 1945*. London: Dent.

Herzel, H. (1993). Bifurcations and chaos in voice signals. *Applied Mechanics Review* 46: 399–413.

Herzel, H., Berry, D.A., Titze, I.R., and Saleh, M. (1994). Analysis of vocal disorders with methods from nonlinear dynamics. *Journal of Speech, Language and Hearing Research* 37: 1008–1019.

Herzel, H. and Reuter, R. (1997). Whistle register and biphonation in a child's voice. *Folia Phoniatrica et Logopaedica* 49: 216–224.

Hübler, K. (1984). Expanding the string technique. *Interface* 13: 187–198.

Jensen, K. (1979). Extensions of mind and voice. *Composer* 2: 13–17.

Kavasch, D. (1980). An introduction to extended vocal techniques: some compositional aspects and performance problems. *Reports from the Center 1* (2). La Jolla: Center for Music Experiment, University of California, San Diego. Available at www.ex-tempore.org/kavash/kavash.htm, accessed 22 November 2013.

Kim, S.H. (1988). *P'ansori: Korea's Epic Vocal Art and Instrumental Music*, compact disc. New York: Nonesuch Explorer Series.

Kimura, M. (1999). How to produce subharmonics. *Journal of New Music Research* 28: 177–184.

Kob, M. (2004). Analysis and modeling of overtone singing in the Sygyt style. *Applied Acoustics* 65(12): 1249–1259.

Kohler, K.J. (1996). Articulatory reduction in German spontaneous speech. *Proceedings of the 4th Speech Production Seminar*. San Diego: Singular Publishing Group.

La Barbara, J. (2003). *Voice is the Original Instrument*, compact disc. New York: Lovely Music.

Ladefoged, P. (1996). *Elements of Acoustic Phonetics*. Chicago: University of Chicago Press.

Large, J. and Murray, T. (1979). Studies of extended vocal techniques: safety. *NATS Bulletin* 34: 30–33.

Laver, J. (1980). *The Phonetic Description of Voice Quality*. Cambridge: Cambridge University Press.

Lee, M.H., Lee, J.N., and Soh, K.S. (1998). Chaos in segments from Korean traditional singing and western singing. *Journal of the Acoustical Society of America* 103: 1175–1182.

Levin, T. and Edgerton, M. (1999). The throat singers of Tuva. *Scientific American* 281(3): 70–77.

Marasovich, W.A., Gopal, H.S., Gerber, S.E., and Gibson, W.S. (1993). Diplophonia in a neonate. *International Journal of Pediatric Otorhinolaryngology* 25: 227–234.

Mazo, M., Erickson, D., and Harvey, T. (1995). Emotion and expression: temporal data on voice quality in Russian lament. In: O. Fujimura and M. Hirano (eds) *Vocal Fold Physiology: Voice Quality Control*, pp. 173–187. San Diego: Singular Press.

McKinney, J.C. (1982). *The Diagnosis and Correction of Vocal Faults*. Nashville: Broadman.

Mende, W., Herzel, H., and Wermke, K. (1990). Bifurcations and chaos in newborn cries. *Physics Letters A*, 145: 418–424.

Mergell, P., Herzel, H., and Titze, I. (2000). Irregular vocal fold vibration: high-speed observation and modeling. *Journal of the Acoustical Society of America* 108: 2996–3002.

Minton, P. (1998). *A Doughnut in One Hand*, compact disc. Berlin: FMP.

Neubauer, J., Edgerton, M., and Herzel, H. (2004). Non-linear phenomena in contemporary vocal music. *Journal of Voice* 18(1): 1–12.

Newell, R.M. (1970). *Writing for Singers in the Sixties*. DMA Thesis, University of California, San Diego, La Jolla.

Nonomura, N., Seki, S., Kawana, M., Okura, T., and Nakano, Y. (1996). Acquired airway obstruction caused by hypertrophic mucosa of the arytenoids and aryepiglottic folds. *American Journal of Otolaryngology* 17: 71–74.

Risset, J.C. (1978). Musical acoustics. In: E.C. Carterette and M.P. Friedman (eds), *Handbook of Perception*, Vol. IV: Hearing, pp. 520–564. New York: Academic Press.

Rose, P. (1988). Phonetics and phonology of Yang Tone phonation types in Zhenhai. First International Conference on Wu Dialects, December 12–14, 1988, Chinese University of Hong Kong, Hong Kong.

Sakakibara, K-I., Fuks, L., Imagawa, H., and Tayama, N. (2004). Growl voice in ethnic and pop styles. *Proceedings of the International Symposium on Musical Acoustics*, 31 March–3 April 2004, Nara, Japan.

Sakakibara, K-I., Imagawa, H., Konishi, T., Kondo, K., Murano, E.Z., Kumada, M., and Niimi, S. (2001). Vocal fold and false vocal fold vibrations in throat singing and synthesis of Khöömei. *Proceedings of the International Computer Music Conference*, Laboratorio Nacional de Musica Electroacustica, La Habana Cuba, September 18– 22.

Steinecke, I. and Herzel, H. (1995). Bifurcations in an asymmetric vocal fold model. *Journal of the Acoustical Society of America* 97: 1571–1578.

Stratos, D. (1978). *Cantare la Voce*, compact disc. Milan: Cramps Records.

Sundberg, J. (1977). The acoustics of the singing voice. *Scientific American* 236(3): 82–91.

Tenney, J. (1988). *Meta-Hodos: A Phenomenology of 20th-Century Musical Materials and an Approach to the Study of Form*. Oakland: Frog Peak Music.

Terrio, L. and Schreibweiss-Merin, D. (1993). Acoustic analysis of diplophonia. *Perceptual and Motor Skills*, 77: 914.

Tigges, M., Mergell, P., Herzel, H., Wittenberg, T., and Eysholdt, U. (1997). Observation and modelling glottal biphonation. *Acustica/Acta Acustica* 83: 707–714.

Titze, I. (1994). *Principles of Voice Production*. Upper Saddle River, NJ: Prentice-Hall.

Titze, I., Baken, R., and Herzel, H. (1993). Evidence of chaos in vocal fold vibration. In: I.R. Titze (ed.), *Vocal Fold Physiology: Frontiers in Basic Science*, pp. 143–188. San Diego: Singular Publishing Group.

Ward, P.H., Sanders, J.W., Goldman, R., and Moore, G.P. (1969). Diplophonia. *Annals of Otology, Rhinology, and Laryngology* 78: 771–7.

Wilden, I., Hanspeter, H., Peters, G., and Tembrock, G. (1998). Subharmonics, biphonation, and deterministic chaos in mammal vocalization. *Bioacoustics* 9: 171–96.

Williams, G.P. (1997). *Chaos Theory Tamed*. Washington: Joseph Henry.

Wishart T. (1983). *On Sonic Art*. London: Gordon and Breach.

CHAPTER 37

VOCAL MUSIC AND PEDAGOGY OF CHINESE, AFRICAN, AND INDIAN GENRES

YANG YANG, AARON CARTER-ÉNYÌ,
NANDHU RADHAKRISHNAN,
SOPHIE GRIMMER, AND JOHN NIX

INTRODUCTION

THE *Oxford Handbook of Singing* would be incomplete without at least a brief discussion of the ancient and rich vocal music traditions of the three largest population centers of the world: China, Africa, and India. Together, more than 4,108,000,000 people live in these diverse societies (http://www.worldpopulationreview.com, 2019)—half the human population of the entire planet. Vocal music has been a vital aspect of these cultures for millennia.

The Internet, popular media, and international commerce have exerted powerful forces upon the unique musical environments in China, Africa, and India in recent decades. Political turmoil has also undoubtedly had an impact. While more Westerners are more aware of or even familiar with aspects of traditional Chinese, African, and Indian music than ever before, the reverse is also true: more Asians and Africans have been exposed to (if not become immersed in) Western music, especially Western popular music. As a result, vocal music traditions which were transmitted from one generation to the next through oral/aural means have in some cases become transformed, been threatened, or have become practically obsolete. New means of teaching vocal music have also appeared, with informal master-apprentice structures being replaced with more formal curricula.

This chapter draws together several investigators, each of which is engaged in research involving the traditional vocal music and vocal instruction in China, Africa, and India, respectively. Each section provides a short description of the country or continent's vocal music and how it has been taught. Current trends and challenges are also presented. Each section then concludes with a summary of the authors' key points.

CHINESE VOCAL MUSIC AND PEDAGOGY

The concept of traditional Chinese singing

Traditional Chinese singing embraces a wide range of art forms. They constitute a living tradition spanning many hundreds of years, and have been officially grouped into three general categories: Quyi, traditional theater, and vocal folk music in the 2006 State Intangible Cultural Heritage List. Quyi is an art form which combines ballad singing, storytelling, and comic dialogues. Its performances are more narrative and improvised in comparison to the formalized traditional theaters that comprised both vocal and instrumental music forms. Vocal folk music, in contrast, is solely an art of singing. As a result, the notion of traditional Chinese singing can be seen as a collection of singing music forms from different regions and ethnic traditions, rather than one type of style. Since 2008, 10 of the 172 state-recognized music forms have been inscribed on the UNESCO Intangible Cultural Heritage list. Amongst these, Kun Qu opera, Yueju opera, Tibetan opera, Peking opera, Uyghur Muqam, and Manas are composite music forms concerning singing, whilst Urtiin Duu (solo), Khoomei (solo), Huàer (solo and antiphonal), and Grand song of the Dong ethnic group (chorus) are also traditional vocal musics.

Musical features of traditional Chinese singing

Apart from diverse musical expressions, most of these traditional folk songs are reported to share, at least, three distinctive features in contrast to Western Classical musics (Du 2003a, 2003b, 2003c, 2003d). First, although some Chinese ethnic folk music (such as Uygar) may present different scale arrangements, the "Wusheng" musical scale has been identified as the key music element in many traditional Chinese songs. This scale, which is a type of pentatonic scale often used in Chinese traditional music, may vary in tunings. The intervals between the five notes (Gong, Shang, Jue, Zhi, Yu) roughly correspond to those between scale degrees 1, 2, 3, 5, and 6 (do, re, mi, sol, la) in the major scale of Western music. In particular, music of the Han ethnic group (the largest ethnic group in China) was originally described as a pentatonic scale (Long 1994; Qian 2007; Ren 1990; Wang 2005), which may also develop into heptatonic (seven-tone) scales in some cases as an expansion of a pentatonic core. The second distinctive characteristic of Chinese folk songs is "unfixed tones" (Du 1991; Shen 1982, 1983), which emphasize that a tone in Chinese traditional music is a combination of timbre and inflection (such as melodic shape and ornamentations) of each musical sound (Du 1991). Such unfixed tones, known as Yin Qiang, are the minimum structural unit and smallest significant unit in the movement of musical sounds. In a broader sense, all Yin, as a kind of generation of tone (or tonal sound) accompanied by Qiang can be called YinQiang. And the so-called Qiang are alterable elements (such as pitch, strength, color, etc.), which are purposely affected in the process of tone generation to express specific musical intent. The third musical feature is associated with heterophonic texture. Chinese vocal musics are mostly presented within a horizontal structure, rather than developing a vertical harmonic structure such as is seen in Western Classical vocal music forms, in particular in choral music. Table 37.1 shows a summarized outline of the reported differences (mostly from Chinese publications) between the Chinese and the Western Classical tonal systems.

Table 37.1 A brief comparison of traditional Chinese and Western classical tonal systems

	Traditional Chinese	Western Classical
Design	1. Unfixed tone 2. A tone of indefinite pitch, namely Qiang	1. "Fixed tone" (Roederer 1995) 2. A tone of definite pitch
Tonality	1. Two three-tone groups constitute the basic elements of a key 2. Pentatonic scale-like features in vocal music (Fu 1997; Li 1981; Qiu 2002; Wang 2005)	1. Tonality originated from four-tone series 2. Mode based on a tonal system consisting of several (usually seven) tones in fixed relationship to a tonic, having a characteristic key signature 3. Melodies have harmonic meaning (Chen 2004)
Time (rhythm and tempo)	1. Ban-qiang system (metrical couplets) 2. "Sanban": beats occurring at irregular intervals; having no pattern or order in time 3. "Non-periodic" downbeat 4. Periodic downbeat	1. Periodic downbeat 2. "Non-periodic" downbeat
Texture	Horizontal structure	Vertical structures
Notation	Gonche, lü Several types of notation were used. Singers used the syllabic symbols for the five notes of the pentatonic scale, as did players of pipes. Players of the stone and bell chimes, which were tuned to the lüs, used symbols that represented the pitch names of the lüs. Players of flutes and zithers used a kind of tablature. None of this notation indicated rhythm (http://www.infoplease.com/ce6/ent/A0857319.html)	Stave (mainly) (Hu 2006)

Amongst the five listed areas of difference, "fixed tone" refers to tones in the Western Classical tradition, which are usually characterized by pitch, a sound whose frequency is clear and stable. As the pitch inflections are periodic and stable in terms of vibration, listeners may not easily perceive subtle changes of fundamental frequency within a tone. In contrast, "Qiang" (unfixed tone) was perceived as the minimum structural unit in the movement of musical sound that comprises a number of alterable musical elements, such as pitch, strength, and timbre, to purposely manipulate the process of tone-making (Shen 1982). In a broader sense, every sound ("音" in Chinese) is a process of tone-making accompanied by "Qiang" to express a specific musical intention. It has also been termed as "Yin Qiang," "a living tone," or "tone flexion" in other studies (Fu and Zhou 1999; Zhang 1987). While the concept of "Qiang" illustrated the complexity of presenting Chinese traditional music in contrast to a "pitch-based system," this holistic, probably ambitious, solution for music-acoustic observation of Chinese music was strongly challenged by later researchers. The term "unfixed" was criticized for being restricted to a 'narrow understanding' of musical sound (such as pitching and tuning), in which intrinsic linguistic elements of Sinitic language such as syllables are not taken as a factor of tone-making (Weng, C. W. 2002). On the other hand, it was argued to be possibly "intrinsically contradictive" and to "exaggerate the musical differences between Western [classical] and Chinese traditional music in terms of pitch perception" (Yang et al. 2013).

Contemporary Chinese traditional singing

Due to the decline of traditional oral practices in a modernizing Chinese society, Chinese traditional music has been threatened by two powerful forces since the twentieth century (Guan 1995; Hu and Wang 2001). The first threat is from the increasing Westernization of the traditional music culture through widespread access to global music media in which Western musics predominate. The potential for a non-Chinese bias in music practice is exacerbated by another by-product of this cultural importation, namely the "translation" of a few token traditional Chinese musical examples, into modern performance idioms by contemporary musicians in China. Although this allows the folk adaptations to become accessible and enjoyed by a wider public, there is a danger that the original source material may be lost. This is because the oral folk tradition, by which succeeding generations of local musicians pass on both the music and its "authentic" performance stylistics, is being overtaken by Westernized musical arrangements that "modernize" this particular art form. For instance, instead of using Chinese traditional musical notations, Western Classical notating methods were adopted and promoted in Chinese music education, alongside numeric notation. Although this was an innovative attempt to notate and represent the Chinese traditional sung musics using a system from Western Classical music, it risks losing the "authentic flavor" of music composed with "unfixed tones." While the Western notation may support researchers further to explore the nature of Chinese traditional singing in comparison with Western music, it is also transforming the way in which indigenous music is accessed and learned by young musicians. Therefore, a more "accurate" representation of these musics may need to embrace musical elements and linguistic features that contribute to the authentic singing style as a whole. Recent researches have explored methods of identifying "genuine" traditional folk songs from the Westernized modern folk song repertoires (Huang 2003; Li 2006; Qiao 2003; Xue 2006; Yu 1994a, 1994b; Zang 2004), which have been taught as indigenous music in colleges.

After the 1990s, traditional Chinese musics increasingly attracted public attention in national music competitions and international music events in China (Huang 2005; Jie 1994). The surviving Chinese traditional music rehabilitated its importance in education after a long period of relative neglect and has become more popular with the support of modern technologies such as television and the Internet. Although no clear answer has emerged to explain why this "old and dying" music was able to survive the radical social movements of twentieth-century China, the "cultural practice and awareness" of music was believed to be one of the impetuses in the revival of traditional musics (Chen 2006; Huang 2003; Mi 2007; Zhang 2004). This "revival" was invoked and greatly influenced by a spontaneous awakening of indigenous musics in contemporary Chinese society, along with a policy change that reflected the increasing demand for musical diversity in China's higher education and commercial music market. In the recent national scheme for the protection of folk music heritage

(Department of Cultural Affairs 2006; President of the People's Republic of China 2011), the continued survival of traditional singing and songs has become a key issue to be addressed, along with pedagogical challenges to transfer "authentic" traditional performances into formal music education.

Pedagogical challenges in the education of traditional singing

A case study of Huàer music

A recent case study of Chinese traditional folk song singing, as exemplified by Huàer music (Yang 2011), suggested that (1) "authentic (or traditional) singing" is a social-cultural construct; and (2) musical authenticity is an evaluation or judgment that people make on particular musical features of performance(s) under the influence of specific social and cultural values. There are several similar acoustic and musical features shared by most of the studied folk singing performances, which differentiate them from the other music styles. However, the standard of "authentic" was discovered to be changeable over time. It was found that:

1. A number of unique vocal ornamentations are used in traditional folk singing within the oral culture, but have not been clearly addressed in any related formal singing training. Combined with an improvisational style in performance, these special vocal features appear to increase the difficulty in both teaching and learning of authentic folk singing.
2. Two different approaches (formal versus informal) are identified in folk singing education. In the approach of formal (the Western conservatory) music training, the current highly organized college curricula are not necessarily compatible with non-classical (both Western and Chinese) music styles.
3. Although college music teachers tend to perceive themselves as well-trained educators and musicians, they are less prepared to deal with other-than-Classical music and frequently appear to feel very protective about their music experiments of traditional folk song teaching.
4. Therefore, the introduction of authentic folk vocal music into colleges may also require a transformation of a teacher-organized learning pedagogy to a more cooperative learning style, which can be developed by the vocal music teacher and students with the support from authentic folk singers. The challenge will be how effectively and efficiently these collaborative efforts can be organized within the current curricula frame and pedagogies for music training. Higher education tutors' strengths are likely to be more pedagogical, while the established folk singer's strengths are more focused on authentic sung practices within the focus musical genre.
5. Accordingly, students' learning routes will be more diverse in this recommended dual-channel input of knowledge from both a college tutor and an expert folk singer. This may require students constantly to balance the two approaches and develop effective learning strategies appropriate for their own stages of learning that draw on the strengths of each perspective.
6. The current college assessment system is neither effective nor valid in evaluating observed collective (shared) teaching experimentation. Therefore, teaching objective(s), methods, and evaluation need to be revised for a better consistency to account for the different (Western and Chinese) music traditions.

Summary of research findings on Chinese vocal music and pedagogy

These research findings indicate that:

1. The challenge of teaching authentic folk singing in higher education is not solely a pedagogical issue; it may also be associated with social taboo, cultural tradition, and academic bias.
2. Compared to Western Classical music styles, the traditional conservatory teaching-learning model may not be as effective when transferred to this particular environment of folk music learning.
3. Effective teaching/learning of authentic singing performance may need cooperation between university music tutor, folk singer, and student within or outside the music classroom, which also implies a transformation in the traditional roles of the classroom participants.
4. A carefully designed teaching plan should embrace necessary knowledge of traditional music repertoire, as well as appropriate pedagogical strategies to achieve the teaching objectives. In addition, the methods for assessment should be compatible with the restructured course design and be able to reflect the teaching/learning outcomes.
5. To promote the practice of authentic folk music not only implies an introduction of indigenous music material into higher education, but also a development of musical and cultural understanding about these music traditions.
6. Computer-based technologies can be useful in analyzing singing performance and supporting the learning (vocal skill and social context) of traditional singing musics.

Given that most, if not all, traditional music heritages are experiencing the same pedagogical challenges in a period of social and cultural transformation, to ensure the continued survival of traditional Chinese singing, the practice of "cultural music" is proposed as a possible solution. This educational model should be based on a student-centered learning environment, in which formal and informal music experiences are encouraged to be integrated with each other to achieve effective learning outcomes.

Sub-Saharan African vocal music and pedagogy

Introduction

In Sub-Saharan Africa, singing has been a casual pastime, formal practice, and specialized profession for centuries. This is embodied in the call-and-response choruses found throughout the continent, involving a fluid exchange between leader (often a professional

praise singer) and an inclusive group of all persons present, building community in perhaps the best way: through singing together. Unlike North America and Europe, in Africa,
one rarely hears the phrase, "I cannot sing." The average singing diet is complex, including
Arabic chant or European hymnody (depending on whether one is Muslim or Christian),
popular music in English or French (depending on the colonial past), and choruses in one or
more of Africa's 2000 languages.

This section surveys vocal arts in Sub-Saharan Africa with special attention to three
countries: Ethiopia in the east, Nigeria in the west, and South Africa. These countries share
similarities in the vocal arts. All have historic practices of praise poetry, chanted and sung,
that thrive to this day: *azmari bet* in Ethiopia, *oríkì* in Nigeria, *izibongi* in South Africa. All
are markets for Jamaican reggae and have responded with home-grown reggae stars like
Lucky Dube of South Africa. There is also great diversity. Ethiopia has a rich inventory of
wind and string instruments and unique scales that have coalesced with African-American
music in *Ethio-jazz*. Singing in Nigeria is often accompanied by talking drums that mimic
the pitch contours of the voice. The complex vocal polyphony of South Africa, notably Zulu
mbube and *isicathamiya*, is the sound often identified with Africa in the West through Paul
Simon's album *Graceland* and Disney's animated musical *The Lion King*. After establishing
some key principles and exploring a few very broad categories of vocal arts, teaching and
learning methods are proposed.

Orality and literacy

The legendary Saint Yared of Ethiopia is reported to have devised a musical notation in the
sixth century. Evidence of notated chant, or *melekket*, exists in the form of manuscripts
dating from the sixteenth century, but this notation is not used outside of the Ethiopian
Orthodox Church (Shelemay and Kimberlin 2013). The vocal arts in Sub-Saharan Africa
remained a predominantly oral tradition into the twentieth century. Missionaries first
introduced Western notation into Sub-Saharan Africa in the nineteenth century, and Tonic
Sol-Fa notation is now widely used (Carter-Ényì 2018), as is shown in Figure 37.1.

Today, vocal forms that were transmitted orally, like praise poetry and choruses, are now
a mix of orality and literacy (Kaschula 1999, p. 56). Digital recording and the Internet have
reinvigorated and transformed oral traditions, and facilitated music and film industries independent from the West that are distinctly African.

FIGURE 37.1 An example of Tonic-Solfa notation from David Àìná's "E̩ jé ká jọ yọ̀" (1988), a
Christmas carol in Yorùbá.

Linguistic diversity

In order to understand the singing cultures of Africa, one must first appreciate the incredible ethno-linguistic diversity of the continent. Several language families are unique to Africa: Niger-Congo A, Niger-Congo B (Bantu), Nilo-Saharan, and Khoe-Saan (Khoisan). There are also large numbers of native and non-native speakers of Afro-Asiatic languages (notably Amharic, Arabic, and Berber) and Indo-European languages (notably Afrikaans, English, and French). All in all, there are over 2000 languages spoken in Africa, over a quarter of the 7000 languages estimated to be spoken in the world today. In Nigeria alone, there are approximately 500 languages spoken, while Ethiopia has a formidable 87 languages. South Africa's language count is lower, but its linguistic climate remains complex with a number of native languages, including Sotho, Xhosa, and Zulu, that are more robust than the colonial offshoot Afrikaans (Lewis et al. 2013).

Language and singing

Many of the languages spoken in Sub-Saharan Africa are tone languages of the Niger-Congo families. These languages use pitch as a contrastive feature to differentiate between otherwise identical words. This is also referred to as *speech melody*. An illustration is the disyllable *igba* from the Yorùbá language of Nigeria and Benin, as is seen in Table 37.2. The Yorùbá orthography uses three tone levels: (´) high, ( ) mid, and (`) low. Note the differing meanings as the tone levels change.

The similarity of Yorùbá speech to *syllabic* (one note per syllable) singing is widely acknowledged by Yorùbá speakers, who compare the three speech tones to the solfege syllables *do-re-mi*.

Since Herzog (1934), ethnomusicologists and linguists have compared the tone contours of speech with the melodic contours of singing and found similarity. However, adherence to speech-melody by musicians varies greatly across and within cultures, revealing a genre-dependent trend, with traditional music as the most faithful and contemporary popular music as the least faithful to linguistic features (Schellenberg 2012, p. 271). The pitch

---

Table 37.2 Speech melody and meaning in Yorùbá

Orthographic variants of the Yorùbá disyllable *igba*	Tone pattern: (´) high, ( ) mid, and (`) low	Meaning
Igbá	mid–high	calabash (a dried gourd cup)
Igba	mid–mid	two hundred
ìgbá	low–high	garden egg (similar to an eggplant)
Igbà	mid–low	climbing-rope for palm trees
Ìgbà	low–low	time

From Abraham (1962), pp. 282–284.

contrasts of speech also influence vocal harmony in Africa because, for the sake of linguistic accuracy, similar contours are usually present in all renderings of a lyric. As nineteenth-century missionaries found, the contrary motion favored by European hymnody, in which the same text is set to varying pitch contours, is at odds with the phonological systems of African tone languages (Agu 1992, p. 14; Ekwueme 1974, p. 337). Similarly, strophic forms are not common in the music of tone languages because it requires different lyrics to follow the same melodic contours. Igbo musician Laz Ekwueme identifies parallelism and antiphony (call-and-response) as harmonic devices sympathetic to tone and thus common in African ensemble singing (Ekwueme 1974, pp. 344–345).

Vocal technique

A wide spectrum of sounds are heard in African vocal arts, from speech to chanting to singing to ululation (a uvular trill) to imitations of percussion and animal sounds. All of these sounds might be heard in a single performance, spread amongst the members of an ensemble, or coming from a single voice, like an *azmari* (Amharic praise poet) in an Ethiopian *tej bēt* (honey-wine tavern) (Kebede 1975, p. 52). However, many forms and the artists who specialize in them are defined by specific vocal techniques.

In describing African vocal arts, it is important to identify the language, the movements involved, accompanying instruments, the content or purpose, and vocal style. Among these, language is the most important because it explains the ethnic and geographic origin as well as the phonetic inventory. Xhosa *izibongi* might include clicks while poetry from West Africa will not. Next in importance after language is vocal style, including the type of phonation, registration, and timbral effects like nasalization. Is it speech-like or sung? Is it full voice or falsetto? Is it tense or relaxed? Whether it is Zulu choral music or Yorùbá poetry, vocal quality is often more important to classification than subject matter (Babalola 1966; Erlmann 1999; Vidal 2012). The same words repeated with a different vocal style become a different type of poetry. For example, while essentially all Yorùbá oral poetry involves *oríkì* (praise), it is varied by the vocal style (Okpewho 1992, p. 129).

Solo performance

Vocal performance has been a profession in Africa for centuries, including the iconic *griots* of the West African Sahel (Hale 1998), the *azmari* of Ethiopia, and the *imbongi* of South Africa. These vocalists use a wide variety of voice production and are variously referred to as oral poets, praise singers, and verbal artists in academic literature depending on the discipline of the researcher. Okpewho explains that precolonial communities were governed by a king or chief who had "absolute authority over all matters" and employed court poets whose "major role was to swell the image of the ruler" (1992, p. 25). Oral poets also carried news from one place to another, recanted folktales, and praised gods. But fundamental changes to African life have drastically changed the role of the poet, who is now largely relegated to "cultural performances" (Okpewho 1992, p. 25). Instead of praising kings, the poet now praises the rich; instead of indigenous gods, he praises Allah or Jehovah. One constant is social critique, which remains an important aspect of African oral poetry. Poetry of dissent can incite listeners to protest, as it did during the apartheid era in South Africa, leading to the imprisonment of poets (Kaschula 1999, pp. 57–60). During the occupation of Ethiopia (1936–1941), the Italians gathered *azmari* and executed them for fear of their sway over public opinion (Shelemay and Kimberlin 2013). One hears echoes of the alternation of praise and social critique in African-American hip-hop (Smitherman 1997, p. 4), and now African hip-hop, which ranges from self-praise and boasting to mocking of competitors and social and political indictments.

Vocal style often distinguishes one type of oral poetry from another. Across the continent, Africans are acutely aware of the many sounds the voice can produce. Yorùbá poetry is "classified according to the manner of voice production employed" (Babalola 1966, p. vi). Vidal aptly describes these:

> *Ijala* is characterized by nasal colouring and acoustically intense open voice tone quality . . . *Ewi* is characterized by a high falsetto and wailing voice quality . . . Tense vocal quality with slight nasal colouring can be observed in *rara* . . . *Iyere Ifa* has the purest tone quality of all the four chants.
>
> (Vidal 2012, pp. 71–72)

To help demonstrate some of the differences, four video links of examples of Yorùbá praise poetry are provided below:

Muri's Ewi (Iwi) Example 1: http://digitalcommons.auctr.edu/adept/22/
Muri's Ijala Example 2: http://digitalcommons.auctr.edu/adept/23/
Mayowa Adeyemo praises Ogun: http://digitalcommons.auctr.edu/adept/5/
Mayowa Adeyemo praises Eledumare: http://digitalcommons.auctr.edu/adept/24/

The recent emergence of women in the largely male field of oral poetry (Kaschula 1999, p. 56) has complicated the identification of genre because male and female voices have registrational differences. A woman performing *ìjálá* in head voice might be misinterpreted as an *ewi* poet, thus a high belt might be more appropriate for *ìjálá*.

Ensemble singing

Similar to solo performance, ensemble singing is often characterized by vocal style. Types of Zulu choral music are "frequently conceptualized by . . . vocal registers and timbres . . . *isikhwelajo* is characterized by high-pitched, almost yelling sounds, *cothoza mfana* and *isicathamiya* . . . generally feature more soft-touched, low-intensity vocals" (Erlmann 1999, p. 189). Recording ensembles drawing on the oral tradition continue to distinguish between the vocal styles that defined the various oral genres. Amateur and semi-professional choirs exist in churches, schools, and universities, and many fine composers who pay close attention to the details of language (such as tone contrasts) have emerged. However, the distinct vocal qualities that define the oral singing tradition have been lost in the written choral tradition.

The less formal *chorus* singing is now disconnected from the praise singers (or oral poets) that traditionally led call-and-response singing. Many Nigerian Christians and Muslims would refuse to listen to an *ìjálá* poet praise the indigenous god of iron, *Ògún*, let alone sing a refrain in affirmation. Call-and-response choruses are now sung in large churches filled with thousands of worshipers, often alongside American contemporary Christian music, which is part of the international growth of evangelical and Pentacostal Christianity.

Popular music

Urban centers are now the attraction for the vocally gifted (Okpewho 1992, p. 41). Youssou N'Dour descended from *griots*, but embarked on an international recording career instead of learning the trade of his forebears (Duran 1989, pp. 277–278). In major cities like Addis Ababa, Dakar, Johannesburg, Kinshasa, Lagos, and Nairobi, there are recording studios everywhere, producing music locally that is consumed locally, sold by compact disc vendors in markets and on street corners. From the 1960s to the 1990s, Africans were largely attracted to imported music like James Brown, Bob Marley, and Michael Jackson. Now, in the small shops that dot the neighborhoods, African-produced music overwhelms music from the outside. Because of the high premium for Internet access, Bluetooth file exchange between cellphones has become a primary means of sharing music. If the youth are going to listen to hip-hop, they would rather it be hip-hop that relates to their lives and the complex linguistic environments they live in. Contrastingly, music on television has more of a Western sensibility with the proliferation of amateur singing competitions, including *Project Fame* and *The X-Factor*.

Implications for practice

For classically trained performers and educators interested in African vocal arts, the most accessible resources are scores, and there are abundant resources in this area. This includes solo and ensemble art music written by African composers, including Ephraim Amu of Ghana, Ayo Bankole of Nigeria, Niel van der Watt of South Africa, and many others. These are often available in university libraries. There is also a growing body of transcriptions and arrangements for choir of varying quality.

Learning an oral tradition poses a greater challenge than a score in Western notation with a CD included, but it is possible. The author interviewed a skilled *ìjálá* poet in Nigeria, and asked how someone so young learned this old practice, convinced that it must have been handed down from generation to generation. "No," she said, "I went to the library and got on the Internet!" Linguistic knowledge is essential: beyond that, the human capacity for vocal imitation is quite astonishing, and very effective in combination with solid research. Interviews of *azmari* in Ethiopia and *imbongi* in South Africa suggest that learning a traditional vocal art is often an independent process (Kebede 1975, pp. 50–51; Scheub 1975, pp. 17–22).

Mary Goetze has applied creative pedagogical methods with an innovative ensemble at Indiana University, using a mix of research and rote learning through watching online videos of performances from around the world (Goetze 2010). So type *azmari bet* (Amharic oral poetry from Ethiopia) or *isicathamiya* (a Zulu choral music from South Africa) in to your preferred search engine, or better yet, go to your local university's library for language resources and high-quality recordings.

Section summary and conclusion

The oral tradition in Africa is really an *aural* and an *oral* tradition. It is a tradition of singers hearing and imitating sound, not just words. Old technologies such as the alphabet and musical notation filter out so many aspects of sound and are inept at representing sounds they were not designed for, such as languages with pitch contrasts or music in non-Western scales. We are fortunate that technology has advanced to make recordings that nearly capture the full range of human hearing and vision, and has provided the means to share information with others around the world. The academic study of African vocal arts has been stunted for years by transcriptions that conform to concepts of Western literature and music. Vocal style is cultivated as much as content or structure. Thus, using the term "poetry" is a misleading way to refer to the historic voice profession in Sub-Saharan Africa. For the student of African singing, whether for research or practice, quality transcriptions and descriptions are merely a supplement to dedicated listening.

INDIAN CLASSICAL VOCAL MUSIC
AND ITS PEDAGOGY

Introduction

Indian classical singing has two main branches or forms: the Hindustani and the Karnatic. Underpinning both traditions for centuries has been a teacher-student system which has enabled the intricacies of both forms to be passed on orally for generations (Ranade 1998). This portion of the chapter will examine the two traditions, first by reviewing major aspects of the styles, then by examining the means of instruction within the style. There are both similarities and striking differences between Hindustani and Karnatic singing and instruction. The section concludes with some observations on modern developments in instruction.

Historical background and traditional pedagogy of Karnatic and Hindustani music traditions

Both forms of Indian classical vocal music have origins dating back to approximately 2000 BC. Thought to have developed from the chanting of old Hindu scriptures, the *vedas* (Rowell 1992; Wulff 1983), these vocal traditions are some of the oldest practiced in Southeast Asia. Though the bifurcation into two traditions, Hindustani and Karnatic, occurred much later in history, the traditional modes of their transmission are related.

Guru-shishya or *ustad-shagird* (in Islam) describes the traditional mode of music transmission that occurred in India within the teacher-pupil relationship. Traditionally, the student became a disciple of the master (*guru* or *ustad*). Regarded as part of the master's family, a member of his household, and provided with food and clothing, the student (*shishya or shagird*) was assimilated into the master's schedule. Ranked higher than a biological parent, a metaphysical entity representing God and both parents, the master assumed ultimate authority, in part predicated upon the student's devotion and total obedience. The student imbibed the atmosphere of the art, inadvertently internalizing both musical knowledge and a broader foundation of contextual information. With "no separation between a 'teacher' and a 'curriculum' to be taught" (Weidman 2006, p. 276), the student learned by emulating the master, "by becoming absorbed in him or her." With no distinction made between "life" and "music," the traditional learning environment provided a social context for two modes of transmission, cognitive and cultural (Booth 1996), in which behaviors and customs necessary to oral/aural learning processes are supported and validated.

Hindustani classical tradition

Though it has strong roots in Hinduism, Hindustani music has also been enriched by Islamic culture. The influence of Persian and Arabian civilization was at its peak during the reign of the Moguls, the Muslim emperors who ruled India (White 1971). The evolution of Hindustani music suggests that it has undergone several changes from its historical *dhrupad* form to the current version called *khayal*. The word *dhrupad* means fixed-verse, and this form was the primary type of Hindustani music between the fifteenth and eighteenth centuries. The austerity of this tradition made it difficult to master and practice. *Khayal*, on the other hand, means imagination or thoughts. It is considered the modern version of the Hindustani genre, and has given composers and singers the opportunity to improvise their *raga*, sets of specific notes characteristic to Indian music, during performance (Raja 2005). *Thumri* is yet another version of Hindustani vocal music, but it is considered semi-classical.

Hindustani classical vocal tradition: performance practices and teaching

Characteristically, a Hindustani vocal performance includes the following sequence of pieces: *aalap, bada khayal* or *vilambit, chota khayal* or *drut, sargam*, and *taan*. *Aalap* is where the performer reveals the *raga* in a slow tempo. This piece is usually performed on the vowel /ɑ/, as in the English "father." *Aalap* is followed by *bol-aalap*, which is similar to *aalap* but performed on verses of the song. The *bada* and *chota khayal* are basically slow and fast renderings of the composition. *Sargam* is a way of exploring the *raga* using sol-fa passagework (Massey and Massey 1976). During this process, performers exhibit their skill in improvisation and increase the tempo. Throughout a typical concert, singers embellish their performances with vocal ornaments like *gamak*, a vibrato-like intonation, and *meend*, a form of glissando. *Taan* provides the singers with an opportunity to reach a peak in their performance (Deva 1973). *Taan*, usually performed on the vowel/ɑ/, is an abrupt fall and rise in pitch contour that is voluntarily controlled by the performer (Radhakrishnan et al. 2011). The rate, extent, pitch, and loudness of *taan* is skillfully controlled within the rules of *raga*. Here the performers showcase their skill and vocal control to the audience.

Hindustani music is not as smooth (legato) as Western classical. Consonants make it easier to shift between notes, but *gurus* believe in training students on vowels to challenge their abilities in rendering compositions. As was previously mentioned, songs rendered in Hindustani vocal music have influences from the two religions, Hinduism and Islam. The vedic hymns practiced by Hindus have been modified by Islamic singers with meaningless rhythmic syllables representing specific musical notes of the *raga*. However, both the Hindu and Islamic schools begin vocal training with *aakar*, singing on a vowel, usually /a/.

It may take several years for a student to graduate; the duration of study depends on the *guru's* discretion. Students accompany their *gurus* during performances; however, only students chosen by the *guru* would appear on stage. Students usually take the task of playing the drone that acts as a pitch guide for the *guru*. The traditions learned by students under the guidance of one *guru* may be different from that learned by students of another *guru* at a different school, usually from a different province. The school of each *guru* in the Hindustani tradition is called a *gharana*. *Gharana* refers to the ancestry of gurus, their *shishya*, and the style of music they practice (Neuman 1980). Traditionally, the name of a *gharana* goes after the state or province occupied by the *guru*, for example, Vishnupur and Gwalior. A trained scholar in Hindustani music can identify a singer's *gharana* by listening to him perform. Though all *gharanas* follow the basic rules, each *gharana* will have a particular style or nuance in rendering their music.

Differences between Hindustani and Karnatic classical singing traditions

While the two classical musics of India share essential elements, including certain *ragas* (melody types), Karnatic music is strikingly different from its Hindustani counterpart: improvisatory boundaries are determined more profoundly by the rendition of compositions; ornamental articulation is given greater emphasis, resulting in a particular vocal production; textual content is predominantly religious, often in Sanskrit, a language written in metric verse rather than prose; the repertoire of *ragas, talas* (rhythmic cycle; for an example, see Nelson 2000), compositions and improvisation techniques vary considerably; and the typical ensemble has some different instrumentation. For example, the melodic accompanying instrument is usually a violin, and the *mrdangam* (double-faced wooden drum) in Karnatic music performance (Brown 1965) replaces the *tabla* of the Hindustani tradition. In addition, the socio-cultural history of each canonical style has given rise to different pedagogies, associated social networks, and cultural developments (Allen 2008; Sankaran and Allen 2000; Subramanian, 2006, 2008a, 2008b; Weidman 2003, 2006).

Karnatic classical tradition

Karnatic music involves an unusual combination of compositions (*kalpita sangita*) and a wide range of improvisatory possibilities (*manodharma sangita*). Rather than being mutually exclusive modes of musical activity, they are integrated and intertwined; the former are perceived as flexible, the latter as structured (recall the *khayl* and *dhrupad*, respectively, in the Hindustani tradition). Within certain boundaries determined by a particular stylistic school called *bani* (recall the *gharana* of the Hindustani tradition), certain freedoms are possible when rendering a composition (Catlin 1980, 1985), while improvisation is profoundly influenced by and structured according to the composition to which it relates (Cormack 1992; Ravikiran 2006; Viswanathan 1977). Developing awareness of the subtle effects of form on *raga* and understanding what is fixed within what is flexible is fundamental in the musical training (Viswanathan and Cormack 1998). There is thus an interesting dialectic that arises in Karnatic music between the concepts of improvisation and composition. While creativity and originality are essential characteristics of vivid performance, with a performer expected to highlight the *bhakti* (spirit) and *bhava* (emotion) within the music, fidelity to the composition is considered critical.

Developmental stages of learning in the Karnatic tradition

While finding a unique "voice" is central to the expression of Karnatic classical music, the early stages of a *shishya*'s training with a single *guru* concern the comprehensive establishment of a musical foundation. Through imitation of the *guru*'s singing over an extended period, a *shishya* begins to embody the music of a particular *bani* (school, style, or lineage). Playing a significant part in distinguishing one musician's rendition from another, the intricate *gamakas* (ornaments) that intertwine with a predominantly devotional *sahitya* (lyrics) (Jackson 1991), so prominent a feature of Karnatic music, are given special attention. Meticulously controlled by the Karnatic singer, these *gamakas* are not optional ornamentations but integral to the life of the notes (*svaras*) and are learned initially through focus on the rendition of the compositional kernel, *kalpita sangita*. At this stage, the imitation process for memorization, involving little if any analysis or depth of musical understanding, facilitates absorption of some fundamental musical elements of the repertoire and its interpretation within a particular stylistic paradigm, and a simultaneous growth of perceptual and technical skill. The accumulation of these musical strengths is thought to be fundamental to development of an individual "voice" later in the training.

As a *shishya*'s listening skills become more sophisticated through learning the compositions (*kalpita sangita*), so the improvisatory dimensions of the music (*manodharma sangita*) can begin to be explored, often via call-and-response exchanges between the *guru* and *shishya*. *Shishyas* might also be encouraged to start listening to other performers. With their listening being guided by the guru in a sense, *shishyas* develop greater awareness of particular musical aspects in the lesson as their listening "tunes in" to those same aspects during a live performance or listening to a recording. One process thus feeds the other. Though encouraged by most of the *gurus*, this broader listening is treated with some caution. The extent to which a *guru* monitors it depends upon the perceived level of a *shishya*'s attunement to the *bani*.

Having become finely attuned to the subtleties of a particular stylistic school (*bani*) with a more sophisticated technical facility developed over many years, a *shishya* can then begin the lifelong journey towards finding an individual "voice." Initially supported by the *guru*, this critical developmental stage involves an essentially autonomous iterative process of music listening and exploration. Remaining within the boundary of the *bani, shishyas* gradually accumulate a personalized bank of musical ideas, of "remembered repertoires" (Neuman 1990, p. 22), from which they can draw in the moment of performance.

This process of creative development, manifest in many different pedagogical settings, both formal and informal, continues throughout a singer's life. With listening central at every stage (Grimmer 2012), Karnatic singers gradually explore and hone their own musical ideas. They develop a unique way of listening that informs the kind of material they absorb into their creative music (from what they hear). This listening is filtered through a number of paradigms: the classical tradition; a particular *bani*; an expanding musical knowledge; an evolving vocal skill; a growing awareness of vocal strengths and weaknesses; and individual musical preferences.

Present adaptive strategies

Despite dramatic societal changes in modern India and influences from the diverse pedagogic approaches of a global diasporic community, the special contact between master (*guru*) and disciple (*shishya*) is still considered fundamental to the transmission of musical expertise in contemporary Karnatic vocal training, as was also seen in Hindustani vocal training. The experience of a *guru–shishya* relationship is thought to go beyond learning the execution of musical details, helping to facilitate a more profound embodiment of the esoteric elusive dimensions of the musical tradition. While *shishyas* today are unlikely to experience the traditional total learning environment of *gurukulavasam*, the *guru–shishya* relationship remains pivotal and is adapted continually to embrace the demands of modern life while still accommodating those aspects considered critical for genuine musical development (Grimmer 2011). For example, a *guru* might provide the focal point for a community in which different modes of learning can occur beyond the one-to-one lesson, such as: informal peer-group practicing sessions amongst fellow *shishyas* (often with mixed ability groups, sometimes online); advanced *shishyas* teaching younger *shishyas*; *shishyas* observing the *guru* in different contexts (performing, teaching other *shishyas*, engaging socially with other musicians); and *shishyas* playing the *tambura* for their *guru* in concerts.

SUMMARY OF SECTION KEY POINTS

1. Like African vocal music, the two traditions of classical singing in India, Hindustani and Karnatic, are both *aural* and *oral* traditions.
2. Both traditions feature more fixed compositions (*dhrupad* in the Hindustani; *kalpita sangita* in the Karnatic) as well as improvisatory aspects (*khayal* in the Hindustani; *manodharma sangita* in the Karnatic).
3. Both traditions are based upon *ragas*, sets of notes which form the melodic basis for compositions and improvisatory elements.
4. Both traditions are based upon a unique teacher–student relationship, the *guru–shishya* system known as *gurukul* in the Hindustani tradition and *gurukulavasam* in the Karnatic. The "school," made up of a *guru* and their *shishyas*, is known as a *gharana* in the Hindustani tradition and a *bani* in the Karnatic.
5. While the traditional immersive learning environment of the *shishya* becoming one with the life and family and musical knowledge of a *guru* is becoming less common, new teaching methods are taking root, including those which take advantage of technology and learning community models to continue the essential elements of the respective traditions.

CLOSING REMARKS

The traditional vocal musics of China, Africa, and India have been in existence for thousands of years. While each vocal tradition faces many challenges, some of which are common across the cultures and some of which are unique to each situation, each tradition continues to survive and to reach new audiences. In some cases, direct government intervention has been used to preserve and teach aspects of the traditional music heritage; in other cases, technology and economic forces are reshaping instructional methods so that students of vocal music can choose between learning traditional styles with a personal mentor, with a group of students who might only meet via the Internet, by working independently, or by some hybrid of all three situations.

RECORDINGS AND SCORES

Adzenyah, A.K., Maraire, D., and Tucker, J.C. (1986). *Let your voice be heard: Songs from Ghana and Zimbabwe*. Wauwatosa, WI: World Music Press.

Agawu, V.K., Nzewi, M., and Herbst, A. (2003). *Musical Arts in Africa: Theory, Practice, and Education*. Pretoria: Unisa Press.

Bankole, Ayo. (1976). *Three Yoruba Songs: For Baritone and Piano*. Ile-Ife, Nigeria: University of Ife Press.

Ekwueme, Laz E.N. (1993). *Choir Training and Choral Conducting for Africans*. Lagos, Nigeria: Lenaus.

Mukuna, K. (1980). *African Children's Songs for American Elementary Schools*. East Lansing, MI: African Studies Center, Michigan State University.

Onovwerosuoke, F. (ed.) (2008). *Songs of Africa: 22 Pieces for Mixed Voices*. New York: Oxford University Press.

REFERENCES

Abraham, R.C. (ed.) (1962). *Dictionary of Modern Yoruba*. London: Hodder and Stoughton.

Agu, D.C.C. (1992). Youth songs: a type of Igbo choral music in Igbo Christian worship. *African Music* 7(2): 13–22.

Allen, M.H. (2008). Standardize, classicize, and nationalize: the scientific work of the Music Academy of Madras, 1930–52. In: I. Viswanathan Peterson and D. Soneji (eds), *Performing Pasts: Reinventing the Arts in Modern South India*, pp. 90–129. New Delhi: Oxford.

Babalola, S.A. (1966). *The Content and Form of Yoruba Ijala*. London: Clarendon.

Booth, G.D. (1996). Cognition and culture: systems of music and music education in India and the "West". In: A. Parikh (ed.), *Indian Music and the West*, pp. 73–83. Mumbai: NCPA Sangeet Research Academy.

Brown, R.E. (1965). *The Mrdanga: A Study of Drumming in South India*. Unpublished PhD dissertation, University of California.

Carter-Ényì, A. (2018). Hooked on Sol-Fa: the do-re-mi heuristic for Yorùbá speech tones. *Africa*, 88(2): 267–290.

Carter-Ényì, A. (2014a). Muri's Ewi (Iwi) Example 1. Africana Digital Ethnography Project, 22. http://digitalcommons.auctr.edu/adept/22

Carter-Ényì, A. (2014b). Muri's Ijala Example 2. Africana Digital Ethnography Project, 23. http://digitalcommons.auctr.edu/adept/23

Carter-Ényì, A. and Adeyomo, M. (2013). Mayowa Adeyomo praises Eledumare. Africana Digital Ethnography Project, 24. http://digitalcommons.auctr.edu/adept/24

Carter-Ényì, A. and Aina, D.O. (2013). Mayowa Adeyomo praises Ogun (God of Iron). Africana Digital Ethnography Project, 5. http://digitalcommons.auctr.edu/adept/5

Catlin, A. (1980). *Variability and Change in Three Karnataka Kritis: A Study of South Indian Classical Music*. Unpublished PhD dissertation, Brown University.

Catlin, A. (1985). Pallavi and kriti of Karnatik music: evolutionary processes and survival strategies. *National Centre for the Performing Arts (NCPA) (Mumbai) Quarterly Journal* 14 (1): 26–44.

Chen, F. [陈芳] (2006). Contemporary Development of authentic folk songs in China [原生态民歌的当代发展]. *Huangzhong-Journal of Wuhan Conservatory of Music [黄钟(中国.武汉音乐学院学报]*(S1): 16–18. doi:cnki:ISSN:1003-7721.0.2006-S1-005

Chen, Q. [陈青]. (2004). Incorporeity and Logic: A Comparison between Chinese and Western Musical Forms [忘形与逻辑——中西音乐曲式构成比较]. *Musical Instrument Magazine [乐器]*(4): 38–39.

Cormack, J.A. (1992). *Svara Kalpana: Melodic and Rhythmic Improvisation in Karnatak Music*. Unpublished PhD dissertation, Wesleyan University.

Department of Cultural Affairs, People's Republic of China (2006). *Interim Measures for the Protection and Administration of National Intangible Cultural Heritage*. Beijing: Department of Culture Affairs.

Deva, C. (1973). *An Introduction to Indian Music*. New Delhi: Government of India Ministry of Information and Broadcasting.

Du, Y.X. [杜亚雄] (1991). The definitions of sound, qiang and rhythm in the traditional Han music [汉族传统音乐中音、腔与节奏的概念]. *Chinese Music [中国音乐]*(04): 12–13. doi:cnki:ISSN:1002-9903.0.1991-04-004

Du, Y.X. [杜亚雄] (2003a). Characteristics of time value in traditional Chinese music [中国传统音乐在时值方面的特征]. Accessed September 20, 2015 from http://en.cnki.com.cn/Article_en/CJFDTOTAL-ZJYS200303008.htm.

Du, Y.X. [杜亚雄] (2003b). Characteristics of pitch in traditional Chinese music [中国传统音乐在音高方面的特征]. *Journal of Zhejiang Vocational Academy of Art [浙江艺术职业学院学报]*(02): 57–62. doi: cnki:ISSN:1672-2795.0.2003-02-004

Du, Y.X. [杜亚雄] (2003c). Characteristics of timbre usage in traditional Chinese music [中国传统音乐在音色运用方面的特征]. *Journal of Zhejiang Vocational Academy of Art [浙江艺术职业学院学报]*(01): 57–60. doi:cnki:ISSN:1672-2795.0.2003-01-009

Du, Y.X. [杜亚雄] (2003d). Characteristics of volume in traditional Chinese music [中国传统音乐在音量方面的特征]. *Journal of Zhejiang Vocational Academy of Art [浙江艺术职业学院学报]*(04): 54–59. doi:cnki:ISSN:1672-2795.0.2003-04-005

Duran, L. (1989). Key to N'dour: roots of the Senegalese Star. *Popular Music* 8(3): 275–284.

Ekwueme, L.E.N. (1974). Linguistic determinants of some Igbo musical properties. *Journal of African Studies* 1(3): 335–353.

Erlmann, V. (1999). *Music, Modernity, and the Global Imagination: South Africa and the West*. London: Oxford University Press.

Fu, F.Q. [付放晴] (1997). The Formation and Development of Chinese Pentatonic and Heptatonic Scales [简述我国五声音阶、七声音阶的形成和发展]. *Journal of Guiyang Teacher's College [贵阳师专学报(社会科学版)]*(03): 78–80. doi:cnki:ISSN:1002-6894.0.1997-03-016

Fu, G.Q. and Zhou, X.M. [付国庆, & 周先明] (1999). The Qiang and tone modulations of Chinese Folk Singing [谈民族唱法的行腔韵味]. *Journal of Daxian Teachers College [达县师范高等专科学校学报]*(01). doi:cnki:ISSN:1008-4886.0.1999-01-026

Goetze, M. (2010). OAKE national conference keynote address. *Kodaly Envoy* (Organization of American Kodaly Educators) Summer 2010: 20–22.

Grimmer, S. (2011). Continuity and change: the guru-shishya relationship in Karnatic classical voice training. In L. Green (ed.), *Learning, Teaching, and Musical Identity: Voices across Cultures*, pp. 91–108. Bloomington and Indianapolis: Indiana University Press.

Grimmer, S. (2012). Creativity in perpetual motion: listening in the development of expertise in the Karnatic classical singing tradition of South India. *Music Performance Research* (CMPCP/Performance Studies Network Special Edition) 5: 70–95. http://mpr-online.net/

Guan, J.H. [管建华] (1995). The crisis of subjectivity in the development of Chinese music culture [中国音乐文化发展主体性危机的思考]. *Music Study [音乐研究]*(4): 28–32. doi:CNKI:SUN:MUSI.0.1995-04-006

Hale, T.A. (1998). *Griots and Griottes: Masters of Words and Music*. Bloomington, IN: Indiana University Press.

Herzog, G. (1934). Speech-melody and primitive music. *Musical Quarterly* 20(4): 452–466.

Hu, C.Y. and Wang, Y.L. [胡传宇, & 王炎龙] (2001). Conceptualization and Subject Reformulation of Musical Culture Study in Globalization [全球化语境下音乐文化学的观念整合与主体重构]. *Ethnic Arts Quarterly [民族艺术]*(3): 29–34. doi:CNKI:SUN:MZYS.0.2001-03-004

Hu, X.L. [胡雪丽] (2006). A Comparison of Chinese and Western Notations [中西音乐记谱法的比较研究]. *Art Education [艺术教育]*(11): 73.

Huang, G.H. [黄国华] (2005). A path to success for the internationalization of China's folk songs—an observation of the integration of Nanning International Folk Songs Festival and China-ASEAN Expo [中国民歌国际化的成功之路——兼谈南宁国际民歌艺术节与中国—东盟博览会的交融]. *Journal of Guangxi Normal University (Philosophy and Social Science Edition) [广西师范大学学报(哲学社会科学版)]*(02): 80–85. doi:cnki:ISSN:1001-6597.0.2005-02-018

Huang, Y.Z. [黄允箴] (2003). Existence and release: traditional functions and concepts of authentic folk songs extant [生存与释放——论遗存原生态民歌的传统功能与观念]. *Art of Music-Journal of the Shanghai Conservatory of Music [音乐艺术-上海音乐学院学报]*(04): 20–27. doi:cnki:ISSN:1000-4270.0.2003-04-005

Jackson, W.J. (1991). *Tyagaraja: Life and Lyrics*. Madras: Oxford.

Jie, Z.H. [解志红] (1994). Culture exchange between China and the world though collision: China's participation in international art competitions [在碰撞中同世界文化接轨——中国参加国际艺术比赛述评]. *Culture Exchange [中外文化交流]*(04): 48-49.

Kaschula, R.H. (1999). Imbongi and griot: toward a comparative analysis of oral poetics in southern and west Africa. *Journal of African Cultural Studies* 12(1): 55–76.

Kebede, A. (1975). "The Azmari, Poet-Musician of Ethiopia." *Musical Quarterly* 61(1): 47-57.

Lewis, M.P., Simons, G.F., and Fennig, C.D. (eds) (2013). *Ethnologue: Languages of the World*, 17th edn. Dallas, TX: SIL International.

Li, H.Y. [黎英海] (1981). An overview of the Chinese pentatonic scale [民族五声性调式概述]. *Chinese Music [中国音乐]*(01): 15–16. doi:cnki:ISSN:1002-9903.0.1981-01-005

Li, S.E. [李素娥] (2006). Drift away from or root in the tradition: a competition between modern and authentic folk song singing [游离与扎根——由现代民族唱法与原生态唱法问题引发的思考]. *Chinese Music [中国音乐]*(02): 100–104. doi:cnki:ISSN:1002-9903.0.2006-02-020

Long, M.H. [龙明洪] (1994). The method of You Gong Jian Pian: the analysis and identification of Chinese pentatonic scales [简论优宫减偏法——关于中国五声及五声以下各种音阶调式分析识别中的一些问题]. *Ethnic Arts Quarterly [民族艺术]*(03): 119–126. doi:cnki:ISSN:10032568.0.1994-03-010

Massey, R. and Massey, J. (1976). *The Music of India.* New York: Crescendo.

Mi, Y.Y. [米永盈] (2007). The protection and development of traditional music: a case study of the authentic music [论传统音乐的保护与发展——以原生态民歌为例]. *Folklore Studies [民俗研究]*(02): 15–23. doi:CNKI:SUN:MSYA.0.2007-02-005

Nelson, D. (2000). Karnatak Tala. In: A. Arnold (ed.), *The Garland Encyclopedia of World Music*, vol. 5, South Asia, pp. 138–161. New York/London: Garland Publishing.

Neuman, D. (1980). *The Life of Music in North India: The Organization of an Artistic Tradition.* Detroit: Wayne State University Press.

Neuman, D.M. (1990). *The Life of Music in North India: The Organization of an Artistic Tradition.* Chicago: University of Chicago Press.

Okpewho, I. (1992). *African Oral Literature: Background, Character, and Continuity.* Bloomington, IN: Indiana University Press.

President of the People's Republic of China (2011). Law of the People's Republic of China on Intangible Cultural Heritage. Order No.42 of the President.

Qian, Y.C. [钱艺春] (2007). The origin and development of Chinese pentatonic and heptatonic scales [浅议中国五声七声音阶的起源发展]. *Drama and Film Monthly [剧影月报]*(05). doi:CNKI:SUN:JYYB.0.2007-05-051

Qiao, J.Z. [乔建中]. (2003). The heritance of contemporary Chinese folk songs: written and oral texts [中国当代民歌的生态与传承——兼谈中国民歌的口头文本与书面文本]. *Fujian Arts [福建艺术]*(03): 5–6. doi:cnki:ISSN:1004-2075.0.2003-03-000

Qiu, H.S. [邱怀生] (2002). A comparison of Chinese Yu pentatonic scale and the European harmonic minor [民族五声羽调式与欧洲和声小调式的几种差异]. *Song of Yellow River [黄河之声]*(02): 17. doi:cnki:ISSN:1004-6127.0.2002-02-014

Radhakrishnan, N., Scherer, R.C., and Bandyopadhyay, S. (2011). Laryngeal dynamics of pedagogical Taan gestures in Indian classical singing. *Journal of Voice* 25(3): 139–147.

Raja, D. (2005). *Hindustani Music: A Tradition in Transition.* New Delhi: D.K. Printworld.

Ranade, A.D. (1998). The Guru-Shishya Parampara: a broader view. *Sangeet Natak Akademi* 129–130: 39–54.

Ravikiran, C.N. (2006). Improvisation in Carnatic music. In: *Improvisation in Music*, pp. 172–175. Mumbai: NCPA, Sangeet Research Academy.

Ren, Y. [任勇] (1990). The note names and solmization of Chinese five Sheng and Twelve Lv [中国五声十二律与音名唱名]. *Chinese Music [中国音乐]*(03): 83. doi:cnki:ISSN:1002-9903.0.1990-03-042

Roederer, J.G. (1995). *The Physics and Psychophysics of Music: An Introduction.* New York: Springer-Verlag.

Rowell, L. (1992). *Music and Musical Thought in Early India.* Chicago and London: University of Chicago Press.

Sankaran, T. and Allen, M. (2000). The social organization of music and musicians: southern area. In: A. Arnold (ed.), *The Garland Encyclopedia of World Music*, vol. 5, South Asia, pp. 383–396. New York/London: Garland Publishing.

Schellenberg, M. (2012). Does language determine music in tone languages? *Ethnomusicology* 56(2): 266–278.

Scheub, H. (1975). *The Xhosa Ntsomi*. London: Clarendon Press.

Shelemay, K.K. and Kimberlin, C.T. (2013). Ethiopia. *Grove Music Online. Oxford Music Online*. Oxford: Oxford University Press. <http://www.oxfordmusiconline.com/subscriber/article/grove/music/42063>, accessed June 13, 2014.

Shen, Q. [沈洽] (1982). Theory of Yin Qiang [音腔论]. *Journal of the Central Conservatory of Music [中央音乐学院学报]*(4): 13-21.

Shen, Q. [沈洽] (1983). Theory of Yin Qiang [音腔论]. *Journal of the Central Conservatory of Music [中央音乐学院学报]*(1): 3-12.

Smitherman, G. (1997). The chain remain the same: communicative practices in the hip hop nation. *Journal of Black Studies* 28(1): 3–25.

Subramanian, L. (2006). *From the Tanjore Court to the Madras Music Academy: a social history of music in South India*. Oxford: Oxford University Press.

Subramanian, L. (2008a). Embracing the canonical: identity, tradition, and modernity in Karnatic music. In: I. Viswanathan Peterson and D. Soneji (eds), *Performing Pasts: Reinventing the Arts in Modern South India*, pp. 43–70. New Delhi: Oxford.

Subramanian, L. (2008b). *New Mansions for Music: Performance, Pedagogy and Criticism*. New Delhi: Social Science Press.

Vidal, A.O. (2012). *Essays on Yoruba Musicology: History, Theory and Practice*. Ile Ife, Nigeria: Obafemi Awolowo University Press.

Viswanathan, T. (1977). The analysis of Raga Alapana in South Indian music. *Asian Music* 9: 13–71.

Viswanathan, T. and Cormack, J. (1998). Melodic improvisation in Karnatak music: the manifestation of rāga. In: B. Nettl and M. Russell (eds), *In the Course of Performance: Studies in the World of Musical Improvisation*, pp. 219–233. Chicago and London: University of Chicago Press.

Wang, J. [王建] (2005). A study of Chinese pentatonic modes [对中国五声性调式的研究]. *Journal of Yl Teachers College [伊犁师范学院学报]*(02): 98–101. doi:cnki:ISSN:1009-1076.0.2005-02-030

Weng, C.W. (2002). New methods for measuring tonality and applications: an example of Abing's The Moon Reflection in Erquan. *The Taiwan Symphony Orchestra of the National* 40: 10.

Weidman, A.J. (2003). Gender and the politics of voice: colonial modernity and classical music in South India. *Cultural Anthropology* 18(2): 194–232.

Weidman, A.J. (2006). *Singing the Classical, Voicing the Modern*. Durham and London: Duke University Press.

White, E. (1971). *Appreciating India's Music: An Introduction, with an Emphasis on the Music of South India*. Boston: Cresendo.

World Population Review (2019). http://worldpopulationreview.com, accessed February 27, 2019.

Wulff, D.M. (1983). On practicing religiously: music as sacred in India. In: J. Irwin (ed.), *Sacred Sound*, pp. 149–172. Chico, CA: Scholars Press.

Xue, L. [薛雷] (2006). On the original state folk music again [原生态民间音乐的再认识]. *Journal of Jiangsu Institute of Education (Social Science Edition)* [江苏教育学院学报(社会科学版)](03): 106–107. doi:cnki:ISSN:1671-1696.0.2006-03-033

Yang, Y. (2011). *The Challenges Inherent in Promoting Traditional Folk Song Performance and Pedagogy in Chinese Higher Education: A Case Study of Hua'er*. PhD thesis, Institute of Education, University of London.

Yang, Y., Welch, G., Sundberg, J., and Himonides, E. (2013). Tuning features of Chinese Folksong singing: a case study of Hua'er song singing. Unpublished manuscript in review.

Yu, Y.Y. [余咏宇] (1994a). Definition of Chinese folk music (part 2) [给中国民歌下个定义？（下）]. *Huangzhong-Journal of Wuhan Music Conservatory* [黄钟-武汉音乐学院学报](04): 16–22. doi:cnki:ISSN:10037721.0.1994-04-003

Yu, Y.Y. [余咏宇] (1994b). Definition of Chinese folk music (part 1) [给中国民歌下个定义？（上）]. *Huangzhong-Journal of Wuhan Music Conservatory* [黄钟-武汉音乐学院学报](03): 1–8. doi:cnki:ISSN:10037721.0.1994-03-000

Zang, Y.B. [臧一冰] (2004). The meaning of paying attention to the original ballad for China today [关注原生态民歌对当今中国的意义]. *Arts Criticism* [艺术评论](10): 20–25. doi:cnki:ISSN:1672-6243.0.2004-10-005

Zhang, S.X. [张淑霞] (1987). The meaning of the Runsheng skill in the Chinese vocal music and its category [润腔技巧在民族声乐中的意义及分类]. *Journal of Jilin College of The Arts* [吉林艺术学院学报](01): 41-49. doi:cnki:SCN:22-5033.0.1987-01-011

Zhang, Y. [张渊] (2004). Folk music: the original state popular music [民歌:原生态的流行音乐]. *China Today* [今日中国(中文版)](12): 48–49. doi:cnki:ISSN:1005-0958.0.2004-12-018

PART 6

THE COLLECTIVE "CHORAL" VOICE

CHAPTER 38

CONTEMPORARY CONCEPTS AND PRACTICES OF CHORAL SINGING

URSULA GEISLER AND KARIN JOHANSSON

THE COLLECTIVE CHORAL VOICE

THE collective choral voice echoes through the centuries. Imagine a Sunday morning in St Peter's, Rome, in the 1580s. Palestrina's music floats through the air in the cathedral. What did it sound like? What did the congregation hear and experience? We will never know, but we can peep through the keyhole to the event by looking at, playing, and listening to his scores. They bear witness to the historically evolving development of choral music as an art form, and give inspiration to contemporary individual voices in performance and compositions. By studying written music and recordings, performers and researchers with an intra-musical focus may widen their musical horizons and listening abilities. Now, imagine the city of Vienna in 1928 with the meeting of 140,000 German choral singers in the "Schubert year" and its unmistakably national-political presage of the subsequent Austrian "Anschluß" to the German Reich (Holzer 1995). Choral music with more than 10,000 singers was performed in the great banqueting hall, while the rest of Europe protested against this musical symbolization of Pan-German thought matter. Such an event reminds us that choral singing is an important part of the changing socio-cultural and political public spheres.

As suggested above, choral singing has a double function as both a musical and a societal phenomenon in Western European culture. From an intra-musical perspective, the choir as an instrument with a specific sound is an important part of European musical culture and heritage. As a societal phenomenon, choirs and choral singing have a culturally constructed value with an impact both on the individual and the collective in terms of health, social benefits, and democracy (Ahlquist 2006; Lurton 2011). This dynamic relationship influences contemporary concepts and practices of choral singing.

We see choral practice as a multifaceted and complex field, which motivates as well as requires a multitude of research strategies in different disciplines. Therefore, it is also a field of great possibilities for research *on, for*, as well as *in* music, in the words of Henk Borgdorff

(2011). In this terminology, research *on* music applies an interpretative perspective and requires the researcher to be at a distance, while research *for* music has an instrumental perspective and is made, so to speak, in the service of art. Research *in* music refers to artistic research studies from a performative or practice-based perspective, where the researcher and the musical practice are not separated. The three perspectives can be described as focusing, respectively, on the context, the process, and the artistic products of choral music-making. With the aim of mirroring and responding to this situation, we initiated the international choral research network Choir in Focus in 2008 (Geisler and Johansson 2010, 2011).

Choir in Focus

Choir in Focus is based at the Southern Choral Centre (Körcentrum Syd), which is a joint venture between Malmö Academy of Music, The Department of Musicology, Odeum (all at Lund University, Sweden), Malmö Symphony Orchestra, and Music South (Musik i Syd).

The overall purpose of Choir in Focus is to encourage debate around the musical and social function of choirs in postmodern society. Moreover, its four main objectives are formulated as to (i) bring together competent European choral researchers, (ii) create a platform for a variety of research perspectives to meet and develop relevant and valuable questions about choir singing, (iii) investigate the need and scope for cross-disciplinary studies, and (iv) develop profiled research questions and common projects in the field of choral research.

The network gathers researchers from 14 universities and music academies in Sweden, Denmark, Norway, Germany, France, and the UK, and has established links to many researchers from other countries with an interest in choral studies. Since 2009, four meetings and conferences have been held in Sweden and Germany. Central points of discussion in all these meetings have been (i) the differing national, socio-economic, and cultural traditions of choral practice and education and, hence, differing conditions for choral singing, and (ii) the relative invisibility of choral research results and their lack of impact on choral life described above. With this in mind, the conference *Concepts and practices of choral singing* was organized in 2012 in close connection and cooperation with Lund Choral Festival, which is an international biannual event and meeting point for choirs, choir singers, and conductors. The purpose of the conference was to highlight interdisciplinary investigations and interaction between practice-based, pedagogical, and historical approaches in choral research. This aim was fulfilled in the realization of the conference, which drew together 45 participants from all over the world, with a variety of disciplinary backgrounds and from different music academies, universities, and museums—in itself a reflection of how the diverse field of choral research is scattered across a range of disciplines.

The two keynote speakers mirrored this diversity: Andreas Lehmann is professor of systematic musicology in Würzburg, Germany, and Karin Rehnqvist is professor of composition at the Royal College of Music in Stockholm, Sweden. In "From vocal grooming to female tenors: A music psychologist's view of choral singing," Lehmann started from the question of why music is so important to humans if it does not have biological benefits. He stated that the current public interest in choral singing motivates an integration of different research perspectives and he pointed out three central relationships for further studies: (i) the individual singers and their use of singing, (ii) singer-conductor and singer-singer interactions, and (iii) the choir-audience relationship. Karin Rehnqvist pictured another crucial relationship in "Courage and resistance: Composing for choir," i.e. that between the composer and the choir as a musical instrument. From her viewpoint as a composer, she discussed what resistance and courage in music may mean to composers and musicians today and connected this to questions about the role of contemporary music in society.

With this underpinning, the conference participants were invited to explore challenges for choral research today and in the future, and the conference established a meeting point for research made from all three perspectives of *on, for*, and *in* music. In the following, we will give an outline of the contemporary development of choral research from our perspective as leaders of Choir in Focus, with examples from the conference presentations and with connections to the chapters in this section on the collective choral voice.

CONCEPTUALIZATIONS OF CHORAL PRACTICES AND MUSICS

Choir singing, choral practice, and singing in general are explored as research objects in a variety of disciplines. Together, they describe a complex and multifaceted field of cultural-historical, pedagogical, sociological, psychological, and music-related topics that carry differing definitions of the concept "choir" (Brusniak 2003; Di Grazia 2013; Durrant 2003; Fagius 2009; Kvist Dahlstedt 2001). So, what is a choir?

In the re-construction of classical antiquity by the Enlightenment during the eighteenth century, "choir" was defined as three different phenomena, but with each associated with the others, namely: (1) a group of people singing, (2) the music performed by the group, and (3) the place in which the group performed the music (Sulzer 1771/2002). These definitions are still widely used and accepted, and have been complemented so as to include notions of performance, audience, and sound (Daugherty 1996; Duchan 2007).

Departing from the conception of a collective choral voice, a brief discussion of definitions is necessary, since all terms describing "choral singing" are situated in national traditions, languages, and specific socio-historical locations. For example, the English language terms choir, chorus, band, ensemble, and singing group may have different, yet sometimes overlapping connotations, depending on the context. Similarly, the German term Chor relates to both *Singgruppe* and to *Gesangverein*. These terms point to the difference between, on the one hand, an ensemble of trained singers giving a staged performance with an esthetic goal to a separate, listening, audience and, on the other hand, a group of singing people for whom music-making can be described as signifying a process of stabilizing local community. Both activities may be described as "choral singing" and, when it comes to choir movements in Europe, terms like "voicing," "sounding," and "visualizing" may be equally suitable. Choirs have always represented "sounding humans," but they have also been used as musical symbols in political and religious rituals, and may thus be interpreted in collectivistic terms. For example, in a study of paradigm shifts during the twentieth century, Geisler (2011) demonstrates how the performance and reception of choral music depends on political and social factors as much as on musical ones. She relates the paradigm shifts of the 1920/30s, the years around 1968, and 1989 in different European countries to changing choral cultures and changing references to singing communities as representatives for "nation," "health," and "individuality/collectivism," respectively. Choral singing can thus be described as a "figurative carrier of meaning" (Kohlhaas and Kürsten 2007, p.13) that can be studied from different disciplinary angles.

Complementing the definition of "choral singing" with aspects of "voicing," "sounding," and "visualizing" means that traditional choral research might need to broaden its perspective to include not only studies of choral sheet music and a presumed one-way communication between the choir and the audience, but also the two-way dialogue between the choir director and the choir. An example of how this can be done is given in Chapter 40 of this volume, "Cultural history and a singing style: 'The English Cathedral tradition'," where Tim Day asks the question of how the relationship between singers and singing styles might be studied from the perspective of cultural history, and what sources can be used for illuminating this relationship. He traces the background to the formation of what is today called "the English cathedral tradition" with a particular focus on the influential and famous singing style of King's College Choir, Cambridge. While their sound is today often believed to be the crowning glory of a long line of historical development, Day shows how the maturation of this style as a musical ideal was connected to the liturgical revolution of the Oxford movement and to socio-economic processes during the nineteenth century, which were followed by changes in attitudes towards education, childhood, and masculinity. During the twentieth century, the middle class notion that an interest in music was to be considered "unmanly" slowly faded away, along with a growing public involvement in music. Highlighting the tension and relationship between research perspectives that focus upon choral *production* and choral *reception*, respectively, may contribute to historically informed studies that contextualize choral practice and performance and reach beyond discipline-specific borders.

Considering the double nature of the collective choral voice, we recommend that the definition of choral singing should not be limited to its *structure*, but should include the social, communicative, and ritual *functions* of choral singing. The functions of music described by Merriam (1964) vary from the expression of emotions to reinforcing the stability of a certain culture. Merriam distinguishes the functions of music from its use: while individuals use music in different situations, its functions concern "the reasons for its employment and particularly the broader purpose which it serves" (p. 210). The functions of music might thus be analyzed and described through studies of its use.

In a study of high-ranking Swedish choir leaders (n = 26), Johansson (2011) poses questions such as: Where is choral activity in Sweden heading? Is it possible to speak of it as one phenomenon? With an analysis of choral practice as an activity system (Engeström 2005; Welch 2007), the study points to how the choir leaders mirror and respond to the contemporary situation in Swedish musical life and to how they, in different ways, relate to what can be called the loss of common grounds. Choral music making is seen as a cultural practice where contemporary Swedish discourses on choral music making illustrate a range of interpretive repertoires (Potter 1996), such as:

- The "traditional" pattern of the choir leader as the subject with the objective of delivering a personal musical expression.
- The choir leader as a subject working on diminishing and dissolving his/her own influence, with the objective of a collective musical expression.
- The choir itself as a subject, with the objective of achieving social change through music.

These repertoires are described against the backdrop of a tacit discourse that concerns the question of what the objective of choir singing in society and musical culture might be on a general level; and if there is one.

A striking observation made in this study (Johansson 2011) was that even though a great amount of choral research exists worldwide, practitioners do not generally use or benefit from these studies. Geisler's bibliography of choral research (2012), which is part of a global inventory project and which at present includes more than 4000 international choral research publications, gives an impression of a wealth of available resources that are apparently both unknown and unused by practitioners. What might be the reasons for this? We suggest that it is due to, for example, (i) underdeveloped forms of communication between theory and practice, that is, between researchers and practitioners, and (ii) the fact that choral research is distributed across a range of disciplines that apply differing methodological and theoretical approaches. This lack of contact between the field of choral practice and traditional research on choral topics is remarkable, but has the advantage that it creates a motivating force for research and music-making to meet.

Historical, Psychological, and Social Dimensions of Choral Singing

The way music is made in a society describes its history and its present, but also foretells its future. Attali (2011) even argues that it is *prophetic* in the sense that "its styles and economic organization are ahead of the rest of society because it explores, much faster than material reality can, the entire range of possibilities in a given code" (p. 11). Naturally, ways of singing, repertories, and choral sound change over space and time. Since Greek antiquity a specific societal status has been attributed to the choir (Bierl 2001); the collective choral voice expresses something else and more than individual needs and feelings, and differing choral representations of societal change can be seen during different periods in the European countries. A contemporary example is how choir-related topics are used in movies. Recent popular film productions such as "Les Choristes" (The Chorus, 2004), "Fighting Temptations" (2003), "Så som i himmelen" (As it is in heaven, 2004), and "Oh, Happy Day" (2004) often portray the choir as a forum through which people are motivated to change their lives, or as a gateway through which otherwise marginalized individuals may enter civil society. Through the participation in a choir, they become part of a community and can achieve more than anyone can do on their own. That is, choral music-making is a symbol, or a means, for participation, community, and the creation of meaning.

The roots of choral singing in both the sacred and the secular are reflected in many topics of research, and studies on singing in churches and in congregations have contributed to the field with knowledge about choral singing and the function of collective vocality (Bernskiöld 1986; Kremer and Werbeck 2007; Niemöller et al. 2002; Scheitler 2000). The specific character of the monastic singing ideal has been emphasized as a form of representation of the individual's role in community (Strinnholm Lagergren 2009). While until the eighteenth century choirs mainly belonged to the domain of the church, amateur choral singing associations became an important element in the development of civil society during the nineteenth century. The uplifting and standardization of choral singing was connected to the emancipation of the bourgeoisie, and singing groups became social meeting places also outside the church, the school, and the opera. Self-organized choirs—mainly students' and male choirs—became visible in the public space. In many European countries, profane choral life since the Enlightenment has been characterized by folk movements, and by student choirs and men's choruses. Mixed choirs, women's choirs, children's choirs, and other specialized choirs developed in the nineteenth century as a response to the need of variable collective singing rituals in modern society.

The French Revolution was a kind of European starting point for the national connotations of community singing (Lurton 2011; Mason 1996), echoing an earlier initiative from the 1820s onwards in Germany, where community singing was promoted to unite the federal states in one nation (Brusniak and Klenke 1995). After the French Revolution, secular choirs gained political and cultural impact that can still be seen today and, in a study on choir singing and socio-musical attitudes from a Swedish-German perspective, Geisler (2011) points out that "choirs in the twentieth century were not 'only' *musical* associations, but to a large extent visible signs that satisfied the need for symbols of transcendence in modern society" (p. 104). Throughout history, choral singing has perhaps had the function of being a bridge builder between different countries and generations, and a facilitator in processes of social transformation. This seems obvious when looking at European history and the role choral movements have played in different nationalization processes (Ahlquist, 2006; Brusniak and Klenke 1995; Fischer and Kürsten 2007; Jonsson 1990). A well-known example of this is the politically ritualized choral singing during National Socialism and Stalinism in the first half of the twentieth century. Another example is the "Singing Revolution" (Vesilind 2008) in the Baltic States around 1989, where collective singing was used as a political instrument, although with altogether different overtones than during the 1930s. Laine Randjärv (2012) pictures the background to this process of liberation in Estonia as heavily dependent on the song celebration tradition. She describes how the musical repertoire was a crucial tool and support on the path to independence. In Sweden, the so-called "Swedish Choral Miracle" is regarded as one of the main cultural achievements of the second half of the 20th century (Fagius 2009; Reimers et al. 1993). Its musical contribution and social recognition may be seen in relation to the welfare state; during large parts of the nineteenth and twentieth century, social institutions like the church, school, unions, and student contexts were stable bases for choir singing and music-making in Sweden (Sparks 1998), and the artistic outcomes of the choral miracle must be seen in this context. Today, the unions, "folkrörelserna," and the church are gradually disintegrating and other, perhaps more temporary, structures appear. In parallel, new kinds of choirs have been established, such as, for example, "complaint choirs," "everyone-can-sing choirs," and choirs that represent minorities. This development can be described as an integrated part of the transformation of the public sphere (Habermas 1962) and as an expression of changing attitudes towards the position of the individual in society.

Research on choral singing in the nineteenth and twentieth centuries has shown that (as implied earlier) choir singing is dependent on contextual factors such as politics, social development, ideologies, and the state of civil society. However, the differences and similarities between different countries have only been highlighted to a small extent. For instance, when Friedhelm Brusniak and Alexander Arlt point out that the German choral society movement of the early nineteenth century should be seen as a driving force in the formation of

Germany's modern civic society, they also underline that previous research about national choral conditions and developments needs to be completed by looking at the organizational interlinking principles that expanded transregionally to other European countries. From a meta-perspective, music and choral singing are thereby understood as a medium of social and political communication, whose contribution to the development of modern society is yet to be determined more closely.

Aspects of constructed national identity can also be illuminated through nineteenth century practices of mass singing, as discussed by Josephine Hoegaerts (2012). She points to the fact that choirs not only passed on patriotic discourses through the lyrics that they sang, but also "represented" the nation as a people singing in unison. Hoegaerts aims to show that:

> this construction of a national identity, with its specific characteristics depending on gender and age, was part of a conscious policy shared by local politicians, educators on the national and the local level (the ministry of education and teachers) and the nation's acclaimed artists.
>
> (Hoegaerts, 2012)

On the one hand, this "conscious policy" constructed ideal types of choral singing and of people's democratic behavior. On the other hand, choral singing in music societies and associations is an expression of changing civil society structures and of a need for a secular representative of transcendence.

Internationally, choir singing is increasingly important as a meeting point for cultural practices and for transcending national and cultural boundaries (e.g. as exampled in international conferences on choral topics such as Ars Choralis, April 2012, Croatia; Choirs transforming our world, June 2012, Yale; International conference on the concepts and practices of choral singing, October 2012, Lund).

PRACTICE-BASED AND PRACTICE-DEVELOPING STUDIES OF CHORAL SINGING

As stated by Haugland Balsnes "the praxis field (i.e. the choir itself) will benefit from research because it can make rehearsals more efficient and improve the quality of conductors" (2010, p. 18). This potential dialogue between practitioners' personal experience and the collective knowledge building represented by research is valuable in situations of contemporary choral music-making, that present musicians with new questions concerning, for example, musical quality, artistic identity, gender positions, economic status, and performance practices. Traditional values are questioned, historically stable structures are developed, and conventional esthetics are continuously challenged (Johansson 2010).

Choir singing and leadership in contemporary musical practice is increasingly explored in the area of music education (e.g. Durrant 2009; Durrant and Varvarigou 2008; Haugland Balsnes 2009; Jansson 2013; Sandberg Jurström 2009). Such studies focus on the complex musical and social interactions in choirs: The choir leader interacts with the choir, which is in turn built up of inter-individual and intra-individual micro-interactions between the voices and between individuals. Apart from focusing on intra-musical aspects, some studies discuss the interaction with audience/listeners and with a wider social context than that from which the choir draws its members. However, as stated by Dag Jansson in Chapter 44 of this volume, "Choral Singers' Perceptions of Leadership," there is a lack of studies that consider the perspective of the members, that is, the singers. He echoes the previously mentioned distinction between research that focuses either on choral production or choral reception when he differentiates between (i) the *intended reality* in choral conducting, aimed at by the maestro writing tradition, (ii) the *observed reality* studied by the social and natural sciences, and (iii) the *perceived reality* experienced by choral singers. His focus is on the latter aspect, that is, on conducting as a lived experience on the part of the singers. Through qualitative interviews made from a phenomenological perspective, he investigates singers' perceptions of conductors and discusses the question: Why is a conductor's leadership needed in a choral ensemble? Even though musical leadership can be enacted in numerous ways and, as Jansson argues, there are no universally applicable best practices when it comes to choral conducting, he presents a legitimacy model (see Figure 44.1 in Jansson's chapter), in which the main theme describes the conductor as a sense-maker of the musical event.

This particular issue—the conductor as a leader who makes sense of a common musical event—is also addressed by Colin Durrant and Maria Varvarigou in Chapter 41 of this volume, "Perspectives on Choral Conducting." They underline the responsibility and power of conductors to facilitate optimal learning, flow, and emotional release with the singers and discuss results from choral research that are relevant for the development of conductors' practice. Apart from an international and historical outline of the background to choral leadership, they give an overview of how the conscious use of non-verbal gestures, varied rehearsal styles, and the combination of modeling, verbal, and visual communication interact in the creation of efficient musical learning and performance. In this context, they emphasize the importance of high quality feedback in education and performance from both tutors and singers. They suggest increasing the possibilities for reflection in action through, for example, peer observation, and the use of video recordings. This might be complemented by Jansson's observation of how the singers' perspective is a neglected yet potentially valuable asset in studies that further investigate the artistic aspects and the complexity of the conductor's role.

An holistic perspective is taken by Caplin and Eriksen (2012), who in cooperation have developed methods for studying "what is really going on" in the communication between the conductor and the choir by merging musical, pedagogical, and psychological knowledge and experience. With the aim of strengthening the interaction between conductors and ensembles, Caplin, a choir conductor, and Eriksen, a researcher in education and psychology, have formed research partnerships with choirs and thus have been able to conduct action research studies that include video recordings and collaborative analyses. Their holistic view of the conductor's competence forms a background to the argument that the musical training of conductors needs to be complemented by, for example, management theory, gestalt psychology, and drama in order to give students a solid foundation for musical leadership. Considering that musicians as well as institutions of higher music education continuously need to relate to the "new basic skills" (Johansson 2012) that are needed for a successful musical career today, this project gives an example of how these may be defined and formulated in interaction between practitioners and researchers.

One such skill might be seen as the ability and will of conductors and singers to question and transform power relations inherent in the situations of choral music practice and performance. Jason Vodicka (2012) points to the necessity of developing new structures for rehearsals and—hereby—choral singers' agency by, for example, (i) engaging singers in verbal dialogue, (ii) teaching singers what it means to think like a musician, (iii) connecting musical material to the singers' lives, and (iv) using choral placing for changing power balance. Positioning singers as one instrument implies an act of subordination where power over emotions, bodies, and voices is given to the conductor, but Vodicka uses Freire's critical pedagogy (Freire 1972) as inspiration for empowering singers. With illustrations from the work on Schubert's Mass in G with a high school choir, he shows how a focus on intramusical factors and artistic quality may interact with an awareness of power structures and transform the rehearsal situation as well as the traditional roles of singers and conductors.

A crucial factor for the development of choral practice is the interaction with repertoire in general, and with newly composed music in particular. Lauren Holmes Frankel (2012) touches upon this issue when she describes how the Tapiola children's choir was instrumental in creating a national identity through choral singing during the last decades of the twentieth century. This was achieved partly through the cooperation with prominent contemporary Finnish composers who wrote for the specific constellation of the Tapiola choir. A similar present-day project is the cooperation between choir conductor Joy Hill (author of Chapter 39 in this volume, "The Youth Choir") and composer Gabriel Jackson, which has been the topic of a developmental project at the Royal College of Music, London. In both these cases, the collaboration between performers and composers through the entire process up unto a musical production can be seen as an aspect of the agency mentioned by Vodicka; music written especially for the singers promotes a sense of ownership and initiative, and the interaction between composer, conductor, and singers constructs the emerging musical work as a field (Stubley 1998) where negotiations about its content and meaning are possible in an on-going "thinking-through-practice" (Östersjö 2008). With her special focus on the young choral voice, Hill describes in Chapter 39 how this can be enacted also by inviting young composer students to write for their chorister peers, hereby promoting an interest and emphasis in new music. Based on evidence from an interview study with prominent youth choir leaders and composers, she suggests that actively working with contemporary composers is an important factor, both in the perspective of singers' and conductors' life-long learning, and for achieving high quality levels in choral performance.

A growing area in recent research concerns gender and health aspects on choir singing (e.g. Ashley 2002; Clift 2011). When Martin Ashley (2012) calls for a turnaround according to female and male participation in choir singing, this builds on his perception of a stated loss of male voices to choral singing practice in the UK today. According to Ashley, there is increasing disagreement between researchers, singing teachers, voice coaches, choir directors, audiences, and "fans" of boys singing concerning the reasons and remedies for this situation, and he outlines its socio-historical background as a combination of "the secular trend" and "secularization." Ashley's research includes a large quantitative survey of boys' voice change in puberty as related to the English choral tradition (Ashley 2013) and studies of how repertoire and social interaction in choirs influence attitudes towards singing (Ashley 2002, 2009). Based on comparisons with Scottish and French contexts for choral singing, he suggests ways ahead for children's singing in a secularized society and emphasizes the importance of professionality in educating choristers and training choir directors.

Against the background of a growing body of research with a focus on the positive health effects of choral singing (see Part 7 in this volume, "The Wider Benefits of Singing"), Anne Haugland Balsnes (2012) describes a study of how chronically ill people perceive their health and life quality. The participation in a choir is seen as (i) an individual resource, (ii) a social resource, and (iii) an existential resource. Haugland Balsnes argues that it is an under-used, cost-effective activity seen from a therapeutic perspective.

While studies *on* arts and music education employ a variety of approaches (Bresler 2007; Colwell and Richardson 2002), research into higher musical education and artistic practice are expanding domains (Jörgensen 2009). Here, choir singing and choral work are of a certain interest, since musical knowledge development and production can be studied from multiple perspectives and in situations where aspects of performance and education overlap and interact. The common denominator for practice-developing studies relating to choral singing is a focus on analyzing and improving contemporary structures, and on developing theory or working methods for achieving artistic and pedagogical goals. Apart from examples such as those mentioned above, this can be studies of non-verbal, gestural transmission of musical intention and expression (Beer 2011; Garnett 2009; Sandberg Jurström 2009), the application of activity theoretical perspectives on cathedral choristers' singing (Welch 2007, 2011), or studies aiming at improving performance practice.

An example of such studies is given by David Howard in Chapter 43, where he addresses the tendency for singers to tune using just temperament when singing *a cappella*. With examples of electrolaryngography-based studies of choristers performing Bach chorales, he demonstrates how this use of just-temperament often causes pitch drift; that is, straying from the original key. Howard discusses possible additional influences on a choir's capacity to stay in key, such as local acoustics, the singers' ability to hear each other, and collective intentions to stay in tune. However, he also points to the inherent dichotomy of aiming at staying in tune when singing *a cappella*: this inevitably produces a pitch drift, which is seen as undesirable. Implications of this paradox include, as stated by Howard, the need for further education and research.

The young discipline of artistic research, which is rapidly growing with examples from Sweden, Holland, England, and Finland (Biggs and Karlsson 2011), holds promises for holistic projects where "the artist makes a difference" (Coessens et al. 2009), and where the musical practice is both the starting point, the method, and the objective of the research. Collaborative studies in which researchers and musicians cooperate (Hultberg 2005; Johansson 2012) have also proved to be a way to raise consciousness and increase the options for making informed choices about future actions. Central to studies of contemporary artistic work is to regard the practice as a meeting point for theory and practice where distinctions between method and process are transparent (Hannula et al. 2005). The concept of research *in* the arts offers interesting options for choral singing as an art form and for developing research strategies that combine the researchers' and the musicians' perspectives in the same person.

Future choral research—a field of possibilities

Choral singing and choral music are a widely spread and integrated part of the leisure time activities of a significant part of the population in Europe. For example, eight to nine percent of Germans participate in choral singing (Agricola 2003); statistics are also readily available for Eastern European countries, such as Estonia (Sahk 2014). However, this popularity stands in stark contrast to the limited amount of in-depth and transnational research studies of choral singing practices. One of the key objectives of the network Choir in Focus has been to encourage international and trans-disciplinary cooperation, and this concluding section presents some thoughts and suggestions for such projects.

Questions that concern the political, educational, and sociological impacts of contemporary choral singing may be for example: How does choral life in different countries depend on and interact with socio-cultural, political, and educational developments and what does this mean for the future of civil societies? What role does contemporary choral activity (in leadership, singing, and listening) play in the construction of social and musical meaning?

Corresponding questions with a focus on intra-musical issues are for example: What can be regarded as "new" knowledge in choral music-making? How can collective, choral, creativity be promoted and expanded? What are possible directions for development of the musical practice of choir singing today?

From a global perspective, the topic of cultural encounters and choral singing is interesting since the different constructions and transformations of choral singing and community ideals are the results of long-term processes that include people, musical ideas, singing ideals, pedagogical transfers, and social paradigms. Looking at choral singing from a transnational point of view would make it possible to focus on questions of, for example, the "Europeanness" of certain choral sounds, or chorality as part of European cultural heritage. Simultaneous and joint research projects in different countries could combine different theoretical perspectives and methodologies; since concepts of cultural transfer are embedded in historically, systematically, and performance-oriented choral studies, several academic disciplines could contribute to a multifaceted picture of choral singing, sociability, and cultural change in Europe since the Enlightenment up to today. Relevant topics would include choir life and practices in border regions and in multicultural regions in comparison with the contextualization of choir life in cities and provinces. Studies of choral societies and associations as an international phenomena with sub-aspects of repertoire, singing practice, gender aspects, and identifications would facilitate drawing institutional parallels in and between different countries and concerning the specificity of choir music from a European perspective.

From a pedagogical and performance-oriented point of view, the relationship between musical "dialects" and educational practices is a suitable area for studies from different perspectives, such as, for example, concerning director-choir communication, singer-singer interaction, or choir-audience contact. An example is a suggestion that was produced during one of the Choir in Focus network meetings as a cross-cultural and genre-crossing project (Durrant 2009). It focuses on the relationship between conductor and choir, which concerns (i) the nature of communication (verbal and non-verbal as well as style and impact of conducing gestures); (ii) the background and training of the conductor; (iii) the organization of the choirs and role of the conductor; (iv) musical preference and choice of repertoire; and (v) the societal role and historical changes of the leadership concept. A transnational project would include a "mapping" of the choral conducting education systems and practices across the participating countries, case studies of those considered as "successful" choirs in each country (from school, church, and community), empirical investigations of the relationship between conductor and choir, analysis of findings to determine the impact of education/training of choral conductors on their "behaviors" and on the musical results, and, finally, recommendations for conductor education and for further research.

The task of describing, analyzing, and developing contemporary choral practices as highly relevant musical and societal contributions to modern society is both a challenge and a source of inspiration. With a widened research perspective and a combination of historical analysis and practice-based approaches, considerable contributions to the development of interdisciplinary theories and methodologies can be made. The area of choral research should, therefore, be seen as a field of possibilities for creating new knowledge and new opportunities for interaction between researchers and practitioners.

References

Agricola, S. (2003). Chorsingen und marketing. In: Friedhelm Brusniak (ed.), *Chor-Visionen in Musik. Essener Thesen zum Chorsingen im 21. Jahrhundert*, pp. 141–165. Kassel: Bärenreiter.

Ahlquist, K. (ed.) (2006). *Chorus and Community*. Urbana: University of Illinois Press.

Ashley, M. (2002). Singing, gender and health: Perspectives from boys singing in a church choir. *Health Education* 102(4): 180–187.

Ashley, M. (2009). *How High Should Boys Sing? Gender, Authenticity and Credibility in the Young Male Voice*. Aldershot: Ashgate.

Ashley, M. (2012). 1000 years and 1000 boys' voices: The crisis and radical challenge for choral singing. Paper given at the conference *Concepts and Practices of Choral Singing*, Lund, Sweden, October 2012.

Ashley, M. (2013). The English choral tradition and the secular trend in boys' pubertal timing. *International Journal of Research in Choral Singing* 4(2): 4–27.

Attali, J. (2011). *Noise. The Political Economy of Music*. Minneapolis/London: University of Minnesota Press.

Beer, E. (2011). *Dirigentische mimik und gestik entschlüsseln—eine experimentelle studie mit sängerinnen*. Unpublished Thesis, Hochschule für Musik Würzburg, Germany.

Bernskiöld, H. (1986). *"Sjung av hjärtat sjung": Församlingssång och musikliv i Svenska Missionsförbundet fram till 1950-talet*. PhD, Gothenburg University.

Bierl, A. (2001). *Der Chor in der alten komödie. Ritual und performativität unter besonderer Berücksichtigung von Aristophanes' "Thesmophoriazusen" und der Phalloslieder fr. 851 PMG*. München: Saur.

Biggs, M. and Karlsson, H. (eds) (2011). *The Routledge Companion to Research in the Arts*. London: Routledge.

Borgdorff, H. (2011). The production of knowledge in artistic research. In: M. Biggs and H. Karlsson (eds), *The Routledge Companion to Research in the Arts*, pp. 44–63. London: Routledge.

Bresler, L. (ed.) (2007). *International Handbook of Research in Arts Education*. Dordrecht: Springer.

Brusniak, F. (ed.) (2003). *Chor—Visionen in Musik. Essener Thesen zum Chorsingen im 21. Jahrhundert*. Kassel: Bärenreiter.

Brusniak, F. and Klenke, D. (eds) (1995). *"Heil deutschem Wort und Sang!" Nationalidentität und Gesangskultur in der deutschen Geschichte—Tagungsbericht Feuchtwangen 1994*. Augsburg: Wißner Augsburg (Feuchtwanger Beiträge zur Musikforschung).

Caplin, T. and Eriksen, S. (2012). How does 2 + 2 become 5, in a musical context? Paper given at the conference *Concepts and Practices of Choral Singing*, Lund, Sweden, October 2012.

Clift, S. (2011). Singing, wellbeing and health. In: R.A.R. MacDonald, G. Kreutz, and L. Mitchell (eds), *Music, Health and Wellbeing*, pp. 113–124. Oxford: Oxford University Press.

Coessens, K., Crispin, D., and Douglas, A. (2009). *The Artistic Turn. A Manifesto.* Ghent: Orpheus Institute.

Colwell, R. and Richardson, C. (eds) (2002). *The New Handbook of Research on Music Teaching and Learning*. Oxford: Oxford University Press.

Daugherty, J.F. (1996). *Spacing, formation, and choral sound: Preferences and perceptions of auditors and choristers*. PhD, The Florida State University.

Di Grazia, D.M. (ed.) (2013). *Nineteenth-Century Choral Music*. New York: Routledge.

Duchan, J.S. (2007). *Powerful voices: Performance and interaction in contemporary collegiate a cappella*. PhD, University of Michigan.

Durrant, C. (2003). *Choral Conducting: Philosophy and Practice*. New York: Routledge.

Durrant, C. (2009). Communicating and accentuating the aestethic and expressive dimension in choral conducting. *International Journal of Music Education* 27: 326–340.

Durrant, C. and Varvarigou, M. (2008). Real time and virtual: Tracking the professional development and reflection of choral conductors. *Reflecting Education* 4(1): 72–80.

Engeström, Y. (2005). *Developmental Work Research: Expanding Activity Theory in Practice*. Berlin: Lehmanns Media.

Fagius, G. (2009). *The Swedish Choral Miracle. On Choir Life in Sweden. Why, How and Where Do People Sing in Choirs?* Uppsala: KÖRSAM.

Fischer, E. and Kürsten, A. (eds) (2007). *Chorgesang als Medium von Interkulturalität: Formen, Kanäle, Diskurse*. Stuttgart: Steiner.

Frankel, L.H. (2012). The Tapiola Choir and Finnishness: Institutional and Government support for contemporary music in Finland. Paper given at the conference *Concepts and Practices of Choral Singing*, Lund, Sweden, October 2012.

Freire, P. (1972). *The Pedagogy of the Oppressed*. London: Penguin.

Garnett, L. (2009). *Choral Conducting and the Construction of Meaning. Gesture, Voice, Identity*. Farnham: Ashgate.

Geisler, U. and Johansson, K. (eds) (2010). *Choir in Focus 2010*. Göteborg: Bo Ejeby Förlag.

Geisler, U. and Johansson, K. (eds) (2011). *Choir in Focus 2011*. Göteborg: Bo Ejeby Förlag.

Geisler, U. (2011). Choir singing and socio-musical attitudes. Continuity and change in a Swedish-German long-term perspective. In: U. Geisler and K. Johansson (eds), *Choir in Focus 2011*, pp. 104–115. Göteborg: Bo Ejeby Förlag.

Geisler, U. (ed.) (2012). *Choral Research 1960–2010 Bibliography*. Malmö: Körcentrum Syd.

Habermas, J. (1962). *Strukturwandel der Öffentlichkeit. Untersuchungen zu einer Kategorie der bürgerlichen Gesellschaft*. Frankfurt a.M.: Suhrkamp.

Hannula, M., Suoranta, J., and Vadén, T. (2005). *Artistic Research—Theories, Methods and Practices*. Espoo: Cosmoprint Oy.

Haugland Balsnes, A. (2009). *Å lære i kor. Belcanto som praksisfellesskap. [Learning in Choir. Belcanto as a community of practice]*. PhD, Norwegian Academy of Music.

Haugland Balsnes, A. (2010). Choir research—a Norwegian perspective. In: U. Geisler and K. Johansson (eds), *Choir in Focus 2011*, pp. 16–19. Göteborg: Bo Ejeby Förlag.

Haugland Balsnes, A. (2012). Choral singing for a better life for persons with chronic illnesses. Paper given at the conference *Concepts and Practices of Choral Singing*, Lund, Sweden, October 2012.

Hoegaerts, J. (2012). Little citizens and "petites patries": Learning patriotism through choral singing in Antwerp in the late nineteenth century. Paper given at the conference *Concepts and Practices of Choral Singing*, Lund, Sweden, October 2012.

Holzer, A. (1995). *Dokumente des Musiklebens. Katalog und Regestenheft zur Ausstellung "Österreich-Ideologie in der Musik"*. Aus dem Archiv des Instituts für Musikgeschichte, 18.

Hultberg, C. (2005). Practitioners and researchers in cooperation—method development for qualitative practice-related studies. *Music Education Research* 7(2): 211–224.

Jansson, D. (2013). *Musical leadership: The choral conductor as sensemaker and liberator*. PhD dissertation, Norwegian Academy of Music.

Johansson, K. (2010). "Practice-related studies of choir: music education and artistic research perspectives." In: U. Geisler and K. Johansson (eds), *Choir in Focus 2010*, pp. 88–94. Göteborg: Bo Ejeby Förlag.

Johansson, K. (2011). Inside views on contemporary Swedish choral practice. In: U. Geisler and K. Johansson (eds), *Choir in Focus 2011*, pp. 15–32. Göteborg: Bo Ejeby Förlag.

Johansson, K. (2012). Experts, entrepreneurs and competence nomads: The skills paradox in higher music education. *Music Education Research* 14(1): 47–64.

Jonsson, L. (1990). *Ljusets riddarvakt: 1800-talets studentsång utövad som offentlig samhällskonst*. PhD dissertation, Uppsala University.

Jörgensen, H. (2009). *Research into Higher Music Education. An Overview from a Quality Improvement Perspective*. Oslo: Novus Press.

Kremer, J. and Werbeck, W. (eds) (2007). *Das Kantorat des Ostseeraums im 18. Jahrhundert. Bewahrung, Ausweitung und Auflösung eines kirchenmusikalischen Amtes*. Berlin: Frank and Timme (Greifswalder Beiträge zur Musikwissenschaft, 15).

Kohlhaas, D. and Kürsten, A. (2007). Chorgesang als medium von interkulturalität—einleitende überlegungen. In: E. Fischer and A. Kürsten (eds), *Chorgesang als Medium von Interkulturalität: Formen, Kanäle, Diskurse*, pp.11–16. Stuttgart: Steiner.

Kvist Dahlstedt, B. (2001). *Suomis sång: kollektiva identiteter i den finländska studentsången 1819–1917*. PhD dissertation, Gothenburg University.

Lurton, G. (2011). *Le Choeur partagé. Le Chant choral en France, intégration socio-économique d'un monde de l'art moyen*. PhD dissertation, Institut d'Études Politiques de Paris.

Mason, L. (1996). *Singing the French Revolution: popular culture and politics, 1787-1799*. Ithaca: Cornell University Press.

Merriam, A.P. (1964). *The Anthropology of Music*. Chicago: Northwestern University Press.

Niemöller, K.W., Loos, H., and Koch, K.-P. (eds) (2002). *Musikgeschichte zwischen Ost- und Westeuropa: Kirchenmusik, geistliche Musik, religiöse Musik. Bericht der Konferenz Chemnitz 28.-30. Oktober 1999 anlässlich des 70. Geburtstages von Klaus Wolfgang Niemöller*. Sinzig: Studio.

Östersjö, S. (2008). *Shut up 'n' play! Negotiating the musical work*. PhD dissertation, Lund University.

Potter, J. (1996). *Representing Reality*. London: Sage.

Randjärv, L. (2012). Estonian song celebrations as driver for political and social change. Paper given at the conference *Concepts and Practices of Choral Singing*, Lund, Sweden, October 2012.

Reimers, L., Wallner, B., and Ericson, E. (eds) (1993). *Choral Music Perspectives. Dedicated to Eric Ericson*. Stockholm: The Royal Academy of Music.

Sahk, K. (ed.) (2014). *Eesti statistika aastaraamet 2014/Statistical Yearbook of Estonia 2014* (Tallin: Statistics Estonia): 16. Available at: <http://www.stat.ee/72571>. Accessed July 30, 2014.

Sandberg Jurström, R. (2009). *Att ge form åt musikaliska gestaltningar. En socialsemiotisk studie av körledares multimodala kommunikation i kör. [Shaping musical performances. A social semiotic study of choir conductors' multimodal communication in choir].* PhD, Gothenburg University.

Scheitler, I. (ed.) (2000). *Geistliches Lied und Kirchenlied im 19. Jahrhundert: Theologische, musikologische, und literaturwissenschaftliche Aspekte.* Tübingen: Francke Verlag (Mainzer hymnologische Studien).

Sparks, R. (1998). *The Swedish Choral Miracle: Swedish A Cappella Music Since 1945.* Pittsboro: Blue Fire Productions.

Strinnholm Lagergren, K. (2009). *Ordet blev sång. Liturgisk sång i katolska kloster 2005–2007.* PhD, Gothenburg University.

Stubley, E. (1998). Being in the body, being in the sound: A tale of modulating identities and lost potential. *Journal of Aesthetic Education* 32(4): 93–105.

Sulzer, J.G. (1771/2002). *Allgemeine Theorie der schönen Künste. Lexikon der Künste und der Ästhetik (1771/1774).* Berlin: Directmedia Publ., p. 792. Cf. Sulzer's lexicon in full text: <http://www.zeno.org/Sulzer-1771/A/Chor>.

Vesilind, P. (2008). *The Singing Revolution: How Culture Saved a Nation.* Tallinn: Varrak.

Vodicka, J. (2012). Empowerment, engagement, and transformation: A new paradigm for the choral rehearsal. Paper given at the conference *Concepts and Practices of Choral Singing,* Lund, Sweden, October 2012.

Welch, G. (2007). Addressing the multifaceted nature of music education: An activity theory research perspective. *Research Studies in Music Education* 28: 23–37.

Welch, G.F. (2011). Culture and gender in a cathedral music context: An activity theory exploration. In: M. Barrett (ed.), *A Cultural Psychology of Music Education,* pp. 225–258. New York: Oxford University Press.

CHAPTER 39

....

THE YOUTH CHOIR

....

JOY HILL

Rhythm and melody enter into the soul of the well-instructed youth and produce there a certain mental harmony hardly obtainable in any other way.

(Plato)

INTRODUCTION

....

PLATO would have been happy with the concept of collective choral singing for young people. Youth choirs are recognized as contributing positively to a young person's general music education, as well as providing an opportunity for them to perform in this unique musical way. For example, in London, at the Royal College of Music Junior Department, it is claimed that singing in their choirs "develops aural awareness, vocal technique and general musical perception" (Junior Department, Royal College of Music 2014).

Ever changing and fresh, unlike adult choirs whose membership is more static, youth choirs tend to be mixed voices aged sixteen to twenty-six. Curiously, several leading international choirs refer to their groups as youth choirs yet they consist of all female singers; for example, the Netherlands Youth Choir consists of twenty female voices.

Once established, some choirs actively promote the cultural identity of the community or country that they represent through the performance of their national music, such as, for example, the Lois Botha Technical High School Choir from Bloemfontein, South Africa (Hill 2009). In addition, the coming together of youth choirs from different cultures in order to share concert programs is recognized as being a positive platform for intercultural dialogue through music. The World Youth Choir, whose members represent many different nations, was given the UNESCO Artist for Peace Award in 1996. Similarly, when the European Choral Association, Europa Cantat (ECA–EC), organized its first Youth Choir Festival (1961), choirs from several countries sang to each other and, importantly, with each other. Europa Cantat's current "Singing the Bridge" events still continue to focus on issues of reconciliation via choral singing with young singers.

Like many who are involved in choral music, I was introduced to singing in choirs while at school, where I was fortunate to have had opportunities to sing at international festivals such as the Llangollen Eisteddfod. Later, as a member of a female youth choir, I had the experience of winning the BBC "Let the Peoples Sing" choir competition. Hearing and seeing excellent youth choirs from all over the world, all performing with total commitment at the highest level was inspirational and opened my ears and eyes to a world of choral music to which I wanted to belong. However, I do not advocate competitive singing as the principal motivation for a choir.

Young musicians relish opportunities to sing good choral repertoire for its own sake and even some years later they recall these experiences of singing collectively with great affection. Conversely, I have also had the experience of observing conductors working with highly competent young musicians in the context of youth choir rehearsals (and sometimes in performances) where the students are not engaged musically and the conductors struggle to enthuse the singers to take part at all, resulting in the students proclaiming that they "do not like singing in choirs."

Like any musical instrument, the extent to which the youth choir can be played successfully or unsuccessfully is dependent on many factors. With choirs, the most important factors are the voices that form the instrument itself, the repertoire that has been selected, and the way that the singers are conducted.

When I have had the opportunity to sit on international juries at youth choir festivals and competitions, jury members (often from extremely diverse cultural backgrounds), will usually be unanimous when judging a choir to be "outstanding," as opposed to "good" or just "average." The most outstanding choirs obviously have something unique about their performances, which cannot be replicated necessarily by other choirs. However, working within the world of choral education, which generally aims to make choral art accessible to all young students, it is perhaps pertinent to consider generic features that might contribute to the making of *some* youth choirs especially good.

As someone who is interested in people and the wealth of diversity regarding how we approach what we do and how we actually do it, I decided to carry out a study involving interviews with singing teachers, composers, and choral conductors who work in the specialized field of youth choirs. Research in the field of how singing teachers, composers, and conductors work with youth choirs is not very apparent, possibly because those who work in this area tend to be actively involved in the actual practice rather than the theory behind it. However, development in the relatively new field of artistic research emphasizes the importance of the artist's inside perspective (e.g. Biggs and Karlsson 2011), on the premise that theory and practice can inform and possibly enhance one another. This creates an opportunity for a dialogue between the practice of choral performance and relevant theoretical perspectives (e.g. Johansson 2011).

FINDINGS FROM AN INTERVIEW STUDY WITH SINGING TEACHERS OF YOUTHS CHOIRS, COMPOSERS, AND CONDUCTORS

With the aim of highlighting various perspectives regarding possible constituent elements that are significant in the creation of excellent youth choirs, I undertook an interview-based study with professional musicians who regularly work with youth choirs. The purpose was to explore their current thinking and ideas relating specifically to the voices in youth choirs, to the repertoire that they perform, and to the ways that the voices are conducted. This chapter offers some results from the study with the aim of giving a picture of the process of producing excellence in collective choral performance with young singers—ultimately leading to outstanding performances of good choral music. The evidence that will be discussed is drawn from interviews carried out with eminent singing teachers, leading choral composers, and choral conductors who work within the field of youth choirs, and aims at being illustrative of contemporary trends rather than exhaustive. Data were collected between 2011 and 2013. Sixteen interviewees were selected on the basis of professional contacts as a choral conductor and my personal respect and admiration for the participants' work in their respective fields. Interviewees chosen for the study came from the UK, Estonia, Sweden, Australia, Switzerland, South Africa, the USA, Israel, and Latvia, and the choirs referred to tend to be formed of selected singers who are mostly from specialized musical backgrounds.

Data presented is in the form of recent observations made by the research participants, all of whom have given their time freely and generously. Audio recordings were made of their responses to written prompt questions that were put to them regarding their professional work, including the specific approaches that they take when working with youth choirs, and their general ideas in relation to this specialized musical area. Their answers were recorded and then edited for readability and categorized according to the focus of the questions, i.e. in relation to the voices of the choir, the repertoire, or specific issues of conducting.

In all cases, colleagues mentioned by name have given written permission to be identified and had the opportunity to give comments on the text.

Taking care of the voices in the youth choir

The interview data suggest that the sound of the voices in youth choirs is perceived to have a unique quality and is something that should be celebrated and not seen merely as a young, not fully developed singing voice due only to reach its potential at some time in the future. Composer Stephen Leek makes this clear in his observations:

> Youth choirs have a unique and distinctive colour and that can be utilised well in new compositions. So often composers think of a youth choir as just an unformed/training adult choir - but I really think that there are particular qualities in the "untrained," "natural" voices of the youth choir that have their own artistic and creative attractions. Most youth choirs are (thankfully) without vibrato and have beautiful natural voice qualities to them. This means that a composer has the potential to extract a more earthy, "world music" type of colour out of them. I believe youth choirs offer a broader spectrum of choral colour that can be explored (or ignored) by composers. Obviously young voices do not necessarily have the same sort of stamina that adult voices do, so this needs to be taken into consideration also.
>
> (Leek 2012)

Conductor Rudolf De Beer, Senior Lecturer in choral conducting at Stellenbosch University, South Africa, who has had extensive experience working with youth choirs in that country, outlined his particular methods when working with young voices. He suggested that the following were essential:

> Correct vocal coaching through appropriate warm ups and voice building sessions; the placing of voices with the same colour next/close to each other; and repertoire which will build the voices and the choir-as-a-whole's musicianship and vocal technique.
>
> (De Beer 2011)

When asked about mistakes that some conductors might make when working with youth choirs, he commented:

> Not looking after the voices, through either singing too long at a time or using the wrong vocal technique when striving to reproduce an adult sound for such young voices, which can ruin them in the long run.
>
> (De Beer 2011)

De Beer's comments resonate with recent research focused on the development of young adolescent singing voices that has highlighted the finding that people working with young voices, i.e. conductors of youth choirs, often have not necessarily had the opportunity to learn about the adolescent singing voice, and the male adolescent voice in particular (see, for example, Harrison et al. 2012; Thurman and Welch 2000; Williams 2013).

I asked conductor Naomi Mora, conductor of the Moran Choirs in Israel, a highly experienced conductor and also a trainer of teachers working with youth choirs, whether she thought there were mistakes made when working with young voices. She responded;

> Many conductors lack real knowledge about the anatomical set-up for voice production . . . this is a special age group in light of the physical, spiritual and musical development that transpires during these years. It is an opportunity to nurture and give the basis for the choir members' musical future.
>
> (Mora 2012)

Working with young singers who may be considering (or are already) studying voice at conservatory level can sometimes lead to a point of contention as to whether the singer should produce a "soloistic sound" and/or a "collective choral sound," and if, in fact, it is of any value at all for the first study singer actually to sing in a choir.

My colleague Liza Hobbs, who teaches some of the singers in my Royal College of Music Junior Department (RCMJD) Chamber Choir, has extensive experience as a professional singer in choirs and in opera house choruses. She is a strong advocate of young singers performing in choirs. She highlights particular gains, musically and vocally, which can present themselves to young first study singers performing in choirs:

> Singing in groups or in choirs presents vocal challenges for all singers. There is a powerful instinctive desire to hear one's own voice within the group. By asking choir members to sing in such a way that they can hear their neighbours is not only good choral singing practice, but is also a first-class way to stop singers listening to their own voices and thereby to sing more effectively.
>
> (Hobbs 2012)

Encouraging first study singers to take part in choral singing, as well as singing on their own, was also commented on by Kate Lewis, another colleague, at the RCMJD, who also teaches the choristers at Canterbury Cathedral:

I can see no reason why developing the techniques needed for choir singing should hinder overall development unless an inordinate amount of time is spent in choir. One rehearsal a week is unlikely to hurt, and ensemble techniques are needed by soloists in both opera and oratorio or in duet recitals on the concert platform. On the positive side, it is also important for the development of musicianship and listening skills. However, a big voice constantly singing piano would find it very hard work, which could lead to some tension issues.

(Lewis 2012)

Kate pointed out the importance of conductors' knowledge of the voices they are working with:

One final thought (and I can safely say this to you as I know how careful you are to get things right): what conductors do can really make or break on this issue. Instructions (however well-meaning but in ignorance of how the voice really works) can be positively harmful, though one would hope that a first study singer would have the sense to keep his/her own integrity.

(Lewis 2012)

Conductor David Lawrence, Artistic Director of the Ulster Youth Choir, Choir Leader of the City of Birmingham Young Voices and Musical Director of the Cambridgeshire County Youth Choir, supports the idea that conductors need to accept the advice of vocal experts: "Some choral conductors have the humility to work with vocal experts—and certainly more of us should" (Lawrence 2012).

Esteemed international soloist, Anne Sofie von Otter, reported that, previously, she had extensive experience of singing in choirs and says that she now has mixed thoughts on the idea of including first study singers in choirs. I asked her what advantages and disadvantages she thought there might be:

Depending on the standard of the choir, it can be very good from the point of view of learning to read music quickly, to sing music from different eras, to learn to blend with the voices around you and to have a great time in general making music with others your own age. I certainly profited enormously, learning repertoire from Palestrina to Ligeti, being made aware about pitch as in singing in tune (fine tuning, really making chords "stand and vibrate"), declaiming as you sing, phrasing, taking a step back to let other parts of the choir through, etc., etc. But it *very much* [her emphasis] depends on the leader/conductor.

(Von Otter 2012)

When I asked her if there is a profit vocally she said:

I don't know . . . it's more that you get to actually use your singing voice, build stamina. I would definitely not say you become a better singer technically by singing in a choir if you want to be a soloist! If you are lucky, i.e. have a good conductor, you will learn to think chamber-musically, to listen to others. But the big risk in choir singing is that you cheat! You will do all sorts of things wrong (technically speaking), and nobody will notice, because one doesn't when one listens to a group of singers. Singing soft, loud, breathing properly, supporting properly is all very hard and needs an awful lot of concentration. In a choir, you don't necessarily concentrate on that, instead it's about pitch, starting and stopping simultaneously etc. A good soloist is also rhythmically quite free, one needs to use rubato . . . an absolute no-no in a choir. It depends totally on the type of voice you have and the type of choir; are you expected to sing with a straight voice or can you wobble all you like? A big voice would have big difficulties, in the soprano and tenor sections particularly. An alto or a bass with a big or "unruly" voice would not be so noticeable or awkward perhaps. I have a lyric voice and am the type who enjoys "fitting in," not the case with everyone. I disagree with those who say it's perfectly OK for every aspiring singer to sing in a choir all the way to becoming a soloist. I eventually got to a point where it was not OK anymore to sit there and try to fit in; the time had come for me to let my voice free of the choir reins. A voice with a lot of "timbre," i.e. individual colour or weight, will be held back, certainly, if they sing frequently in a choir. Others, like myself will have a great time and learn lots . . . up to a certain limit.

(Von Otter 2012)

Among the points made here, Anne Sofie von Otter does acknowledge the benefits that choral experience brought her earlier in her career, in terms of the need to listen to and blend with others. Whatever the view of the conductor regarding the value of the first study singer performing within the context of the collective choral voice, it is widely acknowledged that choral conductors need to have an understanding of how the young voice functions and develops. I would suggest, therefore, that choral conductors should work collaboratively with the singing teachers of their choir members in order that students do not receive conflicting messages from their different mentors. There is also the professional bonus for the singing teachers and the conductors who work in this way to learn from each other and to enhance the effectiveness of their work.

The choice of repertoire for youth choirs

Repertoire choice and programming for youth choirs is something that conductors will acknowledge as occupying a great deal of their time and, in my experience, it never becomes easier! The choice of suitable repertoire for youth choirs was discussed specifically at the World Symposium for Choral Music in Puerto Madryn, Argentina (2011) by choral conductor Michael Gohl. He said that:

the choice of repertoire defines the quality of your choir. To gain knowledge of good repertoire for youth choirs is much more demanding than for adult choirs. Just as a good parent does not let young people only eat and drink what they like in that moment (i.e. chips, coke, and ice cream), the conductor should know what repertoire brings the choir to its highest level. Young people do not have a problem with listening to heavily commercial music during the day, and singing enthusiastically a Renaissance Christmas song or pieces by Britten in the evening. The conductor should be aware of that and keep the repertoire as well as the rhythm of rehearsals very varied.

(Gohl 2011)

The point Michael Gohl makes is an important one—that it is a mistake to limit the repertoire choice to one that is based on what the conductor might perceive as being more attractive to the singers, related to their popular culture and experience. This underpins David Lawrence's view, which seems to be held widely by conductors of successful youth choirs, that "a firm grasp of repertoire is key to a youth choir's development and success" (private correspondence 2012). Indeed, it is widely acknowledged that, ultimately, repertoire is key to young people's enjoyment of the singing experience and future success of the group.

Global access to publishers and repertoire is now possible via new technology, while international festivals, for those who travel, have a significant impact on the way that music and ideas cross borders, reflecting the international nature of much choral music that is performed today. However, it is acknowledged that many places in the world do not have the advantage of established publishing houses to support composers and performing groups. Leading Western European publishers such as Oxford University Press, Music Sales, Edition Peters, Boosey and Hawkes, and Faber Music all have dedicated staff working within the area of choral music for young voices and can advise conductors on repertoire. The International Federation of Choral Music (IFCM) also offers support to members in the area of repertoire choice via publications and a repertoire database.

Adjudicating at choir festivals and competitions both in the UK and abroad, I am always interested in the music chosen by the organizing committee for the "test pieces" for youth choirs and the reasons given for the inclusion of the works. Often these reasons are based on ideas associated with heritage and "what has always been sung." It is important to acknowledge the value of the inclusion of established repertoire and the importance of presenting a range of music so that the young singers can begin to understand the whole historical canon. However, I think that the additional inclusion of newly created music in a choir's repertoire is vital when working with young singers. Young singers are attracted to new ideas and can respond all the more readily to music when it is written especially for them, and when the composer works closely with the choir throughout the writing and performing of the piece. Some choirs may be deterred by the cost but, in my experience, conductors who actually take the first step in trying to create a commission and spend time seeking funding are likely to find it immensely worthwhile in terms of what the choir may gain from the musical experience.

Composing for youth choir/young voices

As part of the interview process, eminent composers whose music is often performed by youth choirs were asked if they make any special consideration when writing for these choirs. John Rutter spoke particularly about the writing of music for young tenors and basses, and the fact that students will rise to the highest levels if you expect it of them:

> I have rarely written specifically for youth or children's choir—it has been more a case of the choral music I have written happening to get performed by young choirs . . . with teenagers and students you don't usually get very high tenors or low basses, which is something to bear in mind. I just write what I write and choirs of all ages seem to deal with it fine . . . Probably the best performances I have ever directed of the Bach motets have been with high school kids. They will rise to the level of the music if you demand that they do.
>
> (Rutter 2012)

Judith Bingham, UK composer and former professional singer, also believes that youth choirs rise to the highest level if given the opportunity. She spoke about the powerful impact of the conductor on the possible performance outcomes:

> I would never dumb down or try and "think young," as to kids I know I am a very old person who cannot possibly understand them! I have written really difficult music for youth choirs, but my experience is that conductors tend to decide on the level of the choir's ability based on their own ability! A change of conductor can bring about a startling change in [the choir's] ability.
>
> (Bingham 2011)

I also asked her what mistakes she thought composers might make when writing for youth choirs:

> Well, what can seem like a mistake now may not seem so in the future, but apart from that, I think composers are too banal in their harmonic world, thinking that it will be too hard for young singers if they do something a bit unexpected. There are thousands of banal pieces, full of pop rhythms, and embarrassing shouty moments—conductors have a lot of choice when it comes to that sort of music, it's a bottomless pit. It's maybe more interesting to think outside the box a bit. But then again, it all comes down to the conductor again and their ideas of what is "appropriate." I think that teenagers are thinking about a very wide range of subjects and don't just want to do the cute stuff, the anaesthetised folk tunes, the pop arrangements. But maybe I think that because I don't want to write that stuff! I would say to a composer that they should try running with a subject that they would enjoy writing about, but make it practical and eminently performable.
>
> (Bingham 2011)

UK Composer Gabriel Jackson also maintains the importance of not "writing down" when composing for youth choirs and discussed the art of writing at an appropriate level:

> I try to write music that is of an appropriate level of difficulty for the abilities of the choir in question. The secret is, I think, to write music that is difficult enough for the singers to have something to "get their teeth into" and to be a bit of a challenge, but to make sure that challenge is not so great that they can't meet it, and that they will enjoy the experience. With young people, particularly, I think it's essential not to patronise them—by "writing down" to them—and to recognise that, while they may not be as technically advanced, vocally, as the top professional groups, they are intelligent people, and in all likelihood, very good musicians . . . The big mistake is writing music that is unnecessarily difficult. There's nothing as soul-destroying for singers than working really hard to get to grips with difficult material that isn't worth the effort. An obvious vocal challenge thrillingly overcome—some of the music in the Bach motets, for example—can be very exciting for the audience and performers alike, but "grey" music that is unrewarding and uninteresting is a curse, and there's too much of it. The other mistake often made when writing for young people, of course, is to underestimate their abilities and bore them, and probably bore the audience, too!
>
> (Jackson 2013)

The specific issue of boys' voices that was raised by John Rutter was addressed by the Estonian composer Urmas Sisask. He considers the specific quality of the young voice in his compositions, particularly in relation to the likely restricted range of boys' voices and the possibility of combining the tenor and bass parts:

> When I am composing choral music for youth choirs, I take into account the distinctive nature of the young voice and, unlike when writing for adult choirs, when I usually create music for four and more parts, I recommend the writing of just three parts.
>
> (Sisask 2011)

Similarly, Australian composer Stephen Leek, known internationally for his compositions for youth choirs, specifically mentioned the issue of writing for boys' changing voices. He said that:

> Probably the most difficult issue is that no two choirs in this age group are the same—many have more sopranos than other voices. If there are boys, often there are some whose voices are changing and usually in different states of change; often there is an imbalance between the

parts. So writing to find compromises that will embrace many of these factors is challenging. Usually this means that, in terms of range, one has to be very careful and err on the side of caution for the ranges of the male parts in particular—not too high nor too low in the tenor range and bass range. The trick is to make it interesting given these limitations!

(Leek 2012)

UK composer and conductor Bob Chilcott has not only written pieces for youth choirs throughout the world, but is also revered as a choral conductor. I asked if he approached writing music for youth choirs in a special way, and, in response, he spoke about the significance of the text:

Young people often have a very open response to text that can be stimulating to both composer and performers. Also, a lot of ideas expressed in text can correspond with the discovery of ideas and feelings that are explored by the enquiring mind and this can help enable an important stimulus for young people. I find that I am able to be more creative with regard to idiom and musical style. I find that young people can be more open in this regard . . . The important thing is that I write something that stimulates a positive musical and vocal response to the music.

(Chilcott 2011)

Another new repertoire option is to include students' own compositions in the choir's repertoire, as this can be a strong musical stimulus and have a strong artistic impact on fellow singers. My RCMJD Chamber Choir has been involved in "Living Song," a collaborative performance and composition project created and led by the English Folk Dance and Song Society (EFDSS) in partnership with the RCMJD. The project introduces young singers and composers to English folk song as a living, evolving tradition, and also gives them opportunities to experience the creation and the performance of new compositions.

Each academic year a group of students from RCMJD attend a folk song workshop at Cecil Sharp House led by leading folk artists. Following this, young composers work, with guidance from their teachers, to create new choral compositions based on the traditional folk songs that they have learnt, originally collected by composers such as Ralph Vaughan Williams and Gustav Holst. The RCMJD Chamber Choir then premieres these new works in concert performances. The challenge for the young composers is to create compositions for collective choral performance from works that are originally monodic.

Students have consequently been involved in the holistic process of creating and performing new choral music. They have since acknowledged how this project has informed their thinking regarding all periods of choral music and extended their understanding of the distinctive way composers write for the collective choral voice. Giving a platform for young composers to have their music performed is also an important way to nurture and value the young composers who might end up composing for choirs in the future.

Conducting youth choirs

Choral conductors come from multifaceted musical backgrounds and may well have additional significant professional experience as composers, singers, instrumentalists, and teachers. Some, depending on their country of origin, may have had opportunities to study as a choral conductor, but for many, the reported journey is often one of learning the craft via osmosis. However, the growing number of choral conducting courses and opportunities to study at graduate and postgraduate levels in this field could obviously impact on this pattern of learning, possibly taking the standard of choral singing and its potential to even greater heights. The choral conductor (working with all age groups), and the effective approaches that they might employ when conducting choirs generally, have been discussed in professional choir symposia, choral articles, and books (see, for example, Carrington 2012; Durrant 2003), and the issue of "evoking" the actual collective choral sound is one area that has also been considered (Jordan 1996).

However, with my interest in understanding the practice of working specifically with young adult voices, I asked leading choral conductors of youth choirs if there were any distinctive approaches that they took when working with this age group. Conductor David Lawrence, Artistic Director of the Ulster Youth Choir and Choir Leader of the City of Birmingham Young Voices, spoke about the necessity for the conductor to understand the possible impact of the choir on the young people's spiritual growth as well as their musical development:

> In my experience, young singers sing for personalities. Everyone has a voice, but a young person's voice usually comes with less insecurities and fear than that of an adult. All young people love to sing in a safe environment where they are respected, valued, and through the development of both their individual voice and the collective voice of which they are a part, value themselves even more. A good youth choir conductor knows this, and sees the music-making as a means to "person-building," understands the extraordinary spiritual (not religious) potential that singing has and takes the long view of developing choral skills, musicianship and of course musicality.
>
> (Lawrence 2012)

Conductor Michael Gohl states that aims and objectives are vital when directing youth choirs. He says that as a conductor you need to:

> be very clear about your visions, your values and your aims with your choirs, if possible before you start a choir. Most difficulties in choirs occur because of different expectations among the singers, their parents and the conductor. Check your "credo": Do you really believe in the potential of your singers? This requests that you are able to realistically estimate the potential of every singer.
>
> (Gohl 2011)

Swedish conductor Gary Graden, former conductor of the Stockholm Gymnasium Youth Choir, World Youth Choir, and European Youth Choir, described his approach to directing youth choirs as follows:

> I try to create a joyful and positive atmosphere in all aspects and stages of the choral experience, from the first moments of a warm-up, through various stages of rehearsal, through to the final moments of a concert. I try to share with singers and choirs the joy that I myself feel in the magical process of making music. I use exclusively the "yes" words and, hopefully, never or rarely the "no" words. [He explains] I try to give information and suggestions as to how singers and choirs can improve; not what they're doing wrong, but how they can improve the beautiful work that they are already doing. I guess it's something like hypnosis—using the infinitely important power of suggestion. If, in fact, some musical idea or particular piece of

music does not work, then I try to find creative ways to solve the problems. It is important to be satisfied with what singers and choirs achieve, given the particular level of individuals' and choirs' talents and abilities. It is surely important to take risks and to challenge a group in various ways (this is part of our job as conductors); and finally it is important to enjoy and love the process regardless of the end result.

(Graden 2012)

André Thomas is widely acknowledged as a leader in the field of teaching choral conducting and working with youth choirs. He has produced two instructional videos along with Rodney Eichenberger (Eichenberger and Thomas 1994). The videos demonstrate how an awareness of the visual, the aural, and the kinetic can promote artistic choral singing, and how the conductor changes the sound of the choir through conducting gestures and individual personality.

Latvian conductor, Maris Sirmais, who founded the youth choir Kamēr, an outstanding international choir that is widely considered to have an extraordinary ability to communicate choral music and to move audiences, spoke of his particular approach to conducting his choir, and his belief in the importance of knowing each singer individually. He said that:

the most important thing we have developed in Kamēr . . . since its very beginning, is personal contact with every singer. Each singer spends individual time with a vocal teacher and also with the conductor where you can get to know this person and find the right way to work with him/her and their ability. This is, of course, in addition to the twice-weekly rehearsals. Due to this intensive personal contact, we achieve strong mutual feeling. The choir is built not as a collective unit, but as a unit of personalities and individual singers. Each one of them is a significant part of the performance with their personal attitude, phrasing and understanding of the lyrics, music and spirit of a particular piece.

When it comes to the sound of the choir—it sounds in my head and is hard to describe. I just know what I want to get and the vocal teachers have learned this sound and work towards it. I would say mutual sensibility is the key word in our performance.

. . . both the full emotional surrender, a characteristic of amateur singers, as well as the strictest criteria for the vocal quality of a performance, are of equal importance for the choir. This is also exemplified by the ellipsis encoded in the choir's name, Kamēr, which means "while" in English. While we are still young, anything is possible.

(Sirmais 2012)

All of these recorded observations made by conductors point to the vital importance of the ability of the conductor to create a rehearsal environment where the young singers feel valued, both socially and musically. Presenting challenging musical programs is also emphasized as being highly significant.

There is a general consensus that conductors need to appreciate that they are motivators of the singers as well as the directors of the music. This, I suggest, is more essential when working with youth choirs, as it is likely to be the students' first experience of singing collectively and they may lack other points of reference. More experienced singers, in choral societies and community choirs, for example, will perhaps be more accepting of a musician who knows the music, but is relatively dull in their conducting approach. The interview responses suggest that young people do not suffer fools gladly and know that they have other options regarding the use of their musicianship and time.

Beyond this, I suggest that the art of successfully conducting youth choirs requires an active interest on the part of the conductor, to listen to other choirs and to observe other conductors working in rehearsals and in performances. I would further suggest that a hunger to seek out repertoire from other cultures as well as our own is also important. Ideally, organizing trips to take young singers to other countries in order to hear and experience other choral performance practices, and to perform with other choirs, can present the opportunity for the singers themselves, as well as the conductors, to extend their understanding and learning regarding choral art and humanity.

A philosophical stance concerning the lifelong professional learning of choral conductors, listening to and watching other choirs as well as their own, is generally supported by the comments from the featured interviewees in this chapter, as well as by other recognized specialists. Simon Carrington, for example, states: "I am confident that there is no substitute for a steady diet of listening to the sounds and styles of choirs of all shapes and sizes while watching and evaluating their conductors" (Carrington 2012).

Conclusions

Within the material presented in this chapter it is generally held that the conductor's understanding of the young voice and its unique nature is essential if the potential of the collective choral voice of the youth choir is to be developed and used appropriately. Selecting suitable repertoire for the group, based on this knowledge, is perhaps an art as well as a skill that takes considerable time and energy outside formal rehearsal time. Along with the inclusion of a broad repertoire, actively working with composers can create an exciting dynamic and can help to ensure that both singers and conductor are an integral part of the creative process, leading to the performance of new choral music. A good rapport between the conductor and the young singers is also essential if the singers are to reach the highest level of collective choral performance. The data, particularly in relation to the role of the conductor, supports the premise that it is important to really know the individual singers and their voices and to appraise the choice as well as the performance of the music.

Finally, there is evidence that a constant curiosity and open-mindedness is needed in relation to all aspects of creating and developing a youth choir, both artistically and musically, including from conductors, singing teachers, and composers, as well as from the singers themselves. When this curiosity is grounded in a personal approach of humility, the ultimate aim of making great music with youth choirs can begin to be realized. As singers in the most outstanding youth choirs in the world know, when professionals working with youth choirs approach their work in this way, everything is possible.

Further Reading

Ericson, E., Ohlin, G. and Spångberg, L. (1974.) *Choral Conducting*. Springfield, MO: Walton Music Corporation.

Rink, J. (2002). *Musical Performance—A Guide to Understanding*. Cambridge: Cambridge University Press.

Scherchen, H. (1989). *Handbook of Conducting*. Oxford: Oxford University Press.

Williamon A. (2004). *Musical Excellence: Strategies and Techniques to Enhance Performance*. Oxford: Oxford University Press.

Websites

Boosey and Hawkes, <http://www.boosey.com>.
Edition Peters, <http://www.edition-peters.com>.
IFCM, <http://www.ifcm.net>.
OUP, <http://ukcatalogue.oup.com>.
Royal College of Music, Junior Department, <http://www.rcm.ac.uk/junior/aboutrcmjd/>.

References

Biggs, M. and Karlsson, H. (eds) (2011). *The Routledge Companion to Research in the Arts*. London: Routledge.

Bingham, J. (2011). Interview. December.

Carrington, S. (2012). *The Cambridge Companion to Choral Music*. Cambridge: Cambridge University Press.

Chilcott, B. (2011). Interview. October.

De Beer, R. (2011). Interview. December.

Durrant, C. (2003). *Choral Conducting: Philosophy and Practice*. New York: Routledge.

Eichenberger, R. and Thomas, A. (1994). *What They See Is What You Get* (DVD). Seminole Productions. Chapel Hill: Hinshaw Music Inc.

Gohl, M. (2011). Interview. November.

Graden, G. (2012). Interview. January.

Harrison, S., Welch, G.F., and Adler, A. (2012). Men, boys and singing. In: S. Harrison, G.F. Welch, and A. Adler (eds), *Perspectives on Males and Singing*, pp. 9–22. London: Springer.

Hill, J. (2009). True colours. *Choir and Organ* September/October: 49–50.

Hobbs, L. (2012). Interview. March.

Jackson, G. (2013). Interview. February.

Johansson, K. (2011). Inside views on contemporary Swedish choral practice. In: U. Geisler and K. Johansson (eds), *Choir in Focus 2011*, pp. 15–32. Gothenburg: Bo Ejeby Förlag.

Jordan, J. (1996). *Evoking Sound: Fundamentals of Choral Conducting and Rehearsing*. Chicago: GIA Publications.

Junior Department, Royal College of Music (2014). <http://www.rcm.ac.uk/junior/aboutrcmjd/>.

Lawrence, D. (2012). Interview. March.

Leek, S. (2012). Interview. April.

Lewis, K. (2012). Interview. November.

Mora, N. (2012). Interview. February.

Rutter, J. (2012). Interview. January.

Sirmais, M. (2012). Interview. January.

Sisask, U. (2011). Interview. January.

Thurman, L. and Welch, G.F. (eds). (2000). *Bodymind and Voice: Foundations of Voice Education* (rev. edn). Iowa City: National Center for Voice and Speech.

Von Otter, A.S. (2012). Interview. March.

Williams, J. (2013). *Teaching Singing to Children and Young Adults*. London: Compton.

....

CHAPTER 40

CULTURAL HISTORY AND A SINGING STYLE
"The English Cathedral Tradition"

....

TIMOTHY DAY

INTRODUCTION

....

MUSICOLOGY has mostly been concerned with texts, with notes on the page, with the canon of European "great works." But many musicologists are now becoming more concerned with music in performance and musical experience and the ways shifting performing styles can reflect changing musical experiences. Such thinking is clearly facilitated by the availability of more than a century of recorded performances and the large amount of comment on these.

Nicholas Cook has reminded us that music "is deeply embedded in human culture ... [is] suffused with human values, with our sense of what is good or bad, right or wrong ... People *think* through music, decide who they are through it, express themselves through it" (Cook 1998, pp. vi, vii). By thinking about their singing a cultural historian will try and understand what particular musicians and music-lovers were about, rather as an anthropologist might examine some faraway and exotic society.

Cultural history can usually prove very little, it can only suggest. It can only succeed to the extent that others feel that an account is plausible, coherent, that it rings true. Such analysis is undertaken on the assumption that, as one anthropologist framed it, "man is an animal suspended in webs of significance he himself has spun," and that this kind of analysis is "not an experimental science in search of law but an interpretive one in search of meaning" (Geertz 1973, p. 5).

Such historical writing may draw on the insights of anthropologists and ethnomusicologists as well as musicologists and all kinds of historians and may take into account the findings of psychologists and scientists engaged in work on music and the brain. But this kind of writing can rarely follow prescribed methodologies since it treats music in human relationships, and human relationships, being complex and intricate, cannot be mathematically deduced or described.

Such writing on singing is not intended to convince anyone of the beauty of a particular singing style, which would inevitably be a vain endeavor, but to try and describe the richness and complexity of the meanings of a certain kind of music in performance on the assumption that anyone who loves any kind of music performed in any kind of style will recognize the potential power and significance of the most minute nuances. The hope would be that such detailed descriptions might perhaps deepen musical experience and our understanding of human lives, including our own.

"THE ENGLISH CATHEDRAL TRADITION"

This chapter concerns itself with a very parochial singing style, but one which had a great influence on all kinds of classical music-making—and not just in England and not on vocal styles alone—in the later decades of the twentieth century. This was the distinctive kind of singing of those English choirs of men and boys in cathedrals, university college chapels, and those churches called royal peculiars of which the best known are Westminster Abbey and St George's Chapel, Windsor. As the style became known all over the world through broadcasting and recording the assumption in the last century often seemed to be that the style was of great antiquity, that these choirs had been singing in this way for hundreds of years. In 1938 a clear-sighted and clear-headed historian concluded that this tradition was probably "more recent than is often thought" (Scholes 1941, p. 146). He was right. This chapter traces the formation of this singing style, usually referred to as "the English cathedral tradition." The one choir that was held by most music-lovers and by most cathedral musicians themselves, either consciously or unconsciously, to represent the quintessence of the style during the later decades of the twentieth century was that of King's College, Cambridge in the 1960s. As we shall see, in one crucial aspect it was quite unlike all the cathedral choirs of that time. Yet it realized ideals about choral singing that had been held at the English choral foundations throughout the twentieth century. It became so famous because of its distinctiveness and distinction and because it was heard everywhere by means of the recently invented long-playing disc. It seemed so new and fresh. It seemed so old.

How might this singing style be described? The ensemble is perfectly disciplined: consonants are clearly enunciated and synchronized with unerring precision. The timbre is unforced and violent changes in dynamic are avoided; even in *forte* there is no sense of strain, or indeed of drama, or at least not of any emotional outpouring. Expressive gestures are intense but subdued. Tempos are almost invariably steady. Vibrato is avoided. The tuning is immaculate. The sounds shine with an unearthly silvery glitter. A very good example of the style can be heard on a recording of Byrd's "Ave Verum corpus" (Gradualia 1605) released in 1959 (King's College, Cambridge 1959).

Why did they sing like that?

An Earlier Singing Style

How did the King's choir sound a century earlier? There is not very much evidence that illuminates this. There are hardly any descriptions of style or tone quality that convey sufficient detail. A little can be deduced. For his voice trial in 1836 one boy was taken out for a stroll by a senior chorister at King's who encouraged him to shout back at lengthening distances in order to strengthen his voice. He did at any rate pass the trial and was admitted (Case 1899, unnumbered fourth and fifth pages of the Preface). The evidence there is suggests that the choir at King's was similar to the choirs at the other English choral foundations in the middle decades of the nineteenth century.

An American visitor in 1852 (who seems not to have visited Cambridge) thought English choirs in cathedrals all far inferior to the best German choirs, particularly the ones in St Thomas's in Leipzig or in the Dom-Kirche in Berlin. The Chapel Royal in London he considered "a poor choir," the choir at Westminster Abbey "very indifferent" (Mason 1853, pp. 167–168). The psalms at Worcester were just gabbled—as they were at St Paul's—with no two members of the choir keeping together, and no attempt by anyone at clear enunciation. All this prevented any attempt at expressiveness (Mason 1853, p. 12). The choir at York was supposed to be the best in England. But the terrible roughness of the boys was enough "to tear out one's soul" (Mason 1853, p. 309). The observer asked an Austrian composer he found in London about English trebles. "Boys' voices," Sigismund Neukomm replied, "are like cats' voices." It was the shrillness and the screeching of English boys, Neukomm told him, that so got on Mendelssohn's nerves on one occasion in Exeter Hall in 1837 as he sat listening to a rehearsal of his oratorio "St Paul." And Mendelssohn had wondered why on earth the English did not follow the Germans and employ women for both soprano and alto parts (Mason 1853, pp. 309–310).

From all kinds of sources, including the parliamentary reports on cathedrals, it is clear that the stipends for the men who sang in all cathedral choirs in the nineteenth century were miserably insufficient and there was almost no provision for pensions to be provided for the old and those whose voices had deteriorated. There might well have been some excellent voices among the eight or ten lay clerks at Durham in the 1850s but there were almost invariably two or three who had grown old and inefficient or had lost their voices completely and did more harm than good (Parliamentary Papers 1854/xxv, p. 972). It was the same in the 1880s at Winchester Cathedral where one of the priests who intoned the services reported that of the nine lay clerks there, "two or three managed to mar all the music of our services, and they cannot be removed" (Parliamentary Papers 1884–1885/ xxi, p. 54). It was the probably the same most of the time in nearly all cathedral choirs. There were also nearly everywhere too few men. Twenty-seven cathedral organists in 1880 suggested to the cathedral commissioners that no cathedral choir should consist of no fewer than twelve men (Parliamentary Papers 1884–1885/xxi: p. 243). At King's in 1877 there were six (Mann 1877).

Who were the lay clerks at King's? All the men singing at the choral foundations were poor and few had usually received much musical or even much general education. At King's in the nineteenth century the gentlemen of the choir earned additional money as a weaver, a piano tuner, a shoemaker, a tailor, the Cook of Pembroke College, a music engraver. The boys too were from poor families. A handwritten sheet in the College archives at King's, Cambridge indicates the occupation of choristers' fathers in the 1870s: the fathers in the earlier years of the decade worked as a builder, a trader at Newmarket, as domestic servants, a coal merchant's clerk, a watchmaker, a tailor, a coach painter, the College Chapel clerk, and the College shoe-black, a butcher, a general laborer, a domestic servant, a millwright, and a tailor. But then, suddenly, at the end of the 1870s, the boys were the sons of clergymen—including the Vicar of St Andrew's, Norwich and the Rector of St John's, Manchester—and a surgeon of Piccadilly in London, and another one in Newport in Essex, a GP, an inspector of schools. For in the autumn of 1878 a boarding school had been opened (King's College, Cambridge 1860).

Changes in Personnel

And then in 1881 an undergraduate came to King's to read Mathematics and to "assist" in the choir, the first choral scholar. By the end of the century there were regularly three choral scholars in the choir at King's. From 1906 until the First World War there were four; in the 1920s—after wartime reductions—the number crept up until there were eleven in 1929 and finally twelve in 1930. The last lay clerk died, in office, in 1928. And, except during the Second World War, twelve more or less it has remained ever since, supplemented with a few, normally two, volunteers singing with the sixteen choristers (*King's College, Cambridge Annual Reports*, 1882–).

Why did the social background and musical training of these musicians at King's change? Because of changes in attitudes towards education. These were driven in part by political and economic factors. England saw other European powers, particularly Germany, developing a state education system and realized the disadvantages in keeping a population uneducated and untrained. By the end of the nineteenth century through a succession of education acts there was compulsory free education for all children up to the age of twelve.

At the same time this period saw the establishment of a great number of new independent schools, including the seven founded by Nathaniel Woodard, all staunchly Anglican foundations. The Woodard Foundation schools were also the result of Thomas Arnold's reforms at Rugby School. King's clearly had to do something. In the middle of the century the choristers were still required not only to sing but also to wait at table on the undergraduates and Fellows every day. They were given a very rudimentary education at the back of the dining hall. At any rate the Fellows of the College had concluded in the 1870s that "Cambridge boys of the lower classes produced a result which was not satisfactory either musically or morally" (Leigh 1899, p. 290).

Spiritual Changes

The changes were also evidence of the spiritual reformation in the Anglican Church. The Oxford Movement changed the spirituality of the English Church. It changed the spirituality of the English. It wanted to restore a sense of the numinous; it was a movement of the heart, not the head; it was a part of the great swing against the neat and tidy spick-and-span Age of Enlightenment. It wanted to recapture the spirit of the medieval church. Some wanted to reinstall the forms of medieval worship.

It began in obscure parish churches, sometimes with the introduction of Gregorian chant. But from the 1870's St Paul's in London began to stimulate change in cathedrals. There, in 1872, prayers began to be said in the vestry before the choir began processing into the stalls. Until that year the choristers had worn long surplices alone; now they wore cassocks under surplices. In 1873 the men also began to wear cassocks. Daily celebrations of communion began in 1877. A three hour devotion on Good Friday was instituted in 1878 (Chadwick 1972, p. 387). The revolution in music at St Paul's began with the appointment of John Stainer in 1872. At the same time public interest in music itself was growing. Earlier in the nineteenth century a succession of local choral societies as well as festivals were established, like the one at Leeds and the Crystal Palace Handel festivals. Some thought that developing interest in music and in singing derived from the example of Queen Victoria and the Prince Consort who was not only a singer but a musician who played the piano and organ and wrote canticle settings and anthems himself (Hueffer 1889, p. 5).

It was a great advantage that cathedral music had as a champion Sir Frederick Gore Ouseley (1825–1889), from a rich family distinguished in military and diplomatic matters, and a godson of the Duke of Wellington, who took a degree in music when "it was utterly derogatory for a man in his social position to entertain such an idea," as the Dean of Christ Church told him (Fellowes 1946, p. 9). He was Precentor of Hereford Cathedral and remonstrated against the ignorance of music of the clergy of his day. But he also became a reforming Professor of Music at Oxford, and through his private wealth he established a boarding school in 1856 specifically to set an example of the daily round of liturgical worship maintained with the utmost care at St Michael's College, at Tenbury in Worcestershire.

How did these social changes affect the singing of cathedral choirs? That American visitor in 1852 considered English boys' voices rough and harsh and horrible; the Norwich Festival Chorus was far inferior to that in Birmingham, where the top line was taken almost entirely by mature women's voices. At Norwich there were forty-one female sopranos but almost thirty-four boys singing alongside, "enough boys," in the American's opinion, "to spoil almost any soprano" (Mason 1853, p. 262).

Half a century later the organist and choirmaster of St Paul's Church, Baltimore visited seventeen English cathedrals and heard sixty choral services. There were certainly still some poor cathedral choirs in England. But three choirs he considered outstanding: Magdalen College, Oxford, St Paul's Cathedral, London, and King's College, Cambridge. He thought these three afforded "the best examples in the world of the possibilities, the beauty, the perfection of vested choirs of men and boys" (Farrow 1900a). Outside of these three, the singing of most boys in English choirs was still harsh. The organist at Southwark at the turn of the century explained that "the average boy neither knows nor cares anything about Voice Production; his one idea is to make as much noise as possible, and in this, unfortunately, he is as a rule only too successful" (Richardson 1900, p. 8).

The choirmasters at both Magdalen and St Paul's wrote manuals on voice training. At Magdalen, Varley Roberts' fundamental principle was to "cultivate soft singing" and to "strengthen the head voice." The so-called chest voice, which some musicians call the "shouting" notes, can be rough and unpleasant in quality, and these notes, according to the organist at Magdalen College, Oxford, "should never be forced, but always sung softly," otherwise the head notes will be ruined (Roberts 1905, pp. 3–4). At King's also the choirmaster did not allow "a single 'chest' tone," the American noticed (Farrow 1900b). The "soft, full tone" that ought to characterize boys' voices: where could you hear it at the turn of the century? Even now it could only be heard in "very few places," the Southwark organist thought. "It would perhaps be safe to say that their number might be counted on the fingers of both hands" (Richardson 1900, p. 8).

Boys' Voices and Anglicanism

Why was it that in the second half of the nineteenth century the outstanding choirmasters were insisting on the use of what many called the *head* voice, that is teaching the boys to use a cricothyroid-dominant production, and so to produce a less assertive tone?

In January 1900, Mr. Augustus Toop, organist to St Peter's, Belsize Park, who made a special feature of training choirboys, advertised vacancies for "gentlemanly boys with pure voices" (Toop 1900). It was now perfectly acceptable that the parents of a gentlemanly boy might encourage him to learn to sing in a gentlemanly way, in a restrained manner. But it was not just that he was a *gentlemanly* boy. Childhood itself was being reimagined. The crucial figure here is Wordsworth. At least Wordsworth's poetic thoughts on this topic were known far better than any other imaginative writer. And most famously of all in the *Intimations of Immortality* (lines 64–67):

> And not in utter nakedness,
> But trailing clouds of glory do we come
> From God, who is our home:
> Heaven lies about us in our infancy!

> (Wordsworth 1919)

A little child has moved so recently out of God's presence that he can irradiate older, sadder people with whom he has contact now. And so childhood is uniquely valuable, and the utterances of a little child and the tone of his or her voice are to be fastened on to, to be listened to with rapt attention.

In 1848, in the very cradle of the Oxford Movement, a Fellow of Magdalen College wrote a book called *The Devout Chorister*, a manual for choirboys. In it he says that "the vocation of a Chorister, although of course inferior to that of a Priest in ministerial power, is yet higher than that of a Priest, so far as the odour of sanctity peculiar to childhood imparts a glory to the office which appertains to no other" (Smith 1848, p. 4).

In 1850, many choirmasters used boys reluctantly, because they had to, and because they thought St Paul had said they must. S.S. Wesley, one of the best and most influential cathedral musicians of the nineteenth century in England, ascribed no particular value to boys' voices at all; he simply regretted that he had to use what he considered a "poor substitute for the vastly superior quality and power of those of women" (Wesley 1849, p. 72). Now, by 1900— and it was to remain so throughout the twentieth century—it was received wisdom among cathedral musicians that boys' voices were the "essence" of the cathedral choir and that the men are at their best when they blended with "that clean white tone" (Dyson 1952, p. 492).

One of the leaders of the Oxford Movement maintained that the Catholic Church tells you to be "inebriated" with the love of God. But, he said, the chief characteristic of the Anglican church was "sobriety" (Ward 1912, p. 66). Reticence and reserve, an avoidance of flamboyance, had been fundamental qualities in the spiritual and devotional life of the Tractarians who inaugurated this nineteenth-century spiritual reformation. Indeed, one of the original *Tracts for the times* had been "On reserve in communicating religious knowledge," "that reserve, or retiring delicacy . . . which exists naturally in a good man." Religious knowledge is always mysterious and requires meditation; it cannot be proclaimed. Reticence and reserve accompany "all strong and deep feeling," this Tractarian explained, and are characteristic of great poetry as well as religious feeling (Williams 1838, p. 55). And in a series of lectures dedicated to Wordsworth, John Keble, one of the most famous reformers of them all, was sure that "Religion and poetry are akin because each is marked by a pure reserve, a kind of modesty or reverence . . . Beauty is shy, is not like a man rushing out in front of crowd" (Keble 1844, p. 815).

In 1899 the Provost of King's considered that the introduction of "an undergraduate element" had undeniably "strengthened the singing" while tending to give the services "a more devotional and less professional character" (Leigh 1899, p. 291). A "less professional" character because the choral scholars were undoubtedly inexperienced, their voices much less mature than the lay clerks. The choral scholars at King's were much less concerned with their own individual vocal prowess. Very few of them had aspirations to become even lay clerks; none of the choral scholars before the Second World War became professional soloists. They were more responsive to calls for cooperative endeavor.

Romantic and anti-Romantic

A.H. Mann, who was born in 1850, was director of the choir at King's from 1876 until he died in 1929. He made only one recording that was issued commercially, right at the end of his life, of two Bach chorales from Schemelli's *Gesangbuch* (King's College, Cambridge 1929). It comes as rather a shock. Certainly an intensity is discernible; to modern ears, however, finesse is lacking, as is the expected blend, though the awareness of individual voices on these early discs and the absence of the famous acoustic may be put down to technological limitations. This is not how it would have sounded to a listener in the Chapel. But what are even more surprising still are the deliberate, slow, plodding speeds and—most surprising of all—the monumental *ritardandi* at cadences, and not just at final cadences. How can these features be understood?

Stylistically, Mann looked backwards. He considered each piece that his choir sung had to be *presented* to the listeners, sung with Dickensian force and emphasis and projection. Mann's tendency to take music very slowly was noticed by everyone; such deliberation, as he explained, was demanded by the famously rich acoustic of King's. But it must also be remembered that he grew up with slow deliberate singing as a chorister at Norwich. A member of the congregation at the enthronement of Bishop Pelham at Norwich in June 1857 thought that the anthem was so slow it sounded more like a farewell to the retiring bishop than a welcome to his successor (Armstrong 1949, p. 53).

For unaccompanied music in services, Mann usually descended to the stalls and stood at the end of the trebles' bench on Decani. Humorously, the days on which this happened were called "scrum" days by the boys because one had to squeeze up (Magee 1987). He might direct the choir with movements of his head, a glance, or even a finger. He would never allow anyone to stand in the center aisle to direct. But for the two full practices in Chapel each week, arrayed in a voluminous silk gown, Mann would mount a conductor's platform with its own desk set up between the choir stalls. Passages were repeated over and over again. "Gesticulations and looks of unspeakable anguish" pleaded for a yet quieter *pianissimo*; rare passages of *fortissimo* were driven on with loud cries and even banging on the desk (Evans 1965). To a new man like Edward Dent, who was professor of music at Cambridge between 1926 and 1941, even in the 1890s Mann's performances had sounded extravagant and self-indulgent. He listened as an undergraduate to the choir at King's singing Mendelssohn's "Hear my prayer" in which the solo treble, in his opinion, "carried out Mann's hysterical and operatic interpretations with a marvellous fidelity . . . everyone thought it extraordinarily beautiful, which it would have been if it had not been so studiedly theatrical" (Dent 1897). "Hysterical" is also the word Dent uses for Mann's playing of an organ Toccata and Fugue by Bach on another occasion. Voluntaries were more dignified, in Dent's opinion, if Mann had no assistant in the organ loft to manipulate the stops and so pile on the drama (Dent 1896). Even to a child, a chorister who came to King's in 1924, everything seemed exaggerated, the *fortes* being too loud and the *pianos* too quiet. And then there were those habitual extended *rallentandi* and Mann's mysterious habit of hanging on to the last pedal note of a chord (Magee, n.d., p. 9).

As was previously stated, Mann was a High Victorian and an extrovert. Boris Ord, his successor, was a man of the deflationary anti-rhetorical 1920s with anti-Romantic esthetic ideals and aspirations. He conducted Stravinsky's *The Soldier's Tale* as a young man; he felt close to the Tudor composers and enthusiastically entered many new works by sixteenth-century composers on the Chapel bills. Mann was a journeyman musician who served an apprenticeship at the hands of a cathedral organist. Ord was the son of a Kingsman, educated at Clifton College, an undergraduate at Cambridge himself, an organ scholar at Corpus Christi College, and a pupil at the Royal College of Music of Sir Walter Parratt. Parratt was renowned for the classicism and refinement and the objectivity of his approach to both organ playing and to training choirs. With his pupils he was harsh in his condemnation of any form of showiness or vulgarity. He rarely directed the choir from between the stalls at Windsor—it would be too theatrical—and when a composition of his own was sung the work's title had no name appended on the music lists (Tovey and Parratt 1941, p. 141).

Ord was already a Fellow of King's when he was appointed choirmaster; Mann was given a Fellowship only when he had been organist for forty-five years. When Mann was appointed he could not enter the senior common room, nor dine with the College Fellows, nor walk in the Fellows' Garden (King's College, Cambridge 1879). Ord and his choral scholars were from the same social background. Their attitudes towards music and education and society and worship were formed through a similar rather earnest and austere education.

Dent was not one to bestow unnecessary praise on his compatriots. And yet when he listened to performances by undergraduate musicians during the Congress of the International Musicological Society in Cambridge in 1933 he had to admit that he was "really quite amazed;" never in all his life, he said, had he heard "such technical excellence of playing and singing in Cambridge before." He was sure that the performances would have "a wonderful reverberation on the Continent and in America" (Carey 1979, p. 143).

It was now possible for the choir at King's to achieve even higher standards in tuning and ensemble simply because it practiced more frequently. There were two full practices each week with Mann; this was at a time when some cathedral choirs hardly ever had full practices. Now, with the involvement of boys and undergraduates alone, young men *in statu pupillari*, Boris Ord could summon them all to rehearse on five or six days each week before services in the Chapel. And being a private chapel, the choir could rehearse in a closed building before evensong, giving the singers regular opportunities to perfect balance and ensemble with each other and with the organ not generally available to cathedral choirs.

Journalists covering the 1933 conference marveled when they remembered that these singers in the King's College Choir and in the undergraduate University Madrigal

Society—women singing with the men in this—were all young amateurs. One reported that the musicians sang "with earnest feeling and understanding, the voices were never forced, the tempi always sensible and natural, the nuances perfectly balanced and the accentuation faultless." Everything was sober, everything was controlled, everything was unexaggerated, nobody tried to excel or to stand out. The journalist was sure that the singers were in fact saturated with "a tradition that has remained latent in certain classes of English men and women since the days of Byrd and Morley" (Pulver 1933, p. 1019). He evidently assumed that most of his readers knew what he meant by his coy phrase "certain classes." He meant middle-class, or upper middle-class, "the educated," those "of gentle birth." But such concepts were almost meaningless when applied to sections of society over centuries. By saying that this tradition of singing had remained "latent" the writer seems to concede that most educated men had in fact taken little interest in music at all, certainly for at least two and a half centuries. Even now, in the 1930s, few from this social background were musical, and fewer still could sing with skill and understanding. But those who did sing did indeed make vocal gestures which reflected the very narrow social stratum which nurtured them and the values they embraced wholeheartedly.

Manliness and Gamesmanship

Most of these singers had been educated—as had Boris Ord—at an independent public school. In his book called *Godliness and Good Learning*, David Newsome includes among the ideals of such schools at this period: "the moral and physical beauty of athleticism; the salutary effects of Spartan habits and discipline; the cultivation of all that is masculine and the expulsion of all that is effeminate, un-English and excessively intellectual" (Newsome 1961, p. 216).

What personal qualities are singled out in the King's College annual report in its obituaries for these generations of students in the first decades of choral scholars from 1881 to the Second World War? Simplicity, straightforwardness, fearlessness, modesty, and reliability are words that keep cropping up: "direct, resolute, and unassuming"(*King's College, Cambridge Annual Report*); "The life of a solider proved thoroughly congenial to him" (*King's College, Cambridge Annual Report*); "In his reserve there was no hauteur and in his silences there was no censoriousness" (*King's College, Cambridge Annual Report* 1933, p. 4). Of one who had a very brilliant career both as athlete and academically: he appeared "wholly unconscious of being in any way a celebrity" (*King's College, Cambridge Annual Report* 1927, p. 5). One of the outstanding rugby players at Cambridge in the 1930s in Cambridge—he was to become a clergyman and a distinguished church historian—explained that he liked to play hooker, because there in the scrum "you can do your good anonymously, with no sense of display;" he did not wish to tear about on the field where people could watch him "doing noble things and all that" (Chadwick 2011). The blend and the impersonality of these singers were features of the style that immediately struck contemporaries.

And these young men, these choral scholars, certainly wished to emphasize their "manliness." A Cambridge undergraduate who asked in the 1890s, "Is he musical?" might be inquiring: "Is he homosexual?"(Annan 1990, p. 143). Homosexuality meant, essentially, effeminacy. Not all these singers at King's were gifted sportsmen, though some of them were. H.W. Thomas, who entered school in 1909, was a good cricketer but a genius at rugby, and he played not only for the University but as an international for Wales (*King's College, Cambridge Annual Report*). But even if they themselves were not sportsmen they all valued the conformity, precision, and teamwork that were encouraged and fostered in this society. "Athleticism" in the choir was team spirit that emphasized the importance of meticulous ensemble and immaculate blending.

Until World War Two, there was always at least one ordinand in the choir. As a Dean of St George's Chapel, Windsor, who was born in 1864, explained to his sons: "whatever we do matters. Moses began to teach that lesson to the Israelites by declaring that there was glory in the perfectness of the service which a man gave even in the fixing of a tent peg" (Anon 1934, p. 46). Or, he might have said, in the timing of the "d" at the end of "Lord" on the third beat of the bar.

Cathedral musicians at this time liked to emphasize the toughness of their duties. At first sight, a distinguished choir-trainer thought just after the First World War, there seemed little connection between the life of a chorister—the peaceful cultivation of music in such severe forms—and the life of a soldier. In fact, the characteristics of a good choir were not at all dissimilar to those of a good regiment. A chorister must demonstrate alertness, thoughtfulness and sustained powers of concentration. So must a soldier. A solider must show discipline, courage, endurance, and a disregard of self. So must a chorister in securing blend and ensemble and in sustaining the daily round of long services and practices without flagging and in undertaking demanding solos. The chorister and the solider required both individual initiative and flexibility and adaptability in precise teamwork, which qualities were nowhere more in evidence than in the singing of psalms. The cultivation of a strong sense of rhythm which underlies all musical training was the very quality which enables a regiment to march effectively. The pride in the performance of the group was shared by chorister and soldier alike. The solider and chorister were spurred on equally by competitive instincts and by the pride in joint successes. Musical ability made a man more companionable. Singing and playing music together lifted spirits and cemented friendship. Listening to music bred patience, gave men hope, made minds sweet. At any rate, the choirmaster pointed out, there were a great number of musicians who had been cathedral choristers who secured the highest rewards for bravery and distinguished service in the World War One (Allen c. 1920).

Sometimes in Mann's day, because of the sickness of choral scholars, temporary singers were drafted in. They had a terrible time at practices, and often went out in tears at the ferociousness of the choirmaster's comments, though they never spoke against him afterwards (Crowder 1986). Having all the vigor of a much younger man, Ord drove the choir even more aggressively and could be bitingly sarcastic. An undergraduate at Cambridge around 1950 remembered him as an irascible and alarming man who "glowed horribly" in the candlelight and moved in processions "with ominous authority" (Steane 1998, pp. 67–68). Singing in this choir was not for the fainthearted. It was not meant to be.

In 1936, King's made its first tour abroad, to Sweden, Denmark, Holland, and Germany. The choir sang to capacity audiences. But they were not really audiences. They felt themselves part of a solemn rite. Everyone was startled by the irresistible beauty of the voices, the concentration, the inwardness, the intensity which seemed to increase during a concert. Local journalists commented on the clarity, transparency, and purity of the sound. They admired the extraordinary delicacy of the singing but at the same time the assurance, the confidence and the dependability of the performers, the matchless accuracy in intonation.

To talk in terms of accuracy though might be misleading, one listener thought: these performances smacked nothing of pedantry or antiquarianism, however meticulously the text might be followed; this was a living dynamic harmony. A Swedish composer marveled at the phenomenal precision of the performances. They noticed that Boris Ord led his choir with tiny movements of his left hand; with his right he held a copy of the music. It appeared that the choir seemed not to need a conductor. When the choirmaster walked away to play an organ piece, the control and unanimity of attack never faltered (King's College, Cambridge 1936).

Such comments are of particular importance because Boris Ord considered that 1930s technology could not convey very much of the experience of hearing the choir in the Chapel; as a result, he did not wish to record. His first commercial recordings were not released until 1949. That he quickly effected profound stylistic changes in the performing style though cannot be doubted.

Around 1960 the choristers at Durham Cathedral listened to the broadcasts of the Christmas Eve service from King's and were awestruck. They knew that their choir could never quite sing in this style nor reach this standard. They had no young choral scholars; they had lay clerks, mostly tradesmen or else stonemasons and plasterers who worked round the Close (Fenton 1992). Why, if the choral scholars at King's were so generally admired, had more choral scholarships not been created by now? The last lay clerks were not retired at St John's, Cambridge until 1949 (St John's College, Cambridge, n.d.) and at Magdalen College, Oxford not until 1960 (Magdalen College, Oxford 1956, 1958). Why had it taken so long?

While King's were just able to recruit enough singers there had never been a superabundance of them. Up to the Second World War nearly all the choral scholars came from minor public schools. A few came from state grammar schools. Very few came from the best-known schools, from the major public schools. A master at one of these explained in the 1920s that the first aim of a music teacher was to identify those boys who were said to be "good at music" and then stop all that dangerous nonsense. You must remember, he said, that "when the normal healthy English boy proves to be musically gifted the smallest overdose of the food he is longing for will turn him into a monstrosity which is neither normal, nor healthy, nor English" (Buck 1922, pp. 183–184). Music was still regarded with suspicion by most middle-class Englishmen; one was likely to be stigmatized automatically as (a) unmanly, (b) simply not a gentleman, or (c) a clergyman in training. None of these impressions were the type one wished to convey. The education given to boys going to university equipped few of them with the special musical expertise that would enable them to take part in performances of a high standard. School choral societies were not for those with beautiful voices, nor for those who had knowledge of sight-reading. They were for everyone who wanted to join, whether he sang like an angel or squealed like a pig. "We are not aiming at perfect performances," said one music master in 1894 (Parker 1893, p. 100).

"Breaking" Voices

But there was a further fundamental difficulty. The advertisements for the first choral scholarships at King's College, Cambridge stipulated that candidates must be "under twenty-five years of age." Should schoolboys between the ages of, say, fifteen and eighteen, be singing at all? Sir George Martin trained the boys at St Paul's from 1874 and was in charge of the choir from 1888 until 1916. His was a widely-held view that the voice should never be used for singing while the treble voice is changing.

> It is likely to injure the vocal tone for ever after. Many otherwise fair musicians had been deprived of vocal power by this reprehensible practice. A boy whose voice is changed or broken, ought no more to be allowed to sing than a man with a fractured limb ought to be permitted to walk or use it. There is no doubt that many valuable voices are lost through overstraining their powers at the period of the break.
>
> (Martin 1892, p. 22)

After Sir Sydney Nicholson had been organist of Manchester Cathedral and Westminster Abbey, he established the School of English Church Music (later known as the Royal School of Church Music). In the first decade or so of the School (1929–1939), Nicholson concentrated on the trebles in parish church choirs. But in the later 1930s he made a special point of encouraging teenage boys to sing; he was perfectly sure that it was possible for boys to sing before the breaking voice had settled. In 1940 he established an annual Festival Service in Gloucester Cathedral for schoolboys from all over the country, and then in 1942 was able to build on the success of that event by arranging a fortnight's summer course for two groups of fifty boys, each group singing daily services in the cathedral for a week, all this while the cathedral choir was on holiday (Evans 1942). So now, in the 1950s, more and more teenage boys were developing vocal expertise earlier, generating an increasing number of potential choral scholars. And there was clear evidence of the changing seriousness with which music was regarded when undergraduate courses in music for a BA degree were established in 1947 at Cambridge and in 1950 at Oxford.

Choirmasters: Temperaments and Characters

The changes that Boris Ord effected after he succeeded A.H. Mann in 1929 can be clearly established. In 1958, Ord was succeeded by David Willcocks. Even though Ord was insistent about accurate tuning, punctilious about the timing of final consonants, and meticulous about details in the score and about ensemble, nonetheless he wished to give any performance sweep and intensity; he valued above all spontaneity and the illusion of improvisation. Before his appointment as organist at King's, he had worked for several months at the Cologne Opera. He was the son of a German mother and christened Bernhard but he took the name Boris because of his enthusiasm for Mussorgsky's opera *Boris Godunov*. He would not be averse to giving the lay clerks free rein on occasion. Howells did not quite become Mussorgsky but he would encourage the singing to take wing on occasion (see Radcliffe 1962).

Boris Ord was not a chorister, though he and David Willcocks were both educated at the same private senior school. David Willcocks was put on a train when he was nine and sent from Cornwall to be a chorister at Westminster Abbey, under the rather severe and distant, reticent and reserved Sir Ernest Bullock; Willcocks described his choirmaster as "not an emotional man" (Owen 2008, p. 18). David Willcocks' mother herself was formal and severe to her grandchildren, as one of them remembered (Owen 2008, p. 24).

Willcocks' parents never visited him when he was a boy in London, even when he was in hospital and having his tonsils out. It was too expensive (Owen 2008, p. 69). He had great natural musicianship; he had perfect pitch. At his organ scholarship examination at King's, Willcocks was asked to play his Bach piece. He said he would play any of a handful of great preludes and fugues he listed; the one selected by the examiners he played from memory (Owen 2008, p. 36). When still a student Willcocks conducted the Cambridge Philharmonic Society, the town chorus and orchestra, in Bach's *St Matthew Passion*, and he did that, too, from memory (Owen 2008, p. 75). After one year as an organ scholar at Cambridge he was called into military service in 1940. When two of his commanding officers were killed in action he took temporary command and his battalion held off ferocious nighttime German bombardment, and retained their positions though at dawn three hundred men of the seven hundred in the battalion lay dead or wounded. Willcocks, bravery in this battle resulted in his being awarded the Military Cross (Owen 2008, p. 69). He returned to Cambridge and afterwards became organist at Salisbury and Worcester Cathedrals before returning to King's.

He ran the choir at King's like an army unit, and his orders were obeyed without question, as he expected them to be. He had the ability to banish everything from his mind except the job in hand. His grandchildren loved the way he played "Grandmother's footsteps," like them completely absorbed in it (Owen 2008, p. 161). He could instill similar intensity in his young singers, and he could instill them with perfect control. Boris Ord once said of him: "Even very good musicians have a tendency to hurry just a little when things get very difficult, when the page gets very black. But listen to David play. When all gets really horribly tricky, he slightly steadies himself"(Owen 2008, p. 165). He was meticulous about tuning, or as some thought, obsessive: he would stop and say: "That note is not flat but it *might* be flat"(Owen 2008, p. 266). One choral scholar said that it felt as though you ceased to be an individual person, a personality in your own right. You were a cog in a wheel. It suited anyone in the 1960s coming from a boys' independent school, he said. You never had any doubt as to what you had to do. He was always very clear and explicit. And you did not forget it if you failed to meet his demands (Owen 2008, pp. 183–184).

The very distinctive changes that Willcocks effected are well-documented in a great number of private recordings made between 1955 and 1960, the last years of Ord and the first of Willcocks (King's College, Cambridge 2006). It was the choir under David Willcocks whose performances were carried round the world on the recently developed long-playing disc.

As early as 1949 the organ scholar and a handful of choral scholars were listening several times to a tape of the Christmas Eve carol service and wrote to the BBC outside broadcasts manager about microphone placings (Harrison 1949). From the late 1940s and through the 1950s, before everyone was home-taping, the choir would go to Broadcasting House in January and listen to the service together (Ord 1953). If a singer had not realized that he had mistimed the "t" in "heart"—*what I can I give him?*—*Give my heart*—he did now.

SUMMARY

This uniquely English singing style was the flowering of ideas that arose through those stupendous changes in historical consciousness we call Romanticism; it was formed because of a musical Queen's consort; because of Wordsworth and the Oxford Movement; because of changing attitudes towards education and boyhood and music and musicians; because of a need for men and boys to display their masculinity; because the sound had to be a Protestant one and not a Catholic one, and an Anglican one and not a non-conformist one; because of the vast acoustic of one of Europe's great buildings; because of particular men's temperaments and personalities and powers of leadership; because of technology; because of convictions about values and ways of living, and about appropriate musical gestures which matched particular speech patterns and physical gestures.

That is why those singers sang as they did.

WEBSITES

<http://www.fcm.org.uk/>
Friends of Cathedral Music is a charity founded in 1956 to increase public knowledge of English cathedral music and to support the work of the choirs. The site includes details of choral services at all the cathedrals.

<http://www.inquiresandplaces.com/>
A very full list of recordings of "choirs of gentlemen and boys singing in the English Cathedral tradition."

<http://www.martin-ashley.com/>
Professor Martin Ashley of Edge Hill University has for many years researched and written on boys and singing. His site gives a full account of his work on this topic and includes useful bibliographies and sound examples.

<http://www.ioe.ac.uk/study/ARHS_69.html>
Professor Graham Welch of the Institute of Education, London University has a special interest in children and singing and his site gives the latest information on his work on boys and girls in cathedral choirs.

FURTHER READING

The ways of cultural history being "devious and uncertain" as one of its most assured practitioners has put it, it is difficult to give a short list of much assistance. Listed here though are two books of essential importance on the nature of the subject, a magisterial cultural history of the first millennium of church music in the West, and one of the few major studies of English cathedral singers. The last book is a recent bold sweeping survey of music in society, full of stimulating and suggestive insights.

Manning, T. (2008). *The Triumph of Music: composers, musicians and their audiences, 1700 to the present*. London: Allen Lane.

Mould, A. (2007) *The English Chorister: a history*. London: Hambledon Continuum.

Murray, M. (ed.) (2002). *A Jacques Barzun Reader*. New York: HarperCollins.

Page, C. (2010). *The Christian west and its singers: the first thousand years*. New Haven and London: Yale University Press.

REFERENCES

Allen, H.P. (c. 1920). "Choral music in wartime," manuscript notes for a speech or article. New College, Oxford Archive PA/ALL, 5/2.

Annan, N. (1990). *Our Age*. London: Weidenfeld and Nicolson.

Anon [A.V. Baillie]. (1934). *The Making of a Man: letters from an old parson to his sons*. London: Nicholson and Watson.

Armstrong, B.J. (1949). *A Norfolk Diary*. Edinburgh: G. Harrap.

Buck. P.C. (1922). Music in public schools. In: H.C. Stewart, P.C. Buck, G. Dyson, et al. (eds), *Music and Letters*, III/2, pp. 179–99 April.

Carey, H. (1979). *Duet for Two Voices: an informal Biography of Edward Dent compiled from his letters to Clive Carey*. Cambridge: Cambridge University Press.

Case, T. (1899). *Memoirs of a King's College Chorister, Cambridge*. Cambridge: Spalding.

Chadwick, O. (1972). *The Victorian Church: Part Two 1860–1901*, 2nd edn. London: Adam and Charles Black.

Chadwick, O. (2011). Interview of Owen Chadwick by Alan Macfarlane on 29 February 2008; DSpace at Cambridge; Department of Social Anthropology, <http://www.dspace.cam.ac.uk/handle/1810/198014>, accessed 3 October 2011.

Cook, N. (1998). *Music: a very short introduction*. Oxford and New York: Oxford University Press.

Crowder, J. (1986). An interview recorded on 21 January 1986 and transcribed by Andrew Parker. King's College, Cambridge Archive Centre KCAR 8/3/24.

Dent, E.J. (1896). Manuscript diary entry for Sunday June 7 [1896]. King's College, Cambridge Archive Centre mark EJD/3/1/1.

Dent, E.J. (1897). Manuscript diary entry for Sunday March 14 [1897]. King's College, Cambridge Archive Centre EJD/3/1/3.

Dyson, G. (1952). Of organs and organists. *The Musical Times* 93/1317: 491–2.

Evans, S. (1942). *English Church Music* XII/4, October 1942, 25–7.

Evans, S. (1965). Typewritten script of a talk given to the Church Music Society in May 1965 by The Very Revd The Dean of Gloucester, Seriol Evans, who was a chorister and choral scholar under Mann. King's College, Cambridge Archive Centre KCAR/8/4/2.

Farrow, M. (1900a). Quoted in *The Musical Times* 41/689, 464.

Farrow, M. (1900b). *Musical Courier*, November 10 1900, 252. A newspaper cutting reprinting what Mr Miles Farrow wrote in *The Baltimore Sun* preserved in *The Presidents' Note Book* beginning June 21, 1898, pp. 251–2. Magdalen College, Oxford Archives PR/2/13.

Fenton, James. (1992). Angelic upstarts. *The Independent on Sunday Sunday Review*, 20 December, 1992, 26.

Fellowes, E.H. (1946). *Memoirs of an Amateur Musician*. London: Methuen and Co.

Geertz, C. (1973). *The Interpretation of Cultures*. New York: Basic Books.

Harrison, K. (1949). Letter to Manager, BBC Outside Broadcasts, Sound dated Boxing Day 1949. BBC Written Archives Centre File R30/233/4.

Hueffer, F. (1889). *Half a Century of Music in England 1837–1887: Essays towards a History*. London: Chapman and Hall.

Keble, J. (1844). *Praelectiones Academicae*. Oxford: J.H. Parker.

King's College, Cambridge. (1882–). *Cambridge Annual Reports*. 1882– Cambridge: King's College.

King's College, Cambridge. (1927). *Cambridge Annual Report*, p. 5. Cambridge: King's College.

King's College, Cambridge. (1860). A Register of the Choir in the Kings (*sic*) College of Blessed Mary and Saint Nicholas in Cambridge 1860. Manuscript. King's College, Cambridge Archive Centre KCAR/8/3/1.

King's College, Cambridge. (1879). Educational Council Minutes (II). 1879–1882. Printed document dated February 15 1879 ("Notice of Business . . . "). King's College, Cambridge Archive Centre KCGB/5/1/1/2.

King's College, Cambridge. (1929). HMV B3707 (10" 78rpm disc).

King's College, Cambridge. (1936). Choir tour. Newspaper cuttings: Ster Broman, *Sydsvenska Dagbladet*, 22 March 1936; N.S-g., *Aftonbladet*, 29 March 1936; C.K., *Svenska Dagbladet*, 29 March 1936. King's College, Cambridge Archive Centre KCAR/8/3/9/1.

King's College, Cambridge. (1959). ARGO RG 226 (mono)/ZRG 7226 (stereo). 12 inch 33⅓ rpm long-playing disc.

King's College, Cambridge. (2006). *The Brian Head King's College Cambridge Collection of recordings*. British Library shelf-mark 1CDR0025637-1CDR0025803.

Leigh, A.A. (1899). *King's College [A History]*. London: Robinson.

Magdalen College, Oxford. (1956). Minutes of the Chapel and Choir Committee meeting of 7 October 1956. Magdalen College Archives CMM/2/17.

Magdalen College, Oxford. (1958). Minutes of the Chapel and Choir Committee meeting of 4 November 1958. Magdalen College Archives CCM/1/3.

Magee, P.C. (n.d.). *A Journal: The Days of Patrick Connor Magee*, typed manuscript. King's College, Cambridge Archive Centre KCHR/8/9.

Magee, P.C. (1987). Letter to King's College, Cambridge [Mrs Cranmer] dated "16.ii.87". King's College Archive Centre KCAR/8/3/24.

Mann, A.H. (1877). Handwritten letter to the Provost of the College, Richard Oakes, dated "8.5.77". King's College, Cambridge Archive Centre KCAR/8/5/1/3.

Martin, G.C. (1892). *The Art of Training Choir Boys*. London: Novello.

Mason, L. (1853). *Musical Letters from abroad: including detailed accounts of the Birmingham, Norwich and Düsseldorf Musical festivals of 1852*. Boston, Mass.: Mason Brothers.

Newsome, D. (1961). *Godliness and Good Learning: four studies on a Victorian ideal*. London: John Murray.

Ord, B. (1953). Letter to Manager, BBC Outside Broadcasts, Sound dated 22 December 1953. BBC Written Archives Centre File R30/233/5.

Owen, W. (2008). *A Life in Music: conversations with Sir David Willcocks and friends*. Oxford: Oxford University Press.

Parker, L.N. (1893). Music in our public schools. *Proceedings of the Musical Association* (1893–1894), pp. 97–113.

Parliamentary Papers [UK: House of Commons] 1854/xxv. London, HMSO.

Parliamentary Papers [UK: House of Commons] 1884-85/xxi. London, HMSO.

Pulver, J. (1933). Society for Musical Research. *Musical Opinion*, September 1933, 1019.

Radcliffe, P. (1962). *Bernhard (Boris) Ord 1897–1961*. Cambridge: King's College.

Richardson, A. Madeley. (1900). *Choir Training based on Voice Production*. London: Vincent Music Co.

Roberts, J. Varley. (1905). *A Treatise on a Practical Method of Training Choristers* 3rd edn. London: Henry Frowde.

St John's College, Cambridge. (n.d.). Minute on the history of "Choral Scholarships." St John's College, Cambridge Archives SBF 50/Chapel/General.

Scholes, P.A. (1941). *Oxford Companion to Music,* 3rd edn. London: Oxford University Press.

Smith, T.F. (1848). *The Devout Chorister.* London: Masters.

Steane, J. (1998). A review of Boris Ord/Choir of King's College, Cambridge. *English Church Music and Favourite Christmas Carols*, TESTAMENT SBT 1121 [CD, mono], *Gramophone,* vol. 76, no. 909, pp. 67–8.

Toop, A. (1900). Advertisement for "gentlemanly boys." *The Musical Times* 41/683: 5.

Tovey, D. and Parratt, G. (1941). *Walter Parratt: Master of the Music.* London: Oxford University Press.

Ward, W. (1912). *William George Ward and the Catholic Revival.* London: Longmans, Green, and Co.

Wesley, S.S. (1849). *A Few Words on Cathedral Music.* London: F. and J. Rivington.

Williams, I. (1838). *On reserve in communicating religious knowledge.* Tracts for the times, no. 80. London: J.G. and F. Rivington.

Wordsworth, W. (1919). Intimations of Immortality (from *Recollections of Early Childhood*). In: A. Quiller-Couch (ed.), *The Oxford Book of English Verse 1250–1900.* Oxford: Clarendon.

CHAPTER 41

PERSPECTIVES ON CHORAL CONDUCTING
Theory and Practice

COLIN DURRANT AND MARIA VARVARIGOU

INTRODUCTION AND HISTORICAL PERSPECTIVE

THIS chapter addresses issues concerning the choral voice and the conductor's role in leading, motivating, and expressing the essence of choral music in rehearsal and performance. We introduce the multi-faceted nature of the choral conductor from historical, musical, philosophical, and sociological perspectives and draw on historical, musical, and educational research. The nature and purpose of the choral conductor in relation to efficient and effective delivery of musical, vocal, and educational outcomes is described. Some of the great monuments of classical civilization are represented in large-scale choral compositions that are interpreted by conductors, who in turn have inspired countless performers and listeners. However, conductors operate in a variety of contexts—in schools, churches, communities—both in an amateur and professional capacity. It is largely in the amateur capacity, however, where conductors have to rehearse as well as perform, that many issues concerning leadership and communication of the musical intent arise (Harrison et al. 2013; Matthews and Kitsantas 2013; Varvarigou 2009).

Evolution of conducting

There are many references to choral conducting in historical sources, stemming from ancient Sumerians c. 2270 BCE evidences in bas-reliefs and wall paintings, the Egyptians c. 1400 BCE and the ancient Greeks, as well as early Christian music. In these instances some form of beating time or extrinsic hand gesture seems to be a notable feature in leading choral singing. Further indication of musical practices from ancient history is provided by Robinson and Winold (1976), who suggest that there may well have been some interpretative gesturing in Vedic music of India as well as in the rhythmically free chanting of early Christian music (also see Durrant 2018).

In the context of Western choral traditions of more recent times, time beaters were present in the Sistine Chapel in the fifteenth century. Here a roll of paper, referred to as a "sol-fa" was used to determine the pulse of the music being sung. In Elizabethan England, similar practices were in evidence, where prints from the fourteenth to the sixteenth century show a person leading musical practice with instrumentalists and singers with a stick or roll of paper. During the baroque period, most choral music was accompanied by instruments or at least by a harpsichord or organ, where singers (and instrumentalists) were kept together by the percussive sounds of the continuo. The performance location would often dictate the nature of the musical composition and consequently the manner in which the performers were kept together. The first large-scale choral performances were probably in St Mark's Venice, where large instrumental and choral forces were brought together in the antiphonal music of the Gabrielis and Monteverdi in the sixteenth and early seventeenth centuries; here the equilateral cross-shaped design of the Basilica in turn inspired the musical architecture of a generation of compositions. Some form of visual time keeping was inevitable in such a location.

Choral conducting took a significant step in its evolution in England, when in 1737 the English composer William Boyce was appointed conductor of the Three Choirs Festival (one of the oldest annual music festivals taking place alternately in Hereford, Gloucester, and Worcester). Samuel Wesley (another noted English composer) later noted that Boyce's method of conducting was "to mark out the measure. . . with a roll of parchment in his hand" (Durrant 2018, p. 65). With the emergence of large-scale choral festivals and the collective singing of the oratorios of Handel, Haydn, and Mendelssohn in particular, the conductor took on an increasingly significant role. Large numbers of singers needed not only controlling in tempo, but also engaging in expressive interpretation of the text, especially with the romantic composers of the late nineteenth and early twentieth centuries. During this time, large-scale choral compositions made increasing demands on the interpretative skills of the conductor with such pieces as the requiems of Berlioz and Verdi, the oratorios of Mendelssohn and Elgar, and even smaller scale liturgical settings and motets of, for example, Bruckner. By the twentieth century, music became more complex rhythmically as well as harmonically, as exemplified in such choral large scale compositions as Elgar's *Dream of Gerontius*, Stravinsky's *Symphony of Psalms*, Walton's *Belshazzar's Feast*, and Britten's *War Requiem*. These demand great technical skills from the conductor and the conductor consequently becomes more than a mere timekeeper.

The modern choral conductor

Choirs throughout the world operate in a variety of formats—very formal concert choirs, symphonic choruses often associated with orchestras, church, and cathedral choirs (some professional) singing the liturgy, choral societies associated with a geographical region or town, small chamber choirs with a leaning for particular repertoire, and a whole raft of more informal groups who come together to sing at certain events or seasons. There are choirs that appeal to particular ethnicities (for example, Welsh male voice choirs can be found across the globe—not just in Wales), those aimed at particular age groups—youth choirs, senior citizen choirs and, more recently, gay and lesbian choirs have become a phenomenon in many cities in Europe and North America. Mostly choirs form as amateur groups who come together for love of singing and socializing (Durrant and Himonides 1998). The role of the conductor has, therefore, become increasingly significant in cementing the socialization of these groups as well as being responsible for musical leadership.

THE CONDUCTOR AND GESTURE

Many choirs have a conductor who leads the choral singing and is involved in rehearsing as well as performing in concerts or other singing events. In England and other countries in Europe, the conductor of church and cathedral choirs has traditionally been the organist, thus conducting almost as a secondary activity to playing the organ. In some instances it is clear that gesture is only represented by some form of tactus—beating time, with little sense of expressive conducting. Until recently, there was very little training for choral conductors in England, contrasting the situation in North America and other parts of northern Europe (Durrant 1996; Varvarigou 2009). This has meant that the quality, standard, and skills of conductors and their understanding and practical application of gesture vary considerably. The relationship between conductor and singers is key to promoting and maintaining high quality singing and vocal and musical development. Research into this relationship has divined that a range of particular knowledge and skills are paramount if the conductor is not only to gain mastery over the art and craft of conducting, but also through enabling the singers to feel capable, sing expressively, improve, and feel good about their singing (Durrant 2009, 2018).

Models of effective choral direction

A model of effective choral conducting established by Durrant and refined has highlighted some of the knowledge and skills necessary for choral conducting. These are classified under: (i) philosophical understanding of the role and esthetic appreciation of music; (ii) musical and technical skills; (iii) communication and interpersonal skills. Previously, Hilary Apfelstadt (1997) refers to the leadership role of the conductor as being integral to the creation of an appropriate environment in which quality singing can take place. She puts forward three elements of leadership: (i) a musical, artistic intuition; (ii) an extra-musical confidence, articulateness, and enthusiasm; (iii) a "gestalt"—combining musical and extra-musical elements artfully. In both models, the conductor needs musical and vocal knowledge, an esthetic awareness, and musical intuition, alongside a raft of musical communication skills. If the conductor cannot convey the music's meaning to the singers, then less convincing musical events will take place. If the conductor cannot hear what the singers are producing, then there will be little in the way of valid and useful feedback in rehearsal.

Types of gestures

One significant characteristic is that conductors operate, certainly in performance, non-verbally. Hence, gesture is the conveyance of musical meaning—not only of starts, stops, and tempo indications, but also with regard to the expressive import of the music. In

Choral Conducting: Philosophy and Practice (Durrant 2018), an attempt is made to convey the meaning of particular gestures. Some are "literal" (giving tempo indication, starting and stopping), some are "connotative" or suggestive of an expressive character or phrase, and other gestures might, particularly in a rehearsal context, be helpful in forming a vocal timbre or assisting with intonation, for example. In brief, conducting gestures are effective if they are: (i) an esthetic reflection and representation of musical expression; (ii) efficient and unambiguous; and (iii) vocally friendly. This suggests that some conducting gestures have the potential to be un-esthetic and inexpressive, inefficient and ambiguous, and vocally un-friendly. Conducting patterns and gestures that are too based on timekeeping at the expense of communicating an esthetic dimension can be counterproductive and generate unmusical singing (Durrant 2009).

Through empirical studies on non-verbal conductor behavior, as well as surveys addressing conducting competency and systematic observations of conducting behavior, researchers and practitioners endeavour to promote ways of furthering skill development on conducting (Cofer 1998; Yarbrough and Madsen 1998). At the same time, precise definitions of conducting skills, opportunities to practice conducting, videotaped feedback, and self-analysis appear to be common and recent basic elements of conducting education in the USA (Sheldon and DeNardo 2005; Zielinski 2005).

Effective communication is an essential attribute of the choral conductor; the impor-tance of developing an adequate gestural vocabulary is put forward by Durrant (2018). In order for choral gestures to be meaningful, they need to be linked with the vocal outcome. Inappropriate gestures can give misleading messages to the performers and can also distract the audience from the enjoyment of listening to the music. Other pedagogies have applied Rudolf Laban's theories on movement to choral conducting gestures, with the aim of de-veloping "stylistic artistry" through creative movement for musical expression. Their work argues that the joy of movement in conducting stems from the critical roles conductors have in influencing and shaping the sound of their ensembles.

Studies on expressive conducting and the impact on musical and vocal outcomes have in some way contributed to our understanding that non-verbal communication through thoughtful conducting gestures is a convincing way to elicit healthy and efficient vocal beha-vior and expressive choral singing. An obsession with technical instruction by the conductor can have a negative impact on singers' perceptions of the music—that it is basically a series of technical exercises to master—and produce mundane performances that often fail to cap-ture the music's expressive character. Expressive singing is more likely the result of expres-sive conducting with the conductor dealing with the expressive character of the music rather than just the technical. Even when learning new music, the conductor needs to communi-cate to the singers the musical character as well as attend to learning the notes. Imagery and analogy is a significant tool in communication.

As part of non-verbal communication, movement, both from the conductor and the singers, is a tool for activating the "kinesthetic" approach to musical expression. Many choirs have movement as a natural part of their musical understanding in rehearsal and performance; notably this is so in African choral singing contexts. Movement is a way of demonstrating musical understanding as is evidenced in young children, whose nat-ural response to music is through movement. Sometimes in Western classical contexts, this freedom to respond through movement is "trained" out. The connection between conducting and energy flow is something that approaches a kinesthetic awareness of gestures and their relationship with the music. Leonard Meyer (1956) refers to tension and resolution as being fundamental to musical movement; one only has to acknowledge the unending sequence of harmonic tensions in Wagner's *Tristan und Isolde*, for example, where the resolution is delayed and delayed. The very essence of physical gesture should be able to reflect these musical structures and sequences. "Resistance" in the gesture is a phenomenon that is articulated in the movement theories of Rudolf Laban—moving through limited space slowly requires a sense of resistance—pushing against the air in a similar way we might push against water when swimming. The energy when swimming is required from the arms underwater, pushing the water out of the way, not splashing needlessly on the surface. A similar approach is usefully employed in conducting gestures—pushing against air, not floundering about with excessive and unnecessary movement. Conductors then have a responsibility to act within the esthetic frame of the music—ugly gestures will generate ugly sounds, whereas beautiful movements and gestures are more likely to generate expressive and beautiful sounds. A smooth legato vocal line will not be the outcome if conducting gestures are not themselves smooth and legato.

THE CONDUCTOR AND REHEARSAL

Facilitating "flow"

The everyday rehearsing of choirs is a craft skill. While the intention here is not to provide an exhaustive list of what to do and what not to do, this section offers some insights into the rehearsal process that are founded in research and practice. As most choral conductors are conducting amateur choral groups, there is a responsibility to educate singers in a range of musical and vocal skills. We are developing singers to attain the highest musical levels within their collective grasp as well as give them individual ownership of their voice and mastery over it. There is a body of research that has looked into the health and well-being benefits of singing, as exemplified in Clift and Hancox (2010). This suggests that the responsibility of the conductor is awesome, in that particular behaviors are likely to influence and impact upon singers' perceptions of themselves and the music. Conductors can motivate and demotivate. The psychologist Csikszentmihalyi (2000) has coined the term "flow" to indicate a high-interest state of being in an activity. He was searching for a theoretical model of enjoyment. Researching with a wide range of people who engage in a wide range of activities, including artistic and sports, he discovered the intrinsic rewards of their activities stimulated and maintained their commitment of time and effort. The main reasons in rank order were:

Enjoyment of the experience and use of skills.
The activity itself: the pattern, the action, and the world it provides.
Development of personal skills.
Friendship, companionship.
Competition, measuring self against others.
Measuring self against own ideals.
Emotional release.
Prestige, regard, glamor.

This suggests that teachers, conductors, and those leading musical activity should seek to facilitate the flow—the optimal learning situation—by providing opportunities for setting challenge and the wherewithal to meet the challenge. Therefore, the interest level in singing a diet of solely easy and familiar songs will pall if no other musical and vocal challenges are offered. Conversely, setting unrealistic musical and vocal challenges will de-motivate and frustrate. For amateur singers especially, the rehearsal is fundamental to the development of musical skills as well as to a range of collective and personal skills. It is also a preparation for emotional release often gained through participating in music, through understanding the expressive import and responding accordingly. Creating the environment in which singers can gain access to the expressive character of the music as well as to technical accomplishment will more likely enhance the well-being and emotional lives of the participants and, ultimately, those listening to their performances.

There are many considerations to be taken into account in providing an effective, efficient, and motivating choral rehearsal. With amateur groups it is useful to approach with seduction techniques more than admonition (Durrant 2000), to give high quality feedback—that is feedback that suggests ways forward for improving, in preference just to indicating what has gone wrong. Indeed, the very feedback a conductor is giving is vital in the rehearsal process as it would be with any activity. Singers need to know how they are doing. While conductors do hold ultimate responsibility for technical accuracy and musical outcomes, a rehearsal that is devoted entirely to a "telling off" for wrong notes can be very intimidating and de-motivating for developing and less confident singers.

Providing an optimal rehearsal experience

Conductors in rehearsal would be wise to address a range of issues in addition to musical accuracy in itself in order that optimal musical and vocal development can take place. These include:

> Creating a welcoming and purposeful environment: singing is an enjoyable activity as well as a musical event.
>
> Concentrating, especially at the beginning of rehearsals, on posture and breathing, which are essential to healthy vocalizing. These can be done through effective and purposeful warm-ups. It is useful to have reminders throughout the rehearsal of appropriate "lengthy" posture, particularly when singers are sitting and singing.
>
> Use of verbal and non-verbal language: imagery and analogy are often more effective ways of getting a desired vocal timbre than an instruction that is entirely technical. This is something that can be effectively used in a warm-up, exploring vocal timbres by imagining styles of singing—an opera diva, a country and western singer, a cathedral choirboy, for example—all using different parts of the body and vocal mechanism in the production of the sound.
>
> Gesture is the conductor's essential tool-kit, so it is important that the conductor uses gesture meaningfully (see above). Again this is something that can be practiced in the context of warm-ups, by including singers in gesturing a particular vocal exercise (e.g. stabbing movements for staccato and smooth brush strokes for legato).

Planning and preparation: this is for the long-term over the year down to the individual rehearsal and is concerned with choosing repertoire that is (i) appropriate for the ability level of the choir, (ii) attractive and balanced perhaps in terms of styles, eras, large and small scale, types of challenges (i.e. expressive, musical, vocal, linguistic, etc.), (iii) a program to appeal to (and challenge) an audience, (iv) the concert venue (its space and acoustics), and (v) the cost.

THE CONDUCTOR AND COMMUNICATION

There are numerous means of communication that a successful conductor employs, both in rehearsal and performance. Naturally, in a concert or other performance context, the essential style of communication will be non-verbal, while in the rehearsal both verbal and non-verbal strategies will be used in order to instruct, to provide feedback, to motivate, to correct, and to praise.

Choral conductors tend to verbalize their instructions during rehearsals for various purposes, such as to question, model, direct, provide feedback, criticism, and praise. Freer's study (2006) investigated teacher discourse and student experience in the middle school choral rehearsal in the USA. The findings indicated that the two choral directors observed tended to use three types of instruction: (i) teacher task presentation, (ii) student response/interaction with the task, and (iii) specific teacher reinforcement, in order to "transfer responsibility for learning from teacher to students" and "offer task-based support" (Freer 2006, p. 87). Hence, there is a perspective that minimal verbalization is related to performance achievement and often associated with ensemble maturity (Price 2006). Davis (1998) put forward the notion that the frequency of verbal communication might simply indicate a conductor's preference and could not necessarily affect the ensemble's performance. Davis's study investigated the amount of non-verbal communication (conducting, approving, and disapproving) between the student singers and the conductor during rehearsals, and found that as the students became more proficient, non-verbal signals were used more often.

Feedback

One cannot over-emphasize the importance of singers receiving reinforcement and qualitative knowledge through verbal and/or visual feedback. Singers of all ages are curious to learn about the function of their vocal mechanism while singing. The qualitative knowledge that conductors can offer them, such as how to use various vocal techniques without damaging their voices, promotes acceptance of individual differences in skills and motivates personal skill development. Singers and particularly student singers are usually appreciative of quality feedback. Indeed, individual feedback can be an important motivational technique in drawing attention to the musical and personal development of singers and provide them with detailed feedback, both on individual progress and on ensemble effort.

Magnitude

Complementing gestures, strategies such as modeling have been shown to influence singers' performance levels. The concept of "magnitude" (Yarbrough 1975; Yarbrough and Madsen 1998) as an attribute of effective teaching and as a stimulus for attentiveness in the interaction between the singers and the conductor has been the topic of various studies. Yarbrough (1975) suggested that the conductor's magnitude is what makes a rehearsal more exciting and that high-magnitude behaviors are those that encompass a dynamic teaching style. Such conditions are, therefore, believed to result in greater student attentiveness, preference, and performance. The conducting and rehearsing strategies observed were: (i) eye contact, (ii) closeness to the choir, (iii) volume and modulation of voice, (iv) gestures, (v) facial expressions, and (vi) rehearsal pace.

> A high magnitude conductor maintains *eye contact* with group and/or individuals throughout rehearsals; frequently walks or leans towards chorus or particular section (*closeness*); has wide range of volume as well as speaking pitch and the voice reflects enthusiasm and vitality (*volume and modulation of voice*); uses arms and hands to aid in musical phrasing, has great variety of movement and varies size of conducting patterns to indicate phrases, dynamics and the like (*gestures*); reflects through the face sharp contrasts between approval disapproval. Approval is expressed by grinning, laughing aloud, raising eyebrows, widening eyes. Disapproval is expressed by frowning, knitting brow, pursing lips, narrowing eyes (*facial expression*). Lastly, high magnitude conductors have "rapid and exciting" rehearsal pace: quick instructions, minimal talking, less than one second between activities and frequently give instructions to the group while it is singing.
>
> (Yarbrough 1975, p. 138)

The results of the study indicated that although magnitude of conductor behavior had no significant effect on the performance, attentiveness, and attitude of the students in mixed choruses, the students did prefer the high magnitude conductor in preference to the low magnitude conductor.

Eye contact and facial expression as reinforcing techniques that affect choral performance and the perception of the overall conductor's effectiveness have also been discussed in Yarbrough's study (1975), who considered the maintenance of eye contact with a group or individuals to be an indication of high magnitude teaching. A later study by Yarbrough and Madsen (1998, p. 477) revealed that "even tedious drill rehearsals can be successful in maintaining student attentiveness if approvals and eye contact are high" and if conductors' talk is efficient, accurate, and "kept to a minimum." Effective communication therefore is judicious use of eye contact and facial expression as well as beat patterns and gesture.

Modeling, used in conjunction with verbal and visual communication, is more likely to improve ensemble performance than just using one mode; the combination of a variety of strategies is more likely to bring about better choral results and enhance individual and collective musical learning.

Summary of methods for effective choral practice

In summary, research studies on effective choral conducting and communication seem to lay emphasis on the fact that leading a choral ensemble requires more than mere technical artistry and instruction. The technical aspects of conducting—the gestural vocabulary, eye contact, and facial expressions, albeit significant, need to be combined with a variety of other methods and approaches such as modeling, verbal instruction that includes qualitative feedback and positive reinforcement, in order for choral practice to be effective and enjoyable. Above all, in order for the communication between the conductor and the singers to be achieved, a positive learning environment through an acceptance and awareness of the singers' abilities should be secured.

LEADERSHIP, REFLECTION, FEEDBACK: APPLICATION OF THEORY AND PRACTICE

Choral conductors often work in isolation in their choral communities, schools, churches and other situations: there is usually only one conductor. Therefore, it is often challenging for a conductor to know whether his or her own musical leadership is effective, whether the choir understands and shares the conductor's vision about the music and sound of the choir and, most importantly, whether the singers really enjoy the choral experience they are creating for themselves and their audiences. Discussions with student conductors on higher education choral conducting programs (Varvarigou 2009; Varvarigou 2014; Varvarigou and Durrant 2010) have revealed that the student conductors generally value the discourse and reactions from members of the choir on their conducting and rehearsal styles and their input on the process and progression of choral rehearsals. They indicated how important it is, yet difficult, to inspire the choir and at the same time maintain a semblance of authority as a conductor and musical leader.

The authoritarian tradition

The traditional perception of a conductor is of an extrovert character that directs and instructs people what to do, pointing out when they make mistakes. The singers and players simply accept the instructions, acknowledge their mistakes, and recognize the authority and leadership of the conductor. The roots of choral conducting are firmly planted in the authoritarian tradition, and choir classrooms [in this case in the North American context] are set up with the director at the front of the room and students sitting obediently in their seats. It is clear that conductors want to be in control of what happens during the choral rehearsal; some argue that giving too much voice to the singers either delays the whole rehearsal process or creates the situation where learners fall into misguided perceptions of their own abilities as singers, conductors, or musicians, often thinking that they are better than they really are (Varvarigou 2009). However, this authoritarian approach limits creativity and the singers' feeling of ownership of the final music product and its process of creation. Research into choral conducting education undertaken by the two authors (Durrant 1996; Durrant and Varvarigou 2008; Varvarigou 2009; Varvarigou and Durrant 2010) has an example to offer in how rules and relationships can be built up and blossom over time. Three key principles, (i) the creation of a safe environment for practice that provides positive reinforcement and encourages collaborative learning, (ii) quality feedback to the conductor from the singers and accompanist, and (iii) encouragement of reflective practice—have emerged from the authors' research and practice and are believed to result in effective choral practice. These principles can be applicable to any choral conducting situation, whether it be the training of choral conductors or actual choral conducting practice.

One way in which choral conductors can continue to develop their professional skills and become increasingly effective leaders in the field is through the receiving of high quality feedback both from tutor conductors and from the singers they are conducting.

The power of feedback

As already mentioned, one way of keeping students motivated is through giving them constant feedback on their progress, as motivation theories advocate that confident students are more likely to try harder and thus perform better. And so the development of expertise requires conductors to become capable of giving constructive and even painful feedback to their learners. In choral conducting settings, the singers themselves can be encouraged and "encultured" to give constructive feedback to their conductor. Does this conductor communicate with me? Has she looked at me? Does her posture give me confidence in singing? Does she convey the meaning and expressive character of this piece of music? In order for any feedback to be useful, it needs to be specific on what requires improvement or change; this is something that singers can offer since they are at the receiving end of all that the conductor conveys. Gathering our own data (both online and in face-to-face seminar settings) has revealed a high level of insight into various aspects of the choral conducting phenomenon. The students represented in the comments here are themselves both conductors in training and singers in the workshop choir for the other student conductors. These examples are from singers to the conductors, where the feedback addresses issues related to posture and gesture, vocal outcome, and rehearsal strategies, and illustrate how the singers can actively contribute to the conductor's development, the rehearsal process, and acquire shared ownership of the whole venture.

- You have a lovely feel for the pulse and movement of the music but just be careful not using the shoulders too much. Make your arm movements communicate more; this could also be clearer with very explicit contrast—big/small, closer to the body, away from the body for optimum dynamic contrast and effect.
- Perhaps don't mouth the words as much. For particular moments, I understand why you would do it—but not for entire phrases. You did improve this as you went!
- [You] are very clear, particularly when teaching words—perhaps the music could come first?
- Once [you] started thinking more about performance and less about explanation, [you] began to "teach" the music and everything started to come together.
- Although [you] mouth the words, this doesn't seem to hinder us, but rather to help us. I noticed that occasionally [you] sing along, which sometimes may be necessary, but might mean that [you] can't really hear the choir.

Such comments as these confirm an understanding of a range of issues pertinent to the choral conductor in the role of teacher and communicator. The comments address posture and the significance of gesture, including the axiom that "less is more" (see Durrant 2018), that unnecessary and excessive movement and gesture can interfere with the music. Furthermore, as suggested, if conductors insist on singing along with their choirs, then they cannot really be listening to what is going on and therefore cannot provide feedback to singers with any valid and reliable comments.

Reflection

Reflection is integral to any professional development: as there is usually only one conductor for each ensemble, so opportunities for reflection can be offered either through asking colleagues to observe one's practice or through video recording rehearsals for reflection "in action" (Schön 1983). The use of video as a tool for reflection is now commonly used in choral conducting education contexts and the following examples show the kinds of comments that student conductors have made after watching themselves through video recordings of their conducting.

- Looking back at the video from session one, I am very aware that my gesture is unnecessarily large. At the end of my go. . . I reduced things a touch but the target I am going to set myself is to reduce this even more, and to make this new scale of gesture my default setting!
- Well that was painful! I need to move less, and not lean forward with my head and body. Also, if doing a jazzy piece like this again, try and get more of a sense of the mood of it, more relaxed even though upbeat and moving the hips rather than the upper body.
- Having watched back my video, I can see that my gestures seemed too large. Perhaps that would be effective at certain points, but my gesture was consistently large. My target will be to minimize my gestures and try to keep my arms closer to my body and near my navel in a relaxed way. I will also try to conduct phrases rather than keep the beat the whole time.

It is quite understandable that student choral conductors (and indeed those more experienced) are concerned about what they look like in front of the choir. Singers are, after all, intentionally looking at the conductor. With media developments of television close-up and YouTube and other videos, it is now not so unusual for conductors to be in front of the camera. This can be a positive step in the development of a conducting esthetic—the beautiful gesture, the expressive gesture, the effective and "vocally friendly" gesture. The conductor can use such media to refine and inform: the posture and gesture can enable vocal efficiency and musical singing. Our message is that conducting matters if approached with understanding of musical esthetics and vocal health and development.

References

Apfelstadt, H. (1997). Applying leadership models in teaching choral conductors. *Choral Journal* 37(8): 23–30.

Clift, S. and Hancox, G. (2010). The significance of choral singing for sustaining psychological wellbeing: Findings from a survey of choristers in England, Australia and Germany. *Music Performance Research* 3(1): 79–96.

Cofer, S.R. (1998). Effects of conducting-gesture instruction on seventh-grade band students' performance response to conducting emblems. *Journal of Research in Music Education* 46(4): 360–373.

Csikszentmihalyi, M. (2000). *Beyond Boredom and Anxiety: Experiencing Flow in Work and Play.* San Francisco: Jossey-Bass.

Davis, A.H. (1998). Performance achievement and analysis of teaching during choral rehearsals. *Journal of Research in Music Education* 46(4): 496–509.

Durrant, C. (1996). *Towards a model of effective choral conducting: Implications for music education, musical communication and curriculum development.* PhD Dissertation, University of Surrey, Surrey.

Durrant, C. (2000). Making choral conducting seductive: Implications for practice and choral education. *Research Studies in Music Education* 1: 40–49.

Durrant, C. (2009). Communicating and accentuating the aesthetic and expressive dimension in choral conducting. *International Journal of Music Education* 27: 326–340.

Durrant, C. (2018). *Choral Conducting: Philosophy and Practice,* 2nd edn. New York: Routledge.

Durrant, C. and Himonides, E. (1998). What makes people sing together? *International Journal of Music Education* 32: 61–70.

Durrant, C. and Varvarigou, M. (2008). Real time and virtual: Tracking the professional development and reflections of choral conductors. *Reflecting Education Journal* 4(1): 72–80.

Freer, P.K. (2006). Dissertation review: Rehearsal discourse of choral conductors: meeting the needs of young adolescents by K.H. Phillips. *Bulletin of the Council for Research in Music Education* 169: 87–89.

Harrison, S., O'Bryan, J., and Lebler, D. (2013). "Playing it like a professional": Approaches to ensemble direction in tertiary institutions. *International Journal of Music Education* 31(2): 173–189.

Matthews, W. and Kitsantas, A. (2013). The role of the conductor's goal orientation and use of shared performance cues on collegiate instrumentalists' motivational beliefs and performance in large musical ensembles. *Psychology of Music* 41(5): 630–646.

Meyer, L. (1956). *Emotion and Meaning in Music.* Chicago: The University of Chicago Press.

Price, H.E. (2006). Relationships among conducting quality, ensemble performance quality and state festival ratings. *Journal of Research in Music Education* 54(3): 203–214.

Robinson, R. and Winold, A. (1976). *The Choral Experience: Literature, Materials and Methods.* New York: Harper's College Press.

Schön, D. (1983). *The Reflective Practitioner: How Professionals Think in Action.* New York: Basic Books.

Sheldon, D.A. and DeNardo, G. (2005). Comparisons of high-order thinking skills among prospective freshmen and upper-level preservice music education majors. *Journal of Research in Music Education* 53(1): 40–50.

Varvarigou, M. (2009). *Modelling effective choral conducting education through an exploration of example teaching and learning in England.* PhD Dissertation, Institute of Education, London.

Varvarigou, M. (2014). "I owe it to my group members who critically commented on my conducting . . ."—cooperative learning in choral conducting education. *International Journal of Music Education* 34(1): 116–130. doi: 10.1177/0255761414535564.

Varvarigou, M. and Durrant, C. (2010). Theoretical perspectives on the education of choral conductors: A suggested framework. *British Journal of Music Education* 28(3): 325–338.

Yarbrough, C. (1975). Effect of magnitude of conductor behaviour on students in selected mixed choruses. *Journal of Research in Music Education* 23: 134–146.

Yarbrough, C. and Madsen, C. K. (1998). The evaluation of teaching in choral rehearsals. *Journal of Research in Music Education* 46(4): 134–146.

Zielinski, R. (2005). The performance pyramid: Building blocks for a successful choral performance. *Music Educators Journal* 92(1): 44–49.

CHAPTER 42

....

GROUP SINGING
AND SOCIAL IDENTITY

....

JANE W. DAVIDSON AND ROBERT FAULKNER

INTRODUCTION

Group singing

Geisler and Johansson (see their chapter in the current volume) broadly refer to choirs as groups of people who sing music of special significance that is typically performed for an audience, often in specially allocated venues. This definition applies to the singers explored in this chapter, with the context of the group and the participants themselves being of interest. Group singing practices interact with socio-cultural underpinning, where specific agendas such as health and social benefit are often found to wax or wane over time and context, which influence the popularity of choirs as social structures at any given point in time. In other words, there is a dynamic relationship between trends in group singing and social context, and this relationship is central to the discussion in the current chapter about social identity.

Geisler and Johansson's survey also underscores the critical importance of musical sound, performance, and audience to the choral experience, and, once more, these elements feature in the current chapter. The other contributing chapters in this section of the book as a whole explore the formal structures of choirs in the Western choral tradition, with its associated arrangement of voices, and compositional practices. The work also draws out the conditions and experiences required to encourage choral singing activity (both vocal methods and group leadership style), as well as the specific types of repertoire developed for different styles of performance, largely for the concert hall or religious context, with some attention being given to audience responses. While the current chapter refers to data that incorporates many of these elements, it moves away from the contexts traditionally associated with the long-established traditions for Western choristers and directors. Exploration includes informal contexts for group singing and the therapeutic impact of choral groups that have developed in response to some of the social trends explained above. Three case studies are investigated, exploring similarities and differences of experience for the singers in these groups.[1]

Social identity

The theoretical frameworks that underpin the case studies presented in this chapter are rooted in Western social psychology, with a starting tenet being that a person's agency or ability to act in the world is expressed in the concept of Self-Identity (Korsgaard 2009). That is, we constitute ourselves as agents, the authors of our actions, and so generate our identities. James's (1890) seminal work on the Self argued that three principal components of Self interact: the *Material Self* (the body and the physical world); the *Social Self* (expressed in social relationships); and the *Spiritual Self* (found in religious or spiritual experience). Weber (2000) has modernized and elaborated this model to argue that individual and cultural factors interact in the production of a Self that has the potential to expand and contract according to personal, material, social, and spiritual concerns. The latter element of the model moves away from the religious one defined by James. Weber's work translates these categories of Self as follows: material becomes *Body*; social becomes *Persona* and spiritual, *Spirit*. Weber argues that these tripartite elements of Self interact in a rich web of individual and cultural circumstance, the overall becoming labeled the *Created Self*. This model offers the analytic framework for the current investigation.

In this chapter it is therefore acknowledged that Selfhood develops firmly within a strong social and cultural milieu and is profoundly shaped by the specific roles we enact, and is thus socially constructed. Identity, though it has core intrapersonal elements, is developed in relation to others, comprising many elements that are not fixed, but changing.

Elsewhere in this volume, Self-Determination Theory (Deci and Ryan 2000), a theory of human motivation and personality that aims to encapsulate people's inherent growth tendencies and psychological needs, is used to frame the experience of singing (see Davidson and Garrido in this volume). The motivational framework—though not the central focus here—can be usefully applied to understand the overarching psychological benefits of singing. By addressing the inherent motivation behind the choices that we make, desire for personal *autonomy*, a sense of *competence* as well as *relatedness* to a social group, is found to be key to ensuring positive engagement in a range of life's experiences, the case of singing being the specific example of focus. The cases presented in the current chapter build from this model of intrapersonal motivation to explore how strong social musical identities are developed dependent on the skills involved in the social activity of the choir.

---

[1] Text and data used in this chapter appear in publications by the authors, some data being used to present a different theoretical discussion.

THREE CASE STUDIES

Karlakórinn Hreimur

The first case study presented emerges from an extensive and detailed study by the second author of this chapter (Faulkner 2013), which draws heavily on Weber's model, focusing on the histories, thought, and sung sounds of a choir from North East Iceland.

So what of the Hreimur choir, and why are they of specific interest when considering group singing and social identity? It is an amateur male voice choir whose membership numbers sixty, ranging in age from eighteen to eighty years old, which draws from a population pool of only 4000 people. It comprises men who represent many different occupations: mechanics, truck drivers, farmers, fishermen, a medical consultant, a headmaster, and others besides. It has been in existence since 1974 and still contains many founding members, though it has had several directors. Robert began working as the choir's director in the 1980s, and conducted them for over two decades.

A significant starting point for our discussion of this group is Icelanders cultural history and the fact that the island has a rich musical past, with records dating back to the modal Epic and Quint Songs of the early medieval period. Although practitioners are now very few and far between, something of that long-term investment in the sung narrative, inflected and supported by an attentive participatory audience, seems to continue to influence how people approach songs, the stories they contain, and collective participation as audience/performer in Iceland today. Indeed, all the singers not only sang with the Hreimur choir, but they also sang all the time: with their families and broader communities, in work, and social activity. So at a cultural level, singing offered a form of agency within their society—a means for shaping and expressing *Persona*.

Of course, we need to be wary of presenting a reductionist view of cultural heritage. A carefully contextualized description of the island's social history explains that after the population diminution through Iceland's medieval and early modern periods (where natural disasters, famines, and epidemics abounded), the nineteenth century produced a realignment of the cultural values towards those of modern Europe, in large part as a result of Danish control. From 1850, songs and singers were to function in diatonic harmony, with church choirs taking up a new and central status in cultural practice. So Icelanders' views of how and why people sing together have shifted over history. In recent times, explicit social and political agendas have been expressed through singing, with support for home rule in 1918 and the founding of the Icelandic Republic in 1944 being examples where group singing brought opportunity for solidarity. Like any cultural group, the Icelanders have a unique set of social factors shaping their cultural practices, but the sum of Icelanders' experience is that group singing has been a crucial marker of social life, albeit in different configurations, over a long history.

The repertoire of Karlakórinn Hreimur reflects Icelander history, with some references back to the modal music of the medieval period, as well as nineteenth-century church music, and nineteenth-century inflected folk music. Additionally, the singers are all male, their style of singing coming from that mid-nineteenth century four-part choral style, a configuration that was popularized above all other styles of singing in Iceland for more than 100 years.

In fact, feminist historian Björnsdóttir (2001) has critiqued Icelandic male voice choirs, arguing that they were adopted to facilitate the maintenance of a hegemonic national identity. It is fair to say that the members of the Hreimur choir both support and challenge this assertion. On the one hand, some of the male choristers see their social identity in the choir as having strong associations with sexual display, as one chorister comments: "I mean in the choir, aren't we guys always the cockerel showing off? You see it in nature; doesn't that happen everywhere in nature? The male always has to display himself . . . has a specific routine" (Faulkner 2013, p. 136).

This is by no means a unanimous view, with some choristers observing that the all-male configuration of the group is simply a historical artifact, and has little in the way of a masculine or power agenda.

A detailed analysis enriches explanations of the complexity of history and current practices, and highlights that whatever the belief, there is an identity script to be performed. For the male singers in this specific choir, many nuanced interactions and histories feed their beliefs, stemming from discourses on masculinity, Saga history, nineteenth-century Romanticism, Christian worship, and many other factors besides. Ideas from Connell's *Masculinities* (1995) enable an exploration of how some constructions of the Hreimur choir's identity can be captured in sex-role theory, where enactments of single-sex group behaviors are linked to a biological root and a fundamental dichotomy between male and female. Readers may disagree with the proposition, but nonetheless, it highlights that identity is most likely shaped around a number of different and perhaps even conflicting factors and/or according to different scripts.

The idea of a social identity script can be explored at several levels in relation to Karlakórinn Hreimur. The first of interest is the family script. Introduced by Byng-Hall (1995), Family Script Theory aimed to capture thinking about how and why family interaction patterns occur and are repeated. In the case of the men studied, the singing was often part of relational fabric of the family: fun songs with the granddaughter, offering a platform to enact intergenerational relationships as well as lineage; celebratory songs within the family; songs about work activities undertaken with family members; and so on. These songs also represented the dynamics of interfamilial and intergenerational relationships, with a solo singer often being an older family member who sang to a younger one, or family groups singing together at celebrations. Using the idea of singing as agency, vocal behavior becomes the regulation and representation of a key Icelandic social construct—kinship.

Owing to the close familial bonds of the Icelandic community, family script was also played out in the choir, with some repertoire being about family relationships, but specifically because five father and sons, four brothers from one family, and two pairs of brothers from other families were all choristers in that vocal community. Outside of this immediate family script, there was also the musico-cultural cohesion experienced in the choir itself. For instance, one chorister traveled three hours in each direction for a two-hour long rehearsal, such was his commitment to the music, the experience of singing, and the group to which he belonged. To all effect, the bonding within the choir was like that of a family.

In addition to the familial social identities scripted within the Hreimur choir, there was the broader script emergent from the opportunity the choir offered to express vocal collectivity, dependent on the unique contribution of each individual. One example of this was the way the men approached learning repertoire, including their parts, which often took place informally outside rehearsal time. The men supported one another's vocal strengths and weaknesses, always playing to positive advantage. For instance, one chorister recognized that he had a weaker voice, yet in the context of the group: "I think I'm pretty good in a team, when we're not singing too loudly, but I can often get pretty high, but it's not a particularly big voice" (Faulkner 2013, p. 76).

This sort of collaboration was an important part of enriching the choir. The *Persona* was also fed by the positive experience of being a performer in front of an audience, frequently described in terms of the pleasure felt at being part of the collective sound and having the opportunity to entertain others. But, for those who took solos, there was gratification in being able to balance individuality alongside the social support of the collective. The detailed vocal life history of one of the choir's soloists provides a layered account of the complex interaction between personal and social identity, between individuals and their personal or solo voice on the one hand, and collectives, or choirs, and their group sound and songs on the other.

Another way that *Persona* was expressed was through a relationship to other vocal groups. One manifestation of this was for the choir to compete informally in regional, national, and international settings, pitting their socio-vocal identity against that of other choirs.

In addition to the social aspect of Self being supported and developed in the Hreimur choir, the *Body* (as it is referred to by Weber) or *Material Self* (James's term) was also powerfully articulated as being crucial to these men's vocal identities: they used their singing voices in their everyday environments to strengthen and inform their broader constructions of Self. For instance, at work in the barn, in the machine shed, or out in the valley, men sang to mark their environment with the sounds of their voice, using voice as an extension of self into the larger space, but also as an activity of endorsing the physical Self:

> I sing by myself and for myself when I'm in the barn . . . maybe you're just testing yourself.
> I was alone in the control room at the power station . . . and it sounds like the very best concert hall. It's impossible not to take a few notes!
>
> (Faulkner 2013, p. 100)

Out in the countryside: "It's pretty good to sing there with the rocks, and the mountain to throw the sound between them" (Faulkner 2013, p. 105).

In relation to the physicality of singing and the *Body* employed, a particularly noteworthy element of the men's experience in the choir was the close physical proximity it afforded— singing together in a huddle was commented on by many of the choristers as being a crucial bonding experience. The activity seemed to function to expand the sense of the individual boundaries of body to the level of the collective, both literally and metaphorically; that is, not just the close tactility when singing, but also through the communion of the sounds of the voices. With vertical harmonies, the voices sit together and move with same or varying rhythmic expressions to give consonant or contrapuntal effect.

More generally, this type of experience acted so powerfully on these men that some referred to a lack of opportunity to sing being like having part of the Self missing:

> after my operation, there was a long period when I couldn't sing . . . Then one day when I came indoors singing, my wife said: "Oh you're back then" and I said "Yeah, I'm back" and came in singing. She meant I was back, me, she thought I was myself again.
>
> (Faulkner 2013, p. 111)

Looking at this data, it could be argued that the choir is perceived by its singers to be a place where the Self expands in order to be healthier. This concept is strongly pursued in other work, and it is worth returning to the chapter by Davidson and Garrido (see this volume) in which the Venda of South Africa are referenced and discussed. In context, we are told that for Venda people singing behaviors are assimilated into many aspects of life, particularly those to do with the regulation of social order and cultural information. Without a singing voice, there is a belief that personhood dies (Emberly 2009). As noted at the very beginning of this chapter, such a belief related to cultural context. But the cultural practices of the Icelanders and indeed the Venda ladies reveal that the bodily/material and social practices of singing invigorate participants, especially in a group context, which in large part enhances and expands Self.

Consideration of the interaction between Material Self or *Body* and Social Self or *Persona* also draws us to the third and crucial element of the tripartite model of Self, the *Spirit*. For the Venda of Limpopo Province collective singing can conjure up the spirits of ancestors, and in different cultural ideologies this sort of rhetoric is not uncommon. In Karlakórinn Hreimur the men talked about Icelandic historical traditions that capture the spirits and characters of former times, often feeling a "presence" of these spirits as they sing.

"Spiritual" aspects of singing also seem to incorporate the idea of the voice traveling outwards beyond the physical and material realm, thus carrying the participant to a place beyond the human realm. On reflection, the vocal experiences described as having "spiritual" purpose and outcome seem to have three key elements: they offer preparation for a change or movement beyond the typical everyday experience (e.g. preparation for death, departure, marriage, life, homecoming); they are used for collective experience (e.g. being together in the vocal music to remember someone, feeling solidarity etc.) and in turn, this results in collective resolution (e.g. expressing a focused collective grief at a funeral). In the study of Icelandic men, this is seen most explicitly in an older chorister who insists on preparing the music for his own funeral. His careful use of song to create deep personal and social meaning (i.e. to reduce senses of psychological entropy in the face of death) seems to be applicable to all spiritual vocal experiences (see Faulkner 2013, p. 118).

These spiritual opportunities seem to be available to audiences too, but the activity of performing the music in the collective offers the most emotionally powerful experience of communion. As choristers comment, after singing:

> You feel completely different afterwards . . . you release something somehow.
>
> (Faulkner 2013, p. 119)

> You feel much better in harmony with others. Then you get that kick, that's how it's supposed to be.
>
> (Faulkner 2013, p. 123)

So, by exploring Karlakórinn Hreimur, it has become apparent that the tripartite elements of Self defined by Weber and James operate powerfully within this close community of singing.

As director of the Hreimur choir, the second author has previously discussed at length his role in shaping and selecting repertoire and the skills he brought to bear on developing sense of identity within the choir. While the Icelandic male voice choir tradition was founded on music that was either imported or composed as part of the European Romantic tradition (see Faulkner 2012), contemporary Icelandic musical tastes tend to be eclectic and relatively intergenerational. The small population has mitigated against subcultural trends or specializations. Singing medieval Icelandic quint songs, nineteenth-century Romantic repertoire, contemporary popular songs, jazz standards, sacred music, opera choruses, and even contemporary works composed by the son of one of the choristers who studied composition at the St. Petersburg Conservatoire, all fulfill different kinds of social and personal needs, giving opportunity for expansion and contraction, for challenge and affirmation. To gain fuller access to the role of the choral director in shaping chorister identity, we turn to two other cases. For the sake of confidentiality, we refer to them adopting the pseudonyms the Sound of Song and the Senior Singers. Before discussing their data in detail, the groups are now introduced.

The Sound of Song

This choir has been running in Australia for a decade. Its members are from backgrounds of homelessness, long-term unemployment, and disability, with histories of substance abuse, mental illness, and social exclusion featuring strongly. Members range in age from eighteen to seventy-five years, with a fairly even gender split. The group is supported by charity workers and is led by a male community musician who has also had a significant career as a solo folk/pop musician. Such community choirs have attracted media attention in recent years. The "Choir of Hard Knocks" was a hit TV series, tracing the lives and experiences musical and otherwise of its members. A pioneering psychological study into such groups came from Betty Bailey, who investigated a choir made up of a group of homeless men who enjoyed significant media success in Montreal, Canada. The results fit within the current theoretical framework, so that, in terms of identity, it was discovered that the Canadian men regarded the choir as the most meaningful thing in their lives (see Bailey and Davidson 2002). The choir offered a structure to otherwise challenged lives, and provided a crucial platform for feelings of self-worth and pride. The heart-wrenching life stories of all participants revealed that the choir offered a workable social structure for these men. It offered a mixture of autonomy and social interdependence that permitted participation without the kind of conformity that other kinds of group structures would have demanded.

Of course, elsewhere in the current volume, community singing groups are explored as they often use a singing intervention to promote physical and psychological well-being. They have been remarkably successful, often reflecting different challenges to those of regular choristers. For instance, community choristers often require a lot of support to approach the activity, or even to identify with it, which is not a typical feature for those who join a choir because of its high musical standards and specific choral singing challenges. So again, the social and cultural agenda shapes its impact on participants.

The Senior Singers

Also from Australia, and like the Sound of Song, the Senior Singers group was created to offer a health promotion opportunity. It is directed by a very experienced female who has both taught music and worked in similar community choir circumstances. The thirty-five choristers largely live alone, receive some sort of homecare service, and are aged between seventy and ninety-four years of age. Two-thirds of the choristers are female, reflecting the gender balance statistic of this age group. It was a challenge to retain members, many of whom find transport to and from the rehearsal venue difficult. Many also lacked confidence around their capacities to sing.

Data from these groups, as for the Icelandic male voice group, were collected through questionnaires and interviews related to experience. Among the emergent themes that are discussed below is that of the role of the conductor or facilitator.

Leadership to secure a vocal identity

The first and most striking factor relating to leadership in the context of these two choirs was how much the director's capacity to manage the group swayed the choristers' beliefs about the quality of their own experience in the choir:

> He's a very good guy. He knows when to tell us to pull into line and he also knows when to encourage us.

> She's a classic. She's just so funny. The way she introduces every session with a joke to get our diaphragms working is just great. She sets a tone. She won't let anyone change that mood. She's very clever. One or two can be a bit awkward at times, but she just encourages them and you know, she works it all out.
>
> (Davidson 2011, p. 81)

These group management skills were extensively reported, with characteristics like: giving freedom as well as offering boundaries; being skilled musicians and singers, but always being ready to allow the participants the space to express themselves from their own starting point. This type of direction is consistent with the commonly reported literature on leadership (e.g. see Avolio 2011). More than this, these strategies seem to mobilize the motivations discussed in Self-Determination Theory (Deci and Ryan 2000). The directors themselves comment: the Senior Singers' director:

> I always believe in fun, but I challenge them a bit too. Not too much though, as I want them to feel safe. You begin with simple things like breathing, then a bit more technique and then, eventually, you can vary the repertoire from very straightforward unison songs, to parts and rounds. It takes a long time to build their confidence and develop the dynamic in a way that they will rise to the new challenges that I set. You learn to follow a routine to give people a structure and a formula. Sometimes I get complaints if I don't do things the same as usual.
>
> (Davidson 2011, p. 81)

The Sound of Song director:

> We talk about all sorts of things from social through to musical and sometimes very personal stuff, but we keep moving, and getting through the singing too, because I need to balance up all their needs with the central role of the group: to sing. It seems that all the other stuff happens, too, quite naturally, but I've got to keep my material in the session. We try to work on creative work, too: bringing some lyrics, writing a new tune and that sort of thing.
>
> (Davidson 2011, p. 82)

These leadership strategies engage with the chorister's *autonomy, competency*, and sense of *relatedness*. In terms of positive Self-Identity, especially owing to a lack of previous experience in the choral context, the impact of the choir on these individuals was profound.

Choristers' sense of Self

The singing activity itself offered a *new* relationship with Self:

> When I was in my "out there" phase as a real alcoholic, I would have never joined anything like a singing group that performs classical music in Latin! But, you reflect on life and you think: "Why not give it a go, you've got nothing else to lose!" When you sing with the others there is a discipline to it. I didn't realize how precise it has to be: come in together; blend in together; pronounce your words clearly; try to sing that high note stronger or softer; watch your tuning. There's a precision and beauty to it. Being a singer is not easy, but it is better and more enjoyable than I imagined. Being a singer also means you've got to be a team player.
>
> (Davidson 2011, p. 77)

> The director lets us fly in the music. I feel like I'm me.
>
> (Davidson 2011, p. 81)

> Expressing through being in the music is very powerful. It is another way of being, it permits you to be together with everyone in the music—part of the harmony, But, you're also independent. So, in music, you can be small and big, contributing in different ways to the whole. Maybe that's particularly true of singing groups?
>
> (Davidson 2011, p. 79)

This impact on identity makes this practice of choral singing powerful and positive. Much seems related to the director's management of the sessions and also through the offering of repertoire appropriate to the group, repertoire that has a specific psychological function:

> I wouldn't say I got teary, but when you haven't heard those songs for so many years and your memory goes back . . . to when you sort of . . . family company and that.
>
> (Davidson 2011, p. 79)

But more than this, there was a complex impact of the choral sound:

> The truth is that as you get older, you're less attractive and there are far fewer opportunities for intimacy. When your husband dies, well you don't get that sort of physical reassurance. I've found with singing that you get close to the people emotionally and physically, you know I can feel the hairs on the back of my neck stand up when the men sing those lower harmonies.
>
> (Davidson 2011, p. 79)

These elements link back to themes discussed in relation to the Icelanders, though those men were steeped in a choral tradition, and the impact is perhaps reported using less emotive language. It could be that rhetoric found among the members of the Sound of Song and the Senior Singers is connected to the aims of the groups—to bring about well-being and positive health impact. As part of this, the choristers felt that their work in group singing expanded their sense of Self and their personal potential, by taking on new musical encounters: "We all like our familiar stuff . . . but we're trying to learn new music: music my kids listened to when they were teenagers. We even did some quite highbrow classical stuff" (Davidson 2011, p. 83). It also seemed to offer a new form of social encounter with old friends, thus changing the nature of interpersonal relations: "In between sessions, I'm going around recording all the songs . . . I made a copy for a friend of mine . . . we sit at her place and we put the tape on and we sing together" (Davidson 2011, p. 83).

Many reported experiences similar to these, with one re-evaluating her relationship with music and defining this as a love of participation through singing.

Performance

Another area that has had a profound impact on the choristers of these two community singing groups was revealed in their experiences of performance. Again, this rather resembled the excitement of the Icelanders, but without the long cultural understanding of singing, the impact seemed even more profound:

> My grandchildren thought it was brilliant that I was going to be performing in a concert. Of course I go and see them at swimming events and in school concerts, but when all the family came to see and hear me in a concert, now that was something special! I've never been one for the spotlight. Getting applause and being praised in public is important recognition. It gives you worth. I don't think I've ever had applause for anything else I do.
>
> (Davidson 2011, p. 76)

> On the streets no one takes notice of you—apart from moving you on and shouting at you because you're homeless. When you get up in a concert and all those eyes are looking at you, then applauding you and praising you; well it is fabulous.
>
> (Davidson 2011, p. 76)

The sense of achievement and control was staggeringly positive:

> I didn't think I had a good voice and then [the facilitator] asked me if I'd try a solo. I panicked, but did it and everyone thought I had this real great and gravelly voice. Then, I started practicing along to rock CDs and stuff. Now, I get up there and sing solos for anyone. I have something good to offer: I sing and people like me in a different sort of way. Performing gives another side to my sense of who I am. I feel good at what I'm doing. I'm no trained musician, but I can do the job and other people tell me that.
>
> (Davidson 2011, p. 76)

This specific example also clearly demonstrates how identity is being expanded and developed.

Agents of change and creation

Despite the contrast between these two choirs, the choristers' responses across topic areas were virtually identical. Singing seemed to be a catalyst to enhance individual confidence and social connection. In other words, there was an incredible sense of group achievement, the group feeling being "a special thing" more important than the individual thrill which led members to being close physically and emotionally. For many this was because of the new situation.

Perhaps the word expansion most neatly encapsulates what the experience of singing together did for these choristers. This is entirely consistent with Weber's theory that pursuits have the potential for the expansion or contraction of Self, for creating Self. Song changed their feelings and experience of themselves in relation to others, showed them that the sense of who they were could be adapted and changed, and indicated that there was a great creative potential in the sung experience:

> We're learning new music . . . We even did some quite high-brow classical stuff.
>
> (Davidson 2011, p. 83)

> I never imagined that I could do this. It is new and exciting. We even make up our own words, try to create new tunes. It is amazing.
>
> (Previously unpublished)

Some choristers took these ideas a step further, speaking about a new spiritual connection to others. It could be that in this expanded sense of spiritual connection, people are describing the phenomenon of peak or transcendent experience captured by Abraham Maslow in his famous social psychological work on self-actualization (Maslow 1970). The underlying feeling is positivity and something that generates a sense of wonderment. The experiences also align with John Sloboda's reflection on the experience of being in music as offering a peak esthetic experience (Sloboda 1991, 1998). It is certainly the case that these data deal with the spiritual, transcendent quality of experience in a non-religious conception, and it is evident that the framing of the experience is dependent on social and individual belief systems.

Audiences per se are not a specific focus in this chapter, but research reported elsewhere (e.g. see Gabrielsson 2011) notes that audiences are susceptible to the powerful experiences of group singing, even when just watching and listening. Very recently, the first author's study of thousands of listeners—modern-day consumers of music available through technological media as well as accessed in live performance—showed how people manage and expand their identity as much through music as any other factor in their lives (see Davidson and Garrido 2014).

REFLECTIONS

This chapter has illustrated the powerful impact of singing on generating and developing social identity. Through the application of Weber's tripartite model of the Created Self, social benefits of singing are found. It is to be added that Levitin (2009) has identified six basic functions of song: knowledge, friendship, religion, joy, comfort, and love. Ruud (2012) has also distinguished four dimensions or categories of quality of life that benefit from musicking: vitality (emotional life, esthetic sensibility, pleasures), agency (sense of mastery and empowerment, social recognition), belonging (network, social capital), and meaning (continuity of tradition, transcendental values, hope). This chapter has indicated that Levitin and Ruud's functions and distinctions apply to the singers whose data have been presented. Crucially, Cohen (2005) has noted that as we progress through life we become increasingly flexible, seeking experiences to challenge ourselves. Arguably then, the *Created Self* becomes more expansive in singing groups because of their multi-level stimulation, and thus we can see them as being particularly useful to society.

When we think of social identity, it is also necessary to consider ways in which some caution and critical reflection is necessary. Looking at the latter two groups considered in this chapter, performance was in some ways a difficult matter in relation to identity, especially because of how this was perceived by others. Unlike the Hreimur choir, who by their cultural standard were highly skilled, well rehearsed, and well tuned, the Sound of Song and Senior Singers groups were committed and enthusiastic, but many of them joined their choir as their very first encounter with singing. It was important for the groups and their leaders to be sensitive to their strengths and limitations, and for those singers not to be placed in situations where the health and well-being benefits of performance in particular could be turned into stressors.

The first author has been supporting senior singing groups for some years. Focusing on the management of performance to maximize positive outcomes and minimalize stress has been a key focus. The choristers revel in the peak positive feelings associated with group singing as well as singing in front of and for others, but a cultural understanding of the role and function of these choirs and their performances is required by audiences—there needs to be an appropriate cultural attunement to the choir. To address this matter, events for choirs to sing for one another have been very useful, in addition to opportunities to sing at organizations where their performances are valued and well supported—for example, singing in seniors' clubs. In this regard, it is vitally important to highlight the important role directors and managers play.

Looking back to the homeless Canadian singing group studied a decade ago, they have now vanished from the public eye. They no longer have CD contracts or experience any of the excitement publicity and fame once offered them. Of course, we could reflect on this sort of situation for many singers, professional or otherwise, but when choristers are particularly vulnerable members of our communities, identity needs should be kept in focus.

Summary

In this chapter, we have seen how choristers from dramatically contrasting geographical and cultural settings use the singing experience to create and perform Self. They revise, reinvent, expand, and represent their social identities individually and together through the choir form and context. The vocal activities they participate in connect them in special ways. For all of these individuals and groups, singing and the songs that they sing are essential life technologies. They are not at all the same songs or genres, nor are they necessarily sung to the same standard, but group singing and social identity become synonyms. The relationship between social identity, well-being, socio-cultural context, and singing is one that managers and developers of social experiences should aim to understand and use for positive outcomes.

FURTHER READING

Csikszentmihayli, M. (1993). *The Evolving Self: A Psychology for the Third Millennium.* New York: Harper Perennial.

Davidson, J.W. (2017). Performance Identity. In: R.A.R. MacDonald, D.E. Miell, and D.J. Hargreaves (eds), *The Oxford Handbook of Musical Identities*, pp. 364–382. Oxford: Oxford University Press.

Deci, E.L. and Ryan, R.M. (eds) (2006). *The Handbook of Self-Determination Research.* Rochester: University of Rochester Press.

Faulkner, R. (2013). *Icelandic Men and Me: Sagas of Singing, Self and Everyday Life.* Aldershot: Ashgate Publishing.

North, A.J. and Hargreaves, D.J (2008). *The Social and Applied Psychology of Music.* Oxford: Oxford University Press.

REFERENCES

Avolio, B.J. (2011). *Full Range Leadership Development.* London: Sage.

Bailey, B. and Davidson, J.W. (2002). Group singing as adaptive behavior: Perceptions from members of a choir of homeless men. *Musicae Scientiae* 6: 221–256.

Björnsdóttir, I.D. (2001). Hin karlmannlega raust og hinn hljóðláti máttur kvenna: Upphaf kórsöngs á Íslandi. *Saga* 39: 7–50.

Cohen, G. (2005). *The Mature Mind.* New York: Basic Books.

Connell, R.W. (1995). *Masculinities.* Cambridge: Polity Press.

Davidson, J.W. (2011). Musical participation: expectations, experiences and outcomes. In: J.W. Davidson and I. Deliège (eds), *Music and the Mind*, pp. 65–87. Oxford: Oxford University Press.

Davidson, J.W. and Garrido, S. (2014). *My Life as a Playlist.* UWA: UWA Publishing.

Deci, E.L. and Ryan, R.M. (2000). The "what" and "why" of goal pursuits: human needs and the self-determination of behavior. *Psychological Inquiry* 11: 227–268.

Emberly, A. (2009). *Mandela went to China . . . and India too: Musical cultures of childhood in South Africa.* PhD thesis, University of Washington.

Faulkner, R. (2013). *Icelandic Men and Me: Sagas of Singing, Self and Everyday Life.* Aldershot: Ashgate Publishing.

Faulkner, R. (2012). Icelandic Men, Male Voice Choirs and Masculine Identity. In: S. Harrison, A. Adler, and G. Welch (eds), *Perspectives on Males and Singing*, pp. 215–231. Berlin: Springer Press.

Gabrielsson, A. (2011). *Strong experiences with music: Music is much more than just music.* Oxford, UK: Oxford University Press.

James, W. (1890). *Principles of Psychology*, 2 vols. New York: Henry Holt.

Korsgaard, C.M. (2009). *Self-Constitution: Agency, Identity and Integrity.* Oxford: Oxford University Press.

Levitin, D.J. (2009). *The World in Six Songs: How the Musical Brain Created Human Nature.* New York: Plume.

Maslow, A. (1970). *Motivation and Personality*, 2nd edn. New York: Harper and Row.

Ruud, E. (2012). The new health musicians. In: R. MacDonald, G. Kreutz, and L. Mitchell (eds), *Music, Health, and Wellbeing*, pp. 87–96. Oxford: Oxford University Press.

Sloboda, J.A. (1991). Music structure and emotional response: some empirical findings. *Psychology of Music* 19: 110–120.

Sloboda (1998). Does music mean anything? *Musicae Scientiae* 2: 21–32.

Weber, R.J. (2000). *The Created Self: Reinventing Body, Persona and Spirit*. New York: W.W. Norton.

CHAPTER 43

....

INTONATION AND STAYING IN TUNE IN *A CAPPELLA* CHORAL SINGING

....

DAVID M. HOWARD

INTRODUCTION

....

WHEN singing unaccompanied or *a cappella*, singers have to tune the notes they are singing to those being produced by singers of other parts. This is a very different situation when compared to singing accompanied, where singers tune their notes to the accompanying instrument(s). In practice, it turns out that the tuning system used to tune a keyboard instrument such as a piano, organ, or electronic keyboard instrument is compromised in terms of how individual notes are tuned in order to retain accurate tuning of the octaves as a doubling or halving in frequency (ascending or descending respectively). During the Baroque era, various compromise tuning systems were developed to enable keyboard instruments to be tuned keeping in-tune octaves and these would typically be implemented such that musical keys with up to three flats or sharps in their key signatures would sound pleasing or *consonant* whereas other keys would tend to sound less pleasing or more *dissonant*. This illustrates directly the reason for the pitch shifts experienced in *a cappella* singing because singers tend towards consonant tuning, but this cannot be maintained as the music changes key and returns to the starting key unless the overall pitch shifts.

The equal tempered tuning system, which was adopted to enable music to be performed in any of the twelve keys, sets each semitone to be equal and this results in all musical intervals except the octave being slightly out of tune. Thus there is another difficulty for singers in that the tuning imposed when there are accompanying instruments is different to that they would naturally adopt when singing *a cappella*. Temperament is therefore a strong driver in terms of overall tuning, particularly since the possibility that the tuning of notes should be different depending on whether there is accompaniment or not is not widely appreciated or understood amongst choirs and their directors. It is, however, very much understood by professional ensemble singers (Potter 2000, Chapter 13). That it is not widely understood is reinforced when one observes the use of a keyboard instrument doubling the parts during rehearsal of an *a cappella* piece, or in performance when a starting chord rather than just the tonic is given on a keyboard. This latter point is particularly important since good *a cappella* singing depends on the tuning (mainly listening) abilities of the singers and for such singers there should be no issue about finding notes of a chord from a single reference note.

This chapter describes how and why intonation can affect directly the overall pitch in *a cappella* choral singing. The chapter explores this issue quantitatively in three ways: (1) In terms of the nature of non-equal tempered tuning based on maximum *consonance* in musical intervals; (2) in the context of predicting the pitch shift effect; and (3) how vocal quartets tune in practice. Use is made of specially written choral exercises which clearly demonstrate the effect, along with items from the *a cappella* choral repertoire which typically exhibit a pitch shift to establish the extent to which intonation is a contributor.

BACKGROUND AND THEORETICAL FRAMEWORK

Music takes advantage of a number of basic attributes relating to how we hear sounds, including dynamic variations in pitch, loudness, timbre, and rhythm. Pitch is controlled in some instruments, such as the piano, harp, or pipe organ, by the instrument itself, which has to be tuned regularly by a specialist. Other instruments, such as wind instruments, non-fretted stringed instruments, and to a degree fretted stringed instruments, leave a degree of fine pitch tuning available to the player. Singers have complete freedom in their pitching when singing *a cappella* since they can produce pitches over a wide range, sometimes as large as three or more octaves, and apart from those with so-called *perfect* or *absolute pitch* (Ward 1998) the majority have no restrictions in terms of pre-set note pitch positions.

During *a cappella* choral singing, relative tuning tends towards just temperament assuming members of the choir are listening carefully to each other (Bohrer 2002; Carlsson et al. 2000; Helmholtz 1954; Howard 2007; Potter 2000). In just temperament the main intervals in a major or minor triad (perfect fifth, major third, minor third) have fundamental frequency ratios between the notes that are in integer ratios (perfect fifth: 3/2; major third: 5/4; minor third: 6/5). The tendency when tuning individual notes of a chord will be in the appropriate integer ratio to the tonic of that chord. What happens as the music progresses in terms of relative tuning between successive chords will depend on the nature of the music itself and what references are available from one chord to the next (for example, if adjacent chords share a unison or octave note in common then there is a basis for relative tuning between the chords).

In practice, it is not possible to tune a keyboard instrument using just temperament throughout and maintain all ascending (descending) octaves with a doubling (halving) in fundamental frequency ratio (Meffen 1982). This effect can be demonstrated mathematically as follows. Keyboard instruments are usually tuned in fifths from a starting note, say middle C, and all octaves are tuned exactly. If all the notes of a keyboard were tuned in ascending integer fundamental frequency ratio fifths of 3:2 (dropping an octave when appropriate to stay within the keyboard's range), there are twelve fifths, known as the *circle of fifths*, required to cover each of the twelve notes in an octave. Twelve fifths have a frequency ratio of $(3/2)$ multiplied by itself twelve times or $(3/2)^{12}$ which equals 129.746. Moving through all twelve fifths in the circle of fifths completes seven octaves, which has a frequency ratio of two multiplied by itself seven times, or $2^7 = 128$. These frequency ratios are not the same and their ratio $(129.746/128.000) = 1.01364$ is known as the *Pythagorean comma*.

To tune a keyboard instrument while preserving the octaves requires that some compromise is made such that completing the fifths covers a frequency ratio of 128. In Baroque times various tuning systems were adopted, such as Werkmeister, Valotti and Young, Kirnenburger (Meffen 1982), in which the Pythagorean comma was distributed around musical keys that are rarely used (usually those with four or more sharps or flats in their key signatures). Today's compromise is the so-called equal-tempered system in which all semitones have the same frequency ratio; the number that when multiplied by itself twelve times equals two, or the twelfth root of two (2^{-12}) or 1.05946. This is the basis of the tuning adopted for Bach's *Das wohltemperierte Klavier* of 1722. However, it can be said of the equal-tempered system that no musical interval is in-tune except for the octave.

Recall that when singers are singing *a cappella* they make use of integer ratio just tuning which is a non-equal tempered tuning system, and if they stick to this as the music modulates to different keys and usually back to the starting key, there will be an overall pitch shift. The theoretical basis for the use of just non-equal tempered tuning arises from knowledge of human hearing and in particular, the bandwidths of the auditory filters (Glasberg and Moore 1990). The use of just tuning ensures that the maximum number of harmonics between the different notes is in unison, and therefore the overall perception for the listener is maximally consonant. Based on the definition of harmonics as an integer multiplied by the fundamental frequency, it is the use of integer ratio tuning between notes (just intonation) that guarantees this is the case. For example, if two notes are a perfect fifth apart, then their fundamental frequencies in just intonation are in the integer ratio (3:2), which ensures that the third harmonic of the lower note and the second harmonic of the upper note are in unison. Overall perceived dissonance of a chord is based on the number of harmonics whose frequencies lie between five and 50 percent of a critical band, and maximum dissonance occurs when the frequency difference is a quarter of a critical bandwidth (Plomp and Levelt 1965).

The potential for an overall pitch shift in *a cappella* choral singing as a result of the use of just intonation is the subject of this chapter and the investigations of others, including Devaney and Ellis (2008); Bohrer (2002); Vurma and Ross (2004); Ternström and Sundberg (1988). Modern clinical technology enables this effect to be investigated experimentally in such a way that the measured output from each singer does not contaminate data from other singers through the use of an electrolaryngograph (Abberton, Howard, and Fourcin, 1989) for each singer (Bohrer 2002; Howard 2007). It would not be possible to make these measurements with sufficient accuracy using microphones unless the singers were in separate sound-isolated recording booths, since without booths all four microphones would pick up a certain proportion of all four singers. These measured fundamental frequency data are presented to demonstrate the existence of the effect and to illustrate how it manifests itself in practice with items from the *a cappella* choral repertoire.

EXPERIMENTAL WORK

Materials, subjects, and procedure

In order to investigate the potential for the use of just tuning to result in an overall pitch shift in *a cappella* choral singing, a number of exercises were written in which a sequence of a

FIGURE 43.1 Example exercise in score form used to investigate pitch drift (upper) and as performed by the quartets (lower).

small group of four-part (SATB) chords moved through various key chords having started in a particular key and ended in the same key (Howard 2007). A tendency for an overall pitch shift would therefore be apparent by comparing the pitches of notes in the first and last chords. Of the exercises written, that shown in Figure 43.1 provided the most straightforward example. The upper part of Figure 43.1 shows the scored version and the lower part shows how the singers were asked to perform it by ensuring that the tied notes were clearly audible to the rest of the group between the chords and that the notes of each chord began and ended together. A single note (middle C: the tonic of the first chord) was given at the start of each exercise as a pitch reference using an electronic tuner.

This exercise has been sung by three vocal quartets, each comprising second or third year first-study singer undergraduates from the Department of Music at the University of York who were experienced performers and good listeners. Each singer wore electrolaryngograph electrodes connected to four electrolaryngographs that were electrically adjusted so as not to interfere with each other. In addition, a cardioid microphone was placed 30 cm from the lips of each singer at an angle of 45 degrees to avoid popping. The resulting eight channels of audio data were recorded onto a Korg D-1600 eight-channel hard disk recorder with 16-bit quantization at a sampling rate of 44.1 kHz. These data were transferred digitally to a PC for analysis.

Data analysis

The predicted fundamental frequencies for each note of the score were calculated in just tuning with reference to the starting note (middle C—the tonic of the first chord which appears in the alto part) using integer ratios (octave as 2:1; perfect fifth as 3:2; perfect fourth as 4:3; major third as 5:4; minor third as 6:5). The tied notes provide a tuning link between

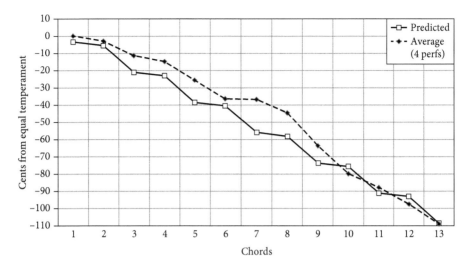

FIGURE 43.2 Plot of predicted pitch drift (solid line) for the exercise shown in Figure 43.1 and the average measured pitch drift (dashed line) for four performances (two performances by each of two quartets).

the chords. In order to analyze for pitch drift, the equal tempered value for each note was also calculated to enable the predicted difference between just tuning and equal temperament to be calculated first as a frequency ratio and then as a difference in cents (one cent is one hundredth of a semitone). A full account of the calculations as well as a table of values is given in Table 1 of Howard (2007). The overall average across the four parts (SATB) was calculated and the results are plotted in Figure 43.2 (solid line) against the 13 chords of the exercise. It can be seen that this exercise exhibits an overall pitch shift of just over a semitone (100 cents) flat.

Measurement of the fundamental frequencies used in practice by a quartet was based on the output from the four electrolaryngographs. These were specially set up by Laryngograph Ltd. (<www.laryngograph.com>) to operate in close proximity without interfering with each other by ensuring that their operating frequencies, which are in the 1–3 MHz range (Howard 2009), were mutually compatible. In order to measure the average fundamental frequency for each note of each chord, the SPEAD software from Laryngograph Ltd. was used. The electrolaryngograph system enables fundamental period measurements to be made to the nearest microsecond, from which the fundamental frequency can be obtained as the reciprocal (fundamental frequency = (1/fundamental period)). The fundamental frequency trace for each individual note can be selected and the average value found which is then recorded on an Excel spreadsheet. Each value is then normalized to the reference note (middle C)—the first alto note—as a frequency ratio, and then compared in cents with the calculated equal tempered values. The results for two performances by each of two quartets are averaged together and plotted as the dashed line in Figure 43.2. It can be seen that the average pitch drift across these four performances is very close to the prediction based on just tuning; confirmation that singers do tend to make use of just non-equal tempered tuning when singing *a cappella*.

Pitch drift in choral repertoire

The original inspiration for this work arose from the choral singing experience of the author who recalls being asked by a choirmaster to sing pieces again because they had drifted in pitch, but without any guidance as to what one should be doing that was different from the previous rendition. In order to test whether this effect is related to the use of just intonation, two Bach chorales (*Ach bleib bei uns, Herr Jesu Christ*—BWV 253 and *Ach Gott und Herr, wie gross und schwer*—BWV 255) were analyzed using the same protocol that was employed for the exercise described above. The chorales were performed on the vowel /a:/in order to remove any word pronunciation distractions and the pauses were ignored in terms of lengthening the notes but they were taken as indicators of the ends of phrases. A pitch reference was provided from an electronic tuner, which was the tonic of the first chord in each case (A4 for BWV 253 and middle C for BWV 255). The SATB scores for these chorales are shown in Figures 43.3 and 43.4.

An Excel spreadsheet was created in which the predicted fundamental frequency values for each note of each chord were calculated based on just tuning for each chorale. In each case the average fundamental frequency drift across the four parts (SATB) was calculated in cents relative to equal temperament. These overall averages are shown as the solid lines in Figures 43.5 and 43.6 for the two chorales BWV 253 and BWV 255 respectively. The chorales were sung on the vowel /a:/ by a semi-professional SATB vocal quartet at the National Centre for Early Music in York in a comfortable acoustic (this room can be set using reversible wall panels and extensive curtaining in the ceiling spaces). Each singer wore electrolaryngograph electrodes. The electrolaryngograph outputs were analyzed using the same procedure described above for the exercise to enable the fundamental frequency values for each sung note of each chord of the chorales to be measured. The overall average fundamental frequency value across all four parts (SATB) for each chord was calculated and the results are shown as the dashed lines in Figures 43.5 and 43.6 for BWV 253 and BWV 255, respectively.

FIGURE 43.3 Score for the chorale *Ach bleib bei uns, Herr Jesu Christ* (BWV 253) by J.S. Bach. (The numbers refer to the chord numbering for analysis shown in Figure 43.5.)

FIGURE 43.4 Score for the chorale *Ach Gott und Herr, wie gross und schwer* (BWV 255) by J.S. Bach. (The numbers refer to the chord numbering for analysis shown in Figure 43.6.)

It can be seen from Figures 43.5 and 43.6 that the singers do drift in pitch during the singing of both of these chorales. For *Ach bleib bei uns, Herr Jesu Christ* (BWV 253), the pitch drift exhibited in performance by the quartet is remarkably close to the prediction, where

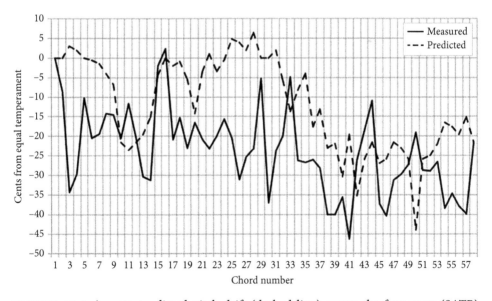

FIGURE 43.5 Average predicted pitch drift (dashed line) across the four parts (SATB) based on just intonation and the average measured pitch drift (solid line) across the four parts (SATB) for a performance by a semi-professional vocal quartet of the chorale *Ach bleib bei uns, Herr Jesu Christ* (BWV 253) by J.S. Bach performed on the vowel /a:/.

FIGURE 43.6 Average predicted pitch drift (dashed line) across the four parts (SATB) based on just intonation and the average measured pitch drift (solid line) across the four parts (SATB) for a performance by a semi-professional vocal quartet of the chorale *Ach Gott und Herr, wie gross und schwer* (BWV 255) by J.S. Bach performed on the vowel /aː/.

both end up 22 cents flat (values taken from the spreadsheet) on average, as compared to equal temperament, where the difference is zero. In addition, although the detailed variation on a chord-by-chord basis is not identical, there is evidence to suggest that the overall trends are to some extent being followed.

For *Ach Gott und Herr, wie gross und schwer* (BWV 255), the fundamental frequency drift is downwards (flattening) as predicted but the quartet ends up at -37 cents relative to equal temperament which is just under half of the -86 cents predicted fundamental frequency drift (values taken from the spreadsheet). In terms of their performance, the quartet has drifted in accordance with the prediction to around chord number 20, which is just prior to the end of the third phrase (see Figure 43.4). From there onwards it appears that they are attempting to hold their tendency to drift in average fundamental frequency. It is also of note that the detailed changes in average fundamental frequency show some similarities between the predicted and performance values in terms of the peak and trough variations.

DISCUSSION

The results indicate that there is evidence to suggest that a pitch drift is associated with *a cappella* performance of both chorales and that this drift does follow the prediction suggested by an analysis of the score based on just intonation in terms of its direction (musically flat or sharp). The fact that the measured pitch drift is in-line with the prediction based on the use of just intonation, which itself is a documented feature of *a cappella* singing, does suggest that its use is a contributory factor. However, it is also clear from these data that the predicted variation is followed neither exactly nor completely, which implies that the use of just temperament cannot be the sole explanation for this tendency to drift in pitch. This begs the question as to whether there are other aspects of *a cappella* singing that might be contributing either for or against pitch drift in performance. The following are possibilities that suggest themselves as possible additional influences:

- *Perfect* or *absolute pitch*. The presence of a member of an *a cappella* choir who has perfect or absolute pitch (Ward 1998) which often means that they are able to sing a note on a score with a reasonable to high degree of accuracy without reference to an external reference, can have a highly significant effect on overall tuning. A singer with perfect or absolute pitch will typically only be able to sing the pitch that they link with the note they see on the score and they will often report that they are unable to tune locally to other singers when the pitch drifts. This effect is particularly strong for example when a piece is transposed to another key but the score remains in the original key. Then some perfect or absolute pitch singers find they are unable to sing in the transposed key unless the score itself is also transposed to the new key. In the context of overall pitch drift, just one singer with perfect or absolute pitch in the group will be effectively working against any tendency that the group has to drift in pitch. This will cause issues for other singers in the group who will not only have the tendency for pitch drift caused by just intonation or temperament to contend with, but will also have the pitch anchoring effect sponsored by the perfect or absolute pitch singer. In practice this can lead to tuning inaccuracies throughout.

- *Ease or otherwise of singing through transition regions*. All singers have regions in their sung output where there are difficulties crossing a pitch transition, sometimes referred to as a register break (e.g. Cowley 2010). For example, pitch transitions exist around D4 to F#4 (adult males and females) and D5 to F5 (adult females), and these can cause production issues which might override fine pitching maneuvers and therefore affect intonation directly. If a singer is unable to achieve the desired pitch for such a vocal reason then this could affect directly the overall drift of the group itself, especially in groups where good listening skills are the norm. In addition, this effect may have a variable effect since it is likely to be different depending on whether the singer is ascending or descending through the transition region, whether the vowels are favorable ones for that singer and that range, and the dynamic level.

- *Singing towards extremes in pitch range*. When a singer is singing towards the upper or lower end of her or his pitch range there will be a tendency for the pitch to flatten or sharpen respectively, and this effect is likely to be greater the closer to the extreme the singer is. High notes in the tenor range, for example around G4 to A4, and high notes in the soprano range, for example around A5 to C6, can be difficult for some choral singers to sing in-tune because they are struggling to achieve these pitches with their voice production technique. Similar issues can exist for low notes, particularly for basses around C2 to F2, which can be less easy for other members of the choir to hear and can often be heard as being somewhat sharp.

- *Local acoustics of the environment.* The local environment will affect the local acoustics which in turn will affect what is heard by each singer. It is particularly important for vocal performers that they are able to hear themselves as well as other members of the group at a reasonable level so they can monitor their own output. To achieve this requires some local reflection of sound back to the ears of the performers due to the geometry of the space (for example, closeness and relative positions of walls and ceiling), the positions of local items within the space (for example, architectural features, large items such as bookcases), and the nature of those surfaces (for example, glass or curtained windows, plaster or panelled walls, carpeted or parquet floor). This is one reason why local fold-back loudspeakers or in-ear monitoring are used in amplified bands to ensure that solo singers can hear themselves at an appropriate level relative to the accompaniment. Apart from the fact that singers are likely to over sing with the potential for vocal fatigue or vocal damage when in the absence of an appropriate level of local acoustic feedback, the ability to hear oneself and the rest of the group is essential for good overall tuning. One would anticipate not only that the pitch shift effect would be greatly reduced in the absence of appropriate local acoustic feedback but also that overall pitching and blend would be compromised.

- *Ability to hear oneself.* In order to be able to sing in-tune, singers have to be able to hear themselves and those around them. Ternström (1999) investigated this and coined the term "self to other ratio" for singers. This is a measurement of the ratio of the sound level output from an individual singer in relation to the other singers. Ternström's results suggested that there are situations in which the levels of the other singers could be too high causing individual singers to over sing with poor intonation; something that could be exacerbated by high levels of reverberation. If on the other hand the level of the other singers is too low, perhaps as a result of spacing the singers too far apart in a non-reverberant environment (Daugherty 2003), then intonation could also suffer.

- *Ubiquity of instruments tuned in or close to equal temperament.* We hear music in many situations: In live concerts; when we choose to listen to recordings; as background in shops and restaurants; on the radio and the television; and in almost every situation in western culture the tuning is based on equal temperament. This is especially the case when electronic musical instruments are employed because their tuning is accurately preserved in equal temperament. Sound will be heard by the unborn baby and will be essentially in equal temperament, which will be established as the underlying musical tuning framework. In addition, early choral experiences are likely to have been accompanied in rehearsal and performance by an acoustic piano, electronic keyboard or organ and this ubiquity of equal temperament will reinforce that underlying framework. Singers in groups tuning in non-equal temperament when singing *a cappella* singing require focused listening as well as conscious awareness and subsequent variation of their own sung output to those of the singers around them. This will be somewhat hampered by everyday experiences over years of equal tempered listening, potentially resulting in a sub-conscious holding back when it comes to pitch shifting. In another experiment using the exercise shown in Figure

43.1, where four sopranos and four altos sang with the other three parts electronically synthesized over headphones, it was found that when the electronic parts were tuned in equal temperament, all eight singers sang on average flat, but when the electronic parts were tuned in just temperament all eight singers sang on average sharp (Howard et al. 2013).

- *Corporate intention to stay in-tune.* In many choirs there is a sense that to go out of tune overall is wrong and any such tendency should be combatted, typically by accompanying *a cappella* sections on a piano or other keyboard instrument a number of times. Such practice mitigates against in-tune singing between parts. It can also build a dependence on the presence of the accompaniment itself, which can prevent the build up of confidence in the group to sing *a cappella* thereby limiting overall development of an important performance skill. The dichotomy here is the overall subject of the chapter; to sing in-tune within a piece requires a shift in pitch overall and this latter point is typically seen at face value to be something that should be avoided at all costs.

Bearing in mind these additional effects, which will vary with singers, their positioning and the local acoustics of the environment, it is clear that the art of choral singing has a number of influencing factors when it comes to a consideration of accuracy in intonation. Investigation of the influence of the use of just intonation on the overall pitch of a piece of music with musical key change will be influenced by such factors, but it would appear based on the experimental data offered above that there is good reason to accept such an influence. It is the case that a number of the influencing factors will be familiar to professional singers who will compensate for some of them by making small changes to their position relative to the other singers and, for example, make use of their music folders as sound reflectors in order to ensure that they can hear themselves and their colleagues appropriately.

The Society for the Preservation and Encouragement of Barber Shop Quartet Singing in America is very aware of this effect and guidance is provided for the *lead* and *harmony* singers in barbershop music as follows:

> The Lead has the responsibility for singing the melody and staying in key. The harmony singers support the Lead by singing harmony in tune with the melody. All singers have the responsibility for preserving the tonal center of the song. Essentially we use just intonation for harmonic tuning while remaining true to the established tonal center.
>
> (Richards 2001, p. 16)

This instruction is clear: The lead singer maintains the overall pitch of the piece while the harmony singers sing in-tune with the lead singer. In the context of choral singing the effect is not well-known and the author is not aware of guidance provided to choral directors or choral singers on this topic. The notion that going out-of-tune is wrong is not necessarily the case and this suggests that some strategy needs to be in the minds of choral directors to deal with this if they want their singers to progress through a piece singing in-tune vertically chord-by-chord.

It is also worth spending a moment dwelling on what the alternative approach might involve if singers sang in equal temperament. Howard (2007, p. 314) suggests that:

Another facet to consider is that tuning intervals in equal temperament would demand the strong conviction of memory based on exposure to equal temperament from an early age to be able to place the notes accurately, because there is no readily available physical guide to be derived, such as the absence of beating. Given how unable most singers tend to be at accurately pitching a specified interval above a reference when singing alone, it is unlikely that such a memory for equal temperament is available. It seems reasonable to suppose that they are making use of some psychoacoustic or psychophysical consequence of singing their note alongside the notes of other parts, such as beating or greater consonance, respectively.

Summary and conclusions

Singing in-tune involves tuning intervals such that they are consonant as opposed to dissonant, with as many individual harmonics as possible of each note being exactly in-tune with those of other notes. This is the definition of just temperament, which singers do appear to use when singing *a cappella*. A direct consequence of this is that the overall pitch of a piece of *a cappella* music will tend to drift in a manner that is predictable mathematically and has been shown herein for a four-part (SATB) exercise and two Bach chorales. Measurements on vocal quartets for these pieces of music, where the fundamental frequencies used by the four individual singers have been accurately measured using four electrolaryngographs, have indicated that the pitch drift exhibited by the groups does follow the tend predicted. In addition, a number of compounding factors that might tend to mitigate against pitch drift in performance have been discussed as a means of suggesting why these trends might not be followed exactly. Overall, it is clear that the tendency to drift in pitch overall with musical key change is strong and its basis can be attributed at least in part to the tendency for *a cappella* singers to tune using just temperament.

This tendency for an overall pitch shift to occur as a fundamental facet of *a cappella* singing is typically not recognized or understood, whether in performance by either amateur or professional choral directors and choral singers, in recording studios by recording engineers and producers, or by singing teachers in singing studios. It is, however, clearly understood in professional ensemble groups working one-to-a-part (Potter 2000, Chapter 13). There is a clear need here for education as to the basis for the effect and what it means in performance practice. While as indicated above, the Society for the Preservation and Encouragement of Barber Shop Quartet Singing in America has taken note of the tendency and promulgated appropriate performance advice (Richards 2001), there is not clear guidance on this point available in contemporary choral pedagogy. Indeed, many choral directors who become aware that the overall pitch is changing in rehearsal will note that this is happening, stop the piece and ask the choir to start again because they are going out-of-tune. Such practice is not an appropriate response to an effect which has its own roots in tuning, the very thing that they are trying to mitigate against.

FURTHER READING

Barbour, J.M. (1953). *Tuning and Temperament: A Historical Survey*. East Lansing: Michigan State College Press.

Iscaoff, S. (2003). *Temperament*. New York: First Vintage Books.

Lloyd, L.S. and Boyle, H. (1978). *Intervals, Scales and Temperaments*. New York: St. Martin's Press.

REFERENCES

Abberton, E.R.M., Howard, D.M., and Fourcin, A.J. (1989). Laryngographic assessment of normal voice: a tutorial. *Clinical Linguistics and Phonetics* 3: 281–296.

Bohrer, J.C.S. (2002). *Intonational strategies in ensemble singing*. PhD dissertation, University of London.

Carlsson, A., Davidsson, H., Ruiter-Feenstra, P., Dunthorne, S., and Speerstra, J. (2000). *Tracing the Organ's Masters' Secret* [GOart publications, No. 2]. Göteborg, Sweden: Göteborg University.

Cowley, R. (2010). Knowledge and skill in teaching registers: A reflection on practice. In: S. Harrison (ed.), *Perspectives on Teaching Singing*, pp. 122–140. Bowen Hills: Australian Academic Press.

Daugherty, J. (2003). Choir spacing and formation: Choral sound preferences in random, synergistic, and gender-specific chamber choir placements. *International Journal of Research in Choral Singing* 1(1): 48–59.

Devaney, J. and Ellis, D.P.W. (2008). empirical approach to studying intonation tendencies in polyphonic vocal performances. *Journal of Interdisciplinary Music Studies* 2(1 and 2): 141–156.

Glasberg, B.R. and Moore, B.C.J. (1990). Derivation of auditory filter shapes from notched-noise data. *Hearing Research* 47: 103–138.

Helmholtz, H. (1954). *On the Sensations of Tone*, 2nd edn. [1885 translation by A.J. Ellis of the 1877 4th edn.]. New York: Dover.

Howard, D.M. (2007). Intonation drift in *a capella* SATB quartet singing with key modulation. *Journal of Voice* 21(3): 300–315.

Howard, D.M. (2009). Electroglottography/electrolaryngography. In: M.P. Fried and A. Ferlito (eds.), *The Larynx*, 3rd edn, pp. 227–243. San Diego: Plural Press.

Howard, D.M., Daffern, H., and Brereton, J. (2013). Four-part choral synthesis system for investigating intonation in a cappella choral singing. *Logopedics Phoniatrics Vocology* 38(3): 135–142. doi:10.3109/14015439.2013.812143.

Meffen, J. (1982). *A Guide to Tuning Musical Instruments*. Newton Abbot, Devon, U.K.: David and Charles.

Plomp, R. and Levelt, W.J.M. (1965). Tonal consonance and critical bandwidth. *Journal of the Acoustical Society of America* 38: 548–560.

Potter, J. (2000). *The Cambridge Companion to Singing*. Cambridge: Cambridge University Press.

Richards, J. (2001). *The Physics of Barbershop Sound* [Stock No. 3083]. Kenosha, WI: Society for the Preservation and Encouragement of Barber Shop Quartet Singing in America Inc.

Ternström, S. (1999). Preferred self-to-other ratios in choir singing. *Journal of the Acoustical Society of America* 105(6): 3563–3574.

Ternström, S. and Sundberg, J. (1988). Intonation precision of choir singers. *Journal of the Acoustical Society of America* 84(1): 59–69.

Vurma, A. and Ross, J. (2004). Intonation accuracy when singing in ensemble. In: *Proceedings of the Conference of Interdisciplinary Musicology* (CIM04), pp. 160–161, Graz, Austria, April 15–18.

Ward, W.D. (1998). Absolute Pitch. In: D. Deutsch (ed.), *The Psychology of Music*, 2nd edn, pp. 265–298. San Diego: Academic Press.

CHAPTER 44

··

CHORAL SINGERS' PERCEPTIONS OF MUSICAL LEADERSHIP

··

DAG JANSSON

WHAT IS CONDUCTING?

··

THIS chapter is about musical leadership and specifically the role of the choral conductor. The conductor role is familiar to anyone who has sung in a school choir or has been in the audience of live or televised concerts. The role is prominent in concert programs and is associated with ensembles whenever they are profiled or critiqued. The presence of a conductor is largely taken for granted by the layman as well as the scholar, as self-evident as the presence of instrumentalists and singers. The purpose of this chapter is to look through this veil of self-evidence by reflecting on what conducting *is*, why we *need* it and what makes it *work*. Contrary to most writing on conducting and conductors, this chapter will take the choral singer's viewpoint, describing how musical leadership is perceived and experienced by those upon whom conducting is intended to impact.

The conductor role, as we know it today, is a product of romanticism in the nineteenth century, although musical leadership is a much older and wider notion (Galkin 1988; Schonberg 1967). The shapers of modern day conducting, Wagner (1869) and Berlioz (1843)—famous conductors of their time—were also those who started to write about it, a tradition that continued into the twentieth century. The early writers on choral conducting were Kurt Thomas (1935) and Pavel Chesnokov (1940). These represent the "maestro writing" tradition: the great master sharing his own experience and ideas. Maestro writing, as it evolved, stayed within an intentional and prescriptive perspective, whether it concentrated on technical skills or took a broader view of the role. Most writing was in the form of handbooks, some even denoted as such in the title, aiming at supporting the training and development of conductors.[1] Scientific research on conducting is a more recent phenomenon, and three

---

[1] Some of the important sources on choral conducting (ordered by publication year) include: Lewis (1945), Ehmann (1949), Inghelbrecht (1949), Åhlen (1949), Lindeman (1957), Uggla (1979), Stanton (1971), Holst (1973), Ericsson and colleagues (1974), Gordon (1977), Kaplan (1985), Dahl (2002), Emmons

important observations can be made on conducting research from the last few decades: (1) it is predominantly US based; (2) it is pedagogy-oriented (mostly in a high school and college setting); and (3) with few exceptions, it takes a "reductionist" view, isolating some particular angle, which is investigated by a quantitative approach. Recent European research takes a more holistic view, recognizing that musical experience also involves meaning making, and is therefore approached more qualitatively. While still having conductor training or conducting practice in mind, some of this research pays significant attention to the philosophical foundations of the conductor role.[2] Others draw on the parallels with general leadership, although to varying degrees assuming that leading art is not necessarily the same as leading anything else.[3]

The maestro writing tradition clearly shows that conductors at the outset took ownership of the notion of musical leadership. Following conductors' definitional powers, *how to do it* becomes the prevalent perspective. As outsiders to the profession take interest in the conducting phenomenon, it becomes the study object of the social sciences, ranging from the complex organization of symphony orchestras[4] to the effects on health and well-being of the community choir[5], and the natural sciences (especially neurology and cognition).[6] There is however little research that asks fundamental questions about what conducting *is* and how we may understand it. Conducting gesture is the most visible aspect of the role, to the extent that it is an iconic feature familiar to everyone, but it is clearly only one out of many features. Durrant (1994) pinpoints that research is inconclusive when it comes to determining the importance of conducting gesture versus other features. Moreover, the applicability of the various features of conducting (like rehearsing style, gestural repertoire, voice teaching and so on) across different contexts is not well understood.

Conductors can no longer claim full ownership of the phenomenon, as pedagogues, sociologists, and cognitive scientists engage with it. Who engages with conducting has strong bearing upon the research perspective and approach, and consequently what knowledge can be generated and which aspect of reality that we are able to see. Maestro writing inevitably attends to the *intended reality*, as it is oriented towards what needs to be done to achieve certain results. The social and natural sciences are able to explain the structures that exist and the processes that take place within and outside the ensemble organizations—an *observed reality*. The most striking aspect about the conducting research literature, in my judgment, has been the absence of the *impact view*, specifically the singer experience as a source of insight into how conducting works. The focus of this chapter is to let the voices of the singers be

and Chase (2006), and Jordan (2009). Lewis (1945) and Inghelbrecht (1949) deal with orchestral as well as choral conducting. Important sources on orchestral conducting in the maestro writing tradition include Boult (1949) and Malko (1950).

  [2] See for example Fowler and Swan (1987), Durrant (2003), Koivunen (2003), Durrant (2009), Garnett (2009), Koivunen and Wennes (2011).

  [3] See for example Goldstein (1987), Allen (1988), Davidson (1995), Armstrong and Armstrong (1996), Guise (2001), Butke (2006), Wis (2007), Springborg (2010), Woodward and Funk (2010), Ladkin and Taylor (2010).

  [4] See for example Schonberg (1967), Lebrecht (1997), Mintzberg (1998), Koivunen (2003).

  [5] See for example Bengtsson and Laxvik (1982), Ruud (1997), Durrant (2005), Langston and Barrett (2008), Balsnes (2009), Parker (2009).

  [6] See for example Godøy and Leman (2010).

heard, in this context their verbally expressed experience with conducting and conductors. It is the choral singers who are allowed to frame conducting and it is their *perceived reality* that is described. The singer experience is conceptualized into three models of how choral singers encounter conductors and conducting: (1) the legitimacy model, (2) the enactment model, and (3) the notion of elusive perfection. The description underlying the models is the result of a recent study of choral singer experience in Norway.[7] Although the interviewees are all musically educated and acting as professional or semi-professional choral singers, the findings are probably valid beyond the researched sample, although to varying degrees. This chapter should offer a starting point for conductors and researchers in terms of how we may think and talk about the conducting phenomenon.

As we begin to investigate what conducting is, a number of questions arise concerning what domain we are in and where its boundaries are. There is something slippery about the whole notion, at the same time being familiar and yet also a mystery. This might be said of leadership in general as well—in fact, leadership is an even slipperier concept, though a pervasive one. The media is obsessed with leadership and leaders, attributing otherwise collective achievements and triumphs to whomever is in charge, whether in business, politics, or music. Conducting's relationship to leadership is evident simply for etymological reasons— *conducere* is the Latin verb to *lead with*—but the nature of that relationship is far from clear. Some scholars simply state that conductors by definition are leaders (Price and Bryo 2002; Wis 2007). But what does it mean that a conductor leads the music, or the ensemble? And is conducting simply a specific realization of a general notion of leadership, or, conversely, is leadership merely one aspect of the conductor's role? Furthermore, what is the relationship between conducting and teaching? Should the conductor be seen as a leader or a teacher, or both? Is it even possible that all of these questions miss the point—that the conductor is in fact nothing more than a co-musician, an ensemble member alongside singers and instrumentalists, a non-sound-producing musician with some special tasks, a specialist like everyone else in the ensemble? This chapter will not offer an answer to all these questions. Still, the choral singer viewpoint does offer important insight into the conducting phenomenon, its legitimacy, its various facets, and boundaries.

[7] The project aims at understanding musical leadership through the lived experience of the choral singer, as expressed in conversation. The study was based on a hermeneutic-phenomenological approach (van Manen 1990). I interviewed 22 singers, 10 male and 12 female, in four cities across Norway. They have college or university degrees in music/musicology with extensive exposure to different conductors, for some of them very many conductors. Together, the singers have been exposed on a regular basis to more than 30 of the most prominent conductors currently operating in Norway. In addition, more than half of the singers have experience with a number of project conductors, including foreign guest conductors. Each interview took place in the form of a free-flowing dialogue about conducting and conductors, departing from one common question: What is great musical leadership, and what's going on when you experience it? I deliberately abstained from definitions—of leadership and conducting—at the outset of this work, developing the themes and categories by how the interviewed singers talked about their experiences. The reflection level and expressivity of the interviewed singers was so strong that I found it fully possible to interpret the interviews largely using their own words and concepts. The three models presented in this chapter are a result of the interview analysis. However, as commented in the text, they partly build on, are inspired by, and complement the writings of Ladkin (2008), Nielsen (2012), Weick (1995), and Durrant (2003).

THE PHENOMENOLOGY OF CONDUCTING IMPACT

When studying the impact of conducting and conductors, we could in principle *observe* how singers are affected. We could assess how we as listeners are *affected* by the sounding music. We could potentially *explain* the impact by some structural theory from the social or natural sciences. But even a whole host of such studies would not produce a comprehensive picture of the conducting phenomenon. The effect of choral leadership will necessarily have to go through those who are directly involved in the leadership act and who create meaning from it: the singers. One avenue to understanding how conducting impacts singers is through their perceptions, their lived experience, as made available through verbal dialogue. This knowledge angle lends itself naturally to phenomenology as a philosophical platform. Although phenomenology is a rather heterogeneous movement that still lacks a unifying definition of the term (Zahavi 2007, p. 122), three important cornerstones remain in place. Phenomenology's first cornerstone is that the prime source of knowledge about the world emerges from the first-person perspective. Every phenomenon is an appearance of something to someone—that is, it is perceptually revealed as opposed to objectively given. The locus of conducting's impact, of course, is the singer/musician. This is where leadership behavior is transformed into musical consequence. The second cornerstone is the immediacy of the phenomenon, which can only be understood by how it appears. In this regard, then, it is the appearance of conducting (and the conductor) that represents the reality, not the structures behind or around it. For the singer, it does not matter what lies behind the conductor's leadership—his or her training, particular style, or intentions. It is how the leadership is perceived that creates the impact: perception is reality. The corporeal, pre-lingual nature of human gestures reinforces the immediacy of the conducting phenomenon. This is not to reject that we are also affected by aspects of leadership outside the immediate present moment, like prior knowledge about the conductor's stylistic preferences, reputation, and public image. Of course it is true that the conducting phenomenon could be investigated primarily via social structures and processes, but an inquiry devoted to what musical leadership *is* and how it *works* must start with what it means for the individual singer in the music-making situation.

The third cornerstone is that phenomenological analysis involves an investigation of the various appearances of an object. Given the richness and multivalence of conducting, its study must reckon with a multitude of appearances—not only situations, music genres, ensemble types, and competencies, but also, at the micro level, breathing, hand movements, musical phrasing, error correction, and so on. Phenomenological thinking copes well with—even favors—complexity and richness over simplicity and unity. The notion of ambiguity is not a problem either, but an inherent characteristic of the phenomenon itself, and it is therefore a research principle and research topic in its own right. The methodological principle of creative variation even uses changing appearances and a lack of unity as a means of uncovering the essential features of the phenomenon. When the same conductor is described by one singer as pompous and by another as sincere, they are together introducing a tension that may in fact characterize the conductor role.

In sum, the three epistemological cornerstones of phenomenology suit the inquiry into how singers perceive conductors and conducting and how we may understand this encounter. The singers' life world is revealed through human consciousness, to which the primary access is human conversation. In fact, the qualitative interview as a methodology is to a large extent based on and shaped by phenomenological thinking.[8] Through this type of interview, qualitative descriptions of the person's life world and interpretations of its meaning are captured—seeking to find the non-trivial in a familiar practice. The interview welcomes the interviewee's own experience, seeking precise descriptions and key significances while suspending the researcher's prior knowledge. With the premise that a pure description is not possible, that interpretation always comes into play, hermeneutic-phenomenology (van Manen 1995) offers a practical approach to investigate conducting as lived experience.

LEGITIMIZING THE CONDUCTOR ROLE AS "SENSE-MAKING"

We are accustomed to seeing the choral leader in front of the performing choir. Even those who have never sung or played in an ensemble are familiar with the role, to the extent that they easily would be able to mimic the visual appearance of a conductor's posture and movements. The conductor has become a highly recognizable, almost iconic figure. At the same time, outsiders may ask questions about what conductors really do and why this figure is needed. The conductor role is at the same time familiar and enigmatic. Choral singers, of course, have at least experienced the practical doings of their conductor, from organizing rehearsals to synchronizing the start of a musical piece during a performance. Most singers will probably also have experienced how the conductor has inspired or demotivated their own singing contribution and affected the choir's musical expression. To varying degrees, choral singers have reflected systematically on why they want someone to lead the music and the music event. Choirs also sing without a conductor, more so in certain musical styles and for smaller ensembles. Still, all choral singers will at least have experienced fragments of singing without a conductor, whether a conductor steps out of the role for a moment in the rehearsing process or as a stage experiment. Although the question of *why we need a conductor* may not be top of mind for every choral singer, singers certainly are able to reflect on the question and provide insight into the *legitimacy* of the role.

The legitimacy of the conductor role (*the why*) is of course a broad theme that will entail different connotations across all the various imaginable and unimaginable choir types and music situations. Often, the legitimacy of the role is defined in administrative terms, by how it is regulated by statutes, employment contracts and so on. Choral leadership may even be a secondary role, embedded in some other activity like primary school teaching and social work. However, *the why* must be rooted in a more fundamental experience of the music-making act, by what contribution the conductor may bring to the music and the ensemble. Despite all the attractive features of direct communication between the choir members when there is no conductor, choral singers experience five distinct reasons for why they

---

[8] See for example Kvale's interview model (Kvale 1996; Kvale, 2001, p. 40).

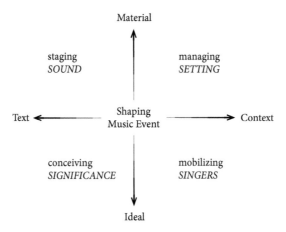

FIGURE 44.1 The legitimacy model of the five dimensions of sense-making.

want a conductor to lead, for which the overarching theme is *making sense* of and from the music event. The five dimensions of sense-making that the singers identify are (1) conceiving significance (the musical idea), (2) mobilizing singers, (3) staging sound, (4) managing the setting, and (5) shaping the overall music event. These dimensions are depicted as the *legitimacy model* in Figure 44.1.

Conceiving significance

The lower left area of the map represents textual meaning—creating the musical idea. The singers expect the conductor to understand the music, discover a purpose within unfamiliar material, act as an excavator of hidden meaning, and be a mediator or spokesperson between the composer and the singers. When singers talk about the musical idea, they are referring to the music as material (as opposed to context) and associate it directly with musical will and musical intention. The musical idea is therefore perceived as something distinctly non-material that exists before the sounding music, then later coexists with it and is adapted by it. A cornerstone of the conductor role is therefore bringing to light the significance latent in the music material. The musical idea is the conductor's conception of the music, but creating musical meaning is not an isolated affair but an act of alignment. This conception process involves understanding and reconceptualizing composer ideas as well as later associations based in performance and reception history. One singer exemplifies how significance underpins the sounding music as well as the link with the ensemble:

> I consider the conductor to be a leader, an interpreter of music on paper, who tries to recreate his or her interpretation of the music—with the instrument available, of course. And then be able to show it. It is one thing to understand the music that you (the conductor) see on paper, but you also need to be able to express it through your own body language and instructions that make the others understand the music, or the perception of the music, and be able to execute it.

Conductors must align their ideas with these past ideas, even when they deliberately choose to break with tradition. Conductors must also align with the ensemble, because the conductor may not be the only one with a musical idea. Every singer represents a possible idea, even if it is largely unarticulated, with which the conductor must negotiate, gesturally, or verbally.

Mobilizing singers

The primary source of meaning outside of the music material itself is the ensemble—the singers produce every sound and every expressive detail. How they think and feel, what drives them or holds them back, and what commitment and understanding they bring to the music-making situation all affect the sounding music. What we hear, in short, reflects the meaning singers infuse into the performance situation. The interviewees recognize the way in which great leadership can unleash their efforts, focus their energy, and liberate their expressiveness. Poor or absent leadership, conversely, tends to result in music that is lifeless and dull. Singers want to be mobilized and yearn for what good leadership can do to their vocal contribution. They have a zest for it, which the conductor may reinforce or destroy. The word zest is chosen to denote something that is more active than inspiration and more pleasurable than enthusiasm. If "significance" denotes meaning associated with the music material, then "mobilized singers" denotes meaning arising from the interpersonal experience between singers and between the individual singer and the conductor. The conductor may mobilize singers in a number of ways, from the display of devotion to achieving the proper balance between control and empowerment, from deep musical knowledge to its corresponding embodiment. A conductor's impact upon the singers in this respect may represent the pivotal point where the legitimacy of the role itself—the legitimacy *by design*—becomes legitimacy *earned* for the individual conductor. One description of such a situation highlights many of the facets of great musical leadership:

> That is a blissful situation. The music is in focus, and the conductor knows exactly what he or she needs to do to make it work. The conductor listens; he hears where to put his finger and fix things. And he unites the ensemble to sound like one choir and pulls everyone to share one thought, so that all concentrate on one thing. Oh, this is life! It could in fact be just two bars, or getting a passage right that you have worked on for a long time, or you hear that it all comes together, or you master everything better than before. Someone who is able to use movements so that as a singer I breathe correctly, who has movements and gestures that make me just flow with the music, who is able to show it in a physical way, so that as a singer I may sing freely. In those moments, I am a happy singer.

This singer exemplifies the three corners of the legitimacy model outlined in the preceding sections. The conductor has a musical idea, is well integrated with the choir (listens and knows what interventions to make), is able to liberate her as a singer, and stages a unified sound. Her statement also exemplifies the sense-making aspect of the experience by the momentary sensation—the split second where it all comes together and deep meaning is created.

Staging sound

The upper left area of the model, the sounding music, represents the manifestation of the musical idea in the form of vibrating sound waves that are audible to those present. But sound is not only material manifestation of the musical idea but also the manifestation of the ensemble's capabilities, will, and effort. The sounding music draws its meaning from the music material (text) as well as the ensemble (context). Or more precisely, while the sounding music is a material manifestation of the musical idea, the latent meaning of the score comes to life as the choir engages with it in the music-making act. The singers see the conductor as well positioned, in terms of physical location as well as role and responsibilities, to stage the sounding music. Staging sound also encompasses error detection and correction over the course of the rehearsing process. The conductor is able to hear what comes out, balance the sound, amplify singer contributions, and ensure that the intended expressivity actually carries over to the audience. He or she stages the ensemble as well as the music, in fact, acting as a sound director—*mettur-en-son* or *klangregisseur*—in the manner of the theatrical director. This dialogue exemplifies the sound directing aspect of the conductor role:

> A little unique for choirs, perhaps, compared to instrumental ensembles is that what is perceived as a lot here is perceived as very little out there. You think you sing distinctly, but you don't sing distinctly. You think you are exaggerating that phrasing, but you aren't.
> *Does that mean that the conductor functions as some sort of amplifier? Amplifier of effects?*
> Yes, absolutely.

Furthermore, the choral leader not only stages the concert sound, as an event specific manifestation, but also the ensemble's sound representing a lasting, potentially long-term feature of musical leadership.

Managing setting

The upper right area represents the material context of the music event—denoted as the *setting*. There are managerial aspects of the conducting role—that is, activities that are not limited to musical leadership but apply in some fashion to all forms of leadership. In terms of conducting, such activities might include a range of near-music activities such as singer auditioning, contract negotiation with external soloists and instrumentalists and tour planning, as well as non-music activities such as ensemble funding and marketing. In some ensemble types, and for certain organizational constructs, it is easy to imagine that managerial structures are non-distinguishable from the music-making organization itself (the opera choir and the opera orchestra would probably represent such cases). For some choral conductors, the setting may be beyond their influence. Iszatt-White (2011) argues that context has traditionally (and wrongly) been seen as external to leadership work, whereas leadership would be better understood as "mutual elaboration," according to "the inseparability of action and context which this entails" (2011, p. 132). Whatever the given conductor's degree of control over the setting, he or she cannot disregard how the setting influences the other sense-making dimensions or disregard it in his or her leadership scope.

Shaping the music event

The fifth legitimacy theme is about unifying the ensemble's efforts. Choral singers find that the conductor does make a difference. Conductors are in a position to influence the music, and their minute cues may have substantial effects on the musical flow. The (effective) conductor unifies the ensemble, both concentrating and amplifying individual expression. Once singers accept the conductor, he or she has the power to shape the music right at the meeting point of significance, sound, singers, and setting. The setting, encompassing venue, acoustics, and repertoire and so on, determines the constraints within which singers may realize their musicality according to the conductor's musical idea, and make salient the significance of the music. In turn, singers are willing to abandon their own musical ideas when the conductor convincingly proposes a different idea. Singers are voluntarily letting themselves be disciplined; in fact, conductors may mobilize a yearning to be caught by and be subject to the musical flow. Henri Bergson (1910, p. 7) points out that music may "suspend the normal flow of our sensations and ideas." This effect is contingent on the invitation (and conviction) of the conductor, and while the efforts of the singers produce the sound, the conductor stages the sound as collective and unified expression. This role is facilitated by the fact that the conductor listens while everyone else must sing, so he or she can control and reconceive meaning during the continuous relay between original musical idea and sounding manifestation. This involves a delicate balancing act between providing central control and empowering singers to sing freely.

Each of the four corners of the legitimacy model represents aspects of meaning in and from the music event. In the absence of a conductor, meaning would also be created. When singers allow for and favor a conductor role, it is because they see its contribution to be unique in two ways: (1) it is more *effective* to have a single, designated leader, and (2) it is more *efficient* to have a single, designated leader.

Effective means that the impact is greater, for example being in the best position to hear the balanced sound, to correct and amplify the music, whether it is diction, phrasing, or timbre, ensuring that the individual singer efforts get out there, beyond the stage front. Although smaller ensembles can sing well without a conductor, the singers experience that singing without a conductor usually leads to a duller and edgeless sound.

Efficient means that energy or time is saved. An example of being more efficient is to have one leader taking care of the rehearsal process, both in terms of how to manage time, but also in terms of esthetic judgment. Even in the performing situation, the conductor provides efficiency. When the singers know that the conductor keeps an overview and guides critical details, the conductor unburdens the singers, allowing them to focus. They don't need to sense absolutely everything all the time. Instead, they can pay more attention to their own vocal technique, bodily preparedness, tone production and musical expression. The combined effectiveness-efficiency advantage is what allows the fifth element of the legitimacy model—the conductor as the overall *shaper* of the music event.

ENACTING CHORAL LEADERSHIP

Singers find the conductor role meaningful because it provides unique contributions to the music event. Choral singers describe their encounter with conductors as a rich experience, encompassing a host of themes, ranging from the most tangible aspects of rehearsing and performing to how the conductor exposes his/her involvement with the music and the ensemble. When everything works at its best, singers experience a deep intersubjectivity where time is standing still and roles are transcended. This section will discuss what constitutes the enactment of choral leadership.

The various themes that describe the encounter between conductor and ensemble arise from conversations about personal experiences. The phenomenology of conducting impact is about understanding these experiences. Singers provide different entry points to their experience, a named conductor, a particular rehearsal, a peak performing moment, or some recurring irritation over a certain conductor behavior. The enactment of choral leadership may be understood as a layered phenomenon. A conceptualization is visualized by the enactment model in Figure 44.2. The three levels are inspired by Donna Ladkin's (2008) notions of mastery, congruence, and purposefulness. Her simple, yet powerful model of "leading beautifully" was developed from a case study of multi-artist Bobby McFerrin.[9] The enactment model also bears resemblance with Frede Nielsen's (2012) model of musical meaning, a stratified spherical model with the most tangible aspects of music in the outer strata and the most personal and existential aspects in its core. The enactment model and Colin Durrant's (2003) "super-model conductor" also have many themes in common. The difference is the viewing angle; Durrant's model is a comprehensive set of "must master" attributes of a conductor, whereas the enactment model captures how these attributes are perceived by the choral singers and made meaningful in the music-making act. Naturally, these two perspectives have significant overlaps.

Mastery

Mastery is about those skills and competences the conductor brings to the choral situation. They become visible through how they are applied. In fact, singers do not experience conductor skills and competences as discrete elements but by how they come into play in the conductor act and the conductor-being in its entirety. Whereas the sum of skills and competences reside as "latent" with the conductor, mastery manifests itself in the present moment where they are put into use. Very importantly, leading beautifully not only requires

---

[9] The innermost layer in the enactment model is denoted "intersubjective space," rather than "purposefulness" in Ladkin's model. This is not meant as a proposed change of Ladkin's model, rather an elaboration that arises from the fact that purpose and meaning are a complex web of relationships between singers and conductor, and that meaning is created and mediated intersubjectively within the ensemble. The middle layer in the enactment model is denoted "coherence" rather than "congruence" in Ladkin's model. This is not meant as a distinction between the two terms, but to reserve "corporeal congruence" as a subset of "coherence," the way in which the various facets of "coherence" come together as bodily manifestation.

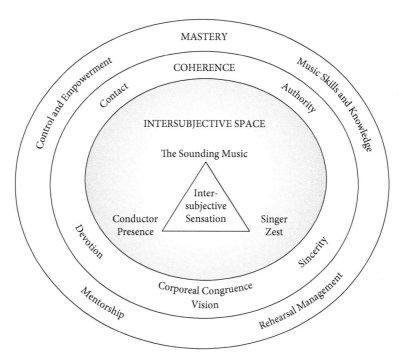

FIGURE 44.2 The enactment model of choral leadership.

knowing what to do, but also blending the various interventions, applying them in the right quantity/strength and choosing the appropriate timing. In Ladkin's words, mastery is about form as well as measure, drawing on Plato's notion of beauty (Ladkin 2008, p. 34).

There are four main themes in the mastery level. *Control and empowerment* and *mentorship* are about how the conductor integrates with the ensemble—blending control, delegation, help, and demands. This applies to the rehearsing situation as well as performance. Control/empowerment is a general leadership theme, but it must also be considered an element of mastery that is strongly tied to the unique features of conducting, as it relies on understanding a music flow, its cues, and its gestural possibilities. In the performing situation, singers expect the conductor to be in control, while not controlling the singers excessively, thereby inhibiting their ability to sing freely and come forward with their own musicality and expressivity. One singer statement exemplifies the value of unobtrusive leadership:

> The conductor has a way of communicating with the singers that is kind of relaxing; you feel that you get the space to be with the music, that it is not too micro-managed, perhaps.

Empowerment may also imply relinquishing control to the point where some ambiguity and "risk" is created in the performing situation, thereby mobilizing singers to assume responsibility and be on the edge. Empowerment in the rehearsing situation is more on the practical level, for example by how instruction is mixed with self-learning.

Mentorship involves the notions of control/empowerment by how the conductor guides singers when rehearsing and performing. But mentorship is a wider and deeper engagement in the development of singers, by assessing what they need and responding to these needs.

Good mentoring is seeing singers exactly where they are, understanding what intervention will make them progress, and achieving optimal timing of the intervention. The two main levers are help and demand and the appropriate application of each requires situational mastery. Singers perceive help that is not needed to be condescending (for example, vocal instruction of skilled singers) and demands to be demotivating where competence is wanting (for example, fixing a difficult pitch problem). Mentorship requires a certain generosity on the part of the conductor, letting singer needs take precedence and avoiding unnecessary lecturing as well as futile expectations.

Rehearsal management shares its characteristics with most other types of projects. The rehearsing project is a goal-oriented endeavor, with any activity set being a means to an end. Musical rehearsing involves time constraints, schedules, milestones, unexpected events, and corrective action, as is found in any other subject matter domain. However, rehearsing as an artistic process may also deviate significantly from a non-artistic process. The most efficient process may not necessarily lead to the most impactful performance. Clear goals may also be counterproductive to an exciting end result. The absence of ambiguity and crisis may bring premature closure to the musical idea. Having said this, choral singers largely appreciate the predictable rehearsing project as well as the single well-run rehearsal.

Music skills and knowledge contain many of the features that are unique for a music project. The sub-themes include:

- Repertoire knowledge
- Score analysis
- Language
- Aural skills and error detection
- Voice technique
- Gestural skills

Music skills and knowledge may be what is most explicitly taught at music academies, and it is hard to imagine rehearsing without them. Still, they are very far from being sufficient— they may not even be the determining factor. While there are examples of conductors whom singers appreciate even when mastery is wanting, there is no question that singers prefer a conductor who comes to the rehearsal situation with a high degree of mastery. Music skills and knowledge is the mastery element that is most specifically related to the music domain, but only gestural skills are specifically related to conducting. The other capability elements are somewhat more generic and are relevant outside the music domain. However, choral leadership mastery is about the situational *application* of capabilities, which goes well beyond the *possession* of capabilities.

The placement of mastery as the outer layer of the model illustrates that these themes are the most outward and worldly features of musical leadership. They are also concrete and tangible, in that that they are part of university curricula, objects of conducting master classes, and foci of research projects. While there is no question about the value of the distinct conductor competences that constitute the mastery level, choral singers describe a depth of experience that cannot be understood only in terms of mastery. The musical leadership for which singers yearn can only be fully grasped via a deeper view of its enactment—by the access to the intersubjective space of musical sense-making that it enables. The mystique and magic commonly associated with great conducting is less of a mystery and more about the difficulty of articulating what goes on in the music-making moment. At its best, musical leadership simply exploits the possibilities latent in the intersubjective sensation to which the conductor and the ensemble commit, and which the conductor has a unique and particular responsibility to enable.

Coherence

The coherence layer is about the integrity of the conductor as human being and includes contact, devotion, sincerity, authority, vision, and will. *Contact* is perceived momentarily by how the conductor meets and engages with the choir. Contact goes beyond the visual, it is also experienced as a willingness on the part of the conductor to *be with* the choir in the musical flow. Contact involves a delicate balance between distance and intimacy. When singers expect the conductor to be *sincere*, it means that there are no false motives or hidden agendas. It requires a certain vulnerability, where the conductor is exposed with whatever faults and weaknesses may exist. Choral singers give of themselves and make themselves vulnerable in order to make great music, and they can only open up if there is reciprocity. A related and slightly overlapping theme is *devotion*, which is about the depth of commitment on the part of the conductor. It appears as passion for the music, but also as faithfulness and generosity towards choral singers—devotion involves a lasting quality of the engagement. *Authority* manifests itself in a number of ways, by competence, vision, will, and a type of forcefulness—there is no question about who is in charge. However, authority also seems to remain intact when conductors demonstrate humility or even make mistakes. There is an important distinction between having authority and being authoritarian, the latter perceived as conductor being centered on the self rather than the cause—the music. Conceiving the musical idea is one of the elements that legitimizes the conductor role. Enacting the idea comes through how the conductor is able to communicate his or her vision and exercise the will to make it happen. Musical *vision and will* therefore seems to be a pair of elements that is very tightly coupled, perhaps more so than in other leadership domains.

The coherence themes are very important for singers—they can be showstoppers or gate openers, as they unlock or shut the gates to the innermost layer. The interviewed singers give examples of high caliber conductors who have not succeeded because of their lack of sincerity or questions about their authority. Conversely, they also give example of a conductor, famous for his poor gestural and communicative skills, but where his devotion and passion is so compelling that he is nevertheless effective.

Because the gate openers are largely non-verbal perceptions, they must be understood as embodied phenomena, which, in order to be valid, require corporeal congruence. This congruence derives from conductor signals that are delivered in different modes (speech, posture, breath, hand movement, eye contact) that contain the same message (or at least do not contradict one another). With some allowance for vision and authority, the gate openers are generally ways of being that are unrelated to competencies. It is therefore possible to open gates when competence is lacking; conversely, gates may be shut even for the highly competent conductor. However, what the conductor does is inseparable from how he or she is being it. For example, devotion is exposed through how a conductor rehearses a certain piece of music. A lack of sincerity is exposed through how a conductor abuses his or her mentoring task. How a conductor technically solves certain gestural challenges may reveal weak authority or lack of contact with the singers. The conductor is continuously and visibly present, fully open for all of the perceptual powers of the singers. Singers talk about what conductors do, and their descriptions are filled with perceptions of how conductor tasks are enacted, which is inseparable from the conductor's embodied being.

The embodied nature of musical leadership makes gesture (in a broad sense) both a skill set (that is included in the mastery category) and a way of being through which the other gate openers are experienced visually. A variant of this duality also appears in Durrant's concept of three types of conducting gesture—literal, expressive, and supporting (Durrant 2003, p. 147). Literal gestures are indexical in that they indicate pulse, location, and direction in the musical flow. Expressive gestures suggest the character and nuances of the music, and they are emotive, in that they seek to elicit a corresponding vocal response on the part of the singers. Supporting gestures are intended to help singers breathe and sustain phrases. They enable favorable bodily conditions via a "mirroring" effect.[10] The conductor's gestural skill set matters, including posture, point of gravity, intense presence, and friendly eye contact. These qualities go beyond mere skilled mastery and blend with coherence themes like devotion, authority, and will.

Intersubjective space

The innermost layer is denoted intersubjective space. This is the common room of music-making. This is where the present moment is experienced, where the *sounding music* becomes past and the music flow is anticipated. This space is where *intersubjective sensation* takes place and meaning is created and shared. Singers expect a strong *conductor presence* to enable and open this space, while recognizing that it is maintained and nurtured by everyone present. Singers describe a yearning for this space. This is the holy grail for choral singers, rare and precious—a room where admittance is not guaranteed, and whose existence cannot be taken for granted. The room for music-making is a fragile and ephemeral construction, and access to it is enabled or disabled by the outer layers of the model. In the intersubjective space where music-making experience happens, distinct roles seem to vanish, boundaries between singers and conductor become blurred, and the leadership role is transcended. Singers refer to this space in different ways, but their descriptions involve a certain simultaneity of meaning and shared anticipation of the continued musical flow. The singers' intersubjective experience is expressed in a number of ways, as fused lives, seeing without eye contact, and understanding at the same time. These are "lived examples" of intersubjectivity, as described by Holgersen (2006) and Zahavi (2003). The space metaphor is suggested by a number of word images: confines in which there is security; a substance in which you are immersed; the music as an inside as opposed to the trivialities outside; an enclosure you can fall out of and get back into; and a proximity that prevents you from disappearing or withdrawing from one another. Intersubjective space is still experienced as a state of mind, of course, and Garnett (2009, p. 197) uses the phrase *common house of being* to denote a communal state of consciousness and the thought processes in which collective

---

[10] The mirroring effect was understood by the major discovery of mirror neurons (Winerman 2005). Mirror neurons represent a coupling between our sensory and motor apparatus, so that a singer's body is engaged when conducting gesture is perceived.

identities are formed, adding, "inhabitance is therefore the means by which the subjective becomes intersubjective."

Sense-making is more enactive than just understanding—it is the continuous relay of responding to new cues and understanding previous responses. When Weick (1995, p. 8) speaks about sense-making as creation, it follows that sense-making in a choir is co-creation, since the stream of cues is collectively produced by conductor and ensemble. Although the conductor may not necessarily make the same sense out of the musical flow as the singers, he or she is nevertheless affected by the actual sounding music. In the performing situation, the conductor must rely on a limited scope of gestural cues only, each of which is loaded with meaning beyond the gesture itself. The singers make sense of the conducting gestures as the cues invoke their own memories. This applies even in the case of prima vista singing, because sight-reading in every present moment involves anticipating the music flow, and once it has been read, musical meaning becomes memory that is then ready to be moderated by conducting cues.

As the conductor is conveying musical meaning in real time, he or she is making sense by providing direction. The conductor is also simultaneously part of the collective sensing of the musical flow. The duality of sense-making has an etymological parallel in the Latin root of sense and is also expressed by Weick as he points out that sense-making is both enactive and retrospective. When Holgersen (2006), in his exploration of musical intersubjectivity, draws on Husserl's distinction between operational intentionality and act-intentionality, this may likewise evoke the dual nature of sense-making. Operational intentionality makes sense by understanding where the musical flow is in any given moment, whereas act-intentionality gives sense by directing the continued flow. In a choral ensemble, the conductor is a sense-maker, creating sense by giving direction and also creating the intersubjective space where everyone may sense the musical flow, upon which renewed direction may be given. This is not to say that the conductor is the only "sensible" person in the midst of bewilderment and ignorance. Everyone in the choir is making sense of the music, and of what they do, but sense-making is a dedicated function of the conductor's position. The conductor has a particular responsibility to give sense to the ensemble and, as importantly, to sense what the ensemble does.

ELUSIVE PERFECTION: BALANCING SINGER NEEDS

It has been pointed out that research is inconclusive when it comes to determining the importance of conducting gesture in relation to other features, as well as the interplay between these features. Interviews with choral singers confirm that it is very difficult to pin down a conductor profile or practice that is universally best, or even good. Perfect choral leadership is simply a slippery notion. We might understand this in light of a series of balancing acts and tradeoffs that the conductor continuously has to make.

The enactment model described in the previous section is about *the how*. The choral singer experiences the musical leader as an integral phenomenon. For this reason, it is difficult to deconstruct the role and investigate singular themes. It is equally difficult to make claims about what great musical leadership is, as singers articulate widely different experiences and conflicting views. However, what could be misconstrued as an inconsistent picture of what good musical leadership is should instead be viewed as a consistent picture of balancing acts, where conductors have to continuously make choices and trade between interventions. The relationships between the various model themes in Figure 44.2 seem to be ephemeral, which can be attributed to the abundance of meaning-making possibilities they represent. The perfect musical leadership is an elusive phenomenon, not only because many of the preferences are situational but also because many of the things conductors are and do involve continuous choices and constant rebalancing, which affects the singers in turn. Some of the most prominent examples include the following:

Control versus empowerment: the conductor faces this balance in the rehearsing process as well as the performance. When to relinquish and when to take command is never predestined as such but is a judgment of the musical moment. Sensing as perception and sense-giving as a directive are both at the heart of such judgments. The notions of pacing and leading are different sides of the same coin.

Knowing versus searching: the general expectation is that the conductor comes to the music-making situation with a musical idea and a rehearsal plan. However, singers also expect the conductor to be adaptable, in terms of (1) reconciling the musical idea to the given ensemble and situation, and (2) adjusting the rehearsal plan in accordance with the actual progress made and the triumphs and difficulties encountered.

Working details versus the whole: the most prominent conductor choice in the rehearsing situation is when to solve specific problems and when to let the ensemble self-correct via the uninterrupted run-through. In a sense, this represents a special case of the control–empowerment balance, in terms of who is made responsible for getting it right.

Demanding versus helping: this balancing act is explicitly captured by the mentoring theme, which is also closely related to control–empowerment, since it deals with deciding what to bring to the ensemble member—specific help, clear expectation of self-improvement, or maybe a blunt "wake-up call."

Telling versus showing: talk can interfere with singers' own music-making and sometimes involve distracting or counterproductive content. At the same time, speech is invaluable for conveying contextual meaning and succinctly addressing specific and detailed problems. This balancing act is closely linked to working with details versus the whole.

Being versus doing: doing, of course, is inseparable from being. On the other hand, conductors may also impact singers through their perceived devotion, an unarticulated but assumed intention, or the empowerment derived from a moment of gestural ambiguity. Action is not the sole instrument of influence.

The pompous versus the meek: singers expect authority and willpower but also modesty and sincerity. None of these things are necessarily in conflict, but too much egocentricity, for example, is usually off-putting, whereas too little may undermine authority.

What is particularly noteworthy about these various balancing acts is that there are no stable balancing points. The perfect blend of actions or behaviors in one moment may not be perfect the next moment. In fact, the choice of one mode immediately invites its opposite. After spending a good portion of a rehearsal working through minute details, singers will long for a run-through of the whole piece. Even a conductor who is extremely effective at showing gesturally what he or she wants may sacrifice some impact if thoughts are never communicated verbally. Singers do appreciate a well-prepared conductor who always knows what the end result should sound like, but the complete absence of experimentation, no possibility for deviation or no risk of failure, can lead to singer complacency.

This apparent lack of stability and precision is captured by Weick's notion of *plausibility* as a characteristic of sense-making. A conductor intervention does not work because it is universally correct but because it is sufficiently meaningful in a given moment. This calls for great caution when we attempt to prescribe what good conducting is. Correctness is not the key point, but what makes sense here and now. The elusiveness of conductor "perfection" and the scope of meaningful realizations of musical leadership underscore the fact that art is ultimately an open-ended process that does not seek unambiguous expression or final closure in terms of understanding. In fact, this may be the point where conducting departs from the adjoining arenas of leadership in general and teaching in particular. The conductor-as-artist is a neglected perspective in literature on choirs and conducting, which favors strictly pedagogical aspects instead. When the interviewed singers acknowledge, accept, and even enjoy the imperfections of these conductor profiles, it is not only because they are generous in spirit but also because those imperfections are inextricable parts of an artistic process and an artful means of leading music. There is a limit to how far we can take the parallel between organizational leadership in general and musical leadership. Despite all of the outwardly set goals of a musical ensemble, from performance quality to financial control, music-making is stuck (and blessed) with being its own reward. Music-making may be a means to another end but nevertheless remains a unique avenue to experience (*Erlebnis*) and insight (*Erkenntnis*). The interviewed singers certainly recognize the importance of mastery. But in the end, it is the intersubjective space that the conductor is able to open up that matters most of all, and they have experienced that even imperfect conductors can enable perfect experiences.

What should singer perceptions mean for conductors?

The history of conducting is dominated by what conductors think about their own practice. Conducting is an art and a craft; knowledge, therefore, tends to be experience based. After all, conductors are exploring what works and what does not in every encounter with a choir. A certain level of reflection is therefore inevitably embedded in every conducting practice. However, the scope of reflection may not be as wide as it could. Reflecting merely on one's own practice may not take into account the full richness of the role and the power of its impact. The role calls for a certain humility with regard to what it takes to fill it, both by questioning what the role is for and by recognizing that it matters how singers experience it. The point of departure should be that the value of musical leadership derives from its impact, not from what is intended, how the conductor is trained, nor what some administrator decides. Although choral singers provide a multitude of experiences with conductors they value highly, the stories being told also indicate widely varying levels of self-awareness on the part of the conductors themselves. In my judgment, a key implication for conducting practice is the recognition that, though the role provides an inherent legitimacy, this legitimacy must be substantiated through the way in which the role is enacted. Understanding the impact of one's own practice, however, is difficult in the absence of conscious verbal exchange. In many ways, being a conductor is lonely, because the role stands apart from the rest of the ensemble and demands a different distance-intimacy blend than that among the singers. The models described in this chapter will hopefully help to nurture a professional exchange around conducting practice and philosophy.

Another key implication of choral singers' perceptions is the conscious and explicit recognition of elusive perfection—that the conductor continuously faces balancing acts that require good situational judgment as well as the ability to choose among and adapt the various approaches and interventions. Few "best practices" are universally and permanently effective. As a complex, personal, and situational phenomenon, great musical leadership would seem to demand significant self-insight. The short version of the singers' expectations towards the conductor could be paraphrased as follows: know the music, know the ensemble, know yourself!

Many of the insights outlined in this chapter may be imbedded in the teachings and practices of various schools of conducting education, although not necessarily visible as curriculum. Four topics are worth reflecting on, independently of school of training or level of teaching. First, viewing conducting as an extension of playing an instrument is too narrow. Music students are naturally obsessed with playing their instruments and dismiss auxiliary subjects that might interfere with this. But conducting as "playing" encompasses a host of auxiliary concerns, including all of the musical leadership themes that are covered in the enactment model. Second, the previous point touches upon the question of core versus supporting curriculum in conductor education. I would advocate for a broadening of the core curriculum beyond what most educators presently apply. Third, more challenging is the degree to which elements of the conductor curriculum should be taught as stand-alone subjects or as integral parts of the act of musical leadership. Based on the findings of this project, the holistic nature of effective musical leadership advocates for the integration of the various features into real music-making situations. The trick, however, would be to make the real ensemble situation accommodate all the various features, in terms of instruction, practicing, coaching, and self-reflection. Lastly, it seems as if conductors could benefit from more systematic and explicit sharing of experience, making use of multiple sources of feedback and reflection beyond tutor feedback and occasional peer chats. The conducted ensemble (and probably also fellow conductors) is an under-utilized asset when it comes to reflecting on the impact of a conductor-in-training. Two obvious themes for such feedback include rehearsal organization and the match between conductor interventions and singer needs. As a summary remark, the importance of the choral singer viewpoint should be reiterated: the singer view is an immediate access to knowledge about conducting impact, it is unavoidable since impact is unimaginable without singer perceptions, and it is the least attended to in conducting research. Luckily, for research purposes as well as conductors' self-development, the singer perspective is also easily accessible.

FURTHER READING

Durrant, C. (2003). *Choral Conducting: Philosophy and Practice*. London: Routledge.

Garnett, L. (2009). *Choral Conducting and the Construction of Meaning: Gesture, Voice, Identity*. Farnham: Ashgate Publishing.

Koivunen, N. and Wennes, G. (2011). Show us the sound! Aesthetic leadership of symphony orchestra conductors. *Leadership* 7 (51): 51–71.

Ladkin, D. (2008). Leading beautifully: How mastery, congruence and purpose create the aesthetic of embodied leadership practice. *Leadership Quarterly* 19: 31–41.

Thomas, K. (1935). *Lehrbuch der Chorleitung*. Wiesbaden: Breitkopf and Härtel.

References

Åhlen, D. (1949). *Kördirigenten: en handbok i körfostran och kördirigering*. Stockholm: Nordiska Musikfölaget.

Allen, S.G. (1988). *Leadership styles of selected successful choral conductors in the United States*. PhD Dissertation, University of North Carolina at Greensboro.

Armstrong, S. and Armstrong, S. (1996). The conductor as transformational leader. *Music Educators Journal* (May): 22–25.

Balsnes, A.H. (2009). *Å lære i kor: Belcanto som praksisfellesskap*. PhD Dissertation, Norwegian Academy of Music, Oslo.

Bengtsson, K. and Laxvik, I. (1982). *Människan i kören*. Stockholm: Carl Ehrmans Musikförlag.

Bergson, H. (1910). The intensity of psychic states. In: *Time and Free Will: An Essay on the Immediate Data of Consciousness*, pp. 1–74. London: George Allen and Unwin.

Berlioz, H. (1843). *Grand Traité d'Instrumentation et D'orchestration Modernes*. Paris: Shoenberger.

Boult, A.C. (1949, 1st edn. 1920). *A Handbook on the Technique of Conducting*. London: Hall the Publisher Limited.

Butke, M.A. (2006). Reflection on practice: A study of five choral educators' reflective journeys. *Update: Applications of Research in Music Education* 25(1) (fall-winter): 57–69.

Chesnokov, P. (2010, 1st ed. Russian 1940). *The Choir and How to Direct it*. Utrecht: Broekmans and Van Poppel.

Dahl, T.B. (2002). *Korkunst*. Stavanger: Cantando Musikkforlag.

Davidson, B.J. (1995). *Leadership styles of successful male and female college choral directors*. PhD Dissertation, Arizona State University.

Durrant, C. (1994). Towards a model of effective communication: a case for structured teaching of conducting. *British Journal of Music Education* 11(1): 57–76.

Durrant, C. (2003). *Choral Conducting: Philosophy and Practice*. London: Routledge.

Durrant, C. (2005). Shaping identity through choral activity: singers' and conductors' perceptions. *Research Studies in Music Education* 24(1): 88–98.

Durrant, C. (2009). Communicating and accentuating the aesthetic and expressive dimension in choral conducting. *International Journal of Music Education* 27(4): 326–340.

Ehmann, W. (1949). *Die Chorführung, Band II: Das künstlerische Singen*. Kassel: Bährenreiter-Verlag Karl Vötterle.

Emmons, S. and Chase, C. (2006). *Prescriptions for Choral Excellence*. New York: Oxford University Press.

Ericsson, E., Ohlin, G., and Spånberg, L. (1974). *Kördirigering*. Stockholm: Sveriges Körförbunds förlag.

Fowler, C. and Swan, H. (1987). *Conscience of a Profession: Howard Swan, Choral Director and Teacher*. Chapel Hill, NC: Hinshaw Music.

Galkin, E.W. (1988). *A History of Orchestral Conducting in Theory and Practice*. Stuyvesant, NY: Pendragon Press.

Garnett, L. (2009). *Choral Conducting and the Construction of Meaning: Gesture, Voice, Identity*. Farnham: Ashgate Publishing.

Godøy, R.I. and Leman, M. (eds) (2010). *Musical Gestures: Sound, Movement, and Meaning*. New York: Routledge.

Goldstein, R.E. (1987). An investigation into the leadership behaviors and descriptive characteristics of high school band directors in the United States. *Journal of Research in Music Education* 35: 13–25.

Gordon, L. (1977). *Choral Director's Complete Handbook*. West Nyack (NY): Parker Pubishing Company.

Guise, P.E. (2001). Director or leader? How to gain control of the choir (and how to give it away). In: A. Rose and K. Adams (eds), *Sharing the Voices: The Phenomenon of Singing III*, pp. 132-137. St. John's: Memorial University of Newfoundland.

Holgersen, S.-E. (2006). Den kroppslige vending: en fænomenologisk undersøgelse av musikalsk intersubjektivitet. *Nordic Research in Music Education Yearbook* 8: 33–57. Oslo: NMH-publikasjoner.

Holst, I. (1973). *Conducting a Choir: A Guide for Amateurs*. London: Oxford University Press.

Inghelbrecht, D.-É. (1949). *Le Chef D'orchestre et Son Équipe*. Paris: Renè Julliard.

Iszatt-White, M. (2011). Methodological crises and contextual solutions: an ethnomethodologically informed approach to understanding leadership. *Leadership* 7(2): 119–135.

Jordan, J.M. (2009). *Evoking Sound: Fundamentals of Choral Conducting and Rehearsing*. Chicago: GIA Publications.

Kaplan, A. (1985). *Choral Conducting*. New York: W.W. Norton and Company.

Koivunen, N. (2003). *Leadership in symphony orchestras: discursive and aesthetic practices*. PhD Dissertation, Tampere, Tampere University Press.

Koivunen, N. and Wennes, G. (2011). Show us the sound! Aesthetic leadership of symphony orchestra conductors. *Leadership* 7(51): 51–71.

Kvale, S. (1996). *Interviews: An Introduction to Qualitative Research Interviewing*. Thousand Oaks, CA: Sage.

Kvale, S. (2001). *Det kvalitative forskningsintervju*. Oslo: Gyldendal Akademisk.

Ladkin, D. (2008). Leading beautifully: how mastery, congruence and purpose create the aesthetic of embodied leadership practice. *Leadership Quarterly* 19: 31–41.

Ladkin, D. and Taylor, S. (2010). Leadership as art: variations on a theme. *Leadership* 6(235): 235–241.

Langston, T.W. and Barrett, M.S. (2008). Capitalizing on community music: a case study of the manifestation of social capital in a community choir. *Research Studies in Music Education* 30(2): 118–138.

Lebrecht, N. (1997). *The Maestro Myth: Great Conductors in Pursuit of Power*. London: Simon and Schuster.

Lewis, J. (1945). *Conducting without Fears, Part II: Choral and Orchestral Conducting*. London: Scherberg, Hopwood and Crew.

Lindeman, T. (1957). *Lærebok i Taktering for Kor-dirigenter*. Oslo: Aschehoug and Co. (W. Nygaard).

Malko, N. (1950). *The Conductor and his Baton: Fundamentals of the Technic of Conducting*. Copenhagen: Wilhelm Hansen.

Mintzberg, H. (1998). Covert leadership: notes on managing professionals. *Harvard Business Review* (November–December): 140–147.

Nielsen, F.V. (2012). How can music contribute to Bildung? On the relationship between Bildung, music and music education from a phenomenological point of view. *Nordic Research in Music Education*, Yearbook 13: 9–32. Oslo: NMH-publikasjoner.

Parker, E.A.C. (2009). *Understanding the process of social identity development in adolescent high school choral singers: a grounded theory*. PhD Dissertation, University of Nebraska.

Ruud, E. (1997). *Musikk og identitet*. Oslo: Universitetsforlaget.

Schonberg, H.C. (1967). *The Great Conductors*. New York: Simon and Schuster.

Springborg, C. (2010). Leadership as art: leaders coming to their senses. *Leadership* 6(3): 243–258.

Stanton, R. (1971). *The Dynamic Choral Conductor*. Delaware Water Gap (Penn.): Shawnee Press.

Thomas, K. (1935). *Lehrbuch der Chorleitung*. Wiesbaden: Breitkopf and Härtel.

Uggla, M. (1979). *För kör: Handbok för Körledare och Körsångare*. Stockholm: Edition Reimers.

Van Manen, M. (1990). *Researching Lived Experience: Human Science for an Action Sensitive Pedagogy*. Albany: The State University of New York.

Van Manen, M. (1995). On the epistemology of reflective practice. *Teachers and Teaching: Theory and Practice* 1(1): 33-50.

Wagner, R. (1869). *Über das Dirigieren*. Leipzig: Verlag von C. F. Kahnt.

Weick, K.E. (1995). *Sensemaking in Organizations*. Thousand Oaks, CA: Sage Publications.

Winerman, L. (2005). The mind's mirror. *Monitor on Psychology* 36(9). Available at: <http://www.apa.org/monitor/oct05/mirror.aspx>, accessed 10 September 2012.

Wis, R.M. (2007). *The Conductor as Leader: Principles of Leadership Applied to Life on the Podium*. Chicago: GIA Publications.

Woodward, B.J. and Funk, C. (2010). Developing the Artist-Leader. *Leadership* 6(3): 295-309.

Zahavi, D. (2003). *Fænomenologi*. Fredriksberg: Roskilde Universitetsforlag.

Zahavi, D. (2007). Fænomenologi. In: *Humanistisk Videnskapsteori*, pp. 121–138. Copenhagen: DR Multimedie.

PART 7

THE WIDER BENEFITS OF SINGING

CHAPTER 45

....

CAN SINGING HAVE A BENEFICIAL EFFECT ON LUNG FUNCTION AND BREATHING FOR PEOPLE WITH RESPIRATORY ILLNESS?

....

STEPHEN CLIFT AND REBEKAH GILBERT

INTRODUCTION

....

AN increasing body of evidence supports the view that group singing can offer participants considerable benefits in terms of their mental, emotional, and social well-being (Clark and Harding 2012; Clift et al. 2010; Gick 2011). A more challenging issue, however, is whether singing can have measurable benefits for physical health, over and above the value it may have for mental and social well-being.

In the first author's experience, when the possibility that group singing can be beneficial for health and well-being is raised in academic contexts, the most common response is to question whether singing per se can give rise to health and well-being benefits, or whether some other mechanism is at work—most likely the effects of cooperating with other people in a group in an enjoyable and creative activity. Perhaps, it is suggested, any activity which has the same social, cooperative, and creative characteristics, whether musical or not, could equally well give rise to benefits for well-being and health.

One way of addressing this challenge is to consider whether regular singing might have specific benefits for the component structures and functions of the body that are an inherent part of the activity of singing. The obvious questions, then, are whether singing can be beneficial for the vocal apparatus and respiratory and muscular processes involved in breathing (Pettersen 2010).

When posed in this way, further questions immediately arise as to whether singing, under certain circumstances, could be harmful to these structures and functions. It is very instructive to reverse the question, because the potential for singing to damage the voice is well known for professional singers. There are many examples that can be given of singers "straining" their voices, or using the vocal apparatus in ways which lead to more serious damage (Connor and Sharp 2011). A relatively recent high-profile case is that of the popular singer Adele, who in 2011 was forced to cancel her US tour due to a hemorrhage of her vocal cords. As Randhawa (2011) reported in the London Evening Standard:

> The London-born star was to perform 10 dates but has been told by medics to cancel the multi-million-pound schedule, leaving hundreds of thousands of her fans bitterly disappointed. Doctors told her she needs a period of extended rest after a hemorrhage on her vocal cords. The Grammy Award-winning performer, renowned for her powerful live performances, said she feared damaging her voice permanently if she did not take a break.

Professor Antony Narula, a UK consultant ear, nose, and throat surgeon, is quoted as saying that hemorrhage of the vocal cords "can happen with very powerful singers who are trying to achieve too much volume but without the correct technique," and that Adele needed to rest her voice for at least two weeks or her vocal cords could be permanently damaged.

By contrast to the situation for the vocal apparatus, the authors are not aware of any evidence that over-strenuous singing could give rise to damage to the lungs, or to the muscular-skeletal framework involved in the cycle of regular inspiration and expiration. Conversely, it may be the case that regular singing activity serves to strengthen or improve the functioning of the respiratory apparatus.

EARLY STUDIES ON SINGING AND LUNG FUNCTION

Clift et al. (2008), in a systematic mapping and review of research on singing and health, found three studies which had investigated the potential value of regular singing for lung function. The two earliest studies by Heller et al. (1960) and Gould and Okamura (1973) report conflicting findings. The former study reported no differences on nine measures of lung function in a comparison of 16 professional singers and 21 participants with no "professional vocal training." The second study by contrast, compared trained professional singers, students of voice, and participants with no vocal training, and found that singers were better able to use their "total lung capacity."

> Specifically, it was found that the ratio of the residual lung volume (RV) (the amount of air remaining in the lungs at the end of a total voluntary expiration) to TLC (total lung capacity) was lower in the trained singers than in the students of voice and that the students in turn, had a lower RV/TLC ratio than untrained subjects.
>
> (Gould and Okamura 1973, p. 89)

Both studies have been strongly criticized by Schorr-Lesnick et al. (1985), however, for methodological weaknesses due to small sample sizes and inappropriate controls. In their study, the groups compared were 34 professional singers from the New York City Opera and Choristers' Union, 48 wind instrumentalists, and 31 string or percussion players with professional ensembles or bands. Comparisons were made on seven measures of pulmonary function and pressure including forced expiratory volume in one second (FEV_1) and forced vital capacity (FVC).

No significant differences were found between groups on any lung function measure when compared directly, nor when controlling for potentially confounding variables such as weight, smoking, and years of performing. As the authors state:

> We compared string and percussion instrumentalists with wind players and with vocalists with and without holding confounding factors constant, and in no case was there any significant difference between them in any of the tests of pulmonary function or pressure studies.
>
> (Schorr-Lesnick et al. 1985, p. 203)

Interesting differences did emerge, however, from a "self-administered questionnaire" designed to assess performance and occupational histories, medical history, and health attitudes and behaviors. Schorr-Lesnick et al.'s summary of the differences found between groups is worth quoting in full:

> While wind players thought they were more subject to stress and nervous conditions, and string and percussion instrumentalists believed that they were more susceptible to muscular aches and fatigue, the singers believed that they were more susceptible to illness, particularly upper-respiratory-tract infections. Singers believed that prevention of illness was possible and actively engaged in exercise and generally abstained from tobacco. This heightened awareness of health may have created or fuelled the belief of improved pulmonary function among singers. Based upon the parameters of pulmonary function studies, we could find no basis in fact for this myth.
>
> (Schorr-Lesnick et al. 1985, p. 204)

QUALITATIVE STUDIES SUGGESTING BENEFITS OF SINGING FOR LUNG FUNCTION IN AMATEUR SINGERS

Despite the conclusion reached by Schorr-Lesnick et al. (1985), subsequent qualitative studies of singers' beliefs about the benefits they experience from singing have revealed that improvements in lung function and breathing are the most commonly cited physical health benefits.

Clift and Hancox (2001) report two studies investigating the perceived benefits associated with choral singing. The first study was qualitative and exploratory in character and involved asking choral singers to write answers to the following open questions about their experience of singing:

> Do you feel you have benefited personally in the following ways (four areas were specified—physically, emotionally, socially, spiritually) from being involved in this choir so far? If "yes" please explain how.
>
> Are there any ways in which you think that participating in this choir could be "good for your health?"
>
> (Clift and Hancock 2001, p. 250)

Table 45.1 Perceived benefits of choral singing—Clift and Hancox (2001) survey (Total n = 84)

Participants specifying benefits from singing	n	%
Social benefits (n = 72)		
Have got to meet/know more people through singing	46	64
Have made new friends	13	18
Emotional benefits (n = 59)		
Makes me feel positive/good/happier/raises mood	36	61
Emotional workout/induces emotions	7	12
Helps to release stress/reduce stress/lessen tension	7	12
Physical benefits (n = 45)		
Increased control over breathing/improves breathing	20	44
Wakes me up/feel more alert/energized/active	9	20
Improved posture/improved stance	8	18
Exercises lungs/improved lung capacity	6	13
Spiritual benefits (n = 37)		
Spiritually uplifting	10	27

Participants in the study were 84 members of a University College Choral Society, and a majority of respondents agreed that singing gave them social (87%), emotional (75%), and physical benefits (58%). Just under half also agreed that singing gave them spiritual benefits (49%). Of particular interest in the context of this chapter are the specific ways in which choristers believed they benefited from singing in a choir. Table 45.1 (based on Table 45.2 in Clift and Hancox, 2001) presents the ten most commonly expressed themes.

Clearly, the three most important issues identified are increased social connectedness, increased positive mood state, and improved breathing. Responses to the second, more specifically focused question on benefits for health reinforce the main themes indicated in Table 45.1. A total of 74 respondents provided answers to this question, and 41% mentioned "improved lung function and breathing," 30% referred to "improved mood and feelings of happiness," and 22% suggested that singing can help to "reduce stress."

Building on the Clift and Hancox (2001) study, Clift et al. (2009) conducted a large-scale study of singers in choirs and choral societies in Australia, England, and Germany. Over 1,000 singers were invited to complete a questionnaire structured in three parts. Section 1 asked for personal data (e.g. sex, age, partnership status, employment) and experience of singing and music making (e.g. time in the choir, ever auditioned, singing lessons). Section 2 included three open questions on the effects of singing on quality of life, well-being, and health, followed by a structured 24-item "Effects of Choral Singing" questionnaire with a

Table 45.2 What effects, if any, does singing have on physical health? Main categories of answers (NB: These categories are not mutually exclusive and percentages cannot be summed)

Categories of effect	n	% of total sample (n = 1064)	% of sample giving a substantive answer (n = 818)
Lung function and breathing	364	34.2	44.5
Posture and body control	101	9.5	12.3
Relaxation, calmness	71	6.7	8.7
Stress relief	52	4.9	6.4
Physical activity, exercise	91	8.6	11.1
Energy levels	54	5.1	6.6
Positive affect and happiness	199	18.7	24.3
Cognitive demands	77	7.2	9.4

five-point "agree–disagree" response format. Section 3 contained the short version of the World Health Organization Quality of Life Questionnaire.

Clift et al. (2009) presented findings from an analysis of written answers to one of the open questions included in the questionnaire, which asked respondents: "What effects, if any, does singing in a choir have on your physical health?" In general, answers to the question on singing and physical health were short and straightforward and required little by way of interpretation. The analysis was supported by MAXQDA2007 qualitative analysis software (see Clift et al. 2009 for details).

Table 45.2 reports the codes employed in categorizing the substantive answers given by respondents to the question on singing and physical health. Only categories used by 50+ participants are reported here. It is clear from the results that the most commonly expressed belief among choristers is that singing improves lung function and promotes deep controlled breathing. Beyond this most common response, singers highlight the impact of engagement in singing on posture and body control, and point to the physical work involved serving to exercise the body, and raise energy levels. A further important theme running through choristers' accounts is the feeling that singing can reduce feelings of "stress" and help to promote a sense of "relaxation," both of which have strong physical and psychological components. In addition, despite the focus on physical health in the open question considered here, choristers commonly made reference to singing promoting positive mood and a sense of happiness, and entailing significant cognitive demands.

Examples of the kinds of comments give a clearer indication of singers' beliefs about how singing can be helpful for breathing and lung function; the significant role of enduring problems experienced with breathing, and the feedback from professionals that supported their beliefs about the beneficial impact of regular singing.

A few respondents noted changes in their pattern of breathing and an increased ability to hold longer notes when singing:

> The normally careless "chest breathing" is replaced by the healthier "stomach breathing."
>
> (German female age 39)

> Also it has helped my breathing, I can now hold notes for much longer.
>
> (English female age 71)

Twenty-six respondents explicitly mentioned problems with asthma, and a few more choristers noted health problems affecting their lungs, and reported improvements with their breathing:

> Have mild asthma (recent recurrence, since childhood) fully under control but I'm sure the necessary controlled breathing in singing has helped when it was worse.
>
> (English female age 61)

> It helps manage my chronic asthma.
>
> (Australian male age 54)

> Regular weekly rehearsals are definitely beneficial health wise. Singing requires lots of breathing exercise and breath control.
>
> (English female age 61)

> My breathing has improved and the bronchitis from which I've often suffered has got a lot better.
>
> (German female age 68)

Some respondents were also able to report on comments they had received from health professionals on the condition or capacity of their lungs:

> I am convinced the breathing has a beneficial effect. At an examination for a life insurance the doctor was surprised and I can put a peak flow meter on the stops.
>
> (English male age 60)

> I am a mild asthmatic and apparently I have fairly good lung function and the doctor believes this is due to breathing improvements from singing.
>
> (Australian female age 50)

> I am unsure, but I imagine there are benefits to my lung function and posture. I am told I have asthmatic, even "tuberculosis" lungs, but still perform well on a lung function test and rarely get sick.
>
> (Australian female age 58)

> Affects and facilitates breathing—have pleural plaques so singing in a choir has a very beneficial effect—anything that keeps the airflow open.
>
> (Australian female age 77)

> Because I've been singing for so many years I've got a very good breathing capacity which is above average for my age group. (It has been measured by a pulmomologist).
>
> (German female age 67)

What emerges very clearly from the cross-national study is that positive benefits for lung function and breathing are the most commonly cited benefits. Indeed, the percentage of singers mentioning this idea (44.5%) is very similar to the figure reported earlier by

Clift and Hancox (2001) in a pilot survey of a singing choral society (44%). It is also clear that many of the singers who perceive benefits are affected by ongoing difficulties with their breathing, particularly asthma.

MORE RECENT QUANTITATIVE STUDIES ON SINGING AND BREATHING PROBLEMS

Qualitative reports of the kind given above are valuable in documenting the beliefs of regular amateur singers regarding the potential benefits of singing. The findings stand in contrast to the conclusions drawn by Schorr-Lesnick et al. (1985) in a study of professional singers compared with professional wind and string instrumentalists; it may be that the amateur singers in the Clift et al. (2009) study have also absorbed the possible "myth" that singing improves pulmonary function. Nevertheless, the qualitative evidence also points to the factor of chronic respiratory illness among amateur singers, and it may be that regular singing can provide some therapeutic benefits for people with long-term lung disease.

It might be expected, given the wide prevalence and potential seriousness of asthma, that the value of singing for this condition would have been widely researched. In fact, only two studies have investigated the potential value of group singing for asthma and both are limited by small samples, incomplete data reporting, and uncontrolled designs (Clift et al. 2010; Gick and Nicol 2015). Wade (2002) compared the value of vocal exercises and singing with music-assisted relaxation for nine children with asthma and reported that exercises and singing improved peak expiratory flow rates, especially when singing followed relaxation. However, the study ran over a very short period of time and no statistical analysis was completed. Eley and Gorman (2010) offered weekly music lessons over six months to Australian aboriginal children and adults with asthma (didgeridoo playing for males and singing lessons for females). They report significant improvements for peak expiratory flow for ten adolescent females who received singing lessons. Qualitative feedback indicated that many participants felt their general health and their understanding and management of their asthma had improved because of the music lessons; however, male and female participant comments were not distinguished and so the impact of group singing for the females is unclear.

Better designed and controlled research studies have recently focused on the potential value of singing for people with COPD. COPD is an umbrella term for a number of specific conditions (primarily chronic bronchitis and emphysema) leading to irreversible airflow obstruction. Diagnosis relies on a combination of history, physical examination, and confirmation of airflow obstruction using spirometry (NICE 2010). Four stages of COPD severity can be distinguished—mild, moderate, severe, and very severe, based on the amount of air an individual can forcefully expel from their lungs in one second (FEV_1) (GOLD 2010). Mild COPD is indicated by an FEV_1 of 80% or more of expected values, moderate by an FEV_1 of <80% and >50%, severe by an FEV_1 of <50% and >30% of expected values for age and sex, and very severe COPD by an FEV_1 value of <30%. The most common debilitating symptom of COPD is breathlessness (Dewar and Curry 2006), which often leads to inactivity, isolation, and dependence. Pulmonary rehabilitation can improve physical activity and quality of life, although the benefits depend upon continued adherence to physical activity (BTS/BLF 2002). COPD is associated with other, often smoking-related long-term health conditions including cardiovascular disease, osteoporosis, and depression (Fletcher et al. 1959).

Engen (2005) recruited participants from a gerontology clinic and pulmonary rehabilitation clinic who had a diagnosis of emphysema. Twelve participants met in small groups twice a week for six weeks. None of the physical health and quality-of-life measures employed showed improvements over the six weeks, but breathing mode changed from predominantly clavicular to diaphragmatic in all cases and this was maintained for two weeks after the treatment sessions ended.

Bonilha et al. (2008) reported a small randomized controlled trial assessing the impact of singing groups on lung function and quality of life among patients diagnosed with COPD. This study randomized 43 patients to a program of singing or handcraft classes. Fifteen participants in each group completed 24 sessions and were comparable at baseline in their mean $FEV_1\%$ predicted values (singing group 48.8; control group 53.4). The singing group showed a small improvement in a measure of maximal expiratory pressure at the end of the study, while the control group showed a larger decline, with the difference being statistically significant. Both groups showed increased quality-of-life scores with no significant difference, emphasizing the benefits of group participation for perceived quality of life.

Two small trials examining the effects of singing lessons for patients with COPD have been completed at the Royal Brompton Hospital in London. In the first (Lord et al. 2010), 36 COPD patients were randomized to either 12 one-hour sessions of singing lessons over six weeks, or usual care. Following attrition, 15 patients in the singing group (mean baseline $FEV_1\%$ predicted 36.8) were compared with 13 controls (mean baseline $FEV_1\%$ predicted 37.7). Significant improvements were found in levels of anxiety and self-assessed physical well-being in the singing group. No differences were found between the groups for single breath counting, incremental shuttle walking test (ISWT) scores, or recovery time following ISWT and intriguingly breath-hold time increased more in the control group than the singing group. In the second study (Lord et al. 2012) 33 patients with COPD participated in either 16 sessions of singing over eight weeks (mean $FEV_1\%$ predicted 44.4), or an active control condition in which participants watch films together and discussed them (mean $FEV_1\%$ predicted 63.5). Although the mean $FEV_1\%$ predicted value was higher for the control group, this difference was not statistically significant. Follow-up assessment showed that the singing group improved significantly in self-assessed physical health compared with the control group, but no differences emerged in direct measures of lung function.

More recently, Goodridge et al. (2013) in a small non-randomized study, compared 14 patients with severe COPD involved in an eight-week singing program with a comparison group receiving standard pulmonary rehabilitation. No differences were found, however, on standardized measures of quality of life or illness perception, nor on distance walked in six minutes. However, the participants reported enjoying the singing. A film about the project can be viewed at: https://www.youtube.com/watch?v=79H9FVWeAHQ, and interestingly, all of the patients featured provide testimony that regular singing has helped them with their breathing.

To date, therefore, research on singing and COPD has involved small groups of patients and short interventions in clinical settings focused on the teaching of singing. While existing research has shown that singing is an acceptable activity for people with COPD and that it can have general well-being benefits, little or no improvement in measures of lung function have been found. It may be that the interventions have not been long enough, and indeed, the increase in singing sessions between the two Royal Brompton studies from 12 to 16 singing sessions was motivated by a concern that the earlier study was too short to reveal positive benefits. It may be that even the increase to 16 sessions was still insufficient to promote measurable improvements in breathing and lung function. In addition, the groups in the Brompton study were small, and individuals may not have experienced the support in singing that comes from being part of a larger choir, nor the impetus to improve that comes from preparation to perform.

A RECENT COMMUNITY SINGING INITIATIVE FOR PEOPLE WITH COPD

Morrison et al. (2013a, 2013b) recently reported findings from an observational study on the value of community-based singing groups for people with COPD. A total of 106 people with COPD were recruited, and a network of six community singing groups were established, meeting weekly for 30 sessions over the course of ten months. The approach adopted in this study was modeled on previously successful community singing for health initiatives undertaken by the De Haan Research Centre in relation to older people (Skingley et al. 2011) and individuals with a history of severe and enduring mental health issues (Clift and Morrison 2011). In addition to teaching good posture, breathing techniques, and engaging in singing, the groups worked towards combined workshop and performance events for family, friends, and health professionals. It was considered important to answer a number of feasibility questions regarding recruitment, retention, and acceptability of the intervention before proceeding to a large community-based randomized controlled trial.

Spirometry was carried out by a qualified health professional to assess forced expiratory volume in one second (FEV1) and as a percentage expected value (FEV$_1$%), forced vital capacity (FVC), and as a percentage expected value (FVC%) both before and at the end of the project. Participants were assessed before each spirometry session to ensure their health was satisfactory prior to commencement of the maneuvers and no contra-indications identified. In addition, participants completed the St. George's Respiratory Questionnaire (SGRQ), a self-assessed measure of health impairment widely employed in research on chronic respiratory illness and COPD. Four scores are produced from the questionnaire: symptoms, activity, impacts, and total (SGRQ 2008), with higher scores indicating poorer health status.

Table 45.3 reports the results from the spirometry undertaken at baseline and the end of the singing program. The results show that participants in the study had on average just over 54% of expected lung function at baseline, but with a wide variation from mild to very severe COPD. Following ten months of the singing program, however, significant increases were found for FEV$_1$%, FVC, and FVC%, suggesting improvements in lung function.

Table 45.4 reports the results from the St. George's Respiratory Questionnaire, for baseline and after the ten-month program of singing. Significant improvements emerged for the SGRQ total and impacts scores between baseline and the end of the program.

Participants had the opportunity to write comments about their experience of the project and their health on the questionnaire. At the end of the project, the large majority gave

Table 45.3 Measures of lung function at baseline and end of a program of community singing for people with COPD

Measure	n	Baseline	End of program	Mean difference (95% CI)	p value
FEV$_1$	66	1.29 (0.49)	1.32 (0.51)	0.03 (−0.01; 0.58)	0.094
FEV$_1$% predicted	67	54.34 (20.45)	56.28 (21.98)	1.94 (0.58; 3.30)	0.006
FVC	64	2.43 (0.75)	2.54 (.075)	0.11 (0.01; 0.20)	0.027
FVC% predicted	65	81.72 (22.60)	85.35 (21.70)	3.63 (0.28; 6.98)	0.034

comments pointing to the social, psychological, and physical health benefits they experienced from taking part. The following examples highlight the benefits experienced from singing, especially in relation to control and ease of breathing.

> Standing to sing helps posture, you think "upright" automatically as this gives maximum output from your lungs. The relaxation exercises do just that, and learning to breathe bringing the muscles of the abdomen into play, as well as controlled exhalation, has helped me enormously.
>
> This is the first winter I have not had to call an ambulance or be on several lots of antibiotics and have taken only maintenance doses of steroids. This may be a coincidence or it may be better because of the breathing help we have received.
>
> Have not for the first time in five years been admitted to hospital or casualty over the winter period. Opened up doors i.e. joining the (BLF) Breathe Easy group.
>
> I have enjoyed the project the singing has helped me to understand how breathing and singing can help me to breathe better.
>
> I believe that the project is teaching me how to understand my breathing and how to control it. This is very useful; it stops me hyperventilating when my breathing is under pressure, i.e. climbing a steep hill.
>
> Have enjoyed being in project and liked the singing bit. I gave up going to the gym as found the singing exhausting and as good as exercise.

A film based on the project can be viewed at: https://www.youtube.com/watch?v=coUK2X3i-FU, and as with the Canadian project video referred to above, people with

Table 45.4 St. George's Respiratory Questionnaire scores at baseline and end of a program of community singing for people with COPD

Measure	n	Baseline	End of program	Mean difference (95% CI)	p value
SGRQ total	71	48.71 (16.95)	45.42 (16.96)	−3.29 (−6.14; −0.45)	0.024
SGRQ symptoms	71	59.16 (23.49)	56.04 (22.05)	−3.13 (−7.35; 1.08)	0.143
SGRQ activities	71	65.46 (22.41)	63.33 (22.14)	−2.13 (−5.44; 1.18)	0.204
SGRQ impact	70	35.65 (17.56)	32.21 (15.90)	−3.45 (−6.77; −0.13)	0.042

COPD who participated talk positively about the benefits they have experienced from regular group singing.

DISCUSSION

Research on the potential value of regular group singing for lung function and breathing began over 50 years ago, with the earliest study undertaken by Heller, Hicks, and Root in 1960. While this study did not report encouraging findings, a further study by Gould and Okamura in 1973 was more encouraging. Both studies, however, were severely criticized by Schorr-Lesnick et al. (1985), and their failure to find any differences in the pulmonary functions of professional singers compared with professional wind and instrumental players appears to have brought research interest in this field to a halt. While an active program of research continued on researching patterns of breathing and muscular activity during singing (Pettersen 2010), there is no evidence of interest in the possible value of singing for breathing from a health perspective until the work of Clift and Hancox (2001), which reported that no fewer than 44% of amateur singers in one university choral society believed that regular singing was beneficial to their breathing. This study provided the starting point for a much more ambitious survey of over 1,000 amateur singers in established choirs and choral societies in Australia, England, and Germany (Clift et al. 2009), which again found that 44.5% of singers reported experience of benefits for breathing. A significant finding was the number of singers reporting long-term problems with asthma and other pulmonary conditions and the benefits they had experienced from regular singing.

Remarkably little research has been conducted on singing and asthma, but three recent randomized controlled trials have explored the potential benefits of singing lessons for people with COPD. These studies all show that singing is an acceptable and enjoyable activity for people with this chronic and progressive lung disease, and it has clear benefits both socially and psychologically. Nevertheless, the benefits of singing lessons for direct measures of lung function and breathing were less clear, and this may reflect the nature and length of the interventions explored in these studies. Group sizes were small, the number of sessions was limited, and participants may not have had the experience typical of amateur singers who are regular members of community choirs and who rehearse in order to perform. The Sidney De Haan Research Centre recruited over 100 people with COPD across the full range of severity from mild to very severe, to test the feasibility of such an approach. Six small singing groups were established which met weekly, with opportunities after five months and at the end of the project for the groups to come together for combined choral workshops and performance events. A further feasibility study to determine whether the approach can be replicated in a multi-ethnic urban context in South London is currently underway.

If the positive qualitative feedback from participants in the East Kent study and the significant improvements found on measures of lung function and self-reported health status are replicated in South London, this will point to the viability of a more robust community randomized trial as the next step in testing the robustness of the findings from the feasibility study. Such a controlled trial is important not only to establish the effectiveness of singing in helping to maintain and even improve the health of people with COPD, but also in providing evidence for the cost-effectiveness of such an intervention. Two of the participants quoted above refer to the fact that during their participation in the project they had not needed to call upon health services to the same degree as in previous years. If a controlled study was able to establish that singing benefited an intervention group in this way when compared with a usual care control group, the potential cost savings to health services could be very great, and would more than exceed the costs associated with running community singing groups.

REFERENCES

Bonilha, A.G., Onofre, F., Vieira, M.L., Prado, M.Y.A., and Martinez, J.A.B. (2008). Effects of singing classes on pulmonary function and quality of life in COPD patients. *International Journal of COPD* 4(1): 1–8.

BTS/BLF. (2002). *Pulmonary Rehabilitation Survey*. London: British Thoracic Society/British Lung Foundation.

Clark, I. and Harding, K. (2012). Psychosocial outcomes of active singing as a therapeutic intervention: a systematic review of the literature. *Nordic Journal of Music Therapy* 21(1): 80–98.

Clift, S.M. and Hancox, G. (2001). The perceived benefits of singing: findings from preliminary surveys of a university college choral society. *Journal of the Royal Society for the Promotion of Health* 121(4): 248–256.

Clift, S., Staricoff, R., and Whitmore, C. (2008). *A Systematic Mapping and Review of Nonclinical Research on Singing and Health*. Canterbury, UK: Sidney De Haan Research Centre for Arts and Health, Canterbury Christ Church University. Available at: http://www.canterbury.ac.uk/Research/Centres/SDHR/Home.aspx

Clift, S., Hancox, G., Morrison, I., Hess, B., Kreutz, G., and Stewart, D. (2009). What do singers say about the effects of choral singing on physical health? Findings from a survey of choristers in Australia, England and Germany. *European Society for the Cognitive Sciences of Music (ESCOM) Conference*, Jyvaskyla, Finland, August 12–16, 2009. Available at: https://jyx.jyu.fi/dspace/handle/123456789/20854

Clift, S., Nicol, J., Raisbeck, M., Whitmore, C., and Morrison, I. (2010). Group singing, wellbeing and health: a systematic mapping of research evidence. *The UNESCO Journal* 2: 1. Available at: http://web.education.unimelb.edu.au/UNESCO/pdfs/ejournals/clift-paper.pdf

Clift, S.M. and Morrison, I. (2011). Group singing fosters mental health and wellbeing findings from the East Kent "singing for health" network project. *Mental Health and Social Inclusion* 15(2): 88–97.

Connor, S. and Sharp, R. (2011). How do you solve a problem like damaged vocal cords? *The Independent*, Thursday, August 11, 2011. Available at: http://www.independent.co.uk/lifestyle/health-and-families/health-news/how-do-you-solve-a-problem-like-damaged-vocal-cords-2335535.html

Dewar, M. and Curry, R.W. (2006). Chronic obstructive pulmonary disease: diagnostic considerations. *American Academy of Family Physicians* 73(4): 669–676.

Eley, R. and Gorman, D. (2010). Didgeridoo playing and singing to support asthma management in Aboriginal Australians. *Journal of Rural Health* 26: 100–104.

Engen, R. (2005). The singer's breath: implications for treatment of persons with emphysema. *Journal of Music Therapy* 42: 20–48.

Fletcher, C.M., Elmes, P.C., Fairbairn, M.B., and Wood, A.S. (1959). The significance of respiratory symptoms and the diagnosis of chronic bronchitis in a working population. *British Medical Journal* 2: 257–266.

Gick, M.L. (2011). Singing, health and well-being: a health psychologist's review. *Psychomusicology* 21(1–2): 176–207.

Gick, M.L. and Nicol, J.J. (2015). Singing for respiratory health: theory, evidence and challenges. *Health Promotion International* 31(3): 725–734. doi: 10.1093/heapro/dav013.

GOLD (2010). *Spirometry for Health Care Providers*. (s.l: Global Initiative for Chronic Obstructive Lung Disease). Available at: http://www.goldcopd.com/

Goodridge, D., Nicol, J., Horvey, K., and Butcher, S. (2013). Therapeutic singing as an adjunct for pulmonary rehabilitation participants with COPD: outcomes from a feasibility study. *Music and Medicine* 5: 169–176.

Gould, W.J. and Okamura, H. (1973). Static lung volumes in singers. *Annals of Otology, Rhinology and Laryngology* 82: 89–95.

Heller, S.S., Hicks, W.R., and Root, W.S. (1960). Lung volumes of singers. *Journal of Applied Physiology* 15(1): 40–42.

Lord, V.M., Cave, P., Hume, V., Flude, E.J., Evans, A., et al. (2010). Singing teaching as a therapy for chronic respiratory disease—randomised controlled trial and qualitative evaluation. *BMC Pulmonary Medicine* 10: 41. Available at: http://www.biomedcentral.com/1471-2466/10/41

Lord, V.M., Hume, V.J., Kelly, J.L., Cave, P., Silver, J., et al. (2012). Singing classes for chronic obstructive pulmonary disease: a randomized controlled trial. *BMC Pulmonary Medicine* 12: 69. Available at: http://www.biomedcentral.com/1471-2466/12/69

Morrison, I., Clift, S., Page, S., Salisbury, I., Shipton, M., et al. (2013a). *A Feasibility Study on the Health Benefits of a Participative Programme of Community Singing for People with Chronic Obstructive Pulmonary Disease (COPD)*. Canterbury, UK: Sidney De Haan Research Centre for Arts and Health, Canterbury Christ Church University.

Morrison, I., Clift, S., Page, S., Salisbury, I., Shipton, M., et al. (2013b). A UK feasibility study on the value of singing for people with chronic obstructive pulmonary disease. *UNESCO Journal* 3(3): 1–19. Available from: http://education.unimelb.edu.au/__data/assets/pdf_file/0003/1067421/003_MORRISON_PAPER.pdf

NICE (2010). *Chronic Obstructive Pulmonary Disease Clinical Guidelines 101*. London: National Institute for Health and Clinical Excellence.

Pettersen, V. (2010). *From Muscles to Singing: Breathing Muscles' Activity in Breathing for Singing*. Saarbrücken: VDM Verlag.

Randhawa, K. (2011). Heartbroken Adele: I can't risk damaging my voice for ever. *The London Evening Standard*, November 5, 2011. Available from: http://www.standard.co.uk/showbiz/heartbroken-adele-i-cant-risk-damaging-my-voice-for-ever-6450327.html

Schorr-Lesnick, B., Teirstein, A.S., Brown, L.K., and Miller, A. (1985). Pulmonary function in singers and wind-instrument players. *Chest* 88(2): 201–205.

Skingley, A., Clift, S.M., Coulton, S.P., and Rodriquez, J. (2011). The effectiveness and cost-effectiveness of a participative community singing programme as a health promotion initiative for older people: protocol for a randomised controlled trial. *BMC Public Health* 11: 142. Available from: http://www.biomedcentral.com/content/pdf/1471-2458-11-142.pdf

Wade, L.M. (2002). A comparison of the effects of vocal exercises/singing versus music-assisted relaxation on peak expiratory flow rates of children with asthma. *Music Therapy Perspectives* 20(1): 31–37.

CHAPTER 46

SINGING AND PSYCHOLOGICAL NEEDS

JANE W. DAVIDSON AND SANDRA GARRIDO

INTRODUCTION

THROUGHOUT our lives we are generally concerned with what motivates us to act. According to self-determination theory (Deci and Ryan 2000), along with physiological needs such as food and water, we all have universal, innate psychological needs that must be met in order for us to thrive. The theory explores the ways intrinsic and varied extrinsic forces interplay to shape our motivations to engage in life. While self-determination theory is a macro-theory of human motivation and personality, the current authors have found it useful to apply the exploration of internal and external motivators to the case of singing. Indeed, core questions underlying the current chapter are: what motivates us to sing? What is it about the activity of singing that can be so psychologically powerful and positive for one person and yet, potentially so difficult for another person? To investigate these questions we trace the ways singing meets our basic psychological needs from birth across the lifespan. The role of singing in traditional communities such as in South Africa is contrasted with its place in Western societies such as Australia and the UK. At the end of this chapter, our own theoretical model is proposed to explain the psychological functions fulfilled by experiences of singing in a variety of contexts.

Deci and Ryan (2000) propose that people's inherent growth tendencies and innate psychological needs come under the umbrella of three key needs: *relatedness*, the need to be connected socially and integrated in that social group; *competence*, the need to be effective in one's efforts; and *autonomy*, the need to feel that one's activities or pursuits are self-endorsed, self-governed, and of free will (but not necessarily autonomous, given the need for relatedness). While other psychological needs are argued such as meaningfulness and self-esteem, Deci and Ryan believe that all of these can be explained as subsets or combinations of *competence*, *relatedness*, and *autonomy* (Ryan and Deci 2002). They propose that when psychological needs are met, feelings of well-being ensue. That is, feelings of happiness, comfort, security, safety, and positive health are promoted (Ryan and Deci 2002), and human behavior and experience is enhanced.

SINGING AND PSYCHOLOGICAL NEEDS

Bailey and Davidson (2005) developed a model of the positive effects of participation in group singing sessions and group singing performances. This identified four discrete areas of value: (1) clinical or therapeutic benefits; (2) benefits related to group process; (3) benefits associated with choir/audience reciprocity, and (4) cognitive benefits. Ruud (2012) has also identified four dimensions or categories of quality of life that benefit from making music: vitality (emotional life, esthetic sensibility, pleasures), agency (sense of mastery and empowerment, social recognition), belonging (network, social capital), and meaning (continuity of tradition, transcendental values, hope). Evidence emerging from other community singing projects and a study of the psychological benefits of musical engagement in general strongly suggests that singing may provide a valuable way of meeting the three key needs proposed by Deci and Ryan (2000). The evidence relating to each will be examined separately below.

Relatedness

As highly social beings, our behavior depends on strong forms of social connections and relatedness. The need for relatedness encourages us to place ourselves in social groups to offer protection and sharing; indeed, so strong is this connectedness that it forms a foundation for the transmission of knowledge (Evans et al. 2013). Given this innate drive, we tend to use and develop activities that are beneficial to us succeeding in a social world, and we tend to reject activities that either prevent or inhibit social interaction (Deci and Ryan 2000).

Singing plays an important role in fostering a sense of relatedness from the earliest stages of life. It is reported in historical texts that singing to an unborn fetus has been practiced for centuries (Garrido and Davidson 2013). For example, reference is made to the mother of Henri IV of France, who reported that she wished to make her unborn child of mild temperament by singing sweet music to him during her pregnancy (Davidson 2001a). In fact, by about the twenty-fourth week of gestation a growing fetus has functional hearing, sounds within the womb being mainly internal such as the mother's heartbeat, the movement of blood, and gastrointestinal sounds. External sounds can also be heard, though attenuated. The mother's own voice is one of the external sounds that is most clearly heard *in utero* since it is also transmitted via internal vibrations (Querleu et al. 1988). Thus newborn infants are able to recognize the sound of their mother's voice after developing a familiarity with it during the pregnancy (see Garrido and Davidson 2013 for a summary).

In utero it is primarily the prosodic element of the mother's voice that is heard, e.g. the rhythm, along with the melodic intonations and dynamic contrasts, rather than the articulation of the actual words or the specifics of subtle pitch variation. In a sense, singing focuses on all of these aspects of speech, and is certainly a stimulus to which even an unborn child can respond (Hepper 1991). Thus, even before birth, singing (or listening to it), promotes a sense of connectedness between mother and child. It can also contribute to the ease with which mother and child relate after birth, for it has been shown that infants not only recognize the contours of their mother's voice, but that they can recognize musical stimuli learned *in utero* (Malloch and Trevarthen 2009), using it most typically as a means to calm the infant.

For the newborn, maternal singing is prevalent and this is across all cultures (Trehub and Trainor 1998). Promoting the value of singing in such interactions, it is important to note that infants do seem to show greater responsiveness to maternal singing than to maternal speech (Nakata and Trehub 2004). Studies have demonstrated significant benefits to preterm infants when their mothers sing to them in their incubators, suggesting that renewed connection to the maternal voice has important implications for the long-term well-being of the most vulnerable infants (Filippa et al. 2013).

Of course, after birth, and the child develops, the act of singing becomes rapidly increasingly interactive, with both mother and child becoming involved in the singing and gestures that may accompany it. The bonding interactions of holding, patting, and bouncing babies for parents to engage in proto-musical behaviors known as infant directed "goo-goo," "ga-ga," "sing-songy" interactions which characterize parent-infant communication in the early months of the infant's life. These interactions are playful and fun, thus developing social interaction, but they also offer soothing, and can be gentle and restful, promoting feelings of comfort and security. Malloch and Trevarthen (2009) regard these interactions as a crucial part of child development, with infants becoming less engaged or even fearful in social contexts when they are deprived of such parental exchanges in their environment.

It has been argued that the relatedness aspect of music more generally is the evolutionary basis for the existence of music as a whole. The major proponents of this idea are Dissanayake (2000) and Cross (2001). Their theories propose that music evolved from pre-verbal vocalizations, as a way of bonding child and parent, enabling them to stay in touch even when the caregiver has to move away at times like gathering food. From an evolutionary point of view, these pre-verbal communications could be seen as being vital to survival given the vulnerability of human babies. Support for this theory rests in the fact that neonates are more responsive to the exaggerated pitch contours, higher pitch, and slow tempo of infant-directed speech than to adult-directed speech (Trehub et al. 1997).

It has been argued that prenatal experiences of maternal singing prime neuro-psychobiological systems to associate particular acoustic features with the expression of certain emotions (Welch 2005). This is described as providing infants with "emotional capital" (Welch 2005, p. 247) with which they can begin to make sense of their sonic environment after birth. Studies have found similarities between the acoustic cues used to signal emotions in music with those found in speech (Juslin and Laukka 2003). In general, the capacity to recognize emotion in music is associated with emotional intelligence, or the ability to identify, understand, and manage emotions in everyday life (Reniscow and Salovey 2004), an ability which is crucial to human relations.

Taken together, these findings tend to support the hypothesis that early singing plays an important role in not only facilitating child-carer bonding, but in ensuring social relatedness throughout life.

Communication of emotion is at the heart of singing performances throughout the lifespan. As discussed by Davidson (2001b, 2006) gestures and facial expressions within singing performances further facilitate the communication of emotion. Singing in groups or in social settings also assists in creating a sense of inclusion with social groups and in identity formation (see Chapter 20 by Walker, Chapter 42 by Davidson and Faulkner, this volume). For example, as a form of cultural practice, pop music offers opportunity for peer identification, and social bonds in sub-cultural practices for generational and trans-generational connection. It is highly pervasive in mass media, bringing a focus for social discussion, if not participation (Clarke et al. 2010).

Competency

Beliefs relating to our ability to do something successfully or efficiently influence us as we approach any learning situation: there has to be a belief that we can attain competency (Deci and Moller 2005). According to Seligman (1995), one of the founders of positive psychology, learning optimism is crucial to avoiding depression and achieving success, and the crucible in which optimism is forged is through "experiences of mastery," that is, learning through experience that it is possible to face challenges and overcome them successfully.

Singing is something that everyone can engage in without specialized training. Despite the idolization given to so-called expert singers especially in Western societies, people everywhere can engage in the most widespread forms of community music-making through singing even without formal training as a singer. For many, this provides a unique opportunity to face previously unknown challenges, and to enjoy the satisfaction of meeting them successfully. Cohen et al. (2006), for example, quote the words of one chorister:

> I'm 94 years old, and wasn't sure I could sing, and was even less sure that I could follow the notes. [Becoming increasingly animated] But I found that I could sing! In fact, I'm improving! And, I can't believe it but I'm finding it easier and easier to read the notes! I am so glad I decided to take a chance and join the chorale. This has been one of the most important experiences of my life. I hope it will never stop.
>
> (p. 728)

Such experiences may then flow on to other areas of life, encouraging the individual to face challenges with more confidence, thus achieving competency and mastery in other activities as well.

When the activity that one is engaged in provides just the right level of challenge to match one's personal abilities, one often experiences "flow," a sense of complete immersion in one's task, deepened concentration, and heightened alertness that is highly satisfying and pleasurable (Csikszentmihalyi 1991). The concept of flow is related to the phenomenon of absorption, a similar capacity to become so immersed in a task so that one is unaware of the passage of time or of things going on in the external environment. Absorption also tends to occur when engaged in tasks in which a certain level of competency has been reached. Not only are absorption and flow pleasurable states to experience, they can act as useful ways to cope with stress and difficulties.

The sense of competency and achievement that singing provides for some can lead them to experience flow-like experiences when engaged in it. A group of marginalized individuals in a study by Bailey and Davidson (2005), for example, described how their participation in a singing group resulted in feelings of increased alertness and mental stimulation. Participants in the study conducted by Hays and Minichiello (2005) also described a sensation of becoming so absorbed in the singing activity that they stopped thinking about their physical ailments or personal worries.

Thus singing can provide an opportunity for people with little or no musical training to experience the satisfaction of mastering something difficult, and the discovery of an activity in which they can achieve a state of flow and absorption which lifts them above the worries of daily life.

Autonomy

The condition of having the freedom and circumstances to self-govern, autonomy is viewed as being vital to learning because it influences the achievement of competence and relatedness, and the level of satisfaction obtained from fulfilling these other psychological needs. In essence, feelings of autonomy aid intrinsic motivation and promote the internalization of regulation. Autonomy is allied to self-regulation, for the more individuals internalize regulation, the more they become intrinsically motivated, and feel that their actions are under their own control (Deci et al. 1996). Autonomy is closely related to the concept of agency, which is the freedom for individuals to act independently and to make their own choices. Lack of agency or helplessness, is a state that can lead to depression (West and George 2002).

Promoting a sense of agency is one of the key aims of music therapy (Ruud 1997). However, it has also been found to be of benefit in studies of community music-making. Bailey and Davidson (2003) have demonstrated that homeless men benefited from a singing group formed in their soup kitchen in Montreal, with the singing experience leading to feelings of pride and personal pride in achievement, as well as increased feelings of agency and self-empowerment. Rapping is a form of singing that is popular particularly with young males and it has been found to promote a sense of empowerment through self-expression among disadvantaged youths who may be overwhelmed with helplessness in other areas of their lives.

The same benefits hold true in non-Western cultures such as the South African Venda culture. The development of autonomy is facilitated with the entry to performance groups only being allowed after basic skills have been accomplished. This learning occurs through a positive set of social practices beginning with very young children being allowed to play freely at the edge of everyday musical group activities to enable them to learn through assimilation. The youngsters are highly motivated and through trial and error, imitation, and a lot of practice, become able to achieve the standard required to gain entry to the performance group. It is very common to see young children engaging in this sort of autonomous learning alongside a musical group (Emberly 2009).

Thus, singing promotes feelings of autonomy by both allowing self-monitoring which is essential for the development of skilled performance, and by facilitating self-expression which empowers individuals who may experience strong feelings of helplessness in other areas of their lives.

Other psychological benefits

Among the other psychological benefits to singing are cognitive benefits. Again, these begin early in life, with infants who are sung to experiencing increased arousal, mental alertness, and engagement with their environment (Shenfield et al. 2003). Studies with singing groups among homeless people have reported benefits from the increased cognitive stimulation, such as improved concentration and more orderly thought processes (Bailey and Davidson 2003, 2005). Others experiencing adverse life events (von Lob et al. 2010), and older people (Clift and Hancox 2010) have reported similar effects. Spatial-temporal reasoning has also been found to be improved in children by singing (Rauscher and LeMieux 2003). The problem-solving skills, language skills, and mental reasoning involved in a serious study of singing, can also flow over into other domains. In dyslexic children, for example, singing can improve phoneme awareness (Overy 2000). Singing has even been found to increase general IQ even more than instrumental instruction (Schellenberg 2004).

Emotion and mood regulation are also prominently cited as benefits from singing in much of the literature (Dingle et al. 2012). In fact it is one of the most prominent reasons given for musical engagement in general (Garrido and Schubert 2011b; Saarikallio 2008). In babies, as mentioned earlier, caregiver singing has a powerful influence on the infant and is one of the most effective methods for regulating arousal (Shenfield et al. 2003). In therapeutic contexts the following examples (among many others) can be found: a mentally ill individual being presented with an opportunity to sing out emotional expressions of anxiety and anger to regulate and calm mood (Ansdell 1995); a terminally ill patient using singing to express their grief and sense of loss (Pavlicevic and Ansdell 2004); group work using singing to explore feelings of empathy and emotional transference (Odell-Miller 2005; Robarts 2006) (see Chapter 48 by Boyce-Tillman in this volume for more information on music therapy).

It has been shown that older people with mood disorders who engaged in the choral participation, in contrast to a comparison group who undertook different activities, reported improved general health and morale, reduced loneliness, had fewer visits to doctors, and reported a reduction in the number of over-the-counter medications taken (Cohen et al. 2006).

In other studies outside of formal therapeutic contexts, singing is reported to possess mood-elevating qualities. Choir singers report perceived increases in positive affect and decreases of negative affect observed after singing (Kreutz et al. 2003). A study of 1124 choral singers from choirs in Australia and the UK also reported positive mood benefits (Clift and Hancox 2010). Adults engaging in singing on a regular basis report feeling happier, more confident, and relaxed after their singing session (Beck et al. 2000; Unwin et al. 2002). It may be of particular benefit for emotion regulation purposes when people are going through challenging times, to assist individuals in processing negative emotions they may be experiencing, or as a form of distraction from personal problems (von Lob et al. 2010). It can be a powerful cathartic mechanism for stress release as well (Smithrim 1997).

A STUDY OF SINGING WITH OLDER PEOPLE

Strong emotional affect through singing clearly offers huge potential for cognitive stimulation as well as the evocation of collective experience. It was with these potentials in mind that the study described here was developed. In order to explore the viability of singing programs for older people in the Australian context, a study was created that used community musicians to conduct the singing groups. The intention was to investigate improvements in the psychological well-being of older people participating in singing groups. It sought to identify factors that may have facilitated any improvements and contributed to the group experience.

Study

The work reported here is part of a larger project involving an examination of six community choirs involving over 200 choristers all over 70 years of age.[1] Some of the choirs involved included people with dementia and their caregivers. Over the six-year period of the program, intermittent questionnaires, face-to-face interviews, and group discussions took place to sample experience. The majority of the surveys were conducted during the group sessions, but in order to minimize interruption to the singing group activities, some data were collected with the researchers attending the participants' homes.

Questions explored underlying psychological needs topics relating to motivation for joining, on-going experience, positive and negative aspects of involvement, and the impact of the choir experience on each participant's self-confidence and social connection. The interviews were transcribed for analytical purposes and subjected to Interpretative Phenomenological Analysis Techniques (Smith 2003; Smith et al. 2009).

Results

Thematic analysis identified a number of key themes including: relatedness, mood regulation, expression and validation of emotions, life review, and competency.

Relatedness

While a negative relationship between aging and social isolation, depression, and other chronic health problems has been reported (Bunker et al. 2003; Sorkin et al. 2002), meaningful social engagement is one way in which well-being for older people might be enhanced (Greaves and Farbus 2006).

In our singing groups, participants had the opportunity to meet and work along with new people. Singing together also provided opportunities to enhance relationships between caregivers and the cared-for. This was built on the group activities we encouraged that included cooperating together in warm-ups or small-group singing, and also choosing songs. Singing together also helped people to feel connected via a sense of group cohesion and the immediacy of emotions shared in the music. Participants reported feeling a strong sense of friendship, even intimacy with their fellow singers.

> "Sometimes I just sit there and think: this music is helping us all to be together. It puts you into the same space and on the same wave-length. Gets you into the here and now."

> Being in a group and singing is a deeply physical and emotional experience. I can feel the hairs rise on the back of my neck as I feel the vibrations of the low male bass voices singing behind

[1] This chapter includes previously published writing' including Davidson, J.W. (2011). Musical participation: expectations, experiences and outcomes. In: J.W. Davidson and I. Deliege, eds., Music and the Mind, 65-87. Oxford: Oxford University Press.

me. When people get older, they don't experience physical contact the way they used to when they were young. When I sing, I can literally feel the caress of the breath of others close to me; I can feel us all breathing together, being close and intimate in the harmonies.

Mood regulation

As discussed above, music is one of the most effective means for improving one's mood (Thayer et al. 1994). Participants in this study also reported feeling more relaxed after singing, and found it to be an effective means for elevating their moods.

> "Before I did the singing group I used to get stuck in my mood and in one of those times. Singing helps to see that life isn't so bad."

Expression and validation of emotion

Singing can also enable expression of emotions that individuals have not otherwise been able to express (Magee and Davidson 2004). In fact studies show that even when language skills have deteriorated, dementia patients may still be capable of singing (Cuddy 2005; Prickett and Moore 1991). At times, the music itself seems to offer understanding.

> "Without words we can understand one another in the music."
> "Sometimes you just understand your neighbor through the tone of their voice and the look they give you."
> "Our members living with dementia certainly understand the group atmosphere, the sensitivity of the music (sometimes they laugh, sometimes they cry—often very appropriately), the melody, the harmonies."

Life review

Participation in group singing can also help the elderly to make sense of their lives and to imbue past events with meaning and worth. Magee and Davidson (2004) describe the use of singing activities with older individuals in the late-stages of multiple sclerosis to permit the use of songs for reminiscence value. Familiar song repertoire in particular, has been shown to be useful in one-to-one therapeutic contexts for life review in palliative care (Aldridge 1999).

> I wouldn't say I got teary, but when you haven't heard those songs for so many years and your memory goes back... to when you sort of... family company and that.
> "I used the tune from 'Tea for Two' and wrote about 'me and you!,' talking about when me and my old man met."

Competency

As people age, they tend not to have opportunities to learn new skills, yet research shows that the challenge of new skills helps people to feel able and valued. Attendance at the singing groups provided opportunities for participants to develop new skills. Performing added considerably to the experience. Participants gained a sense of pride in the achievement and increased feelings of self-worth and being valued by others. The renewed sense of hope enabled participants to have a reinvigorated interest in life and to further value relationships with others (Mystakidou et al. 2009).

> "I used to sing all the time as a child: in the playground, with my Mum at the park. But, that is different to being in a proper choir. I mean, being at home isn't really proper singing—you know, being able to sing scales, harmonies, hold a line. . . It is a great new challenge."
>
> ". . . You reflect on life and you think: 'Why not give it a go, you've got nothing else to lose!' When you sing with the others there is a discipline to it. I didn't realize how precise it has to be: come in together; blend in together; pronounce your words clearly; try to sing that high note stronger or softer; watch your tuning. There's a precision and beauty to it. Being a singer is not easy, but it is better and more enjoyable that I imagined. Being a singer also means you've got to be a team player. Team-building can be challenging." [smirks]
>
> "Something inside me said: 'Have a go, because if you don't do it now, you'll never do it.' So, I did, and I've never regretted it for a second. I plucked up the courage to go and I did it."
>
> "When you get up in a concert and all those eyes are looking at you, then applauding you and praising you; well it is fabulous."
>
> "Performing gives another side to my sense of who I am. I feel good at what I'm doing. I'm no trained musician, but I can do the job and other people tell me that."

A NEW MODEL OF THE PSYCHOLOGICAL BENEFITS OF SINGING

Taken together, the literature explored and the data presented reveal that singing can offer effective means of providing social connection and emotional experience which satisfy psychological needs of the participants and so lead to positive well-being impact. It is clear that the psychological needs for relatedness, competency, and autonomy can be fulfilled through participation in singing activities. Further benefits include the power that singing has to elevate the mood, relax, and to increase mental alertness and cognitive performance in other domains.

However, while singing has a lower participatory threshold than many other forms of music-making, in many Western cultures, opportunities for people to engage in music-making and singing together are relatively limited (Sloboda et al. 1994). In many traditional non-Western cultures, by contract, wider opportunities are available. The Messengers' work with the Anang Ibibo tribe of West Africa (Nigeria) demonstrates the high value given to music in that culture. Across four decades of study they noted that everyone in the tribe demonstrated an understanding of their specific musical practices (Messenger and Messenger 1992). Similar extensive musical prowess was found in Venda musical culture. The Venda people of Limpopo Province in South Africa were the topic of extensive study by Blacking (1962, 1964, 1965, 1969, 1973). Fine musical arts practices were found to be used for special ceremonial occasions as well as everyday activities, such as undertaking manual work or in playful improvised drinking songs and dances. The musical arts practices were sites for personal expression, social communication, and sharing.

Compared with African and other cultures across the globe, people in contemporary Western culture—Anglophones of European heritage in the UK, US, and Australia in particular—experience very limited and limiting experiences of musical participation. Their principal exposure to music is through listening. Sloboda (2005) notes that in fact music listening is a huge industry, and it is a voraciously consumed commodity, frequently used for self-administered mood regulation, social sharing, and often even used to denote social identification and status. The overarching lack of exposure to and experience of musical performance opportunity in Western culture has meant that for those relatively few who do engage as performers, they tend to be placed in a specialist niche with incumbent pressures associated with acquiring expertise.

But one might say that this cannot be the case for vocal performance, as it is something we can all do: you open your mouth and it happens fairly spontaneously. Indeed the majority of us can hum a tune to ourselves or sing out loud in the shower. Also it is important to remember the power of singing for the everyday person, and nowhere is this more strongly characterized than in the four-year period, 1987–1991, when song was to stir people into revolution against Soviet rule in Estonia, Latvia, and Lithuania. "The Singing Revolution," the term adopted by an Estonian activist Heinz Valk to describe the spontaneous mass night-singing demonstrations that took place, showed that people used national songs and Roman Catholic hymns to share in the powerful emotional experience of being together in the music to promote their solidarity (Thompson 1992). Yet the practice of singing, at least in the Anglophone part of Western culture, has diminished and the overarching benefits, especially the psychological ones, have been sorely overlooked.

In a series of qualitative interviews with Australian adults aged 65 and over, participants were asked to reflect on their memories of singing (Hays and Minichiello 2005). Several could recall social activities where people would sing around the piano, and regretted that the frequency of such practices had declined. Smithrim (1997) reports in her study of the role of singing in the lives of women of various ages, that from the turn of the century into the 1950s, singing around the piano played a large role in teenagers' and adults' social lives. Older participants report singing hymns with family and friends and holding parties that centered around singing. In the sixties and seventies, rather than gathering around the piano, youths gathered around the campfire with guitars, singing folk songs and the songs of the peace movement. Little social singing was reported by the participants who were teenagers in the 1980s and 1990s. Smithrim reports that going to concerts seems to have replaced gathering to sing as a social music activity. However, she argues that "singing has changed considerably in context, and perhaps not so much in quantity" (p. 230). She cites as evidence the fact that access to recorded music has now increased. People may now carry music around and listen to it wherever they may be and this has only increased since the publication of Smithrim's study. The compulsion to sing along is strong. Smithrim states that: "The context of singing has changed from social and family gatherings to more private singing. Young women are far more likely to sing along with recorded music by themselves or with one or two others than to sing with a social group for entertainment" (p. 231). She cautions against holding a biased interpretation of what constitutes singing.

Whether Smithin's view, that the quantity of singing has not changed in Western societies, is true or not, it is clear that the social benefits to be gained from singing in social contexts are not present when people sing alone. We propose in this chapter that the mechanisms by which singing can improve psychological and social well-being are, at least in part, by fulfilling the three overarching psychological needs of relatedness, competency, and autonomy (see Figure 46.1). However, it could be argued that much of the competency benefits to be

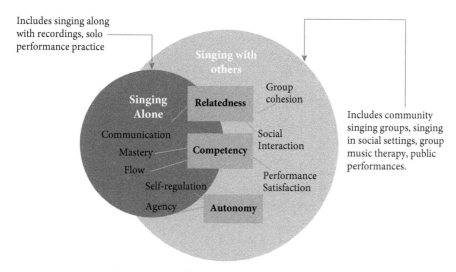

Includes singing along with recordings, solo performance practice

Includes community singing groups, singing in social settings, group music therapy, public performances.

FIGURE 46.1 A model of the mechanisms underpinning the psychological benefits of singing.

derived come from the satisfaction of performing much more than they would from singing along to recorded music in private. As can be seen from Figure 46.1, opportunities for public and communal singing hold the greatest power to enrich the lives of participants. While there is some overlap between the psychological benefits that can be obtained from singing alone and singing with others, there are virtually no psychological benefits to singing alone which cannot be enjoyed by singing with others. It could be argued that singing alone avoids the need to confront a fear of singing with others, or a fear of performance. Indeed, the singer can express all the emotions of the song's content, the inner feelings they are experiencing and "let it all out" without any sense of ridicule, the cathartic effects thus perhaps being greater in a private setting in which release of emotions need not be restrained.

Additionally, of course, as singing is a capacity we have innately and when encouraged in infancy, it is strongly associated with the warmth of early bonding. As singing alone (without parent support) persists, it might be retained by us as a technology to produce an imaginary social encounter. Add to this the fact that people who sing alone nowadays often do it with a CD or to a radio voice. As we know that singing offers shared socio-emotional opportunity, it could be that singing along to the radio offers a sense of communion with the recorded singer as well. In sum, however, the multiple benefits of singing in a group cannot be underestimated, as it can provide a relatively non-threatening environment in which to overcome a fear of public performance or a fear of expressing emotions in public, all of which lead to a sense of competency and relatedness.

In terms of developmental processes and conditions for learning, it seems that given the desire for expansion and liberation experienced by the participants in the studies discussed above, we should be working towards expanding conceptions of human development as a lifelong process. While some skills are perhaps more difficult to acquire in later life owing to some of the degenerative conditions associated with aging—arthritis being a difficult challenge to overcome if trying to learn the piano or guitar, for instance—singing and other instruments such as harmonica, flute, some percussion instruments and drums are instantaneous providers of new opportunity, quick progress in learning, and potential for group integration and experience, which can assist individuals in finding liberation and developing new interests and opportunities for positive musical experience.

Anglophone Westerners, despite the naturalness of singing and the importance of singing in infancy, have rather impoverished access to musical participation through performance, even though evidence in Western contexts is beginning to reveal the important social, musical, and personal benefits simple activities like group singing can afford. It is also very important to note that in the Western context singing programs can be offered at little cost and that a simple and effective program can be developed along basic principles, such as introductory exercises to warm the voice and establish good group relations; work on repertoire; then finishing with summarizing work for memorization and closure of the session. It is proposed in this chapter that we can and should all benefit psychologically from singing.

Further reading

Cohen, G. (2005). *The Mature Mind*. New York: Basic Books.

Csikszentmihayli, M. (1993). *The Evolving Self: A Psychology for the Third Millennium*. New York: Harper Perennial.

Deci, E.L. and Ryan, R.M. (eds) (2006). *The Handbook of Self-Determination Research*. Rochester: University of Rochester Press.

North, A.J. and Hargreaves, D.J (2008). *The Social and Applied Psychology of Music*. Oxford: Oxford University Press.

References

Aldridge, D. (1999). *Music Therapy in Palliative Care: New Voices*. London: Jessica Kingsley Publishers.

Ansdell, G. (1995). *Music for Life*. London: Jessica Kingsley Publications.

Bailey, B.A. and Davidson, J.W. (2003). Amateur group singing as a therapeutic instrument. *Nordic Journal of Music Therapy* 12(1): 18–32.

Bailey, B.A. and Davidson, J.W. (2005). Effects of group singing and performance for marginalized and middle-class singers. *Psychology of Music* 33(3): 269–303.

Beck, R.J., Cesario, T.C., Yousefi, A., and Enamoto, H. (2000). Choral singing, performance perception, and immune system changes in salivary immunoglobin A and cortisol. *Music Perception* 18(1): 87–106.

Blacking, J. (1962). Musical expeditions of the Venda. *African Music* 3(1): 54–72.

Blacking, J. (1964). *Black Background: The Childhood of a South African Girl*. London and New York: Abelard Schuman.

Blacking, J. (1965). The role of music in the culture of the Venda of the Northern Transvaal. In: M. Kolinski (ed.), *Studies in Ethnomusicology*, pp. 20–52. New York: Oak Publications.

Blacking, J. (1969). Songs, dance, mimes and symbolism of Venda girls' initiation schools, Parts 1–4. *African Studies* 28(1–4): 3–35, 69–118, 149–199, 215–266.

Blacking, J. (1973). *How Musical is Man?* Seattle: University of Washington Press.

Bunker, S., Colquhoun, D., and Murrary, D. (2003). Stress and coronary heart disease: Psychosocial risk factors, National Heart Foundation position statement update. *Medical Journal of Australia* 178: 272–276.

Clarke, E.F., Dibben, N., and Pitts, S.E. (2010). *Music and the Mind in Everyday Life.* Oxford: Oxford University Press.

Clift, S.M. and Hancox, G. (2010). The significance of choral singing for sustaining psychological wellbeing: Findings from a survey of choristers in England, Australia and Germany. *Music Performance Research* 3(1): 79–96.

Cohen, G.D., Perlstein, S., Chapline, J., Kelly, J., Firth, K.M., and Simmens, S. (2006). The impact of professionally conducted cultural programs on the physical health, mental health, and social functioning of older adults. *The Gerontologist* 46(6): 726–734.

Cross, I. (2001). Music; Cognition; Culture; Evolution. *Annals of the New York Academy of Science* 930: 28–42.

Csikszentmihalyi, M. (1991). *Flow: The Psychology of Optimal Experience.* New York: Harper Collins.

Cuddy, L.A. (2005). Music, memory, and Alzheimer's disease: is music recognition spared in dementia and how can it be assessed? *Medical Hypothesis* 64(2): 229–235.

Davidson, J. (2001a). The role of the body in the production and perception of solo vocal performance: A case study of Annie Lennox. *Musicae Scientiae* 5(2): 235–256.

Davidson, J.W. (2001b). Music and the body. In: C. Blakemore and S. Jennett (eds), *Oxford Companion to the Body*, pp. 465–466. Oxford: Oxford University Press.

Davidson, J.W. (2006). "She's the One": Multiple functions of body movement in a stage performance by Robbie Williams. In: A. Gritten and E.C. King (eds), *Music and Gesture*, pp. 208–226. Aldershot: Ashgate.

Deci, E.L. and Moller, A.C. (2005). The concept of competence: A starting place for understanding intrinsic motivation and self-determined extrinsic motivation. In: A.J. Elliot and C.S. Dweck (eds), *Handbook of Competence and Motivation*, pp. 579–597. New York, NY: Guilford Publications.

Deci, E.L. and Ryan, R.M. (2000). The "what" and "why" of goal pursuits: Human needs and the self-determination of behavior. *Psychological Inquiry* 11: 227–268.

Deci, E.L., Ryan, R.M., and Williams, G.C. (1996). Need satisfaction and the self-regulation of learning. *Learning and Individual Differences* 8: 165–183.

Dingle, G.A., Brander, C., Ballantyne, J., and Baker, F. (2012). "To be heard": The social and mental health benefits of choir singing for disadvantaged adults. *Psychology of Music* 41 (4): 405–421. doi: 10.1177/0305735611430081

Dissanayake, E. (2000). Antecedents of the temporal arts in early mother-infant interactions. In: N.L. Wallin, B. Merker, and S. Brown (eds), *The Origins of Music*, pp. 389–410. Cambridge, MA: MIT Press.

Emberly, A. (2009). *Mandela went to China . . . and India too: Musical cultures of childhood in South Africa.* PhD, University of Washington.

Evans, P.E., McPherson, G.E., and Davidson, J. (2013). Psychological needs and motivation to continue or cease playing a musical instrument. *Psychology of Music* 41: 595–633.

Filippa, M., Devouche, E., Arioni, C., Imberty, M., and Gratier, M. (2013). Live maternal speech and singing have beneficial effects on hospitalized preterm infants. *Acta Paediatrica* 102(10): 1017–1020.

Garrido, S. and Davidson, J. (2013). Music and mood regulation: A historical enquiry into individual differences and musical prescriptions through the ages. *Australian Journal of Music Therapy* 24: 89–109.

Garrido, S. and Schubert, E. (2011b). Negative emotion in music: What is the attraction? A qualitative study. *Empirical Musicology Review* 6(4): 214–230.

Greaves, C.J. and Farbus, L. (2006). Effects of creative and social activity on the health and well-being of socially isolated people: Outcomes from a multi-method observational study. *The Journal of the Royal Society for the Promotion of Health* 126: 134–142.

Hays, T. and Minichiello, V. (2005). The contribution of music to quality of life in older people: An Australian qualitative study. *Ageing and Society* 25: 261–278.

Hepper, P.G. (1991). An examination of fetal learning before and after birth. *Irish Journal of Psychology* 12: 95–107.

Juslin, P.N. and Laukka, P. (2003). Emotional expression in speech and music: evidence of cross-modal similarities. *Annals of the New York Academy of Science* 1000: 279–282.

Kreutz, G., Bongard, S., Rohrmann, S., Grebe, D., Bastian, H.G., and Hodapp, V. (2003). *Does singing provide health benefits?* Paper presented at the 5th Triennial ESCOM Conference, Hanover University of Music and Drama, Hanover, Germany, September 8–13.

Magee, W.L. and Davidson, J.W. (2004). Music therapy in Multiple Sclerosis: Results of a systematic qualitative analysis. *Music Therapy Perspectives* 22: 39–51.

Malloch, S. and Trevarthen, C. (2009). Musicality: Communicating the vitality and interests of life. In: S. Malloch and C. Trevarthen (eds), *Communicative Musicality: Exploring the Basis of Human Companionship*, pp. 1–15. New York: Oxford University Press.

Messenger, J.C. and Messenger, B. (1992). Sexuality in folklore in a Nigerian society. *Central Issues in Anthropology* 3(1): 29–50.

Mystakidou, K., Tsilika, E., Parpa, E., Athanasouli, P., Galanos, A., Pagoropoulou, A., and Vlahos, L. (2009). Illness-related hopelessness in advanced cancer: Influence of anxiety, depression and preparatory grief. *Archives of Psychiatric Nursing* 23(2): 138–147.

Nakata, T. and Trehub, S. (2004). Infants' responsiveness to maternal speech and singing. *Infant Behavior and Development* 27: 455–464.

Odell-Miller, H. (2005). Why provide music therapy in the community for adults with mental health problems? *Voices* 5(1). <https://voices.no/index.php/voices/article/view/220/164>. Accessed on January 18, 2015. Originally published in *British Journal of Music Therapy* 9(1) (1995).

Overy, K. (2000). Dyslexia, temporal processing and music: The potential of music as an early learning aid for dyslexic children. *Psychology of Music* 28: 218–229. doi: 10.1177/0305735600282010

Pavlicevic, M. and Ansdell, G. (eds) (2004). *Community Music Therapy*. London and New York: Jessica Kingsley Publishers.

Prickett, C.A. and Moore, R.S. (1991). The use of music to aid memory of Alzheimer's patients. *Journal of Music Therapy* 28: 101–110.

Querleu, D., Renard, X., Versyp, F., Paris-Delrue, L., and Crepin, G. (1988). Fetal hearing. *European Journal of Obstetrics and Gynecology and Reproductive Biology* 28(3): 191–212.

Rauscher, F.H. and LeMieux, M.T. (2003). *Piano, rhythm, and singing instruction improve different aspects of spatial-temporal reasoning in Head Start children*. Paper presented at the Annual Meeting of the Cognitive Neuroscience Society, New York, NY, 29 March–1 April.

Reniscow, J.E. and Salovey, P. (2004). Is recognition of emotion in music performance an aspect of emotional intelligence? *Music Perception* 22(1): 145–158.

Robarts, J. (2006). Music therapy with sexually abused children. *Clinical Child Psychology and Psychiatry* 11(2): 249–269.

Ruud, E. (1997). Music and identity. *Nordic Journal of Music Therapy* 6(1): 3–13.

Ruud, E. (2012). The new health musicians. In: R. MacDonald, G. Kreutz, and L. Mitchell (eds), *Music, Health, and Wellbeing*, pp. 87–96. Oxford: Oxford University Press.

Ryan, R.M. and Deci, E.L. (2002). Overview of self-determination theory: An organismic dialectical perspective. In: E.L. Deci and R.M. Ryan (eds), *Handbook of Self-Determination Research*, pp. 3–33. Rochester, NY: University of Rochester Press.

Saarikallio, S. (2008). Music in mood regulation: initial scale development. *Musicae Scientiae* 12(2): 291–309.

Schellenberg, E.G. (2004). Music lessons enhance IQ. *Psychological Science* 15: 511–514. doi: 10.1111/j.0956-7976.2004.00711.x

Seligman, M. (1995). *The Optimistic Child*. Milson's Point: Random House.

Shenfield, T., Trehub, S., and Nakata, T. (2003). Maternal singing modulates infant arousal. *Psychology of Music* 31(4): 365–375. doi: 10. 1177/03057356030314002

Sloboda, J.A. (2005). *Exploring the Musical Mind*. New York: Oxford University Press.

Sloboda, J.A., Davidson, J.W., and Howe, M.J.A. (1994). Is everyone musical? *The Psychologist* 7: 349–354.

Smith, J.A. (ed.) (2003). *Qualitative Psychology: A Practical Guide to Research Methods*. London: SAGE.

Smith, J.A., Flowers, P., and Larkin, M. (2009). *Interpretive Phenomenological Analysis: Theory, Method and Research*. London: SAGE.

Smithrim, K.L. (1997). Singing for our lives: Singing in the everyday lives of women through this century. *The Phenomenon of Singing* 1: 217–232. Retrieved from: <http://journals.library.mun.ca/ojs/index.php/singing/article/view/947>

Sorkin, D., Rook, K.S., and Lu, J.L. (2002). Loneliness, lack of emotional support, lack of companionship, and the likelihood of having a heart condition in an elderly sample. *Annals of Behavioral Medicine* 24: 290–298.

Thayer, R.E., Newman, R., and McClain, T.M. (1994). Self-regulation of mood: Strategies for changing a bad mood, raising energy, and reducing tension. *Journal of Personality and Social Psychology* 67: 910–925.

Thompson, C. (1992). *The Singing Revolution: A Political Journey through the Baltic States*. London: Joseph.

Trehub, S. and Trainor, L. (1998). Singing to infants: Lullabies and play songs. In: L. P. Lipsitt, C.K. Tovee-Collier, and H. Hayne (eds), *Advances in Infancy Research*, Vol. 12, pp. 43–78. Portsmouth, NH: Greenwood Publishing Group.

Trehub, S., Unyk, A.M., Kamenetsky, S.B., Hill, D.S., Trainor, L., Henderson, J.L., and Saraza, M. (1997). Mothers' and fathers' singing to infants. *Developmental Psychology* 33(3): 500–507.

Unwin, M.M., Kenny, D.T., and Davis, P.J. (2002). "The effects of group singing on mood." *Psychology of Music* 30(2): 175–185.

von Lob, G., Camic, P., and Clift, S. (2010). The use of singing in a group as a response to adverse life events. *International Journal of Mental Health Promotion* 12(3): 45–53.

Welch, G.F. (2005). Singing as communication. In: D. Miell, R.A.R. MacDonald, and D.J. Hargreaves (eds), *Musical Communication*, pp. 239–259. Oxford: Oxford University Press.

West, M. and George, C. (2002). Attachment and dysthymia: The contributions of preoccupied attachment and agency of self to depression in women. *Attachment and Human Development* 4(3): 278–293.

CHAPTER 47

THE EFFECTS AND BENEFITS OF SINGING INDIVIDUALLY AND IN A GROUP

TÖRES THEORELL

INTRODUCTION

SINGING affects muscular activities, breathing, cardiovascular functions, and hormones. It is difficult to disentangle these different kinds of effects. Accordingly, the only thing we can do is to describe the "total" effect of singing, although, as researchers, we still try to tease apart key factors. It is also almost impossible to know whether the effects that we observe are due to esthetic and emotional influences, or to bodily processes associated with the physical production of the singing sounds. During the past 20 years, an increasing number of scientific publications have discussed the bodily effects of singing and almost all of them deal with the immediate effects. In these studies, psychological states, as well as effects on hormonal systems, on immunological and cardiovascular functions, and on other biological stress parameters (such as sweating) have been assessed. The most frequently assessed physiological parameter in studies of singing is heart rate. Heart rate always tells us something about the body's level of activation. This chapter will discuss how much heart rate change is associated with singing activity and what the conditions are that may influence this.

PSYCHOLOGICAL CHANGES ASSOCIATED WITH SINGING

An illustration of how variable the experience of singing can be is a study performed in our Institute some years ago (Grape et al. 2003). The experimental subjects were eight professional and eight amateur singers. Careful measurements were performed before, during, and after a regular singing lesson. The study showed that the professionals and the amateurs reacted differently to this situation, both somatically and psychologically, although they also had some reactions in common, which will be described.

In order to understand the *biological* reactions that we found in the study of the singing lesson, we have to know what the *psychological* reactions were in the singing situation. All the participants in the study were accustomed to the situation of the singing lesson. Even the amateurs had at least half a year's experience of singing lessons. During normal conditions, a singing lesson is a "safe" situation. Teacher and pupil know one another well and there is no disturbing audience. Although there may be "strict" teachers and "scared" pupils, they share the same goal, namely to improve the pupil's singing technique. Male and female singers were included in both groups. The age ranged from 25 to 45 years. Before the start of the singing lesson, and after it had ended, all participants filled in a short questionnaire, which included responses to visual analogue scales (VAS) on which they recorded in a simple way three aspects of their emotional state. The scale consisted of a 10 cm horizontal line on which the subjects were asked to put a cross in the place corresponding to their state in that particular moment. The maximally bad position was located at the left end of the line and the maximally good one in the right end. The three emotional states were: sad–joyful, tired–energetic, and tense–relaxed.

So what changes did the singers report on the VAS scales? With regard to the sad–joyful dimension, there was no change at all after the singing lesson in the professional singers, whereas the amateurs reported increased joy. Both groups started to the right of the middle of the VAS, i.e. more joyful than sad, but the results showed that the amateurs became happier whereas the professionals stayed at the starting level. The difference was also obvious in interviews performed after the singing lessons. The singers were asked to describe in their own words how they had perceived their singing lesson. While the amateurs described the joy of singing and how they appreciated the opportunity to enrich their lives, the professionals were concerned with technical details in their singing and often described it in self-derogatory terms. Examples included: "Was not able to keep the note long enough;" "Was not in good shape;" and "Did not support the notes with my diaphragm."

For the other two emotional states, tired–energetic and tense–relaxed, however, both groups reported improvements, with no significant difference between amateurs and professionals. Participants became more energetic and more relaxed after the singing lesson, regardless of professional status. This particular effect has been described in many other studies, for instance by Sandgren and Borg (2009). These studies were examinations of how "expert" and "non-expert" choir singers in Stockholm experienced a choir rehearsal in Stockholm. Experts as well as non-expert choir singers reported increased joy and relaxation during the rehearsals and there was no striking difference between the groups. The rehearsals are probably calibrated to the level of the choir. This may mean that challenges and frustrations are experienced to the same extent, regardless of level of expertise in the choir situation, although for one and the same choir this will vary across rehearsals depending on repertoire. It will also vary between individuals. But to a great extent the choir rehearsal is a collective experience. In the individual singing lesson, on the other hand, the professional singer who earns their living from singing has to work hard to maintain a high level of quality. And there is no doubt that the qualities of the voice in the professional differ in several ways from those of the amateur (Sundberg 1989). The professionals have a wider pitch range and a wider control of volume, for instance.

According to modern neurobiological research, the brains of professional singers differ from the brains of other people. A neurobiological examination (Kleber et al. 2010—see also Kleber and Zarate, "The Neuroscience of Singing," in this volume) of functional activation in relation to accumulated singing practice has been performed. Highly accomplished opera singers, conservatory-level vocal students, and laymen were examined while singing an Italian aria in a neuroimaging experiment. The results showed that singing training increases activation of those parts of the brain that are important for enhanced control of voice muscles and for regulating the sensory function in those muscles. In addition, such training is associated with increased activity in memory areas for these muscles and for the coordination of their movements.

Other research (Wilson et al. 2011) has shown that expert and non-expert singers differ with regard to engagement of the language network in the brain. Non-expert singers engage their brain's language network to a greater extent than expert singers. These findings indicate that singing expertise promotes independence from the language network, with this "decoupling" producing more tuneful performance.

From the evidence considered so far, we can conclude that professional singing training influences the experience of singing and also changes the brain function in several important ways. But does singing also influence cardiovascular function?

CARDIOVASCULAR EFFECTS OF SINGING

First of all, cardiovascular function is intimately associated with breathing, which is different during singing than in most other activities. During normal breathing, inhalation and exhalation are of approximately the same duration. Singing, on the other hand, is characterized by a rapid inhalation and a slow exhalation, the latter also taking place with some resistance because the vocal folds form a narrow passage for the air coming from the lungs. These facts are of importance to the analysis of heart rate and rate variability.

Heart rate and heart rate variability

During the study of the singing lesson (Grape et al. 2003), an electrocardiogram was recorded continuously. We observed that the heart rate at rest was normally between 60 and 80 beats per minute. During singing, the average heart rate increased by 20 beats per minute and this did not differ between professionals and amateurs. But it was possible also to follow heart rate variability (HRV). This is important because HRV mirrors the balance in activity between the sympathetic nervous system (SS) and the parasympathetic nervous system (PSS). Why is this important in relation to singing? It is important because, broadly speaking, the sympathetic nervous system corresponds to arousal and nervousness, whereas the parasympathetic nervous activity corresponds to relaxation and calmness. The parasympathetic system could, therefore, be regarded as an anti-stress system. Interestingly, the most important vehicle for the parasympathetic activity in the body is the vagus nerve that starts in the lower part of the brain and extends to the lungs and the gastrointestinal system. It has sometimes been labeled the "big lung and stomach nerve." Deep slow activation of diaphragmatic breathing activates the vagus nerve and so accounts for common reports from singers that singing is "relaxing" (Clift and Hancox 2001; Clift et al. 2010).

One of the reasons why heart rate varies is that the heart rate increases when we inhale air and decreases when the air is exhaled. This makes sense physiologically because when oxygenated air enters the lungs it is useful to have a large volume of blood pumped into them. On the other hand, a slower heart rhythm during exhalation allows the heart to "rest" for a short period. The professional singer who has learnt a good breathing technique adapted to singing may be more able than others to take a deep breath before the singing phrase and perhaps also utilize this kind of heart rate variability which is referred to as respiratory sinus arrhythmia (RSA).

Heart rate variability is not solely due to breathing. The PSS has rhythmic oscillations in its activity and so does the SS, but the frequencies of these variations are not the same and also not the same as the breathing cycle. Every time PSS activity peaks, the heart rate decreases and, correspondingly, heart rate increases when SS activity peaks. The result is a complicated heart rate variability pattern with several components that can be disentangled through mathematical analysis. This means that, within a given time interval, it is possible to assess the activity of the PSS and the SS respectively. When we breath normally, the HRV components in this complicated web of variations can be divided into high frequency power (HFP: 0.15–0.5 Hz corresponding to 9 to 30 cycles per minute), low frequency power (LFP: 0.04–0.15 Hz corresponding to 2.4 to 9 cycles per minute), and very low frequency power (VLFP: below 0.04 Hz corresponding to less than 2.4 cycles per minute). HFP is determined almost exclusively by the PSS and by breathing (which is in itself a stimulus to parasympathetic activity). A mixture of sympathetic and parasympathetic activity is believed to determine the LFP. The VLFP, finally, is again determined by the PSS. For most people when awake, the breathing rate is 12–18 breaths per minute if there is no psychological or physical exertion. During solo singing a lower breathing rate of fewer than 9 cycles per minute is sometimes demanded, since phrases could occasionally last for more than seven seconds (corresponding to 8.6 breaths per minute or slower). This means that some of the breathing-related HRV during singing is moved from the HFP to the LFP spectrum. In addition, the difference in pressure regulation during the breathing process is different in singing than in normal breathing and, therefore, the rules of thumb applied in HRV research may not always apply to singing. Accordingly, during singing the inhalation is rapid and relatively forced and the exhalation is relatively slow and the pressure controlled. During normal breathing the inhalation is slow and there is no pressure control. Although speculative, such factors may explain why LFP seems to be a more important component than HFP in some studies of singing.

What happens to HRV during singing? As mentioned previously, it is likely that the breathing-related HRV is important. The professional singer who is able to take a deep breath using their diaphragm effectively (that may result in a particularly strong parasympathetic stimulus) may also be more able than others to oxygenate blood during inhalation and allow the heart to rest during exhalation. This may result in improved ability to save energy and to maintain long phrases during singing. There is evidence from our own research supporting this view (Grape et al. 2003). Awareness of the importance of diaphragm breathing in people who have been taught how to sing may help them in other everyday situations when they are not singing. This may be one possible health promoting mechanism associated with choir singing. Findings from research with people affected by lung disease show that individuals do generalize these breathing/singing techniques to daily life (Morrison et al. 2013).

The ECG recordings during the singing lesson in the study of amateurs and professionals (Grape et al. 2003) showed that the HRV increased more in professionals than in amateurs when they were singing. This was particularly evident and statistically significant for LFP. At the same time, the professionals had an increased ratio between LFP and HFP. This is assumed to mirror a more pronounced activation of the SS. Accordingly, the professionals had a greater skill in handling the collaboration between breathing and circulation than the amateurs, but they also showed more evidence of a biological stress reaction that is consistent with the discussion above, as for them the singing lesson was not for joy only. An interesting observation was that the mean heart rate during five-minute periods did not differ between the two groups—the differences were observed only when the more sophisticated measures of HRV were analyzed.

HORMONES AND THE IMMUNE SYSTEM

Before and after the singing lesson, venous blood was drawn for the analysis of hormonal changes after the singing lesson (Grape et al. 2003). An important observation was that the blood plasma concentration of oxytocin increased significantly both in amateurs and professionals. Oxytocin concentration increases in many situations, as for example, during massage. Oxytocin also starts the contractions of the uterus when a child is to be born. Accordingly, the effect in singing is not a specific one. Animal experiments have shown (e.g. Uvnäs Moberg 1997) that oxytocin stimulates learning. Oxytocin, because of its role in learning, may stimulate curiosity. In addition, animal research (Grippo et al. 2012) has shown that oxytocin injections during a period of isolation may protect the body from adverse effects of a stressful situation. In other words, oxytocin seems to have a protective role in relation to adverse effects of negative stress reactions. Most of this is highly speculative and exactly how we can link learning and singing to oxytocin is not known. It is likely that lullabies and caressing may be of great importance to brain functions in the small child and that some of this may be mediated by oxytocin.

Oxytocin and singing

The oxytocin effect of the singing lesson was the same in amateurs and professionals. There were, however, differences in other biological systems. The most striking difference was observed for TNF alpha. This is a pro-inflammatory cytokine, a group of immune-chemical agents in the body stimulating inflammatory reactions that are part of the defense in stress situations. TNF alpha is a chemical substance that increases fatigue. A speculative interpretation of this is that the peripheral (immune) system regulating inflammation wants to give a chemical signal to the brain that there is need for a rest! The blood concentration of TNF alpha increased significantly in the professional singers during the singing lesson, but not at all in the amateurs. Perhaps this means that the stress reaction in the professional singers was also activating the immune system.

How can we interpret the "good" performance of the HRV during singing with the biological stress reaction in the SS and in the pro-inflammatory immune system in the professional singers, while the amateur singers perform more poorly with regard to HRV while they have no stress reaction? The explanation may be that the professionals are more skillful, but also more engaged in their task and, therefore, more stressed in this particular situation. Stress is here defined as bodily arousal in a situation that requires greater levels of exertion and consequently high levels of energy. The professionals have learned how to activate the PSS with large variations in heart rate while they have a high sympathetic arousal; the two opposing systems are activated at the same time! This is a relatively underdeveloped research field and so we have no clear answers.

A German study (Kreutz et al. 2004) examined changes in the immune system in choir singers from before a choir rehearsal to after its completion. The concentration of plasma immunoglobulin A increased significantly after the choir rehearsal, while no such effect was observed after listening to the same music. Accordingly, the immune system is engaged while we sing. This finding is interpreted as positive since immunoglobulin A contributes to the defense against infections. We do not know how long lasting such effects are and whether a repeated activation of this part of the immune system once a week has a beneficial general effect on health.

HEART RATE—PHYSICAL WORK

How much elevation of heart rate does singing give rise to? The previously mentioned small study of singers in a singing lesson shows that the effects on average heart rate per five-minute period are relatively small. The maximal heart rate was between 105 and 115 beats per minute and the effect was the same for amateurs and professionals. A real audience, however, does make a considerable difference with much more pronounced heart rate elevation. Many experience nervousness when they are going to sing in front of an audience. This has frequently been labeled stage fright, which is sometimes an adequate description of a frequent feeling. Another way of describing it is to say that the performer wants the audience to love the song just as much as the singer does and that they want to transmit an emotional message. This causes considerable arousal. However, if the singer forgets themselves and devotes all their effort to the message in the song, then the audience is more likely to get engaged and a wordless communication arises. Such a state is labeled "flow" (cf. Csikszentmihalyi 1990). It is characterized by a high level of arousal, a feeling that the performer is successfully managing something that is difficult, and finally an elated emotion (Ullén et al. 2010). Its physiological correlates will be described below.

In a further study (Harmat and Theorell 2010), we performed continuous ECG recordings during ten pairs of performances of one "strenuous" piece (long phrases, high intensity levels, high notes) and one "easy" piece (shorter phrases, lower intensity levels, no high notes), with and without an audience. The musicians were professional singers and flute players (flute playing is very similar to singing).

Effects on heart rate

Both the degree of difficulty and the audience had an effect on the average heart rate, but it was clear that the audience effect was stronger (+22 beats per minute in the easy and +27 beats per minute in the strenuous piece) than the effect of the strenuous versus easy piece (+4 beats per minute without audience and +9 beats per minute with audience). A parallel phenomenon was observed for HRV, with a very strong effect of the audience and a small effect of the easy vs. strenuous piece. Another interesting observation was that the effect of the audience during the performance of the strenuous piece was particularly strong when the performer felt nervous before the concert (average 206 for the nervous vs. 1620 in the non-nervous; technically, these measures are based upon a logarithmic transformation of the original data, since the distributions are strongly skewed). HRV showed a much stronger correlation with nervousness than heart rate did.

LFP was the component of HRV that discriminated the most clearly. This may be due to the fact that we recorded professional performances and some of the musical phrases were long. According to the discussion above, long phrases exceeding seven seconds could cause drifting of HRV from the high frequency to the low frequency domain. In addition, a successful concert performance by a professional singer may be characterized by a mixture of parasympathetic and sympathetic arousal. The high skill level makes it possible for the professional to focus on the emotional message and the totality of the performance despite a high arousal level, since little conscious attention has to be paid to the technical details of the performance.

From these descriptions it may be possible to identify a few factors that may be of importance to the biological effects of singing:

1. The singer's skill.
2. The human surrounding, if there is an audience and how the audience behaves (supportive or critical).
3. The technical demands in the song (dynamics or intensity level, pitch, difficult or simple intervals, complicated or simple rhythms, length of phrases).
4. The emotional engagement of the singer (flow or negative feelings).

A more detailed study of the flow state (de Manzano et al. 2010) as it arises in pianists has also been published. Twenty-one professional solo pianists participated. They were asked to play in the laboratory a difficult self-selected piece that they liked. After each performance they were asked with the use of a standardized questionnaire to rate the degree of flow that they had experienced. The performances were ranked with regard to flow and online physiological recordings were also analyzed in relation to the flow experience. The flow experience was characterized by a high heart rate, relaxed chewing muscles, and deep breathing. This could be interpreted as evidence of concomitant sympathetic and parasympathetic arousal. That such concomitant arousal of these "accelerator" and "decelerator" systems may take place during flow has received additional support from another experiment in our research group (Harmat et al. 2012) in which 42 experimental subjects were performing a videogame. The setup was such that, in random order, players were exposed to three video playing situations: easy, difficult, and optimal. In the optimal situation, the speed was adapted to the player, whereas in the difficult situation it exceeded the player's optimal speed and in the easy situation it was below the optimal. Both the difficult and the optimal situations were characterized by high heart rate, but in the optimal situation the activation of the PSS (mirrored in slower and deeper breaths) was significantly more pronounced than in the other conditions. Accordingly, in this non-music situation, the state corresponding to flow may also have been characterized by the double arousal of both the accelerator and decelerator systems.

GROUP SINGING AND ITS EFFECTS

Many people report that they feel increased well-being when they sing in a choir. Several studies have been published in which choir members have been asked about their experiences (see also Davidson and Faulkner, "Group Singing and Social Identity," Clift and Gilbert, "Can Singing have a Beneficial Effect on Lung Function and Breathing for People with Respiratory Illness?" and Davidson and Murray, "Voice Management and the Older Singer," all in this volume). For example, Clift and Hancox (2010) gathered written comments from a cross-national sample of over 1,000 older choir singers, while Sandgren and Borg (2009) interviewed mixed-age adult choir singers of varying degrees of expertise ranging from professionals to less advanced amateurs, all singing classical music. An increasingly popular kind of choir is one for those who have never sung before, or "beginner choirs" (see Knight, "Addressing the Needs of the Adult 'Non-Singer,'" in this volume).

Joint breathing

As expected, slow deep breathing occurs when singers perform in unison easily structured songs with long phrases and without words. This breathing pattern is related to variations in heart rate, which slows down during exhalation and speeds up during inhalation. Such variations occur in a concerted way in choir singers (Vickhoff et al. 2013). Breathing and heart rate effects are the same, for instance, as those arising when mantras are recited, the difference of course being that the song in itself strengthens the possibility of the participants following the rhythm. The music provides a strong motivation for joint breathing cycles. When more complicated songs are performed and when the singers sing in different voices (soprano, alto, tenor, and bass), this strong coordination is likely to disappear. When words are added to the sound the psychophysiological patterns become even more complicated (Olsson et al. 2013). Following this reasoning, slow unison wordless singing (or singing with few simple words) may be of particular importance to group cohesiveness. But, of course, more complicated choir singing may be very powerful in triggering joint strong emotions, despite individual differences in physiological phase.

Education, gender, and participation

As a general rule, a high level of education increases the likelihood of participation in cultural activities. There are interesting exceptions to this rule, however. In a Norwegian study, for example (Vaag et al. 2012), all staff in two county hospitals were offered the opportunity to participate in joint rock singing (i.e. a kind of well-being choir at work). After rehearsals, the participants gave a concert and 1,431 employees completed a survey questionnaire after the performance (57 percent participation). Thirty percent of the respondents had participated in the singing. Lower participation was found among men, employees above 62 and below 38 years of age, part-time employees, university-educated workers, and health-care workers. The likelihood of participation was determined by a number of factors. The kind of music activity is a factor of decisive importance that interacts with age, gender, ethnic group, and type of employment. In the Norwegian study, singing rock music appealed particularly to middle-aged women without higher education.

Age and participation in choirs

In interviews with older people singing in a choir, spontaneous statements of relevance to well-being have been systematically analyzed (Clift and Hancox 2001, 2010). The most common kinds of well-being statements relate to the reports of joy and togetherness that subjects experience when they sing. This is a powerful amplifier of social support and is of importance to health because these people feel a strengthened motivation to adopt a healthy lifestyle. The singing brings meaning to their lives. In many of these choral groups organized for older and elderly people we are frequently talking about unison singing without different parts. Elite goals are unimportant. On the other hand, it is important not to trivialize the choice of music, nor to underestimate the ability of the participants. To find a reasonable goal that is accepted by the majority is a challenge for the leader. The collective effect is most important and it will be discussed more in detail below. The importance of music choice, attitude towards the participants' singing ability, and socio-economic conditions is substantial. Negative associations with choir singing have also been described in written responses to open-ended questions in a large-scale survey with 3,145 subjects (Kreutz and Brünger 2012). Social problems as well as conflicting esthetic goals dominate in such negative statements.

It should be remembered that statements from choir singers that they feel healthier than people in general is not proof that choir singing gives rise to good health. Those who develop certain kinds of illnesses are likely to stop participating in their choir. Accordingly, some of this association could be due to reversed causality—healthy singers are more likely to continue to sing in a choir! Therefore, studies are needed which are based upon subjects who start singing in a choir and are followed for longer periods of time, and not only when they sing. A wide range of health parameters could be studied.

Health benefits of choir singing include such effects as discussed above:

- esthetic and emotional surprises resulting in changed life goals and coping patterns;
- physical training;
- improved coordination between breathing and circulation;
- balance between the sympathetic and parasympathetic systems; and
- hormonal changes (such as related to cortisol, oxytocin, beta-endorphins).

But in choir singing there is also the collective effect. Perhaps we are even genetically programmed to feel strong togetherness when we make sounds together? Throughout mankind's history, human beings have performed dance and music in their religious rituals. Perhaps the overriding goal of this has been to strengthen cohesiveness in order to make group members collaborate effectively? Individuals who have not been able to participate in such activities may have had a smaller survival chance than others. It could even be that, after tens of thousands of years, this has resulted in genetic selection of subjects with the ability to participate in music and dance? It may explain why tone deafness is very uncommon in the general population (see Wise, "Defining and Explaining Singing Difficulties in Adults," in this volume).

Oxytocin and choir singing

Kreutz (2014) studied variations in the saliva concentration of oxytocin in a group of choir singers. The concentration was assessed before and after two activities: the first was a choir rehearsal and the second was conversation in pairs. The saliva oxytocin concentration was significantly higher after the choir singing than it was after chatting. At the same time, positive feelings increased significantly and negative feelings decreased significantly after the choir rehearsal, whereas no such changes were observed in the speaking condition. This is an example that illustrates that group singing has stronger hormonal effects than talking in pairs. Oxytocin is particularly interesting since it has been assumed to have a role in group cohesion and bonding between child and parents (Feldman et al. 2011).

Challenges may be important for health effects. A choir may face a difficult piece and may initially doubt its ability to perform it (perhaps in a concert). If it succeeds well, the feeling of achievement may be a strong health promotion factor in itself. If it fails, there may be opposite effects.

GROUP SINGING AND IRRITABLE
BOWEL SYNDROME

Grape et al. (2008, 2010) report an experiment to assess the potential value of group singing for people with irritable bowel syndrome (IBS). We examined whether choir singing once a week during a whole year had the same effect as a comparison program in which participants received small lectures and discussions (also once a week). The time allotted to the lectures and the singing was the same in the two groups during the study period. None of the participants with IBS had sung in a choir before, but wanted to start doing so. For participation in the study, they had to accept that they would be allocated randomly to one of the two groups. IBS symptoms (oscillation between constipation and diarrhea, flatulence, and pain) are partly determined by psychological reactions to stress and partly by a number of physical factors, such as aberrations in meal rhythm and diet. IBS is a common illness (Gulewitsch et al. 2011 report prevalence of 18 percent among German students) and may periodically be incapacitating, although it is not life threatening. IBS patients have been described in the literature as having increased bodily sensitivity to external stimuli and stress. Since participants in both groups were involved in group activities, cohesiveness effects could have been obtained in both, and if the choir group would turn out to differ from the other group, the difference would be likely to be due to the group singing as such.

Several factors were assessed in the two IBS groups, before the start of the groups, as well as after six, nine, and 12 months. Firstly, there were findings (Grape et al. 2010) on a factor that is of importance because it reflects the body's regenerative activity. Regeneration is important because there is a constant breakdown of cells in all tissues in the body—in the skin, the immune system, the mucosa, the muscles, the connective tissue, the bones, and the cells supporting the brain cells (Horvitz 2003). If this repair and supportive activity is reduced (which tends to happen during periods of excessive negative stress), the body suffers and illness will arise sooner or later. In order to give the reader a concrete idea of this, it has been calculated that—on average—we need to replace 1.5 kg of cells every day. The half-life of cells differs across different organ systems. There is a very slow turnover of skeletal cells (years) and a rapid destruction of white blood cells (days), for instance. One important theory regarding music's possible health-promoting effect is that it may stimulate regenerative activity, just like regular moderate physical exercise may do.

Testosterone levels as an indicator

A regenerative hormone that is relatively easy to assess is testosterone. This is one of the male sex hormones (anabolic steroids) that constitute a problem in sports. We associate them with men and with illegal administration of high dosages. However, both men and women have testosterone. Men have 10 to 20 times more testosterone in their blood than women, but most of the excess testosterone in men is tied to globulins and not immediately accessible. Free testosterone, on the other hand, is released into saliva, where the levels are more similar in men and women (although, men have approximately 50–100 percent higher concentration in saliva than women). In addition, the concentration of testosterone in saliva is regulated physiologically in such a way that when the individual feels fine and has a good psychosocial situation, the salivary testosterone concentration increases (mirroring increasing regeneration) and vice versa, both in men and women.

In the study of choir singing and IBS, the participants were asked to collect saliva on six occasions during an assessment day—when they woke up, half an hour after waking up, at lunch, before the activity (choir or group talk), after the activity, and finally before going to bed. Means were calculated from those six assessments. This testosterone mean showed a 60 percent increase during the first six months of choir singing group, whereas no such change was observed in the talk group. When the development was analyzed, the difference between the groups was shown to have decreased from six to nine months and then further from nine to 12 months after the beginning of the program. Visual analogue scales were used for the IBS participants who were asked to rate the degree of tiredness/vitality that they felt before and after choir/talk. These assessments showed that after four months there was no vitality effect in the talk group, but a pronounced and highly significant such effect after the choir activity.

In summary, the "vitality" effect (so frequently reported after choir rehearsals in other studies, such as Grape et al. 2003, Sandgren and Borg 2009) was obvious four months after these beginners had started choral singing. The testosterone effect that was measured after six months is consistent with this and may mirror an increased regeneration activity in the participants. However, the effect did not last until the end of the study year. We can only speculate about the reasons for this—perhaps the choir group was not as stimulating at the end as it was in the beginning? We have to know more about how to make the choir effect last longer.

Indicators of inflammation

Samples of venous blood were also collected from the IBS participants before and after the study year (Grape et al. 2008) for the assessment of fibrinogen. Fibrinogen mirrors the activity in the pro-inflammatory part of the immune system. During periods of arousal its concentration in blood plasma increases and vice versa. High levels of plasma fibrinogen are associated with increased risk of developing cardiovascular disease. There was a significant difference between the groups with regard to fibrinogen lasting through the whole study year. After half a year, the concentration had decreased in the choir group, while it had increased in the talk group. Twelve months after starting, the choir group still had a significant advantage over the talk group, although the difference had decreased. Similarly, after 12 months, a hormone regulating the bowel movements and therefore of direct significance for the IBS itself, motilin, showed a slight decrease in the choir group and a slight increase in the talk group (though the difference was not statistically significant). An exact parallel was observed during the study year with regard to pain related to IBS: a slight decrease in the choir group and a slight increase in the talk group (again, however, the difference was not statistically significant).

The IBS choir experiment as described here in some detail was not a perfect one. In both study groups, there was a drop-out—only 50 percent in both groups participated until the end of the study year. The final number of participants after 12 months was relatively small: 13 in the choir group and 14 in the other group. Even at the start, our participants were not representative of the normal population—all of them had IBS, all wanted to start singing in a choir, and all had accepted the special study conditions, including random allocation. It could perhaps be argued that the activity in the comparison group may have been a disappointment for those participants. However, this was not the case. They reported themselves as being quite satisfied with the lectures and group discussions that they had experienced during the study year. More studies of this kind are needed. Choir singing once a week may not only have temporary effects during and immediately after the choir activity. Effects in the direction of reduced catabolism (reduced fibrinogen mirroring "negative stress") and improved anabolism (increased testosterone mirroring improved resistance against stress) may take place.

The IBS study type does not give us any clue as to what it is in choir singing that may have positive health effects. Is it the training of the collaboration between lungs and heart? Is it the esthetic experience that starts a new orientation in life? What is the significance of the joint bodily movements that the members are making during singing? A study of the neurohormonal effects of tango dancing (Quiroga Murcia et al. 2009) has shown that the presence of a partner stimulates the saliva secretion of testosterone—a finding in line with our finding on testosterone. At any rate, the results of our study indicate that group singing may add something important psychologically and biologically to the general group effect arising when people meet once a week to talk.

CONCLUSION

....

The evidence in the scientific literature on the possible positive health effects of choir singing hitherto is actually scant. In a review, Clift (2012) has recently concluded that the support from experimental studies of health effects of choral singing is modest. Most of the evidence for a health effect is indirect. The findings in Hyyppä's (2007) research indicate that choir singing may be an important ingredient in the greater level of social capital that may explain the higher longevity of Swedish-speaking vs. Finnish-speaking East Bothnians. Choir singing of a specific kind in a given social context may contribute to longevity.

Another study (Cohen et al. 2007; Cohen, 2009) which supports the position that regular choir singing may have real health effects is the study performed on elderly subjects in Washington DC. All potential participants wanted to start singing in a choir. Two comparable groups were established. Half of them started singing in a choir once a week for two years while the other half had to wait for two years. Standardized questionnaires were used before the study, after one year and after two years, for the assessment of health. The findings showed that the choir singing subjects were favored with regard to health development.

The ability of the music to make "short cuts" to the emotional brain and to trigger unexpected psychological processes has been discussed above in the section "Psychological changes associated with singing." The combination of this with a strong social experience arising within group singing may explain why it is possible rapidly to establish a vitalizing effect, both psychologically and biologically, when a choral group is set up. As I have pointed out, there are also direct physical effects of training large muscle groups (diaphragm and breathing muscles) as takes place in regular physical exercise, and of coordinating breathing and circulation.

Inexperienced singers, however, may experience fear when they are singing in a small group. This may threaten the good effects of group singing. It may also be one explanation why some of the good health effects were attenuated during the latter part of the study year in the IBS study. Since there were relatively few participants in some of the rehearsals, it may be that some individuals may have felt "exposed" when singing.

Different kinds of choirs, such as gospel choirs, rehabilitation choirs, choirs for the elderly, or beginners' choirs, may work in very different ways. They also operate in a way that is completely different from that of a professional radio choir, for example. In a gospel choir, rhythm, religious experiences, and improvisation are in focus. In a rehabilitation choir, the choir leader has the responsibility of finding out what the needs of the participants are and to build the activities in relation to those. A music therapist may have the required knowledge and expertise to do this effectively. As yet, little research has explored these various dimensions, but clearly there is considerable scope for further work to add to our knowledge of the potential value of singing for health and well-being.

REFERENCES

Clift, S. and Hancox, G. (2001). The perceived benefits of singing: findings from a preliminary survey of a university college choral society. *Journal of the Royal Society for the Promotion of Health* 121(4): 248–256.

Clift, S., Hancox, G., Morrison, I., Hess, B., Kreutz, G., et al. (2010). Choral singing and psychological wellbeing: Quantitative and qualitative findings from English choirs in a cross-national survey. *Journal of Applied Arts and Health* 1(1): 19–34. doi:10.1386/jaah.1.1.19/1

Clift, S.M. (2012). Singing, wellbeing, and health. In: R. Macdonald, G. Kreutz, and L. Mitchell (eds), *Music, Health and Wellbeing*, pp. 113–124. Oxford: Oxford University Press.

Cohen, G., Perlstein, S., Chapline, J., Kelly, J., Firth, K.M., and Simmens, S. (2007). The impact of professional conducted cultural programs on the physical health, mental health and social functioning of older adults – 2-year results. *Journal of Aging, Humanities and the Arts* 1: 5–22.

Cohen, G. (2009). New theories and research findings on the positive influence of music and art on health with ageing. *Arts and Health* 1: 48–62.

Csikszentmihalyi, M. (1990). *Flow: The Psychology of Optimal Experience*. New York: Harper and Row.

De Manzano, Ö., Harmat, L., Theorell, T., and Ullén, F. (2010). The psychophysiology of flow during piano playing. *Emotion* 10(3): 301–311.

Feldman, R., Gordon, I., and Zagoory-Sharon, O. (2011). Maternal and paternal plasma, salivary and urinary oxytocin and parent-infant synchrony considering stress and affiliation components of human bonding. *Developmental Science* 14: 752–761.

Grape, C., Sandgren, M., Hansson, L.O., Ericson, M., and Theorell, T. (2003). Does singing promote well-being? An empirical study of professional and amateur singers during a singing lesson. *Integrative Physiological and Behavioral Science* 38(1): 65–74.

Grape, C., Theorell, T., Wikström, B.M., and Ekman, R. (2008). Choir singing and fibrinogen. VEGF, cholecystokinin and motilin in IBS patients. *Medical Hypotheses* 72: 223–234.

Grape, C., Wikström, B-M., Ekman, R., Hasson, D., and Theorell, T. (2010). Comparison between choir singing and group discussion in irritable bowel syndrome patients over one year: saliva testosterone increases in new choir singers. *Journal of Psychotherapy and Psychosomatics* 79: 196–198.

Grippo, A.J., Pournajafi-Nazarloo, H., Sanzenbacher, L., Trahanas, D.M., McNeal, N., et al. (2012). Peripheral oxytocin administration buffers autonomic but not behavioral responses to environmental stressors in isolated prairie voles. *Stress* 15: 149–161.

Gulewitsch, M.D., Enck, P., Hautzinger, M., and Schlarb, A.A. (2011). Irritable bowel syndrome symptoms among German students: prevalence, characteristics and associations to somatic complaints, sleep, quality of life and childhood abdominal pain. *European Journal of Gastroenterology and Hepatolology* 23: 311–316.

Harmat, L. and Theorell, T. (2010). Heart rate variability during singing and flute playing. *Music and Medicine* 2: 10–17.

Harmat, L, de Manzano, Ö., Theorell, T., and Ullén, F. (2012). The psychophysiology of optimal experience: parasympathetic activation is higher during flow states than during effortful attention. In review.

Horvitz, H.R. (2003). Worms, life, and death. (Nobel lecture—review). *Chem BioChem* 4(8): 697–711.

Hyyppä, M. (2007). *Livskraft ur gemenskap (Life power from cohesiveness)*. Lund: Studentlitteratur.

Kleber, B., Veit, R., Birbaumer, N., Gruzelier, J., and Lotze, M. (2010). The brain of opera singers: experience-dependent changes in functional activation. *Cerebral Cortex* 20: 1144–1152.

Kreutz, G., Bongard, S., Rohrmann, S., Hodapp, V., and Grebe, D. (2004). Effects of choir singing or listening on secretory immunoglobulin A, cortisol and emotional state. *Journal of Behavioral Medicine* 27: 623–635.

Kreutz, G. and Brünger, P. (2012). A shade of grey: negative associations with amateur choral singing. *Arts and Health* 4: 230–238.

Kreutz, G. (2014). Does singing facilitate group bonding? *Music and Medicine* 6: 51–60.

Morrison, I., Clift, S., Page, S., Salisbury, I., Shipton, M., et al. (2013). A UK feasibility study on the value of singing for people with chronic obstructive pulmonary disease (COPD). *UNESCO Journal* 3: 3. Available at: http://web.education.unimelb.edu.au/UNESCO/pdfs/ejournals/vol3iss3_2013/003_MORRISON_PAPER.pdf, last accessed October 23, 2017.

Olsson, E.M.G., von Schéele, B., and Theorell, T. (2013). Heart rate variability during choral singing. *Music and Medicine* 5: 52–59; published online 10 January 2013 doi: 10.1177/1943862112471399

Quiroga Murcia, C., Bongard, S., and Kreutz, G. (2009). Emotional and neurohumoral responses to dancing tango argentino: the effects of music and partner. *Music and Medicine* 1: 14–21.

Sandgren, M. and Borg, E. (2009). Immediate effects of choral singing on emotional states: differences between groups with lower and higher health status. Unpublished. Department of Psychology, Stockholm University.

Sundberg, J. (1989). *The Science of the Singing Voice*. Dekalb, IL: Northern Illinois University Press.

Ullén, F., de Manzano, Ö., Harmat, L., and Theorell, T. (2010). The physiology of effortless attention: correlates of state flow and flow proneness. In: B. Bruya (ed.), *Effortless Attention: A New Perspective in the Cognitive Science of Attention and Action*, pp. 205–217. Cambridge, MA: MIT Press.

Uvnäs Moberg, K. (1997). Oxytocin linked antistress effects—the relaxation and growth response. *Acta Physiologica Scandanavica* 161(suppl. 640): 38–42.

Vaag, J., Saksvik, P.Ö., Theorell, T., Skillingstad, T., and Bjerkeset, O. (2012). Sound of well-being—choir singing as an intervention to improve well-being among employees in two Norwegian county hospitals. *Arts and Health* doi:10.1080/17533015.2012.727838

Vickhoff, B., Malmgren, H., Åström, R., Nyberg, G., Engvall, M., et al. (2013). Music determines heart rate variability of singers. *Frontiers in Cognitive Neuroscience* doi: 10.3389/psyg.2013.00334

Wilson, S.J., Abbott, D.F., Lusher, D., Gentle, E.C., and Jackson, G.D. (2011). Finding your voice: a singing lesson from functional imaging. *Human Brain Mapping* 32: 2115–2130.

CHAPTER 48

UNCHAINED MELODY

The Rise of Orality and Therapeutic Singing

THE REV DR. JUNE BOYCE-TILLMAN

INTRODUCTION

> No one knows what music is. It is performed, listened to, composed, and talked about; but its essential reality is as little understood as that of its cousin, electricity. We know it detaches the understanding, enabling thoughts to turn inward upon themselves and clarify; we know that it releases the human spirit into some solitude of meditation where the creative process can freely act; we know that it can soothe pain, relieve anxiety, comfort distress, exhilarate health, confirm courage, inspire clear and bold thinking, ennoble the will, refine taste, uplift the heart, stimulate intellect, and do many another interesting and beautiful things. And yet, when all is said and done, no one knows what music is. Perhaps the explanation is that music is the very stuff of creation itself.
>
> (Lucien Price 1883–1964, quoted in Exley 1991, n.p.)

Such writing occurs regularly in the history of Western philosophy/theology but often fails to inform the way we see singing in music education or in the wider culture. In this chapter I will explore therapeutic approaches to singing related to personal and cultural developments and including various areas of musicking (Small 1998)—creating/composing, performing, and listening. I will explore some of these claims in the light of contemporary culture and research, particularly the rise of orate singing traditions (Ong 1982).[1] This chapter is an interdisciplinary weaving together of philosophy, music,

---

[1] I have used the word orate throughout rather than aural or oral because I have drawn heavily on Walter Ong's thinking in this area. It seems to be a word to describe a complete tradition which does not use a written notation system of some kind for its musicking in contrast with a literate tradition which is transmitted and learned through the medium of a written notation. This seems clearer than the words oral/aural which can simply describe a way of teaching rather than a complete tradition.

poetry, musical practice, and experience in the form of a crystallization project as described by Ellingson:

> Crystallization combines multiple forms of analysis and multiple genres of representation into a coherent text or series of related texts, building a rich and openly partial account of a phenomenon that problematizes its own construction, highlights researchers' vulnerabilities and positionality, makes claims about socially constructed meanings, and reveals the indeterminacy of knowledge claims even as it makes them.
>
> (Ellingson 2009, p. 4)

I will start by examining the social context in which the esthetics of singing have developed in Western culture and the changes in this context that have enabled therapeutic approaches to singing to develop.

VALUE SYSTEMS

The upsurge of new themes in relation to singing in contemporary society represents a rise of value systems which have traditionally been subjugated in Western culture (Foucault/ Gordon 1980). In the early twenty-first century attempts are being made to restore an imbalance that has developed within the intensely rationalistic culture of the West. Following a social constructionist view of knowledge (Gergen 1985), a culture is seen as favoring (in terms of financial support, publicity, indices of esteem, educational curricula) a particular set of values. Within any culture, a diversity of value systems will exist, but some are subjugated and embraced by groups of people who are not, in general, in positions of power (whether economic, political, or military). Individuals within a culture will also have a preference for a particular way of knowing/valuing based on their enculturation and personality characteristics. In a society where an individual's way of knowing is in tune with those in power in the wider society the person is more likely to be seen as well adjusted and will suffer less stress and disease (Boyce-Tillman 2000a). Table 48.1 (based on Boyce-Tillman 2007) shows the values that have been subjugated by the dominant classical music tradition. The dominant value systems in the UK are on the right-hand side of this table and the subjugated value systems are on the left-hand side (based upon Boyce-Tillman 2006, p. xiv).

The development of the singing traditions with therapeutic intention can be seen as an upsurge in the previously subjugated value systems in an effort to find acceptance by those in authority. It is most clearly seen in the growth of community choirs:

> Unfortunately despite the availability of music as a consumer item in many different formats, it is extraordinarily easy for people to become separated or cut off from music making and singing, as indeed from other direct experiences of the arts.
>
> (Morgan and Boyce-Tillman 2016, pp. 53–4)

The dominant singing traditions—often called classical—valued products rather than process, individual achievement over community building, challenging entry routes divorced from nurture, and unity within its structures rather than the encompassing of diverse traditions and styles. So in the early twenty-first century there are two esthetics alive that are associated with singing in UK society:

Table 48.1 Dominant and subjugated value systems in the UK. These value systems need to regarded in relationship with one another; there needs to be a flow between them rather than a polarization. The rise of orality and therapeutic approaches to singing represents an attempt to bring some of these subjugated values into relationship with the dominant value systems

Subjugated value systems	Dominant value systems
Community	Individual
Private	Public
Process	Product
Embodied	Disembodied
Intuitive	Rational
Nurture	Challenge
Diversity	Unity
Relaxation	Excitement

- The classical perspective on singing emphasizes performance, perfection, and virtuosity—the standard or "taproot" esthetic[2] that has been recognized in music education since its inception in the mid-1800s.
- The second esthetic for singing stresses community building, diversity, group collaboration and relationship (Pascale 2005, p. 167, author's quotation marks).

The title of this chapter is designed to show that the dominance of the classical perspective has resulted in the imprisoning of people's natural ability to sing. In the opinion of the author, in line with Christopher Small's idea of musicking (1998), singing is a universal human attribute. Turino describes this process of musical disempowerment as demusicalization (Small 1998, p. 210; Turino 2008, p. 25). Sarah Morgan describe her own "demusicalization" and concludes: "Those involved in less formal music making (often identified as music making 'just for fun'), will say 'I'm not really a musician,' regardless of how significant a part music plays in their lives" (Morgan and Boyce-Tillman 2016, p. 53).

The result is the downplaying of orate traditions which are regarded as of less value than the dominant literate tradition. It is this dominance that causes people who may be skilled in orate traditions to define themselves as not musical. However, although this chapter is largely concerned with the re-establishment of the valuing of orality in therapeutic approaches to singing, it does not deny that many people participating in the literate classical esthetic would claim similar benefits to those that this chapter explores. It is not a binary opposition but an acknowledgment of difference and an acceptance of the validity of the two esthetics discussed above, as well as a desire to have both traditions valued by the dominant culture.

---

[2] Described earlier as the dominant value system.

The revision of the value system from a product-based esthetic to one more inclusive of process led to the inclusion of intention in the planning and description of musicking. This led to research into the broadly therapeutic effects of musicking.[3] Gradually, in the latter part of the twentieth century, a variety of intentions emerged in the area of the orate traditions of singing:

- *Restoring*: healing, strengthening individuals and communities, as in community music and music therapy using the benefits of the music itself, which can contribute to inner peace, learning how to transform energies, improving self-esteem, developing the capacity to create; also giving persons the possibility to question their ways to act, or to react, changing their way to be.
- *Affirming*: legitimizing and stabilizing societies, as in national anthems and giving groups of people an identity.
- *Resisting*: opposing, protesting against perceived injustices, as in such phenomena as protest songs.
- *Creating*: inventing, promoting new ways of organizing society, as in music as a way of conflict transformation by peaceful means (Urbain 2008).

There is now considerable research on the way these intentions play out in contemporary society in areas like sociology, therapy, and ethnomusicology. Since the middle of the twentieth century this has resulted in an increase in literature researching that singing in various contexts can:

- provide social, emotional, and physical benefits (Clift and Hancox 2001)
- improve life-satisfaction (VanderArk et al. 1983)
- improve well-being, social benefits, lifestyle, functional ability, improvements in breathing, breath control, and physical health for people with COPD (Clift et al. 2013)
- improve well-being, communication, cognition and understanding, relations with others, organization and structure, skills and physical ability for people with Parkinson's (Vella-Burrows and Hancox 2012)
- decrease stress and promote relaxation
- decrease behavioral and psychological symptoms of dementia (i.e. delusions, agitation, anxiety, apathy, irritability, and night-time disturbances)
- promote the recall of personal histories; improve mood, orientation, remote episodic memory, and to a lesser extent also general cognition
- enhance caregiver well-being, when they are engaged in the singing activities.

As can be seen, there is considerable Western interest in the therapeutic effects of singing.

The rest of this chapter will explore the development of the area of the therapeutic use of singing under the following themes, which connect with the emerging subjugated value systems described above:

---

[3] It was as early as 1939 that music was recommended as a prescription to be given by a doctor (Podolsky 1939).

- orality and the valuing of process
- embodiment
- transformation within the self: de-integration and re-integration and the valuing of the more chaotic
- expression and the valuing of the emotional
- empowerment associated with the rise of nurturing in a challenging tradition
- transformative relationships—building community including the birth of new choirs
- getting it together—musical inclusion, rather than exclusivity
- liminality, which may be seen as representing the restoration of spirituality to musicking.

THERAPEUTIC USES OF SINGING

Orality and the valuing of process

In all of this therapeutic literature the processes that are being described are mostly orate ones. The establishment of the dominance of literacy over orality in the area of words is well described by Walter Ong (1982) as part of the colonial enterprise; the result is that orate traditions are regarded as inferior. This is also true in singing:

> The concept of informal or amateur as the "lesser version" points us back to the comments of John Julius Norwich, or to our unachievable ideal. The worth and status of oral, improvised, informal or amateur music making can be eroded both explicitly . . . and in more subtle ways, by use of terminology such as high or low culture, amateur and professional musician, national, or local performer, and so on.
>
> (Morgan and Boyce-Tillman 2016, p. 57)

In the UK, Frankie Armstrong played an important part in the re-valuing of the orate through establishing the welcoming climate of the Natural Voice Network:

> Natural Voice is about celebrating the voice you were born with, rather than trying to train it to an ideal of perfection. It's about building accepting, non-judgmental communities that sing together. It's about welcoming all voices into a group without audition and working from there to make a group sound. It's about making learning by ear accessible to the whole group so that nobody needs to be able to read music.
>
> (Natural Voice Network 2014)

So now there is a more of a sense of valuing the orate for itself and not simply as a stepping-stone to the literate traditions. It is a continually changing tradition always being recontextualized; in it there is scope for creative re-interpretation of material on the part of performers. We see this process of contextualization in the adaptations made to a literate tradition of hymnody in black singing traditions:

> The oral tradition introduces itself again; the "standard" or well-known, Euro-American hymns require no special instruction for black rendition. The Black religious community instinctively knows how to sing them. The mode of singing is common to the Black religious experience and is passed from one generation to another via an oral tradition in Black sacred

music. Rather than retaining the Euro-American structure, hymns were reshaped or improvised or "blackenized" as a means of contextualization.

(Cited in Costen 1993, p. 43)

The orate traditions are much more fluid, ever changing, and capable of being re-
adapted: "Because much of my material is folk based, I also explain that the music is usually just
a guideline or a reminder, not a set of precise instructions—a river rather than a road" (Morgan
and Boyce-Tillman 2016, p. 60). This fluidity enables the therapeutic approach to singing to
flourish in a variety of contexts; it is flexible and adaptable to a variety of circumstances.

To summarize, the rise of the valuing of process as well as product has enabled orate
traditions to be re-evaluated; this freed up singing for many people who had been trapped by
their inability to grasp the principles of the literate musical traditions.

Embodiment

The dominance of the literate tradition in singing has meant that a great deal of energy in
music teaching has been on the cognitive aspects of deciphering the notation. Consequently,
the physical effects of singing have sometimes been lost. A work that I created (*PeaceSong*
2005) included a procession carrying candles in which the participants sang the word *shalom*
on a single note. One of the participants reflected on her own experience of singing:

> I have sung for many years but it always meant working out if the next note was a G sharp or G
> natural and a crotchet or a quaver. Because you only asked me to sing a single note I was aware
> of the breath entering and leaving my body and it became a meditative experience.
>
> (Morgan and Boyce-Tillman 2016, p. 210)

A holistic approach to singing sees it as a physical, mental, and spiritual activity. Brendan
Doyle describes the physical effects of singing the chants of Hildegard of Bingen. When they
are sung, the control of the breath required to manage the long phrases is seen as a physical
meditation associated with the Holy Spirit (Doyle 1987, p. 364).

Striking work has been done in this area at the Sidney De Haan Research Centre for Arts
and Health at Christchurch Canterbury University (see the chapter by Clift and Gilbert in
this volume).[4] One project consisted of setting up a weekly community singing session for
people with chronic obstructive pulmonary disease (COPD). They assessed impact on lung
function, functional capacity, breathlessness, and quality of life over the period September
2011 to June 2012. The St Georges Respiratory Questionnaire (SGRQ), MRC breathlessness
scale, EQ-5D, and York SF-12 were administered at baseline, mid-point, and end of study; spirometry was used to assess lung function at baseline and study end. Written feedback from
participants was also analyzed. The results were that health-related quality of life assessed
by SGRQ showed a 3.3 point change in the direction of health improvement. Improvements
were also found in FEV1 percent (a percentage between the measured and statistically expected value for an individual on the forced expiratory volume in one second test), FVC
(forced vital capacity), and FVC percent (a percentage between the measured and expected

---

[4] http://www.canterbury.ac.uk/Research/Documents/COPDSummaryReport.pdf, contacted
January 2015.

value for an individual on the forced vital capacity test). Qualitative evidence showed that the singing groups were enjoyable social events and participants reported improvements in their breathing, activity levels, and well-being. A decline in health would normally have been expected over a ten-month period with this disease; so the study supports the physical effects of regular singing.

Similar effects were found in the Elevate project in Salisbury hospital (Preti and Boyce-Tillman 2014). Artists working in Salisbury hospital saw physical changes in patients when they sang:

> you create something either out of memory or imagination; you create or recreate another world in the place between the two of you . . . I've seen people, the muscles on their faces change as they follow the path into the wood, you know, as they begin to recollect the place where they used to swing or something that had happened there. And they can very physically change in front of you when that happens, and that's wonderful.
>
> (Preti and Boyce-Tillman 2014)

Kate Numger describes the physical aspects of the Threshold choir singing at the bedside of the dying:

> Two to three singers will go to a bedside, and they pick songs based upon what a patient or the patient's family wants . . . Sometimes, the recipient will move a finger, mouth a "thank you" or will change their breathing and relax their muscles. At the end of life, when human functions began to slow and cease, the signal for "I like this" can be as simple as a blink.
>
> (Threshold Choir 2014)

Here we see how psychological and spiritual changes are reflected physically and brought together by singing.

To summarize, in the literate Western classical music tradition much stress has been laid on the cognitive aspects of musicking. The rise of the orate traditions and their therapeutic possibilities has enabled an increased awareness of the physicality of singing.

Transformation within the self: de-integration and re-integration

All descriptions of the processes of creativity include a measure of chaos or darkness—a time when the whole appears to fragment before it re-establishes itself again in a different configuration (Wallas 1927). The notion of a steady progress towards an integrated self underpinned Jungian psychotherapy; but psychologists like Thomas Fordham have challenged this, suggesting that the process of living is more one of de-integration and re-integration (Jennings 1999, p. 45). Because of the high premium placed on integration, de-integration is frequently pathologized and people who are diagnosed as ill are experiencing a de-integration of the self.

A classic example of de-integration is the grieving process. When a loved person, animal, or object disappears, the integration within the self is disturbed. The self has to de-integrate in order to re-integrate with a previously essential part missing. In former times protected time was given for this process to happen with rituals associated with grieving. With the contemporary requirement that life go on as "normal," the self has huge problems in re-integrating, which it would do quite naturally, given time and support. I have found in my workshops that the acceptance of multiplicity within the self enables people to see singing, especially song creation, as a way of re-integrating the self. The philosopher Gillian Rose calls us to work in what she calls "the broken middle," which has within it the necessity of living with the contradictions:

> In the middle of imposed and negated identities and truths, in the uncertainty about who we are and what we should do. [. . .] She [Gillian Rose] commends us to work with these contradictions, with the roaring and the roasting of the broken middle, and to know that it is "I".
>
> (Tubbs 1998, p. 34)

The acceptance of the more fragmented aspects of the personality leads to a "re-membering" of the person. In Beethoven's sketchbooks, for example, we have a record of Beethoven wrestling with the process of "re-membering" himself. The use of fragments generated by improvisation is used in music therapy in a process that is essentially one of self-transformation. The ability to enter that chaos, with tools for handling it, would seem to be what differentiates the experienced composer or music therapist from the less experienced musician or music therapy client:

> What we need is to fumble around in the darkness because that's where our lives (not necessarily all the time, but at least some of the time, and particularly when life gets problematical for us) take place; in the darkness, or, as we say in Christianity, "the dark night of the soul." It is in these situations that Art must act and then it won't be judged Art but will be useful to our lives.
>
> (John Cage, quoted in Ross 1978, p. 10)

In encouraging people to make up their own songs or even just improvise freely with no product they are entering into a process familiar to established composers (Boyce-Tillman 2018, p. 406). Sometimes the songs generated in this way can be empowering not only for the person themselves but also their carers and relations: "I have worked with a number of groups in the hospice Day Unit and in a variety of care homes . . . One group wrote three songs, the melodies came from music we improvised as a group" (Dives in Hartley et al. 2008, n.p.).

In a recent project with young people with special needs run by La Folia[5] in Salisbury Cathedral, I saw how small sung motifs could create impressive musical structures. The motifs, which had been created by the youngsters in response to the Magna Carta document on display at the cathedral, formed the basis of a number of improvisatory pieces in various parts of the cathedral. Around the themes of protest, reflection, asking for help, power, struggle, feeling safe, protection, and freedom participants sang fragments with texts such as:

> We need a system bigger than we are
> We need lots of help
> We have a voice that's strong enough to say "no"!

With the help of an actor, dancer, and various instrumentalists, these were impressively woven into fascinating soundscapes that empowered the participants and also fascinated the

---

[5] http://lafoliamusic.org/about/creative-projects/

visitors to the cathedral. It was a real example of the process of reintegration of ideas, people, and musical motifs achieved through group improvisation.

The process of humming and whistling, which was more common in past ages, allowed people to play with small motifs and so reconstruct themselves:

> *The Symphony*
>
> He sits beside his mother
> Cuddling his four years on the planet
>
> The train bleats
> And he improvises a symphony
> Around its falling minor third
>
> He has yet to learn
> That he cannot compose.
>
> But we will soon teach him.

(Boyce-Tillman 2004)

The process of listening to singing can enable the listener to participate in this process of the composer; listeners are called to enter into the processes of the performer and composer. The listener shares their journey and is reassured by the fact that another person has been into that chaotic place that they are experiencing. In listening we can be taken into a different world by a composer/guide, who leads us through it musically. The composer, together with performer, becomes a therapist. Millie Taylor (2013) illustrates this with the example of Stephen Sondheim showing how his song "Into the Woods" (Sondheim and Lapine 1987) takes the audience on a journey into difficult places. Here musical theater becomes a form of companionship along the journeys of life, and a guide in negotiating them. Discovering this in times of de-integration can provide people with a tool for handling chaotic times in their lives.

In a similar way, singing particular songs has long been a way of establishing and maintaining identity in difficult circumstances. Ruth Westheimer, writing of her experience of being taken away from her Jewish parents at the beginning of life, writes: "I sang that lullaby—which has a melody written by Heinrich Isaak back in 1490—to my children. And maybe I mangled the melody, but I felt—and still feel –the sweetness of it in my bones" (Westheimer 2003, p. 13).

A letter from the trenches in World War I shows how hymn singing was used to maintain an identity in difficult conditions: "Here we try to keep our spirits up through all the firing. We have short services here in the trenches and in all the mud. I turn to sing the verses that I learnt at dear Mynydd Gwyn. I hope that I will be back there soon" (Griffith Roberts, quoted in Boyce-Tillman 2000a).[6]

Within this essentially orate process lies the possibility of redeeming and surviving the damaging experiences through the two processes of vocal improvising and the singing of significant songs. In one music at the bedside project an Irish family was strengthened by a singer enabling them to sing the well-known Irish song "Cockles and Mussels." Such experiences enable us to recreate our selfhood. Listening can also aid this inner journey of transformation.

---

[6] Letter from Griffith Roberts given by John Roberts.

To summarize, singing can play a significant part in the central life processes of de-integration and re-integration. By playing with small fragments of melody and text people can create new songs that give new meaning and integrity to their lives.

Expression and meaning

This process of self-transformation has another aspect. The Western literature on music and creativity stresses the area of self-expression (Boyce-Tillman 2018, pp. 327–8). It is often linked with human emotion. Traditions of word-based psychotherapy have developed ways of accessing deep areas of feeling and painfully traumatic experiences; but they can leave people with difficult memories allied to powerful feelings, such as anger and despair, with no strategies for dealing with them. Not only does music offer the possibility of expressing these but also of remaking them into an esthetically satisfying object. Ray Charles confirms this in his own use of song;

> I'd like to think that when I sing a song, I can let you all know about the heartbreak, struggle, lie and kicks in the ass I've gotten over the years for being black and everything else, without actually saying a word about it.
>
> (Quoted in Moore 1986/1992, p. 123)

The process of acceptance of one's expression by a group creates the possibility of growth; a person can gain acceptance of their private trauma through expression through music. Music can express what is inexpressible in words: "Words are good for many things, but they don't seem sufficient when it comes to death. The feelings are just too deeply intense and words are too inadequate . . . But music can reach those places where words alone can't go" (Threshold Choir 2014). This characteristic of inaccessibility makes it, by definition, a confidential medium as well as being expressive. It is a "veiled" medium. As Lévi-Strauss writes, "music is the only language with the contradictory attributes of being at once intelligible and untranslatable" (Levi-Strauss 1970, p. 18). The process of expression can lead to the construction of new meaning by awakening a broader awareness, and expanding personal horizons: "[Music] does not offer meaning but triggers the effort to produce the meaning" (Voegelin 2010, p. 165).

Around this area of meaning and expression lies its use in reminiscence therapy. This exploits the mystery surrounding the precise meaning of music, where this is situated and how it is communicated. It has increasingly become clear that there is an element of cultural and personal interpretation in the process of decoding the meaning of music. Within a piece of music there is not only the meaning encoded by the creator in the sounds themselves—intrinsic meaning. For example, a piece that is slow and soft will have an expressive meaning associated with being calm. However, there is also meaning that has been locked on to a piece by particular circumstances in our lives—extrinsic meaning (Green 1988, but using the author's terms). An example of the latter is the phenomenon of "they're playing our tune"—a melody that has been associated with a particularly emotional moment.

It is this phenomenon of explicit meaning, which enables music to be used to unlock painful and pleasant areas of memory. No other person can know what memories are locked onto a piece by someone else. Sometimes the person themselves is not aware. This area of meaning is one used widely in music therapy especially in reminiscence with older patients.

Costanza Preti writes how skillfully the artists in the Elevate programs in Salisbury hospital were able to handle sensitively the implications of extrinsic musical meaning:

> The artists were not intimidated by the patients' emotional reactions; they welcomed them instead as an expression of emotional release that was perceived as beneficial and somehow therapeutic. They were observed to take immediate notice of these reactions addressing the patients asking if they wanted them to stop playing a certain song or reading a certain poem.
>
> (Preti and Boyce-Tillman 2014)

Overall, the patients were very appreciative about the opportunity to release their emotions: "Her final choice reduced me to tears but I can only describe them as good tears" (Preti and Boyce-Tillman 2014).

Music was seen in Salisbury Hospital to work with the elderly as an extremely important way of unlocking painful memories—making the private more public so that it can be healed. Patients would request a song that they were keen to hear, such as "The White Cliffs of Dover," "It's a Long Way to Tipperary," "Edelweiss," "Oh What a Beautiful Morning!" The varied repertoire of the artists allowed patients to engage actively with the songs, singing along, recognizing the tunes.

Most therapeutic studies of singing highlight a significant effect on mood. This was clear in Salisbury in patients with dementia who were suffering from depression, anxiety, and various mental health issues, or experiencing boredom and frustration from their long stay in the hospital. It helped them and their families to focus on something constructive, different from the illness:

> The rewards are the smiles on the faces . . . a woman who always asks for "Que Sera Sera", every time she does, and she's beautiful, she's very, very effusive in her praise, you know, she always says "Oh, you've cheered me up so much", "Oh, you've made my day."
>
> (Preti and Boyce-Tillman 2014)

This often opened a new perspective on the patient for the hospital staff who remarked on these unexpected effects—their awareness of the patient was broadened.

The element of expression was also true in the area of singing and mental health, as in the East Kent Singing for Health Network Project. In this project 137 participants were involved, of which 32 participants provided sufficiently complete data at three assessments. EQ-5D and CORE questionnaires were used. Qualitative accounts were gathered and a DVD produced based on a performance event involving all singing groups in the network. Substantial reduction was found in CORE-OM scores over a period of eight months. Changes were found in functioning, problems, and well-being. This account shows how the process of expression also manages extreme emotions:

> I have bipolar disorder. When I am depressed, singing in the group and coming together with other people lifts my mood and gives me something positive and productive to focus on. When I am manic, singing is something I can channel my extra energy into and express my enthusiasm for life through. The choir provides structure and purpose in an otherwise sometimes empty life.
>
> (Woman aged 30)

It is this sort of research that has led to an increasing number of Recovery Choirs for people with mental health problems which help them bridge the gap between hospital and life beyond it, as well as giving them a strategy for handling their problems. The range and scope of these will be examined later in this chapter.

The summary of this section is contained in this quotation from *Songwriting for Music Therapists*:

> Songs reflect on the past, present and future. They give us an immediate context. They are a container for thoughts, feelings—a way to explore emotions. They express who we are and how we feel, they bring us closer to others, they keep us closer together, they keep us company when we are alone. They articulate our beliefs and values. As the years pass songs bear witness to our lives. They are our musical diaries, our life stories.
>
> (Bruscia quoted in Hartley et al. 2008, n.p.)

Empowerment—nurturing with singing

Singing in the classical esthetic has followed Western culture's love of challenge with programs of examinations, competitive events, and auditions. The revaluing of music as empowerment has meant a rediscovery of the nurturing power of singing. In this changing value system there has been a revisiting of ancient traditions:

> While bedside singers may be unique in American culture, it's not unprecedented. In some Hindu and Buddhist practices, hymns are sung near those who are dying, while mantras are chanted into the ear at the moment of death. In the Middle Ages, French Benedictine monks became famous for establishing infirmaries across Europe for the terminally ill, where they used Gregorian chants to soothe the dying.
>
> (Ellen Synakowski in Threshold Choir 2014)

The decline of organized religion and regular attendance once a week at a place of worship—in which singing would have played a prominent part—meant that there was a loss of an inclusive singing tradition that forged community. The burgeoning community choir movement regularly has empowerment and nurture as core values. As church attendance declined, other choirs grew up in the mid to late twentieth century to nurture people. This was apparent in titles like: the Can't Sing Choir (Joan Taylor at Morley College); Singing for the Terrified (Polly Bolton)

Most importantly into this field came Frankie Armstrong and the Natural Voice Network (1988), as mentioned above. Estelle Jorgensen (1996) highlights the role of the itinerant singing masters in empowering the poor and the women in eighteenth-century society. These delivered the only formal education open to groups of people from otherwise disenfranchised groups, especially women and girls who were excluded from much music-making in the churches and communities. She claims that the nineteenth-century political movements, which encouraged the inclusion of music in the school curriculum of the emerging state-supported schools, were inspired by the work of these singing schools.

However, in the name of music education in a normalizing curriculum we have sometimes cheated people out of their birthright to sing; the use of a culture of musical challenges has engendered a process of demusicalization for many people. The map of singing as presented in the average school is one of a restricted range of pitches and tone colors, and a concern to make children musically literate. What this denies is the premise that we all have our own note, the note that is easiest for us to sing at any time

(Boyce-Tillman 1996, p. 215). The limited horizons of the curriculum have excluded people from their singing birthright. Their own note needs validating before they can move forward in acquiring a wider range of pitches.

When people have found their singing power they can use it to survive their darkest moments. It becomes a valuable coping strategy. From the El Mozote massacre in El Salvador in 1981 comes the remarkable story of a young girl, an evangelical Christian, who was raped several times in one afternoon. Through it all she sang:

> She had kept on singing, too, even after they had done what had to be done, and shot her in the chest. She had lain there on La Cruz [the hill on which the soldiers carried out their killings]—with the blood flowing from her chest and had kept on singing—a bit weaker than before, but still singing. And the soldiers, stupefied, had watched, and pointed. Then they had grown tired of the game and shot her again, and she sang still, and their wonder turned to fear, until they had unsheathed their machetes, and hacked her through the neck, and at last the singing stopped.
>
> (Danner 1994, pp. 78–79)

When I was leading a workshop on the power of music in Australia, I met a nun who felt overwhelmed by her work in a community that concerned itself with violations of human rights. After the course I was leading, in which she had sung some of her songs, she said: "I know what I had forgotten; I had forgotten to sing. If I remember to sing I can survive the stories that our community is receiving and even transform them in some way." Similarly, a woman in a difficult marriage used the song "One Day at a Time Sweet Jesus" as her prime strategy for survival.

There are many accounts of the relation of singing and healing. Many of these involve hymns of some kind—possibly because of their extrinsic meaning or possibly because they bring a spiritual dimension to the situation:

> After the address came the hymn, "All hail the power of Jesus' name." During the singing of it I felt the power of God falling upon me. My sister felt it too, and said "Floie, you're going to walk." The Lord gave me faith then.
>
> (RERC Accounts of Religious Experience 1970)

Other accounts include singing as a strategy for retaining/regaining power:

> A woman . . . had turned on the gas in her home heaters in order to commit suicide . . . She had forgotten to turn off the radio in the kitchen. As the music continued she heard someone singing the familiar hymn,
>
> > What a Friend we have in Jesus,
> > All our sins and griefs to bear!
>
> The impact of that hymn changed that woman's mind and saved her life.
>
> (Carnegie 1944, pp. 154–156)

Singing can be a transmission of love and strength. In Gugulethu, South Africa, I was present at a service where people could come forward for healing. They told the pastor their problem. He relayed this to the congregation. The congregation then sang to support the healing. What was interesting here was that the songs were not soft and gentle but strong louder pieces accompanied by drumming patterns made on hymnbooks. The greater the need, the greater the strength of the singing of the thousand people present. The song appeared to transmit a sense of loving holding through its power. I have seen this phenomenon working beautifully in funeral and memorial services for certain ethnic groups in London.

An exercise that I do in workshops is a humming bath. In this a group surrounds two people in the middle with a group hum executed with loving intention. Participants hum whatever note is easy for them taking a breath when necessary. This gives the people in the middle a sense of being held, warmed, supported, and loved.

Singing can also play a significant part of holding people with memory loss which I attempted to express in a poem:

> *Cry from the Depths*
> 1. Hold me! My eyes are dim, my memory faltering
> My sense of past and future now are fused
> I cannot recognise much any longer
> Except the music that the choir intones.
>
> 2. Help me! My limbs are frail and arms that once worked strongly
> Hang limp and useless, will not respond to me;
> I cannot understand the puzzling world around me
> Except the music that the choir intones.
>
> 3. Hear me! My earthly usefulness is fading
> And nurture that I once gave freely, now I need;
> I can make sense of little any longer
> Except the music that the choir intones.
>
> 4. Heal me! You whom I loved and who once loved me
> How can I feel that caring love right now?
> Where can I still lay hold of warm acceptance?
> Ah! In the music that the choir intones.
> So now I flow within the river of that song.

(Boyce-Tillman 2014)

Music in the area of memory loss both holds and empowers. In one Singing for Wellbeing choir with which I am familiar, for example, an ex-soldier led the same song each week. Just for a moment he was able to exercise the power he had used for all his working life. In the same group one woman had suffered the onset of her dementia for several years, so she was the most advanced in our group. After two sessions, she walked steadily into the room, and showed no signs of anxiety, and started humming along, perfectly in pitch. She also developed over the term her own "tune," which occurred at certain songs. She locked eyes and said "Thank you" with a smile.[7]

The earliest bonding between mother and child through improvised singing has been carefully researched by Colwyn Trevarthen (2002) and has a nurturing, empathetic, bonding function. But the demusicalized parent often needs freeing from their preconceived view of themselves as a singer—to unchain their own melody. Work by Sheila Woodward in her doctoral thesis showed that this process starts in the uterus by placing microphones in a mother's womb:

---

[7] I am grateful to Sandra Thibault and Jackie Shipster for these accounts.

You still hear the sound of the music, but it's a little like listening to music say, underwater. And, with the human voice, we still hear that it's a woman or a man, we can hear the particular tone quality of that voice, and we can hear the notes that are being sung.

(Woodward 2015, n.p.)

She investigated whether this singing to the child in the uterus will affect their development from about four to five months onwards. She encouraged mothers to establish a relationship with their unborn child through song. This was also carried out in the UK at St Mary's Hospital on the Isle of Wight.

The lullaby is an area where traditionally children have been held musically. In child-rearing there have been indications that children use the songs sung to them by their parents as comforters, rather like teddy bears and comfort blankets. My own young son comforted himself in the night with his version of "Twinkle, Twinkle, Little Star." The publicity for the Threshold Choir links the processes of birth and dying with singing, which is often led by women:

> A mother's heartbeat is the first sound that each of us hears. It feels to me that women's bodies are the guardians of life entering this world and it feels right that we will be guardians of the gate out. Experienced soloists are often not the best fit because "projection of voice is not the goal; softness and comfort are," says Munger. She, Synakowski and other choir leaders encourage those who like to sing but lack professional experience to join. It's easier to teach them to mix their voices into the groups, sing softly and focus on the dying instead of themselves.

(Threshold Choir 2014)

Although self-efficacy was a perceived benefit of community choir participation, Sarah Morgan prefers not to use the word "empowerment":

> I prefer not to use the term "empowering," as to me that implies that people lack a power which I can mysteriously bestow on them. I do strongly believe that everyone has the ability to experience and enjoy singing in some way, and I see my role as helping to remind people of that, and trying to remove barriers, where they exist, whether they relate to musical technicality, terminology, accessibility or skills.

(Morgan and Boyce-Tillman 2016, pp. 59–60)

Much of this nurturing is about process-based musicking; in this area of the valuing of process, singing groups are sometimes divided about whether to present performances at all, with some members preferring simply to come and sing once a week—valuing the process over the product. However, some of the literature sets out the potential value of performance, in this case with people with mental health problems:

> Such performances demonstrate the power of singing to bring people together and support recovery from mental ill-health; they promote social inclusion, social capital and normalization for people with mental health issues, and serve to challenge misconceptions, stigma and prejudice associated with mental illness.

(Morrison and Clift 2012b, p. 16)

The need for a sense of nurturing runs through all the literature on the characteristics of leadership in community singing groups. Sarah Morgan writes about the need to be aware of people's state of mind:

> At a practical level, one of the most useful skills I acquired was an ability to look around a group and quickly notice people who looked uneasy or uncomfortable, and make it acceptable for people to voice their unease, as well as finding ways of making mistakes an accepted and even a positive part of the process of learning.
>
> (Morgan and Boyce-Tillman 2016, p. 21)

Rehearsals are often seen as uplifting and friendly (Birmingham Wellbeing Choir 2014). In the Elevate program in Salisbury hospital, the nurturing and empowerment was not only for the patients but also for the staff. Members of the hospital staff were actively observed taking part in the artists' sessions, just by singing a song with the musicians or improvising a little dance in the middle of the bay:

> It was also noticed that the staff would sing or hum the tune of a song in a variety of situations, for example while they were washing a patient behind the curtains, when they were taking the blood pressure of a patient or giving them their medications. Furthermore, it became increasingly evident that some of the staff was using music to distract the patients from the procedure they were carrying out.
>
> (Preti and Boyce-Tillman 2014)

The possibility for empowerment for caregivers is also commented on in project evaluations. One caregiver associated with the Winchester Singing for Well-being choir described how taking her husband with dementia to the choir enabled her to find her own singing voice. Indeed, in the Centre for the Arts as Wellbeing at Winchester University we have a motto—Discovery in Recovery. In one program that we planned, older patients will have taster sessions of singing, movement, painting, and drama while in hospital which they can continue after they have been discharged. So their time in hospital will be a time when they can discover new abilities such as their ability to sing.

The role of musical skill in all of this is regularly a subject for discussion and the literature on music therapy does not see itself as giving skills but simply as using existing skills. However, in the wider world this distinction is often blurred. The Can't Sing Choir in Morley College, London from the late twentieth century saw people wanting to use the choir as a stepping stone to the literate tradition, as these comments from members illustrate:

> I have found learning very hard, but very rewarding. It is difficult for a non-reader to pick up a tune . . . I hope to learn to read music and to sing from a score. My ambition would be to join a choir which sings "oratorical" music and it is the older music which we sing that I enjoy most.
> I like singing, but cannot sight-read very well, so I joined the Can't Sing Choir to improve my standard of singing and sight-reading. Also to get some practice in four-part singing for enjoyment. Without the responsibility of preparing for concerts.[8]

Giving musical skills through education of some kind can improve people's independence. I arranged music lessons for four children diagnosed with chronic anxiety as part of a treatment program in conjunction with Winchester Child Guidance Unit (Walker and Boyce-Tillman 2002). All of them were re-empowered to return to normal life through the development of musical skills that included improvisation.

To summarize, singing can contribute to personal growth and can allow people both individually and corporately to claim their power. Often this is by validating more process-based,

---

[8] Unpublished interviews from the Can't Sing Choir, thanks to Joan Taylor.

orate traditions. The development of community choirs can be seen as enabling people to overcome past negative musical experiences and regain their musical heritage.

Transforming relationships—building community

Words are designed to classify and identify differences that divide, but singing can unite and has united many cultures (Storr 1993). When a group of people makes music together their unity is restored. The chief loss resulting from the decline of Western Judaeo-Christian theology in our culture may not be the theology but the whole community coming together once a week to make music. The Western classical tradition in the Middle Ages had a notion of community that included the cosmos and, in particular, God, up to the Renaissance. During this period notions of healing through the creation of community were widely found in the literature:

> Musical harmony softens hard hearts. It brings in them the moisture of reconciliation, and it invokes the Holy Spirit. When different voices sing in unity, they symbolize the simple tenderness of mutual love. When different voices blend in song, they symbolize the blending of thoughts and feelings which is the highest pleasure human beings can know. Let the sweet sound of music enter your breast, and let it speak to your heart. It will drive out all darkness, and spread spiritual light to every part of you.
>
> (Hildegard of Bingen in Boyce-Tillman 2000b, p. 138)

In post-Enlightenment Europe, the heroic journey model gained prominence (Boyce-Tillman 2007) with the individual composer set over and perhaps against the community. The individual performer often suffered an isolated hot-housing process (Kemp 1996, p. 248) and community music-making was devalued by the literate High Art traditions as we saw above. There is a vision today of a society that establishes peace by giving value to all:

> We support the development of a culture of transformative personal, organizational, and social change that fosters and celebrates the highest human qualities and practices, including empathy, altruism, peaceful conflict resolution, and restorative justice.
>
> (Schulman 2012)

From many sources comes the idea that singing can play a significant part as a community-building exercise to defeat the loneliness, isolation, fragmentation, and meaninglessness of our society:

> What then does aesthetic experience mean for Dewey? Together with aspects of artistic doings and contextualism of this doing, the aesthetic aspect of experience means a qualitatively different, fulfilling and inherently meaningful mode of engagement in contrast to the mechanical, the fragmentary, the non-integrated and all other non-meaningful forms of engagement.
>
> (Westerlund 2002, p. 191)

We see these elements present in this account from the East Kent Singing for Mental Health Project:

> It's a chance to do something in a group without being competitive. Meeting different people and joining with them in a co-operative venture. It has helped me deal with bouts of depression. I've rediscovered the pleasure of singing. I'd become inhibited about singing for several years. I've felt more relaxed having found a way to get out of a downward spiral.
>
> (Woman aged 63)

The tolerance of diversity is an important element in the way a community defines itself; the admitting of diversity has enabled new societies and new ways of conceiving society to emerge. The process of readjusting this balance can be seen in a post-apartheid South Africa where musicians have played a part in this process. For example, West Nkosi released a 1992 CD entitled *The Rhythm of Healing* that brings together a variety of different musical traditions from all over the country. Many other musicians have engaged in peace-making projects to contain diverse elements respectfully within musical structures, well illustrated in *Music and Conflict Transformation: Harmonies and Dissonances in Geopolitics* (Urbain 2008).

The increase in community singing projects has opened up new horizons for reconciliations across cultures and between groups of people out of contact with one another in a single geographical area, including interfaith dialogue (Illman 2010):

> [It may] involve learning new skills and expanding the meaning of concepts, often "unlearning" what was formerly believed to be true . . . Through performance, communities are finding ways of seeking truth and also recognizing its multiple faces.
>
> (Cohen 2008, p. 31)

My own event Space for Peace (Boyce-Tillman 2011, 2012) shows this. It is a radically innovative event designed to bring faiths together through the arts—a vigil for peace. It started in Winchester Cathedral but has been tried in other venues, including a Hindu temple, as a means of interfaith dialogue. The age range of participants is 7 to 85 years with people from many traditions. The way the event is structured creates a resonant meditative space able to contain and merge diversity in a way that accepts it without obliterating it. The groups are situated around the cathedral in various chapels. Each chooses in advance what they would sing—some of their favorite pieces.

This is the middle section of the vigil, which is created by the participants on the basis of choice. Each group chooses when to sing; the audience/congregation moves around the building, lighting candles, praying, being quiet, as they choose, but also participating in creating the musical sound.

The vigil is designed therefore to reflect a new model of peace-making; this is based on the principle that we all do what we want to do but then also have the responsibility of working out how far it fits with what other people want to do. Everyone present has a part in the creation of an experience of beauty and togetherness; they experience intuitive ways of relating to and cooperating with others, as these comments illustrate:

> What surprises me also was that an Imam climbed the pulpit and chanted the call for peace in Islamic religion. I would not have thought that such a thing could be possible in a cathedral. The same Imam and a Rabbi chanted together in the same place. If only because of this, I think the performance was truly remarkable.
>
> It was for me poignantly, beautiful and moving, cross-generational and as multi-cultural as is possible in immediate vicinity.

There are many deeply moving personal stories from the informal process-based structure of this event. One person says that in the midst of a violent landscape it enables him to keep alive a vision of peace. In one of the events a woman in a wheelchair who said that the reason for her paralysis was hatred of Islam dating from events in her childhood, parked her chair beneath the pulpit where the imam was singing and cried away all her hatred listening to the imam's chanting. Other people ask any of the faiths to sing on behalf of someone who needs support, like singing Kaddish for a dead friend. There are also times when everyone sings together, including opening chants which fit together as a Quodlibet and the singing of peace in a variety of languages on a single note. This project opens up a new possibility of improvisation as a route to community building based on giving difference dignity (Boyce-Tillman 2012; Jordaan 2015).

To summarize, singing is a community-building exercise. We need to examine new ways of exploring an increasingly diverse community and enabling both similarity and difference to flourish musically.

Community building—the birth of new choirs

The revaluing of the orate meant a reworking of the concept of choir. We have already seen how in the late twentieth century people were experiencing the opening of the self and relationships with a wider community within the community choir movement; the wider culture too was discovering that everyone could sing. The community generated new singing groups—for the homeless, for the mentally ill, people with memory loss, stroke victims. The next section outlines just a few of them.

The Seaview Singers in Kent were set up for people with dementia and included sufferers and carers. It included not only singing songs but lyric writing and improvisational activities. It did, however, develop relationships, via Christchurch Canterbury University, with other groups including university students and an intergenerational project with the local school (Vella-Burrows 2012, pp. 11–13).

Recovery choirs enable people to be rehabilitated after hospitalization for mental health issues. An example is the Wellbeing Community Choir which was formed in 2009 by Birmingham and Solihull Mental Health NHS Trust for people with mental ill health, carers, friends of the trust, community members, and staff. Originally it performed at community and trust events, but it became an example of the partnerships developing between the two esthetic traditions when it joined with the Handsworth Choir, forming a partnership between the Health Trust and the City of Birmingham Symphony Orchestra and the CBSO Selly Oak Choir, for a pre-concert performance on Friday July 12, 2013 at Symphony Hall, Birmingham. The website declares "This was a fantastic opportunity for all choir members to sing at Symphony Hall, one of the world's greatest concert halls!" (Wellbeing Community Choir 2014). This sort of project, which involves singing in what the community regards as a significant venue, is always regarded as profoundly empowering. I have experienced the same phenomenon in events taking place in Winchester Cathedral.

Another Recovery choir is called the Raucous Caucus Recovery Chorus, based at Sharp, Liverpool. It is made up of people in active recovery from drug and alcohol addiction. It uses a wide range of musics, including chants, mantras, folk, and pop songs (Raucous Recovery Choir 2014a) and is run by Action on Addiction which sponsors many creative arts projects. Its home is a non-residential recovery center which offers a 48-day recovery program—and includes families as well as recovering addicts. It has performed in other treatment centers. The head of the charity sees it as an unusual treatment but cannot deny its success:

> Most people would say people need to be doing group therapy, they need to be doing counselling. But you'll notice a lot of the guys saying that they didn't really feel that they

belonged anywhere. Taking part in a choir they begin to understand all about communities just through singing.

(Raucous Recovery Choir 2014b)

Again, it is the sense of belonging that is highlighted. One member describes how it enables him to keep connected to other people in recovery who are struggling like him. The space is described as magical and one in which confidence can be built.

The East Kent Singing for Health project includes similar reflections:

> For some years, due to numerous life events/close losses, I've undergone depression—feeling sometimes life not worth living—despite trying to count my blessings compared to so many in the world. Obviously any activity cannot change the fact that now I'm alone. Yet the singing has made a definite improvement in how I feel, if only while singing and intermittently. It's a very uplifting thing and I like all the people in the group. Look forward to it.

(Woman aged 66)

Threshold choirs support the process of dying through bringing ease and comfort to clients, family, and caregivers. Their calm focused presence revealed in their songs soothed and reassured (Threshold Choir 2014). This movement is largely in North America, although there are people singing with the dying in hospices in the UK. Again it is about connection with a community; in the past death happened in the context of a community, but dying now often takes place in the separate environment of a hospital or hospice.

The Amies Project works with trafficked women. It was established in 2011 to provide a creative outlet for young women trafficked into the UK for prostitution or domestic labor. In the UK victims of such trafficking receive just 45 days of "compulsory reflection and recovery." This project has given them much longer support. Here, singing is combined with dancing, sharing stories, and laughter. At the time of the writing of this chapter 60 young women have been helped by the project to move forward in their lives into education, training, and employment. Comments from participants showed its transformative effect and its ability to help people trust again (Amies Choir 2014).

To summarize, the rise of orate singing traditions has resulted in new groups of people finding a sense of belonging through group singing. These groups have sometimes been able to combine with the literate tradition to produce performances that form new communities of empowerment.

Getting it together: inclusion versus exclusivity

Singing groups and inclusive community

Since we have, as a community, recovered the notion that everyone can sing, we have seen how choirs have been established for particular groups within a culture as listed above. Winchester Singing for Wellbeing Choir was originally conceived as being for people with memory loss; but subsequently it was moved to the Winchester Live-at-home scheme and then included a variety of people who had not been diagnosed with memory loss. It still included the original group but the character of the singing changed when a greater variety of people was included.

So can we have people singing together with a variety of needs in order to reintegrate a fragmented society? "Music could be a genuine way to create situations, to construct social relations in situations, to communicate in a holistic way that combines body and ethics, individual and community" (Westerlund 2002, p. 144).

The challenges are considerable, for present in these groups are a variety of bodies and culturally constructed sounds. There needs to be a concern for the expressive elements in music including extrinsic meaning and the use of musical constructions that are orate in origin, as well as musical scores that are notated, and musical structures that embrace both. There needs to be an inclusive value system underpinning an inclusive musical project, valuing diversity and different cultural forms of singing as well as nurturing leadership styles. The research literature is beginning to set out what practicalities are helpful in these contexts. They include:

- recorded CDs and websites with mp3 files of individual parts
- a system of mentoring in the choir—a buddy system
- seating with blocks of singers rather than men behind women
- a diverse repertoire
- the use of a variety of criteria for success so that accuracy and uplift are balanced.

In an article entitled "Adapting choral singing experiences for older adults: The implications of sensory, perceptual and cognitive changes," Yinger Swedberg (2014) provides helpful advice for the inclusion of a variety of needs, such as attention to lighting (many sources and no glare), the use of a 12-point sized typeface in a simple font, large conducting gestures, and fewer rows to help people with visual impairment. People challenged haptically (at risk of falling) need clear floors, the permission to use assistive devices, and the use of a slower tempo for pieces with fast articulation. People with hearing problems need to use their hearing aids, make sure they can see the leader who needs to use a lower-pitched voice, decrease talking, repeat points, give clear instructions and non-verbal cues such as gestures, while keeping their mouth visible for lip reading. People with cognitive impairment (with memory problems) need to be allowed to use copies and have written reminders for rehearsals, etc. They need to use cues from words, not musical notation, and be able to relate music to their experiences by tapping into extrinsic meaning. They need to be allowed to generate some familiar repertoire from the participants, and terminology needs explaining carefully. People with visual attention and spatial cognition problems need a slow instruction pace with only one thing at a time being dealt with and directions repeated. It helps if texts are projected with highlighting important things in color. All choirs need to allow participants to use chairs while singing.

To summarize, the inclusion of people with a variety of needs in a singing group requires a rethinking of the way choral groups have functioned, and some considerable adaption in leadership styles, yet all can benefit from being in a group with people who are different from them, for it creates new communities.

A vision for community—musical inclusion

It is in this general esthetic landscape that the radically inclusive musical event is located. There is a risk that these specific groupings still serve the cause of marginalizing groups of people whom others might deem unacceptable. In my own composing (Boyce-Tillman 2016, pp. 313–33) I have gradually edged towards this inclusiveness. *The Healing of the Earth* (1997) included professional instrumentalists as well as children who also had a chance to improvise their own pieces. *The Call of the Ancestors* for Winchester Cathedral from 1998 included three orate groups (Thai gongs, Kenyan drums, and a rock group) alongside a large choir singing from notation. Gradually, I developed in my composing spaces for improvised episodes and a greater variety of performers. *The Great Turning*, a work on ecological themes in 2014, saw the number and range of community choirs increased. *From Conflict to Chorus: An Intermezzo for Peace* for March 14, 2015 is a remembering of World War I. Guns were converted into musical instruments for the orchestra. One was in the shape of a battered soldier and was both an artwork and a sounding source played by the children in the school choirs. A flute was made out of a rifle barrel. The concept of the piece is radical inclusivity, which is in my thinking a model for peace. It included the Southern Sinfonia (a professional orchestra), the Singing for Well-being choir (including people with diagnosed memory loss), as well as a school for pupils with profound and multiple learning difficulties, five Hampshire schools, community choirs, notated choral parts for Winchester university choirs and soloists, a young singer songwriter who is visually impaired and has learning difficulties, and a dance performance by a group of young adults with learning difficulties. My vision is of a choral/orchestral event that can include whoever wishes to be involved and their carers. This provides a model of a truly inclusive society where the organizer (previously composer) is a frame-builder in which everyone can participate fully in accordance with ability. The inclusion of this great diversity of people with a variety of abilities has involved substantially more individual work and careful scoring of the accompaniment. Composing becomes not the imprinting of one person's ideas on a group of people, but the building of a scaffold (Holzman 2008) in which everyone can realize their full potential.

To summarize, I have set out another way of including people with diverse needs, experiences, and traditions in a single performance in which the notion of "composer" needs rethinking into one of enabler. I have set out a musical way of rethinking community by mutual empowerment.

The liminal space

The transformative properties of musicking involve the creation of a liminal space (sometimes called a spiritual space). The notion of the transformative properties of the sacred or liminal space has been explored in various contexts (Boyce-Tillman 2001a, 2007, 2009, 2016, pp. 265–83) including healthcare (Wright and Sayre-Adams 2000/2009). Isabel Clarke's (Clarke 2005, p. 93) notion of the transliminal way of knowing is drawn from cognitive psychology (Thalbourne et al. 1997). In her thinking, this way of knowing is to do with our "porous" relation to other beings and tolerating paradox. It is in contrast to "propositional knowing," which gives us the analytically sophisticated individualized way of knowing that "our culture has perhaps mistaken for the whole." To access the other way of knowing we cross an internal "limen" or threshold to a space which is potentially transformative. The important aspect here is that difference co-exists easily here. It becomes a way for discovery of this alterity within the self (Jackson 1998, p. 119) and accepting it; another example of this is the practice of mindfulness.[9] This can extend to encountering others who are different (Derrida 1972; Levinas 1969), as we saw in the communities in the choral groups above. The following characteristics of the spiritual/liminal domain emerge from various sources:

- a limen that is crossed from ordinary knowing especially in the space/time dimension
- a sense of encounter
- a paradoxical knowing so that diversity can exist within it easily
- a sense of empowerment, bliss, realization
- a sense of the beyond, infinity
- a feeling of an opening-up in the experiencer as boundaries start to dissolve
- a sense of transformation, change
- an evanescent and fleeting quality that cannot be controlled, which may result in a sense of givenness
- a feeling of unity with other beings, people, the cosmos.

We have already heard the word "uplift" being used in descriptions of the singing experience. Within the Elevate project staff described this feeling:

> Sometimes, members of the hospital staff would come into the bay pretending to dance, or joining in the sing along, creating amusement among the patients. These occasions appeared to break the hospital routine and create a free space where, even for few minutes, everyone was interacting in a different way.
>
> (Preti and Boyce-Tillman 2014)

The Elevate music sessions in the wards of Salisbury Hospital appeared to create a relaxing atmosphere, consequently facilitating the work of the hospital staff. "It relaxes us . . . Our stressful day becomes calm" (Nurse interview in Preti and Boyce-Tillman 2014). Staff invariably responded that they would have liked artistic work to be more frequent because of the relaxing effect on the staff and the patients. The Chief Executive of Salisbury NHS Foundation Trust identified the transformative impact of Elevate on the hospital environment as one of the main features of the program: "It has a very positive impact on the environment both for the individual patient and the patients around them and the staff on the ward and the environment, and it also leaves behind a kind of lasting footprint" (Preti and Boyce-Tillman 2014).

Other authors have described how singing "fills us with awe, with joy, with wellbeing, that which adds meaning to our lives" (Agwin 1998, p. 6) and so helps to deal with burnout in healthcare contexts. Wright and Sayre-Adams describe music as a soul food along with art, nature, and scripture (Wright and Sayre-Adams 2009, p. 29). They summarize the history of music in healing contexts:

> From the relaxation effect of soft background music, to patient participation in music making, there are many opportunities for carers to find a path for music in holding the sacred in right relationship. Music, the "food of love" has inspired people to the heights of

---

[9] At the University of Winchester we are examining the potential relationship between this practice and musicking.

human achievement, and has been used in all cultures as a meditative and contemplative tool to alter states of consciousness, from the repetitive drumming of the shaman to the ragas of India and the complex and intricate qawaal songs of the Sufis . . . A whole new (some might argue, renewed) science and art is emerging of "music thanatology." (Schroeder-Sheker 1994), bringing prescriptive music to the dying and seriously ill, with profound beneficial and spiritual effects being reported.

(Wright and Sayre-Adams 2009, p. 94)

Within this thinking we have the concept of being able to hold a sacred (potentially transformative) space:

When you and the choir sang to my mom, I felt your singing was able to hold a space open that we all fear. That "space" could be death or just the struggle of sickness, and when it's held open like that, we are less alone in it . . . When you sang, your voices had a kind of wisdom of being in dark places or feared places.

(Threshold Choir 2014)

Earlier in the chapter we saw how hymns have been featured in some healing contexts. It is possible that it is through singing that the spiritual can be awakened in healing contexts (Beattie 2007; de Botton 2012) with transformative effect.

To summarize, singing has the potential to take us to a different way of knowing and perceiving the world in which all is connected and transformed by this process. This is beginning to be understood in health contexts and needs further exploration.

Summary

This chapter has set out how the re-valuing of orate singing traditions has freed up many therapeutic possibilities and unchained the innate singing power of numerous people. I have explored contexts in which people have found singing to be physically strengthening, psychologically empowering, socially enriching, expressive, and mood improving. We have seen how these effects operate at a cultural level as well and how cultural singing events might interact with personal healing. I have opened up the possibility that singing might restore a spiritual dimension to healing contexts. The chapter has drawn on a wide variety of sources for these findings, which has enabled us to explore therapeutic singing through a number of lenses. There is sufficient evidence for the inclusion of singing formally in health-care programs and the possibility of establishing sustainable programs of well-being through singing that will be extremely cost-effective and sustainable. This is particularly true of the interface between the personal and psychosocial; it acknowledges that often therapeutic work needs to operate to bring the individual and communal together to provide healing at the deepest level for our society, and in so doing it can effect profound social change.

References

Agwin, R. (1998). Creating sacred space. *Positive Health* Dec./Jan.: 6–7.
Amies Choir, available at: http://pan-arts.net/pages/amies.html. Accessed June 15, 2014.
Beattie, T. (2007). *The New Atheists: The Twilight of Reason and the War on Religion*. London: Darton, Longman and Todd.

Birmingham Wellbeing Choir. (2014). Available at: http://www.thewellbeingcommunitychoir.org/about.php. Accessed February 12, 2016.

Boyce-Tillman, J. (1996). Getting our acts together: Conflict resolution through Music. In: M. Liebmann (ed.), *Arts Approaches to Conflict*, pp. 209–236. London: Jessica Kingsley.

Boyce-Tillman, J. (1997). *The Healing of the Earth*. London: Hildegard Press.

Boyce-Tillman, J. (2000a). *Constructing Musical Healing: The Wounds that Sing*. London: Jessica Kingsley.

Boyce-Tillman, J. (2000b). *The Creative Spirit: Harmonious Living with Hildegard of Bingen*. Norwich: Canterbury Press.

Boyce-Tillman, J. (2001a). Sounding the sacred: music as sacred site. In: K. Ralls-MacLeod and G. Harvey (eds), *Indigenous Religious Musics*, pp. 136–166. Farnborough: Scolar.

Boyce-Tillman, J. (2005). *Peacesong*. London: Hildegard Press.

Boyce-Tillman, J. (2006). *A Rainbow to Heaven*. London: Stainer and Bell.

Boyce-Tillman, J. (2007). *Unconventional Wisdom*. London: Equinox.

Boyce-Tillman, J. (2009). The transformative qualities of a liminal space created by musicking. *Philosophy of Music Education Review* 17(2): 184–202.

Boyce-Tillman, J. (2011). Making musical space for peace. In F. Laurence and O. Urbain (eds), *Peace and Policy Dialogue of Civilization for Global Citizenship, Vol 15, Music and Solidarity: Questions of Universality, Consciousness and Connection*, pp. 185–201. London: Transaction Publishers.

Boyce-Tillman, J. (2012). Music and the dignity of difference. *Philosophy of Music Education Review* 20(1): 25–44.

Boyce-Tillman, J. (2016). *Experiencing Music—Restoring the Spiritual*. Oxford, Bern, Brussels, Frankfurt am Main, New York, and Vienna: Peter Lang.

Boyce-Tillman, J. (2018). *Freedom Song: Faith, Abuse, Music and Spirituality: A Lived Experience of Celebration*. Oxford, Bern, Brussels, Frankfurt am Main, New York, and Vienna: Peter Lang.

Carnegie, D. (1944). *How to Stop Worrying and Start Living*. New York: Simon and Schuster.

Clarke, I. (2005). There is a crack in everything--that's how the light gets in. In: C. Clarke (ed.), *Ways of Knowing: Science and Mysticism Today*, pp. 93–96. Exeter, UK: Imprint Academic.

Clift, S.M. and Hancox, G. (2001). The perceived benefits of singing: findings from preliminary surveys of a university choral society. *Journal of the Royal Society for the Promotion of Health* 121: 248–256.

Clift, S., Morrison, I., Coulton, S., Treadwell, P., Page, S., Vella-Burrows, T., et al. (2013). *A Feasibility Study on the Health Benefits of a Participative Community Singing Programme for Older People with Chronic Obstructive Pulmonary Disease*. Canterbury: Canterbury Christchurch University.

Cohen, C. (2008). Music: a universal language? In: *Music and Conflict Transformation: Harmonies and Dissonances in Geopolitics*, pp. 26–39. London: I. B. Tauris.

Costen, M.W. (1993). *African American Christian Worship*. Nashville: Abingdon Press.

Danner, M. (1994). *The Massacre at El Mozote*. New York: Vintage.

De Botton, A. (2012). *Religion for Atheists: A Non-Believer's Guide to the Uses of Religion*. London: Hamish Hamilton.

Derrida, J. (1972). *Margins of Philosophy*. Chicago: University of Chicago Press.

Doyle, B. (1987). Introduction to the Songs. In: M. Fox (ed.), *Hildegard of Bingen's Book of Divine Works, with Letters and Songs*, pp. 360–367. Santa Fe: Bear and Co.

Ellingson, L. (2009). *Engaging Crystallization in Qualitative Research: An Introduction*. London: Sage.

Exley, H. (ed.) (1991). *Music Lovers Quotations*. Watford: Exley.

Foucault M. with Gordon, C. (ed.) (1980). *Power/Knowledge: Selected Interviews and Other Writings 1972–77*. Hemel Hempstead: Harvester Wheatsheaf.

Gergen, K.J. (1985). The social constructionist movement in modern psychology. *American Psychologist* 40(3): 266–275.

Green, L. (1988). *Music on Deaf Ears: Musical Meaning, Ideology and Education*. Manchester: Manchester University Press.

Hartley, N., Butchers, A., Dives, T., Hearth, G., Li, J., Prince, G., Sanchez-Camus, R., et al. (2008). *Over 40 years of care and innovation 1967–2008*. London: St Christopher's Hospice.

Holzman, L. (2008). *Vygotsky at Work and Play*. London: Taylor and Francis.

Illman, R. (2010). Plurality and peace: interreligious dialogue in a creative perspective. *International Journal of Public Theology* 4: 175–192.

Jackson, P.W. (1998). *John Dewey and the Lessons of Art*. New Haven: Yale University Press.

Jennings, S. (1999). *Introduction to Developmental Play Therapy: Playing and Health*. London: Jessica Kingsley.

Jordaan, G. (2015). Improvisation in a spiritual context of a religious community. Paper given at *Spirituality and Music Education Conference*, North West University, Potchefstroom, South Africa, March 25–27.

Jorgensen E. (1996). The artist and the pedagogy of hope. *International Journal for Music Education* 27: 36–50.

Kemp, A.E. (1996). *The Musical Temperament*. Oxford: Oxford University Press.

Levinas, E. (1969). *Totality and Infinity: An Essay in Exteriority*. Pittsburgh: Duquesne University Press.

Levi-Strauss, C. (1970). *The Raw and the Cooked*, trans. D. Weightman and J. Weightman. London: Cape.

Moore, D. (1986/1992). *Off Beat: Dudley Moore's Musical Anecdotes*. London: Robson Books.

Morgan, S. and Boyce-Tillman, J. (2016). *A River Rather Than a Road: The Community Choir as Spiritual Experience*. Oxford, Bern, Brussels, Frankfurt am Main, New York, and Vienna: Peter Lang.

Morrison, I. and Clift, S. (2012b). *Singing and Mental Health*. Canterbury: Canterbury Christchurch University.

Natural Voice Network. (1988). http://www.naturalvoice.net/ (accessed May 11, 2014).

Nkosi, W. (1992). *The Rhythm of Healing*. London: British Museum National Sound Archive, 1CD004251.

Ong, W. (1982). *Orality and Literacy: The Technologizing of the Word*. London: Methuen.

Pascale, L. (2005). Dispelling the myth of the non-singer—embracing two aesthetics for singing. *Philosophy of Music Education Review* 13(2): 165–175.

Podolsky, E. (1939). *The Doctor Prescribes Music: The Influence of Music on Health and Personality*. New York: Frederick A. Stokes Company.

Preti, C. and Boyce-Tillman, J. (2014). *Elevate, Using the Arts to Uplift People in Hospital*, Research Report. Winchester: University of Winchester.

Raucous Recovery Choir. (2014a). http://naturalvoice-net.greenstrata.com/choir_profile/779/Raucous%20Caucus%20Recovery%20Chorus (accessed October 1, 2014).

Raucous Recovery Choir. (2014b). http://news.bbc.co.uk/today/hi/today/newsid_9696000/9696262.stm (accessed October 1, 2014).

RERC Accounts of Religious Experience (1970). Held at the Religious Experience Research Centre, Lampeter University, Wales. Available at: https://alisterhardytrust.uwtsd.ac.uk.

Ross, M. (1978). *The Creative Arts*. London: Heinemann.

Schulman, M. (2012). How to combat a culture of violence—and maybe save lives. *Huffington Post: The Blog*. December 27. Available at: http://www.huffingtonpost.com/mark-schulman/combat-culture-of-violence_b_2371661.html (accessed November 22, 2015).

Small, C. (1998). *Musicking: The Meanings of Performing and Listening*. Middletown, CT: Wesleyan University Press.

Sondheim, S. and Lapine, J. (1987). Into the Woods. Available at: http://theatre-musical.com/intothewoods/libretto.html (accessed October 15, 2013).

Storr, A. (1993). *Music and the Mind*. London: HarperCollins.

Taylor, M. (2013). *Humanity, Community and Excess: Feel the Flow in Musical Theatre Performance*. Inaugural lecture as Professor of Music Theatre, University of Winchester, Winchester, UK, April 29.

Thalbourne, M.A., Bartemucci, L., Delin, P.S., Fox, B., and Nofi, O. (1997). Transliminality: its nature and correlates. *Journal of the American Society for Psychical Research* 91: 305–331.

Threshold Choirs, http://thresholdchoir.org/ (accessed June 30, 2014).

Trevarthen, C. (2002). Origins of musical identity: evidence from infancy for musical social awareness. In: R.A.R. Macdonald, D. Hargreaves, and D. Miell (eds), *Musical Identities*, pp. 21–38. New York: Oxford University Press.

Tubbs, N. (1998). What is love's work? *Women: A Cultural* Review 9(1): 34–46.

Turino, T. (2008). *Music as Social Life: The Politics of Participation*. Chicago: University of Chicago Press.

Urbain. O. (2008). *Music and Conflict Transformation: Harmonies and Dissonances in geopolitics*. London: I. B. Tauris.

VanderArk, S., Newman, I., and Bell S. (1983). The effects of music participation on quality of life of the elderly. *Music Therapy* 3: 71–81.

Vella-Burrows, T. (2012). *Singing with People with Dementia*. Canterbury: Canterbury Christchurch University.

Vella-Burrows, T. and Hancox, G. (2012). *Singing and People with Parkinson's*. Canterbury: Canterbury Christchurch University.

Voegelin, S. (2010). *Listening to Noise and Silence*. London: Continuum.

Walker, J. and Boyce-Tillman, J. (2002). Music lessons on prescription? The impact of music lessons for children with chronic anxiety problems. *Health Education* 102(4): 172–179.

Wallas, C. (1927). The art of thought. In: P. Vernon (ed.), *Creativity*, pp. 91–97. Harmondsworth: Penguin.

Wellbeing Community Choir, http://www.ukrw2013.co.uk/wellbeingcommunitychoir. (accessed October 1, 2014).

Westerlund, H. (2002). *Bridging Experience, Action, and Culture in Music Education*. Helsinki: Sibelius Academy.

Westheimer, R. (2003). *Musically Speaking: A Life through Song*. Philadelphia: University of Pennsylvania Press.

Woodward, S. (2015). The music instinct: womb sounds. Available at: http://www.pulseplanet.com/dailyprogram/dailies.php?POP=4516 (accessed January 20, 2015).

Wright, S.G. and Sayre-Adams, J. (2009, first published 2000). *Sacred Space—Right Relationship and Spirituality in Healthcare*. Cumbria: Sacred Space Publications.

Yinger, O. Swedberg (2014), Adapting choral singing experiences for older adults: The implications of sensory, perceptual and cognitive changes, *International Journal of Music Education*, 32(2): May pp. 203–12.

PART 8

SINGING AND TECHNOLOGY

....

CHAPTER 49

HISTORICAL APPROACHES IN REVEALING THE SINGING VOICE, PART 1

....

HARM K. SCHUTTE

INTRODUCTION

THIS chapter reports on the development over past centuries of how we think about the human voice and of how early physiologists influenced thinking on voice production. In particular, the invention of the laryngological mirror by Garcia was a landmark event in the visualization of the inner side of the larynx and the vibrating vocal folds. This device had a great influence on the development of a new branch in medicine, laryngology, leading to a related innovation in stroboscopy. Under the influence of the technical improvements and the application of optical endoscopes, (video)stroboscopy became the gold standard in laryngological practice. In addition, high-speed camera registrations appeared, resulting in a high-quality data stream for voice evaluation.

The results of stroboscopic findings are presented below, in particular with regard to the opening and closing vibratory pattern in the different main registers. It will be shown that the results, continuing to the present day, are infused by an underlying belief in certain theories concerning the vibration pattern and voiced sound production. The specific and inherent drawback of stroboscopy, being its illusionary character, was not seen as a serious problem initially. The recognition of this neglect, however, led to other imaging advances, such as our studies in Groningen on fast and irregular vibratory events that led to the development of videokymography.

Within this historical perspective, vocal registers have also been a prime focus in much singing voice research. In Groningen, for example, chest voice and falsetto registers were studied in detail, and this work led to interesting results. Garcia's novel approach gave a boost to such investigations, and his work is therefore seen as being very influential for research into singing behaviors, even though he struggled to see the importance of his findings.

How is the voice generated?

Voice, in a physical sense, is relatively low-frequency, audible vibrating air. That voice has to do with air has been known since Hippocrates (c. 460–370 BC), Aristotle (384–322 BC), and Galen of Pergamon (AD 130–200). They also talked about the voice being created in the larynx, but did not know how. The "myoelastic-aerodynamic theory," formulated in 1958 by my teacher in voice physiology, Janwillem Van den Berg, is the current paradigm, being generally accepted and commonly referenced in some form wherever the physical basis of vocal behavior is being discussed (Van den Berg 1958). In some instances, it is skipped over in textbooks, probably because it is deemed "obvious." Where there are exceptions, it is probably on the part of those who reject the theory because it is a theory of "not a living larynx" (Garde 1970).

The myoelastic-aerodynamic theory, in summary, is as follows: The vocal folds are brought together by muscles that move the arytenoid cartilages; air pressure from the lungs is built up below the closed vocal folds until a threshold is reached, when the glottis opens and a pulse of air escapes or is driven through. Due to the resulting lowering of the pressure and the elastic forces that are built up by the stretching of the outward movement, the vocal folds spring back and the glottis closes. In this closing act—when the vocal folds are near to one another—the Bernoulli-effect helps the closing, specifically affecting the mucosal tissue, and the cycle starts anew.

However, in experimental measurements in the Groningen Voice Research Lab, where we used high-frequency pressure transducers above and below the glottis (Miller and Schutte 1985), we established a deviation from the theory. Instead of a peak in subglottal pressure that opens the vocal folds, the pressure peaks at the moment of closure and then drops immediately, even in the short period that the glottis is still closed. This means that the pulse excitation takes place at the moment of closure and not in the open glottis phase. How can there be a pulse excitation of the vocal tract when the glottis is still closed?

What was the situation at the start of the eighteenth century?

Denis Dodart (1634–1707)

The first scientific reports on the physiology of the human larynx were produced by Denis Dodart. Unfortunately, we do not know why Dodart became interested. He was known as an expert in mouth whistling and perhaps this initiated his fascination with the voice. In 1700, he presented his ideas in the weekly session at the Académie Royale des Sciences in Paris (Dodart 1700).[1] Dodart first explained that the sound was caused in the same way as a striking wind makes a piece of paper flap against a broken glass in a window. In such cases, the sound is caused by the repeatedly changing force making the paper move, whereas the pitch is changed by the speed at which the paper flaps and the vocal folds vibrate. Dodart's explanation had its critics, but the Academy members accepted his treatise.

---

[1] Dodart was a French naturalist and botanist; he got a doctorate in medicine in 1660 and was elected as an early member of the French Academy of Sciences in 1673. The Académie was founded in 1666.

Dodart gave strong reasons for believing that the larynx is the proper organ of the voice, as the trachea could not play an important role because of its constant dimensions. It is clear from Dodart's writings that he was groping in the dark somewhat. Dodart was not sure about his ideas on the working mechanism and changed his mind in his later writings. Subsequently, he concluded that the vocal folds worked like the mouthpiece of a flute, where the air is blown against the rim of the glottis, i.e. the edge of the vocal folds. This position is already closer to the correct working theory compared to earlier writings, in which the narrowing and widening of the windpipe, the trachea, was considered to lead to pitch changes. Dodart switched to the idea that the tone is dependent on the air pressure and the size of the glottis opening; elsewhere, he explains that tone is dependent on the vocal folds. Thus he switches from considering the larynx as a pipe with a tongue (the "flapping" vocal folds) to a flute (with vocal folds as the labia).

Dodart was probably misled by an inappropriate analogy: the analogy with mouth whistling (Van den Berg 1968). Dodart explained everything in an aerodynamic sense by comparing the vocal folds during phonation with the lips during whistling. Essential to the argument is that the pitch variations should be due to the variations of the glottal area, by proper muscular adjustment of the vocal folds. Air coming from the lungs is pressed from below against the vocal folds, leading to eddies because of the friction of the air with the vocal folds. Vibrations of the vocal folds would be secondary and actually negligible. We need to realize that Dodart had no scientific instruments: no laryngoscope, no stroboscopy, no bright light to observe the vocal folds while phonating; in his eyes the vocal folds took a certain position and seemed to stand still, like his lips. Dodart did some more experiments on excised larynges, probably of cows, and came back with modified explanations (Dodart 1706a, 1706b, 1707).

Antoine Ferrein (1693–1769)

About 40 years after Dodart, in 1741, Antoine Ferrein picked up the voice topic. Ferrein was an anatomist and became a member of the Académie Royale des Sciences in 1742. He undertook acoustic investigations on excised larynges; like Dodart, they were most probably taken from a cow (Ferrein 1741a, 1741b). The understanding of acoustics was barely developed at that time, but he determined that the sound varied in strength, depending on how close the vocal folds were positioned to each other. He concluded that pitch is not dependent on the width of the glottis, but on the longitudinal tension of the vocal folds and also their length. He believed that the length of the vocal folds was the most important feature, in that they resemble the strings of a musical instrument such as, for instance, an Aeolus harp, in which movement in the air puts the strings into vibration. As a consequence, it is not the air alone that gives the tones; rather, it is the vocal folds, or *cordes vocales*, as he called them. Therefore, he talked of an instrument *à cordes et à vent*, strings and air, and also offered a theory that *vent* (wind/air) and the "cords" work together to produce voice. He indeed coined the term vocal folds, but his incorrect explanation became popular and is still in use nowadays.[2]

---

[2] Surgical operations have been performed in recent years to shorten the length of the vocal folds in, for example, transgender treatment to get a higher pitch in male to female transitions. The application of a concept of strings seems obvious.

Von Haller (1708–1777): the working of the arytenoids

In *Primae liniae Physiologiae Halleri* (1747) Von Haller wrote about the working of the arytenoids: that these can be brought together and also separated. If there is a vertical movement of the larynx, the glottis will become narrower and the vocal folds approach each other. For example, the lowering of the larynx enables the glottis to become wider and the resultant tone is lower. Von Haller mentioned that the voice itself is created if the air is pressed against the vocal folds of the glottis, by which the larynx is set into vibration, and that by elasticity the pattern of the vibrations is reinforced. There is no stable sound without a vibration, otherwise there only will be noise. However, von Haller did not focus on the vibration of the vocal folds, but equated the glottis with the slit of a flute-like organ pipe. Narrowing of the glottis occurs by pressing tissue inwards in the larynx; if one presses the middle part, the remaining free part will sound an octave higher; pressing at a third of the length gives a fifth higher, as if they are strings.

PHYSIOLOGISTS OF THE NINETEENTH CENTURY

One of the earliest theses on voice is probably from R.A. Vogel's *Dissertatio de larynge Humano et Vocis formatione* from around 1770. Vogel did not seem satisfied with the work of Dodart, nor that of Ferrein, but adhered to a notion that both were probably correct. That was also the opinion of von Kempelen (1791) (see also Dudley and Tarnóczy 1950). It is not clear whether the theories that likened voicing to a flute, strings, and air were accepted. It seems evident, however, that not much progress was made in the second half of the eighteenth century, perhaps due to the lack of a proper assessment protocol and evaluation instruments. Although the anatomy of the larynx had been correctly described at the beginning of the nineteenth century, the action of the laryngeal muscles and the production of the voice were understood imperfectly and inconclusively.

At that time, the prevailing theory of voice production was that the glottis formed a slit, which can be made more or less open, as well as longer and shorter. This flute-like analogous theory lasted for more than a hundred years and, in many instances, has continued to exert an influence on popular conception to the present day. However, the first objections, historically, began to emerge at the beginning of the nineteenth century. At that time, the physiologists Francois Magendy (1783–1855)[3] and Malgaigne (1806–1865) brought new insights into the production of voice. These Frenchmen introduced another possibility to explain the nature of voice production, namely the reed or tongue idea. Magendy wrote in his 1816 physiology textbook that the larynx works as a reed pipe, in which the reed, changeable in form and size, is able to produce all the tones of the human voice. When the vocal folds vibrate over their full length, then low notes are formed; in contrast, higher notes are produced when only the posterior parts of the vocal folds vibrate. Higher notes are also reported as possible if the other parts are pressed together by a forceful muscle action. This explanation was easy to comprehend because the theorized action was then comparable to the trusted understanding of the working of violin strings.

---

[3] We will meet him in 1841 as reporter for the work of Garcia.

Magendy was a pioneer of experimental physiology[4] and held the Chair in Paris in physiology from 1830 to 1855. Although he was interested in voice in general, he concentrated on the function of the epiglottis. He believed that the airstream would hit the epiglottis and set it into vibration. To test the effect, he cut the epiglottis of living dogs to see whether there was an effect on the barking sound of the dog. He concluded that the parts of the body above the larynx do not contribute much, nor have an essential influence, on vocal pitch, but are enabled through changes in size and form to be in harmony with the working of the larynx.

Malgaigne, in 1831, viewed this differently. He reported that the voice works as a tube with double membranous reeds and that voice is produced in the anterior part of the vocal folds. This is in contrast to the contribution of the vocal tract, particularly the nasal cavities, which can be opened and closed off by the soft palate, and are very important for modifying the ultimate sound character of the perceived output.

The resulting summative knowledge was that, in general, the larynx and vocal folds, maybe also with an effect from the false vocal folds (forming the top of the Morgagni sinus), were all closely related in voice production. This knowledge was to a large extent based on experiments with dogs and excised human larynges, as had been undertaken in the previous century by Dodart and Ferrein. From these collective observations, it was concluded that the open space between the vocal folds—the glottis—was related to pitch. So, at this time the flute concept, as well as the string concept of air striking the vocal folds (as in an Aeolus harp), were still dominant. The influence of the false vocal folds above the Morgagni sinus was still mysterious; also the epiglottis, to which the stream of air was projected, was considered to play an important role in voice production.[5]

Furthermore, this theory was considered to be conclusive, as demonstrated in 1923 by Eykman, Dutch phonetician and co-author with the physiologist Zwaardemaker, in their writing on the theory of voice production. He wrote that Magendy and Malgaigne "present a fully clear and correct insight in the origin of voice" (Eykman 1923; Zwaardemaker Cz and Eijkman 1928).

Specific studies

Johannes Müller (1801–1858)

It is this great physiologist who, in addition to addressing many other topics in medical physiology, published the results of his experiments with artificial membranes and specially prepared excised larynges (Müller 1839). He objected to many of the contemporary findings of Malgaigne through his quantitative study of the relationship between vocal fold tension and subglottal pressure in the control of fundamental frequency. He focused on glottis closure and how it was possible through concurrent physical forces that the glottis remained open at the dorsal part but closed on the frontal side during phonation. He did not question the principle of the slit for voicing, such as in a flute. While space does not allow a detailed discussion

---

[4] He was a devoted vivisectionist. His activities led to the start of the antivivisection movement.

[5] Flowing air was mixed up with sound propagation. It was considered the same phenomenon. Sound could "hit" the epiglottis, the palate, the teeth, etc. And in many treatises of today this misconception on directing sound can still be found.

of Müller's findings, his approach in experiments acted as a guideline for excised laryngeal research over the following 150 years.[6]

Carl Ludwig Merkel (1812–1876)

In 1856, Merkel published[7] an extensive work, *Antropophonik*, on the working of the larynx, but he did not doubt the vocal fold position concept (Merkel 1863). He believed that a glottis opening of a certain size allows air coming through; this air strikes the vocal folds and sets these in vibration and thus the out-streaming air is modulated in air pressure. The changes in air pressure are perceived as sound. The glottis opening is varied in size by the internal laryngeal muscles and, by this action, the pitch and sound volume can be altered. If this explanation sounds quite familiar, it is because this is how most handbooks nowadays describe the formation of voice. As we will see later, this concept is only partly correct, but for many colleagues it seems to suffice.

Hermann L.F. Helmholtz (1821–1894)

Helmholtz paid attention to voice production, even though his main interest was the perception of tones and music theory, as the title of his book indicates. However, in talking about the vocal folds, he considered them to be membranous tongues, stretched across the windpipe that leave a small slit, the glottis, between them.[8] Helmholtz wrote: "If the vocal chords (*sic*)[9] are examined from above with a laryngoscope, while producing a tone, they will be seen to make very large vibrations for the deeper breast (*sic*) voice, shutting the glottis tightly whenever they strike inwards" (Helmholtz 1954). Helmholtz also stated, as cited in Van den Berg (1955), that the glottis opens to get a pulse of air to excite the vocal tract, implicitly suggesting that the instance of the opening of the glottis is the sound-producing act.

C.F.S. Liscovius (1780–1844)

Also of interest in the nineteenth century is the work of Liscovius, both in an early thesis of 1814 and another in 1846. It is clear from his later published work that Liscovius followed all the pertinent publications over a period of more than 30 years. He collected together all the writings across these decades and annotated them in detail. He could not make up his mind whether the voice organ was a flute or a reed instrument. He experimented by making organ pipes with flexible walls to study the effect of these walls on the sound. The conclusion emerged that, in general, the glottis is formed as a slit by appropriate positioning of the arytenoids. The glottis can be adjusted in size (i.e. width and length), with air coming from the lungs setting the vocal folds in vibration to produce sound. In chest voice, the vocal folds are rather thick and broad; in middle voice a bit thinner; and in falsetto, thin and stretched.

---

[6] More can be found in Barth (1911) and Cooper (1986).

[7] Second printing in 1863, following first printing in 1856.

[8] Somewhere he should have said that, in speaking, the glottis comes to closure, but in singing the glottis remains open, but I could not verify this statement in the literature.

[9] Probably this is a translation error in the translated edition I used. Also the term "breast" is used instead of "chest"/"Brust."

The prevailing theory, however, about voice production during this period was based on a flute concept. The size of the glottis opening was considered in the flute concept to be the pitch-determining factor. This opening was seen to be adjusted by the arytenoids, which put both vocal folds in an appropriate position. The arytenoids in the German language were probably therefore named *Stellknorpel*, meaning cartilages that put (the vocal folds) into position.

Additional sources

Objections to the flute theory came from Henri Dutrochet (René Joachim Henri) (1776–1847), botanist and physiologist, who, guided by the vibrations, especially in the lower notes of a human voice, assumed not only that the tone was produced by air, as is the case in a flute pipe, but also that a solid mass had to contribute to the formation of the lower voice sound. He stated that the human voice organ resembles a horn in the playing of which the origin for the sound is the vibration of the (muscles of the) lips.[10] But there was no better alternative than the flute concept, although varying tongues were suggested by Malgaigne and Magendy around 1845; this concept is also apparent in the work of MacKenzie (1890).

A new idea was promoted by Savart (1791–1841), who suggested that the Morgagni sinus was the sound generator for the voice, resembling in parallel the functioning principle of his "hunter's whistle." At the end of the nineteenth century this notion was picked up and defended by Guillemin.[11] Morat and Dyon, in their *Traité de Physiologie* of 1918 also strongly defended this theory; both Eykman and Zwaardemaker accepted this explanation too. However, when Röntgen-tomograms became available in the 1930s, these were used to study variability in ventricle size and sound character. Zimmermann, Luchsinger, and Husson each found differing results or gave different explanations. Van den Berg (1955) discussed several possibilities, leading to a refutation of Negus' statement that the ventricle had no function at all, while also refuting Savart/Guillemin/Morat and Dyon's opinions that the ventricle was the voice source. Based on theoretical approaches and some existing (tomographic) evidence and his own experiments, Van den Berg came to the conclusion that the ventricle could work as a low-pass filter. Russell observed a close approximation to the "Wrisberg region" (Russell 1929). As the relatively weak tissue of the larynx did not show much on X-ray photographs, it was only with the application in the 1950s of tomography (among other measures) that conclusive details emerged that made it possible for Van den Berg (1953, 1955) to refute[12] the "hunter's whistle theory" of Savart and Guillemin (Guillemin 1888, 1897).

---

[10] We will meet Dutrochet as the secretary of the report committee reviewing the work of Garcia for the Académie in 1841.

[11] The original literature of Guillemin from 1897 has recently been reprinted, but the physiologists Morat and Dyon supported the theory strongly in 1918.

[12] It is interesting how a Dutch MD, Louise Kaiser, who became a leading phonetician, described the working of the larynx. She was internationally renowned and a pioneer in the field. She published much and was the prime mover in a committee to publish two editions of the *Manual of Phonetics* (Kaiser 1957, 1964). In 1950, she published a Dutch Introduction to phonetics, in which she explains

Zimmermann (1938) gave extensive descriptions of his experiments, together with Nadoleczny, on measuring the length of the vocal folds in male and female professional singers. The literature review is exceptionally well done and covers the pertinent literature of the 50 years prior to 1938. The generally accepted differences in the length of the vocal folds between males and females were obvious. However, the determination of the length is not really conclusive when related to the differences in *Fach*, such as between a soprano's and a mezzo-soprano's voice. (*Fach* is a specific term denoting and relating a specific voice type (soprano, baritone, etc.) to specific roles in musical performances, e.g. tenore lyrico, basso buffo, soprano dramatico.) Zimmerman stated: "The human larynx shows, like other body organs, individually qualitative different capabilities, which primarily seem to be based on the anatomical build. One should, however, not forget, that a large range of other factors also have a co-determining influence." The other factors that Zimmermann summarized include a specific symmetrical shape of the cartilages in singers, as suggested by Zuckerkandl (1900), especially of the cricoid, because this would determine the form and width of the glottis. In a related study, Thost (1913, 1924) postulated, based on X-rays, that there is a gradual transition of the trachea to the larynx, as well as the ratio of the trachea lumen to the larynx. The Morgagni sinus is again mentioned as being remarkable in singers (e.g. an "open" sinus is always present in singers). Avellis (1906) even talked about a "singer ventricle."

One might conclude from these various contributions that the vocal folds were still considered to be strings and that thus it was important to study their length. Savart's idea of the Morgagni sinus as a representation of his hunter's whistle also appeared to be present in readers' minds. The vocal tract and the larynx position were discussed by Zimmerman in 1938, referring back to Hellat (1898), who wrote that basses have long vocal folds, a wide pharynx, and low positioned larynx; this all being in contrast to the equivalent anatomical features of sopranos. However, there are exceptions. Zimmermann carefully concluded that many researchers were doubtful about the possibility of determining the type and *Fach* by observing and measuring the larynx/vocal folds. Imhofer (1904) in Prague and Negus (1929) were certain: it was not possible; this was a task for the teacher of singing.

Zimmerman's 1938 evaluation of concepts emerging from the previous years indicates that not much theoretical progress was made during this period. The vocal folds do not behave like strings, as was implicit in the efforts to measure the length of the vocal folds. Nevertheless, Thost (1924), who had also written on this subject earlier in 1913 (based on X-rays), was still of the opinion that a singer's larynx is deviant from that of non-singers: the singer's larynx has a beautiful architecture and a symmetrical build. He also stated that the development of the vocal folds in singers is deviant from the usual. The fact that Zimmermann referred back to work from the beginning of the twentieth century suggests that there was a weakness, scarcity, or poverty in the progress of research into singing.

In summary, by the end of the nineteenth century, there were different ideas prevalent about the physiology of voice production: (1) Ferrein's *à cordes et à vent*—the strings; (2) the flute concept; (3) the reed concept; (4) the horn with vibrating lips; and (5) Savart's hunter's whistle.

voice production on the basis of Savart's "hunter's whistle." Curiously, it was the reading of this text that induced Van den Berg in about 1950 to start his study of the physical aspects of voice production, which resulted in his thesis in 1953.

Thus it is probably not unreasonable to say that, at this point in history, the prevailing theory of voice production was that of air blowing against the rims of the vocal folds to create eddies (air pressure changes) such as in an organ pipe with labia. These air vibrations also resulted in the vibration of the vocal folds. Such theoretical explanations seem to have longevity. For example, the conclusion of Helmholtz, cited in Van den Berg (1955), was that the glottis opens to get a pulse of air to excite the vocal tract. Current textbooks and modern results still follow this patterning, as in the case of voice-source/vocal tract theory, a theory developed by technicians to tackle the problem of vowel production and transmission engineering. "Change a factor, other factors remaining the same." This approach in thinking nowadays seems to signal the final stage of voice research, whereas it should be the starting point of thinking. Only in this way can new insights find their way into the science of voice production (e.g. Schwartz 1993).

Modern approaches to the visualization of the vibrating vocal folds

At the beginning of the 1990s, my student and colleague Jan G. Švec came to the Voice Research Lab in Groningen with a plan to study in greater detail what happens to the vocal folds when a voice tone with an audible subharmonic is produced. A preparative study had already been published (Švec and Pesák 1992). The idea was to study the phenomenon with stroboscopic light and record it on videotape for further evaluation. We discovered quite soon that the usual video recordings did not have sufficient time resolution to allow a reliable explanation of the phenomenon. It was clear to us that this inherent feature of stroboscopy was not helpful in observing this irregular vibration pattern. Stroboscopy needs a steady, regular vibration pattern with triggering from a clean, regular signal. However, we wanted to study voice signals of an irregular character, as this is more often the case than not in pathological voices. In addition, the fast transitions that occur in register flips could not be studied with stroboscopy. This led to the implementation of a prepared video camera to form what was called videokymography, first presented at the COMET meeting of 1994.

As reported above, the study of the gross movements of the vocal folds started with the invention of the laryngeal mirror by Garcia (1855). The vibration pattern could be observed and evaluated by the application of stroboscopy, in a primitive form, by Oertel (1878). One might have expected, at this point, that our understanding of the creation of the voice was likely to have been solved quite soon, not least because stroboscopy was called the microscope of the voice. In fact this was doubtful. The researchers were far too influenced by dominant theories to come to an acceptable explanation.

The narrative below charts the development of laryngoscopy and stroboscopy over one and a half centuries in order to understand how it became the gold standard of today.

Invention of the laryngeal mirror

In 1855, Garcia described his invention of the laryngeal mirror and mentioned that what he had observed confirmed his ideas about registers from the mirror examination of his own voice and that of his students (a form of inductive research, Garcia 1855). Garcia was looking at the working of the vocal folds as a confirmation of what he "knew" already. The mirror idea was picked up quickly by many investigators and essentially formed the start of laryngology. Garcia's work and the reactions to it can be found in the works of Stark (1991, 1999) and Radomski (2005). While it is beyond the scope of this historical overview of research on singing to discuss Garcia's work in any detail, it should be noted that he reported on registers, described the vocal folds, the size of the glottis, pinching, the control of precise "positions" of the vocal folds, and complete approximation or non-complete closure of the vocal folds. Although Garcia wrote about the vibrating parts of the vocal folds, and correlated this to brilliancy and dullness of the voice, there is no evidence of how he thought the vocal folds were involved in sound production.

Laryngoscopy at the end of the nineteenth century

The invention of the laryngeal mirror, as presented in 1855, marks the beginning of the specialization of laryngology. Until then doctors could not inspect what happened behind the curvature of the tongue in the pharynx and windpipe. The advent of this new technology enabled the physician to observe the vocal folds in their working state and this visualization method has had relevance for singing voice research subsequently. Visualization of the vibration pattern for sung registers, such as chest and falsetto, was restricted to observing the position of the vocal folds. With the concepts of those days being dominated by metaphors related to the flute, reed, and/or strings, the size of the glottis was of primary concern, and that was easy to see with a laryngeal mirror. Consequently, the need for better observations was hardly felt. The vocal folds move too fast to see the vibrations; but this became possible by applying stroboscopy.

Nevertheless, doctors in the second part of the nineteenth century had to be convinced that the new piece of equipment (stroboscope) was of great practical value, although it was not easy to do stroboscopy in practice. In an overview by Weiss (1932b), a lot of attention was given to adjusting the stroboscopic illumination of the voice, as this was still rather tricky. Similarly, many researchers were reported as mentioning sources of possible errors (Weiss 1932a). As a result, the contribution of stroboscopy to understanding singing at that time was low according to Loebell (1926) and Weiss (1932b).

Stroboscopy

Oertel (1835–1897) is important in the history of stroboscopy because of his publication in 1878 of a preliminary message about using the stroboscopic principle in laryngology (Oertel 1878). Although he was the first to do so, it was not until 1895 that he found time to describe his experiences and present the stroboscope that he developed. However, it was not immediately clear that this could be of help for the diagnostics and understanding of the working of the larynx, although MacKenzie (1890) mentions using it for his laryngoscopic investigations on singers. Oertel saw a big future for the stroboscope, although other investigators did not see much influence on the prevalent understanding of voice physiology (Moore 1991). Oertel's main interest was in the differences in voice registers, and he published a monograph on this topic in 1882: *On the Mechanism of Chest Voice and Falsetto Voice* (Oertel 1882). He described that the vibrations of the vocal folds resembled the movements of a thin, flexible rubber membrane. His interpretations seem to be heavily dependent on the theory of strings, such as by dividing the vocal folds to a half or a third of their total length in order to explain higher frequencies. He also reported that when vocal pitch rises, the vocal folds come closer to each other, such as in agreement with the lip (labia of a flute) concept. It has to be said that what Oertel saw in 1882 was mostly derived from his artificial models, so that when he viewed a living larynx, he was probably influenced by what he had seen in the models. Here again is a likely example of inductive research: just like Garcia looking at his mirror, Oertel saw what he expected to see. For an excellent overview of the historical development of stroboscopy, see Moore (1937a, reprinted 1991).

For several decades, Musehold (1898, 1913) set the tone for what would be visible in photography and stroboscopy. He concluded that the glottis does not work as a membrane, but that the vocal folds move outwards and somewhat upwards. Musehold also saw in his photographs a rather long closed phase in chest register, which he correlated with air pressure building up in the trachea, in accordance with Garcia's descriptions. He investigated the differences in sung registers and came to a conclusion that had significant consequences for later researchers by stating that, in falsetto, the glottis does not close. He also described himself as in agreement with Garcia's "pinching" observation regarding the posterior sections of the vocal folds becoming tightly pressed together and pushing the glottis anteriorly (see also Stark 1999).

In an important contribution to our historical understanding of the development of stroboscopy use, Moore (1937a) reported that the principal functional problem being experienced by the leading stroboscopists in the Interbellum (Stern, Weiss, Maljutin, and Heymann) was the variation in movements between the two folds.[13] With infiltration of the tissue, the functioning is always disturbed. In many normal participants, the motion in one fold was frequently much reduced in relation to the other. Maljutin (1931), for example, used stroboscopy to examine over two hundred students of singing of the Moscow Conservatory. He found great variation from singer to singer, such as in length, color, and mass. In addition, he often observed unequal vibration of the two sides. His opinion was that the vocal fold on the "preferred side" was the more active. Moore (1937b, p. 563) concluded that: "Differences of belief have accompanied almost every conclusion drawn" on the working of the larynx, especially in terms of confusion on the type of closure, which still often seems to be the case.

Electronic strobes

After the Second World War, it was Richard Luchsinger (1900–1993) who strongly advocated stroboscopy, as had Tarneaud earlier in Paris.[14] Luchsinger developed a stroboscope in Zürich on an electronic basis (Luchsinger 1946). He wrote on stroboscopy (Luchsinger 1948, 1950) and also designed stroboscopic filming equipment (Luchsinger 1964; Luchsinger and Nielsen 1961; Luchsinger et al. 1958). An extensive description of stroboscopic principles was

[13] Moore writes lips.   [14] A laryngologist working at the Paris Opera.

subsequently published by Winckel (1957).[15] It is complete, describing all modalities and possibilities, but unfortunately no clinical (ENT) specialist is able to undertake all of these possibilities in already overfilled consultation hours.

Luchsinger trusted his equipment sufficiently to get a clear answer to an old question, "Does the glottis close (also) in falsetto? as in chest voice, or "Is the vocal folds' behavior in falsetto like a flute opening?" This had been a question since Musehold, although Tonndorf doubted that this could be the case on the basis of his own experience with stroboscopy (Tonndorf 1926). Luchsinger (1950) came to a *categorical judgment* that in falsetto, the vocal folds do not close the glottal space. This statement has been rarely critiqued since then, and even Van den Berg in his thesis of 1953 copied this finding. It is probable that the stroboscopic filming equipment of the 1950s did not have sufficient time resolution; from recent experiments, such as with VoceVista which includes electroglottography (EGG), it is easy to demonstrate that there is a closure, although sometimes this is of a very short nature. Many teachers of voice and modern physiologists still accept the theory (or "belief") that the glottis in falsetto does not close. Also more recent books on stroboscopy suggest that in falsetto the glottis does not come to a closure. It is, of course, true that a tone with a falsetto character can be produced without any moment of closure, but the statement that there is no closure at all is not valid, particularly when applied to understanding the professional countertenor voice.

Stroboscopic equipment improved quickly through the application of electronics (see Beck and Schönhärl 1954; Timcke 1956; and Van den Berg 1959) and a much-cited monograph on stroboscopy which was issued by Schönhärl (1960). The content offers a great variety of images, with some singers being described, but no conclusions are given, only suggestions for doing better stroboscopy. In the years after 1960, the equipment improved considerably: the flashes became shorter and brighter, the triggering improved, and the automatic delta-f principle was implemented. Using this electronic device the stroboscope not only followed the fundamental frequency (pitch) of the voice, but by subtracting a small value from the measured fundamental (delta-f), it became possible to observe the apparent movements of the vocal folds by slowing down virtually. In the 1980s, it became possible to make video recordings for slow-speed observations.

Hirano and Bless (1993) published a book on stroboscopy with stills of stroboscopic images that were taken from videos. It is noticeable that there are three possibilities in the images: normal, not normal, and blurred. The latter possibility implies that the stroboscopic approach does not work, or at least is unreliable. Any irregularity in vocal movement leads to a blurred image, but this blurred image literally obscures. The monograph shows images, but offers no conclusions on physiology. Similarly, the book by Boehme and Gross (2005) provides a great deal of historical information, but no new insights. In falsetto, according to these authors, the glottis still does not come to closure!

All in all, the use of stroboscopy in laryngoscopy, although nowadays considered to be the gold standard for voice source imaging, is not well defined. Left/right differences in vibrating patterns are not so easy to observe as we might expect; in irregular vibrations, one only sees

---

[15] In 1968, Fritz Winckel was Director of the Electronic Music Studio at the Technical University of Berlin. He succeeded in getting Maria Callas to come to in his studio to sing a *messa di voce* and to depict the strong "singer's" (3 kHz) formant; see Winckel (1953).

blurring; in the 1950s this was already called "Symptom der Unschärfe," a euphemistic description of not being able to observe the vibration pattern.

Is stroboscopy useless?

Stroboscopy is not useless, but the application should be used for what it is really able to show. It is indispensable, for instance, in evaluating the physiological nature and extent of the dynamic glottis closure,[16] i.e. how complete the glottis closure is in a cycle; how abruptly the glottis closes; that there is a gradual closure from ventral to dorsal (zipper); that there remains an opening in the best closure, often at the dorsal part; and that there are so many differences between left and right that the vocal folds follow each other in a "lambada" pattern. Only with stroboscopic evaluation/standstill in the correct phase can maximum closure of the glottis at the same moment be evaluated reliably. According to our experience, the norm for Western classical singers is an abrupt, full closure.

In voice clinics, modern stroboscopic evaluations have in recent years been shown to be of great importance, for example in discovering the existence of sulci in the vocal folds, or to establish the presence of small epithelial lesions. Irregular movements are fundamental in an unclear voice. On the other hand, it is not possible to infer that a good voice is always based on regular movements, as was suggested by researchers of singing around 1900.

Visualization of irregular vibrations

In our research, we were faced with the impossibility of registering fast transition phenomena in voice production by stroboscopy, such as in chest-falsetto register transitions, or in the production of (audible) subharmonic tones. Triggering of the strobe appeared impossible, although a trick with a pulse divider did make this possible, as published in Švec et al. (1996). A signal of an irregular character is essentially not appropriate for stroboscopy, which only works well with a regular signal.

This was the starting point in our Voice Research Lab investigation for an additional way to record and assess fast phenomena in voice production. We invented what was called "videokymography" (see Švec and Schutte 1995, 1996). In videokymography, the images of the vocal folds, obtained by an endoscope (preferably a rigid type) are recorded with a customized video camera. By selecting only one image line of the total number of horizontal lines and giving up the time needed for scanning the rest of the lines, the spatial resolution of the total image (usually 25 images per second) is replaced by a higher time resolution of up to 7,000 (line) images per second. This is much higher than the 25 images per second of a PAL video registration, or 4,000 images per second in video high speed. Digital kymography is derived from the video high speed approach. Examples of videokymographic images are given in Švec et al. (2008, 2009), and Švec and Šram (2011); an example is included with this chapter as Figure 49.1.

---

[16] Dynamic glottis closure is the evaluation of closure of the glottis during phonation. Using the option of standstill, the maximally closed and maximally open position can be evaluated.

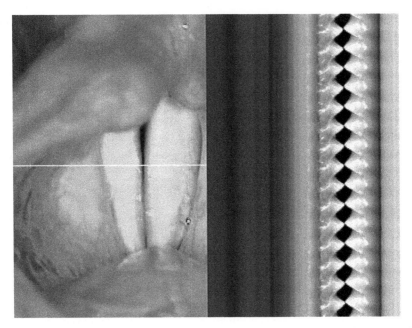

FIGURE 49.1 The image combines a view of the vibrating vocal folds obtained per-orally by a 90-degree rigid endoscope of a singer, producing a tone of approximately 400 Hz, sung in falsetto mode. The panel on the right side shows a videokymogram (vkg), obtained at the white line in the left panel, about in the middle of the vocal folds. The vkg shows clearly that there is a very short contact of the vocal folds at this place, with possibly slightly longer contact nearer to the frontal side (lower in this image). The vkg also shows a slight phase shift (left vocal fold ahead of the right vocal fold) and a traveling mucosal wave. The vkg on the white line is recorded at a frequency of about 7000 Hz, denoting 16 vibrational periods.

Courtesy of Prof. Dr. Felix de Jong.

The time resolution of the images of the videokymography makes it possible to see fast phenomena, or—in a steady phonation—the development and movements of the vocal fold mucosa. The importance of the mucosa has become more and more apparent and will be a topic of much research in the near future. Meanwhile, Švec et al. (1999) have described the possibilities of establishing differences between sung registers. Through using videokymography, we have also been able to show that in falsetto the glottis may come to a (short) moment of closure.

The advantage of videokymography over stroboscopy is that the images of the vibrating vocal folds are no longer dependent on triggering. Irregular vibrations, such as a difference in the vibration pattern of the left and right vocal fold, as well as fast register transitions, can easily be followed. In the clinic, where irregular patterns are most often related to voice disturbances, the obtained independence of triggering is a big advantage. Second-generation videokymography shows an overview image, where the place of the scan line is depicted, next to the videokymography image (Qiu and Schutte 2006). It may be that the advantages of videokymography will lead to this technology supplanting stroboscopy for the study of vocal fold vibrations. Further investigations using the videokymography signal have included the development of an evaluation system, based on the glottis opening and closing patterns, and including the observation of mucosal trajectories.

With a specially developed endoscope connected to kymography, in Groningen we were also able to register the vertical movements of the vocal folds in phonation, in a process called depth kymography (George et al. 2008, 2009). By combining the data from the horizontally oriented videokymography with the data from the depth kymography, a 3D (moving) image of the vocal folds in action can be obtained. The results have formed the basis of a simulation program to study the effects of the changing tension of the vocal folds and other factors (de Mul et al. 2009).

VOCAL REGISTERS IN SINGING

In the early 1980s, Donald Miller visited Van den Berg in Groningen, following a tradition initiated by other researchers/singers in the 1960s such as Vennard, Isshiki, Stark, and Richard Miller, in order to study the phenomena related to voice registers. We knew about chest and falsetto, in that we had Van den Berg's explanation in the instructional film, *The Vibrating Larynx* (Van den Berg 1958; Van den Berg et al. 1960). I also gathered information on registers from singers for my own thesis (James Stark, Richard Miller (1977), Johannes Pahn, and a few Dutch professional singers). Don Miller came back to Groningen, but the first orientating experiments were not very successful. Van den Berg advised us to use a miniature dual pressure transducer to be placed transglottally, as he had done with a subglottally placed tube of glass in his earlier studies (Van den Berg 1956). Van den Berg could provide the catheter, so we started, admittedly with some hesitancy at the prospect of moving a catheter through the glottis in a still-performing professional singer.[17]

The signals recorded included electroglottography (EGG), but it took a while before we could read, understand, and evaluate the data curves in a trustworthy fashion. The signals were studied in detail by Fast Fourier Transform spectrography, written out one by one on an X–Y writer/plotter. A big step forward was the availability of a PC that was fast enough to display real-time spectra. Of further importance was the development of a dedicated computer program for this purpose: VoceVista,[18] by Dick Horne.

The measurements formed the data for several detailed studies on topics that would contribute to a better understanding of vocal registers. The studies led to a thesis (Miller 2000) and to a monograph on VoceVista (Miller 2008). It is striking that many singers do not appear to "believe" in such findings and also that they think they do not need to know. Maybe the latter is true: history shows that understanding the physiology of singing is not necessary for singing well, although such knowledge is probably crucial when things go wrong. What follows is an examination of the history of register exploration.

---

[17] In fact, this was an instrument in use in the Department of Medical Physics to study the activity of the urine bladder sphincter. But we cleaned it first!

[18] See www.VoceVista.com.

An overview of the study of registers

The study of registers gained impetus from the writings of Garcia (1805–1906), as mentioned earlier. A teacher of singing of Spanish origin, he wrote a treatise on singing also based on the teaching of his father Manuel Garcia Sr., who was a well-known baritone for whom Rossini wrote specific arias. Thus, Garcia was a member of a very important family in the history of singing (see Stark 1999; Radomski 2005; Stevenson 1949). A biography written a few years after Garcia's death by the husband of one of Garcia's students also contains interesting information (Mackinlay 1908).

Garcia Jr. stopped his professional singing career early at 23 years old after a critical evaluation of a performance. He left home and started a career in the army. There he met wounded soldiers, observed the anatomy of the larynx, and became interested in how the larynx works. He began to undertake experiments with animals of all kinds. His sister Pauline Viardot-Garcia (1821–1910), a renowned singer, helped him by blowing a pair of bellows; she was surprised by the different sounds that were emitted (Mackinlay 1908; Radomski 2005).

From this experience, it is understandable that Garcia was very eager to see his own vocal folds in a working state, as he wrote in 1855 in his presentation to the Royal Academy in London. He got his chance when he followed an impulse to get two mirrors and arranged these successfully to allow him to see the vocal folds in action. Garcia taught singing at the Paris Conservatory and while there wrote his *Traité complet de l'Art du Chant en deux parties*. He had written about registers in 1837, prior to the invention of the laryngeal mirror. The first edition of the *Traité* was intended as a tribute to his father, and as such, he reproduced his father's instructions on teaching. However, Garcia Jr. wanted to give pedagogical practice a more theoretical form; his own method would be more analytical and would establish the teaching of singing on a physiological basis.

In 1840, Garcia Jr. wrote about three registers in the same singer: *voix de fausset, la voix de poitrine*, and what was then called, as in the deep Russian basses, *la voix sombre*, a sort of voice which "was for a long time unknown and often not distinguished in France." Then in 1841, Garcia Jr. presented his treatise to the Académie Royale des Sciences in Paris, the *Memoire sur la voix humaine*. His ideas—"Cet habile professeur de chant"—were only accepted after a committee of members of the Académie had provided their comments in a report, the *Rapport sur le Mémoire sur la voix humaine*, of which an extract appeared in the *Comptes rendus des séances de l'Académie des Sciences* of April 12, 1841. The text of Garcia's *Memoire* was subsequently printed in 1847 (Garcia 1847). The three academy members in Paris who formed the 1841 committee were Magendy, Savart, and Dutrochet (each mentioned earlier). However, Félix Savart (born 1797) was critically ill and died in July 1841, which is why Savary was asked to replace him. The secretary, Dutrochet, had earlier published a thesis on voice in 1806: *Essai sur une nouvelle théorie de la voix, avec l'exposé de divers systèmes qui ont paru jusqu'à ce jour sur cet objet*. The third member of the committee, Francois Magendy (1783–1855), was a pioneer of experimental physiology, as reported earlier. Félix Savart, originally scheduled to be on the committee, was known as an acoustician and was not really in favor of the insights of Manuel Garcia. Almost all of the voice researchers of that time were convinced that the human voice belonged to the family of wind instruments, in which the tone is produced by vibrations of solid as well as elastic bodies. The other two scientists in the report hastened to say that, in spite of the scientific qualities of Savart, he did not have many followers on that idea. A few days before he died, he accepted the purport of the contrasting argument.

Overall, this was an expert committee (for that time) to study the value of Garcia's 1841 work, and they were not easily convinced. The live presentations by Garcia's students did not convince the committee of new facts. Furthermore, Garcia's ideas on registers were not considered to be new by the reviewers. They wrote that a lot of Garcia's ideas had already been presented by other researchers. For example, Bennati (1798–1834) used a translated text by Rush in his physiology book of 1833 (Bennati 1834). Rush (1746–1820) had already written on both registers: *la voix naturelle* (*la voix de poitrine*) and *la fausette* (Rush 1845). In the end, it seems that Garcia had to accept that he was not the first. Nevertheless, Garcia finally received the compliments of the Académie and was assured that his work certainly would be important in furthering the knowledge and understanding of the voice. The Académie accepted Garcia's *Memoire* and the report on it.

Stark (1999) writes that Garcia had to have made a strong impact in order to secure his place at the Conservatory, headed by the composer Luigi Cherubini, and it is probably correct to say that Garcia, although appointed to the Paris Conservatory of Music in 1835, was not taken seriously as a scientist. Garcia left Paris in 1848 due to political unrest in France at the time and settled in London, where he taught until 1895 (at age 90), when he retired (he died in 1906, at age 101). According to Scripture (1927), he lived his final years in the house of the father of Hermann Klein, who became known as a singer and who was a student of Garcia. Klein wrote on singing and of Garcia's time in London (Klein 1903, 1923).

Garcia did not write a single word on laryngoscopy in his *Memoire* of 1841, but only gives a description in detail of the registers that he had discerned. He did not write about observing the vocal folds until his *Observations on the Human Voice*, presented in 1855 to the Royal Academy in London (Garcia 1855). The report contained an English translation of the *Traité*, and several translations were published subsequently. A translation was issued by his second wife, Beate, in 1894 and reprinted in 1982 (Garcia 1894, 1982). In 1924, his son Albert, also a professional singer, republished the work of his father with only marginal changes. The works were reprinted in 1980 (Garcia 1980), and also by Paschke (1975, 1984). Garcia talks about the vibrating parts of the vocal folds and correlates these to brilliancy and dullness in the voice. However, there is no indication of how he thinks the vocal folds come to produce sound.

Physiologists and singing

Until the middle of the nineteenth century, physiologists scarcely paid attention to singing. They restricted themselves to trying to explain voice production and the difference between two obvious registers, chest and falsetto. Nevertheless, in the nineteenth century much commentary on singing was published, as illustrated in review articles by Grützner (1879) and Nagel (1909). However, the books on singing do not contain much information on voice production. In the last decades of the nineteenth century and the early twentieth century, much attention was being given to hygiene and general advice on "how to sing," such as in the (translated) books of Lilly Lehman of 1902/1922 and Martienssen-Lohmann, with both authors often being reprinted (Hewitt 1978; Lehmann 1985; Martienssen-Lohmann 1923, 1943, 1957, 1981).

There was barely a doubt amongst the voice researchers that the vocal folds acted as a membrane. Koschlakoff (1886) was one of the first to describe that the vocal folds appeared thicker and wider in chest register than in falsetto and that in chest the vocal folds vibrated as a whole. Oertel (1882), talking of the differences between the registers, said that the vocal folds in chest register were vibrating as a whole, whereas in the "middle"[19] register a nodal line would be seen on the upper surface of the whole length of each fold.[20] In falsetto, several nodal lines on each fold were described. At first, Réthi (1896) accepted the existence of nodal lines, but after more careful work, he changed his mind. He was the first to describe his observation of waves that were running from the edges of the glottis to the ventricles over the vocal folds. The physiologist Nagel (1909) disagreed about the differences between the registers and stated his belief that the vocal folds probably never touched each other during phonation, not even in chest register. He reasoned that they were unable to stand such frequent contact without damage (reported by Moore 1937b). This "belief" still resonates in other literature to the present day. For example, a "vocal folds banging" theory is offered for the supposed creation of vocal fold nodules.[21]

Teachers of singing and physiology

From early in the Western classical music tradition (around 1600), singers reportedly knew about voice registers, called *chest voice* and *falsetto*, and that these could be distinguished from each other by proprioceptive and auditory differences. This knowledge was included in the early books on singing that were written by the teachers of the time, such as Tosi (1723), but almost nothing was included on the physiology of the larynx. Information is more focused on aspects of sung performance, such as ornamentation and correct singing. Such books formed the basis of available written knowledge on (Western classical) singing and were translated into many languages, such as the German translation of Tosi by Agricola that was reprinted in 1966 (Tosi and Agricola 1966; see also Mancini 1777, 1969; Tosi 1987), implying perhaps not just a historical interest in previous methods, but also an attraction towards a contemporary pedagogical application of the content.

Gradually, a greater sense of cooperation was evidenced between singers and laryngologists. For example, Seiler, a famous singer of the nineteenth century, guided Morell Mackenzie in his hygiene work of 1890. The medical doctor Lennox Brown was a co-author of Behnke's first edition on singing (Behnke 1880; Browne and Behnke 1921). This book was well received and appeared to have dominated singing pedagogy practice for decades, as it ran to some 25 editions. Similarly, the *Treatise complet* of Garcia (Garcia 1840) was first printed in 1847, translated by his second wife Beate in 1894 and reprinted in 1911 (Garcia 1911). Other reprints included one by Garcia's grandson, Albert, in 1924 (Garcia 1924). Modern

---

[19] Middle is here conceptualized as something in pitch between chest and falsetto.

[20] How this "nodal" line looked is nowadays unclear. I did not find any image in the literature.

[21] It is easy to hold a "belief" that banging the vocal folds into each other leads to vocal nodules. But on careful observation under stroboscopy, the vocal folds do not bang; rather, they nestle—as far as is possible—into each other. One can even see that as soon as the vocal folds touch each other, the movement changes from inward to outward, thus opening the glottis.

reprints are also available (Garcia 1980, 1982). For many singers (and singing teachers), therefore, it would seem that Garcia's pedagogically related advice is more than just an anecdotal or historical work. The general approach to singing is characterized by what Behnke (1880) wrote in his opening chapter to the ninth edition of his book (noting that his book got its first printing in the same year).[22] We take this volume as an example because, apparently, it was still very much in use at the end of the nineteenth century, with Behnke's daughter, Emil, editing the sixteenth edition[23] and adding a new chapter "Voice Failure." She was also a teacher of singing.

After having provided a short historical introduction focused on the "lost beautiful singing in recent times," Behnke declared that the experiments of "great physiologists" such as Johannes Müller (1839) were undertaken on excised larynges.[24] However, this generated significant concern:

> But . . . as various teachers . . . treated the voices of their pupils accordingly, these investigations have perhaps on the whole done more harm than good. Science was made responsible for the blunders of those who attempted to be guided by it. And thus it happened that when at a later period further trials were made, but this time upon the living subject, and in the act of singing, they were received with indifference and distrust. Only very lately teachers of vocal music have begun to find out that here are facts put before them which cannot be gainsaid, and that if these investigations do nothing else, they at any rate make them acquainted with the exact nature of the vocal organ, and what it will bear and what it will not bear.
>
> (Behnke 1880 (Gutenberg ebook 2010), p. 7)

It was not important for Behnke to know precisely how the larynx works. This is best illustrated in the following citation:

> "Physiologists," says Dr. Witkowski, "are quite at issue when they endeavour to determine what kind of instrument the vocal organ resembles . . . indeed, Galien compares it to a flute, Magendie to a hautboy, Despiney to a trombone, Diday to a hunting-horn, Savart to a bird-catcher's call, Biot to an organ-pipe, Malgaigne to the little instrument used by the exhibitors of Punch, and Ferrein to a spinet or harpsichord. The last-named compared the lips of the glottis to the strings of a violin; hence . . . the name Vocal Cords, which they have since retained. The current of air was the bow, the exertion of the chest and lungs the hand which carried the bow, the thyroid cartilages the points d'appui, the arytenoids the pegs, and lastly, the muscles inserted in them the power which tensed or relaxed the cords." It must be admitted that the human voice bears more resemblance to a reed instrument than to any other; but when the comparison is pushed to its legitimate consequences, it is found to break down. We cannot resist the conclusion that the vocal organ is infinitely superior to any instrument made by human hands. Its mechanism is so wonderful as to excite the profoundest admiration, and the more we continue to study it the more we marvel at the wisdom of the Divine Maker who planned it. I shall, therefore, speak of it simply as a wind instrument composed of . . . the bellows, the windpipe, the voice box or larynx and the resonator.
>
> (Behnke 1880 (Gutenberg ebook 2010), pp. 8–9)

---

[22] This is the same year that Sir Morell Mackenzie published his textbook on laryngology.

[23] It would be interesting to compare the first and last edition, and how much has been changed over the years in relation to the physiology of singing.

[24] This approach in using excised "dead" larynges as a basis for physiological knowledge became central in the controversy: a dead vs alive larynx, which was strongly influenced by Husson—promotor of the neurochronaxy theory—and followers like Garde and others, even up to today.

It will be clear that this viewpoint saved the author from discussing the difficult and still (at that time) mysterious working of the larynx. Despite the co-authorship in the first edition with Lennox Browne, a laryngologist, it is not noticeably strong on physiology, but more focused on anatomy. Other books on singing published in the opening decades of the twentieth century include one by Wesley Mills (1906), an MD and singer, and the books of Lilly Lehman, first printed in 1902, which are marked by an approach in which the resonances in chest and head register have to be felt. The book is still read and the approach is still advocated, now as then (see Lehmann 1902a, 1902b, 1922). Similarly, Martienssen-Lohmann's book of 1923 is still considered to contain valuable advice for developing a correct singing technique.

CRITICAL EVALUATION AND SUMMARY

The nature of voice production in relation to the activity of the larynx in speech and singing has been shrouded in mystery for decades, something that has changed only relatively recently. Different physiological conceptions emerged within the dominant treatises of the time, often with contrary explanations of how the voice was produced. These theories, although different, remained alive over the years, leading to confusion and even to incorrect concepts when applied to surgery. Laryngoscopy, introduced by Garcia, and then later the application of stroboscopy were expected to make a large contribution and to promote a greater consensus and a better understanding of the voice for singing. However, stroboscopy, even in its modern form, did not lead to a better understanding of how the voice worked in all particular circumstances, such as registers. Furthermore, a general reading of the literature cited here suggests that the concepts, or "beliefs" as Moore called them, were often strongly resistant to new data. In falsetto, for example, it was said that the glottis did not come to a closure because in the flute pipe concept of high tones the glottis did not need to close. Furthermore, key conceptualizations of voice that were promoted by leading physiologists of the early nineteenth century were still being adhered to in the mid twentieth century, such as Savart's hunter's whistle concept of larynx functioning. Following the description of the myoelastic-aerodynamic theory of the 1950s, nobody seems to have any doubt. The vocal folds are placed in a certain position—"Stellknorpel"—and the glottis is changed in size and width by the working of the elastic tissue and the action of the muscles. In the second part of this discussion (Chapter 50), an overview is given of the results of singing voice physiology in the second part of the twentieth century.

REFERENCES

Avellis, G. (1906). Die Ventrikelform beim Sängerkehlkopf. *Archiv für Laryngologie und Rhinologie (Fränkel)* 18: 115–127.

Barth, E. (1911). *Einführung in die Physiologie, Pathologie und Hygiene der menschlichen Stimme.* Leipzig: Thieme Verlag.

Beck, J.D. and Schönhärl, E. (1954). Ein neues mikrophongesteuertes Lichtblitzstroboskop. *HNO-Wegweiser* 4: 212.

Behnke, E. (1880). *The Mechanism of the Human Voice*, 15th edition. London: J. Curwen and Sons Ltd, http://www.gutenberg.org/files/30889/30889-h/30889-h.htm.

Bennati, F. (1834). *Mémoire sur un cas particulier d'anomalie de la voix humaine pendant le chant*. Paris: Imprimerie de H. Dupuy.

Boehme, G. and Gross, M. (2005). *Stroboscopy and Other Techniques for the Analysis of Vocal Fold Vibration*. London: Whurr Publishers.

Browne, L. and Behnke, E. (1921). *Voice, Song, and Speech*. New York: G.P. Putnam's Sons.

Cooper, D.S. (1986). Research in laryngeal physiology with excised larynges. In: C. W. Cummings et al. (eds), *Otolaryngology—Head and Neck Surgery*, 2nd edn, Vol. 3, pp. 1728–1737. Toronto: C. V. Mosby.

de Mul, F.F.M., George, N.A., Qiu, Q., Rakhorst, G., and Schutte, H.K. (2009). Depth-kymography of vocal fold vibrations: part II. Simulations and direct comparisons with 3D profiles measurements. *Physics in Medicine and Biology* 54(13): 3955–3977.

Dodart, M. (1700). Sur les causes de la voix de l'Homme, et de ses différent tons. In: *Histoire de l'Académie Royale des Sciences. Avec les Mémoires de Mathématique & de Physique pour la même Année*, pp. 244–289, Paris: Chez Gabriel Martin, https://hal.archives-ouvertes.fr/ads-00104281.

Dodart, M. (1706a). Suite de la Premiere Partie du Supplement au Memoire sur la Voix et sur les Tons de la premiere. In: *Histoire de l'Académie Royale des Sciences. Avec les Mémoires de Mathématique & de Physique pour la même Année*, p. 388. Paris: Chez Gabriel Martin, https://books.google.com/books?id=gm1TFuw3jq4C.

Dodart, M. (1706b). Supplement au Memoire sur la voix et sur les tons. Premiere partie. *Histoire de l'Académie Royale des Sciences. Avec les Mémoires de Mathématique & de Physique pour la même Année*, pp. 136–148. Paris: Chez Gabriel Martin, https://books.google.com/books?id=gm1TFuw3jq4C.

Dodart, M. (1707). Supplement au Memoire sur la voix et les tons. Seconde Partie. In: *Histoire de l'Académie Royale des Sciences. Avec les Mémoires de Mathématique & de Physique pour la même Année*, pp. 66–81. Paris: Chez Gabriel Martin, https://books.google.com/books?id=TgUOAAAAQAAJ.

Dudley, H. and Tarnóczy, T.H.v. (1950). The speaking machine of Wolfgang von Kempelen. *Journal of the Acoustical Society of America* 22(2): 151–166.

Eykman, L.P.H. (1923). Geschiedkundig Overzicht van de klankleer in Nederland. *De Nieuwe Taalgids* 17–18: 161–174; 225–243; 283–293; 17–33.

Ferrein, A. (1741a). De la formation de la voix de l'homme. In: *Histoire de l'Académie Royale des Sciences. Avec les Mémoires de Mathématique & de Physique pour la même Année*, pp. 409–432. Paris: Chez Gabriel Martin, https://books.google.com/books?id=gm1TFuw3jq4C.

Ferrein, A. (1741b). Sur l'Organe immediate de la voix et de ses différent tons. In: *Histoire de l'Académie Royale des Sciences.Avec les Mémoires de Mathématique & de Physique pour la même Année*, pp. 51–56. Paris: Chez Gabriel Martin, https://books.google.com/books?id=gm1TFuw3jq4C.

Garcia, A. (1924). *Garcia's Treatise on the Art of Singing: A Compendious Method of Instruction. with Examples and Exercise for the Cultivation of the Voice by Manuel Garcia*. London: Leonard and Co.

Garcia, B. (1982). *Hints on Singing by Manual Garcia*. New York: Joseph Patelson.

Garcia, M. (1840). Description des produits du phonateur humain. *Comptes Rendus* 11(20): 815–816.

Garcia, M. (1847). *Traité complet de l'art du chant. In Two Parts*. Paris: Chez l'Auteur.

Garcia, M. (1855). Observations on the human voice. *Proceedings of the Royal Society of London* 1854–1855: 399–410.

Garcia, M. (1894). *Hints on Singing*. New York: Joseph Patelson.

Garcia, M. (1911). *Hints on Singing*. New York: Joseph Patelson.

Garcia, M. (1980). Observations on the human voice. In: J.W. Large and J. Large (eds), *Contributions of Voice Research to Singing*, pp. 123–133. Houston: College-Hill Press.

Garde, E.J. (1970). *La Voix*. Paris: Presses Universitaires de France.

George, N., de Mul, F.F.M., Qiu, Q., Rakhorst, G., and Schutte, H.K. (2008). New laryngoscope for quantitative high-speed imaging of human vocal folds vibration in the horizontal and vertical direction. *Journal of Biomedical Optics* 13(6): 064024-1–064024-5.

George, N., de Mul, F.F.M., Qiu, Q., Rakhorst, G., and Schutte, H.K. (2009). Depth-kymography: high-speed calibrated 3D imaging of human vocal fold vibration dynamics. *Physics in Medicine and Biology* 53: 2667–2675.

Grützner, P. (1879). Physiologie der Stimme und Sprache. In: L. Hermann (ed.), *Handbuch der Physiologie*, pp. 1–236. Leipzig: F.C.W. Vogel.

Guillemin, A. (1888). *Étude sur la voix humaine*. Lyon: Impremature Novelle.

Guillemin, A. ([1897], 1902). *Sur la génération de la voix et du timbre*, 2nd edn. Paris: F. Alcan.

Hellat, P. (1898). Von der Stellung des Kehlkopfes beim Singen. *Archiv für Laryngologie und Rhinologie (Fränkel)* 8.

Helmholtz, H. (1954). *On the Sensations of Tone*. New York: Dover.

Hewitt, G. (1978). *How to Sing*. London: EMI Music Publishing Ltd.

Hirano, M. and Bless, D.M. (1993). *Videostroboscopic Examination of the Larynx*. San Diego: Singular.

Imhofer, R. (1904). *Die Krankheiten der Singstimme für Ärzte*. Berlin: Verlag Otto Enslin.

Kaiser, L. (1957). *Manual of Phonetics*. Amsterdam: North-Holland Publishing.

Kaiser, L. (1964). *Een inleiding tot de Phonetiek*. Den Haag: Servire.

Klein, H. (1903). *Thirty Years of Musical Life in London, 1870–1900*. London: Heinemann.

Klein, H. (1923). *The Bel Canto, with Particular Reference to the Singing of Mozart*. London: Humphrey Milford.

Koschlakoff, D.J. (1886). Ueber die Schwingungstypen der Stimmbänder. *Pflügers Archiv für die gesamte Physiologie des Menschen und der Tiere* 38: 428–476.

Lehmann, L. (1985). *More than Singing*. New York: Dover.

Lehmann, L. (1902a). *How to Sing*. New York: Macmillan.

Lehmann, L. (1902b). *Meine Gesangkunst*. Berlin: Zukunft.

Lehmann, L. (1922). *Meine Gesangkunst*. Berlin: Bote and Bock.

Liscovius, C.F.S. (1814). *Dissertatio physiologica sistens theoriam vocis*. Leipzig: Breitkopf et Haertel.

Liskovius, K.F.S. (1846). *Physiologie der menschlichen Stimme für Aerzte und Nichtärzte*. Leipzig: Verlag von Joh. Amb. Barth.

Loebell, H. (1926). Ein neues Stroboskop. *Zeitschrift für Hals-, Nasen- und Ohrenheilkunde* 15: 371–373.

Luchsinger, R. (1946). Beitrag zur stroboskopischen Registrierung der Stimmstärke. *Practica Oto-Rhino-Laryngologica* 8: 436–440.

Luchsinger, R. (1948). Zur stroboskopischen Symptomatik. *Practica Oto-Rhino-Laryngologica* 10: 209–214.

Luchsinger, R. (1950). Zur Kenntnis der Mechanismus der Brust- und Kopfstimme. *Practica Oto-Rhino-Laryngologica* 12: 311–314.

Luchsinger, R., Schweizer, C., and Nielsen, E. (1958). Eine neuartige stroboskopische Kurzfilmapparatur für den klinischen Gebrauch in der Kehlkopfheilkunde. *Arch Ohren usw Heilk u Z Hals usw Heilk* 172: 411–418.

Luchsinger, R. and Nielsen, E. (1961). Über den Ausbau einer neuartigen Kurzfilmapparatur für die Laryngo-Stroboskopie. *Folia Phoniatrica* 13: 93–98.

Luchsinger, R. (1964). In: D.W. Brewer (ed.), *Research Potentials in Voice Physiology*, pp. 185–189. New York: State University of New York.

MacKenzie, M. (1890). *The Hygiene of the Vocal Organs*, 7th edn. London: Macmillan.

Mackinlay, M.S. (1908). *Garcia: The Centenarian and his Time*. London: William Blackwood and sons.

Magendie, F., Savary, P., and Dutrochet, H., (1841). Rapport sur la Mémoire sur la voix humaine, présenté à l'Academie des Sciences par Manuel Garcia. *Comptes Rendu des séances de l'Academie des Sciences, séance du 12 avril 1841*, 25–26.

Maljutin, E.N. (1931). Stroboskopische Erscheinungen bei Gesangschülern. *Acta Oto-laryngologica (Stockholm)* 15: 109–119.

Mancini, G.B. (1777). *Pensieri e Riflessioni sopra il Canto figurato*, 3rd edn. Milan: Giuseppe Galeazzi.

Mancini, R. (1969). *L'Art du chant*. Paris: Presses Universitaires de France.

Martienssen-Lohmann, F. (1923). *Das Bewusste Singen*. Leipzig: C.F. Kahnt.

Martienssen-Lohmann, F. (1943). *Der Opernsängers, Berufung und Bewährung*. Mainz: B Schott's Söhne.

Martienssen-Lohmann, F. (1957). *Ausbildung der Gesangsstimme*. Wiesbaden: Rud Erdmann Musikverlag.

Martienssen-Lohmann, F. (1981). *Der Wissende Sänger. Gesangslexikon in Skizzen* Zürich: Atlantis Musikbuch-Verlag AG.

Merkel, K.L. (1863). *Anatomie und Physiologie des menschlichen Stimm- und Sprachorgans (Antropophonik)*. Leipzig: Verlag von Ambrosius Abel.

Miller, D.G. and Schutte, H.K. (1985). Characteristic patterns of sub- and supraglottal pressure variations within the glottal cycle. In: V.L. Lawrence (ed.), *Transcripts of the 13th Symposium on the Care of the Professional Voice*, pp. 70–75. New York: Voice Foundation.

Miller, D.G. (2000). *Registers in Singing. Empirical and Systematic Studies in the Theory of the Singing Voice*. PhD dissertation, University of Groningen.

Miller, D.G. (2008). *Resonance in Singing: Voice Building through Acoustic Feedback*. Princeton, NJ: Inside View Press.

Miller, R. (1977). *English, French, German and Italian Techniques of Singing: A Study in National Tonal Preferences and How They Relate to Functional Efficiency*. Metuchen, NJ: Scarecrow Press.

Moore, G.P. (1937a). Vocal fold movement during vocalization. *Speech Monograph Research Annual* 4: 44–55.

Moore, G.P. (1991). Voice: a historical perspective. A short history of laryngeal investigation. *Journal of Voice* 5(3): 166–281.

Moore, G.P. (1937b). A short history of laryngeal investigation. *Quarterly Journal of Speech* 23(4): 531–564.

Morat, J.-P. (1918). Phonation. In: J.-P. Morat and M. Doyon (eds), *Traité de Physiologie*, pp. 347–383. Paris: Masson et Cie.

Müller, J. (1839). *Über die Compensation der physischen Kräfte am menschlichen Stimmorgan, mit Bemerkungen über die Stimme der Säugetiere, Vögel und Amphibiien*. Berlin: August Hirschwald.

Musehold, A. (1898). Stroboskopische und photographische Studien über die Stellung der Stimmlippen im Brust- und Falsett-Register. *Archiv für Laryngologie und Rhinologie (Fränkel)* 7: 1–21.

Musehold, A. (1913). *Allgemeine Akustik und Mechanik des menschlichen Stimmorgans*. Berlin: J. Springer.

Nagel, W. (1909). Physiologie der Stimmwerkzeuge. In: W. Nagel (ed.), *Handbuch der Physiologie des Mensche*, pp. 691–792. Braunschweig: Friedrich Vieweg und Sohn.

Negus, V.E. (1929). *The Mechanism of the Larynx*. London: Heinemann.

Oertel, M.J. (1878). Über eine neue "laryngostroboskopische" Untersuchungsmethode des Kehlkopfes. *Centralblatt für die Medizinische Wissenschaften* 5: 81–82.

Oertel, M.J. (1882). *Über den Mechanismus des Brust- und Falsettregisters*. Stuttgart: Cottaschen Buchhandlung.

Paschke, D.V.A. (1975). *Complete Treatise on the Art of Singing: Part Two*. New York: Da Capo Press.

Paschke, D.V.A. (1984). *Complete Treatise on the Art of Singing: Part One*. New York: Da Capo Press.

Qiu, Q. and Schutte, H.K. (2006). A new generation videokymography for routine clinical vocal fold examination. *Laryngoscope* 116(10): 1824–1828.

Radomski, T. (2005). Manuel Garcia (1805–1906): a bicentenary reflection. *Australian Voice* 11: 25–41.

Réthi, L. (1896). Experimentelle Untersuchungen über den Schwingungstypus und den Mechanismus der Stimmbänder bei der Falsettstimme. *Sitzb.d.k.Akad.Wiss.Wien.Math.-Naturw.Kl.* 105(Pt 3): 197.

Rush, J. (1845). *The Philosophy of the Human Voice: embracing its Physiological History; together with a system of principles, by which Criticism in the art of Elocution may be rendered intelligible, and instruction, definite and comprehensive. To which is added a brief analysis of Song and Recitative*. Philadelphia: J. Crissy.

Russell, G.O. (1929). The mechanism of speech. *Journal of the Acoustical Society of America* 1: 83–120.

Schönhärl, E. (1960). *Die Stroboskopie in der praktischen Laryngologie*. Stuttgart: Georg Thieme Verlag.

Schwartz, J. (1993). *The Creative Moment—Het creatieve moment. Hoe de wetenschap zichzelf vervreemdde van de modern cultuur* (Dutch translation edn). Amsterdam: Prometheus.

Scripture, E.W. (1927). Eine bel-canto-Aufnahme von einem Schüler Garcias. *Zeitschrift für Hals-, Nasen- und Ohrenheilkunde* 17: 196–199.

Stark, J. (1999). *Bel Canto: A History of Vocal Pedagogy*. Toronto: University of Toronto Press.

Stark, J.A. (1991). Garcia in perspective: his *Traité* after 150 years. *Journal of Research in Singing* 15(1): 2–56.

Stevenson, R.S. (1949). *A History of Oto-Laryngology*. Edinburgh: E. and S. Livingstone.

Švec, J.G. and Pesák, J. (1992). Vlastnosti hlasov¥ch p2eskokà. [Properties of vocal breaks]. *Bulletin of the Acoustical Society of Czechoslovakia* 2: 1–5.

Švec, J.G. and Schutte, H.K. (1995). High-speed line-scanning technique for investigation of vocal fold vibration (videokymography). In: A. Melka, Z. Otcenášek, and J. Štěpánek (eds), *Proceedings of the 32nd Czech Conference on Acoustics Speech—Music—Hearing, Prague, September 23–26, 1995*, pp. 71–74. Prague: Czech Acoustical Society.

Švec, J.G. and Schutte, H.K. (1996). Videokymography: high-speed line scanning of vocal fold vibration. *Journal of Voice* 10(2): 201–205.

Švec, J.G., Schutte, H.K., and Miller, D.G. (1996). A subharmonic vibratory pattern in normal vocal folds. *Journal of Speech and Hearing Research* 39: 135–143.

Švec, J.G., Schutte, H.K., and Miller, D.G. (1999). On pitch jumps between chest and falsetto registers in voice: data from living and excised human larynges. *Journal of the Acoustical Society of America* 106(3) (Pt.1): 1523–1531.

Švec, J.G., Sundberg, J., and Hertegård, S. (2008). Three registers in an untrained female singer analyzed by videokymography, strobolaryngoscopy and sound spectrography. *Journal of the Acoustical Society of America* 123(1): 347–353.

Švec, J.G., Šram, F., and Schutte, H.K. (2009). Videokymography. In: M.P. Fried and A. Ferlito (eds), *The Larynx Volume 1*, 3rd edn, p. 253. San Diego: Plural Publishing.

Švec, J.G. and Šram, F. (2011). Videokymographic examination of voice. In: E.P.M. Ma and E.M.L. Yiu (eds), *Handbook of Voice Assessments*, pp. 129–146. San Diego: Plural Publishing.

Thost, A. (1913). *Archive und Atlas der normalen und pathologischen Anatomie in typischen Röntgenbildern: Der normale und kranke Kehlkopf des Lebenden im Röntgenbild*. Hamburg: Universität Hamburg.

Thost, A. (1924). Feinere pathologischen Veränderungen des Kehlkopfes im Röntgenbild. *Zeitschrift für Hals-, Nasen- und Ohrenheilkunde* 22.

Timcke, R. (1956). Die Synchron-Stroboskopie von menschlichen Stimmlippen. *Zeitschrift für Laryngologie, Rhinologie, und Otologie* 35: 331.

Tonndorf, W. (1926). Die Schwingungszahl der Stimmlippen. *Zeitschrift für Hals-, Nasen- und Ohrenheilkunde* 15: 363–371.

Tosi, P.F. (1723). *Opinioni de`cantori antichi, e moderni o sieno Osservaio ni Sopra il canto figurato*. Gran Brettagna: Accademico Filarmonico.

Tosi, P.F. and Agricola, J.F. (1966). *Anleitung zur Singkunst*. Leipzig: VEB Deutscher Verlag für Musik.

Tosi, P.F. (1987). *Observations on the Florid Song*. London: Stainer and Bell.

Van den Berg, Jw. (1953). *Physica van de stemvorming, met toepassingen*. Groningen: Rijksuniversiteit Groningen.

Van den Berg, Jw. (1955). On the role of the laryngeal ventricle in voice production. *Folia Phoniatrica* 7(2): 57–69.

Van den Berg, Jw. (1956). Zur Identifizierung der Phoneme durch das Ohr. *Archiv für Ohren, Nasen, und Kehlkopfheilkunde* 169(2): 253–255.

Van den Berg, Jw. (1958). Oesophageal speech. *Folia Phoniatrica* 10(2): 65–84.

Van den Berg, Jw. (1959). A delta-f-generator and movie- adapter unit for laryngostroboscopy. *Practica Oto-Rhino-Laryngologica* 21(5): 355–363.

Van den Berg, Jw., Vennard, W.D., Burger, D., and Shervanian, C.C. (1960). *Voice Production: The vibrating larynx (Instructional Film)*. Utrecht: Stichting Film en Wetenschap.

Van den Berg, Jw. (1968). Mechanism of the larynx and the laryngeal vibrations. In: B. Malmberg (ed.), *Manual of Phonetics*, pp. 278–308. Amsterdam: North-Holland Publishing Co.

Von Kempelen, W.R. (1791). *Mechanismus der menschlichen Sprache nebst Beschreibung einer sprechenden Maschine*. Wien: J.B. Degen.

Weiss, D. (1932a). Die Laryngostroboskopie. *Zeitschrift für Laryngologie, Rhinologie, und Otologie und ihre Grenzgebiete* 22(5/6): 391–418.

Weiss, D. (1932b). Ein Resonanzphanomen der Singstimme. *Monatsschrift für Ohrenheilkunde und Laryngo-Rhinologie* 66: 964–967.

Wesley Mills, T. (1906). *Voice Production in Singing and Speaking, based on Scientific Principles*, 4th edn. Philadelphia: J.B. Lippincott.

Winckel, F. (1953). Physikalische Kriterien für objektive Stimmbeurteilung. *Folia Phoniatrica* 5(4): 232–252.

Winckel, F. (1957). Technik und Anwendung der Laryngo-Stroboskopie. *Zeitschrift für Laryngologie, Rhinologie, Otologie und ihre Grenzgebiete* 36: 574–585.

Zimmermann, R. (1938). Stimmlippenlängen bei Sängern und Sängerinnen. *Archive Sprache und Stimmphysiologie Sprache und Stimmheilkunde* 2: 103–129.

Zuckerkandl, E. (1900). Zur Anatomie des Sängerkehlkopfes. *Monatsschrift für Ohrenheilkunde und Laryngo-Rhinologie*, 34 (1): 5–16.

Zwaardemaker Cz, H. and Eijkman, L.P.H. (1928). *Leerboek der Phonetiek: inzonderheid met betrekking tot het Standaard-Nederlandsch*. Haarlem: De Erven F Bohn.

....

CHAPTER 50

HISTORICAL APPROACHES IN REVEALING THE SINGING VOICE, PART 2

....

HARM K. SCHUTTE

INTRODUCTION

....

MANUEL P. Garcia, the focus of much discussion in the previous chapter (please see Schutte, chapter 49, in this volume), died in 1906 at the age of 101. In that same year, interest in medical speech pathology became more formalized when Hermann Gutzmann started to pay medical attention to physiological aspects of the speech of the deaf, of stuttering, and, some decades later, of voice. Other books and reviews on voice and singing had already been published.[1]

The previous chapter described how research on the singing voice was factually restricted by existing concepts on voice production, such as the flute principle[2] or the folds acting as strings.[3] Many teachers of singing did not care about the physiology of singing, as Behnke (1880) wrote. They relied upon their trained ears, which they felt were sufficient for participating in musical tasks. Many teachers even held the opinion that informing students about how the vocal folds looked and about which muscles participate in phonation might distract singers and might have a negative influence on subsequent artistic singing.

Developments in experimental phonetics at the start of the twentieth century contributed much to the understanding of voice and speech physiology. Singing became the focus of new

---

[1] See the books by Grützner (1879) and Nagel (1909) for lists of sources.

[2] The vocal folds, when considered to work like labia in a flue pipe, creating eddies, led to the opinion that the vocal folds needed to have a smooth surface. If the rims of the vocal folds were smooth, operations on the folds were considered successful, and the voice was expected to be better (this opinion continued until the 1970s and occasionally even later). This probably led to the surgical procedure of stripping the vocal folds.

[3] When the vocal folds were considered to work like the string of a violin, for which the string formula for fundamental frequency can be applied, with length and tension determining the pitch, it is not surprising that a surgical procedure followed by which the vocal folds were knitted together at the frontal side to shorten the vibrating vocal folds to achieve a higher pitch, e.g. in transgender-related surgery.

scientific techniques, such as girdle pneumography (and subsequently pressure and flow measurements), X-rays, and X-ray tomography. Aerodynamics stood central in the minds of investigators of the physiology of voice and singing. Later in the century, sound analysis equipment started to play a role.

Specific contributions to the understanding of the physiology of voice production were obtained by using miniature transducers around the glottis in order to gather simultaneous pressure measurements. These latter experiments helped to discredit the glottal pulses concept, which had been in use since Helmholtz. This led to our analysis in Groningen that the flow-stopping event at the moment of vocal fold closure is the active mechanism in voice production. Electroglottography, a non-invasive means of tracking vocal fold contact (editors note: see Herbst, Howard, and Švec, "The Sound Source in Singing: Basic Principles and Muscular Adjustments for Fine-tuning Vocal Timbre," this volume), became a crucial part of research equipment. It has proved to be a very valuable tool, especially when used in tandem with other recorded signals, such as the audio signal.

In Groningen, advances in computing led to the development of the software package VoceVista, which became important for understanding the effect of glottis closing and the resonance effects of the vocal tract in professional singing. Attention will be paid to the shift from resonance-based singing voice explanations to Bernoulli (flow)-oriented approaches. Our personal research on voice will be discussed in this context, as will be the shift back to resonance orientation.

In this chapter we will summarize the areas of singing voice research published in the second half of the twentieth century. We have limited ourselves to specific research on the singing voice, through which we will follow the most important lines. According to Kuhn (1970), most research is paradigm-confirming in nature. Following this principle, we have to conclude that the number of published innovative research results is rather low.

State of singing voice investigation at the end of World War II

Until the middle of the twentieth century, there was little scientific literature which led to a better understanding of the singing voice. This is understandable given the technological limitations of the time: laryngostroboscopy demands properly working equipment, good sources of illumination, and excellent musical skills from both the examiner and the subject. Achieving frozen or slow-motion images became easier in subsequent decades.

Another challenge was the devastation of World War II. Most of the labs in Europe were gone. Some important researchers and physicians took refuge in America, such as G.E. Arnold, F.S. Brodnitz, and E. Froeschels. Other European voice physiologists/pathologists died; for example, Imhofer in Prague committed suicide, and Branco van Dantzig, a professional soprano, and an important advocate of voice hygiene and speech on schools in the Netherlands, died in Auschwitz. She was important for her translation of the work of Gutzmann, which included the new discoveries of phonetics.

What was predominant in the years just after the war? Innovations in electronics were very helpful. New equipment made new types of research possible, e.g. electromyography. However, it should be noted that often a new device is applied, but the newly acquired data do not contribute to new insights. In general, it can be said that when a new type of equipment became available, researchers started applying it to singing usually without a new idea or scientific questions.

A new start

After World War II it was Richard Luchsinger (1900–1993) who showed interest in aspects of speech and voice. Luchsinger earned his doctoral degree in Lausanne, focusing his research on investigating the isoelectric point of blood. He studied in several places in Europe (Cooper 1997). His interest in phoniatric research was challenged by a stay in Munich in the lab of Nadoleczny, who had been a student of Gutzmann Sr. Luchsinger's first publication on voice appeared in 1942, and was on analyzing the human voice by using spectrography (Luchsinger 1942). Shortly after the war, in collaboration with the Basel, Switzerland-based publisher Karger, he founded a new journal, *Folia Phoniatrica*, which was devoted to voice and speech. All the pre-war journals in the field had either ceased to exist or had converted to journals with an emphasis on ear, nose, and throat, but little on voice.

Luchsinger's greatest influence on the field was as the co-author of the first post-war handbook on voice, *Lehrbuch der Stimm-und Sprachheilkunde* (Luchsinger and Arnold 1949), which he published with G.E. Arnold (1914–1989). In the handbook, an overview is given of the knowledge on voice, speech, and articulation. Luchsinger wrote on voice (with a few other authors), while his co-author Godfrey Arnold wrote specifically on speech and articulation. This book set the standard for the profession.

This book also marked the final separation from the ENT handbooks. Luchsinger and Arnold's handbooks served until the Berlin-based phoniatricians Wendler and Seidner from Berlin published in 1977, with others, the first edition of *Lehrbuch der Phoniatrie* (1977, 1987, 1996, 2005). A stream of other specialized books on voice and speech was issued after these.

A number of methods for exploring voice function were published in *Folia Phoniatrica* and later also in the *Journal of Voice*. Many of these methods found a clinical application; however, only a few appear suitable for also investigating the singing voice. Luchsinger was quite honest when he evaluated the difficulties of performing research on the singing voice and the level of knowledge about singing. He wrote in a review of a book by Tarneaud: *La chant, sa construction, sa destruction*:

> Although singing is already the subject of a rich series of literature it seems that singing pedagogy has not taken advantage of it. However, one may not forget that singing is not learned from books, but rather by practical training. Many teachers of singing are skeptical of phoniatric literature because they point to the disagreement between scientists over important questions in laryngology. When a student said to the author that there had never been a book about singing that showed what is normal or abnormal with any precision and valid proofs, he was correct.
>
> (Luchsinger 1946, reviewing Tarneaud 1946)

One area of research that began after the war was airflow measurements. Measurements in singers were published after the war by Luchsinger and Vogelsanger (Luchsinger 1951; Vogelsanger 1954). They were followed in the early 1960s by Von Leden and Isshiki in Los Angeles (Isshiki and Von Leden 1964). These preliminary studies were the start of a series of flow measurements which will be discussed later in this chapter.

WORK ON PHYSIOLOGY IN THE 1950S AND 1960S

Janwillem Van den Berg (1920–1985)

The work of the physicist Janwillem Van den Berg is notable for many reasons. His thesis *Physica van de stemvorming, met toepassingen* (Van den Berg 1953) touched upon a number of voice physiology items. His subsequent myoelastic-aerodynamic theory of 1958 became the leading theory of phonation for many years (Van den Berg 1958).

His study on the characterization of vowels, a vocal tract issue, helped him make a contribution to research questions of communication engineers. But in studying voice aspects, he realized that the prevailing description of voice production showed lots of imprecision and needed corrections. Van den Berg even described his new approach as: "an attempt at a fully elaborated, balanced and physically founded theory of the voice production . . . ." (Van den Berg 1953, p. 15). His thesis described the state of research between the years 1900 and 1950, which provided little that was new in voice production. Van den Berg, however, described new aspects: the Bernoulli effect; coupling between the glottis and vocal tract; and coupling between both vocal folds.

Van den Berg initially became interested in voice following the publications of Louise Kaiser;[4] he questioned her explanation of voice production as based on the hunter's whistle theory of Savart editors note: (see Schutte, "Historical Approaches in Revealing the Singing Voice, Part 1," chapter 49, this volume) and made this a topic of a chapter in his thesis.

Savart and Morgagni's ventricle

In the 1950s the role of the laryngeal ventricle was still under discussion. Savart (1825a, 1825b) and Guillemin (1897) considered the ventricle as the sound generator itself, in analogy to the function of a hunter's whistle. Morat and Dyon strongly defended this theory in their *Traité de Physiologie* (Morat 1918). So it is unsurprising that Eykman (1923; Zwaardemaker Cz and Eijkman 1928) accepted this explanation as well.

With the advent of X-ray tomography in the 1930s, variability in laryngeal ventricle size, vocal fold length in relation to pitch, and sound character were studied (Husson 1933, 1952, 1954). Zimmermann (1938) obtained differing results or gave different explanations for what was observed. Van den Berg discussed several possibilities, also leading to a refutation of Negus' statement that the ventricle has no function at all. Based on theoretical approaches and some existing (tomographic) evidence and his experiments, Van den Berg came to the conclusion that the ventricle could work as a low-pass filter. The soft tissue of the larynx is poorly defined on X-ray photographs; conclusive details only became possible in the 1950s,

---

[4] Louise Kaiser (1891–1973) was an MD-pediatrician who early in the twentieth century became interested in speech and phonetics. She finally became lector in phonetics at the University of Amsterdam. She was strongly involved in international phonetics and published in *Archives Néerlandaises de Phonetique Experimentelle*. She also edited two editions of the *Manual of Phonetics* (Kaiser 1957; Kaiser 1968). On voice production she followed the explanation of Savart. The new insights of Van den Berg were not included, however, until the second edition of the *Manual*.

with tomograms and other techniques being used by Van den Berg to refute the hunter's whistle theory of Savart and Guillemin (Van den Berg 1955).

Husson

Another alternative theory triggered Van den Berg's interest: the neurochronaxic theory of the French singer and physicist Raoul Husson. Before World War II, he had developed a new theory on the production of voice (Husson 1933, 1936; Husson and Tarneaud 1933). This led Van den Berg to a chapter in his thesis, in which he, in French, declared the neurochronaxic theory totally invalid (Van den Berg 1953; Van den Berg 1961; Van den Berg and Tan 1959). The level of imprecision and outright guesswork on voice production led Van den Berg to formulate the myoelastic-aerodynamic theory of voice production.

Myoelastic-aerodynamic theory of voice production

The myoelastic-aerodynamic theory of voice production was published in the first volume of the *Journal of Speech and Hearing Research* (Van den Berg 1958). It received world-wide acceptance.[5] The theory is still regarded as a leading one, but it needs some modifications based on modern findings, such as those indicated by Titze (1980) and others found in our own research in Groningen (Miller and Schutte 1985; Schutte and Miller 1988). However, few modifications of this theory have been published.

Van den Berg's new formulation of the physiology of voice production received much attention. He was invited to present the main lecture at the International Congress of the International Association of Logopedics and Phoniatrics in Padua in 1962. In this presentation, he gave an overview of experimental possibilities for voice and speech (Van den Berg 1962).

Instructional film The Vibrating Larynx by Van den Berg, Vennard, and others (1960)

William Vennard, professional singer and voice teacher at the University of Southern California, visited Van den Berg towards the end of the 1950s to participate in making the instructional film *The Vibrating Larynx*, which was released in 1960 (Van den Berg, Vennard, Burger, and Shervanian 1960). One of the key principles explained in the film, the Bernoulli effect, was integrated into the teaching of singing through the work of Vennard (1967) and many other voice physiologists, voice/speech trainers, and therapists.

Van den Berg's formulation of the myoelastic-aerodynamic theory in 1958 also had a large effect on the type of research which occurred in the following years and even decades. The aerodynamic factors, especially the Bernoulli effect, led to an emphasis on measuring air-flow rates, subglottic pressure, and efficiency, in professional singers as well. The results and consequences of these experiments will be discussed later (see the section "Aerodynamics of phonation, including singing"). The myoelastic part of the theory led to studies on the activity of the intrinsic muscles. See the section "Electromyography of the muscles of the larynx," later in this chapter.

---

[5] The Bell Telephone Laboratories Technical Library Publication Department immediately made a translation of the voice chapter of Van den Berg's thesis for their own purposes.

RESEARCH ON SINGING IN AND AFTER THE 1960S

In the 1960s and later, research on the physiological aspects of voice increased, but there were still relatively few articles specifically dealing with the singing voice. Luchsinger stopped publishing after turning 65 in 1965, with the exception of one study on singing (Luchsinger 1975). Other writers published articles on specific aspects of singing, such as nasal resonance, airflow rate (Isshiki 1961, 1965), and aerodynamic relations to fundamental frequency (McGlone, Richmond, and Bosma 1966). Several Japanese researchers, on sabbatical in Los Angeles and working with Von Leden, published a series of aerodynamic measurements. These typically dealt with airflow rate and featured datasets for a limited number of subjects, including Hirano, Koike, and Von Leden (1968); Koike, Hirano, and Von Leden (1967); Koike and Hirano (1968); Yanagihara and Koike (1967); Faaborg-Andersen, Yanagihara, and Von Leden (1967); Yanagihara (1967); Yanagihara and Von Leden (1967); Yanagihara (1970); Isshiki (1961, 1964, 1965, 1981, 1985); Isshiki, Okamura, and Morimoto (1967); Iwata and Von Leden (1970a, 1970b); Iwata, Von Leden, and Williams (1972); and Iwata 1988. They developed a series of quotients, also in relation to the vital capacity measured. In each of the successive series of publications one more individual was added to the group of "normals." Normative values[6] were developed, but all of these were, in my opinion, questionably based only on the measurement of airflow rate.[7]

Numerous published studies demonstrated the usage of new equipment. Table 50.1 gives a brief listing of some of the types of equipment used and a sampling of the most significant papers.

Early articles by Johan Sundberg appeared in 1973 (Sundberg 1973), and this author's first presentation of aerodynamic results was published in 1974 (Schutte and Van den Berg 1974).

Most of the articles cited here were published in *Folia Phoniatrica*, but relatively few really dealt with singing, except for some which we produced in Groningen together with the American pedagogue Richard Miller (Miller and Schutte 1994; Miller and Schutte 1981; Miller and Schutte 1983; Rothenberg 1988; Schutte and Miller 1983; Schutte and Miller 1984a; Schutte and Miller 1984b; Schutte and Miller 1985).

In 1987 the *Journal of Voice* began publication. A number of articles on voice and some on singing also appeared in the *Journal of Speech and Hearing Research*. Most of these articles deal with related aspects of voice and singing, perception of singing, and vocal registers: Bjorkner et al. (2006); Echternach, Dippold et al. (2010); Echternach Sundberg, Arndt, et al. (2010); Echternach, Sundberg, Markl, et al. (2010); Echternach et al. (2011); Echternach et al. (2012); Echternach and Richter (2012); Herbst, Fitch, and Švec (2010); Herbst, Howard, and Schlömicher-Thier (2010); Herbst et al. (2011); Herbst et al. (2013); Herbst and Švec (2014); Herbst et al. (2014); Herbst et al. (2015); Sundberg (1990); Titze (1988).

From the Voice Research Lab in Groningen a series of publications appeared from 1990 onwards. The remainder of this chapter will focus on these publications, which are based upon the author's work in Groningen and which began under the guidance of Van den Berg.

---

[6] The presentation of mean normative values for flow by these authors, even leading to a minimal difference between male and female, is a statistical error. The arithmetical values (without paying attention to the spread of the data) suggest a precision that is unrelated to the measured values and misleading.

[7] In 1994 Isshiki also came to the same conclusion, expressing to me that "airflow is over-estimated."

Table 50.1 Voice analysis equipment or analysis topics and significant research papers

Electromyography	Laryngography	Vocal register studies	Imaging the larynx
Hirose (1977)	E. Allen (1980); E.L. Allen and Hollien (1973); Damsté, Hollien, and Moore (1968); Hollien (1964, 1965); Hollien, Coleman, and Moore (1968)	Colton and Hollien (1972, 1973a, 1973b); Colton (1972, 1973); Colton, Estill, and Gould (1977); Large and Iwata (1971); Large (1972, 1973, 1979); Large, Iwata, and Von Leden (1972); editors note: see also "The Sound Source in Singing" by Herbst, Howard, and Švec in this volume	Laryngokymography: Gall, Gall, and Hanson (1971); High speed film: Tanabe et al. (1975); Photoglottography: Kitzing and Sonesson (1974); Kitzing (1977; 1982); Kitzing, Carlborg, and Löfqvist (1982); Sonesson (1959)
Vocal fold movement	Voice range profile/ phonetogram	Jitter and shimmer measurements	Magnetic resonance imaging
Electroglottography: Askenfelt et al. (1980); Childers and Krishnamurthy (1985); Kitzing et al. 1982); Herbst and Ternström (2006); editors note: see also "The Sound Source in Singing" by Herbst, Howard, and Švec in this volume	Dejonckere (1977); Schutte and Seidner (1983; 1988); Schutte (2009); Sulter et al. (1994); editors note: see also "Voice Range Profile based voice quality feedback" by Peter Pabon within "Future Perspectives" in this volume	Horii (1979; 1982; 1985); Leonard et al. (1987); Wendahl (1966)	Baer et al. (1987); Baer et al. (1988, 1991); Echternach et al. (2010); Ford et al. (1995); Honda et al. (1995); Miller et al. (1997); Neuschaefer-Rube et al. (1996); Story, Titze, and Hoffman (1996, 1998, 2001); Sulter et al. (1992); editors note: see also "The Vocal Tract in Singing" by Story in this volume

Research conducted in the Groningen Voice Research Lab

Introduction

In the second year of my medical education I came to work in the Laboratory of Medical Physics, which was chaired by Prof. dr. Janwillem (Jw) Van den Berg.

Phonetograms

I started at the end of the 1960s by studying the value and practicality of registering a so-called phonetogram, which is also known as a *courbe vocale* (Calvet and Malhiac 1952)

or a voice range profile (VRP). A phonetogram is a registration of the frequency and intensity, as measured by a microphone at a fixed distance from the mouth (editors note: see the section by Peter Pabon within the multi-author chapter 53, "Future Perspectives," in this volume). Because the acoustics of a room can influence the measuring results, we did some fundamental tests on the reliability of the measurement procedure and designed supporting equipment to assist with the process.

The results of these experiments and our technical advice were published in *Folia Phoniatrica* (Schutte 1975; Schutte and Seidner 1983). Next, I aimed to get education and experience in performing indirect laryngoscopy with a mirror and a 1955 type-Ahrend-van Gogh stroboscope which was designed by Van den Berg, but which I had to repair first. This enabled me to combine the phonetogram with images of the larynx in action. The availability of the Von Stuckradt endoscope in 1977 made it possible to take photographs (slides) of larynges of patients and non-patients/singers; after 1984, video recordings were possible. From these results in combination with the phonetogram, conclusions could be drawn about a singer's possibilities.

The individual possibilities of a (professional) singer's voice can be made visual in a registration of the phonetogram, which as previously mentioned, graphically relates the voice's frequency (f_o, in Hertz) and intensity (Sound Pressure Level (SPL), in dB). In general, the maximum curve shows the (frequency) places where a transition from one register to another of the voice happens. It shows where a female voice is capable of a strong, loud sound in the higher notes of the frequency range, or where a bass can still produce a low, well-sounding note and is able to make a crescendo, whereas other voices appear to lose power due to the relaxation of the muscles, as needed for a low note, but also concomitantly leading to a loss of efficient glottis closure to make a sound.

Potential pitfalls

In some instances, especially when in a research project several phonetograms need to be compared for some reason, researchers transform the horizontal frequency axis, which by nature and in musical practice is logarithmic, like on a keyboard, into a linear scale (Coleman 1977; Coleman et al. 1977). While this might make calculating the statistics easier, the resulting phonetogram loses a lot of information for the musician/singer. Further, by putting many phonetograms over each other to derive mean values, the individual phonetogram as a description of the capacities of an individual singer's voice is totally lost.

The use of a C weighting curve of the sound pressure meter, instead of a curve A[8] or B, as we proposed in Schutte and Seidner (1983), has a negative influence on the interpretation of a phonetogram. Curve A was proposed to avoid the influence of low-frequency sound components in surrounding noise (like air ventilators) on the measurements of the sound pressure level (SPL). Indeed, curve C runs flat from 31.5 Hz to 8000 Hz (+/– 3 dB), and curve A is in the same way defined as flat from 500 Hz to 10 kHz. Curve B is flat from 160 Hz to 8000 Hz. The relatively small loss of the lower part of the range is not crucial for voice. In

---

[8] As proposed in IEC Recommendation 179 for precision sound level meters, 1970.

chest voice the intensity of the fundamental is not strong (sometimes even 15–20 dB lower in SPL), so that for the male voice with a fundamental lower than 250 Hz, the contribution of the fundamental to the total SPL is not great; this is even more true in a female voice with a higher, low-frequency fundamental.

Details of voice registrations and even some support for determining a voice classification can be found in Schutte (1975, 1987, 2009); Sulter et al. (1994); Titze et al. (1995) and Lycke, (2012).

Thesis work

In my own case, when it came to a topic for my thesis, it seemed as if Van den Berg already had a plan prepared. In a one-hour session he wrote down a research plan. No phonetogram, no electroglottography, but aerodynamics based in principle on his own work (Van den Berg 1956). That was a single case study with himself as a subject and steered by his knowledge of lung mechanics, as expressed in the varying pressure in the esophagus with varying lung volume. Now, about twenty years later, with improved possibilities and up-to-date equipment, he saw the possibility of measuring simultaneously mean airflow rate and mean subglottal pressure, using the esophageal balloon in sustained phonation on a single vowel. Values had to be measured on different fundamental frequencies and sound pressure levels in patients and, for reference purposes, in "normal-sounding" voices. By measuring the sound pressure levels and the aerodynamic values the efficiency of these larynges could then be calculated. The idea, of course, was to find that a diseased voice was less efficient in voice production, and after voice therapy or surgery the efficiency would be better. This led to a thesis, *The Efficiency of Voice Production* (Schutte 1980).

As was previously mentioned, Luchsinger (1951) used the pneumotach by Fleisch to study airflow in singers, a study he published in *Folia Phoniatrica*. Van den Berg (1956) applied the esophageal balloon to determine the subglottal pressure. After Isshiki and Von Leden (1964) had published on the pneumotachograph with better equipment, under the guidance of Van den Berg, I applied both the esophageal balloon and the pneumotachograph in my thesis study.

We obtained data from patients of several kinds, and a number of them were remeasured after treatment, which was either a surgical intervention or voice training. Further, for reference values, 45 non-patients (24 male and 21 female), among them six professional singers, were measured. From my aerodynamic research work we established in singers[9] that the pressure can be rather high, up to 75 or even 100 cm H2O during a sustained phonation.

The singers also showed an individual pattern. Unusual high pressures[10] were established in tenors, up to 100 cm H2O, which some colleagues would call "unbelievable and

[9] In non-trained persons the subglottic pressure seldom reaches values above 30 cm H2O. This is probably correlated with the untrained body unacquainted with a situation where the venous blood stream to the heart is more difficult to maintain as a result of the higher intra-thoracic pressure (i.e. the subglottic pressure) above 30 cm H2O. Singing voice training also involves the preparative training of the body (i.e. the breathing mechanism) for these higher pressures.

[10] Such high pressures cannot be measured reliably with the /baeb/ method using intra-oral pressure changes, as promoted by Rothenberg (1968), but are still unfortunately often used in singing voice studies (see Nieboer, Schutte, and de Graaf 1984). Voice production needs time to build up, to get resonance; the intra-oral pressure method cuts the voicing off too early in the mouth closed phase.

(a)

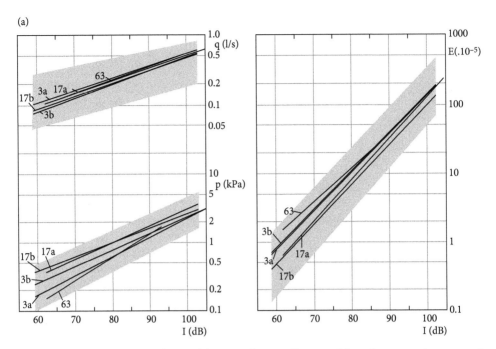

FIGURE 50.1A Regression lines of three professionally trained bass-baritones (#3, #17 and #63; #3 and #17 measured 2 times), for flow and subglottic pressure (left panel) and the calculated efficiency (right panel), each over the total SPL range measured at 30 cm in front of the mouth.

Considerable differences exist in the values of subglottic pressure between the singers, leading also the differences in efficiency.

hyperfunctional," and a reproducible flow within the "normal" range, together leading to low efficiency (Figure 50.1a). Twenty years later, one of the professional singers from the study showed that by changing his training strategies he was able considerably to reduce his subglottic pressure values, while maintaining and even improving the desired voice quality. Much of the change observed seemed to be related to the closed quotient (Stark 1999). Another singer showed a flow pattern over the whole dynamic range of c. 300 ml/sec. (see Figure 50.1b, left graph, upper portion, lines 62a, 62b, and 62c). A close relationship between flow and pressure was not established (Schutte 1980). All patients tested for the thesis work used a higher subglottic pressure than the arithmetic mean of the subglottic pressure of the non-patients; however, flow rates were very similar in both groups. This meant the efficiency values varied in patients just as in non-patients.

The relation with the SPL was also individually determined. Generally, the rule as given in the literature, of flow increasing with SPL, was found, although the opposite applied in some cases. Voicing is a very individual phenomenon; a person has an individual larynx with its own working pattern. A comparison with the data established by Vogelsanger (1954) showed the same pattern. However, this study only measured flow in 25 singers and four patient singers. This comparison is published in Schutte (1980).

(b)

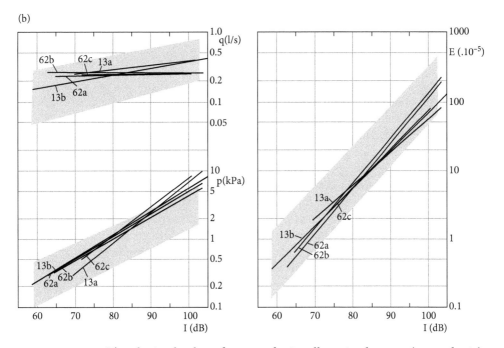

FIGURE 50.1B The obtained value of two professionally trained tenors (#13 and #62). Note the high subglottic pressure in tenor #13; up to 100 cmH2O (10 kPa).

The lines are placed in reference areas to compare with the male and female subjects with "normal", i.e. non-deviant, sounding voices. The shaded areas depict normative values for flow, subglottic pressure, and efficiency based on the authors' study (Schutte 1980).

A statistical method was used to determine the shaded areas. For each value of the SPL, in steps of 0.5 dB, obtained in Schutte (1980), confidence levels of 95% were calculated, based on the data obtained for that specific SPL of all test persons (male and female lumped together, because no statistical difference was established).

The end points of these lines (vertical for each 0.5 dB—not depicted here) were used to calculate the upper and lower limits of the reference areas.

The reference areas occupy a large field. This means that if an aerodynamic value or efficiency measured falls within this area it can be considered normal or non-deviant with 95% confidence. Values outside the reference area can be denoted abnormal with 95% confidence.

The reference areas have been initially published in Schutte (1986). The measured values of the professional singers, here for the first time published in relation to the reference areas, show clearly that singers do not show a higher efficiency in voice production. The desired voice quality is not efficiency-driven!

The often-mentioned difference in calculated mean values for male and female by the Von Leden group in the 1970s and recently by Björklund and Sundberg (2016) are based on faulty applied statistics, not keeping in account the large spread in normal values.

For further detail on this research, readers may wish to consult my dissertation, which may be accessed online (Schutte 1980, pp. 75–79).

Aerodynamics of phonation, including singing

Air usage in singing: mean values

Air expelled from the lungs is the power source for voice production in all speaking and singing. Understandably, breathing also received a great deal of attention in the research on singing. At the end of the nineteenth century lung physiology research had developed and the volume compartments, such as vital capacity, residual volume, etc., had been described. Of course, breath management is a central issue in singing and some fundamental knowledge was present: "A candle flame in front of the mouth should not flicker while producing a tone," though the reason why this was a valid instruction was unclear.

Important studies had been published by Luchsinger (1951) and Vogelsanger (1954) on air usage in singing in relation to sound pressure level. The Fleisch pneumotach, invented in 1925, was available at the time and sound pressure measurements could be performed with electronic equipment. This kind of research was continued by the group led by Hans von Leden in Los Angeles in the 1960s, and was a part of my own dissertation.

My own scientific work was determined by Van den Berg's wish to study the flow and pressure relations in patients and between different patient categories. Following the concept of the valve principle of the glottis, flow and pressure were counterbalanced: a low airflow would mean a high (subglottic) pressure. Pressure and flow are the energy source and the outcome is sound pressure. In medical patients, the balance was thought to be disturbed, and in general it was thought that if patients could be trained to reduce the pressure without losing too much air (or reduce the airflow without drastically increasing the pressure), the sound production would essentially be more efficient—i.e. more effective.

It is important to note that these measurements were based on mean values from a stable portion of an instance of phonation on the vowel /a/, with a mouthpiece to restrict mouth-opening variation. The measurements were done aiming at measuring at fixed,[11] somewhat arbitrarily chosen pitches, and on each pitch, in as many steps of 5 dB as possible. A nose clamp[12] prevented "air escaping from the nose," but in the vowel used the nasal port was considered closed anyway. Almost none of the patients could do falsetto; this register was then excluded from the data. From the resulting data for each measurement a regression line through the data for airflow rate, subglottic pressure, and efficiency was determined. The lines were bundled to get an overview of the data; we could thus derive normative values for phonation (Schutte 1980, 1986a, 1986b).

---

[11] This was a mistake: for some voices the pitches did not match well with the individual voice structure. A fixed pitch meant neglecting the individual voice type; a pitch chosen guided by a phonetogram would have been better.

[12] This was another mistake in the test design. Through the extension of the vocal tract by connecting tubing to the pneumotachograph, the resonance characteristics changed considerably. All the professional singers commented on this resonance frustrating interference. Isshiki mentions this problem, but decided to neglect it (Isshiki 1964).

Direct high-frequency aerodynamic measurements

Measurements to achieve high-frequency resolution of the aerodynamic events around the glottis, specifically the pressure (which was an old wish of Van den Berg), brought new aspects to discover. The results led us to a new vision, in particular of singing, which is why we will describe in certain detail the procedure followed. It led to a discrepancy in knowledge between flow and resonance.

In Groningen at the end of the 1970s we established that there was not a conclusively different mean airflow rate between professional singers and non-professional voice users (Schutte and Van den Berg 1980). Following the definition of Van den Berg (1956), efficiency also showed little difference; subglottic pressure was the only primary aspect that differed. This was especially true in tenors, where subglottal pressure was higher than in non-singers. At the beginning of the 1980s, we decided that we had to look more closely at pressure, flow, and acoustical effects in a more time-detailed fashion.

We began making measurements in the early 1980s, and Donald G. Miller first presented the results at the Voice Foundation meeting, which was then held in New York (Miller and Schutte 1985). This first publication from 1985 describes in detail the procedure we followed, including the discovery that a certain habituation time is necessary for getting the body (inner larynx) adapted to the insertion and presence of a catheter.

Research was done on fifteen professional singers trained in the Western Operatic Tradition. We were registering different types of phonations, pitches, and different maneuvers. Evaluation of the curves was a time-consuming and tedious affair, but this effort formed the basis for the later development of VoceVista. At the start, spectrograms were made from selected parts by an FFT analyzer with printouts on paper. The time-stretched recordings offered the possibility of easy time correction between the microphone (audio) signal (positioned at 30 cm from the mouth opening) and the signals from below and above the glottis. Understanding grew, in particular of the EGG signal, and we were surprised to establish that the moment of glottis closure fell in time with the highest peak in the subglottic pressure and with the moment of lowest pressure at the supraglottic spot at the entrance of the vocal tract, immediately above the vocal folds (Miller and Schutte 1985). This was in great contrast with the prevailing theory of "the glottis is pushed open by the higher subglottal pressure and then a puff of air escapes."[13] In fact, our measurements formed the experimental proof of the statement by Fant (1979) that the closing of the glottis is the excitation moment.

It is significant to point out some of the key differences between our work in Groningen and that of other prominent laboratories. In Groningen, the singing voice research aimed at studying the acoustical effects in professional singing via direct measurements of the glottis pressure changes, whereas other researchers emphasized the glottal pulse annex open quotient using inverse filtering.

---

[13] Helmholtz was the first to state that the puffs of air through the glottis generate the sound (Van den Berg 1955, fn p. 58).

Methods

Measuring the pressure variations in the air below and above the vocal folds was possible using miniature pressure transducers[14] placed 6 cm apart from each other on a catheter. The transducers could nominally be used to register up to 10 kHz. The catheter was guided through a lower nasal passage and placed transglottally in the posterior cartilaginous part of the glottis. After a while, the catheter, due to its thermoplasticity, folded itself in the tissue of the posterior glottis, leaving the vocal folds unhampered in their vibratory movements. By proper positioning of the catheter and checking the signals on an oscilloscope, air pressure events in the subglottal and supraglottal regions near the vocal folds could be measured. It was a lucky shot that we also used an electroglottographic device, because that appeared to be crucial in evaluating and understanding the pressure signals. On a fourth channel the audio signal was recorded. Sound pressure levels derived from the audio signal were registered when the signals were written out on Mingograph paper.

We used a DC-instrumentation tape recorder and an ink writer, the Mingograph, which was in general use in electroencephalographic (EEG) studies and in phonetics. By recording at high tape speed on the instrumentation recorder and replaying the signals at 64 times reduced speed while using fast paper speed on the ink writer, we could obtain a frequency resolution up to 10000 Hz (Miller and Schutte 1985).

In our protocol design (in 1984, prior to the development of personal computers), we chose to record all the calibrated data on a DC-instrumentation recorder. We began with a four-channel recorder, which was later replaced with a 16-channel recorder. In the latter, the audio signal could be recorded with different level settings, meaning that, in case of a large dynamic range in a measuring series, an undistorted audio signal would be available. All the signals were monitored on an oscilloscope during a recording session. All these signals were analogue signals.

Using the tape recordings which were later converted into multiple channel digital signals, one could afterwards make a selection to study specific research issues. This was done far more easily after development of the software package VoceVista.

With the protocol based on test experiments we started measurements. Herewith a new phase started in singing voice research. Donald Miller was looking for a description of registers, based on the common experience of singers of sensing a noticeable back pressure at specific spots in the mouth cavity. Perhaps this is related to the "point de Maran" mentioned in French-oriented pedagogical literature.

There are many possible tasks one can use to investigate the singing voice, depending upon what types of data are desired: Sustained phonations at designated pitches and loudness levels; scales, arpeggios, and other patterns; and different registers. Where to start? Fixed pitches and loudness were considered not to be the optimal approach, as mentioned in the section on aerodynamics.

---

[14] The transducer was loaned to us by Van den Berg's lab. It was originally used in experiments to measure the pressure gradient over the sphincter of a urine bladder. We made sure to clean it first!

Transglottal pressures

Selections of the recordings were chosen to study in detail the relationships between the signals. We had supraglottal and subglottal pressures, EGG and audio signals. First the graphs were studied on paper with a Ubiquitous spectrum analyzer with recordings made on a slow X-Y writer. This tedious and time-consuming work was no longer necessary when personal computers became available. Moreover, the evaluation of the signals, in particular following the relationships between formant(s) and harmonic(s), as well as the singer's formant, became much easier using the computer program VoceVista which was developed (see www. Vocevista.com).

Earlier researchers using transglottally placed pressure transducers included Kitzing and Löfqvist (1975); Koike and Perkins (1968); and Koike (1969). They presented the same pressure patterns, but did not use EGG and therefore lacked information about the actual opening and closing of the glottis. From our material it is difficult to support the statement that there is a "puff" of air escaping to excite the vocal tract. This can be seen in Figure 50.2.

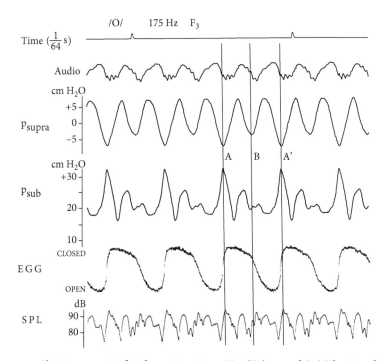

FIGURE 50.2 Short segment of a phonation at 175 Hz. (F3), vowel /o/. The time line shows 1/64 sec. between marks, as the tape was played back at 1/64 of the recording speed of 60 inch per second speed of the tape. The position of the audio signal and SPL level has been adjusted to compensate for the lag of 1.5 milliseconds caused by the distance from the glottis to the microphone. The electroglottograph signal is displayed so that upward movement indicates closing. Vertical lines A and A1 indicate moments of closure of the glottis, and line B indicates an opening moment.

From Miller, D.G. and Schutte, H.K. (1985). Characteristic patterns of sub- and supraglottal pressure variations within the glottal cycle. In: V.L. Lawrence (ed.), *Transcripts of the XIIIth Symposium on the Care of the Professional Voice*, 70–75. New York: Voice Foundation.

We found that the lowest pressure transducer did not necessarily need to be placed transglottally. It was sometimes a difficult procedure. The same signal information of the subglottal tract could be obtained by placing the tip of the transducer just below the entrance of the esophagus. This also meant a sort of fixation for the supraglottal transducer just above the vocal folds. The above-mentioned research results showed that the excitation moment for the vocal tract is the moment of the closing of the glottis, which led us to re-evaluate the concept of the often-used term "open quotient." It is not surprising that the concept, formulated by Helmholtz in the nineteenth century, held that the pulses, escaping under subglottic pressure at the moment the glottis is open would then excite and bring the air in the vocal tract in resonance, of course, fitting to the size of the vocal tract. It seemed no more than logical that the researchers, evaluating the high-speed Bell film of 1940 (Farnsworth 1940; Timcke, Von Leden, and Moore 1958; Timcke, Von Leden, and Moore 1959; Von Leden, Moore, and Timcke 1960), used the open quotient notion in their work. In the following decades this remained the norm, the usual way of presenting glottal cycle information. The opening of the glottis logically gave pulses. It seemed trivial to advocate for the closed quotient, because it is the reciprocal of OQ, but, from our experimental experience, we concluded that a slightly larger closure time of the glottis in a cycle can be beneficial to the resonating standing wave in the vocal tract and thus for the ensuing sound. Examples of this can be found in the work of Donald G. Miller (2000, 2008). The material gathered formed the basis for a series of presentations and publications on several topics which were relevant to the better understanding of professional singing voice production, and which will be presented later in the section "For singers, formants are the basis of the power and quality of the voice."

Crucial in our investigations was our discovery of the placement or tuning of the first two formants on harmonics of the fundamental, achieved by training and listening. Not all investigators agree with our view; some, like Titze (2001) state that best resonance is achieved with tuning the formant slightly above the desired harmonic. Raising the first formant with increasing pitch in female singers was already known by the work of Sundberg (1973, 1977a, 1977b). Gradually, we discovered that a second tuning effect plays an important role, that of the alignment of the second formant with the third harmonic, specifically in the *passaggio* region.

The discovery of formant tuning by sopranos in high f_o singing paved the way to the specification of secondary registers that are characterized by acoustic, rather than laryngeal, features. This was based on the increasing possibilities of spectral analysis, referring to knowledge obtained in the related theory of speech. Moreover, the technological development of electroglottography proved to be very useful as a non-invasive means for tracking vocal fold vibratory patterns.

Differences in the timing of the resonances in the vocal tract might be correlated with the use of a larger CQ, showing a longer closure time of the glottis. Not only can subglottic pressure be sustained at higher levels because of this, but also the time-wise longer closure of the glottis may act as a "sounding board" to reflect the sound wave at a proper moment, helping to create a stronger standing wave in the vocal tract (Miller 2008).

Spectral analysis studies

Sundberg gave the first description of the first formant following a rising fundamental in a soprano's high note region with spectral analysis (Sundberg 1973). He also published an important work on the singer's formant (Sundberg 1977a), and wrote a book in which the knowledge on singing at that moment was condensed (Sundberg 1987). He and colleagues in Stockholm have made use of "analysis by synthesis" for some of their acoustical research. This method involves synthesizing sounds and subsequently analyzing eventual differences by a listeners' panel. In Groningen, we took a different direction, as has already been stated, concentrating on data directly obtained from singers in our laboratory. Selections were taken from the tape recordings described above (see the previous section "Methods") and studied in detail. The topics that were studied in this way were reflected in a series of publications the key elements of which we will present in the following sections. Several aspects, like spectral phenomena, as well as EGG and timing issues, have been investigated.

For singers, formants are the basis of the power and quality of the voice

The close grouping of the 3rd, 4th, and 5th formants leads to a phenomenon known as the singer's formant. This was first mentioned by Bartholomew (1934). The phenomenon was extensively studied by Sundberg (1977a). The presence of the singer's formant has been demonstrated to be specific to professional singers. Its existence is more apparent in male voices than in female professionals.

In 2000, Donald Miller defended his thesis in Groningen on voice registers (Miller 2000). The thesis gave an annotation of some articles published through 2000 and a synthesis of the scheme of registers we have developed for male and female singers. The first chapter attempts to locate the position of the theory of the singing voice among the academic disciplines, and gives a historic overview of the problem of registers.

The fundamental difference between chest register and falsetto register, which forms the basis of the very concept of register, is given. This concept is then extended to other discontinuities or transitions aiming at the goal of an integral and even voice. Such transitions could have their basis in a different vibration pattern of the vocal folds or in the acoustics of the vocal tract. Four of the most prominent vocal discontinuities are identified for both male and female professional singers.

Often it is very difficult to determine the frequency position of a formant. It is much easier to determine the harmonics of the glottal sound. In fact, the first five formants are important in the singing voice. A practical method was developed, found by serendipity, for determining the formant frequencies of the singing voice. With this method the determination of the formant frequencies of the vocal tract in singing could be done with sufficient accuracy (Miller and Schutte 1990a, 1990b). The method uses non-periodical vibrations of the vocal folds, meanwhile maintaining the vocal tract position of the sung vowel in question. The sound produced delivers a full spectrum, rich in harmonics. This made it easier to determine the frequency place of a formant. We compared our method against several other sources (Miller and Schutte 1990a).

In a study using MRI to correlate the resonance characteristics and dimensions of the vocal tract, Miller took the opportunity to re-validate the method of using non-periodic sounds (Sulter et al. 1992). MRI was used to determine the extent to which constant posture of the vocal tract is responsible for the accuracy of the determination of formant frequencies through the use of non-periodic phonation. It was concluded that the accurate reproduction of the first two formant frequencies in non-periodic phonation has an aural rather than a postural basis. This calls into question the concept of proprioceptive control of singing, which is still a paradigm in singing theory. Important for tuning purposes, next to the frequency location of formants, is the bandwidth aspect of formants; results of a study of this topic were published in Schutte, Miller, and Švec (1995).

The method of non-periodic sound production was then used to compare "classical" singing techniques with "pop" and "belting." Belting can be defined by its typical physiology (extended chest register to higher frequencies) and acoustics (first formant aligned with the second harmonic). This type of phonation is significant because of the rising frequency of the second harmonic and the needed adjustment of the vocal tract to get the first formant so high. The first formant is mainly determined by the total length of the vocal tract (between vocal folds and lip opening). In belting, this length needs to be made as short as possible to get the frequency of the first formant aligned with the high second harmonic. This second harmonic of pitches between D4 and G5 lies between 588 Hz and 1184 Hz. It is a kind of art to obtain well-vibrating vocal folds along with this small space of the total vocal tract. Pedagogues of classical singing are usually not very enthusiastic about this art of constricting the throat. It is totally different from a "classical singing" approach (Schutte and Miller 1993).

Another line of research of transglottal pressure events examined how a well-trained soprano achieved maximal resonance efficiency by singing high notes with a "falsetto" voice source while matching the first formant to the fundamental frequency. The pressure modulation above and below the glottis revealed a remarkable acoustic phenomenon, in which the pressure across the glottis actually reversed during the open phase of the glottis (Schutte and Miller 1986). This led to a much more recent article (Rothenberg and Schutte 2016) in which a comparison was made between the soprano strategy and the tuning strategy in a power-end-stage amplifier of a high frequency ham radio transmitter.

Features of the flageolet register were also described. Non-periodic sounds appeared very helpful in understanding this highest useful register in singing. It showed reliably that in this case the fundamental frequency passes beyond the first formant frequency. However, the voice still seems resonant because both first and second formants draw close to each other, forming a broader, composite formant (Miller and Schutte 1993). This is similar to what we see in the creation of the singer's formant.

Another article in Miller's thesis discusses one of the most conspicuous problems in traditional vocal pedagogy: the male *passaggio*, including "cover" and the extension into the upper end of the singing range. This had attracted a lot of discussion in the past. Alternative strategies are considered in dealing with this situation, including "register violation." The solution is identified as primarily an acoustic adjustment of the vocal tract, rather than an adjustment of the intrinsic muscles of the larynx (Miller and Schutte 1994).

Individually varying discontinuities are encountered in singers when they attempt to diminish from forte to pianissimo and when male singers use *mezza voce*. Two highly accomplished tenors were studied, each meeting the challenge in his own way, according to what the biomechanical structure of his vocal folds would allow. Objective criteria for a proposed distinct register, *mezza voce*, including an opening of the typically constricted laryngeal collar and incomplete closure of the glottis were given (Miller, Schutte, and Doing 2001).

Register discontinuities where the singer has the task of smoothing and disguising them were approached from another view. We studied the chest-falsetto transition in its maximally abrupt form. The size of the interval leaps between the two registers was measured, and the data showed a tendency for the leap to be larger in male than in female voices (Miller, Švec, and Schutte 2002).

After 2000, a few more articles were published, finally leading to a monograph (Miller 2008); further presentations continue to be given by Miller on different aspects of singing at the Voice Foundation Conference in Philadelphia each year.

It became clear to us in Groningen that an engineering-driven model of voice did not predict specific features we observed in singing; for example, consider closed quotients exceeding 70 percent and the second-formant tuning strategy. These aspects turn up repeatedly in the strategies of some highly accomplished singers, while other singers take quite different measures to satisfy an esthetic ideal. From the speech model the complex habitual pattern of vocal behavior found in singers of high quality cannot be extrapolated (Miller 2008; Miller and Schutte 2005; Schutte, Miller, and Duijnstee 2005).

Dynamic glottis closure

A second item that needs to be discussed is the variation in dynamic glottis closure as is revealed under stroboscopic light during phonation. Dynamic glottis closure denotes how far and how completely the glottis comes to full closure by the movement of the mucosa. This is not the same as what is usually called adduction. The latter is the consequence of adhering to the valve principle. The concept of adduction variations leads to terms such as adduction forces and adduction quotients. The mucosal wave of the cover of the vocal folds is the leading factor in this process.

The vocal folds indeed are brought into a certain position for phonation, but not in a way that resembles a valve, more or less open. It is the mucosa that really shut the glottis leading to closure. It became obvious from doing laryngoscopy by mirror and endoscope that if the dynamic glottis closure is complete, as observed under a properly executed stroboscopy, the air passage is fully stopped by the mucosa of each side touching each other. By this, as we will explain later, the acoustics of both sides of the glottis can follow according to their own, different acoustical laws. The supraglottic and subglottic spaces are then acoustically separated. The better and more complete the closure is, the better the sound that is produced. This quality of the glottis closure is strongly correlated with the maximum flow declination rate (Bjorkner 2008; Holmberg et al. 1995; Sapienza and Stathopoulos 1994; Sulter and Schutte 1991; Titze 2006).

The finding we had that a slightly larger closure time of the glottis might be beneficial for the desired sound in Classical (Western Operatic) singing tradition, led us to question the often-heard statement that a closed quotient (CQ) of more than about 60 percent is a sign of "hyperfunction." In our measurements of tenors, a high CQ, up to 75 percent, was found to be needed for a properly built-up resonance. Perhaps "hyperfunction" (and its counterpart, "hypofunction") have some other physiological basis besides adduction muscular forces.

GENERAL EVALUATION OF RESEARCH ON THE SINGING VOICE

What have we learned in the past 150 years? The results of our research in Groningen in aerodynamic and spectral analysis research, including EGG, helped redefine the correct moment of excitation of the vocal tract and more. This brings us to some interesting and important conclusions.

Stop the flowing air at once

The data from the high-frequency pressure measurements show clearly that the crucial pressure change for creating the vocal sound is the stopping of the airflow at the moment of glottis closing. This blockage is crucial and essential. Moreover, the transglottal pressure is reinforced by the effect of the still outwards moving column of air in the vocal tract. This movement cannot stop at once due to the air column having mass (and thus inertia), and leads to a skewing of the glottal air pulse, as was demonstrated by Rothenberg in several studies (Rothenberg 1981a, 1981b, 1983a, 1983b, 1988; Rothenberg, Miller, and Molitor 1988).

The (short) continuation of the movement of the air column above the glottis leads to a rarefaction of the air just above the glottis, as can be seen in the lowering peak in pressure in the supra-curves in Figure 50.2. The blockage/stopping and the rarefaction reinforce each other to create a pressure change at the frequency of the opening and closing of the glottis, creating the fundamental of the complex sound. It is also important to note that at the moment of opening of the glottis, the blockage and rarefaction ceases, the pressures over the glottis equalize, and the process starts anew.

Let us now consider the degree of abrupt closure of the glottis. A (dorsal) incomplete glottis closure will have a negative influence on the stopping of the air column. As expected in (professional) singers, where the voice is excellent, the dynamic glottis closure is optimal. There is a gradual development in dynamic glottis closure from weak voices to optimal voices. This correlates with the voice possibilities depicted in the general size of the phonetogram.

A dorsal (mostly dorsal) incomplete dynamic glottis closure usually shows fewer voice capacities, and if such a voice is subjected to high demands, no matter how "the voice is used," a discrepancy is present which may lead to voice problems. A better adjustment balance between capacities and demands is then needed. Our publications on this topic have unfortunately gained relatively little attention.

In singers, especially classical singers in the Western Operatic Tradition, the dynamic glottis closure is complete. Usually the phonetogram shows rich capacities: a wide f_o range, and over this whole range a high difference in dynamics between soft and loud. In closer evaluation register differences can often be observed in the place and extent of a "dip" in the maximum SPL-level; one can also observe preferable pitches, supporting ideas about most appropriate voice classification or *Fach*.

Open and closed quotient

That the excitation moment is the moment of closing of the glottis brings us to re-evaluate the concept of the often-used term "open quotient." As stated above in the section "Transglottal pressures," it is not strange that people adopted the open quotient as an important factor in voice, especially after the results of the high-speed Bell Telephone Company film of 1940 were published. However, we need to understand that the perfectness, abruptness of closure, and duration of closure are some of the most or even more important aspects of well-trained singing.

Returning to the higher CQs: it is found that a slightly larger CQ, if physiologically possible[15] for the larynx in question, often also helps the singer to achieve proper second formant tuning (Miller and Schutte 1990a). Second formant tuning was discovered from our high-frequency pressure measurements and from our research carried out in later years.

Bernoulli vs. resonance

Due to the work of Van den Berg in the 1950s, the influence of the Bernoulli effect in the functioning of the vocal folds became a leading theory. As the Bernoulli effect needs flow to be effective, it is not surprising that in the 1950s airflow became important for voice physiology, with consequences for research and clinic. Although Titze did bring forward some questions, for decades the Bernoulli effect remained central to the physiology of voice production (Titze 1980). Titze remarked in 1980 that physically the Bernoulli effect will only be significant when the vocal folds are rather close to each other.

The Bernoulli effect was rather new in the middle of the twentieth century, although clever researchers like Tonndorf (1925, 1926, 1927, 1929) described its possible influence 30 years before Van den Berg. In those days, however, proper resonance building in voicing was considered the most important aspect. The earlier work of Vennard, in the second edition of his book, stressed the resonance approach, but after having visited Van den Berg in Groningen in 1960 and having contributed to the film *The Vibrating Larynx*, he changed his mind, and in the third edition Vennard turned from "resonance" to "Bernoulli." (Vennard 1967). Coffin (1980), another leading American teacher of singing, advocated resonances in his book. His descriptions were based on observing and listening, as Helmholtz[16] and Donders did. Coffin was also remarkable because he had no fancy equipment, although he did collaborate with Pierre DeLattre, a phonetician. Much of his work could have been much more easily accomplished nowadays by using VoceVista. Working with VoceVista underlined the importance of resonance.

I do not want to suggest that the Bernoulli effect is *not* important. The over-estimation of Bernoulli's importance is today being replaced slowly by the importance of resonance, as it was in the first half of the twentieth century. Vennard's book marks the pedagogical transition from resonance to Bernoulli. Stark also questioned the influence of Bernoulli, which

[15] It is not always a matter of "use the larynx in such and such way" or "do this and that." In many cases a larynx is not optimally built for all desired actions. Some larynges simply cannot reach a closed quotient above 55 percent, because of thin vocal folds or because of an incomplete dynamic glottis closure. Remember that evaluating the voice possibilities of a student's larynx by the voice pedagogue is a standard procedure. Why not in all voice patients taking the phonetogram?

[16] Helmholtz (1954; first German edn 1862), only mentions voice production in a few words in passing in his book: *Die Lehre von der Tonempfindingen*. Helmholtz concentrated his work on perception, not on production. Helmholtz held the opinion that a Fourier analysis of the primary glottal tone shows a fundamental and harmonics of the same fundamental. He constructed a series of electrically driven tuning forks to mimic a vowel and believed that transmission by the vocal tract is maximal around the harmonic frequencies, thus formant tuning.

means aerodynamics with muscularity (myoelastic) as the counter-player. He called it the infatuation of an idea (Stark 1991, 1999).

Paradigms

Two paradigms, blocking scientific progress, have already been discussed: (1) the moment of excitation; (2) the Bernoulli effect.

Kuhn (1970) wrote that 95 percent of research work is paradigm confirming. This means that only 5 percent of all research leads to new discoveries. Nevertheless, even the smallest steps can have their influence. Kuhn observes that a paradigm first needs to be "shaken" before it can be changed.

This is certainly the case in (singing) voice research. It happens frequently that new equipment determines the topic for a new study. It unmistakably leads to new information, but often does not answer any fundamental questions. An example: at the beginning of the twentieth century the airflow rate was measured using a spirometer. In 1951, Luchsinger made use of the pneumotachograph, which had been developed in 1925 by Fleisch. Luchsinger spotted the potential and utility of the pneumotachograph, but the results were not fundamentally different from the data obtained by spirometry and certainly did not lead to new insights. Luchsinger's results were accepted and used from then on. Airflow measurements became routine and Isshiki started a line of flow research in the 1960s. Flow measurements still are *en vogue*.

Air usage in the larynx is a very individual phenomenon, depending a great deal on the individual build of the organ. Each larynx has its own pattern of air usage, in the same way that each phonetogram shows the individual possibilities. Of course, some variation is possible, but the basis is the anatomic configuration, e.g. the tissue structure of the vocal folds and the form of the participating laryngeal cartilages.

I take the opportunity to state here:

(1) Flow is less important than was thought; (2) a low flow does not mean high subglottic pressure and high flow does not necessarily mean low subglottic pressure; (3) aerodynamic behavior is individually determined by the build of the larynx.

Electromyography of the muscles of the larynx

The development of electromyography (EMG) in voice and phonetics by Faaborg-Andersen (1957) and Basmajian and De Luca (1985) led to a series of investigations in voice and speech, but hardly any were undertaken for singing. Soon after the first studies were published in *Folia Phoniatrica* (Faaborg-Andersen 1958), EMG was picked up by investigators in Japan (Hirano and Ohala 1967; Hirano, Ohala, and Smith 1967; Hiroto, Hirano, Toyozumi, and Shin 1967). Hirano developed bipolar hook electrodes to measure the activity of the intrinsic muscles of the larynx. Several studies by other investigators followed (Kotby 1975; Kotby and Haugen 1970; Kotby et al. 1992).

A few years later William Vennard and Hans von Leden organized a session in Los Angeles along with a few other singers to perform an EMG study of professional singers. The courage of Vennard and others in undergoing such an invasive investigation is admirable. It led to a series of four publications in the *Journal of Singing/NATS Journal/NATS Bulletin*, which were later re-issued by the Voice Foundation (Vennard and Hirano 1971; Vennard, Hirano, and Ohala 1970). After this publication not much EMG research was carried out on singers, except for some in Norway using surface electrodes and specialized equipment (Pettersen 2005, 2006; Pettersen et al. 2005).

The results showed that there is a close cooperation of the different muscles. It leads to a reinforcement of the (expected) knowledge, also showing different patterns in different registers, but there is no specificity.

Does hyperfunction exist?

This term is derived from voice pedagogy and was already in use before voice physiology started, near the end of the nineteenth century. Our experiences and results, which were obtained from aerodynamic studies, led to some deliberations. I bring this up because some singers' performance styles ask for a laryngeal and glottis configuration that is sometimes considered hyperfunctional. These configurations are mandatory in view of the desired sound quality and cannot therefore be considered pathological or less efficient.

Vocal folds not exclusively important in singing

In voice clinics and research, viewing and observing the movements of the vocal folds was focused on the vibrational behavior and on the movements by stroboscopy of the vocal folds.

In singing, however, this is only a part of the action. In 1977 photographs were taken of the well-known tenor and teacher Richard Miller, an author of many books on singing and editor of the *Journal of Singing* for years. In some of his books he included results of our common work on professional singing. Richard Miller found it difficult to obtain acceptable photographs of the vocal folds in optimal singing action. When we succeeded in getting the epiglottis out of sight and saw the vocal folds, the singer was not satisfied with the sound produced and vice versa. When making a "good" and "ringing" sound, the epiglottis covered the laryngeal outlet almost completely; it almost touched the back wall of the pharynx.

Russell (1928) had much earlier observed a close approximation of the "Wrisberg region," which was corroborated by my own observations with photographs of Miller and others. Titze and others researching the use of semi-occluded vocal tract exercises in voice therapy and singing training observed similar narrowing in the epilaryngeal area to the narrowing seen with Richard Miller.

The explanation and so the consequence of this came to my mind later and was presented in 2004 in Denver at the PAS II[17] conference. Singing is more than just an action of the vocal folds; it is also coordinating their vibratory patterns with the resonance characteristics of the vocal tract. In Richard Miller's case, his epiglottis movements probably related to the formation of the singer's formant, which appeared to be rather strong (Miller and Schutte 1983; Schutte and Miller 1984a; Schutte and Miller 1984b). This fact is

---

[17] Presented at the PAS-II in Denver 2004. www.ncvs.org/pas/2004/pres/schutte/schutte.htm

easy to understand for singers, but was often neglected and insufficiently understood by ENTs, laryngologists/phoniatricians, and speech-language pathologists over the years in the twentieth century.

Airflow measurements

Airflow measurements are still carried out, but neither researchers nor reviewers queried if these measurements have a real value for understanding voice (patho) physiology.

Vocal fold length and f_o

Research on the mysterious relation between vocal fold lengths and fundamental frequency received attention also in the period after WWII using a wide range of newly developed instruments and approaches. These experiments were reported in several important articles (Sonninen 1954, 1956; Vennard 1959; Zenker and Zenker 1960). Recently ultrasound equipment was used (Woojin 2014). This study did not show a clear relationship between fundamental frequency and vocal fold length. See also chapter 49 on this topic. The main reason for these failing studies is the wrong paradigm, claiming that vocal folds work like violin strings.

The larynx is not a valve, by which the "adduction" can be varied

Our results strongly deny the notion that the larynx works as a valve, as a kind of resistive device in which a high pressure relates to a low airflow rate and vice versa. The larynx does not behave in a linear, Ohm's law of resistance manner (editors note: see also the chapter by Herbst, Howard, and Švec, "The Sound Source in Singing: Basic Principles and Muscular Adjustments for Fine-tuning Vocal Timbre" in this volume).

Airflow puts the vocal folds into movement, and it is therefore important. However, my research has shown that airflow measurements are of questionable value, as the amount of flow is not important and differs on an individual basis. It certainly has no diagnostic value. As soon as the moving volume of air has passed the glottis the air is not important anymore. Everything depends on the individual larynx, i.e. the constitution of the vocal folds; in other words, the dynamic process of voice production.

The larynx is not a valve with a variable size glottis opening. Our results have also shown that flow and pressure are not linearly related, like currency and voltage in Ohm's law. Years ago, Van den Berg assumed that there was no more than 5 percent flow or pressure modulation (Van den Berg 1956), but in singers this is definitely not the case, as even a 100 percent modulation is possible, as we established later in our work (Schutte and Miller 1986). Singers are also not more aerodynamically efficient (Schutte 1984), which is also in contrast to what people expect. This is obvious from the previously given Figures 50.1a and 50.1b, where data of airflow rate, subglottic pressure, and efficiency of five professional singers are shown in comparison to lumped data of 2,745 instances of phonation of non-patients over a wide SPL-range of about 40 dB measured at 30 cm in front of the mouth.

EPILOGUE

Air is not the important issue. Yes, it drives the larynx, it is the energy source for phonation, and in singing, the phrase and text determine how much air is needed in a single inhalation, but the individual larynx determines how much pressure and flow is needed for a proper performance. The outcome, particularly in (professional) singing, is determined by the sound quality, which is driven by the demands of the musical culture and style. The real adjustments are made by the closed period of the glottal cycle and in appropriate resonance adjustments of the vocal tract acoustics.

Is this a demystification of the Berlin (Gutzmann) and Vienna (Froeschels, Stern) schools? What about later researchers, like Van den Berg, von Leden, Moore, Isshiki, and Hirano? Yes and no!

No, because they were searching in the dark, pioneering in an unknown field. There were no prior research results; they presented the very first results in a part of a medical field where no one had experience. They started with no equipment; they had to invent equipment, in which the surrounding fields (physics, physiology, phonetics, and other medical specialties) were very helpful—but they had to do it themselves. Gutzmann and Froeschels started with the deaf mutes, because this population had the first cases in which the researchers could understand where the problems were. They began with teaching methods to give deaf mutes speech and to make them understandable; meanwhile, otologists would try to find what was the cause of the deafness.

And yes, it is a demystification, but Van den Berg and others cannot be blamed for what they gave as suggestions, beliefs, and opinions. Many of their successors seemed to take everything for granted as settled and true. When someone said "this is phonasthenia," "this is hyperfunctional," it was accepted and promulgated further. For these successors, it may come as a disappointment, because they also firmly believed, even after decades, what had been written earlier. In Kuhn's terms, the paradigms were confirmed.

For over half a century no one questioned the physiological significance of vital capacity in singing (Gould 1973) and other pneumographic data. There remains no scientific proof of their importance for singing. The concepts that are assumed to explain function are still used in clinical voice books. Lung pressure is needed to drive the vocal folds, but how much pressure and how much flow is very individual, depending on the laryngeal build. Further, exhaled air loses its importance at the moment the air has had its influence on the glottis; from that moment on, the vibrating sound waves created are the only remaining important factor.

There are two aspects that in the near future need to be investigated further: the dynamic glottis closure and resonance interactions between glottis and vocal tract. As I stated earlier, high closed quotients do not necessarily mean "hyperfunction," whatever that might be, nor does flow phonation guarantee freedom. The timely adjustments between the closing moment and the proper resonances in the vocal tract need to be studied further. The study of the mixed voice in females and *mezza voce* are also still wide open for discoveries; the phenomenon appears to be more vocal tract than vocal folds (Miller 2008). Although almost all books on singing start with a discussion on the importance of breathing, breath and breathing seem to be overestimated. This is not to say that breathing for singing is not at all important, but proper breathing and breath support are pedagogical issues.

Is it not remarkable that many of the medical doctors working in voice research have also studied music or sing themselves? It is unknown what impact, positive or negative, this has on what these doctors write. Certainly, it helps to be musical as a voice doctor doing clinical examinations, in order to understand what the patient singer means terminology-wise as he or she speaks about his or her voice, and to give appropriate advice about what is in the singer's best interests career-wise (all the more reason why the phonetogram is indispensable, because it shows the possibilities of a specific voice). On the other hand, singing, more than other genres of music, is very person-specific, from the point of view of the teacher as well as of the singer student. Singing is strongly connected to the individual person, to the individual build of a larynx, and to the individual build of pharynx/mouth.

General rules for singing are therefore very difficult to promulgate. Concentrating upon the Western classical musical style there are esthetic norms, e.g. final sound products, in which the margins are relatively small. How to achieve this with an individual larynx and still get the appreciation of the spoiled public is the final task for the ears and taste of the teacher, and the ears and struggle of the student to achieve what needs to be heard. That is teaching, and there lies the problem, especially if the teacher overuses his or her own experiences in the teaching method for students. Since 1600, when solo singing started, the ears have been guiding change.[18] In general, small changes in outcome make the difference between ordinary and special (think of Pavarotti singing his high C), but generally the sound should fit to the Western operatic tradition.

The association between laryngology and phoniatrics has become looser in the decades after World War II. Voice is no longer a topic for the general ENT doctors, and cancer is the primary concern of the laryngologist nowadays. Medical education concerning voice is minimal in most countries, although there are some exceptions, happily enough.

It is striking that a well-functioning voice research lab in Groningen was abandoned and closed by an otologist, and non-cancer laryngology was given up in almost all ENT clinics in the Netherlands. The controversies and sometimes conflicting views between general ENT physicians and phoniatricians in Europe should have led to more possibilities for medical voice and voice-related research.

The progression from otology, rhinology via laryngology to voice clinics may indeed be leading to a profession sometimes called vocology, a possible solution. However, a warning is justified: in my opinion fewer medical specialists seem to be involved in voice clinics and voice research. This might lead to a situation where the medical aspects remain in the hands of the surgery-oriented laryngologists, as was the case a hundred years ago, and that, in my view, would be a large step backwards in time.

---

[18] Proprioception-oriented ideas and explanations appeared much later in history.

REFERENCES

Allen, E. (1980). An integration of research in singing. In: V.L. Lawrence and B. Weinberg (eds), *Transcripts of the IXth Symposium on the Care of the Professional Voice*, pp. 66–71. New York: The Voice Foundation.

Allen, E.L. and Hollien, H. (1973). A laminagraphic study of pulse (vocal fry) register phonation. *Folia Phoniatrica* 25: 241–250.

Askenfelt, A., Gauffin, J., Sundberg, J., and Kitzing, P. (1980). A comparison of contact microphone and electroglottograph for the measurement of vocal fundamental frequency. *Journal of Speech and Hearing Research* 23(2): 258–273.

Baer, T., Gore, J.C., Boyce, S., and Nye, P.W. (1987). Application of MRI to the analysis of speech production. *Magnetic Resonance Imaging* 5(1): 1–7.

Baer, T., Gore, J. C., Gracco, V.L., and Nye, P.W. (1988). Vocal tract dimensions obtained from magnetic resonances images. *Journal of the Acoustical Society of America* 84: S125.

Baer, T., Gore, J.C., Gracco, L.C., and Nye, P.W. (1991). Analysis of vocal tract shape and dimensions using magnetic resonance imaging: Vowels. *Journal of the Acoustical Society of America* 90(2): 799–828.

Bartholomew, W.T. (1934). A physical definition of "good voice-quality" in the male voice. *Journal of the Acoustical Society of America* 6: 25–33.

Basmajian, J.V. and De Luca, C.J. (1985). *Muscles Alive: Their Functions Revealed by Electromyography*, 5th edn. Baltimore: Williams and Wilkins.

Behnke, E. (1880). *The Mechanism of the Human Voice*. London: J. Curwen and Sons Ltd.

Björklund, S. and Sundberg, J. (2016). Relationship between subglottal pressure and sound pressure level in untrained voices. *Journal of Voice*, 30(1): 15–20.

Bjorkner, E. (2008). Musical theater and opera singing—why so different? A study of subglottal pressure, voice source, and formant frequency characteristics. *Journal of Voice* 22(5): 533–540.

Bjorkner, E., Sundberg, J., Cleveland, T., and Stone, E. (2006). Voice source differences between registers in female musical theater singers. *Journal of Voice*, 20(2): 187–197.

Calvet, P.J. and Malhiac, G. (1952). Courbes vocales et mue de la voix. *Journal of French Otorhinolaryngology Chirurgie Maxillo-faciale* 1(2): 115–124.

Childers, D.G. and Krishnamurthy, A.K. (1985). A critical review of electroglottography. *Critical Reviews in Biomedical Engineering* 12(2): 131–161.

Coffin, B. (1980). *Overtones of bel canto*. London: The Scarecrow Press.

Coleman, R.F. (1977). Dynamic vocal ranges: results of tracking female adolescent voices. In: V.L. Lawrence (ed.), *Transcripts of the VIth Symposium on the Care of the Professional Voice*, pp. 11–13. New York: The Voice Foundation.

Coleman, R. F., Henn Mabis, J., and Kidd Hinson, J. (1977). Fundamental frequency-sound pressure level profiles of adult male and female voices. *Journal of Speech and Hearing Disorders* 20(2): 197–204.

Colton, R.H. (1972). Spectral characteristics of the modal and falsetto registers. *Folia Phoniatrica* 24: 337–344.

Colton, R.H. (1973). Vocal intensity in the modal and falsetto registers. *Folia Phoniatrica* 39: 62–70.

Colton, R.H., Estill, J.A., and Gould, L.V. (1977). Physiology of voice modes: vocal tract characteristics. In: V.L. Lawrence (ed.), *Transcripts of the VIth Symposium on the Care of the Professional Voice*, pp. 37–41. New York: The Voice Foundation.

Colton, R.H. and Hollien, H. (1972). Phonation range in the modal and falsetto registers. *Journal of Speech and Hearing Research* 15(4): 708–713.

Colton, R.H. and Hollien, H. (1973a). Perceptual differentiation of the modal and falsetto registers. *Folia Phoniatrica* 25: 270–280.

Colton, R.H. and Hollien, H. (1973b). Physiology of vocal registers in singers and non-singers. In: J.W. Large (ed.), *Vocal Registers in Singing*, pp. 105–136. The Hague/Paris: Mouton and Co.

Cooper, D.S. (1997). Richard Luchsinger (1900–1993): an appreciation. *Journal of Voice* 11(3): 249–253.

Damsté, P. H., Hollien, H., and Moore, G.P. (1968). An x-ray study of vocal fold length. *Folia Phoniatrica* 20(6): 349–359.

Dejonckere, P. (1977). Phonetogramme, son intérêt clinique. *Les Cahiers d'Oto-Rhino-Laryngologie* 12: 865–872.

Echternach, M., Dippold, S., Sundberg, J., Arndt, S., Zander, M.F., and Richter, B. (2010). High-speed imaging and electroglottography measurements of the open quotient in untrained male voices' register transitions. *Journal of Voice* 24(6): 644–650.

Echternach, M., Sundberg, J., Arndt, S., Markl, M., Schumacher, M., and Richter, B. (2010). Vocal tract in female registers—a dynamic real-time MRI study. *Journal of Voice* 24(2): 133–139.

Echternach, M., Sundberg, J., Markl, M., and Richter, B. (2010). Professional opera tenors' vocal tract configurations in registers. *Folia Phoniatrica et Logopaedica* 62: 278–287.

Echternach, M., Traser, L., Markl, M., and Richter, B. (2011). Vocal tract configurations in male alto register functions. *Journal of Voice* 25(6): 670–677.

Echternach, M., Traser, L., and Richter, B. (2012). Perturbation of voice signals in register transitions on sustained frequency in professional tenors. *Journal of Voice* 26(5): 674.e9–674.e15. doi:10.1016/j.jvoice.2012.02.003

Echternach, M. and Richter, B. (2012). Passaggio in the professional tenor voice—evaluation of perturbation measures. *Journal of Voice* 26(4): 440–446.

Eykman, L.P.H. (1923). Geschiedkundig overzicht van de klankleer in Nederland. *De Nieuwe Taalgids, XVII–XVIII*, 161–174; 225–243; 283–293; 17–33.

Faaborg-Andersen, K. (1957). Electromyographic investigation of intrinsic laryngeal muscles in human: an investigation of subjects with normally movable vocal cords and patients with vocal cords paresis. *Acta Physiologica Scandinavica Supplement* 140: 9–147.

Faaborg-Andersen, K. (1958). Elektromyographische Untersuchungen der inneren Kehlkopfmuskeln des menschen. *Folia Phoniatrica* 10: 54–57.

Faaborg-Andersen, K. and Vennard, W.D. (1964). Electromyography of extrinsic laryngeal muscles during phonation of different vowels. *Annals of Otology, Rhinology and Laryngology (St Louis)* 73(1): 1–7.

Faaborg-Andersen, K., Yanagihara, N., and Von Leden, H. (1967). Vocal pitch and intensity regulation. *Archives of Otolaryngology (Chicago)* 85: 122–128.

Fant, G. (1979). Glottal source and excitation analysis. *STL-QPSR KTH Stockholm* 20: 85–107.

Farnsworth, D.W. (1940). High-speed motion pictures of the human vocal cords. *Bell Laboratories Record* 18(7): 203–208.

Ford, C.N., Unger, J.M., Zundel, R.S., and Bless, D.M. (1995). Magnetic resonance imaging (MRI) assessment of vocal fold medialization surgery. *Laryngoscope* 105(5): 498–504.

Gall, V., Gall, D., and Hanson, J. (1971). [Laryngeal photokymography]. *Archiv Fur Klinische Und Experimentelle Ohren- Nasen- Und Kehlkopfheilkunde* 200(1): 34–41.

Gould, W.J. (1973). Static lung volumes in singers. *Annals of Otology, Rhinology and Laryngology (St Louis)* 82: 89–95.

Grützner, P. (1879). Physiologie der Stimme und Sprache. In: L. Hermann (ed.), *Handbuch der Physiologie*, pp. 1–236. Leipzig: F.C.W. Vogel.

Guillemin, A. (1897). *Sur la génération de la voix et du timbre*. Paris: Société d'Études Scientifiques. Kessinger Legacy Reprints.

Helmholtz, H. von. (1954). *On the Sensations of Tone*. New York. Dover Publications, Inc. The 2nd English edition conformal to the 4th (and last) German edition of 1877, translated by Alexander J. Ellis.

Herbst, C.T., Fitch, W.T., and Švec, J.G. (2010). Electroglottographic wavegrams: A technique for visualizing vocal fold dynamics noninvasively. *Journal of the Acoustical Society of America* 128(5): 3070–3078.

Herbst, C.T., Herzel, H., Švec, J.G., Wyman, M.T., and Fitch, W.T. (2013). Visualization of system dynamics using phasegrams. *Journal of the Royal Society Interface* 10(85): 20130288.

Herbst, C.T., Hess, M., Müller, F., Švec, J.G., and Sundberg, J. (2015). Glottal adduction and subglottal pressure in singing. *Journal of Voice* 29(4): 391–402.

Herbst, C.T., Howard, D., and Schlömicher-Thier, J. (2010). Using electroglottographic real-time feedback to control posterior glottal adduction during phonation. *Journal of Voice* 24(1): 72–85.

Herbst, C.T., Lohscheller, J., Švec, J.G., Henrich, N., Weissengruber, G., and Tecumseh Fitch, W. (2014). Glottal opening and closing events investigated by electroglottography and super-high-speed video recordings. *Journal of Experimental Biology* 217: 955–963.

Herbst, C.T., Qiu, Q., Schutte, H.K., and Švec, J.G. (2011). Membranous and cartilaginous vocal fold adduction in singing. *Journal of the Acoustical Society of America* 129(4): 2253–2262.

Herbst, C.T. and Švec, J.G. (2014). Adjustment of glottal configurations in singing. *Journal of Singing* 70(3): 301–308.

Herbst, C.T. and Ternström, S. (2006). A comparison of different methods to measure the EGG contact quotient. *Logopedics-Phoniatrics-Vocology* 31(3): 126–138.

Hirano, M., Koike, Y., and Von Leden, H. (1968). Maximum phonation time and air usage during phonation. *Folia Phoniatrica* 20: 185–201.

Hirano, M. and Ohala, J.J. (1967). Use of hooked-wire electrodes for electromyography of the intrinsic laryngeal muscles. *Working Papers in Phonetics* 7: 35–55.

Hirano, M., Ohala, J.J., and Smith, T. (1967). Current techniques used in obtaining EMG data. *Working Papers in Phonetics* 7(20): 24.

Hirose, H. (1977). Electromyographic of the larynx and other speech organs. In: M. Sawashima and F.S. Cooper (eds), *Dynamic Aspects of Speech Production: Current Results, Emerging Problems, and New Instrumentation*, pp. 49–65. Tokyo: University of Tokyo Press.

Hiroto, I., Hirano, M., Toyozumi, Y., and Shin, T. (1967). Electromyographic investigation of the intrinsic laryngeal muscles related to speech sounds. *Annals of Otology, Rhinology and Laryngology (St Louis)* 76(4): 861.

Hollien, H. (1964). Laryngeal research by means of laminagraphy. *Archives of Otolaryngology (Chicago)* 80: 303–308.

Hollien, H. (1965). Stroboscopic laminagraphy of the vocal folds. In: E. Zwirner and W. Bethge (eds), *Proceedings of the Fifth International Congress of Phonetic Sciences, Münster 1964*, pp. 362–364. Basel: Karger.

Hollien, H., Coleman, R.F., and Moore, G.P. (1968). Stroboscopic laminagraphy of the larynx during phonation. *Acta Otolaryngologica (Stockholm)* 65: 209–215.

Holmberg, E.B., Hillman, R.E., Perkell, J.S., Guiod, P.C., and Goldman, S.L. (1995). Comparisons among aerodynamic, electroglottographic, and acoustic spectral measures of female voice. *Journal of Speech and Hearing Research* 38(6): 1212–1223.

Honda, K., Hirai, H., Estill, J.A., and Tohkura, Y. (1995). Contributions of vocal tract shape to voice quality: MRI data and articulatory modelling. In: O. Fujimura and M. Hirano (eds), *Vocal Fold Physiology: Voice Quality Control*, pp. 23–38. San Diego, California: Singular Publishing Group.

Horii, Y. (1979). Fundamental frequency perturbation observed in sustained phonation. *Journal of Speech and Hearing Research* 22(1): 5–19.

Horii, Y. (1982). Jitter and shimmer differences among sustained vowel phonations. *Journal of Speech and Hearing Research* 25: 12–14.

Horii, Y. (1985). Automatic transcription of the singing voice. In: V.L. Lawrence (ed.), *Transcripts of the XIVth Symposium on the Care of the Professional Voice*, pp. 44–49. New York: The Voice Foundation.

Husson, R.M. (1933). Étude théorique et expérimentale de la réaction du résonateur pharyngien sur la vibration des cordes vocales pendant la phonation. *Review Française de Phoniatrie* 1: 106–167.

Husson, R.M. and Tarneaud, J. (1933). Les phénomènes réactionnels de la voix. étude physique, physiologique et pathologique. *Review Française de Phoniatrie* 1: 251–310.

Husson, R.M. (1936). La phonation. quelgues aspects energetiques des principaux phenomes acoustiques et dissipatifs. *Review Française de Phoniatrie* 4: 19–48.

Husson, R.M. (1952). Étude expérimentale, au cours de la phonation, des organs phonateurs en tant que récepteurs intéroceptifs et proprioceptifs et des régulations efférentes. *Journal of Applied Physiology* 44: 1–2.

Husson, R. M. (1954). La commande et la régulation centrales de l'activité récurrentielle pendant la phonation. *Journal of Physiology* 46: 388–390.

Isshiki, N. (1961). Voice and subglottic pressure. *Studia Phonologica* 1: 86–94.

Isshiki, N. (1964). Regulatory mechanism of voice intensity variations. *Journal of Speech and Hearing Research* 7: 17–29.

Isshiki, N. (1965). Vocal intensity and airflow rate. *Folia Phoniatrica* 17: 92–104.

Isshiki, N. (1981). Vocal efficiency index. In: K.N. Stevens and M. Hirano (eds), *Vocal Fold Physiology*, pp. 193–204. Tokyo: University of Tokyo Press.

Isshiki, N. (1985). Clinical significance of a vocal efficiency index. In: I.R. Titze and R.C. Scherer (eds), *Vocal Fold Physiology: Biomechanics, Acoustics and Phonatory Control*, pp. 230–238. Denver: Denver Center for the Performing Arts.

Isshiki, N., Okamura, H., and Morimoto, M. (1967). Maximum phonation time and airflow rate during phonation: simple clinical tests for vocal function. *Annals of Otology, Rhinology and Laryngology (St Louis)* 76: 998–1007.

Isshiki, N. and Von Leden, H. (1964). Hoarseness: Aerodynamic studies. *Archives of Otolaryngology (Chicago)* 80: 206–213.

Iwata, S. (1988). Aerodynamic aspects for phonation in normal and pathologic larynges. In: O. Fujimura (ed.), *Vocal Physiology: Voice Production, Mechanisms and Functions*, pp. 423–432. New York: Raven Press Ltd.

Iwata, S. and Von Leden, H. (1970a). Clinical evaluation of vocal velocity index in laryngeal disease. *Annals of Otology, Rhinology and Laryngology (St Louis)* 79: 259–269.

Iwata, S. and Von Leden, H. (1970b). Phonation quotient in patients with laryngeal diseases. *Folia Phoniatrica* 22: 117–128.

Iwata, S., Von Leden, H., and Williams, D. (1972). Airflow measurement during phonation. *Journal of Communication Disorders* 5: 67–79.

Kaiser, L. (1957). *Manual of Phonetics*. Amsterdam: North-Holland Publishing Company.

Kaiser, L. (1968). *Manual of Phonetics*, 2nd edn. Amsterdam: North-Holland Publishing Company.

Kitzing, P. and Sonesson, B. (1974). A photoglottographical study of the female vocal folds during phonation. *Folia Phoniatrica* 26(2): 138–149.

Kitzing, P. (1977). Methode zur kombinierten photo- und elektroglottographischen Registrierung von Stimmlippenschwingungen. *Folia Phoniatrica* 29: 249–260.

Kitzing, P. (1982). Photo- and electroglottographical recording of the laryngeal vibratory pattern during different registers. *Folia Phoniatrica* 34: 234–241.

Kitzing, P., Carlborg, B., and Löfqvist, A.G. (1982). Aerodynamic and glottographic studies of the laryngeal vibratory cycle. *Folia Phoniatrica* 34: 216–224.

Kitzing, P. and Löfqvist, A.G. (1975). Subglottal and oral air pressure during phonation: Preliminary investigation using a miniature transducer system. *Medical and Biological Engineering* 13(5): 644–648.

Koike, Y. (1969). A method for direct determination of subglottal pressure. *Journal of the Acoustical Society of America* 46(1): 96–97.

Koike, Y. and Hirano, M. (1968). Significance of vocal velocity index. *Folia Phoniatrica* 20: 285–296.

Koike, Y., Hirano, M., and Von Leden, H. (1967). Vocal initiation: acoustic and aerodynamic investigations of normal subjects. *Folia Phoniatrica* 19: 173–182.

Koike, Y. and Perkins, W.H. (1968). Application of a miniaturized pressure transducer for experimental speech research. *Folia Phoniatrica* 20: 360–368.

Kotby, M.N. (1975). Percutaneous laryngeal electromyography: standardization of the technique. *Folia Phoniatrica* 27: 116–127.

Kotby, M.N., Fadly, E., Madkour, O., Barakah, M., Khidr, A., Alloush, T., and Saleh, M. (1992). Electromyography and neurography in neurolaryngology. *Journal of Voice* 6(2): 159–187.

Kotby, M.N. and Haugen, L.K. (1970). Attempts at evaluation of the function of various laryngeal muscles in the light of muscle and nerve stimulation experiments in man. *Acta Otolaryngologica (Stockholm)* 70: 419–427.

Kuhn, T.S. (1970). *The Structure of Scientific Revolutions*, 2nd edn. Chicago, London: University of Chicago Press.

Large, J.W. (1972). Towards an integrated physiologic-acoustic theory of vocal registers. *The NATS Bulletin* 29: 18–40.

Large, J.W. (1973). Acoustic study of register equalization in singing. *Folia Phoniatrica* 25: 39–61.

Large, J.W. (1979). Airflow study of vocal vibrato. In: V.L. Lawrence and B. Weinberg (eds), *Transcripts of the VIIIth Symposium on the Care of the Professional Voice*, pp. 39–45. New York: Voice Foundation.

Large, J.W. and Iwata, S. (1971). Aerodynamic study of vibrato and voluntary "straight tone" pairs in singing. *Folia Phoniatrica* 23: 50–65.

Large, J.W., Iwata, S., and Von Leden, H. (1972). The male operatic head register versus falsetto. *Folia Phoniatrica* 24: 19–29.

Leonard, R.J., Ringel, R.L., Daniloff, R.G., and Horii, Y. (1987). Vocal frequency changes in singers and nonsingers. *Journal of Voice* 1(3): 234–239.

Luchsinger, R. (1942). Untersuchungen über die Klangfarbe der menschlichen Stimme. *Arch.Sprach.Stimmphysiol.Sprach.Stimmheilkunde* 6: 1–39.

Luchsinger, R. (1946). Book review: Le chant, sa construction, sa destruction. J. Tarneaud. *Practica Oto-Rhino-Laryngologica* 8(1): 60.

Luchsinger, R. (1951). Schalldruck- und Geschwindigkeitsregistrierung der Atemluft beim Singen. *Folia Phoniatrica* 3: 25–51.

Luchsinger, R. (1975). Zeitdehneraufnahmen der Stimmlippenbewegungen beim offenen und gedeckten Singen. *Folia Phoniatrica* 27: 88–92.

Luchsinger, R. and Arnold, G.E. (1949). *Lehrbuch der Stimm- und Sprachheilkunde.* Wien, Springer.

Luchsinger, R. and Faaborg-Andersen, K. (1966). Phonetische und elektromyographische Registrierungen beim Tonhalten. *Folia Phoniatrica* 18: 91–97.

Lycke, H., Decoster, W., Ivanova, A., Van Hulle, M.M. and De Jong, F.I.C.R.S. (2012). Discrimination of three basic female voice types in female singing students by voice range profile-derived parameters. *Folia Phoniatrica et Logopaedica* 64: 80–86.

McGlone, R.E., Richmond, W.H., and Bosma, J.F. (1966). A physiological model for investigation of the fundamental frequency of phonation. *Folia Phoniatrica* 18: 109–116.

Miller, D.G. (2000). *Registers in singing. Empirical and systematic studies in the theory of the singing voice.* PhD Thesis, University of Groningen. http://hdl.handle.net/11370/86aa05db-fc14-4d42-b814-4e1ca9a03010

Miller, D.G. (2008). *Resonance in Singing. Voice Building through Acoustic Feedback.* Princeton, NJ: Inside View Press.

Miller, D.G. and Schutte, H.K. (1985). Characteristic patterns of sub- and supraglottal pressure variations within the glottal cycle. In: V. L. Lawrence (ed.), *Transcripts of the XIIIth Symposium on the Care of the Professional Voice,* pp. 70–75. New York: The Voice Foundation.

Miller, D.G. and Schutte, H.K. (1990a). Feedback from spectrum analysis applied to the singing voice. *Journal of Voice* 4(4): 329–334.

Miller, D.G. and Schutte, H.K. (1990b). Formant tuning in a professional baritone. *Journal of Voice* 4(2): 231–237.

Miller, D.G. and Schutte, H.K. (1993). Physical definition of the "flageolet register." *Journal of Voice* 7(3): 206–212.

Miller, D.G. and Schutte, H.K. (1994). Toward a definition of male "head" register, passaggio, and "cover" in western operatic singing. *Folia Phoniatrica et Logopaedica* 46(4): 157–170.

Miller, D.G. and Schutte, H.K. (2005). "Mixing" the registers: glottal source or vocal tract? *Folia Phoniatrica et Logopaedica* 57(5–6): 278–291.

Miller, D.G., Schutte, H.K., and Doing, J. (2001). Soft phonation in the male singing voice: a preliminary study. *Journal of Voice* 15(4): 483–491.

Miller, D.G., Sulter, A.M., Schutte, H.K., and Wolf, R.F. (1997). Comparison of vocal tract formants in singing and nonperiodic phonation. *Journal of Voice* 11(1): 1–11.

Miller, D.G., Švec, J.G., and Schutte, H.K. (2002). Measurement of characteristic leap interval between chest and falsetto registers. *Journal of Voice* 16(1): 8–19.

Miller, R. and Schutte, H.K. (1981). The effect of tongue position on spectra in singing. *NATS Bulletin* 34: 26–27.

Miller, R. and Schutte, H.K. (1983). Spectral analysis of several categories of timbre in a professional male (tenor) voice. *Journal of Experimental Research in Singing* 7: 6–10.

Morat, J.-P. (1918). Phonation. In: J.-P. Morat, and M. Doyon (eds), *Traité de physiologie,* pp. 347–383. Paris: Masson et Cie.

Nagel, W. (1909). Physiologie der Stimmwerkzeuge. In: W. Nagel (ed.), *Handbuch de Physiologie des Menschen,* pp. 691–792. Braunschweig: Friedrich Vieweg und Sohn.

Neuschaefer-Rube, C., Wein, B., Angerstein, W., and Klajman, S. (1996). Kernspintomographische Untersuchung der Kehlkopfstellungen beim Singen von Vokalen. *Folia Phoniatrica et Logopaedica* 48(4): 201–209.

Nieboer, G.L.J., Schutte, H.K., and de Graaf, T. (1984). On the reliability of the intraoral measuring of subglottal pressure. In: M.P.R. van den Broecke and A. Cohen (eds), *Proc. Xth Int Congress of Phonetics Sciences*, pp. 367–371. Utrecht.

Pettersen, V. (2005). Muscular patterns and activation levels of auxiliary breathing muscles and thorax movement in classical singing. *Folia Phoniatrica et Logopaedica* 57(5–6): 255–277.

Pettersen, V. (2006). Preliminary findings on the classical singer's use of the pectoralis major muscle. *Folia Phoniatrica et Logopaedica* 58(6): 427–439.

Pettersen, V., Bjorkoy, K., Torp, H., and Westgaard, R. H. (2005). Neck and shoulder muscle activity and thorax movement in singing and speaking tasks with variation in vocal loudness and pitch. *Journal of Voice* 19(4): 623–634.

Rothenberg, M. (1968). *The Breath-Stream Dynamics of Simple-Released Plosive Production*. Basel: Karger.

Rothenberg, M. (1981a). Acoustic interaction between the glottal source and the vocal tract. In: K.N. Stevens, and M. Hirano (eds), *Vocal Fold Physiology*, pp. 305–328. Tokyo: University of Tokyo Press.

Rothenberg, M. (1981b). The voice source in singing. In: J. Sundberg (ed.), *Research Aspects on Singing*, pp. 15–33. Stockholm, Sweden: Royal Swedish Academy of Music.

Rothenberg, M. (1983a). An interactive model for the voice source. In: D.M. Bless and J. H. Abbs (eds), *Vocal Fold Physiology: Contemporary Research and Clinical Issues*, pp. 155–165. San Diego: College-Hill Press.

Rothenberg, M. (1983b). Source-tract acoustic interaction. In: V.L. Lawrence (ed.), *Transcripts of the XIIth Symposium on the Care of the Professional Voice*, pp. 25–31. New York: The Voice Foundation.

Rothenberg, M. (1988). Acoustic reinforcement of vocal fold vibratory behavior in singing. In: O. Fujimura (ed.), *Vocal Physiology: Voice Production, Mechanisms and Functions*, pp. 379–389. New York: Raven Press.

Rothenberg, M., Miller, D.G., and Molitor, R. (1988). Aerodynamic investigation of sources of vibrato. *Folia Phoniatrica* 40: 244–260.

Rothenberg, M. and Schutte, H.K. (2016). Interactive augmentation of voice quality and reduction of breath airflow in the soprano voice. *Journal of Voice*, doi:http://dx.doi.org/10.1016/j.jvoice.2015.09.016

Russell, G.O. (1928). *The Vowel, Its Physiological Mechanism as Shown by X-ray*. Ohio: Ohio State University Press.

Sapienza, C.M. and Stathopoulos, E.T. (1994). Comparison of maximum flow declination rate: Children versus adults. *Journal of Voice* 8(3): 240–247.

Savart, F. (1825a). Nouvelles recerces sur les vibrations de l'air. In: J. Gay-Lussac and M. Arrago (eds), *Annales de Chimie et de Physique*, Series 2, Vol. XXIX, pp. 404–426. Paris: Crochard.

Savart, F. (1825b). Mémoire sur la voix humaine. In: J. Gay-Lussac and M. Arrago (eds), *Annales de Chimie et de Physique*, Series 2, Vol. XXX, pp. 64–87. Paris: Crochard.

Schutte, H.K. (1975). Over het fonetogram. *Tijdschrift voor Logopedie en Foniatrie* 47: 82–92.

Schutte, H.K. (1980). *The Efficiency of Voice Production*. Thesis, University of Groningen. http://www.rug.nl/research/portal/en/publications/the-efficiency-of-voice-production(859a910f-f03b-4084-9cec-aeea3c66caf0).html http://hdl.handle.net/11370/859a910f-f03b-4084-9cec-aeea3c66caf0

Schutte, H.K. (1984). Efficiency of professional singing voices in terms of energy ratio. *Folia Phoniatrica* 36: 267–272.

Schutte, H.K. (1986a). Aerodynamics of phonation. *Acta oto-rhino-laryng. Belg.* 40: 344–357.

Schutte, H.K. (1986b). Transglottal pressures. *Acta oto-rhino-laryng. Belg.* 40: 395–404.

Schutte, H.K. (1987). De zangstem. *Natuur en Techniek* 55: 810–821.

Schutte, H.K. (2009). The phonetogram; measurements and interpretation. In: M.P. Fried and A. Ferlito (eds), *The Larynx*, pp. 245–252. San Diego: Plural Publishing.

Schutte, H.K. and Miller, R. (1983). Differences in spectral analysis of trained and untrained voices. *NATS Bulletin* 40: 22–23.

Schutte, H.K. and Miller, R. (1984a). Breath management in repeated vocal onset. *Folia Phoniatrica* 36: 225–232.

Schutte, H.K. and Miller, R. (1984b). Resonance balance in register categories of the singing voice: A spectral analysis study. *Folia Phoniatrica* 36: 289–295.

Schutte, H.K. and Miller, R. (1985). Intraindividual parameters of the singer's formant. *Folia Phoniatrica* 37: 31–35.

Schutte, H.K. and Miller, D.G. (1986). The effect of f_0/F_1 coincidence in soprano high notes on pressure at the glottis. *Journal of Phonetics* 14: 385–392.

Schutte, H.K. and Miller, D.G. (1988). Resonanzspiele der Gesangsstimme in ihren Beziehungen zu supra- und subglottalen Druckverläufen: Konsequenzen für die Stimmbildungstheorie. *Folia Phoniatrica* 40: 65–73.

Schutte, H.K. and Miller, D.G. (1993). Belting and pop, nonclassical approaches to the female middle voice: Some preliminary considerations. *Journal of Voice* 7(2): 142–150.

Schutte, H.K., Miller, D.G., and Švec, J.G. (1995). Measurement of formant frequencies and bandwidths in singing. *Journal of Voice* 9(3): 290–296.

Schutte, H.K., Miller, D.G., and Duijnstee, M. (2005). Resonance strategies revealed in recorded tenor high notes. *Folia Phoniatrica et Logopaedica* 57: 292–307.

Schutte, H.K. and Seidner, W.W. (1983). Recommendation by the Union of European Phoniatricians (UEP): standardizing voice area measurement/phonetography. *Folia Phoniatrica* 35: 286–288.

Schutte, H.K. and Seidner, W.W. (1988). Registerabhängige differenzierung von elektroglottogrammen. *Sprache-Stimme-Gehör* 12: 59–62.

Schutte, H.K and Van den Berg, J. (1974). Estimation of the subglottic pressure and the efficiency of sound production in patients with a disturbed voice production. *Folia Phoniatrica* 26: 220–221.

Schutte, H.K. and Van den Berg, J. (1980). The efficiency of voice production. *Folia Phoniatrica* 32: 238–239.

Sonesson, B. (1959). A method for studying the vibratory movements of the vocal cords. A preliminary report. *Journal of Laryngology and Otology (Ashford)* 73(11): 732–737.

Sonninen, A. (1954). Is the length of the vocal cords the same at all different levels of singing? *Acta Otolaryngologica Supplement (Stockholm)* 118: 219–231.

Sonninen, A. (1956). The role of the external laryngeal muscles in length-adjustment of the vocal cords in singing. *Acta Otolaryngologica Supplement (Stockholm)* 130: 1–102.

Stark, J.A. (1991). Garcia in perspective. His *Traité* after 150 years. *Journal of Research in Singing* 15(1): 2–56.

Stark, J.A. (1999). *Bel canto: A History of Vocal Pedagogy*. Toronto: University of Toronto Press.

Story, B.H., Titze, I.R., and Hoffman, E.A. (1996). Vocal tract area functions from magnetic resonance imaging. *Journal of the Acoustical Society of America* 100(1): 537–554.

Story, B.H., Titze, I.R., and Hoffman, E.A. (1998). Vocal tract area functions for an adult female speaker based on volumetric imaging. *Journal of the Acoustical Society of America* 104(0001–4966; 1): 471–487.

Story, B.H., Titze, I.R., and Hoffman, E.A. (2001). The relationship of vocal tract shape to three voice qualities. *Journal of the Acoustical Society of America* 109(4): 1651–1667.

Sulter, A.M., Miller, D.G., Wolf, R.F., Schutte, H.K., Wit, H.P., and Mooyaart, E.L. (1992). On the relation between the dimensions and resonance characteristics of the vocal tract: A study with MRI. *Magnetic Resonance Imaging* 10(3): 365–373.

Sulter, A.M. and Schutte, H.K. (1991). On the existence of speaker-specific maximum flow declination rate (MFDR)—sound pressure level (SPL) profiles. *Journal of the Acoustical Society of America* 91: 2420.

Sulter, A.M., Wit, H.P., Schutte, H.K., and Miller, D.G. (1994). A structured approach to voice range profile (phonetogram) analysis. *Journal of Speech and Hearing Research* 37(5): 1076–1085.

Sundberg, J. (1973). The source spectrum in professional singing. *Folia Phoniatrica* 25: 71–90.

Sundberg, J. (1977a). The acoustics of the singing voice. *Scientific American* 236(3): 82–92.

Sundberg, J. (1977b). Studies of the soprano voice. *Journal of Research in Singing* 1(1): 25–35.

Sundberg, J. (1987). *The Science of the Singing Voice*. Dekalb, IL: Nothern Illinois University Press.

Sundberg, J. (1990). What's so special about singers? *Journal of Voice* 4(2): 107–119.

Tanabe, M., Kitajima, K., Gould, W.J., and Lambiase, A. (1975). Analysis of high-speed motion pictures of the vocal folds. *Folia Phoniatrica* 27: 77–87.

Tarneaud, J. (1946). *Le chant, sa construction, sa destruction*. Paris: Librairie Maloine SA.

Timcke, R., Von Leden, H., and Moore, G.P. (1958). Laryngeal vibrations: Measurements of the glottic wave: Part 1. the normal vibratory cycle. *AMA Archives of Otolaryngology* 68: 1–19.

Timcke, R., Von Leden, H., and Moore, G.P. (1959). Laryngeal vibrations: Measurements of the glottic wave: Part 2. physiologic variations. *AMA Archives of Otolaryngology* 69: 438–444.

Titze, I.R. (1980). Comments on the myoelastic-aerodynamic theory of phonation. *Journal of Speech and Hearing Research* 23(3): 495–510.

Titze, I.R. (1988). A framework for the study of vocal registers. *Journal of Voice* 2(3): 183–194.

Titze, I. (2001). Acoustic interpretation of resonant voice. *Journal of Voice* 15(4): 519–528.

Titze, I.R. (2006). Theoretical analysis of maximum flow declination rate versus maximum area declination rate in phonation. *Journal of Speech Language and Hearing Research* 49(2): 439–447.

Titze, I.R., Wong, D., Milder, M.A., Hensley, S.R., and Ramig, L.O. (1995). Comparison between clinician-assisted and fully automated procedures for obtaining a voice range profile. *Journal of Speech and Hearing Research* 38: 526–535.

Tonndorf, W. (1925). Die Mechanik bei der Stimmlippenschwingung und beim Schnarchen. *Zeitschrift für Hals-, Nasen- und Ohrenheilkunde* 11: 241–245.

Tonndorf, W. (1926). Die Schwingungszahl der Stimmlippen. *Zeitschrift für Hals-, Nasen- und Ohrenheilkunde* 15: 363–371.

Tonndorf, W. (1927). Die Wechselbeziehungen zwischen dem Kehlkopf und seinem Ansatzrohr bei der Bildung der Sprachlaute. *Zeitschrift für Hals-, Nasen- und Ohrenheilkunde* 18: 490–497.

Tonndorf, W. (1929). Zur Physiologie des menschlichen Stimmorgans. *Zeitschrift für Hals-, Nasen- und Ohrenheilkunde* 22: 412–423.

Van den Berg, Jw. (1953). *Physica van de stemvorming, met toepassingen*. PhD Thesis, University of Groningen.

Van den Berg, Jw. (1955). On the role of the laryngeal ventricle in voice production. *Folia Phoniatrica* 7(2): 57–69.

Van den Berg, J. (1956). Direct and indirect determination of the mean subglottic pressure. *Folia Phoniatrica* 8(1): 1–24.

Van den Berg, J. (1958). Myoelastic-aerodynamic theory of voice production. *Journal of Speech and Hearing Research* 1(3): 227–244.

Van den Berg, J. (1961). Physiological basis of language. *Logos* 4(2): 56–66.

Van den Berg, J. (1962). Modern research in experimental phoniatrics. *Folia Phoniatrica* 14: 81–149.

Van den Berg, J. and Tan, T.S. (1959). Données nouvelles sur la fonction laryngée. *Journal of French Otorhinolaryngology Chirurgie Maxillo-faciale* 3(1): 103–111.

Van den Berg, Jw., Vennard, W.D., Burger, D., and Shervanian, C.C. (1960). *Voice production: The Vibrating Larynx (instructional film)*. Stichting Film en Wetenschap.

Vennard, W.D. (1959). Some implications of the Sonninen research. *NATS Bulletin* 18: 8–13.

Vennard, W.D. (1967). *Singing: The mechanism and the technic*. New York: Fischer.

Vennard, W.D. and Hirano, M. (1971). Varieties of voice production. *NATS Bulletin* 27: 26–32.

Vennard, W.D., Hirano, M., and Ohala, J. (1970). Chest, head, and falsetto. *NATS Bulletin* 31: 30–37.

Vogelsanger, G.T. (1954). Experimentelle Prüfung der Stimmleistung beim Singen. *Folia Phoniatrica* 6(4): 193–227.

Von Leden, H., Moore, G.P., and Timcke, R. (1960). Laryngeal vibrations: Measurements of the glottic wave: Part 3. the pathologic larynx. *Archives of Otolaryngology (Chicago)* 71: 16–35.

Wendahl, R.W. (1966). Laryngeal analog synthesis of jitter and shimmer auditory parameters of harshness. *Folia Phoniatrica* 18: 98–108.

Woojin, C., Juhye, H. and Hachoon P., (2014). Real-time ultrasonographic assessment in professional singers. *Journal of Voice* 26(6): 819.e1–819.e3.

Yanagihara, N. (1967). Hoarseness: Investigation of the physiological mechanism. *Annals of Otology, Rhinology and Laryngology (St Louis)* 76: 472–488.

Yanagihara, N. (1970). Aerodynamic examination of the laryngeal function. *Studia Phonologica* 5: 45–51.

Yanagihara, N. and Koike, Y. (1967). The regulation of sustained phonation. *Folia Phoniatrica* 19: 1–18.

Yanagihara, N. and Von Leden, H. (1967). Respiration and phonation: the functional examination of laryngeal disease. *Folia Phoniatrica* 19(3): 153–166.

Zenker, W. and Zenker, A. (1960). Über die Regelung der Stimmlippenspannung durch von außen am Kehlkopf angreifende Mechanismen. *Folia Phoniatrica* 12(1): 1–36.

Zimmermann, R. (1938). Stimmlippenlängen bei Sängern und Sängerinnen. *Arch. Sprach. Stimmphysiol. Sprach. Stimmheilkunde* 2: 103–129.

Zwaardemaker Cz, H. and Eijkman, L.P.H. (1928). *Leerboek der phonetiek: Inzonderheid met betrekking tot het standaard-nederlandsch*. Haarlem: De Erven F Bohn.

CHAPTER 51

....

AVE VERUM PENTIUM

Singing, recording, archiving, and analyzing within the digital domain

....

EVANGELOS HIMONIDES

INTRODUCTION

In this chapter, I consider the role of technology in recording, processing, and archiving the singing voice. The novel conceptual "compass" for the present discussion is that the recording chain (i.e. the set of individual technologies involved between the singer's lips and the listener's ears, during recording and playback) is often presented in the literature as deterministic and free of context. In reality, practicing singers and recording performers, music producers, teaching practitioners, educators, researchers, and/or people that play multiple roles, often have different needs both in terms of the technological solutions that they require but also in terms of the level of scientific understanding required for effective practice. With this chapter we do not attempt to trivialize the complex worlds of acoustics, psychoacoustics, mathematics, engineering, computer science, performance, pedagogy, and production, nor offer a *passe-partout* that unlocks all possible practices and creative foci. It is hoped that this work offers a bridge between the sciences, arts, and the humanities, thus allowing readers from different backgrounds to form a somewhat broader understanding about the wonderfully diverse world of the recorded voice and offer insights into (and share challenges about) proximate worlds and practices. It is emphasized that outside the highly specialized worlds of research and scholarship in acoustics, electronics engineering, and physics, it is perfectly achievable to perform successful recordings given that we maintain a systematic approach to our methodologies and praxes.

WHAT IS SOUND?

Sound! In almost every book on acoustics and psychoacoustics, there is an opening section that refers to "sound" being around us, "with" us, constantly. Even before we are born, during the last trimester of pregnancy, our auditory system is functioning (Malloch and Trevarthen 2010; Welch 2005a). Research also suggests that due to our connection with our mothers pre-birth and the ability to hear sounds coupled with their emotional "potential" through the bloodstream, during the last trimester in the womb, we enter this world "pre-programmed" to like and dislike particular sounds, certain melodies and to recognize familiar timbres. Our understanding of the outside world is strongly connected to how things "feel," "look" and "sound."

But what is "sound"? What are its properties? How do we perceive "sound"? How do we visualize "sound"? Are there common misunderstandings regarding "sound" and its representation?

According to Everest (2001), depending on the perspective used (what Everest calls "the approach," either physical or psychophysical), sound can be defined as a wave motion in air or other elastic media (stimulus) or as an excitation of the hearing mechanism that carries out a preliminary analysis of the incoming sound for the perception of sound (sensation). He further explains that "the type of problem dictates the approach to sound. If the interest is in the disturbance in air created by a loudspeaker, it is a problem in physics. If the interest is how it sounds to a person near the loudspeaker, psychophysical methods must be used" (Everest 2001, p. 1). Similarly, Howard and Angus (2016) suggest that

> at a physical level sound is simply a mechanical disturbance of the medium, which may be air, or a solid, liquid or other gas. However, such a simplistic description is not very useful as it provides no information about the way the disturbance travels, or any of its characteristics other than the requirement for a medium in order for it to propagate.
>
> (Howard and Angus 2016, p. 2)

A useful metaphor employed within numerous textbooks on physics and acoustics, that can help people understand the propagation of sound, is that of the "slinky." The slinky is a very good way to aid understanding of and to demonstrate wave motion. This visual (and haptic) metaphor can exemplify the two major categories of waves; the "longitudinal" waves (sound waves are longitudinal waves) and the "transverse" waves (often found in the vibrations of strings or membranes). The difference between the two can perhaps be clarified using (or imagining using) a slinky in two different ways (see also: *The Physics Classroom*, n.d.): first, if we rested the slinky on a table surface and held each end with our hands and —while keeping one of our two hands steady— started moving the other hand back and forth, we would achieve a motion that is similar to a longitudinal wave. Alternatively, if instead of moving one of the ends back and forth (i.e. to the axis defined by the length of the slinky), we tried to make small perpendicular movements (i.e. perpendicular to the length of the slinky) we would be seeing something that is close to what some might know as a "sinusoidal curve," as long as we tried to keep our movements uniform. This is a good representation of a transverse wave. As mentioned earlier, sound waves are longitudinal waves (i.e. what was achieved with the first slinky experiment).

> Sound is readily conducted in gases, liquids, and solids such as air, water, steel, concrete, etc., which are all elastic media. Perhaps one remembers as a child hearing two sounds of a rock striking a railroad in the distance, one sound coming through the air and one through the rail. As Everest (2001) explains: "The sound through the rail arrives first because the speed of sound in the dense steel is greater than that of tenuous air. Sound has been detected after it has travelled thousands of miles through the ocean. Without a medium, sound cannot be propagated. In the laboratory, an electric buzzer is suspended in a heavy glass bell jar. As the button is pushed, the sound of the buzzer is readily heard through the glass. As the

air is pumped out of the bell jar, the sound becomes fainter and fainter until it is no longer audible. The sound-conducting medium, air, has been removed between the source and the ear. Because air is such a common agent for the conduction of sound, it is easy to forget that other gases as well as solids and liquids are also conductors of sound."

(p. 5)

Capturing sound

Background

In order to form a better understanding about current recording techniques, it might be useful to look at the history of recording. At the time of publication (i.e. 2019), recording sound for later playback had been available to humanity for 140 years. Given a plethora of evidence (e.g. Mithen 2006) or hypotheses (Himonides 2012; Welch 2005b) that humans are musical by design and have been singing and making music since the very beginning of their phylogenetic journey, sound recording can be viewed as an affordance that is practically contemporary. In 1877, Thomas Alva Edison applied to the United States Patent and Trademark Office in order to register his invention that could record sound. On February 19 of the following year, Edison's invention received official approval as patented technology, with Patent Number 200521 and the official title "The Phonograph or Speaking Machine." Edison's technology was rather crude, and the quality of playback was quite poor and ephemeral by today's standards, due to the choice of tin-foil as the material on which the vibrations of a needle/stylus caused indentations. A decade later, and thanks to the development work by Alexander Graham Bell and Charles Tainter, a significantly better material, wax, spread on the rotating cylinder of the phonograph, allowed for much better recording and reproduction qualities, as well as longer "shelf life." Following on from Edison's original invention, its advancement by Bell and Tainter, and further polish by Edison, a different technology appeared that changed the face of music and sound forever. This was the "gramophone," invented by Emil Berliner (1887). It is remarkable that the vinyl record, a direct offspring of the gramophone, is still used today, and surprisingly seeing an impressive increase in global sales (O'Connor 2018). It is a celebration of the importance of the human voice that both technologies that marked the beginning of the era of sound recording used *phono-* and *-phone* in their names, where the ancient Greek word φωνή (i.e. phōnḗ) means "voice." Therefore, at birth, *sound recording* was seen by its forebearers as *voice recording*.

Analog domain

In the natural world, as briefly described earlier, sound exists within what we call "the acoustic domain," as a strictly mechanical phenomenon. It is important to understand that no different types of sound exist (e.g. analog sound and/or digital sound) as is often misunderstood. Different "representations" of sound though do exist. These "representations" allow us to capture, store, edit and replicate performances at different levels of accuracy, at different costs and logistical complexity, with varying levels of reproduction fidelity, at varying levels of perceived warmth and perceived quality, with different levels of complexity with editing and manipulation, and with varying technical and logistical requirements for storage, archiving, and communication.

As a first step onward from the acoustic domain, we have the "analog domain" (nb: the American spelling is almost exclusively used globally in this context). Within the analog domain, sound vibrations are converted into varying electrical signals, which are then usually stored onto a magnetic medium, like tape (e.g. reel to reel tape, 8-track tapes, standard cassette tapes). Interestingly, magnetic media are also being used for the storage of digital information (see next section). This introduces multiple advantages, as these electrical signals can be created using other than traditional voice and/or instrument recordings, like for example with the use of analog synthesizers (i.e. where we do not convert actual sound into signals, but where we create signals artificially in order to convert them later into sound). At the stage of playback, whatever domain we have been working in, we *always* need to move onto the acoustic domain; otherwise we will not hear an audible result. Within the analog domain, in order to play representations of sound back we need to convert electrical signals back into vibrations. A typical means for achieving this is the ubiquitous "loud-speaker" (or speaker). The speaker is a typical example of what is called a "transducer," where one form of energy (electrical) is converted into another one (mechanical— the vibration of the speaker membrane, which results in the production of sound).

Microphones

A very important technology within the analog domain is the microphone. The microphone essentially performs exactly the opposite job of that of the speaker. It converts mechanical energy (i.e. sound—vibrations) into electrical energy (i.e. a fluctuating electrical signal).

Paul White's introduction within his short book *Basic Microphones* (2003) is a very helpful starting point and essential reading for the reader who would like to discover more detail about how microphones work, and how they are used in various recording contexts and situations. He explains:

> no matter how sophisticated computers or synthesizers become, the recording of "real" sound always starts with a microphone. The problem is that, unlike the human ear, there is no single microphone that is ideal for all jobs—microphones come in many types and sizes, and all are designed to handle a specific range of tasks. The problem is in deciding what microphone to choose for a particular application. Having selected an appropriate microphone, there is still the question of how best to position it relative to the sound source in order to capture the desired sound.
>
> (White 2003, p. 11)

Within this overview chapter, we shall not go through the different technologies and designs of microphones in detail. We will simply mention the two major classification factors and briefly explain their basic differences, as they are quite important within the voice recording studio.

One important classification factor for microphones is "directionality" (Figure 51.1). Not all microphones pick up sound in the same way, and the type you choose will depend on the task at hand. Some pick up sound efficiently regardless of the direction from which the sound is coming—in other words you don't have to point the microphone directly at the sound source because it can "hear" equally well in all directions. Some microphones may be designed to capture mainly sounds from a single direction while others may pick up sounds from the both front and the rear but not from the sides. These basic directional characteristics are known as:

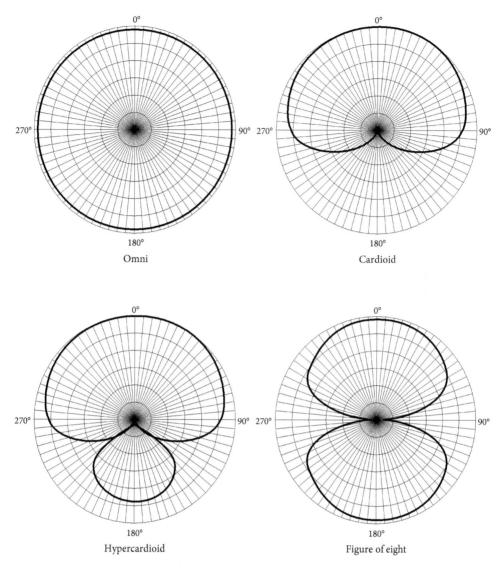

FIGURE 51.1 Common microphone polar patterns.

- omni-directional (all directions)
- cardioid (uni-directional—literally, "heart-shaped")
- figure-of-eight (mics which pick up from both front and rear but not from the sides).

(White 2003, p. 16)

Secondly, based on the construction of the microphone itself (i.e. its topology) we can have:

- dynamic microphones
- ribbon microphones
- capacitor (or condenser) microphones.

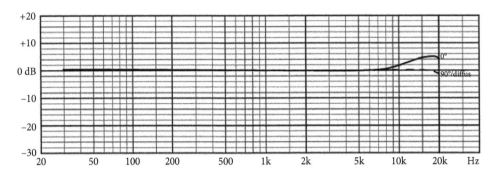

FIGURE 51.2 The frequency response of the Beyerdynamic MM 1 professional grade measurement microphone. Here we can see the remarkably flat frequency response throughout the device's entire range (20 Hz–20000 Hz).

The differences between the three are related to the slightly different topologies employed in order to convert sound to electricity.

Different designs result in not all microphones behaving similarly, and not all microphones showing similar qualities in their operation, the accuracy of the signal that they generate (see above, as the *representation* of the recorded sound). Microphone design is a very complex science, but also a praxial battlefield for very passionate exchanges based on empirical convictions that recordists, engineers, singers, researchers, and practitioners possess (Figure 51.2). Remarkably, microphone technology is also not a plateau where we have seen much progress and innovation in the past century. Some of the most expensive, valued, and cherished studio microphones to date are microphones that were manufactured before WWII with countless contemporaries trying to imitate their design, at varying levels of success (e.g. Neumann/Telefunken and Gefell microphones, see Figure 51.3).

As with other contexts where we attempt to "capture" a phenomenon, like photography for example, there is no ultimate or definitive tool that we can use in order to achieve optimal results. In reality, we always need to perform certain compromises in one area in order to gain better results in another; we need to consider the cost of our decisions; we need to adjust our "gains" in order to achieve optimum "yield" within our set of logistical constraints and affordances. Since we mentioned "photography" above, it would be interesting to perhaps remind ourselves that the definitive lens for a camera does not exist. A lens that is extremely fast, sharp, and responsive at larger distances is a lens that would require extremely expensive optics, but also a lens that would need to be terribly heavy and large in size compared to a standard fixed 50mm lens. On the other hand, a lens that would work brilliantly for long distances could never outperform a lens that was designed for macro photography (i.e. close up photography) or a lens that would produce acceptable results for most photography tasks (an "all rounder") and a range of foci.

In recording, a microphone that has been designed for ultimate "accuracy" in capturing sound (in this context, meaning a microphone that has as flat a frequency response as possible) is not necessarily a device that would be appropriate for recording real singing performances. Singers and producers only care about perceived "warmth," "presence," "punch," "distortion," "color," and "character." All these properties are usually opponents to "accuracy." One would therefore not find a lab "measurement microphone" in a commercial

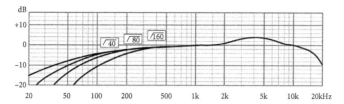

FIGURE 51.3 The frequency response of the Neumann M149 tube microphone at a figure-of-eight configuration and four different low frequency roll-off settings. Here we can observe how the microphone is tuned to boost frequencies within the 2–6 kHz band, which is something that is perceived to add warmth and presence to vocal recordings.

recording studio used for recording artists. This is why we would rarely see an omni-directional microphone being used for recording studio vocals, as opposed to cardioid or hyper-cardioid designs, whilst it would be inappropriate to use anything but an omni-directional microphone for acoustic analyses, measurement, and research.

Similar "compromises" (or "tactical decisions") have to be performed with the choice of microphone capsule or diaphragm size. Once again, no definitive answers can be offered to the question "which microphone should I use?" There are numerous factors at play with the different capsule designs and sizes, that result in varying ability to handle large sound pressure levels, but also in varying self-noise levels, and in varying success levels for perceived proximity effect (i.e. the perceptual assessment of how close to the capturing device the sound source had been). For example, tiny diaphragms can handle much higher sound pressure levels, yet at the same time they would suffer much higher self-noise levels.

To date, one of the most comprehensive scholarly works that presents the complexity of microphone technology within the voice research context is that of Jan Švec and Svante Granqvist (2010) for the American Speech-Language-Hearing Association. Therein, the authors offer evidence about how different design aspects of microphones impact systematic acquisition of recorded data in great detail.

In the present context, it is useful to consider the following, depending on the recording task.

For *educators* and *practitioners*, when recording singers for reference, and/or in order to gauge development longitudinally, the most important thing to safeguard is a replicable and systematic recording, as it is perceived change that matters, as does keeping the underlying technologies for recording it constant. Nowadays, it is possible to achieve something like this with very accessible and affordable technologies. Things to consider when trying to keep a constant include:

- selection of microphone;
- microphone placement;
- recording venue/room (i.e. room acoustics);
- positioning of the singer in relation to the microphone and the room;
- pre-amplifier gain settings (see "Microphone pre-amplifiers (Mic PREs)"); and
- remaining recording chain (see "Digital domain").

Following the previously offered argument that very little has changed in microphone design within the past century, it is interesting that what this author perceives as one of the most exciting recent developments in microphone designs since the introduction of the microphone is not really related to the sound capturing technology. It is the introduction, by British manufacturer Aston, of a laser pointing device built onto the body of their "Starlight" model microphones, thus enabling the user to perform very accurate positioning and replicate placement from one recording to another.

For *researchers* and *scientists*, within systematically researched contexts, vocal recordings need to be calibrated, systematically designed, set up and conducted, but also using high quality and reference technologies that enable the researchers to "capture" sound (i.e. the acoustical phenomenon) as accurately as possible within the analog and digital (see below) domains. In this respect, researchers should solely be using high quality reference microphones, with omni-directional response patterns, extremely flat response curves, very low self-noise, and placed systematically at the appropriate distance from the singers' lips and within carefully controlled singer placement and room acoustics. Beyond the microphone, the remainder of the "recording chain" would also need to be carefully controlled. This means that we need to understand the role of microphone pre-amplification, as well as how the analog signal becomes converted into digital "information" (nowadays, almost exclusively!).

For *artists* and *producers*, it is oft celebrated by successful producers and sound engineers that "if it sounds right, it is right." Experience and studio practice suggest that there really is no point in immersing ourselves into science in order to achieve a successful recording. Any microphone is a potential candidate in this context, especially within popular music genres. Accuracy, transparency, fidelity, and/or clarity are often not seen as important, when distorted, colored, lo-fi, or branded sound recordings are sought under a specific esthetic paradigm. This can further become exaggerated within editing and post-production. Within this context, the technological continuum is so vast that one can witness multi-platinum vocals that had been recorded using the microphone of a discarded telephone handset, but also recordings that were performed using vintage Neumann U47 large diaphragm condenser microphones (often selling for close to 10,000 American dollars).

Microphone pre-amplifiers (also known as Mic PREs)

Microphones put out small voltages; mixing desks and outboard gear work at much higher voltages. A pre-amplifier is therefore needed between a microphone and whatever capturing device to turn the millivolts at the mic output (mic level) into volts for processing (line level). This simple task is absolutely central to the recording process. Any signal that leaves the microphone will be affected by the design and quality of the mic PRE that receives it, and any noise, distortion, or inaccuracy introduced to the sound at this point will become a permanent part of the signal (i.e. the information within the digital domain past conversion to digital data). Once again, the neighboring paradigm of photography has been used by English producer and engineer John Leckie to demonstrate the importance of the microphone pre-amplifier within the recording chain. Leckie often compared the microphone pre-amplifier with camera lenses, highlighting how important their quality is in determining the quality of the final captured photograph. Within professional recording circles, the importance of microphone pre-amplifiers is often seen as greater than that of the microphone: a high-quality mic PRE affects the performance of microphones very directly, and an ordinary mic through a top-quality mic PRE will sound better than a good mic through a poor mic PRE (Pro Audio n.d.).

It is worth noting that microphone pre-amplifiers are not always present as dedicated, stand-alone devices within the recording chain. Often, microphone pre-amplifiers are built into mixing desks, computer recording interfaces, solid-state recorders, live or studio vocal performance units and/or pedals, dedicated recording strips, mobile phones, and even concealed within devices that appear to be traditional microphones (e.g. contemporary USB microphones). The latter will also feature built-in analog-to-digital converters (something discussed later in the chapter). In light of this, it is important to consider the different needs for the three general recording "umbrellas" that we identified earlier.

Educators and *practitioners*: similar to employing an appropriate microphone, the choice of microphone pre-amplifier is not a complicated exercise, and its use should be focused on being systematic rather than being scientific. As mentioned earlier, it is important to try to filter out possible variables and/or contaminants when we aim to monitor singing development and singing performance practice longitudinally. Therefore, the use of a decent quality microphone pre-amplifier, even if built into a standalone solid-state recording device, is perfectly acceptable as long as the practitioner has control over its gain settings. Although there is no real need for properly controlled calibration of sound pressure levels for the recording within this context, it is essential that the gain settings are set (i.e. not automatically adjusted by the recorder, known as auto-gain). Additional care needs to be offered in ensuring that the amplified signal is not overloading the analog to digital converter (we shall clarify this in the following section).

Researchers and *scientists*: a microphone pre-amplifier within the scientific research context needs to be as close as possible to what many sound engineers call the hypothetical "straight piece of wire with gain." This is presented as hypothetical because, once again, practice suggests that no hardware design topology can actually result in an amplifier that can achieve this perfectly (i.e. to take a low-level signal generated by the microphone, and simply make it louder without any alteration). Simplistically, if we performed comparisons (i.e. spectral analyses) between the un-amplified and the amplified microphone signals using a theoretically perfect microphone pre-amplifier, we should not be able to see any spectral differences. Practically, this is not achievable. The design of any amplifier will have an impact on the distortion and/or coloration (i.e. the *change*) of the resulting amplified signal. Once again, a compromise is required so that we can use a sensible, but also affordable, technical solution. Additionally, sound pressure level (SPL) calibration within this context is absolutely essential. This is not only because pre-amplifiers will affect/brand the resulting signal differently depending on the device's gain settings, but because a valid assessment about singing energy, energy slope, and/or subglottal pressure levels during singing isn't possible unless there exists a systematic reference of what the amplifier contributed to the final signal (or digital representation of it) at the time of analysis (for further details, see Švec and Granqvist 2010).

Artists and *producers*: similar to the microphone paradigm, we once again face a praxis where "everything goes." Any type of amplifying technology can be used—often misused or abused—in order to foster creativity. Producers and engineers have been known to utilize any type of amplification technology in trying to create novel sonic products, from guitar amplifiers to old vacuum tube (aka valve) radios, from PA systems to low-fidelity amplifiers, all the way up to boutique and significantly expensive topologies that can be found in professional mixing desks (e.g. SSL, API) and dedicated, stand-alone, pre-amplification units (e.g. Manley, Great

River, Millennia, etc.). Different esthetic schools exist within the recording and audio production worlds, and these are strongly reliant on different types of microphone pre-amplification designs (e.g. from the glassy and transparent pop diva-type vocals, to the edgy and punchy Nashville country vocals, to the "brown" and oversaturated British pop vocals).

DIGITAL DOMAIN

One can be quite confident in claiming that we have all used the term digital—some of us on a daily basis! Nevertheless, it would be useful to remind ourselves what we actually mean when we refer to digital technologies and (somewhat erratically) digital audio.

How many times have you heard the phrase "we live in a digital age"? Salespeople often term a product "better" if it is digital. Discussions abound about analog vs digital that describe the purity (warmth, thickness, creaminess, substance, color, quality, depth, richness, etc.) of vinyl compared to CDs. But what is digital? And, consequently, what is digital audio?

A digital system is one that uses discrete values rather than continuous. The word comes from the same source as the word digit: the Latin word for finger (counting on the fingers) as these are used for discrete counting.[1] In circuitry, a digital circuit is one in which data-carrying signals are restricted to either of two voltage levels, corresponding to logic 1 or 0 (see among others: http://www.wgcu.org). In terms of technology in general, digital describes electronic technology that generates, stores, and processes data in terms of two states: positive and non-positive. These two states are described by the two available symbols of the binary system. Thus, data transmitted or stored with digital technology is expressed as a string of 0s and 1s. Each of these state digits is referred to as a bit (and a string of 8 bits that a computer can address individually as a group is a byte).[2]

No matter how complicated the software running on a computer, ultimately everything is being translated into zeros and ones. This is how computers work. Machines with digital circuits only operate on this binary logic (1–0, yes–no, positive–negative).

Some inventions prior to the appearance of computers have claimed to be the ideas that led to the conception of the first computer. Based on the same binary logic, industrial sewing machines could be programmed in order to produce different designs and patterns. The sewing heads were controlled by a perforated paper-tape. When the tape that was feeding the head at a given moment had a hole, the head would move down, otherwise it would stand still. Many devices used this hole/not-hole technology, either in a single linear fashion (just one line of holes or gaps) or in a multiple line fashion.

It is very important to understand that digital is nothing but a *representation* of data. In the case of audio and sound, digital audio is a *representation* of sound and *not the sound itself*. According to what we presented within the introductory section, sound is a physical (mechanical) phenomenon—there is no such thing as "digital sound." If we are able to hear something, then it is definitely an acoustic (i.e. mechanical) phenomenon.

Fundamentally, a representation of a phenomenon cannot possibly be better than the actual phenomenon; it can be, though, an extremely accurate representation of the

[1] wikipedia.org   [2] iptv.org

phenomenon, and in many cases, it can be so accurate that the benefits for utilizing such a representation can be immense:

- the representation (successful or not) can be replicated faithfully and effortlessly;
- the representation can be distributed through various channels of communication;
- the representation will not change;
- the representation can be easily manipulated, edited, and altered deterministically;
- the representation can be easily archived; and
- the representation can be easily retrieved.

Sampling

Since we have established that digital is a representation of a phenomenon and not the actual phenomenon, we need to be a little bit more analytical about how we represent a phenomenon. There are various metaphors to explain *digital* and over the years this author has developed and become particularly accustomed to using one in particular with his students.

Imagine that you witness a crime.

You go to the nearest police station in order to report it.

Some police stations employ sketch artists who liaise with the witnesses in order to draw images of the criminals.

You have to describe the person that you've seen to the artist and you have to do it in a fixed period of time. Obviously, the best thing that could possibly happen would be for you to produce the actual criminal and show them to the artist. But this is not usually possible. Given that you have a fixed amount of time to describe the person, it seems that two issues are of the essence: The amount of information that you will give to the artist each time (i.e. how long your sentences are going to be every time you open your mouth) and the number of times that you will do this (i.e. how many sentences of XXX length per unit of time). In theory, if you possess a photographic memory as well as remarkable linguistic skills, your description could lead to an extremely accurate representation of the criminal . . . you could go into so much detail that you are describing each pore of their skin! In any case, the more information you provide and the more times you provide this information will produce a better (in terms of a more realistic) result.

This leads us to the two most important aspects of sampling (i.e. what we do in order to produce a digital representation of an analog phenomenon):

- bit-depth or word-length: the amount/size of information that is provided/stored each time the phenomenon is described; and,
- sampling rate or sampling frequency: the number of times per second that the above-mentioned chunks of information are provided per second.

Binary, bits, and bytes

Since computers can only process things in a binary fashion, all information that is being input needs to be translated to binary code. Understanding how this works requires a very short refresher from our primary school years, as augmented by the introduction of reme-dial algebra during high school!

Since our early years, we have been educated and "branded" to understand numbers using the decimal system. The decimal system is nothing more than another convention to provide a common ground for describing, exchanging, and utilizing information. The base of the decimal system is, of course, the number ten (10). The numbers (digits) that can be used in the decimal system are 0, 1, 2, 3, 4, 5, 6, 7, 8, and 9. Everything else is a composite using these ten available components.

Take for example the number 157. What does 157 actually mean? Primary school children learn that 157 means: 1 set of a hundred + 5 sets of ten + 7 units. Later in our lives, most of us learn the algebraic interpretation of the same definition which is $157 = (1\text{x}10^2) + (5\text{x}10^1) + (7\text{x}10^0)$.

The binary system only uses two digits, 0 and 1. In order to represent a number in the binary system we follow the same line of thought as presented for the decimal system, with the obvious limitation that we can only work with 0 and 1 and the powers of our base (the number 2, see Table 51.1). Therefore, the decimal number 157 can be represented as 10011101: $10011101 = (1\text{x}2^7) + (0\text{x}2^6) + (0\text{x}2^5) + (1\text{x}2^4) + (1\text{x}2^3) + (1\text{x}2^2) + (0\text{x}2^1) + (1\text{x}2^0)$.

Digital audio

With this understanding about how computers process and understand data we can con-tinue with our introduction to audio in the digital domain. As mentioned, in the real world, the sound of our voices is an acoustic phenomenon. During recording, and with the use of microphones, these acoustic phenomena are converted into electrical signals. To process these signals in computers, we need to convert the signals to digital form.

Table 51.1 The first ten powers of 2

power	symbolism	decimal result
0	2^0	1
1	2^1	2
2	2^2	4
3	2^3	8
4	2^4	16
5	2^5	32
6	2^6	64
7	2^7	128
8	2^8	256
9	2^9	512
10	2^{10}	1024

While an analog signal is continuous in both time and amplitude, a digital signal is discrete in both time and amplitude. Converting a signal from continuous time to discrete time uses a process called sampling. The value of the signal is measured at certain intervals in time, and each measurement is referred to as a sample.[3] In order to convert an analogue signal into a digital representation of it, we practically perform thousands of amplitude measurements per second and store the amplitude values. Please note that the term sampling is also being used in modern music production with reference to the recall of pre-programmed samples (audio snippets) with various triggers (buttons, controllers, keyboards, etc.). A modern sampler is a device that stores recorded sounds and is able to manipulate them and reproduce them; they can then be distributed across a keyboard and played back at various pitches (sample-based Synthesis is an appropriate keyword for further research). Both sampling-rate and word-length are absolutely *essential* factors concerning the accurate representation of the signal.

Sampling-rate (or sampling-frequency)

Imagine that you have to describe (or paint) how bright the sky is during a twenty-four-hour period. You go outside, fix your photo-camera on a tripod, point to the sky, and take one photograph at 11pm and just one more after twenty-four hours. For this example, we won't worry about color—just brightness—and we will assume that we have a monochrome film. Therefore, Figure 51.4 shows how our photographs will look.

If we decided to shoot another one at mid-day, then we would probably have something like Figure 51.5.

And, of course, the higher the number of photos we take during the 24 hours, the better our understanding about brightness will be (Figure 51.6).

A video camera (which is nothing more than a camera that shoots anything between 30 and 50 photos per second) would produce something similar to Figure 51.7.

How many samples are necessary to ensure that we are preserving the information contained in the (audio) signal? If the signal contains high frequency components, we will need to sample at a higher rate to avoid losing information that is in the signal. In general, to preserve the full information in the signal, it is necessary to sample at twice the maximum frequency of the signal. This is known as the Nyquist rate. The Sampling Theorem states that

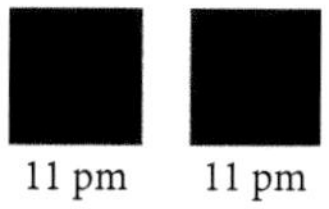

11 pm   11 pm

FIGURE 51.4 Two snapshots taken 24 hours apart.

---

[3] Zawistowski, T. and Shah, P. Engineering Computing Center, University of Houston.

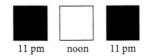

11 pm   noon   11 pm

FIGURE 51.5 Three snapshots throughout the 24-hour period spread 12 hours apart.

a signal can be exactly reproduced if it is sampled at a frequency F, where F is greater than twice the maximum frequency in the signal.[4]

Some of us perhaps know that CD-quality audio is sampled at 44.1 kHz. This is connected to the fact that our ears are able to process frequencies between 20 Hz and 22,000 Hz. According to the Nyquist theorem, in order to represent frequencies up to 22 kHz we need to use a sampling frequency greater than twice the frequency in the signal, hence 44.1 kHz.

People with "golden ears" claim that 44.1 kHz sampling frequency is simply not high enough. New, high-definition recording and production is using 96 kHz (DVD audio standard) and—more extreme—192 kHz sampling frequencies. In theory, the latter is adequate for the exact representation of audio signals up to 96 kHz (when human ears cannot possibly hear frequencies above 22 kHz). Why go to so much trouble? Psychoacoustics is a very complicated field; in a nutshell, it is believed (and continually researched) that although it is not possible to "hear" frequencies above the 22 kHz limit, the interaction and masking of higher frequency components with the audible frequencies produces blended results that "affect" the listener and/or "trigger" different esthetic experiences when higher sampling rates are being employed.

Bit-Depth (or word-length)

CD-quality audio uses 16-bit words for each channel (16-bit, 44.1 kHz, stereo). What does this mean? When we are sampling, we store in our machines (44,100 times per second) information (words) that describe the amplitude of the waveform at each given time. Since each word is 16 bits long, this means that we are able to represent a minimum value of 0 and a maximum value of 65,535 when describing the amplitude at a given time. What happens

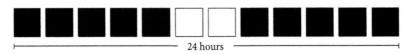

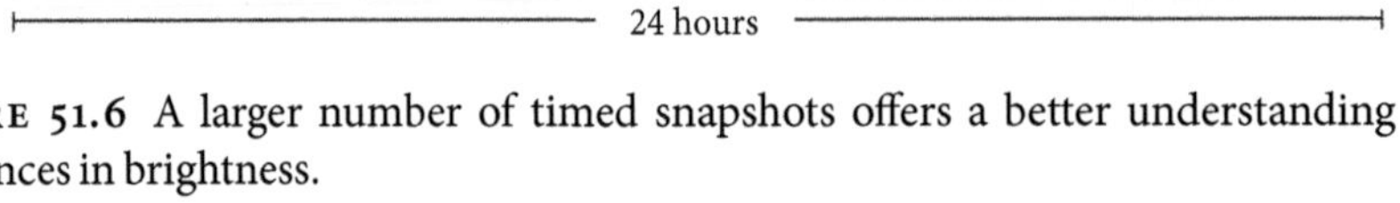

24 hours

FIGURE 51.6 A larger number of timed snapshots offers a better understanding of the differences in brightness.

[4] Ibid.

24 hours

FIGURE 51.7 A high-resolution (i.e. using high sampling frequency) recording of the phenomenon.

when we sample audio using 8-bit words? You can see that the possible amplitude values that we can use are significantly less.

Create a parallel with this to the visual world again, and try to recall very old computer graphics printouts, where a pixel could either be blank (white) or black (couldn't we call this a 1-bit sampling?). This allowed the reproduction of quite crude images where detail was lost due to the limited amount of available colors (or shades of grey). Figure 51.8 shows the difference between a low resolution and low bit depth image and the same image sampled with a higher resolution and bit depth.

If you open your computer's display properties you will see that your Windows (or Macintosh) system is configured to run at either 24- or 32-bit (!!!) color quality; they cannot be bothered any longer to give you the actual number, which is why they say "millions of colors."

Exactly the same occurs when we are sampling audio. Depending on the level of detail, we can achieve different levels of accuracy/quality if we tried to sample a sinewave. Figure 51.9 shows a graphical representation of such an exercise.

The quality of the representation is strongly related to the sampling word-length. The bigger the word, the better the sampling.

Entering the digital domain

Moving on from a superficial crash course to digital theory and sampling, this section offers an overview of how this occurs in practice. As mentioned, the acoustic phenomenon (i.e. vibrations, sound) excite a surface on the microphone (the transducer) which converts mechanical energy (the sound) to electrical energy (electrical signal). This electrical signal is then fed to an amplification device (the microphone pre-amplifier) in order to become stronger. The amplified signal is consequently fed into a device that

FIGURE 51.8 Comparison between low and high bit depth.

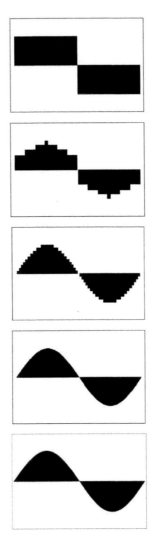

FIGURE 51.9 An example of sampling the same waveform at different bit depths.

performs sampling (as described earlier) at the sampling rate that we have determined (44.1 thousand times per second for CD-quality audio) generating chunks of information (words) of an also pre-determined size (bit depth or word length—16 bits for CD-quality audio). The device that performs this type of conversion is called an analog-to-digital converter (or A/D converter). As with previous components in the recording chain, A/D converters can be stand-alone devices, but they can also be bundled inside other devices, even modern microphones (e.g. new generation USB microphones are essentially bundles of a microphone, a microphone pre-amplifier, and an A/D converter). A/D converters are in most new technologies, mobile phones (either used as phones or as recording devices), solid-state voice recorders, video cameras, computer soundcards, built-in audio interfaces for laptop computers, RaspberryPi and Arduino "shields" and "hats," wearable electronic components, even cheap plastic toys that allow voice recording (albeit sometimes unpleasantly "lo-fi").

Past the A/D converter, we solely deal with zeros and ones. There is no raw information about sounds or frequencies—only thousands of measurements of amplitude values stored sequentially. This is an important thing to remember and stresses the need for processing (see "Processing within the digital domain") as some of the processes in editing digital audio are related to frequency and timbre. This automatically suggests that one more transformation is somehow necessary in order for us to work with spectral aspects of sound (more accurately, the digital representation of it!). One mathematical process that allows us to compute frequency information from amplitude/time sequences is called a Fourier Transformation after the French mathematician Joseph Fourier. Currently, digital data is processed using fast Fourier transformations (FFT). These sit under the thematic umbrella of Digital Signal Processing (DSP). Some readers might have come across music technology equipment reviews where a particular synthesizer's or effect unit's DSP engine was reviewed.

Processing within the digital domain

We have produced a sound (perhaps a beautiful singing performance), captured it with a microphone by converting it to electrical signal, amplified the signal with a microphone pre-amplifier, fed the amplified signal to a computer soundcard's analog-to-digital-converter, and captured (recorded) the resulting *data* on our computer with the appropriate software (e.g. a dedicated "wave editor" like the free software Audacity, or part of a digital audio workstation (DAW), e.g. Cubase, Logic, Sonar, Nuendo, Reaper, ProTools, Live, Garage Band, etc.). What happens past this point depends upon the type of operation performed on the stored stream of digital data, exactly like manipulating different columns of numbers on a software spreadsheet. There are countless processes that could be applied to the digitally stored data. Some examples of popular effects (Fx) available with most software tools are offered below.

Compression

Compressors are sophisticated dynamics processors that sound engineers use, especially for instruments that produce sounds with a great variability in dynamic range (the voice being the most representative). With modern production, practically everything goes through a compressor. In a nutshell, a compressor reduces the dynamic range (making the distance between the loudest and the quietest part smaller). Think of a compressor like being an invisible hand that increases or reduces the gain of a signal in milliseconds (according to our needs). Compressors are also used when we want to remedy recording problems that occur with aspirated consonants (e.g. T and P) and can also work in tandem with equalizers when on some occasions sibilants (e.g. S) sound harsh (then we call them De-essers).

Equalization (EQ)

Equalization is an essential part of recording and production. By increasing the energy within specific bands in the spectrum we can facilitate the placement as well as the clarity of the different sounds in the final mix. Some might have heard or interacted with software equalizers and might have also come across different types that somehow resembled (or presented visual metaphors of?) old analog parametric and graphic equalizers.

Reverb

Reverberators are processors (or algorithms when used as effects within sound-editing or production software) that change the recording by branding it (i.e. applying to it) the acoustical characteristics of different physical spaces (e.g. room, chamber, cathedral, etc.). This is achieved in a number of ways, the most dominant being either by attempting to model the acoustical properties of a venue algorithmically, or by using an actual digital-sonic "imprint" of the physical space itself (known as a sound impulse of the space). The latter is achieved by performing a controlled recording of a prescribed sound (e.g. a passage of white or pink noise, or the burst of a balloon) and comparing the recorded result in that venue with the original (dry) signal.

Echo

Echo is a family of digital effects inspired by the natural phenomenon of the same name. The only difference with artificial echo is that the repetitions (timing, number of repetitions, amplitude) can be controlled, sometimes resulting in extremes, and often used as novel esthetic artifacts.

Delay

Delays are also time-based effects. Very impressive results can be achieved with careful usage (and programming) of delay effects. This is especially so when the repetitions are carefully planned to correspond with the musical time, i.e. time signatures and tempi. Known popular musicians that have mastered delay technology are musicians David Gilmour (and his famous delayed guitar sounds for Pink Floyd) and Edge of U2 ("Where the Streets Nave No Name" is a very good example of creative delay programming).

Pitch shifting

Pitch shifters affect the pitch of a recording. This is very handy with some loop-based modern music-making technologies. Modern, sophisticated algorithms can affect the pitch of a recording without affecting the time (if that is what is wanted). Pitch-shifters can change the pitch of an entire recording or use even more sophisticated algorithms for correcting out-of-tune singing (a ubiquitous technology for the recording of musically challenged pop-idols, it seems). Sophisticated, new-technology pitch-shifting software are sensitive to formant-shifting in order to enable us to perform more realistic correction of sung performances.

Chorus

Chorus effects are based on both pitch-shifting as well as time processing. This is somewhat similar to what occurs within an actual choir. You cannot possibly have two singers sing in unison producing exactly the same sound, in the exact same time. This is what the chorus effect is trying to simulate. This effect has been very successful with guitar and piano sounds.

Harmonization

Harmonizers are very similar to pitch-shifters. The difference is that harmonizers output the original recording mixed with additional voices as well. Such devices (or algorithms) can be programmed in different ways (e.g. number of additional voices, how many harmony parts, mix levels), but they can also be programmed to either work within a predefined chord or as dynamic harmonizers either triggered by real-time performers (e.g. using a MIDI keyboard or controller), or with a fluctuating harmonic envelope programmed in advance (for a live performance) or post hoc (during editing vocal performances on a computer).

Audio compression to reduce file size

Audio compression is a form of data compression designed to reduce the size of audio data files. As mentioned, audio compression should not be confused with the compression effect (part of dynamics processing). Streams of data (in our case digital audio-related data) are passed through audio compression algorithms that have been designed in order to render the original datasets into lighter (i.e. smaller) datasets. The two main categories of compression are lossless and lossy.

Lossless compression is perfectly reversible (i.e. where we can re-create the exact, unchanged, original dataset from the lighter, compressed one). *Lossy* compression happens where the original dataset (i.e. as it was exactly past A/D conversion) cannot be recreated. The most popular audio compression algorithm to date is the MP3 compression algorithm (also known as MPEG layer 3). What is important for the present discussion is that MP3 is a *lossy* compression format. This means that in order to reduce the file size information is removed that *cannot* be retrieved at a later stage. Known *lossless* compression formats are FLAC and Apple Lossless formats.

For *educators* and *practitioners*, as with earlier suggestions, it is important to safeguard the systematic approach to recording, capturing, editing, and storing audio recordings. Where there is no real logistical burden to employ lossy compression (e.g. a singing school that performs digital recordings of all taught sessions, in multiple rooms, and therefore needs a vast amount of digital storage), it would be advisable to archive recordings either uncompressed or, at the least, using a lossless compression algorithm. When compression is unavoidable, it is advisable to perform it at 128 kilobytes per second (Kbps) at the least. Kbps is the *compression rate*, which essentially determines the quality of the resulting compressed file, and it is either strongly or perfectly correlated to its final size. This will ensure that practitioners can listen to reference recordings and assess singing development longitudinally without experiencing problems and without audible artifacts in the digital files.

For *researchers* and *scientists*, again within scientific research and in tandem with a systematic approach, it is vital to ensure that the datasets are in their purest form and to maintain (and monitor) their integrity. Researchers therefore need to ensure that past the appropriate microphone, and the transparent microphone pre-amplifier, sits a high-quality, high-dynamic range A/D converter. It is important to note that not all A/D converters are built the same and therefore not all A/D converters perform conversion of the same quality. This is why the previously mentioned argument that "digital is good quality" is somewhat flawed, as conversion of an analog signal to a stream of digital information is not a deterministic task. Thus, professional recording studios have to perform major investments in their A/D (as well as D/A sections, see below). Past the A/D conversion, researchers should avoid data compression. Finally, the affordances that digital audio introduces and the opportunities for fast, sometimes instantaneous, processing of digital files, harbors the threat of mishandling of those files and the erratic monitoring of their different versions at different junctures. This was not a common threat when people had to utilize physical tape, the manipulation of which could almost certainly not occur on a whim. Within the digital domain, researchers and practitioners need to introduce strict systems on versioning, tagging, file naming, storing, and archiving in order to avoid the risk of losing their work, or jeopardizing the integrity of their data.

For *artists* and *producers*, regardless of the liberty to experiment with available technologies within the digital domain, it is also vital to be systematic to ensure that their work is safe, but also replicable. Most people have suffered the horror of lost work. Often, producers and artists achieve novel sonic products, but lose track of the different steps and processes involved in achieving a particular sound or effect; they are left unable to replicate the previous steps taken. Evolution and versioning in this context are beneficial, and useful principles from the field of computer science and software engineering could be adopted to prevent such roadblocks. While it has artistic value, it could also be valuable to safeguard intellectual property.

As explained earlier, within the digital domain all three groups deal with information. In order to perform any action within the digital domain, valid information is essential, but having any kind of information is actually vital. *Clipping* is one final notion of this complex world and is presented here in a somewhat naïve (accessible) way. Clipping occurs when the A/D converter is overloaded with a signal that would need to be converted to a numerical value greater than the converter could handle at a given setting. This, to some, might sound similar to the phenomenon of saturation, overdrive, and/or distortion that

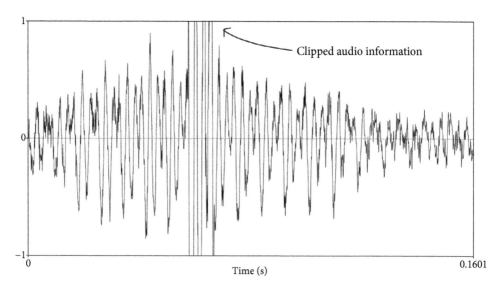

FIGURE 51.10 A waveform representation of digital audio data where clipping is visible.

one might experience with analog circuitry (which many people actually try to achieve intentionally in order to introduce character or warmth). Within the digital domain, however, this introduces unpleasant audible artifacts, and, unfortunately, complete loss of data past the clipping point. It is disheartening to witness researchers presenting sound waveform visualizations that show clipping artifacts (easily identified as straight horizontal lines at 0 dBFS) even within published research papers and/or presentation slides at conferences (Figure 51.10).

OUTTRO

Music technology is a continually evolving concept. Historically, having access to specific equipment could really make a difference, not only in the recording world but also in the production and composing worlds. The things that people could do in the old RCA studios, the innovatory techniques that the Beatles used for their albums, the music of Vangelis were—to a great extent—connected to the technologies that were available and at hand. When the *Chariots of Fire* soundtrack was produced in 1981, the places in the world that could be used for the production of the specific sounds that were used for the album could be counted on the fingers of one hand. Today, those sounds can be produced with a handful of free software plug-ins. Gaining the knowledge to be able to create those sounds and be able to put them together in a composition is a different process that results in a different art, craft, and science.

In the singing studio, having access to novel technology that allows real-time analyses of singing output and high-resolution digital recording of each lesson offers wonderful new opportunities. The effective use of the available technologies, however, is not self-evident. Similarly, in the world of research, novel tools allow us to perform complex analyses in real time; just two decades ago, some of these analyses could have taken months to complete. Analytical software can perform numerous analyses of complex datasets regardless of whether certain analyses are meaningful and/or in violation of basic scientific principles. This introduces new challenges for the practitioners, researchers, and digital natives that we are not necessarily fully equipped to deal with. This introduces the need for new, systematic educational praxes that are context sensitive and in line with what tools and affordances are now available. The future studio—be it recording, production, educational, or research—will almost certainly center on computers, with only the microphone as tangible equipment "outside the box." Future generations of recordists, producers, musicians, practitioners, researchers, scientists, and enthusiasts are likely to benefit from sound education in the systematic acquisition and handling, as well as the critical processing and assessment, of digital information.

REFERENCES

Berliner, E. (1887). *U.S. Patent No. 372786A*. Washington, DC: U.S. Patent and Trademark Office. Retrieved from; https://patents.google.com/patent/US372786A/en

Edison, T.A. (1878). *U.S. Patent No. 200521*. Washington, DC: U.S. Patent and Trademark Office. Retrieved from; https://patents.google.com/patent/US200521A/en

Everest, F.A. (2001). *The Master Handbook of Acoustics*, 4th edn. New York: McGraw-Hill.

Himonides, E. (2012). The misunderstanding of music-technology-education: A meta-perspective. In G. McPherson and G.F. Welch (eds.), *The Oxford Handbook of Music Education*, Vol. 2, pp. 433–456. New York: Oxford University Press.

Howard, D.M., and Angus, J. (2016). *Acoustics and Psychoacoustics*, 5th edn. New York: Routledge.

Malloch, S. and Trevarthen, C. (eds) (2010). *Communicative Musicality: Exploring the Basis of Human Companionship*. Oxford: Oxford University Press.

Mithen, S. (2006). *The Singing Neanderthals: The Origin of Music, Language, Mind and Body*. London: Phoenix.

O'Connor, R. (2018). Vinyl sales increased again in 2017. *Independent*. 3 January. [online]. Retrieved February 11, 2018, from http://www.independent.co.uk/arts-entertainment/music/news/vinyl-sales-2017-bpi-music-report-uk-industry-ed-sheeran-rag-n-bone-man-amy-winehouse-most-popular-a8140261.html

The Physics Classroom (n.d.). Retrieved February 10, 2018, from http://www.physicsclassroom.com/

Pro Audio (n.d.). SNAP! [Blog]. Available at: http://www.proaudioeurope.com

Švec, J.G., and Granqvist, S. (2010). Guidelines for selecting microphones for human voice production research. *American Journal of Speech-Language Pathology* 19(4): 356–368.

Welch, G.F. (2005a). Singing as communication. In: D. Miell, R. MacDonald, and D.J. Hargreaves (eds), *Musical Communication*, pp. 239–259. New York: Oxford University Press.

Welch, G.F. (2005b). We are musical. *International Journal of Music Education* 23(2): 117–120.

White, P. (2003). *Basic Microphones*. London: SMT.

....

CHAPTER 52

PRACTICAL VOICE ANALYSES AND THEIR APPLICATION IN THE STUDIO

....

GARYTH NAIR, DAVID M. HOWARD, AND GRAHAM F. WELCH

IN MEMORIAM

DURING the preparation of this chapter our colleague Garyth Nair passed away. The editors felt that we owed it to Garyth and his legacy in his work with his students to complete this chapter. Graham Welch kindly agreed to complete his sections. Garyth will be sorely missed within the voice pedagogy community. We present this chapter in his memory.

INTRODUCTION

Singing fulfills a basic human need in common expression, communication of ideas, and innermost thoughts and performance. Whether at a professional or amateur level, the desire to sing can be very strong in many people who are aware that gaining a measure of technical guidance will improve their vocal output, whether for karaoke, singing in a church or concert choir, barbershop singing, solo singing in the theater, operatic performance, singing in the local club, bar, or studio, recording vocal backing tracks, or singing with a jazz, pop, rock, or country band. In addition, the acquisition of some vocal skills through singing or speech coaching can also enhance vocal stamina and promote vocal health for those who use their voices regularly in daily life, including teachers, lecturers, politicians, interviewers, town criers, market traders, youth club leaders, scout and guide leaders, committee officers, driving instructors, and sports coaches. In practice, everyone can benefit from having some basic vocal knowledge in terms of keeping their voices healthy and being able to increase vocal functionality for everyday life.

Computers are now ubiquitous in everyday life and, as a consequence, there is growing interest, particularly amongst the younger generation of singers and teachers, in the potential use of computers in supporting the process of learning to sing. Today's multimedia desktop and laptop computers are quite capable of carrying out standard voice laboratory analysis routines in real time, and this means that it is now quite feasible to make use of such data in the singing studio as well as in the voice laboratory. Inexpensive software is available that has been written specifically for this purpose, along with various items of freeware that can be employed in this context with suitable background guidance. It should be noted that there is no computer system that can teach all necessary singing skills. This is likely to remain the case, since there are so many qualitative aspects relating to the process of developing a voice, including focused listening, as well as the guidance and experience of a professional singing pedagogue.

To date there is no computer program that can provide subjective listening, which by definition requires a human listener; moreover, the detailed processes involved are far from being understood. In addition, there is no computer program that can provide the detailed analysis with which each ear provides the brain, and again the detailed processes involved are far from being understood. Therefore, it is important to bear in mind that any computer program used in the context of singing training can only be a useful tool to be brought out as required during lessons or practice in the same way that a mirror might be employed, and that any use of a computer for improving singing technique should be under the guidance of a professional singing teacher with experience of such technology.

This chapter introduces the outputs from the main voice analysis techniques that are used to support singing pedagogy and have been shown to have practical application. In particular, the use and interpretation of real-time spectrography is presented in the context of its practical application in the singing studio.

ACOUSTIC ANALYSES FOR REAL-TIME VISUAL FEEDBACK

When considering the nature of a *real-time* output, it is important to bear in mind that theoretically there is no such thing. Any analysis requires a finite amount of time for it to be carried out and, therefore, it is not possible ever to provide an output contemporaneously with the input upon which it is based. The key to defining *real-time* in the context of visual displays is whether the actual processing time is noticeable by the user. If it is not, then the program can be said to be working in real-time, and this is the principle that should be applied when making "real-time" claims for a particular system. In practice, experience suggests that, providing the processing takes no longer than about a twentieth of a second, or 50 ms, a user will not perceive a delay between their vocal input and the appearance of the graphical on-screen output. In the case of voice analysis algorithms that are typically found to be useful in practice as visual displays in the singing studio, they can both operate and be rendered graphically on screen within this time and therefore they can be employed in a real-time display system.

In the context of singing, the following acoustic parameters have been found to be useful for examining, monitoring, and quantifying voice change with training (Howard et al. 2004; Nair 1999; Rossiter and Howard 1996; Thorpe et al. 1999):

- fundamental frequency, which relates directly to perceived musical pitch;
- spectrogram, which shows spectral variation of the vocal output over time;
- formant analysis, which tracks variation in the vocal tract resonances with time;
- spectrum, which relates to the nature of the vocal output and the perceived timbre at an instant;
- oral tract, which tracks changes in the vocal tract tube shape with time;
- side camera, which presents a side view of the upper back, shoulder, and head.

The processing techniques used for these measurements are beyond the scope for this chapter (more details can be found in Childers 2000; Gold and Morgan 2000; Howard 1998), but what is relevant here is consideration of the nature of each of the real-time outputs themselves and how to interpret them.

Fundamental frequency

The fundamental frequency (f_0) of a vocal output is the number of cycles per second completed by the vibrating vocal folds during a pitched sound and it has the unit *Hertz* or *Hz*. Since f_0 is always varying in a human sung output (we cannot produce a completely monotone output which would have a fixed number of cycles per second), f_0 can be measured on a cycle-by-cycle basis. There can be issues with f_0 measurements for singing; chiefly, this is because of the wide range of f_0 that can be found across singers from a low bass note (e.g. C2, whose f_0 is around 65 Hz) to high soprano notes (e.g. F6, whose f_0 is around 1,400 Hz), a total range of four octaves and a fourth. f_0 is usually plotted graphically on the Y axis against time on the X axis in a real-time display, as illustrated in the upper plot in Figure 52.1.

Spectrogram

To view how the nature of the acoustic output varies with time during the production, for example of sung lyrics, a plot of the frequency components against time, or a spectrogram, is used, which plots frequency on the vertical (Y) axis, time on the horizontal (X) axis, and the blackness of marking or the change in color indicating the energy at that frequency and time. It is worth noting that the use of a color spectrogram can lead to potentially misleading conclusions being made, since there will be places in the spectrogram where the color changes, say from yellow to orange. Such places stand out to the eye and can suggest that they are areas of significant acoustic change when in fact they are not; they just happen to be where there is a change in energy level, say from 60.1 dB to 60.2 dB. Unless calibrated, such a change does not mean anything significant; for example, it could be the result of a small

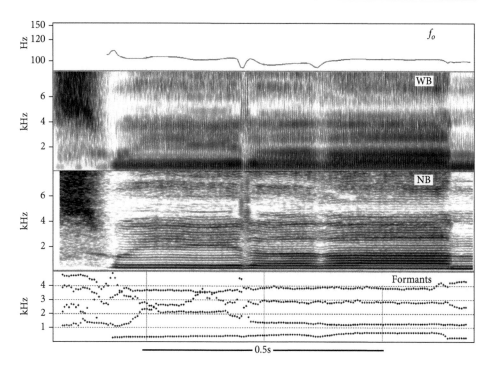

FIGURE 52.1 Displays of fundamental frequency (f_0), wide-band spectrogram (WB), narrow-band spectrogram (NB), and formants for *sweeter than* from "My Evaline" (Hall 1953, p. 118) first bass part as sung by an adult male.

change in lip to microphone distance. For this reason, the use of a gray scale or any other single color intensity variation is recommended in practice.

Types of spectrograms

Spectrograms are usually either wide band or narrow band, depending on whether one is interested in good time accuracy or frequency accuracy respectively (Howard and Murphy 2008, p. 15). Example wide- and narrow-band spectrograms are plotted in the second and third plots in Figure 52.1. Note that the main underlying detail for a pitched sound (one that has a clear note associated with it) is vertical lines, or *striations*, in wide-band spectrograms, and horizontal lines, or *harmonics*, on narrow-band spectrograms.

Each striation is the result of a single vocal fold closure, so changes in pitch would result in variation of the spacing between the striations (lower pitch when they are further apart and higher pitch when they are closer together). The harmonics are the individual frequency components in the sound and they are evenly spaced in a narrow-band spectrogram because the Y axis is plotted on a linear scale. Wide-band spectrograms show acoustic features accurately in time and narrow-band spectrograms show detail accurately in frequency. If, for example, one wants visual feedback on changes in fundamental frequency such as vibrato, then a narrow-band spectrogram would be most appropriate because the harmonics of the sound are shown. However, if one wanted to study rhythmic time onsets of consonants, a wide-band spectrogram would be most appropriate.

Formant analysis

A formant analysis plots frequency on the Y axis against time on the X axis; an example is shown in the lower plot of Figure 52.1. The formants relate to the vocal tract resonances, and different vowels have different formant frequencies due to their different vocal tract shapes (Howard and Murphy 2008, ch. 2). The frequency positions of the formants relative to one another in frequency enable listeners' vowel perception. As a singer varies articulation and hence the vocal tract shape, the formant frequencies change and therefore a display of formants against time indicates vocal tract shape changes.

Spectrum

The spectrum (an example is shown in the upper part of Figure 52.2) shows the energies of the frequency components that make up a sound at a chosen instant in time (frequency and energy are plotted on the X and Y axes respectively). If the sound is pitched, the key features on the spectrum will be individual frequency components, which are harmonics (integer multiples of f_o) whose energy levels will depend on the acoustic resonant properties of the vocal tract, which in turn depend on the vocal tract (pharynx, mouth, and nose) shape above the larynx. A spectrum is, in effect, a vertical slice through a spectrogram, showing the detailed nature of the frequency components of the acoustic signal graphically at a single instant in time. A long-term average spectrum (LTAS) is often used to study the differences between sounds, where an average of many spectra during the sound of interest is taken. By taking a long-term average, the main features of interest in the sound are enhanced since they are present all the time while any background noise, which is essentially a random process and so varies all the time, is reduced in level by the averaging process.

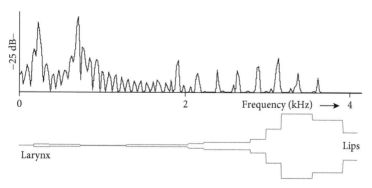

FIGURE 52.2 Narrow-band spectrum (upper) and associated oral tract area (lower) for the vowel as in *cat* spoken by an adult male from the WinSingad real-time visual feedback program (Howard et al. 2004).

Oral tract

The acoustic output changes primarily as a result of the shape of the oral tract (mouth) being altered during the production of sounds, and the area of the oral tract tube from the larynx to the lips can be plotted in real time. An example is shown in the lower plot of Figure 52.2 for the same sound for which the spectrum is plotted. Like the spectrum, an oral tract area plot is for a single instant in time, and such a display enables the nature of articulatory variation to be viewed while singing.

Side-view camera

An essential part of healthy and efficient singing relates to body posture and, while traditionally the use of a mirror is commonplace, it has the drawback that it only shows a front view. Generally there are no particular issues with left/right asymmetry; the priority is vertical alignment, which cannot be seen when viewed frontally. A side camera provides a useful addition to the front-view mirror, enabling the shape of the spine and the head-to-spine relationship to be seen directly by teacher and singer alike (Howard et al. 2004).

The role of the teacher

With any real-time visual display for voice development, it is important that the user understands what is expected of them in terms of what the display is showing and how that display relates to their vocal output. This aspect customarily needs to be considered in conjunction with feedback from a technologically sensitive professional singing teacher as part of a structured lesson; at present, there is no display system that can in itself teach someone to sing. A key reason for this is that it is often possible to achieve what is demanded in terms of changes to the screen plot in a particular display by making sounds that are inappropriate to singing performance and, at worst, unhealthy for the voice. Therefore, such displays should be used in consultation with a professional singing teacher, since the display itself is of a physical or *objective* visual metaphor of the acoustic reality; improvements in singing can only be judged "in the round" by human ears—a *subjective* measurement. Real-time displays will never replace a good singing teacher, but they can provide excellent additional supportive information that illustrates pedagogical points. Given that much singing pedagogy relies on metaphor to enhance awareness, having additional visual feedback that is systematic and consistent supports the singer's interpretation of the verbal guidance and feedback from the teacher.

What real-time displays can aid is speed of learning and progress during practice, leaving the teacher time to concentrate on more musical matters that no display can currently contribute to including: stagecraft, interpreting the score, understanding the words and how to tell the story, singing with an accompanist, and when to use different voice qualities.

THE CUSTOMARY PRACTICE OF VOCAL STUDY

The sounds emanating from a great singer are louder, more resonant, and have less co-articulation of consonants with vowels than that person's everyday speech. The sung sounds are produced with incredible consistency and display a phoneme-to-phoneme movement of enormous accuracy and speed. Contrary to the old adage, those great singers are not singing the way they speak—they have had massively to alter their speech habits to achieve the singing sounds that we admire. Additionally, each had to accomplish an extra-linguistic habituation in posture, breathing, pitch control, and vocal tract shape. Then, as performers on stage they add acting, stage movement, interpretation of the score, and the enormous mental and emotional demands of performing music night after night. It is miraculous that anyone can accomplish such a constellation of tasks, let alone at the high levels attained by our best artists.

The process of learning to sing well involves a massive retraining of phonemic production. This explains why it can take so long to educate a singer to such lofty levels. Much of what takes place in the voice studio is on a par with attempts to retrain a stroke victim to speak; singing requires serious neuromuscular reprogramming.

The voice pedagogue's primary habilitative technique has traditionally been a process of *example imitation*, where the teacher sings an *example* of the desired vocal behavior and the student attempts an *imitation* of it. This is followed by a trial and error process until the student can replicate the example to the teacher's satisfaction.

Any attempt to habituate neuromuscular behaviors, especially concerning a skill as complex as singing, must have at its core *accurate* knowledge of results or KR (Maas et al. 2008; Verdolini and Krebs 1999). Without accurate KR, the learner embarks on something of a hit-or-miss process. Thus, both teacher and student must strive to utilize the best KR possible. However, achieving accurate KR in the voice studio is no easy task, for there are two impediments to address when learning to sing, which make the seemingly simple task of converting speech habits exponentially more difficult to achieve. These are truth in hearing and speech template rules.

Truth in hearing

In terms of our hearing, we mostly hear our own voices internally within our skulls via bone conduction (see the chapter by Howard and Hunter in this volume). The sounds that we hear from our own voice are predominantly those conveyed from the vibrating vocal folds via the bones of our skull. Some acoustic output is also heard, but it is a predominantly bass-heavy version of our vocal output, as the treble part leaves the mouth in a directional manner essentially straight ahead while the bass part travels in all directions (e.g. Howard and Murphy 2008) with acoustic reflections from surfaces in the room (see the chapter by Jers in this volume).

The first experience of this external acoustic component for most people is when they hear their voice recorded and played back on a recording device. In most cases, the resulting sound is unexpected and usually not liked because of its unfamiliarity. This response gives some idea of just how skewed our internal perception is compared to the acoustic signal that actually leaves our mouth. Because this internal KR is limited, it can present a handicap when first learning to sing. Without accurate KR, it becomes much more difficult to alter neuromuscular behavior without an outside observer (usually a voice teacher) providing offsetting KR and KP (knowledge of performance).

Speech template rules

As if faulty aural perception were not enough, a second, equally powerful force interferes with the would-be singer's attempts: the speech template. Our speech template is an amalgam of the totality of the neuromuscular habits that we have assembled during a lifetime of speaking language. As small children, we begin acquiring speech by imitating the speech of those around us. A baby's babble is actually an intense trial and error process by which it learns to execute the building blocks of language, the phonemes. By the time the child acquires enough phonemes to begin to form words, their speech template is already a formidable neurological entity.

Later on, the first individual words, then phrases, then sentences appear; the speech template morphs into a very powerful set of neuromuscular instructions. When the child learns to express thoughts, they assemble the needed phonemic sequencing in *background neural processing*; they do not consciously have to do the assembly because the thoughts are there, ready to use.

A neural network powerful enough to construct complex thoughts in the background must be able to exert an equally powerful effect on the foreground processing when we attempt to sing. After all, because singing utilizes the same language building blocks as speech, the brain naturally wants to do much of the work in the background using speech norms. Thus, the phoneme set acquired and reinforced since birth routinely hijacks attempts to make suitable adaptions in order to sing well, at least in Western classical singing. Even though the singer tries to sing a word or even a single phoneme that duplicates a teacher's example, the speech template background processing intervenes and the attempt is often unacceptable to the teacher's ear.

These two problems (skewed internal hearing and deeply ingrained speech template) make the job of learning to sing difficult. Even when the teacher indicates that a sound is appropriate, these twin barriers can cause the singer subconsciously to doubt the teacher's judgment. In the case of the internal hearing skew, a teacher's indication that a sound is bright enough may be strongly countered by the singer's internal perception that the sound is not bright at all as a direct consequence of the ears being behind our mouth (see Hunter and Howard, this volume). As for speech template interference, a common occurrence in all voice studios concerns the presence of final consonants for words. The teacher might indicate that a final /t/ is needed, for example in the word "that," and the singer, making subconscious judgments based on their speech habits says, "But I sang it." The teacher heard almost no final /t/ that had any chance of matching the preceding vowel in terms of overall volume, and yet the singer may be convinced the /t/ was gloriously present. It is not that the singer necessarily doubts the teacher on a conscious level; it is the background processing that is interfering with the pedagogical process. Furthermore, the feedback from the teacher follows the singer's utterance, unfolding over time, and, in order to make sense of the instruction, the singer has to remember the nature of their own vocal product as well as the teacher's response.

Prior to the introduction of sound and video recording equipment in the second half of the twentieth century, voice teachers had only their own stated judgments with which to attempt to adjust the singer's perception of their own product. When recording technology was employed, while helpful, it had the same serious drawback that is inherent in the customary lesson model: the KR it offered was presented *after* the fact. The student could listen to the result of the habituation only after having sung and recorded it. What was needed was real-time biofeedback (more recently labeled as neurofeedback), something that could inform the singer's efforts immediately.

Today, one finds multitudinous examples of biofeedback being employed to habituate and rehabituate behavior in the practice of medicine. The critical principle germane to biofeedback is that it is delivered in real time. Thus, if one is trying to teach a patient to relax certain muscles, by observing a graphic, real-time display that shows the extent to which the muscles are tense, the patient has a viable KR with which to learn the required muscular control.

Because learning to sing well is also the habituation of muscular behavior, it stands to reason that real-time KR can be used in the pedagogical process to great benefit. Relatedly, with the increasing ubiquity of computers, singers and teachers now have such virtual real-time KR available. All one has to do is accept its validity in the process and march forward into the twenty-first century to explore its potential for learning.

This chapter reveals some of the principal kinds of biofeedback available via today's technology—biofeedback that can greatly accelerate the retraining of the phonemic production needed to sing well.

REAL-TIME VISUAL FEEDBACK IN THE VOICE STUDIO

Before delving into the subject of voice studio biofeedback any deeper, let us deal with a problem many have with the introduction of this technology to the voice studio: the *teacher's* possible subconscious fears of being replaced by the machine. The root of this assumption stems from a deep fear that the computer must be able to make normative *qualitative* decisions (such as making the decision that some vocal sound is good or bad, sufficient or not).

Nothing could be further from the truth, because virtual real-time spectrography simply presents a graphical display that shows the acoustic *quantitative* components present in the sound emanating from the singer. The program's algorithms are unable to make any qualitative judgments concerning the efficacy, *appropriateness*, or *contextual* use of those sounds. *All* of the qualitative determinations to be made must still be provided by a human being based on what they are *hearing* from the singer. After detecting a vocal problem, the teacher can look at the spectrogram on the monitor and use the results to illustrate or reinforce a point with the singer. In Robert Sataloff's words: "The best acoustic analyzers are still the human ear and brain" (Sataloff 1997, p. 756).

While the computer is particularly suited to ferret out and reveal minute quantitative detail, the place of that detail in the totality of the voice is still the province of the human mind.

To reinforce the point, a spectrogram of singer A's /i/ vowel may be rich in upper harmonics (see Figure 52.3, left), and listeners may perceive it to possess a marvelous blend between rich bottom resonance and the brilliance of the upper harmonics that can be so thrilling to an audience. By contrast, singer B may present an image that looks nominally the same (Figure 52.3, right). However, when we listen to the radiated sound that the spectrograph analyzed for singer B, we are startled to find that the tone is spread and harsh.

How can the two singers' spectrograms appear so similar visually but represent such disparate results to the listener? The reason is that those sounds are being produced by two different human bodies, bodies whose resonance chambers and even vocal fold cellular makeup may be minutely different; however, these differences may be enough to produce these different results. The totality of all of the acoustic elements at any given point in time is what we perceive as vocal timbre.

The precept that there must be an educated, informed, vocally experienced human being (normally the teacher) available to interpret what elements of the spectrogram are relevant or desirable (or not) for a *particular* singer sits at the core of our use of the spectrograph as biofeedback in the training of singers. As of the time of this writing, there are no known algorithmic formulae that can replicate the function of the human ear, something that in practice may never be realized.

A simple principle sits at the heart of the rationale for using this technology in the voice studio: *every* sound we make with the human vocal apparatus has its own unique acoustic signature. Because the spectrograph analyzes the singer's output and graphically presents it in real time, a singer's eyes can glean more objective KR (with copious guidance from the teacher) to balance any relatively inaccurate KR stemming from either their hearing skew and/or speech template interference.

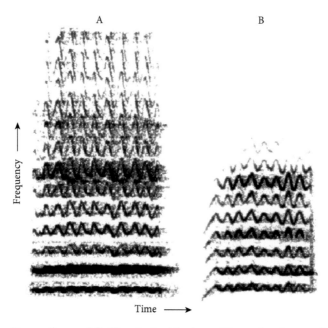

FIGURE 52.3 Singer A's vowel (left) paired with singer B's production on the same pitch, same vowel.

Figure 52.4 presents three different stop plosive /t/ consonants. Note that the display for each is somewhat different. As one can easily see (and hear), these are three entirely different variants of the same phoneme. The left /t/ is rich in harmonics and even shows strong formants resonating from the oral/pharyngeal cavities, typical of the resonant-rich production expected from a trained singer. The middle example represents a typical, jaw-high, speech /t/ in which much of the pharyngeal resonance of the instrument is missing. The /t/ on the right shows a significant loss of harmonics (i.e. carrying power) due to unwanted space in front of the tongue as well as concomitant tongue massing in the back of the mouth due to the singer's posterior point of articulation.

With the aid of spectrography, the teacher could model a desired /t/ and point out the elements in the graphic that make the consonant sound the way it should. As the singer attempts to imitate the production, the teacher can continue to call attention to the elements of the display relevant to the student's quest to find the proper physical configuration of their articulators. Such a visual adjunct offers a huge advantage: the student has a more objective display which shows the acoustic results of subtle vocal tract shape changes which can help the singer overcome both their skewed hearing and the speech template.

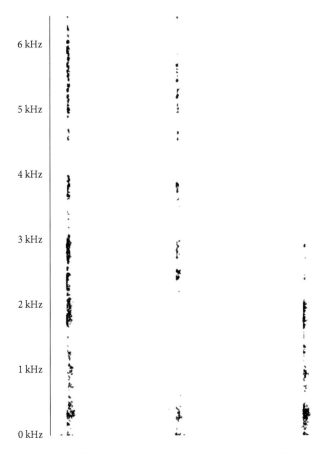

FIGURE 52.4 Spectrograms of three/t/s made by the same person: (left) a normal, resonant singer's sung /t/; (middle) /t/without the requisite resonance from an open oral/pharyngeal cavity; (right) /t/produced with the tongue placed far back in the mouth.

Let us now present a few more of the many ways in which spectrography can be a learning aid in the voice studio and can significantly accelerate a student's progress in the process.

Vibrato

In the classical singing community, a desirable vibrato (one that falls within communally agreed norms of rate and extent—the amount of pitch variation above and below the notated pitch) is a required quality in trained Western classical voices for both reasons of style and technique (Dejonkere et al. 1995; Sundberg 1987). One generally agreed upon factor is that vibrato is present when the extra-laryngeal muscles are adequately relaxed. Therefore, the presence or absence of vibrato can be utilized as a fairly accurate barometer of the state of muscular tension in and around the larynx.

Referring back to Figure 52.3, which shows spectrograms of sung /i/ vowels by two singers, it can be seen that, due to the regular undulations in frequency of the harmonics, these have been produced with vibrato. All the harmonics move "locked" together as integer (2, 3, 4, 5 . . .) multiples of the fundamental frequency.

Figure 52.5 shows a spectrogram for a soprano singing "The Lord of hosts" from *The Messiah*, and here she intentionally alters her production on the words "The" and "hosts." The result is a tell-tale, almost straight-line (constant frequency) of the harmonics for these two words, directly contrasting with the vibrato seen in the other two words of the phrase, "Lord" and "of."

If this were to occur in the voice studio, the teacher might try to facilitate greater (matching) freedom on those two words (e.g. the underlying causes might include issues with the execution of the initial "th" of "The" and the "h" of "hosts"). Once the singer learns to recognize the acoustic signature of sounds without vibrato, they learn to hear the appropriate subtle differences and should be able to self-correct most of the incidences of this type of production in either the voice studio or the practice room.

Scooping

Almost every singer in training scoops at one time or another (a scoop is beginning voicing slightly under the target pitch and then quickly sliding up to the required note).

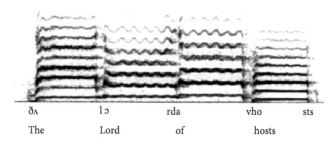

FIGURE 52.5 The phrase "The Lord of hosts" from Handel's *Messiah* where the singer alters her production on the first and last syllables.

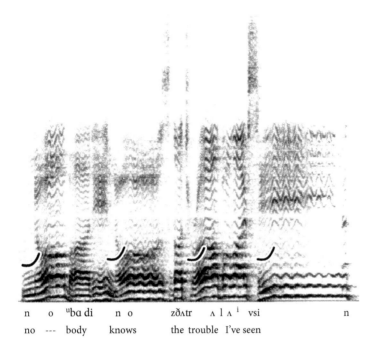

n   o   ᵘbɑ di   n o   zðʌtr   ʌ l ʌ ⁱ vsi   n

no --- body   knows   the trouble I've seen

FIGURE 52.6 The passage "Nobody knows the trouble I've seen" sung with scoops in the positions indicated graphically.

This behavior frequently occurs on consonants that are pitched (such as m, n, g, b) and often happens when the singer is trying to add emotion to the performance. Depending on the style and historical period, some judicious scooping may be perfectly acceptable. However, when scooping becomes an unconscious habit or a technical crutch, it morphs into a real and disturbing problem for the listener. Often, the singer is not consciously aware that they are scooping.

Figure 52.6 illustrates a singer scooping; note the tell-tale little upward driving slopes. Once a singer recognizes this visual signal and associates it with the vocal behavior, they become conscious of the problem and better equipped to banish the unwanted habit.

Slides versus vocal glissandi

Downward glissandi are considered to be part of the technique of any singer who sings Romantic opera. It is a way of making downward leaps less angular. Figure 52.7 reveals a singer performing an incorrect downward slide (left) and then a properly executed glissando (right). In the right-hand example, the male singer times the slide so that his vibrato gives the illusion that he is singing discrete half-steps on the way down.

Note the word "illusion" in the above sentence. If the singer actually tried to sing the constituent half-steps in this interval of a third, it would sound stilted and awkward. The operatic

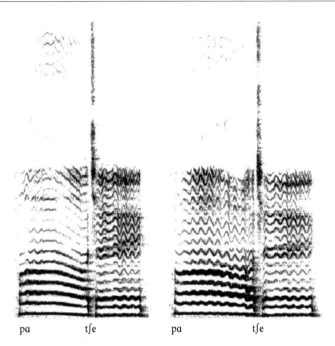

FIGURE 52.7 The word "pace" sung as a vocal slide (left), a singing glissando (right).

effect we know and love must be timed precisely with the singer's vibrato speed in order to be effective. The spectrograph is a wonderful aid in refining this skill.

Blooming tone

While some phonemes require a jaw-up position (e.g. /t/), most well-sung phonemes in Western classical singing are executed with the jaw in an optimally down position. Blooming occurs when an inexperienced or maltrained singer begins singing a sustained phoneme with the jaw in the up (speech) position and then quickly drops their jaw to more closely produce the resonance and openness of the classical model. The end result is a gradual development of the tone that the first author terms "blooming." No matter where it occurs in the sung line, blooming gives the illusion that the singer's tone is going in and out of focus. This can be a pervasive problem because the singer rarely actually achieves optimal resonance and openness.

Blooming is very easy to spot in the spectrographic display (Figure 52.8) because the upper harmonics gain intensity as the vowel progresses.

This problem indicates evidence of the pervasiveness of the speech template because this singer begins the /m/ utilizing speech norms and then, moving on to the vowel, modifies the production to gradually achieve the singing norm. In the properly produced sample on the right, notice that the harmonic structure of the vowel /e/ is instantly present upon releasing the /m/.

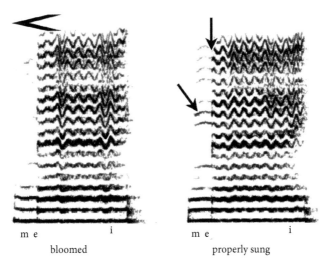

m e   i   m e   i
  bloomed   properly sung

FIGURE 52.8 The word "may" in which the singer "blooms" the primary vowel (/e/) of the diphthong (left), and then properly executes the word using singing norms throughout (right).

Presence of final consonants

Diction is another huge area where the spectrogram can reveal critical differences in vocal production in virtual real time. Here are just a few of the more obvious studio applications in this area. One of the most common issues in the voice studio, especially with beginning singers, concerns the production of final consonants. While a singer may sing a line beautifully, the final consonants of words are often perceptually absent.

Although a beginning singer may produce occasionally wonderful diction during a phrase, consonants (especially plosives) are routinely inadequate. This is because the singer's brain relies on the speech template for the myo-sequential instructions for these briefly occurring sounds. We sing most consonants at the same speed as they are spoken in everyday speech and so it is natural that the brain applies speech norms; it is easier to concentrate on singing norms in Western classical singing when sounds, like the vowels, are more sustained.

When this happens, the singer often fails to make final consonants clear. Consider the passage shown in Figure 52.9. Because of the way the music is notated by the composer, the vowels occupy the vast majority of the execution time. On the other hand, the consonants occur at *basically the same speed* as speech. The phonemes are:

As printed: Thus saith the Lord
IPA: ðʌs seᶦəə ðʌ lɔrd

The most predictable problem in this passage occurs on the final prevoiced stop plosive /d/. Most often, a beginning singer will fail to provide an adequate /d/ so that the passage will sound like /ðʌs seᶦəə ðʌ lɔr/ (see Figure 52.10). It is almost a given that, once having been coached into a proper /d/, the male singer will feel that he is over-exaggerating to an

Thus saith the Lord,

FIGURE 52.9 Score of the opening of recitative, "Thus saith the Lord" from Handel's *Messiah*.

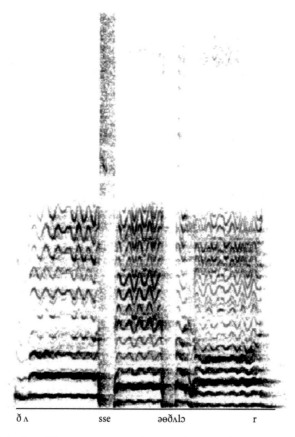

ð ʌ   sse   clʌʊəə   r

FIGURE 52.10 The Handel passage sung with an inadequate final *speech* /d/ at the end of the word "Lord."

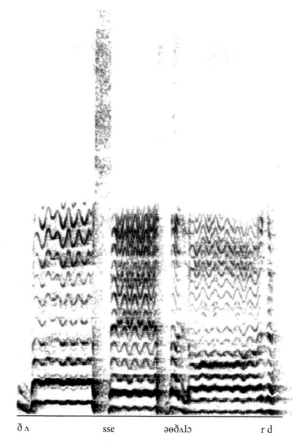

ð ʌ   sse   əəðʌlɔ   r d

FIGURE 52.11   The Handel passage sung with a final *singer's* /d/ at the end of the word "Lord."

extent that he may feel foolish. Meanwhile, the listeners will understand the text perfectly because the singer has produced a /d/ of sufficient power and resonance to match the rest of the phonemes in the passage. Voice teachers have been heard to muse that they might earn more if they charged for missing final consonants! When properly produced, that same singer's spectrogram would appear as it does in Figure 52.11.

The singer may be convinced by the teacher that his performance in Figure 52.11 is fine, but after seeing the difference on the monitor and hearing the result, it should be far easier to convince him of the efficacy of the requested production. Not only can the student instantly understand the difference from looking at the display on the monitor, the teacher can save the student's best effort as a file so the student can practice achieving that new standard.

Diphthongs

Almost every singer has trouble with diphthongs at one time or another. A diphthong consists of two contiguous vowels, one taking up approximately 90–95 percent of the execution time, and the other 5–10 percent. Figure 52.12 shows the common English word "may" (/meⁱ/).

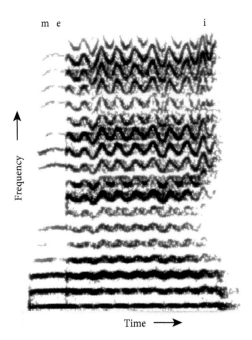

FIGURE 52.12 The English word "may" showing a clear distinction between the primary (/e/) and secondary vowel (/i/).

As the singer's tongue shifts from the /e/ to the /i/, one can clearly see evidence in the gradual shift of the strength of higher harmonics as the second formant rises as the tongue moves forward and higher in the oral cavity. Queries such as the identity of the constituent vowels and timing of the diphthong are more easily addressed with the visual evidence on the monitor. Even an Irish folk singer's love of reversing the timing of the diphthong /meɪ/ (where the /e/ lasts 5–10 percent of the total duration and the /i/ receives the remainder) is an easy concept to coach utilizing the visual technology should this idiomatic dialectal device be desired.

It is only natural for the speech habits present in one's native speech to become a hindrance during attempts to sing foreign languages. Such a common cross-contamination occurs between English and Italian and involves the phonemes /e/ and /o/. In Figure 52.12, we encountered the long /e/ of the word "may," and demonstrated how to recognize the diphthong on the spectrogram. In an Italian word such as "che," the primary vowel /e/ *must* be sung, not as the English diphthong (/eⁱ/), but as a solitary /e/. The same applies for the /o/ vowel, where in the Italian word "ora," the /o/ vowel must be sung, rather than the English diphthong /oᵘ/. A native English-speaking singer will generally unconsciously resort to their speech template and improperly convert "che" (/ke/) to a very un-idiomatic /keⁱ/. Thus, the passage, "Che faro senza Euridice" will sound as /keⁱ faroᵘ sɛnza ʲʊriditʃeⁱ/ instead of the proper Italian /ke faro senza ʲʊriditʃe/.

Look at Figure 52.12 and notice the evidence of the little "tail" of rising intensity in higher harmonics that indicates the tongue movement from the primary vowel /e/ to the secondary /i/, caused by the higher second formant found in /i/. In Figure 52.13, the spectrogram easily reveals the presence of these improper diphthongs in the sung Italian passage

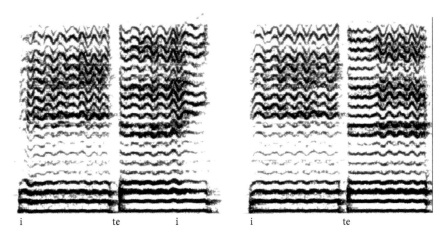

FIGURE 52.13 An Italian passage sung with improper English diphthongs (left) and with the proper Italian diction (right).

(left) and then shows the correct idiomatic Italian diction (right). Singers can quickly learn to recognize the acoustic signature of this problem, which can then put them on the way to solving it whether in the voice studio or in the practice rooms.

Insertion of nasals at the beginning of prevoiced stops

A subtler diction problem often occurs when singers improperly produce the muffled phonemes that begin all prevoiced stops (/b/, /d/, /g/, and /dʒ/). A proper prevoicing is made by totally blocking all exit points in the mouth and nose and then voicing on pitch. Figure 52.14

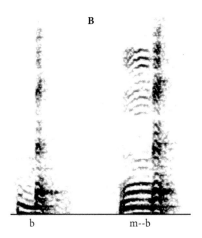

FIGURE 52.14 The prevoiced stop /b/(left) showing the short prevoicing (on pitch) that precedes the plosive release for the consonant to be contrasted with the inserted bilabial nasal (/m/) prior to the /b/(right).

Table 52.1 Prevoiced stops and the homorganic nasal consonants that singers often attempt to substitute for the proper prevoicing

Prevoiced stop	In IPA	Prevoicing homorganic with
b	/b/	/m/
d	/d/	/n/
g	/g/	/ŋ/
j	/dʒ/	/n/

shows properly produced prevoicing for /b/ (left) contrasted with an inserted bilabial nasal (/m/) prior to the /b/ (right).

It is important to note that, with all air pressure escape routes blocked, the vocal folds can vibrate for only a very short time before the airstream can no longer move and the sound ceases. Just before this muffled vocalization stops, the brain command releases the built up pressure as the plosive component of /b/ (with its concomitant pitch overlay from that brief vocalization).

At some point, many singers consciously or unconsciously discover that the total closures that are the hallmark of the prevoicing for these phonemes are all homorganic (produced with the oral articulators in the same position) with the nasal consonants /m n ŋ/ (see Table 52.1). Because the nasal consonants are (1) easier to produce, (2) sound richer and louder to the singer internally, and (3) are easier to time in the production of the phoneme, the temptation to use these unwanted substitutions is almost inevitable. Figure 52.15 shows these consonant in pairs; each pair is sung with the proper prevoicing on the left and the improper nasal on the right.

Listeners easily detect the improper substitutions and reject the artifice. Using the spectrogram, once a singer learns the visual difference on the monitor and associates the image

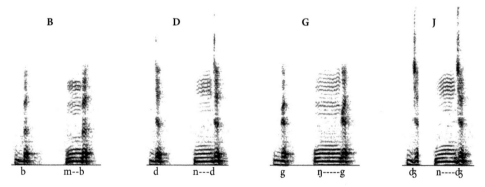

FIGURE 52.15 The set of prevoiced stops performed in pairs showing the proper prevoicing on the left and the improper substitution of the accompanying nasals on the right of each pair.

with the vocal behavior, he or she will be well on the way to hearing the difference and producing the sung language more idiomatically.

SUMMARY AND CONCLUSIONS

The availability of real-time visual displays resulting from the acoustic analysis of the vocal output on standard home multimedia computers has led to their application as a tool in the singing studio (Howard et al. 2007). A number of possible displays exist, but one of the most useful is the spectrogram since it provides a display that is based on the nature of the output to the brain from the peripheral hearing system. Any interpretation based on the spectrogram is, therefore, likely to be directly related to the manner in which we perceive the sound.

The practical examples that have been given represent only a minute sample of what can be seen on the spectrogram during a voice lesson or practice session. Teachers and students new to spectrographic analysis may exclaim initially that the display scrolling across the screen is too complex and alien for them to understand and apply. However, if they sit down with a microphone and play with their own voice while watching the analyzed results appear in real time on the screen, they will quickly begin to correlate their own anatomical-physiological processes with the display. As they play with their articulators, they can quickly get a sense of how the technology can be used. This playtime is recommended *prior* to the singer or teacher tackling the suggested reading found at the end of this chapter.

A veteran voice teacher with many years experience once scoffed at the idea of using spectrography in the voice studio. After much effort, she was convinced just to try out the technology with her own voice and, three hours later, exclaimed that she had learned more about how the voice worked during that short time than in all of her years of study. This technology provides singers with a vast resource that so easily reveals the psychoacoustics of the voice.

REFERENCES

Childers, D.G. (2000). *Speech Processing and Synthesis Toolbox*. New York: Wiley.

Dejonkere, P.H., Hirano, M., and Sundberg, J. (1995). *Vibrato*. San Diego: Singular Publishing Group.

Gold, B. and Morgan, N. (2000). *Speech and Audio Signal Processing*. New York: Wiley.

Hall, A.E. (1953). My Evaline. In: *Songs of Yale*. New York: G. Schirmer, dist. Hal Leonard.

Howard, D.M. (1998). Equipment for measuring voice: uses and limitations. In: T. Harris, S. Harris, J.S. Rubin, and D.M. Howard (eds), *The Voice Clinic Handbook*. London: Whurr Publishers.

Howard, D.M., Welch, G.F., Brereton, J., Himonides, E., DeCosta, M., et al. (2004). WinSingad: a real-time display for the singing studio. *Logopedics Phoniatrics Vocology* 29(3): 135–144.

Howard, D.M., Brereton, J., Welch, G.F., Himonides, E., DeCosta, M., et al. (2007). Are real-time displays of benefit in the singing studio? An exploratory study. *Journal of Voice* 21(1): 20–34.

Howard, D.M. and Murphy, D.T. (2008). *Voice Science Acoustics and Recording*. San Diego: Plural Press.

Maas, E., Robin, D.A., Austermann Hula, S., Freedman, S.E., Wulf, G., et al. (2008). Principles of motor learning in treatment of motor speech disorders. *American Journal of Speech-Language Pathology* 17: 277–298.

Nair, G. (1999). *Voice—Tradition and Technology: A State-of-the-Art Studio*. San Diego: Singular Publishing Group.

Rossiter, D. and Howard, D.M. (1996). ALBERT: a real-time visual feedback computer tool for professional vocal development. *Journal of Voice* 10(4): 321–336.

Sataloff, R.T. (1997). *Professional Voice: The Science and Art of Clinical Care*. San Diego: Singular Publishing Group.

Thorpe, C.W., Callaghan, J., and Doorn, J.V. (1999). Visual feedback of acoustic voice features for the teaching of singing. *Australian Voice* 5: 32–39.

Verdolini, K. and Krebs, D.E. (1999). Some considerations on the science of special challenges in voice training. In: G. Nair (ed.), *Voice Tradition and Technology: A State-of-the-Art Studio*. San Diego: Singular.

Additional resources

Bunch, M. (1995). *Dynamics of the Singing Voice*. Vienna: Springer Verlag.

Callaghan, J. and Wilson, P. (2004). *How to Sing and See: Singing Pedagogy in the Digital Era*. Surry Hills, AUS: Cantare Systems.

Chapman, J. (2006). *Singing and Teaching Singing: A Holistic Approach to Classical Voice*. San Diego: Plural Press.

Doscher, B.M. (1994). *The Functional Unity of the Singing Voice*. Metuchen, NJ: Scarecrow Press.

McCoy, S. (2012). *Your Voice: An Inside View*, 2nd edn. Delaware, OH: Inside View Press.

Miller, R. (1996). *The Structure of Singing*. New York: Schirmer.

Miller, D.G. (2008). *Resonance in Singing: Voice Building Through Acoustic Feedback*. Princeton, NJ: Inside View Press.

Sundberg, J. (1987). *The Science of the Singing Voice*. Evanston, IL: Northern Illinois University Press.

Websites

Sing and See: http://www.singandsee.com, accessed October 15, 2017.

Voce Vista: http://www.vocevista.com, accessed October 15, 2017.

KTH: http://www.speech.kth.se/software, accessed October 15, 2017.

CHAPTER 53

FUTURE PERSPECTIVES

PETER PABON, DAVID M. HOWARD, STEN TERNSTRÖM, MALTE KOB, AND GERHARD ECKEL

INTRODUCTION

THE purpose behind this "future perspectives" chapter is to provide a look at activities in hand that could greatly affect future ways of interacting with each other vocally as well as musically. These activities include vocal masterclasses at a distance, furthering understanding of the acoustics of the singing voice in the future with reference to what is known about the hearing system, creating electronic voices, and, last but not least, changing the acoustics of spaces for rehearsal and performance. Research in voice is an ongoing activity in a number of laboratories around the world. This chapter is a snapshot of just some of the key activities in progress, presented to give a flavor of some important areas under investigation at present. The chances are that all or some of these will impact on practical voice performance in the future, whether in terms of voice analysis or new ways of performing vocally.

The specific areas selected for presentation are not exhaustive but are reckoned to provide a cross-section of interesting work that has the potential to become more mainstream in the foreseeable future. They are: the Voice Range Profile and its use for voice assessment; hearing modeling spectrography for voice analysis; electronic voice synthesis techniques; 3D printed vocal tracts; teaching in a masterclass situation at a distance; the use of virtual acoustics for singers, and the place of the voice in music composition.

VOICE RANGE PROFILE-BASED VOICE QUALITY FEEDBACK

Peter Pabon

The Voice Range Profile (VRP) is a graph of the intensity range of the voice as a function of its fundamental frequency (f_o). The representation is generally used with clinical voice assessment (Pabon 1991). In singing, the VRP is used as a means to quantify the voice classification and to document and monitor the effects of singing voice training. Modern automated VRP recording systems can augment the VRP area with additional parameters relating to voice quality, and these offer unique feedback possibilities for the singer as well as navigation options that are especially relevant and useful for voice training in practice. This section focuses on uses of the VRP, and employs a case study as a means of presentation.

It will be evident from earlier chapters that much is known about the spectrum and waveform properties relating to the acoustic nature of the singing voice. However, interactively using a real-time spectrum analyzer or waveform display to simultaneously match a perceived aspect of voice quality can prove to be far from simple. Consider for example the idea of monitoring of the spectrum around 3 kHz to estimate the strength of the singer's formant cluster (see also the chapter by Sundberg on the acoustics of different genres in this volume). Especially singers of classical genre consider this singer's formant a desired property of their voice. Its presence is seen as a sign of a proper singing technique, where a strong acoustical power is radiated without forcing the voice. As this acoustical power appears in a relatively unexcited or unoccupied part of the spectrum range, it adds to the presence of the voice (Sundberg 1987). The current scientific model explains the singer's formant structure to be the result of a formant clustering process, where it should be said that this is a rather patchy model. In this section the phenomenon is approached in a more pragmatic manner.

When a real-time spectrum display is reviewed while singing, it will not be difficult to spot a peak in the region around 3 kHz. But is this truly the singer's formant structure? In practice, the observed spectral shape will seldom match the textbook example. Curiously, it is also rather difficult not to obtain a spectrum shape that already roughly approximates a singer's formant silhouette. The real problem is false positives; how to decide if the observed spectrum shape actually matches the essential properties of the singer's formant? These properties seem evident or straightforward, but actually there is no accurate criterion. Our idea on what a singer's formant should look like stems from an archetypical shape that is regularly observed with classically trained male voices. When these males sing loud, their voice spectra typically show a single undifferentiated spectrum peak around 3 kHz that is now called the singer's formant. The high power associated with this spectrum bulge often exceeds the level boost that could be expected to result from a single formant. Science found an answer to this incongruity by explaining this singer's formant structure to result from a clustering of several formants.

This explanatory model implies that by a proper vocal-tract articulation the right amount of clustering can be reached to obtain the anticipated boost. What this proper articulatory setting is, how the vocal tract should be adjusted, and how the articulatory setting can be maintained under largely varying dynamic conditions, science does not have a clear answer for. It is cleverly considered to be the domain of the singer or singing teacher.

The clustering model would also imply that there is a particular vocal tract adjustment that, in theory, anyone could approximate to produce a singer's formant. It is debatable if this is actually true. Moreover, it is questionable to what degree the notion of a continuous controllable articulatory adjustment is applicable. The suddenness by which the singer's formant generally introduces itself, or may vanish, presents an argument to treat the attribute more as a voice state, or mode, that has a status comparable to that of a register mechanism. Some voices have this distinct attribute more than others; some voices acquire more of it by training. Some voices always had it; some voices cannot sing without it. Many singers and teachers have their own account of it, but still on the short run one thing stays: at a certain moment the voice has it or not. There just seems no gradual emergence or any precise vowel tuning connected with the phenomenon.

Given this unpredictable, state-like behavior and knowing that a concise or definite spectral detection criterion is missing, is it still wise to advise a real-time spectrum display as a visual feedback instrument to train for a singer's formant quality? What to instruct if there is actually no clear articulatory directive that will make the alleged clustering emerge before our eyes?

Despite all knowledge and experience that an experienced spectrum reader may have acquired, any connection of the observed spectrum shape with the singer's formant quality will always be subjective. A machine that objectively measures a singer's formant metric will not simply perform better at this task. The underlying problem is that the characteristic spectrum features that express the presence of the singer's formant are likely to transform or reshape when the pitch, the level, the vowel, or the register changes. A dedicated metric would need a continuous rescaling and adaptation to compensate for these changes in context, something that our perception naturally deals with.

The just sketched problematic is not exclusively seen with the singer's formant only. The expression of voice quality in general is highly conditional on the dynamic context! Without some dynamic reference all aspects we measure may drift, float, or submerge in this sea of change. To truly judge if there is an improvement on a certain quality aspect, we need a reference. Thus, one of the most important prerequisites with interactive training using visual feedback is to have means to narrow in, to precondition, or in some way "freeze" the dynamic setting.

The VRP

The VRP offers a framework that is dynamically sharp and reproducible. It has two absolute coordinates, f_o and intensity (Sound Pressure Level or SPL), and these are the two main dimensions over which most voice quality aspects expose their major dependencies. With an ordering along these two scales, the majority of parameter variation is accounted for and largely narrowed down. Moreover, a parameter linked to a VRP inherits a powerful attribute: dynamic reproducibility

Figure 53.1 shows the VRP recording of a trained female singer. The horizontal scale gives the f_o either logarithmically in Hz (lower X axis) or in semitones (upper X axis). The vertical scale gives voice intensity as Sound Pressure Level (SPL). The objective with a VRP recording is to detect for each sung tone in the singer's range the minimum SPL and the maximum SPL that can be produced. It is standard practice that only the vowel /a/ is sustained during a VRP recording. The recording system measures f_o and SPL in real time and provides visual feedback of their instantaneous values via an on-screen pointer. The singer can directly monitor the VRP area as it builds up and thus freely explore the dynamic extent of the voice interactively. In addition, the total time spent at each specific cell in the VRP plane is measured as "phonation density" (see the legend). Those cells where the tone was sustained longer or visited more often will thus be plotted towards the red end of the scale. The jagged contour marks the outline or VRP contour that encloses the overall area where phonation can be sustained. Inside this contour there may be open (blank) areas that the singer very likely could also cover, but they simply were not tested for. The jagged contour along the lower margin of the plot outlines the SPL level where a voice sound could just be detected, even if it was for a very short moment. Just above the lower margin in Figure 53.1, there is a red zone with increased density

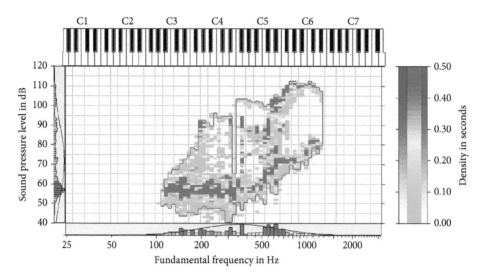

FIGURE 53.1   VRP for a trained female singer.

that reflects where the voice stalled during the dynamic search process for the threshold. The slanted red band from D5/100 dB SPL to E6/110 dB SPL indicates that for this high part of the pitch range the loudest extremes were also well explored, but for the lower part of the frequency range (B2 to C5), this search for the loudest extremes was not very thorough. Only at G3/90 dB SPL was more time spent. The rushing in this test was for a specific reason as there was a hidden agenda with the VRP recording of the female singer shown above.

In addition to the measurement of the f_o and the SPL, the recording system also calculates and stores the average spectrum for each cell in the VRP. Thus, by inspecting the spectrum areas around 3 kHz it is possible to spot the presence of the singer's formant for any cell in the VRP. At the moment of the recording, the singer was in her opinion not mastering this specific quality and she was very motivated to discover if her voice "had it." The abstraction used to quantify the presence of the singer's formant is a measure of the energy in the band from 2 to 5 kHz (a wide zone around the 3 kHz target area) that is compared to the total energy level. In Figure 53.2, the legend indicates a red color whenever the level in the 3 kHz band went above –12 dB compared to the overall energy. Note that this energy balancing parameter is a relatively blunt measure; it takes no account of the bandwidth or sharpness of the singer's formant structure. Therefore pressed voice for example, or adding some twang could increase the overall high frequency energy and this could lead to a false (but still useful) suggestion of a raised singer's formant structure.

The color coding in the VRP in Figure 53.2 reported that only in a narrow horizontal zone at around 88 dB SPL that ranges from F4 to B4 did the singer reach a relatively high value in the 2 to 5 kHz band. Figure 53.3 shows a typical spectrum sample taken from one of the cells in this zone. Note that there is a steep downward sloping to a notch just before 4 kHz, but the expected clustering to a single pronounced singer's formant peak is however not very convincing.

If only a sharply peaked cluster was searched for, the above spectrum sample would have been disregarded. However, in this case such a selective strategy would have been

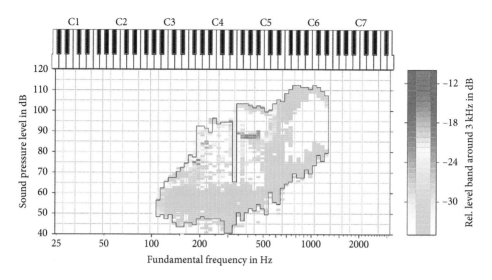

FIGURE 53.2 VRP for the same female singer's data shown in Figure 53.1 showing the dB level in the 3 kHz band compared to the overall level of the spectrum (color scaling shown).

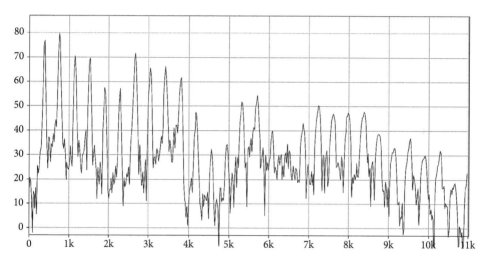

FIGURE 53.3 The average spectrum that was stored in the cell at G4 (392 Hz) and 88 dB SPL in the middle of the red stripe seen in Figure 53.2.

unfavorable, as both singer and instructor claimed to have noticed the desired singer's formant sound quality right at the spot. It is not unthinkable that the current scientific conception of the clustering as distinctive property needs revision, as an overall raised level around 3 kHz with a steep cut-off by a deep notch seems to be enough to determine the production and perception of the singer's formant. As long as this issue is not settled, we are better off with a more blunt, open metric.

The singer in this case study was eager to attain an explicit singer's formant quality and considered it not a regular attribute of her voice. A new recording session was started with the specific aim to enhance the singer's formant level. Instead of using a spectrum analyzer, a real-time color mapping of the above parameter was used. This kind of interactive use of the VRP recording system for voice training remains a relatively new phenomenon in singing voice training. It is however much more common in clinical settings. There, the typical approach is to use the real time visual feedback to navigate to a quality optimum detected earlier. From such a starting point small alterations in f_o and SPL are instructed. A core voice quality can thus be ported to neighboring pitch and level settings and the range of the optimum is thus expanded on.

The singer in this example followed the same rationale. Starting from the designated zone around G3/88 dB SPL that showed an initial trace of this quality (see Figure 53.2), the singer managed to rapidly extend on the enhanced singer's formant area, as acknowledged by the larger, red-colored area that is projected on top of the initial VRP (see Figure 53.4).

The actual exploratory process that went on during this interactive recording session is best characterized as a focus switching between monitoring the red color emerging in the the VRP target area, listening, and a proprioceptive awareness of the articulation, this all while at the same time gradually adjusting the settings. Once on hold, she was able to establish singer's formant qualities with an even more pronounced timbre and higher relative level in the 2 to 5 kHz band, as is for instance seen in the spectrum sample (see Figure 53.5) that was selected from one of the deep red-colored cells in Figure 53.4. Surprisingly and frustratingly, this was all accomplished without any direct clue of the precise articulatory factor she was gaining control on.

Changes in singing voice quality or in vocal behavior are seldom gradual. They begin accidentally, with sudden insights and small discoveries of a certain core quality. After the first acknowledgment, such an event is generally accompanied by uncertainties of its

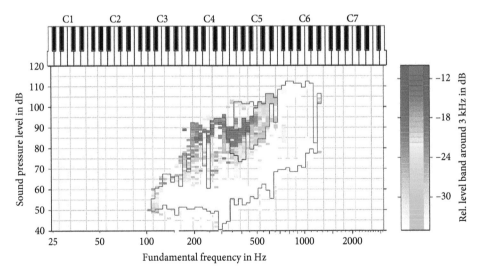

FIGURE 53.4 Markings of an exploratory session where the singer used the interactive visual feedback of the VRP recording system to improve on her energy in the singer's formant region. For initial targeting the result of the initial VRP recording session (see Figure 53.2) was projected at the background using a white-to-blue color mapping.

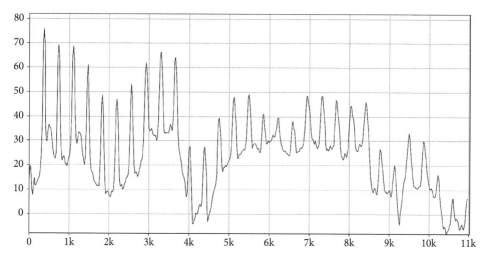

FIGURE 53.5 The average spectrum stored in the cell at E4 (329 Hz) 83 dB SPL in the VRP of Figure 53.4.

appearance, and the desire to have clues that will guarantee again reaching the same setting. The recording system will always assure that any new established acoustic alternatives will instantly leave their imprint on the displayed VRP. The direct visual feedback within the VRP space offers a look-up and trace-back possibility, to return to the dynamic conditions that previously worked to express a certain quality. Voice change is primarily established through the ears. Still, any voice change has a better chance to persist and to be understood and also valued when it is confirmed by visual proof.

HEARING MODELING SPECTROGRAPHY

David M. Howard

When analyzing the acoustic output from the singing voice, the most commonly used display is the spectrogram. Traditionally spectrograms are either wide band or narrowband, which refers to the bandwidth of the equivalent band pass filter used in the analysis of the acoustic pressure waveform captured with a microphone. The terms "wide" and "narrow" in this context refer to whether the analysis filter bandwidth is greater (wider) or smaller (narrower) than the fundamental frequency (f_o) of the sound being analyzed. Traditionally, the filter bandwidths used in wide- and narrow-band spectrographic analysis are set to 300 Hz and 45 Hz respectively. The wide-band spectrogram provides "good" time response, with its structure being based on vertical lines or striations, while the narrow-band spectrogram provides "good" frequency response, with its main structure being based on horizontal lines or harmonics when analyzing periodic sounds (Baken and Orlikoff 1990; Howard and Murphy 2008). Therefore the choice of spectrogram for a particular situation would usually be based on the nature of the acoustic features of interest in terms of whether the need is for accurate time or frequency estimates.

In the context of analyzing the output from the singing voice, the range of f_o that is covered when analyzing the singing voice will usually extend well above 300 Hz which is around D4 (the D above middle C). All singers, except possibly very low second basses, will frequently be singing notes above D4. For such notes the use of a traditional wide-band spectrogram will not result in "good" time response since the filter's bandwidth will be smaller than the f_o, resulting in a spectrogram that will exhibit the characteristics of a narrow-band output albeit with limited frequency resolution due to the wide analysis bandwidth. One possible remedy would be to widen further the bandwidth of the analysis filter, but this cannot usefully be done to any great extent in practice because the formants become merged together as frequency definition is lost.

This is illustrated in the plot A of Figure 53.6 which shows a wide-band spectrogram for the phrase *sweeter than the honey* sung by an adult male as the second bass part of "My Evaline" (Bartholomew 1953, p. 118) starting on G#3 (207 Hz). As expected, the wide-band

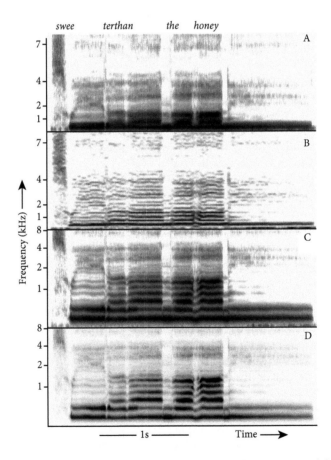

FIGURE 53.6 Wide-band (A), narrow-band (B), standard hearing modeling (C), and sone-based hearing modeling (D) spectrograms for the words *sweeter than the honey* sung by an adult male as second bass from the four-part male voice song "My Evaline" starting on G#3 (207 Hz).

spectrogram (plot A) exhibits essentially vertical structure (striations) because the f_o is less than 300 Hz (but it should be noted that this is often not the case when analyzing singing). Plot B in the figure shows the narrow-band spectrogram, which consists of horizontal lines (in this case these are harmonics since the sound is periodic).

The traditional spectrogram was originally designed to provide a graphical illustration that approximates to the sort of frequency analysis that each ear provides to the brain of the listener. However, there is an important difference between the implementation of the traditional wide- and narrow-band spectrograms and the way in which the ear analyzes incoming sounds. The basilar membrane in the cochlea of each ear carries out a frequency analysis of the incoming sound based on its mechanical properties, and this process is usually thought of in terms of a bank of band pass filters (Moore 2003). The bandwidths of the individual filters vary as a function of their center frequencies, becoming wider as the center frequency increases. This characteristic is measured in practice as the "equivalent rectangular bandwidth" or "ERB" (Glasberg and Moore 1990), and it rises from around 35 Hz for a filter centered at 100 Hz to around 1 kHz for a filter centered at 10 kHz. Thus the time and frequency resolution in a hearing modeling spectrogram varies with frequency.

As a consequence, the output from a spectrogram that is based upon hearing modeling will exhibit the characteristics of a narrow-band filter at low frequencies (harmonics for periodic sounds) and those of a wide-band filter at high frequencies (striations). This is illustrated in plots C and D in figure 53.6, which show hearing modeling spectrograms for the words *sweeter than the honey* sung by an adult male as second bass from the four-part male voice song "My Evaline" starting on G#3 (207 Hz). There are a number of features exhibited by a hearing modeling spectrogram that distinguish it from a wide- or a narrow-band spectrogram, including the following (based on Howard 2005).

1. Traditional spectrograms usually make use of linear axes while that of a hearing modeling spectrogram is based on the ERB scale, which is approximately logarithmic above 1 kHz and linear below 1 kHz. This gives the lower formants more prominence in the plot while fricatives take up less space, which is in keeping with their relative importance perceptually.

2. The plot is a mixture of harmonics towards the low frequency end and striations towards high frequencies thus encompassing the key features of both traditional spectrograms. This reinforces the basic feature of the human hearing system that it has good frequency resolution at low frequencies and good time resolution at high frequencies.

3. No matter what the f_o of a periodic sound being analyzed, the lowest five to seven harmonics will be isolated separately, showing up as harmonic structure on the spectrogram (e.g. Howard and Angus 2009). Higher harmonics are not resolved and therefore the underlying structure is striated. For singing, where the f_o is commonly greater than 300 Hz, the hearing modeling spectrogram is always useful while the wide band ceases to be very informative when f_o is above about 300 Hz.

4. The effect of the sone scaling of the amplitudes, which plots them in accordance with the ear's equal loudness curves, can be observed in plot D in Figure 53.6. This demonstrates how the ear hears the sound and it can be seen that one effect is to enhance the singer's formant (Sundberg 1987) cluster with respect to the other components.

VOICE SYNTHESIS

Sten Ternström

Synthesizing the human voice in an illusory way is notoriously difficult. After decades of intensive research, a general speech or singing synthesis of illusory quality remains to be achieved. This is simply because it is so hard to model in sufficient detail the intricate physics of the voice, where acoustic waves are generated by the interaction of motions of elastic solids, liquids, and air. Although we consider here only the sound-producing mechanism, it should be understood that synthesis from scratch of natural speech or song would also require models of auditory perception and memory, so as to incorporate feedback and learning. Our voice apparatus is intimately controlled by the brain, itself perhaps the most complex object/agent known to science.

Nevertheless, modeling the human voice through synthesis is an indispensable tool for research, with numerous promising applications in voice pedagogy, composition, music production, voice prostheses, robotics, and virtual environments such as games. There are currently three main approaches which are used for both speech and song: source-filter synthesis, concatenative synthesis, and articulatory synthesis. These are illustrated in Figures 53.7, 53.8, and 53.9. In the near future, direct physics-based modeling will probably become more common, as computing power continues to fall in price.

Principles

The human voice can be machine imitated in a variety of ways. The first useable electronic voices were based on the so-called source-filter theory of voice production (Fant 1960).

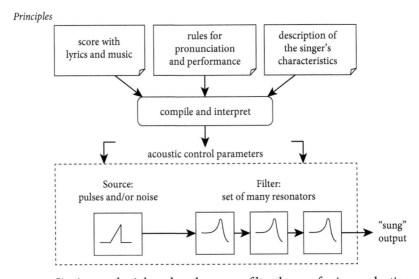

FIGURE 53.7 Singing synthesis based on the source-filter theory of voice production.

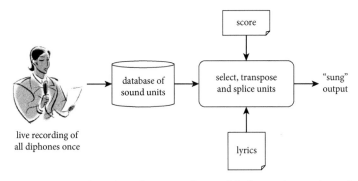

FIGURE 53.8 Singing synthesis based on recordings of diphones (or triphones).

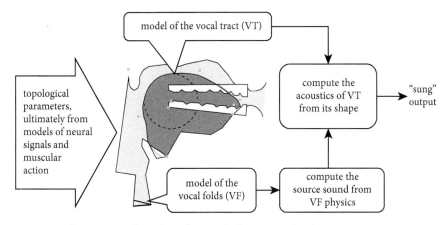

FIGURE 53.9 Singing synthesis based on articulatory synthesis.

Adapted from Birkholz's VocalTractLab.

These were *terminal analogues* that model only the signal emerging from the mouth (the "terminal"), and not the way in which the human voice actually produces those sounds. While source-filter or formant synthesizers can readily produce a useful range of convincing vowel sounds, it is difficult to mimic articulatory gestures and transitions, particularly those for consonants, using a mechanism that is ignorant of human physiology.

As computing power became cheaper in the 1990s, more natural-sounding speech was devised using machine *concatenation* of pre-recorded voice sounds. This method, it can be argued, is not really synthesis, but rather a very sophisticated jukebox for short units such as diphones or triphones that encompass the sensitive transitions between sounds. With considerable ingenuity, concatenative synthesis has been refined to a point where it is currently the prevalent approach. A few such systems for singing are available (e.g. Yamaha Vocaloid). Further, systems have been demonstrated that generate a form of singing by transforming a recorded spoken lyric to follow a musical score (such as Japanese Interspeech), the idea being that even non-singers might thus produce a passable rendition of a song. While pitch and timbre can be modified to some extent, such methods are inherently rigid, in that they require human voices to pre-record every required combination of sounds.

The term *articulatory synthesis* refers to approaches that do account for the shape and position of the speaker's or singer's articulators. This information can be used to control a conventional formant synthesizer, or to control various forms of direct physical simulation of how sound is generated by the glottis and shaped by the vocal tract. In order to represent a useful range of human vocal expression, reams of biomechanical and phonetic data must be acquired and systematized. Such measurements are cumbersome to make, which makes articulatory synthesis a challenging approach.

In the 2010s, commercial speech synthesis has made remarkable strides toward usability, driven by the huge data volumes that are available to the dominating infotech companies, and by new methods in machine learning. After marathons of automatic training, some large so-called neural networks are capable of generating speech audio output directly from an input text. The mechanisms for this are opaquely self-organized in "black box" algorithms, and offer little in the way of explanations. Nevertheless, the future perspective of similar techniques applied to the singing voice is rapidly becoming clearer.

Synthesis in Research

When any synthesis of vocal sounds is initially attempted, some things are bound to sound less than perfect. Still, these failures, when properly understood, will point the researcher in the direction of a more refined theoretical analysis. In singing research, such *analysis by synthesis* is a popular paradigm. Once a model is devised that can synthesize convincingly some core aspect of singing voice, over an appropriate range of conditions, then it is likely that the analysis underlying the model is valid and represents accurate knowledge. An advantage of this paradigm is that it tends to focus the research effort on the perceptually most obvious deficiencies of the research model, which leads to an efficient iterative refinement.

The human voice is hugely variable, not only between singers, but also even in the same singer, from one day to the next. Therefore, it is a challenge to perform experiments using live singers with closely controlled factors, especially if subtle effects are to be explored. Here, synthesis is an invaluable tool, when it can be made realistic enough to be appropriate for the scientific question at hand. For instance, a terminal analog synthesizer is very useful for isolating and reproducing consistently the audible effects of changes in signal properties, such as formant frequencies or fundamental frequency contours. On its own, however, it does not help us to explain how such changes are achieved by the singer. A simulation based more directly on the physics of the human body would have a greater explanatory power in relating the produced sound to, say, lung pressure, larynx height, vocal fold adduction, or tongue position—in other words, things over which the singer can exert some conscious control. Here we may expect future systems soon to become more and more ambitious, thereby narrowing the "gap of understanding" between what goes on at the physical level and what is happening at the level of musical performance and expression.

A special case of research is the work being done by composers and performers seeking new forms of artistic expression through what are often very creative variants of voice synthesis (see the section below on composition).

Applications

Commercial Music Production

The instrumental sounds in the music of shopping malls, elevators, film soundtracks, and much of rock and pop today are mostly generated using synthesizers controlled by software. To keep costs down, the material is often produced by just one or two studio musicians, even if on casual listening it may sound like a full orchestra. Recently, even backing vocals such as *oooh* and *doo-daah* are appearing, that have been rendered using voice sampling. Still, the lead vocals remain very much alive. Today's tools are not yet expressive enough to be cost-effective for controlling all the desirable aspects of a song with verbal and emotional content. Curiously, around the turn of the millennium, there emerged a pop music esthetic for roboticized vocals, using pitching devices based on the vocoder.

Singing Pedagogy

Computer simulations with acoustic output can be used to illustrate aspects of voice production that are difficult to verbalize. For example, the interaction of formants and partial tones can be clarified using a source-filter synthesizer with a graphical display of the partial frequencies, overlaid by the formant frequencies (such as Madde). A more sophisticated example could be a direct physics simulation of how the vowel timbre is modified by small changes in vocal tract shape, or of how the vibration of the vocal folds is affected by the laryngeal posturing. If a sufficiently expressive synthesis were available, it could also be used by the teacher to illustrate issues of *musical rendition* in a controlled, reproducible manner.

Virtual Environments

The burgeoning computer games industry has led the technology for creating realistic video. It is now gradually turning to audio, and ultimately will address also simulated voices. Real-time voice synthesis would enable an even more responsive and naturally interactive environment between gamers and simulated characters, so perhaps the resources for developing illusory voice synthesis will come from these quarters. Virtual acoustics have already been used in research concerning vocal ensemble performance. For example, all voices (synthetic or recorded), except that of a live subject, may be synthesized and presented in a virtual acoustic environment, complete with artificial reverberation (see also the section by Kob in this chapter), thus providing a choral situation over which the experimenter has complete control.

3D Printed Vocal Tracts

David M. Howard

Achieving a clear picture of the internal structure of the vocal tract and how it changes during speech or singing is a basic requirement for understanding its acoustic properties.

In particular, it provides a basis for understanding which acoustic properties relate to the differences between the underlying sounds of the language concerned and which relate to variations between individual speakers or singers. The former provide the listener with the message (*intelligibility*) and the latter with speaker characteristics and identity (*naturalness*). Such knowledge informs attempts to synthesize human speech or singing that is not only highly intelligible (today's synthesis systems achieve this quite effectively), but also very natural sounding (today's synthesis systems rarely if ever achieve this).

As part of ongoing research into improving the naturalness of singing and speech synthesis, the technique being used is a three dimensional (3D) digital waveguide mesh (Speed et al. 2014). Vocal tract shapes for specific spoken and sung vowels and consonants are measured in 3D using magnetic resonance imaging (MRI) of human subjects, and from these, the 3D shape of the airway can be recovered. At present, these do not include the teeth since they are invisible to MRI, and the overall accuracy of the 3D shapes recovered depend on the subject's ability to remain still for the 16 seconds required to take the images as a sound is sustained. The availability of 3D printing has facilitated the production of 3D printed replicas of the oral cavity for various vowel sounds to be produced, and these provide a basis for enhancing understanding of the internal shapes of the throat and mouth to be explored in a tactile and visible manner. In addition, a suitable loudspeaker drive unit has been found. The 3D printed tracts are terminated at the glottis with a coupling collar that mates with the loudspeaker (Adastra 952.210). Doing so enables an electronic sound source to be input to the 3D tracts so that their output sounds can be heard. Figure 53.10 shows 3D printed tracts for the vowels /i:/ (left) and /a:/ (right) sitting atop their loudspeakers. Noting that there is some similarity between the printed tracts and the pipes of a pipe organ, the author has implemented a new prototype musical instrument based on the 3D printed tracts of various vowels, which is called the *Vocal Tract Organ* (Howard 2015, 2017).

The 3D printed vocal tract sits on a loudspeaker that is driven with an appropriate sound source for voiced speech or singing; the acoustic excitation provided by the vibrating vocal folds. The LF model (Fant et al. 1985) is employed, in keeping with what is done in other synthesis systems, and it is implemented using Pure data or Pd (Puckette 2007), which is a freeware music programming environment. Pd includes the standard MIDI (musical instrument digital interface) that enables musical controllers such as keyboards to be connected; this is basic to the operation of the Vocal Tract Organ. An additional advantage is that waveforms to be synthesized can be set up as hand-drawn wavetables, and this works very effectively for the LF model (Howard et al. 2013). When synthesizing speech or singing, the fundamental frequency is controllable as appropriate to either the intonation patterns of speech or the notes of the sung music, and for a sung output, there is an option to add vibrato with variable rate and depth. Depending on the application, Pd allows these parameters to be controlled either via on-screen sliders, by prestored time-organized values in a Pd file, or via real-time performance standard or purpose-built MIDI controllers. For example, the Vocal Tract Organ makes use of a MIDI keyboard, while joysticks have been implemented via an Arduino microcomputer to control fundamental frequency and overall volume (joystick 1) and vibrato rate and depth (joystick 2). The latter provides a basis for demonstrating the principles of the function of the sound source in singing in an interactive manner as well as a virtual singer performance instrument.

The availability of 3D printed vocal tracts provides an engaging and practical way to demonstrate the different vocal tract shapes involved in speech and singing, both visually to

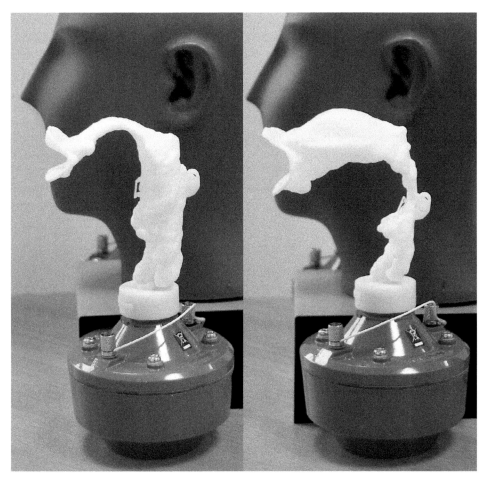

FIGURE 53.10 3D printed vocal tracts for the vowels /iː/ (left) and /aː/ (right) for an adult male sitting atop Adastra (952.210) loudspeakers.

highlight shape variation between vowels and how the articulators function, and acoustically to hear the differences. Singing teachers and those teaching phonetics are able to show actual shapes of tracts for different spoken or sung sounds to give students an appreciation of how the tongue in particular is used to articulate the different sounds of language. In addition, the ability to hear the output from the 3D tracts means that a full appreciation of the overall effects of tract shape changes can be gained while providing a clear indication of what changes are needed to produce different sounds. Because the shape of the vocal tract is far from being a simple tube, especially close to the larynx end, an appreciation of some of the complexity of the detailed tract shape can be gained through reference to the 3D models. For example, the piriform sinuses can be clearly seen and the variation in their shapes can be appreciated by comparing 3D tracts for different vowels. This can be discussed with regard to their acoustic properties through the introduction of acoustic zeroes around 4 to 4.5 kHz (Delvaux and Howard 2014). In addition, the fact that the two piriform sinuses are usually of different volumes can also be readily appreciated with reference to the 3D models.

The use of 3D printing for creating models of the vocal tract provides a new way to show the nature of the various shapes of tract used in different spoken and sung sounds, and placing the tract on a suitable loudspeaker enables the acoustic output to be heard. The pedagogical advantage offered by being able to bring the vocal tract shape "out into the open" is huge. Clearly 3D printed tracts are static models and the human vocal tract is a dynamic system. Trials with flexible 3D printed tracts have so far not been successful in terms of the acoustic output, and anyway true volume changes cannot be realized simply by squeezing a flexible tract since tract muscular changes will vary the shape by changing wall circumference, a task which cannot be achieved readily with a flexible-walled model. A way to overcome this might well be found in the future, but in the meantime, the Vocal Tract Organ is a new musical instrument that brings vocalise to the keyboard player on the musical stage.

MASTERCLASS TEACHING AT A DISTANCE

Research Center for Opera and Technology KTH Stockholm

Introduction

In the education of singers of opera and classical music the masterclass concept is an important element. During a masterclass session an experienced singer, in many cases a renowned artist, observes, instructs, and coaches a student, usually with other students as an audience. The interaction between teacher and student is close and intense and may address all levels of singing performance, from posture, breathing, tone formation and sound projection, to phrasing and interpretation. The interaction includes numerous kinds of hands-on feedback from the teacher, who demonstrates by singing, "conducting" the student's singing, physically correcting body posture, and checking breathing function and muscular tensions. Ideally, the masterclass session makes a lasting impact on the student's development.

However, there is a flip-side. Masterclass teaching is an expensive form of training and difficult to organize efficiently. Qualified singers with developed pedagogical talents are scarce, heavily booked, and constantly traveling. Ambitious students often have to travel a considerable distance to attend, and meetings with famous teachers are often infrequent and irregular. Further, a single masterclass session is far from sufficient in order to enable the student to profit from the teacher's feedback and views on performance technique and musical interpretation. In all, masterclass instruction may well result in being an isolated one-shot performance shift experience of rather limited value rather than an opportunity for learning, one which barely complements regular teaching at the home conservatory.

The idea of using state-of-the-art electronic communication technologies for allowing more masterclass sessions with the same teacher to the same group of students, or offering a wider circle of students access to qualified teaching is an appealing alternative. However, serious doubts may be raised in relation to masterclass teaching at a distance. Will it be possible to maintain the close communication, interaction, and sense of presence required for emotionally intense instruction when the student and teacher are not in the same room? The answer is, rather surprisingly, yes! Proof-of-concept experiments (see the section below) show that masterclass teaching at a distance can involve good student–teacher interaction. A situation can be foreseen where masterclasses with teachers greatly in demand are made available to students at various locations around the world without incurring time-consuming and expensive travel and accommodation needs for teacher and students.

Proof-of-Concept Experiments

Experiments with masterclass teaching at a distance have been run between students and teachers at the University College of Opera in Stockholm and the Sibelius Academy in Helsinki. In the first experiment, the audio quality was varied in order to assess how technical quality affected the interaction. The communication was based on the state-of-the-art video concept using a large semi-transparent mirror with camera and presentation screen, which allows the student and teacher to see each other in natural half-length portrait size and with direct eye contact. In addition, a full-length view of the student in profile allowed the teacher to observe body posture. Two students and one teacher participated and a panel of professional singing teachers evaluated the teaching situation. In the experiment, actual distance was simulated by connecting two separate and non-adjacent rooms in the same building with a two-way video and audio connection (e.g. see Figure 53.11) in order to allow a comparison with a normal masterclass situation with teacher and student face to face.

FIGURE 53.11 Practical interaction situation.

Scores on questions on the ability of the teacher to assess the physical performance (posture, facial expressions, breathing, tensions, etc.) received scores only one unit below the face-to-face condition on a six-point scale. Similar scores were obtained for the questions "To what extent do you experience emotional contact and intimacy between teacher and student?" and "How well does the pedagogical situation work out?" Surprisingly, the audio quality appeared to be of little importance. Even telephone transmission quality (300–3000 Hz) and headphone listening gave no major changes in scores.

Comments made by participants included: "After a while, you completely forget that the student is inside a box" (panel); "There were moments when I actually felt like being in the same room as the teacher." He "stepped out of the box" (student); "In a certain sense the contact becomes more intense in a mediated situation since matters that could be expressed physically in a non-mediated situation will have to be formulated in words" (panel); "The communication between teacher and student is much better than could be expected. As a complement to actual meetings, this is very valuable" (participating student); "the technology is quite acceptable and useful as a complement to—but not a replacement for—live interaction" (teacher).

With the encouragement of these results, a second step was taken. The dependence on the teacher's and student's personalities for an efficient and emotional intense interaction at a distance was studied in a full-scale experiment between Stockholm and Helsinki. In particular, the importance of the teacher's ability to be "there beside you," although actually at a distance, was studied. The experiment involved four teachers and eight students almost equally distributed between Stockholm and Helsinki. An expert panel at each location, consisting of ten experienced singing teachers and advanced students, made observations and answered questionnaires. In about half of the teacher–student combinations, this distance-teaching session was their first contact. The teachers were very different in terms of their approaches, their involvement with the student during performance, and the type of feedback they provided.

The same technology as before was used but with a slight reduction in video quality due to the transmission over regular internet (semi-HD video quality, 2 x 27 Mbit/s, up to 30 ms latency). Pianists were present at both locations in order to circumvent synchronization problems caused by latency in transmission.

The results were very satisfying in this experiment as well. Questions on how the teaching situation worked out, the contact between teacher and student, and the quality of picture received scores around 5 on a six-point scale. In this experiment there was no face-to-face case with which to compare. The panel members observed (and teachers confirmed afterwards) that the teachers adapted their teaching somewhat because of the latency in transmission. For example, "conducting" when the student was singing was problematic. However, the teachers did not report that they were severely hindered by this technical constraint.

The critical question to the panels "Would you be willing to participate in this form of distance teaching on a regular basis?" received very positive answers (89 percent of 144 responses). The remaining answers were more negative due to the specific combination of teacher and student.

The students did not experience that the physical distance from the teacher was a major hindrance in the teaching situation. As one soprano student put it: "It was an intimate situation. I experienced a good contact with the teacher almost as if we had been together at the same location in Finland, a feeling of that she was close to me. I got the impression of singing in a large room with good acoustics."

Panels and teachers emphasized that this teaching situation worked very well, particularly for more experienced students who have established a sound basic singing technique. The main limitation is that the teacher and student have no physical contact, so the teacher cannot feel and correct breathing, posture, and tension. Some teachers expressed a concern about their ability to judge how the voice carried in a large hall. All involved did stress that distance teaching should be used as a complement to traditional face-to-face sessions, not as a replacement. A representative comment was: "A very good and exciting complement to my traditional teaching." A highly promising observation was that the differences between the teachers' personalities and ways of teaching were not reflected in the results. This suggests that successful distance teaching is not limited to a small group of teachers with exceptionally charismatic talents.

Conclusions

In conclusion, the results of the proof-of-concept experiments clearly indicate that masterclass teaching at a distance using video communication over a normal Internet channel may work well. A high-definition close-up image with eye-to-eye contact, supported by a full-length image in profile, and in combination with a stereo sound of consumer electronics quality is sufficient for an efficient masterclass education. The technology is also capable of creating a sense of emotional contact and intimacy between teacher and student. Audio quality plays only a limited role in the evaluation of the student's vocal performance and the creation of the emotional intensity of the learning situation.

Almost all teachers and students who have been involved in these experiments see great potential in introducing distance-teaching technology, including being able to widen the circle of students who can get access to high-quality teachers; students receiving guidance from more teachers and on a more regular basis; and reduced travel time and costs from the points of view of economy and sustainability. Students were particularly positive.

Finally, masterclass-at-a-distance sessions should not replace the traditional face-to-face sessions. They are a complement providing more intense teaching on a regular basis. It is suggested that teacher and student need to meet after five to eight distance sessions in order to maintain a close personal contact.

VIRTUAL ACOUSTICS

Malte Kob

The singing voice is characterized by several domains of acoustics. Voice is initiated by the generation of sound waves in the larynx as a fluid-dynamical process which generates self-sustained oscillations of the vocal folds. These vibrations are controlled by boundary conditions such as muscular tensions and laryngeal geometry (Titze 1994). The sound wave propagates through the vocal and nasal tracts. The acoustics of small rooms can be applied to characterize the filter effect of these tracts in terms of vocal tract modes or formants (Baken and Orlikoff 1990; Fant 1970). The radiation of the singer into the surrounding room is an example of room acoustics, which extends to the psychoacoustic interaction of the singer with his or her reflected voice and the sounds from other musicians (Kob 2002).

Attempts to mimic the human voice by mechanical or numerical models are motivated by two wishes: on the one hand, models are used to validate and illustrate theories of physical principles of voice production; alternatively, the other idea would be the synthesis of voice signals for practical applications such as text-to-speech (TTS) systems or sounds for music. Examples would be automatic translation or navigation systems or the voice sounds of synthesizers.

Mechanical Voice Models

An early attempt to create synthetic voice signals was the speaking machine of Ritter von Kempelen. This device could produce realistic-sounding simple words using a bellow as lungs, a reed pipe as glottis, and a flexible leather tube as vocal tract (von Kempelen 1791; DailyMotion 2017). MRI and electroacoustic technology allow for more realistic models realized using rapid prototyping technology (see Fujita & Honda 2005; YouTube 2007 and section "3D Printed Vocal Tracts" in this chapter). Recent models of the vocal folds are produced in 1:1 scale and are used for investigation of fluid dynamic processes (Farley & Thomson 2011).

Numerical Voice Models

Thanks to the availability of fast computers, the simulation of voice acoustics is feasible at several stages. First models that could produce realistic vocal fold area functions were built by Ishisaka and Flanagan (Ishizaka and Flanagan 1972), Brad Story and Ingo Titze (Titze 1973; Story and Titze 1995). Extensions to the concept of the discrete mass model approach for more specialized and/or accurate simulations including voice pathologies and singing voice registers were developed (Erath et al. 2013; Kob 2002; Tokuda et al. 2010). For modeling of the vocal tract function the classical approach is the wave-guide method that is based upon a concept of Kelly and Lochbaum (1962). The concept uses segmented vocal tract area functions for the calculation of plane waves that travel back and forth due to reflections and transmissions at the transitions between the segments. More recent approaches such as the TLM method (El-Masri et al. 1998; Maeda 1982) take into account the effect of lateral extensions of the vocal tract that can have a significant impact on the vocal tract transfer function above 4 kHz, which is important for the quality of the singing voice. The combination of more oscillating systems such as the ventricular folds or focalization of vocal tract resonances can be used to synthesize under- and overtone singing (Fuks 1999; Kob 2004).

Concatenative Voice Synthesis

The most successful method of singing voice synthesis makes use of the sophisticated combination of small voice signal samples—so-called phonemes—that have been pre-recorded for a huge number of different singing styles and text fragments. The concept has been successfully adapted to a number of text-to-speech applications such as navigation systems or automatic call-answering machines. For a synthetic voice track the appropriate phonemes need to be assembled according to the textual and musical context of the score. The result of such a synthesis system can be surprisingly good.

Virtual Room Acoustics—Auralization

When a virtual voice signal has been created a major task still remains. The radiation of the signal into space and the effect of room acoustics on the voice signal provide the engulfment of the listener. The realism of voice synthesis essentially depends on the quality of such acoustic immersion. Successful approaches make use of mirror-source and ray-tracing methods and binaural auralization using headphones or loudspeakers (Vorländer 2008, Pelzer 2014).

Currently, most singing voice synthesis methods are either limited in voice quality, musical applicability, or real-time processing. It may be expected that each of these aspects will improve with increased knowledge about the acoustic nature of singing voice production (Kob et al. 2011).

THE VOICE IN COMPUTER MUSIC COMPOSITION

Gerhard Eckel

Music composition may be understood as the task of conceiving sound capable of evoking sonic identities.[1] In this sense, composing also means negotiating the conditions under which sonic identities may emerge in the imagination of the listener. This negotiation is a complex process constrained by cultural conventions, individual experience, the human senses, and the instruments of sound production implied or applied. This section concentrates on the latter two aspects, perception and sound production, and argues how and why the human voice, understood as a particular system of constraints, is of importance for computer music composition.

As human beings we are all equipped with a unique sound source, which serves as our main means of expression and communication. This sound source can be understood as the most embodied[2] form of sound production available to musicians. Unlike musical instruments, the connection of the human body and the sound production mechanism is as direct as it can be since the vocal organs form an integral part of the body. As opposed to the voice, a musical instrument can be thought of as an inanimate sound production device. The human body may extend into an instrument in a way similar to how it extends into a tool (Merleau-Ponty 1945). But this extension comes at the expense of requiring a mechanical

---

[1] Sonic identities are imaginary entities that may be recognized consistently as units in a context. They are the objects a particular music is made of and can virtually take any form that may emerge from the perception of sound.

[2] Embodiment is understood here as the extension of the human body into an artifact. Being part of the body, the voice can, strictly speaking, not be subject to embodiment. Speaking of it as embodied makes sense only when looking at it as an instrument (Benade 1976, chapter 19) for the sake of comparison.

mediation of the player's motion with the instrument's sound production mechanism, nec-essarily resulting in a reduced degree of possible embodiment. Although most musical instruments are modeled after the human voice in one way or another, trying to overcome some of the voice's limitations, they cannot reach the same degree of embodiment as the voice. This has been a basic condition of music-making for millennia.

With the advent of new media technology (such as electro-acoustic transducers, analog/digital converters, signal processing, and computer modeling), new possibilities of conceiving sound and making music arose. Nowadays, sound can be modeled math-ematically and dealt with in a non-mechanical form as an analog or digital signal. This has liberated music composition from the constraints imposed by traditional musical instruments and their performance. It has also allowed for a part of the above-mentioned mediation process to become subject to modeling and thus musical composition (Magnusson 2010). Digital synthesis can be employed to produce sounds with the least imaginable degree of embodiment, an option realized by so-called "non-standard syn-thesis" (Döbereiner 2011). Composers, performers, and their audience are nowadays confronted with the full extent of achievable degrees of embodiment in music making, which ranges from sound production without any significant bodily intervention, such as algorithmically controlled digital sound synthesis, to the human voice, the instrument embedded in our body.

Aspects of embodiment in sound production are highly relevant for music-making be-cause human perception is specialized in detecting and tracking traces of embodied inter-action, traces of the body in the sound (Peters 2012). Just as we are able to tell with stunning accuracy which inanimate objects are involved in a physically produced sound, we are able to sense the minutest details of human agency shaping sound production using mechano-acoustical or digital instruments. This is another basic condition of music-making, which, as we will see, needs special consideration in computer music composition.

In order to illustrate the potential role of the voice in computer music, it is useful to con-ceive of composition as a modeling process (Eckel 2012) targeted at evoking sonic identities. The production of such identities in enactive perceptual processes is based on exploiting traces of constraints constituent of the sound model, constraints that are crucial in shaping the sound. Such constraints result in perceptual invariants typically exploited by our senses in perceptual processes. In order for a sonic identity to emerge, usually many constraints have to be operative in a sound model. Hence composition can be understood as modeling systems of constraints, as the targeted sonic entities cannot be modeled directly.

From an artistic point of view, no restrictions should apply with respect to the constraints to be modeled. But it is a fact that the constraints introduced by physics and through human physiology and behavior are especially relevant to human perception. It is in this respect that the voice is of central interest as a system of constraints highly rel-evant for human auditory perception, which is assumed to be specially adapted to voice sounds. An important particularity of voice sounds is that we are able to reproduce or imi-tate what we hear, which also illustrates the embodiment aspect in perception. As the body extends into the instrument when producing a sound, the listener extends into the sound when experiencing it (Peters 2012). Also here we can assume that the reachable level of embodiment is highest with voice sounds, as they are so familiar to us that we can embody them best.

Taking the voice as a model for composing systems of constraints does not necessarily mean aiming at composing voice sounds, but rather at evoking sonic identities with voice-like qualities. The voice is an interesting object of study if we want to understand and explore the difference between sonic entities emerging from sounds that are shaped through human agency, i.e. bodily movement, and others that are not. Research questions related to this problem are a perfect example of an interdisciplinary approach combining artistic and scientific research, bearing a rich potential for cross-fertilization. Also here an *analysis-by-synthesis* approach is very promising—for the same reasons pointed out in the section in this chapter by Ternström on "Voice Synthesis." Composers need to understand how meaningful systems of constraints can be established and voice scientists are currently attempting to establish voice models based more directly on the physics of the human body in order to overcome the limitations of existing approaches, especially with respect to their explanatory value. Making explicit a part of the tacit behavioral knowledge that we all have of our voice and which allows us to speak and sing will enable composers to enter new domains of sound synthesis control. Experimenting with systems of constraints modeling the dynamics and kinematics of articulator movements will help us to better understand the difference between embodied and disembodied sound production. Being able to establish continua between these two extremes is of great artistic interest.

Acknowledgments

The authors wish to recognize the members of the Research Center for Opera and Technology, which is based at KTH Royal Institute of Technology and at University College of Opera in Stockholm, Sweden, for their contribution to this chapter: Anders Askenfelt, Nils Enlund, Sten Ternström, Mark Tatlow, Mats Erixon, Leif Handberg, Greger Henriksson, and Minna Räsänen.

References

Baken, R.J. and Orlikoff, R.F. (1990). *Clinical Measurement of Speech and Voice*, 2nd edn. San Diego: Singular Press.

Bartholomew, M. (1953). *Songs of Yale*. New York: Schirmer.

Benade, A.H. (1976). *Fundamentals of Musical Acoustics*. New York: Oxford University Press.

Delvaux, B. and Howard, D.M. (2014). A new method to explore the spectral impact of the piriform fossae on the singing voice: benchmarking using MRI-based 3D-printed vocal tracts. *PLOS ONE* 9(7): 1–15.

Döbereiner, L. (2011). Models of constructed sound: nonstandard synthesis as an aesthetic perspective. *Computer Music Journal* 35(3): 28–39.

Eckel, G. (2012). Embodied generative music. In: D. Peters, G. Eckel, and A. Dorschel (eds.), *Bodily Expression in Electronic Music: Perspectives on a Reclaimed Performativity*, pp. 143–151. London, New York: Routledge.

El-Masri, S., Pelorson, X., Saguet, P., and Badin, P. (1998). Development of the transmission line matrix method in acoustics applications to higher modes in the vocal tract and other complex ducts. *International Journal of Numerical Modelling Electronic Network Devices and Fields* 11: 133–151.

Erath, B.D., Zañartu, M., Stewart, K.C., Plesniak, M.W., Sommer, D.E., and Peterson, S.D. (2013). A review of lumped-element numerical models of voiced speech. *Speech Communication* doi: http://dx.doi.org/10.1016/j.specom.2013.02.002

Fant, G. (1970). *Acoustic Theory of Speech Production*, 2nd edn. Paris: Mouton.

Fant, G., Liljencrants, J., and Lin, Q. G. (1985). A four-parameter model of glottal flow. *STL-QPSR* 2(3): 1512–1522.

Farley, J. and Thomson, S.L. (2011). Acquisition of detailed laryngeal flow measurements in geometrically realistic laryngeal models. *Journal of the Acoustical Society of America* 130(2): EL82–EL86.

Fujita, S., Honda, K. (2005). An experimental study of acoustic characteristics of hypopharyngeal cavities using vocal tract solid models. *Acoustical Science and Technology* 26(4):353–357. DOI: https://doi.org/10.1250/ast.26.353, URL: https://www.jstage.jst.go.jp/article/ast/26/4/26_4_353/_article

Fuks, L. (1999). *From air to music—acoustical, physiological and perceptual aspects of reed wind instrument playing and vocal-ventricular fold phonation*. PhD thesis, Royal Institute of Technology.

Glasberg, B.R. and Moore, B.C.J. (1990). Derivation of auditory filter shapes from notched-noise data. *Hearing Research* 47: 103–138.

Howard, D.M. and Murphy, D.T. (2008). *Voice Science Acoustics and Recording*. San Diego: Plural Press.

Howard, D.M. and Angus, J.A.S. (2009). *Acoustics and Psychoacoustics*, 4th edn. Oxford: Focal Press.

Howard, D.M., Daffern, H., and Brereton, J. (2013). Four-part choral synthesis system for investigating intonation in a cappella choral singing. *Logopedics Phoniatrics Vocology* 38(3): 135–142.

Howard, D.M. (2005). Human hearing modelling real-time spectrography for visual feedback in singing training. *Folia Phoniatrica et Logopaedica* 57(5/6): 328–341.

Howard, D.M. (2015). The vocal tract organ and the vox humana organ stop. *Special Issue of the Journal of Music, Technology and Education* 7(3): 265–277.

Howard, D.M. (2017). The Vocal Tract Organ: A new musical instrument using 3-D printed vocal tracts, Journal of Voice, https://doi.org/10.1016/j.jvoice.2017.09.014

Ishizaka, K. and Flanagan, J.L. (1972). Synthesis of voiced sounds from a two-mass model of the vocal cords. *Bell System Technical Journal* 50(3): 1233–1268.

Kelly, J.L. and Lochbaum, C.C. (1962). Speech synthesis. In: Nielsen, A.K. (ed.), *Proceedings of the 4th International Congress on Acoustics* August 21–28 1962, Copenhagen, DEN, pp. 1–4. Copenhagen: Organizational Committee of the 4th International Congress on Acoustics.

Kob, M. (2002). *Physical modeling of the singing voice*. PhD thesis, RWTH Aachen University.

Kob, M. (2004). Analysis and modeling of overtone singing in the Sygyt style. *Applied Acoustics* 65: 1249–1259.

Kob, M., Henrich, N., Herzel, H., Howard, D., Tokuda, I., Wolfe, J. (2011). Analysing and Understanding the Singing Voice: Recent Progress and Open Questions. *Current Bioinformatics* 6(3), 362–374.

Maeda, S. (1982). A digital simulation method of the vocal-tract system. *Speech Communication* 1: 199–229.

Magnusson, T. (2010). Designing constraints: composing and performing with digital musical systems. *Computer Music Journal* 34(4): 62–73.

Merleau-Ponty, M. (1945). *Phénoménologie de la perception*. Paris: Gallimard.

Moore, B.C.J. (2003). *An Introduction to the Psychology of Hearing*, 5th edn. San Diego: Academic Press.

Pabon, J.P.H. (1991). Objective acoustic voice-quality parameters in the computer phonetogram. *Journal of Voice* 5: 203–216.

Sönke Pelzer, Lukas Aspöck, Dirk Schröder, Michael Vorlaender (2014). Interactive Real-Time Simulation and Auralization for Modifiable Rooms. Building Acoustics 21(1):65–73. DOI10.1260/1351-010X.21.1.65

Pelzer, S., Aspöck, L., Schröder, D., Vorländer, M. (2014). Interactive real time simulation and auralization for modifiable rooms. *Building Acoustics* 21(1):65–73.

Peters, D. (2012). Touch: real, apparent, and absent on bodily expression in electronic music. In: D. Peters, G. Eckel, and A. Dorschel (eds.), *Bodily Expression in Electronic Music: Perspectives on a Reclaimed Performativity*, pp. 17–34. London, New York: Routledge.

Puckette, M. (2007). *The Theory and Technique of Electronic Music*. London: World Scientific Publishing.

Speed, M., Murphy, D.T., and Howard, D.M. (2014). Modeling the vocal tract transfer function using a 3D digital waveguide mesh. *IEEE Transactions in Audio, Speech and Language Processing* 22(2): 453–464.

Story, B.H. and Titze, I.R. (1995). Voice simulation with a body-cover model of the vocal folds. *Journal of the Acoustical Society of America* 97: 1249–1260.

Sundberg, J. (1987). *The Science of the Singing Voice*. Dekalb, Illinois: Northern Illinois University Press.

Titze, I.R. (1973). The human vocal cords: a mathematical model. *Phonetica* 28: 129–170.

Titze, I.R. (1994). *Principles of Voice Production*. Englewood Cliffs, NJ: Prentice-Hall.

Tokuda, I.T., Zemke, M., Kob, M., and Herzel, H. (2010). Biomechanical modeling of register transitions and the role of vocal tract resonators. *Journal of the Acoustical Society of America* 127: 1528–1536.

von Kempelen, W. (1791). *Mechanismus der menschlichen Sprache nebst der Beschreibung seiner sprechenden Maschine*. Wien: J.B. Degen.

Vorländer, M. (2008). *Auralization*. Berlin: Springer.

Websites

http://www.tolvan.com/index.php?page=/madde/madde.php for a download of the freeware Madde singing synthesizer. Accessed July 25, 2015.

http://www.vocaloid.com Yamaha Corporation: VOCALOID Singing Synthesis Software. Accessed July 25, 2015.

http://vocaltractlab.de/ for a download of the freeware Vocaltractlab area function-based voice synthesizer (developed by Birkholz). Accessed July 25, 2015.

Youtube (2007) https://www.youtube.com/watch?v=TVYYnJ_9258 Vocal tract quartet DEMO by ATR BPI members. Accessed February 26, 2019.

DailyMotion (2017) https://www.dailymotion.com/video/x363xkr Demonstration of a replica of Von Kempelen's Speaking Machine. Accessed February 26, 2019.

Author Index

Note: Tables are indicated by an italic *t* following the page number.

SUBJECT INDEX

Note: Tables and figures are indicated by an italic *t* and *f* following the page number.